| Year | (13) Price Level GDP Deflator (1987 = 100) | (14) Consumer Price Index (1987–84 = 100) | (15) Real Average Hourly Earnings (1982 dollars) | (16) Population (millions) | (17) Labor Force* | (18) Civilian Unemployment Rate (percent) | (19) Money Supply M1 (in December) (billions of dollars) | (20) M2 | (21) Interest Rates Treasury Bills (percent) | (22) Corporate Bonds† | (23) Exchange Value of U.S. Dollar[a] (March 1973 = 100) | (24) Federal Budget Surplus (+) or Deficit (−) (billions of dollars) |
|---|---|---|---|---|---|---|---|---|---|---|---|---|
| 1929 | 12.5 | 17.1 | — | 121,767 | 49.2 | 3.2 | — | — | — | 4.73 | — | +1.2 |
| 1933 | 9.5 | 13.0 | — | 125,579 | 51.6 | 24.9 | — | — | 0.52 | 4.49 | — | −1.3 |
| 1939 | 11.0 | 13.8 | — | 130,880 | 55.2 | 17.2 | — | — | 0.02 | 3.01 | — | −2.2 |
| 1945 | 13.3 | 18.0 | — | 139,928 | 53.9 | 1.9 | — | — | 0.38 | 2.62 | — | −42.1 |
| 1950 | 20.2 | 24.1 | 5.34 | 152,271 | 62.2 | 5.3 | — | — | 1.22 | 2.62 | — | +9.2 |
| 1955 | 22.9 | 26.8 | 6.15 | 165,931 | 65.0 | 4.4 | — | — | 1.75 | 3.06 | — | +4.4 |
| 1960 | 26.0 | 29.6 | 6.79 | 180,671 | 69.6 | 5.5 | 140.7 | 312.3 | 2.93 | 4.41 | — | 3.5 |
| 1961 | 26.3 | 29.9 | 6.88 | 183,691 | 70.5 | 6.7 | 145.2 | 335.5 | 2.38 | 4.35 | — | −2.6 |
| 1962 | 26.9 | 30.2 | 7.07 | 186,538 | 70.6 | 5.5 | 147.8 | 362.7 | 2.78 | 4.33 | — | −3.4 |
| 1963 | 27.2 | 30.6 | 7.17 | 189,242 | 71.8 | 5.7 | 153.3 | 393.2 | 3.16 | 4.26 | — | 1.1 |
| 1964 | 27.7 | 31.0 | 7.33 | 191,889 | 73.1 | 5.2 | 160.3 | 424.8 | 3.55 | 4.40 | — | −2.6 |
| 1965 | 28.4 | 31.5 | 7.52 | 194,303 | 74.4 | 4.5 | 167.9 | 459.3 | 3.95 | 4.49 | — | 1.3 |
| 1966 | 29.4 | 32.4 | 7.62 | 196,560 | 75.7 | 3.8 | 172.0 | 480.0 | 4.88 | 5.13 | — | −1.4 |
| 1967 | 30.3 | 33.4 | 7.72 | 198,712 | 77.3 | 3.8 | 183.3 | 524.3 | 4.32 | 5.51 | 120.0 | −12.7 |
| 1968 | 31.8 | 34.8 | 7.89 | 200,706 | 78.7 | 3.6 | 197.4 | 566.3 | 5.34 | 6.18 | 122.1 | −4.7 |
| 1969 | 33.4 | 36.7 | 7.98 | 202,677 | 80.7 | 3.5 | 203.9 | 589.5 | 6.68 | 7.03 | 122.4 | 8.5 |
| 1970 | 35.2 | 38.8 | 8.03 | 205,052 | 82.8 | 4.9 | 214.4 | 628.0 | 6.46 | 8.04 | 121.1 | −13.3 |
| 1971 | 37.1 | 40.5 | 8.21 | 207.661 | 84.4 | 5.9 | 228.3 | 712.6 | 4.35 | 7.39 | 117.8 | −21.7 |
| 1972 | 38.8 | 41.8 | 8.53 | 209,896 | 87.0 | 5.6 | 249.2 | 805.1 | 4.07 | 7.21 | 109.1 | −17.3 |
| 1973 | 41.3 | 44.4 | 8.55 | 211,909 | 89.4 | 4.9 | 262.8 | 860.9 | 7.04 | 7.44 | 99.1 | −6.6 |
| 1974 | 44.9 | 49.3 | 8.28 | 213,854 | 91.9 | 5.6 | 274.3 | 908.4 | 7.89 | 8.57 | 101.4 | −11.6 |
| 1975 | 49.2 | 53.8 | 8.12 | 215,973 | 93.8 | 8.5 | 287.5 | 1023.1 | 5.84 | 8.83 | 98.5 | −69.4 |
| 1976 | 52.3 | 56.9 | 8.24 | 218,035 | 96.2 | 7.7 | 306.3 | 1163.5 | 4.99 | 8.43 | 105.6 | −52.9 |
| 1977 | 55.9 | 60.6 | 8.36 | 220,239 | 99.0 | 7.1 | 331.1 | 1286.4 | 5.27 | 8.02 | 103.4 | −42.4 |
| 1978 | 60.3 | 65.2 | 8.40 | 222,585 | 102.3 | 6.1 | 358.2 | 1388.5 | 7.22 | 8.73 | 92.4 | −28.1 |
| 1979 | 65.5 | 72.6 | 8.17 | 225,055 | 105.0 | 5.8 | 382.5 | 1496.4 | 10.04 | 9.63 | 88.1 | −15.7 |
| 1980 | 71.7 | 82.4 | 7.78 | 227,726 | 106.9 | 7.1 | 408.5 | 1629.2 | 11.51 | 11.94 | 87.4 | −60.1 |
| 1981 | 78.9 | 90.9 | 7.69 | 229,966 | 108.7 | 7.6 | 436.3 | 1792.6 | 14.03 | 14.17 | 103.4 | −58.8 |
| 1982 | 83.8 | 96.5 | 7.68 | 232,188 | 110.2 | 9.7 | 474.4 | 1952.7 | 10.69 | 13.79 | 116.6 | −135.5 |
| 1983 | 87.2 | 99.6 | 7.79 | 234,307 | 111.6 | 9.6 | 521.2 | 2186.5 | 8.63 | 12.04 | 125.3 | −180.1 |
| 1984 | 91.0 | 103.9 | 7.80 | 236,348 | 113.5 | 7.5 | 552.4 | 2376.0 | 9.58 | 12.71 | 138.2 | −166.9 |
| 1985 | 94.4 | 107.6 | 7.77 | 238,466 | 115.5 | 7.2 | 620.1 | 2572.4 | 7.48 | 11.37 | 143.0 | −181.4 |
| 1986 | 96.9 | 109.6 | 7.81 | 240,651 | 117.8 | 7.0 | 724.5 | 2816.0 | 5.98 | 9.02 | 112.2 | −201.0 |
| 1987 | 100.0 | 113.6 | 7.73 | 242,804 | 119.9 | 6.2 | 750.0 | 2917.2 | 5.82 | 9.38 | 96.9 | −151.8 |
| 1988 | 103.9 | 118.3 | 7.69 | 245,021 | 121.7 | 5.5 | 787.1 | 3078.3 | 6.69 | 9.71 | 92.7 | −136.6 |
| 1989 | 108.5 | 124.0 | 7.64 | 247,342 | 123.9 | 5.3 | 794.6 | 3233.3 | 8.12 | 9.26 | 98.6 | −122.3 |
| 1990 | 113.3 | 130.7 | 7.52 | 249,924 | 124.8 | 5.5 | 827.2 | 3345.5 | 7.51 | 9.32 | 89.1 | −163.5 |
| 1991 | 117.7 | 136.2 | 7.45 | 252,688 | 125.3 | 6.7 | 899.3 | 3445.8 | 5.42 | 8.77 | 89.8 | −203.4 |
| 1992 | 121.1 | 140.3 | 7.42 | 255,414 | 127.0 | 7.4 | 1026.6 | 3494.9 | 3.45 | 8.14 | 86.6 | −276.3 |

*Counts persons 14 years and older 1929–1946, 16 years and older 1947–present.
†Moody's Aaa rating.
[a]Multilateral trade-weighted average. Federal Reserve series.

SIXTH EDITION

# ECONOMICS

## PRINCIPLES AND POLICY

WILLIAM J. BAUMOL

C.V. STARR CENTER
FOR APPLIED ECONOMICS,
NEW YORK UNIVERSITY

ALAN S. BLINDER

PRINCETON UNIVERSITY

THE DRYDEN PRESS
HARCOURT BRACE & COMPANY

FORT WORTH PHILADELPHIA SAN DIEGO NEW YORK ORLANDO AUSTIN SAN ANTONIO
TORONTO MONTREAL LONDON SYDNEY TOKYO

**Publisher** Liz Widdicombe
**Senior Acquisitions Editor** Rick Hammonds
**Senior Developmental Editor** Daryl Fox
**Manuscript Editor** Margie Rogers
**Production Manager** Mandy Manzano
**Designer** Linda Miller
**Director of Editing, Design, and Production** Diane Southworth
**Photo Editor** Elizabeth Banks
**Literary Permissions** Shirley Webster
**Indexer** Leslie Leland Frank
**Compositor** Monotype Composition Company, Inc.
**Text Type** Palatino 10/12

**About the Cover** The curve in the left-hand corner represents a production possibilities frontier. As Chapter 3 tells us, any point on or inside this frontier is attainable. Notice that the icons representing the *Twelve Ideas for Beyond the Final Exam* are outside the frontier. It is the mission of this text to help each student move these important ideas into his or her frontier. Within this text, students will find the resources and technology to master core economic concepts and expand their frontier.



*Address for Editorial Correspondence*
The Dryden Press, 301 Commerce Street, Suite 3700, Fort Worth, TX 76102

*Address for Orders*
The Dryden Press, 6277 Sea Harbor Drive, Orlando, FL 32887
1-800-782-4479, or 1-800-433-0001 (in Florida)

ISBN: 0-03-098927-2

Library of Congress Catalog Card Number: 93-74232

Printed in the United States of America

3 4 5 6 7 8 9 0 1 2 048 9 8 7 6 5 4 3 2 1

The Dryden Press
Harcourt Brace College Publishers

Illustration credits appear on page **C-1**, which constitutes a continuation of the copyright page.

# ABOUT THE AUTHORS

William J. Baumol was born and raised in New York City. He received his undergraduate degree in economics with a minor in art from the City University of New York and his Ph.D. in economics from the London School of Economics.

He taught at Princeton University for over forty years, and he is now at New York University where he is the director of the C. V. Starr Center for Applied Economics.

Professor Baumol has published over five hundred scholarly articles and more than twenty books that have been translated into a dozen languages.

He has been president of four professional societies, including the American Economic Association. He is also a member of the Board of Trustees of the Joint Council on Economic Education and a member of the National Academy of Sciences.

He is married and has two children and two grandchildren. Besides courses in economics, Professor Baumol also taught wood sculpture at Princeton University.

Alan S. Blinder was born in New York City and earned his A.B. at Princeton University, his M.Sc. at the London School of Economics, and his Ph.D. at Massachusetts Institute of Technology—all in economics.

Since 1971, he has taught at Princeton University, where he is now the Gordon S. Rentschler Memorial Professor of Economics. Professor Blinder chaired the department of economics from 1988 to 1990, and he is also the founder and director of Princeton's Center for Economic Policy Studies.

Professor Blinder is the author of ten books and scores of scholarly articles. He is currently a member of the Council of Economic Advisers and president-elect of the Eastern Economic Association.

Professor Blinder is married, has two sons, and currently lives in Washington, D.C.

# THE DRYDEN PRESS SERIES IN ECONOMICS

ASCH AND SENECA
*Government and the Marketplace*
Second Edition

BAKER
*An Introduction to International Economics*

BAUMOL AND BLINDER
*Economics: Principles and Policy*
Sixth Edition (Also available in micro and macro paperbacks)

BAUMOL, PANZAR, AND WILLIG
*Contestable Markets and the Theory of Industry Structure*
Revised Edition

BERCH
*The Endless Day: The Political Economy of Women and Work*

BREIT AND ELZINGA
*The Antitrust Casebook: Milestones in Economic Regulation*
Second Edition

BRUE
*The Evolution of Economic Thought*
Fifth Edition

CAMPBELL, CAMPBELL, AND DOLAN
*Money, Banking, and Monetary Policy*

CLAUDON AND OLSEN
*Eco Talk*

DEMMERT
*Economics: Understanding the Market Process*

DOLAN AND LINDSEY
*Economics*
Seventh Edition (Also available in micro and macro paperbacks)

ECKERT AND LEFTWICH
*The Price System and Resource Allocation*
Tenth Edition

EDGMAND, MOOMAW, AND OLSON
*Economics and Contemporary Issues*
Second Edition

ESTEY
*The Unions: Structure, Development, and Management*
Third Edition

FRIEDMAN
*Milton Friedman Speaks (Video)*

GARDNER
*Comparative Economic Systems*

GLAHE
*Microeconomics: Theory and Application*
Second Edition

GREEN
*Macroeconomics: Analysis and Applications*

GWARTNEY AND STROUP
*Economics: Private and Public Choice*
Sixth Edition (Also available in micro and macro paperbacks)

GWARTNEY AND STROUP
*Introduction to Economics: The Wealth and Poverty of Nations*

HEILBRONER AND SINGER
*The Economic Transformation of America: 1600 to the Present*
Second Edition

HIRSCH AND RUFOLO
*Public Finance and Expenditure in a Federal System*

HIRSCHEY AND PAPPAS
*Fundamentals of Managerial Economics*
Fourth Edition

HIRSCHEY AND PAPPAS
*Managerial Economics*
Seventh Edition

HOERNEMAN, HOWARD, WILSON, AND COLE
*CAPER: Computer Assisted Program for Economic Review*

HYMAN
*Public Finance: A Contemporary Application of Theory to Policy*
Fourth Edition

JOHNSON AND ROBERTS
*Money and Banking: A Market-Oriented Approach*
Third Edition

KAUFMAN
*The Economics of Labor Markets*
Fourth Edition

KEATING AND WILSON
*Fundamentals of Managerial Economics*

KEATING AND WILSON
*Managerial Economics*
Second Edition

KENNETT AND LIEBERMAN
*The Road to Capitalism: The Economic Transformation of Eastern Europe and the Former Soviet Union*

KIDWELL, PETERSON, AND BLACKWELL
*Financial Institutions, Markets, and Money*
Fifth Edition

KOHN
*Money, Banking, and Financial Markets*
Second Edition

KREININ
*International Economics: A Policy Approach*
Sixth Edition

LANDSBURG
*Price Theory and Applications*
Second Edition

LINK, MILLER, AND BERGMAN
*EconoGraph II: Interactive Software for Principles of Economics*

LOTT AND RAY
*Applied Econometrics with Data Sets*

NICHOLSON
*Intermediate Microeconomics and Its Application*
Sixth Edition

NICHOLSON
*Microeconomic Theory: Basic Principles and Extensions*
Fifth Edition

ORMISTON
*Intermediate Microeconomics*

PUTH
*American Economic History*
Third Edition

RAGAN AND THOMAS
*Principles of Economics*
Second Edition (Also available in micro and macro paperbacks)

RAMANATHAN
*Introductory Econometrics with Applications*
Second Edition

RUKSTAD
*Corporate Decision Making in the World Economy: Company Case Studies*

RUKSTAD
*Macroeconomic Decision Making in the World Economy: Text and Cases*
Third Edition

SAMUELSON AND MARKS
*Managerial Economics*

SCARTH
*Macroeconomics: An Introduction to Advanced Methods*
Third Edition

SMITH AND SPUDECK
*Interest Rates: Principles and Applications*

THOMAS
*Economics: Principles and Applications*
(Also available in micro and macro paperbacks)

WACHTEL
*Labor and the Economy*
Third Edition

WALTON AND ROCKOFF
*History of the American Economy*
Seventh Edition

WELCH AND WELCH
*Economics: Theory and Practice*
Fourth Edition

YARBROUGH AND YARBROUGH
*The World Economy: Trade and Finance*
Third Edition

ZIMBALIST, SHERMAN, AND BROWN
*Comparing Economic Systems: A Political-Economic Approach*
Second Edition

## THE HARCOURT BRACE COLLEGE OUTLINE SERIES

Emery
*Principles of Economics: Macroeconomics*

Emery
*Principles of Economics: Microeconomics*

Emery
*Intermediate Microeconomics*

*To my four children,*
*Ellen, Daniel,*
*and now Sabrina and Jim*

W.J.B.

*For Scott, who is now*
*Beyond the Final Exam,*
*and William, who is on his way*

A.S.B.

# PREFACE

Economic analysis has continued to progress since the writing of the previous edition; but it has produced no revolutionary upheavals requiring major changes in this book. However, the world about us has changed in ways that were beyond belief just a few years ago. Who would have dreamed five years ago that the Berlin Wall would be chopped up and sold as souvenirs in shops throughout the world, that the Soviet Union would disintegrate, and that even Russia itself would be headed by leaders eager to declare their commitment to the market mechanism?

For us, the fundamental importance of these events stems not only from their negative verdict on the workability of central planning, nor from the fact that the free market has won the competitive struggle with "Marxism," sensational though that victory clearly is. Perhaps equally important for the long run is the fact that these cataclysmic developments are sure to affect our economy in a variety of ways. U.S. military spending is being cut substantially, under powerful public pressure. The reunification of Germany has implications for the U.S. balance of payments and for American competitiveness in world markets. U.S. business is now offered substantial marketing and investment opportunities in the newly reopened economies of Eastern Europe that competition does not permit it to ignore.

These and other related developments hammer home the fact that American workers and American firms carry out their economic activities *in a market that is fundamentally international*. Half a century ago, the rest of the world mattered far less to the U.S. economy than it does today. Back then, General Motors was primarily concerned with competition from Ford and Chrysler; foreign cars were hardly worth worrying about. In almost all industries, the bulk of U.S. production was sold to other Americans. Imports and exports constituted a far smaller share of GDP than they do today. But all this has changed. American producers of computers, airplanes, and TV programs make a large proportion of their sales and profits outside our borders. Television sets in U.S. homes come almost entirely from abroad, and Japanese cars are the primary competitive threat to our automobile industry.

For these reasons, it made sense in the past for most of the pages of an *American* textbook to treat the U.S. economy as an isolated world complete in itself, and, for the sake of expository simplicity, that is how most books were written. Only in later chapters were international economic linkages introduced as a necessary but troublesome complication, modifying somewhat the isolated-country analysis of the remainder of the volume.

The Sixth Edition of our book represents a major reorientation and rewriting task. In addition to substantial editing, we have devoted an enormous amount of effort to improving the logical coherence and flow of the microeconomic analysis. As usual, we have begun with the firm providing products to households. But we sought to make it easier for the student to recognize that the circular flow of the economy is completed by the household's supply of inputs to the firm. For this purpose, we brought the chapters on distribution of income and determination of wages, interest, rent, and profit closer to the chapters on production and consumer demand.

In addition, we reordered the four chapters on production and demand, starting out with the firm's output and pricing decisions. We did so for two reasons. In the chapters on the firm, it is easier to provide real applications of the analysis, and we hoped thereby to stimulate the reader's interest. Perhaps even more important pedagogically, this permits us to begin the core micro discussion with the chapter that explains the logic and use of *marginal analysis*, thus providing the student at a very early stage with the tools that will be needed throughout the book.

We also changed completely the figures and tables in the chapters on the firm and production, making them entirely unified both in terms of the subject and the numerical relationships. We believe that you will find that this substantially improves these sections as teaching materials.

Accordingly, in this Sixth Edition, our book continues the reorientation introduced in the Fifth Edition, seeking to provide the reader with a depiction of the workings of an economy firmly intertwined with many others. The international interconnections of our economy are embedded throughout the book rather than appended as an afterthought. Illustrative cases, descriptive factual materials, analytic tools, and end-of-chapter problems have all been modified in this way. We trust the result will give the reader an enhanced sense of pertinence, and offer him or her more illuminating insights into the way the economy really works.

This edition, however, continues the basic philosophy of its predecessors. In particular, we avoid the fiction, so popular among textbook writers, that everything is of the utmost importance—a pretense that students are sufficiently intelligent to see through in any event. We try, instead, to highlight those important ideas that are likely to be of lasting significance—principles that students will want to remember long after the course is over because they offer insights that are far from obvious, because they are of practical importance, and because they are widely misunderstood by intelligent laymen. A dozen of the most important of these ideas are selected as **12 Ideas for Beyond the Final Exam** and are called to the reader's attention when they occur through the use of the book's logo.

All modern economics textbooks abound with "real world" examples. We try to go beyond this by elevating the examples to preeminence for, in our view, the policy issue or everyday economic problem ought to lead the student naturally to the economic principle, not the other way around. For this reason, many chapters start with a real policy issue or a practical problem, sometimes drawn from our own experience, that may seem puzzling or paradoxical to noneconomists. We then proceed to describe the economic analysis required to remove the mystery.

In so doing, we use technical terminology and diagrams only where there is a clear need for them, never for their own sake. Still, economics is a technical subject and so this is, unavoidably, a book for the desk, and not for the bed. We make, however, strenuous efforts to simplify the technical level of the discussion as much as possible without sacrificing content. Fortunately, almost every important idea in economics can be explained in plain English, and this is what we try to do.

Finally, in addition to a host of minor changes throughout the volume, we have, with some invaluable help (see below) gone over the book with considerable care, seeking to emphasize issues related to discrimination against minority groups and women. It should be emphasized that this is no attempt to impart political correctness into the book. We frankly do not care whether what we have written is or is not deemed "politically correct" by any particular observer. Moreover, we are deeply dedicated to academic freedom, meaning that we are prepared to defend the right of any writer on economics to take positions, political and economic, very different from our own. However, we also believe that the economic issues raised by discrimination against women or the members of any minority group are of profound significance and, in addition, our own value judgments emphatically call for the devotion of effort to the elimination of all such discrimination. We have sought to act accordingly in the revision of the book, while meticulously seeking to avoid any attempt to foist our own political views or value judgments upon anyone.

As a last personal note, we must mention that completion of the work has had to be carried out under the handicap of a divorce between the coauthors. Happily, their separation entails neither disagreement nor rancor, and there is every reason to expect it to be temporary. However, when Alan Blinder left for Washington to join President Clinton's Council of Economic Advisers, though that undoubtedly contributed to the relevance of this book's materials to the real world, it made communication between us far more challenging. Besides, we simply miss one another.

However, there is a silver lining to this inconvenience. Blinder reports renewed and enhanced respect for Herb Stein's observation that "most of the economics that is usable for advising on public policy is at about the level of the introductory undergraduate course."

## NOTE TO THE STUDENT

We would like to offer one suggestion for success in your economics course. Unlike some of the other courses you may be taking, economics is cumulative—each week's lesson builds on what you have learned before. You will save yourself both a lot of frustration and a lot of work by keeping up on a week-to-week basis. To help you do this, there is a chapter summary, a list of important terms and concepts, and a selection of questions to help you review at the end of each chapter. Making use of these learning aids will increase your success in your economics course. For additional assistance, see the following list of ancillary materials.

## ANCILLARIES

As economic education incorporates new technologies, our extensive learning package has been expanded to accommodate the needs of students and instructors. Each of the following items can be ordered through your bookstore or your local Dryden representative.

**Study Guide** by Craig Swan, University of Minnesota (for students)

- Available in macro or micro splits, as well as a combined version.
- Chapter reviews and "Basic Exercises" have been updated and revised.
- More multiple-choice questions in "Self Test for Understanding."

- New "Economics in Action" sections in all chapters.
- New "Supplementary Exercises" based on external reading that emphasize critical thinking.

**Instructor's Manual** by John Isbister, University of California–Santa Cruz

Each chapter corresponds to a text chapter and opens with a brief summary, pointing out highlights and principal goals. Each chapter contains the following instructional elements:

- The "Chapter Outline" section contains major and minor headings. Instructors can use this to get a quick and comprehensive overview.
- Two "Major Ideas" are listed and explained.
- "On Teaching the Chapter" contains ideas for presenting the material. It helps the instructor think about new pedagogical strategies.
- An additional set of "Problems" requires numerical, graphical or theoretical answers.
- "Discussion Questions" are available which may be assigned for written responses or for classroom discussion.
- Available in micro, macro, and combined versions.

**New Test Bank A** by Peter Schwarz and Julia Mobley, University of North Carolina–Charlotte

- Consists of 2,700+ questions of True/False, Multiple Choice, and 10 essay questions per chapter with an emphasis on problem solving.
- Combined micro/macro versions are available.

**Computerized Test Bank A** by Peter Schwarz and Julia Mobley, University of North Carolina–Charlotte

- Appears in combined version.
- Available in IBM 3.5, 5.25, and Mac versions.
- EXAMASTER+ allows you to add and edit your own questions, create and edit graphics, print scrambled versions of tests, convert multiple-choice questions to open-ended questions, plus much more.

**New Test Bank B** by John Dodge, Sioux Falls College

- Available in micro and combined versions.
- For instructors who want additional questions.
- Consists of 2,700+ questions of True/False, Multiple Choice, and 10 essay questions per chapter with an emphasis on problem solving.

**Computerized Test Bank B** by John Dodge, Sioux Falls College

- Available in IBM 3.5, 5.25, and Mac versions.

**Transparency Acetates and Masters**

- Full color acetates provide exact graphics from the text.
- "Sequenced" acetates allow the instructor to build in curve shifts and changes, facilitating student understanding.
- One color Transparency Masters for all text figures can be duplicated for students.

**Economics in Focus Videos** by Media Solutions

- Facilitate multi-level learning and critical thinking through its up-to-date coverage of current events in our society, while focusing on economic issues important to students and their understanding of the economy.
- Recent segments from MacNeil / Lehrer's *News Hour* program are updated quarterly.
- **Economics in Focus** looks at three major themes:
  - *International Economic Scene* covers free trade, foreign policy, and other related issues.
  - *Economic Challenges and Problems* explores such topics as declining incomes, the budget deficit, and inflation.
  - *The Political Economy* looks at the role of the government, free enterprise, and economic stabilization.
  - Each issue of **Economics in Focus** closes with a special feature story or one-to-one interview with a noted economist.

**Laser Discs**

This package contains both a microeconomics disc and a macroeconomics disc. Each focuses on the core principles and presents the information interactively. A brief 5–7 minute video from CBS begins each learning section. Related animated graphics then follow. With an understanding of the concepts, the student is challenged with critical thinking questions. A printed *Media Instructor's Manual* explains how the laser discs coordinate with *Economics: Principles and Policy, Sixth Edition*.

**TAG Software (Tututorial and Graphing) Software** by Todd Porter and Teresa Riley, Youngstown State University (for students)

- This award-winning software has been significantly enhanced to contain an extensive chapter-by-chapter tutorial, a hands-on graphing section where students are actually required to draw curves (with key strokes or a mouse) and a practice exam for each section. Students receive feedback on their answers. Available in IBM versions.

**Macintosh Tutorial Software** (for students)

- This user-friendly interface allows students to revisit and apply concepts from the text.

**Lecture Presentation Software**

- Menu-driven presentation software.
- Each video clip and still frame image on laser disc has a specific page and/or figure reference to the text.
- Allows instructor to add lecture notes, video, and laser disc material.
- Available in IBM Windows and Apple Macintosh formats, with supporting documentation.

**Mathematics Supplement** by Denise Kummer, St. Louis Community College–Meramec

- Walks the student through basic math and algebra.

- Structured lessons allow for review and practice with variables, averages, ratios, percentages, and simple equations.
- A real help to students with varied math backgrounds.

**Dryden's *News-by-Fax*** by John Isbister, University of California–Santa Cruz

- Provides instructors with updates regarding current issues on a monthly basis.
- Includes source of the article under discussion, a brief summary of the article, and questions for classroom discussion.
- Establishes close links to the text by providing page / topic references to the text.

## NOTE TO THE INSTRUCTOR

In trying to improve the book from one edition to the next, we rely heavily on our experiences as teachers. But our experience using the book is minuscule compared with that of the hundreds of instructors who use it nationwide. If you encounter problems, or have suggestions for improving the book, we urge you to let us know by writing to either one of us in care of The Dryden Press, 301 Commerce Street, Suite 3700, Fort Worth, TX 76102. Such letters are invaluable, and we are glad to receive them, even if they are critical (but not *too* critical!). Many such suggestions accumulated over the past three years found their way into the Sixth Edition.

What follows are suggested course outlines for a one-semester and a one-quarter course in microeconomics.

## OUTLINE FOR A ONE-SEMESTER COURSE IN MICROECONOMICS

| CHAPTER NUMBER | TITLE |
|---|---|
| 1 | What Is Economics? |
| 2 | A Profile of the U.S. Economy |
| 3 | Scarcity and Choice: *The* Economic Problem |
| 4 | Supply and Demand: An Initial Look |
| 5 | Deciding on Output and Price: The Importance of Marginal Analysis |
| 6 | Input Decisions and Production Costs |
| 7 | Demand and Elasticity |
| 8 | The Consumer Choice: Origins of the Demand Curve |
| 9 | The Firm and the Industry under Perfect Competition |
| 10 | The Price System and the Case for Laissez Faire |
| 11 | Monopoly |
| 12 | Between Competition and Monopoly |
| 13 | The Market Mechanism: Shortcomings and Remedies |
| 14 | Real Firms and Their Financing: Stocks and Bonds |
| 15 | Pricing the Factors of Production |
| 16 | Labor: The Human Input |
| 18 | Limiting Market Power: Regulation of Industry |
| 19 | Limiting Market Power: Antitrust Policy |
| 20 | Taxation and Resource Allocation |

**Plus any two of the following:**

| | |
|---|---|
| 17 | Poverty, Inequality, and Discrimination |
| 21 | Environmental Protection and Resource Conservation |
| 22 | International Trade and Comparative Advantage |
| 23 | Comparative Economic Systems: What Are the Choices? |

## OUTLINE FOR A ONE-SEMESTER COURSE IN MACROECONOMICS

| CHAPTER NUMBER | TITLE |
|---|---|
| 1 | What Is Economics? |
| 2 | A Profile of the U.S. Economy |
| 3 | Scarcity and Choice: *The* Economic Problem |
| 4 | Supply and Demand: An Initial Look |
| 22 | The Realm of Macroeconomics |
| 23 | Unemployment and Inflation: The Twin Evils of Macroeconomics |
| 24 | Income and Spending: The Powerful Consumer |
| 25 | Demand-Side Equilibrium: Unemployment or Inflation? |
| 26 | Changes on the Demand Side: Multiplier Analysis |
| 27 | Supply-Side Equilibrium: Unemployment *and* Inflation? |
| 28 | Managing Aggregate Demand: Fiscal Policy |
| 29 | Money and the Banking System |
| 30 | Monetary Policy and the National Economy |
| 31 | The Debate over Monetary Policy |
| 32 | Budget Deficits and the National Debt: Fact and Fiction |
| 33 | The Trade-Off between Inflation and Unemployment |
| 34 | Productivity and Growth in the Wealth of Nations |
| 35 | International Trade and Comparative Advantage |
| 36 | The International Monetary System: Order or Disorder? |
| 37 | Macroeconomics in a World Economy |
| 38 | Growth in Developed and Developing Countries |

## OUTLINE FOR A ONE-SEMESTER COURSE COVERING BOTH MACRO AND MICRO

| CHAPTER NUMBER | TITLE |
|---|---|
| 1 | What Is Economics? |
| 2 | A Profile of the U.S. Economy |
| 3 | Scarcity and Choice: *The* Economic Problem |
| 4 | Supply and Demand: An Initial Look |
| 5 | Deciding on Output and Price: The Importance of Marginal Analysis |
| 6 | Input Decisions and Production Costs |
| 7 | Demand and Elasticity |
| 8 | The Consumer Choice: Origins of the Demand Curve |
| 11 | Monopoly |
| 12 | Between Competition and Monopoly |
| 15 | Pricing the Factors of Production |

| | |
|---|---|
| 16 | The Labor Market and Wages |
| 22 | The Realm of Macroeconomics |
| 24 | Income and Spending: The Powerful Consumer |
| 25 | Demand-Side Equilibrium: Unemployment or Inflation? |
| 27 | Supply-Side Equilibrium: Unemployment *and* Inflation? |

## OUTLINE FOR A ONE-QUARTER COURSE IN MICROECONOMICS

| CHAPTER NUMBER | TITLE |
|---|---|
| 3 | Scarcity and Choice: *The* Economic Problem |
| 4 | Supply and Demand: An Initial Look |
| 5 | Deciding on Output and Price: The Importance of Marginal Analysis |
| 6 | Input Decisions and Production Costs |
| 7 | Demand and Elasticity |
| 8 | Consumer Choice: Origins of the Demand Curve |
| 9 | The Firm and the Industry under Perfect Competition |
| 10 | The Price System and the Case for Laissez Faire |
| 11 | Monopoly |
| 12 | Between Competition and Monopoly |
| 13 | The Market Mechanism: Shortcomings and Remedies |
| 14 | Real Firms and Their Financing: Stocks and Bonds |
| 15 | Pricing the Factors of Production |
| 16 | Labor: The Human Input |
| 20 | Taxation and Resource Allocation |

## OUTLINE FOR A ONE-QUARTER COURSE IN MACROECONOMICS

| CHAPTER NUMBER | TITLE |
|---|---|
| 1 | What Is Economics? |
| 2 | A Profile of the U.S. Economy |
| 3 | Scarcity and Choice: *The* Economic Problem |
| 4 | Supply and Demand: An Initial Look |
| 22 | The Realm of Macroeconomics |
| 23 | Unemployment and Inflation: The Twin Evils of Macroeconomics |
| 24 | Income and Spending: The Powerful Consumer |
| 25 | Demand-Side Equilibrium: Unemployment or Inflation? |
| 26 | Changes on the Demand Side: Multiplier Analysis |
| 27 | Supply-Side Equilibrium: Unemployment *and* Inflation? |
| 28 | Managing Aggregate Demand: Fiscal Policy |
| 29 | Money and the Banking System |
| 30 | Monetary Policy and the National Economy |
| 31 | The Debate over Monetary Policy |
| 32 | Budget Deficits and the National Debt: Fact and Fiction |
| 33 | The Trade-Off between Inflation and Unemployment |

## OUTLINE FOR A ONE-QUARTER COURSE ON APPLICATIONS OF BOTH MACRO AND MICRO

| CHAPTER NUMBER | TITLE |
|---|---|
| 17 | Poverty, Inequality, and Discrimination |
| 18 | Limiting Market Power: Regulation of Industry |
| 19 | Limiting Market Power: Antritrust Policy |
| 20 | Taxation and Resource Allocation |
| 21 | Environmental Protection and Resource Conservation |
| 23 | Unemployment and Inflation: The Twin Evils of Macroeconomics |
| 32 | Budget Deficits and the National Debt: Fact and Fiction |
| 34 | Productivity and Growth in the Wealth of Nations |
| 35 | International Trade and Comparative Advantage |
| 36 | The International Monetary System: Order or Disorder? |
| 38 | Growth in Developed and Developing Countries |
| 40 | Comparative Economic Systems: What Are the Choices? |

# WITH THANKS

Finally, and with great pleasure, we turn to the customary acknowledgments of indebtedness. Ours have been accumulating now through six editions. In these days of specialization, not even a pair of authors can master every subject that an introductory text must cover. Our friends and colleagues Albert Ando, Charles Berry, Rebecca Blank, William Branson, the late Lester Chandler, Gregory Chow, Avinash Dixit, Robert Eisner, Stephen Goldfeld, Claudia Goldin, Ronald Grieson, Daniel Hamermesh, Yuzo Honda, Peter Kenen, Melvin Krauss, Herbert Levine, the late Arthur Lewis, Burton Malkiel, Edwin Mills, Janusz Ordover, Uwe Reinhardt, Harvey Rosen, Laura Tyson, and Martin Weitzman have all given generously of their knowledge in particular areas over the course of six editions. We have learned much from them, and only wish we had learned more.

In this Sixth Edition we owe a particularly heavy debt to Professor Susan Feiner of Hampton University who went over the book with terrifyingly meticulous and thoughtful care, catching errors, pointing out expository shortcomings, and suggesting fundamental revisions. She was also enormously helpful in suggesting places where the book did not deal adequately or appropriately with issues relating to discrimination by sex or ethnic group. In all matters we have adopted most of her suggestions. Perhaps it would have been a better book if we had adopted all of them.

Many economists and students at other colleges and universities offered useful suggestions for improvements, many of which we have incorporated into the Sixth Edition. We wish to thank Robert C. Stuart, Rutgers University; David Aschaur, Bates College; Tom Beveridge, North Carolina State University; Ivan Keith Cohen, Trinity College; Norman L. Dalsted, Colorado Sate University; Larry DeBrock, University of Illinois–Urbana-Champaign; John Edgren, Eastern Michigan University; Robert Eisner, Northwestern University; Chris Ellis, University of Oregon; Shelby Gerking, University of Wyoming; Ami Glazer, University of California–Irvine; Doug Greenley, Moorhead State University; Harry Holzer, Michigan State University; Michael Kupilik, University of Montana; Woo Bong Lee, Bloomsburg University; Charles Okeke, Community College of Southern Nevada; Kevin Rask, Colgate University; Bob Sharp, Eastern Kentucky University; Ernst Stromsdorfer, Washington State University; Roy Van Til, University of Maine at Farmington; Walter Wessels, North Carolina State University; Louise Wolitz, University of Texas at Austin; Prof. Wong, California State University–Fullerton; Ali Zadeh, Susquehanna University; and Michael Zweig, SUNY–Stony Brook.

We also wish to thank the many economists who responded to our questionnaire; their responses were invaluable in planning this revision: Peter Adelsheim, St. Martin's College; Carlos Aguilar, El Paso County Community College; Carolyn Ahern, Monterey Peninsula College; Samuel Kojo Andoh, Southern Connecticut State University; M. Aokoi, University of Rhode Island; K. Arakelian, University of Rhode Island; Roger Atkins, Marshall University; Chris Austin, Normandale Community College; John Azer, Normandale Community College; Robert A. Baade, Lake Forest College; Mohsen Bahmani-Oskooee, University of Wisconsin at Milwaukee; Donald Baum, University of Nebraska; Prof. Baye, Penn State; D.V.T. Bear, University of California–San Diego; Klaus Becker, Texas Tech University; Dallas Blevins, University of Montevallo; Scott Bloom, North Dakota State Univesity; Prof. Brent, Fordham University; John Bungum, University of Minnesota; Evert Campbell, Point Loma Nazarene College; Michael Carter, University of Lowell (MA); Prof. Ceyhun, University of North Dakota; Anthony Chan, Woodbury University; Dan Cobb, St. Louis Community College; Steven Cobb, Xavier University; Joyce Cooper, Boston University; Claude Cox, St. Louis Community College; Ward Curran, Trinity College; Prof. Diulio, Fordham University; Cliff Dobitz, North Dakota State University; Robert Dunn, George Washington University; John C. Dutton, North Carolina State University; Prof. Dziadosz, St. Joseph's University; Alfredo Esposto, Eastern Michigan University; Prof. Fardminash, Temple University; Michael Ferrantino, Southern Methodist University; Prof. Fesmeire, University of Tampa; Rudy Fichtenbaum, Wright State University; Prof. Field-Hendry, CUNY–Queens; Warren Fisher, Susquehanna University; Nancy R. Fox, St. Joseph's University; Richard Fryman, West Georgia College; Yilma Gebremariam, Southern Connecticut State University; Prof. George, LaSalle University; Prof. Ghosh, Tulane University; Prof. Gimmell,

Gettysburg College; Leon Graubard, Worcester Polytechnic Institute; John Green, University of Northern Colorado; Robert Gustavson, Washburn University of Topeka; Rick Hafer, Southern Illinois University; Rebecca Havens, Point Loma Nazarene College; Mark Herander, University of South Florida; Roger Hinderliter, Ithaca College; Dennis Hoffman, Arizona State University; Shane Hunt, Boston University; Beth Ingram, University of Iowa; Walter Johnson, University of Missouri; Prof. Jones, McNeese State University; Frederick Joutz, George Washington University; Prof. Kane, Fordham University; Robert Kerchner, Washington University of Topeka; Jerry Kingston, Arizona State University; Evan Kraft, Salisbury State University; Prof. Kreider, Beloit University; Dale Kuntz, Bentley College; Tae-Hwy Lee, Louisiana State University; Jon G. Lindgren, North Dakota State University; Adam Lutzker, Albion College; Diane Macunovich, Williams College; Michael Manove, Boston University; Robert Marcott, University of St. Thomas; Jeff Marin, Boston University; Jay Martin, Longwood College; John McDowell, Arizona State University; Erica McGrath, Monterey Peninsula College; Ron McNamara, Bentley College; A. Mead, University of Rhode Island; B. Nahata, University of Louisville; Thomas A. Odegaard, Baylor University; Ronald Oldson, University of Kansas; Prof. O'Niel, University of North Dakota; Prof. O'Reilley, North Dakota State University; Theodore Paulos, Wallace State Community College; Prof. Pavlivls, Pennsylvania State University; Helen Popper, Santa Clara University; A. T. Powell, Los Angeles Southwest College; Ali Pyarali, University of South Carolina–Salkehatchie; Prof. Rahman, McNeese State University; Prof. Railing, Gettysburg College; G. Ramsay, University of Rhode Island; John Rappaport, Mount Holyoke College; Prof. Ratkus, LaSalle University; Steven Resnick, University of Massachusetts; Greg Rhodus, Bentley College; Nancy Roberts, Arizona State University; John E. L. Robertson, Paducah Community College; Malcolm Robinson, University of Cincinnati; Gary Rourke, Lakewood Community College; Thomas Sav, Wright State University; Elizabeth Savoca, Smith College; John Schorn, Georgetown University; Steven Shapiro, University of North Florida; John Shaw, California State University–Fresno; John Shea, University of Wisconsin; Earl Shinn, University of Montevallo; Harlan Smith, Marshall University; Janet Smith, Arizona State University; Stephen Smith, Bakersfield College; Paul Snoonian, University of Lowell; Prof. Solon, CUNY–Queens; Steven Spartan, Kansas City, Kansas Community College; J. Starkey, University of Rhode Island; James A. Stephenson, Iowa State University; William Stolte, Berea College; Scott Stradley, University of North Dakota; Richard Sutch, University of California–Berkeley; Prof. Thomas, University of South Florida; James Thornblade, Bentley College; Robert Turner, Colgate University; Lynn Usher, University of Louisville; Prof. Vaz, CUNY–Queens; Lori Warner, University of the Pacific; Rob Wassner, Wayne State University; George Wasson, St. Louis Community College; Art Woolf, University of Vermont; and Dirk Yandell, University of San Diego.

Obviously, the book you hold in your hand was not produced by us alone. An essential role was played by the fine people at The Dryden Press including Rick Hammonds, Daryl Fox, Linda Miller, Mandy Manzano and Elizabeth Banks. In particular, our very capable manuscript editor, Margie Rogers, who has, we feel, become a friend, again worked hard and well to turn our manuscript into the book you see. We appreciate all their efforts.

We also thank our intelligent and delightful secretaries and research co-workers at Princeton and New York University. Phyllis Durepos and Janeece Roderick struggled successfully with the chaos of manuscript exchange, management of proofs, and the simple but difficult task of keeping track of the myriad and all too easily scattered pieces of the uncompleted work. Above all, one of us owes an unrepayable debt to his longstanding partner in crime, Sue Anne Batey Blackman, who carried out much of the updating of materials and who contributed draft paragraphs, illustrative items, and far more with her usual insight and diligence. By now, she undoubtedly knows more about the book than the authors do.

And finally there are our wives, Hilda Baumol and Madeline Blinder. They have now participated and helped in this project for eighteen years. Over that period, if possible, our affection has grown.

William J. Baumol
Alan S. Blinder

# BRIEF CONTENTS

# CONTENTS

## THE DISTRIBUTION OF INCOME 359

## THE UNITED STATES IN THE WORLD ECONOMY 851

# PART I

# *Getting Acquainted with Economics*

Chapter 1

# WHAT IS ECONOMICS?

*Why does public discussion of economic policy so often show the abysmal ignorance of the participants? Why do I so often want to cry at what public figures, the press, and television commentators say about economic affairs?*

**ROBERT M. SOLOW**

Economics is a broad-ranging discipline, both in the questions it asks and the methods it uses to seek answers. Rather than try to define the discipline in a single sentence or paragraph, we will instead introduce you to economics by letting the subject matter speak for itself. ¶ The first part of the chapter is intended to give you some idea of the sorts of issues economic analysis helps clarify and the kinds of solutions that economic principles suggest. Many of the world's most pressing problems are economic in nature. So a little knowledge of basic economics is essential to anyone who wants to understand the world in which we live. ¶ The second part briefly introduces the methods of economic inquiry and the tools that economists use. These are tools you may find useful in your career, personal life, and role as an informed citizen, long after the course is over. ¶ A good deal of economic analysis is carried out with the help of graphs, and so this book is replete with them. For those of you who are unfamiliar with graphs and their properties, the appendix to this chapter provides a brief introduction that will enable you to follow the discussion in the remainder of this volume.

## IDEAS FOR BEYOND THE FINAL EXAM

As college professors, we realize it is inevitable that you will forget much of what you learn in this course—perhaps with a sense of relief—soon after the final exam. There is not much point bemoaning this fact; elephants may never forget, but people do.

Nevertheless, some economic ideas are so important that you will want to remember them well beyond the final exam, for if you do not, you will have shortchanged your education. To help you pick out a few of the most crucial concepts, we have selected 12 from among the many contained in this book. Some offer critical and enduring insights into the workings of the economy. Others bear on important policy issues that appear in newspapers. Others point out common misunderstandings that occur among even the most thoughtful lay observers. As the opening quotation of this chapter suggests, many learned judges, politicians, business leaders, and university administrators who failed to understand or misused these economic principles could have made wiser decisions than they did.

Each of the **12 Ideas for Beyond the Final Exam** will be discussed in depth as it occurs in the course of the book, so you should not expect to master them after reading this opening chapter. Nonetheless, it is useful to sketch them briefly here, both to introduce you to economics and to provide a selective preview of what is to come.

### THE TRADE-OFF BETWEEN INFLATION AND UNEMPLOYMENT

Inflation these days is running a bit below 3 percent per year. In 1990, it was just over 5 percent. What made the inflation rate fall? Most economists believe the answer is simple: In mid-1990, the U.S. economy entered a recession that proved to be deeper and longer than policymakers anticipated. The unemployment rate rose from a low of 5.2 percent in June 1990 to a peak of 7.8 percent in June 1992, and then receded only slowly.

Economists maintain that this conjunction of events—falling inflation and high unemployment—was no coincidence. Owing to features of our economy that we will study in *Macroeconomics* Parts 2 and 3, there is an agonizing *trade-off between inflation and unemployment*, meaning that most policies that lower inflation also cause higher unemployment for a while.

Since this trade-off poses one of the fundamental dilemmas of national economic policy, we will devote all of *Macroeconomics* Chapter 16 to examining it in detail. And we shall also consider some suggestions for escaping from the trade-off, such as supply-side economics (*Macroeconomics* Chapter 10) and wage-price controls (*Macroeconomics* Chapter 16).

### THE ILLUSION OF HIGH INTEREST RATES

Is it more costly to borrow money at 12 percent interest or at 8 percent? That would seem an easy question to answer, even without a course in economics. But, in fact, it is not. An example will show why.

In 1992, banks were lending money to home buyers at annual interest rates as low as 8 percent. In 1981, these rates had been over 12 percent. Yet economists maintain that it was actually cheaper to borrow in 1980 than in 1992. Why? Because inflation in 1980 was running at about 10 percent per year while it was down to about 3 percent by 1992.

But why is information on inflation relevant for deciding how costly it is to borrow? Consider the position of a person who borrows $100 for one year at a 12 percent rate of interest while prices are rising at 10 percent per year. At the end of the year the borrower pays back her $100 plus $12 interest. But over that same year her indebtedness declines by $10 *in terms of what that money will buy*. Thus, in terms of *purchasing power*, the borrower really pays only $2 in interest on her $100 loan, or 2 percent.

Now consider someone who borrows $100 at 8 percent interest when inflation is only 3 percent. This borrower pays back the original $100 plus $8 in interest and sees the purchasing power of his debt decline by $3 due to inflation—for a net payment in purchasing-power terms of $5, or 5 percent. Thus, in the economically relevant sense, the 8 percent loan at 3 percent inflation is actually more expensive than the 12 percent loan at 10 percent inflation.

As we will learn in *Macroeconomics* Chapter 6, the failure to understand this principle has caused troubles for our tax laws, for the financial system, and for the housing and public utility industries. In *Macroeconomics* Chapter 15 we will see that it has even led to misunderstanding of the size and nature of the government budget deficit.

Idea 3

## DO BUDGET DEFICITS BURDEN FUTURE GENERATIONS?

Large federal budget deficits have been in the news for more than a decade now. Congress has struggled continually to cut the deficit and has failed to comply with several deficit-reduction laws that it set for itself (the Gramm-Rudman-Hollings Act). First President Reagan and then President Bush argued that raising taxes is worse than tolerating the deficit, a claim disputed by many. Critics have objected that deficits hold dire consequences—including higher interest rates, more inflation, a stagnant economy, and an irksome burden on future Americans.

The conflicting claims and counterclaims that have marked this debate are bound to confuse the layperson. Who is right? Are deficits really malign or benign influences on our economy? The answers, economists insist, are so complicated that the only correct short answer is: it all depends. The precise factors on which the answers depend, and the reasons why, are sufficiently important that they merit an entire chapter of *Macroeconomics* (Chapter 15). There we will learn that a budget deficit may or may not burden future generations, depending on its size and on the reasons for its existence.

## THE OVERWHELMING IMPORTANCE OF PRODUCTIVITY GROWTH IN THE LONG RUN

In Geneva, a worker in a watch factory now turns out roughly one hundred times as many mechanical watches per year as her ancestors did three centuries earlier. The **productivity** of labor (output per hour of work) in cotton production has probably gone up more than a thousandfold in two hundred years. It is estimated that rising labor productivity has increased the standard of living of a typical American worker about sevenfold in the past century. This means that Americans now enjoy about seven times as much clothing, housewares, and luxury goods as did a typical inhabitant of the United States one hundred years ago.

Economic issues such as inflation, unemployment, and monopoly are important to us all, and will receive much attention in this book. But in the long run nothing has as great an effect on our material well-being and the amounts society can afford to spend on hospitals, schools, and social amenities as the rate of growth of productivity. *Macroeconomics* Chapter 17 points out that what appears to be a small increase in productivity growth can have a huge effect on a country's standard of living over a long period of time because productivity compounds like the interest on savings in a bank.

Similarly, a slowdown in productivity growth that persists for a substantial number of years can have a devastating effect on standards of living. After 1973, productivity growth in the United States, *like that of other industrial countries*, suffered a serious decline. Between 1950 and 1973, the productivity of American workers rose at an annual rate of about 1.9 percent, but since then that growth rate has averaged only about 0.6 percent per year. If productivity growth in the latter period had matched that of the earlier period, average income per person in the United States would now be about 27 percent greater than it actually is!

Idea 5

## MUTUAL GAINS FROM VOLUNTARY EXCHANGE

One of the most fundamental ideas of economics is that in a voluntary exchange *both* parties must gain something, or at least expect to gain something. Otherwise why would they both agree to trade? This principle may seem self-evident, and it probably is. Yet it is amazing how often it is ignored in practice.

For example, it was widely believed for centuries that governments should interfere with international trade because one country's gain from a swap must be the other country's loss. (Chapter 22.) Analogously, some people feel instinctively that if Mr. A profits handsomely from a deal with Ms. B, then Ms. B must have been exploited. Laws sometimes prohibit mutually beneficial exchanges between buyers and sellers—as when a loan transaction is banned because the interest rate is "too high" (*Macroeconomics* Chapter 6), or when a willing worker cannot be hired because the wage rate is "too low" (Chapter 16), or when the resale of tickets to sporting events ("ticket scalping") is outlawed even though the buyer is happy to pay the high price (Chapter 4).

In every one of these cases, and many more, well-intentioned but misguided reasoning blocks the mutual gains that arise from voluntary exchange—and thereby interferes with one of the most basic functions of an economic system (see Chapter 3).

## THE SURPRISING PRINCIPLE OF COMPARATIVE ADVANTAGE

The Japanese economy produces many products that Americans buy in huge quantities—including cars, TV sets, cameras, and electronic equipment. American manufacturers often complain about the competition and demand protection from the flood of imports that, in their view, threatens American standards of living. Is this view justified?

Economists think not. They maintain, as suggested in the last Idea, that both sides must gain from international trade. But what if the Japanese were able to produce *everything* more cheaply than we can? Would it not then be true that Americans would be thrown out of work and that our nation would be impoverished?

A remarkable result, called the law of **comparative advantage**, shows that even in this extreme case the two nations can still benefit by trading and that each can gain as a result! We will explain this principle fully in Chapter 22, where we will also note some potentially valid arguments in favor of providing special incentives for particular domestic industries. But for now a simple parable will make the reason clear.

Suppose Sally grows up on a farm and is a whiz at plowing, but is also a successful country singer who earns $4000 a performance. Should Sally turn down singing engagements to leave time for plowing? Of course not. Instead she should hire Alfie, a much less efficient farmer, to do the plowing for her. Sally may be a better farmer. But she earns so much more by specializing in singing that it makes sense to leave the farming to Alfie. Alfie, though a less skilled farmer than Sally, is an even worse singer. Thus Alfie earns a living by specializing in the job at which he at least has a *comparative* advantage (his farming is not as bad as his singing), and both Alfie and Sally gain. The same is true of two countries. Even if one of them is more efficient at everything, both countries can gain by producing the things they do best *comparatively*.

## ATTEMPTS TO REPEAL THE LAWS OF SUPPLY AND DEMAND: THE MARKET STRIKES BACK

When a commodity is in short supply, its price naturally tends to rise. Sometimes disgruntled consumers badger politicians into "solving" the problem by imposing a legal ceiling on the price. Similarly, when supplies are abundant—say, when fine weather produces extraordinarily abundant crops—prices tend to fall. This naturally dismays producers, who often succeed in getting legislation to prohibit low prices by imposing price floors.

But such attempts to repeal the laws of supply and demand usually backfire and sometimes produce results virtually the opposite of those that were intended. Where rent controls are adopted to protect tenants, housing grows scarce because the law makes it unprofitable to build and maintain apartments. When price floors are placed under agricultural products, surpluses pile up.

History provides some spectacular examples of the free market's ability to strike back at attempts to interfere with it. In Chapter 4, we will see that price controls contributed to the hardships of George Washington's army at Valley Forge. Two centuries earlier, when the armies of Spain surrounded Antwerp in 1584, hoping to starve the city into submission, profiteers kept Antwerp going by smuggling food and supplies through enemy lines. However, when the city fathers adopted price controls to end these "unconscionable" prices, supplies dried up and the city soon surrendered.

As we will see in Chapter 4 and elsewhere in this book, such consequences of interfering with the price mechanism are no accident. They follow inevitably from the way free markets work.

## EXTERNALITIES: A SHORTCOMING OF THE MARKET CURED BY MARKET METHODS

Markets are very efficient at producing just the goods that consumers want, and in the quantities they desire. They do so by rewarding those who respond to what consumers want and who produce these products economically. Similarly, the market mechanism ferrets out waste and inefficiency by seeing to it that inefficient producers lose money.

This works well as long as an exchange between a seller and a buyer affects only those two parties. But often an economic transaction affects uninvolved third parties. Examples abound. The electric utility that generates power for the Midwest also produces pollution which kills freshwater fish in New York State. A farmer sprays crops with toxic pesticides, but the poison seeps into the ground water and affects the health of neighboring communities.

Such social costs—called **externalities** because they affect parties *external* to the economic transaction that causes them—escape the control of the market mechanism. As we will learn in Chapters 13 and 21, there is no financial incentive to motivate polluters to minimize the damage they do. Hence, business firms make their products as cheaply as possible, disregarding externalities that may damage the quality of life.

Yet Chapters 13 and 21 point out a way for the government to use the market mechanism to control undesirable externalities. If the electric utility and the farmer are charged for the harm they cause the public, just as they are charged when they use tangible resources such as coal and fertilizer, then they will have an incentive to reduce the amount of pollution they generate. Thus, in this case, economists believe that market methods are often the best way to cure one of the market's most important shortcomings.

*Idea* 9

## RATIONAL CHOICE AND TRUE ECONOMIC COSTS: THE ROLE OF OPPORTUNITY COST

Despite dramatic improvements in our standard of living since the Industrial Revolution, we have not come anywhere near a state of unlimited abundance, and so we must constantly make choices. If you purchase a new home, you may not be able to afford to eat at expensive restaurants as often as you used to. If a firm decides to retool its factories, it may have to postpone plans for new executive offices. If a government expands its defense program, it may be forced to reduce its outlays on roads or school buildings.

Economists say that the true costs of such decisions are not the number of dollars spent on the house, the new equipment, or the military establishment, but rather *the value of what must be given up in order to acquire the item*—the restaurant meals, the new executive offices, the improved roads, and new schools. These are called **opportunity costs** because they represent the *opportunities* the individual, firm, or government must forgo to make the desired expenditure. Economists maintain that rational decision-making requires that opportunity costs be considered (see Chapter 3).

The **OPPORTUNITY COST** of some decision is the value of the next best alternative which you have to give up because of that decision (for example, working instead of going to school).

The cost of a college education provides a vivid example that is probably close to your heart. How much do you think it *costs* to go to college? Most likely you would answer this question by adding together your expenditures on tuition, room and board, books, and the like, and then deducting any scholarship funds you may receive. Economists would not. They would first want to know how much you could be earning if you were not attending college. This may sound like an irrelevant question; but because you give up these earnings by attending college, they must be added to your tuition bill as a cost of your education. Nor would economists accept the university's bill for room and board as a measure of your living costs. They would want to know by how much this exceeds what it would have cost you to live at home, and only this extra cost would be counted as an expense. On balance, a college education probably costs more than you think.

Idea 10

## THE IMPORTANCE OF MARGINAL ANALYSIS

Many pages in this book will be spent explaining, and extolling the virtues of, a type of decision-making process called **marginal analysis** (see especially Chapters 5 and 6), which can best be illustrated by an example.

Suppose an airline is told by its accountants that the full cost of transporting one passenger from Los Angeles to New York is $300. Can the airline profit by offering a reduced rate of $200 to students who fly on a standby basis? The surprising answer is: probably yes. And the reason is that most of the costs will be paid whether the plane carries 20 passengers or 120 passengers.

Marginal analysis points out that costs such as maintenance, landing rights, and ground crews are irrelevant to the decision whether to carry standby passengers for reduced rates. The only costs that *are* relevant are the *extra* costs of writing and processing additional tickets, the food and beverages these passengers consume, the additional fuel required, and so on. These costs are called **marginal costs** and are probably quite small in this example. Any passenger who pays the airline more than its marginal cost will add something to the company's profit. So it probably is more profitable to let the students ride at low fares than to let the plane fly with empty seats.

There are many real cases in which decision makers, not understanding marginal analysis, have rejected such advantageous possibilities as the reduced fare in our hypothetical example. These people were misled by calculating in terms of *average* rather than *marginal* cost figures—an error that can be quite costly.

## THE COST DISEASE OF THE PERSONAL SERVICES

A distressing phenomenon is occurring throughout the industrialized world. Many community services have been deteriorating—fewer postal deliveries and garbage pickups, larger classes in public schools—even though the public is paying more for them. The costs of providing many services have risen consistently faster than the rate of inflation.

Perhaps the most prominent examples are medical care and education, which constitute a large percentage of many government and household budgets, and which many consider to be indispensable products for society. For example, over the 44-year period since 1948 the daily cost of a stay at a hospital outstripped the rate of inflation by more than 700 percent! A natural response is to attribute the problem to greed, inefficiency, and political corruption. But this cannot be the whole story, because the scenario has been repeated in virtually every other industrialized country, despite great differences in the way these services are provided.

As we shall see in Chapter 13, one of the major causes of the problem is economic. And it has nothing to do with either corruption or inefficiency; rather, it stems from the dazzling growth in efficiency of private manufacturing industries! Because technological improvements make workers more productive in manufacturing, costs go down and wages rise. But wages rise not only for the manufacturing workers but also for postal workers, teachers, and other service workers (because, otherwise these workers would leave their low-paying service jobs and compete for jobs in high-paying industries). But the technology of labor-intensive personal services is not easily changed. Since it still takes one person to drive a postal truck and one teacher to teach a class, the cost of these services is forced to rise in step with wage increases. This is what has been called the "cost disease" of the personal services, a malady that affects many services, including medical care, university teaching, restaurant cooking, retailing, and automobile repairs.

This is important to understand not because it excuses the financial record of our governments, but because an understanding of the problem suggests what we should expect the future to bring and, perhaps, indicates what policies should be advocated to deal with it.

Idea 12

## THE TRADE-OFF BETWEEN OUTPUT AND EQUALITY

"Supply-side" economics was one of the cornerstones of the so-called Reagan revolution, and was embraced by President Bush. The basic idea behind supply-side tax cuts (*Macroeconomics* Chapter 11) is to spur productivity and efficiency by providing greater incentives for working, saving, and investing. Often, that means lowering tax rates. There are important elements of truth in this position. No one doubts that proper economic incentives are critical.

Yet many people feel that the unequal distribution of income in our society is unjust; that it is inequitable for the super rich to sail yachts while poor people go homeless. Such people are disturbed by the fact that supply-side tax cuts are likely to make the distribution of income even more unequal than it already is. During the 1992 presidential campaign, challenger Bill Clinton attacked the strategy as "trickle down" economics, meaning that it offered mere crumbs to working people while serving heaping portions to the rich. This position, too, has elements of truth.

In fact, we have a genuine dilemma. To provide stronger incentives for success in the economic game, the gaps between the "winners" and the "losers" must necessarily be widened. It is these gaps, after all, that provide the incentives to work harder, to save more, and to invest productively. But such programs also breed inequality. Thus, economists say there is a *trade-off* between the *size* of a nation's output and the degree of *equality* with which that output is distributed. Supply-side tax cuts are one example. Another is anti-poverty programs. As we will see in Chapter 17, many policies designed to divide the proverbial economic pie more equally inadvertently cause the size of the pie to shrink.

## EPILOGUE

These, then, are a dozen of the more fundamental concepts to be found in this book—ideas that we hope you will retain **Beyond the Final Exam**. There is no need to master them right now, for you will hear much more about each as the book progresses. Instead, keep them in mind as you read—we will point them out to you as they occur by the use of the book's logo —and look back over this list at the end of the course. You may be amazed to see how natural, or even obvious, they will seem then.

# INSIDE THE ECONOMIST'S TOOL KIT

Now that you have some idea of the kinds of issues economists deal with, you should know something about the way they grapple with these problems.

## ECONOMICS AS A DISCIPLINE

Economics has something of a split personality. Although clearly the most rigorous of the social sciences, it nevertheless looks decidedly more "social" than "scientific" when compared with, say, physics. An economist must be a jack of several trades, borrowing modes of investigation from numerous fields. Usefulness, not methodological purity, is the criterion for inclusion in the economist's tool kit.

Mathematical reasoning is used extensively in economics, but so is historical study. And neither looks quite the same as when practiced by a mathematician or a historian. Statistical inference plays a major role in modern economic inquiry; but economists have had to modify standard statistical procedures to fit the kinds of data they deal with. In 1926, John Maynard Keynes, the great British economist, summed up the many faces of economic inquiry in a statement that still rings true today.

> *The master-economist . . . must understand symbols and speak in words. He must contemplate the particular in terms of the general, and touch abstract and concrete in the same flight of thought. He must study the present in the light of the past for the purposes of the future. No part of man's nature or his institutions must lie entirely outside his regard. He must be purposeful and disinterested in a simultaneous mood; as aloof and incorruptible as an artist, yet sometimes as near the earth as a politician.*[1]

An introductory course in economics will not make you a master-economist; but it should help you approach social problems from a pragmatic and dispassionate point of view. You will not find solutions to all society's economic problems in this book. But you should learn how to pose questions in ways that will help produce answers that are both useful and illuminating.

## THE NEED FOR ABSTRACTION

Some students find economics unduly abstract and "unrealistic." The stylized world envisioned by economic theory seems only a distant cousin to the world they know. There is an old joke about three people—a chemist, a physicist, and an economist—stranded on an isolated island with an ample supply of canned food but no implements to open the cans. In debating what to do, the chemist suggested lighting a fire under the cans, thus expanding their contents and causing the cans to burst. The physicist doubted that this would work. She advocated building a catapult with which they could smash the cans against some nearby boulders. Then they turned to the economist for his suggestion. After a moment's thought, he announced his solution: "Let's assume we have a can opener."

---

[1]See his *Essays in Biography* (New York: Norton, 1951), pages 140–141.

Economic theory *does* make unrealistic assumptions; you will encounter many of them in the pages that follow. But this propensity to abstract from reality results from the incredible complexity of the economic world, not from any fondness economists have for sounding absurd.

Compare the chemist's simple task of explaining the interactions of compounds in a chemical reaction with the economist's complex task of explaining the interactions of people in an economy. Are molecules motivated by greed or altruism, by envy or ambition? Do they ever emulate other molecules? Do forecasts about them influence their behavior? People, of course, do all these things, and many, many more. It is therefore immeasurably more difficult to predict human behavior than to predict chemical reactions. But, if economists tried to keep track of every aspect of human behavior, they would never get anywhere. Thus:

Abstraction from unimportant details is necessary to understand the functioning of anything as complex as the economy.

**ABSTRACTION** means ignoring many details in order to focus on the most important elements of a problem.

To appreciate why economists **abstract** from details, imagine the following hypothetical situation. You have just arrived, for the first time in your life, in Los Angeles. You are now at the Los Angeles Civic Center. This is the point marked *A* in Figures 1–1 and 1–2, which are alternative maps of part of Los Angeles. You

**Figure 1–1** **MAP 1**

Map 1 gives complete details of the road system of Los Angeles. If you are like most people, you will find it hard to read and not very useful for figuring out how to get from the Civic Center (point *A*) to the La Brea tar pits (point *B*). For this purpose, the map carries far too much detail, though for some other purposes (for example, locating some small street in Hollywood), it may be the best map available.

**Figure 1–2** **MAP 2**

Map 2 shows a different perspective of Los Angeles. Minor roads are eliminated—we might say, *assumed away*—in order to present a clearer picture of where the major arteries and freeways go. As a result of this simplification, several ways of getting from the Civic Center (point *A*) to the La Brea tar pits (point *B*) stand out clearly. For example, we can take the Hollywood freeway west to Alvarado Blvd south, then west on Wilshire Blvd. The Tar Pits are on the right. While we might find a shorter route by poring over the details of Map 1, most of us will feel more comfortable with Map 2.

want to drive to the famous La Brea tar pits, marked *B* on each map. Which map would you find more useful? You will notice that Map 1 (Figure 1–1) has the full details of the Los Angeles road system. Consequently, it requires a major effort to read it. In contrast, Map 2 (Figure 1–2) omits many minor roads so that the freeways and major arteries stand out more clearly.

Most strangers to the city would prefer Map 2. With its guidance they are likely to find the tar pits in a reasonable amount of time, even though a slightly shorter route might have been found by careful calculation and planning using Map 1. Map 2 seems to *abstract* successfully from a lot of confusing details while retaining the essential aspects of the city's geography. Economic theories strive to do the same thing.

Map 3 (Figure 1–3), which shows little more than the major interstate routes that pass through the greater Los Angeles area, illustrates a danger of which all theorists must beware. Armed only with the information provided on this map, you might never find the La Brea tar pits. Instead of a useful idealization of the Los Angeles road network, the map makers have produced a map that is oversimplified for our purpose. Too much has been assumed away. Of course, this map was never intended to be used as a guide to the La Brea tar pits, which brings us to an important point:

There is no such thing as one "right" degree of abstraction for all analytic purposes. The proper degree of abstraction depends on the objective of the analysis. A model that is a gross oversimplification for one purpose may be needlessly complicated for another.

**Figure 1-3** MAP 3

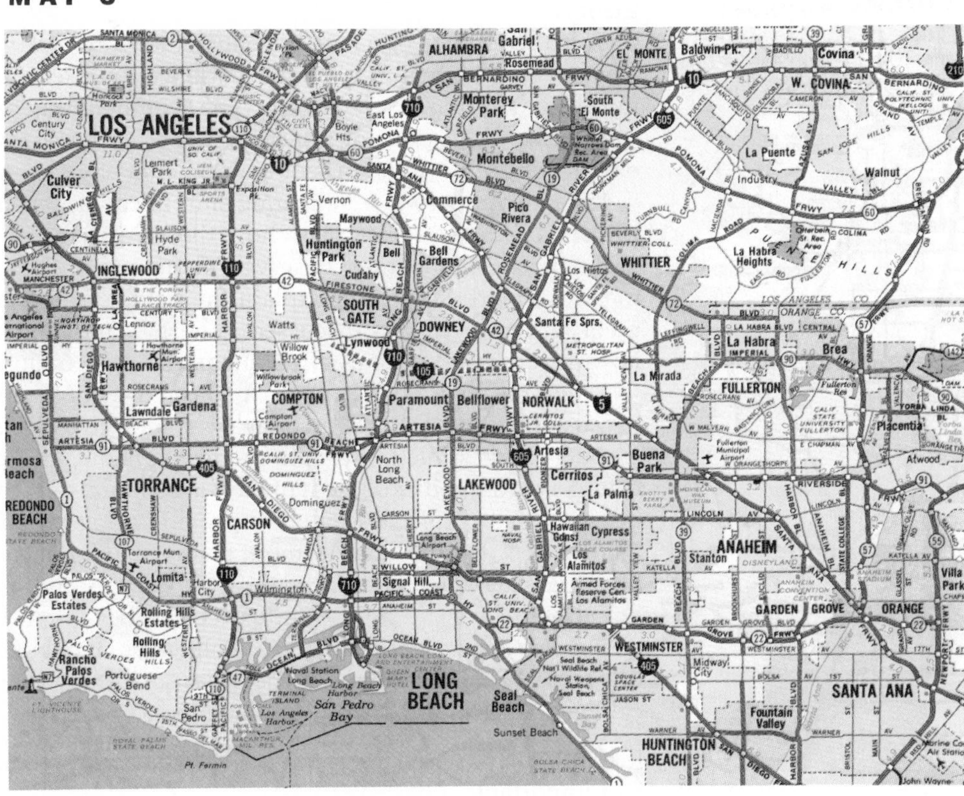


Map 3 strips away still more details of the Los Angeles road system. In fact, only major trunk roads and freeways remain. This map may be useful for passing through the city or getting around it, but it will not help the tourist who wants to see the sights of Los Angeles. For this purpose, too many details are missing.

Economists are constantly treading the thin line between Map 2 and Map 3, between useful generalization about complex issues and gross distortions of the pertinent facts. How can they tell when they have abstracted from reality just enough? There is no objective answer to this question, which is why applied economics is as much art as science. One of the things distinguishing good economics from bad economics is the degree to which analysts are able to find the factors that constitute the equivalent of Map 2 (rather than Maps 1 or 3) for the problem at hand. It is not always easy to do.

For example, suppose you want to learn why different people have different incomes, why some are fabulously rich while others are abjectly poor. People differ in many ways, too many to enumerate, much less to study. The economist must ignore most of these details in order to focus on the important ones. The color of a person's hair or eyes is probably unimportant to the problem at hand, but the color of his or her skin certainly is. Height and weight may not matter, but education probably does. Proceeding in this way, we pare Map 1 down to the manageable dimensions of Map 2. But there is a danger of going too far, stripping away some of the crucial factors, and winding up with Map 3.

## THE ROLE OF ECONOMIC THEORY

A person "can stare stupidly at phenomena; but in the absence of imagination they will not connect themselves together in any rational way." These words of the renowned American philosopher-scientist C.S. Peirce succinctly express the crucial role of theory in scientific inquiry. What, precisely, do we mean by a **theory**?

A **THEORY** is a deliberate simplification of relationships whose purpose is to explain how those relationships work.

To an economist or natural scientist, the word *theory* means something different from what it means in common parlance. In scientific usage, a theory is *not* an untested assertion of alleged fact. The statement that oat bran provides protection from heart disease is not a theory; it is a *hypothesis*, which will prove to be true or false once the right sorts of experiments have been completed.

Instead, a theory is a deliberate simplification (abstraction) of factual relationships that attempts to explain how those relationships work. It is an *explanation* of the mechanism behind observed phenomena. Thus, gravity forms the basis of theories that describe and explain the paths of the planets. Similarly, Keynesian theory (*Macroeconomics* discussed in Parts 2 and 3) seeks to describe and explain how government policies affect the path of the national economy.

Economic theory has acquired an unsavory public image in recent years—partly because of inaccurate predictions by some economists, partly because doctrinal disputes have spilled over into the news media, and partly because some politicians have found it expedient to scoff at economists. This bad image is unfortunate because theorizing is essential to provide a logical structure for organizing and analyzing economic data. Without theory, economists could only "stare stupidly" at the world. With theory, they can attempt to understand it.

People who have never studied economics often draw a false distinction between *theory* and *practical policy*. Politicians and business people, in particular, often reject abstract economic theory as something that is best ignored by "practical" people. The irony of these statements is that:

It is precisely the concern for policy that makes economic theory so necessary and important.

If we could not change the economy through public policy, economics could be a historical and descriptive discipline, asking, for example, what happened in the United States during the Great Depression of the 1930s or how is it that industrial pollution got to be so serious in the twentieth century. But deep concern about public policy forces economists to go beyond historical questions. To analyze policy options, they are forced to deal with possibilities *that have not actually occurred*.

For example, to learn how to prevent depressions, they must investigate whether the Great Depression of the 1930s could have been avoided by more astute government policies. Or to determine what environmental programs will be most effective, they must understand how and why a market economy produces pollution and what might happen if government placed taxes on industrial waste discharges and automobile emissions. As Peirce suggested, not even a lifetime of ogling at real-world data will answer such questions.

Two variables are said to be **CORRELATED** if they tend to go up or down together. But correlation need not imply causation.

Indeed, the facts can sometimes be highly misleading. Data often indicate that two variables move up and down together. But this statistical **correlation** does not prove that either variable *causes* the other. For example, people drive their cars more slowly when it rains, and there are also more traffic accidents. But this correlation does not mean that slow driving causes accidents. Rather, we understand that both phenomena are caused by a common underlying factor—more rain. How do we know this? Not just by looking at the correlation (the degree of similarity) between data on accidents and driving speeds. Data alone tell us little about cause and effect. We must use some simple theory as part of our analysis.

Similarly, most economic issues hinge on some question of cause and effect. So simply observing correlations in data is not enough. Only a combination of theoretical reasoning and data analysis can hope to provide meaningful answers. We must first proceed deductively from assumptions to conclusions and then test the conclusions against data. In that way, we may hope to understand *how*, if at all, different government policies will lead to a lower unemployment rate or *how* a tax on emissions will reduce pollution.

Statistical correlation need not imply causation. Some theory is usually needed to interpret data.

## WHAT IS AN ECONOMIC "MODEL"?

An **ECONOMIC MODEL** is a simplified, small-scale version of some aspect of the economy. Economic models are often expressed in equations, by graphs, or in words.

An **economic model** is a representation of a theory or a part of a theory, often used to gain insight into cause and effect. The notion of a "model" is familiar enough to children; and economists—like other scientists—use the term in much the same way that children do.

A child's model automobile or airplane looks and operates much like the real thing, but it is much smaller and much simpler, and so it is easier to manipulate and understand. Engineers for General Motors and Boeing also build models of cars and planes. While their models are far bigger and much more elaborate than a child's toy, they use them for much the same purposes: to observe the workings of these vehicles "up close," to experiment with them in order to see how they might behave under different circumstances. ("What happens if I do this?") From these experiments, they make educated guesses as to how the real-life version will perform.

Economists use models for similar purposes. A.W. Phillips, the famous engineer-turned-economist who discovered the "Phillips curve" (discussed in Chapter 33), was talented enough to construct a working model of the determination of national income in a simple economy, using colored water flowing through pipes. For years this contraption, depicted in Figure 1–4, has graced the basement of the London School of Economics. However, most economists lack Phillips's manual dexterity, so economic models are generally built with paper and pencil rather than with hammer and nails.

Because many of the models used in this book are depicted in diagrams, we explain the construction and use of various types of graphs in the appendix to this chapter. But sometimes economic models are expressed only in words. The statement "Business firms produce the level of output that maximizes their profits," is the basis for a behavioral model whose consequences are explored in some detail in Parts 2 through 5. Don't be put off by seemingly abstract models. Think of them as useful road maps. And remember how hard it would be to find your way around Los Angeles without one.

## REASONS FOR DISAGREEMENTS: IMPERFECT INFORMATION AND VALUE JUDGMENTS

"If all the earth's economists were laid end to end, they could not reach an agreement," or so the saying goes. Politicians and reporters are fond of pointing out that economists can be found on both sides of many issues of public policy. If economics is a science, why do economists quarrel so much? After all, astronomers do not debate whether the earth revolves around the sun or vice versa.

The question reflects a misunderstanding of the nature of science. Disputes are normal at the frontier of any science. For example, astronomers once did argue,

**Figure 1–4 THE PHILLIPS MACHINE**

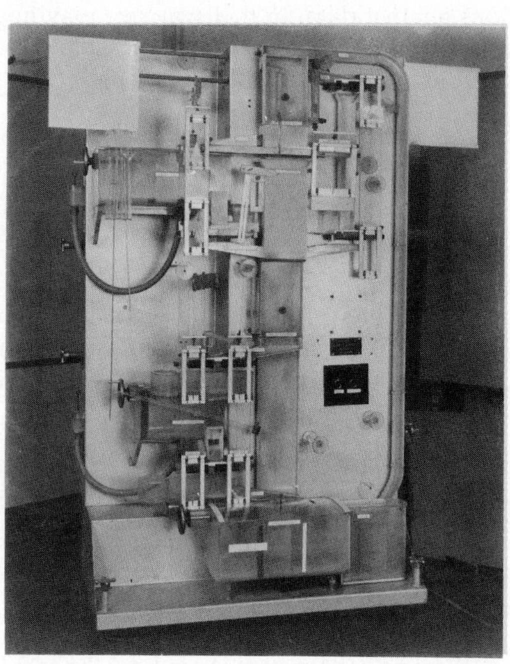

The late Professor A.W. Phillips, while teaching at the London School of Economics in the early 1950s, built this machine to illustrate Keynesian theory. This is the same theory that we will explain with words and diagrams later in the book; but Phillips's background as an engineer enabled him to depict the theory with the help of tubes, valves, and pumps. Because economists are not very good plumbers, few of them try to build models of this sort; most rely on paper and pencil instead. But the two sorts of models fulfill precisely the same role. They simplify reality in order to make it understandable.

and quite vociferously, over whether the earth revolves around the sun. Nowadays, they argue about black holes, gamma-ray bursts, neutrinos, and other esoterica. These arguments go mostly unnoticed by the public because few of us understand what they are talking about. But economics is a *social* science, so its disputes are aired in public. All sorts of people are eager to join economic debates about inflation, pollution, poverty, and the like. Sometimes it seems as if anyone who has ever bought or sold anything fancies himself an amateur economist.

Furthermore, the fact is that economists agree on much more than is commonly supposed. Virtually all economists, regardless of their politics, agree that taxing polluters is one of the best ways to protect the environment (see Chapters 13 and 21), that rent controls can ruin a city (Chapter 4), and that free trade among nations is preferable to the erection of barriers through tariffs and quotas (see Chapter 22). The list could go on and on. It is probably true that the issues about which economists agree *far* exceed the subjects on which they disagree.

Finally, many disputes among economists are not scientific disputes at all. Sometimes the pertinent facts are simply unknown. For example, you will learn in Chapter 21 that the proper tax to levy on industrial wastes depends on quantitative estimates of the harm done by the pollutant. Unfortunately, for most waste products, good estimates are not yet available. This makes it difficult to agree on a concrete policy proposal.

Another important source of disagreements is that economists, like other people, come in all political stripes: conservative, middle-of-the-road, liberal, radical. Each may have different values and a different view of what constitutes the good society. So each may hold a different view of the "right" solution to a public policy problem, even if they agree on the underlying analysis.

For example, we noted early in this chapter that anti-inflation policies are likely to cause recessions. Using tools we will describe in *Macroeconomics* Part 3, many economists believe they can even measure how deep a recession we must endure to reduce inflation by a given amount. Is it worth having 2.6 million more people out of work for a year to cut the inflation rate by 1 percent? An economist cannot answer this any more than a nuclear physicist could have determined whether dropping the atomic bomb on Hiroshima was a good idea. The decision rests on judgments about the moral trade-off between inflation and unemployment, judgments that can be made only by the citizenry through its elected officials.

While economic science can contribute the best theoretical and factual knowledge there is on a particular issue, the final decision on policy questions often rests either on information that is not currently available or on tastes and ethical opinions about which people differ (the things we call "value judgments"), or on both.

Earlier in this chapter, we said that economics cannot provide all the *answers* but can teach you how to ask the right *questions*. Now you know some reasons why. By the time you finish studying this book, you should have a good understanding of when the right course of action turns on disputed facts, when on value judgments, and when on some combination of the two.

## LAST WORD: COMMON SENSE IS NOT ALWAYS RELIABLE

Many people think sound decisions are just a matter of "common sense." If that were so—if untrained but intelligent observers could reach the right economic decisions using only their instincts and intuition—there would be little reason to study economics. Unfortunately, common sense is not always a reliable guide in economics.

True, there are many cases where it is not misleading. Most people undoubtedly realize, for example, that a surge in demand for a product is likely to raise its price, at least for a while. They also understand that increases in the prices of American goods will reduce the quantity we can export to foreign countries.

But many economic relationships are counterintuitive. Try your intuition on this one, for example. You own a widget manufacturing company that rents a warehouse. Your landlord raises your rent by $10,000 per year. Should you raise the price of your widgets to try to recoup some of your higher costs? Or should you lower your price to try to sell more and "spread your overhead?" We shall see in Chapter 6 that both answers are probably wrong!

When intuition fails, common sense will lead to error—sometimes serious error. We have seen, for example, that an interest rate of 8 percent under some circumstances may make borrowing more expensive than a 12 percent interest rate under other circumstances. We have seen that the fact that the costs of public services keep rising faster than inflation may have nothing to do with mismanagement or wrongdoing by government officials but may, instead, be a side effect of technological improvement. We will see later that rent controls on low-rent apartments may make the lives of the poor more miserable, not less.

All these and many more counterintuitive economic relationships will be explained in this book. By the end, you will have a better sense of when common sense works and when it fails. You will be able to recognize common fallacies that are all too often offered as pearls of wisdom by public figures, the press, and television commentators.

## Summary

1. To help you get the most out of your first course in economics, we have devised a list of 12 important ideas that you will want to remember **Beyond the Final Exam**. Here we list them briefly, indicating where each idea occurs in the book.

   (1) Most government policies that reduce inflation are likely to intensify the unemployment problem, and vice versa. (*Macroeconomics* Chapter 16)
   (2) Interest rates that appear very high may actually be very low if they are accompanied by high inflation. (*Macroeconomics* Chapter 6)
   (3) Budget deficits may or may not be advisable, depending on the circumstances. (*Macroeconomics* Chapter 15)
   (4) In a **voluntary exchange**, both parties must expect to benefit. (Chapters 3 and 22)
   (5) Two nations can gain from international trade, even if one is more efficient at making everything. (Chapter 22)
   (6) In the long run, **productivity** is almost the only thing that matters for a nation's material well-being. (*Macroeconomics* Chapter 17)
   (7) Lawmakers who try to repeal the "law" of supply and demand are liable to open a Pandora's box of troubles they never expected. (Chapter 4)
   (8) **Externalities** cause the market mechanism to misfire, but this defect of the market can be remedied by market-oriented policies. (Chapters 13 and 21)
   (9) To make a rational decision, the opportunity cost of an action must be measured, because only this calculation will tell the decision maker what she has given up. (Chapter 3)
   (10) Decision-making often requires the use of **marginal analysis** to isolate the costs and benefits of that particular decision. (Chapter 5)
   (11) The operation of free markets is likely to lead to rising prices for public and private services. (Chapter 13)
   (12) Most policies that equalize income will exact a cost by reducing the nation's output. (Chapter 17)

2. Economics is a broad-ranging discipline that uses a variety of techniques and approaches to address important social questions.
3. Because of the great complexity of human behavior, economists are forced to **abstract** from many details, to make **generalizations** that they know are not quite true, and to organize what knowledge they have according to some theoretical structure.
4. **Correlation** need not imply **causation**.
5. Economists use simplified models to understand the real world and predict its behavior, much as a child uses a **model** railroad to learn how trains work.
6. While these models, if skillfully constructed, can illuminate important economic problems, they rarely can answer the questions that policymakers are confronted with. For this purpose, value judgments are needed, and the economist is no better equipped to make them than is anyone else.
7. Common sense is often an unreliable guide to the right economic decision.

## Key Concepts and Terms

Voluntary exchange
Comparative advantage
Productivity
Externalities
Marginal analysis
Marginal costs
Abstraction and generalization
Theory
Correlation versus causation
Economic model
Opportunity cost

## Questions for Review

1. Think about how you would construct a "model" of how your college is governed. Which officers and administrators would you include and exclude from your model if the objective were

   a. to explain how decisions on financial aid are made?
   b. to explain the quality of the faculty?

   Relate this to the map example in the chapter.
2. Relate the process of "abstraction" to the way you take notes in a lecture. Why do you not try to transcribe every word the lecturer utters? Why do you not just write down the title of the lecture and stop there? How do you decide, roughly speaking, on the correct amount of detail?
3. Explain why a government policymaker cannot afford to ignore economic theory.

# *Appendix* THE GRAPHS USED IN ECONOMIC ANALYSIS[2]

Economic models are frequently analyzed and explained with the help of graphs; and this book is full of graphs. But that is not the only reason for you to study how they work. Most of you will deal with graphs in the future, perhaps frequently. They appear in newspapers. Doctors use graphs to keep track of patients' progress. Governments use them to keep track of the amount of money that they owe to foreign countries. Business firms use them to check their profit and sales performance. Persons concerned with social issues use them to examine trends in ethnic composition of cities and the relation of felonies to family income.

Graphs are invaluable because of the way they facilitate interpretation and analysis of both data and ideas. They enable the eye to take in at a glance important relationships that would be far less apparent from prose descriptions or long lists of numbers. But badly constructed graphs can confuse and mislead.

In this appendix we show, first, how to read a graph that depicts a relationship between two variables. Second, we define the term *slope* and describe how it is measured and interpreted. Third, we explain how the behavior of three variables can be shown on a two-dimensional graph. More detail on graphs of statistical data are provided in the appendix to Chapter 2.

## TWO-VARIABLE DIAGRAMS

Much of the economic analysis to be found in this and other books requires that we keep track of two **variables** simultaneously. For example, in studying the operation of markets, we will want to keep one eye on the *price* of a commodity and the other on the *quantity* that is bought and sold.

For this reason, economists frequently find it useful to display real or imaginary figures in a *two-dimensional graph*, which simultaneously represents the behavior of two economic variables. The numerical value of one variable is measured along the bottom of the graph (called the *horizontal axis*), starting from the **origin** (the point labeled "0"), and the numerical value of the other is measured up the side of the graph (called the *vertical axis*), also starting from the origin.

Figures 1–5(a) and 1–5(b) are typical graphs of economic analysis. They depict an (imaginary) *demand curve*, represented by the blue dots in Figure 1–5(a) and the heavy blue line in Figure 1–5(b). The graphs show the price of natural gas on their vertical axes and the quantity of gas people want to buy at each such price on the horizontal axes. The dots in Figure 1–5(b) are connected by the continuous blue curve labeled DD.

Economic diagrams are generally read as one reads latitudes and longitudes on a map. On the demand curve in Figure 1–5, the point marked *a* represents a hypothetical combination of price and quantity demanded in St. Louis. By drawing a horizontal line leftward from that point to the vertical axis, we learn that the average price for gas in St. Louis is $3 per thousand cubic feet. By dropping a line straight down to the horizontal axis, we find that 80 billion cubic feet are wanted by consumers at this price, just as the statistics in Table 1–1 show. The other points on the graph give similar information. For example, point *b* indicates that if natural gas in St. Louis cost only $2 per thousand cubic feet, quantity demanded would be higher—it would reach 120 billion cubic feet.

Notice that information about price and quantity is *all* we can learn from the diagram. The demand curve will not tell us about the kinds of people who live in St. Louis, the size of their homes, or the condition of their furnaces. It tells us about the price and the quantity demanded at that price; no more, no less. Specifically, it does tell us that when price declines there is an increase in the amount of gas consumers are willing and able to buy.

A diagram abstracts from many details, some of which may be quite interesting, in order to focus on the two variables of primary interest—in this case, the price of natural gas and the amount of gas that is demanded at each price. All the diagrams used in this book share this basic feature. They cannot tell the reader the "whole story" any more than a map's latitude and longitude figures for a particular city can make someone an authority on that city.

---

[2]Students who have a nodding acquaintance with geometry and feel quite comfortable with graphs can safely skip this appendix. See page 25 for appendix definitions.

**Figure 1-5 A DEMAND CURVE FOR NATURAL GAS IN ST. LOUIS**

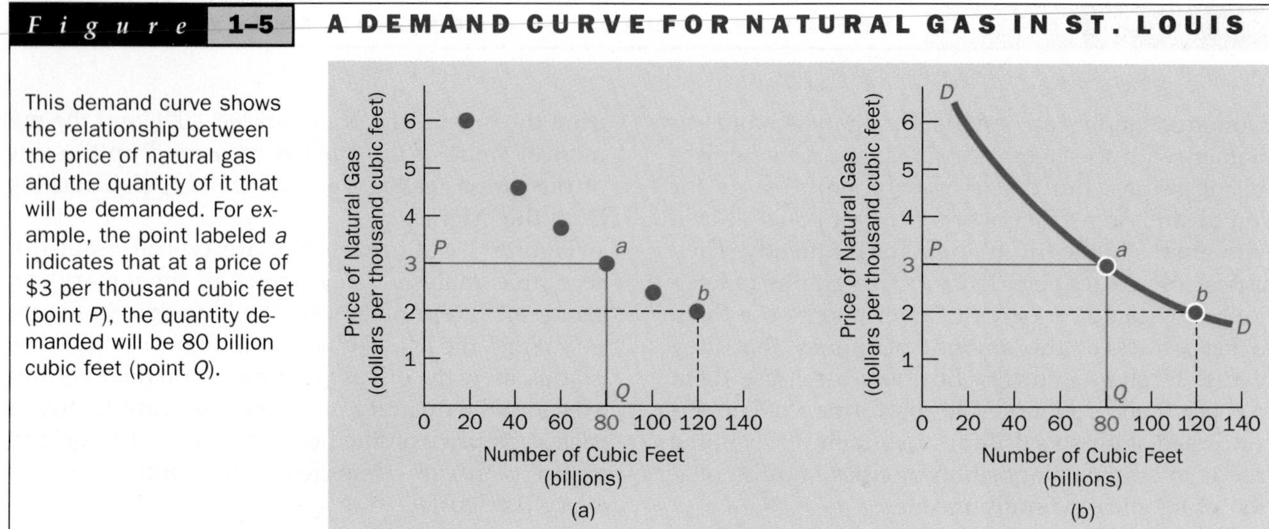


This demand curve shows the relationship between the price of natural gas and the quantity of it that will be demanded. For example, the point labeled *a* indicates that at a price of $3 per thousand cubic feet (point *P*), the quantity demanded will be 80 billion cubic feet (point *Q*).

## THE DEFINITION AND MEASUREMENT OF SLOPE

One of the most important features of the diagrams used by economists is the pace with which the line, or curve, being sketched runs uphill or downhill as we move to the right. The demand curve in Figure 1–5 clearly slopes downhill (the price falls) as we follow it to the right (that is, if more gas is to be demanded). In such instances we say that *the curve has a negative slope, or is negatively sloped, because one variable falls as the other one rises.*

The **slope of a straight line** is the ratio of the vertical change to the corresponding horizontal change as we move to the right along the line, or as it is often said, the ratio of the "rise" over the "run."

The four panels of Figure 1–6 show all the possible slopes for a straight-line relationship between two unnamed variables called *Y* (measured along the vertical axis) and *X* (measured along the horizontal axis). Figure 1–6(a) shows a negative slope, much like our demand curve. Figure 1–6(b) shows a positive slope, because variable *Y* rises (we go uphill) as variable *X* rises (as we move to the right). Figure 1–6(c) shows a *zero* slope, where the value of *Y* is the same irrespective of the value of *X*. Figure 1–6(d) shows an *infinite* slope, meaning that the value of *X* is the same irrespective of the value of *Y*.

Slope is a numerical concept, not just a qualitative one. The two panels of Figure 1–7 show two positively sloped straight lines with different slopes. The line in Figure 1–7(b) is clearly steeper. But by how much? The labels should help you compute the answer. In Figure 1–7(a) a horizontal movement, *AB*, of 10 units (13–3) corresponds to a vertical movement, *BC*, of 1 unit (9 − 8). So the slope is *BC*/*AB* $= \frac{1}{10}$. In Figure 1–7(b), the same horizontal movement of 10 units corresponds to a vertical movement of 3 units (11 − 8). So the slope is $\frac{3}{10}$, which is larger.

By definition, the slope of any particular straight line is the same no matter where on that line we choose to measure it. That is why we can pick any

**Table 1-1 QUANTITIES OF NATURAL GAS DEMANDED AT VARIOUS PRICES**

| | | | | | |
|---|---|---|---|---|---|
| Price ($ per thousand cubic ft.) | $2 | 3 | 4 | 5 | 6 |
| Quantity Demanded (billions of cubic feet) | 120 | 80 | 56 | 38 | 20 |

**Figure 1-6 DIFFERENT TYPES OF SLOPE OF A STRAIGHT-LINE GRAPH**

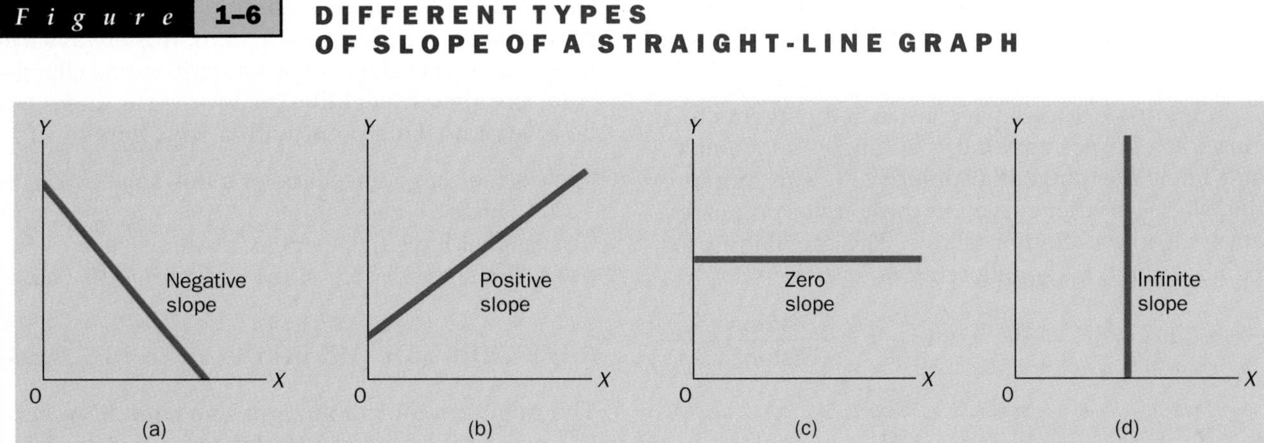


In Figure 1–6(a), the curve goes downward as we read from left to right, so we say it has a negative slope. The slopes in the other figures can be interpreted similarly.

horizontal distance, *AB*, and the corresponding slope triangle, *ABC*, to measure slope. But this is not true of lines that are curved.

Curved lines also have slopes, but the numerical value of the slope is different at every point.

The four panels of Figure 1–8 provide some examples of slopes of curved lines. The curve in Figure 1–8(a) has a negative slope everywhere, while the curve in Figure 1–8(b) has a positive slope everywhere. But these are not the only possibilities. In Figure 1–8(c) we encounter a curve that has a positive slope at first but a negative slope later on. Figure 1–8(d) shows the opposite case: a negative slope followed by a positive slope.

It is possible to measure the slope of a smooth curved line numerically *at any particular point*. This is done by drawing a *straight* line that *touches*, but does not *cut*, the curve at the point in question. Such a line is called a tangent to the curve.

**Figure 1-7 HOW TO MEASURE SLOPE**

Slope indicates how much the graph rises per unit move from left to right. Thus, in Figure 1–7(b), as we go from point *A* to point *B*, we go 13 − 3 = 10 units to the right. But in that interval, the graph rises from the height of point *B* to the height of point *C*; that is, it rises 3 units. Consequently, the slope of the line is *BC*/*AB* = 3/10.

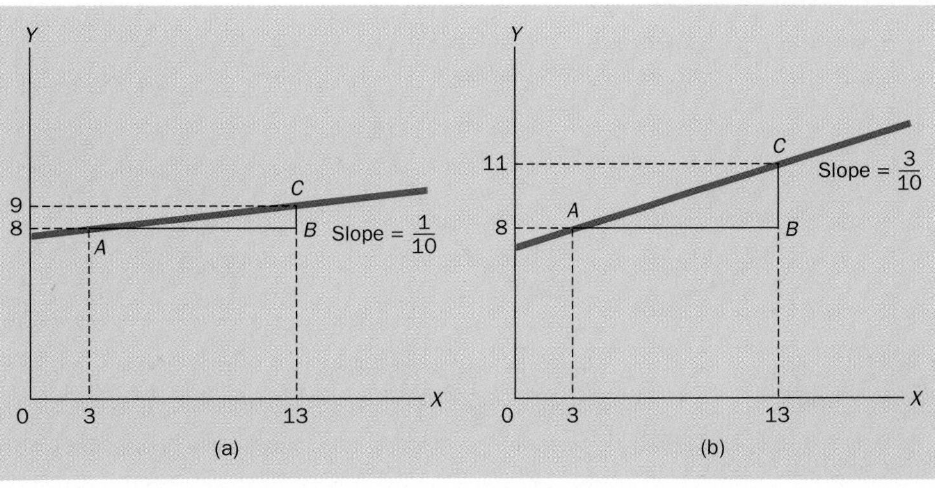

The slope of a curved line at a particular point is the slope of the straight line that is tangent to the curve at that point.

In Figure 1–9 we have constructed tangents to a curve at two points. Line *tt* is tangent at point *C*, and line *TT* is tangent at point *F*. We can measure the slope of the curve at these two points by applying the definition above. The calculation for point *C*, then, is the following:

$$\text{Slope at point } C = \text{Slope of line } tt = \frac{(\text{Distance } BC)}{(\text{Distance } BA)}$$

$$= \frac{(3-6)}{(3-2)} = \frac{(-3)}{(1)} = -3.$$

A similar calculation yields the slope of the curve at point *F*, which, as we can see from Figure 1–9, must be numerically smaller:

$$\text{Slope at Point } F = \text{Slope of line}$$

$$TT = \frac{(1.5-2)}{(8-5)} = \frac{(-0.5)}{(3)} = -0.16.$$

**EXERCISE**

Show that the slope of the curve at point *G* is between −0.16 and −3.

What would happen if we tried to apply this graphical technique to the high point in Figure 1–8(c) or to the low point in Figure 1–8(d)? Take a ruler and try it. The tangents that you construct should be horizontal, meaning that they should have a slope exactly equal to zero. It is always true that where the slope of a smooth curve changes from positive to negative, or vice versa, there will be at least a single point with a zero slope.

Curves that have the shape of a hill, such as Figure 1–8(c), have a zero slope at their *highest* point. Curves that have the shape of a valley, such as Figure 1-8(d), have a zero slope at their *lowest* point.

## RAYS THROUGH THE ORIGIN AND 45° LINES

The point at which a straight line cuts the vertical (*Y*) axis is called the *Y-intercept*. For example, the *Y*-intercept of the line in Figure 1–7(a) is a bit less than 8. Lines whose *Y*-intercept is zero have so many special uses that they have been given a special name, a **ray through the origin**, or a **ray**.

Figure 1–10 contains three rays through the origin, and the slope of each is indicated in the diagram. The ray in the center—whose slope is 1—is particularly useful in many economic applications because it marks off points where *X* and *Y* are equal (as long as *X* and *Y* are measured in the same units). For example, at point *A* we have $X = 3$ and $Y = 3$, at point *B*, $X = 4$ and $Y = 4$, and a similar relation holds at any other point on that ray.

How do we know that this is always true for a ray whose slope is 1? If we start from the origin

Figure 1-8 BEHAVIOR OF SLOPES IN CURVED GRAPHS

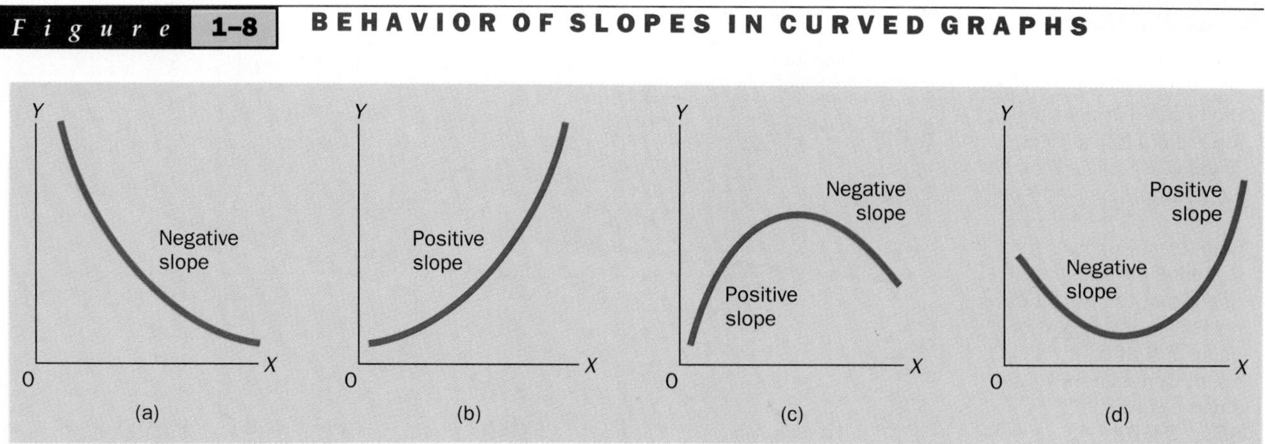


As Figures 1–8(c) and 1–8(d) indicate, where a graph is not a straight line it may have a slope that starts off as positive but that becomes negative farther to the right, or vice versa.

**Figure 1–9**

## HOW TO MEASURE SLOPE AT A POINT ON A CURVED GRAPH

To find the slope at point *F*, draw the line *TT*, which is tangent to the curve at point *F*; then measure the slope of the straight-line tangent *TT*, as in Figure 1–7. The slope of the tangent is the same as the slope of the curve at point *F*.

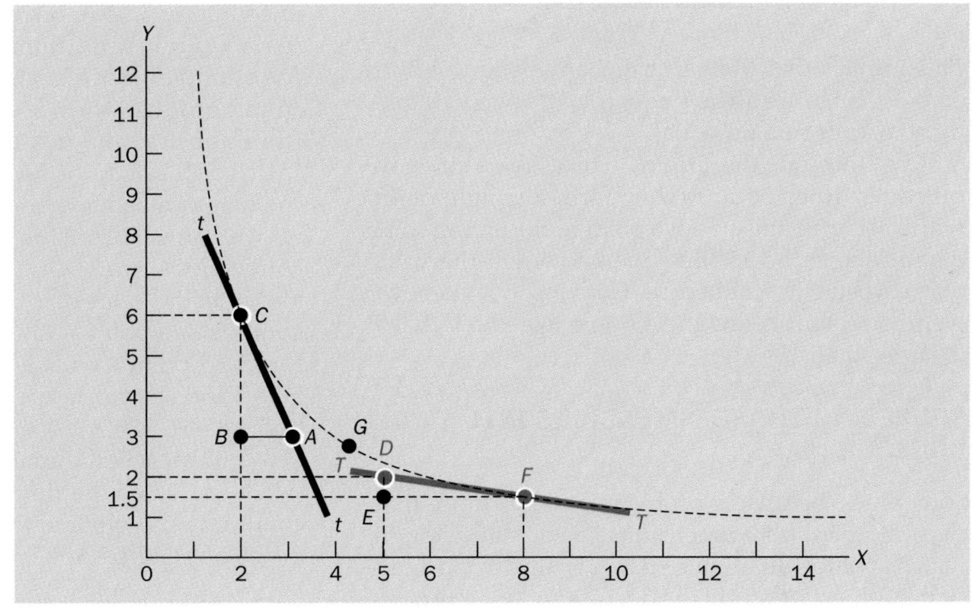


**Figure 1–10**

## RAYS THROUGH THE ORIGIN

Rays are straight lines drawn through the zero point on the graph (*the origin*). Three rays with different slopes are shown. The middle ray, the one with slope = +1, has two properties that make it particularly useful in economics: (1) it makes a 45° angle with either axis, and (2) any point on that ray (for example, point *A*) is exactly equal in distance from the horizontal and vertical axes (length *DA* = length *CA*). So if the items measured on the two axes are in equal units, then at any point on that ray, such as *A*, the number on the *X*-axis (the abscissa) will be the same as the number on the *Y*-axis (the ordinate).

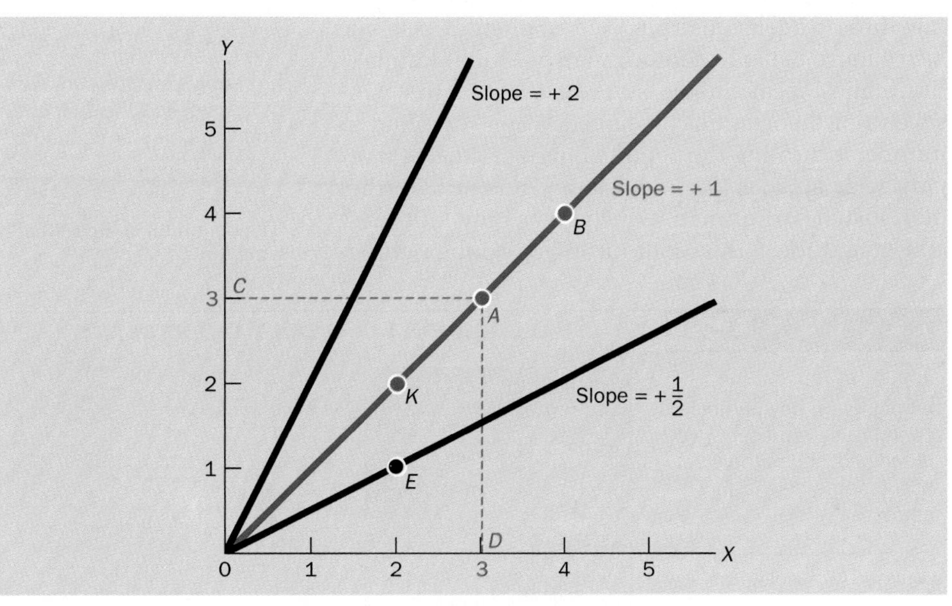

(where both $X$ and $Y$ are zero) and the slope of the ray is 1, we know from the definition of slope that:

$$\text{Slope} = \frac{\text{(Vertical change)}}{\text{(Horizontal change)}} = 1.$$

This implies that the vertical change and the horizontal change are always equal, so the two variables must always remain equal.

Rays through the origin with a slope of 1 are called **45° lines** because they form an angle of 45° with the horizontal axis. If a point representing some data is above the 45° line, we know that the value of $Y$ exceeds the value of $X$. Conversely, whenever we find a point below the 45° line, we know that $X$ is larger than $Y$.

## SQUEEZING THREE DIMENSIONS INTO TWO: CONTOUR MAPS

Sometimes, because a problem involves more than two variables, two dimensions just are not enough, which is unfortunate since paper is only two dimensional. When we study the decision-making process of a business firm, for example, we may want to keep track simultaneously of three variables: how much labor the firm employs, how much raw material it imports from foreign countries, and how much output it creates.

Luckily, there is a well-known device for collapsing three dimensions into two, namely a *contour map*. Figure 1–11 is a contour map of Mount Rainier, the highest peak in the state of Washington. On several of the irregularly shaped "rings" we find a number indicating the height above sea level at that particular spot on the mountain. Thus, unlike the more usual sort of map, which gives only latitudes and longitudes, this contour map exhibits three pieces of information about each point: latitude, longitude, and altitude.

Figure 1–12 looks more like the contour maps encountered in economics. It shows how some third variable, called $Z$ (think of it as a firm's output, for example), varies as we change either variable $X$ (think of it as a firm's employment) or variable $Y$ (think of it as the use of imported raw material). Just like the map of Mount Rainier, any point on the diagram conveys three pieces of data. At point $A$, we can read off the values of $X$ and $Y$ in the conventional way ($X$ is 30 and $Y$ is 40), and we can also note the value of $Z$ by checking to see on which contour line point $A$ falls. (It is on the $Z = 20$ contour.) So point $A$ is able to tell us that 30 hours of labor and 40 yards of cloth produce 20 units of output.

While most of the analyses presented in this book will be based on the simpler two-variable diagrams, contour maps will find their applications, especially in the appendixes to Chapters 6 and 8.

A **VARIABLE** is something, such as price, whose magnitude is measured by a number; it is used to analyze what happens to other things when the size of that number changes (varies).

The lower left-hand corner of a graph where the two axes meet is called the **ORIGIN**. Both variables are equal to zero at the origin.

A straight line emanating from the origin, or zero point on a graph, is called a ray through the origin or, sometimes, just a **RAY**.

A **45° LINE** is a ray through the origin with a slope of +1. It marks off points where the variables measured on each axis have equal values.[3]

[3]The definition assumes that both variables are measured in the same units.

**Figure 1–11** A GEOGRAPHIC CONTOUR MAP

All points on any particular contour line represent geographic locations that are at the same height above sea level.

SOURCE: U.S. Geological Survey.

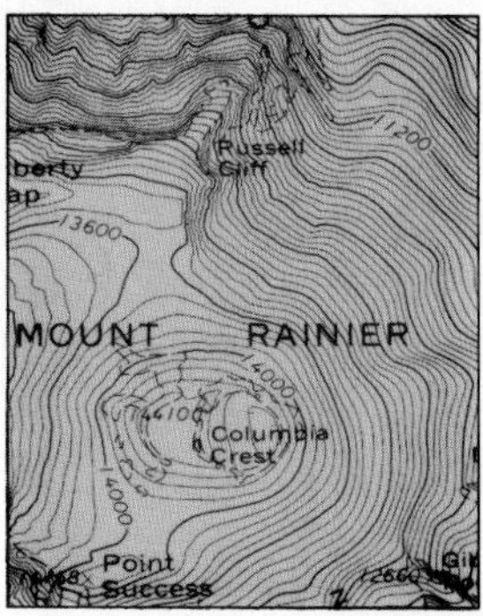

Figure 1–12 **AN ECONOMIC CONTOUR MAP**

In this contour map, all points on a given contour line represent different combinations of labor and raw materials capable of producing a given output. For example, all points on the curve $Z = 20$ represent input combinations that can produce 20 units of output. Point $A$ on that line means that the 20 units of output can be produced using 30 labor hours and 40 yards of cloth. Economists call such maps *production indifference maps.*

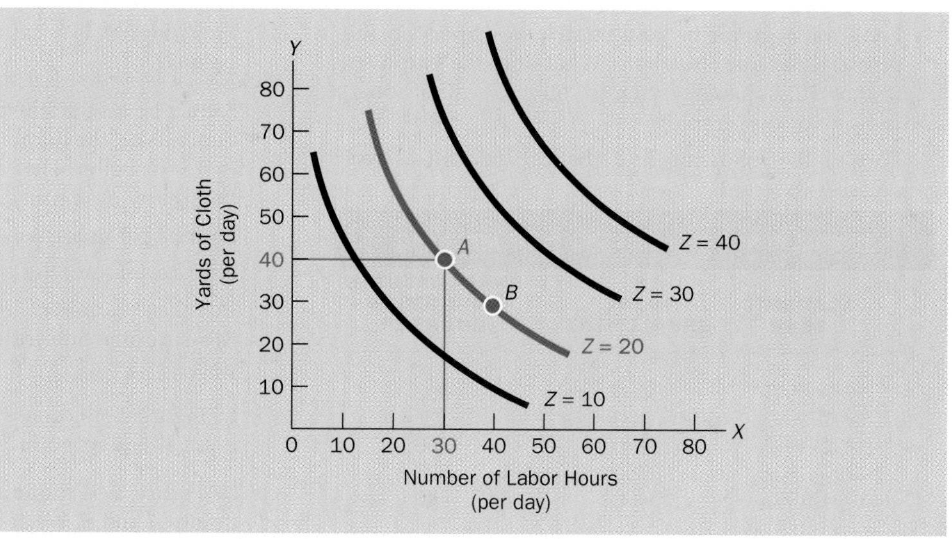


## *Summary*

1. Because graphs are used so often to portray economic models, it is important for students to acquire some understanding of their construction and use. Fortunately, the graphics used in economics are usually not very complex.
2. Most economic models are depicted in **two-variable diagrams**. We read data from these diagrams just as we read the latitude and longitude on a map: each point represents the values of two **variables** at the same time.
3. In some instances, three variables must be shown at once. In these cases, economists use contour maps, which, as the name suggests, show "latitude," "longitude," and "altitude" all at the same time.
4. Often, the most important property of a line or curve drawn on a diagram will be its slope, which is defined as the ratio of the "rise" over the "run," or the vertical change divided by the horizontal change. Curves that go uphill as we move to the right have **positive slopes**, while curves that go downhill have **negative slopes**.
5. By definition, a **straight line** has the same **slope** wherever we choose to measure it. The **slope of a curved line** changes, but the slope at any point on the curve can be calculated by measuring the slope of a straight line **tangent to the curve** at that point.

## *Key Concepts and Terms*

Variable
Two-variable diagram
Horizontal and vertical axes
Origin (of a graph)
Slope of a straight (or curved) line
Negative, positive, zero, and infinite slope
Tangent to a curve
$Y$-intercept
Ray through the origin, or ray
45° line
Contour map

## Questions for Review

1. Look for a graph in your local newspaper, on the financial page or elsewhere. What does the graph try to show? Is someone trying to convince you of something with this graph?
2. Portray the following hypothetical data on a two-variable diagram:

**ENROLLMENT DATA: UNIVERSITY OF NOWHERE**

| ACADEMIC YEAR | TOTAL ENROLLMENT | ENROLLMENT IN ECONOMICS COURSES |
|---|---|---|
| 1990–1991 | 3000 | 300 |
| 1991–1992 | 3100 | 325 |
| 1992–1993 | 3200 | 350 |
| 1993–1994 | 3300 | 375 |
| 1994–1995 | 3400 | 400 |

   Measure the slope of the resulting line, and explain what this number means.
3. From Figure 1–9, calculate the slope of the curve at point *G*.
4. Sam believes that the number of job offers he will get depends on the number of courses in which his grade is B+ or better. He concludes from observation that the following figures are typical:

   | | | | | | |
   |---|---|---|---|---|---|
   | Number of grades of B+ or better | 0 | 1 | 2 | 3 | 4 |
   | Number of job offers | 1 | 3 | 4 | 5 | 6 |

   Put these numbers into a graph like Figure 1–5(a). Measure and interpret the slopes between adjacent dots.
5. In Figure 1–10, determine the values of *X* and *Y* at point *K* and at point *E*. What do you conclude?
6. In Figure 1–12, interpret the economic meaning of points *A* and *B*. What do the two points have in common? What is the difference in their economic interpretation?

Chapter 2

# A PROFILE OF THE U.S. ECONOMY

*E pluribus unum.*

**MOTTO ON U.S. CURRENCY**

This chapter introduces you to the U.S. economy. It might seem that no such introduction is necessary, for you have probably lived your entire life in the United States. Every time you work at a summer or term-time job, pay your college bills, or buy a hot dog, you not only participate in the American economy but observe something factual about it. ¶ But the casual impressions we acquire in our everyday lives, while sometimes correct, are at other times quite misleading. Experience shows that most Americans—not just students—are either unaware of, or harbor grave misconceptions about, some of the most basic facts about our economy. For example, one popular myth holds that America is inundated with imported goods, mostly from Japan. According to another myth, business profits account for something like a third of the price we pay for a typical good or service. Also, "everyone knows" that federal civilian employment has grown rapidly over the last few decades. In fact, none of these things are true. ¶ So, before we begin to construct elaborate theories about how the economy works, it is useful to get a clear—*and accurate*—picture of just what our economy looks like. What *is* the U.S. economy?

## THE AMERICAN ECONOMY: A THUMBNAIL SKETCH

An **ECONOMY** is a collection of markets in a defined geographical area.

A logically prior question is: What is an **economy**? An economy is a collection of markets in a defined geographical area. Usually, that area is a nation-state; so we speak, for example, of the U.S. economy or the Japanese economy. But sometimes the area is considerably smaller—such as the economy of the Northeast, or of New York City. And sometimes the area is bigger than a nation, such as the European Community or the economy of South America.

The markets that comprise an economy generally number in the hundreds or even thousands, and cover a bewildering variety of goods and services. Some of these markets are closely related—such as those for automobiles and tires. But others may be almost totally unrelated—such as the markets for lawyers and breakfast cereals.

### A BIG, RICH COUNTRY

The U.S. economy is the biggest national economy on earth, but for two very different reasons.

First, there are a lot of us. The population of the United States is nearly 260 million—making it, now that the former Soviet Union has split apart, the third most populous nation on earth. That vast total includes children, retirees, full-time students, institutionalized people, and the unemployed, none of whom produce much output. But even the working population of the United States numbers over 120 million. As long as they are reasonably productive, that many people are bound to produce a vast outpouring of goods and services. And they do.

But population is not the main reason why the U.S. economy is the biggest in the world by far. After all, India has about three and a half times the population of the United States but an economy smaller than that of Texas. The second reason why the U.S. economy is so large is that we are a very rich country. Because American workers are among the most productive in the world, our economy produces more than $24,000 worth of goods and services for every living American. If each of the 50 states was a separate country, California would be the eighth largest national economy on earth!

**OUTPUTS** are the goods and services that consumers want to acquire. **INPUTS** or **FACTORS OF PRODUCTION** are the labor, machinery, buildings, and natural resources used to make these outputs.

Understanding why some countries (like the United States) are so rich and others (like India) are so poor is one of the central questions of economics. It is useful to think of an economic system as a *social mechanism*—a machine, if you like—which takes as **inputs** labor and other things we call **factors of production** and transforms them into **outputs**, the things people want to consume. The American economic machine performs this task with extraordinary efficiency, while the Indian machine runs quite inefficiently. Learning why is one of the chief reasons to study economics.

Thus what makes the American economy the center of world attention is our unique combination of prosperity and population. There are other rich countries in the world. At current exchange rates, Germany and Switzerland, among others, have higher per capita outputs than we do.[1] And there are other countries with huge populations, like China and Indonesia. But no nation combines huge popula-

[1]Many economists caution that we should not simply use exchange rates in making international comparisons, but should adjust for the different purchasing power of money within each country. On a purchasing-power basis, German per capita income was estimated to be 21 percent below U.S. per capita income in 1989 (the most recent year available for international comparisons).

Figure 2–1 **POPULATION DENSITIES BY STATE, 1991**

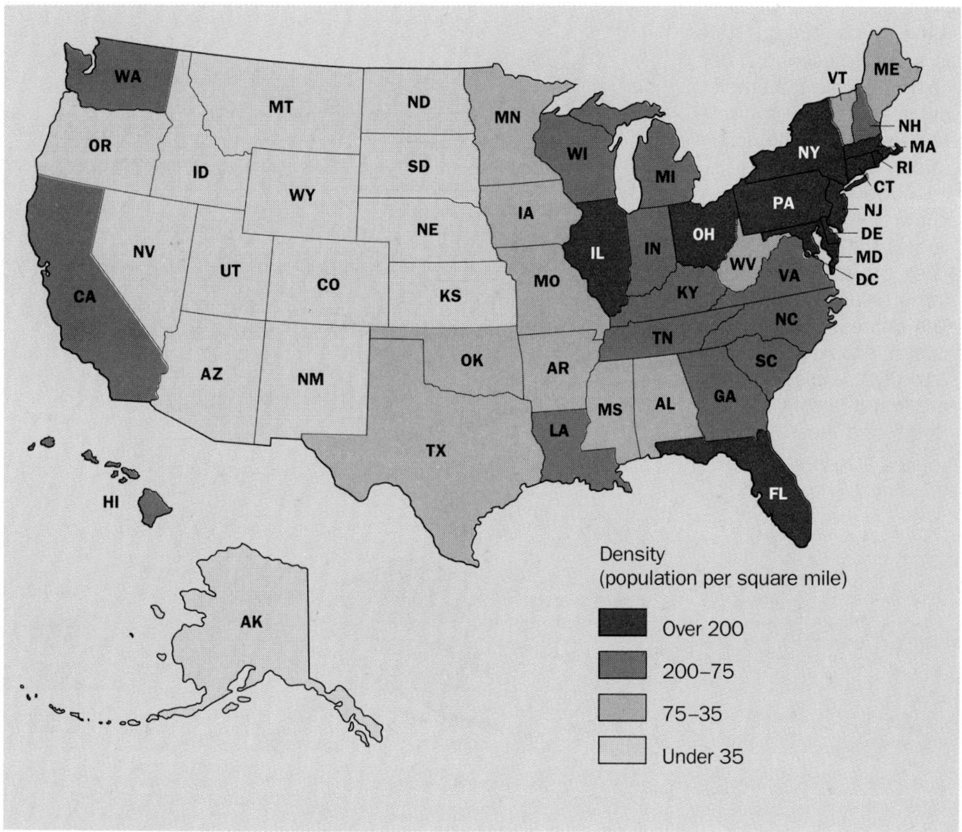


This map divides the states of the United States into four groups according to population density. The most densely populated states (over 200 people per square mile) are displayed in dark blue; they are clearly concentrated in the Northeast. States with intermediate population densities (75–200 people and 35–75 people per square mile, respectively) are shown in medium blue and light blue. They are found all over the nation, but especially in the Midwest and South. The most sparsely populated states, shown in tan, are mainly in the West.

SOURCE: *Statistical Abstract of the United States, 1992.*

tion with high per capita income the way the United States does. Japan, with an economy about 60 percent as large as ours, is the only nation that comes close.

While we are a rich and populous country, the 50 states certainly have not been created equal. Population density varies enormously across the country—from a high of more than 1000 people per square mile in crowded New Jersey to a low of just one person per square mile in Alaska. Figure 2–1 shows where population density is highest and lowest. Income variations are much less pronounced. But, still, average incomes in Mississippi are less than half that of Connecticut. Figure 2–2 shows how per capita income varies among the 50 states.

## A PRIVATE ENTERPRISE ECONOMY

Part of the secret of America's economic success is that free markets and private enterprise have flourished here. America is not unique in these respects. These days more than ever, private enterprise and capitalism are the rule, not the exception, around the globe. But the United States has taken the idea of the free market further than almost any other country.[2] It remains "the land of opportunity."

[2]The tiny city-state of Hong Kong is often held up as an even more extreme example than the United States.

**Figure 2-2 DISPOSABLE INCOME PER CAPITA BY STATE, 1991**

Although the United States is a unified economy, per capita income nonetheless differs substantially from state to state. The richest states (incomes over $17,000 per capita), shown in dark blue, are concentrated in the Northeast, but also include California, Alaska, and Hawaii. The poorest states (per capita incomes under $14,000), indicated in tan, are found mainly in the South and West.

SOURCE: *Statistical Abstract of the United States, 1992.*

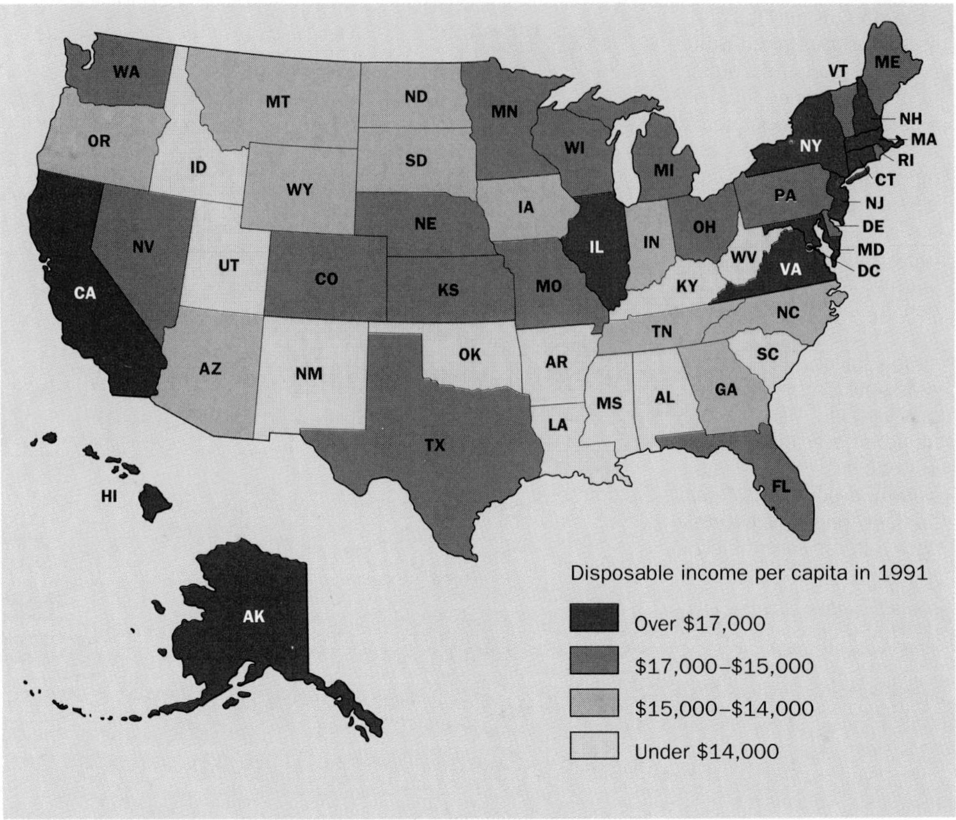


Every country has a mixture of public and private ownership of property. Even in the darkest days of communism, people owned their own personal possessions. In our country, the post office and Tennessee Valley Authority are enterprises of the federal government, and many cities and states own and operate mass transit facilities and sports stadiums. But the United States stands out among the world's nations as among the most "privatized." Hardly any industrial assets are publicly owned in America. Even many city bus companies, and almost all utilities (such as electricity, gas, and telephones), are run as private companies in the United States; in Europe, they are normally government enterprises.

**GROSS DOMESTIC PRODUCT (GDP)** is a measure of the size of an economy. It is, roughly speaking, the money value of all the goods and services produced in a year.

We are also one of the most "marketized" economies on earth. The standard measure of the total output of an economy is called **Gross Domestic Product (or GDP)**, a term which appears frequently in the news. The share of GDP that passes through markets in the United States is enormous. While government purchases of goods and services amount to almost 20 percent of GDP, much of that is purchased from private businesses. Direct government *production* of goods is extremely rare in our society, and government services amount to only about 11 percent of GDP.

## A RELATIVELY "CLOSED" ECONOMY

All nations trade with other nations, and we are no exception. Our annual exports exceed $650 billion and our annual imports exceed $700 billion. That's a lot of money. But America's international trade often gets more attention than it deserves. The fact is that we produce most of what we consume and consume most of what we produce.

Among the most severe misconceptions about the U.S. economy is the myth that this country no longer manufactures anything, but rather imports everything from, say, Japan. In fact, only about 11 percent of America's GDP is imported, and only about a fifth of that comes from Japan. Contrary to a second myth, once we include *services* as well as *goods* in the total, America's exports—at about 10.5 percent of our GDP—are almost (but not quite) as large as our imports.

An economy is called relatively **OPEN** if its exports and imports constitute a large share of its GDP. An economy is considered relatively **CLOSED** if they constitute a small share.

Economists use the terms *open* and *closed* to indicate how important international trade is to a nation. A common measure of "openness" is the average of exports and imports, expressed as a share of GDP. Thus, the Netherlands is considered an extremely **open economy** because it imports and exports about 53 percent of its GDP. (See Table 2–1.) On the other hand, the old Soviet Union was a relatively **closed economy**; it exported and imported merely 7 percent of its production. By this criterion, the United States stands out as among the most closed of the advanced, industrial nations (see Table 2–1). We export and import a smaller share of GDP than most of the countries listed in the table.

Yes, it's a small world and growing smaller. But the United States—with its vast size and geographical isolation—remains relatively insular by world standards, even today. Nonetheless, it is important to realize that this insularity is receding from the peak it attained just after World War II. Exports rose from just 5.5 percent of GDP in 1972 to 9.0 percent in 1982 and 10.7 percent in 1992. We are a great trading nation, and increasingly so.

# A GROWING ECONOMY . . . BUT WITH INFLATION

The next salient fact about the U.S. economy is its growth; it gets bigger almost every year. Gross domestic product in 1992 was $5950 billion, more than ten times as much as in 1962. Figure 2–3 charts the upward march of GDP in the United States since 1950. The rise looks impressive indeed; GDP increased more than

*Table* **2–1** **OPENNESS OF VARIOUS NATIONAL ECONOMIES (average of exports and imports, as share of GDP)**

| | |
|---|---|
| The Netherlands | 53% |
| Germany | 35% |
| Canada | 25% |
| United Kingdom | 24% |
| Mexico | 11% |
| United States | 11% |
| Japan | 9% |
| Soviet Union (1990) | 7% |

SOURCE: IMF, World Bank, and CIA.

Figure 2–3 THE GDP OF THE UNITED STATES SINCE 1950

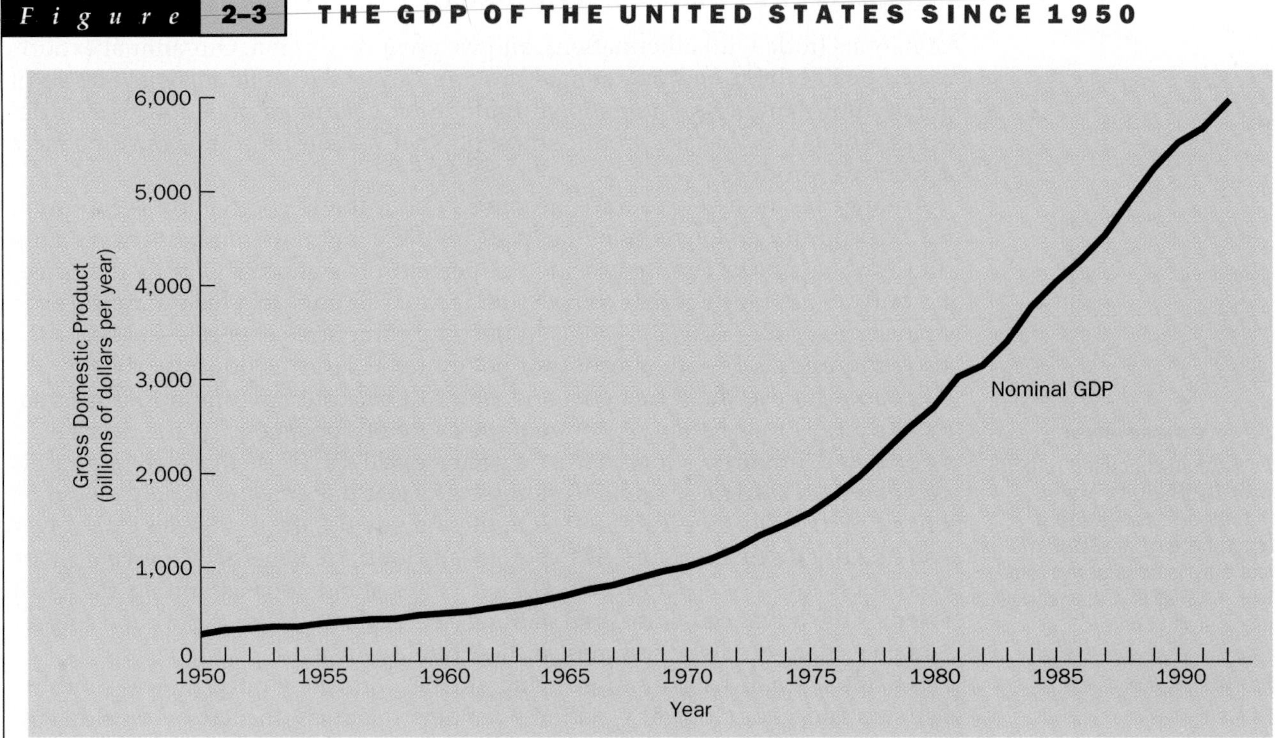


This time-series graph shows that the gross domestic product (GDP) of the United States, measured in dollars, has grown about twenty-fold since 1950.

SOURCE: Department of Commerce.

twenty-fold over the period. But the impression left by the graph is misleading. There is less here than meets the eye, and we need to understand why.

## SOME PERILS IN READING GRAPHS: A DIGRESSION[3]

A **TIME SERIES GRAPH** is a type of two-variable diagram in which time is the variable measured along the horizontal axis. It shows how some variable changed as time passed.

Charts like Figure 2–3, in which time is measured horizontally and some economic variable (in this case GDP) is measured vertically, are used all the time to portray economic data. They are called **time series graphs.** You will find many of them in this book and many more in newspapers and magazines. Quite a number of you will wind up reading time series charts routinely in your work after college. So it is vital to understand what they do and do not show.

By summarizing an immense amount of data in compact form, time series graphs can be invaluable—offering an instant visual grasp of the course of events. However, if misused, such graphs are very dangerous. They can easily mislead persons who are not experienced in dealing with them. Perhaps even more dangerous are the lies perpetrated accidentally and unintentionally by people who draw graphs without sufficient care and who may innocently mislead themselves as well as others. Consider Figure 2–3 as an example.

[3]Some further problems, beyond those discussed in the text, are dealt with in an appendix to this chapter.

**INFLATION** refers to a sustained increase in the average level of prices.

**REAL GDP** is the value of all the goods and services produced by an economy in a year, evaluated in dollars of constant purchasing power. Hence, inflation does not raise real GDP.

Most of the spectacular growth in GDP over this 42-year period was a reflection of two rather mundane facts. First, the price of almost everything rose between 1950 and 1992 because of **inflation**; in fact, average prices in 1992 were about six times higher than in 1950. Since each dollar in 1992 bought only about one-sixth of what it did in 1950, the dollar makes a rather poor measuring rod for comparing *production* in the two years. Most of the "growth" of GDP depicted in Figure 2–3 reflects inflation, not increases in output.

Economists correct for inflation by a process called *deflating by a price index,* which is explained fully in the appendix to Chapter 6 of *Macroeconomics*. Proper deflation leads to the blue line in Figure 2–4, which shows the growth of GDP *in dollars of constant purchasing power*. Economists call this **real GDP**. By this truer measure, we find that output in 1992 was about 3.4 times as high as in 1950, not twenty times as high.

Second, there were many more Americans alive in 1992 than in 1950—69 percent more to be exact. So output *per person* rose by considerably less than even the blue line in Figure 2–4 indicates. The brown line corrects for *both* inflation *and* population growth by charting the time series behavior of GDP *per capita* in dollars of constant purchasing power. Americans were indeed richer in 1992 than

*Figure* **2–4** **NOMINAL GDP, REAL GDP, AND REAL GDP PER CAPITA**

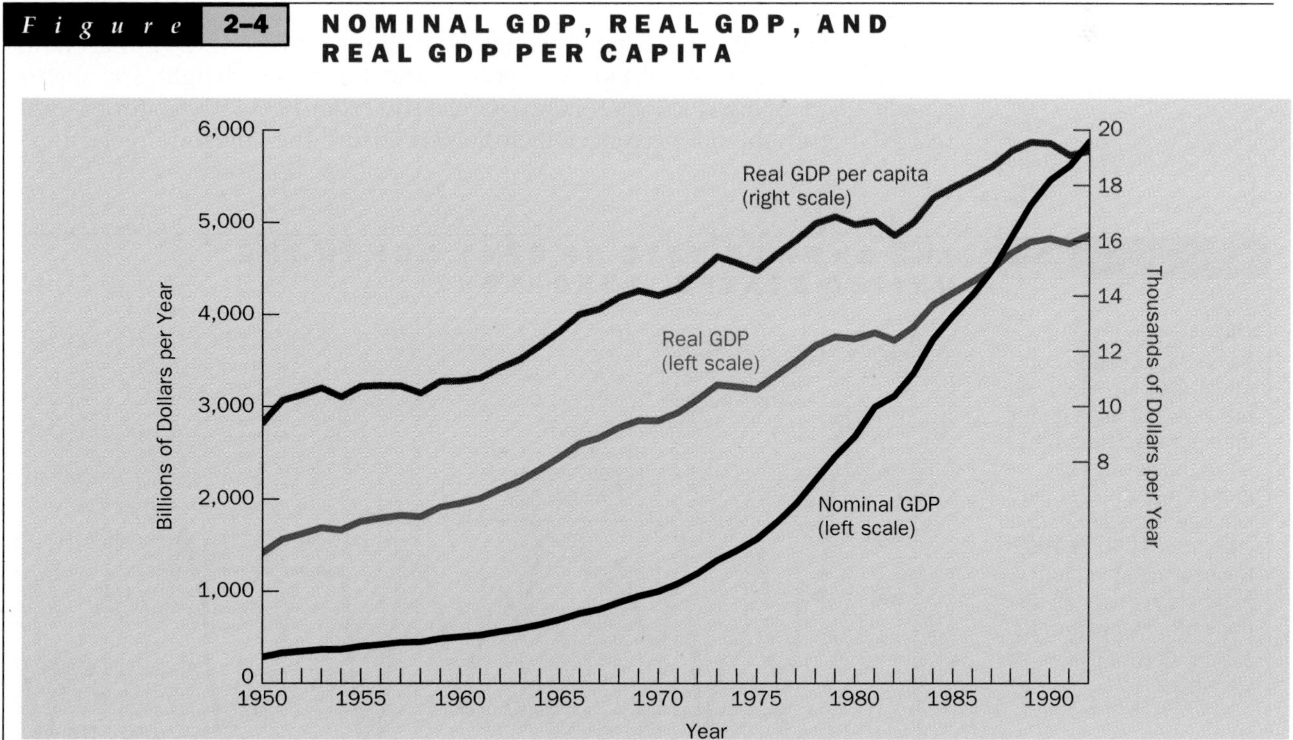


The blue line shows that real GDP, that is GDP measured in dollars of constant purchasing power, has grown much less than GDP in current dollars (black line). Thus most of the "growth" indicated by Figure 2–3 was just inflation. The brown line takes the next step and corrects for the fact that America was a much bigger place—in terms of population—in 1992 than in 1950. It therefore gives a more accurate picture of the increase in standards of living.

SOURCE: Department of Commerce.

in 1950, but not by nearly as much as a naive look at Figure 2–3 suggested. In fact, the American standard of living roughly doubled over this period, rather than rising twenty-fold. How misleading it can be simply to "look at the facts!" There is a general lesson to be learned from this example:

The facts, as portrayed in a time series graph, most assuredly do not "speak for themselves." Because almost everything grows in a growing economy, one must use judgment in interpreting growth trends. Depending on what kind of data are being analyzed, and for what purpose, it may be essential to correct for population growth, for rising prices, or for other distorting or misleading influences.

## BUMPS ALONG THE GROWTH PATH: RECESSIONS

The bird's-eye view offered by Figure 2–4 conceals one more important fact: When you inspect the data more closely, America's economic growth has been quite irregular. We experience alternating periods of good and bad times which are called *economic fluctuations* or sometimes just *business cycles*. In some years—eight since 1950, to be exact—GDP actually declines. Such periods of *declining* economic activity are called **recessions**.

A **RECESSION** is a period of time during which the total output of the economy falls.

The bumps along the American economy's historic growth path are visible in Figure 2–4 but stand out more clearly in Figure 2–5, which displays the same data in a different way. Here we plot not the *level* of real GDP each year, but rather its *growth rate*—the percent change from one year to the next. Now economic life looks anything but placid. The booms and busts that delight and distress people—and swing elections—stand out clearly. From 1983 to 1984, for example, real GDP grew by 6.2 percent, which helped ensure the landslide reelection of

**Figure 2–5**

**THE GROWTH RATE OF REAL GDP IN THE UNITED STATES, 1950–1992**

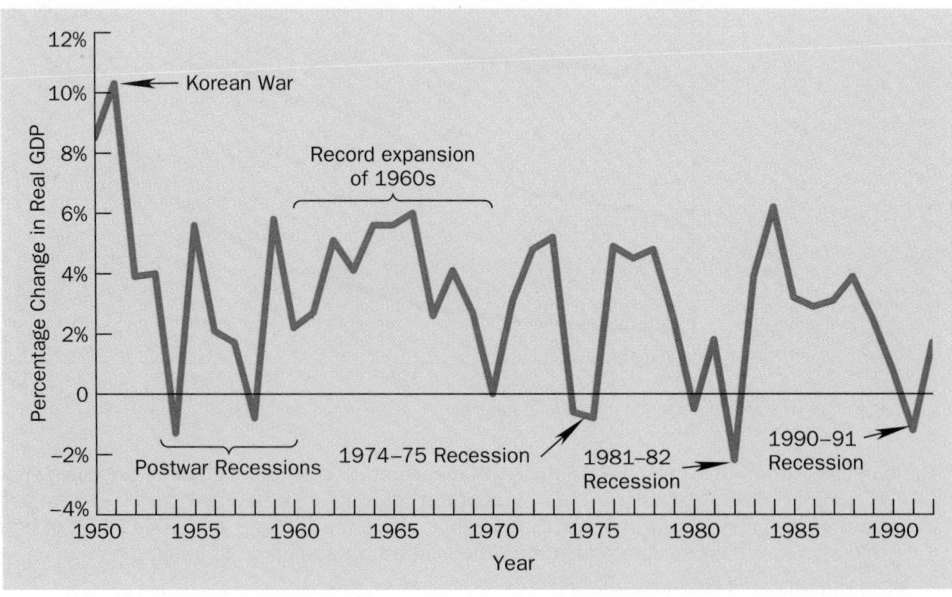


This diagram takes the same data used to construct the blue line in Figure 2–4, but uses it in a different way. Here we show the year-to-year growth rate (that is, percentage increase) in real GDP from 1950 to 1992. Recessions stand out more clearly here as periods of *negative* growth.

SOURCE: Department of Commerce.

Figure 2-6 **THE UNEMPLOYMENT RATE IN THE UNITED STATES, 1929–1992**

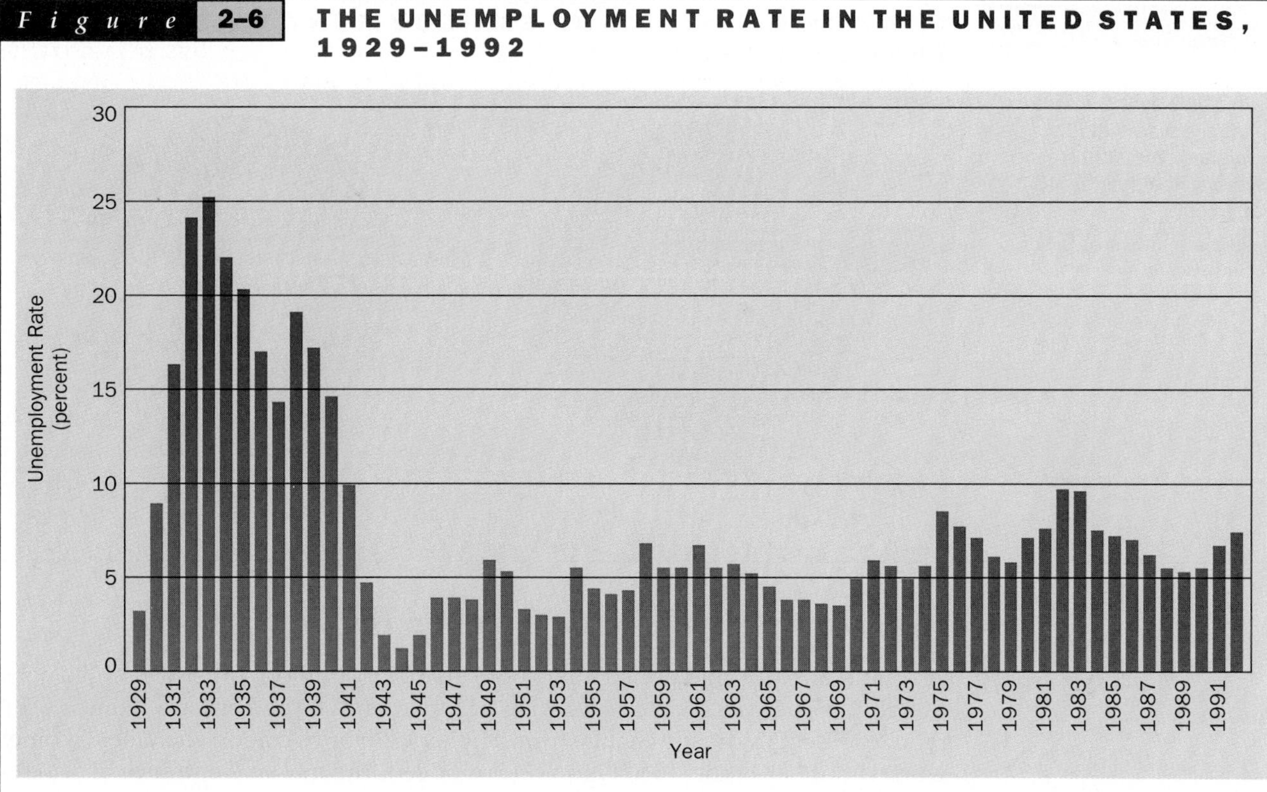


This time series chart shows the ups and downs of the U.S. civilian unemployment rate, annually since 1929. The Great Depression and World War II stand out as most unusual events.

SOURCE: Bureau of Labor Statistics.

Ronald Reagan. But from 1990 to 1991, real GDP actually fell by 1.2 percent, which helped Bill Clinton defeat George Bush.

One important consequence of these ups and downs in economic growth is that *unemployment* varies considerably from one year to the next. (See Figure 2–6.) During the Great Depression of the 1930s, unemployment ran as high as 25 percent of the work force. But it fell to barely over 1 percent during World War II. Just within the last few years, the national unemployment rate has been as low as 5.2 percent (in June 1990) and as high as 7.8 percent (in June 1992). In human terms, that 2.6 percentage point difference meant about 3.5 million *more* jobless workers. Understanding why joblessness varies so dramatically, and what we can do about it, is another major reason for studying economics.

## THE INPUTS: LABOR AND CAPITAL

Let us now return to the analogy of an economy as a machine turning inputs into outputs. The most important input is human labor: the men and women who run the machines, work behind the desks, and serve you in the stores.

*Figure* **2–7** **THE COMPOSITION OF EMPLOYMENT BY SEX, 1950 AND 1992**

In 1950, just 29 percent of jobs were held by women. By 1992, this share had risen to 45 percent.

SOURCE: Bureau of Labor Statistics.

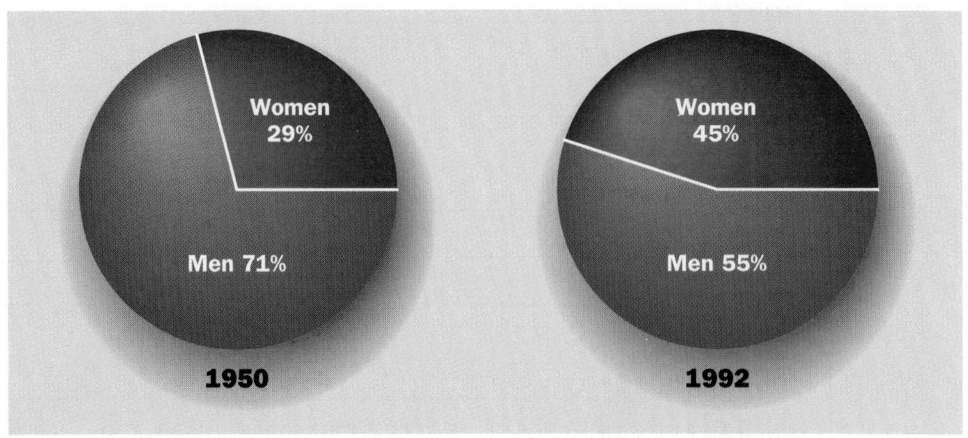


## THE AMERICAN WORKFORCE: WHO IS IT?

We have already mentioned that more than 120 million Americans hold jobs. Roughly 55 percent of these workers are men and 45 percent are women. This ratio represents a drastic change from a generation or two ago, when most women worked only at home. (See Figure 2–7.) Indeed, the massive entrance of women into the paid labor force has been one of the major social transformations of American life during the second half of the twentieth century. In 1950, just 29 percent of women worked in the marketplace; now more than 45 percent do. In truth, we are probably still adapting to this change. The expanding role of women in the labor market has raised many controversial questions—such as whether they are discriminated against (the evidence suggests that they are), whether employers should be compelled to provide maternity leave, and so on.

In contrast to women, teenagers represent a dwindling share of the American workforce. (See Figure 2–8.) Young men and women aged 16–19 accounted for 8.6 percent of employment in 1974 but only 4.6 percent in 1992. As the baby boom gave way to the baby bust, people under 20 became scarce resources! Still, about 6 million teenagers hold jobs in the U.S. economy today. Most of them are in low-wage jobs like working in fast-food restaurants, amusement parks, and the like. Relatively few teenagers can be found in the nation's factories.

## THE AMERICAN WORKFORCE: WHAT IT DOES

What do these 120 million people do? The only real answer is: Almost anything you can imagine. In 1991, America had 772,000 lawyers, 481,000 bank tellers, 685,000 private security guards, and 77,000 professional athletes. Figures 2–9 and 2–10 look at the data somewhat more systematically.

Figure 2–9 shows the breakdown by sector. It holds some surprises for most people. The majority of American workers—like workers in all advanced nations—are engaged in producing services, not goods. In 1992, about 85 million people were employed by service industries, including 25 million in retail and wholesale trade, while only 23.5 million produced goods. The popular image of the typical American worker as a factory hand—Homer Simpson, if you will—

Figure 2–8

## TEENAGE EMPLOYMENT AS A SHARE OF TOTAL EMPLOYMENT, 1960–1992

The share of teenagers (ages 16–19) in total employment rose from 1960 to a peak in 1974. Since then, it has generally been falling.

SOURCE: *Economic Report of the President, 1993.*

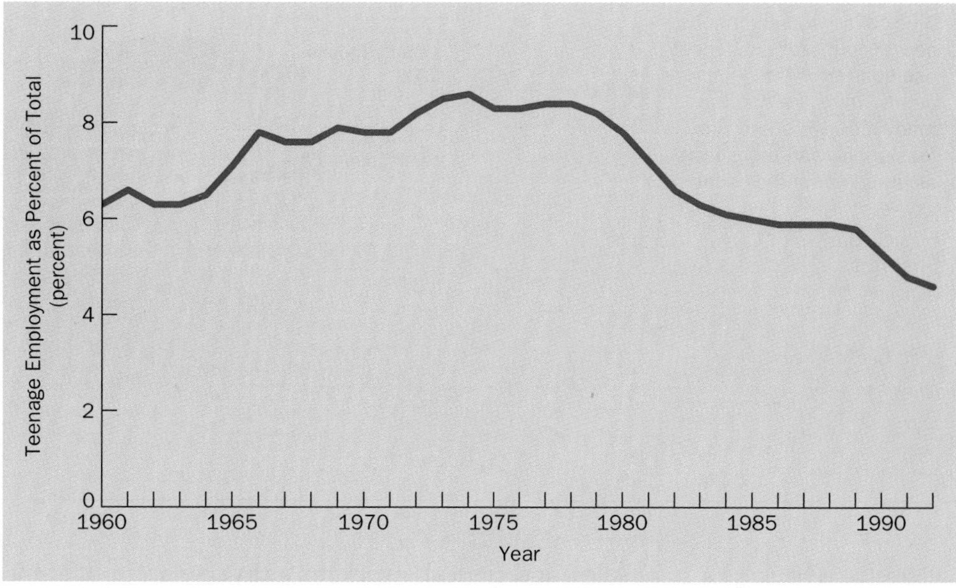


is really quite misleading. Manufacturing companies employ only about 18 million people, and more than a third of them work in offices rather than in the factory. Governments at all levels employ about 21.5 million people. Contrary to another popular misconception, few of these civil servants work for the *federal* government. Federal *civilian* employment is just under 3 million—and has barely grown in two decades. Finally, about 3.2 million Americans work on farms, and the armed forces employ about 1.5 million soldiers.

Most Americans engage in *physical* labor only incidentally. Figure 2–10 breaks down the workforce by occupation. We see that the biggest category is "technical,

Figure 2–9

## CIVILIAN EMPLOYMENT BY SECTOR, 1992

More Americans produce services than goods. In fact, all levels of government now employ more workers than the manufacturing sector, and almost as many as the entire goods-producing sector.

SOURCE: Bureau of Labor Statistics.

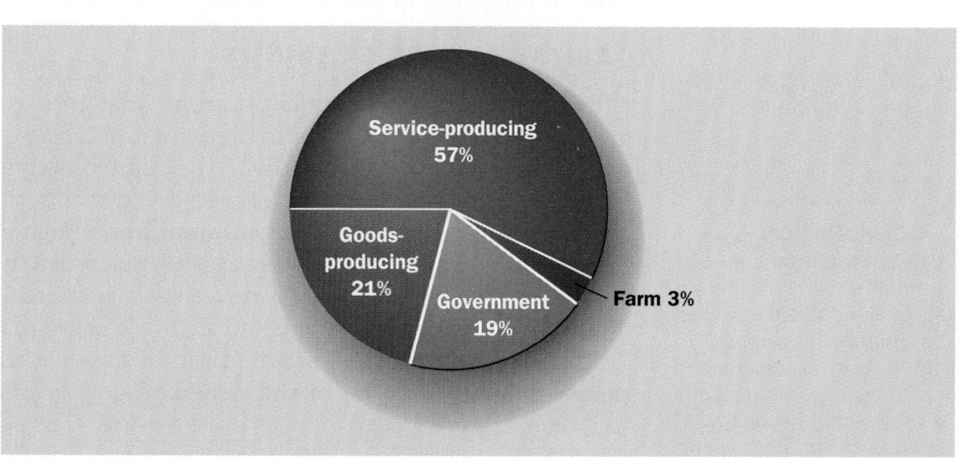

Figure 2-10 **THE OCCUPATIONAL BREAKDOWN OF THE WORKFORCE**

Blue-collar production jobs now account for only about one-quarter of U.S. employment. There are about as many managers and professionals, and more technical, sales, and clerical workers.

SOURCE: Bureau of Labor Statistics.

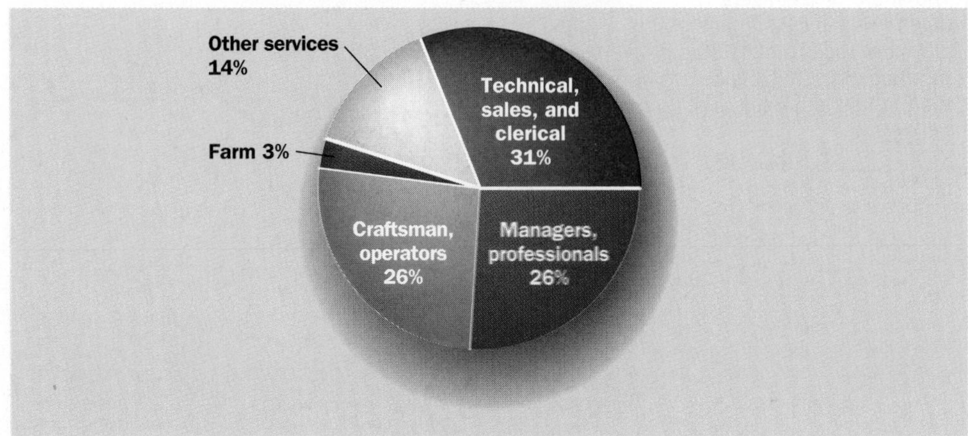


sales, and clerical" workers, a diverse group that includes, among other occupations, secretaries and sales people. About 26 percent of Americans are managers or professionals—a category that includes doctors, lawyers, and college professors. Other service workers comprise another 14 percent, leaving just 26 percent in the traditional blue-collar occupations: craftsmen and operators.

## THE AMERICAN WORKFORCE: WHAT IT EARNS

All together, these workers earn almost three-quarters of the income generated by the production process. That figures up to an average hourly wage of about $11—plus fringe benefits like health insurance and pensions, which can add an additional 30–40 percent for people holding what are often called "good jobs." Since the average work week is about 35 hours long, a typical weekly pay check is about $385 before taxes. That is hardly a princely sum, and most college graduates can expect to earn more.[4] But that is what wage rates are like in a rich country. Wages in Japan and throughout northern Europe are similar.

## CAPITAL AND ITS EARNINGS

After deducting the tiny sliver of income that goes to land and natural resources, most of the remainder accrues to the owners of *capital*—the machines and buildings that make up the nation's industrial plant. Sometimes the ownership of capital is obvious: Edna's Sub Shop is owned by Edna. But the great majority of business assets are owned *indirectly*, via **corporations**. When Phil Ballard buys 100 shares of AT&T stock for $4300, he becomes the owner of a tiny fraction of the company's vast assets. Phil probably will never see the switching systems and fiber optic lines that he "owns," but he is entitled to a share of the company's profits.

A **CORPORATION** is a firm that has the legal status of a fictional individual. This fictional individual is owned by a number of persons, called its stockholders, and is run by a set of elected officers (usually headed by a president) and a board of directors.

The total market value of American business assets—a tough number to estimate—is believed to be in the neighborhood of $11 trillion. Since that capital

[4]These days, college graduates typically earn about 70 percent more than those with only a high school diploma.

## *Public Opinion on Profits*

Most Americans think corporate profits are much higher than they actually are. A recent public opinion poll, for example, found that the average citizen thought that corporate profits *after tax* amounted to 32 percent of sales for the typical manufacturing company. The actual profit rate at the time was closer to 4 percent! Interestingly, when a previous poll asked how much profit was "reasonable," the response was 26 cents on every dollar of sales—over six times as large as profits actually were.

SOURCE: "Public Attitudes Toward Corporate Profits," Opinion Research Corporation, *Public Opinion Index*, Princeton, N.J., June 1986.

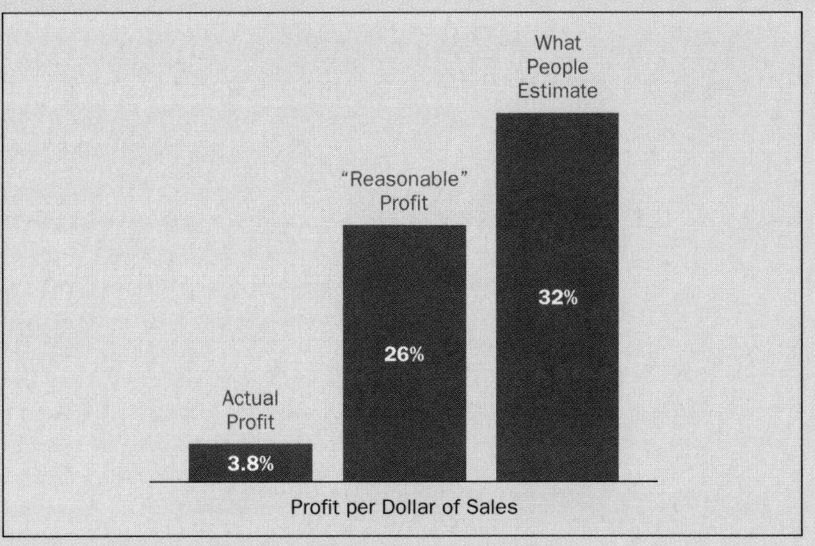


earns an average rate of return of about 10 percent before taxes, the total earnings of capital come to about $1100 billion. Of this, profits are less than half; the rest is mainly interest.

Public opinion polls routinely show that Americans have a distorted view of the level of business profits in our society. The man and woman in the street believes that profits account for 30 percent or so of the price of a typical product. In fact, when you spend a dollar in our economy, about 66 cents is for labor costs, 11 cents goes to cover the wear and tear on the capital stock,[5] 13 cents is for taxes, and 4 cents is for interest. That leaves about 6 cents for after-tax profits.

## THE OUTPUTS: WHAT DOES AMERICA PRODUCE?

What does all this labor and capital produce? Consumer spending accounts for more than two-thirds of GDP. And what an amazing variety of goods and services that is! American households spend roughly 45 percent of their budgets on goods—ranging from $112 billion per year on new cars to $50 billion on tobacco products. Expenditures on services absorb the other 55 percent of household budgets, of which housing commands the largest share. But Americans also spend $61 billion annually on their telephone bills, $29 billion on air tickets, and $36 billion on dentists.

[5]Economists and accountants call this *depreciation*. It is a well-known cost of doing business.

This leaves roughly a third of GDP for all nonconsumption uses. The government buys almost 20 percent: such things as airplanes, guns, and the services of soldiers, teachers, and bureaucrats. The rest is mainly business purchases of machinery and industrial structures (about 10 percent of GDP) and household purchases of new houses (about 4 percent).

## THE CENTRAL ROLE OF BUSINESS FIRMS

Calvin Coolidge once said that "the business of America is business." He was largely right. When we peer inside the economic machine that turns inputs into outputs, we see mainly private companies—literally millions of them. We mentioned earlier that the United States has about 260 million people and 120 million workers. Astonishingly, it also has about 19 million business firms—about one for every 14 people!

The owners and managers of these businesses hire people, acquire or rent capital goods, and arrange for the production of the things people want to buy. Sound simple? It isn't. About 50,000–60,000 businesses fail every year. A few succeed spectacularly. Some do both. Wang Laboratories, an early entrant into the calculator and word processing business, was founded by a brilliant Chinese immigrant in the 1950s and grew to have annual sales of $3 billion and 30,000 employees by 1984. Eight years later, it was bankrupt. Fortunately for the U.S. economy, however, the lure of riches induces hundreds of thousands of people to start new businesses every year—against the odds.

A **PROPRIETORSHIP** is a business firm owned by a single person.

Most business firms are very small. If we simply count firms, the greatest number are what are called **sole proprietorships**—businesses owned by a single individual or family. There are more than 14 million of them in the United States, including most farms and small retail establishments. (Sometimes called "Mom and Pop" stores.) But the average annual sales of a proprietorship is about $50,000—less than the salary of most college professors! Altogether, these 14 million companies account for just 6 percent of total business sales.

A **PARTNERSHIP** is a firm whose ownership is shared by a fixed number of partners.

There are also about 1.7 million **partnerships** in America. Most of them are also very small; the average partnership has under $300,000 in annual revenue. But a few, such as the nation's biggest law and accounting firms, are enormous. The giant law firm of Baker & McKenzie has annual revenues of about $500 million.

Finally, of course, we have the nation's *corporations*—about 4 million of them. Many of these companies are also small; about three-quarters have annual sales under $1 million. But all of America's largest companies—including such household names as Exxon, IBM, General Motors, Proctor & Gamble, and Merck—are corporations. Corporations account for about 90 percent of America's output.

A number of these giant firms do business all over the world, just as foreign-based *multinational corporations* do business here. Indeed, some people claim that it is now impossible to determine the true "nationality" of a multinational corporation—which may have factories in ten or more countries, sell its wares all over the world, and have stockholders in dozens of nations. (See the accompanying boxed insert.) Most of General Motors' profits are generated abroad, for example. And the Honda you drive was probably made in Ohio.

Firms compete with other companies in their *industry*. Many economists believe that this *competition* is the key to industrial efficiency. The sole supplier of a commodity will find it easy to make money, and may therefore fail to innovate or control costs. Its management is liable to become relaxed and sloppy. But a

## Is That an American Company?

Robert Reich, who is currently serving as Secretary of Labor to President Clinton, has argued that it is almost impossible to define the nationality of a multinational company these days. While many scholars think Reich exaggerates the point, no one doubts that he has one. Here are some examples:

What's the difference between an "American" corporation that makes or buys abroad much of what it sells around the world and a "foreign" corporation that makes or buys in the United States much of what it sells? . . . The mind struggles to keep the players straight. In 1990, Canada's Northern Telecom was selling to its American customers telecommunications equipment made by Japan's NTT at NTT's factory in North Carolina.

If you found that one too easy, try this: Beginning in 1991, Japan's Mazda would be producing Ford Probes at Mazda's plant in Flat Rock, Michigan. Some of these cars would be exported to Japan and sold there under Ford's trademark. A Mazda-designed compact utility vehicle would be built at a Ford plant in Louisville, Kentucky, and then sold at Mazda dealerships in the United States. Nissan, meanwhile, was designing a new light truck at its San Diego, California, design center. The trucks would be assembled at Ford's Ohio truck plant, using panel parts fabricated by Nissan at its Tennessee factory, and then marketed by both Ford and Nissan in the United States and in Japan. Who is Ford? Nissan? Mazda? . . .

SOURCE: Robert B. Reich, *The Work of Nations* (New York: Knopf), 1991, pages 131, 124.

company besieged by dozens of competitors eager for its business must keep alert at all times. The rewards for success in business can be magnificent. But the punishment for failure is severe.

The **CONCENTRATION RATIO** is the percentage of an industry's output produced by its *four* largest firms. It is intended to measure the degree to which the industry is dominated by a few large firms.

American industries differ substantially in how competitive they are. One commonly used measure is the four-firm **concentration ratio**, that is, the fraction of an industry's output produced by its four largest firms. Table 2–2 shows this figure for a selection of American industries. The range is enormous. At one extreme, four firms control 90 percent of the market for manufacturing new cars; at the other extreme, the four largest firms account for barely 1 percent of the retail sales of those cars.

Many economists, however, feel that the concentration ratio is a misleading indicator of competitiveness in a *global* economy. General Motors, Ford, and Chrysler together may produce virtually all the cars that carry American nameplates. But the managements of these companies know very well that they face ferocious competition from Toyota, Honda, and Volkswagen, to name just a few. As long as a national economy is *open to trade*, its goods-producing industries are bound to be highly competitive.[6]

[6]International competition in services is more difficult. A Russian barber would gladly cut your hair for $1. But try getting to his shop!

**Table 2–2 CONCENTRATION RATIOS IN SELECTED INDUSTRIES, 1987**

| INDUSTRY | FOUR-FIRM RATIO |
|---|---|
| Motor vehicles | 90% |
| Malt beverages | 87% |
| Photographic equipment | 77% |
| Tires and inner tubes | 69% |
| Department stores | 44% |
| Computers | 22% |
| Men's and boy's clothing | 19% |
| Chemicals | 14% |
| Travel agencies | 8% |
| New and used car dealers | 1% |

SOURCE: Bureau of the Census.

## WHAT'S MISSING FROM THE PICTURE? GOVERNMENT

Thus far we have the following capsule summary of how the U.S. economy works:

- About 19 million private businesses, energized by the profit motive, employ about 120 million workers and about $11 trillion of capital. A theory of how they make these decisions will be presented in Chapters 5 and 6.
- These firms bring their enormously diverse wares to market, where they try to sell them to about 260 million consumers. The theory of how consumers decide what to buy is the subject of Chapters 7 and 8.
- Households and businesses are linked together in a tight circle, depicted in Figure 2–11. Firms use their receipts from sales to pay wages to their employees and interest and profits to the people who provide them with capital. These income flows, in turn, enable consumers to purchase the goods and services that companies produce. This circular flow of money and goods is central to the analysis of how the national economy works—the main subject of *Macroeconomics*.
- All these activities are linked together by a series of interconnected markets, some of which are highly competitive and others of which are less so. Various market forms are studied in Chapters 9–12.

All very well and good. But the story leaves out something important: the role of *government*, which is pervasive even in our decidedly free-market economy. Just what does government do in the U.S. economy—and why?

While an increasing number of tasks seem to get assigned to the state each year, the traditional role of government in a market economy revolves around five jobs: providing certain goods and services such as national defense, raising taxes to pay for these services, redistributing income, regulating business, and making and enforcing the rules. Every one of these is steeped in controversy and surrounded by intense political debate. Each will be discussed at length later in the book. But we conclude this chapter with a brief look at the role of government, nonetheless.

**Figure 2-11** **THE CIRCULAR FLOW OF GOODS AND MONEY**

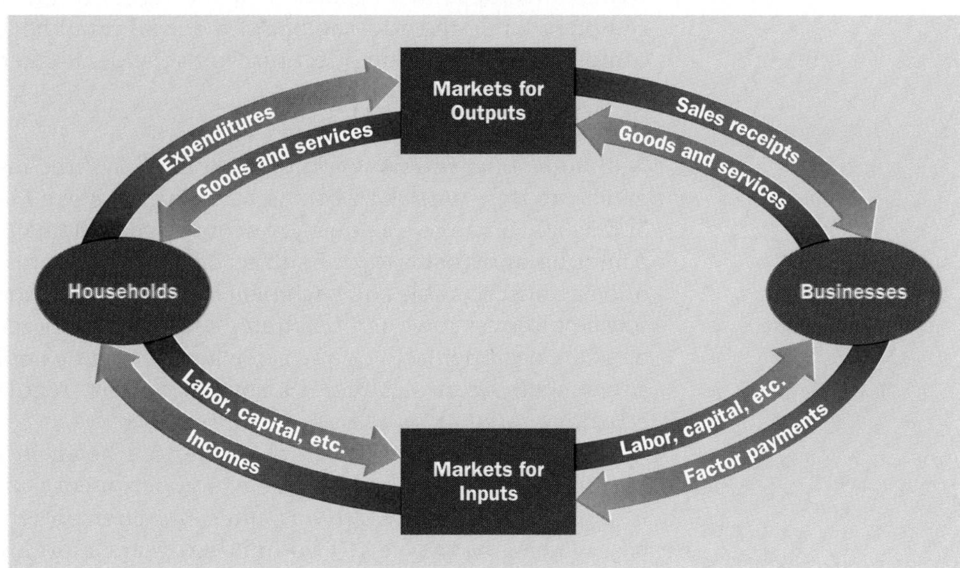


This diagram depicts the ways in which households and firms interact in markets. The upper half signifies the markets for outputs—the goods and services that firms produce and households purchase. The lower half illustrates the markets for inputs like labor and capital that households sell (or rent) to businesses. In each case, the outer loop indicates the flow of money while the inner loop signifies the flow of physical goods and services.

## THE GOVERNMENT AS REFEREE

The economic game can be thought of as a contest. Businesses want to sell their wares for the highest possible prices; consumers want to buy them as cheaply as possible. Each firm wants to gain some advantage over its competitors. For the most part, power is diffused in our economy, and people "play by the rules." But, in the scramble for competitive advantage, disputes are bound to arise. Did Company A live up to its contract? Who owns that disputed piece of property? In addition, some unscrupulous businesses are liable to step over the line now and then—via misleading advertising, attempts to monopolize markets, employment of child labor, and the like.

Enter the government as rulemaker, referee, and arbitrator. Congress and state and local legislatures pass the laws that define the rules of the economic game. The executive branches of all three levels of government have the responsibility for enforcing them. And the courts interpret the laws and adjudicate disputes. All this is familiar.

One particular aspect of the government's rulemaking function is, in fact, *so* familiar that Americans are apt to forget it entirely. But it is proving to be a crushing burden to the formerly socialist economies as they try to make the transition to capitalism. We refer to the *definition and enforcement of property rights.* The answer to the question, *Who owns that*? is usually clear and unambiguous in our country. Your mother and father probably own your family house, Edna owns Edna's Sub Shop, and the shareholders of IBM own the company.

Now think about Russia, where almost everything until recently belonged to the state. Who now owns all the apartment buildings, trucks, industrial machinery, and factories? Is it the tenants, the truck drivers, and the workers? Or is it the managers who ran the enterprises? Or the government? Or the people as a whole? Until such questions are answered, and property rights are clearly defined, it will be difficult or impossible to conduct business in these countries. For example, in one infamous incident a few years ago, the central government of the Commonwealth of Independent States sold the rights to an oilfield to one Western oil company while the government of the local republic sold them to another! Such confusion has a chilling effect on would-be dealmakers.

## REGULATING BUSINESS

Nothing is pure in this world of ours. Even in "free-market" economies, governments interfere with the workings of free markets in many ways and for a myriad of reasons. Some regulations grow out of the rulemaking function. For example, America's **antitrust laws**, the subject of Chapter 19, are designed to protect competition against possible encroachment by monopoly. Others are aimed at promoting social objectives to which unfettered markets do not tend. Environmental regulations are a particularly clear case, which we will examine in Chapter 21. Finally, as we shall see in Chapter 18, some economic regulations have *no* persuasive economic rationale at all!

We mentioned earlier that the American belief in free enterprise runs deep. For this reason, the regulatory role of government is more contentious here than in most other countries. It was, after all, Jefferson who said that government is best which governs least. Two hundred years later, Presidents Reagan and Bush constantly pledged to dismantle regulations—and sometimes did.

## GOVERNMENT EXPENDITURES

During the 1992 presidential election, incumbent George Bush incessantly attacked challenger Bill Clinton's plans as more "tax and spend." He had a point. Taxing and spending are the government's most prominent roles.

During fiscal year 1993, the federal government spent about $1.5 *trillion*—a sum that is literally beyond comprehension. Figure 2–12 shows where the money went. Over one-third went for *pensions and income security* programs, which include both social insurance programs, like social security and unemployment compensation, and programs designed to assist the poor. About 19 percent went for *national defense.* Another 16 percent was absorbed by *health care* expenditures, mainly on Medicare and Medicaid. Adding in *interest on the national debt*, these four functions alone accounted for about 84 percent of federal spending. The rest went for a miscellany of other purposes including education, transportation, agriculture, housing, and foreign aid.

Government spending at the state and local levels was over $1 trillion. Education claimed the biggest share of state and local government budgets (30 percent), with health and public welfare programs in second place (19 percent).

Despite this vast outpouring of public funds, many observers believe that serious social needs remain unmet. Critics claim that our public infrastructure (such as bridges and roads) is inadequate, that our educational system is lacking, that we do not do enough for the poor and homeless, and so on. Many of these claims were echoed during the 1992 presidential campaign. Other critics argue that government tries to do too much—and does it too inefficiently.

## TAXES IN AMERICA

To finance this array of goods and services, taxes are required. Sometimes it seems that the tax collector is everywhere. We have income and payroll taxes withheld from our paychecks, sales taxes added to our purchases, property taxes levied on our homes; we pay gasoline taxes, liquor taxes, and telephone taxes.

**Figure 2-12** **THE ALLOCATION OF GOVERNMENT EXPENDITURES**

These graphs show how the government dollar is spent. The federal government spends most of its money on national defense (19 percent) and on transfer payments to retirees, the poor, the unemployed, and veterans (35 percent). The biggest share of state and local government spending goes for education (30 percent), with health and welfare expenditures (19 percent) in second place.

SOURCE: *Economic Report of the President, 1993* and *Statistical Abstract of the United States, 1992.*

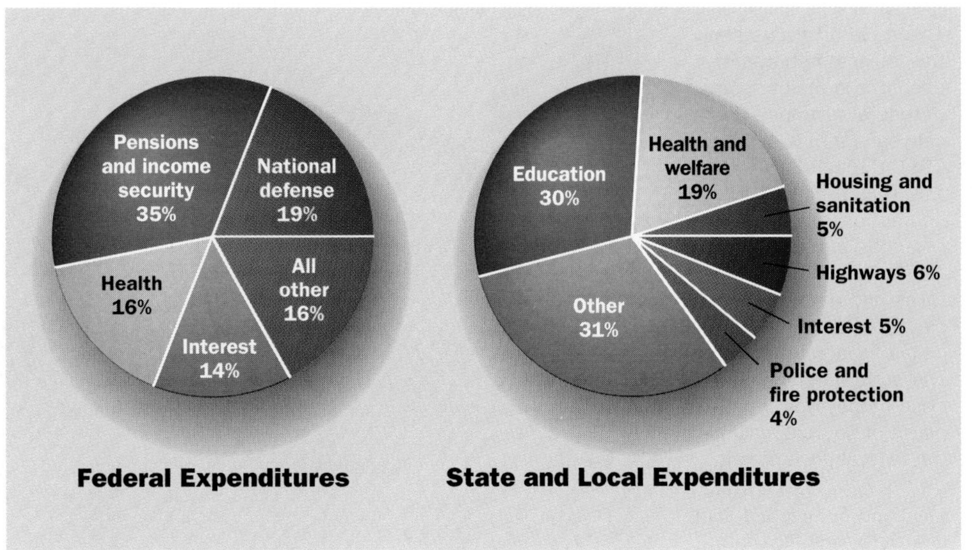


Americans, it seems, have always felt that there are too many taxes and that they are too high. In the 1970s and 1980s, anti-tax sentiment became a dominant feature of the U.S. political scene. The old slogan "no taxation without representation" gave way to the new slogan "no new taxes." Yet by international standards, Americans are among the most lightly taxed people in the world. Figure 2–13

**Figure 2-13** **THE BURDEN OF TAXATION IN SELECTED COUNTRIES, 1989**

Americans are lightly taxed in comparison with the citizens of other advanced industrial countries. The Swedes and the Dutch, for example, pay far higher taxes than we do. Even the Japanese and the Swiss, two countries traditionally noted for their low taxes, pay lower average tax rates than the Americans.

SOURCE: *Statistical Abstract of the United States, 1992.*

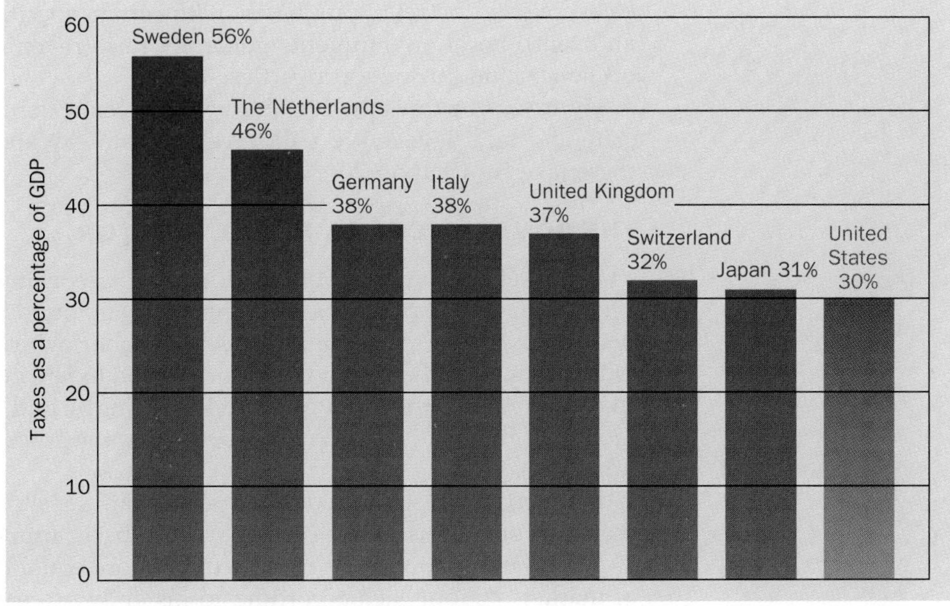

Figure 2–14 **SOURCES OF GOVERNMENT REVENUE**

These pie diagrams show the projected shares of each of the major sources of federal revenues for fiscal year 1993 (October 1992 through September 1993) and the actual shares for state and local revenues in fiscal year 1990. Personal income taxes and payroll taxes clearly account for the majority of federal revenues. The states and localities raise money from a potpourri of sources, including the federal government.

SOURCE: Office of Management and Budget and *Statistical Abstract of the United States, 1992*.

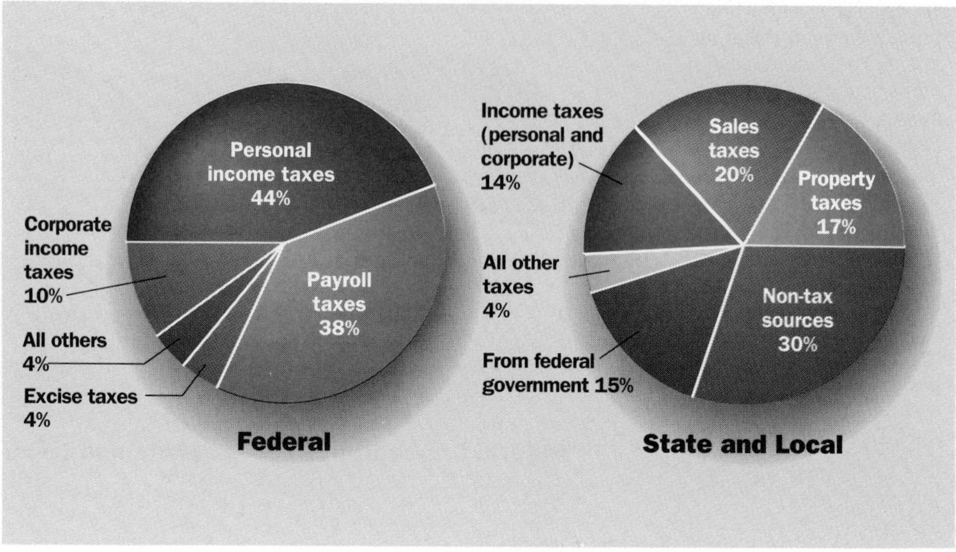


compares the fraction of income paid in taxes in the United States with that paid by residents of other wealthy nations. Americans shoulder the lowest tax burdens in the industrialized world.

How is this money raised? The *personal income tax* is the federal government's biggest revenue source, though the *payroll tax*—a flat-rate tax on wages and salaries up to a certain limit—is not far behind. The rest of federal revenue comes mainly from the *corporate income tax*. Most states and many large cities levy a broad-based *sales tax* on retail purchases, with certain specific exemptions (such as food and rent). Local governments generally raise revenue by levying *property taxes* on homes and business properties.

Figure 2–14 shows the breakdown of revenue sources at both the federal and state and local levels. We will have much to say about the economic effects of these taxes in Chapter 20.

## THE GOVERNMENT AS REDISTRIBUTOR

In a market economy, people earn incomes according to what they have to sell. The details of this process are examined in Chapters 15–17. Unfortunately, many people have nothing to sell but unskilled labor, which commands a paltry price. Others lack even that. Such people are bound to fare poorly in unfettered markets. In extreme cases, they will go homeless, hungry, and ill. Robin Hood transferred money from rich to poor. Some people think the government should do the same; others disagree.

If poverty amidst riches offends your moral sensibilities—a personal judgment that each of us must make—there are two basic approaches. The socialist idea is to force the distribution of income to be more equal by overriding the workings of markets. "From each according to his ability to each according to his needs" was Marx's ideal. In practice, things were not quite so noble under socialism. But there is little doubt that incomes in the old Soviet Union were more equally distributed than in the United States.

**TRANSFER PAYMENTS** are sums of money that certain individuals receive as outright grants from the government rather than as payments for services rendered.

A tax is **PROGRESSIVE** if the ratio of taxes to income rises as income rises.

The liberal idea is to let free markets determine the distribution of *before-tax* incomes, but then to use the tax system and **transfer payments** to reduce inequality—just as Robin Hood did. This is the rationale for, among other things, **progressive taxation** and the anti-poverty programs colloquially known as "welfare." Americans who support redistribution line up solidly behind the liberal approach. But which ways are the best, and how much is enough? These highly contentious questions will be addressed in Chapter 17.

## CONCLUSION: THE MIXED ECONOMY

A **MIXED ECONOMY** is one in which there is some public influence over the workings of free markets. There may also be some public ownership mixed in with private property.

Ideology notwithstanding, all nations at all times blend public and private economic ownership of property in some proportions. All rely on markets for some purposes; but all also assign some role to government. Hence people speak of the ubiquity of **mixed economies**. But mixing is not homogenization; different countries can and do blend state and market in different ways. Even today, the Russian economy is a far cry from the Italian economy, much less from that of Hong Kong.

While most of you were in high school, communism collapsed all over Europe. It was one of the most stunning events in world history. Now the formerly socialist economies are in the midst of a painful transition from a system in which private property, free enterprise, and markets played subsidiary roles to one in which they are central. These nations are changing the mix, if you will—and dramatically so. To understand why this transformation is at once so difficult and so important, we need to explore the main theme of this book: **What does the market do well, and what does it do poorly**? This task begins in the next chapter.

## *Summary*

1. An **economy** is a collection of markets in a defined geographical area. It can be thought of as a social mechanism for transforming **inputs (factors of production)** into **outputs**.
2. The U.S. economy is the biggest national economy on earth both because Americans are rich by world standards and because we are a populous nation. Relative to most other advanced countries, our economy is also exceptionally "privatized" and **closed**.
3. The U.S. economy has grown dramatically over the years. But this growth is exaggerated by looking at dollar figures, which are distorted by both **inflation** and population growth. To get a better understanding of the growth of living standards, we must look at **real GDP** *per capita*.
4. The growth path of the United States economy has been interrupted by periodic **recessions**, during which unemployment rises.
5. America has a big, diverse workforce whose composition by age and sex has been changing substantially. Relatively few workers these days work in factories or on farms; most work in service industries.
6. Employees take home most of the nation's income. Most of the rest goes, in the forms of interest and profits, to those who provide the capital.
7. There are about 19 million businesses in the United States. Most of these are small **sole proprietorships** or **partnerships**. But most of the output is produced by **corporations**, some of which are gigantic and operate on a global scale.
8. Governments at the federal, state, and local levels employ almost a fifth of the America workforce and

produce about a fifth of the GDP. They finance their expenditures by taxes, which account for about 30 percent of GDP. This percentage is the lowest in the industrialized world.

9. In addition to raising taxes and making expenditures, the government in a market economy serves as referee and enforcer of the rules, regulates business in a variety of ways, and redistributes income through taxes and **transfer payments**. For all these reasons, we say that we have a **mixed economy** which blends private and public elements.

## *Key Concepts and Terms*

Economy
Inputs (factors of production)
Outputs
Gross Domestic Product (GDP)
Real GDP
Open economy
Closed economy
Inflation
Recession
Sole proprietorship
Partnership
Corporation
Transfer payments
Mixed economy

## *Questions for Review*

1. Which are the two biggest national economies on earth? Why are they so much bigger than the others?
2. What is meant by a "factor of production?" Have you ever sold any on a market?
3. Do you have any ideas why per capita income in Connecticut is roughly double that of Mississippi?
4. What is the difference between nominal gross domestic product and real gross domestic product? Why is this distinction important?
5. Roughly speaking, what fraction of American labor works in factories? In service businesses? In government?
6. It sounds paradoxical to say that most American businesses are small, but most of the output is produced by large businesses. How can this be true?
7. What is the role of government in a mixed economy?

# Appendix FURTHER PERILS IN THE INTERPRETATION OF GRAPHS

The chapter warned you against certain dangers that arise in interpreting time series graphs. But there are others. This appendix deals with three of them.

## DISTORTING TRENDS BY CHOICE OF THE TIME PERIOD

Users of statistical data must be on guard for distortions of trends caused by unskillful or unscrupulous choice of the beginning and ending periods for the graph. This is best explained by an example.

Figure 2–15 shows the behavior of average stock market prices over the period January 1966–June 1982. The numbers have been corrected for inflation; that is, they are expressed in dollars of constant purchasing power. The graph displays a clear downhill movement that would suggest to anyone not familiar with other information that stocks are a terrible investment.

However, an unscrupulous seller of stocks could use similar stock market statistics for a different group of years to tell exactly the opposite story. Figure 2–16 shows the behavior of average stock in 1989 and 1990. Stocks now look like a superb investment.

A much longer and less-biased choice of period (Figure 2–17) gives a less distorted picture. It indicates that investments in stocks are sometimes profitable, sometimes unprofitable. The lesson is that:

The deliberate or inadvertent distortion resulting from an unfortunate or unscrupulous choice of time period for a graph must constantly be watched for.

While no ironclad rules can give absolute protection from this difficulty, several precautions can be helpful.

1. Make sure the first date on the graph is not an exceptionally high or low point. By comparison with 1966, a year of unusually high stock prices, the years immediately following are bound to give the impression of a downward trend.

Figure 2–15 STOCK PRICES, JANUARY 1966–JUNE 1982

This graph seems to show that stock market prices generally go down.

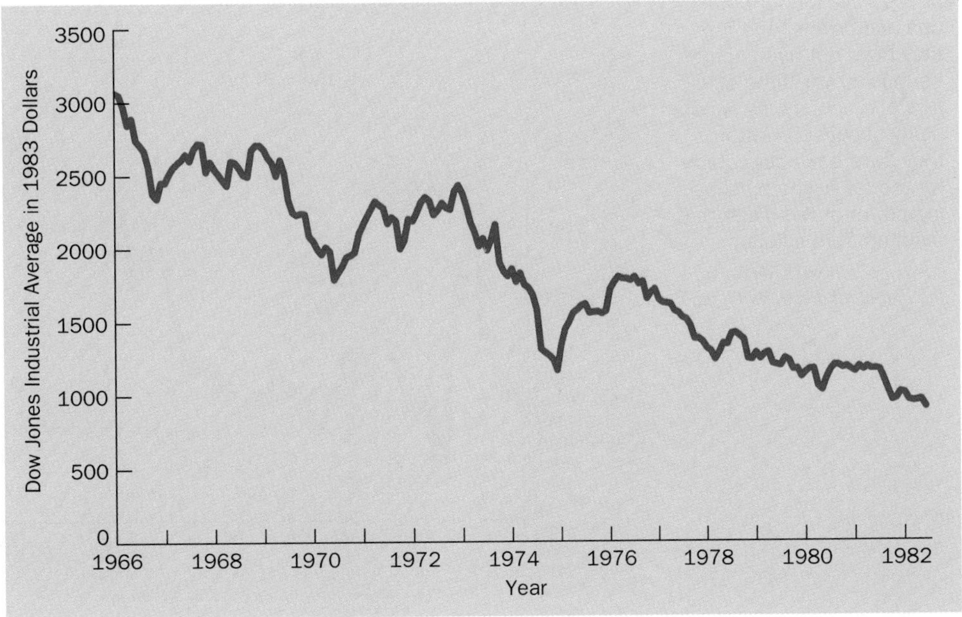

**Figure 2-16** **STOCK PRICES, JANUARY 1988–JULY 1990**

This graph seems to indicate that the value of stocks is steadily climbing.

SOURCE: *Economic Report of the President 1991.*

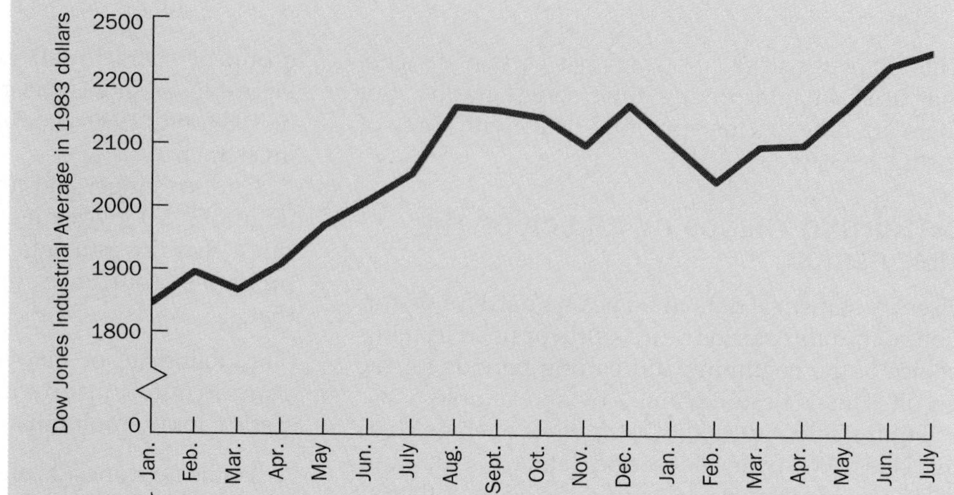


**Figure 2-17** **FULL HISTORY OF STOCK PRICES, CORRECTED FOR INFLATION, 1925–1992**

Here we see that stock prices have lots of *both* ups and downs, and that they have not risen nearly as much, over three quarters of a century, as is popularly supposed—after they have been corrected for the fall in the purchasing power of the dollar that resulted from inflation.

SOURCE: *Economic Report of the President 1990, 1991,* and *1992.*

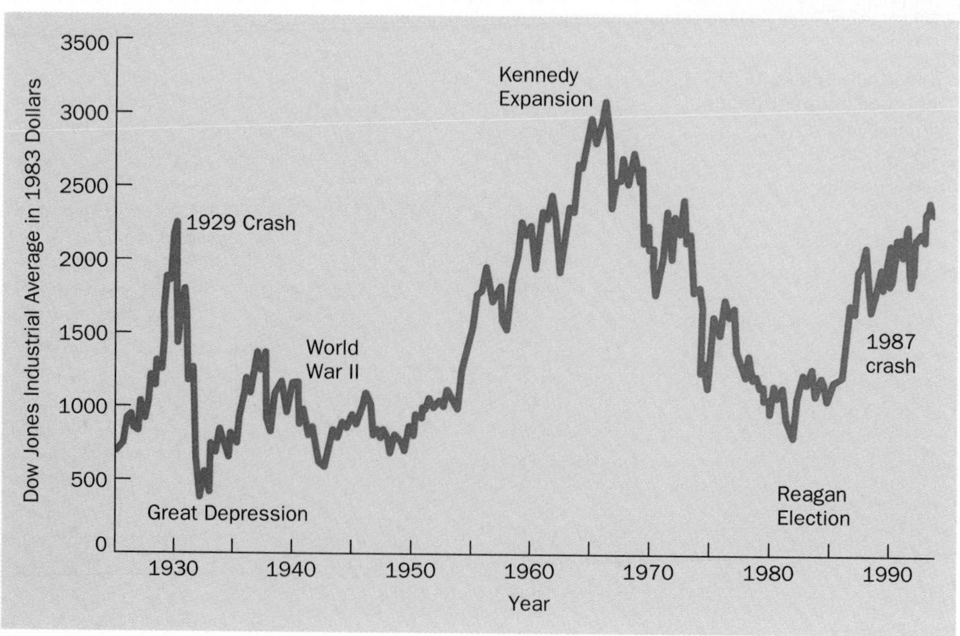

2. For the same reason, make sure the graph does not end in a year that is extraordinarily high or low (although this may be unavoidable if the graph simply ends with the most recent data).
3. Make sure that (in the absence of some special justification) the graph does not depict only a very brief period of time, which can easily be atypical—like Figure 2–16.

## DANGERS OF OMITTING THE ORIGIN

Frequently, the value of an economic variable described by a graph does not fall anywhere near zero during the period under consideration. For example, between 1988 and 1992 the civilian unemployment rate never fell below 5 percent. This means that a time series graph showing unemployment over time would have much wasted space between the horizontal axis (where the unemployment rate is zero) and the level of the graph representing 5 percent. There are simply no data points to plot in that range. It is therefore tempting to eliminate this wasted space by beginning the graph at 5 percent, as the magazine *The International Economy* did when it published Figure 2–18 in 1992.

What is wrong with the drawing? Nothing, if you read carefully. But a hasty glance would vastly exaggerate the rise in unemployment. Figure 2–18 makes it look like the United States experienced an economic catastrophe from 1990 to 1992, with unemployment exploding. A less misleading graph, which includes the origin as well as all the "wasted space" in between, is shown in Figure 2–19. Note how this alternative presentation gives a dramatically different visual impression.

Omitting the origin in a graph is dangerous because it exaggerates the magnitudes of the changes that have taken place.

Sometimes, it is true, the inclusion of the origin would waste so much space that it is undesirable to include it. In that case, a good practice is to put a clear warning on the graph to remind the reader that this has been done. Figure 2–20 shows one way to do so.

## UNRELIABILITY OF STEEPNESS AND CHOICE OF UNITS

The last pitfall we will consider has consequences similar to the one we have just discussed. The problem is that we can never trust the visual impression we get from the steepness of a graph. A graph of stock market prices that moves uphill sharply (has a large positive slope) appears to suggest that prices are rising rapidly, while another graph in which the rate of climb is much slower seems to imply that prices are going up sluggishly. Yet, depending on how one draws the graph, exactly the same statistics can produce a graph that is rising quickly or slowly.

**Figure 2–18** A GRAPH DISTORTED BY OMISSION OF THE ORIGIN

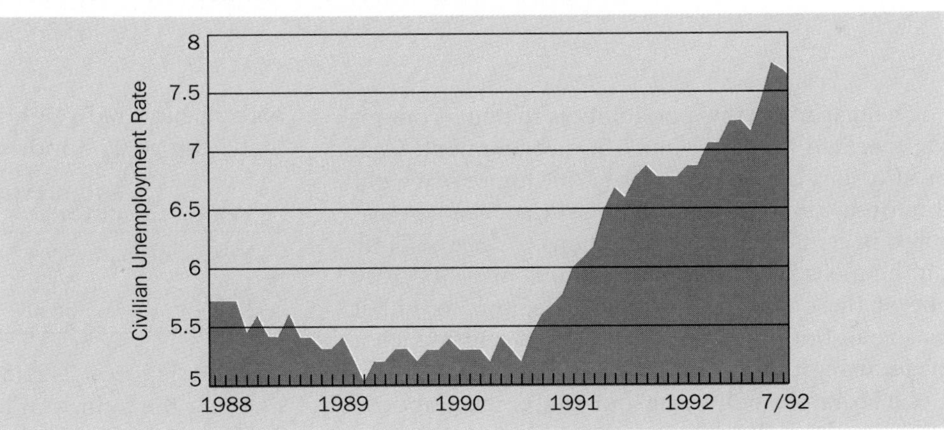


A hasty glance at this figure seems to show that, from mid-1990 to mid-1992, unemployment in the United States soared to disastrous heights.

SOURCE: *The International Economy*, September/October 1992, p. 10.

Figure 2–19 THE SAME GRAPH WITH ORIGIN POINT INCLUDED

Extending the previous graph all the way to zero unemployment shows that the rise in unemployment, while significant, was not so enormous as the previous graph suggested.

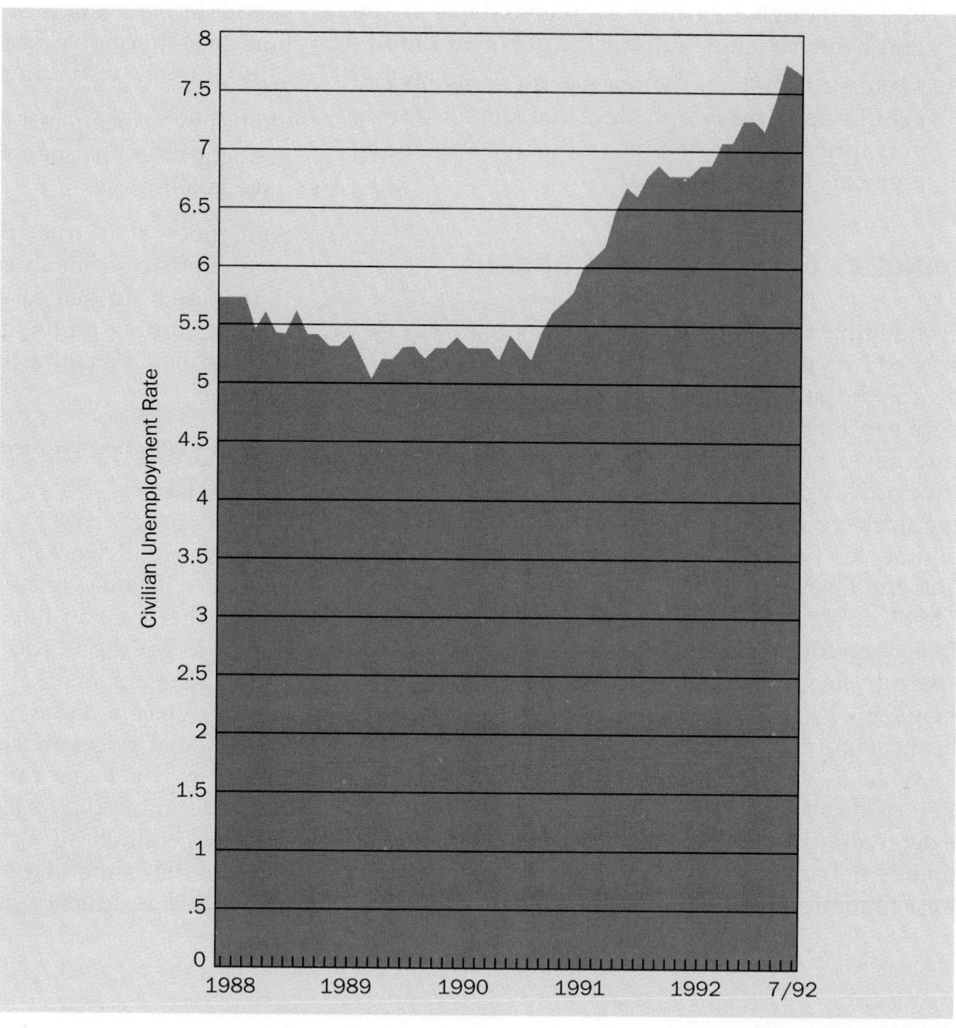


The reason for this possibility is that, in economics, there are no fixed units of measurement. Coal production can be measured in hundredweight (hundreds of pounds) or in tons. Prices can be measured in cents or dollars or millions of dollars. Time can be measured in days or months or years. Any one of these choices is perfectly legitimate, but it makes all the difference to the speed with which a graph using the resulting figures rises or falls.

An example will bring out the point. Suppose we have the following imaginary figures on daily production from a coal mine, which we measure both in hundredweight and in tons (remembering that 1 ton = 20 hundredweight):

| YEAR | PRODUCTION IN TONS | PRODUCTION IN HUNDREDWEIGHT |
|---|---|---|
| 1980 | 5000 | 100,000 |
| 1985 | 5050 | 101,000 |
| 1990 | 5090 | 101,800 |

Look at Figures 2–21(a) and 2–21(b), one graph showing the figures in tons and the other showing the figures in hundredweight. The line looks quite flat in one panel, but quite steep in the other.

**Figure 2-20** **THE SAME GRAPH WITH A WARNING BREAK**

An alternative way to warn the reader that the zero point has been left out is to put a break in the graph, as illustrated here.

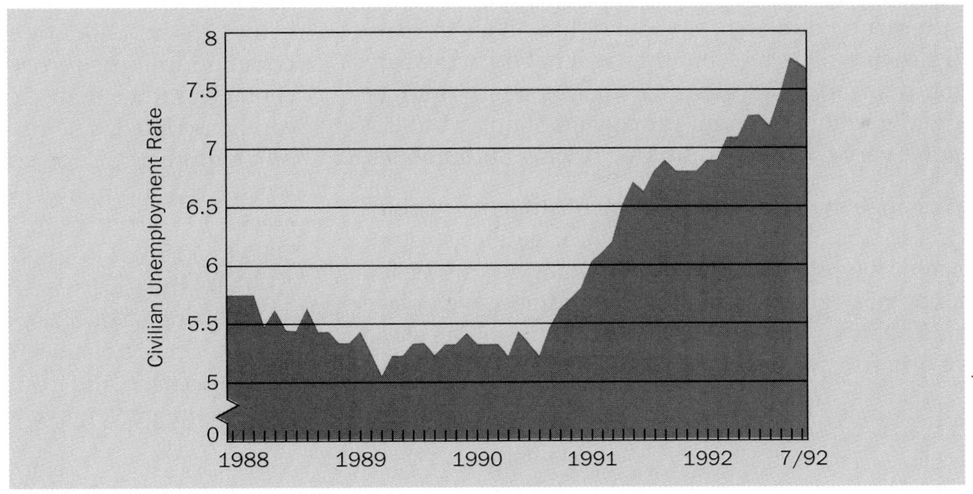


**Figure 2-21** **SLOPE DEPENDS ON UNITS OF MEASUREMENT**



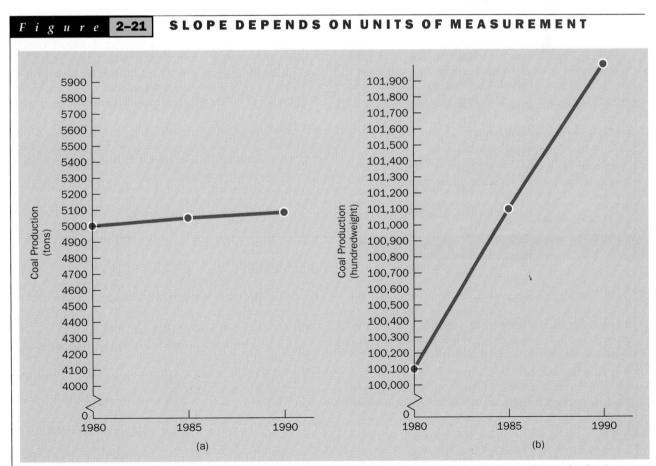

In part (a), coal production is measured in tons, and production seems to be rising very slowly. In part (b), production is measured in hundredweight (hundred-pound units) so the same facts now seem to say that production is rising spectacularly.

Unfortunately, we cannot solve the problem by agreeing always to stick to the same units of measurement. Pounds may be the right unit for measuring demand for beef, but they will not do in measuring demand for cloth or for coal. A penny may be the right monetary unit for postage stamps, but it is not a very convenient unit for pricing automobiles.

A change in units of measurement stretches or compresses the axis on which the information is represented, which automatically changes the visual slope of a graph. Therefore, we must never place much faith in the apparent implications of the slope of an ordinary graph in economics.

Chapter 7 on demand analysis will offer a useful approach that economists have adopted to deal with this problem. Instead of calculating changes in "absolute" terms—like tons of coal—they use as their common unit the *percentage* increase. By using percentages rather than absolute figures, the problem can be avoided. The reason is simple. If we look at our hypothetical figures on coal production again, we see that no matter whether we measure the increase in output from 1980 to 1985 in tons (from 5000 to 5050) or in hundredweight (from 100,000 to 101,000), the *percentage* increase was the same. Fifty is one percent of 5000, and 1000 is one percent of 100,000. Since a change in units affects both numbers *proportionately*, the result is a wash; it does not change the percentage calculation.

## *Summary*

1. A time series graph is a particular type of two-variable diagram that is useful in depicting statistical data. Time is measured along the horizontal axis, and some variable of interest is measured along the vertical axis.
2. While time series graphs are invaluable in helping us condense a great deal of information in a single picture, they can be quite misleading if they are not drawn and interpreted with care.
3. For example, growth trends can be exaggerated by inappropriate choice of units of measurement or by failure to correct for some obvious source of growth (such as rising population). Omitting the origin can make the ups and downs in a time series appear much more extreme than they actually are. Or, by a clever choice of the starting and ending points for the graphs, the same data can be made to tell very different stories. Readers of such graphs—and this includes anyone who ever reads a newspaper—must be on guard for problems like these or they may find themselves misled by "the facts."

## *Questions for Review*

1. Look for a graph in your local newspaper, on the financial page or elsewhere. What does the graph try to show? Is someone trying to convince you of something? Check to see if the graph is distorted in any of the ways mentioned in this chapter.
2. Suppose that between 1992 and 1993 expenditures on dog food rose from $60 million to $70 million, and that the price of dog food went up by 20 percent. What do these facts imply about the popularity of dog food?
3. Suppose that between 1983 and 1993 the U.S. population went up 10 percent and that the number of silk neckties imported from Thailand rose from 3,000,000 to 3,600,000. What do these facts imply about the growth in popularity of Thai ties?

Chapter 3

# SCARCITY AND CHOICE: *the* ECONOMIC PROBLEM

*Our necessities are few but our wants are endless.*

**INSCRIPTION FOUND IN A FORTUNE COOKIE**

The market—what it does well, and what it does badly—is, as we noted in concluding the previous chapter, the central issue of this book. But before we delve into the details of this complex subject, we must first ask a preliminary question: What is the basic task that economists expect the market to carry out? ¶ The answer economists most frequently give is that the market resolves *the* fundamental problem of the economy: the fact that all decisions are constrained by the scarcity of available resources. A science-fiction writer can depict a world in which everyone travels about in a petroleum-powered yacht, but the earth almost certainly lacks the resources needed to make that dream come true. The scarcity of resources, both natural and man-made, makes it vital that we stretch our limited resources as far as possible. Even millionaires, monarchs, and wealthy nations constantly find themselves frustrated by the fact that they lack sufficient purchasing power, labor, and natural resources to do everything they would like. So they, like you and we, must constantly make hard choices. ¶ Because of scarcity, every economic decision involves a trade-off. Should you use that $5 bill to buy a hoagie or some new diskettes for your computer files? Should Chrysler Corporation invest more money in assembly lines or in research on auto design and fuel efficiency? The key role of the market is to facilitate and guide such decisions, assigning each hour of labor and each kilowatt-hour of electricity to the task where, it is hoped, input will serve the public most effectively. Scarcity, then, is the fundamental fact with which the market (or the central planner) must grapple.

The chapter introduces a way to analyze the limited choices available to any decision maker. The same sort of analysis, based on the concept of *opportunity cost*, will be shown to apply to the decisions of business firms, of governments, and of society as a whole. Many of the most basic ideas of economics—such as *efficiency, division of labor, exchange*, and the *role of markets*—are introduced here for the first time. These concepts are useful in analyzing the unpleasant choices forced upon us by scarcity.

### PROBLEM: THE "INDISPENSABLE NECESSITY" SYNDROME

It is natural, but not rational, for people to try to avoid facing up to the hard choices that scarcity makes necessary. This happened, for example, when countries such as Russia and Poland were forced by extreme scarcity of foreign currency to tighten their belts sharply during the 1990s. Shortages of foreign currency meant that these governments and their people had to cut down severely on consumer goods and productive inputs purchased from abroad. But most proposals for cuts were met with demonstrations and the cry that each item slated for reduction was *absolutely* essential.

In the same period, something similar went on in the United States. Taxpayers' revolts made it impossible, politically, for federal, state, and local revenues to increase very much while government services were growing more expensive because of inflation and for other reasons (see Chapter 13, pages 326–29). Belt-tightening was the order of the day. But as politicians and administrators struggled with these decisions, they learned that their constituents often were unwilling to accept *any* reductions. Whether the proposal was to reduce payments to the elderly, expenditure on libraries, outlays on schools, or even defense spending, protest groups argued that the cut in question would destroy American society.

Yet, regrettable as it is to have to give up anything, reduced budgets mean that *something* must go. If everyone reacts by declaring *everything* to be indispensable, the decision maker is in the dark and is likely to end up making cuts that are bad for everyone. When the budget must be reduced, it is critical to determine which cuts are likely to prove *least damaging* to the people affected.

It is nonsense to assign top priority to everything. No one can afford everything. An optimal decision is one that chooses the most desirable alternative *among the possibilities permitted by the quantities of scarce resources available.*

## SCARCITY, CHOICE, AND OPPORTUNITY COST

**RESOURCES** are the instruments provided by nature or by people that are used to create the goods and services humans want. Natural resources include minerals, the soil (usable for agriculture, building plots, and so on), water, and air. Labor is a scarce resource partly because of time limitations (the day has only 24 hours), and partly because the number of skilled workers is limited. Factories and machines are resources made by people. These three types of resources are often referred to as "land," "labor," and "capital." They are also called the inputs used in production processes or **FACTORS OF PRODUCTION**.

One of the basic themes of economics is that the **resources** of decision makers, no matter how large they may be, are always limited, and that as a result everyone has some hard decisions to make. The U.S. government has been agonizing over difficult budget decisions for years, though it spends about a trillion and a half dollars annually! Even Philip II, of Spanish Armada fame, ruler of one of the greatest empires in history, frequently had to cope with rebellion on the part of his troops, whom he was often unable to pay or to supply with even the most basic provisions. His government actually went bankrupt about a half-dozen times.

But far more fundamental than the scarcity of funds is the scarcity of physical resources. The supply of fuel, for example, has never been limitless, and some environmentalists claim that we should now be making some hard choices, such as keeping our homes cooler in winter and warmer in summer, living closer to our jobs, or giving up such fuel-using conveniences as dishwashers. While energy is the most widely discussed scarcity these days, the general principle of scarcity applies to all the earth's resources—iron, copper, uranium, and so on.

A **RATIONAL DECISION** is one that best serves the objective of the decision maker, whatever that objective may be. Such objectives may include a firm's desire to maximize its profits, a government's desire to maximize the welfare of its citizens, or another government's desire to maximize its military might. The term "rational" connotes neither approval nor disapproval of the objective itself.

The **OPPORTUNITY COST** of any decision is the forgone value of the next best alternative that is not chosen.

Even goods that can be produced are in limited supply because their production requires fuel, labor, and other scarce resources. Wheat and rice can be grown. But nations have nonetheless suffered famines because the land, labor, fertilizer, and water needed to grow these crops were unavailable. We can increase our output of cars, but the increased use of labor, steel, and fuel in auto production will mean that something else, perhaps the production of refrigerators, will have to be cut back. This all adds up to the following fundamental principle of economics, one we will encounter again and again in this text.

Virtually all resources are *scarce*, meaning that humanity has less of them than we would like. So choices must be made among a *limited* set of possibilities, in full recognition of the inescapable fact that a decision to have more of one thing means we will have less of something else.

In fact, one popular definition of economics is that it is the study of how best to use limited means in the pursuit of unlimited ends. While this definition, like any short statement, cannot possibly cover the sweep of the entire discipline, it does convey the flavor of the type of problem that is the economist's stock in trade.

**THE PRINCIPLE OF OPPORTUNITY COST**

Economics examines the options available to households, business firms, governments, and entire societies given the limited resources at their command, and it studies the logic of how **rational decisions** can be made from among the competing alternatives. One overriding principle governs this logic—a principle we have already introduced in Chapter 1 as one of the **12 Ideas for Beyond the Final Exam**. With limited resources, a decision to have more of something is simultaneously a decision to have less of something else. Hence, the relevant *cost* of any decision is its **opportunity cost**—the value of the next best alternative that is given up. Rational decision making, be it in industry, government, or households, must be based on opportunity-cost calculations.

To illustrate opportunity cost, we continue the example in which production of additional cars requires the production of fewer refrigerators. While the production of a car may cost $15,000 per vehicle, or some other money amount, *its real cost to society is the refrigerators it must forgo to get an additional car.* If the labor, steel, and fuel needed to make a car are sufficient to make twelve refrigerators, we say that the opportunity cost of a car is twelve refrigerators. The principle of opportunity cost is of such general applicability that we devote most of this chapter to elaborating it.

## OPPORTUNITY COST AND MONEY COST

Since we live in a market economy where (almost) everything "has its price," students often wonder about the connection between the opportunity cost of an item and its market price. What we just said seems to divorce the two concepts. We stressed that the true cost of a car is not its market price but the value of the other things (like refrigerators) that could have been made instead. This *opportunity cost* is the true sacrifice the economy must incur to get a car.

But isn't the opportunity cost of a car related to its money cost? The answer is that the two are often closely tied because of the way a market economy sets the prices of the steel and electricity that go into the production of cars. Steel is valuable because it can be used to make other goods. If the items that steel can make are themselves valuable (that is, if those items are valued highly by consumers), the price of steel will be high. But if the goods that steel can make have little value, the price of steel will be low. Thus, if a car has a high opportunity cost, then a well-functioning price system will assign high prices to the resources that are needed to produce cars, and therefore a car will also command a high price. In sum:

If the market is functioning well, goods that have high opportunity costs will tend to have high money costs, and goods whose opportunity costs are low will tend to have low money costs.

Yet it would be a mistake to treat opportunity costs and explicit monetary costs as identical. For one thing, there are times when the market does not function well and hence does not assign prices that accurately reflect opportunity costs. Many such examples will be encountered in this book, especially in Chapters 13 and 21.

Moreover, some valuable items may not bear explicit price tags at all. We have already encountered one such example in Chapter 1, where we contrasted the opportunity cost of going to college with the explicit money cost. We learned that one important item typically omitted from the money-cost calculation is the *market* value of your time; that is, the wages you could be earning by working instead of attending college. These forgone wages, which you give up in order to acquire an education, are part of the opportunity cost of your college education just as surely as are tuition payments.

Other common examples are goods and services that are given away "free." You incur no explicit monetary cost to acquire such an item. But you may have to pay implicitly by waiting in line. If so, you incur an opportunity cost equal to the value of the next best use of your time.

## PRODUCTION, SCARCITY, AND RESOURCE ALLOCATION

Consumers do not obtain all the goods and services they would want to acquire if those goods and services were provided free; that is what we mean when we say that outputs are scarce. Scarcity forces consumers to make choices. If Fred buys a motorboat, he may be unable to replace his old coat. The scarcity of goods and services, in turn, is attributed to the scarcity of the land, labor, and capital needed to produce them.

The scarcity of such input resources, then, means that the economy cannot produce all the bread, hats, cars, and computers that consumers would want if they were available at a zero price. Somehow it must be decided whether or not to assign more fuel to the production of refrigerators, which will mean there is less fuel to use in the production of airplanes or washing machines.

The **ALLOCATION OF RESOURCES** refers to the decision on how to divide up the economy's scarce input resources among the different outputs produced in the economy and among the different firms or other organizations that produce those outputs.

The decision on how to **allocate resources** among the production of different commodities is made in different ways in different types of economies. In a centrally controlled economy such as the former Soviet Union, many such decisions were made by government bureaus. In a market economy such as the United States, Canada, or Great Britain, no one group or individual makes such resource allocation decisions explicitly. Rather, they are made automatically, often unobserved, by what are called the "forces of supply and demand." For example, if consumers want more beef than ranchers now supply, that will make it profitable for ranchers to hire more labor to increase their cattle herds, thus reallocating labor and other inputs away from other production activities and into increased production of beef.

## SCARCITY AND CHOICE FOR A SINGLE FIRM

The nature of opportunity cost is perhaps clearest in the case of a single business firm that produces two outputs from a fixed supply of inputs. Given the existing technology and the limited resources at its disposal, the more of one good the firm produces, the less of the other it will be able to produce. And unless management carries out an explicit comparison of the available choices, weighing the desirability of each against the others, it is unlikely that it will make rational production decisions.

Consider the example of a farmer whose available supplies of land, machinery, labor, and fertilizer are capable of producing the various combinations of soybeans and wheat listed in Table 3–1. Obviously, the more land and other resources she devotes to production of soybeans, the less wheat she will be able to produce. Table 3–1 indicates, for example, that if she produces only soybeans, she can harvest 40,000 bushels. But, if soybean production is reduced to only 30,000 bushels, the farmer can also grow 38,000 bushels of wheat. Thus the opportunity

*Table* **3–1** **PRODUCTION POSSIBILITIES OPEN TO A FARMER**

| BUSHELS OF SOYBEANS | BUSHELS OF WHEAT | LABEL IN FIGURE 3-1 |
|---|---|---|
| 40,000 | 0 | *A* |
| 30,000 | 38,000 | *B* |
| 20,000 | 52,000 | *C* |
| 10,000 | 60,000 | *D* |
| 0 | 65,000 | *E* |

cost of obtaining 38,000 bushels of wheat is 10,000 fewer bushels of soybeans. Or, put another way, the opportunity cost of 10,000 more bushels of soybeans is 38,000 bushels of wheat. The other numbers in Table 3–1 have similar interpretations.

Figure 3–1 is a graphical representation of this same information. Point *A* corresponds to the first line of Table 3–1, point *B* to the second line, and so on. Curves similar to *AE* appear frequently in this book; they are called **production possibilities frontiers**. Any point *on or inside* the production possibilities frontier is attainable. Points outside the frontier cannot be achieved with the available resources and technology.

A **PRODUCTION POSSIBILITIES** frontier shows the different combinations of various goods that a producer can turn out, given the available resources and existing technology.

The production possibilities frontier always slopes downward to the right. Why? Because resources are limited. The farmer can *increase* her wheat production (move to the right in Figure 3–1) only by devoting more of her land and labor to growing wheat, meaning that she must simultaneously *reduce* her soybean production (move downward) because less of her land and labor remain available for growing soybeans.

Notice that in addition to having a negative slope, our production possibilities frontier *AE* has another characteristic—it is "bowed outward." Let us consider a bit carefully what this curvature means.

Suppose our farmer is initially producing only soybeans, so that she uses for this purpose even land that is much more suitable for wheat cultivation (point *A*). Now suppose she decides to switch some of her land from soybean production to wheat production. Which part of her land will she switch? Obviously, if she is sensible, she will use the part best suited to wheat growing. If she shifts to point *B*, soybean production falls from 40,000 bushels to 30,000 bushels as wheat production rises from zero to 38,000 bushels. A sacrifice of only 10,000 bushels of soybeans "buys" 38,000 bushels of wheat.

Imagine now that the farmer wants to produce still more wheat. Figure 3–1 tells us that the sacrifice of an additional 10,000 bushels of soybeans (from 30,000

*Figure* **3–1** **PRODUCTION POSSIBILITIES FRONTIER FOR PRODUCTION BY A SINGLE FIRM**

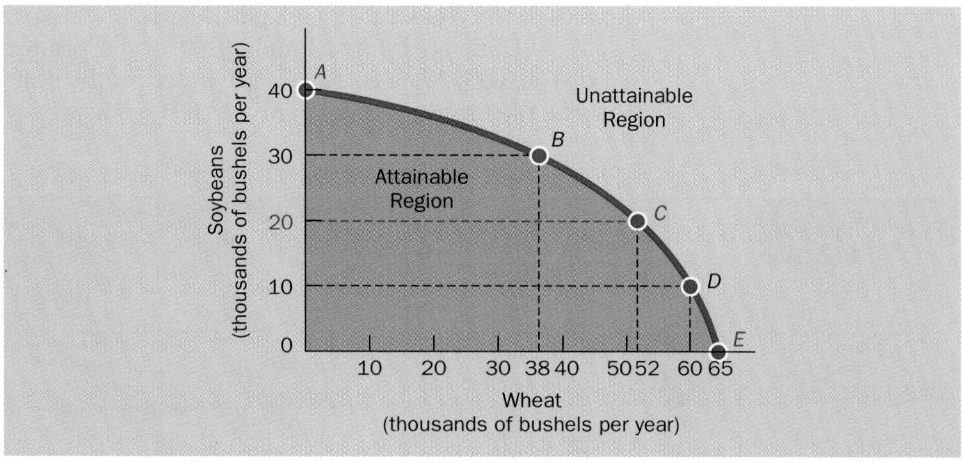


With a given set of inputs, the firm can produce only those output combinations given by points in the shaded area. The production possibilities frontier, *AE*, is not a straight line but one that curves more and more as it nears the axes. That is, when the firm specializes in only one product, those inputs that are especially adapted to the production of the other good lose at least part of their productivity.

down to 20,000) will yield only 14,000 more bushels of wheat (see point *C*). Why? The main reason is that inputs tend to be specialized. As we noted, at point *A* the farmer was using resources for soybean production that were much more suitable for growing wheat. Consequently, their productivity in soybeans was relatively low, and when they were switched to wheat production, the yield was very high. But this cannot continue forever. As more wheat is produced, the farmer must utilize land and machinery that are better suited to producing soybeans and less well-suited to producing wheat. This is why the first 10,000 bushels of soybeans forgone "buys" the farmer 38,000 bushels of wheat while the second 10,000 bushels of soybeans "buys" her only 14,000 bushels of wheat. Figure 3–1 and Table 3–1 show that these returns continue to decline as wheat production expands: the next 10,000-bushel reduction in soybean production yields only 8000 bushels of additional wheat, and so on.

We can now see that the *slope* of the production possibilities frontier represents graphically the concept of *opportunity cost*. Between points *C* and *B*, for example, the opportunity cost of acquiring 10,000 additional bushels of soybeans is 14,000 bushels of forgone wheat; and between points *B* and *A*, the opportunity cost of 10,000 bushels of soybeans is 38,000 bushels of forgone wheat. In general, as we move upward to the left along the production possibilities frontier (toward more soybeans and less wheat), the opportunity cost of soybeans in terms of wheat increases. Or, putting the same thing differently, as we move downward to the right, the opportunity cost of acquiring wheat by giving up soybeans increases.

## THE PRINCIPLE OF INCREASING COSTS

The **PRINCIPLE OF INCREASING COSTS** states that as the production of a good expands, the opportunity cost of producing another unit generally increases.

We have just described a very general phenomenon, which is applicable well beyond farming. The **principle of increasing costs** states that as the production of one good expands, the opportunity cost of producing another unit of this good generally increases.

This principle is not a universal fact; there can be exceptions to it. But it does seem to be a technological regularity that applies to a wide range of economic activities. As our example of the farmer suggests, the principle of increasing costs is based on the fact that resources tend to be specialized, at least in part, so that some of their productivity is lost when they are transferred from doing what they are relatively good at to what they are relatively bad at. In terms of diagrams such as Figure 3–1, the principle simply asserts that the production possibilities frontier is bowed outward.

Perhaps the best way to understand this idea is to contrast it with a case in which there are no specialized resources. Figure 3–2 depicts a production possibilities frontier for producing black shoes and brown shoes. Because the labor and capital used to produce black shoes are just as good at producing brown shoes, the frontier is a straight line. If the firm cuts back its production of black shoes by 10,000 pairs, it always gets 10,000 additional pairs of brown shoes. No productivity is lost in the switch because resources are not specialized.

More typically, however, as a firm switches more and more of its productive capacity from commodity *X* to commodity *Y*, it will eventually be forced to employ in Y production more and more inputs that are better suited to making X. This

*Figure* **3-2** **PRODUCTION POSSIBILITIES FRONTIER WITH NO SPECIALIZED RESOURCES**

Resources that produce black shoes are just as good at producing brown shoes. So there is no loss of productivity when black shoe production is decreased in order to increase brown shoe production. For example, if the firm moves from point *A* to point *B*, black shoe output falls by 10,000 pairs and brown shoe output rises by 10,000 pairs. The same would be true if it moved from point *B* to point *C*, or from point *C* to point *D*. The production possibilities frontier is therefore a straight line.

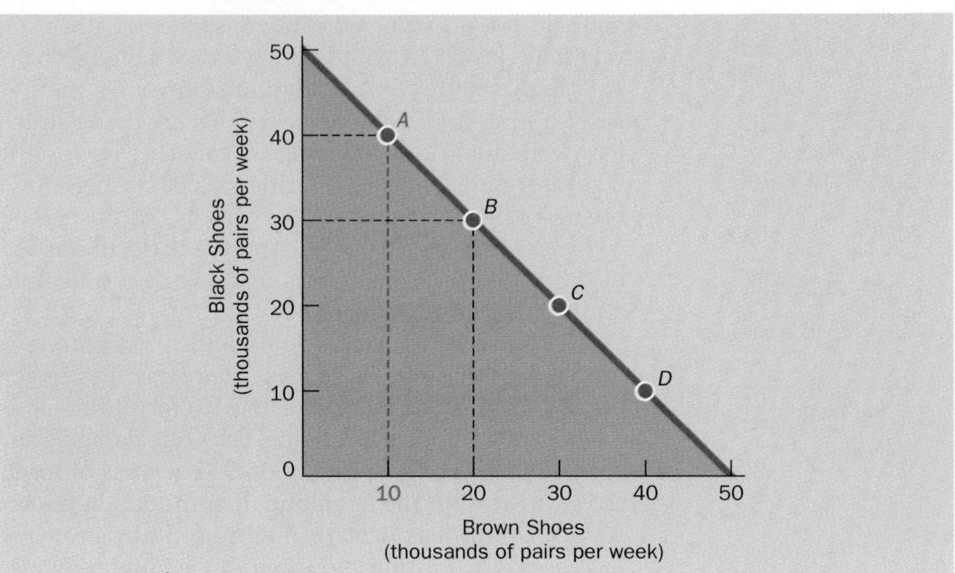


variation in the *proportions* in which inputs are used is forced on the firm by the limited quantities of some of the inputs it uses. It explains the typical curvature of the firm's production possibilities frontier.

## SCARCITY AND CHOICE FOR THE ENTIRE SOCIETY

Like an individual firm, the entire economy is also constrained by its limited resources and technology. If society wants more aircraft and tanks, it will have to give up some boats and automobiles. If it wants to build more factories and stores, it will have to build fewer homes and sports arenas. In general:

The position and shape of the production possibilities frontier that constrains the choices of the economy are determined by the economy's physical resources, its skills and technology, its willingness to work, and how much it has devoted in the past to the construction of factories, research, and innovation.

Since the debate over reducing military strength has been so much on the agenda of several nations recently (see box on page 64), let us illustrate the nature of society's choices by the example of choosing between military might (represented by missiles) and civilian consumption (represented by automobiles). Just like a single firm, the economy as a whole has a production possibilities frontier for missiles and automobiles determined by its technology and the available resources of land, labor, capital, and raw materials. This production possibilities frontier may look like curve *BC* in Figure 3–3.

**Figure 3-3** **THE PRODUCTION POSSIBILITIES FRONTIER FOR THE ENTIRE ECONOMY**

This production possibilities frontier is curved because resources are not perfectly transferable from automobile production to missile production. The limits on available resources place a ceiling, *C*, on the output of one product and a different ceiling, *B*, on the output of the other product.

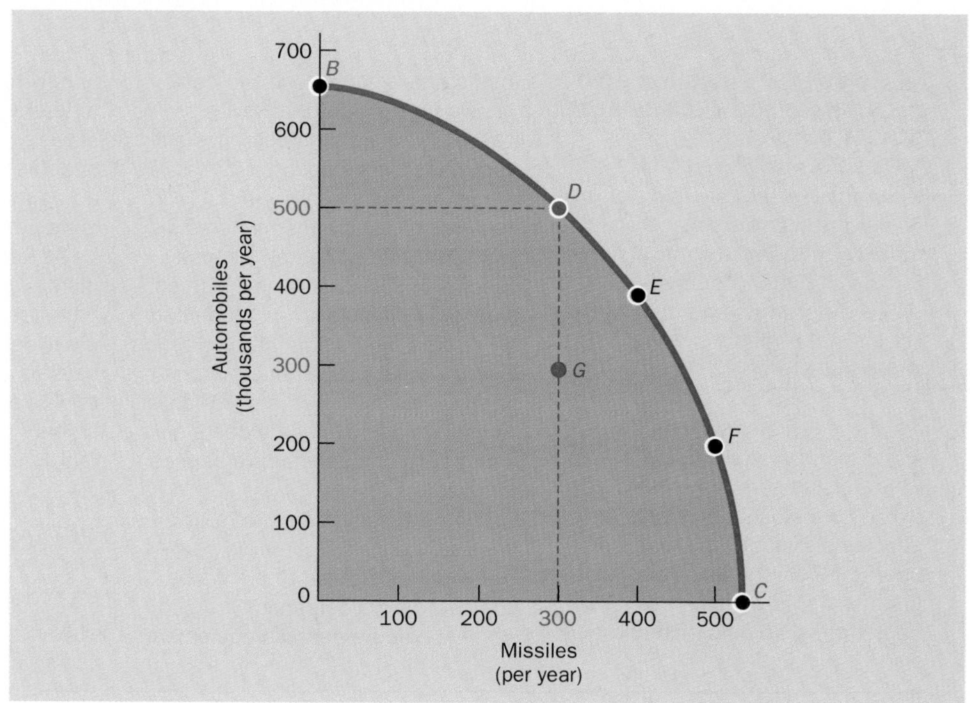


If most workers are employed in auto manufacturing, the production of automobiles will be large but the output of missiles will be small. If resources are transferred in the other direction, the mix of output can be shifted toward increased production of missiles at some sacrifice of automobiles (the move from *D* to *E*). However, something is likely to be lost in the transfer process—the seat fabric that went into the cars will not help much in missile production. As summarized in the principle of increasing costs, physical resources tend to be specialized, so the production possibilities frontier probably curves downward toward the axes.

We may even reach a point where the only resources left are items that are not very useful outside auto building facilities. In that case, even a very large additional sacrifice of automobiles will enable the economy to produce very few more missiles. That is the meaning of the steep segment, *FC*, on the frontier. At point *C* there is very little more output of missiles than at *F*, even though at *C* *automobile* production has been given up entirely.

The downward slope of society's production possibilities frontier implies that hard choices must be made. Our civilian consumption ("automobiles") can be increased only by decreasing military expenditure, not by rhetoric nor by wishing it so. The curvature of the production possibilities frontier implies that, as defense spending increases, it becomes progressively more expensive to "buy" additional military strength ("missiles") by sacrificing civilian consumption.

## *A Military–Civilian Output Trade-Off in Reality*

**"KONVERTSIA": SWORDS INTO PLOWSHARES IN THE FORMER SOVIET UNION**

The effort to convert large chunks of the massive Soviet military armaments industry into production for the civilian economy is proceeding in fits and starts, as the following excerpts illlustrate:

Izhevsk, Russia—Guns have always been Izhevsk's business, even when this city on the western edge of the Ural Mountains was a ramshackle outpost of the czar's empire. In 1947, the city produced the first AK-47 rifle, which became perhaps the world's most popular automatic and arguably one the best known products of the Soviet Union's vaunted and secretive military-industrial complex . . . .

So far, the evidence is that conversion [of such arms manufacturing centers], pushed by Moscow since 1988, is proceeding with considerable difficulty . . . . 20 percent of military production [has] switched over to consumer products in the last two years, but that still [has] left the economy heavily dependent on both the military and the space program.

Some factory directors have tried hard to find new niches for their workers. Motozavod, a plant with 20,000 employees specializing in sophisticated electronic equipment, is now turning out a grab bag of 60 different goods, from stereo tape players to clothing labels, from disposable syringes to cardiograms to an apparatus that helps men overcome impotence.

At Radiozavod, another large plant, which produced sophisticated [satellite] tracking systems, the most profitable business these days is in high-quality, high-priced bricks, a commodity which, unlike military hardware, is in both high demand and short supply.

SOURCE: Celestine Bohlen, "Arms Factory Can Make Bricks, But, Russia Asks, Is That Smart?," *The New York Times*, February 24, 1992, pp. A1 and A10.

## SCARCITY AND CHOICE ELSEWHERE IN THE ECONOMY

We have stressed that limited resources force hard choices upon business managers and society as a whole. But the same type of choices arise elsewhere—in households, in universities and other nonprofit organizations, as well as the government.

The nature of opportunity cost is perhaps most obvious for a household that must decide how to divide its income among the goods and services that compete for the family's trade. If the Simpson family buys an expensive new car, it may be forced to cut back sharply on some of its other purchases. This does not make it unwise to buy the car. But it does make it unwise to buy the car until the full implications of the purchase for the family's overall budget are considered. If the Simpson family is to use its limited resources most effectively, it must explicitly acknowledge that the opportunity costs of the car are the things it will actually choose to forgo as a result; for example, a shorter vacation and making do with the old TV set.

Even a rich and powerful nation like the United States or Japan must cope with the limitations implied by scarce resources. The necessity for choice imposed on the governments of these nations by their limited budgets is similar in character to the problems faced by business firms and households. For the goods and services it buys from others, a government has to prepare a budget similar to that of a very large household. For the items it produces itself—education, police protection, libraries, and so on—it faces a production possibilities frontier much like that of a business firm. Even though the U.S. government will spend about $1.5 trillion in 1993, some of the most acrimonious debates between *every* U.S. president and his critics have been over how to allocate the government's limited resources among competing uses.

## APPLICATION: ECONOMIC GROWTH IN THE UNITED STATES AND JAPAN

**ECONOMIC GROWTH** occurs when an economy is able to produce more goods and services for each consumer.

Among the economic choices that any society must make, there is one extremely important choice that illustrates well the concept of opportunity cost. This choice is embodied in the question "How fast should the economy grow?"[1] At first, the question may seem ridiculous. Since **economic growth** means, roughly speaking, that the average citizen gets larger and larger quantities of goods and services, is it not self-evident that faster growth is always better?

Again, the fundamental problem of scarcity intervenes. Economies do not grow by magic. Scarce resources must be devoted to the process of growth. Cement and steel that could be used to make swimming pools and stadiums must be diverted to the construction of more machinery and factories. Wood that could have been used to make furniture and skis must be used for hammers and ladders instead. Grain that could have been eaten must be used as seed to plant additional acres. By deciding how large a quantity of resources to devote to future needs rather than to current consumption, society in effect *chooses* (within limits) how fast it will grow.

In diagrammatic terms, economic growth means that the economy's production possibilities frontier shifts outward over time—like the move from *FF* to *GG* in Figure 3–4(a). Why? Because such a shift means that the economy can produce more of both of the outputs shown in the graph. Thus, in the figure, after growth has occurred, it is possible to produce the combination of products represented by points like *N*. Before growth had occurred, point *N* was beyond the economy's means because it was outside the production possibilities frontier.

A **CONSUMPTION GOOD** is an item that is available for immediate use by households, and that satisfies wants of members of households without contributing directly to future production by the economy.

A **CAPITAL GOOD** is an item that is used to produce other goods and services in the future, rather than being consumed today. Factories and machines are examples.

How does growth occur? That is, what shifts an economy's production frontier outward? There are many ways. For example, workers may acquire greater skill and learn to produce more output in an hour. Such increases in labor's productivity are discussed in Chapter 34. Perhaps even more important, the economy may construct more capital goods, temporarily giving up some consumption goods to provide the resources to build the factories and machines. Finally, inventions like the steam engine, AC electricity, and industrial robots can and do increase the economy's productive capacity, thereby shifting its production frontier outward.

Figure 3–4 illustrates, for two different countries, the nature of the choice by depicting production possibilities frontiers for **consumption goods** that are consumed today (like food and electricity) versus **capital goods** that can produce larger outputs for future consumption (like drill presses and electricity-generating plants). Figure 3–4(a) depicts a society, such as the United States, that devotes a relatively small quantity of resources to growth, preferring current consumption instead. It chooses a point like *A* on this year's production possibilities frontier, *FF*. At *A*, consumption is relatively high and production of capital is relatively low, so the production possibilities frontier shifts only to *GG* next year. Figure 3–4(b) depicts a society, such as Japan, much more enamored of growth. It selects a point like *B* on its production possibilities frontier, *ff*. At *B*, consumption is

[1]Economic growth will be studied in detail in Chapter 21 of *Macroeconomics*.

Figure 3-4 **GROWTH IN TWO ECONOMIES**

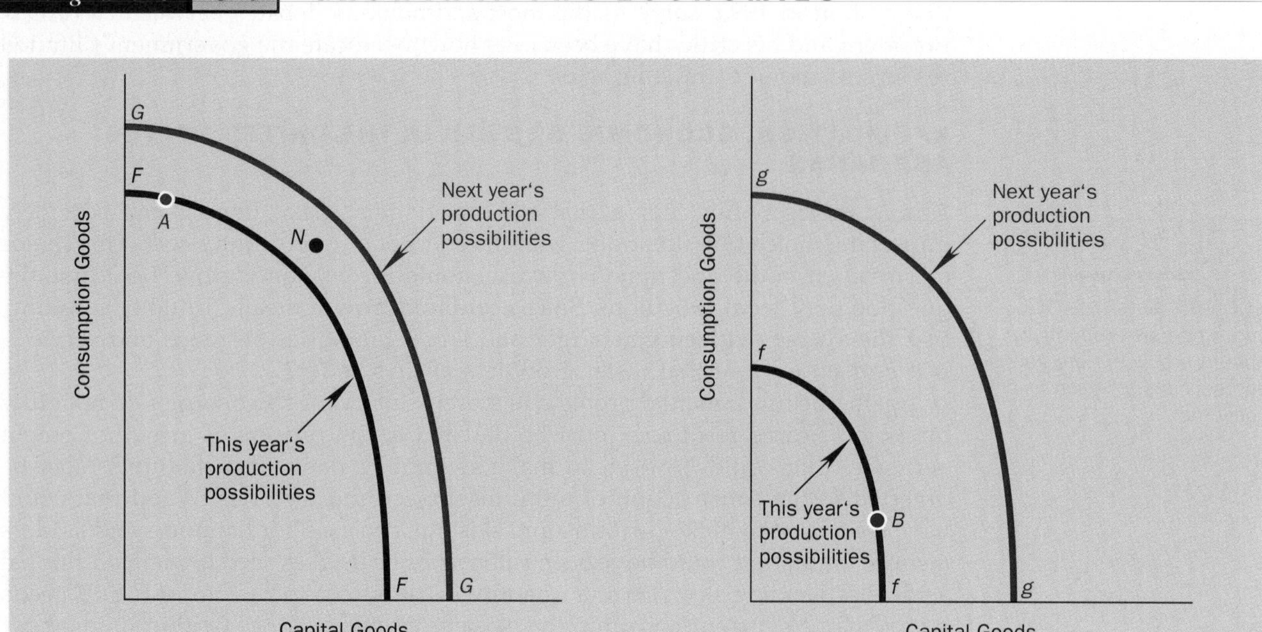


Growth shifts the black production possibilities frontiers *FF* and *ff* outward to the blue frontiers *GG* and *gg*, meaning that each economy can produce more of both goods than it could before. If the shift in both economies occurs in the same period of time, then the Japanese economy [part (b)] is growing faster than the U.S. economy [part (a)] because the outward shift in (b) is much greater than the one in (a).

much lower and production of capital goods is much higher, so its production possibilities frontier moves all the way to *gg* by next year. Japan grows faster than the U.S. But the more rapid growth has a price—an *opportunity cost*: The Japanese must give up some of the current consumption that Americans enjoy.

An economy grows by giving up some current consumption and producing capital goods for the future instead. The more capital it produces, the faster will its production possibilities frontier shift outward over time.

It should be noted that the production of capital goods is not the only way to shift the economy's production possibilities frontier outward. New technology—the process of invention and innovation—is probably the primary means by which economies have increased the output they can produce with a given quantity of resources. Increased education and training of the labor force is generally believed to yield a similar result.

## THE CONCEPT OF EFFICIENCY

So far in our discussion of scarcity and choice, we have assumed that either the single firm or the whole economy always operates on its production possibilities frontier rather than *below* it. In other words, we have tacitly assumed that, whatever it decides to do, the firm or economy does so *efficiently*. Economists define *efficiency* as the absence of waste. An efficient economy utilizes all of its available resources and produces the maximum amount of output that its technology permits.[2]

To see why any point on the economy's production possibilities frontier in Figure 3–3 represents an efficient decision, suppose for a moment that society has decided to produce 300 missiles. According to the production possibilities frontier, if 300 missiles are to be produced, then the maximum number of automobiles that can be made is 500,000 (point *D* in Figure 3–3). The economy is therefore operating efficiently if it actually produces 500,000 automobiles rather than some smaller amount such as 300,000 (as at point *G*). While point *D* is efficient, point *G* is not. This is so because the economy is capable of moving from *G* to *D*, thereby producing 200,000 more automobiles without giving up any missiles (or anything else). Clearly, failure to take advantage of the option of choosing point *D* rather than point *G* constitutes a wasted opportunity.

Note that the concept of efficiency does not tell us which point on the production possibilities frontier is *best*; it only tells us that no point that is *not* on the frontier can be best, because any such point represents wasted resources. For example, should society ever find itself at point *G*, the necessity of making hard choices would (temporarily) disappear. It would be possible to increase production of *both* missiles *and* automobiles by moving to a point such as *E*.

Why, then, would a society ever find itself at a point below its production possibilities frontier? There are a number of ways in which resources are wasted in real life. The most important of them, unemployment, is an issue that will take up a substantial part of this book (especially in Parts 6 and 7). When many workers are unemployed, the economy finds itself at a point like *G*, below the frontier, because by putting the unemployed to work in both industries, the economy could produce more missiles *and* more automobiles. The economy would then move from point *G* to the right (more missiles) and upward (more automobiles) toward a point like *E* on the production possibilities frontier. Only when no resources are wasted by unemployment or misuse is the economy on the frontier.

Inefficiency occurs in other ways as well. One prime example is when inputs are not assigned to the right task—as when wheat is grown on land best suited to soybean cultivation, while soybeans are grown on land more appropriate for wheat production. Another important type of inefficiency occurs where large firms produce goods or services that are best turned out by small enterprises that can pay closer attention to detail, or when small firms produce outputs best suited to large-scale production. Other examples are the outright waste that occurs because of favoritism (e.g., promotion of an incompetent brother-in-law) or restrictive labor practices (e.g., union rules that require a railroad to keep a fireman on a diesel locomotive where there is nothing for a fireman to do).

A particularly serious form of waste is caused by discrimination against African-American, Hispanic, or female workers. When a job is given to a white male in preference to a more qualified African-American woman, output is sacrificed and the entire community is apt to be affected adversely. Every one of these inefficiencies means that the community obtains less output than it could have, given the available inputs.

---

[2]A more formal definition of *efficiency* is offered in Chapter 10.

## THE THREE COORDINATION TASKS OF ANY ECONOMY

In deciding how to use its scarce resources, society must somehow make three sorts of decisions. First, as we have just emphasized, it must figure out **how to utilize its resources efficiently**; that is, it must find a way to get *on* its production possibilities frontier. Second, it must decide **what combination of goods to produce**—how many missiles, automobiles, and so on; that is, it must select one specific point on the production possibilities frontier. Finally, it must decide **how much of each good to distribute to each person**, doing so in a sensible way that does not assign meat to vegetarians and wine to teetotalers.

Certainly, each of these decisions—*which are often referred to as "how?" "what?" and "to whom?"*—can be made in many ways. For example, a central planner can tell people how to produce, what to produce, and what to consume, as used to be done, at least to some extent, in the former Soviet Union and the other countries of Eastern Europe.[3] But these decisions also can be made without central direction, through a system of prices and markets *whose directions are dictated by the demands of consumers and by the costs of producers*. As the formerly socialist countries have learned, markets can do an impressively effective job in carrying out these tasks. To see how markets can do this, let us consider each task in turn.

## SPECIALIZATION, DIVISION OF LABOR, AND EXCHANGE

Efficiency in production is one of the economy's three basic tasks. Many features of society contribute to efficiency; others interfere with it. While different societies pursue the goal of economic efficiency in different ways, one source of efficiency is so fundamental that we must single it out for special attention: the tremendous gains in productivity that stem from **specialization** and the consequent **division of labor**.

**DIVISION OF LABOR** means breaking up a task into a number of smaller, more specialized tasks so that each worker can become more adept at a particular job.

Adam Smith, the founder of modern economics, first marveled at this mainspring of efficiency and productivity on a visit to a pin factory. In a famous passage near the beginning of his monumental book, *The Wealth of Nations* (1776), he described what he saw:

> *One man draws out the wire, another straightens it, a third cuts it, a fourth points it, a fifth grinds it at the top for receiving the head; to make the head requires two or three distinct operations; to put it on is a peculiar business, to whiten the pins is another; it is even a trade by itself to put them into the paper . . .* .[4]

Smith observed that by dividing the work to be done in this way, each worker became quite skilled in a particular specialty, and the productivity of the group of workers as a whole was enhanced enormously. As Smith related it:

> *I have seen a small manufactory of this kind where ten men only were employed . . . . Those ten persons . . . could make among them upwards of forty-eight thousand pins in a day . . . . But if they had all wrought separately and independently . . . they certainly could not each of them have made twenty, perhaps not one pin in a day . . . .*[5]

---

[3]Central planning will be considered in some detail in Chapter 23.

[4]Adam Smith, *The Wealth of Nations* (New York: Random House, Modern Library Edition, 1937), page 4.

[5]*Ibid.*, page 5.

*Biographical Note*

**ADAM SMITH (1723–1790)**

Adam Smith, the philosopher of the market system, was born the son of a customs official in 1723 and ended his career in the well-paid post of collector of customs for Scotland. He received an excellent education at Glasgow College, where, for the first time, some lectures were being given in English rather than Latin. A fellowship to Oxford University followed, and for six years he studied there mostly by himself, since, at that time, teaching at Oxford was virtually nonexistent.

After completing his studies, Smith was appointed professor of logic at Glasgow College and, later, professor of moral philosophy, a field which then included economics. Fortunately, he was a popular lecturer because, in those days, a professor's pay in Glasgow depended on the number of students who chose to attend his lectures. At Glasgow, Smith was responsible for helping young James Watt find a job as an instrument maker. Watt later invented a key improvement in the steam engine that made its use possible in factories, trains, and ships. So in this and many other respects, Smith was present virtually at the birth of the Industrial Revolution, whose prophet he was destined to become.

After 13 years at Glasgow, Smith accepted a highly paid post as a tutor to a young Scottish nobleman with whom he spent several years in France, a customary way of educating nobles in the eighteenth century. Primarily because he was bored during these years, Smith began working on *The Wealth of Nations*. Several years after his return to England, in 1776, the book was published and rapidly achieved popularity.

*The Wealth of Nations* was one of the first systematic treatises in economics, contributing to both theoretical and factual knowledge about the subject. Among the main points made in the book are the importance for a nation's prosperity of free trade and the division of labor; the dangers of tariffs and government-protected monopolies; and the superiority of self-interest—the instrument of the "invisible hand"—over altruism as a means of making the economy serve the public interest.

The British government was grateful for the ideas for new tax legislation Smith proposed, and to show its appreciation appointed him to the lucrative sinecure of collector of customs. The salary from this post together with the lifetime pension awarded him by his former pupil left him very well-off financially, although he eventually gave away most of his money to charitable causes.

The intellectual world was small in the eighteenth century, and Smith's acquaintances included David Hume, Samuel Johnson, James Boswell, Jean Jacques Rousseau, and (probably) Benjamin Franklin. Smith got along well with everyone except Samuel Johnson, who was noted for his dislike of Scots. Smith was absent-minded and apparently timid with women, being visibly embarrassed by the public attention of the eminent ladies of Paris during his visits there. He never married, and he lived with his mother most of his life. When he died, the Edinburgh newspapers recalled only that Smith was kidnapped by gypsies when he was four years old. But thanks to his writings, he is remembered for a good deal more than that.

In other words, through the miracle of division of labor and specialization, ten workers accomplished what would otherwise have required thousands. This was one of the secrets of the Industrial Revolution, which helped lift humanity out of the abject poverty that had for so long been its lot.

But specialization created a problem. With division of labor, people no longer produced only what they wanted to consume themselves. The workers in the pin factory had no use for the thousands of pins they produced each day; they wanted to trade them for things like food, clothing, and shelter. Specialization thus made it necessary to have some mechanism by which workers producing pins could **exchange** their wares with workers producing such things as cloth and potatoes.

Without a system of exchange, the productivity miracle achieved by the division of labor would have done society little good. With it, standards of living rose enormously. As we observed in Chapter 1, such exchange benefits *all* participants.

**MUTUAL GAINS FROM VOLUNTARY EXCHANGE**

Unless there is deception or misunderstanding of the facts, a *voluntary* exchange between two parties must make both parties better off. Even though no additional goods are produced by the act of trading, the welfare of society is increased because each individual acquires goods that are more suited to his or her needs and tastes. This simple but fundamental precept of economics is one of our **12 Ideas for Beyond the Final Exam.**

While goods can be traded for other goods, a system of exchange works better when everyone agrees to use some common item (such as pieces of paper with unique markings printed on them) for buying and selling goods and services. Enter *money*. Then workers in pin factories, for example, can be paid in money rather than in pins, and they can use this money to purchase cloth and potatoes. Textile workers and farmers can do the same.

These two phenomena—specialization and exchange (assisted by money)—working in tandem led to a vast improvement in the well-being of humanity. But what forces induce workers to join together so that the fruits of the division of labor can be enjoyed? And what forces establish a smoothly functioning system of exchange so that each person can acquire what she or he wants to consume? One alternative is to have a central authority telling people what to do. But Adam Smith explained and extolled another way of organizing and coordinating economic activity—the use of markets and prices.

## MARKETS, PRICES, AND THE THREE COORDINATION TASKS

A **MARKET SYSTEM** is a form of organization of the economy in which decisions on resource allocation are left to the independent decisions of individual producers and consumers acting in their own best interests without central direction.

Smith noted that people are adept at pursuing their own self-interest, and that a **market system** is a fine way to harness this self-interest. As he put it—with pretty clear religious overtones—in doing what is best for themselves, people are "led by an invisible hand" to promote the economic well-being of society as a whole.

People who live in a well-functioning market economy like ours tend to take the achievements of the market for granted, much like the daily rising and setting of the sun. Few bother to think about, say, what makes Florida oranges show up daily in South Dakota supermarkets. While the process by which the market guides the economy and leads it to work in such an orderly fashion is far from obvious to most of the public, the general principles are not exceedingly complex.[6]

[6]This topic is studied in detail in Chapter 10.

Firms are encouraged by the profit motive to use inputs efficiently. Valuable resources (such as energy) command high prices, and so producers have a strong incentive not to use them wastefully. The market mechanism also guides firms' output decisions, and hence those of society. A rise in the price of wheat, for example, will persuade farmers to produce more wheat and to devote less of their land to soybeans. Finally, a price system uses a series of voluntary exchanges to determine what goods go to which consumers. Consumers use their income to buy the things they like best among those they can afford. But the ability to buy goods is not divided equally. Workers with valuable skills and owners of scarce resources are able to sell what they have at attractive prices. With the incomes they earn, they can then purchase the goods and services they want most, within the limits of their budgets. Those who are less successful in selling what they own receive lower incomes, and so cannot afford to buy much. In some cases, they suffer severe deprivation.

This, in broad terms, is how a market economy solves the three basic problems facing any society: how to produce any given combination of goods efficiently, how to select an appropriate combination of goods, and how to distribute these goods sensibly among the people. As we proceed through the following chapters, you will learn much more about these issues. You will see that they constitute the central theme that permeates not only this text, but the work of economists in general. As you progress through the book, keep in mind the following two questions: **What does the market do well, and what does it do poorly**? There are numerous answers to both questions, as you will learn in subsequent chapters.

1. Society has many important goals. Some of them, such as producing goods and services with maximum efficiency (minimum waste), can be achieved extraordinarily well by letting markets operate more or less freely.
2. Free markets will not, however, achieve all of society's goals. For example, they often have trouble keeping unemployment and inflation low. And there are even some goals—such as protection of the environment—for which the unfettered operation of markets may be positively harmful. Many observers also believe that markets do not necessarily lead to an equitable distribution of income.
3. But even in cases where the market does not perform at all well, there may be ways of harnessing the power of the market mechanism to remedy its own deficiencies, as you will learn in Chapters 13 and 18.

## RADICAL AND CONSERVATIVE GOALS CAN BOTH BE SERVED BY THE MARKET MECHANISM

Since economic debates often have political and ideological overtones, we think it important to close this chapter by emphasizing that the central theme that we have just outlined is neither a defense of nor an attack on the capitalist system. Nor is it a "conservative" position. One does not have to be a conservative to recognize that the market mechanism can be an extraordinarily helpful instrument for the pursuit of economic goals. Most of the formerly staunch socialist countries of Europe are now working hard to "marketize" their economies, and even the People's Republic of China now seems to be moving in that direction.

The point is not to confuse means and ends in deciding on how much to rely on market forces. Radicals and conservatives surely have different goals, and they may also differ in the means they advocate to pursue these goals. But means should be chosen on the basis of how effective they are in achieving the adopted goals, not on some ideological prejudgments.

Even Karl Marx recognized, indeed emphasized, that the market is a remarkably efficient mechanism for producing an abundance of goods and services unparalleled in pre-capitalist history. Such wealth can be used to promote conservative goals, such as reducing tax rates. Or it can be used to facilitate the achievement of the goals of liberals or even radicals, such as more generous public support of the impoverished, the construction of more public schools and hospitals, and the provision of amenities such as national parks and museums.

Certainly, there are economic problems with which the market cannot deal. Indeed, we have just noted that the market is the *source* of a number of significant problems. But the evidence leads economists to believe that many economic problems are best handled by market techniques. The analysis in this book is intended to help you identify the objectives which we can rely upon the market mechanism to achieve, and those which it will fail to promote, or at least not promote very effectively. We urge you to forget the slogans you have heard—whether from the left or from the right—and make up your own mind after you have learned the materials covered in this book.

## *Summary*

1. Supplies of all **resources** are limited. Because resources are **scarce**, a **rational decision** is one that chooses the best alternative among the options that are possible with the available resources.
2. It is irrational to assign highest priority to everything. No one can afford everything, and so hard choices must be made.
3. With limited resources, a decision to obtain more of one item is also a decision to give up some of another. What we give up is called the **opportunity cost** of what we get. The opportunity cost is the true cost of any decision. This is one of the **12 Ideas for Beyond the Final Exam**.
4. The allocation of resources refers to division of the economy's scarce **inputs** (fuel, minerals, machines, labor, and so on) among the economy's alternative uses for them.
5. When the market is functioning effectively, firms are led to use resources efficiently and to produce the things that consumers want most. In such cases, opportunity costs and money costs (prices) correspond closely. When the market performs poorly, or when important costly items do not get price tags, opportunity costs and money costs can be quite different.
6. A firm's **production possibilities frontier** shows the combinations of goods the firm can produce with a designated quantity of resources, given the state of technology. The frontier usually is not a straight line, but is bowed outward because resources tend to be specialized.
7. The principle of increasing costs states that as the production of one good expands, the opportunity cost of producing another unit of this good generally increases.
8. The economy as a whole has a production possibilities frontier whose position is determined by its technology and by the available resources of land, labor, capital, and raw materials.
9. If a firm or an economy ends up at a point below its production possibilities frontier, it is using its resources inefficiently or wastefully. This is what happens, for example, when there is unemployment.
10. **Economic growth** means there is an outward shift in the economy's production possibilities frontier. The faster the growth, the faster this shift occurs. But growth requires a sacrifice of current consumption, and this is its opportunity cost.
11. **Efficiency** is defined by economists as the absence of waste. It is achieved primarily by gains in productivity brought about through **specialization**, **division of labor**, and a **system of exchange**.
12. If an exchange is voluntary, both parties must benefit even though no new goods are produced. This is another of the **12 Ideas for Beyond the Final Exam**.

13. Every economic system must find a way to answer three basic questions: How can goods be produced most efficiently? How much of each good should be produced? How should goods be distributed?
14. The market system works very well in solving some of society's basic problems, but it fails to remedy others and may, indeed, create some of its own. Where and how it succeeds and fails constitute the theme of this book and characterize the work of economists in general.

## *Key Concepts and Terms*

Resources
Scarcity
Choice
Rational decision
Opportunity cost
Outputs
Inputs (means of production)
Production possibilities frontier
Allocation of resources
Principle of increasing costs
Economic growth
Consumption goods
Capital goods
Efficiency
Specialization
Division of labor
Exchange market system
Three coordination tasks

## *Questions for Review*

1. Discuss the resource limitations that affect
   a. the poorest person on earth
   b. the richest person on earth
   c. a firm in Switzerland
   d. a government agency in China
   e. the population of the world.
2. If you were president of your college, what would you change if your budget were cut by 10 percent? By 25 percent? By 50 percent?
3. If you were to drop out of college, what things would change in your life? What, then, is the opportunity cost of your education?
4. A person rents a house for which she pays the landlord $8000 a year. The house can be purchased for $100,000, and the tenant has this much money in a bank account that pays 4 percent interest per year. Is buying the house a good deal for the tenant? Where does opportunity cost enter the picture?
5. Construct graphically the production possibilities frontier for the Grand Republic of Glubstania, using the data given in the following table. Does the principle of increasing cost hold in the Glubstanian economy?
6. Consider two alternatives for Glubstania in the year 1994. In case (a), its inhabitants eat 60 million pork muffins and build only 12,000 noodle-making machines. In case (b), the population eats only 15 million pork muffins but builds 36,000 noodle machines. Which case will lead to a more generous production possibilities frontier for Glubstania in 1995? (*Note*: In Glubstania, noodle machines are used to produce pork muffins.)

**GLUBSTANIA'S 1994 PRODUCTION POSSIBILITIES**

| PORK MUFFINS (millions per year) | NOODLE MACHINES (thousands per year) |
|---|---|
| 75 | 0 |
| 60 | 12 |
| 45 | 22 |
| 30 | 30 |
| 15 | 36 |
| 0 | 40 |

7. Sarah's Snack Shop sells two brands of potato chips. Brand X costs Sarah 75 cents per bag, and Brand Y costs Sarah $1. Draw Sarah's production possibilities frontier if she has $60 budgeted to spend on potato chips. Why is it not "bowed out"?
8. To raise chickens, it is necessary to use many types of feed, such as corn and soy meal. Consider a farm in the former Soviet Union, and try to describe how decisions on the number of chickens to be raised, and the amount of each feed to use in raising them, was made under the old communist regime. If the farm is now a private enterprise, how does the market guide the decisions that used to be made by the central planning agency?
9. The United States is one of the world's wealthiest countries. Think of a recent case in which the decisions of the U.S. government were severely constrained by scarcity. Describe the trade-offs that were involved. What was the opportunity cost of the decisions that were actually made?

Chapter 4

# SUPPLY AND DEMAND: AN INITIAL LOOK

*The free enterprise system is absolutely too important to be left to the voluntary action of the marketplace.*

**CONGRESSMAN RICHARD KELLY OF FLORIDA (1979)**

If the issues of scarcity, choice, and coordination constitute the basic *problem* of economics, then the mechanism of supply and demand is its basic investigative *tool.* Whether your course concentrates on macroeconomics or microeconomics, you will find that the so-called law of supply and demand is the fundamental tool of economic analysis. Supply and demand analysis is used in this book to study issues seemingly as diverse as inflation and unemployment, the international value of the dollar, government regulation of business, and protection of the environment. So careful study of this chapter will pay rich dividends. ¶ The chapter describes the rudiments of supply and demand analysis in steps. We begin with demand, then add supply, and finally put the two sides together. *Supply and demand curves*—graphs that relate price to quantity supplied and quantity demanded, respectively—are explained and used to show how prices and quantities are determined in a free market. Influences that shift either the demand curve or the supply curve are catalogued briefly, and the analysis is used to explain why airlines often run "sales" and how computers found their way into the home.

One major theme of the chapter is that governments around the world and throughout recorded history have attempted to tamper with the price mechanism. We will see that these bouts with Adam Smith's invisible hand often have produced undesired side effects that surprised and dismayed the authorities. These unfortunate effects were no accidents, but were inherent consequences of interfering with the operation of free markets. The invisible hand fights back!

Finally, a word of caution. This chapter makes heavy use of graphs such as those described in the appendix to Chapter 1. If you encounter difficulties with these graphs, we suggest you review pages 19–26 before proceeding.

## FIGHTING THE INVISIBLE HAND

Adam Smith was a great admirer of the price system. He marveled at its intricacies and extolled its accomplishments—both as a producer of goods and a guarantor of individual freedom. Many people since Smith's time have shared his enthusiasm, but many others have not. His contemporaries in the American colonies, for example, were often unhappy with the prices produced by free markets and thought they could do better by legislative decree. (They could not, as the accompanying boxed insert shows.) And there have been countless other instances in which the public's sense of justice was outraged by the prices charged on the

### *Price Controls at Valley Forge*

George Washington, the history books tell us, was beset by many enemies during the winter of 1777–1778—including the British, their Hessian mercenaries, and the merciless winter weather. But he had another enemy that the history books ignore, an enemy that meant well but almost destroyed his army at Valley Forge. As the following excerpt explains, that enemy was the Pennsylvania legislature.

In Pennsylvania, where the main force of Washington's army was quartered . . . the legislature . . . decided to try a period of price control limited to those commodities needed for use by the army. . . . The result might have been anticipated by those with some knowledge of the trials and tribulations of other states. The prices of uncontrolled goods, mostly imported, rose to record heights. Most farmers kept back their produce, refusing to sell at what they regarded as an unfair price. Some who had large families to take care of even secretly sold their food to the British who paid in gold.

After the disastrous winter at Valley Forge when Washington's army nearly starved to death (thanks largely to these well-intentioned but misdirected laws), the ill-fated experiment in price controls was finally ended. The Continental Congress on June 4, 1778, adopted the following resolution:

"Whereas . . . it hath been found by experience that limitations upon the prices of commodities are not only ineffectual for the purposes proposed, but likewise productive of very evil consequences . . . resolved, that it be recommended to the several states to repeal or suspend all laws or resolutions within the said states respectively limiting, regulating or restraining the Price of any Article, Manufacture or Commodity."

SOURCE: Robert L. Schuettinger and Eamonn F. Butler, *Forty Centuries of Wage and Price Controls* (Washington, D.C.: Heritage Foundation, 1979), page 41. Reprinted by permission.

open market, particularly when the sellers of the expensive items did not enjoy great popularity—landlords, moneylenders, and oil companies are good examples.

Attempts to control interest rates (which may be thought of as the price of borrowing money) go back hundreds of years before the birth of Christ, at least to the code of laws compiled under Hammurabi in Babylonia about 1800 B.C. Our historical legacy also includes a rather long list of price ceilings on foods and other products imposed in the reign of Diocletian, emperor of the declining Roman Empire. More recently, Americans have been offered the "protection" of a variety of price controls. Ceilings have been placed on some prices (such as rents) to protect buyers, while floors have been placed under other prices (such as farm products) to protect sellers. Many if not most of these measures were adopted in response to popular opinion, and there was a great outcry whenever it was proposed that any of them be weakened or eliminated.

Yet, somehow, everything such regulation touches seems to end up in even greater disarray than it was before. Despite rent controls, rents in New York City soared. Despite laws against ticket "scalping," tickets for popular shows and sports events sell at tremendous premiums—tickets to the Super Bowl, for example, are often scalped for $1000 or more. Taxis cost much more in New York City (where they are tightly regulated) than in Washington, D.C. (where they are not). And the list could go on.

Still, legislators continue to turn to controls whenever the economy does not work to their satisfaction, just as they did in 1777. The 1970s and 1980s saw a return to rent controls in many American cities, a brief experiment with overall price controls by a Republican administration that had vowed never to turn to them, a web of controls over energy prices, and a revival of agricultural price supports.

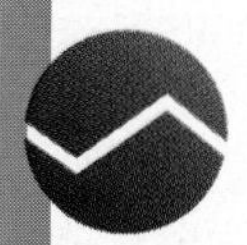

**INTERFERENCES WITH THE "LAW" OF SUPPLY AND DEMAND**

Public opinion frequently encourages legislative attempts to "repeal the law of supply and demand" by controlling prices. The consequences usually are quite unfortunate, exacting heavy costs from the general public and often aggravating the problem the legislation was intended to cure. This is another of the **12 Ideas for Beyond the Final Exam**, and it will occupy our attention throughout this chapter.

To understand what goes wrong when markets are tampered with, we must first learn how they operate when they are unfettered. This chapter takes a first step in that direction by studying the machinery of supply and demand. Then, at the end of the chapter, we return to the issue of price controls, illustrating the problems that can arise by case studies of rent controls in New York City and price supports for milk.

Every market has both buyers and sellers. We begin our analysis on the consumers' side of the market.

## DEMAND AND QUANTITY DEMANDED

Noneconomists are apt to think of consumer demands as fixed amounts. For example, when the production of a new model of computer is proposed, management asks "What is its market potential? How many will we be able to sell?" Similarly, government bureaus conduct studies to determine how many engineers will be "required" in succeeding years.

Economists respond that such questions are not well posed—that there is no *single* answer to such a question. Rather, they say, the "market potential" for computers or the number of engineers that will be "required" depends on a great number of things, *including the price that will be charged for each.*

The **QUANTITY DEMANDED** is the number of units consumers want to buy over a specified period of time.

The **quantity demanded** of any product normally depends on its price. Quantity demanded also has a number of other determinants, including population size, consumer incomes, tastes, and the prices of other products.

Because of the central role of prices in a market economy, we begin our study of demand by focusing on the dependence of quantity demanded on price. Shortly, we will bring the other determinants of quantity demanded back into the picture.

Consider, as an example, the quantity of milk demanded. Almost everyone purchases at least some milk. However, if the price of milk is very high, its "market potential" may be very small. People will find ways to get along with less milk, perhaps by switching to tea or coffee. If the price declines, people will be encouraged to drink more milk. They may give their children larger portions or switch away from juices and sodas. Thus:

There is no *one* demand figure for milk, for computers, or for engineers. Rather, there is a different quantity demanded for each possible price.

## THE DEMAND SCHEDULE

A **DEMAND SCHEDULE** is a table showing how the quantity demanded of some product during a specified period of time changes as the price of that product changes, holding all other determinants of quantity demanded constant.

Table 4–1 displays this information for milk in what we call a **demand schedule,** which indicates how much consumers are willing and able to buy at different possible prices during a specified period of time. The table shows the quantity of milk that will be demanded in a year at each possible price ranging from $1 to 40¢ per quart. We see, for example, that at a relatively low price, like 50¢ per quart, customers wish to purchase 70 billion quarts per year. But if the price were to rise to, say, 90¢ per quart, quantity demanded would fall to 50 billion quarts.

Common sense tells us why this should be so.[1] First, as prices rise, some customers will reduce their consumption of milk. Second, higher prices will induce

*Table* **4–1** **DEMAND SCHEDULE FOR MILK**

| PRICE (dollars per quart) | QUANTITY DEMANDED (billions of quarts per year) | LABEL IN FIGURE 4–1 |
|---|---|---|
| 1.00 | 45 | *A* |
| 0.90 | 50 | *B* |
| 0.80 | 55 | *C* |
| 0.70 | 60 | *E* |
| 0.60 | 65 | *F* |
| 0.50 | 70 | *G* |
| 0.40 | 75 | *H* |

[1]This common-sense answer is examined more fully in Chapters 7 and 8.

**Figure 4–1** DEMAND CURVE FOR MILK

This curve shows the relationship between price and quantity demanded. To sell 70 billion quarts per year, the price must be only 50¢ (point *G*). If, instead, price is 90¢, only 50 billion quarts will be demanded (point *B*). To sell more milk, the price must be reduced. That is what the negative slope of the demand curve means.

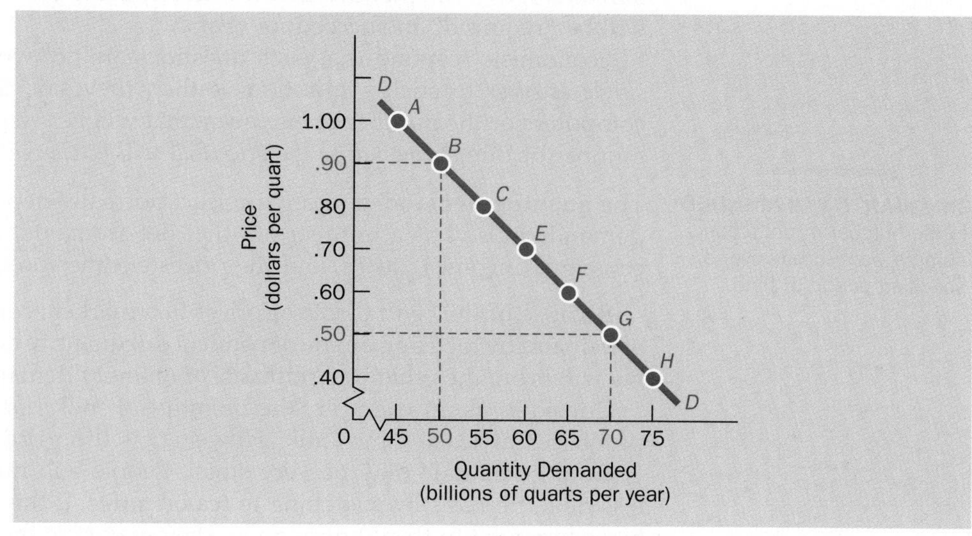


some customers to drop out of the market entirely—for example, by switching to soda or juice. On both counts, quantity demanded will decline as the price rises.

As the price of an item rises, the quantity demanded normally falls. As the price falls, the quantity demanded normally rises.

### THE DEMAND CURVE

A **DEMAND CURVE** is a graphical depiction of a demand schedule. It shows how the quantity demanded of some product during a specified period of time will change as the price of that product changes, holding all other determinants of quantity demanded constant.

The information contained in Table 4–1 can be summarized in a graph like Figure 4–1, which we call a **demand curve**. Each point in the graph corresponds to a line in the table. For example, point *B* corresponds to the second line in the table, indicating that at a price of 90¢ per quart, 50 billion quarts per year will be demanded. Since the quantity demanded declines as the price increases, the demand curve has a negative slope.[2]

Notice the last phrase in the definitions of the demand schedule and the demand curve: "holding all other determinants of quantity demanded constant." These "other things" include consumer incomes and preferences, the prices of soda and orange juice, and perhaps even advertising by the dairy association. We will examine the influences of these factors later in the chapter. First, however, let's look at the sellers' side of the market.

## SUPPLY AND QUANTITY SUPPLIED

Like quantity demanded, the quantity of milk that is supplied by dairy farmers is not a fixed number; it also depends on many things. Obviously, we expect

[2]If you need to review the concept of *slope*, refer back to the appendix to Chapter 1, especially pages 20–23.

The **QUANTITY SUPPLIED** is the number of units sellers want to sell over a specified period of time.

more milk to be supplied if there are more dairy farms, or more cows per farm. Or cows may give less milk if bad weather deprives them of their feed. As before, however, let's turn our attention first to the relationship between **quantity supplied** and one of its major determinants—the price of milk.

Economists generally suppose that a higher price calls forth a greater quantity supplied. Why? Remember our analysis of the principle of increasing cost in Chapter 3 (page 61). According to that principle, as more of any farmer's (or the nation's) resources are devoted to milk production, the opportunity cost of obtaining another quart of milk increases. Farmers will therefore find it profitable to raise milk production only if they can sell the milk at a higher price—high enough to cover the additional costs incurred to expand production.

Looked at the other way around, we have just concluded that higher prices normally will be required to persuade farmers to raise milk production. This idea is quite general and applies to the supply of most goods and services.[3] As long as suppliers want to make profits and the principle of increasing costs holds:

As the price of an item rises, the quantity supplied normally rises. As the price falls, the quantity supplied normally falls.

A **SUPPLY SCHEDULE** is a table showing how the quantity supplied of some product during a specified period of time changes as the price of that product changes, holding all other determinants of quantity supplied constant.

A **SUPPLY CURVE** is a graphical depiction of a supply schedule. It shows how the quantity supplied of some product during a specified period of time will change as the price of that product changes, holding all other determinants of quantity supplied constant.

## THE SUPPLY SCHEDULE AND THE SUPPLY CURVE

The relationship between the price of milk and its quantity supplied is recorded in Table 4–2. Tables like this are called **supply schedules**; they show how much sellers are willing to provide during a specified period at alternative possible prices. This particular supply schedule shows that a low price like 50¢ per quart will induce suppliers to provide only 40 billion quarts, while a higher price like 80¢ will induce them to provide much more—70 billion quarts.

As you might have guessed, when information like this is plotted on a graph, it is called a **supply curve**. Figure 4–2 is the supply curve corresponding to the supply schedule in Table 4–2. It slopes upward because quantity supplied is higher when price is higher.

Notice again the same phrase in the definition: "holding all other determinants of quantity supplied constant." We will return to these "other determinants" a bit later in the discussion. But first we are ready to put demand and supply together.

**Table 4–2 SUPPLY SCHEDULE FOR MILK**

| PRICE (dollars per quart) | QUANTITY SUPPLIED (billions of quarts per year) | LABEL IN FIGURE 4–2 |
|---|---|---|
| 1.00 | 90 | *a* |
| 0.90 | 80 | *b* |
| 0.80 | 70 | *c* |
| 0.70 | 60 | *e* |
| 0.60 | 50 | *f* |
| 0.50 | 40 | *g* |
| 0.40 | 30 | *h* |

[3]This analysis is carried out in much greater detail in the next two chapters.

*Figure* **4-2** **SUPPLY CURVE FOR MILK**

This curve shows the relationship between the price of milk and the quantity supplied. To stimulate a greater quantity supplied, price must be increased. That is the meaning of the positive slope of the supply curve.

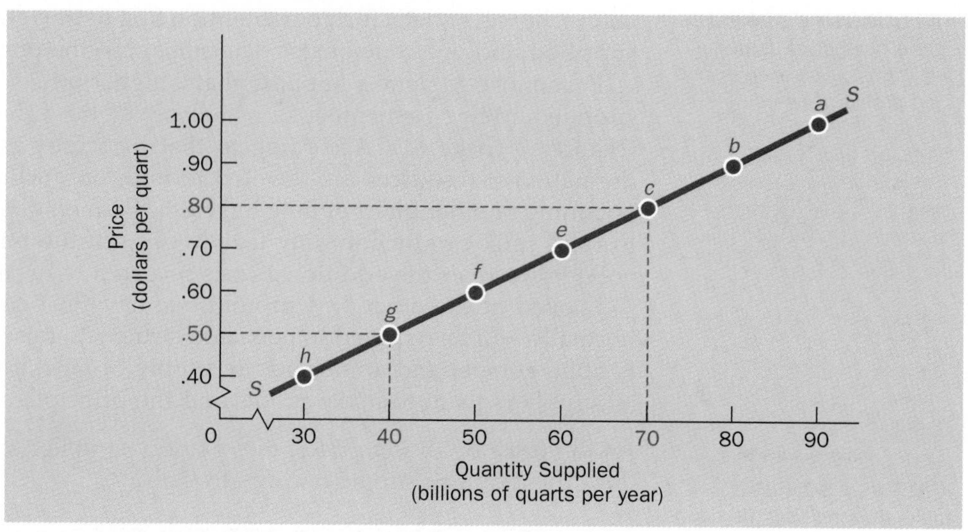


## EQUILIBRIUM OF SUPPLY AND DEMAND

To analyze how price is determined in a free market, we must compare the desires of consumers (demand) with the desires of producers (supply) and see whether the two plans are consistent. Table 4–3 and Figure 4–3 help us do this.

Table 4–3 brings together the demand schedule from Table 4–1 and the supply schedule from Table 4–2. Similarly, Figure 4–3 puts the demand curve from Figure 4–1 and the supply curve from Figure 4–2 on a single graph. Such a graphic device is called a **supply–demand diagram**, and you will encounter many of them in this book. Notice that, for reasons already discussed, the demand curve has a negative slope and the supply curve has a positive slope. Most supply–demand diagrams are drawn with slopes like these.

*Table* **4-3** **DETERMINATION OF THE EQUILIBRIUM PRICE AND QUANTITY OF MILK**

| PRICE (dollars per quart) | QUANTITY DEMANDED (billions of quarts per year) | QUANTITY SUPPLIED (billions of quarts per year) | SURPLUS OR SHORTAGE? | PRICE WILL |
|---|---|---|---|---|
| 1.00 | 45 | 90 | Surplus | Fall |
| 0.90 | 50 | 80 | Surplus | Fall |
| 0.80 | 55 | 70 | Surplus | Fall |
| 0.70 | 60 | 60 | Neither | Remain the same |
| 0.60 | 65 | 50 | Shortage | Rise |
| 0.50 | 70 | 40 | Shortage | Rise |
| 0.40 | 75 | 30 | Shortage | Rise |

**Figure 4-3** **SUPPLY-DEMAND EQUILIBRIUM**

In a free market, price and quantity are determined by the intersection of the supply curve and the demand curve. In this example, the equilibrium price is 70¢ and the equilibrium quantity is 60 billion quarts of milk per year. Any other price is inconsistent with equilibrium. For example, at a price of 50¢, quantity demanded is 70 billion (point *G*), while quantity supplied is only 40 billion (point *g*), so that price will be driven up by the unsatisfied demand.

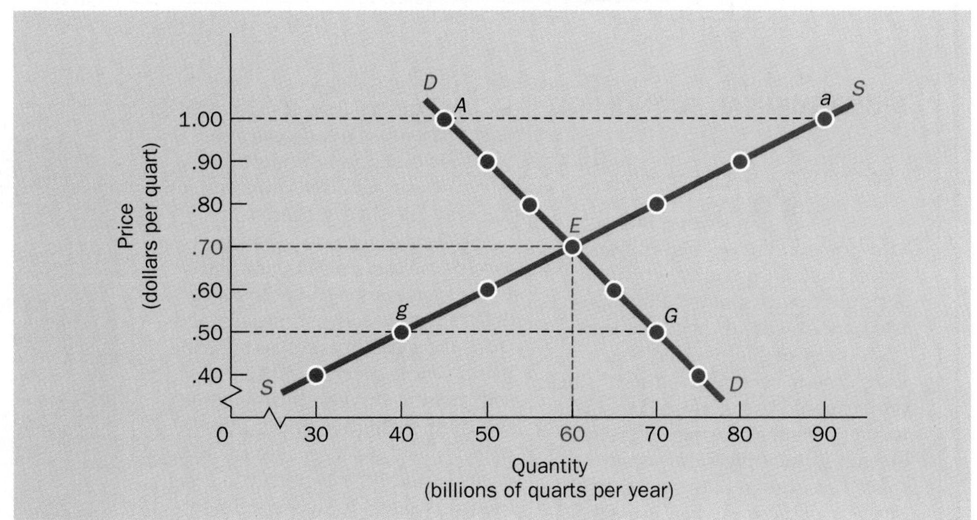


A **SHORTAGE** is an excess of quantity demanded over quantity supplied. When there is a shortage, buyers cannot purchase the quantities they desire.

A **SURPLUS** is an excess of quantity supplied over quantity demanded. When there is a surplus, sellers cannot sell the quantities they desire to supply.

An **EQUILIBRIUM** is a situation in which there are no inherent forces that produce change. Changes away from an equilibrium position will occur only as a result of "outside events" that disturb the status quo.

There is only one point in Figure 4–3, point *E*, at which the supply curve and the demand curve intersect. At the price corresponding to point *E*, which is 70¢ per quart, the quantity supplied and the quantity demanded are both 60 billion quarts per year. This means that, at a price of 70¢ per quart, consumers are willing to buy just what producers are willing to sell.

At any lower price, such as 50¢, only 40 billion quarts of milk will be supplied (point *g*) whereas 70 billion quarts will be demanded (point *G*). Thus quantity demanded will exceed quantity supplied. There will be a **shortage** equal to 70 − 40 = 30 billion quarts. Alternatively, at a higher price like $1, quantity supplied will be 90 billion quarts (point *a*) while quantity demanded will be only 45 billion (point *A*). Quantity supplied will exceed quantity demanded, so there will be a **surplus** equal to 90 − 45 = 45 billion quarts.

Since 70¢ is the price at which quantity supplied and quantity demanded are equal, we say that 70¢ per quart is the **equilibrium price** in this market. Similarly, 60 billion quarts per year is the **equilibrium quantity** of milk. The term "equilibrium" merits a little explanation, since it arises so frequently in economic analysis.

An **equilibrium** is a situation in which there are no inherent forces that produce change; that is, a situation that does not contain the seeds of its own destruction. Think, for example, of a pendulum at rest at its center point. If no outside force (such as a person's hand) comes to push it, the pendulum will remain where it is; it is in *equilibrium*. But if you give the pendulum a shove, its equilibrium will be disturbed and it will start to move upward. When it reaches the top of its arc, the pendulum will, for an instant, be at rest again. But this is not an equilibrium position, for a force known as gravity will pull the pendulum downward. Thereafter, its motion from side to side will be governed by gravity and friction. Eventually, we know, the pendulum will return to the point at which it started, which is its only equilibrium position. At any other point, inherent forces will cause the pendulum to move.

At The FRONTIER

## EXPERIMENTAL ECONOMICS

In theory, supply and demand curves determine prices. But does reality work the way the theory claims? Physicists use experiments to help answer such questions. However, for a long time it was believed that economists could not perform laboratory experiments. After all, people are not guinea pigs. Can economists recreate an entire economy, or even a single market, in a laboratory? And, even if this is done, how can the experimenter get the "guinea pigs" to act as they would in making real decisions—with real money at stake?

For a long time, economists felt that experimental methods were beyond their reach. So they relied almost exclusively on statistical inference to test their theories. But the statistical approach is an imperfect solution because it does not allow us to isolate just *one* influence at a time, as a scientifically controlled experiment does.

Lately, this view of experimentation in economics has begun to change. While economists still rely mainly on statistical analysis, they have also begun to experiment. Market experiments are now conducted to test theories about the behavior of large firms, about government programs that provide financial assistance to poor people, and about a wide variety of other subjects.

Who are the subjects of these experiments? You guessed it. They are often college students who volunteer to participate. Some may volunteer because the experiments are interesting; but there is also money to be earned. In fact, that is what motivates participants to act as they would in a real market. One such experiment was conducted at UCLA and Los Angeles City College*. The objective was to see whether demand and supply curves do in fact determine price in the way the theory claims.

Students were divided into two groups: sellers and buyers. Each was given some money to start. Sellers purchased fictitious "goods" from the experimenter (who acted like a wholesaler), and then tried to sell them to buyers. If they could sell them at higher prices than they paid, sellers got to pocket the difference. Similarly, buyers could resell their purchases to the experimenter, who would pay according to a fixed schedule. They, too, got to keep any profits they made.

For example, seller A was able to buy from the wholesaler at the following prices:

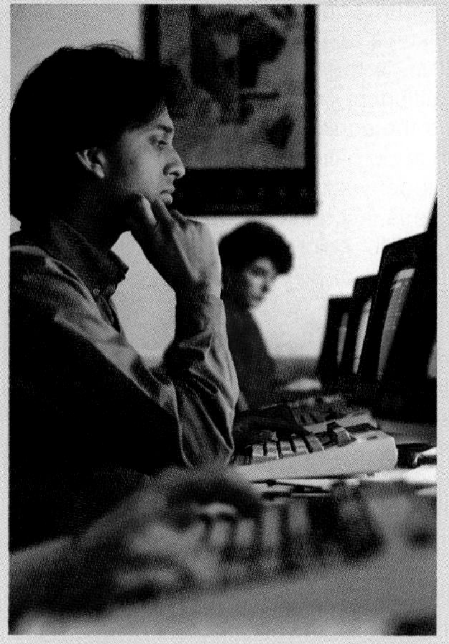

| Unit | 1st | 2nd | 3rd | 4th | 5th | 6th | 7th | 8th |
|---|---|---|---|---|---|---|---|---|
| Price | $2.30 | 2.30 | 2.30 | 2.31 | 2.31 | 2.36 | 2.50 | 2.70 |

That is, she could purchase up to three units of the commodity at a price of $2.30 per unit. However, if she bought a fourth unit, the price would go up to $2.31, and so on. It is clear that, if the market price was, say $2.35, seller A should want to supply five units, because she can obtain this many units from the wholesaler at lower prices. But seller A would be irrational to acquire the sixth unit from the wholesaler for $2.36 and then sell it for $2.35.

So the experimenters knew that, at a price of $2.35, seller A's theoretical quantity supplied was five units. And they could reach a similar conclusion for every other price and every other seller. Analogously, the experimenters were able to calculate the theoretical quantities demanded for each buyer. The theoretical price at which the supply and demand curves intersected was $2.44.

How did the actual prices turn out in the experiment? The experiment was repeated five times, each repetition involving about 20 transactions. The average actual price was slightly lower than the theoretical equilibrium price of $2.44, but the experimental price almost always fell in the $2.40–$2.50 range. And the price came closer and closer to $2.44 as students acquired more experience. In the last two experiments, the average prices were $2.418 and $2.434—within 2.2 percent of the predicted equilibrium. Apparently, the experiments do work, and so does the theory—as a reasonable *approximation* to reality.

*See C.R. Plott, "Externalities and Corrective Policies in Experimental Markets," *The Economic Journal*, vol. 93, March 1983, pages 106–127.

The concept of equilibrium in economics is similar and can be illustrated by our supply and demand example. Why is no price other than 70¢ an equilibrium price in Table 4–3 or Figure 4–3? What forces will change any other price?

Consider first a low price like 50¢, at which quantity demanded (70 billion) exceeds quantity supplied (40 billion). If the price were this low, many frustrated customers would be unable to purchase the quantities they desired. In their scramble for the available supply of milk, some would offer to pay more. As customers sought to outbid one another, the market price would be forced up. Thus a price below the equilibrium price cannot persist in a free market because a shortage sets in motion powerful economic forces that push price upward.

Similar forces operate if the market price is *above* the equilibrium price. If, for example, the price should somehow get to be $1, Table 4–3 tells us that quantity supplied (90 billion) would far exceed quantity demanded (45 billion). Producers would be unable to sell their desired quantities of milk at the prevailing price, and some would find it in their interest to undercut their competitors by reducing price. Such competitive price-cutting would continue as long as the surplus persisted, that is, as long as quantity supplied exceeded quantity demanded. Thus a price above the equilibrium price cannot persist indefinitely.

We are left with only one conclusion. The price 70¢ per quart and the quantity 60 billion quarts per year is the only price-quantity combination that does not sow the seeds of its own destruction. It is the only *equilibrium*. Any lower price must rise, and any higher price must fall. It is as if natural economic forces place a magnet at point *E* that attracts the market just like gravity attracts a pendulum.

The analogy to a pendulum is worth pursuing further. Most pendulums are more frequently in motion than at rest. However, unless they are repeatedly buffeted by outside forces (which, of course, is exactly what happens to pendulums used in clocks), pendulums gradually return to their resting points. The same is true of price and quantity in a free market. Markets are not always in equilibrium, but, if they are not interfered with, experience shows that they normally *move toward equilibrium*.

**THE LAW OF SUPPLY AND DEMAND**

In a free market, the forces of supply and demand generally push the price toward its equilibrium level, the price at which quantity supplied and quantity demanded are equal.

Like most economic "laws," the **law of supply and demand** is occasionally disobeyed. Markets sometimes display shortages or surpluses for long periods of time. Prices sometimes fail to move toward equilibrium. But the "law" is a fair generalization that is right far more often than it is wrong.

The **LAW OF SUPPLY AND DEMAND** states that, in a free market, the forces of supply and demand generally push the price toward the level at which quantity supplied and quantity demanded are equal.

The last interesting aspect of the pendulum analogy concerns the "outside forces" of which we have spoken. A pendulum that is blown by the wind or pushed by a hand does not remain in equilibrium. Similarly, many outside forces can disturb equilibrium in a market. In 1990–1991, the world oil market was disturbed by a war in the Persian Gulf. In 1992, Hurricane Andrew struck Florida and disturbed equilibrium in the market for oranges.

Often these outside influences *change the equilibrium price and quantity* by shifting either the supply curve or the demand curve. If you look again at Figure 4–3, you can see clearly that any event that causes *either* the demand curve *or* the supply curve to shift will also change the equilibrium price and quantity. Such events constitute the "other things" that were held constant in our definitions of supply and demand curves. We are now ready to analyze how these outside forces affect the equilibrium of supply and demand, beginning on the demand side.

## SHIFTS OF THE DEMAND CURVE

Returning to our example of milk, we noted earlier that the quantity of milk demanded is influenced by a variety of things other than the price of milk. Changes in population, consumer income, and the prices of alternative beverages such as soda and orange juice presumably change the quantity of milk demanded even if the price of milk is unchanged.

Since the demand curve for milk depicts only the relationship between the quantity of milk demanded and the price of milk, holding all other factors constant, a change in any of these other factors produces a *shift of the entire demand curve.* More generally:

A change in the price of a good produces a **movement along a fixed demand curve**. By contrast, a change in any other variable that influences quantity demanded produces a **shift of the entire demand curve**. If consumers want to buy *more* at any given price than they wanted previously, the demand curve shifts to the right (or outward). If they desire *less* at any given price, the demand curve shifts to the left (or inward).

Figure 4–4 shows this distinction graphically. If the price of a quart of milk falls from 80¢ to 60¢ and quantity demanded rises accordingly, we move *along demand curve* $D_0D_0$ from point *C* to point *F*, as shown by the blue arrow. If, on the other hand, consumers suddenly decide that they like milk better than they did formerly, *the entire demand curve shifts outward from* $D_0D_0$ *to* $D_1D_1$, as indicated by the blue arrows. To make this general idea more concrete and to show some of its many applications, let us consider some specific examples.

1. ***Consumer incomes***. If average incomes increase, consumers will purchase more of most foods, including milk, even if the price of milk remains the same. That is, *increases in income normally shift demand curves outward to the right*, as depicted in Figure 4–5(a). In this example, the quantity demanded at the old equilibrium price of 70¢ increases from 60 billion quarts per year (point *E* on demand curve $D_0D_0$) to 75 billion (point *R* on demand curve $D_1D_1$). We know that 70¢ is no longer the equilibrium price, since at this price quantity demanded (75 billion) exceeds quantity supplied (60 billion). To restore equilibrium, price will have to rise. The diagram shows the new equilibrium at point *T*, where the price is 80¢ per quart and both quantities demanded and supplied are 70 billion quarts per year. This illustrates a general result.

   Any factor that causes the demand curve to shift outward to the right, and does not affect the supply curve, will raise the equilibrium price and the equilibrium quantity.[4]

[4]This statement, like many others in the text, assumes that the demand curve is downward-sloping and the supply curve is upward-sloping.

**Figure 4–4** **MOVEMENTS ALONG VERSUS SHIFTS OF A DEMAND CURVE**

If quantity demanded increases because the price of a commodity falls, the market moves along a fixed demand curve such as $D_0D_0$ (see the movement from *C* to *F*). If, on the other hand, quantity demanded increases due to a change in one of its other determinants (such as consumer tastes or incomes), the entire demand curve shifts outward, as shown here by the shift from $D_0D_0$ to $D_1D_1$.

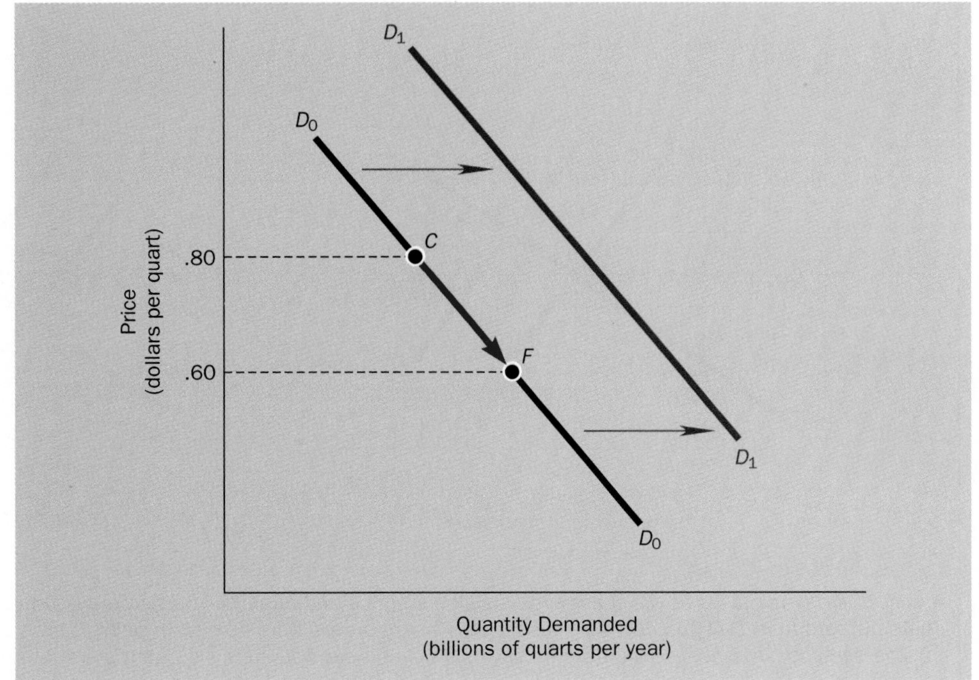


Everything works in reverse if consumer incomes fall. Figure 4–5(b) depicts a leftward (inward) shift of the demand curve that results from a decline in consumer incomes. For example, the quantity demanded at the previous equilibrium price (70¢) falls from 60 billion quarts (point *E*) to 45 billion (point *L* on demand curve $D_2D_2$). At the initial price, quantity supplied must begin to fall. The new equilibrium will eventually be established at point *M*, where the price is 60¢ and both quantity demanded and quantity supplied are 50 billion. In general:

Any factor that shifts the demand curve inward to the left, and does not affect the supply curve, will lower both the equilibrium price and the equilibrium quantity.

2. ***Population***. Population growth affects quantity demanded in more or less the same way as increases in average incomes. A larger population will presumably wish to consume more milk, even if the price of milk and average incomes are unchanged, thus shifting the entire demand curve to the right as in Figure 4–5(a). The equilibrium price and quantity both rise. Similarly, a decrease in population should shift the demand curve for milk to the left, as in Figure 4–5(b), causing equilibrium price and quantity to fall.

3. ***Consumer preferences***. If the dairy industry mounts a successful advertising campaign extolling the benefits of drinking milk, families may decide to raise their quantities demanded. This would shift the entire demand curve

**Figure 4–5 THE EFFECTS OF SHIFTS OF THE DEMAND CURVE**

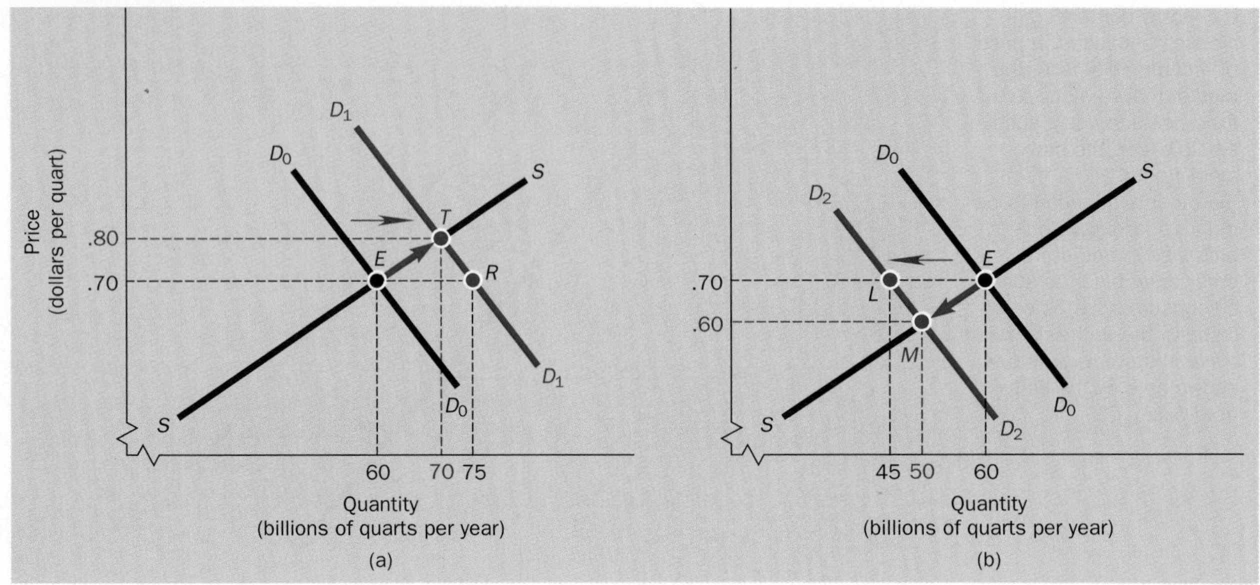


A shift of the demand curve will change the equilibrium price and quantity in a free market. In part (a), the demand curve shifts outward from $D_0D_0$ to $D_1D_1$. As a result, equilibrium moves from point *E* to point *T*; both price and quantity rise. In part (b), the demand curve shifts inward from $D_0D_0$ to $D_2D_2$, and equilibrium moves from point *E* to point *M*; both price and quantity fall.

for milk to the right, as in Figure 4–5(a). Alternatively, a medical report on the dangers of kidney stones may persuade consumers to drink less milk, thereby shifting the demand curve to the left, as in Figure 4–5(b). Again, these are general phenomena.

If consumer preferences shift in favor of a particular item, that item's demand curve will shift outward to the right, causing both equilibrium price and quantity to rise (Figure 4–5[a]). Conversely, if consumer preferences shift against a particular item, that item's demand curve will shift inward to the left, causing equilibrium price and quantity to fall (Figure 4–5[b]).

4. ***Prices and availability of related goods***. Because soda, orange juice, and coffee are popular drinks that compete with milk, a change in the price of any of these beverages can be expected to shift the demand curve for milk. If any of these alternative drinks become cheaper, some consumers will switch away from milk. Thus the demand curve for milk will shift to the left, as in Figure 4–5(b). Other price changes shift the demand curve for milk in the opposite direction. For example, suppose that cookies, a commodity that goes well with milk, become less expensive. This may induce some consumers to drink more milk and thus shift the demand curve for milk to the right, as in Figure 4–5(a).

Increases in the prices of goods that are substitutes for the good in question (as soda is for milk) move the demand curve to the right, thus raising both the equilibrium price and quantity. Increases in the prices of goods that are normally used together with the good in question (such as cookies and milk) shift the demand curve to the left, thus lowering both the equilibrium price and quantity.

While the preceding list does not exhaust the possible influences on quantity demanded, enough has been said to indicate the principles involved. Let us therefore turn to a concrete example.

### APPLICATION: WHY AIRLINES RUN SALES

Anyone who travels knows that airline companies reduce fares sharply to attract more customers at certain times of the year—particularly in winter (excluding the holiday period), when air traffic is light. There is no reason to think that air transportation gets cheaper in winter. Why, then, do airlines run such "sales"? A simple supply and demand diagram (see Figure 4–6) holds the answer.

Given the number of planes in airlines' fleets, the supply of seats is relatively fixed, as indicated by the steep supply curve *SS* in Figure 4–6, and is more or less the same in summer and winter. During seasons when people want to travel less, the demand curve for seats shifts leftward from its normal position, $D_0D_0$, to a position such as $D_1D_1$. Hence, equilibrium in the air-traffic market shifts from point *E* to point *A*. Thus both price and quantity decline at certain times of the year, not because flying gets cheaper or airlines get more generous, but because of the discipline of the market.

## SHIFTS OF THE SUPPLY CURVE

Like quantity demanded, the quantity supplied on a market typically responds to a great number of influences other than price. The weather, the cost of feed,

**Figure 4–6** SEASONAL CHANGES IN AIRLINE FARES

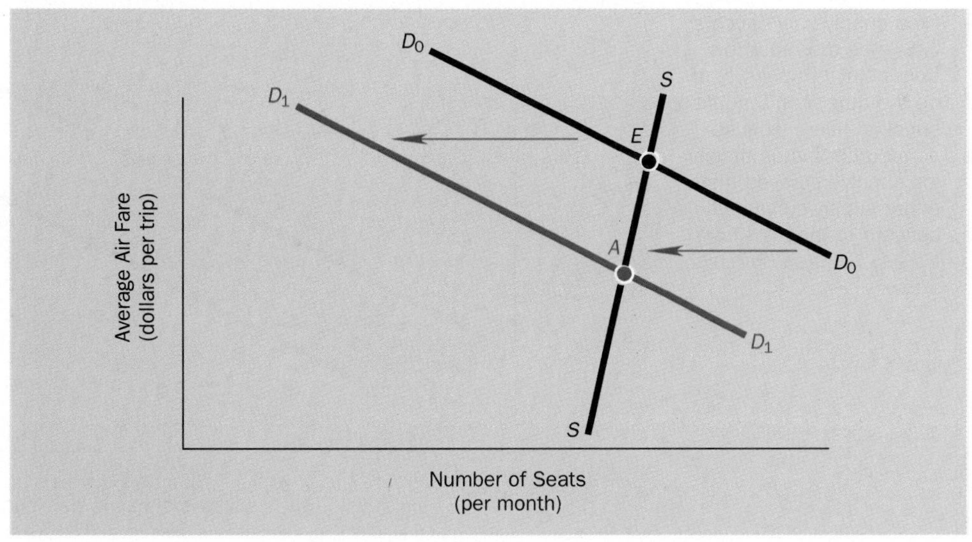


During seasons of slack demand for air travel, the demand curve shifts leftward from $D_0D_0$ to $D_1D_1$. In consequence, the market equilibrium point shifts from *E* to *A*, causing both price and quantity to decline.

the number and size of dairy farms, and a variety of other factors all influence how much milk will be brought to market. Since the supply curve depicts only the relationship between the price of milk and the quantity of milk supplied, holding all other factors constant, a change in any of these other factors will cause the entire supply curve to shift. That is:

A change in the price of the good causes a **movement along a fixed supply curve**. But price is not the only influence on quantity supplied. And, if any of these other influences changes, the **entire supply curve shifts**.

Figure 4–7 once again depicts the distinction graphically. A rise in price from 60¢ to 80¢ will raise quantity supplied by *moving along supply curve* $S_0S_0$ from point f to point c. But any rise in quantity supplied attributable to a factor other than price will *shift the entire supply curve outward to the right* from $S_0S_0$ to $S_1S_1$, as shown by the blue arrows. Let us consider what some of these other factors are, and how they shift the supply curve.

1. ***Size of the industry***. We begin with the most obvious factor. If more farmers enter the milk industry, the quantity supplied at any given price will increase. For example, if each farm provides 600,000 quarts of milk per year when the price is 70¢ per quart, then 100,000 farmers provide 60 billion quarts, but 130,000 farmers provide 78 billion. Thus, when more farms are in the industry, the quantity of milk supplied will be greater at any given price—and hence the supply curve will be farther to the right.

   Figure 4–8(a) illustrates the effect of an expansion of the industry from 100,000 farms to 130,000 farms—a rightward shift of the supply curve from $S_0S_0$ to $S_1S_1$. Notice that at the initial price of 70¢, the quantity supplied after

*Figure* **4–7** **MOVEMENTS ALONG VERSUS SHIFTS OF A SUPPLY CURVE**

If quantity supplied rises because the price increases, we move along a fixed supply curve such as $S_0S_0$ (see the red arrow from point *f* to point *c*). If, on the other hand, quantity supplied rises because some other factor influencing supply improves, the entire supply curve shifts outward to the right from $S_0S_0$ to $S_1S_1$ (see the blue arrows).

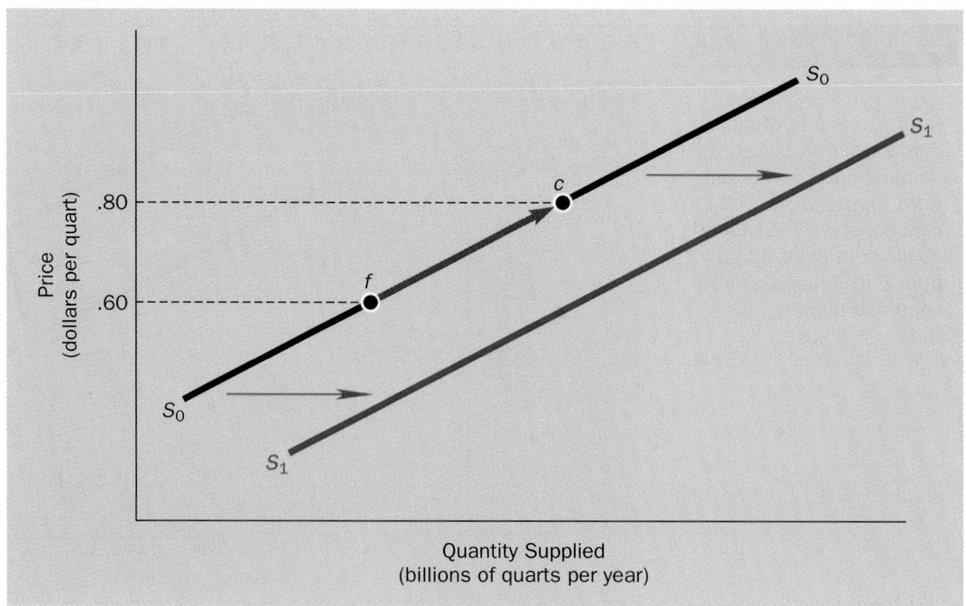

Figure 4–8 EFFECTS OF SHIFTS OF THE SUPPLY CURVE

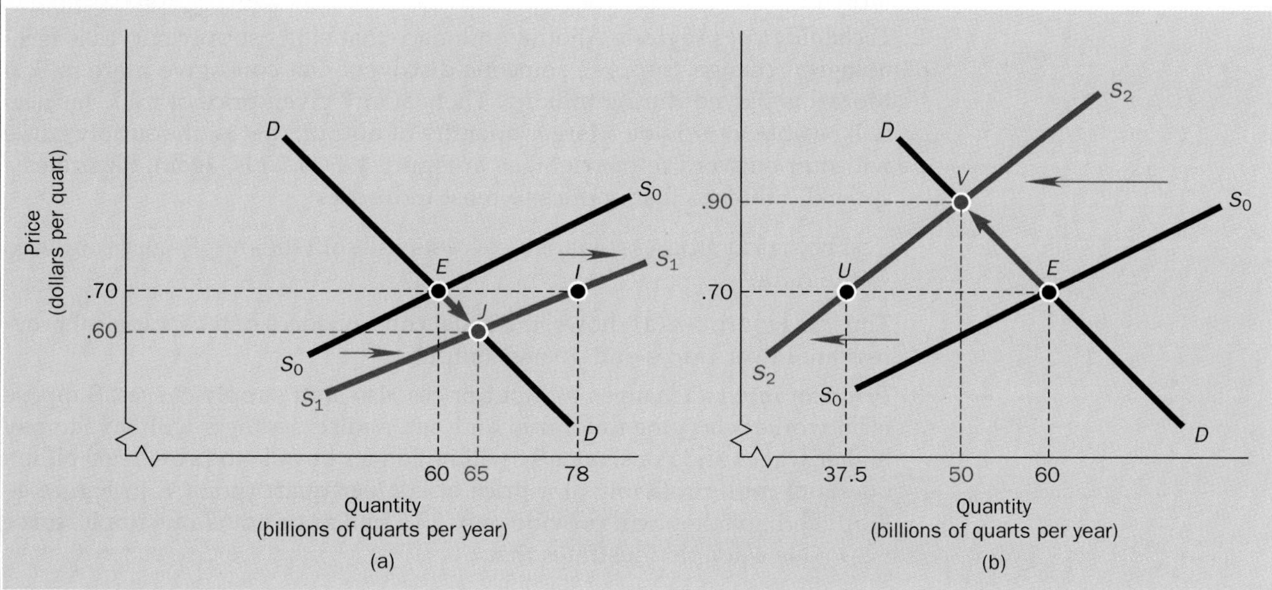


A shift of the supply curve will change the equilibrium price and quantity in a market. In part (a), the supply curve shifts outward to the right, from $S_0S_0$ to $S_1S_1$. As a result, equilibrium moves from point *E* to point *J*; price falls as quantity increases. Part (b) illustrates the opposite case—an inward shift of the supply curve from $S_0S_0$ to $S_2S_2$. Equilibrium moves from point *E* to point *V*, which means that price rises as quantity falls.

the shift is 78 billion quarts (point *I* on supply curve $S_1S_1$), which exceeds the quantity demanded of 60 billion (point *E* on supply curve $S_0S_0$).

We can see in the graph that the price of 70¢ is too high to be the equilibrium price; so the price must fall. The diagram shows the new equilibrium at point *J*, where the price is 60¢ per quart and the quantity is 65 billion quarts per year. The general point is that:

Any factor that shifts the supply curve outward to the right, and does not affect the demand curve, will lower the equilibrium price and raise the equilibrium quantity.

This must *always* be true if the industry's demand curve has a negative slope, because the greater quantity supplied can be sold only if price is decreased to induce customers to buy more.[5]

Figure 4–8(b) illustrates the opposite case: a contraction of the industry from 100,000 farms to 62,500 farms. The supply curve shifts inward to the left and equilibrium moves from point *E* to point *V*, where price is 90¢ and quantity is 50 billion quarts per year. In general:

Any factor that shifts the supply curve inward to the left, and does not affect the demand curve, will raise the equilibrium price and reduce the equilibrium quantity.

[5]Graphically, whenever a positively sloped curve shifts to the right, its intersection point with a negatively sloping curve must always move lower. Just try drawing it yourself.

Even if no farmers enter or leave the industry, results like those depicted in Figure 4–8 can be produced by expansion or contraction of the existing farms.

2. ***Technological progress.*** Another influence that shifts supply curves is technological change. Suppose someone discovers that cows give more milk if Mozart is played during milking. Then, at any given price of milk, farmers will be able to provide a larger quantity of output; that is, the supply curve will shift outward to the right, as in Figure 4–8(a). This, again, illustrates a general influence that applies to most industries:

   Technological progress that reduces costs will shift the supply curve outward to the right.

   Thus, as Figure 4–8(a) shows, the usual consequences of technological progress are lower prices and greater output.

3. ***Prices of inputs.*** Changes in input prices also shift supply curves. Suppose farm workers become unionized and win a raise. Farmers will have to pay higher wages and consequently will no longer be able to provide 60 billion quarts of milk profitably at a price of 70¢ per quart (point *E* in Figure 4–8[b]). Perhaps they will provide only 37.5 billion (point *U* on supply curve $S_2S_2$). This example illustrates that:

   Increases in the prices of inputs that suppliers must buy will shift the supply curve inward to the left.

4. ***Prices of related outputs.*** Dairy farms produce more than milk. If cheese prices rise sharply, farmers may decide to use some raw milk to make cheese, thereby reducing the quantity of milk supplied. On a supply-demand diagram, the supply curve would shift inward, as in Figure 4–8(b).

   Similar phenomena occur in other industries, and sometimes the effect goes the other way. For example, suppose the price of beef goes up, which increases the quantity of meat supplied. That, in turn, will raise the number of cowhides supplied even without any change in price of leather. Thus, a rise in the price of beef will lead to a rightward shift in the supply curve of leather. In general:

   A change in the price of one good produced by a multiproduct industry may be expected to shift the supply curves of all the other goods produced by that industry.

## APPLICATION: A COMPUTER IN EVERY HOME?

Twenty years ago, no one owned a home computer. Now there are tens of millions of them, and enthusiasts look forward to the day when computers will be as commonplace as television sets. What brought the computer from the laboratory into the home? Did Americans suddenly develop a craving for computers?

Hardly. What actually happened is that scientists in the 1970s invented the microchip—a stunning technological breakthrough that sharply reduced both the size and cost of computers. Within a few years, microcomputers were in commercial production. And, as the technology continued to improve, the cost of computers fell and fell and fell. Today, $1500 will buy you more computing power than a multi-million dollar computer could deliver two decades ago—and the machine will play games, too!

Figure 4–9 THE EFFECTS OF RAPID TECHNOLOGICAL CHANGE ON THE COMPUTER MARKET

The invention of the microchip and other technological breakthroughs caused the supply curve of computers to shift outward to the right—moving from $S_0S_0$ to $S_1S_1$. Consequently, equilibrium shifted from point *E* to point *A*. The price of microcomputers fell from $10,000 to $1500, and the quantity increased from 100,000 to 3 million per year.

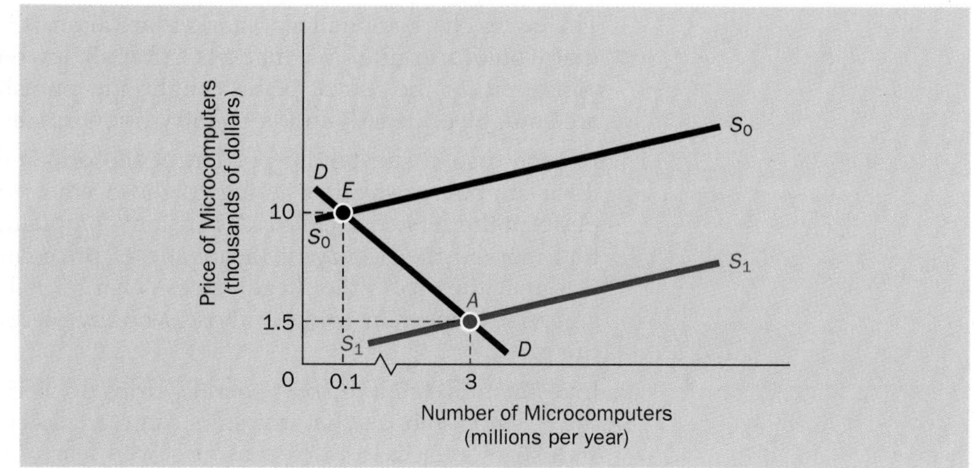


In terms of our supply and demand diagrams, the rapid technological improvement in computer manufacturing shifted the supply curve dramatically to the right. As Figure 4–9 shows, a large outward shift of the supply curve should lower the equilibrium price and raise the equilibrium quantity—which is just what happened to the computer industry. It was not the *demand curve* that shifted out, but the *supply curve*.

## RESTRAINING THE MARKET MECHANISM: PRICE CEILINGS

As we have noted already, lawmakers and rulers have often been dissatisfied with the outcomes of free markets. From Rome to Pennsylvania and from biblical times to the space age, they have battled the invisible hand. Sometimes, rather than trying to make adjustments in the workings of the market, governments have sought to raise or lower the prices of specific commodities *by decree*. In many of these cases, those in authority felt that the prices set by the market mechanism were, in some sense, immorally low or immorally high. Penalties were therefore imposed on anyone offering the commodities in question at prices lower or higher than those determined by the authorities.

A **PRICE CEILING** is a legal maximum on the price that may be charged for a commodity.

But the market has proven itself a formidable foe that strongly resists attempts to circumvent its workings. In case after case where legal **price ceilings** are imposed, virtually the same set of consequences ensues:

1. A persistent shortage develops. Queuing, direct rationing, or any of a variety of other devices, usually inefficient and unpleasant, have to be substituted for the distribution process provided by the price mechanism. *Example*: Rampant shortages in Eastern Europe and the former Soviet Union helped precipitate the revolts that ended communism.
2. An illegal, or "black," market often arises to supply the commodity. There are usually some individuals who are willing to take the risks involved in

meeting unsatisfied demands illegally, if legal means will not do the job. *Example*: Although most states ban the practice, ticket "scalping" occurs at most popular sporting events and rock concerts.

3. The prices charged on illegal markets are almost certainly higher than those that would prevail in free markets. After all, lawbreakers expect some compensation for the risk of being caught and punished. *Example*: Goods that are smuggled illegally into a country are normally quite expensive.
4. In each case, a substantial portion of the price falls into the hands of the illicit supplier instead of going to those who produce the good or who perform the service. *Example*: A constant complaint in the series of hearings that marked the history of theater ticket price controls in New York City was that the "ice" (the illegal excess charge) fell into the hands of ticket scalpers rather than going to those who invested in, produced, or acted in the play.
5. Investment in the industry generally dries up. Because price ceilings reduce the potential returns that investors can earn, less capital will be invested in industries subject to price controls. Even fear of impending price controls can have this effect. *Example*: Tight limits on the prices that public utilities could charge for power led to underinvestment in power-generating stations in the late 1970s and early 1980s, and thus to power shortages in the 1980s.

These points and others are best illustrated by considering a concrete example of price ceilings.

## A CASE STUDY: RENT CONTROLS IN NEW YORK CITY

New York is the only major city in the United States that has had rent controls continuously since World War II. The objective of rent control is, of course, to protect the consumer from high rents. But most economists believe that rent control does not help the cities or their inhabitants and that, in the long run, it makes almost everyone worse off. Elementary supply–demand analysis shows us what actually happens.

Figure 4–10 is a supply–demand diagram for rental units in New York. Curve *DD* is the demand curve and curve *SS* is the supply curve. Without controls, equilibrium would be at point *E*, where rents average $1200 per month and 3 million units are occupied. If rent controls are effective, they must set a ceiling price *below* the equilibrium price of $1200. But with a low rent ceiling, such as $800, the quantity of housing demanded will be 3.5 million (point *B*) while the quantity supplied will be only 2.5 million (point *C*).

The diagram shows a shortage of 1,000,000 apartments. This theoretical concept of a "shortage" manifests itself in New York City as an abnormally low vacancy rate—typically about half the national urban average.

As we expect, rent controls have spawned a lively black market in New York. The black market raises the effective price of rent-controlled apartments in many ways, including bribes, "key money" paid to move up on the waiting list, and requiring prospective tenants to purchase worthless furniture at inflated prices.

According to the diagram, rent controls reduce the quantity supplied from 3 million to 2.5 million apartments. How does this show up in New York? First, some property owners, discouraged by the low rents, have converted apartment buildings into office space or other uses. Second, some apartments have been inadequately maintained. After all, rent controls create a shortage which makes

Figure 4–10 **SUPPLY–DEMAND DIAGRAM FOR RENTAL HOUSING**

When market forces are permitted to set rents, the quantity of dwellings supplied will equal the quantity demanded. But when a rent ceiling forces rent below the market level, the number of dwellings supplied (point *C*) will be less than the number demanded (point *B*). Thus, rent ceilings induce housing shortages.

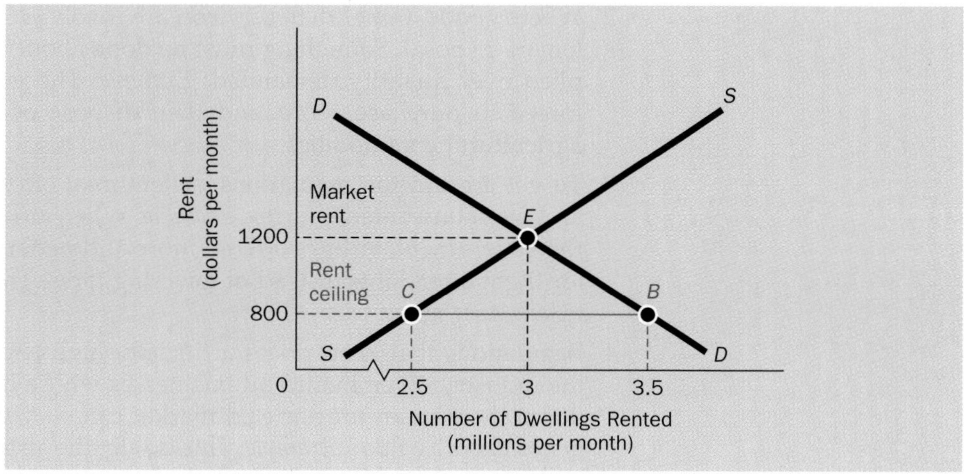


even dilapidated apartments easy to rent. Third, some landlords have actually abandoned their buildings rather than pay rising tax and fuel bills. These abandoned buildings rapidly become eyesores and eventually pose threats to public health and safety.

With all these problems, why do rent controls persist in New York City? And why are some other cities moving in the same direction? Part of the explanation is that most people simply do not understand the problems that rent controls create. Another part is that landlords are unpopular politically. But a third, and important, part of the explanation is that not everyone is hurt by rent controls. Those who benefit from controls fight hard to preserve them. In New York, for example, many tenants pay rents that are only a fraction of what their apartments would fetch on the open market. They are, naturally enough, quite happy with this situation. This last point illustrates another very general phenomenon:

Virtually every price ceiling or floor creates a class of people with a vested interest in preserving the regulations because they benefit from them. These people naturally use their political influence to protect their gains, which is one reason why it is so hard to eliminate price ceilings or floors.

## RESTRAINING THE MARKET MECHANISM: PRICE FLOORS

A **PRICE FLOOR** is a legal minimum on the price that may be charged for a commodity.

Interferences with the market mechanism are not always designed to keep prices *low*. Agricultural price supports and minimum wages are two notable examples in which the law keeps prices *above* free-market levels. **Price floors** are typically accompanied by a standard set of symptoms:

1. A surplus develops as sellers cannot find enough buyers. *Example*: Surpluses of various agricultural products have been a persistent—and costly—problem for the U.S. government. The problem is even more severe in the Euro-

pean Community, where the so-called common agricultural policy holds prices even higher.

2. Where goods, rather than services, are involved, the surplus creates a problem of disposal. Something must be done about the excess of quantity supplied over quantity demanded. *Example*: The government has often been forced to purchase, store, and then dispose of large amounts of surplus agricultural commodities.
3. To get around the regulations, sellers may offer discounts in disguised—and often unwanted—forms. *Example*: When airline fares were regulated by the government, airlines offered more and better food and stylish uniforms for flight attendants instead of lowering fares. Today, the food is worse but tickets cost much less.
4. Regulations that keep prices artificially high encourage overinvestment in the industry. Even inefficient businesses whose high operating costs would doom them in an unrestricted market can survive beneath the shelter of a generous price floor. *Example*: This is why the airline and trucking industries both went through painful "shake outs" of the weaker companies in the 1980s.

Once again, a specific example is useful.

## A CASE STUDY: MILK PRICE SUPPORTS

America's extensive program of farm price supports began in 1933 as "a temporary method of dealing with an emergency"—farmers were going broke in droves. It is with us still today, even though the farm population of the United States is less than a sixth of what it was then.

One of the more absurd legacies of that "temporary emergency" is a maze of milk-marketing orders covering the pricing and distribution of milk in 44 milk-producing regions of the country. By setting the prices of milk, butter, and cheese as high as three times those on world markets, the government ensures that America will suffer from chronic overproduction—as Figure 4–11 shows.

In the diagram, the equilibrium price for milk is 70¢ per quart, but we assume that the government sets a *price floor* at 90¢. At this high price, farmers produce 80 billion quarts per year—20 billion above the equilibrium quantity. But consumers want to purchase only 50 billion—10 billion below the equilibrium quantity. The result is a huge *surplus* of milk—30 billion quarts per year in the example.

In a market economy like ours, Congress cannot simply set prices by decree; it must do something to enforce the price floor. Normally, that "something" is buying up the surplus, that is, adding 30 billion quarts per year in *government demand* to the private demand shown in Figure 4–11.[6] That, of course, requires a lot of the taxpayers' money. In addition, all the surplus milk must be stored somewhere—usually as cheese, for milk does not keep well. That creates another bill for the taxpayer to pick up. But there is more. We pay again as consumers in the form of higher prices for milk—90¢ rather than 70¢ in the example. According to current estimates, milk price supports cost American taxpayers and consumers together about $10–$12 billion a year.

---

[6]Draw a new demand curve into Figure 4–11 which includes this government demand. It must be parallel to DD but 30 billion quarts farther to the right. If you draw it accurately, it will pass exactly through point *B*.

Figure 4-11 **ANALYSIS OF MILK PRICE SUPPORTS**

In this diagram, which repeats the supply and demand curves from Figure 4–3, the support price for milk (90¢ per quart) exceeds the equilibrium price (which is 70¢). Quantity supplied at the support price is 80 billion quarts per year (point *B*) while quantity demanded is only 50 billion (point *A*). To keep the price at 90¢, the government must buy up the 30-billion-quart surplus each year.

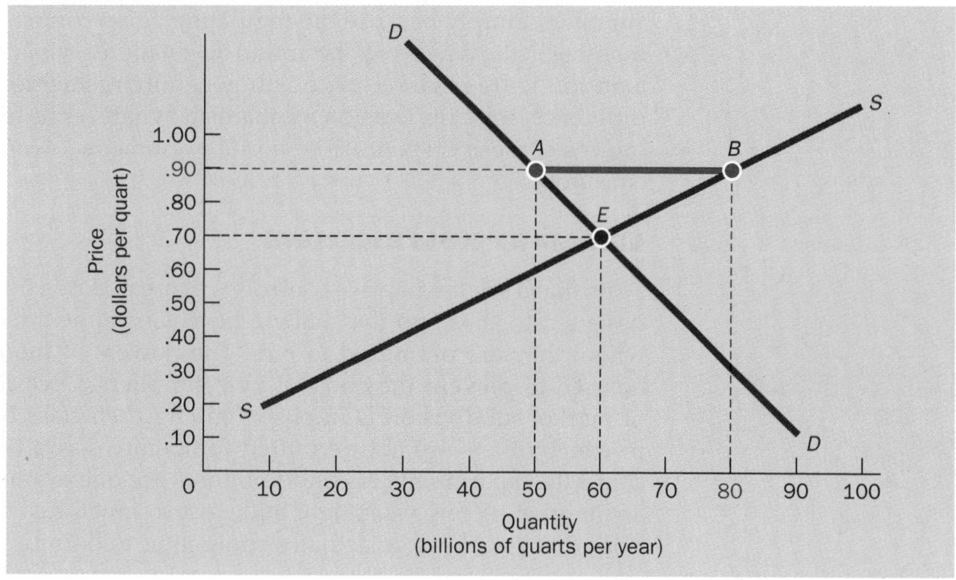


Sometimes the government tires of all this and tries something else. For example, in 1986 it offered to pay dairy farmers to slaughter 1.6 million cows. The result? An uproar from beef raisers as meat prices collapsed.[7] As we said earlier, those who would flaunt the will of the market had better be prepared for unforeseen consequences.

## A CAN OF WORMS

Our two case studies—rent controls and milk price supports—illustrate some of the major side effects of price floors and ceilings, but barely hint at others. There are difficulties that we have not even mentioned, for the market mechanism is a tough bird that imposes suitable retribution on those who seek to circumvent it by legislative decree. Here is a partial list of other problems that may arise when prices are controlled.

### FAVORITISM AND CORRUPTION

When price ceilings or floors create shortages or surpluses, someone must decide who gets to buy or sell the limited quantity that is available. This can lead to discrimination along racial or religious lines, political favoritism, or corruption in government. For example, it has been argued that the high U.S. support price for sugar has led to widespread corruption in Caribbean nations, as foreign producers vie for the valuable right to export sugar cane to the United States.

[7]See Review Question **8** at the end of the chapter.

### UNENFORCEABILITY

Attempts to limit prices are almost certain to fail in industries with numerous suppliers, simply because the regulating agency must monitor the behavior of so many sellers. Ways will be found to evade or violate the law, and something akin to the free-market price will generally reemerge. But there is an important difference: since the evasion mechanism, whatever its form, will have some operating costs, those costs must be borne by someone. Normally, that someone is the consumer.

### AUXILIARY RESTRICTIONS

Fears that a system of price controls will break down invariably lead to regulations designed to shore up the shaky edifice. Consumers may be told when and from whom they are permitted to buy. The powers of the police and the courts may be used to prevent the entry of new suppliers. Occasionally, an intricate system of market subdivision is imposed, giving each class of firms a protected sphere in which others are not permitted to operate. Laws banning conversion of rent-controlled apartments to condominiums are one example. Milk-marketing orders are another. A few years ago, milk cost so much less in New Jersey than in New York that people were actually smuggling milk into New York State!

### LIMITATION OF VOLUME OF TRANSACTIONS

To the extent that controls succeed in affecting prices, they can be expected to reduce the volume of transactions. Curiously, this is true regardless of whether the regulated price is *above* or *below* the free-market equilibrium price. If it is set above the equilibrium price, quantity demanded will be below the equilibrium quantity. On the other hand, if the imposed price is set below the free-market level, quantity supplied will be cut down. Since sales volume cannot exceed either the quantity supplied or the quantity demanded, a reduction in the volume of transactions is the result.[8]

### MISALLOCATION OF RESOURCES

Departures from free-market prices are likely to produce misuse of the economy's resources because the connection between production costs and prices is broken. For example, Russian farmers used to feed their farm animals bread, instead of unprocessed grains, because price ceilings kept the price of bread ludicrously low. In addition, just as more complex locks lead to more sophisticated burglary tools, more complex regulations lead to the use of yet more resources for their avoidance. New jobs are created for executives, lawyers, and economists. It may well be conjectured that at least some of these expensive professionals could be put to better use elsewhere.

Economists put it this way. Free markets are capable of dealing with the three basic coordination tasks outlined in Chapter 3: deciding *what* to produce, *how* to produce it, and *to whom* the goods should be distributed. Price controls throw a monkey wrench into the market mechanism. Though the market is surely not flawless, and government interferences often have praiseworthy goals, good intentions are not enough. Any government that sets out to repair what it sees as a

---

[8]See Review Question **9** at the end of the chapter.

## Economic Aspects of the War on Drugs

For years now, the U.S. government has engaged in a highly publicized "war on drugs." At part of this effort, billions of dollars have been spent on trying to stop illegal drugs at the border. In some sense, interdiction has succeeded: literally tons of cocaine and other drugs have been seized by federal agents. Yet all these efforts have made barely a dent in the flow of drugs to America's city streets. Simple economic reasoning explains why.

When drug interdiction works, it shifts the supply curve of drugs to the left, thereby driving up street prices. But that, in turn, raises the rewards for potential smugglers and attracts more criminals into the "industry," which shifts the supply curve back to the right. The net result is that increased shipments of drugs to our shores replace much of what the authorities confiscate. This is why many economists believe that any successful anti-drug program must concentrate on reducing *demand*, which would lower the street price of drugs, not on reducing *supply*, which can only raise it.

Some economists—and some noneconomists as well—would go even further and advocate *legalization* of many drugs. While this remains a highly controversial position which few are ready to endorse, the reasoning behind it is straightforward. A stunningly high fraction of all the violent crimes committed in America—especially robberies and murders—are drug-related. One major reason is that street prices of drugs are so high that addicts must steal to get the money and drug traffickers are all too willing to kill to protect their highly profitable "businesses."

How would things differ if drugs were legal? Since Colombian farmers earn pennies for drugs that sell for hundreds of dollars on the streets of Los Angeles and New York, we may safely assume that drugs would be vastly cheaper under legalization. And that, proponents point out, would reduce drug-related crimes dramatically. When, for example, was the last time you heard of a gang killing connected with the distribution of cigarettes or alcoholic beverages?

The argument against legalization of drugs is largely moral: Should the state sanction potential lethal substances? But there is also an economic aspect. The vastly lower street prices of drugs that would surely follow legalization would increase drug use. Thus, while legalization would almost certainly reduce crime, it would also produce more addicts. The key question here—to which no one has a good answer—is: How many more addicts? If you think the increase in quantity demanded would be large, you are unlikely to find legalization an attractive option.

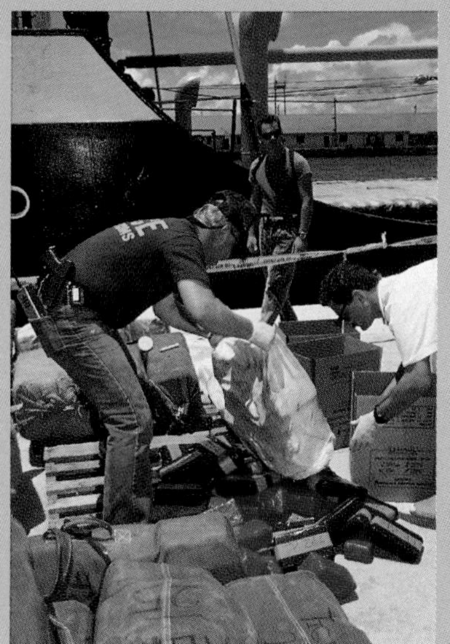

defect in the market mechanism must take care lest it cause even more serious damage elsewhere. As a prominent economist once quipped, societies that are too willing to interfere with the operation of free markets soon find that the invisible hand is nowhere to be seen—a point that the formerly communist nations grew to understand in a very painful way.

## A SIMPLE BUT POWERFUL LESSON

The lessons you have learned in this chapter may seem elementary, even obvious. In many respects, they are. But they are also very important, indeed, indispensable. Although the law of supply and demand is one of the simplest principles in economics, it is also one of the most powerful. Astonishing as it may seem, many people in authority, even highly intelligent people, fail to understand the law of supply and demand or cannot apply it to concrete situations.

For example, a few years ago the *New York Times* carried a dramatic front page picture of the president of Kenya setting fire to a large pile of elephant tusks that had been confiscated from poachers. The accompanying story explained that the burning was intended as a symbolic act to persuade the world to halt the ivory trade.[9] Economists claim no expertise on the likely psychological effect of burning elephant tusks, though one may doubt that it touched the hearts of criminal poachers. However, one economic effect was clear. By reducing the supply of ivory on the world market, the burning of tusks forced up the price of ivory, which raised the illicit rewards reaped by those who slaughter elephants. That could only encourage more poaching—precisely the opposite of what the Kenyan government sought to accomplish.

[9]The *New York Times*, July 19, 1989.

## Summary

1. The quantity of a product that is demanded is not a fixed number. Rather, **quantity demanded** depends on such factors as the price of the product, consumer incomes, and the prices of other products.
2. The relationship between quantity demanded and price, holding all other things constant, can be displayed graphically on a **demand curve**.
3. For most products, the higher the price, the lower the quantity demanded. So the demand curve usually has a negative slope.
4. The quantity of a product that is supplied also depends on its price and many other influences. A **supply curve** is a graphical representation of the relationship between **quantity supplied** and price, holding all other influences constant.
5. For most products, the supply curve has a positive slope, meaning that higher prices call forth greater quantities supplied.
6. A market is said to be in **equilibrium** when quantity supplied is equal to quantity demanded. The equilibrium price and quantity are shown by the point on a graph where the supply and demand curves intersect. The **law of supply and demand** states that price and quantity tend to gravitate to this point in a free market.
7. A change in quantity demanded that is caused by a change in the price of the good is represented by a **movement along a fixed demand curve**. A change in quantity demanded that is caused by a change in any other determinant of quantity demanded is represented by a **shift of the demand curve**.
8. This same distinction applies to the supply curve: Changes in price lead to **movements along a fixed supply curve**; changes in other determinants of quantity supplied lead to **shifts of the whole supply curve**.
9. Changes in consumer incomes, tastes, technology, prices of competing products, and many other influences cause shifts in either the demand curve or the supply curve and produce changes in price and quantity that can be determined from **supply–demand diagrams**.
10. An attempt by government regulations to force prices above or below their equilibrium levels is likely to lead to **shortages** or **surpluses**, black markets in which goods are sold at illegal prices, and to a variety of other problems. This is one of the **12 Ideas for Beyond the Final Exam.**

## Key Concepts and Terms

Quantity demanded
Demand schedule
Demand curve
Quantity supplied
Supply schedule
Supply curve
Supply–demand diagram
Shortage
Surplus
Equilibrium price and quantity
Equilibrium
Law of supply and demand
Shifts in vs. movements along supply and demand curves
Price ceiling
Price floor

## Questions for Review

1. How often do you go to the movies? Would you go more often if a ticket cost half as much? Distinguish between your demand curve for movie tickets and your "quantity demanded" at the current price.
2. What would you expect to be the shape of a demand curve
   a. for a medicine that means life or death for a patient?
   b. for gasoline at an intersection with four gas stations?
3. The following are the assumed supply and demand schedules for footballs in Anytown, USA:

| DEMAND SCHEDULE | | SUPPLY SCHEDULE | |
|---|---|---|---|
| PRICE | QUANTITY DEMANDED (per year) | PRICE | QUANTITY SUPPLIED (per year) |
| $13 | 6,000 | $13 | 71,000 |
| 11 | 13,000 | 11 | 63,000 |
| 9 | 29,000 | 9 | 29,000 |
| 7 | 50,000 | 7 | 11,000 |
| 5 | 61,000 | 5 | 0 |

   a. Plot the supply and demand curves and indicate the equilibrium price and quantity.
   b. What effect will an increase in the price of leather (a factor of production) have on the equilibrium price and quantity of footballs, assuming all other things remain constant? Explain your answer with the help of a diagram.
   c. What effect will a decrease in the price of soccer balls (a substitute commodity) have on the equilibrium price and quantity of footballs, assuming again that all other things are held constant? Use a diagram in your answer.
4. Suppose the supply and demand schedules for Japanese cars in the United States are as follows:

| PRICE (thousands) | QUANTITY DEMANDED (millions per year) | QUANTITY SUPPLIED (millions per year) |
|---|---|---|
| $8 | 2.75 | 1.25 |
| $10 | 2.50 | 1.50 |
| $12 | 2.25 | 1.75 |
| $14 | 2.00 | 2.00 |
| $16 | 1.75 | 2.25 |
| $18 | 1.50 | 2.50 |
| $20 | 1.25 | 2.75 |

   a. Graph these curves and show the equilibrium price and quantity.
   b. Now suppose that a rise in anti-Japanese sentiment in the U.S. reduces the quantity demanded at each price by 500,000 (0.5 million) cars per year. What is the new equilibrium price and quantity? Show this solution graphically. Explain why the quantity falls by less than 500,000 cars per year.
   c. Suppose *instead* that anti-American sentiment in Japan induces the Japanese to reduce their shipments to the U.S. by 500,000 cars per year (at each price). Find the new equilibrium price and quantity, and show it graphically. Explain again why quantity falls by less than 500,000.
   d. What are the equilibrium price and quantity if the shifts described in parts (b) and (c) happen at the same time?
5. The table below summarizes information about the market for principles of economics textbooks:

| PRICE | QUANTITY DEMANDED (per year) | QUANTITY SUPPLIED (per year) |
|---|---|---|
| $20 | 2000 | 0 |
| 30 | 1000 | 200 |
| 40 | 500 | 500 |
| 50 | 250 | 900 |
| 60 | 125 | 1400 |

a. What is the market equilibrium price and quantity of textbooks?
b. In order to quell outrage over tuition increases, the college places a $30 limit on the price of textbooks. How many textbooks will be sold now?
c. While the price limit is still in effect, automated publishing increases the efficiency of textbook production. Show graphically the likely effect of this innovation on the market price and quantity.

6. Show how the following demand curves are likely to shift in response to the indicated changes:
   a. The effect on the demand curve for snow shovels when a heavy snow falls.
   b. The effect on the demand curve for nachos when the price of potato chips declines.
   c. The effect on the demand curve for butter when bread prices fall.
7. Discuss the likely effects of
   a. rent ceilings on the supply of apartments.
   b. minimum wages on the employment of unskilled labor.

   Use supply–demand diagrams to show what may happen in each case.
8. On page 95, it is asserted that reducing milk surpluses by slaughtering cows would lower the price of meat. Use two diagrams, one for the milk market and one for the meat market, to illustrate this. (Assume that meat is sold in an unregulated market.)
9. On page 96, it is claimed that either price floors or price ceilings reduce the actual quantity exchanged in a market. Use a diagram or diagrams to support this conclusion, and explain the common sense behind it.
10. The same rightward shift of the demand curve may produce a very small or a very large increase in quantity, depending on the slope of the supply curve. Explain with diagrams.
11. In 1981, when regulations were holding the price of natural gas below its free-market level, then-Congressman Jack Kemp of New York said the following in an interview with the *New York Times*: "We need to decontrol natural gas, and get production of natural gas up to a higher level so we can bring down the price."[10] Evaluate the congressman's statement.
12. From 1979 to 1989 in the United States, the number of working men grew 12% while the number of working women grew 29%. During this time, average wages for men fell slightly while average wages for women rose about 7%. Which of the following two explanations seems most consistent with the data?
    a. Women decided to work more, raising their relative supply (relative to men).
    b. Discrimination against women declined, raising the relative (to men) demand for female workers.
13. The two diagrams below show supply and demand curves for two substitute commodities: tapes and compact disks (CDs).
    a. On the left-hand diagram, show what happens when technological progress makes it cheaper to produce CDs.
    b. On the right-hand diagram, show what happens to the market for tapes.
14. (More difficult) Consider the market for milk discussed in this chapter (Tables 4–1 through 4–3 and Figures 4–1 through 4–3). Suppose the government decides to fight kidney stones by levying a tax of 30¢ per quart on sales of milk. Follow these steps to analyze the effects of the tax:

[10]The *New York Times*, December 23, 1981.

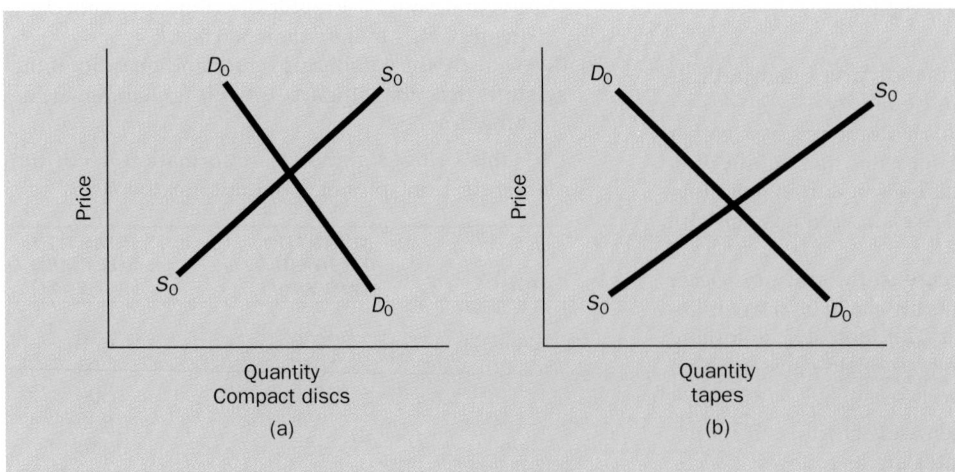

a. Construct the new supply curve (to replace Table 4–2) that relates quantity supplied to the price consumers pay. (*Hint*: Before the tax, when consumers paid 70¢, farmers supplied 60 billion quarts. With a 30¢ tax, when consumers pay 70¢ farmers will receive only 40¢. Table 4–2 tells us they will provide only 30 billion quarts at this price. This is one point on the new supply curve. The rest of the curve can be constructed in the same way.)
b. Graph the new supply curve constructed in part (a) on the supply–demand diagram depicted in Figure 4–3. What are the new equilibrium price and quantity?
c. Does the tax succeed in its goal of reducing the consumption of milk?
d. How much does the equilibrium price increase? Is the price rise greater than, equal to, or less than the 30¢ tax?
e. Who actually pays the tax, consumers or producers? (This may be a good question to discuss in class.)

15. (More difficult) The demand and supply curves for hoagies in Collegetown are given by the following two equations:

$$Q = 8{,}000 - 500P \qquad Q = 2{,}000 + 1000P,$$

where $P$ is measured in dollars and $Q$ is the number of hoagies per month.

a. Find the equilibrium price and quantity algebraically.
b. If Collegetowners decide they do not really like hoagies that much, which of the following might be the new demand curve?

$$Q = 6{,}500 - 500P \qquad Q = 9{,}500 - 500P$$

Find the equilibrium price and quantity after the shift of the demand curve.

c. If, *instead*, two new stores that sell hoagies open up in town, which of the following might be the new supply curve?

$$Q = 1{,}250 + 1000P \qquad Q = 2{,}750 + 1000P$$

Find the equilibrium price and quantity after the shift of the supply curve.

PART II

# Essentials of Microeconomics: Consumers and Firms

Chapter 5

# DECIDING ON OUTPUT AND PRICE: THE IMPORTANCE OF MARGINAL ANALYSIS

*Business is a good game. . . . You keep score with money.*

**NOLAN BUSHNELL, FOUNDER OF ATARI.**

Chapter 4 made extensive use of supply and demand curves without probing very deeply into the origins of either. It is now time to remedy this deficiency by analyzing what underlies the supply and demand curves. The four chapters of Part 2 describe how firms and consumers can make decisions that are **optimal**, meaning that they go as far as is possible, given the circumstances, to promote the goals that the decision maker happens to have selected. As is generally done in economics, we will assume that the goal of the business firm is maximization of its **total profit**, a fairly well-defined concept, while the objective of the consumer is maximization of his or her **utility**, a much more nebulous concept, which we will not even attempt to define until Chapter 7. ¶ Our illustrations in these four chapters will be tied to the efforts in the formerly communist countries to transform themselves into market economies because that will help keep us aware of the pertinence of the analysis that follows to the workings of the market. ¶ This chapter starts off our discussion of microeconomic theory by analyzing the decisions a business

An **OPTIMAL** decision is one which, among all the decisions that are actually possible, is best for the decision maker. For example, if profit is the sole objective of some firm, the price that makes the firm's profit as large as possible is optimal for that company.

firm makes about how much of its products to produce and at what prices to offer them for sale. When firms such as Apple introduce a new line of computers, they must decide on the prices at which each will be offered and the number of each to produce. These are clearly crucial decisions. They have a vital influence on the firm's labor requirements, on the reception given the products by its consumers, and indeed, on the future success of the company. This chapter describes tools that firms like Apple can use to choose the price–output combination that makes its operations as profitable as they can be.

It turns out that these same tools are equally useful to government agencies and nonprofit organizations in making similar decisions. We will also find that the basic analytic tool introduced here, **marginal analysis**, is essential to the analysis of production and costs in the following chapter, in the investigation of consumer decisions in Chapters 7 and 8, and virtually throughout the book. This is indeed one of the most fundamental analytic weapons of economics.

The analysis will also lead to a conclusion which may be somewhat surprising, and shows that unaided common sense can sometimes be misleading in business decisions. Specifically, we will see that it is possible for a firm to make a profit by selling at a price that is, apparently, below cost!

## TWO ILLUSTRATIVE CASES[1]

Price and output decisions can perplex even the most experienced business people, as the following real-life illustrations show. At the end of the chapter we will see how the tools described here helped solve the problems.

*CASE 1: PRICING A SIX-PACK* The managers of one of America's largest manufacturers of soft drinks became concerned when a rival company introduced a cheaper substitute for one of their leading products. As a result, some of the firm's managers advocated a reduction in the price of a six-pack from $1.50 to $1.35. This stimulated a heated debate. It was agreed that the price should be cut if it was not likely to reduce the company's profits. Although some of the managers maintained that the cut made sense because of the additional sales it would stimulate, others held that the price cut would hurt the company by cutting profit per unit of output. The company had reliable information about costs, but knew rather little about the shape of its demand curve. At this point a group of consultants, including one of the authors of this book, was called in to offer their suggestions. We will see how economic analysis enabled them to solve the problem even though the vital demand elasticity figures were unavailable.

*CASE 2: MAKING PROFITS BY SELLING BELOW COSTS* In a recent legal battle between two manufacturers of pocket calculators, which we will call Company A and Company B, the latter accused the former of selling 10 million sophisticated calculators at a price of $12 which A allegedly knew was too low to cover its costs. B claimed that A was doing this only to drive B out of business. Company A's records, which were revealed to the court, appeared at first glance to confirm B's accusation. The cost of materials, labor, fuel, direct advertising of the calculator, and other such direct costs, came to $10.30 per calculator. Company A's accountants also assigned to this product its share of the company's annual expenditure on administration, research, advertising, and the like (which were

[1]The figures in these examples are doctored to help preserve the confidentiality of the information and to simplify the calculations. The cases, however, are real.

referred to as "overhead")—a total of $4.25 per calculator. The $12.00 price clearly did not cover the $14.55 cost attributed to each calculator sold. Yet, economists representing Company A were able to convince the court that manufacture of the calculator was a profitable activity for Company A, so that there was no basis on which to conclude that its only purpose was to destroy B. At the end of the chapter we will explain just how this was possible.

## PRICE AND QUANTITY: ONE DECISION, NOT TWO

This chapter is about how firms like those in the preceding cases select a *price* and a *quantity* of output that best serve their financial interests. While it would seem that firms must choose two numbers, in fact they can pick only one. Once they have selected the *price*, the *quantity* they will sell is up to consumers. Alternatively, firms may decide *how much* they want to sell, but then they must leave it to the market to determine the *price* at which this quantity can be sold.

Management gets its two numbers by making only one decision because the firm's demand curve tells it, for any quantity it may decide to market, the highest possible price its product can fetch. For purposes of illustration, consider a hypothetical Ukrainian firm, Ivana and Ivan's poultry farm (henceforth I&I). The farm is exploring what it can do to provide a living to its owners on the newly freed poultry market in its village, with little competition as yet available. Whether they are aware of it or not, there is a demand curve for Ivana and Ivan's chickens, *DD* in Figure 5–1. This curve shows that if these farmers become greedy and

**Figure 5–1** **I&I'S DEMAND CURVE**

This graph shows the quantity of product demanded at each price. For example, the curve shows that at a price of $15 (point *e*), five units will be demanded.

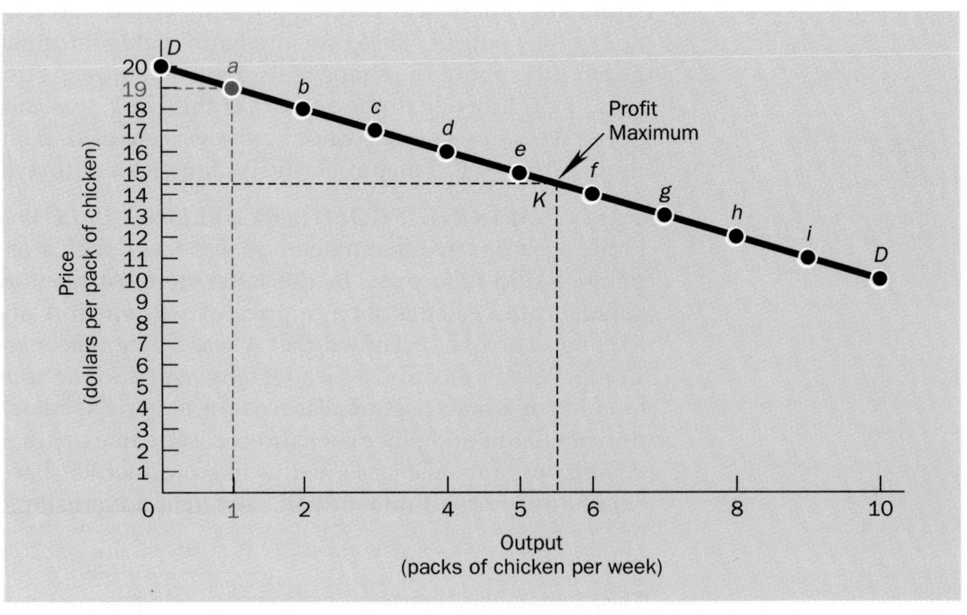

decide to charge the relatively high price of $19 for a 10-kilo package (about 22 pounds) of chicken (point *a* on the curve), they will find that they can sell only one package per week.[2] On the other hand, if they want to sell as many as 5.5 packages per week they can find the required number of customers only by offering chicken at the lower price of $14.50 (point *K*). In summary:

Each point on the demand curve represents a price-quantity pair. The firm can pick any such pair. But it can never pick the price corresponding to one point on the demand curve and the quantity corresponding to another point, since such an output could not be sold at the selected price.

Throughout this chapter, then, we will not discuss price and output decisions separately, for they are merely two different aspects of the same decision. To analyze this decision, we will make a strong assumption about the behavior of business firms—the assumption that firms strive for the largest possible total profit, to the exclusion of any other goal. While not literally correct, this seems to be a useful simplification of a much more complex reality. At least economists have long believed so.

## DO FIRMS REALLY MAXIMIZE PROFITS?

Naturally, many people have questioned whether firms really try to maximize profits, to the exclusion of all other goals. Business people are like other human beings: their motives are varied and complex. Given the choice, many executives might prefer to control the largest firm rather than the most profitable one. Some may be fascinated by technology and therefore may spend so much on R&D that it cuts down profit. Others may be motivated by a desire to "do good" and therefore give away some of the stockholders' money to hospitals and colleges. Different managers within the same firm may not always agree with one another on goals, so that it may not even make sense to speak about "*the* goal of the firm." Thus, any attempt to summarize the objectives of management in terms of a single number (profit) is bound to be an oversimplification.

In addition, the exacting requirements for maximizing profits are tough to satisfy. In practice, the required calculations are rarely carried out fully. In deciding how much to invest, what price to set for a product, or how much to allocate to the advertising budget, the range of available alternatives is enormous. And information about each alternative is often expensive and difficult to acquire. As a result, when a firm's management decides on an $18 million construction budget, it rarely compares the consequences of that decision in any detail with the consequences of all the possible alternatives—such as budgets of $17 million or $19 million. But unless *all* the available possibilities are compared, there is no way management can be sure it has chosen the one that brings in the highest possible profit.

Often management studies with care only the likely effects of the proposed decision itself: What sort of plant will it obtain for the money? How costly will

---

[2]It may seem strange to report I&I's transactions in dollars rather than rubles, the Russian and the Ukrainian national currency. However, because inflation in those countries is so rapid, the ruble is quickly losing its power to purchase goods. The item that cost 100 rubles yesterday may be priced at 120 rubles today. In order to avoid being stuck with currency that is continuously losing value, many market transactions in the former Soviet Union are, consequently, being carried out with dollars. This has happened in a number of countries suffering from rapid inflation.

it be to operate the plant? How much revenue is it likely to obtain from the sale of the plant's output? Management's concern is *whether the decision's results are likely to be acceptable*—whether its risks will not be unacceptably great, whether its profits will not be unacceptably low—so that the company can live satisfactorily with the outcome. Such analysis cannot be expected to bring in the maximum possible profit because, although the decision may be good, some unexplored alternative may be even better.

Decision making that seeks only solutions that are *acceptable* has been called **satisficing**, to contrast it with optimizing (profit maximization). Some analysts, such as Carnegie-Mellon University's Nobel Prize winner Herbert Simon, have concluded that decision making in industry and government is often of the satisficing variety.

But even if this is true, it does not necessarily make profit maximization a bad assumption. Recall our discussion of abstraction and model-building in Chapter 1. A map of Los Angeles that omits thousands of roads is no doubt "wrong" if interpreted as a literal description of the city. Nonetheless, by capturing the most important elements of reality, it may help us understand the city better than a map that is cluttered with too much detail. Similarly, we can learn much about the behavior of business firms by assuming that they try to maximize profits, even though we know that not *all* of them act this way *all* of the time.

We will therefore assume throughout this chapter and for most of the book that the firm has only one objective. It wants to make its *total* profit as large as possible. Our analytic strategy will be to determine what output level (or price) achieves this goal. But you should keep in mind the fact that many of the results depend on a simplifying assumption, so the general conclusions will not apply to every case. Our decision to base the analysis on the assumption that the firm maximizes profits gives us sharper insights, but we pay with some loss of realism.

## TOTAL PROFIT: KEEP YOUR EYE ON THE GOAL

The **TOTAL PROFIT** of a firm is its net earnings during some period of time. It is equal to the total amount of money the firm gets from the sale of its products (the firm's **total revenue**) minus the total amount it spends to make those products (**total cost**).

**Total profit**, then, is assumed here to be *the* goal of the firm. It is, by definition, the difference between what the company earns in the form of sales revenue and what it pays out in the form of costs:

$$\text{Total profit} = \text{Total revenue} - \text{Total costs.}$$

Total profit defined in this way is called **economic profit**, to distinguish it from the accountant's definition of profit. The two concepts of profit differ because total cost, in the economist's definition, includes the opportunity cost of any capital, labor, or other inputs supplied by the owner of the firm. Thus, if a small business earns just enough to pay the owner the fees (say, $35,000 per year) that her labor and capital could have earned if they had been sold to others, economists say she is earning zero *economic* profit. (She is just covering *all* her costs, including her opportunity costs). In contrast, most accountants will say her profit is $35,000.

To analyze how total profit depends on output, we must therefore study the behavior of the two components of total profit: total revenue (TR) and total cost (TC). It should be obvious that both **total revenue** and **total cost** depend on the output-price combination the firm selects; it is these relationships that we study next.

**Table 5–1 I&I'S DEMAND SCHEDULE, TOTAL REVENUE SCHEDULE, AND MARGINAL REVENUE SCHEDULE**

**(data corresponding to Figure 5–1)**

| NUMBER OF CHICKEN PACKS (per week) | PRICE = AVERAGE REVENUE (dollars per pack) | TOTAL REVENUE (dollars per week) | MARGINAL REVENUE 10-KILO PACKS (dollars per pack) |
|---|---|---|---|
| 0 | — | 0 | |
| 1 | 19 | 19 | 19 |
| 2 | 18 | 36 | 17 |
| 3 | 17 | 51 | 15 |
| 4 | 16 | 64 | 13 |
| 5 | 15 | 75 | 11 |
| 6 | 14 | 84 | 9 |
| 7 | 13 | 91 | 7 |
| 8 | 12 | 96 | 5 |
| 9 | 11 | 99 | 3 |
| 10 | 10 | 100 | 1 |

## TOTAL, AVERAGE, AND MARGINAL REVENUE

Total revenue can be calculated directly from the demand curve since, by definition, it is the product of price times the quantity that will be bought at that price:

$$\text{TR} = P \times Q.$$

Table 5–1 shows how the total revenue schedule is derived from the demand schedule for our illustrative firm, I&I. The first two columns simply express the demand curve of Figure 5–1 in tabular form. The third column gives, for each quantity, the product of price times quantity. For example, if Ivana and Ivan market six packages of chicken at a price of $14 per pack, their weekly sales revenue will be 6 packages × $14 = $84.

Figure 5–2 displays I&I's total revenue schedule in graphical form as the black TR curve. This graph shows precisely the same information as the demand curve in Figure 5–1, but in a somewhat different form. For example, point *e* on the demand curve in Figure 5–1, which shows a price–quantity combination of $P$ = $15 per pack and $Q$ = 5 packs of chicken per week, appears as point $E$ in Figure 5–2 as a total revenue of $75 per week ($15 per pack times 5 packs). Similarly, each point on the TR curve in Figure 5–2 corresponds to the similarly labeled point in Figure 5–1.

**AVERAGE REVENUE (AR)** is total revenue (TR) divided by quantity.

The relationship between the demand curve and the TR curve can be rephrased in a slightly different way. Since the price of the product is the revenue *per unit* that the firm receives, we can view the demand curve as the curve of **average revenue**. Average revenue (AR) and total revenue (TR) are related to one another in a simple way.[3] Specifically, since

$$\text{AR} = \frac{\text{TR}}{Q} = \frac{P \times Q}{Q} = P,$$

average revenue and price are two names for the same thing.

[3]See the appendix to this chapter for a general discussion of the relationship between totals and averages.

**Figure 5–2** I&I'S TOTAL REVENUE CURVE

The total revenue curve for I&I is derived directly from the demand curve, since total revenue is the product of price times quantity. Points *A, B, C, D, E,* and *F* in this diagram correspond to points *a, b, c, d, e,* and *f,* respectively, in Figure 5–1.

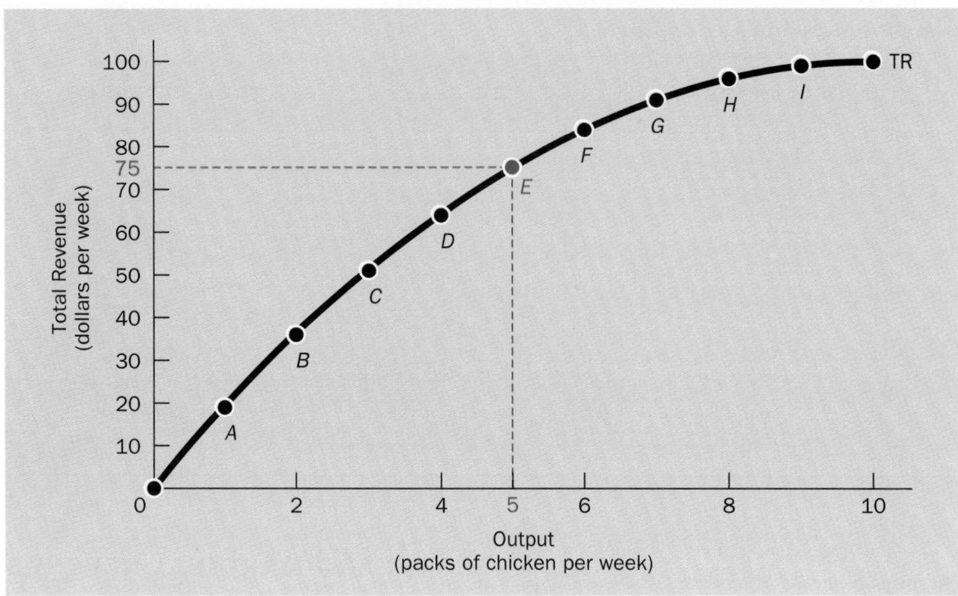


**MARGINAL REVENUE,** often abbreviated MR, is the *addition* to total revenue resulting from the addition of one unit to total output. Geometrically, marginal revenue is the *slope* of the total revenue curve. Its formula is $MR_1 = TR_1 - TR_0$, and so on.

Finally, the last column of Table 5–1 shows what is called the **marginal revenue** for each level of output—an analytic tool whose use will be explained presently. This concept refers to the *addition* to total revenue that results from raising output by one unit. Its definition and calculation are straightforward. The marginal revenue that is generated when the output of I&I increases by one unit is defined as the difference between the total revenue of the larger output and the total revenue of the smaller output. Thus, in Table 5–1 we see that when output rises from two to three units, total revenue goes up from \$36 to \$51, so that marginal revenue is \$51 − \$36 = \$15. Notice, for example, that the \$15 marginal revenue figure corresponding to the move from the sale of two units of output to the sale of three units of output is printed in the table in a way meant to indicate that it lies *between* an output of two units and an output of three units, indicating that the marginal figure corresponds to the transition between those two sales volumes (the zigzag lines between the total and marginal revenue columns). Similarly, and for the same reason, all the other marginal revenue figures in the table are printed to indicate that they show the effect of such a *change* in sales quantities. To return to the concept itself, we may summarize by saying that the marginal revenue accruing to the firm when it is producing some given output (say two packages of chicken) is the resulting addition to the firm's total revenue (\$15).

A firm's **TOTAL COST (TC)** curve shows, for each possible quantity of output at some given point in time, the total amount which the firm must spend for its inputs to produce that amount of output plus any opportunity cost incurred in the process.

## TOTAL, AVERAGE, AND MARGINAL COST

The revenue side is, of course, only half of the firm's profit picture. We must turn to the cost side for the other half. By analogy with the three revenue concepts we have just explained—total revenue (TR), average revenue (AR), and marginal revenue (MR)—there are three corresponding tools of cost analysis, **total cost**

**Table 5–2** TOTAL, AVERAGE, AND MARGINAL COSTS FOR I&I

| NUMBER OF CHICKEN PACKS (per week) | TOTAL COST (dollars per week) | MARGINAL COST (dollars per pack) | AVERAGE COST (dollars per week) |
|---|---|---|---|
| 0 | 0 | | — |
| | | 17 | |
| 1 | 17 | | 17 |
| | | 9 | |
| 2 | 26 | | 13 |
| | | 7 | |
| 3 | 33 | | 11 |
| | | 7 | |
| 4 | 40 | | 10 |
| | | 8 | |
| 5 | 48 | | 9.6 |
| | | 9 | |
| 6 | 57 | | 9.5 |
| | | 10.2 | |
| 7 | 67.2 | | 9.6 |
| | | 12.8 | |
| 8 | 80 | | 10 |
| | | 19 | |
| 9 | 99 | | 11 |
| | | 26 | |
| 10 | 125 | | 12.5 |

A firm's **AVERAGE COST (AC)** curve shows, for each output, the cost per unit, that is, total cost divided by output.

A firm's **MARGINAL COST (MC)** curve shows, for each output, the increase in the firm's total cost required if it increases its output by an additional unit.

**(TC), average cost (AC), and marginal cost (MC)**. As we shall see shortly, average and marginal cost are obtained directly from total cost in exactly the same way that average and marginal revenue were calculated from total revenue.

The *total cost* of some quantity of output is simply the sum of the amounts of money that the firm must spend on labor, fuel, raw materials, etc., to produce that given output. Thus, I&I's total cost curve reports, for each relevant quantity of chicken production for the point of time in question, *the smallest* amount the firm can spend in total and still produce the given quantity of poultry meat.[4]

*Average cost* (AC), also called unit cost, is simply total cost divided by output; that is:

$$\text{Average cost} = \frac{\text{Total cost}}{\text{Quantity of output}}$$

or in symbols:

$$AC = \frac{TC}{Q}.$$

For example, we see in Table 5–2 that the total cost of producing three packs of chicken per week is \$33, making the average cost equal to \$33/3 = \$11.

To determine the *marginal cost* (MC), we must know what would happen to TC if output were to increase by one unit. For example, the marginal cost of a fifth unit of output is the amount by which production of this unit would increase total cost. That is, it is equal to the total cost of producing five units (\$48) minus the total cost of producing four units (\$40). Thus, the marginal cost of a fifth pack of chicken is \$48 − \$40 = \$8. In general:

Once we know a firm's total cost for its various outputs, we can calculate its average cost and its marginal cost directly.

[4]It is, of course, always possible that the firm will be wasteful and spend more. The next chapter studies how firms minimize the total cost of producing any given level of output.

Figure 5–3 plots the numbers in this table and thus shows the total, average, and marginal cost curves for the poultry farm. The shapes of the curves depicted here are considered typical. The TC curve is generally assumed to rise fairly steadily as the firm's output increases. After all, one cannot expect to produce three packs of meat at a lower total cost than two packs. The AC curve and the MC curve are both shaped roughly like the letter U—first going downhill, then gradually turning uphill again. The reasons economists consider these shapes to be plausible will be discussed in the next chapter, where the nature of costs will be examined in some detail. For now we need merely note that the shapes mean that, in any given industry, there is some size of firm that is most efficient in producing the output. Smaller enterprises lose any advantages that derive from a large volume of production, and so their average cost (the cost per unit of output) will be greater than that of a firm operating at the most efficient size of output. Similarly, firms that are too large will suffer from difficulties of supervision, coordination, and perhaps bureaucratic controls, so that their cost per unit of output will also be higher than that of a firm of most efficient size.

## MAXIMIZATION OF TOTAL PROFIT

We now have all the analytic equipment we need to answer our central question: What combination of output and price will yield the largest obtainable total profit?

To study how total profit depends on output, we bring together in Table 5–3 the total revenue and total cost schedules from the two previous tables. The last column in Table 5–3—called, naturally enough, total profit—is just the difference between total revenue and total cost at each level of output. Remembering that I&I's assumed objective is to maximize its profits, it is a simple matter to determine the level of production it will choose. By producing and selling between 5 and 6 packages of meat per week, I&I achieves the highest level of profits it is capable of achieving—some $27 per week. Any higher or lower rate of production would lead to lower profits. For example, weekly profits would drop to $16 if output were expanded to 8 packs. And, if the farm were to make the error of producing 10 packs per week, it would actually emerge with a net weekly loss of $25.

### PROFIT MAXIMIZATION: A GRAPHICAL INTERPRETATION

Precisely the same analysis can be presented graphically. In the upper portion of Figure 5–4 we bring together into a single diagram the total revenue curve from Figure 5–2 and the total cost curve from Figure 5–3. Total profit, which is the difference between total revenue and total cost, appears in the diagram as the *vertical* distance between the TR and TC curves. For example, when output is four units, total revenue is $64 (point *A*), total cost is $40 (point *B*), and total profit is the distance between points *A* and *B*, or $24 per week.

In this graphical view of the problem, I&I wants to maximize total profit, which is the vertical distance between the TR and TC curves. To make total profit more apparent, the curve of total profit—that is, TR − TC—is drawn explicitly in the lower portion of Figure 5–4. We see that it reaches its maximum value, about

## Figure 5-3 I&I'S COST CURVES

The graphs show, for each possible level of output, I&I's total cost, average cost, and marginal cost.

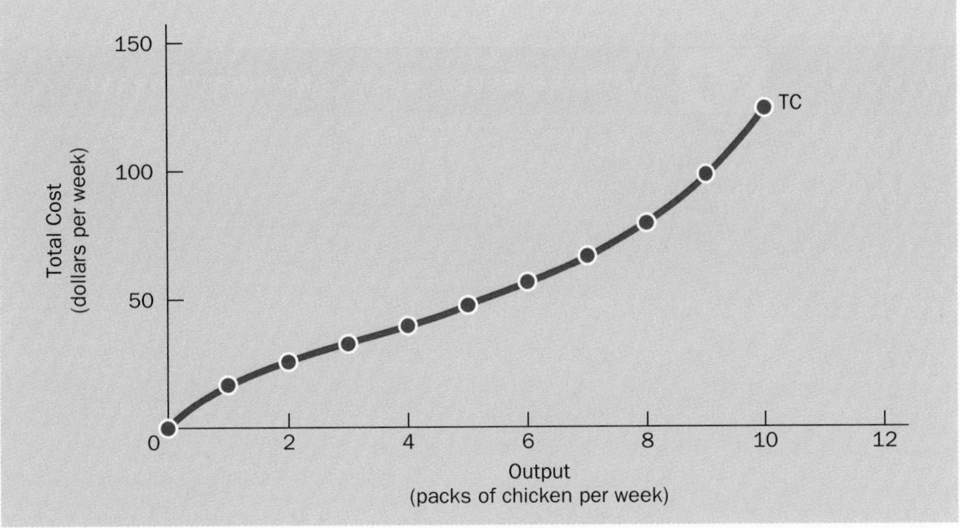


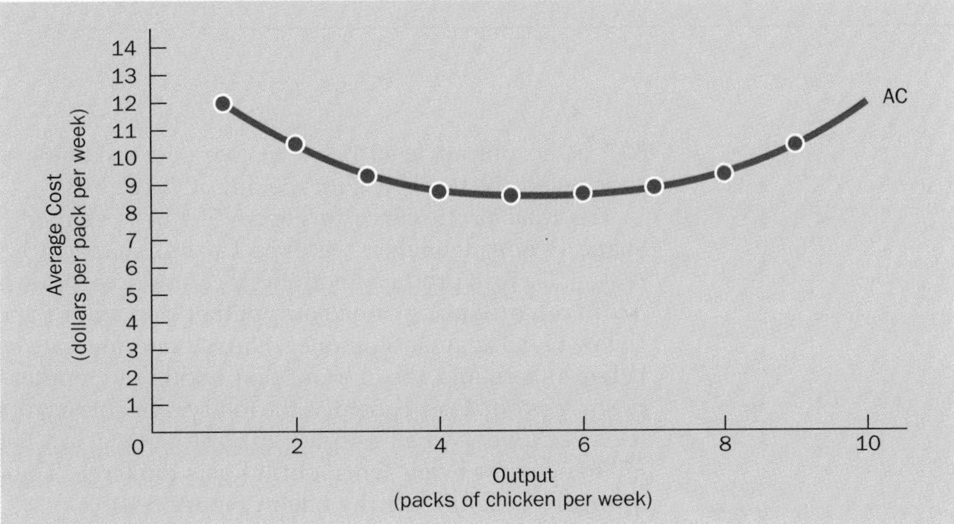


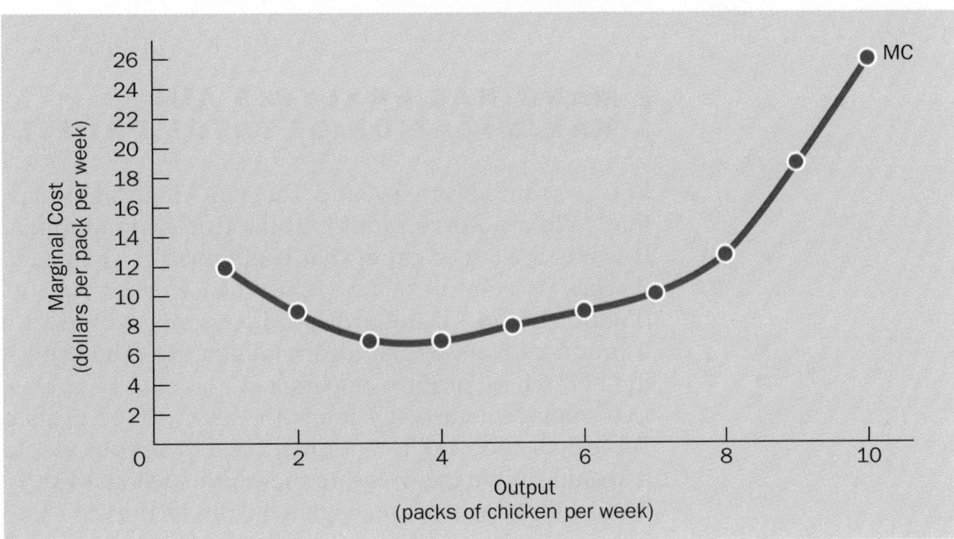

Table 5–3 TOTAL REVENUES, COSTS, AND PROFIT FOR I&I

| NUMBER OF CHICKEN PACKS (per week) | TOTAL REVENUE | TOTAL COST (dollars per week) | TOTAL PROFIT |
|---|---|---|---|
| 0 | 0 | 0 | 0 |
| 1 | 19 | 17 | 2 |
| 2 | 36 | 26 | 10 |
| 3 | 51 | 33 | 18 |
| 4 | 64 | 40 | 24 |
| 5 | 75 | 48 | 27 |
| 6 | 84 | 57 | 27 |
| 7 | 91 | 67.2 | 23.8 |
| 8 | 96 | 80 | 16 |
| 9 | 99 | 99 | 0 |
| 10 | 100 | 125 | −25 |

$27, at an output level between five and six units per week. This is the same conclusion we reached with the aid of Table 5–3.

The total profit curve in Figure 5–4(b) is shaped like a hill. Though such a shape is not inevitable, we expect a hill shape to be typical for the following reason. If a firm produces nothing, it certainly earns no profit. At the other extreme, a firm can produce so much output that it swamps the market, forcing price down so low that it again loses money. Only at intermediate levels of output—something between zero and the amount that floods the market—will the company earn a positive profit. Consequently, the total profit curve will rise from zero (or negative) levels at a very small output, to positive levels in between; and, finally, it will fall to negative levels when output gets too large. Thus, the total profit curve will normally be a hill like the one in Figure 5–4(b).

## MARGINAL ANALYSIS AND MAXIMIZATION OF TOTAL PROFIT

We see from Figure 5–4 and Table 5–3 that there may be many levels of output that yield a positive profit. But the firm is not aiming for just *any* level of profit. It wants the *largest* profit that is obtainable. The profit graph shows that the hill reaches its summit (about $27) when weekly output is between 5 and 6 units [Figure 5–4(b)]. If the firm produces only 4 units, it earns only $24 in profit. If it produces 8, its weekly profit falls to $16. The firm's goal is to get to the top of the hill, where profit is maximized.

If management really knew the exact shape of its profit hill, that is, if it had Table 5–3, choosing the optimal level of output would be a simple task indeed. It would only have to locate the point such as *M* in Figure 5–4(b), the top of its profit hill. However, management rarely if ever has so much information, so a different technique for finding the optimum is required. That technique is **mar-**

Figure 5–4

## PROFIT MAXIMIZATION: A GRAPHICAL INTERPRETATION

I&I's profits are maximized when the vertical distance between its total revenue curve, TR, and its total cost curve, TC, is at its maximum. In the diagram, this occurs at an output of 5.5 units per week; total profits are CR, or $27. The total profit curve is also shown in the figure. Naturally, it reaches its maximum value (about $27) at 5.5 units (point *M*).

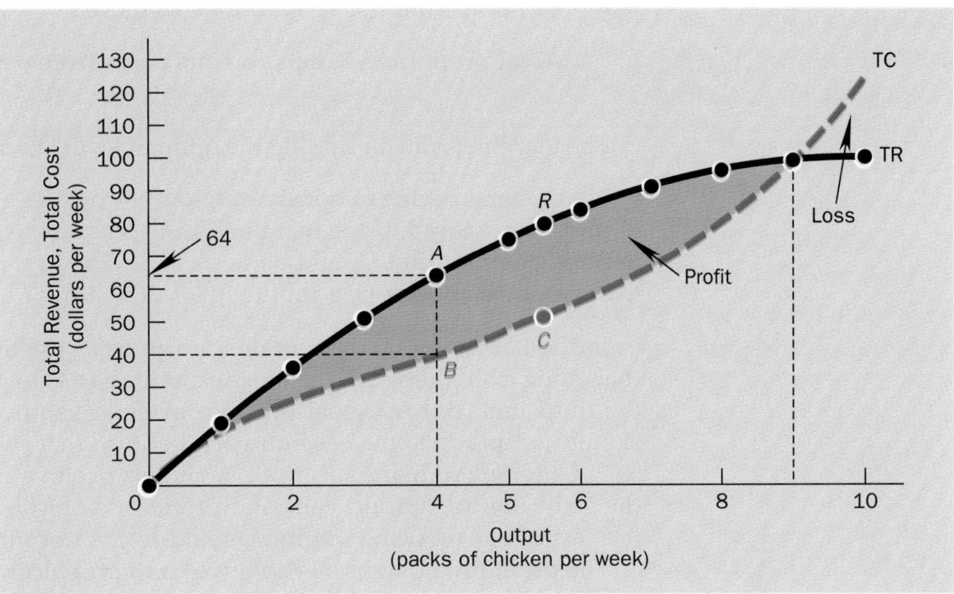


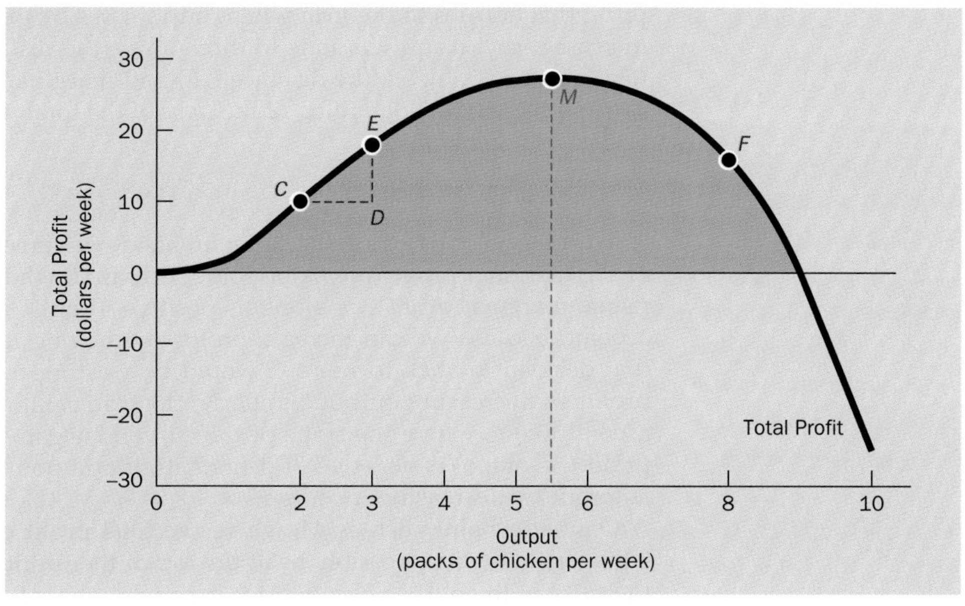


**MARGINAL PROFIT** is the *addition* to total profit resulting from one more unit of output.

**ginal analysis**—the same set of tools we will use later to analyze the firm's input purchase decisions in Chapter 6 and the consumer's buying decisions in Chapters 7 and 8.

To see how marginal analysis helps solve I&I's problem, we introduce an expository concept: **marginal profit**. Referring back to Table 5–3, we see that an increase in I&I's weekly output from two to three packs of chicken would raise total profit from \$10 to \$18; that is, it would generate \$8 in *additional* profit. We call this the *marginal profit* resulting from the addition of the third unit. Similarly, marginal profit from the seventh unit would be

$$\begin{aligned}\text{Total profit from 7 units} - \text{Total profit from 6 units} &= \$23.8 - \$27\\ &= -\$3.2.\end{aligned}$$

The marginal rule for finding the optimal level of output is easy to understand:

If the marginal profit from increasing output by one unit is positive, then output should be increased. If the marginal profit from increasing output by one unit is negative, then output should be decreased. Thus, an output level can maximize *total* profit only if *marginal* profit equals zero at that output.

In the I&I example, the marginal profit from the third unit is \$8. This means that going from the second to the third unit *adds* \$8 to profit, so it pays to produce the third unit. But marginal profit from the seventh unit is − \$3.2, so the firm should not produce the seventh pack because that would reduce total profit by \$3.2. Only where marginal profit is neither positive nor negative (as is true for the sixth unit of output) can total profit be as big as possible, because neither increasing nor reducing output can add to total profit.

The profit hill in Figure 5–4(b) gives us a graphical interpretation of the "marginal profit equals zero" condition. Marginal profit is defined as the additional profit that accrues to the firm when output rises by one unit. So, when output is increased, say, from two units to three units [the distance *CD* in Figure 5–4(b)], total profit rises by \$8 (the distance *DE*) and marginal profit is therefore *DE*/*CD*. This is precisely the definition of the *slope* of the total profit curve between points *C* and *E*. In general:

Marginal profit is the slope of the total profit curve.

With this geometric interpretation in hand, we can easily understand the logic of the marginal profit rule. At a point such as *C*, where the total profit curve is rising, marginal profit ( = slope) is positive. Profits cannot be maximal at such a point, because we can increase profits by moving farther to the right. A firm that decided to stick to point *C* would be wasting the opportunity to increase profits by increasing output. Similarly, the firm cannot be maximizing profits at a point like *F*, where the slope of the curve is negative, because there marginal profit ( = slope) is negative. If it finds itself at a point like *F*, the firm can raise its profit by decreasing its output.

Only at a point such as *M*, where the total profit curve is neither rising nor falling, can the firm possibly be at the top of the profit hill rather than on one of the sides of the hill. And point *M* is precisely where the slope of the curve—and hence the marginal profit—is zero. Thus:

An output decision cannot be optimal unless the corresponding marginal profit is zero.

The firm is not interested in marginal profit for its own sake, but rather for what it implies about *total* profit. Marginal profit is like the needle on the pressure gauge of a boiler: the needle itself is of no concern to anyone, but if one fails to watch it the consequences may be quite dramatic.

One common misunderstanding that arises in discussions of the marginal criterion of optimality is the idea that it seems foolish to go to a point where marginal profit is zero. "Isn't it better to earn a positive marginal profit?" This notion springs from a confusion between the quantity one is seeking to maximize (*total* profit) and the gauge that indicates whether such a maximum has in fact been attained (*marginal* profit). Of course, it is better to have a positive *total* profit than zero total profit. But a zero value on the *marginal* profit gauge merely indicates that all is apparently well, that *total* profit may be at its maximum.

## MARGINAL REVENUE AND MARGINAL COST: GUIDES TO AN OPTIMUM

There is an alternative version of the marginal analysis of profit maximization, couched directly in terms of the cost and revenue components of profit. For this purpose, refer back to Figure 5–4, where the profit hill was constructed from the total revenue (TR) and total cost (TC) curves. Observe that there is another way of finding the profit-maximizing solution. We want to maximize the vertical distance between the TR and TC curves. This distance, we see, is not maximal at an output level such as two units, because there the two curves are growing farther apart. If we move farther to the right, the vertical distance between them (which is total profit) will increase. Conversely, we have not maximized the vertical distance between TR and TC at an output level such as eight units, because there the two curves are coming closer together. We can add to profits by moving farther to the left (reducing output).

The conclusion from the graph, then, is that total profit—the vertical distance between TR and TC—is maximized only when the two curves are neither growing farther apart nor coming closer together; that is, when their *slopes* are equal. While this conclusion is rather mechanical, we can breathe some life into it by interpreting the slopes of the two curves as **marginal revenue** and **marginal cost**. These concepts have been defined and illustrated previously (see pages 109–10 and 110–113). For precisely the same reason that marginal profit is the slope of the total profit curve, marginal revenue is the slope of the total revenue curve, since it represents the increase in total revenue resulting from the sale of one additional unit. And for the same reason, marginal cost is equal to the slope of the total cost curve. This interpretation of marginal revenue and marginal cost, respectively, as the *slopes* of total revenue and total cost permit us to restate the geometric conclusion we have just reached in an economically significant way:

Profit can be maximized only at an output level at which marginal revenue is (approximately) equal to marginal cost. In symbols:

$$MR = MC.$$

The logic of the MC = MR rule for profit maximization is straightforward.[5] When MR is *not* equal to MC, profits cannot possibly be maximized because the firm can increase its profits either by raising its output or by reducing it. For

[5]You may have surmised by now that just as total profit = total revenue − total cost, it must be true that marginal profit = marginal revenue − marginal cost. This is in fact correct. It also shows that when marginal profit = 0, we must have MR = MC.

**Table 5–4 MARGINAL REVENUE AND MARGINAL COST FOR I&I**

| NUMBER OF CHICKEN PACKS (per week) | MARGINAL REVENUE (dollars per pack per week) | MARGINAL COST (dollars per pack per week) |
|---|---|---|
| 0 | | |
| | 19 | 17 |
| 1 | | |
| | 17 | 9 |
| 2 | | |
| | 15 | 7 |
| 3 | | |
| | 13 | 7 |
| 4 | | |
| | 11 | 8 |
| 5 | | |
| | 9 | 9 |
| 6 | | |
| | 7 | 10.2 |
| 7 | | |
| | 5 | 12.8 |
| 8 | | |
| | 3 | 19 |
| 9 | | |
| | 1 | 26 |
| 10 | | |

example if MR = $15 and MC = $7, an additional unit of output *adds* $15 to revenues but only $7 to cost. Hence the firm can increase its net profit by $8 by producing and selling one more unit. Similarly, if MC exceeds MR, say MR = $3 and MC = $19, then the firm loses $16 on its marginal unit, so it can add $16 to its profit by reducing output by one unit. Only when MR = MC is it impossible for the firm to add to its profit by changing its output level.

Table 5–4 reproduces marginal revenue and marginal cost data for I&I from Tables 5–1 and 5–2. The table shows, as must be true, that the MR = MC rule leads us to the same conclusion as Figure 5–4 and Table 5–3. If they want to maximize their profits, I&I should produce and sell 5 or 6 packs of chicken per week.

The marginal revenue of the fifth pack of chicken is $11 (75 dollars from the sale of 5 packs less $64 from selling 4) while the marginal cost is only $8 ($48 – $40). So the firm should produce the fifth unit. But the seventh pack brings in only $7 in marginal revenue while its marginal cost is $10.2—clearly a losing proposition. Only between 5 and 6 units of output does MR = MC = ($9).

Because the graphs of marginal analysis will prove so useful in later chapters, Figure 5–5(a) shows the MR = MC condition for profit maximization graphically. The black curve labeled MR in the figure is the marginal revenue schedule from Table 5–4. The blue curve labeled MC is the marginal cost schedule. They intersect at point *E*, which is therefore the point where marginal revenue and marginal cost are equal. The optimal output for I&I is between five and six units.[6] Figures 5–5(b) and 5–5(c), respectively, are reproductions of the TR and TC curves from the upper part of Figure 5–4 and the total profit curve from the lower portion of that figure. Note how MC and MR intersect at the same output at which the distance of TR above TC is greatest, which is the output at which the profit hill reaches its summit.

[6]One important qualification must be entered. Sometimes marginal revenue and marginal cost curves do not have the nice shapes depicted in Figure 5–5(a), and they may intersect more than once. In such cases, while it remains true that MC = MR at the output level that maximizes profits, there may be other output levels at which MC is also equal to MR but at which profits are not maximized.

**Figure 5–5** **PROFIT MAXIMIZATION: ANOTHER GRAPHICAL INTERPRETATION**

Profits are maximized where marginal revenue (MR) is (approximately) equal to marginal cost (MC), for only at such a point will *marginal profit* be zero. Part (a) shows the MR = MC condition for profit maximization graphically as point *E*, where output is 5.5 packs of chicken per week. The diagram also reproduces from Figure 5–4 the TR and TC curves [(part (b)] and the total profit curve [(part (c)], showing how all three agree that the profit-maximizing output is between 5 and 6 units.

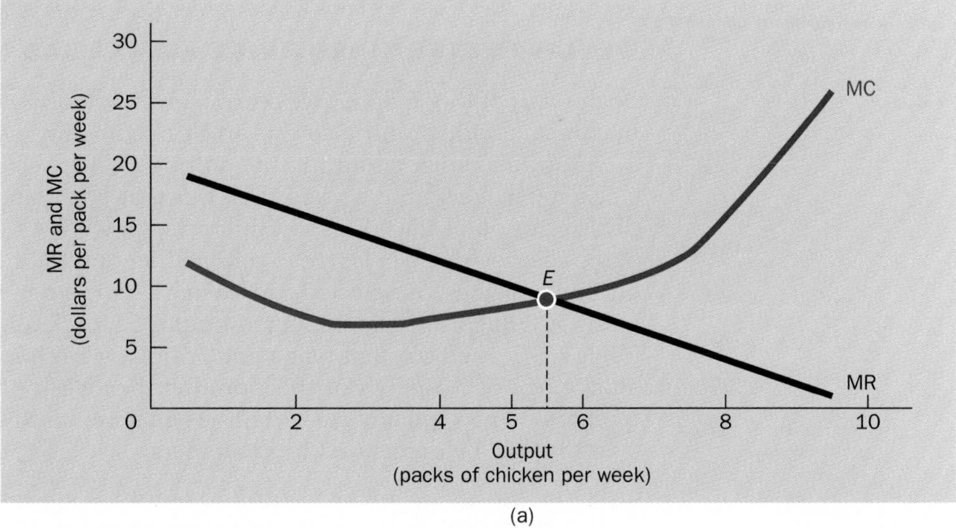


(a)

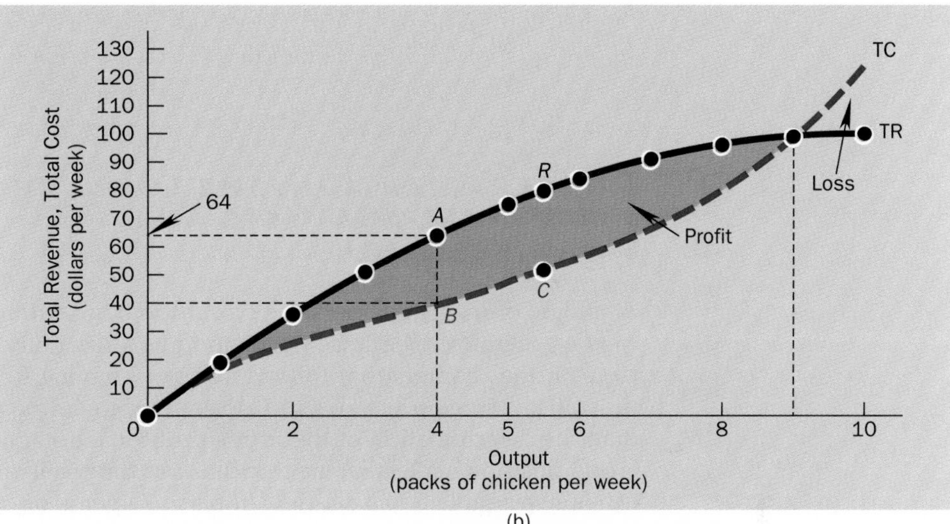


(b)

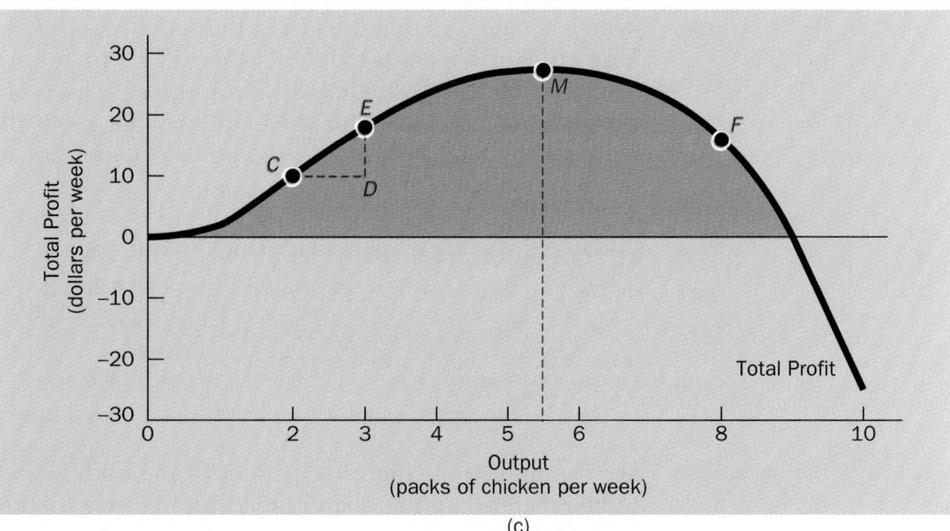


(c)

### WE HAVE DETERMINED PRICE AS WELL AS OUTPUT

At the start of this chapter, we set ourselves a double goal: to determine the profit maximizing *output* and also the profit maximizing *price*. So far, we have found the profit-maximizing output, the output level at which MC = MR (5.5 packs of chicken per week in our example). But that has gotten us almost all the way to determination of the corresponding price as well. As was noted at the beginning of the chapter, the firm is free to select either output or price, but not both, because once one of these is selected, the demand curve determines the other. Once we know that the profit-maximizing output is 5.5 packs of chicken, the demand curve in Figure 5–1 tells us that Ivana and Ivan have no further choice on price. To sell an average of 5.5 packs of their product per week, they must price it at $14.50 (point *K*). The demand curve tells us that this is the only price at which this quantity will be demanded by customers.

Once the profit-maximizing output quantity has been determined with the help of the MC = MR requirement, it is easy to find the profit-maximizing price with the help of the demand curve. Just use that curve to find out at what price the *optimal* quantity will be demanded.

## GENERALIZATION: THE LOGIC OF MARGINAL ANALYSIS AND MAXIMIZATION

The logic of marginal analysis of profit maximization that we have just studied can be generalized, because what amounts, essentially, to the same argument will recur in the chapters that follow. To avoid having to master the argument each time all over again it is useful to see how it can be applied in problems other than the determination of the firm's profit maximizing output. The general issue is this: decision makers often are faced with the problem of selecting the magnitude of some variable, such as how much to spend on advertising, or how many bananas to buy, or how many school buildings to construct. Each of these acts brings benefits, so that the larger the number selected by the decision maker, the larger the total benefits that will be derived. But, unfortunately, as larger numbers are selected, the associated costs also grow. The problem is to take the tradeoff properly into account and calculate at what point the net gain—the difference between the total benefit and the total cost—will be greatest. Thus, we have the following general principle:

If a decision is to be taken about the quantity of some variable, then to maximize

$$\text{net benefit} = \text{total benefit} - \text{total cost}$$

the decision maker must select a value of the variable at which

$$\text{marginal benefit} = \text{marginal cost}.$$

For example, if the marginal benefit from building an additional school is judged to be greater than the cost of an additional school, the community would clearly be better off if it increased the number of schools it undertook to build. On the

## *Moving to a Market Economy: The Perils of Privatization*

In this chapter and the next, we illustrate the workings of a firm in a market economy, making use of Ivana's and Ivan's poultry farm as an example. There are now many such new little enterprises in Eastern Europe. While quite a few of them will, no doubt, run into trouble, they are, at least, relatively easy to get started. One farms a piece of land, or runs a sewing machine, and peddles the product on the street, from home, or in a makeshift retail shop. It is reported, for example, that the number of private farms in Russia grew from approximately zero at the beginning of 1991 to 120,000 farms in July of 1992.*

But that still leaves a major and highly intractable problem for the process of transition from a centrally directed to a market economy. Much of each industrialized nation's GDP comes not from tiny enterprises, but from giant ones—steel works, car factories, electricity generating stations, and the like. The former Soviet Union and the previously associated countries have a large number of such enterprises; but they are all owned by the governments and operated by bureaucrats. Just how does one go about turning them into private enterprises? That may sound easy, but the difficulties are incredible.

First, who will buy them? Most of them are obsolete, inefficient and unprofitable. Second, if they are simply put up for sale, along with some sort of purchase incentives (tax breaks, subsidies, or a grant of monopoly, for example) the buyers are liable to be foreigners, for they are the only ones who have that kind of money. But massive foreign ownership may be politically unacceptable. If you were a Polish citizen, would you like all of the country's large firms to be owned by Japanese, Americans, and Germans?

Third, you can, instead, just give the firms away to the country's citizens. But how? Several of the governments in Eastern Europe have tried to solve this problem by distributing vouchers to all of their citizens. These vouchers are a special kind of money that can be used to buy stocks in the firms undergoing privatization, or they can, instead, be resold to other citizens of the country in question. However, that raises another problem. If each factory's ownership is divided, more or less evenly, among thousands or even millions of citizens, no one will be in a position to influence or control management, and an incompetent or unscrupulous management will be able to run the firm into the ground.

Fourth, how do you prevent the bureaucrats from interfering with the operations of the privatized firm, and regulating it to death?

This is only the beginning of the problem. It is no wonder that Great Britain, in a decade of privatization effort, succeeded in privatizing perhaps fifty large firms. Britain had centuries of experience in the operation of a market economy, yet many competent observers feel that its privatization was carried out clumsily and with results that were far from ideal. How much more difficult will the task be in Russia, for example, with thousands of firms to be privatized and virtually no experience in the workings of the market?

The moral is clear. It is not easy to dismantle a centrally directed economy and transform it into a market.

*The *New York Times*, October 6, 1992, p. A10.

other hand, if it were building so many schools that the marginal benefit was less than the marginal cost, it would be better off with a more limited construction program. Only if the marginal benefit and cost are as close as possible to being equal will neither an increase nor a reduction in the number of buildings be beneficial.

Throughout the chapters of Parts 2–5 we will find this logic repeated frequently. We will find ourselves, again and again, analyzing a quantitative decision that brings together both benefits and costs and concluding that the optimal decision occurs at the point where the marginal benefit equals the marginal cost. The logic, incidentally, is the same whether we are considering the net gains to a firm, to a consumer, or to society as a whole.

## MARGINAL ANALYSIS IN REAL DECISION PROBLEMS

We can now put the marginal analysis of profit determination to work to unravel the puzzles with which we began this chapter. These are both examples drawn from reality, and reality never works as neatly as a textbook illustration. In particular, neither example involves a mechanical application of the MC = MR rule. However, as these cases show, the underlying reasoning *does* help to deal with real problems.

***CASE 1: THE SODA-PRICING PROBLEM*** Our first problem dealt with a firm's choice between keeping the price of a brand of soda at $1.50 per six-pack or reducing it to $1.35 when a competitor entered the market. The trouble was that to know what to do, the firm needed to know its demand curve (and hence its marginal revenue curve). However, the firm did not have enough data to determine the shape of its demand curve. How, then, could a rational decision be made?

As we indicated, the debate among the firm's managers finally reached agreement on one point: the price should be cut if, as a result, profits were not likely to decline; that is, if marginal profit were not negative. Fortunately, the data needed to determine whether marginal profit was positive were obtainable. Initial annual sales were 10 million units, and the firm's engineers maintained emphatically that marginal costs were very close to constant at $1.20 per six-pack over the output range in question. Instead of trying to determine the *actual* increase in sales that would result from the price cut, the team of consultants decided to try to determine the *minimum necessary* increase in quantity demanded that would be required to avoid a decrease in profits.

It was clear that the firm needed additional revenue at least as great as the additional cost of supplying the added volume, if profits were not to decline; that is, MR had to exceed MC. The consultants knew that sales at the initial price of $1.50 per six-pack were $15 million ($1.50 per unit times 10 million units). Letting $Q$ represent the (unknown) quantity of six-packs that would be sold at the proposed new price of $1.35, the economists compared the added revenue with the added cost of providing the $Q$ new units. Since MC was constant at $1.20 per unit, the added cost amounted to

$$\text{Added cost} = \$1.20 \times (Q - 10 \text{ million}).$$

This was to be compared with the added revenue:

$$\text{Added revenue} = \text{New revenue} - \text{Old revenue} = \$1.35Q - \$15 \text{ million.}$$

No loss would result from the price change if the added revenue was greater than or equal to the added cost. The minimum $Q$ necessary to avoid a loss therefore was that at which added revenue equaled added cost, or

$$1.35Q - 15 \text{ million} = 1.2Q - 12 \text{ million,}$$

or

$$0.15Q = 3 \text{ million.}$$

This would be true if, and only if, $Q$, the quantity sold at the lower price, would be

$$Q = 20 \text{ million units.}$$

In other words, this calculation showed that the firm could break even from the 15-cent price reduction only if the quantity of its product demanded rose at least 100 percent (from 10 to 20 million units). Since past experience indicated that such a rise in quantity demanded was hardly possible, the price reduction proposal was quickly abandoned. Thus the logic of the MC = MR rule, plus a little ingenuity, enabled the consultants to deal with a problem that at first seemed baffling—even though they had no estimate of marginal revenue.

***CASE 2: THE "UNPROFITABLE" CALCULATOR*** Our second case study concerned a firm that was apparently losing money on calculator sales because its $12.00 price was less than the $14.55 average cost which the company's accountants assigned to the product. This $14.55 included $10.30 of costs caused directly by manufacture and marketing of the calculators plus a $4.25 per-calculator share of the company's overall general expenses ("overhead"). Accused of deliberately selling below cost in order to drive a competitor out of business, the company turned to marginal analysis to show that this was not true. The price at which the calculators were sold was in fact profitable.

To demonstrate this, the company's witness explained that, if the sales were really unprofitable, the company would have been able to raise its net earnings by ceasing production and sale of the calculators. A moment's consideration shows, however, that the opposite would have happened: profits would have decreased if the company gave up its annual sale of 10 million calculators.

The company's revenues would have been reduced by the (marginal) figure of $12.00 on each of its 10 million units sold—a revenue reduction of $120 million. But how much cost would it have saved? The answer is that the cost outlay actually *caused* by the production of the calculator was only the $10.30 in direct cost. The company president would not have been fired if the product were discontinued, and general expenditures on new product research probably would even have been increased. Thus, none of the company's overhead would have been saved by ending calculator production. Rather, the (marginal) saving would have been the direct cost of $10.30 per calculator times the 10 million calculator output—a total saving of $103 million.

Thus, elimination of the product would have reduced total company profit by $17 million per year—the $103 million cost saving minus the $120 million in revenue forgone. In other words, continued production of the calculators was not causing losses; on the contrary, it was contributing $17 million in profits every year. The court concluded that this reasoning was correct, and used this conclusion in its decision.

This case illustrates a point that is encountered frequently. The calculator producer was selling its product at a price that appeared not to cover costs but really did. The same sort of issue frequently faces a firm considering the introduction of a new product or the opening of a new branch office. In many such cases, the new operation may not cover *average* costs as measured by standard accounting methods. Yet to follow the apparent implications of those cost figures would amount to throwing away a valuable opportunity to add to the net earnings of the firm (because added revenues exceed added costs) and, perhaps, to contribute to the welfare of the economy. Only *marginal* analysis can reveal whether the contemplated action is really worthwhile.

## CONCLUSION: THE FUNDAMENTAL ROLE OF MARGINAL ANALYSIS

We will see in the next chapter how marginal analysis helps us to understand the firm's input choices. Similarly, in Chapters 7 and 8 it will cast indispensable light on the consumer's purchase decisions. And in this chapter it enabled us to analyze output and pricing decisions. The logic of marginal analysis applies not only to economic decisions by consumers and firms, but also to those of governments, universities, hospitals, and other organizations. In short, the analysis applies to any individual or group that must make economic choices for the use of scarce resources. Thus, one of the most important conclusions that can be drawn from this chapter, a conclusion brought out vividly by the two examples we have just discussed, is:

**THE IMPORTANCE OF MARGINAL ANALYSIS**

In any decision about whether to expand an activity, it is always the *marginal* cost and *marginal* benefit that are the relevant factors. A calculation based on *average* figures is likely to lead the decision maker to miss all sorts of opportunities, some of them critical. ¶ More generally, if one wants to make *optimal* decisions, *marginal analysis* should be used in the planning calculations. This is true whether the decision applies to a business firm seeking to maximize profit or minimize cost, to a consumer trying to maximize utility, or to a less developed country striving to maximize per capita output. It applies as much to decisions on input proportions and advertising as to decisions about output levels and prices. Indeed, this is such a general principle of economics that it is one of the **12 Ideas for Beyond the Final Exam.**

A real-life example far removed from profit maximization will illustrate the way in which marginal criteria are useful in decision making. For some years before women were admitted to Princeton University (and to several other colleges), the cost of the proposed change was frequently cited as a major obstacle. It had been decided in advance that any women coming to the university would constitute a net addition to the student body because, for a variety of reasons involving relations with alumni and other groups, a reduction in the number of male students was not feasible. Presumably on the basis of a calculation of average cost, some critics spoke of cost figures as high as $80 million.

To economists it was clear, however, that the relevant figure was the *marginal cost*, the addition to total cost that would result from the introduction of the additional students. The women students would, of course, bring to Princeton additional tuition fees (marginal revenues). If these fees were just sufficient to cover the amount they would add to costs, the admission of the women would leave the university's financial picture unaffected.

A careful calculation showed that the admission of women would add far less to the university's financial problems than the *average cost* figures indicated. One reason was that women's course preferences are characteristically different from men's and hence women frequently elect courses that are undersubscribed in exclusively male institutions. Therefore, the admission of one thousand women to a formerly all-male institution may require fewer additional classes than if one thousand more men had been admitted.[7] More important, it was found that a number of classroom buildings were underutilized. The cost of operating these buildings was nearly fixed—their total utilization cost would be changed only slightly by the influx of women. The corresponding marginal cost was therefore almost zero and certainly well below the average cost (cost per student).

For all these reasons, it turned out that the relevant marginal cost was much smaller than the figures that had been bandied about earlier. Indeed, this cost was something like a third of the earlier estimates. There is little doubt that this careful marginal calculation played a critical role in the admission of women to Princeton and to some other institutions that made use of the calculations in the Princeton analysis. Subsequent data, incidentally, confirmed that the marginal calculations were amply justified.

## A LOOK FORWARD

We have now completed a chapter describing how business managers can make optimal decisions. Can you go to Wall Street or Main Street and find executives calculating marginal cost and marginal revenue in order to decide how much to produce? Hardly. Not any more than you can find consumers in stores using marginal analysis in order to decide what to buy. Like consumers, successful business people often rely heavily on intuition and "hunches" that cannot be described by any set of rules.

However, we have not sought a literal *description* of business behavior, but rather a *model* to help us analyze and predict this behavior. Just as astronomers construct models of the behavior of objects that do not think at all, economists construct models of consumers and business people who do think, but whose thought processes may be rather different from those of economists. In the chapters that follow, which together with the chapter we have just completed constitute the core of microeconomics, we will find ourselves repeatedly using the same sort of approach offered in the same spirit.

---

[7]See Gardner Patterson, "The Education of Women at Princeton," *Princeton Alumni Weekly*, vol. 69, September 24, 1968.

## *Summary*

1. A firm can choose the quantity of its product it wants to sell or the price it wants to charge. But it cannot choose both because price affects the quantity demanded.
2. In economic theory, it is usually assumed that firms seek to maximize profits. This should not be taken literally, but rather interpreted as a useful simplification of reality.
3. Marginal revenue is the additional revenue earned by increasing sales by one unit. **Marginal cost** is the additional cost incurred by increasing production by one unit.
4. Maximum profit requires the firm to choose the level of output at which marginal revenue is equal to marginal cost.
5. Geometrically, the profit-maximizing output level occurs at the highest point of the total profit curve. There the slope of the total profit curve is zero, meaning that marginal profit is zero.
7. It may pay a firm to expand its output if it is selling at a price greater than marginal cost, even if that price happens to be below average cost.
8. Optimal decisions must be made on the basis of marginal cost and marginal revenue figures, not **average cost and average revenue** figures. This is one of the **12 Ideas for Beyond the Final Exam.**

## *Key Concepts and Terms*

Profit maximization
Satisficing
Total profit
Economic profit
Total revenue and cost
Average revenue and cost
Marginal revenue and cost
Marginal analysis

## *Questions for Review*

1. "It may be rational for a firm not to try to maximize profits." Discuss the circumstances under which this statement may be true.
2. Suppose the firm's demand curve indicates that at a price of $12 per unit, customers will demand two million units of its product. Suppose management decides to pick *both* price and output, produces three million units of its product, and prices it at $20. What will happen?
3. Suppose a firm's management would be pleased to increase its share of the market, but if it expands its production the price of its product will fall and so its profits will decline somewhat. What choices are available to this firm? What would you do if you were president of this company?
4. Why does it make sense for a firm to seek to maximize *total* profit, rather than to maximize *marginal* profit?
5. A firm's marginal revenue is $97 and its marginal cost is $80. What amount of profit does the firm fail to pick up by refusing to increase output by one unit?
6. Calculate average revenue (AR) and average cost (AC) in Table 5–3. How much profit does the firm earn at the output at which AC = AR? Why?
7. A firm's total cost is $400 if it produces one unit, $700 if it produces two units, and $900 if it produces three units of output. Draw up a table of total, average, and marginal costs for this firm.
8. Draw an average and marginal cost curve for the firm in Question 7. Describe the relationship between the two curves.
9. A firm has the demand and total cost schedules given in the table below. If it wants to maximize profits, how much output should it produce?

| QUANTITY | PRICE (dollars) | TOTAL COST (dollars) |
|---|---|---|
| 1 | 6 | 1 |
| 2 | 5 | 2.5 |
| 3 | 4 | 6 |
| 4 | 3 | 7 |
| 5 | 2 | 11 |

## *Appendix* THE RELATIONSHIPS AMONG TOTAL, AVERAGE, AND MARGINAL DATA

You may have surmised that there is a close connection between the *average* revenue curve and the *marginal* revenue curve, and that there must be a similar relationship between the average cost and the marginal cost curve. After all, we deduced our total revenue figures from the average revenue and then calculated our marginal revenue figures from the total revenues; and a similar chain of deduction applied to costs. In fact:

Marginal, average, and total figures are inextricably bound together. From any one of the three, the other two can be calculated. The relationships among total, average, and marginal figures are exactly the same for *any* variable—such as revenue, cost, or profit—to which the concepts apply.

To illustrate and emphasize the wide applicability of marginal analysis, we switch our example from profits, revenues, and costs to a noneconomic variable, human body weights, to which the same concepts can also be applied, as we will see next. We switch to this example because calculation of weights is more familiar to most people than calculation of profits, revenues, or costs, and we can use it to illustrate several fundamental relationships between average and marginal figures. The necessary data are in Table 5–5.[8] We begin with an empty room (total weight of occupants is equal to zero). A person weighing 100 pounds enters; marginal and average weight are both 100 pounds. If the person is followed by a person weighing 140 pounds (marginal weight equals 140 pounds), the average weight rises to 120 pounds (240/2), and so on.

The way to calculate average weight from total weight is quite clear. When, for example, there are four persons in the room with a total weight of 500 pounds, the average weight must be 500/4 = 125 pounds, as shown in the corresponding entry of the third column. In general, the rule for converting totals to averages, and vice versa, is

**Rule 1a**. Average weight equals total weight divided by number of persons.

**Rule 1b**. Total weight equals average weight times number of persons.

And this rule naturally applies equally well to cost, revenue, profit, or any other variable of interest.

Calculation of *marginal* weight from *total* weight follows the *subtraction* process we have already encountered in the calculation of marginal cost and marginal revenue. Specifically,

**Rule 2a**. The marginal weight of, say, the third person equals the total weight of three people minus the total weight of two people.

For example, when the fourth person enters the room, *total* weight rises from 375 to 500 pounds, and hence the corresponding marginal weight is

[8]Note that in this illustration, "persons in room" is analogous to units of output, and "total weight" is analogous to total revenue or cost, and "marginal weight" is analogous to marginal revenue or cost, in the discussions of marginal analysis in the body of the chapter.

*Table* **5–5** WEIGHTS OF PERSONS IN A ROOM

| NUMBER OF PERSONS IN ROOM | TOTAL WEIGHT | AVERAGE WEIGHT (pounds) | MARGINAL WEIGHT |
|---|---|---|---|
| 0 | 0 | — | |
| | | | 100 |
| 1 | 100 | 100 | |
| | | | 140 |
| 2 | 240 | 120 | |
| | | | 135 |
| 3 | 375 | 125 | |
| | | | 125 |
| 4 | 500 | 125 | |
| | | | 100 |
| 5 | 600 | 120 | |
| | | | 60 |
| 6 | 660 | 110 | |

500 − 375 = 125 pounds, as is shown in the last column of Table 5–5. We can also go in the opposite direction—from marginal to total—by the reverse, *addition*, process.

**Rule 2b**. The total weight of, say, three people equals the (marginal) weight brought into the room by the first person plus the (marginal) weight of the second person, plus the (marginal) weight of the third person.

Rule 2b can be checked by referring to Table 5–5. There it can be seen that the total weight of three persons, 375 pounds, is indeed equal to 100 + 140 + 135 pounds, the sum of the preceding marginal weights. A similar relation holds for any other total weight figure in the table, as the reader should verify.

In addition to these familiar arithmetic relationships, there are two other useful relationships. The first of these may be stated as

**Rule 3**. (With an exception discussed in the next chapter) the marginal, average, and total figures for the first person must all be equal.

This rule holds because when there is only one person in the room, whose weight is X pounds, the average weight will obviously be X, the total weight must be X, and the marginal weight must also be X (since the total must have risen from 0 to X pounds). Put another way, when the marginal person is alone, he or she is obviously also the average person, and also represents the totality of all relevant persons.

Now for the final and very important relationship:

**Rule 4**. If marginal weight is lower than average weight, then average weight must fall when the number of persons increases. If marginal weight exceeds average weight, average weight must rise when the number of persons increases; and if marginal and average weight are equal, the average weight must remain constant when the number of persons increases.

These three possibilities are all illustrated in Table 5–5. Notice, for example, that when the third person enters the room, the average weight rises from 120 to 125 pounds. That is because this person's (marginal) weight is 135 pounds, which is above the average, as Rule 4 requires. Similarly, when the sixth person—who is a 60-pound child—enters the room, the average falls from 120 to 110 pounds because marginal weight, 60 pounds, is below average weight.

The reason Rule 4 works is easily explained with the aid of our example. When the third person enters, we see that the average rises. At once we know that this person must be above average weight, for otherwise his arrival would not have pulled up the average. Similarly, the average will be pulled down by the arrival of a person whose weight is below the average (marginal weight is less than average weight). And the arrival of a person of average weight (marginal equals average weight) will leave the old average figure unchanged. That is all there is to the matter.

It is essential to avoid a common misunderstanding of this rule: it does *not* state, for example, that if the average figure is rising, the marginal figure must be rising. When the average rises, the marginal figure may rise, fall, or remain unchanged. The arrival of two persons both well above average will push the average up in two successive steps even if the second new arrival is lighter than the first. We see such a case in Table 5–5, where the arithmetic shows that while average weight rises successively from 100 to 120 to 125, the marginal weight falls from 140 to 135 to 125.

## GRAPHICAL REPRESENTATION OF MARGINAL AND AVERAGE CURVES

We have shown how, from a curve of total profit (or total cost or total anything else), one can determine the corresponding marginal figure. We noted several times in the chapter that the marginal value at any particular point is equal to the *slope* of the corresponding total curve at that point. But for some purposes it is convenient to use a graph that records marginal and average values directly rather than deriving them from the curve of totals.

We can obtain such a graph by plotting the data in a table of average and marginal figures, such as Table 5–5. The result looks like the graph shown in Figure 5–6. Here we have indicated the number of persons in the room on the horizontal axis and the corresponding average and marginal figures on the vertical axis. The solid dots represent average weights; the small circles represent marginal weights. Thus, for example, point *A* shows that

Figure 5–6 **THE RELATIONSHIP BETWEEN MARGINAL AND AVERAGE CURVES**

If the marginal curve is above the average curve, the average curve will be pulled upward. Thus, wherever the marginal is above the average, the average must be going upward (blue segment of the curves). The opposite is true where the marginal curve is below the average curve.

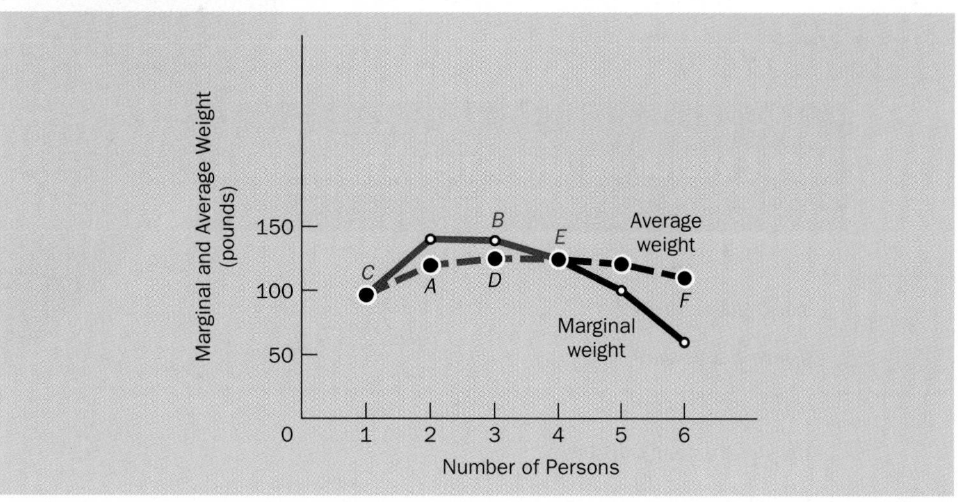


when two persons are in the room, their average weight is 120 pounds, as was reported on the third line of Table 5–5. Similarly, point *B* on the graph represents information provided in the next column of the table; that is, that the marginal weight of the third person who enters the room is 135 pounds. For visual convenience these points have been connected into a marginal curve and an average curve, represented respectively by the solid and the broken curves in the diagram. This is the representation of marginal and average values that economists most frequently use.

Figure 5–6 illustrates two of our rules. Rule 3 says that, for the first unit, the marginal and average values will be the same. And that is precisely why the two curves start out together at point *C*. When there is only one person in the room, marginal and average weight *must* be the same. The graph also obeys Rule 4: between points *C* and *E*, where the average curve is *rising*, the marginal curve lies *above* the average. (Notice, however, that over part of this range the marginal curve *falls* even though the average curve is rising—Rule 4 says nothing about the rise or fall of the marginal curve.) We see also that over range *EF*, where the average curve is falling, the marginal curve is below the average curve, again in accord with Rule 4. Finally, at point *E*, where the average curve is neither rising nor falling, the marginal curve meets the average curve: average and marginal weights are equal at that point.

## *Questions for Review*

1. Suppose the following is your record of exam grades in Principles of Economics:

| EXAM DATE | GRADE | COMMENT |
|---|---|---|
| September 30 | 65 | A slow start. |
| October 28 | 75 | A big improvement. |
| November 26 | 90 | Happy Thanksgiving! |
| December 13 | 85 | Slipped a little. |
| January 24 | 95 | A fast finish! |

Use these data to make up a table of total, average, and marginal grades for the five exams.

2. From the data in your table, illustrate each of the rules mentioned in this appendix. Be sure to point out an instance where marginal grade falls but average grade rises.

*Chapter* **6**

# INPUT DECISIONS AND PRODUCTION COSTS

*You realize this cost figure is only an estimate. Of course, the actual cost will be higher.*

**ARCHITECT TO HIS CLIENT IN AN OLD *NEW YORKER* CARTOON**

We know from the preceding chapter that a firm's output decision depends critically on its costs of production, especially its marginal cost curve. But where do the cost curves used in Chapter 5 come from? This chapter provides the answer. ¶ At one level, of course, the answer is obvious. A firm's costs depend on the quantities of labor, raw materials, machinery, and other inputs it buys, and on the prices of each. But that just raises another question: How does the firm decide how much of each of the various *inputs* to buy? This chapter examines how the firm can select the optimal combination of inputs, that is, the combination that enables it to produce whatever output it decides upon with minimum cost and, hence, with maximum profitability. ¶ To make the analysis easier to follow, we approach this task in two stages. The first part of the chapter deals with the simple case in which the firm only considers varying the quantity of a single input. This vastly simplifies the analysis and enables us to see more easily how to analyze the three key issues of this chapter: how the quantity of input affects the quantity of output, how the firm selects the optimal quantity of an input, and how these input decisions give the firm the cost information it needs to determine output and price.

The second part of the chapter goes over the same territory—production, optimal input use, and the determination of the firm's cost curves—in the more realistic case in which the firm is free to choose the quantities of several inputs. Many new insights emerge from the multi-input analysis.[1] To stay in familiar territory, we will continue to use Ivana and Ivan's poultry farm to illustrate the analysis. That way, we will see precisely where the cost curves that underlay the analysis of the previous chapter come from.

The analysis of this chapter also provides a striking illustration of how common sense can sometimes be misleading in economics. The issue is this: Suppose a firm suffers a sharp increase in its fixed cost, that is, the amount it has to pay no matter how much or little it sells. For example, its rent might double from $6000 to $12,000 dollars per year: How should the firm react? Some would argue that the firm should raise the price of its product to cover the higher rent. But others would argue that it should cut its price in order to increase its sales enough to pay the higher rent. We will show later in this chapter that *both* of these answers are incorrect! A profit-maximizing firm faced with an increase in its rent should neither raise nor lower its price.

## A PRACTICAL APPLICATION: TESTING WHETHER A LARGER FIRM IS MORE EFFICIENT

Economies of large-scale production are thought to be a pervasive feature of modern industrial society. Automation, assembly lines, and sophisticated machinery are widely believed to reduce production costs dramatically. But if such equipment has enormous capacity and requires a very large investment, small companies will be unable to reap many of the benefits of modern technology. Only large firms will be able to take advantage of the associated savings in costs. Where such *economies of scale*, as economists call them, exist, production costs per unit will decline as output expands.

But this favorable relationship between low costs and large size does not characterize every industry. Sometimes a court of law is called upon to decide whether a giant firm should be broken up into smaller units. In such cases, the judges need to know whether the industry has significant economies of scale. Those who want to break up the large firm argue that industrial giants concentrate economic power, which is something these individuals wish to avoid. But those who oppose such breakups point out that, if significant economies of scale are present, smaller firms will be much less efficient producers than larger ones. It therefore becomes crucial to decide whether economies of scale are present. What kind of evidence speaks to this issue?

Sometimes data like those shown in Figure 6–1 are offered to the courts when they consider such cases. These figures, provided by AT&T, indicate that as the volume of messages rose since 1942, the capital cost of long-distance communication by telephone dropped enormously. Yet economists maintain that while this graph may be valid evidence of efficiency, innovation, and perhaps other virtues of the telecommunications industry, it does *not* constitute legitimate evidence, one way or another, about the presence of economies of scale. At the end of this

---

[1]*NOTE*: Some instructors may prefer to postpone this part until later in the course.

**Figure 6–1** **HISTORICAL COSTS FOR LONG-DISTANCE TELEPHONE TRANSMISSION**

By 1987, the dollar cost per circuit mile had fallen below 8 percent of what it was in 1942. Because prices had more than tripled in that period the decline in *real* cost was even more sensational. Yet this diagram of historical costs is not legitimate evidence *one way or the other* about economies of scale in telecommunications.

SOURCE: AT&T.

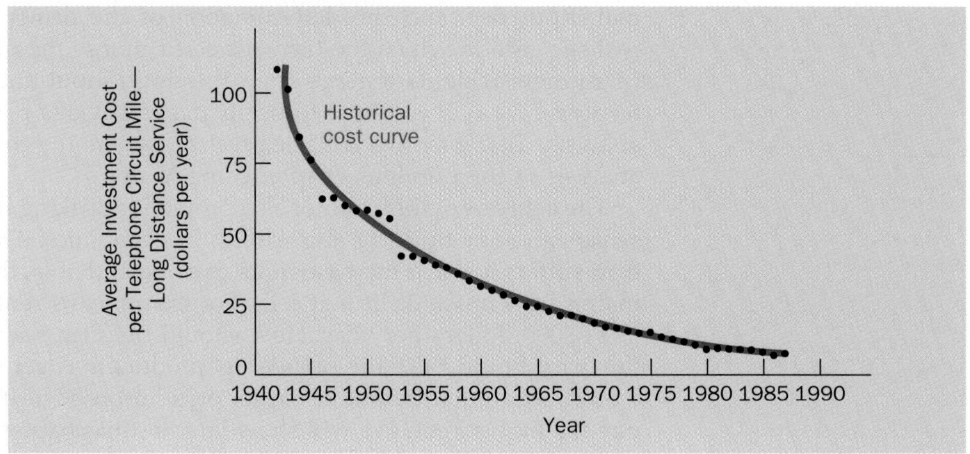


chapter, we will see precisely what is wrong with such evidence and what sort of evidence really is required to determine whether production by a very large firm *is* more efficient.

## PRODUCTION, INPUT CHOICE, AND COST WITH ONE VARIABLE INPUT

While all real businesses use many different inputs, we will begin our discussion with the unrealistic case where there is just a single variable input. In doing so, we are trying to replicate in our theoretical analysis what a physicist or a biologist does in the laboratory when she conducts a *controlled* experiment in which only one variable is permitted to change at a time. This is done in order to study the influence of that variable in isolation.

### THE TOTAL, AVERAGE, AND MARGINAL PHYSICAL PRODUCTS OF AN INPUT

We begin the analysis with the first of our three topics: the relation between the quantity of production and the quantity of input utilized. Consider, as an example, the amount of corn that Ivana and Ivan feed to their chickens. Ultimately, they can vary all their input quantities: they can buy more baby chicks, they can feed them other grains, they can give the chickens larger (or smaller) quantities of growth hormone, they can buy more land and chicken coops, and so on. But suppose for the moment that Ivana and Ivan have purchased all the non-food inputs they need to grow their flock of chickens and all other types of chicken feed other than corn. Thus their only choice is how much corn to feed the flock.

Ivana and Ivan have studied the relationship between the quantity of corn **input** and the **output** of poultry meat. In doing so, they have learned that more corn leads to more output, at least up to a point. The relevant data are displayed in Table 6–1. The table begins by confirming the common sense observation that chickens cannot be raised without food. Thus the total physical product of zero corn input is zero (first entry in the second column). After that, the table shows the increase in chicken output that additional corn yields. For instance, with an input of four 20-kilo bags of corn per week, output is 50 kilos of chicken. Eventually, however, a saturation point is reached beyond which additional corn overfeeds the chickens and causes some to become ill. After 9 bags of corn per week, more corn actually reduces the chicken output (from 92.7 to 90 kilos). The data in Table 6–1 are portrayed graphically in Figure 6–2, which is called a **total physical product (TPP) curve**. This curve shows how much chicken Ivana and Ivan can produce with different quantities of corn, given the quantities of all nonfood inputs.

The firm's **TOTAL PHYSICAL PRODUCT (TPP) CURVE** shows what happens to output when the firm changes the quantity of one of its inputs while holding all other input quantities constant.

Two other physical product concepts are added in Table 6–2. **Average physical product (APP)** measures output per unit of input; it is simply total physical product divided by the quantity of variable input used. In our example, it is total chicken output divided by number of bags of corn used. APP is shown in the next to last column of Table 6–2, in which the TPP schedule is reproduced for convenience. For example, since 4 bags of corn yield 50 kilos of chicken, the APP of 4 bags of corn is 50/4 = 12.5 kilos per bag of corn.

The **AVERAGE PHYSICAL PRODUCT (APP)** is the total physical product (TPP) divided by the quantity of input used. Thus, APP = TPP/X where X = the quantity of input.

If Ivana and Ivan are to decide how much corn to use, they must know how much *additional* chicken output they can expect from each *additional* bag of corn. This concept is known as **marginal physical product (MPP)**. For example, the marginal physical product of the fourth bag of corn is the total output of chicken when four bags of corn are used *minus* the total output when three bags are used, or 50 − 33 = 17 kilos. The other MPP entries for I&I's farm, given in the third column of Table 6–2, are calculated from the total product data in exactly the same way. Figure 6–3 displays these numbers graphically in a **marginal physical product curve**.

The **MARGINAL PHYSICAL PRODUCT (MPP)** of an input is the increase in total output that results from a one-unit increase in the input, holding the amounts of all other inputs constant.

*Table* **6–1** **IVANA AND IVAN'S TOTAL PHYSICAL PRODUCT SCHEDULE**

| CORN INPUT (20-kilo bags) | CHICKEN OUTPUT (kilos) |
|---|---|
| 0 | 0 |
| 1 | 7 |
| 2 | 18 |
| 3 | 33 |
| 4 | 50 |
| 5 | 65 |
| 6 | 78 |
| 7 | 87.5 |
| 8 | 92 |
| 9 | 92.7 |
| 10 | 90 |
| 11 | 82.5 |
| 12 | 72 |

*Data of the sort provided in this table do not represent the farmers' subjective opinion. They are objective information of the sort a poultry scientist can and does supply from experimental evidence.

**Figure 6–2** TOTAL PHYSICAL PRODUCT WITH DIFFERENT QUANTITIES OF CORN

This graph shows how Ivana and Ivan's chicken output varies as they use more and more corn. (Other inputs, such as labor, are held constant in this graph.)

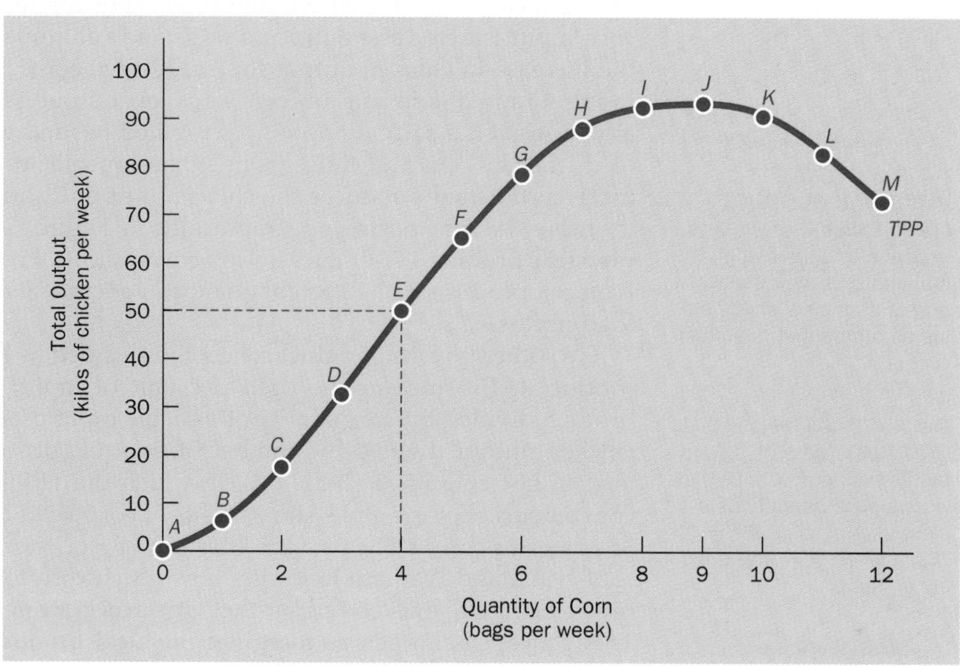


**Table 6–2** IVANA AND IVAN'S SCHEDULES FOR TOTAL PHYSICAL PRODUCT, MARGINAL PHYSICAL PRODUCT, AVERAGE PHYSICAL PRODUCT, AND MARGINAL REVENUE PRODUCT OF CORN

| CORN INPUT (bags) | TOTAL PHYSICAL PRODUCT (chicken output in kilos) | MARGINAL PHYSICAL PRODUCT (kilos per bag) | AVERAGE PHYSICAL PRODUCT (kilos per bag) | MARGINAL REVENUE PRODUCT (dollars) |
|---|---|---|---|---|
| 0 | 0 | | — | |
| | | 7 | | 10.15 |
| 1 | 7 | | 7 | |
| | | 11 | | 15.95 |
| 2 | 18 | | 9 | |
| | | 15 | | 21.75 |
| 3 | 33 | | 11 | |
| | | 17 | | 24.65 |
| 4 | 50 | | 12.5 | |
| | | 15 | | 21.75 |
| 5 | 65 | | 13 | |
| | | 13 | | 18.85 |
| 6 | 78 | | 13 | |
| | | 9.5 | | 13.78 |
| 7 | 87.5 | | 12.5 | |
| | | 4.5 | | 6.53 |
| 8 | 92 | | 11.5 | |
| | | 0.7 | | 1.02 |
| 9 | 92.7 | | 10.3 | |
| | | –2.7 | | –3.92 |
| 10 | 90 | | 9 | |
| | | –7.5 | | –10.88 |
| 11 | 82.5 | | 7.5 | |
| | | –10.5 | | –15.23 |
| 12 | 72 | | 6 | |

**Figure 6–3** **IVANA AND IVAN'S MARGINAL PHYSICAL PRODUCT (MPP) CURVE**

This graph of marginal physical product (MPP) shows how much *additional* chicken Ivana and Ivan get from each application of an additional bag of corn.

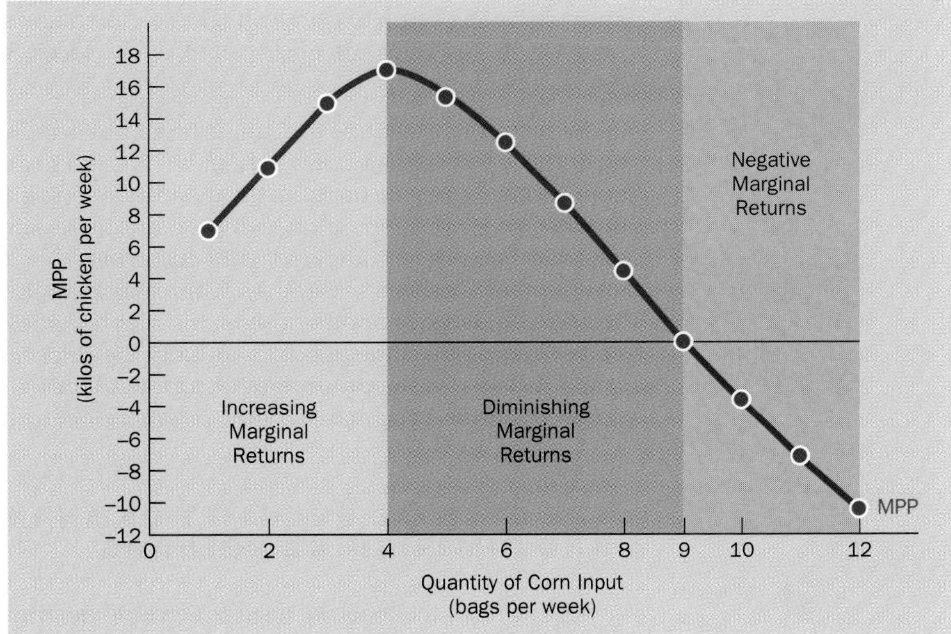


## THE "LAW" OF DIMINISHING MARGINAL RETURNS

The marginal physical product curve in Figure 6–3 shows a pattern that will prove significant for our analysis. Until four bags of corn are used, the marginal physical product of corn is *increasing*; between four bags and nine bags it is *decreasing*, but still *positive*; and beyond nine bags the MPP of corn actually becomes *negative*. The graph has been divided into three zones to illustrate these three cases. The left zone is called the region of increasing marginal returns, the middle zone is the region of diminishing marginal returns, and the right zone is the region of negative marginal returns. In this graph, the marginal returns to corn increase at first and then diminish. This is the typical pattern.

In the increasing returns zone, each additional bag of corn adds more to TPP than the previous bag did. This corresponds to points *A* through *E* in Figure 6–2, where the curve is rising with increasing rapidity. In the diminishing returns area, each additional bag of corn adds less to TPP than the previous bag added. This corresponds to points *E* through *J*, where the TPP curve in Figure 6–2 is still rising, but at a diminishing rate. Finally, in the zone of negative marginal returns (input quantities greater than 9) additional corn actually reduces production by making the chickens ill.

The "law" of diminishing marginal returns, which has played a key role in economics for two centuries,[2] asserts that when we increase the amount of any one input, *holding the amounts of all others constant*, the marginal returns to the expanding input ultimately begin to diminish. The so-called law is no more than an empirical regularity based on some observation of the facts; it is not a theorem deduced analytically.

The reason why returns to a single input are usually diminishing is straightforward. It is a consequence of what can be referred to as the "law" of variable input proportions. When we increase the quantity of one input while holding all others constant, the input whose quantity we are increasing gradually becomes more and more abundant compared with the others (for example, the proportion of corn to other foods increases). As Ivana and Ivan use more and more corn with their fixed quantities of other foods, the diet becomes unbalanced so that adding yet more corn does little good. Eventually the chickens eat so much corn that any further increase in the proportion of corn to other foods will actually harm them. At this point the marginal physical product of corn becomes *negative*.

## THE OPTIMAL QUANTITY OF AN INPUT AND DIMINISHING RETURNS

We now have all the tools we need to see how the firm can decide on the quantity of input that is consistent with maximization of its profits. For this purpose, let us look again at the first and third columns of Table 6–2, showing Ivana and Ivan's marginal physical product schedule. Suppose corn costs $10 per bag, and that chicken sells for $1.45 per kilo ($14.50 per 10-kilo pack) and the farmers consider using one bag of corn. Is this optimal—that is, does it maximize profits? The answer is no, because the marginal physical product of a second bag of corn is 11 kilos of chicken (third entry in the marginal physical product column of Table 6–2). This means that although a second bag of corn would cost $10, it would yield an additional 11 kilos, which at the price of $1.45 per kilo, would add $15.95 to revenue. Thus the farm comes out $15.95 − $10 = $5.95 ahead if it adds a second bag of corn.

The **MARGINAL REVENUE PRODUCT (MRP)** of an input is the additional revenue the producer earns from the increased sales when it uses an additional unit of the input.

It is convenient to have a specific name for the additional *money revenue* that accrues to a firm when it increases the quantity of some input by one unit; we call that the input's **marginal revenue product**. So if Ivana and Ivan's chicken sells at a fixed price (say, $1.45 per kilo), the marginal revenue product (MRP) of the input equals its marginal physical product (MPP) multiplied by the price of the product:

$$\text{MRP} = \text{MPP} \times \text{Price of output}.$$

For example, we have just seen that the marginal revenue product of the second bag of corn to Ivana and Ivan is $15.95, which we obtained by multiplying the MPP of 11 kilos by the price of $1.45 per kilo. The other (MRP) entries in the last column of Table 6–2 are obtained in precisely the same way. The concept of MRP enables us to formulate a simple rule for the optimal use of any input. Specifically:

[2]The "law" is generally credited to Anne Robert Jacques Turgot (1727–1781), one of the great Comptrollers-General of France before the Revolution, whose liberal policies, it is said, represented the old regime's last chance to save itself. But, with characteristic foresight, the king fired him.

When the marginal revenue product of an input exceeds its price, it pays the firm to use more of that input. Similarly, when the marginal revenue product of the input is less than its price, it pays the firm to use less.

Let us test this rule in the case of Ivana and Ivan's farm. We have observed that two bags of corn cannot be enough because the MRP of a second bag ($15.95) exceeds its price ($10). What about a third bag? Table 6–2 tells us that the MRP of the third bag ($21.75) also exceeds its price; thus, stopping at three bags also cannot be optimal. This is equally true of a seventh bag of corn whose MRP ($13.78) still exceeds the $10 price of a bag of corn. The same cannot be said of an eighth bag, however. An eighth bag is not a good idea because its MRP is only $6.53, which is clearly less than its $10 cost. Thus, the optimal quantity of corn for I&I to purchase each week is seven bags, yielding a total output of 87.5 kilos of chicken.[3]

Notice the crucial role of diminishing returns in this analysis. That is why the marginal *physical* product of corn eventually begins to decline. When marginal physical product declines we can also expect the money value of that product to fall; that is, the marginal revenue product will decrease as well. At the point where MRP falls below the price of corn, it is appropriate for Ivana and Ivan to stop increasing their corn purchases. In sum, it always pays the producer to expand input use until diminishing returns set in and reduce the MRP to the price of the input.

A common expression suggests that it does not pay to continue doing something "beyond the point of diminishing returns." As we see from this analysis, quite to the contrary, it normally *does* pay to do so! Only when the marginal revenue product of an input has been reduced (by diminishing returns) to the level of the input's price has the proper amount of the input been employed, because then the firm will be wasting no opportunity to *add* to its total profit. Thus, the optimal quantity of an input is that at which the MRP is equal to its price (P). In symbols,

$$\text{MRP} = \text{P of input.}$$

Notice that the logic of the analysis is exactly the same as in our discussion of marginal analysis in Chapter 5. The farmers are trying to maximize the difference between the *total* revenue their corn input yields and the *total* cost of buying that input. To do so, they must increase their usage of corn up to the point where its *marginal* cost (the price of an additional bag) equals its marginal revenue product.

## COST CURVES AND INPUT QUANTITIES

We turn now to the third of the three main topics of this chapter: How the firm's cost curves, which played such a crucial role in the previous chapter, are derived from the input decisions we have just studied. To do so, we use our two basic assumptions—that the price of corn is beyond the control of the firm and that

[3]Some readers may notice that the profit-maximizing output of chicken that was determined in Chapter 5 is smaller than the figure obtained here. These two results are, however, not really comparable, because the calculation carried out at this point in the text is based on a number of temporary assumptions adopted to simplify the exposition—notably, the premise that the prices of all inputs other than corn are all zero (see below). Later in the chapter we will see what happens when this premise is dropped.

the quantities of all inputs other than corn are fixed—to deduce the firm's total costs from its physical product schedule.

The method is simple: For each quantity of output, record from Table 6–1 or Figure 6–2 the amount of corn required to produce it. Then multiply that quantity of corn by its price. Here, it is critical to recognize that these additional costs must include the *opportunity costs* of any quantities of input the farmers contribute themselves—such as corn that they have grown themselves, and which they could have sold to other farmers instead of using it up themselves.

In addition to the cost of their corn, Ivana and Ivan must spend money on other inputs. But since, to keep the discussion from becoming too complex, we are focussing exclusively on corn input in this first part of the chapter, let us assume for the next several pages that all other inputs are free, so that corn is the only expense that needs to be considered. Later, we will see that we calculate the cost of each other input just as we do that of corn, by multiplying its quantity by its price, and adding the result to the farm's total cost number.

So, suppose, once more, that corn costs $10 per bag. Then, from Table 6–1, we have the table of total costs shown in Table 6–3. For example, to produce 33 kilos of chicken, we know from the fourth row of Table 6–1 that it requires 3 bags of corn at $10 per bag, which gives us the total cost, $30. The point of this exercise is that:

The total product curve tells us the input quantities needed to produce any given output. And from those input quantities and the price of the inputs, we can determine the *total cost* (TC) of producing any level of output. This is the amount the firm spends on the inputs needed to produce the output, plus any opportunity costs that arise in that production activity. Thus, the relation of total cost to output is determined by the technological production relations between inputs and outputs, and by input prices.

As we learned in the previous chapter (pages 110–113), the firm's other two cost curves—**average cost** and **marginal cost**—are calculated directly from the total cost curve which we have just determined. All three curves are shown here in Figure 6–4.

So far, by assuming that the price of every other input is zero, we have omitted from our calculations the costs of all of Ivana and Ivan's inputs other than corn,

**Table 6–3 A PORTION OF IVANA AND IVAN'S TOTAL COST SCHEDULE**

**(Obtained from the production data in Table 6–1, assuming corn is the only variable input)**

| CHICKEN OUTPUT (kilos per week) | CORN INPUT (bags per week) | TOTAL COST (cost of corn, dollars per week) |
|---|---|---|
| 7 | 1 | 10 |
| 18 | 2 | 20 |
| 33 | 3 | 30 |
| 50 | 4 | 40 |
| 65 | 5 | 50 |
| 78 | 6 | 60 |
| 87.5 | 7 | 70 |
| 92 | 8 | 80 |

## Figure 6-4 TOTAL, AVERAGE, AND MARGINAL COSTS

Ivana and Ivan's costs are derived from the Total Cost schedule in Table 6–3. They are reproduced from Figure 5–3 in the preceding chapter.

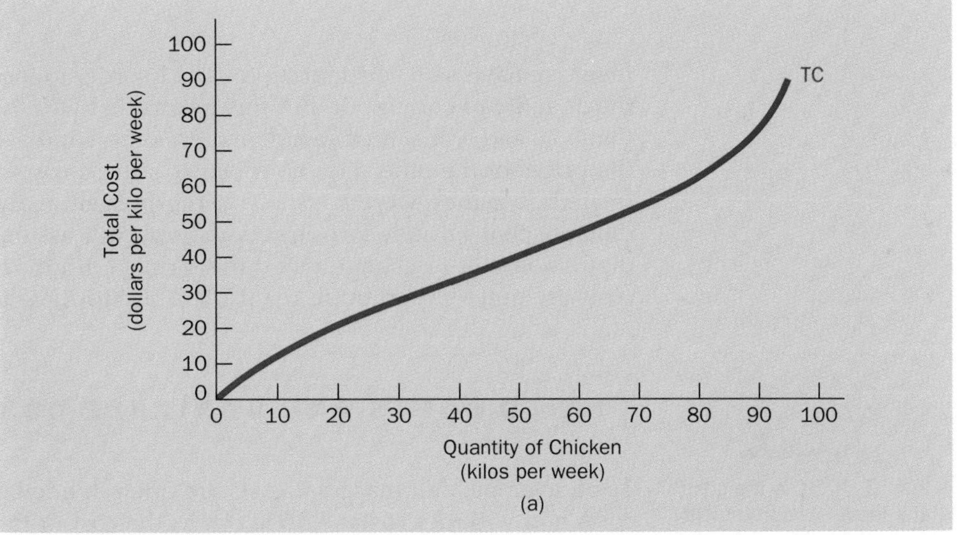

(a)

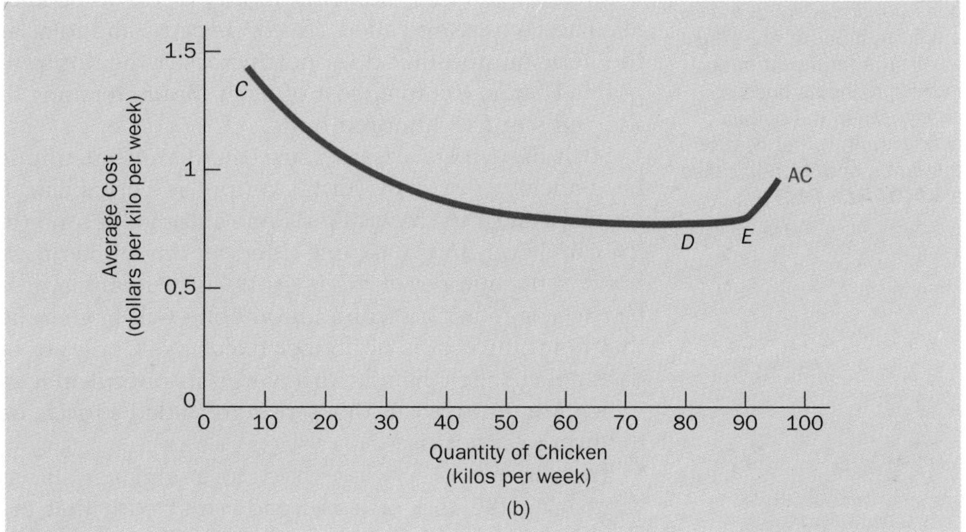

(b)

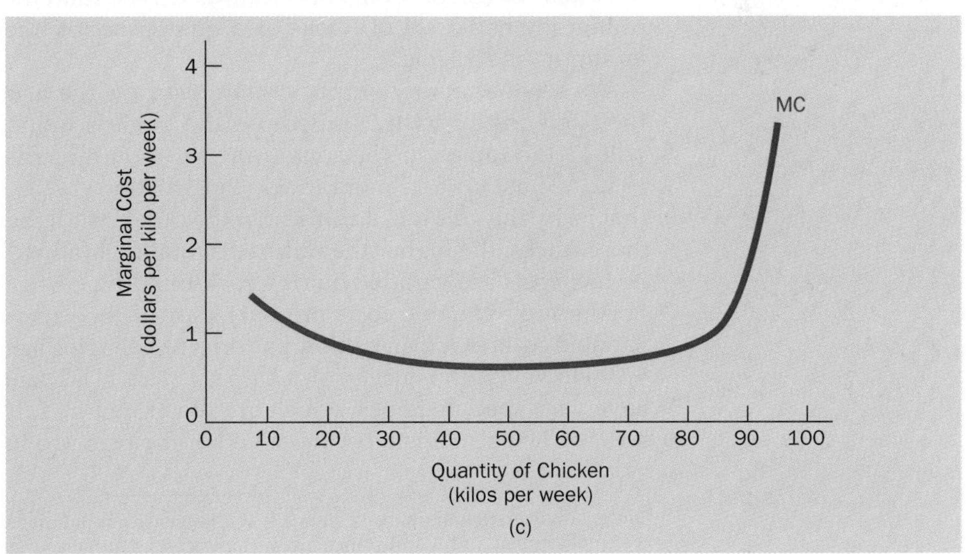

(c)

items we have held constant up to now in order to focus on the effect of changing the quantity of corn input. But this means that we have so far ignored the money that Ivan and Ivana must spend on those other inputs. Even if we had not assumed the prices of the other inputs to be zero, these costs would therefore have been treated as if they were constant in the present analysis; that is, the number of dollars spent on non-corn inputs is implicitly assumed, up to this point in the discussion, not to change when the farm's output varies. Since such unvarying costs are quite important in reality, it is appropriate to examine their properties.

## FIXED COSTS AND VARIABLE COSTS

A **FIXED COST** is the cost of the inputs whose quantity does not rise when output goes up, and which are required to produce any output at all. The total cost of such indivisible inputs does not change when the output changes. Any other cost of the firm's operation is called a **VARIABLE COST**.

Total, average, and marginal costs are often divided into two components: **fixed costs** and **variable costs**. A *fixed cost* is the cost of the smallest (least expensive) batch of inputs that the firm can buy if it is to be able to produce any output at all. These costs are called "fixed" because the total amount of money spent on the items in question does not increase when output rises, at least up to some point. That is, the total cost of such inputs remains the same whether output is five units or five hundred units.

Such fixed costs arise because there are some inputs whose quantities cannot be reduced, even if the firm's output is very small. For example, to run a taxi business one must have at least one automobile, and that cost is the same whether the cab driver finds only one rider per day or 50 riders. (Of course, beyond some point, if the number of riders grows sufficiently large, the capacity of the cab will be exceeded, and a second automobile will have to be acquired, so that beyond that point the cost is no longer fixed). Naturally, the total cost of such an input does not change when the firm varies its output, at least within some range. Costs which are not fixed in this sense are called *variable* because they increase when the firm's output rises.

The difference between fixed costs and variable costs can be illustrated by comparing the cost of a railroad's fuel with that of its track construction. To operate between St. Louis and Kansas City, a railroad must lay a set of tracks. It cannot lay half a set of tracks or a quarter set of tracks. We therefore call such an input "indivisible."

We see that at any output *greater than zero* the firm has no choice but to pay the fixed cost of its track. Because the track is indivisible, its construction cost will be the same whether one train per month or five trains per day travel the route.[4] Thus, up to a point, track construction cost is unaffected by output size, that is, by the volume of traffic. On the other hand, the more trains that pass over those tracks, the higher the railroad's total fuel bill will be. We therefore say that its fuel costs are variable but its track-building cost is fixed.

Although variable costs are only part of total (fixed plus variable) costs, the variable costs of a firm exhibit patterns of behavior just like those shown in Table 6–3. However, the curves of *total fixed costs* (TFC) and *average fixed costs* (AFC) have very special shapes, which are illustrated in Table 6–4 and Figure 6–5. We see that TFC remains the same whether the firm produces a lot or a little, so long

[4]Note, however, that an increase in traffic will increase annual maintenance and replacement cost, so that replacement and maintenance are variable costs. Note also that opportunity costs can be fixed, variable, or a combination of the two.

**Table 6–4 TOTAL AND AVERAGE FIXED COSTS ON IVANA AND IVAN'S CHICKEN FARM**

| OUTPUT PER PERIOD (10-kilo packages per week) | TOTAL FIXED COST (TFC) (dollars) | AVERAGE FIXED COST (AFC) (dollars) |
|---|---|---|
| 0 | 5 | — |
| 1 | 5 | 5 |
| 2 | 5 | 2.5 |
| 3 | 5 | 1.7 |
| 4 | 5 | 1.3 |
| 5 | 5 | 1.0 |
| 6 | 5 | 0.8 |
| 7 | 5 | 0.7 |
| 8 | 5 | 0.6 |

as it produces anything at all.[5] As a result, any TFC curve, like the one in Figure 6–5(a), is horizontal—it has the same height at every output.

Average fixed cost, however, gets smaller and smaller as output increases because, with TFC constant, AFC = TFC/Q gets smaller and smaller as output (the denominator) increases. Business people typically put the point another way: any increase in output permits the fixed cost to be spread among more units, leaving less of it to be carried by any one unit. For example, suppose the fixed cost incurred by Ivana and Ivan is $5 per week. When only one ten-kilo package of chicken is sold, the entire $5 of fixed cost must be borne by that one unit of output. But if the farm produces two ten-kilo packages, each of them need only cover half the total—$2.5 each (Table 6–4).

However, AFC can never reach zero since, even if the farm were to produce, say, a million packages of chicken per week, each unit would have to bear, on the average, one millionth of the TFC—which is still a positive (though very small) number. It follows that the AFC curve gets lower and lower as output increases, moving closer and closer to the horizontal axis, but never crossing it. This is the pattern shown in Figure 6–5(b).

The total fixed cost curve is always horizontal because, by definition, total fixed cost does not change when output changes. The average fixed cost curve declines when output increases, moving closer and closer to the horizontal axis, but never crossing it.

Since we have simply divided costs into two parts, fixed costs (FC) and variable costs (VC), we also have the rules:[6]

$$TC = TFC + TVC \qquad AC = AFC + AVC$$

[5]Here we assume that the fixed costs are also what economists call "sunk," meaning that the firm has already spent the money in question or signed a contract to do so. Consequently, if the firm decides to go out of business (produce zero output), it must still spend the money.

[6]The reader may wonder if there is such a thing as marginal fixed cost. The answer is "yes," but it doesn't matter because marginal fixed cost must generally equal zero. Why? Because, by definition, an increase in output never adds anything to total fixed cost. For example, for both 2 and 3 units of output TFC must be the same, so that $MFC_3 = TFC_3 - TFC_2 = 0$.

*Figure* **6–5** **FIXED COSTS: TOTAL AND AVERAGE**

The total fixed cost curve [part (a)] is horizontal because, by definition, TFC does not change when output changes. AFC in part (b) decreases steadily as the TFC is spread among more and more units of output, but because AFC never reaches zero, the AFC curve never crosses the horizontal axis.

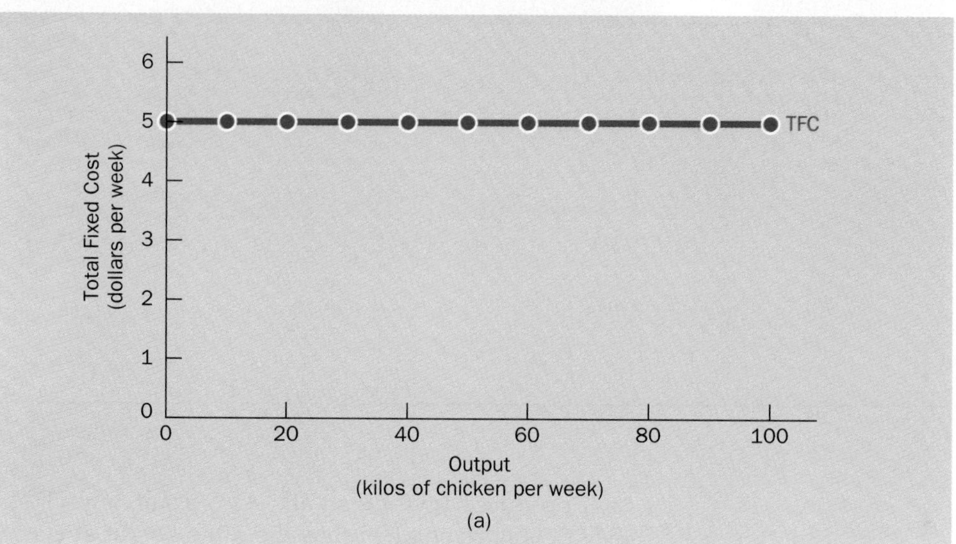


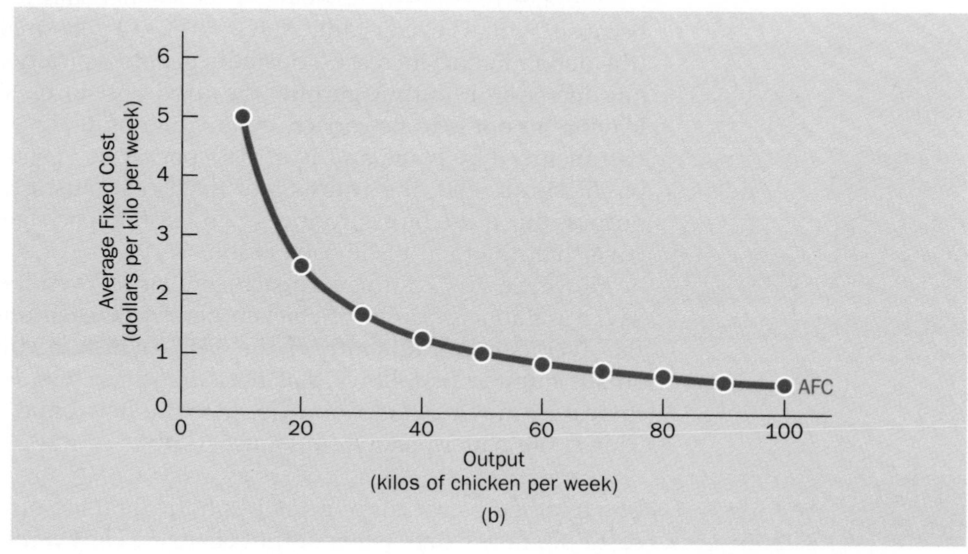


## APPLICATION: FIXED COST AND THE PROFIT-MAXIMIZING PRICE

Our analytic apparatus can now be used to offer a surprising insight. Suppose there is a rise in the firm's fixed cost; say, the rental cost of an indispensable dust-filtering machine doubles. What will happen to the profit-maximizing price and output? Should price go up to cover the increased cost? Should the firm push for a larger output even if that requires a fall in price? The surprising answer is: Neither!

When a firm's fixed cost increases, its profit-maximizing price and output remain completely unchanged, so long as it pays the firm to stay in business.

In other words, there is nothing the firm's management can do to offset the effect of the rise in fixed cost. It must just put up with it. This is surely a case where common sense is not a reliable guide to the right decision.

Why is this so? Remember that, by definition, a fixed cost is a cost that does not change when output changes. If I&I suffer an increase in their fixed costs, that increase is the same whether business is slow or booming, whether production is 2 packs of chicken or 200. This is illustrated in Table 6–5, which also reproduces I&I's total profits from Table 5–3 of the previous chapter. The third column of the table shows that total fixed cost has risen from zero to $5 per week. As a result, total profit is $5 less than what it would have been otherwise—no matter what the firm's output. For example, when output is four units, we see that total profit falls from $24 (second column) to $19 (last column).

Now, because profit is reduced by the same amount at each and every output level, whatever output was most profitable before the increase in fixed costs must still be most profitable. In Table 6–5, we see that $22 is the largest entry in the last column, which shows profits after the rise in fixed cost. This highest possible profit is attained, as it was before, when output is between five and six units. In other words, the firm's profit-maximizing price and quantity will remain exactly as they were before.

All of this is shown in Figure 6–6, which displays the firm's total profit hill before and after the rise in fixed cost (reproducing I&I's initial profit hill from Figure 5–4 in the previous chapter). We see that the cost increase simply moves the profit hill straight downward by $5, so the highest point on the hill is just lowered from point $M$ to point $N$. But the top of the hill is shifted neither toward the left nor toward the right. It remains at the 55 kilo (or, 5.5 packages) output level, just as Table 6–5 indicated.

## SHAPE OF THE AVERAGE COST CURVE

The preceding discussion of fixed and variable costs enables us to complete a topic we began in the last chapter: the investigation of the shapes of the average cost curve.

**Table 6–5 TOTAL PROFIT SHARING BEFORE AND AFTER A RISE IN FIXED COST**

| CHICKEN INPUT (10 kilo packages per week) | TOTAL PROFIT WITHOUT FIXED COST (dollars per week) | TOTAL FIXED COSTS (dollars per week) | TOTAL PROFIT AFTER FIXED COST (dollars per week) |
|---|---|---|---|
| 0 | 0 | 5 | –5 |
| 1 | 2 | 5 | –3 |
| 2 | 10 | 5 | 5 |
| 3 | 18 | 5 | 13 |
| 4 | 24 | 5 | 19 |
| 5 | 27 | 5 | 22 |
| 6 | 27 | 5 | 22 |
| 7 | 23.8 | 5 | 18.8 |
| 8 | 16 | 5 | 11 |
| 9 | 0 | 5 | –5 |
| 10 | –25 | 5 | –30 |

**Figure 6–6 FIXED COST DOES NOT AFFECT PROFIT-MAXIMIZING OUTPUT**

The graph reproduces I&I's initial profit hill from Figure 5–4 (the black curve labeled "profit with zero fixed cost"). A $5 per week increase in fixed cost shifts the profit hill downward, to the blue curve marked "profit when there is a fixed cost." But the original point of maximum profit (point *M*) and the new one (point *N*) are at the same output level. This is so because the cost increase pushes the profit hill straight downward.

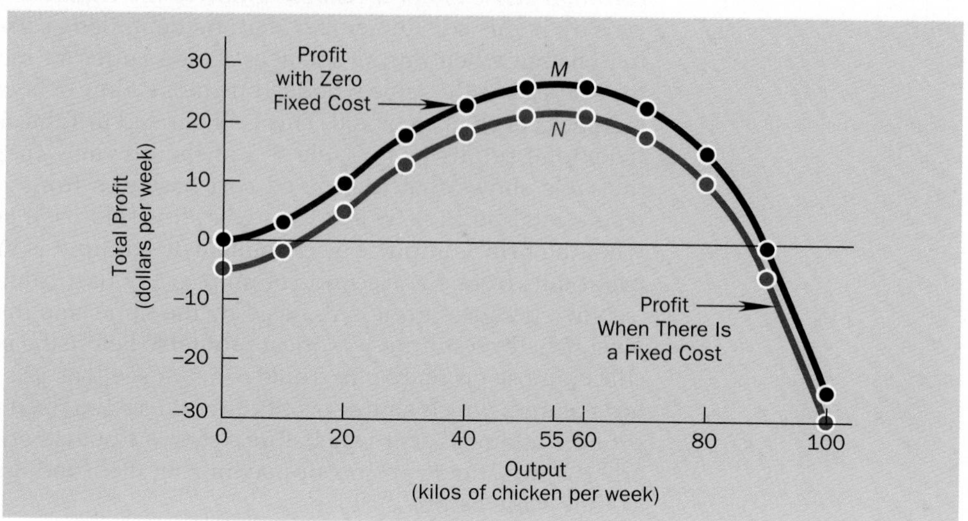


We have drawn the AC curve to be U-shaped in Figure 6–4(b): the leftward portion of the curve is downward sloping, and the rightward portion is upward sloping. There are two main reasons to expect AC to decline when output increases in the leftward portion of the AC curve.

The first is the role of changing input proportions as we increase the quantity of only one input, holding the others constant. We have seen that, if Ivana and Ivan are using very little corn relative to the amounts of the other inputs they employ, a rise in the quantity of corn can, up to a point, yield increasing additions to output (increasing marginal physical product of corn, as illustrated in the leftward part of Figure 6–3). This tends to reduce the average cost of output as the quantity increases.

The second reason why the lefthand portion of the firm's average cost curve tends to decline pertains to fixed costs. As we see in Figure 6–5(b), the average *fixed* cost curve always falls as output increases, and it falls very sharply at the leftward end of the AFC curve. But since AC = AFC + AVC, the AC curve of virtually any product contains a fixed cost portion, AFC, which falls steeply at first when output increases. That is the main reason we can expect the AC curve for any product to have a downward sloping portion such as *CD* in Figure 6–4(b)—a portion which is said to be characterized by decreasing average cost.

To the right of point *E* in the same figure—the zone of increasing average cost—the AC curve is rising as output increases. This means that a given percentage rise in output requires a greater percentage rise in TC, so that AC = TC/*Q* must rise.

Why does the portion of the AC curve with decreasing average cost come to an end? There are two reasons: (1) the law of diminishing returns, and (2) the administrative (bureaucratic) problems of large organizations.

The first of these phenomena is crucial for our present discussion in which we are expanding one input (the quantity of corn) while holding all others constant. In that case, we can be sure that the law of diminishing returns will work to increase marginal (and average) costs, for reasons already discussed.

The second, and probably more important, source of increasing average cost in practice is sheer size. As was noted very briefly in Chapter 5, large firms tend to be relatively bureaucratic, impersonal, and costly to manage. As the firm becomes very large and the personal touch of top management is lost, costs will ultimately rise disproportionately. So average cost will ultimately be driven upward.

The point at which average cost begins to rise varies from industry to industry. It occurs at a much larger volume of output in automobile production than in farming—which is why no farms are as big as even the smallest auto producer. A large part of the reason is that the fixed costs of automobile production are far greater than those in farming, so the resulting spreading of the fixed cost over an increasing number of units of output keeps AC falling in auto production far longer than it does in farming. Thus, although firms may have U-shaped AC curves in both industries, the bottom of the U occurs at a far larger output in auto production than in farming.

The typical AC curve of a firm is U-shaped. Its downward sloping segment is attributable to increasing marginal returns and/or to the fact that the firm's fixed costs are spread over larger and larger outputs. The upward sloping segment is attributable to decreasing marginal returns and to the disproportionate rise in administrative cost that occurs as firms grow large. The output at which decreasing average cost ends and increasing average cost begins varies from industry to industry. Other things equal, the greater the relative size of fixed costs, the higher will be the output at which the switchover occurs.[7]

**SUNK COST** is a cost to which a firm is precommitted for some limited period, either because the firm has signed a contract to make the payments or because the firm has already paid for some durable item (such as a machine or a factory) and cannot get its money back except by using that item to produce output for some period of time.

The **SHORT RUN** is a shorter period of time than the long run, so that some, but not all, of the firm's commitments may have ended.

The **LONG RUN** is a period of time long enough for all the firm's sunk commitments to come to an end.

## LONG-RUN VERSUS SHORT-RUN COSTS

The cost to the firm of a change in its output depends very much on the period of time under consideration. The reason is that, at any point in time, many input choices are *precommitted* by past decisions. If, for example, the firm purchased machinery a year ago, it is committed to that decision for the remainder of the machine's economic life, unless the company is willing to take the loss involved in getting rid of it sooner. The cost is then said to be **sunk**.

Whether or not a cost is sunk depends on the planning horizon being considered. For example, a two-year-old machine with a nine-year economic life is an inescapable commitment, and therefore a sunk cost, for the next seven years. But it is not an unchangeable (sunk) commitment in plans that extend beyond seven years, for the machine will have to be replaced in any case. Economists summarize this notion by speaking of two different "runs" for decision making—the **short run** and the **long run**.

These terms will recur time and again in this book. They interest us now because of their relationship to the shape of the cost curve. In the short run, there is relatively little opportunity for the firm to adapt its production processes to the size of its current output because the size of its plant has largely been predeter-

[7]Empirical evidence confirms this view, though it suggests that the bottom of the U is often long and flat. That is to say, there is often a considerable range of outputs between the regions of decreasing and increasing average cost. In this intermediate region the AC curve is approximately horizontal, meaning that, in that range, AC does not change when output increases.

mined by its past decisions. Over the long run, however, all inputs, including the size of the plant, become adjustable.

Consider the example of Ivana and Ivan. Once they have constructed their chicken coop, they have relatively little discretion over their production capacity. They can build an addition, but that may be considerably more expensive than building a bigger coop in the first place. Cutting the size of the coop is even more costly. Over a somewhat longer planning horizon, however, the original chicken coop will need to be replaced, and Ivana and Ivan will be free to decide all over again how large a building to construct.

Much the same is true of big industrial firms. In the short run, management has little control over its plant and equipment. But with some advance planning, different types of machines using different amounts of labor and energy can be acquired, factories can be redesigned, and other choices can be made. Indeed, over the longest run, no inputs remain committed; all of them can be varied in both quantity and design.

It should be noted that the short and long runs do not refer to the same period of time for all firms; rather, they vary in length, depending on the nature of the firm's sunk commitments. If, for example, the firm can change its work force every week, its machines every two years, and its factory every 20 years, then 20 years will be the long run, and any period less than 20 years will constitute the short run.

## THE AVERAGE COST CURVE IN THE SHORT AND LONG RUNS

As we just observed, which inputs can be varied and which are precommitted depends on the time horizon under consideration. It follows that:

The average (and marginal and total) cost curve depends on the firm's planning horizon. The average (and total) cost curve pertinent to the long run differs from that for the short run because in the long run more inputs become variable.

We can, in fact, be much more specific about the relationships between short-run and long-run average cost (AC) curves. Consider, as an example, Ivana and Ivan's chicken coop capacity. In the short run, after the coop is built, the owners can choose only the number of chickens they crowd into its capacity. But, in the long run, they can also choose among different size buildings.

If they construct a smaller building, the AC curve looks like curve *SL* in Figure 6–7. That means that if I&I are pleasantly surprised, and their sales grow to 50 kilos per week, their average cost will be $12 per week (point *V*). They may then wish they had built the bigger chicken coop (whose AC curve is shown as *BG*), which would have enabled them to cut unit cost to $9 (point *W*). However, in the short run nothing can be done about this decision; the AC curve remains *SL*. Similarly, had they built the larger chicken coop, the short-run AC curve would be *BG*, and the farm would be committed to this cost curve even if business declined sharply.

In the long run, however, the building must be replaced, and management has its choice once again. If Ivana and Ivan expect sales of 50 kilos per week, they will construct the larger building and have an average cost of $9 per kilo of

**Figure 6–7** **SHORT- AND LONG-RUN AVERAGE COST CURVES**

In the graph Ivana and Ivan have a choice of two sizes of chicken coop, a small one with AC curve *SL*, and a big one with AC curve *BG*. These are the short-run curves that apply as long as the farm is stuck with its chosen plant. But in the long run, when it has its choice of plant size, it can pick any point on the blue lower boundary of these curves. This lower boundary, *STG*, is the long-run average cost curve.

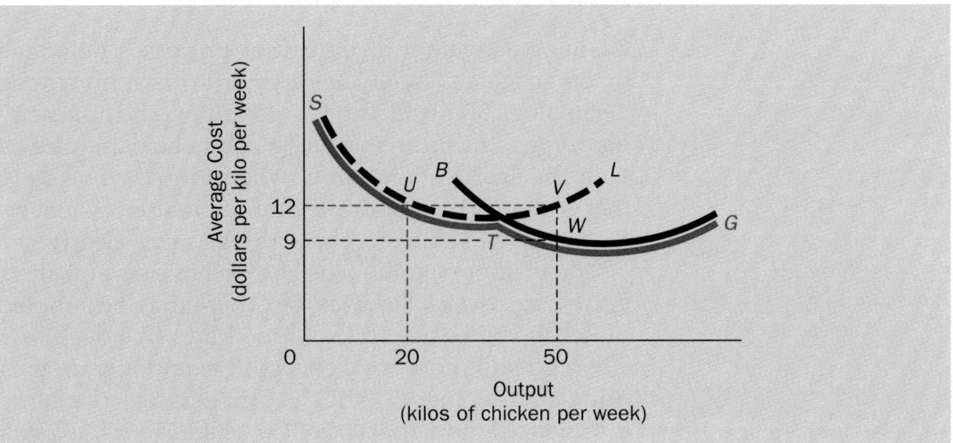


chicken. Similarly, if they expect sales of only 20 kilos, they will arrange for the smaller building and for average costs of $12 (point *U*). In sum, in the long run, the firm will select the plant size (that is, the short-run AC curve) that is most economical for the output level it expects to produce. The long-run average cost curve then consists of all the *lower* segments of the short-run AC curves. In Figure 6–7, this composite curve is the blue curve *STG*.

The long-run average cost curve shows the lowest possible short-run average cost corresponding to each output level.

## MULTIPLE INPUT DECISIONS: THE CHOICE OF OPTIMAL INPUT COMBINATION[8]

Up to this point in the chapter we have simplified the analysis by assuming that the firm only considers changing the quantity of one of its inputs. We come next to the more realistic case in which the firm can and does decide on the quantities of several inputs at once—labor, land, capital, as well as the amount of corn and other animal feeds. We will once again examine our three basic subjects—production, optimal choice of input quantities, and the costs of the firm—but this time considering the fact that the firm must select the quantities of *many* inputs. This generalization of the analysis enables us to study a key issue: how a firm, by its choice of production method, can make up for decreased use of one input by using more of another.

[8]Instructors may want to teach this part of the chapter (up to page 153) now, or they may prefer to wait until they come to Chapters 15 and 16 on the determination of wages, interest rates, profit, and rent.

## SUBSTITUTABILITY: THE CHOICE OF INPUT PROPORTIONS

Casual observation of industrial processes deludes many people into thinking that management really has very little discretion in choosing its input proportions. Technological considerations alone, it would appear, dictate such choices. A particular type of furniture-cutting machine may require two operators working for an hour on a certain amount of wood to make five desks, no more and no less. But this is an overly narrow view of the matter; whoever first declared that there are many ways to skin a cat saw things more clearly.

The furniture manufacturer may have several alternative production processes for making desks. For example, there may be simpler and cheaper machines that can change the same pile of wood into five desks using more than two hours of labor. Or still more workers could eventually do the job with simple hand tools, using no machinery at all. The firm will seek the *least costly* method of production. In advanced industrial societies, where labor is expensive and machinery is cheap, it may pay to use the most automated process; in more primitive societies, where machinery is scarce and labor abundant, making desks by hand may be the most economical solution.

We conclude that one input can generally be *substituted* for another. A firm can produce the same number of desks with less labor, *if* it is prepared to sink more money into machinery. But whether it *pays* to make such a substitution depends on the relative costs of labor and machinery. Several general conclusions follow from this discussion.

1. Normally, there are different options available to a firm wanting to produce a particular volume of output. Input proportions are rarely fixed immutably by technological considerations.
2. Given a target level of production, if a firm cuts down on the use of one input (say, labor), it will normally have to increase its use of another input (say, machinery). This is what we mean when we speak of *substituting* one input for another.
3. Which combination of inputs represents the *least costly* way to produce the desired level of output depends on the relative prices of the various inputs.

The purpose of the analysis of the next few pages is to see how that most-economical input combination can be determined by the firm. But you should know at the outset that the analysis is applicable well beyond the confines of business enterprises. Nonprofit organizations, like your own college, are interested in finding the least costly ways to accomplish a variety of tasks (for example, maintaining the grounds and buildings); government agencies are concerned with meeting their objectives at minimum costs. Even in the household, there are many "cats" that can be "skinned" in different ways. Thus our present analysis of **cost minimization** is widely applicable.

## THE MARGINAL RULE FOR OPTIMAL INPUT PROPORTIONS: INTRODUCTION

Choosing the input proportions that minimize the cost of producing a given output is really a matter of common sense. To bring out the logic, let us turn, once again, to our concrete example. Suppose Ivana and Ivan are considering whether to use more corn and less soy meal, or vice versa, to feed their flock. The two feeds are

## *Input Choice in Times of Shortage*

The story of Ivana and Ivan thinking over their optimal input proportions is told here as though they lived in a well-functioning market economy. It imagines grain markets with clearly known prices, so that buyers of grain need simply decide on the quantities they want, knowing they can get delivery on demand.

But in economies in turmoil, like those in the former Soviet Union, things can be much more chaotic and complex. Deliveries can be unreliable. Some items can be out of stock altogether, or available one day and gone the next. In Russia, formerly a big exporter of petroleum, shortages of fuel have reportedly led to sharp cutbacks in air transportation. Under such chaotic conditions, the prices of many inputs may be extremely high—a dependable sign that the item in question is very scarce. An economy in which the central command mechanism has broken down, but no mature market mechanism has yet taken its place, can revert to conditions that the western world has not experienced for many decades, perhaps for centuries. Farmers who can no longer find the inputs they need in markets may be forced to make everything themselves—including their own tools, buildings, and clothing. Of course, technology is likely to be primitive in such an economy. Farmers, after all, are not likely to be expert in the production of sophisticated farm equipment, nor to have the machinery to make it. Self-sufficiency and isolation are apt to be the hallmarks of such a near-medieval economy, which can even bring back the perils of earlier centuries when localized famines brought death to one district while crops were abundant in another a few hundred miles away.

Eastern Europe is not irretrievably condemned to such a fate, though it is surely not immune from it. One can hope that the market economy will quickly grow strong, and that Ivana and Ivan will have reliable input markets available to them, markets where prices are known to all and where orders placed at the going price are quickly filled.

substitutes: if the chickens get more soy meal, they need less corn. *But the feeds are not perfect substitutes.* Soy meal provides more protein but less energy than corn, so there is considerable benefit in providing the chickens with a balanced diet. If their diet contains too much of one feed and too little of the other, the output of chicken meat will suffer. In other words, it is reasonable to assume that there are *diminishing returns* to excessive substitution of either type of feed for the other.

Now suppose corn costs $10 per 20-kilo bag, as in our earlier example, while an equally heavy bag of soy meal costs twice as much in the Ukrainian grain market. Given this fact, and the $10 and $20 prices for corn and soy, how much of each feed should I&I use? To answer this, we obviously must compare the prices of each feed with information on what each of them yields—their marginal physical products. If the marginal physical product of a bag of corn is 15 kilos of meat, but the marginal physical product (MPP) of an additional package of soy meal is 25 kilos, what should Ivana and Ivan do?

A little thought indicates the answer: Ivana and Ivan should cut down on soy meal and increase their use of corn. Why? Because soy meal costs twice as much as corn ($20 is twice as much as $10), but yields only 67 percent more meat (25 is 67 percent more than 15). Let us examine the reasoning a bit more carefully.

Our claim is that, when the ratios of prices and MPPs are as in our example, the farmers can produce the same output of chicken at lower input cost by spending less on soy meal and more on corn. To see why, suppose Ivan and Ivana buy one less bag of soy meal, thus saving $20. This reduces their output by 25 kilos of chicken—the marginal product of soy meal. How much more corn do they need to replace the lost output? Since the MPP of corn is 15 kilos, it will take 25/15 = 1.67 additional bags of corn to make up the shortfall. But, at a price of $10 per bag, the 1.67 bags of corn will cost the farmers just $16.70. Thus, by using one less bag of soy meal and 1.67 more bags of corn, the farmers end up saving $20 − $16.70 = $3.30 and producing the same output—a good deal!

What makes this example work out the way it does is that *the ratio of the marginal product of soy meal to price of soy meal is less than the ratio of the marginal product of corn to the price of corn.* Specifically, the MPP of soy meal is 25 kilos and its price is $20, so the MPP per dollar is 25/20 = 1.25. By contrast, the MPP per dollar of expenditure on corn is 15/10 = 1.50, which is larger. This means that the farmers get more for their money—at the margin—by spending on corn rather than on soy meal.

This discussion is readily generalized. We can interpret the ratio

MPP of any input/price of that input

as the marginal product of investing $1 in the input in question. It should be fairly clear that it always pays to reduce spending on input *A* if its MPP per dollar *is* less than the MPP per dollar of input *B*. That dollar should be spent on *B* instead. Such a move must *always* reduce the firm's costs. By switching away from the input with the *lower* marginal product per dollar, and buying enough more of the input with the *higher* marginal product per dollar, the firm can reduce the money it spends without reducing its output.

We have thus derived the basic rule for attainment of the most economical way to produce any given output:

A firm can reduce the cost of producing a given output by using less of some input, *A*, and making up for it by using more of another input, *B*, whenever the ratio of marginal physical product of *A* to the price of *A* is less than the ratio of the marginal physical product of *B* to the price of *B*, *that is, whenever:*

$$\mathrm{MPP}_a/P_a < \mathrm{MPP}_b/P_b.$$

Obviously, the opposite will be true if the MPP per dollar spent on *A* is higher than the MPP per dollar spent on *B*. Putting these two together, we conclude that input proportions *cannot* be optimal if the ratio of the marginal physical product to the price differs for any two inputs, that is:

The proportions of any two inputs, *A* and *B*, used by the firm can be optimal only if

$$\mathrm{MPP}_a/P_a = \mathrm{MPP}_b/P_b.$$

This rule, as we have noted, is simply common sense. If a unit of input *A* has a marginal product that is, say, three times as big as that of input *B*, the firm should be willing to pay exactly three times as much money for an additional unit of *A* as it does for *B*, no more and no less.

But what if the market happens to set input prices so that this doesn't work? Suppose the market price of *A* happens to be twice as large as that of *B*, as in our chicken-growing example. What can the farmer do about it? We have seen that in this case the farmer should buy less of *A* (soy meal, in our example) and more of *B* (corn). That will not change the market *prices* of corn and soy meal. But it will change the *marginal physical products* of the two inputs because of the law of diminishing returns. As Ivana and Ivan buy more corn and less soy meal, the marginal product of corn will fall and the marginal product of soy meal will rise. When the farmers have gone just far enough in switching money from soy meal to corn, the ratio of their marginal products will rise from 25:15 = 1.67 up to, say, 28:14 = 2. At that point, it will equal the ratio of the prices of the two inputs, so the rule for cost minimization will be satisfied.

## CHANGES IN INPUT PRICES AND OPTIMAL INPUT PROPORTIONS

The common-sense reasoning behind the rule for optimal input proportions leads to an important conclusion. Suppose I&I are producing 60 kilos of chicken per week and the price of corn rises while the price of soy meal remains the same. The rule

$$\text{MPP of corn}/P \text{ of corn} = \text{MPP of soy meal}/P \text{ of soy meal}$$

### Input Substitution on the Range

When the second fuel crisis hit the United States at the end of the 1970s, the newspapers reported that ranchers in the Southwest were hiring additional cowhands to drive cattle on the hoof instead of carrying them on trucks. In other words, the rising price of oil had led ranchers to substitute the labor of cowhands for the gasoline formerly used in driving cattle-carrying trucks. This is no scenario from a Wild West movie, but an illustration of the way in which life follows the principles described in the text: Real-life firms substitute inputs whose relative prices fall for inputs whose relative prices rise.

There are many other illustrations of this phenomenon. It helps to explain the virtual disappearance, in merely half a century, of personal servants—who were once commonplace in the homes of even middle-class American families. Because of rising real wages, washing machines, clothes dryers, and dishwashers now do the jobs that household workers used to do. It also helps to account for the disappearance of wooden houses in England: as forests disappeared, wood became increasingly expensive compared with other building materials. You can undoubtedly come up with other examples.

tells us that optimal use of corn now requires that the MPP of corn must rise. But, by the "law" of diminishing returns, the MPP of corn is *higher* only when the use of corn is lower. Thus a rise in the price of corn leads the farmers to use *less* corn and, if they still want to produce 60 kilos of chicken, to use *more* soy meal. In general:

As any one input becomes more costly relative to competing inputs, the firm is likely to substitute one input for another; that is, to reduce its use of the input that has become more expensive and to increase its use of competing inputs.

This general principle of input substitution applies in industry just as it does on Ivana and Ivan's farm. For an unusual application of the analysis, see the box on page 151.

## THE PRODUCTION FUNCTION AND CHOICE OF OPTIMAL INPUT PROPORTIONS

The **PRODUCTION FUNCTION** indicates the *maximum* amount of product that can be obtained from any specified *combination* of inputs, given the current state of knowledge. That is, it shows the *largest* quantity of goods that any particular collection of inputs is capable of producing.

To help select the combination of inputs that can produce the desired output at least cost, economists have invented a concept they call the **production function**. The production function summarizes the technical and engineering information about the relationship between inputs and output in a given firm, taking *all* the firm's inputs into account. It indicates, for example, just how much chicken meat Ivana and Ivan can produce with given amounts of land, labor, corn, and so on. If, as we normally assume, there are many ways to produce the desired amount of output, the production function tells us all the input combinations that will do the job.

If there are only two inputs—which are enough to indicate the basic principles—a production function can be represented graphically (which we do in the appendix to this chapter) or by a simple table. Table 6–6 shows part of Ivana and Ivan's production function for the use of soy meal. It shows some of the combinations of soy meal and corn that are capable of yielding 40 kilos of chicken per week, as well as the input combinations that yield 60 kilos. So, for example, if I&I want to produce 60 kilos, they can examine the menu of choices offered by the production function table. They can then select the least-cost combination of inputs by using the rule that MPPs per dollar must be equal.

How much labor and corn should Ivana and Ivan use if they want to produce 60 kilos of chicken? The production function table shows us that there are a variety

**Table 6–6 ALTERNATIVE INPUT COMBINATIONS FOR PRODUCTION OF GIVEN OUTPUT QUANTITIES**

| WAYS TO PRODUCE FORTY KILOS OF CHICKEN PER WEEK | | | WAYS TO PRODUCE SIXTY KILOS OF CHICKEN PER WEEK | | |
|---|---|---|---|---|---|
| Corn (bags per week) | Soy Meal (bags per week) | Total Cost* (dollars per week) | Corn (bags per week) | Soy Meal (bags per week) | Total Cost* (dollars per week) |
| 5.0 | 0 | 50 | 7.0 | 0 | 70 |
| 3.5 | 0.5 | 45 | 4.5 | 0.7 | 59 |
| 2.0 | 1.0 | 40 | 2.9 | 1.4 | 57 |
| 1.5 | 2.1 | 57 | 2.0 | 2.8 | 76 |
| 0 | 4.1 | 80 | | 5.5 | 110 |

*NOTE: Total Cost is calculated from the formula TC = price of corn × quantity of corn + price of soy meal × quantity of soy meal, with corn priced at $10 per bag and soy meal at $20 per bag.

of options. They can, for example, use 7 bags of corn per week and no soy meal. Or they can use 4.5 bags of corn and 0.7 bags of soy meal. Or, at the other extreme, they can raise the 60 kilos of chicken without any corn by using 5.5 bags of soy meal. Thus, the numbers in Table 6–6 indicate the different ways in which Ivana and Ivan can meet a 60-kilo production target.

Which will they choose? Naturally, the one that costs them the least. This can be done directly with the help of the table and the information that corn costs $10 per bag, while soy meal is priced at $20. Thus, for example, we see that if the 60 kilos of chicken are produced with the aid of 4.5 bags of corn and 0.7 bags of soy meal, the total cost will be $10 x 4.5 + $20 x 0.7 = $59 (second entry in the last column in Table 6–6, in blue). The last column in the table also reports the total cost of each of the other input combinations capable of producing 60 kilos of chicken (the reader can verify that each entry is obtained, as before, by multiplying the input quantities by the input prices and adding). We see (brown numbers) that the lowest entry in the last column is $57, corresponding to the use of 2.9 bags of corn and 1.4 bags of soy meal. That implies that this input combination is the most economical way to produce the 60 kilos of chicken. Similarly, the third column in the table indicates that 40 kilos of chicken can be produced most inexpensively using 2 bags of corn and one bag of soy meal, costing $10 x 2 + $20 x 1 = $40.

Alternatively, if we had the data, we could determine the most economical input combination to produce each given quantity of output with the aid of the rule that MPP/price should be the same for all inputs at the input quantities selected. This will yield the same result as the calculation in the preceding paragraph. This second method of calculation requires more data, but is more effective when the problem involves more inputs than the simple two-input example we are using here. More generally, when there are more than the two inputs to be selected, suppose it remains true that 2 bags of corn and 1 bag of soy meal is the least-cost combination for production of 40 kilos of chicken. Then the minimum total cost of producing that quantity of chicken will be 2 bags of corn at $10 each plus 1 bag of soy meal at $20, or:

$$\text{TC} = 2 \times \$10 + 1 \times \$20 + \text{cost of any other inputs.}$$

In other words, the total cost of producing the given quantity of output equals the sum of the cost-minimizing quantities of each of the inputs, with each input quantity multiplied by the price of that input.

## THE FIRM'S COST CURVES

We can now revisit the third main topic of this chapter: the relationship between input choice and the firm's production costs. Earlier we calculated the firm's cost curves in the special case where the firm selected only one input quantity—corn. Now we can see how the cost curves are derived in the more realistic case where all input quantities are adjusted to keep the costs of any given output as low as possible. We have just seen how the total cost figure for different output quantities can be calculated. Thus, with the aid of the production function table (Table 6–6), we have just determined that the total cost of efficient production of 40 kilos of chicken is $40, while the corresponding total cost of 60 kilos is $57. This gives us two points on Ivana and Ivan's total cost curve.

In deciding on the quantity of output that serves its objectives best, the firm must consider alternative production levels and compare their costs. Consequently, outputs of 40 and 60 kilos per week are not the only production levels that Ivana and Ivan should consider. They can be expected to consider also, for example, the least costly way to produce 30 kilos or 90 kilos, and so on.

Using the procedures outlined in the previous section, Ivana and Ivan can compute the minimum cost of producing *any* quantity of output. Let us now suppose that they have done this. We would then have all the information Ivana and Ivan need to plot their *total cost curve*. As before, dividing the total cost for each output by the quantity of output, would give the corresponding *average cost*; that is, the cost per unit of output. Similarly, we can deduce the marginal cost curve from the total cost figures, just as we did before.

## ECONOMIES OF SCALE

Production is said to involve **ECONOMIES OF SCALE,** also referred to as **INCREASING RETURNS TO SCALE**, if, when all input quantities are doubled, the quantity of output is more than doubled.

We are now beginning to put together the apparatus we need to address the question posed at the start of this chapter: How can we tell if a firm has substantial **economies of scale**? First we need a precise definition of this concept.

The scale of operation of a business enterprise is defined by the quantities of the various inputs it uses. To see what happens when the firm doubles its scale of operations, we must consult the production function. For an example of economies of scale, turn back to the production function table for Ivana and Ivan, given in Table 6–6, and assume that soy meal and corn are the only two inputs.[9] Notice that with 1.5 bags of corn and 2.1 bags of soy meal, output is 40 kilos of chicken. But if they increase both inputs by 33-1/3 percent—to 2 bags of corn and 2.8 bags of soy meal—the table shows that output rises by 50 percent (to 60 kilos). Since output goes up by a greater percentage than all the inputs, Ivana and Ivan's production function displays **increasing returns to scale** (also knows as *economies of scale*), at least in this range.

Economies of scale seem to be present in many modern industries. Where they exist, they foster large firm size because larger firms have a cost advantage over smaller ones. Automobile production and telecommunications are examples commonly cited. The firms in these industries are, indeed, huge.

Technology generally determines whether or not a specific economic activity is characterized by economies of scale. One particularly clear example is warehouse space. Imagine two warehouses, each shaped like perfect cubes. But the length, width, and height of warehouse 2 are twice as large as those of warehouse 1. Now remember your high-school geometry. The surface area of any side of a cube is equal to the *square* of its length. So the amount of material needed to build warehouse 2 will be $2^2 = 4$ times as great as that of warehouse 1. However, since the volume of a cube is equal to the *cube* of its length, warehouse 2 will have $2^3 = 8$ times as much storage space as warehouse 1. Thus, multiplying the inputs by 4 leads to 8 times the storage space—an example of strongly increasing returns to scale.

This example is, of course, oversimplified. It omits such complications as the need for stronger supports in taller buildings, the increased difficulty of moving goods in and out of higher stories, and the like. Still, the basic idea is correct, and shows why, up to a point, the very nature of warehousing creates technological relationships that lead to economies of scale.

[9]This is necessary because the table deals with only two inputs and the definition requires that *all* inputs be doubled simultaneously. So, to be true to the definition, because labor, corn, *land, and machinery* were all used by the farmer, their quantities would all have to be doubled.

We can relate our definition of economies of scale to the shape of the *long-run* average cost curve instead of the production function. Notice that the definition requires that a doubling of *every* input bring about more than a doubling of output. If all input quantities are doubled, total cost must double. But if output *more* than doubles, then cost per unit (average cost) must decline. In other words:

Production functions with economies of scale lead to long-run average cost curves that decline as output expands.

Figure 6–8(a) depicts a decreasing average cost curve. But this is only one of three possible shapes the long-run average cost curve can take. The case of constant returns to scale is shown in part (b) of the figure. Here, if all input quantities, say, double, both total cost (TC) and the quantity of output ($Q$) double, so average cost (AC $=$ TC$/Q$) remains constant. Finally, it is possible that output less than doubles when all inputs double. This would be a case of decreasing returns to scale, which leads to a rising long-run average cost curve like the one depicted in part (c). Thus there is a close association between the slope of the AC curve and the nature of the firm's returns to scale.

It should be pointed out that the same production function can display increasing returns to scale in some ranges, constant returns to scale in others, and decreasing returns to scale in yet others. This is true of all the U-shaped average cost curves we have shown [see, for example, Figure 6–4(b)].

## THE "LAW" OF DIMINISHING RETURNS AND RETURNS TO SCALE

Earlier in this chapter, we discussed the "law" of diminishing marginal returns. Is there any relationship between economies of scale and the phenomenon of diminishing returns? It may seem at first that the two are contradictory. After all,

**Figure 6–8 THREE POSSIBLE SHAPES FOR THE LONG-RUN AVERAGE COST CURVE**

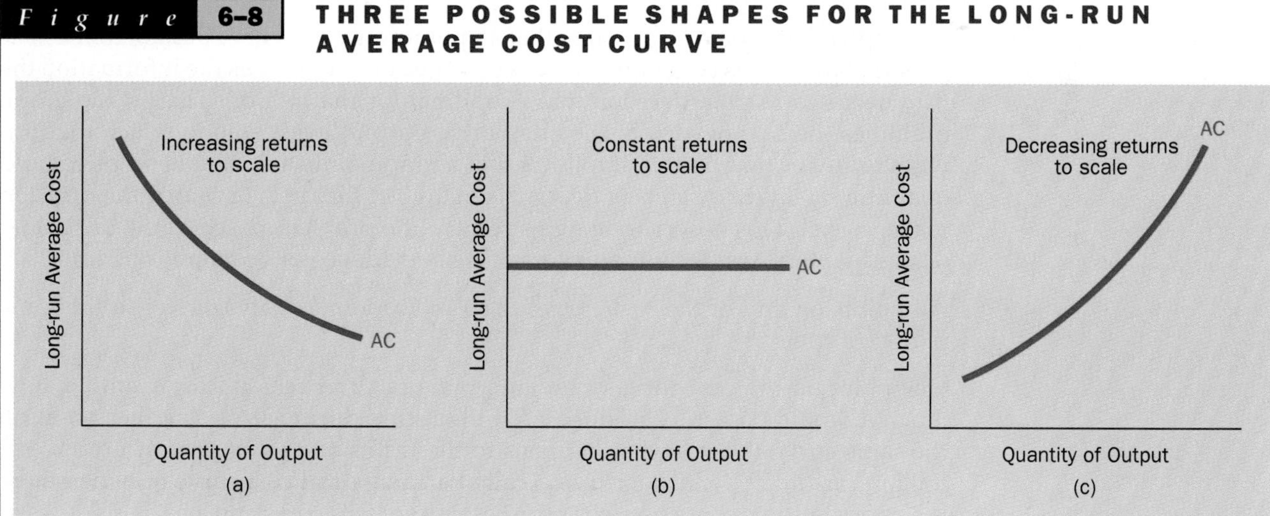


In part (a), long-run average costs are decreasing as output expands because the firm has significant economies of scale (increasing returns to scale). In part (b), constant returns to scale lead to a long-run AC curve that is flat; costs per unit are the same for any level of output. In part (c), which pertains to a firm with decreasing returns to scale, long-run average costs rise as output expands.

if a producer gets diminishing returns from his inputs as he uses more of each of them, doesn't it follow that by using more of *every* input, he must encounter decreasing returns to scale? The answer is that there is no contradiction, for the two principles deal with fundamentally different issues.

1. ***Returns to a single input.*** Here we ask the question: How much does output expand if we increase the quantity of just *one* input, *holding all other input quantities unchanged*?
2. ***Returns to scale.*** Here the question is: How much does output expand if *all* inputs are increased *simultaneously* by the same percentage?

The "law" of diminishing returns pertains to the first question since it examines the effects of increasing only one input at a time. It is plausible that the firm will encounter diminishing returns as this one input becomes relatively abundant. Thus, for example, the addition of too much soy meal to a given quantity of corn will contribute too much protein and too little energy to the chickens, yielding diminishing returns.

Returns to scale pertain to a proportionate increase in *all* inputs, and therefore answer the second question. If we double the quantities of both corn and soy meal, the diet need not become unbalanced. Thus the "law" of diminishing returns (to a single input) is compatible with *any* sort of returns to scale. In summary:

Returns to scale and returns to a single input (holding all other inputs constant) refer to two distinct aspects of a firm's technology. A production function that displays diminishing returns to *a single input* may show diminishing, constant, or increasing returns when *all input quantities are increased proportionately.*

## HISTORICAL COSTS VERSUS ANALYTICAL COST CURVES

In Chapter 5 we noted, in passing, that all points on a cost curve pertain to the *same* period of time. This common period is used because it gives us the information the firm needs to reach a decision that is optimal for that period. That is, the graph examines the cost of each of the alternative output levels among which the firm will decide for that period. It follows that a graph of historical data on prices and quantities at *different points in time* is normally *not* the cost curve that the decision maker needs. This observation helps resolve the problem posed at the beginning of the chapter: Are declining historical costs evidence of economies of scale?

All points on any of the cost curves used in economic analysis refer to the same period of time.

One point on the cost curve of an auto manufacturer tells us, for example, how much it would cost it to produce 2.5 million cars during 1994. Another point on the same curve tells us what happens to the firm's costs if, *instead*, it produces 3 million cars in 1994. Such a curve is called an analytical cost curve or, when there is no possibility of confusion, simply a cost curve. This curve must be distinguished from a diagram of **historical costs**, which shows how costs changed from year to year.

The different points on an analytical cost curve represent *alternative possibilities*, all for the same time period. In 1994, the car manufacturer will produce either 2.5 or 3 million cars (or some other amount), but certainly not both. Thus, at most, only one point on this cost curve will ever be observed. The company may, indeed, produce 2.5 million in 1994 and 3 million in 1995; but the latter is not relevant to the 1994 cost curve. By the time 1995 comes around, the cost curve may have shifted, so the 1994 cost figure will not apply to the 1995 cost curve.

We can, of course, draw a different sort of graph that indicates, year by year, how costs and outputs have varied. Such a graph, which gathers together the statistics for a number of different periods, is not, however, a *cost curve* as that term is used by economists. An example of such a diagram of historical costs was given in Figure 6–1.

But why do economists rarely use historical cost diagrams and instead deal primarily with analytical cost curves, which are more abstract, harder to explain, and difficult to obtain statistically? The answer is that analysis of real policy problems—such as the desirability of having a single supplier of telephone services—leaves no choice in the matter. Rational decisions require analytical cost curves. Let us see why.

## RESOLVING THE ECONOMIES OF SCALE PUZZLE

Since the 1940s there has been great technical progress in the telephone industry. From ordinary open wire, the industry has gone to microwave systems, telecommunications satellites, and coaxial cables of enormous capacity. Now new techniques using fiber optics are being adopted widely. Innovations in switching techniques and in the use of computers to search out and quickly redirect messages along uncrowded routes are equally impressive. All of this means that the *entire* analytical cost curve of telecommunications must have shifted downward quite dramatically from year to year. Innovation must have reduced not only the cost of large-scale operations *but also the cost of smaller-scale operations.*

Now, if we are to determine whether a single supplier can provide telephone service more cheaply than can a number of smaller firms in 1994, we must compare the costs of *both* large-scale and small-scale production *in 1994*. It does no good to compare the cost of a large supplier in 1994 with its own costs as a smaller firm back in 1942, because that cannot possibly give us the information we need. The cost situation in 1942 is irrelevant for today's decision between large and small suppliers because no small firm today would use the obsolete techniques of 1942. Until we compare the costs of large and small suppliers *today,* we cannot make a rational choice between single-firm and multifirm production. It is the analytical cost curve, all of whose points refer to the same period, that, by definition, supplies this information.

Figures 6–9 and 6–10 show two extreme hypothetical cases, one in which economies of scale are present and one in which they are not. Yet both of them are based on the same historical cost data (in black) with their very sharply declining costs. (This curve is reproduced from Figure 6–1.) They also show (in blue and brown) two possible average cost curves, one for 1942 and one for 1994. In Figure 6–9, the analytical AC curve has shifted downward very sharply from 1942 to 1994, as technological change reduced all costs. Moreover, both of the AC curves slope downward to the right, meaning that, in either year, the larger the firm the lower its average costs. Thus, the situation shown in Figure 6–9 really does represent a case in which there are economies of scale, so that one firm can serve the market at lower cost than many.

But now look at Figure 6–10, which shows exactly the same historical costs as Figure 6–9. Here, however, both analytical AC curves are U-shaped. In particular,

**Figure 6–9** **DECLINING HISTORICAL COST CURVE WITH THE ANALYTICAL AVERAGE COST CURVE ALSO DECLINING IN EACH YEAR**

The two analytical cost curves shown indicate how the corresponding points (*A* and *B*) on the historical cost diagram are generated by that year's analytical curve. Because the analytical cost curves are declining, we know that there are economies of scale in the production activity whose costs are shown.

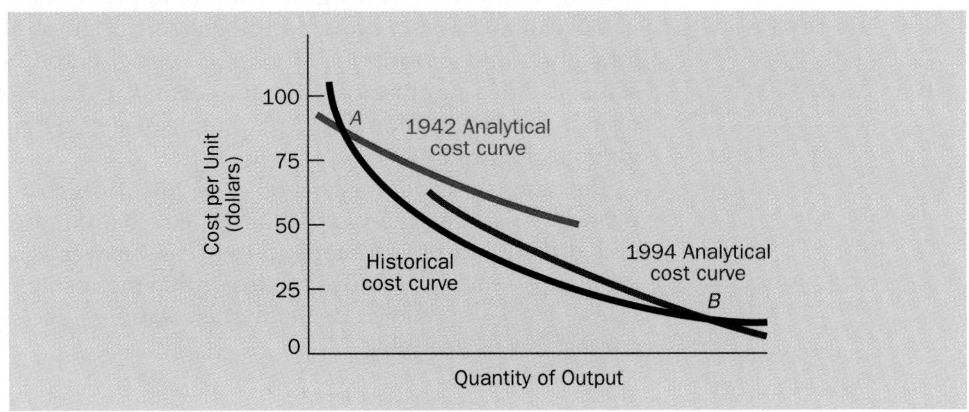


we note that the 1994 AC curve has its minimum point at an output level, *A*, that is less than one-half the current output, *B*, of the large supplier. This means that, in the situation shown in Figure 6–10, a smaller company can produce more cheaply than a large one. In this case, one cannot justify domination of the market by a single large firm on the grounds that its costs are lower—despite the sharp downward trend of historical costs. In sum, the behavior of historical costs tells us nothing about the cost advantages or disadvantages of a single large firm. More generally:

Because a diagram of historical costs does not compare the costs of large and small firms at the same point in time, it cannot be used to determine whether there are economies of large-scale production. Only the analytical cost curve can supply this information.

**Figure 6–10** **DECLINING HISTORICAL COST CURVE WITH U-SHAPED ANALYTICAL COST CURVES IN EACH YEAR**

Here the shape of the analytical average cost curves do not show economies of scale.

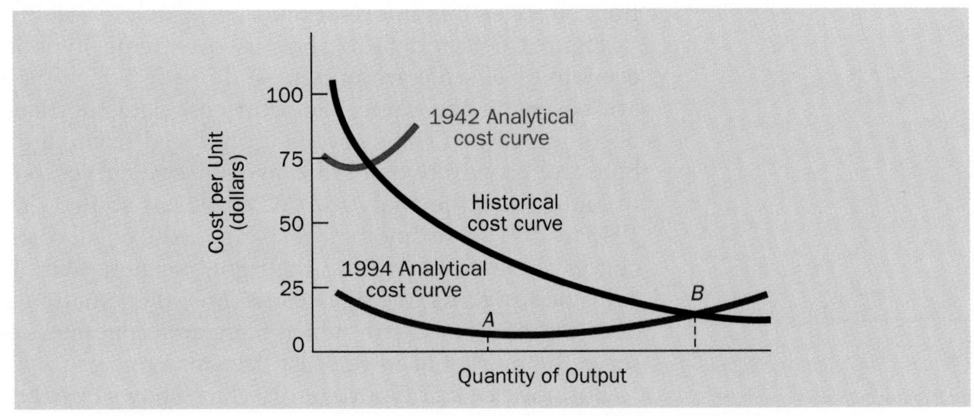

## COST MINIMIZATION IN THEORY AND PRACTICE

Lest you be tempted to run out and open a business, confident that you now understand how to minimize costs, we should point out that decision making in business is a good deal harder than we have indicated here. Rare is the business executive who knows for sure what her production function looks like, or the exact shapes of her marginal physical product schedules, or the precise nature of her cost curves. No one can provide a cookbook for instant success in business. What we have presented here is, instead, a set of principles that constitutes a guide to good decision making.

Business management has been described as the art of making critical decisions on the basis of inadequate information, and in our complex and ever-changing world there is often no alternative to an educated guess. Actual business decisions will at best approximate the cost-minimizing ideal outlined in this chapter. Certainly, there will be mistakes. But when management does its job well and the market system functions smoothly, the approximation may prove amazingly good. While no system is perfect, inducing firms to produce at the lowest possible cost is undoubtedly one of the jobs the market system does best.

## *Summary*

1. A firm's total cost curve shows the lowest possible cost of producing any given level of output. It is derived from the input combination used to produce any given output and the prices of the inputs.
2. The **marginal physical product** of an input is the increase in total output resulting from a one-unit increase in the use of that input, holding the quantities of all other inputs constant.
3. The **"law" of diminishing marginal returns** states that if we increase the amount of one input (holding all other input quantities constant), the marginal physical product of the expanding input will eventually begin to decline.
4. To maximize profits, a firm must purchase an input up to point at which diminishing returns reduce the input's **marginal revenue product** to its price.
5. The **long run** is a period sufficiently long for the firm's plant to require replacement and for all its current contractual commitments to expire. The **short run** is any period briefer than that.
6. **Fixed costs** are costs whose total amounts do not vary when output increases. All other costs are called *variable.*
7. At all outputs the total fixed cost (TFC) curve is horizontal and the average fixed cost (AFC) curve declines toward the horizontal axis but never crosses it.
8. TC = TFC + TVC; AC = AFC + AVC.
9. A change in fixed cost will not change the profit-maximizing level of output.
10. It is normally possible to produce the same quantity of output in a variety of ways by substituting more of one input for less of another. Firms normally seek the least costly way to produce any given output.
11. A firm that wants to minimize costs will select input quantities at which the ratios of the **marginal physical product** of each input to its price—its MPP per dollar—are equal for all inputs.
12. The **production function** shows the relationship between inputs and output. It indicates the maximum quantity of output obtainable from any given combination of inputs.
13. If a doubling of all the firm's inputs *just* doubles its output, the firm is said to have **constant returns to scale**. If a doubling of all inputs leads to *more than* twice as much output, it has **increasing returns to scale** (or, **economies of scale**). If a doubling of inputs produces *less than* double the output, the firm has **decreasing returns to scale**.
14. With increasing returns to scale, the firm's long-run average costs are decreasing; constant returns to scale are associated with constant long-run average costs; and decreasing returns to scale are associated with increasing long-run average costs.
15. We cannot tell if there are economies of scale (increasing returns to scale) simply by inspecting a diagram of historical cost data. Only the underlying analytical cost curve can supply this information.

## *Key Concepts and Terms*

Total physical product (TPP)
Average physical product (APP)
Marginal physical product (MPP)
Marginal revenue product (MRP)
"Law" of diminishing marginal returns
Fixed cost
Variable cost
Sunk Cost
Increasing (decreasing) average cost
Short and long runs
Substitutability of inputs
Cost minimization
Rule for optimal input use
Production function
Economies of scale (increasing returns to scale)
Constant returns to scale
Decreasing returns to scale
Historical versus analytical cost relationships

## *Questions for Review*

1. A firm's total fixed cost is $120,000. Construct a table of total and average fixed costs for this firm for output levels varying from 0 to 6 units. Draw the corresponding TFC and AFC curves.

2. With the following data, calculate the firm's AVC and MVC and draw the graphs for TVC, AVC, and MVC.

| QUANTITY | TOTAL VARIABLE COSTS (thousands of dollars) |
|---|---|
| 1 | $ 80 |
| 2 | 160 |
| 3 | 240 |
| 4 | 352 |
| 5 | 480 |
| 6 | 720 |

3. From the figures in Questions 1 and 2, calculate TC and AC for each of the output levels from 1 to 6, and draw the two graphs.

4. If a firm's commitments in 1994 include machinery that will need replacement in five years, a factory building rented for 8 years, and a three-year union contract specifying how many workers it must employ, when, from its point of view in 1994, does the firm's long run begin?

5. If the marginal revenue product of a kilowatt hour of electric power is 8 cents and the marginal cost of a kilowatt hour is 12 cents, what can a firm do to increase its profits?

6. A firm hires two workers and rents 15 acres of land for a season. It produces 150,000 bushels of crop. If it had doubled its land and labor, production would have been 280,000 bushels. Does it have constant, decreasing, or increasing returns to scale?

7. Suppose wages are $20,000 per season and land rent per acre is $3000. Calculate the average cost of 150,000 bushels and the average cost of 280,000 bushels, using the figures in Question 6 above. (Note that average costs diminish when output increases.) What connection do these figures have with the firm's returns to scale?

8. Ivana and Ivan have bought a great deal of corn. Suppose they now buy more *land*, but not more corn, and spread the corn evenly over all this land. What is likely to happen to the marginal physical product of corn? What, therefore, is the role of input proportions in the determination of marginal physical product?

9. Labor costs $10 per hour. Nine workers produce 180 bushels of product per hour. Ten workers produce 196 bushels. Land rents for $1000 per acre per year. With ten acres worked by nine workers, the marginal physical product of an acre of land is 1400 bushels per year. Does the farmer minimize costs by hiring nine workers and renting ten acres of land? If not, which input should he use in larger relative quantity?

10. Suppose I&I's total costs are increased by $10 per week at every output level. Show in Table 6–2 how this affects their total and average costs.

11. In the wave of acquisitions of the 1980s, in which many firms bought other companies, many of the acquirers were left with heavy debts that amounted to huge additions to their fixed costs. Why did this not affect the output levels that maximized their profits?

12. (More difficult) A firm finds there is a sudden increase in the demand for its product. In the short run, it must operate longer hours and pay higher overtime wage rates. In the long run, however, the firm can install more machines instead of operating them for longer hours. Which do you think will be lower, the short-run or the long-run average cost of the increased output? How is your answer affected by the fact that the long-run average cost includes the new machines the firm buys, while the short-run average cost includes no machine purchases?

# *Appendix* PRODUCTION INDIFFERENCE CURVES

To describe a production function—that is, the relationship between input combinations and size of total output—we can use a graphic device called the **production indifference curve** instead of the sort of numerical information described in Table 6–6 in the chapter.

A **production indifference curve** (sometimes called an *isoquant*) is a curve in a graph showing quantities of *inputs* on its axes. Each indifference curve indicates *all* combinations of input quantities capable of producing *a given* quantity of output; thus, there must be a separate indifference curve for each quantity of output.

Figure 6–11 represents different quantities of labor and capital capable of producing given amounts of wheat. The indifference curve labeled 220,000 bushels indicates that an output of 220,000 bushels of wheat can be obtained with the aid of *any one* of the combinations of inputs represented by points on that curve. For example, it can be produced by 10 years of labor and 200 acres of land (point *A*) or, instead, it can be produced by the labor-capital combination shown by point *B* on the same curve. Because it lies considerably below and to the right of point *B*, point *A* represents a productive process that uses more labor and less land than shown at point *B*.

Points *A* and *B* can be considered *technologically* indifferent because each represents a bundle of inputs capable of yielding the same quantity of finished goods. However, "indifference" in this sense does not mean that the producer will be unable to make up his mind between input combinations *A* and *B*. Input prices will permit him to arrive at that decision, because the two input choices are not *economically* indifferent.

The production indifference curves in a diagram such as Figure 6–11 constitute a complete description of the production function. For each combination of inputs, they show how much output can be produced. Since it is drawn in two dimensions, the diagram can deal with only two inputs at a time. In more realistic situations, there may be more than two inputs, and an algebraic analysis must be used. But all the principles we need to analyze such a situation can be derived from the two-variable case.

## CHARACTERISTICS OF THE PRODUCTION INDIFFERENCE CURVES

Before discussing input pricing and quantity decisions, we first examine what is known about the shapes of production indifference curves.

*Characteristic 1: Higher curves correspond to larger outputs.* Points on a higher indifference curve rep-

### *Figure* 6–11 A PRODUCTION INDIFFERENCE MAP

The figure shows three indifference curves, one for the production of 220,000 bushels of wheat, one for 240,000 bushels, and one for 260,000 bushels. For example, the lowest curve shows all combinations of land and labor capable of producing 220,000 bushels of wheat. Point *A* on that curve shows that 10 person-years of labor and 200 acres of land are enough to do the job.

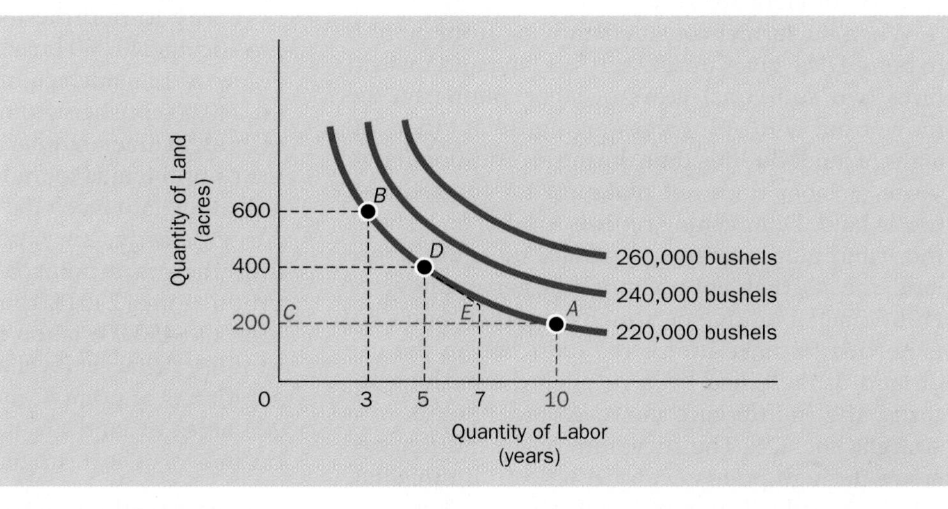

resent larger quantities of *both* inputs than the corresponding points on a lower curve. Thus, the higher the curve, the larger the *output* it represents.

*Characteristic 2: The indifference curve will generally have a negative slope.* It goes downhill as we move toward the right. This means that if we reduce the quantity of one input used, and we do not want to cut production, we must use more of another input. For example, if we want to use less land to produce 220,000 bushels of wheat, we will have to use more labor to make up for the reduced land input.

*Characteristic 3: The curves are typically assumed to curve inward toward the origin near their "middle."* This is a reflection of the "law" of diminishing returns to a single input. For example, in Figure 6–11, points *B*, *D*, and *A* represent three different input combinations capable of producing the same quantity of output. At point *B* a large amount of land and relatively little labor is used, while the opposite is true at point *A*. Point *D* is intermediate between the two. Indeed, point *D* is chosen so that its use of land is exactly halfway between the amounts of land used at *A* and at *B*.

Now consider the choice among these input combinations. As the farmer considers first the input combination at *B*, then the one at *D*, and finally the one at *A*, he is considering the use of less and less land, making up for it by the use of more and more labor so that he can continue to produce the same output. But the trade-off does not proceed at a constant rate because of diminishing returns in the substitution of labor for land.

When the farmer considers moving from point *B* to point *D*, he gives up 200 acres of land and instead hires two additional years of labor. Similarly, the move from *D* to *A* involves giving up another 200 acres of land. But this time, hiring an additional two years of labor does not make up for the reduced use of land. Diminishing returns to labor as he hires more and more workers to replace more and more land means that now a much larger quantity of additional labor, five person-years rather than two, is needed to make up for the reduction in the use of land. If there had been no such diminishing returns, the indifference curve would have been a straight line, *DE*. The curvature of the indifference curve through points *D* and *A* reflects diminishing returns to substitution of inputs.

## THE CHOICE OF INPUT COMBINATIONS

A production indifference curve only describes what input combinations *can* produce a given output; it indicates the technological possibilities. A business cannot decide which of the available options suits its purposes best without the corresponding cost information: that is, the relative prices of the inputs.

Next, we construct a **budget line**—a representation of equally costly input combinations—for the firm. For example, if farmhands are paid $9000 a year and land rents for $1000 per acre a year, then a farmer who spends $360,000 can hire 40 farmhands but rent no land (point *K* in Figure 6–12), or he can rent 360 acres but have no money left for farmhands (point *J*). But it is undoubtedly more sensible for him to pick some intermediate point on his budget line, *JK*, at which he divides the $360,000 between the two inputs.

If the prices of the inputs do not change, then the slope of the budget line for a $360,000 expenditure will be the same as that for $400,000 or for any other level of spending. For if the price of hiring a worker is nine times as high as the cost of renting an acre then the farmer can rent 9 times as many acres as he can hire farmhands, with any given amount of money. Thus, with input prices given, the budget line for different amounts of expenditure will all be parallel, as in Figure 6-13.

In studying the firm's problem in minimizing costs one cannot assume that the position of the budget line is given. Its budget is not fixed. Instead, it wants to produce a given quantity of output (say, 240,000 bushels) with the *smallest possible budget*.

A way to find the minimum budget capable of producing 240,000 bushels of wheat is illustrated in Figure 6–13, which combines the indifference curve for 240,000 bushels from Figure 6–11 with a variety of budget lines similar to *JK* in Figure 6–12. The firm's problem is to find the lowest budget line that will allow it to reach the 240,000-bushel indifference curve. Clearly, an expenditure of $270,000 is too little; there is no point on budget line *AB* that permits production of 240,000 bushels. Similarly, an expenditure of $450,000 is too much, because the firm can produce its target level of output more cheaply. The solution is at point *T*, meaning that 15 workers and 225 acres of land are used to produce the 240,000 bushels of wheat. In general:

The least costly way to produce any given level of

Figure 6–12 A BUDGET LINE

The firm's budget line, *JK*, shows all the combinations of inputs it can purchase with a fixed amount of money—in this case $360,000.

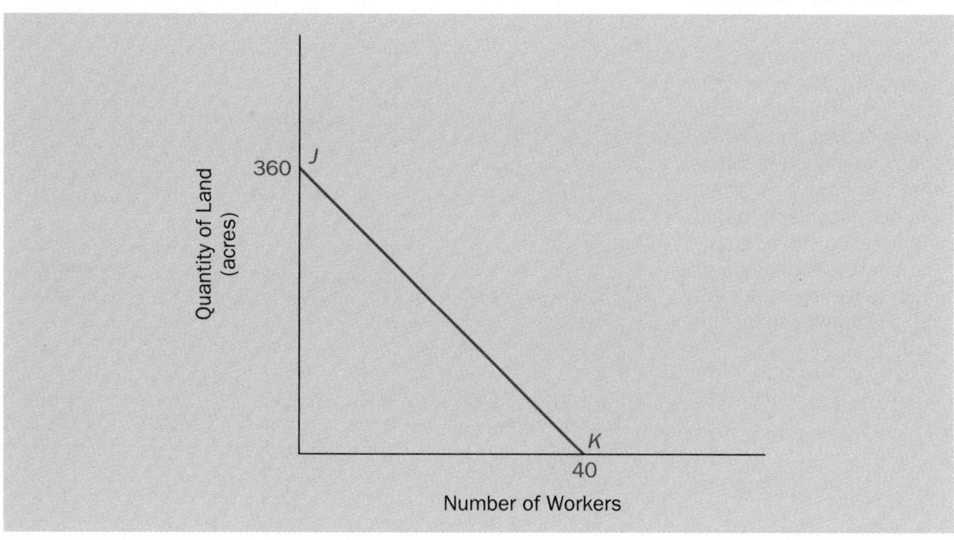

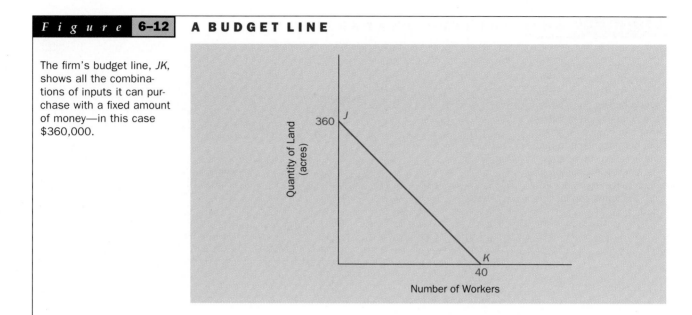

output is indicated by the point of tangency between a budget line and the production indifference curve corresponding to that level of output.

## COST MINIMIZATION, EXPANSION PATH, AND COST CURVES

Figure 6–13 shows how to determine the input combination that minimizes the cost of producing 240,000 bushels of output. We can repeat this procedure exactly for any other output quantity, such as 200,000 bushels or 300,000 bushels. In each case, we draw the corresponding production indifference curve and find the lowest budget line that permits it to be produced. For example, in Figure 6–14, budget line *BB* is tangent to the indifference curve for 200,000 units of output and budget line *B′B′* is tangent to the indifference curve for 300,000 units of

Figure 6–13 COST MINIMIZATION

The least costly way to produce 240,000 bushels of wheat is shown by point *T*, where the production indifference curve is tangent to budget line *JK*. Here the farmer is employing 15 workers and using 225 acres of land. It is not possible to produce 240,000 bushels on a smaller budget, and any larger budget would be wasteful.

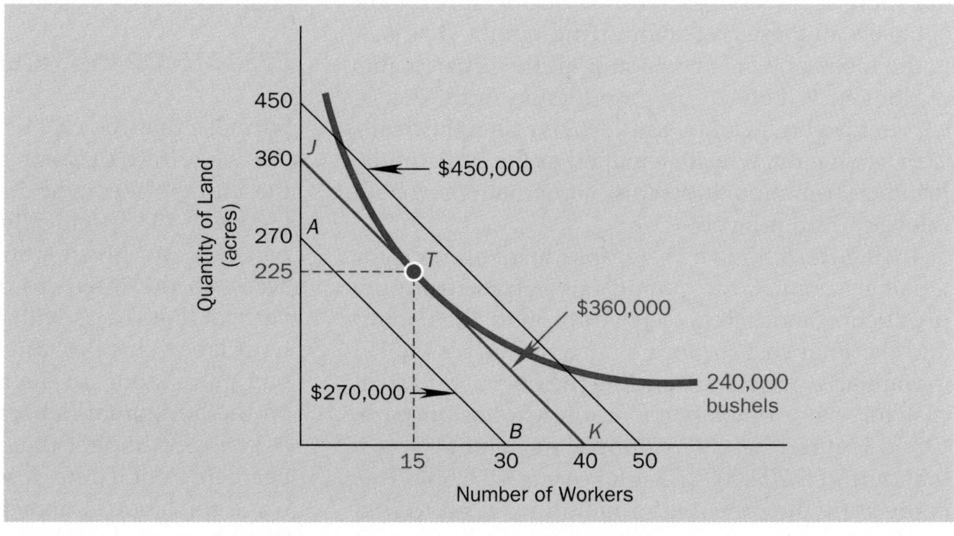

Figure 6–14 THE FIRM'S EXPANSION PATH

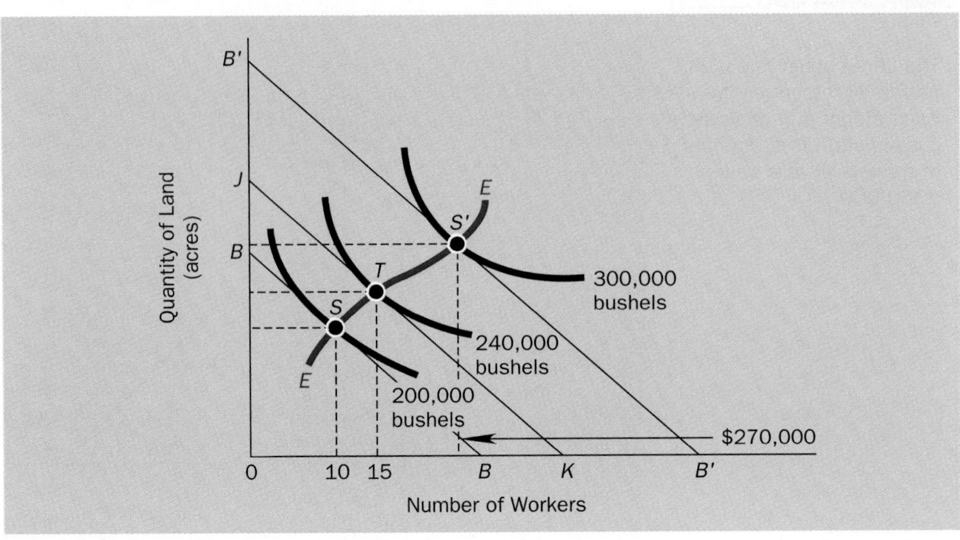


Each point of tangency such as *S*, between a production indifference curve and a budget line shows the combination of inputs that can produce the output corresponding to that indifference curve at lowest cost. The locus of all such tangency points is *EE*, the firm's expansion path.

output. In this way, we obtain three tangency points: *S*, which gives us the input combination that produces a 200,000-bushel output at lowest cost; *T*, which gives the same information for a 240,000-bushel output; and *S′*, which indicates the cost-minimizing input combination for the production of 300,000 bushels. This process can be repeated for as many other levels of output as we like. For each such output we draw the corresponding production indifference curve and find its point of tangency with a budget line. That tangency point will show the input combination that produces the output in question at lowest cost. Curve *EE* in Figure 6–14 connects all these cost-minimizing points, that is, it is the locus of *S*, *T*, and *S′* and all the other points of tangency between a production indifference curve and a budget line. Curve *EE* is called the firm's expansion path, which is defined as the locus of the firm's cost-minimizing input combinations for all relevant output levels.

In Figure 6–13 we were able to determine for tangency point *T* the quantity of output (from the production indifference curve through that point) and the total cost (from the tangent budget line).

Similarly, we can determine the output and total cost for every other point on the expansion path, *EE*, in Figure 6–14. For example, at point *S* we see that output is 200,000 and total cost is $270,000. This is precisely the sort of information we need to find the firm's total cost curve; that is, it is just the sort of information contained in Table 6–4, from which we first calculated the total cost curve and then the average and marginal cost curves in Figure 6–4. Thus we see that:

The points of tangency between a firm's production indifference curves and its budget lines yield its **expansion path**. The expansion path shows the firm's cost-minimizing input combination for each pertinent output level. This information also yields the output and total cost for each point on the expansion path, which is just what we need to draw the firm's cost curves.

## EFFECTS OF CHANGES IN INPUT PRICES

Suppose that the cost of renting land increases and the wage rate of labor decreases. This means that the budget lines will differ from those depicted in Figure 6–13. Specifically, with land now more expensive, any given sum of money will rent fewer acres, so the intercept of each budget line on the vertical (land) axis will shift *downward*. Conversely, with labor cheaper, any given sum of money will buy more labor, so the intercept of the budget line on the horizontal (labor) axis will shift to the *right*. A series of budget lines corresponding to a $1500 per acre rental rate for land and a $6000 annual wage for labor is depicted in Figure 6–15. We see that these budget lines are less steep than those

Figure 6–15 **OPTIMAL INPUT CHOICE AT A DIFFERENT SET OF INPUT PRICES**

If input prices change, the combination of inputs that minimizes costs will normally change, too. In this diagram, land rents for $1500 per acre (more than in Figure 6–13) while labor costs $6000 per year (less than in Figure 6–13). As a result, the least costly way to produce 240,000 bushels of wheat shifts from point *T* in Figure 6–13 to point *E* here.

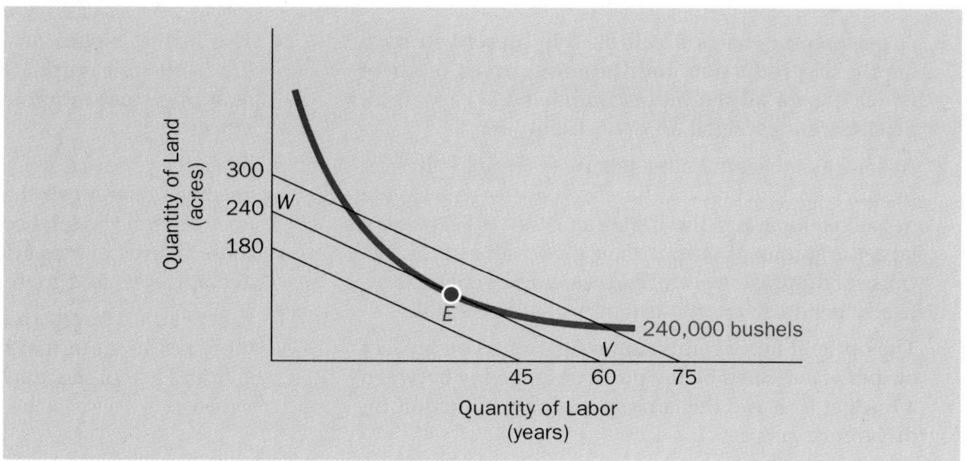


shown in Figure 6–13, and that the least costly way to produce 240,000 bushels of wheat is now given by point *E*.

To assist you in seeing how things change, Figure 6–16 combines, in a single graph, budget line *JK* and tangency point *T* from Figure 6–13 and budget line *WV* and tangency point *E* from Figure 6–15. Notice that point *E* lies below and to the right of *T*, meaning that as wages decrease and rents increase, the firm will hire more labor and rent less land. As common sense suggests, when the price of one input rises in comparison with that of others, it will pay the firm to hire less of this input and more of other inputs to make up for its reduced use of the more expensive input.

In addition to this substitution of one input for another, a change in the price of an input may induce the firm to alter the level of output that it decides to produce. This is a subject that was studied in the previous chapter.

Figure 6–16 **HOW CHANGES IN INPUT PRICES AFFECT INPUT PROPORTIONS**

When land becomes more expensive and labor becomes cheaper, the budget lines (such as *JK*) become less steep than they were previously (see *WV*). As a result, the least costly way to produce 240,000 bushels shifts from point *T* to point *E*. The firm uses more labor and less land.

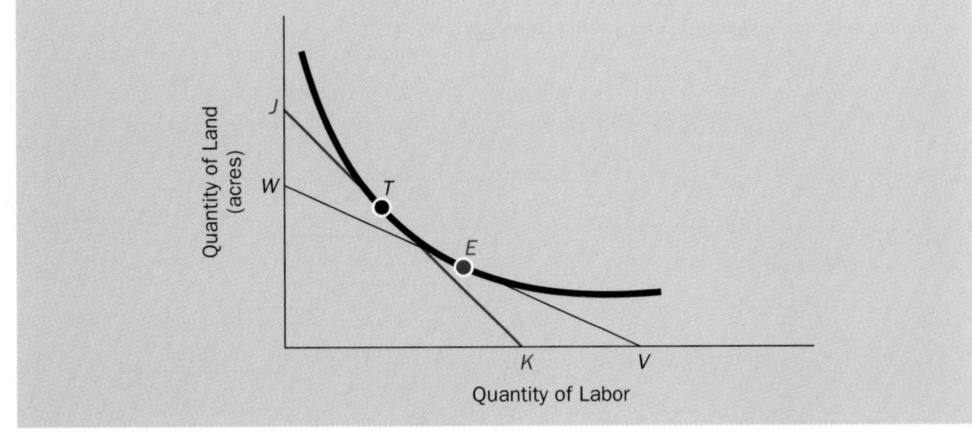

## *Summary*

1. A production function can be fully described by a family of **production indifference curves**, each of which shows all the input combinations capable of producing a specified amount of output.
2. As long as each input has a positive marginal physical product, production indifference curves will have a negative slope and the higher curves will represent larger amounts of output than the lower curves. Because of diminishing returns, these curves characteristically bend toward the origin near their middle.
3. The optimal input combination for any given level of output is indicated by the **point of tangency between a budget line and the corresponding production indifference curve**.
4. The firm's **expansion path** shows, for each of the firm's possible output levels, the combination of input quantities that minimizes the cost of producing that output.
5. From the production indifference curves and the budget lines tangent to them along the expansion path, one can find the total cost for each output level. From these figures one can determine the firm's total cost, average cost, and marginal cost curves.
6. When input prices change, firms will normally use more of the input that becomes relatively less expensive and less of the input that becomes relatively more expensive.

## *Key Concepts and Terms*

Production indifference curve
Budget line
Expansion path
Point of tangency between the budget line and the corresponding production indifference curve

## *Questions for Review*

1. Compound Consolidated Corporation (CCC) produces containers with the aid of two inputs: labor and glue. If labor costs $5 per hour and glue costs $5 per gallon, draw CCC's budget line for a total expenditure of $100,000. In this same diagram, sketch a production indifference curve indicating that CCC can produce no more than 1000 containers with this expenditure.
2. With respect to Question 1, suppose that wages rise to $10 per hour and glue prices rise to $6 per gallon. How are CCC's optimal input proportions likely to change? (Use a diagram to explain your answer.)
3. What happens to the expansion path of the firm in Question 2?

*Chapter* **7**

# DEMAND AND ELASTICITY

*A high cross elasticity of demand [between two goods indicates that they] compete in the same market. [This can prevent a supplier of one of the products] from possessing monopoly power over price.*

**SUPREME COURT OF THE UNITED STATES (the Dupont Cellophane Decision, 1956)**

Our study of decision making by business firms was based on two pieces of information: the cost curves and the demand curve. Chapter 6 examined in some detail the origins of the firm's cost curves. This chapter and the next provide the material needed to understand the demand curve. ¶ The quantity of a good demanded in a market depends on many things: the incomes of consumers, the price of the good, the prices of other goods, the volume and effectiveness of advertising, and so on. Demand analysis deals with all these influences, but it has traditionally focused on the *price* of the good in question. The reason is that the market price of a commodity plays a crucial role in influencing both quantity supplied and quantity demanded. As we saw in Chapter 5, the demand curve that enters the firm's profit-maximizing price and output decisions relates the price of the product to the quantity that will be demanded. That relationship is the focus of most of the next two chapters. ¶ In Chapter 8, we will study decision making by consumers and show how demand curves depend on their attitudes toward the commodities they purchase and how much money they have to spend. But first, in this chapter, we examine certain critical properties of the demand curve—especially how the responsiveness of quantity demanded to price is measured. In particular, we introduce and explain an important concept called *elasticity* which is almost always used for this purpose. Next, we apply that concept to measuring the strength of the interconnection between the demands for related commodities, such as hamburgers and ketchup. Finally, in an appendix, we explain the importance of the time period to which a demand curve applies and how this can create problems in obtaining demand information from statistical data.

## TWO ILLUSTRATIVE CASES

Two examples—one hypothetical, the other concrete—will illustrate why measuring the responsiveness of quantity demanded to price is an issue of critical interest to decision makers in business and government. As usual, we start by laying out the issues, postponing resolution until the required analytical tools have been explained.

***Example I: The Glubstanian Tariff Decisions.*** Our first example is hypothetical, but it deals with real issues. The Treasury Department of the Republic of Glubstania, a notorious dictatorship, became acutely aware of its growing budget deficit. As a major step toward elimination of the deficit, the Treasury Department decided to impose what was referred to as a "revenue tariff" on the importation of English china and French cheese; that is, a tax was imposed on every set of dishes imported from England and on every pound of cheese imported from France. Hearing of this new idea, the Department of Public Morals decided that it also could impose a tax to be used for an even nobler purpose. To combat the chronic drunkenness of Glubstanians, it put a large tariff on imports of Russian vodka—the favorite drink in the country—calling it a "morality protective tariff."

The results surprised both the Treasury Department and the Department of Public Morals. The tariff on English china and French cheese brought in very little revenue. But the tariff on vodka yielded huge sums while utterly failing to curb inebriation. What had gone wrong in the Glubstanian decisions?

***Example II: Polaroid v. Kodak.*** Our second example involves a multibillion dollar court case involving two well-known U.S. firms in which one of the authors of this volume was deeply involved as an expert witness. Polaroid sued Kodak for infringement of its instant-photography patents, and won. A second court case was then launched to determine how much Kodak should be required to pay Polaroid in compensation. The issue was: How much financial damage had Polaroid suffered as a result of Kodak's infringement?

Polaroid claimed that it would have charged higher prices for its film and cameras if Kodak had not infringed its patents and had consequently been unable to compete with Polaroid. Witnesses for Kodak pointed out, however, that such price increases would have reduced the quantity of film and cameras demanded. The court was therefore faced with a clear question: how would Polaroid's total revenue have been affected as a result of the price increases it claims it would have instituted?

To take a first step toward answering the question, we must recognize that it depends on the responsiveness of quantity demanded to price changes, that is, on the shape of the demand curve for Polaroid film. To illustrate the principles involved, we start with a hypothetical case in which demand is relatively unresponsive to price [see part (a) of Figure 7–1]; that is, a given (vertical) change in

Figure 7–1 TWO HYPOTHETICAL DEMAND CURVES FOR POLAROID FILM

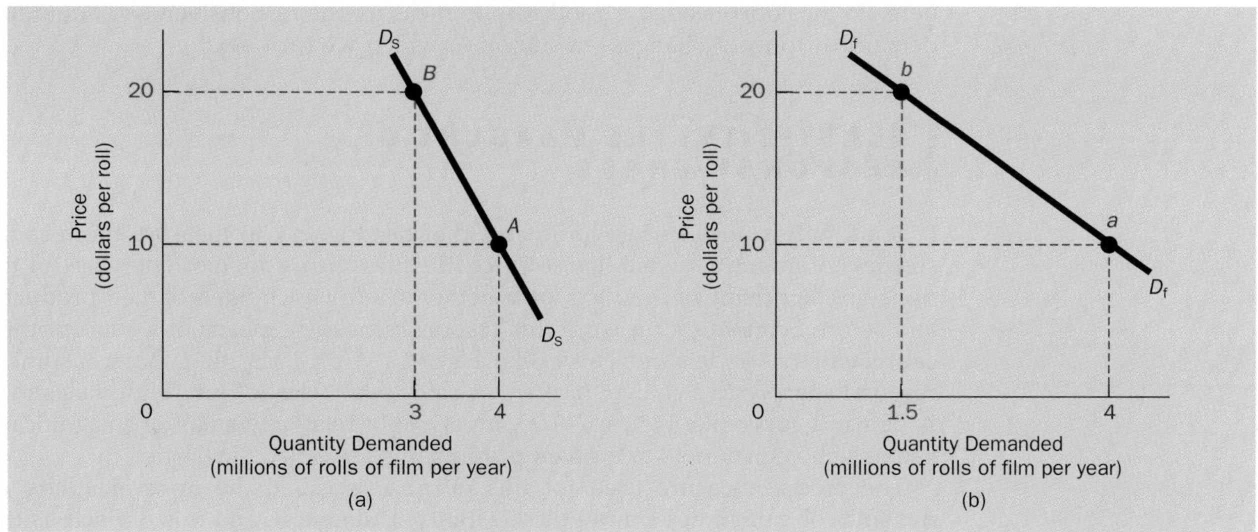


The demand curve in (a) is comparatively steep, so that a rise in price leads to only a small change in quantity demanded. Consequently, the price increase raises Polaroid's total revenue. In contrast, the demand curve in (b) is relatively flat, so that the same rise in price produces a sharp cut in quantity demanded and decreases total revenue.

price leads to a small (horizontal) change in quantity, making the demand curve rather steep. Figure 7–1(a) shows that in this case, if Polaroid had doubled its price, from \$10 per roll of film to \$20, this would have lowered the quantity sold from 4 million to 3 million rolls per year—the move from point A to point B on the steep demand curve.

According to their testimony at the trial, Polaroid's management believed that such a price rise would increase the company's total sales revenue. The graph suggests that they were right. If the demand curve is indeed very steep, a rise in price causes only a small drop in quantity sold. At the lower price of \$10 per roll, 4 million rolls per year can be sold, bringing a total revenue of \$10 × 4 million = \$40 million per year. At the higher price of \$20 per roll, only 3 million film rolls would be sold annually. But this modest drop in sales would yield annual revenue of \$20 × 3 million = \$60 million. Thus, in this example, a doubling of price would lead to a 50 percent rise in Polaroid's total revenue.

Part (b) of Figure 7–1 shows that things work out quite differently if quantity demanded is much more responsive to price. Demand curve $D_fD_f$ is much flatter than demand curve $D_sD_s$, meaning that a given change in price elicits a much greater quantity response. As a result, if the price of film rises from \$10 to \$20, as it did in the previous graph, quantity demanded falls far more sharply than before—from 4 million rolls per year all the way down to 1.5 million. Consequently, the rise in price now actually *reduces* Polaroid's total revenue from \$40 million at point *a* down to \$30 million (\$20 × 1.5 million) at point *b*. Thus, when the demand curve is relatively flat, as in part (b) of the graph, a rise in price actually decreases total revenue. In this example, doubling the price produces a 25 percent drop in total revenue. So the court had to decide whether the situation depicted in part (a) or in part (b) was more relevant to the dispute between Polaroid and Kodak.

Clearly, the *responsiveness* of quantity demanded to price was the key influence here. So the court needed a good way to measure the responsiveness of quantity demanded to price changes—a subject to which we turn next.

## ELASTICITY: THE MEASURE OF RESPONSIVENESS

It is not only courts and governments that need a way to measure the responsiveness of quantity demanded to price. Business firms do, too. They need it for decisions on pricing of products, on whether to add new models of their products, and so on. Economists measure this responsiveness by means of a concept they call **elasticity**. A demand curve like Figure 7–1(b), indicating that consumers respond sharply to a change in price, is said to be "elastic" (or "highly elastic"). A demand curve like Figure 7–1(a), involving a relatively small or insignificant response by consumers to a given price change, is called "inelastic."

The precise measure used for this purpose is called the **price elasticity of demand**, or sometimes simply the **elasticity of demand**, and it is defined as the ratio of the *percentage* change in quantity demanded to the associated *percentage* change in price. Specifically:

$$\text{Elasticity of demand} = \frac{\%\text{ change in quantity demanded}}{\%\text{ change in price}}.$$

Thus, demand is called **elastic** if, say, a 10 percent rise in price leads to a reduction in quantity demanded of more than 10 percent. The demand is called **inelastic** if such a rise in price reduces quantity demanded by less than 10 percent.

Let us now consider how these definitions can be used to analyze a demand curve. At first, it may seem that the *slope* of the demand curve conveys the information we need: curve $D_sD_s$ is much steeper than curve $D_fD_f$ in Figure 7–1, so that any given change in price appears to correspond to a much smaller change in quantity demanded in Figure 7–1(a) than in Figure 7–1(b). So it is tempting to call (b) "more elastic." But slope will not do the job because the slope of any curve depends on the units of measurement, as we saw in Chapter 2; and in economics there are no standardized units of measurement. Cloth output may be measured in yards or in meters; milk in quarts or liters; and coal in tons or kilograms.

Figure 7–2 brings out the point explicitly. In this graph, we return to the parable of Ivana and Ivan's poultry farm. It will be recalled that in earlier chapters we measured output in ten-kilo packs of chicken, as is done in Figure 7–2(a). We see that a fall in price from $17 to $16 per pack (points A and B) raises quantity demanded from 3 packs to 4 packs per week. Now look at Figure 7–2(b), which provides *exactly* the same information, but measures chicken output in kilos, rather than in 10-kilo packs. Thus, the same price change as before is shown to increase quantity demanded by 10 units, that is, by 10 kilos, rather than by 1 unit (one 10-kilo pack).

To the eye, the increase in quantity demanded looks 10 times as great in part (b) as in part (a). But all that has changed is the unit of measurement. The 10-unit increase in Figure 7–2(b) represents the same 10-kilo increase in quantity demanded as the one unit increase in Figure 7–2(a). Just as we get different

Figure 7-2

## THE SENSITIVITY OF SLOPE TO UNITS OF MEASUREMENT

The slope of a curve changes whenever we change units of measurement. Part (a)'s demand curve looks very steep because we measure output in 10-kilo packs of chicken. In Part (b) we measure quantity in kilos instead, so all the quantities are multiplied by 10. As a result, the demand curve looks rather flat. But the two demand curves present exactly the same information.

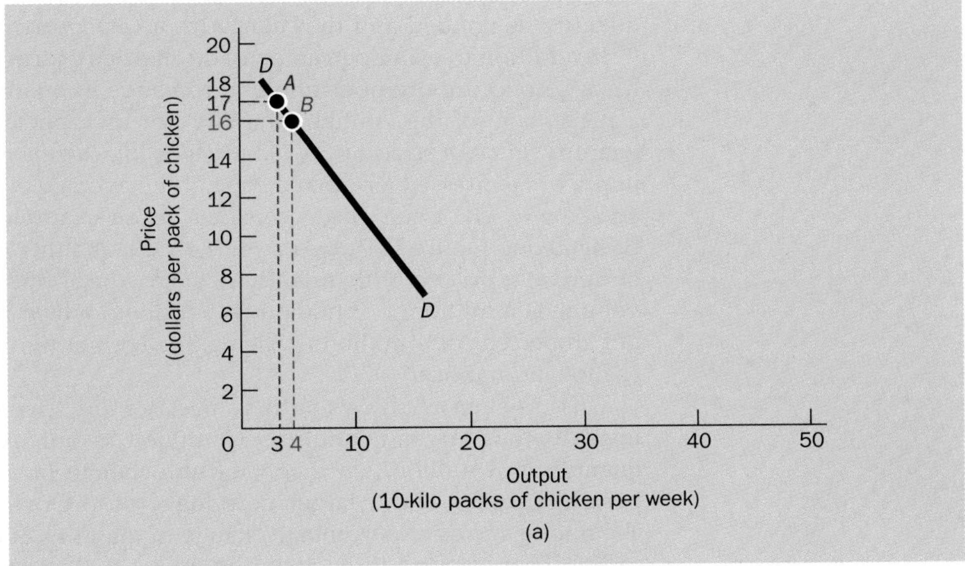


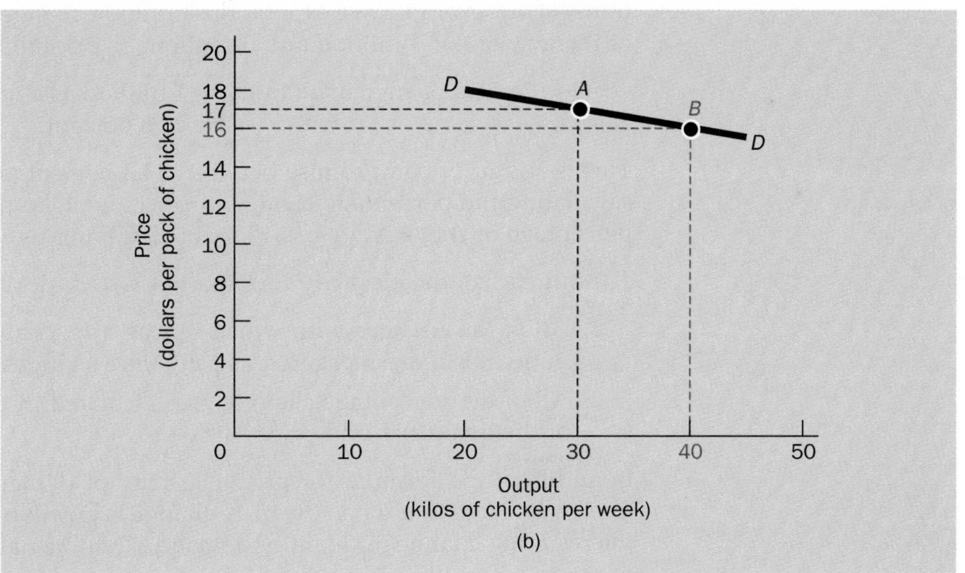


numbers for a given rise in temperature depending on whether we measure it in centigrade or in Fahrenheit, the slope of the demand curve is different depending on whether we measure quantity in packs or in kilos. Clearly, then, slope is not a good measure of the responsiveness of quantity demanded to price, because the measure changes whenever the units of measurement change.

It is because of this problem that economists use the elasticity measure, which is based on *percentage* changes in price and quantity rather than on *absolute* changes. The elasticity formula solves the units problem because percentages are unaffected by units of measurement. If the defense budget doubles, it goes up by 100 percent, whether measured in millions or billions of dollars. If a person's height doubles between the ages of 5 and 15, it goes up 100 percent, whether measured in inches or centimeters. The elasticity formula given above expresses both the change in quantity demanded and the change in price as *percentages*.[1]

In addition to using percentages, the elasticity formula usually used in practice has a second important attribute: the change in quantity is calculated neither as a percentage of the "initial" quantity nor as a percentage of the "subsequent" quantity, but *as a percentage of the average of the two quantities*. Similarly, the change in price is expressed as a percentage of the average of the two prices in question. To see why the issue arises, consider, as an example, the demand information presented in Figure 7–1(a). At a price of $20, quantity demanded is 3 million rolls of film; at a price of $10, quantity demanded is 4 million. The difference in sales volume is 4 million − 3 million = 1 million, which is 33.3 percent of 3 million, but 25 percent of 4 million. Which is the correct figure to use as the percentage change in quantity?

This problem is always with us because any given change in quantity must involve some larger quantity $Q$ (4 million in our example) and some smaller quantity $q$ (3 million), so that the same change in quantity must be a smaller percentage of $Q$ and a larger percentage of $q$. Obviously, neither of these can claim to be *the* right percentage change in quantity. It turns out to be convenient to use what appears to be a compromise—the *average* of the two quantities. In terms of our example, we express the 1 million change in quantity as a percentage of the average of 4 million and 3 million, or 3.5 million. Thus:

$$\begin{aligned}\text{Percent change in quantity} &= \text{1 million as a percent of 3.5 million}\\ &= \text{28.6 percent.}\end{aligned}$$

This is a kind of compromise between 33.3 percent and 25 percent. Similarly, in calculating the percentage change in price, we take the $10 change in price as a percentage of the average of $10 and $20, giving us $10/$15, or 66.7 percent.

To summarize, the elasticity formula has two basic attributes:

1. All of the changes with which it deals (the change in price and the change in quantity) are measured as *percentage* changes.
2. All of the percentage changes are calculated in terms of the average values of the quantities and prices at issue.

In addition, the formula for price elasticity of demand usually is adjusted in a third way. Note that when the price change is positive (that is, the price increases) the resulting change in quantity demanded will usually be negative. So the ratio of the two would be negative. However, it is customary to express elasticity as a positive number. Hence:

3. All of the percentage changes are taken as "absolute values," meaning that we drop all minus signs.[2]

---

[1]The remainder of this section involves fairly technical computational issues, so that on a first reading you may prefer to go directly to the new section that begins on page 174.

[2]This third attribute of the elasticity formula—the removal of all minus signs—applies only when the formula is used to measure the responsiveness of *quantity demanded* to a change in *price*. Later in the chapter, we will see that equivalent formulas are used to measure the responsiveness between other pairs of variables. For example, the elasticity of supply uses a similar formula to measure the responsiveness of quantity supplied to price. In such other uses, it is not customary to drop minus signs when calculating elasticity. The reasons will become clearer later in the chapter.

## An Illustration of an Elasticity Calculation

Suppose the quantity demanded, $Q$, is 17 when the price, $P$, is \$12; and the quantity demanded is 23 when price is \$8. Then the change in $P$ is \$12 − \$8 = \$4, and average $P$ is (\$12 + \$8)/2 = \$10, so the percentage change in $P$ is 40 percent. Similarly, the change in $Q$ is 23 − 17 = 6, and average $Q$ is (23 + 17)/2 = 20, so the change in $Q$ is 6 as a percentage of 20, or 30 percent. Hence:

$$\text{Elasticity} = \frac{30}{40} = 0.75.$$

This calculation is summarized in tabular form below.

**CALCULATION OF PRICE ELASTICITY OF DEMAND**

| | PRICE | QUANTITY |
|---|---|---|
| Situation 1 | $P_1 = 12$ | $Q_1 = 17$ |
| Situation 2 | $P_2 = 8$ | $Q_2 = 23$ |
| Change | $P_1 - P_2 = 12 - 8 = 4$ | $Q_2 - Q_1 = 23 - 17 = 6$ |
| Average | $(P_1 + P_2)/2 = 20/2 = 10$ | $(Q_2 + Q_1)/2 = 40/2 = 20$ |
| % change | 4 as % of 10 = 40% | 6 as % of 20 = 30% |

$$\text{Elasticity} = \frac{\%\text{ change in quantity}}{\%\text{ change in price}} = \frac{30}{40} = 0.75$$

We can now restate the formula for price elasticity of demand, keeping in mind all three features of the formula. We have

$$\text{Price elasticity of demand} = \frac{\text{change in quantity as \% of average of the two quantities in question}}{\text{change in price as \% of average of the two prices in question}}.$$

In our example of Polaroid film:

$$\text{Elasticity} = \frac{\text{1 million as \% of 3.5 million}}{\text{\$10 as \% of \$15}}$$

$$= 28.6\%/66.7\% = 0.43.$$

The calculation in the box is also written out in algebraic symbols. That permits us to express elasticity as a formula into which we can insert price and quantity numbers directly to calculate the elasticity. This standard formula is easily derived by means of some simple algebra, and its proof is found in intermediate microeconomics texts. We use $P_1$ and $P_2$ to represent the two prices, and $Q_1$ and $Q_2$ to represent the corresponding quantities on the demand curve. Then we have

$$\text{Price elasticity of demand} = \frac{(Q_2 - Q_1)(P_2 + P_1)}{(P_2 - P_1)(Q_2 + Q_1).}$$

The reader can readily check out the formula by inserting four illustrative numbers in the table, $P_1 = 12$, $P_2 = 8$, $Q_1 = 17$, $Q_2 = 23$, to obtain

$$\begin{aligned}\text{Elasticity} &= (23 - 17)(8 + 12) \text{ divided by } (8 - 12)(23 + 17)\\ &= 6 \text{ times } 20 \text{ divided by } -4 \text{ times } 40\\ &= 120/-160 = 3/-4, \text{ or, if we drop the minus sign,}\\ \text{Elasticity} &= 0.75.\end{aligned}$$

## PRICE ELASTICITY OF DEMAND AND THE SHAPE OF DEMAND CURVES

Figure 7–3 indicates how elasticity of demand is related to the shape of the demand curve. We begin with two extreme but important cases. Part (a) depicts a demand curve that is simply a vertical line. This curve is called *perfectly inelastic* throughout because its elasticity is zero. That is, since quantity demanded remains at 90 units no matter what the price, the percentage change in quantity is always zero, and hence the elasticity is zero. Thus, in this case, consumer purchases do not respond at all to any change in price.

Demand curves like this are quite unusual. It may perhaps be expected when the price range being considered already involves very low prices from the point of view of the consumer. (Will anyone use more salt if its price is lowered?) It may also occur when the item (such as medicine) is considered absolutely essential by the consumer, although even here the demand curve will remain vertical only so long as price does not exceed what the consumer can afford.

Part (b) of Figure 7–3 shows the opposite extreme: a horizontal demand curve. It is said to be *perfectly elastic* (or "infinitely elastic"). If there is the slightest rise in price, quantity demanded will drop to zero; that is, the percentage change in quantity demanded will be infinitely large. This may be expected to occur where a rival product that is just as good in the consumer's view is available at the going price ($5 in our diagram). In cases where no one will pay more than the going price, the seller will lose all her customers if she raises her price even one penny.

**Figure 7–3 DEMAND CURVES WITH DIFFERENT ELASTICITIES**

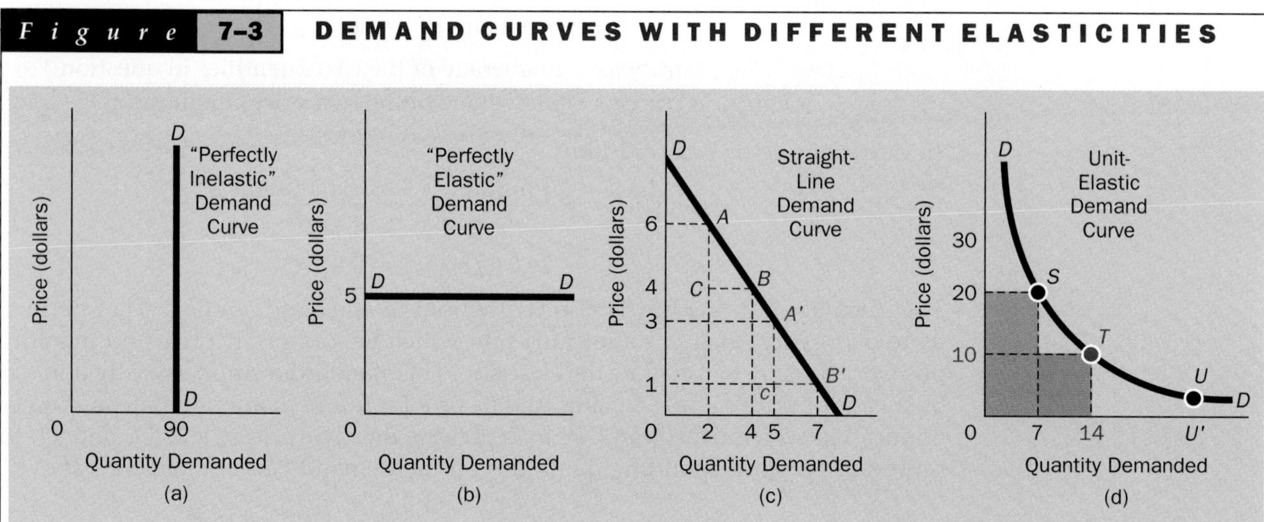


The vertical demand curve in part (a) is *perfectly inelastic* (elasticity = 0)—quantity demanded remains the same regardless of price. The horizontal demand curve in part (b) is *perfectly elastic*—at any price above $5, quantity demanded falls to zero. Part (c) shows a *straight-line demand curve.* Its *slope* is constant, but its *elasticity* is not. Part (d) depicts a *unit-elastic* demand curve whose constant elasticity is 1.0 throughout. A change in price pushes quantity demanded in the opposite direction but does not affect total expenditure. When price equals $20, total expenditure is price times quantity, or $20 × 7 = $140; and when price equals $10, expenditure equals $10 × 14 = $140.

Part (c) depicts a case between these two extremes: a *straight-line* demand curve, which is neither vertical nor horizontal. Though the *slope* of a straight-line demand curve is constant throughout its length, its *elasticity* is not. For example, the elasticity of demand between points $A$ and $B$ in Figure 7–3(c) is

$$\frac{\text{Change in } Q \text{ as \% of average } Q}{\text{Change in } P \text{ as \% of average } P} = \frac{2 \text{ as \% of } (2+4)/2}{2 \text{ as \% of } (4+6)/2}$$

$$= \frac{2/3}{2/5} = \frac{66\ 2/3\%}{40\%} = 1.67.$$

But the elasticity of demand between points $A'$ and $B'$ is

$$\frac{2 \text{ as \% of } (5+7)/2}{2 \text{ as \% of } (3+1)/2} = \frac{2/6}{2/2} = \frac{33\ 1/3\%}{100\%} = 0.33.$$

Along a straight-line demand curve, the price elasticity of demand grows steadily smaller as we move from left to right. That is so because the quantity keeps getting larger, so that a given *numerical* change in quantity becomes an ever smaller *percentage* change. But the price keeps going lower, so that a given numerical change in price becomes an ever larger percentage change.

If the elasticity of a straight-line demand curve varies from one part of the curve to another, what is the appearance of a demand curve with the same elasticity throughout its length? For reasons explained in the next section, it looks like the curve in Figure 7–3(d), which is a curve with elasticity equal to one throughout (a *unit-elastic* demand curve). That is, a unit-elastic demand curve bends in the middle toward the origin of the graph, and at either end moves closer and closer to the axes but never touches or crosses the axes.

As we have seen, it is conventional to speak of a curve whose elasticity is greater than one (percentage change in quantity greater than percentage change in price) as an *elastic* demand curve, and of one whose elasticity is less than one as an *inelastic* curve. When elasticity is exactly one, we say the curve is *unit elastic*. This terminology is convenient for discussing the last important property of the elasticity measure.

Real-world price elasticities of demand seem to vary considerably from product to product. Luxury goods are generally more price-elastic than goods that are considered necessities. Products with close substitutes tend to have relatively high elasticities. And the elasticities of demand for producers' goods such as raw materials and machinery tend to be greater on the whole than those for consumers' goods. Table 7–1 gives some actual statistically estimated elasticities for some commodities in the economy.

## THE RELATION BETWEEN ELASTICITY AND SLOPE

We have emphasized that elasticity and slope are not the same thing. But the two are closely related, and it is this relationship that helps to explain the shapes of the curves in Figure 7–3. Remember that the formula for elasticity is

$$\text{Price elasticity of demand} = \frac{\Delta Q/Q}{\Delta P/P}$$

**Table 7-1 ESTIMATES OF LONG-RUN PRICE ELASTICITY OF DEMAND: 1947–64***

| COMMODITY | LONG-RUN PRICE ELASTICITY |
|---|---|
| Aluminum | 0.4 |
| Shoe repairs and cleaning | 0.4 |
| Newspapers and magazines | 0.5 |
| Medical care and hospitalization insurance | 0.8 |
| Purchased meals (excluding alcoholic beverages) | 1.6 |
| Electricity (household utility) | 1.9 |
| Boats, pleasure aircraft | 2.4 |
| Public transportation | 3.5 |
| China, tableware | 8.8 |

*The aluminum figure is from Franklin M. Fisher, *A Priori Information and Time Series Analysis, Essays in Economic Theory and Management*, Amsterdam: North Holland Publishing Company, 1962, page 112. All other figures are from H.S. Houthakker and Lester D. Taylor, *Consumer Demand in the United States*, 2nd edition, Cambridge: Harvard University Press, 1970, pages 153–58.

where $\Delta Q$ and $\Delta P$ are the changes in quantity and price, respectively, $P$ is the average of the prices in question, and $Q$ is the average of the quantities.[3] This formula can be rewritten as

The **(PRICE) ELASTICITY OF DEMAND** is the ratio of the *percentage* change in quantity demanded to the *percentage* change in price that brings about the change in quantity demanded.

$$\text{Price elasticity of demand} = (\Delta Q/\Delta P)(P/Q)$$

where $\Delta Q/\Delta P$ is the reciprocal of the slope of the demand curve, which is $\Delta P/\Delta Q$. So slope is part of the elasticity formula. But it is only part: the ratio $P/Q$ is involved as well.

Going back to Figure 7–3(a), we see that this last formula tells us why a vertical demand curve has an elasticity of zero. When the demand curve is vertical, a change in price never changes quantity one iota. So $\Delta Q$ always equals zero. Since anything multiplied by zero equals zero, we see from the last formula that the elasticity is always zero. Similarly, if the demand curve is horizontal, as in Figure 7–3(b), price never changes—so $\Delta P = 0$. But any number divided by zero is, roughly speaking, infinity; so we say that a horizontal demand curve has infinite elasticity.

The varying elasticity of the straight line demand curve in Figure 7–3(c) is also explained by the new version of the elasticity formula. Along a straight line, by definition, slope is the same everywhere, so $\Delta Q/\Delta P$ must be constant. But, as we move from one part of the straight-line demand curve to another, the ratio $P/Q$ is changing. Toward the left-hand end of the demand curve, $P$ is relatively large and $Q$ is relatively small, so the ratio $P/Q$ is large. Our formula thus calls for a high elasticity. The opposite is clearly true toward the right-hand end.

[3] It is easy to derive this formula from the definition of elasticity as the percentage change in $Q$ divided by the percentage change in $P$, or

$$\%\Delta Q/\%\Delta P.$$

Just note that the two percentage changes can be written $\Delta Q/Q$ and $\Delta P/P$ and write the ratio.

## PRICE ELASTICITY OF DEMAND AND TOTAL EXPENDITURE

Aside from its role as a measure of the responsiveness of demand to a change in price, elasticity is convenient for a second purpose. Often, as in the Polaroid example at the beginning of this chapter, a firm wants to know if a rise in price will increase or decrease its revenue. The price elasticity of demand provides a simple guide to the answer:

If demand for the seller's product is elastic, a rise in price will decrease total revenue. If demand is exactly unit elastic, a rise in price will leave total revenue unaffected. If demand is inelastic, a rise in price will raise total revenue. The opposite will be true when price falls.

It should be noted that a corresponding story must hold true about the expenditures made by the *buyers* of the product. After all, the expenditures of the buyers are exactly the same thing as the revenue of the seller.

These relationships hold because total revenue (or expenditure) equals price times quantity demanded, $P \times Q$, and a fall in price has two opposing effects on $P \times Q$. It decreases $P$ and, if the demand curve is negatively sloped, it increases $Q$. The first effect decreases revenues by cutting the amount of money a consumer spends on each unit of the good. But the second effect increases revenue by raising the number of units of the good that is sold.

The net consequence for total revenue (or total expenditure) depends on the elasticity. If price goes down 10 percent and quantity demanded increases 10 percent (a case of *unit elasticity*), the two effects just cancel out: $P \times Q$ remains constant. On the other hand, if price goes down 10 percent and quantity demanded rises 15 percent (a case of *elastic* demand), $P \times Q$ increases. Finally, if a 10 percent price fall leads to a 5 percent rise in quantity demanded (an *inelastic* case), $P \times Q$ falls.

The connection between elasticity and total revenue is easily seen in a graph. First we note that:

The total revenue (or expenditure) represented by any point on a demand curve (any price-quantity combination), such as point $S$ in Figure 7–4, is equal to the area of the rectangle under that point (the area of rectangle $ORST$ in the figure). This is so because the area of a rectangle equals height times width = $OR$ times $RS$ = price times quantity—which is exactly total revenue.

To illustrate the connection between elasticity and consumer expenditure, Figure 7–4 shows an elastic portion of a demand curve, $DD$. At a price of \$6 per unit, the quantity sold is four units, so total expenditure is 4 × \$6 = \$24. This is represented by the vertical rectangle whose upper right corner is point $S$, because the formula for the area of a rectangle is area = height × width, which in this case is equal to 4 × \$6 = \$24. When price falls to \$5 per unit, 12 units are bought. Consequently, the new expenditure (\$60 = \$5 × 12), now measured by the blue rectangle, will be larger than the old.

In contrast, Figure 7–3(d), the unit elastic demand curve, shows a case in which expenditure remains constant even though selling price changes. Total spending is \$140 whether the price is \$20 and 7 units are sold (point $S$) or the price is \$10 and 14 units are sold (point $T$).

Figure 7–4 **AN ELASTIC DEMAND CURVE**

When price falls, quantity demanded rises by a greater percentage, increasing the total expenditure. Thus when the price falls from $6 to $5, quantity demanded rises from 4 to 12, and total expenditure rises from $6 × 4 = $24 to $5 × 12 = $60.

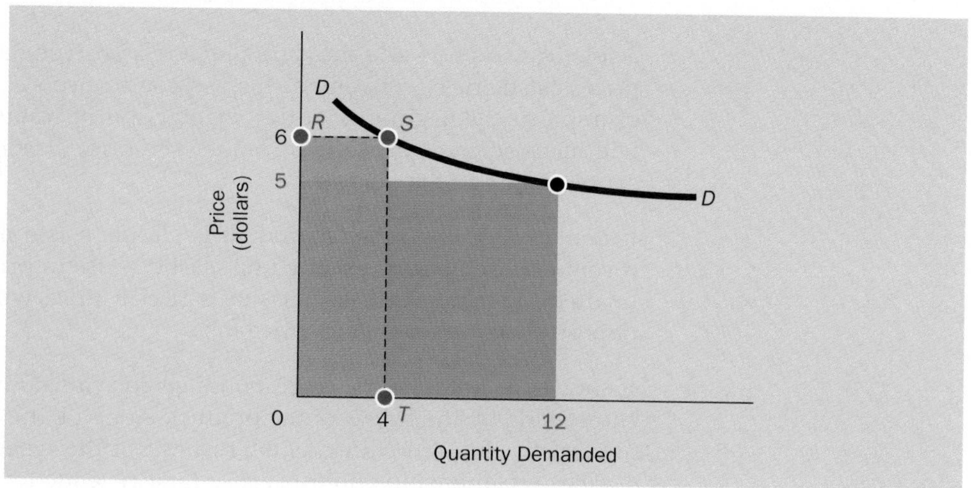


This discussion also indicates why a unit-elastic demand curve must have the shape depicted in Figure 7–3(d), hugging the axes closer and closer but never touching or crossing them. We have seen that when demand is unit-elastic, total expenditure must be the same at every point on the curve. It must be the same ($140) at point *S* and point *T* and point *U*. Suppose that at point *U* (or some other point), the demand curve were to touch the horizontal axis, meaning that the price was zero. Then total expenditure would be zero, not $140. Therefore, we conclude that if the demand curve is unit-elastic throughout, it can never cross the horizontal axis (where $P = 0$). By the same reasoning, it cannot cross the vertical axis (where $Q = 0$). Since the slope of the demand curve is negative, the curve simply must get closer and closer to the axes as one moves away from its middle points, as illustrated in Figure 7–3(d).

All of this indicates why elasticity of demand is so important for business decisions. A firm should not jump to the conclusion that an increase in price will add to its profits, for it may find that consumers take their revenge by cutting back on their purchases. In fact, if the demand curve is elastic, the firm will end up selling so many fewer units that its total revenue must actually fall, even though it makes more money than before on each unit it sells. In sum, whether a price rise or a price cut will be the better strategic move for a business firm depends very much on the elasticity of demand for its product.

## WHAT DETERMINES ELASTICITY OF DEMAND?

What kinds of goods have elastic demand curves, meaning that quantity demanded responds strongly to price? And what kinds of goods have inelastic demand curves? Several considerations are relevant.

### NATURE OF THE GOODS

*Necessities*, such as basic foodstuffs, have very inelastic demand curves, meaning they are not very responsive to changes in prices. For example, the quantity of potatoes demanded does not decline much when the price of potatoes rises. One study estimates that the price elasticity of demand for potatoes is as low as 0.3, meaning that when their price rises 10 percent, the quantity of potatoes purchased falls only 3 percent. In contrast, many *luxury goods*, such as restaurant meals, have rather elastic demand curves. One estimate is that the price elasticity of demand for restaurant meals is 1.6, so that a 10 percent rise in their price will cut purchases of such meals by 16 percent.

### AVAILABILITY OF CLOSE SUBSTITUTES

If consumers can easily get a good substitute, Y, for a product, X, they will switch readily to Y if the price of X rises. Thus the closer the substitutes for X that are available, the more elastic its demand will be. This factor is a critical determinant of elasticity. The demand for gasoline is inelastic because it is not easy to run a car without it. But the demand for *any particular brand* of gasoline is quite elastic, because another brand will work just as well. This example suggests a general principle: the demand for narrowly defined commodities (such as iceberg lettuce) is more elastic than the demand for more broadly defined commodities (such as vegetables).

### FRACTION OF INCOME ABSORBED

The fraction of income absorbed by a particular item is also important. Who will buy fewer shoelaces if the price of shoelaces rises? But many families will buy fewer cars if auto prices go up.

### PASSAGE OF TIME

This factor is relevant because the demand for many products is more elastic in the long run than in the short run. For example, when the price of home heating oil rose in the 1970s, some homeowners switched from oil heat to gas heat. But, at first, very few homeowners switched; so the demand for oil was quite inelastic. As time passed and more homeowners had the opportunity to purchase and install new equipment, the demand curve gradually became more elastic.

We will see in the appendix to this chapter that the price elasticity of demand is not easy to calculate statistically. But first we give some other examples of important elasticity measures.

## ELASTICITY IS A GENERAL CONCEPT

While we have spent much time studying the *price* elasticity of demand, elasticity is a very general measure of the responsiveness of one economic variable to another.

It is clear from what we have said that a firm will be very interested in the price elasticity of its demand curve. But this is not where its interest in demand ends, for as we have noted, quantity demanded depends on other things besides price. Business firms will be interested in consumer responsiveness to changes in these variables as well.

For example, we know that quantity demanded depends on the consumers' incomes. The firm's management will therefore want to know how much a change in consumer income affects the demand for its product. Fortunately, the elasticity measure can be helpful here too. An increase in consumer incomes clearly raises the quantity demanded of most goods. To measure the response we use the *income elasticity of demand*, defined as the ratio of the percentage change in quantity demanded to the percentage change in income.

Economists also use elasticity to measure other analogous responses. For example, to measure the response of quantity *supplied* to a change in price, economists use the *price elasticity of supply*, defined as the ratio of the percentage change in quantity supplied to the percentage change in price. The logic and analysis of all such elasticity concepts are, of course, perfectly analogous to those for price elasticity of demand.

## CROSS ELASTICITY OF DEMAND: SUBSTITUTES AND COMPLEMENTS

There are many products whose quantities demanded depend on the quantities and prices of other products. Certain goods make others more desirable. For example, cream and sugar increase the desirability of coffee, and vice versa. The same is true of mustard or ketchup and hamburgers. In some extreme cases, neither of two products ordinarily has any use without the other—an automobile and tires, a pair of shoes and shoelaces, and so on. Such goods, each of which makes the other more valuable, are called **complements**.

Two goods are called **COMPLEMENTS** if an increase in the quantity consumed of one increases the quantity demanded of the other, all other things remaining constant.

The demand curves of complements are interrelated; specifically, a rise in the price of coffee is likely to reduce the quantity of sugar demanded. Why? When coffee prices rise, less coffee will be drunk and therefore less sugar will be demanded. The opposite will be true of a fall in coffee prices. A similar relationship holds for other complementary goods.

At the other extreme, there are goods that make one another *less* valuable. These are called **substitutes**. Ownership of a motorcycle, for example, may decrease the desire for a bicycle. If your pantry is stocked with cans of tuna fish, you are less likely to rush out and buy cans of salmon. As you might expect, demand curves for substitutes are also interrelated, but in the opposite direction. When the price of motorcycles falls people may demand fewer bicycles, so the quantity demanded falls. When the price of salmon goes up, people eat more tuna.

Two goods are called **SUBSTITUTES** if an increase in the quantity consumed of one cuts the quantity demanded of the other, all other things remaining constant.

There is another elasticity measure which can be used to determine whether two products are substitutes or complements: their **cross elasticity of demand**. This measure is defined much like the ordinary price elasticity of demand, only instead of measuring the responsiveness of the quantity demanded of, say, coffee to a change in the price of coffee, cross elasticity of demand measures the responsiveness of the quantity demanded of coffee to a change in the price of, say, sugar. For example, if a 20 percent rise in the price of sugar reduces the quantity of coffee demanded by 5 percent (a change of *minus* 5 percent in quantity demanded), then the cross elasticity of demand will be

The **CROSS ELASTICITY OF DEMAND** for product X to a change in the price of another product, Y, is the ratio of the percentage change in quantity demanded of product X to the percentage change in the price of product Y that brings about the change in quantity demanded.

$$\frac{\%\text{ change in quantity of coffee demanded}}{\%\text{ change in sugar price}} = \frac{-5\%}{20\%} = -.25.$$

Obviously, cross elasticity is important for business firms. The producers of breakfast cereal X care a great deal about the cross elasticity of the demand for product X with respect to the price of rival cereal Y.

Using the cross elasticity of demand measure, we come to the following rule about complements and substitutes:

If two goods are substitutes, a rise in the price of one of them tends to raise the quantity demanded of the other; so their cross elasticities of demand will normally be positive. If two goods are complements, a rise in the price of one of them tends to decrease the quantity demanded of the other item, so their cross elasticities will normally be negative.[4]

This result is really a matter of common sense. If the price of a good goes up and there is a substitute available, people will tend to switch to the substitute. If the price of Japanese cameras goes up and the price of American cameras does not, at least some people will switch to the American product. Thus, a *rise* in the price of Japanese cameras causes a *rise* in the quantity of American cameras demanded. Both percentage changes are positive numbers and so their ratio, the cross elasticity of demand, is also positive.

On the other hand, if two goods are complements, a rise in the price of one will discourage its own use and will also discourage use of the complementary good. Automobiles and car radios are obviously complements. A large increase in the price of cars will depress the sale of cars, and this in turn will reduce the sale of car radios. Thus, a positive percentage change in the price of cars leads to a negative percentage change in the quantity of car radios demanded. The ratio of these numbers, the cross elasticity of demand for cars and radios, is therefore negative.

In practice, cross elasticity of demand is often used by courts of law (see the quotation from a U.S. Supreme Court decision at the beginning of this chapter) to measure whether a firm faces strong competition that can prevent the firm from overcharging consumers. If a rise in the price of firm X causes consumers of its product to switch in droves to competitive product Y, then the cross elasticity of demand for product Y with respect to the price of X is high. That, in turn, means that competition is really powerful enough to prevent firm X from raising its price arbitrarily. This is why cross elasticity is used so often in litigation before courts or governmental regulatory agencies when the degree of competition is an important issue.

## SHIFTS OF THE DEMAND CURVE: ADVERTISING, INCOME, AND PRICES OF COMPLEMENTS AND SUBSTITUTES

Demand is obviously a complex phenomenon. We have studied in detail the dependence of quantity demanded on price, and we have just seen that quantity demanded depends on other variables such as incomes and the prices of complementary and substitute products. Because of these "other variables," demand curves often do not retain the same shape and position as time passes. Instead, they shift about. And, as we learned in Chapter 4, shifts in demand curves have predictable consequences for both quantity and price.

But in public or business discussions, we often hear vague references to a "change in demand." By itself, this expression does not really mean anything. Remember from our discussion in Chapter 4 that it is vital to distinguish between a response to a price change (*which is a movement along the demand curve*) and a change in the relationship between price and quantity demanded (*which is a shift in the demand curve*).

[4]Because cross elasticities can be positive or negative, it is *not* customary to drop minus signs as we do when calculating the ordinary price elasticity of demand.

When price falls, quantity demanded generally responds by rising. This is a movement *along* the demand curve. On the other hand, an effective advertising campaign may mean that more goods will be bought at *any given price*. This would be a rightward *shift* in the demand curve. In fact, such a shift can be caused by a change in the value of any of the variables affecting quantity demanded other than price. While the distinction between a shift in a demand curve and a movement along it may at first seem trivial, it is a significant difference in practice and can cause confusion if it is ignored. So let us pause for a moment to consider how changes in some of these other variables shift the demand curve.

As an example, consider the effect of a change in consumer income on the demand curve for jeans. In Figure 7–5(a), the black curve $D_0D_0$ is the original demand curve for jeans. Now suppose that parents start sending more money to their needy sons and daughters in college. If the price of jeans were to stay the same, we would expect students to use some of their increased income to buy more jeans. For example, if the price were to remain at $25, quantity demanded might rise from 40,000 (point *R*) to 60,000 (point *S*). Similarly, if price had instead been $18, and had remained at that level, there might be a corresponding change from *T* to *U*. In other words, the rise in income would be expected to *shift* the entire demand curve to the right from $D_0D_0$ to $D_1D_1$. In exactly the same way, a fall in consumer income can be expected to lead to a leftward shift in the demand curve for jeans, as shown in Figure 7–5(b).

**Figure 7–5 SHIFTS IN A DEMAND CURVE**

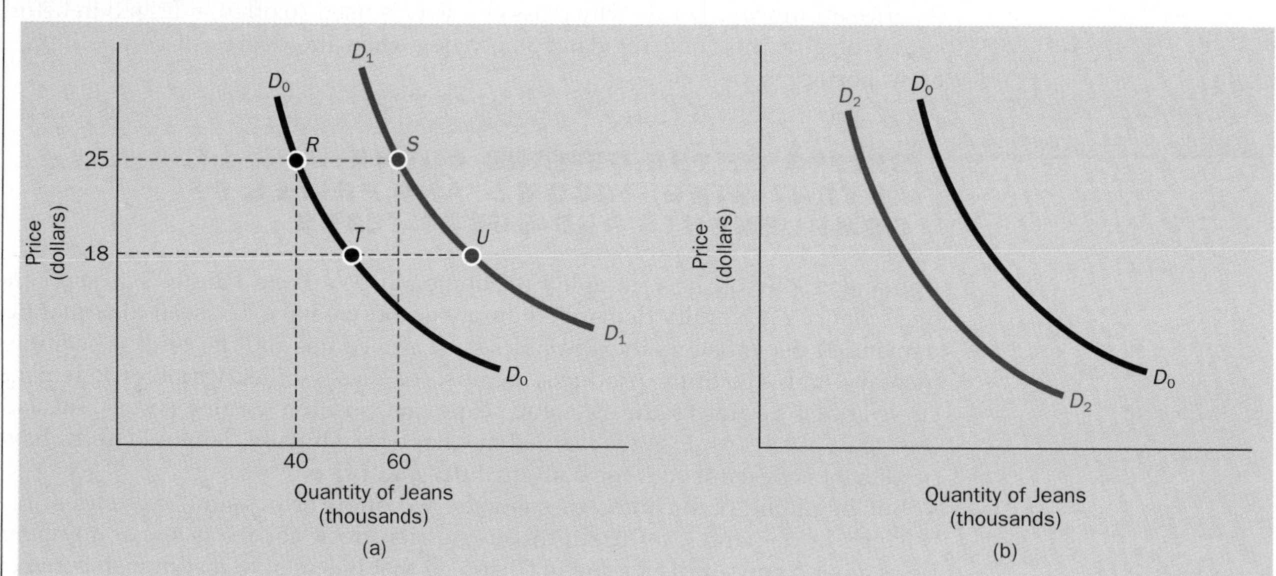


A rise in consumer income or an increase in advertising or a rise in the price of a competing product can all produce a rightward (outward) shift of the demand curve for a product, as depicted by the shift from the black curve $D_0D_0$ to the blue curve $D_1D_1$ in part (a). This means that at any fixed price (say, $25), the quantity of the product demanded will rise. (In the figure, it rises from 40,000 to 60,000 units.) Similarly, a fall in any of the variables, such as consumer income, will produce a leftward (inward) shift in the demand curve, as in part (b) of the figure.

Other variables that affect quantity demanded can be analyzed in the same way. For example, a rise in TV advertising for jeans might lead to a rightward (outward) shift in the demand curve for jeans, as in Figure 7–5(a). The same thing might occur if there were an increase in the price of a substitute product, such as skirts or corduroy trousers, because that would put jeans at a competitive advantage. That is, if two goods are substitutes, a rise in the price of one of them will tend to cause the demand curve for the other one to shift outward (to the right). Conversely, if a product that is complementary to jeans (perhaps a certain type of belt) becomes more expensive, we would expect the demand curve for jeans to shift to the left, as in Figure 7–5(b). In summary:

A demand curve is expected to shift to the right (outward) if consumer incomes rise, if tastes change in favor of the product, if substitute goods become more expensive, or if complementary goods become cheaper. A demand curve is expected to shift to the left (inward) if any of these factors goes in the opposite direction.

## THE TIME DIMENSION OF THE DEMAND CURVE AND DECISION MAKING

There is one more feature of a demand curve that does not show up on a graph but is important nevertheless. A demand curve indicates, at each possible price, the quantity of the good that is demanded *during a particular period of time*. That is, all the alternative prices considered in a demand curve must refer to *the same* time period. We do not compare a price of $10 for January with a price of $8 for September.

This feature imparts a peculiar character to the demand curve and makes statistical estimates more difficult to obtain because the data we actually observe show different prices and quantities only for different dates. Why, then, do economists adopt this apparently peculiar approach? The answer is that the time dimension of the demand curve is dictated inescapably by the logic of decision making.

When a business undertakes to find the best price for one of its products for, say, the next six months, it must consider the range of alternative prices available to it for that six-month period and the consequences of each possible choice. For example, if management is reasonably certain that the best price lies somewhere between $3.50 and $5.00, it should perhaps consider each of the four possibilities, $3.50, $4.00, $4.50, and $5.00, and estimate how much it can expect to sell at each of these potential prices during the six-month period in question. The result of these estimates may appear in a format similar to that shown in the table below.

| Potential price | $3.50 | $4.00 | $4.50 | $5.00 |
|---|---|---|---|---|
| Expected quantity demanded | 75,000 | 73,000 | 70,000 | 60,000 |

This table, which supplies management with what it needs to know to make an optimal pricing decision, also contains precisely the information an economist uses to draw a demand curve.

The demand curve describes a set of hypothetical responses to a set of potential prices, only one of which can actually be charged. All of the points on the demand curve refer to alternative possibilities for the *same* period of time—the period for which the decision is to be made.

Thus the demand curve as just described is no abstract notion that is useful primarily in academic discussion. Rather it offers precisely the information that businesses need for rational decision making. However, as already noted, the fact that all points on the demand curve are hypothetical possibilities, all for the same period of time, causes problems for statistical evaluation of demand curves. These problems are discussed in the appendix to this chapter.

## THE TWO ILLUSTRATIVE APPLICATIONS OF ELASTICITY ANALYSIS

This chapter started out with two illustrative issues. We are now in a position to show how the elasticity concept helps resolve them.

***Example I: The Glubstanian Tariff Problem.*** The story, it will be recalled, involved the imposition of a tax (a "revenue tariff") on imports of French cheese and British dishes in order to increase the Glubstanian government's tax revenue. Another tax was levied on imports of Russian vodka in order to reduce alcohol consumption. Both taxes failed in their purposes. The taxes on cheese and china brought in little revenue, and the tax on vodka did little to reduce its importation (but brought in a lot of revenue).

You should by now see the explanation. The Glubstanian government had simply failed to evaluate the elasticities of demand for the three products. Evidently, the demand curves for French cheese and English tableware were elastic. So the increases in their selling prices caused by the tax reduced imports sharply. Perhaps this was because close substitute products were available—for example, cheese from Italy and dishes from France. The consequence of this was that the tariffs produced little government revenue. Instead, they reduced quantities demanded sharply. In contrast, the demand for vodka was evidently very inelastic. So the rise in price resulting from the tax brought a sharp increase in government revenues, but little increase in Glubstanian sobriety.

***Example II: Polaroid v. Kodak.*** In 1989, there was a lengthy trial to determine how much money Kodak owed Polaroid for its patent infringement when it began to sell instant cameras and film in 1976 and sold them until 1986. The key issue was to estimate just how much profit Polaroid had lost as a result of Kodak's entry into this field. The concepts of price elasticity of demand and cross elasticity of demand both played crucial roles on three different issues.

Estimates of the price elasticity of demand were important in determining whether the explosive growth in instant camera sales from 1976 to 1979 was mainly attributable to the fall in price that resulted from Kodak's competition, or mainly to Kodak's reputation and its access to additional retail outlets. In the latter case, Polaroid might actually have benefited from Kodak's entry, rather than lost profit as a result.

After 1980, sales of instant cameras and film began to drop sharply. On this issue, it was *cross elasticity* of demand between instant and noninstant cameras (and film) that was crucial to the explanation. Why? Because, at the same time the decline in the instant camera market occurred, the prices of 35 millimeter cameras, film, developing, and printing all began to fall significantly. If the decrease in cost of 35 millimeter photography was the cause of the decline in Polaroid's overall sales, then it was not the fault of Kodak's instant photography activity. Consequently, the amount that Kodak would be required to pay to Polaroid would be significantly smaller. On the other hand, if the cross elasticity of demand between conventional photography prices and the demand for instant cameras and film was low, then the cause of the decline in Polaroid's sales might have been Kodak's patent-infringing activity—adding to the damage payments to which Polaroid was entitled.

The third elasticity issue in the case was raised at the beginning of the chapter. By how much would Polaroid's total revenue have been increased by the rise in film price that Polaroid claimed it would have adopted had not Kodak illegally competed with it? You now know that the crucial matter here was the price elasticity of demand for instant camera film. Polaroid tried to show that this elasticity figure was small because, in that case, the rise in price would have raised its revenues a great deal—meaning that Kodak had damaged it quite severely. Kodak, on the other hand, tried to show that the statistical evidence suggested that the elasticity of demand for instant film was large. For, in that case, a rise in price would have brought in little additional revenue and might possibly even have reduced it.

On the basis of its calculation of all of the elasticities it deemed relevant, Polaroid at one point claimed that Kodak was obligated to pay it $9 billion or more. Kodak claimed that it owed Polaroid only (!) something in the neighborhood of $450 million. Much was obviously at stake. The judge's verdict came out with a number very close to Kodak's figure.

## *Summary*

1. To measure the responsiveness of quantity demanded to price, we use the **elasticity of demand**, which is defined as the percentage change in quantity demanded divided by the percentage change in price.
2. If demand is **elastic** (elasticity greater than one), a rise in price will reduce total expenditure. If demand is **unit elastic** (elasticity equal to one), a rise in price will not change total expenditure. If demand is **inelastic** (elasticity less than one), a rise in price will increase total expenditure.
3. Demand is not a fixed number. Rather, it is a relationship showing how quantity demanded is affected by price and other pertinent influences. If one or more of these other variables change, the demand curve will shift.
4. Goods that make each other more desirable (hot dogs and mustard, wristwatches and watch straps) are called **complements**. Goods such that if we have more of one we usually want less of another (steaks and hamburgers, Coke and Pepsi) are called **substitutes**.
5. **Cross elasticity of demand** is defined as the percentage change in the quantity demanded of one good divided by the percentage change in the price of the other good. Two substitute products normally have a positive cross elasticity of demand. Two complementary products normally have a negative cross elasticity of demand.
6. A rise in the price of one of two substitute commodities can be expected to **shift the demand curve** of the other commodity to the right. A rise in the price of one of two complementary goods is apt to shift the other's demand curve to the left.
7. All points on a demand curve refer to the *same* time period—the time during which the price will be in effect.

## *Key Concepts and Terms*

(Price) elasticity of demand
Elastic, inelastic, and unit-elastic demand curves
Complements
Substitutes
Cross elasticity of demand
Shift in a demand curve

## *Questions for Review*

1. What variables besides price and advertising are likely to affect the quantity of a product that is demanded?
2. Describe the probable shifts in the demand curves for
   a. airplane trips when there is an improvement in the airplanes' on-time performance.
   b. automobiles when airplane fares rise.
   c. automobiles when gasoline prices rise.
   d. electricity when average temperature in the United States falls during a particular year. (Note: The demand curve for electricity in Maine and the demand curve for electricity in Florida should respond in different ways. Why?)
3. Taxes on particular goods discourage their consumption. Economists therefore say that such taxes "distort consumer demands." In terms of the elasticity of demand for the commodities in question, what sort of goods would you choose to tax if your objective were to
   a. Collect a large amount of tax revenue?
   b. Distort demand as little as possible?
   c. Discourage consumption of harmful commodities?
   d. Discourage production of polluting commodities?
4. Explain why elasticity of demand is measured in *percentages*.
5. Explain why the elasticity of demand formula normally eliminates minus signs.
6. Give examples of commodities whose demand you expect to be elastic and some you expect to be inelastic.
7. Explain why the elasticity of a straight-line demand curve varies from one part of the curve to another.
8. A rise in the price of a certain commodity from $15 to $20 reduces quantity demanded from 20,000 to 5,000 units. Calculate the price elasticity of demand.
9. If the price elasticity of demand for gasoline is 0.3, and the current price is $1.20 a gallon, what rise in the price of gasoline will reduce its consumption by 10 percent?
10. A rise in the price of a product whose demand is elastic will reduce the total revenue of the firm. Explain.
11. Name some things that will cause a demand curve to shift.
12. Which of the following product pairs would you expect to be substitutes and which would you expect to be complements?
    a. Shoes and sneakers.
    b. Gasoline and big cars.
    c. Bread and butter.
    d. Instant camera film and regular camera film.
13. For each of the previous product pairs, what would you guess about their cross elasticity of demand?
    a. Do you expect it to be positive or negative?
    b. Do you expect it to be a large or small number? Why?
14. Explain why the following statement is true. "A firm with a demand curve that is inelastic at its current output level can always increase its profits by raising its price and selling less." (*Hint*: Refer back to the discussion of elasticity and total expenditure on pages 177–78)

# *Appendix* STATISTICAL ANALYSIS OF DEMAND RELATIONSHIPS

The peculiar time dimension of the demand curve, in conjunction with the fact that many variables other than price can influence quantity demanded, makes it surprisingly hard to discover the shape of the demand curve from statistical data. It can be done, but the task is full of booby traps and can usually be carried out successfully only by using advanced statistical methods. Let us see why these two characteristics of demand curves cause problems.

The most obvious way to go about estimating a demand curve statistically is to collect a set of figures on prices and quantities sold in different periods, like those given in Table 7–2. These points can then be plotted on a diagram with price and quantity on the axes, as shown in Figure 7–6. One can then proceed to draw in a line (the dotted line *TT*) that connects these points reasonably well and that appears to be the demand curve. Unfortunately, line *TT*, which summarizes the historical data, may bear no relationship to the demand curve we are after.

You may notice at once that the prices and quantities represented by the historical points in Figure 7–6 refer to different periods of time and that they all have been *actual*, not *hypothetical*, prices and quantities at some time. The distinction is not insignificant. Over the period covered by the historical data, the true demand curve, which is what we re-

*Table* 7–2 HISTORICAL DATA ON PRICE AND QUANTITY

| | JANUARY | FEBRUARY | MARCH | APRIL | MAY |
|---|---|---|---|---|---|
| Quantity sold | 95,000 | 91,500 | 95,000 | 90,000 | 91,000 |
| Price | $7.20 | $8.00 | $7.70 | $8.00 | $8.20 |

*Figure* 7–6 PLOT OF HISTORICAL DATA ON PRICE AND QUANTITY

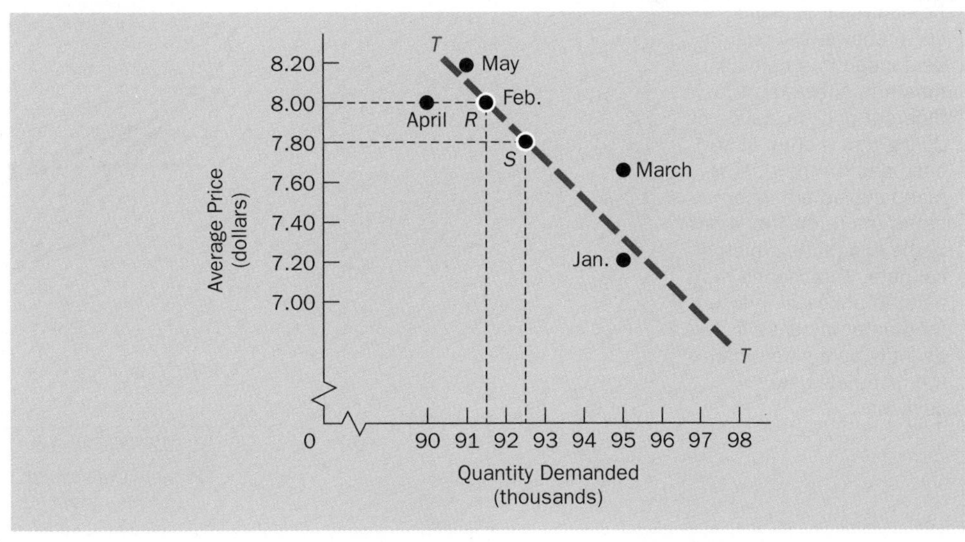


The dots labeled Jan., Feb., and so on represent actual prices and quantities sold in the months indicated. The blue line *TT* is drawn to approximate the dots as closely as possible.

ally want, may well have shifted because some of the other variables affecting quantity demanded changed.

What actually happened may be as shown in Figure 7–7. Here we see that in January the demand curve was given by *JJ*, but by February the curve had shifted to *FF*, by March to *MM*, and so on. That is, there was a separate and distinct demand curve for each of the relevant months, and none of them need have any resemblance to the plot of historical data, *TT*.

In fact, the slope of the historical plot curve, *TT*, can be very different from the slopes of the true underlying demand curves, as is the case in Figure 7–7. This means that the decision maker can be seriously misled if she selects her price on the basis of the historical data. She may, for example, think that demand is quite insensitive to changes in price (as line *TT* in the diagram seems to indicate), and so she may reject the possibility of a price reduction when in fact the true demand curves show that a price reduction will increase quantity demanded substantially.

For example, if in February she were to charge a price of $7.80 rather than $8, the historical plot would suggest to her a rise in quantity demanded of only 1000 units. (Compare point *R*, with sales of 91,500 units, and point *S*, with sales of 92,500 units, in Figure 7–6.) However, as can be seen in Figure 7–7, the true demand curve for February (line *FF* in Figure 7–7) promises her an increment in sales of 2500 units (from point *R*, with sales of 91,500, to point *W*, with sales of 94,000) if she reduces February's price from $8 to $7.80. A manager who based her decision on the historical plot, rather than on the true demand curve, might be led into serious error.

In light of this discussion, it is astonishing how often in practice one encounters demand studies that use apparently sophisticated techniques to arrive at no more than a graph of historical data. One must not allow oneself to be misled by the apparent complexity of the procedures employed to fit a curve to historical data. If these merely plot historical quantities against historical prices, the true underlying demand curve is unlikely to be found.

## AN ILLUSTRATION: DID THE ADVERTISING PROGRAM WORK?

Some years ago one of the nation's largest producers of packaged foods conducted a statistical study to determine the effectiveness of its advertising expenditures, which amounted to nearly $100 million a year. A company statistician collected year-by-

**Figure 7–7** **PLOT OF HISTORICAL DATA AND TRUE DEMAND CURVES FOR JANUARY, FEBRUARY, AND MARCH**

An analytical demand curve shows how quantity demanded in a particular month is affected by the different prices considered during that month. In the case shown, the true demand curves are much flatter (more elastic) than is the line plotting historical data. This means that a cut in price will induce a far greater increase in quantity demanded than the historical data suggest.

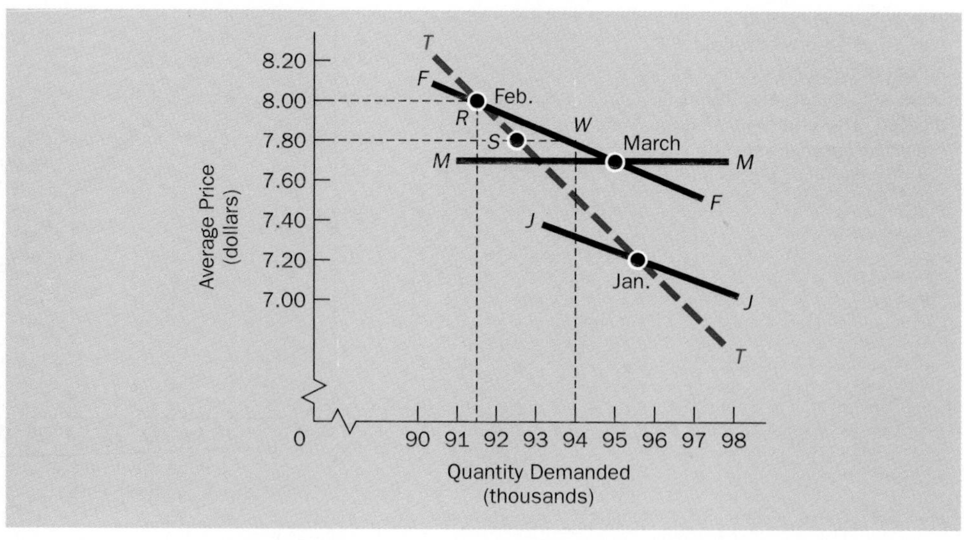

year figures on company sales and advertising outlays and discovered, to his delight, that they showed a remarkably close relationship to one another: quantity demanded rose as advertising rose. The trouble was that the relationship seemed just too perfect. In economics, data about demand and any one of the elements that influence it almost never make such a neat pattern. Human tastes and other pertinent influences are just too variable to permit such regularity.

Suspicious company executives asked one of the authors of this book to examine the analysis. A little thought showed that the suspiciously close statistical relationship between sales and advertising expenditure resulted from a disregard for the principles just presented. The investigator had in fact constructed a graph of *historical* data on sales and advertising expenditure, analogous to *TT* in Figures 7–6 and 7–7 and therefore not necessarily similar to the truly relevant relationship.

The stability of the relationship actually arose from the fact that, in the past, the company had based its advertising outlays on its sales, automatically allocating a fixed percentage of its sales revenues to advertising. The *historical* advertising-demand relationship therefore described only the company's budgeting practices, not the effectiveness of its advertising program. If management had used this curve in planning its advertising campaigns, it might have made some regrettable decisions. *Moral*: Avoid the use of historical curves like *TT* in making economic decisions.

Chapter 

# THE CONSUMER'S CHOICE: ORIGINS OF THE DEMAND CURVES

*Everything is worth what its purchaser will pay for it.*

**PUBLILIUS SYRUS (1ST CENTURY B.C.)**

The market demand curves we have been using in previous chapters depend on choices made by individual consumers. Here, we explore the logic underlying those choices. Just as Chapter 6 undertook to explain the economic relationships that underlie the cost curves, we will now complete the story by probing the underpinnings of demand curves. ¶ In contrast with Chapters 4 and 7, where we dealt with curves describing the combined demand of *all consumers in the market*, here we will focus upon the demand curve of *an individual consumer*. Since such a demand curve tells us how much of a good a consumer wants to purchase at each possible price, its origins must in some sense rest in consumer psychology. But since economists claim no special qualifications for making deep pronouncements about consumer psychology, our exploration will not go very far below the surface. It will, however, describe some powerful tools used in the analysis of consumer choice and cast some light on a number of important issues, including the consequences of scarcity for consumer behavior. Here, as throughout the book, marginal analysis will prove to be the primary tool of the analysis.

The chapter ends with a discussion of the relation of the demand curve for an entire market to the demand curves of the individual purchasers who participate in that market, showing explicitly how the market demand curves of earlier chapters can be determined from the individuals' demand curves.

### PARADOX: SHOULD BREAD BE WORTH MORE THAN CAVIAR?

When Adam Smith was lecturing at the University of Glasgow in the 1760s, he introduced the study of demand by posing a puzzle. Common sense, he said, suggests that the price of a commodity must somehow depend on what that good is worth to consumers—on the amount of *utility* that commodity offers. Yet, Smith pointed out, there are cases which suggest that a good's utility apparently has little influence on its price.

Smith's example was diamonds and water. It can be brought up to date, and aligned with the Eastern European theme of this section of the book, by considering instead two food products that everyone associates with Russia—bread and caviar. In line with Smith's argument, we note that bread (which is called the "staff of life" because it is regarded as the most basic food) is of enormous value to most consumers, but generally sells at a very low price, while caviar, on the other hand, may sell for $500 per pound even though it hardly constitutes anything resembling a necessity. In a few pages we will be in a position to see how marginal analysis helps to resolve the paradox.

## TOTAL AND MARGINAL UTILITY

In the American economy, millions of consumers make millions of decisions every day. You decide to buy a movie ticket instead of a paperback novel. Your roommate decides to buy two pounds of imported cheese rather than one or three. How are these decisions made?

Economists have constructed a simple theory of consumer choice based on the hypothesis that each consumer spends his or her income in the way that yields the greatest amount of satisfaction, or *utility*. This seems a reasonable starting point, since it says little more than that people do what they prefer. But, to make the theory operational, we need a way to measure utility.

A century ago, economists envisioned utility as an indicator of the pleasure a person derives from the consumption of some set of goods, and they thought that utility could be measured directly in some kind of psychological units (sometimes called "utils"), after somehow reading the consumer's mind. But gradually it came to be realized that this was an unnecessary and, perhaps, impossible task. How many utils did you get from the last movie you saw? You probably cannot answer that question because you have no idea what a util is. And neither does anyone else.

But you may be able to answer a different question like, "How many hamburgers would you give up to get that movie ticket?" If you answer "three," we still do not know how many utils you get from seeing a film. But we do know that you get more than you get from a single hamburger. When the issue is approached in this way, hamburgers, rather than utils, become the unit of measurement. We can say that the utility of a movie (to you) is three hamburgers.

Early in the twentieth century, economists concluded that this more indirect way of measuring utility was all they needed to build a theory of consumer choice.

**Table 8–1** TOTAL AND MARGINAL UTILITY OF CHICKEN (MEASURED IN MONEY TERMS)

| (1) QUANTITY (*Q*) (kilos per month) | (2) TOTAL UTILITY (TU) (in dollars) | (3) MARGINAL UTILITY (MU)* = (ΔTU/Δ*Q*) (in dollars) | (4) POINT FIGURE 8–1 |
|---|---|---|---|
| 0 | 00 | | *A* |
| 1 | 6.00 | 6.00 | *B* |
| 2 | 11.60 | 5.60 | *C* |
| 3 | 16.00 | 4.40 | *D* |
| 4 | 19.60 | 3.60 | *E* |
| 5 | 21.40 | 1.80 | *F* |
| 6 | 22.20 | .80 | *G* |
| 7 | 22.60 | .40 | *H* |
| 8 | 2.26 | 0 | |

*Each entry in this column is the difference between successive entries in column (2)

We can measure the utility of a movie ticket by asking how much of some other commodity (like hamburgers) you are willing to give up for it. Any commodity will do for this purpose. But the simplest choice, and the one we will use in this book, is money.[1]

The **TOTAL UTILITY** of a quantity of goods to a consumer (measured in money terms) is the maximum amount of money he or she is willing to give in exchange for it.

Thus we are led to define the **total utility** of some bundle of goods to some consumer as *the largest sum of money he will voluntarily give up in exchange for it*. For example, suppose Vladimir, one of the customers of Ivana and Ivan's poultry farm, is considering purchasing six kilos of chicken during the next month. He has determined that he will not buy them if they cost more than $22.20, but he will buy them if they cost $22.20 or less.[2] Then the *total utility* of six kilos of chicken to him is $22.20—the maximum amount he is willing to spend to have them.

The **MARGINAL UTILITY** of a commodity to a consumer (measured in money terms) is the maximum amount of money he or she is willing pay *for one more unit* of it.

Total utility measures the benefit Vladimir derives from his purchases. It is total utility that really matters. But to understand which decisions most effectively promote *total* utility we must consider the related concept of **marginal utility**. By now it should be obvious that this term refers to *the addition to total utility that an individual derives by consuming one more unit of any good*.

Table 8–1 helps clarify the distinction between marginal and total utility and shows how the two are related. The first two columns show how much *total* utility (measured in money terms) Vladimir derives from various quantities of chicken, ranging from zero to eight kilos per month. For example, a single kilo is worth (no more than) $6 to him, two kilos are worth $11.60, in total, and so on. The *marginal* utility is the *difference* between any two successive total utility figures.

[1]NOTE TO INSTRUCTORS: You will recognize that, while not using the terms, we are distinguishing here between *neoclassical cardinal utility* and *ordinal utility*. Moreover, throughout the book, *"marginal utility in money terms"* (or "money marginal utility") is simply used as a synonym for the *marginal rate of substitution* between money and the commodity in question.

[2]It seems strange to use dollars to calculate chicken prices in the former Soviet Union. However, as was pointed out in Chapter 5, inflation in these countries is so rapid, that prices expressed in local currency simply cannot be kept up to date, and so many transactions are now actually carried out in terms of dollars, as in the text here.

For example, if Vladimir already has three kilos (worth $16 to him), an *additional* kilo brings his total utility up to $19.60. His marginal utility is thus the difference between the two, or $3.60.

*Remember*: Whenever we use the terms *total utility* and *marginal utility*, we are defining them in terms of the consumer's willingness to part with money for the commodity—not in some unobservable (and imaginary) psychological units.

## THE "LAW" OF DIMINISHING MARGINAL UTILITY

With these definitions, we can now propose a simple hypothesis about consumer tastes: The more of a good a consumer has, the less will be the *marginal* utility of an additional unit.

In general, this is a plausible proposition, and it is utilized widely in economics. The idea is based on the assertion that every person has a hierarchy of uses to which he or she will put a particular commodity. All of these uses are valuable, but some are more valuable than others. Let's consider chicken again. Vladimir may use chicken meat to feed his children, to feed his wife and his mother, or to give to a brother-in-law for whom he has no deep affection. If he has only one kilo per month, it will all go to the children. The second and third may be shared with mother and wife. If a fourth kilo is available, Vladimir may join in with the other adults in eating the meat. A fifth kilo, if purchased, may lead to an invitation to the brother-in-law, with his large appetite, to join the family at dinner.

The point is obvious. Each kilo of chicken contributes something to the satisfaction of the needs of Vladimir's household. But each additional kilo contributes less (relative to money) than its predecessor because the use to which it can be put has a lower priority. This, in essence, is the logic behind the **"law" of diminishing marginal utility**.

The **"LAW" OF DIMINISHING MARGINAL UTILITY** asserts that additional units of a commodity are worth less and less to a consumer in money terms. As the individual's consumption increases, the marginal utility of each additional unit declines.

The third column of Table 8–1 illustrates this concept. The marginal utility (abbreviated MU) of the first kilo of chicken is $6; that is, Vladimir is willing to pay *up to* $6 for the first kilo. The second kilo is worth no more than $5.60, the third kilo only $4.40, and so on until, for the sixth kilo, Vladimir is willing to pay only 80 cents (the MU of the sixth kilo is 80 cents).

The numbers in the first and third columns in the table are shown in Figure 8–1 by points *A*, *B*, *C*, and so on. We note that the graph of marginal utility is negatively sloped; this again illustrates how marginal utility diminishes as the quantity of product rises.

The assumption upon which this "law" is based is plausible for most consumers and for most commodities. But, like most laws, there are exceptions. For some people, the more they have of some good that is particularly significant to them, the more they want. The needs of alcoholics and stamp collectors are good examples. The stamp collector who has a few stamps may consider the acquisition of one more to be mildly amusing. The person who has a large and valuable collection may be prepared to go to the ends of the earth for another stamp. Similarly, the alcoholic who finds a dry martini quite pleasant when he first starts drinking may find one more to be absolutely irresistible once he has already consumed four or five. Economists, however, generally treat such cases of *increasing marginal utility* as anomalies. For most goods and most people, marginal utility probably declines as consumption increases.

Table 8–1 illustrates another noteworthy relationship. We notice that as more and more units of the commodity are bought, that is, as we move further down the table, the total utility numbers keep getting larger and larger, while the marginal utility numbers get smaller and smaller. The reasons should now be

Figure 8–1 A TYPICAL MARGINAL UTILITY OR DEMAND CURVE: VLADIMIR'S DEMAND FOR CHICKEN

This demand curve is derived from the consumer's table of marginal utilities by following the optimal purchase rule. The points in the graph correspond to the numbers in Table 8–1.

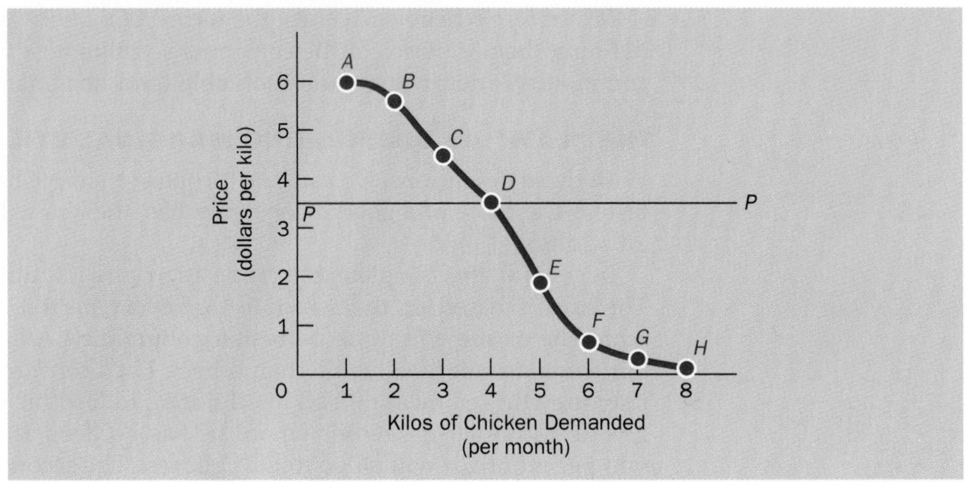


fairly straightforward. The marginal utility numbers keep declining as a result of the "law" of diminishing marginal utility, as was just explained. But *total* utility keeps rising, so long as marginal utility is positive. A woman who owns ten business suits, other things being equal, is better off (she has higher total utility) than a woman who possesses only nine, so long as the MU of the 10th suit is positive. In summary

As a rule, the more of a commodity a consumer acquires, the greater will be her total utility and the smaller her marginal utility from that good, all other things being equal. In particular, when a commodity is very scarce we can expect it to have a high marginal utility, even though it may provide little total utility.

## THE OPTIMAL PURCHASE RULE

Now let us put the concept of marginal utility to work in analyzing consumer choice. Every consumer has a limited amount of money to spend. There are always choices to be made among the many commodities that compete for the consumer's dollar. Which items will he buy, and in what quantities? The theory of consumer choice is based on the hypothesis that he will spend his money on some commodity, say, chicken, in the way that *maximizes* his net gain in *total utility* from that purchase. For, in buying a quantity, $Q$, of that commodity at its current price, $P$, the consumer gains the utility that this amount of the product offers him, but in exchange he gives up the quantity of money, $P$, for each unit of the commodity that he buys. That is, $P$ is the cost of an additional unit of the product to the consumer—it is the product's marginal cost. Consequently, the hypothesis that the consumer chooses in a way that makes the largest net contribution to total utility, leads to the following **optimal purchase rule**:

It always pays the consumer to buy more of any commodity whose marginal utility (measured in money) exceeds its price (the marginal cost of the commodity to the consumer), and less of any commodity whose marginal utility is less than its price. When possible, the consumer should buy the quantity of each good at which price ($P$) and marginal utility (MU) are exactly equal, that is, at which

$$\text{MU} = P,$$

because only these quantities will maximize the *net total utility* he gains from his purchases, given the fact that the money he has available must be divided among all the goods he buys.[3]

Put another way, the consumer is trying to maximize the money value of the total utility he derives from his purchase *minus* the amount he must spend to make that purchase. Economists give the name **consumer's surplus** to that difference, that is, to the net gain in total utility that his purchase brings him. Thus, the consumer is trying to make the purchase decisions that maximize

$$\text{consumer's surplus} = \text{total utility (in money terms)} - \text{total expenditure.}$$

Thus, just as a firm can be taken to maximize total profit = total revenue − total cost, the consumer can be assumed to maximize consumer's surplus, that is, the difference between total utility of the purchased commodity and the amount that is spent on it. Later in the chapter, more will be said about the concept of consumer's surplus. But for now, let us see what the consumer must do to maximize this quantity.

By now, it should be obvious that we must use marginal analysis for this purpose. By analogy with the discussions found in the three preceding chapters, the principles of marginal analysis tell us that to maximize the difference between the total utility of good X and the total expenditure on good X, we must make the *marginal* utility equal to the marginal expenditure on X. But it should be obvious that the consumer's marginal expenditure on X is simply the price; so we obtain in a different way than before the optimal purchase rule for a consumer:

The consumer will have purchased the optimal quantity of some good only if the money marginal utility of that good is equal to its price, or MU = $P$.

Notice that, as usual, while our concern is with *total* utility and total expenditure, the rule is framed in terms of *marginal* utility and price (= marginal expenditure). Marginal utility and marginal expenditure are not important for their own sakes, but rather as the instruments used to calculate the level of purchases that maximizes total utility minus total expenditure.

To see why this rule works, refer back to the table and graph of marginal utilities of chicken (Table 8–1 and Figure 8–1). Suppose that Ivana and Ivan's chicken is *retailing* in the town market for $3.60 a kilo (line *PP* in the graph) and Vladimir considers buying only two kilos. We see that this is not a wise decision, because the marginal utility of the third kilo of chicken ($4.40, point C) is greater than its $3.60 price. If Vladimir were to increase his purchase to three kilos, the additional kilo would cost $3.60 cents but yield $4.40 in marginal utility; thus the additional purchase would bring a clear net gain of 80 cents. Obviously, at the $3.60 price he is better off with three kilos of chicken than with two.

---

[3]We can equate a dollar price with marginal utility only because we measure marginal utility in money terms (or, as the matter is more usually put by economists, because we deal with the marginal rate of substitution of money for the commodity in question). If marginal utility were measured in some psychological units not directly translatable into money terms, a comparison of $P$ and MU would have no meaning. However, MU could also be measured in terms of any commodity other than money. (Example: How much bread is Vladimir willing to trade for an additional kilo of chicken?)

Similarly, at this price, five kilos (point *E*) is *not* an optimal purchase because the \$1.80 marginal utility of the fifth kilo is less than its \$3.60 price. Vladimir would be better off with only four kilos, since that would save \$3.60 with only a \$1.80 loss in utility—a net gain of \$3.60 − \$1.80 = \$1.80 from the decision to buy one kilo less. In sum, our rule for optimal purchases tells us that Vladimir should *not* end up buying a quantity at which MU is higher than price (points like *A*, *B*, and *C*) because a larger purchase would make him better off. Similarly, he should not end up at points *E*, *F*, *G*, and *H*, at which MU is below price because he would be better off buying less. Rather, Vladimir should buy four kilos (point *D*), where $P$ = MU.

It should be noted that price is an objective, observable figure determined by the market, while marginal utility is subjective and reflects the tastes of the consumer. Since the consumer lacks the power to influence the price, he must adjust his purchases to make the marginal utility of each good equal to the price given by the market.

It may strike you that the preceding discussion does not really represent the thought processes of any consumer you have ever met. Buyers' decisions are made much more instinctively and without any formal calculation of marginal utilities, or anything like them. That is true, and yet it need not undermine the pertinence of the discussion. When you give a command to your computer, you actually activate some electronic switches and start them on some operations in what is referred to as binary code. Most computer users do not know they are doing this and do not care. Yet they are doing it nevertheless, and the analysis of the computation process does not misrepresent the fact by describing this sequence. In the same way, if the shopper divides his purchasing power among the various available purchase options in a way that yields the largest possible satisfaction from his money, he *must* be following the rules of marginal analysis, even though he is totally unaware of this. Still, there is growing experimental evidence that points out some persistent deviations in reality from the picture of consumer behavior provided by marginal analysis (see box on page 197).

## FROM MARGINAL UTILITY TO THE DEMAND CURVE

We can use the optimal purchase rule to show that the "law" of diminishing marginal utility implies that demand curves typically slope downward to the right, that is, they have negative slopes.[4] For example, it is possible to use the list of marginal utilities in Table 8–1 to determine how much chicken Vladimir would buy at any particular price. Table 8–2 gives several alternative prices, and the optimal purchase quantity corresponding to each. (To make sure you understand the logic behind the optimal purchase rule, verify that the entries in the right-hand column of Table 8–2 are in fact correct.) This *demand schedule* is depicted graphically in Vladimir's *demand curve* shown in Figure 8–1. This demand curve is simply the blue marginal utility curve. You can see that it has the characteristic negative slope commonly associated with demand curves.

Let us examine the logic underlying the negatively sloped demand curve a bit more carefully. If Vladimir is purchasing the optimal amount of chicken, and then the price falls, he will find that his marginal utility of chicken is now above the suddenly reduced price. For example, Table 8–1 tells us that at a price of \$4.40

[4]If you need to review the concept of slope, turn back to pages 20–24 in the appendix to Chapter 1.

*At The* **FRONTIER**

## DO CONSUMERS REALLY BEHAVE "RATIONALLY" AND MAXIMIZE UTILITY?

Recent experimental studies by groups of economists and psychologists have questioned whether consumers really behave as "rationally" as the optimal purchase rule describes. Their results, obtained by asking groups of respondents to fill out questionnaires about how they would act in various hypothetical situations, have revealed a variety of "anomalies" in behavior which seem to contradict the assumptions of calculating rationality that underlie the economist's model. The following two examples illustrate what seem to be violations of the optimal purchase rule.

In both cases, two groups of respondents were offered what are really identical options, presumably yielding similar marginal utilities. Yet, depending on differences in some irrelevant information that was also provided to the participants in the experiments, the two groups made very different choices.

. . . One group of subjects received the information in parentheses and the other received the information in brackets . . . .

[*Problem 1*]. Imagine that you are about to purchase . . . a calculator for ($15)[$125]. The calculator salesman informs you that the calculator you wish to buy is on sale for ($10)[$120] at the other branch of the store, located a 20-minute drive away. Would you make the trip to the other store?

. . . The responses to the two versions of this problem were quite different. When the calculator cost $125 only 29% of the subjects said they would make the trip, whereas 68% said they would go when the calculator cost only $15.

Thus, in the first problem the two groups were told they could save $5 on the price of a product if they took a 20 minute trip to another store. Yet, depending on whether the product was a cheap or an expensive one, the number of persons willing to make the trip to save the same amount of money was very different.

[*Problem 2*]. You are lying on the beach on a hot day. All you have to drink is ice water. For the last hour you have been thinking about how much you would enjoy a nice cold bottle of your favorite brand of beer. A companion gets up to go make a phone call and offers to bring back a beer from the only nearby place where beer is sold (a fancy resort hotel) [a small, run-down grocery store]. He says that the beer may be expensive and so asks how much you are willing to pay for the beer. He says that he will buy the beer if it costs as much or less than the price you state, but if it costs more than the price you state he will not buy it. You trust your friend and there is no possibility of bargaining with (the bartender) [the store owner].

When this questionnaire was administered to the participants in an executive education program, the median responses were $2.65 in the hotel version and $1.50 in the grocery store version.

Thus, in the second example, the two groups were offered a chance to buy one can of the same brand of beer. Yet, the price they were willing to pay differed very much, depending on the type of outlet from which it was to be delivered.

SOURCE: Richard H. Thaler, *Quasi Rational Economics*, New York: Russell Sage Foundation, 1992, pp. 148–150.

**Table 8–2 LIST OF OPTIMAL QUANTITIES OF CHICKEN FOR VLADIMIR TO PURCHASE AT ALTERNATIVE PRICES**

| PRICE* (in dollars) | QUANTITY OF PURCHASE (kilos per month) |
|---|---|
| .40 | 7 |
| .86 | 6 |
| 1.80 | 5 |
| 3.60 | 4 |
| 4.40 | 3 |
| 5.60 | 2 |
| 6.00 | 1 |

*Note that for simplicity of explanation the prices shown have been chosen to equal the marginal utilities in Table 8–1. In-between prices would make the optimal choices involve fractions of a kilo (say 2.6 kilos).

per kilo it is optimal to buy three kilos, because the marginal utility (MU) of the fourth kilo is $3.60. But, if price is reduced to anything less than $3.60, it then pays to purchase the fourth kilo because its MU exceeds its price. This additional kilo of chicken will lower the marginal utility of the next (fifth) kilo of chicken (to $1.80 in the example), and so if the price is above $1.80 it will not pay the consumer to buy that fifth kilo, just as prescribed in the optimal purchase rule.

Note the critical role of the "law" of diminishing marginal utility. If *P* falls, a consumer who wishes to maximize total utility will see to it that MU falls. According to the "law" of diminishing marginal utility, the only way to do this is to increase the quantity purchased.

While this explanation is a bit abstract and mechanical, it can easily be rephrased in practical terms. We have noted that the various uses to which an individual puts a commodity have different priorities. For Vladimir, giving chicken to his children has a higher priority than using the chicken to feed the adults in the family. If the price of chicken is high, Vladimir will buy only enough for the high-priority uses—those that offer a high marginal utility. When price declines, however, it pays to purchase more of the good—enough for some low-priority uses. This is the essence of the analysis. It tells us that the same assumption about consumer psychology underlies both the "law" of diminishing marginal utility and the negative slope of the demand curve. They are really two different ways of describing the assumed attitudes of consumers.

## CONSUMER CHOICE AS A TRADE-OFF

The optimal purchase rule has been expressed as a decision about how much of some *one* commodity to buy. However, lurking behind this decision is the scarcity of income that turns every such decision into a trade-off. Given the consumer's limited income, a decision to buy a new car may mean that some travel will have to be given up, or the purchase of some furniture will have to be postponed. The purchase of a dozen video tapes may mean fewer trips to the movies. The money that the consumer gives up when she makes a purchase—her expenditure on that purchase—simply represents the true underlying cost to her. That real cost is the *opportunity cost* of the purchase—the commodities she must give up as a result of the purchase decision in question.

Any decision to buy must involve such a trade-off. That is the consequence of the scarcity that constrains any and all economic decisions. Even a multimillionaire faces such trade-offs, which are very real, even if they do not make us sorry for her. If she decides to buy a factory, she cannot afford to buy the office building in which she had previously been planning to invest.

This last example has one other important implication. The trade-off resulting from a consumer's purchase decision does not always involve giving up another consumers' good. Instead, it may be an investment opportunity or something else that has to be forgone as a result. Here is an important example:

***Consumption versus Saving*** A significant trade-off facing most consumers is that between consumption now and consumption later. A decision to cut down consumption now and to put the money into the bank means that the consumer will be wealthier one year from now because of the interest earned. This means that he will be able to afford more consumers' goods at that future date. But the opportunity cost of that enhanced future consumption will be the consumption he must give up in exchange today.

Thus, every purchase decision entails a trade-off. The trade-off requires the consumer to balance the benefits offered by two bundles of commodities or two other items between which she must choose. If she is buying two goods, X and Y, optimality requires that the purchase of an *additional* dollar's worth of X contribute just as much utility as does a dollar's worth of Y. This is another way of saying that the opportunity cost incurred when she spends an additional dollar on X is the utility of the amount of Y she could have gotten by spending that dollar on the latter.

## CONSUMER'S SURPLUS: THE NET GAIN FROM A PURCHASE

**CONSUMER'S SURPLUS** is the difference between the amount that the quantity of commodity *X* purchased is worth to the consumer and the amount that the market requires the consumer to pay for that quantity of *X*.

Earlier, we discussed the concept of *consumer's surplus,* taking the goal of the consumer in making a purchase decision to be to try to get as large a surplus as possible. There is, however, something counterintuitive about the notion that you receive a sort of free bonus, a *surplus,* whenever you acquire some good by buying it or swapping something for it. How can this be true, particularly for those goods whose prices seem to be outrageous? And how can a fair exchange—a swap—possibly produce a surplus for *both* parties? It used to be thought that neither party to a fair exchange can make a net gain, because each must pay the other just what the good is worth. But this view of the matter really makes no sense. If neither Naomi nor Alex makes a net gain from a trade, why would she or he take the time and trouble to carry out the transaction? Economists recognized several centuries ago that, whenever an exchange is entirely voluntary and there is no cheating or misrepresentation, then there must be a net gain for *both* parties. *There must be mutual gains from trade.*

That sounds too good to be true. Suppose Naomi gives Alex four books and gets two pounds of apples in exchange. No additional goods are created in the process. Yet, magically, both end up better off than when they began. How can this be so? The explanation is simple. It is true that they make no overall gain in the *physical quantities* of the commodities; they end up with as many books and apples, between them, as they possessed to begin with. What *has* increased, however, is the total *utility* that each of them enjoys. If Naomi had read the books and had no desire to reread them, and if Alex had so many apples that they were in danger of rotting, then the source of the mutual gain would be clear. But this can also happen where the circumstances are less extreme. All that is necessary is that Naomi like the two pounds of apples more than the four books, and that the opposite be true for Alex. But this must always be so in a voluntary trade. Otherwise one of the parties would refuse to participate.

The same must be true when the consumer makes a *voluntary* purchase from a supermarket or an appliance store. The consumer must expect a net gain from the transaction, or else he will simply not bother to buy. Even if the seller overcharges, by some standard, that will reduce the size of the consumer's net gain, but it cannot eliminate it altogether. If the seller is so greedy as to charge a price that wipes out the net gain altogether, the punishment will fit the crime. The consumer will refuse to buy, and the greedy seller's would-be gains will never materialize.

## RESOLVING THE CAVIAR–BREAD PARADOX

We can now use marginal utility analysis to solve the paradox that caviar is very expensive while bread is comparatively very cheap, even though bread seems to offer far more utility. The resolution of the caviar–bread paradox is based on the distinction between marginal and total utility.

The *total* utility of bread—its role as the "staff of life"—is indeed much higher than that of caviar. But price, as we have seen, is not related directly to *total* utility. Rather, the optimal purchase rule tells us that price will tend to be equal to *marginal* utility. And there is every reason to expect the marginal utility of bread to be very low while the marginal utility of caviar is very high.

Bread is comparatively cheap to produce, and so its price is generally quite low. Consumers thus use correspondingly large quantities of bread. By the principle of diminishing marginal utility, therefore, the marginal utility of bread to a typical household will be pushed down to a low level, though, as we saw earlier, this also means that its *total* utility is likely to be high.

On the other hand, high-quality caviar is scarce (and becoming scarcer). As a result, the quantity of caviar consumed is not large enough to drive the MU of caviar down very far, and so buyers of such luxuries are willing to pay high prices for them. The scarcer the commodity, the higher its *marginal* utility and its market price will be, regardless of the size of its *total* utility. And, as we have seen, because there is so little of it consumed, its total utility is likely to be comparatively low, despite its large marginal utility.

Thus, like many paradoxes, the caviar–bread puzzle has a straightforward explanation. In this case, all one has to remember is that:

Scarcity raises price and *marginal* utility but generally reduces *total* utility.

## PRICES, INCOME, AND QUANTITY DEMANDED

Our study of marginal analysis has enabled us to examine the relation between the price of a commodity and the quantity that will be purchased. Let us next consider briefly how quantity demanded responds to a change in income.

## THE DEMAND CONSEQUENCES OF A CHANGE IN INCOME

As a concrete example, let us consider what happens to the number of basketball tickets a consumer will buy when her real income rises. It may seem almost certain that she will buy more tickets than before, but that is not necessarily so. A rise in real income can either increase or decrease the quantity of tickets purchased.

Why might it do the latter? There are some goods and services that people buy only because they cannot afford any better. They eat chicken three days a week and lobster twice a year, but they would rather have it the other way around. They use plastic handbags instead of leather, or purchase most of their clothing secondhand. If their real income rises, they may then buy more lobster and less chicken, more leather and less plastic, more new shirts and fewer secondhand shirts. Thus, a rise in real income will reduce the quantities of chicken, cheap plastic handbags, and secondhand shirts demanded. Economists have given the rather descriptive name **inferior goods** to the class of commodities for which quantity demanded falls when income rises.

An **INFERIOR GOOD** is a commodity whose quantity demanded falls when the purchaser's real income rises, all other things remaining equal.

The upshot of this discussion is that we cannot draw definite conclusions about the effects of a rise in consumer incomes on quantity demanded. For most commodities, if incomes rise and prices do not change, there will be an increase in quantity demanded. (Such an item is often called a *"normal good,"* meaning a good whose quantity demanded goes up when the consumer's income rises.) But for the inferior goods there will be a decrease in quantity demanded.

## THE TWO EFFECTS OF A CHANGE IN PRICE[5]

When the price of some good, say heating oil, falls, it has two consequences. First, it makes fuel oil cheaper relative to electricity, gas, or coal. We say, then, that the *relative price* of fuel oil has fallen. Second, this price decrease leaves homeowners with more money to spend on movie admissions, soft drinks, or clothing. In other words, the decrease in the price of fuel oil *increases the consumer's real income*—her power to purchase other goods.

While a fall in the price of a commodity always produces these two effects simultaneously, our analysis will be easier if we separate the effects from one another and study them one at a time.

1. **The income effect of a change in price**. As we have just noted, a fall in the price of a commodity leads to a rise in the consumer's *real* income—the amount that her wages will purchase. The consequent effect on quantity demanded is called the **income effect** of the price fall. The income effect caused by a fall in a commodity's price is much the same as if the consumer's wages had risen: she will buy more of any commodity that is not an inferior good. The process producing the income effect thus has three stages: (1) the price of the good falls; causing (2) an increase in the consumer's real income; which leads to (3) a change in quantity demanded. Of course, a price increase will produce the same effect in reverse. The consumer's real income will decline, leading to the opposite change in quantity demanded.

The **INCOME EFFECT** is a *portion* of the change in quantity of a good demanded when its price changes. A rise in price cuts the consumer's purchasing power (real income), which leads to a change in the quantity demanded of that commodity. That change is the income effect.

2. **The substitution effect of a change in price**. A change in the price of a commodity produces another effect on quantity demanded that is rather

[5]This section contains rather more difficult material, which, in shorter courses, may be omitted without loss of continuity.

The **SUBSTITUTION EFFECT** is the change in quantity demanded of a good resulting from a change in its relative price, exclusive of whatever change in quantity demanded may be attributable to the associated change in real income.

different from the income effect. This is the **substitution effect**, which is the effect on quantity demanded attributable to the fact that the new price is now higher or lower than before *relative to the prices of other goods*. The substitution effect of a price change is the portion of the change in quantity demanded that can be attributed *exclusively* to the resulting change in relative prices rather than to the associated change in real income.

There is nothing mysterious or surprising about the effect of a change in relative prices when the consumer's real income remains unchanged. Whenever it is possible for the consumer to switch between two commodities, she can be expected to buy more of the good whose relative price has fallen and less of the good whose relative price has risen. For example, a few years ago AT&T instituted sharp reductions in the prices of evening long-distance telephone calls relative to daytime calls. The big decrease in the relative price of evening calls brought about a large increase in calling during the evening hours and a decrease in daytime calling, just as the telephone company had hoped. Similarly, a fall in the relative price of fuel oil will induce more people who are building new homes to install oil heat instead of gas heat.

When the price of any commodity X rises relative to the price of some other commodity Y, a consumer whose real income has remained unchanged can be expected to buy less X and more Y than before. Thus, *if we consider the substitution effect alone*, a decline in price always increases quantity demanded and a rise in price always reduces quantity demanded.

These two concepts, the income effect and the substitution effect, which many beginning economics students think were invented to torture them, are really quite useful. They really become *very* important when we consider the prices of inputs, for example, wages as the price of labor. Since a rise in wages really affects incomes very substantially, the income effect of such a price change is large and can make a very substantial difference, as we will see in Chapters 15 and 16. But the two concepts we are studying also throw some light on the consequences of a change in the price of an ordinary consumers' good. Suppose the price of hamburgers declines while the price of cheese remains unchanged. The *substitution effect* clearly induces the consumer to buy more hamburgers in place of grilled cheese sandwiches, because hamburgers are now comparatively cheaper. What of the *income effect*? Unless hamburger is an inferior good, it leads to the same decision. The fall in price makes consumers richer, which induces them to increase their purchases of all but inferior goods. This example alerts us to two general points:

If a good is not inferior, it must have a downward-sloping demand curve, since income and substitution effects reinforce each other. However, an inferior good may violate this pattern of demand behavior because the income effect of a decline in price leads consumers to buy less.

Do *all* inferior goods, then, have upward-sloping demand curves? Certainly not, for we have the substitution effect to reckon with; and the substitution effect always favors a downward-sloping demand curve. Thus we have a kind of tug-of-war in the case of an inferior good. If the *income effect* predominates, the demand curve will slope upward; if the *substitution effect* prevails, the demand curve will slope downward.

Economists have concluded that the substitution effect generally wins out; so while there are many examples of inferior goods, there are few examples of upward-sloping demand curves. When might the income effect prevail over the substitution effect? Certainly not when the good in question (say, plastic handbags) is a very small fraction of the consumer's budget, for then a fall in price makes the consumer only slightly "richer," and therefore creates a very small income effect. But the demand curve could slope upward if an inferior good constitutes a substantial portion of the consumer's budget.

We conclude this discussion of income and substitution effects with a warning against an error that is frequently made. Many students mistakenly close their books thinking that price changes cause substitution effects while income changes cause income effects. This is incorrect. As the forgoing example of hamburgers made clear:

Any change in price sets in motion *both* a substitution effect *and* an income effect, each of which affects quantity demanded.

## FROM INDIVIDUAL DEMAND CURVES TO MARKET DEMAND CURVES

A **MARKET DEMAND CURVE** shows how the total quantity demanded of some product during a specified period of time changes as the price of that product changes, holding other things constant.

So far, in this chapter, we have studied how *individual demand curves* are derived from the logic of consumer choice. But to understand how the market system works we must derive the relationship between price and quantity demanded *in the market as a whole*—the **market demand curve**.

If each individual pays no attention to other people's purchase decisions when making his own, it is straightforward to derive the market demand curve from the customers' individual demand curves. We simply *add* the negatively sloping individual demand curves *horizontally* as shown in Figure 8–2. There we see the

Figure 8–2 **THE RELATIONSHIP BETWEEN TOTAL MARKET DEMAND AND THE DEMAND OF INDIVIDUAL CONSUMERS WITHIN THAT MARKET**

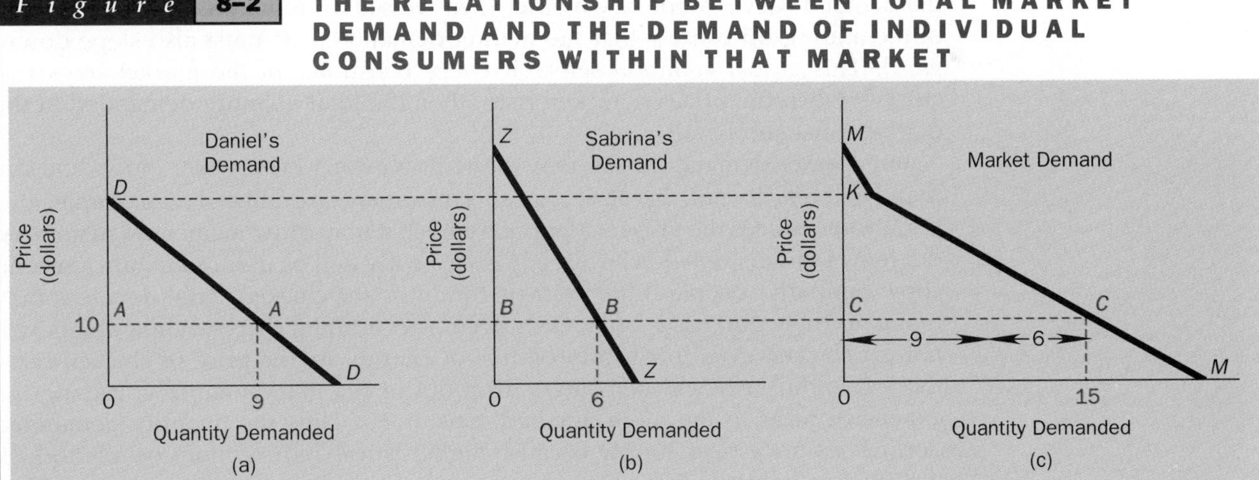


If Daniel and Sabrina are the customers of a product, and at a price of $10 Daniel demands 9 units [line *AA* in part (a)] and Sabrina demands 6 units [line *BB* in part (b)], then total quantity demanded by the market at that price is 9 + 6 = 15 [line *CC* in part (c)]. In other words, we obtain the market demand curve by adding horizontally all points on each consumer's demand curve at each given price. Thus, at a $10 price we have length *CC* on the market demand curve, which is equal to *AA* + *BB* on the individual demand curves. (The sharp angle at point *K* on the market curve occurs because it corresponds to the price at which Daniel, whose demand pattern is different from Sabrina's, first enters the market. At any higher price, only Sabrina is willing to buy anything.)

individual demand curves *DD* and *ZZ* for two people, Daniel and Sabrina, and the total (market) demand curve *MM*.

Specifically, this market demand curve is constructed as follows. *Step 1*: Pick any relevant price, say $10. *Step 2*: At that price, determine Daniel's quantity demanded (9 units) from Daniel's demand curve in part (a) and Sabrina's quantity demanded (6 units) from Sabrina's demand curve in part (b). Note that these quantities are indicated by line segment *AA* for Daniel and line segment *BB* for Sabrina. *Step 3*: Add Sabrina's and Daniel's quantities demanded at the $10 price (segment $AA +$ segment $BB = 9 + 6 = 15$) to yield the total quantity demanded by the market at that price [line segment *CC*, with total quantity demanded equal to 15 units, in part (c)]. Now repeat the process for all alternative prices to obtain other points on the market demand curve until the shape of the entire curve *MM* is indicated. That is all there is to the adding-up process. (Question: What happens to the market demand curve if, say, population grows, and another consumer enters the market?)

## THE "LAW" OF DEMAND

The **"LAW" OF DEMAND** states that a lower price generally increases the amount of a commodity that people in a market are willing to buy. So, for most goods, demand curves have a negative slope.

As in the case of the individual's demand curve, we expect the total quantity demanded by the market normally to move in the opposite direction from price. Economists call this relationship the **"law" of demand.**

Notice that we have put the word *law* in quotation marks. By now you will have observed that economic laws are not always obeyed, and we shall see in a moment that the "law" of demand is not without its exceptions. But first let us see why the "law" usually holds.

Earlier in this chapter we learned that individual demand curves are usually downward sloping because of the "law" of diminishing marginal utility. If individual demand curves slope downward, then we see from the preceding discussion of the adding-up process that the market demand curve must also slope downward. This is just common sense: if every consumer in the market buys less chicken when the price of chicken rises, then the total quantity demanded in the market must surely fall.

But market demand curves may slope downward even when individual demand curves do not, because not all consumers are alike. For example, if a bookstore reduces the price of a popular novel, it may draw many new customers, but few of the customers who already own a copy will be induced to buy a second copy. Similarly, people differ in their fondness for chicken. True devotees may maintain their purchases of chicken even at exorbitant prices, while others will not eat chicken even if it is offered free of charge. As the price of chicken rises, the less enthusiastic chicken eaters drop out of the market entirely, leaving the expensive meat to the more devoted consumers. Thus the quantity demanded declines as price rises simply because higher prices induce more people to kick the chicken habit. Indeed, for many commodities, it is the appearance of new customers in the *market* when prices are lower, rather than the negative slope of *individual* demand curves, that accounts for the law of demand.

This is also illustrated in Figure 8–2 where we see that at a price higher than *D* only Sabrina will buy the product. However, at a price below *D* Daniel is also induced to make some purchases. Hence, below point *K* the market demand curve lies further to the right than it would have if Daniel had not been induced to enter the market. Put the other way, a rise in price from a level below *D* to a level above $D$ will cut quantity demanded for two reasons: first because Sabrina's demand curve has a negative slope and, second, because it drives Daniel out of the market.

We conclude, therefore, that the law of demand stands on fairly solid ground. If individual demand curves are downward sloping, then the market demand curve surely will be, too. And the market demand curve may slope downward even when individual demand curves do not.

Nevertheless, exceptions to the law of demand have been noted. One common exception occurs when quality is judged on the basis of price—the more expensive the commodity, the better it is perceived to be. For example, many people buy "name-brand" aspirin, even if right next to it on the drugstore shelf there is an unbranded "generic" aspirin, with an identical chemical formula, sold at half the price. The consumers who do buy the name-brand aspirin may well use comparative price to judge the relative qualities of different brands. They may prefer brand X to brand Y because X is slightly more expensive. If brand X were to reduce its price below that of Y, consumers might assume that it was no longer superior and actually reduce their purchases.

Another possible cause of an upward-sloping demand curve is snob appeal. If part of the reason for purchasing a Rolls Royce is to advertise one's wealth, a decrease in the car's price may actually reduce sales, even if the quality of the car is unchanged. Other types of exceptions have also been noted by economists. But, for most commodities, it seems quite reasonable to assume that demand curves have a negative slope, an assumption that is supported by the data.

## THREE TYPES OF DEMAND CURVE: FOR INDIVIDUALS, FOR MARKETS, FOR FIRMS

We have, so far, dealt with two different but closely interrelated types of demand curve: the market demand curve, and the demand curve of an individual consumer. The market demand curve is, so to speak, built up from the demand curves of all the individuals (households) who shop in the market in question. Thus, market demand is an aggregative concept; it is determined by summing the demand curves of the pertinent individual consumers.

There is, however, a third type of demand curve—the demand curve for the firm. It is this third type that was used in Chapters 5 and 6 in analyzing the decisions of business firms. A firm normally has many customers. But any one firm will usually capture only a portion of the purchasers in the market, because some customers will do their shopping at competing firms. Thus, the demand curve for the firm is derived by *dividing* the market demand curve up among the firms that serve the market. In general, this is a complicated matter. But the next chapter will illustrate how the firm's demand curve can be obtained from the market demand curve in one special case.

## *Summary*

1. Economists distinguish between total and marginal utility. **Total utility**, or the benefit a consumer derives from a purchase, is measured by the maximum amount of money he or she would give up in order to have the good in question. Rational consumers seek to maximize (net) total utility, that is, consumer's surplus = total utility derived from a commodity − the value of the money spent in buying it.

2. **Marginal utility** is the maximum amount of money a consumer is willing to pay for an additional unit of a particular commodity. Marginal utility is useful in calculating what set of purchases maximizes net total utility.
3. **The "law" of diminishing marginal utility** is a psychological hypothesis stating that as a consumer acquires more and more of a commodity, the marginal utility of additional units of the commodity will decrease.
4. To maximize the total utility obtained by spending money on some commodity X, given the fact that other goods can be purchased only with the money that remains after buying X, the consumer must purchase a quantity of X such that the price is equal to the commodity's marginal utility (in money terms).
5. If the consumer acts to maximize utility, and if his marginal utility of some good declines when larger quantities are purchased, then his demand curve for the good will have a negative slope. A reduction in price will induce the purchase of more units, leading to a lower marginal utility.
6. Abundant goods tend to have a low price and low marginal utility regardless of whether their total utility is high or low. That is why bread can have a low price despite its high total utility.
7. An **inferior good**, such as secondhand clothing, is a commodity consumers buy less of when they get richer, all other things held equal.
8. Consumers usually earn a surplus when they purchase a commodity voluntarily. This means that the quantity of the good that they buy is worth more to them than the money they give up in exchange.
9. A rise in the price of a commodity has two effects on quantity demanded: (a) a **substitution effect**, which makes the good less attractive because it has become more expensive than it was previously, and (b) an **income effect**, which decreases the consumer's total utility because higher prices cut her purchasing power.
10. Any increase in the price of a good always has a *negative* substitution effect; that is, considering only the substitution effect, a rise in price must reduce the quantity demanded.
11. The **income effect** of a rise in price may, however, push quantity demanded up or down. For normal goods, the income effect of a higher price (which makes consumers poorer) reduces quantity demanded; for inferior goods, the income effect of higher prices actually increases quantity demanded.
12. The demand curve for an entire market is obtained by (horizontal) summation of the demand curves of all of the individuals who buy or consider buying in that market. This summation is obtained by adding up, for each price, the quantity of the commodity in question that every such consumer is willing to purchase at that price.

## Key Concepts and Terms

Marginal analysis
Total utility
Marginal utility
The "law" of diminishing marginal utility
Optimal purchase rule ($P$ = MU)
Scarcity and marginal utility
Consumer's surplus
Inferior goods
Income effect
Substitution effect
Individual and market demand.

## Questions for Review

1. Describe some of the different things you do with water. Which would you give up if the price of water rose a little? If it rose by a fairly large amount? If it rose by a very large amount?
2. Which is greater: your *total* utility from 12 gallons of water per day or from 20 gallons per day? Why?
3. Which is greater: your *marginal* utility at 12 gallons per day or your marginal utility at 20 gallons per day? Why?
4. Suppose you wanted to measure the marginal utility of a commodity to a consumer by determining the consumer's psychological attitude or strength of feeling for the commodity directly, rather than by seeing how much money the consumer is willing to give up

for the commodity. How might you go about such a psychological measurement? (*Note*: No one has a good answer to this question.)

5. Some people who do not understand the optimal purchase rule argue that if a consumer buys so much of a good that its price equals its marginal utility, she could not possibly be behaving optimally. Rather, they say, she would be better off quitting when ahead; that is, buying a quantity such that marginal utility is much greater than price. What is wrong with this argument? (*Hint*: What opportunity does the consumer then miss? Is it maximization of marginal or total utility that serves the consumer's interests?)

6. What inferior goods do you purchase? Why do you buy them? Do you think you will continue to buy them when your income is higher?

7. Which of the following items are likely to be normal goods to a typical consumer? Which are likely to be inferior goods?

   a. Expensive perfume
   b. Paper plates
   c. Secondhand clothing
   d. Overseas trips

8. Suppose that electricity and paper clips each rise in price by 40 percent. Which will have the larger income effect on the purchases of a typical consumer? Why?

9. Around 1850, Sir Robert Giffen observed that Irish peasants actually consumed more potatoes as the price of potatoes increased. Use the concepts of income and substitution effects to explain this phenomenon.

10. Suppose strawberries sell for $2 per basket. Jim is considering whether to buy 0, 1, 2, 3, or 4 baskets. Construct a table of total, marginal, and average expenditures for the different quantities of strawberries. Draw the graph of the three curves.

11. Why are the average and marginal expenditure curves in question 10 identical? What is their relation to the price of strawberries? Why?

12. Consider a market with two consumers, Jasmine and Jim. Draw a demand curve for each of the two consumers and use those curves to construct the demand curve for the entire market.

# *Appendix* INDIFFERENCE CURVE ANALYSIS

The analysis of consumer demand presented in this chapter, while correct as far as it goes, has one shortcoming: by treating the consumer's decision about the purchase of each commodity as an isolated event, it conceals the necessity of choice imposed on the consumer by his limited budget. It does not indicate explicitly the hard choice behind every purchase decision—the sacrifice of some goods to obtain others. The idea, of course, is included implicitly because the purchase of a commodity involves a trade-off between that good and money. If you spend more money on rent, you have less to spend on entertainment. If you buy more clothing, you have less money for food. But to represent the consumer's *choice* problem explicitly, economists have invented two geometric devices, the **budget line** and the **indifference curve**, which this appendix describes.

## GEOMETRY OF THE AVAILABLE CHOICES: THE BUDGET LINE

Suppose, for simplicity, that there were only two commodities produced in the world, cheese and rubber bands. The decision problem of any household then would be to determine the allocation of its income between these two goods. Clearly, the more it spends on one, the less it can have of the other. But just what is the trade-off? A numerical example will answer this question and also introduce the graphical device that economists use to portray the trade-off.

Suppose that cheese costs $2 per pound, boxes of rubber bands sell at $3 each, and our consumer has $12 at her disposal. She obviously has a variety of choices—as displayed in Table 8–3. For example, if she buys no rubber bands, she can go home with six pounds of cheese, and so on. Each of the combinations of cheese and rubber bands that the consumer can afford can be shown in a diagram in which the axes measure the quantities of each commodity that are purchased. In Figure 8–3, pounds of cheese are measured along the vertical axis, number of boxes of rubber bands is measured along the horizontal axis, and each of the combinations enumerated in Table 8–3 is represented by a labeled point. For example, point *A* corresponds to spending everything on cheese, point *E* corresponds to spending everything on rubber bands, and point *C* corresponds to buying two boxes of rubber bands and three pounds of cheese.

If we connect points *A* through *E* by a straight line, the blue line in the diagram, we can trace all the possible ways to divide the $12 between the two goods. For example, point *D* tells us that if the consumer buys three boxes of rubber bands, there will be only enough money left to purchase one and one-half pounds of cheese. This is readily seen to be correct from Table 8–3. Line *AE* is therefore called the **budget line**.

The **budget line** for a household represents graphically all the possible combinations of two commodities that it can purchase, given the prices of the commodities and some fixed amount of money at its disposal.

*Table* **8–3** ALTERNATIVE PURCHASE COMBINATIONS FOR A $12 BUDGET

| NUMBER OF BOXES OF RUBBER BANDS (at $3 each) | EXPENDITURE ON RUBBER BANDS (in dollars) | REMAINING FUNDS (in dollars) | NUMBER OF POUNDS OF CHEESE (at $2 each) | LABEL IN FIGURE 8–3 |
|---|---|---|---|---|
| 0 | 0 | 12 | 6 | *A* |
| 1 | 3 | 9 | 4½ | *B* |
| 2 | 6 | 6 | 3 | *C* |
| 3 | 9 | 3 | 1½ | *D* |
| 4 | 12 | 0 | 0 | *E* |

**Figure 8–3** **A BUDGET LINE**

This budget line shows the different combinations of cheese and rubber bands the consumer can buy with $12 if cheese costs $2 per pound and a box of rubber bands cost $3 each. At point *A* the consumer buys six pounds of cheese and has nothing left over for rubber bands. At point *E* she spends the entire budget on rubber bands. At intermediate points (such as *C*) on the budget line, the consumer buys some of both goods (two boxes of rubber bands and three pounds of cheese).

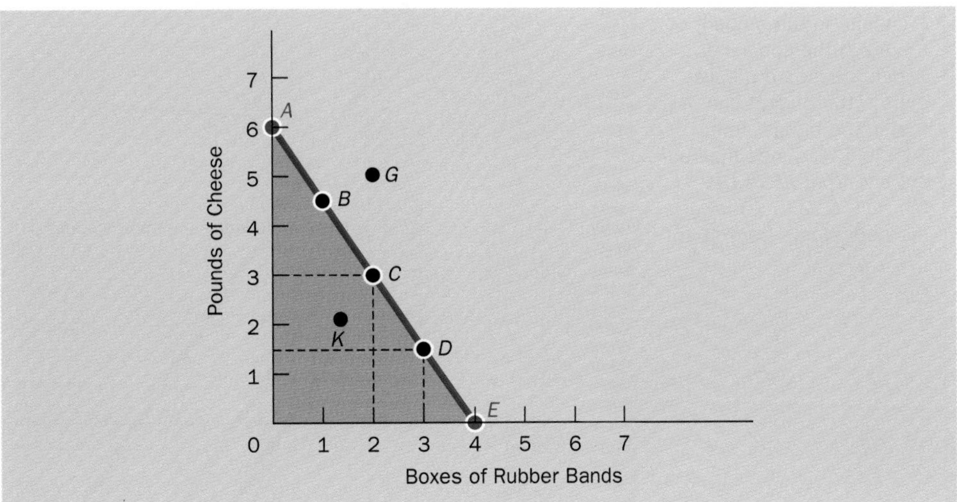


## PROPERTIES OF THE BUDGET LINE

Let us now use $r$ to represent the number of boxes of rubber bands purchased by our consumer and $c$ to indicate the amount of cheese she acquires. Thus, at $2 per pound, she spends on cheese a total of 2 × (number of pounds of cheese bought) = $2c$ dollars. Similarly, she spends $3r$ dollars on rubber bands, making a total of $2c + 3r$ = $12, if the entire $12 is spent on the two commodities. This is the equation of the budget line. It is also the equation of the straight line drawn in the diagram.[6]

We note also that the budget line represents the *maximal* amounts of the commodities that the consumer can afford. Thus, for any given purchase of rubber bands, it tells us the greatest amount of cheese her money can buy. If our consumer wants to be thrifty, she can choose to end up at a point below the budget line, such as *K*. Clearly, then, the choices she has available include not only those points on the budget line *AE*, but also any point in the shaded triangle formed by the budget line *AE* and the two axes. By contrast, points above the budget line, such as *G*, are not available to the consumer given her limited budget. A bundle consisting of five pounds of cheese and two boxes of rubber bands would cost $16, which is more than she has to spend.

The position of the budget line is determined by two types of data: the prices of the commodities purchased and the income at the buyer's disposal. We can complete our discussion of the graphics of the budget line by examining briefly how a change in either of these magnitudes affects its location.

Obviously, any increase in the income of the household increases the range of options available to it. Specifically, *increases in income produce parallel shifts in the budget line*, as shown in Figure 8–4. The reason is simply that a, say, 50 percent increase in available income, if entirely spent on the two goods in question, would permit the family to purchase exactly 50 percent more of *either* commodity. Point *A* in Figure 8–3 would shift upward by 50 percent of its distance from the origin, while point *E* would move to the right by 50 percent.[7] Figure 8–4 shows

[6]The reader may have noticed one problem that arises in this formulation. If every point on the budget line *AE* is a possible way for the consumer to spend her money, there must be some manner in which she can buy fractional boxes of rubber bands. Perhaps the purchase of one and one-half boxes can be interpreted to include a down payment of $1.50 on a box of rubber bands on her next shopping trip! Throughout this book it is convenient to assume that commodities are available in fractional quantities when drawing diagrams. This makes the graphs clearer and does not really affect the analysis.

[7]An algebraic proof is simple. Let $M$ (which is initially $12) be the amount of money available to our household. The equation of the budget line can be solved for $c$, obtaining $c = -(3/2)r + M/2$. This is the equation of a straight line with a slope of

Figure 8–4 **THE EFFECT OF INCOME CHANGES ON THE BUDGET LINE**

A change in the amount of money in the consumer's budget causes a parallel shift in the budget line. A rise in the budget from \$12 to \$18 raises the budget line from *AE* to *UP*. A fall from \$12 to \$9 lowers the budget line from *AE* to *DN*.

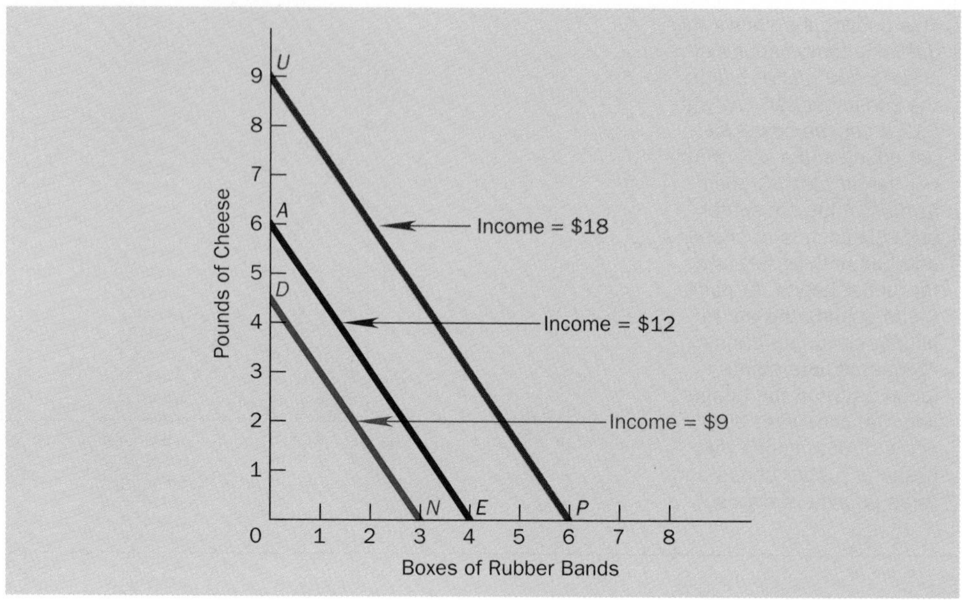


three such budget lines corresponding to incomes of \$9, \$12, and \$18, respectively.

Finally, we can ask what happens to the budget line when there is a change in the price of some commodity. In Figure 8–5, we see that when the price of the rubber bands *decreases*, the budget line moves outward, but the move is no longer parallel because the point on the cheese axis remains fixed. Once again, the reason is fairly straightforward. A 50 percent reduction in the price of rubber bands permits the family's \$12 to buy twice as many boxes of rubber bands as before: point *E* is moved rightward to point *H*, at which eight boxes of rubber bands are shown to be obtainable. However, since the price of cheese has not changed, point *A*, the amount of cheese that can be bought for \$12, is unaffected. Thus we have the general result that *a reduction in the price of one of the two commodities swings the budget line outward along the axis representing the quantity of that item while leaving the location of the other end of the line unchanged.*

(continued) $-$ 3/2 and a vertical intercept of $M/2$. A change in $M$, the quantity of money available, will not change the *slope* of the budget line; it will lead only to parallel shifts in that line.

## WHAT THE CONSUMER PREFERS: THE INDIFFERENCE CURVE

The budget line tells us what choices are *available* to the consumer, given the size of her income and the commodity prices fixed by the market. We next must examine the consumer's *preferences* in order to determine which of these available possibilities she will want to choose.

After much investigation, economists have determined what they believe to be the minimum amount of information they need about a purchaser in order to analyze her choices. This information consists of the consumer's *ranking* of the alternative bundles of commodities that are available. Suppose, for instance, the consumer is offered a choice between two bundles of goods, bundle *W*, which contains three boxes of rubber bands and one pound of cheese, and bundle *T*, which contains two boxes of rubber bands and three pounds of cheese. The economist wants to know for this purpose only whether the consumer prefers *W* to *T*, *T* to *W*, or whether she is *indifferent* about which one she gets. Note that the analysis requires no information about *degree* of preference—whether the consumer is

Figure 8–5 **THE EFFECT OF PRICE CHANGES ON THE BUDGET LINE**

A fall in the price of rubber bands causes the end of the budget line on the rubber bands axis to swing away from the origin. A fall in rubber bands price from \$3 to \$1.50 swings the price line from *AE* to blue line *AH*. This happens because at the higher price, \$12 buys only four boxes of rubber bands, but at the lower price, it can buy eight boxes of rubber bands.

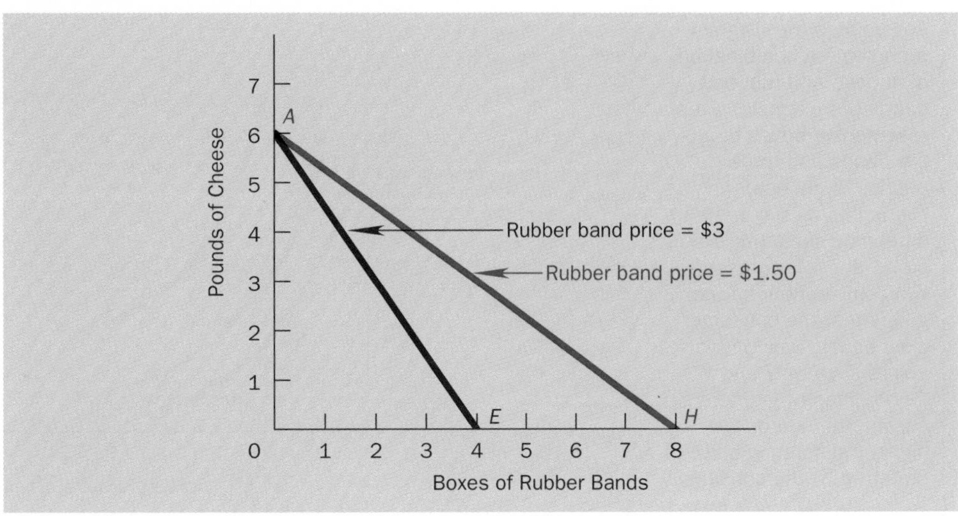


wildly more enthusiastic about one of the bundles or just prefers it slightly.

Graphically, the preference information is provided by a group of curves called **indifference curves** (Figure 8–6).

An **indifference curve** is a line connecting all combinations of the commodities in question that are equally desirable to the consumer.

But before we examine these curves, let us see how such a curve is interpreted. A single point on an indifference curve tells us nothing about preferences. For example, point *R* on curve $I_a$ simply represents the bundle of goods composed of four boxes of rubber bands and one-half pound of cheese. It does *not* suggest that the consumer is indifferent between one-half pound of cheese and four boxes of rubber bands. For the curve to tell us anything, we must consider at least two of its points, for example, points *S* and *W*. Since they represent two different combinations that are on the same indifference curve, they are equally desirable to our consumer.

## PROPERTIES OF THE INDIFFERENCE CURVES

We do not know yet which bundle, among all the bundles she can afford, our consumer prefers; we know only that a choice between certain bundles will lead to indifference. So before we can use an indifference curve to analyze the consumer's choice, we must examine a few of its properties. Most important for us is the fact that:

As long as the consumer desires *more* of each of the goods in question, *every* point on a higher indifference curve (that is, a curve farther from the origin in the graph) will be preferred to *any* point on a lower indifference curve.

In other words, among indifference curves, higher is better. The reason is obvious. Given two indifference curves, say $I_b$ and $I_c$ in Figure 8–6, the higher curve will contain points lying above and to the right of some points on the lower curve. Thus, point *U* on curve $I_c$ lies above and to the right of point *T* on curve $I_b$. This means that at *U* the consumer gets more rubber bands *and* more cheese than at *T*. Assuming that she desires both commodities, our consumer must prefer *U* to *T*. Since every point on curve $I_c$ is, by definition, equal in preference to point *U*, and the same relation holds for point *T* and all other points along curve $I_b$, *every* point on curve $I_c$ will be preferred to *any* point on curve $I_b$.

This at once implies a second property of indifference curves: they never intersect. This is so because if an indifference curve, say $I_b$, is anywhere above another, say $I_a$, then $I_b$ must be above $I_a$ everywhere,

Figure 8–6 THREE INDIFFERENCE CURVES FOR CHEESE AND RUBBER BANDS

Any point in the diagram represents a combination of cheese and rubber bands (for example, *T* represents two boxes of rubber bands and three pounds of cheese). Any two points on the same indifference curve (for example, *S* and *W*) represent two combinations of the goods that the consumer likes equally well. If two points such as *T* and *W*, lie on different indifference curves, the one on the higher indifference curve is preferred by the consumer.

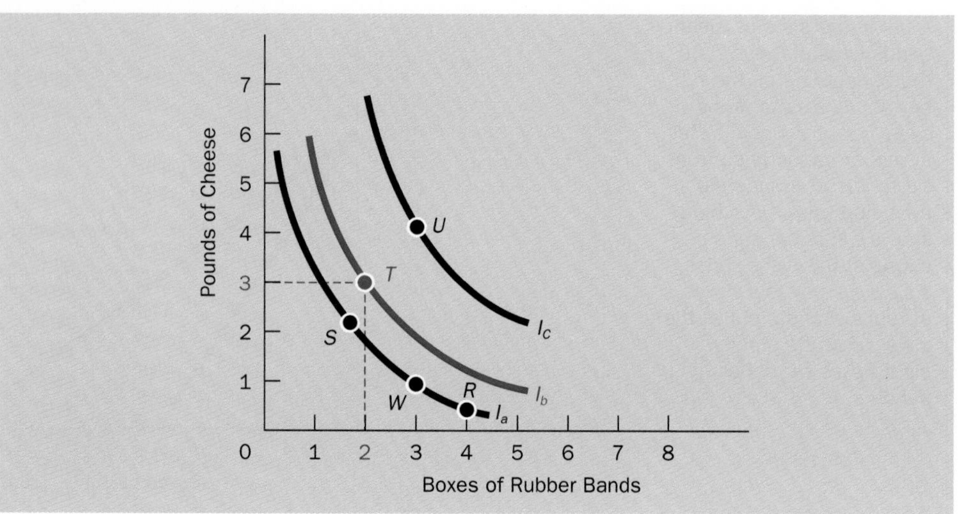


since every point on $I_b$ is preferred to every point on $I_a$.

Another property that characterizes the indifference curve is its *negative slope*. Again, this holds only if the consumer wants more of both commodities. Consider two points, such as *S* and *R*, on the same indifference curve. If the consumer is indifferent between them, one cannot contain more of *both* commodities than the other. Since point *S* contains more cheese than *R*, *R* must offer more rubber bands than *S*, or the consumer would not be indifferent about which she gets. This means that if, say, we move toward the one with the larger number of rubber bands, the quantity of cheese must decrease. The curve will always slope downhill toward the right, a negative slope.

A final property of indifference curves is the nature of their curvature—the way they round toward the axes. As drawn, they are "bowed in"—they flatten out (their slopes decrease in absolute value) as they extend from left to right. To understand why this is so we must first examine the economic interpretation of the slope of an indifference curve.

## THE SLOPES OF AN INDIFFERENCE CURVE AND OF A BUDGET LINE

In Figure 8–7 the average slope of the indifference curve between points *M* and *N* is represented by *RM*/*RN*. *RM* is the quantity of cheese the consumer gives up in moving from *M* to *N*. Similarly, *RN* is the increased number of boxes of rubber bands acquired in this move. Since the consumer is indifferent between bundles *M* and *N*, the gain of *RN* rubber bands must just suffice to compensate her for the loss of *RM* pounds of cheese. Thus the ratio *RM*/*RN* represents the terms on which the consumer is just willing—*according to her own preference*—to trade one good for the other. If *RM*/*RN* equals two, the consumer is willing to give up (no more than) two pounds of cheese for one additional boxes of rubber bands.

The **slope of an indifference curve**, referred to as the **marginal rate of substitution** between the commodities involved, represents the maximum amount of one commodity the consumer is willing to give up in exchange for one more unit of another commodity.

The slope of budget line *BB* in Figure 8–7 is also a rate of exchange between cheese and rubber bands. But it no longer reflects the consumer's subjective willingness to trade. Rather, the slope represents the rate of exchange *the market* offers to the consumer when she gives up money in exchange for cheese and rubber bands. Recall that the budget line represents all commodity combinations a consumer can get by spending a fixed amount of money. The bud-

Figure 8–7 **SLOPES OF A BUDGET LINE AND AN INDIFFERENCE CURVE**

The slope of the budget line shows how many pounds of cheese, *ED*, can be exchanged for *EF* boxes of rubber bands. The slope of the indifference curve shows how many pounds of cheese, *RM*, the consumer is just willing to exchange for *RN* boxes of rubber bands. When the consumer has more rubber bands and less cheese (point *m* as compared with *M*), the slope of the indifference curve decreases, meaning that the consumer is only willing to give up *rm* pounds of cheese for *rn* boxes of rubber bands.

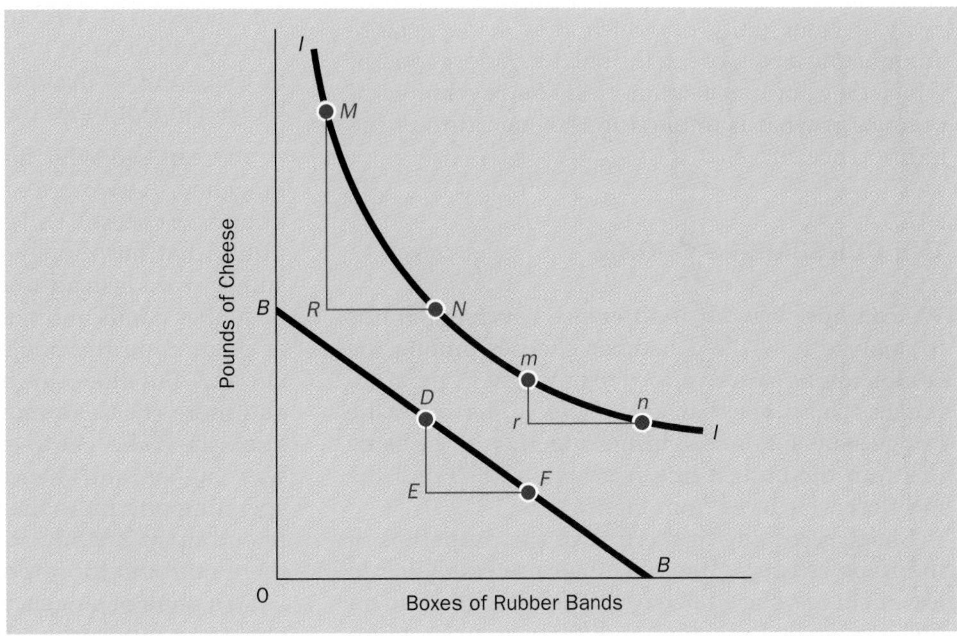


get line is thus a curve of constant expenditure. At current prices, if the consumer reduces her purchase of cheese by amount *DE* in Figure 8–7, she will save just enough money to buy an additional amount, *EF*, of rubber bands, since at points *D* and *F* she is spending the same total number of dollars.

The **slope of a budget line** is the amount of one commodity the market requires an individual to give up in order to obtain one additional unit of another commodity without any change in the amount of money spent.

The slopes of the two types of curves, then, are perfectly analogous in their meaning. The slope of the indifference curve tells us the terms on which the *consumer* is willing to trade one commodity for another, while the slope of the budget line reports the *market* terms on which the consumer can trade one good for another.

It is useful to carry our interpretation of the slope of the budget line one step further. Common sense tells us that the market's rate of exchange between cheese and rubber bands would be related to their prices, $p_c$ and $p_r$, and it is easy to show that this is so. Specifically, the slope of the budget line is equal to the ratio of the prices of the two commodities. The reason is straightforward. If the consumer gives up one box of rubber bands, she has $p_r$ more dollars to spend on cheese. But the lower the price of cheese the greater the quantity of cheese this money will enable her to buy—that is, her cheese purchasing power will be inversely related to its price. Since the price of cheese is $p_c$ per pound, the additional $p_r$ dollars permit her to buy $p_r/p_c$ more pounds of cheese. Thus the slope of the budget line is $p_r/p_c$.

Before returning to our main subject, the study of consumer choice, we pause briefly and use our interpretation of the slope of the indifference curve to discuss the third of the properties of the indifference curve—its characteristic curvature—which we left unexplained earlier. With indifference curves being the shape shown, the slope decreases as we move from left to right. We can see in Figure 8–7 that at point *m*, toward the right of the diagram, the consumer is willing to give up far less cheese for one more box of rubber bands (quantity *rm*) than she is willing to trade at point *M*, toward the left. This is because at *M* she initially has a large quantity of cheese and few rubber bands, while at *m* her initial stock of cheese is low and she has many rubber bands. In general terms, the curvature premise on which indifference curves are usually drawn asserts that consumers are relatively eager to trade away a commodity of which they have a large amount but are more reluctant to trade goods of which they hold small quantities. This psychological premise is what is implied in the curvature of the indifference curve.

## THE CONSUMER'S CHOICE

We can now use our indifference curve apparatus to analyze how the consumer chooses among the combinations she can afford to buy; that is, the combinations of rubber bands and cheese shown by the budget line. Figure 8–8 brings together in the same diagram the budget line from Figure 8–3 and the indifference curves from Figure 8–6.

Since, according to the first of the properties of indifference curves, the consumer prefers higher to lower curves, she will go to the point on the budget line that lies on the highest indifference curve attainable. This will be point *T* on indifference curve $I_b$. She can afford no other point that she likes as well. For example, neither point *K* below the budget line nor point *Z* on the budget line gets her on as high an indifference curve, and any point on an indifference curve above $I_b$, such as point *U*, is out of the question because it lies beyond her financial means. We end up with a simple rule of consumer choice:

Consumers will select the most desired combination of goods obtainable for their money. The choice will be that point on the budget line at which the budget line is tangent to an indifference curve.

We can see why no point except the point of tangency, *T* (two boxes of rubber bands and three pounds of cheese), will give the consumer the largest utility that her money can buy. Suppose the consumer were instead to consider buying four boxes of rubber bands and no cheese. This would put her at point *Z* on the budget line and on indifference curve *I*. But then, by buying fewer rubber bands and more cheese (a move to the left on the budget line), she could get to an indifference curve $I_a$, that was higher and hence more desirable without spending any more money. It clearly does not pay to end up at *Z*. Only at the point of tangency, *T*, is there no room for improvement.

At a point of tangency where the consumer's benefits from purchasing cheese and rubber bands are maximized, the slope of the budget line equals the slope of the indifference curve. This is true by the definition of a point of tangency. We have just seen that the slope of the indifference curve is the marginal rate of substitution between cheese and rubber bands, and that the slope of the budget line is the

**Figure 8–8** **OPTIMAL CONSUMER CHOICE**

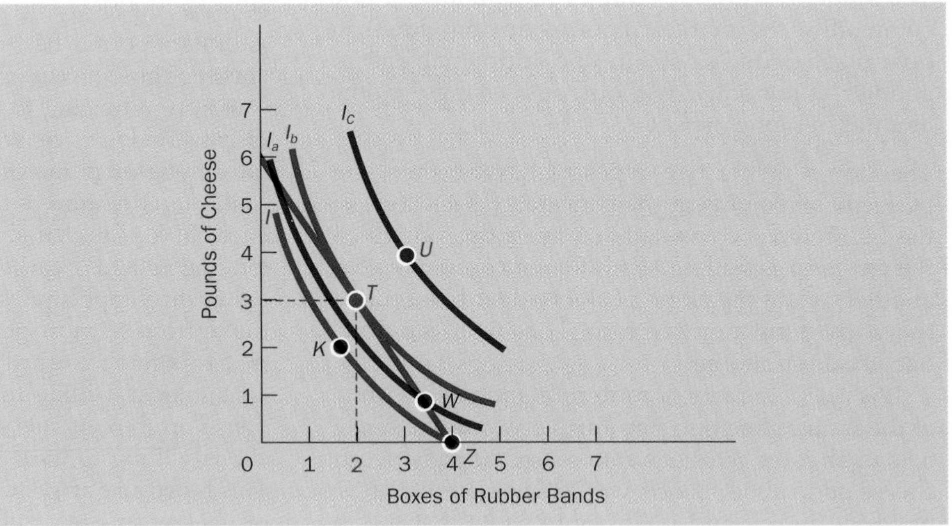


Point *T* is the combination of rubber bands and cheese that gives the consumer the greatest benefit for her money. $I_b$ is the highest indifference curve that can be reached from the budget line. *T* is the point of tangency between the budget line and $I_b$.

ratio of the prices of rubber bands and cheese. We can therefore restate the requirement for the optimal division of the consumer's money between the two commodities in slightly more technical language:

Consumers will get the most benefit from their money by choosing a combination of commodities whose marginal rate of substitution is equal to the ratio of their prices.

It is worth reviewing the logic behind this conclusion. Why is it not advisable for the consumer to stop at a point like *Z*, where the marginal rate of substitution (slope of the indifference curve) is less than the price ratio (slope of the budget line)? Because by moving upward and to the left along her budget line, she can take advantage of market opportunities to obtain a commodity bundle that she likes better. And this will always be the case if the rate at which the consumer is *personally* willing to exchange cheese for rubber bands (her marginal rate of substitution) differs from the rate of exchange offered *on the market* (the slope of the budget line).

## CONSEQUENCES OF INCOME CHANGES: INFERIOR GOODS

Next, consider what happens to the consumer's purchases when there is a rise in income. We know that a rise in income produces a parallel outward shift in the budget line, such as the shift from *BB* to *CC* in Figure 8–9. This moves the consumer's equilibrium from tangency point *T* to tangency point *E* on a higher indifference curve.

A rise in income may or may not increase the demand for a commodity. In the case shown in Figure 8–9, the rise in income does lead the consumer to buy more cheese *and* more rubber bands. But indifference curves need not always be positioned in a way that yields this sort of result. In Figure 8–10 we see that as the consumer's budget line rises from *BB* to *CC*, the tangency point moves leftward from *H* to *G*, so that when her income rises she actually buys *fewer* rubber bands. In this case we infer that rubber bands are an **inferior good**.

## CONSEQUENCES OF PRICE CHANGES: DERIVING THE DEMAND CURVE

Finally, we come to the main question underlying demand curves: how does our consumer's choice change if the price of one good changes? We learned earlier that a reduction in the price of a box of rubber bands causes the budget line to swing outward along the horizontal axis while leaving its vertical intercept unchanged. In Figure 8–11, we depict the effect of a decline in the price of rubber bands on the

*Figure* **8–9** **EFFECTS OF A RISE IN INCOME WHEN NEITHER GOOD IS INFERIOR**

The rise in income causes a parallel shift in the budget line from *BB* to *CC*. The quantity of rubber bands demanded rises from three to four boxes, and the quantity demanded of cheese also increases.

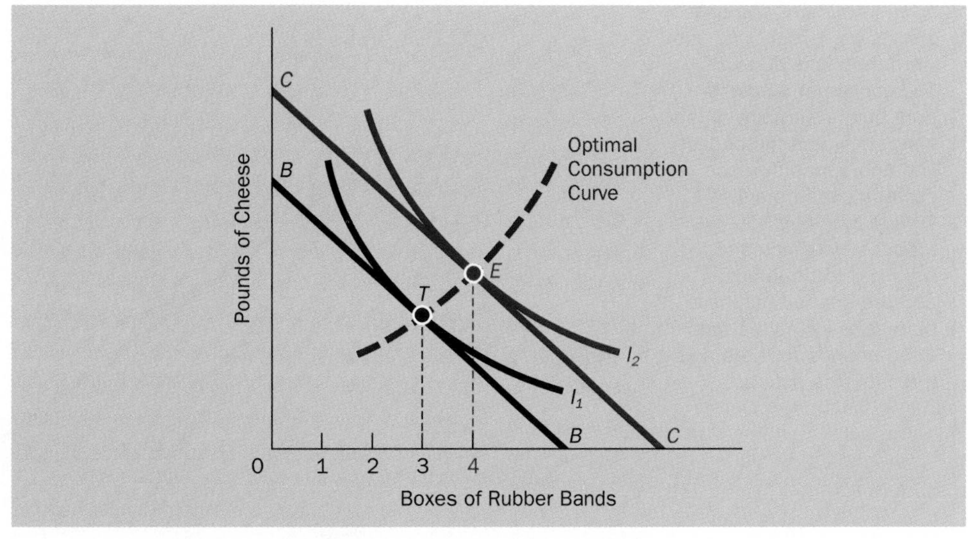

**Figure 8–10** **EFFECTS OF A RISE IN INCOME WHEN RUBBER BANDS ARE AN INFERIOR GOOD**

The upward shift in the budget line from *BB* to *CC* causes the quantity of rubber bands demanded to fall from four boxes (point *H*) to three (point *G*).

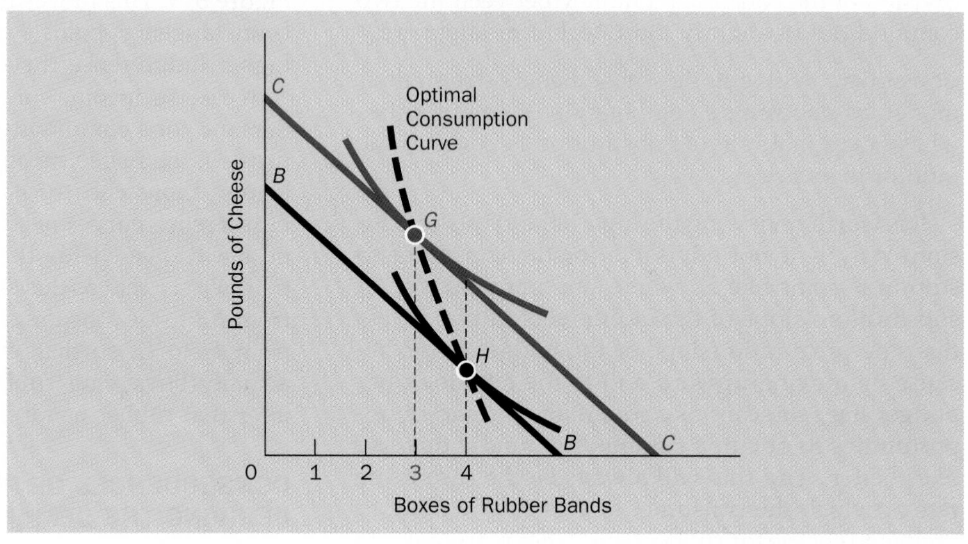


quantity of rubber bands demanded. As the price of rubber bands falls, the budget line swings from *BC* to *BD*. The tangency points, *T* and *E*, also move in a corresponding direction, causing the quantity demanded to rise from two to three. The price of rubber bands has fallen, and the quantity demanded has risen: the demand curve for rubber bands is negatively sloped.

The demand curve for rubber bands can be constructed directly from Figure 8–11. Point *T* tells us that two boxes of rubber bands will be bought when the price of a box of rubber bands is $3. Point *E* tells

**Figure 8–11** **CONSEQUENCES OF PRICE CHANGES**

A fall in rubber band price swings the budget line outward from line *BC* to *BD*. The consumer's equilibrium point (the point of tangency between the budget line and an indifference curve) moves from *T* to *E*. The desired purchase of rubber bands increases from two to three boxes, and the desired purchase of cheese increases from three pounds to three and three-fourths pounds.

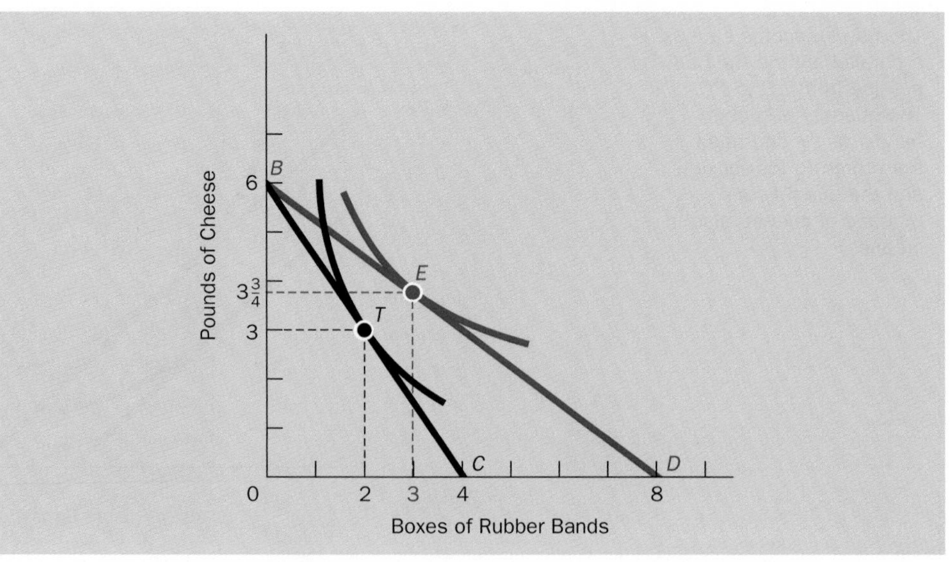

*Figure* **8–12** **DERIVING THE DEMAND CURVE FOR RUBBER BANDS**

The demand curve is derived from the indifference curve diagram by varying the price of the commodity in question. Specifically, when the price is \$3 per box of rubber bands, we know from Figure 8–11 that the optimal purchase is two boxes (point *T*). This information is recorded here as point *t*. Similarly, the optimal purchase is three boxes when the price of rubber bands is \$1.50 (point *E* in Figure 8–11). This is shown here as point *e*.

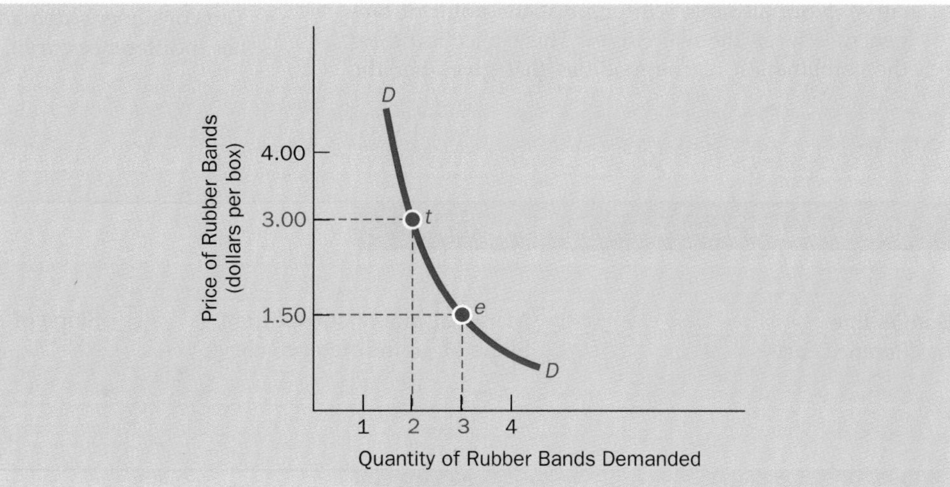


us that when the price of a box of rubber bands falls to \$1.50, quantity demanded rises to three boxes of rubber bands.[8] These two pieces of information are shown in Figure 8–12 as points *t* and *e* on the demand curve for rubber bands. By examining the effects of other possible prices for rubber bands (other budget lines emanating from point *B* in Figure 8–11), we can find all the other points on the demand curve in exactly the same way.

The indifference curve diagram also brings out an important point that the demand curve does not show. A change in the *price of rubber bands* also has consequences for the *quantity of cheese demanded* because it affects the amount of money left over for cheese purchases. In the example illustrated in Figure 8–11, the decrease in the price of rubber bands increases the demand for cheese from three to three and three-fourths pounds.

## *Summary*

1. Indifference-curve analysis permits us to study the interrelationships of the demands for two (or more) commodities.
2. The basic tools of indifference-curve analysis are the consumer's **budget line** and **indifference curves**.
3. A budget line shows all combinations of two commodities that the consumer can afford, given the prices of the commodities and the amount of money the consumer has available to spend.
4. The budget line is a straight line whose slope equals the ratio of the prices of the commodities. A change in price changes the slope of the budget line. A change in the consumer's income causes a parallel shift in the budget line.
5. Two points on an indifference curve represent two combinations of commodities such that the consumer does not prefer one of the combinations over the other.
6. Indifference curves normally have negative slopes and are "bowed in" toward the origin. The **slope of an indifference curve** indicates how much of one commodity the consumer is willing to give up in order to get an additional unit of the other commodity.

[8]How do we know that the price of rubber bands corresponding to budget line *BD* is \$1.50? Since the \$12 total budget will purchase at most eight boxes (point *D*), the price per box must be \$12 ÷ 8 = \$1.50.

7. The consumer will choose the point on her budget line that gets her to the highest attainable indifference curve. Normally this will occur at the point of tangency between the two curves. This choice indicates the combination of commodities that gives her the greatest benefits for the amount of money she has available to spend.
8. The consumer's demand curve can be derived from her indifference curve.

## Key Concepts and Terms

Budget line
Indifference curves
Marginal rate of substitution
Slope of an indifference curve
Slope of a budget line

## Questions for Review

1. John Q. Public spends all his income on gasoline and hot dogs. Draw his budget line when:
   a. his income is \$80 and the cost of one gallon of gasoline and one hot dog is \$1.60 each.
   b. his income is \$120 and the two prices are as in part (a).
   c. his income is \$80 and hot dogs cost \$1.60 each and gasoline costs \$1.20 per gallon.
2. Draw some hypothetical indifference curves for John Q. Public on a diagram identical to the one you constructed for part (a) of Question 1.
   a. Approximately how much gasoline and how many hot dogs will Public buy?
   b. How will these choices change if his income increases to \$120, as in part (b) of Question 1? Is either good an inferior good?
   c. How will these choices change if gasoline prices fall to \$1.20 per gallon, as in part (c) of Question 1?
3. Explain what information the *slope* of an indifference curve conveys about a consumer's preferences. Use this to explain the typical U-shaped curvature of indifference curves.

# PART III

# The Market System: Virtues and Vices

Chapter 9

# THE FIRM AND THE INDUSTRY UNDER PERFECT COMPETITION

*Competition . . . brings about the only . . . arrangement of social production which is possible . . . . [Otherwise] what guarantee [do] we have that the necessary quantity and not more of each product will be produced, that we shall not go hungry in regard to corn and meat while we are choked in beet sugar and drowned in potato spirit, that we shall not lack trousers to cover our nakedness while buttons flood us in millions.*

**FRIEDRICH ENGELS**

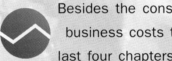

Besides the consumer demands and the business costs that were studied in the last four chapters, the decisions of firms also depend on the number, size, and behavior of the other firms in the industry. The strength of the competition faced by a company can profoundly affect its pricing, its output decisions, and its input purchases. Strong competitive pressures, sometimes taking subtle forms, can severely limit the freedom of choice of management in setting prices and, in the process, protect the interests of consumers. Giant corporations may also find themselves under this sort of pressure, even where there are few rival domestic firms. In recent years, for example, many American companies have found themselves facing stiffening competition from foreign companies, including Japanese, German, and Swedish firms. ¶ This chapter and the four chapters that follow it analyze some of the forms that competition—or its absence—can take, and examine some of the implications for the general welfare. ¶ Industries differ dramatically in how populated they are and in the size of a typical firm. Some industries, such as fishing, contain a great many very small firms; others, like automobile manufacturing, are composed of a few industrial giants. This chapter deals with a very special type of market structure—called *perfect competition*—in which firms are numerous and small. The chapter begins by comparing alternative market forms and defining perfect competition precisely. We then use the tools acquired in Chapter 5 to analyze the behavior of the perfectly competitive firm. Next, we consider *all* the firms in an industry as a group, and we investigate how developments in the industry affect the individual firms.

### TWO PRACTICAL PUZZLES

We begin this chapter, once again, with two puzzling but important applications. By the end of the chapter the analysis will have supplemented your common sense sufficiently to supply the required insights to the problems.

***ISSUE 1. POLLUTION–REDUCTION INCENTIVES THAT INCREASE POLLUTION*** Many economists and others who are concerned with the environment believe that cleaner air and water can be achieved cheaply and effectively if polluters are required to pay for the damages they cause. If a polluting firm can escape the emissions charge by emitting less, that will provide the required incentive. (See Chapter 21, pages 526–27 for more details.)

Yet such charges are often viewed as taxes, and that can make them political poison. Some politicians have reasoned that the donkey can be made to move as effectively by means of the carrot as by the stick. Consequently, it has been proposed to provide rewards to firms that cut down their emissions of pollutants. Instead of charging them money for every gallon of crud they emit, the idea is to give them money for every gallon by which they cut their emissions.

There is at least theoretical evidence that this system of bribes (or subsidies) does work, *at least up to a point*. Polluting firms, will, indeed, respond by cutting pollution. But, when everything settles down, it turns out that society will end up with more pollution than before! Payments to the firms actually make the pollution problem worse. How can it be that each firm pollutes less, and yet total pollution is worse?

***ISSUE 2. CAN FIRMS SHIFT THE BURDEN OF TAXATION TO CONSUMERS?*** It is widely believed that a tax on business is not borne by the firm. According to this view, any such tax will be passed on to consumers. "Firms don't pay taxes, people do." Yet whenever a tax on some product is proposed, the affected industry's lobbyists invariably show up at the legislature, arguing against the program. If firms can simply pass on the tax to the consuming public, why should they waste money and effort fighting it?

## VARIETIES OF MARKET STRUCTURE: A SNEAK PREVIEW

A **MARKET** refers to the set of all sale and purchase transactions that affect the price of some commodity.

It will be helpful to open our discussion by explaining clearly what is meant by the word "**market**." Economists do not reserve the term to denote only an organized exchange operating in a well-defined physical location. In its more general and abstract usage, "a market" refers to a set of sellers and buyers whose activities affect the price at which a *particular commodity* is sold. For example, two separate sales of General Motors stock in different parts of the country may be considered as taking place on the same market, while the sale of bread and carrots in neighboring stalls of a market square may, in our sense, occur on totally different markets.

So far, we have talked only about firms in general, without worrying about the sort of market in which they operate. But in this chapter and the next few we will see that the type of market in which the firm operates makes a great deal of difference for the way in which it can and does behave. Under some market forms, for example, the firm has no control over its price. In others, the firm has the power to adjust its price in a way that adds to its profits and which, in the opinion of some, constitutes exploitation of consumers.

Economists distinguish among different kinds of markets according to (1) how many firms they include, (2) whether the products of the different firms are identical or somewhat different, and (3) how easy it is for new firms to enter the market. *Perfect competition* is at one extreme (many small firms selling an identical product), while *pure monopoly* (a single firm) is at the other. In between are hybrid forms—called *monopolistic competition* (many small firms each selling products slightly different from the others') and *oligopoly* (a few large rival firms)—that share some of the characteristics of perfect competition and some of the characteristics of monopoly.

Perfect competition is far from the typical market form in the U.S. economy. Indeed, it is quite rare. Many farming and fishing industries approximate perfect competition, as do many financial markets (such as the New York Stock Exchange).

Pure monopoly—literally *one* firm—is also infrequently encountered. Most of the products you buy are no doubt supplied by oligopolies or monopolistic competitors—terms we will be defining precisely in Chapter 12.

## PERFECT COMPETITION DEFINED

You can appreciate just how special perfect competition is once we provide a comprehensive definition. A market is said to operate under **perfect competition** when the following four conditions are satisfied:

1. *Numerous Small Firms and Customers.* So many buyers and sellers that each one constitutes a negligible portion of the market—so small, in fact, that its decisions have no effect on the price. This requirement rules out trade associations or other collusive arrangements strong enough to affect price.
2. *Homogeneity of product.* The product offered by any seller is identical to that supplied by any other seller. (Example: wheat of a given grade is a homogeneous product; different brands of toothpaste are not.) Because the product is homogeneous, consumers do not care from which firm they buy.
3. *Freedom of entry and exit.* New firms desiring to enter the market face no impediments that the existing firms can avoid. Similarly, if production and sale of the good proves unprofitable, there are no barriers preventing firms from leaving the market.
4. *Perfect information.* Each firm and each customer is well informed about the available products and their prices. They know whether one supplier is selling at a price lower than another is.

These are obviously exacting requirements that are met infrequently in practice. One example might be a market for common stock: there are literally millions of buyers and sellers of AT&T stock; all of the shares are exactly alike; anyone who wishes can enter the market easily; and most of the relevant information is readily available in the daily newspaper. But it is hard to find many other examples. Our interest in perfect competition is surely not for its descriptive realism.

Why, then, do we spend time studying perfect competition? The answer takes us back to the central theme of this book. It is under perfect competition that the market mechanism performs best. So, if we want to learn what markets do well, we can put the market's best foot forward by beginning with perfect competition.

As Adam Smith suggested some two centuries ago, perfectly competitive firms use society's scarce resources with maximum efficiency. And as Friedrich Engels (the closest friend of and coauthor with Karl Marx) suggested in the opening quotation of this chapter, only perfect competition can ensure that the economy turns out just those varieties and relative quantities of the various goods that match the preferences of consumers. So by studying perfect competition, we can learn just what an *ideally functioning* market system can accomplish. This is the topic of the present chapter and the next one. Then, in Chapters 11 and 12, we will consider other market forms and see how they deviate from the perfectly competitive ideal. Still later chapters (especially Chapter 13 and the chapters in Parts 4 and 5) will examine many important tasks that the market does not perform at all well, even under perfect competition. These chapters combined should provide a balanced assessment of the virtues and vices of the market mechanism.

## THE COMPETITIVE FIRM AND ITS DEMAND CURVE

To discover what happens in a market in which perfect competition prevails, we must deal separately with the behavior of the *individual firms* and the behavior of the *industry* that is constituted by those firms. One basic difference between the firm and the industry under competition relates to *pricing*. We say that:

Under perfect competition, the firm is a pure *price taker*. It has no choice but to accept the price that has been determined in the market.

The fact that a firm in a perfectly competitive market has no control over the price it charges follows from the definition of perfect competition. The presence of a vast number of competitors, each offering identical products, forces each firm to meet but not exceed the price charged by the others. Like a stockholder with 100 shares of General Electric, the firm simply finds out the prevailing price on the market and either accepts that price or refuses to sell. But while the individual firm has no influence over price under perfect competition, the industry does. This influence is not conscious or planned. It happens spontaneously through the impersonal forces of supply and demand, as we observed in Chapter 4.

With two important exceptions, the analysis of the behavior of the firm under perfect competition is exactly the same as that pertaining to any other firm, so the tools described in Chapters 5 and 6 can be applied directly. The two exceptions are the special shape of the competitive firm's demand curve and the effects of freedom of entry and exit on the firm's profits. We will consider them in turn, beginning with the demand curve.

In Chapter 5, we always assumed that the firm's demand curve sloped downward; if a firm wished to sell more (without increasing its advertising or changing its product specifications), it had to reduce the price of its product. The competitive firm is an exception to this general principle.

A perfectly competitive firm has a **horizontal demand curve**. This means it can sell as much as it wants at the prevailing market price. It can double or triple its sales without any reduction in the price of its product.

How is this possible? The answer is that the competitive firm is so insignificant relative to the market as a whole that it has absolutely no influence over price. The farmer who sells his corn through an exchange in Chicago must accept the current quotation his broker reports to him. Because there are thousands of farmers, the Chicago price per bushel will not budge because Farmer Jones decides he doesn't like the price and holds back a truckload for storage.

Thus, the demand curve for Farmer Jones's corn is as shown in Figure 9–1; the price he is paid in Chicago will be $8 per bushel whether he sells one truckload (point *A*) or two (point *B*) or three (point *C*). That is so because price is determined by the *industry's* supply and demand curves shown in the right-hand portion of the graph.

Notice that, in the case of perfect competition, the downward-sloping industry demand curve in Figure 9–1(b) leads to the horizontal demand curve for the individual firm in Figure 9–1(a). The firm's demand is obtained by subdivision of the total quantity demanded in the market into the quantities demanded from each of the individual firms in the industry. The demand curve for an individual firm, however, need not resemble the demand curve for the industry.

## SHORT-RUN EQUILIBRIUM OF THE PERFECTLY COMPETITIVE FIRM

We have pointed out that economists define the short run to be a period so brief that some commitments cannot be changed. For example, if the firm has signed

**Figure 9–1** DEMAND CURVE FOR A FIRM UNDER PERFECT COMPETITION

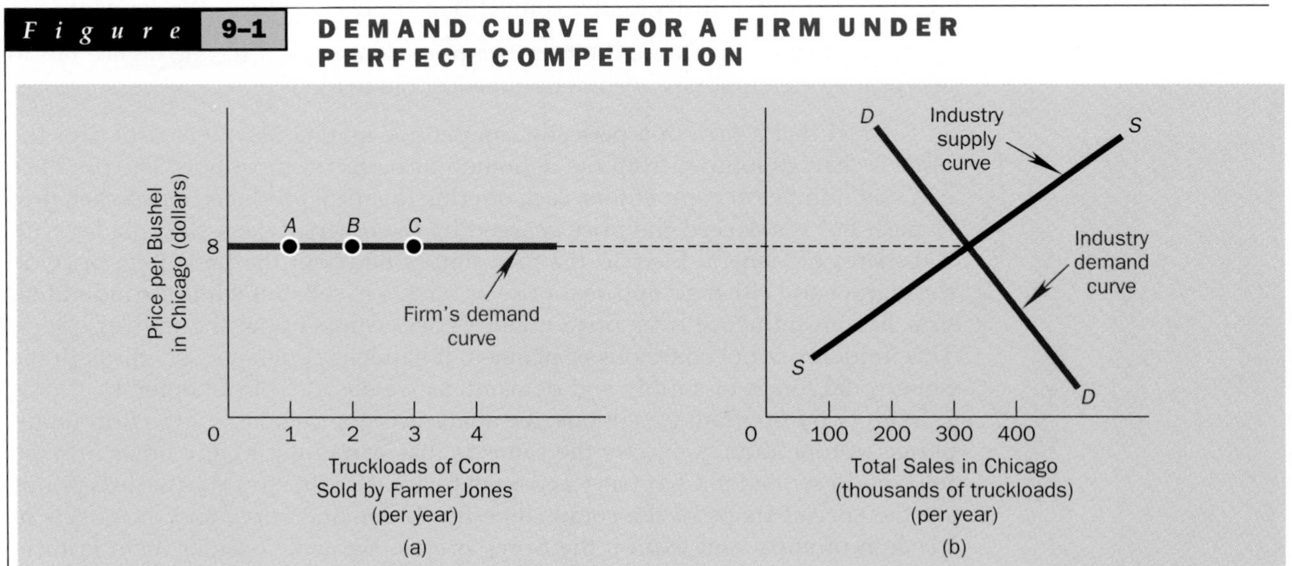


Under perfect competition the size of the output of a firm is so small a portion of the total industry output that it cannot affect the market price of the product. Even if the firm's output increases many times, market price remains $8, where it is set by industry supply and demand.

a five-year rental lease, its long run must be at least five years. A second critical element that cannot change in the short run is the number of firms in the industry. Even if an industry is making profits so high that new entrants are attracted into the business, that will usually take time. In the short run, then, we can ignore the possibility of entry or exit and study the decisions of the firms already in the industry.

We already have sufficient background to do this. Recall from Chapter 5 that profit maximization requires the firm to pick an output level that makes its *marginal cost equal to its marginal revenue*: MC = MR. The only feature that distinguishes the profit-maximizing equilibrium of the competitive firm from that of any other type of firm is its horizontal demand curve.

Because the demand curve (the average revenue curve) is horizontal, the competitive firm's marginal revenue curve is a horizontal straight line that coincides with its demand curve; hence, MR = price (*P*). It is easy to see why this is so. If the price does not depend on how much the firm sells (which is what a horizontal demand curve means), then each *additional* unit sold brings in an amount of revenue (the *marginal* revenue) exactly equal to the market price. So marginal revenue always equals price under perfect competition; the demand curve and the MR curve coincide because the firm is a price taker. That is, the firm must simply accept as a given the price that is determined by supply and demand in the market in which it sells its product [Figure 9–1(b)].

Once we know the shape and position of a firm's marginal revenue curve, we can use this information and the marginal cost curve to determine its optimal output and profit, as shown in Figure 9–2. As usual, the profit-maximizing output is that at which MC = MR (point *B*). This competitive firm produces 50,000 bushels per year—the output level at which MC and MR are both equal to the market price, $8. Thus:

Because it is a price taker, the *equilibrium* of a profit-maximizing firm in a perfectly competitive market must occur at an output level at which marginal cost is equal

*Figure* **9–2**

**SHORT-RUN EQUILIBRIUM OF THE COMPETITIVE FIRM**

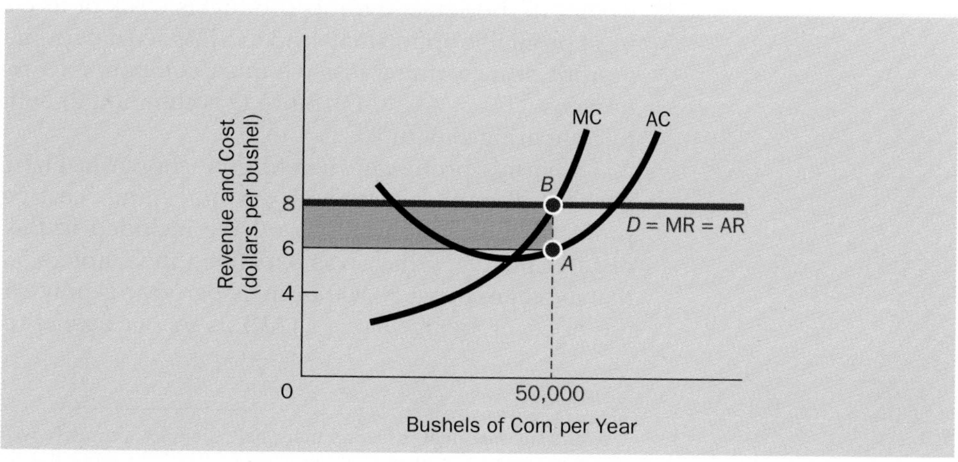


The profit-maximizing firm will select the output (50,000 bushels per year) at which marginal cost equals marginal revenue (point *B*). The demand curve, *D*, is horizontal because the firm's output is too small to affect market price, thus it is also the marginal revenue curve. In the short run, demand may be either high or low in relation to cost. Therefore each unit it sells may return a profit (*AB*) or a loss.

**Table 9–1 REVENUES, COSTS, AND PROFITS OF A COMPITETIVE FIRM**

| TOTAL QUANTITY (thousands of bushels) | TOTAL REVENUE | MARGINAL REVENUE | TOTAL COST | MARGINAL COST | TOTAL PROFIT |
|---|---|---|---|---|---|
| | | | (thousands of dollars) | | |
| 0 | 0 | | | | |
| | | 80 | | | |
| 10 | 80 | | 85 | | −5 |
| | | 80 | | 65 | |
| 20 | 160 | | 150 | | 10 |
| | | 80 | | 30 | |
| 30 | 240 | | 180 | | 60 |
| | | 80 | | 50 | |
| 40 | 320 | | 230 | | 90 |
| | | 80 | | 70 | |
| 50 | 400 | | 300 | | 100 |
| | | 80 | | 150 | |
| 60 | 480 | | 450 | | 30 |
| | | 80 | | 250 | |
| 70 | 560 | | 700 | | −140 |

to price. This is because a horizontal demand curve makes price and MR equal and, therefore, both equal to marginal cost. In symbols:

$$MC = P.$$

This idea is illustrated in Table 9–1, which gives the firm's total and marginal revenue, total and marginal cost, and profit for different output quantities. We see from the last column that total profit is maximized at an output of about 50,000 bushels, where total profit is $100,000. An increase in output from 40,000 to 50,000 bushels incurs a marginal cost ($70,000) which is approximately equal to the corresponding marginal revenue ($80,000),[1] confirming that 50,000 bushels is the profit-maximizing output.

## SHORT-RUN PROFIT: GRAPHIC REPRESENTATION

Our analysis so far tells us how the firm can pick the output that maximizes its profit. But even if it succeeds in doing so, the firm may conceivably find itself in trouble. If the demand for its product is weak or its costs are high, even the firm's most profitable option may lead to a loss. To determine whether the firm is making a profit or incurring a loss we must compare *total* revenue ($TR = P \times Q$) with *total* cost ($TC = AC \times Q$). Since $Q$ is common to both of these, that is equivalent to comparing $P$ with AC.

The firm's profit can therefore be shown in Figure 9–2. By definition, profit per unit of output is revenue per unit minus cost per unit. To enable us to see profit per unit graphically, we have included in the diagram the firm's *average cost* (AC) curve, which was explained in Chapters 5 and 6. We see in the figure that average cost at 50,000 bushels per year is only $6 per bushel (point *A*). Since the price, or *average revenue* (AR), is $8 per bushel (point *B*), the firm is making

[1]To calculate marginal costs and marginal revenues accurately we should increase output one bushel at a time, instead of proceeding in leaps of 10,000 bushels. But that would require too much space! In any event, that is why MR and MC are not exactly equal.

Figure 9–3 **SHORT-RUN EQUILIBRIUM OF THE COMPETITIVE FIRM WITH A LOWER PRICE**

In this diagram, the cost curves are the same as in Figure 9–2 but the demand curve (*D*) has shifted down to a market price of $4 per bushel. The firm still does the best it can by setting MC = *P* (point *B*). But since its average cost at 30,000 bushels per year is $6 per bushel, it runs a loss (shown by the shaded rectangle).

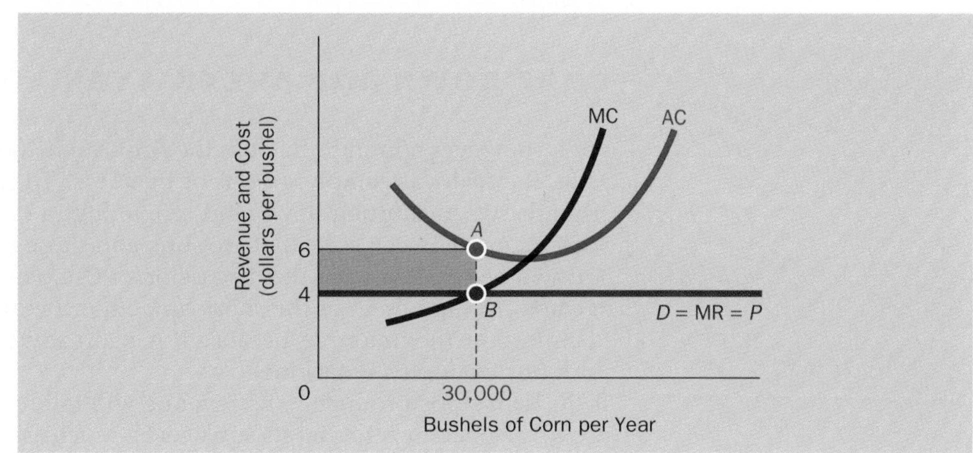


a profit of AR − AC = $2 per bushel. This profit margin appears in the graph as the vertical distance between points *A* and *B*.

Notice that in addition to showing the *profit per unit*, the graph can be used to show the firm's *total profit*. Total profit is the profit per unit ($2 in this example) times the number of units (50,000 per year). Therefore, total profit is represented as the *area* of the tan rectangle whose height is the profit per unit ($2) and whose width is the number of units (50,000).[2] That is, total profit at any output is the area of the rectangle whose base equals the level of output and whose height equals AR − AC. Thus, in this case, profits are $100,000 per year.

The MC = *P* condition gives us the output that maximizes the perfectly competitive firm's profit. It does not, however, tell us whether the firm is making a profit or incurring a loss. To determine this, we must compare price with average cost.

## THE CASE OF SHORT-TERM LOSSES

The market is obviously treating the farmer in the graph rather nicely. But what if the market were not so generous in its rewards? What if, for example, the market price were only $4 per bushel instead of $8? Figure 9–3 shows the equilibrium of the firm under these circumstances. The firm still maximizes profits by producing the level of output at which marginal cost is equal to price—point *B* in the diagram. But this time "maximizing" profits really means keeping the loss as small as possible.

At the optimal level of output (30,000 bushels per year), average cost is $6 per bushel (point *A*), which exceeds the $4 per bushel price (point *B*). The firm is therefore running a loss of $2 per bushel times 30,000 bushels, or $60,000 per

[2]Recall that the formula for the area of a rectangle is area = height × width.

year. This loss, which is represented by the area of the tan rectangle in Figure 9–3, is the best the firm can do. If it selected any other output level, its loss would be even greater.

## SHUT-DOWN AND BREAK-EVEN ANALYSIS

There is, however a limit to the loss the firm can be forced to accept. If losses get too big, the firm can simply go out of business. To understand the logic of the decision between shutting down and remaining in operation, we must return to the distinction between costs that are sunk and those that are variable in the short run. It will be recalled from the discussion of Chapter 6 that costs are sunk if the firm cannot escape them in the short run, either because of a contract (say, with the landlord or the union) or because it has already bought the item whose cost is sunk (for example, a machine).

If the firm stops producing, its revenue will fall to zero. Its short-run variable costs will also fall to zero. But its sunk costs—such as rent—will remain to plague it. If the firm is losing money, sometimes it will be better off continuing to operate until its obligations to pay sunk costs expire; but sometimes it will do better by shutting down and producing nothing. Two rules govern the decision:

***Rule 1.*** The firm will make a profit if total revenue (TR) exceeds total cost (TC). In that case, it should not plan to shut down either in the short run or in the long run.

***Rule 2.*** The firm should continue to operate in the short run if TR exceeds total short-run variable cost (TVC). It should nevertheless plan to close in the long run if TR is less than TC.

The first rule is obvious. If the firm's revenues cover its total costs, then it does not lose money.

The second rule is a bit more subtle. Suppose TR is less than TC. If our unfortunate firm continues in operation, it will lose the difference between total cost and total revenue, that is:

$$\text{Loss if the firm stays in business} = \text{TC} - \text{TR}.$$

However, if the firm stops producing, both its revenues and short-run variable costs become zero, leaving only the *sunk* costs to be paid:

$$\text{Loss if the firm shuts down} = \text{sunk costs} = \text{TC} - \text{TVC}.$$

Hence, it is best to keep operating as long as:

$$\text{TC} - \text{TR} < \text{TC} - \text{TVC},$$

or

$$\text{TVC} < \text{TR}.$$

That is Rule 2.

Rule 2 is illustrated by the two cases in Table 9–2. Case A deals with a firm that loses money but is better off staying in business in the short run. If it closes down, it will lose its $60,000 sunk cost. But if it continues to operate, it will lose only $40,000 because TR = $100,000 exceeds total variable cost (TVC = $80,000) by $20,000, so that its operation contributes $20,000 toward meeting its sunk costs. In case B, on the other hand, it pays the firm to shut down because continued operation only adds to its losses. If the firm operates, it will lose $90,000 (last

**Table 9–2 THE SHUT-DOWN DECISION**

| | CASE A (thousands of dollars) | CASE B |
|---|---|---|
| Total revenue (TR) | $100 | $100 |
| Total variable cost (TVC) | 80 | 130 |
| Sunk cost | 60 | 60 |
| Total cost (TC) | 140 | 190 |
| Loss if firm shuts down ( = sunk cost) | 60 | 60 |
| Loss if firm does not shut down | 40 | 90 |

entry in Table 9–2), whereas if it shuts down, it will lose only the $60,000 in sunk costs which it must pay whether it operates or not.

The shut-down decision can also be analyzed graphically. In Figure 9–4 the firm will run a loss whether the price is $P_1$, $P_2$, or $P_3$, because none of these prices is high enough to reach the minimum level of average cost (AC). The *lowest* price that keeps the firm from shutting down can be shown in the graph by introducing one more short-run cost curve: the **average variable cost** (AVC) curve. Why is this curve relevant? Because, as we have just seen, it pays the firm to remain in operation if its total revenue (TR) exceeds its total short-run variable cost (TVC). If we divide both TR and TVC by quantity ($Q$), we get TR/$Q$ = $P$ and TVC/$Q$ = AVC, so this condition may be stated equivalently as the requirement that price exceed AVC. The conclusion is:

The firm will produce nothing unless price lies above the minimum point on the AVC curve.

**Figure 9–4 SHUT-DOWN ANALYSIS**

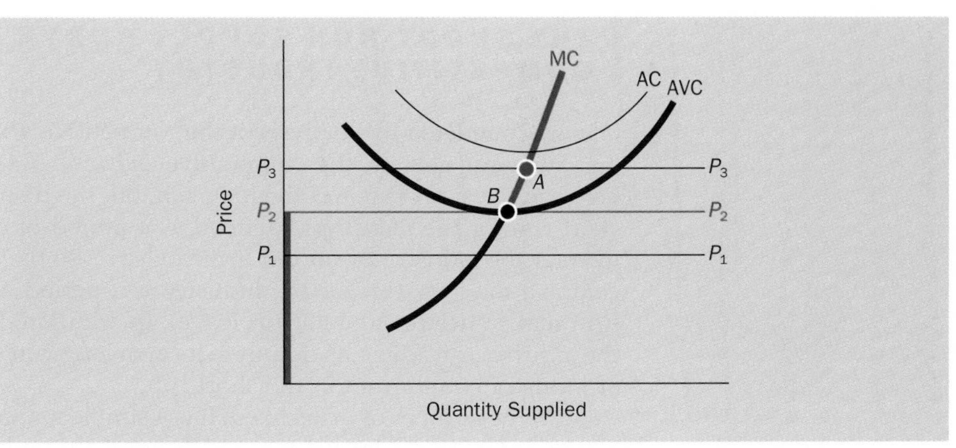


At a price as low as $P_1$, the firm cannot even cover its short-run average variable costs, and it is better off shutting down entirely. At a price as high as $P_3$, the firm selects point *A* but operates at a loss (because $P_3$ is below AC). However, it is more than covering its average variable costs (since $P_3$ exceeds AVC), so it pays to keep producing. Price $P_2$ is the borderline case. With this price, the firm selects point *B* and is indifferent between shutting down and staying open.

Figure 9–4 illustrates this principle by showing an MC curve, an AVC curve, and several alternative demand curves corresponding to different possible prices. Price $P_1$ is below the minimum average variable cost. With this price, the firm cannot even cover its variable costs and is better off shutting down (producing zero output). Price $P_3$ is higher. While the firm still runs a loss if it sets MC $=$ $P$ at point $A$ (because AC exceeds $P_3$), it is at least covering its short-run variable costs, and so it pays to keep operating in the short run. Price $P_2$ is the borderline case. If the price is $P_2$, the firm is indifferent between shutting down and staying in business and producing at a level where MC $=$ $P$ (point $B$). $P_2$ is thus the *lowest* price at which the firm will produce anything. As we see from the graph, $P_2$ corresponds to the minimum point on the AVC curve.

## THE SHORT-RUN SUPPLY CURVE OF THE COMPETITIVE FIRM

Without realizing it, we have now derived the **supply curve of the competitive firm** in the short run. Why? Recall that a supply curve summarizes in a graph answers to questions such as, "If the price is so and so, how much output will the firm offer for sale?" We have now discovered that there are two possibilities, as indicated by the thick blue line in Figure 9–4.

1. In the short run, if the price exceeds the minimum AVC, it pays a competitive firm to produce the level of output that equates MC and $P$. Thus, for any price above point $B$, we can read the corresponding quantity supplied from the firm's MC curve.
2. If the price falls below the minimum AVC, then it pays the firm to produce nothing. Quantity supplied falls to zero.

Putting these two observations together, we conclude that:

The short-run supply curve of the perfectly competitive firm is the portion of its marginal cost curve that is above the point where it intersects the average (short-run) variable cost curve; that is, above the minimum level of AVC. If price falls below this level, the firm's quantity supplied drops to zero.

## THE SHORT-RUN SUPPLY CURVE OF THE COMPETITIVE INDUSTRY

Having completed the analysis of the competitive *firm's* supply decision, we turn our attention next to the competitive *industry*. Again we need to distinguish between the short run and the long run, but the distinction is different here. The short run for the *industry* is defined as a period of time too brief for new firms to enter the industry or for old firms to leave, so the number of firms is fixed. By contrast, the long run for the industry is a period of time long enough for any firm that so desires to enter (or leave). In addition, in the long run each firm in the industry can adjust its output to its own long-run costs.[3] We begin our analysis of industry equilibrium in the short run.

With the number of firms fixed, it is a simple matter to derive the **supply curve of the competitive industry** from those of the individual firms. At any given

[3]The relationship between short-run and long-run cost curves for the firm was discussed in Chapter 6, pages 145–47.

price, we simply *add up* the quantities supplied by each of the firms to arrive at the industry-wide quantity supplied. For example, if each of 1000 identical firms in the corn industry supplies 45,000 bushels when the price is $6 per bushel, then the quantity supplied by the industry at a $6 price will be 45,000 bushels per firm × 1000 firms = 45 million bushels.

This process of deriving the *market* supply curve from the *individual* supply curves of firms is perfectly analogous to the way we derived the *market* demand curve from the *individual* demand curves of consumers in Chapter 7. Graphically, what we are doing is *summing the individual supply curves horizontally,* as illustrated in Figure 9–5. At a price of $6, each of the 1,000 firms in the industry supplies 45,000 bushels [point *c* in part (a)], so the industry supplies 45 million bushels [point *C* in part (b)]. At a price of $8, each firm supplies 50,000 bushels [point *e* in part (a)], and so the industry supplies 50 million bushels [point *E* in part (b)]. Similar calculations can be carried out for any other price. This adding-up process indicates, incidentally, that the supply curve of the industry will shift to the right whenever a new firm enters the industry.

The supply curve of the competitive industry in the short run is derived by *summing* the short-run supply curves of all the firms in the industry *horizontally.*

Notice that if the short-run supply curves of individual firms are upward sloping, then the short-run supply curve of the competitive industry will be upward sloping, too. We have seen that the firm's supply curve is its marginal cost curve (above the level of minimum average variable cost), so it follows that rising marginal costs lead to an upward sloping short-run *industry* supply curve.

## INDUSTRY EQUILIBRIUM IN THE SHORT RUN

Now that we have derived the industry supply curve, we need only add a market demand curve to determine the price and quantity that will emerge. This is done

**Figure 9–5**

**DERIVATION OF THE INDUSTRY SUPPLY CURVE FROM THE SUPPLY CURVES OF THE INDIVIDUAL FIRMS**

In this hypothetical industry of 1000 identical firms, each individual firm has the supply curve *ss* in part (a). For example, quantity supplied is 45,000 bushels when the price is $6 per unit (point *c*). By *adding up* the quantities supplied by each firm at each possible price, we arrive at the industry supply curve *SS* in part (b). For example, at a unit price of $6, total quantity supplied by the industry is 45 million units (point *C*).

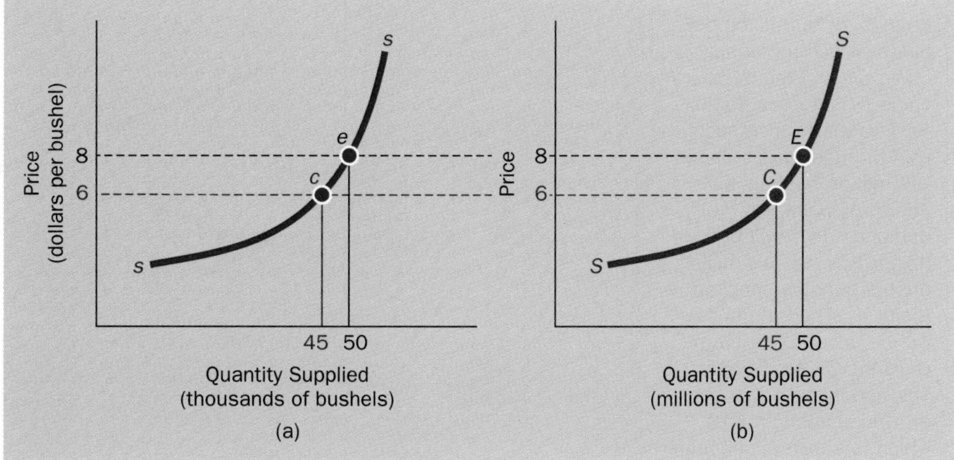

for our illustrative corn industry in Figure 9–6, where the blue industry supply curve [carried over from Figure 9–5(b)] is *SS* and the demand curve is *DD*. Note that for the competitive industry, unlike the competitive firm, the demand curve is normally downward sloping. Why? Each firm by itself is so small that, if it alone were to double its output, the effect would hardly be noticeable. But if *every* firm in the industry were to expand its output, that would make a substantial difference. Customers can be induced to buy the additional quantities arriving at the market only if the price of the good falls.

Point *E* is the equilibrium point for the competitive industry, because only at a price of $8 and a quantity of 50 million bushels are neither purchasers nor sellers motivated to upset matters. At a price of $8, sellers are willing to offer exactly the amount consumers want to purchase.

Should we expect price actually to reach, or at least to approximate, this equilibrium level? The answer is yes. To see why, we must consider what happens when price is not at its equilibrium level. Suppose it takes a lower value, such as $6. The low price will stimulate customers to buy more; and it will also lead firms to produce less than at a price of $8. Our diagram confirms that at a price of $6, quantity supplied (45 million bushels) is lower than quantity demanded (72 million bushels). Thus, unsatisfied buyers will probably offer to pay higher prices, which will force price *upward* in the direction of its equilibrium value, $8.

Similarly, if we begin with a price higher than the equilibrium price, we may readily verify that quantity supplied will exceed quantity demanded. Under these circumstances, frustrated sellers are likely to reduce their prices, so price will be forced downward. In the circumstances depicted in Figure 9–6, then, there is in effect a magnet at the equilibrium price of $8 that will pull the actual price in its direction if for some reason the actual price starts out at some other level.

In practice, there are few cases in which competitive markets, over a long period of time, seem not to have moved toward equilibrium prices. Matters

**Figure 9–6**

**SUPPLY–DEMAND EQUILIBRIUM OF A COMPETITIVE INDUSTRY**

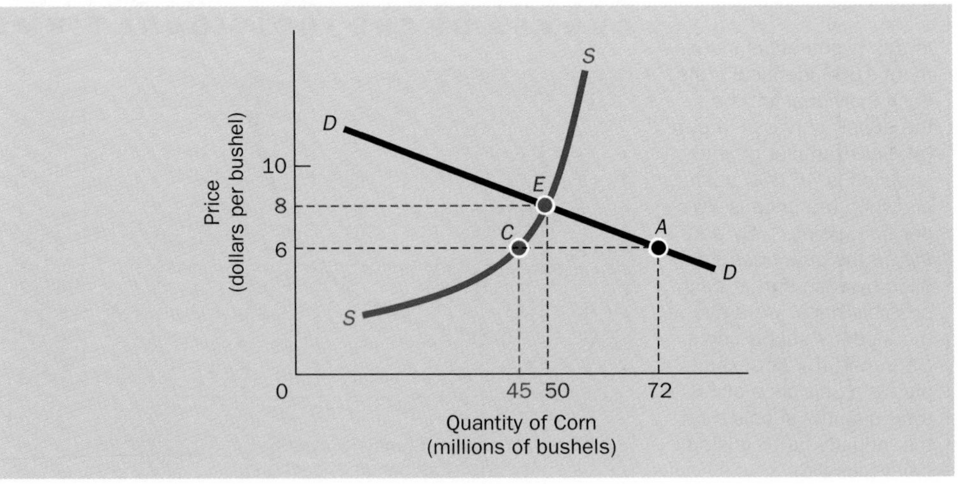


The only equilibrium combination of price and quantity is a price of $8 and a quantity of 50 million bushels, at which the supply curve *SS* and the demand curve *DD* intersect (point *E*). At a lower price such as $6, quantity demanded (72 million bushels as shown by point *A* on the demand curve) will be higher than the 45 million bushel quantity supplied (point *C*). Thus the price will be driven back up toward the $8 equilibrium. The opposite will happen at a price such as $10, which is above equilibrium.

eventually appear to work out as depicted in Figure 9–6. Of course, numerous transitory influences can jolt any real-world market away from its equilibrium point—a strike that cuts production, a sudden change in consumer tastes, and so on.

Yet, as we have just seen, there are powerful forces that do push prices back toward equilibrium—toward the level at which the supply and demand curves intersect. These forces are of fundamental importance for economic analysis, for if there were no such forces, prices in the real world would bear little resemblance to equilibrium prices, and there would be little reason to study supply-demand analysis. Fortunately, the required equilibrating forces do exist.

## INDUSTRY AND FIRM EQUILIBRIUM IN THE LONG RUN

The equilibrium of a competitive industry in the long run may differ from the short-run equilibrium that we have just studied for two reasons. First, the number of firms in the industry (1000 in our example) is not fixed in the long run. Second, as we saw in Chapter 6 (pages 145–47), the firm can vary its plant size and make other changes in the long run that were prevented by temporary commitments in the short run. Hence the firm's (and the industry's) long-run cost curves are not the same as its short-run cost curves.

What will lure new firms into the industry or repel old ones? Profits. Remember that when a firm selects its optimal level of output by setting MC $=$ $P$ it may wind up with either a profit or a loss. Such profits or losses must be *temporary* for a competitive firm, because the freedom of new firms to enter the industry or of old firms to leave it will, in the long run, eliminate them.

Suppose very high profits accrue to firms in the industry. Then new companies will find it attractive to enter the business, and expanded production will force the market price to fall from its initial level. Why? Recall that the industry supply curve is the horizontal sum of the supply curves of individual firms. Under perfect competition, new firms can enter the industry *on the same terms as existing firms.* This means that new entrants will have the *same* individual supply curves as old firms. If the market price did not fall, entry of new firms would lead to an increased number of firms with no change in output *per firm*. Consequently, the total quantity supplied on the market would be higher, and would exceed quantity demanded. But, of course, this means that in a free market entry of new firms *must* push the price down.

Figure 9–7 shows how the entry process works. In this diagram, the demand curve *DD* and the original (short-run) supply curve $S_0S_0$ are carried over from Figure 9–6. The entry of new firms seeking high profits *shifts the industry's short-run supply curve outward to the right,* to $S_1S_1$. The new market equilibrium is at point *A* (rather than at point *E*), where price is \$6 per bushel and 72 million bushels are produced and consumed. Entry of new firms reduces price and raises total output. (Had the price not fallen, quantity supplied after entry would have been 80 million bushels—point *F*.) Why must the price fall? Because the demand curve for the industry is downward sloping—an increase in output will be purchased by consumers only if the price is reduced.

To see where the entry process stops, we must consider how the entry of new firms affects the behavior of old firms. At first, this may seem to contradict the notion of perfect competition; perfectly competitive firms are not supposed to care what their competitors are doing. Indeed, these corn farmers do not care. But they *do* care very much about the market price of corn, and, as we have just

*Figure* **9–7** **A SHIFT IN THE INDUSTRY SUPPLY CURVE CAUSED BY THE ENTRY OF NEW FIRMS**

This diagram shows what happens to the industry equilibrium when new firms enter the industry. Quantity supplied at any given price increases; that is, the supply curve shifts to the right, from $S_0S_0$ to $S_1S_1$ in the figure. As a result the market price falls (from \$8 to \$6) and the quantity increases (from 50 million bushels to 72 million bushels).

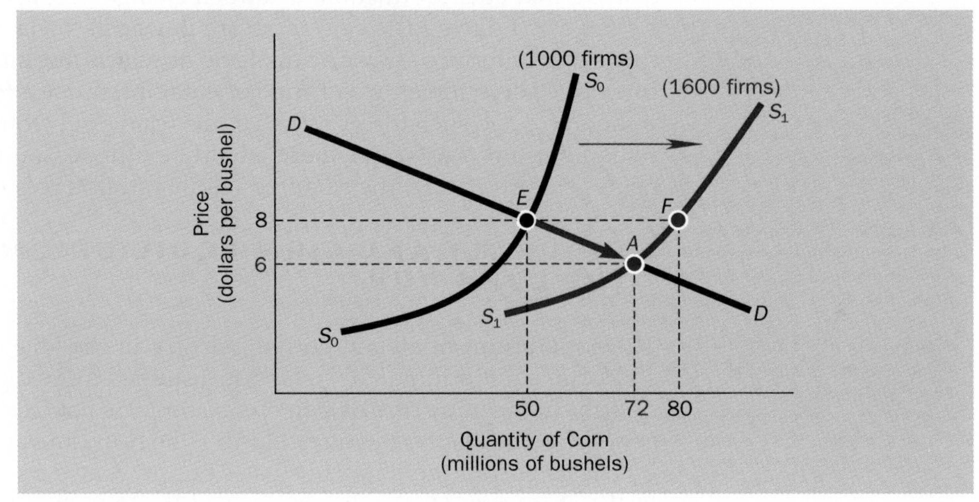


seen, the entry of new firms into the corn-farming industry lowers the price of corn.

In Figure 9–8, we juxtapose the diagram of the equilibrium of the competitive firm (Figure 9–2 on page 225) and the diagram of the equilibrium of the competitive industry (Figure 9–7). Before entry, the market price was \$8 [point *E* in Figure 9–8(b)] and each of the 1000 firms was producing 50,000 bushels—the point where marginal cost and price were equal [point *e* in Figure 9–8(a)]. The demand curve facing each firm was the horizontal line $D_0$ in Figure 9–8(a). There were profits because average costs (AC) at 50,000 bushels per firm were less than price.

Now suppose 600 new firms are attracted by these high profits and enter the industry. Each has the cost structure indicated by the AC and MC curves in Figure 9–8(a). As we have noted, the industry supply curve in Figure 9–8(b) shifts to the right, and price falls to \$6 per bushel. Firms in the industry cannot fail to notice this lower price. As we see in Figure 9–8(a), each firm reduces its output to 45,000 bushels in reaction to the lower price (point a). But now there are 1600 firms, so total industry output is 45,000 $\times$ 1600 $=$ 72 million bushels [point *A* in Figure 9–8(b)].

At point *a* in Figure 9–8(a), there are still profits to be made because the \$6 price exceeds average cost. Thus the entry process is not yet complete. When will it end? Only when all profits have been competed away. Only when entry shifts the industry supply curve so far to the right [$S_2S_2$ in Figure 9–9(b)] that the demand curve facing individual firms falls to the level of minimum average cost [point *m* in Figure 9–9(a)] will all profits be eradicated and entry cease.

The two panels of Figure 9–9 show the competitive firm and the competitive industry in long-run equilibrium.[4] Notice that at the equilibrium point [*m* in part (a)], each firm picks its own output level so as to maximize its profit. This means

[4]If the original short-run equilibrium had involved losses instead of profits, firms would have exited from the industry, shifting the industry supply curve inward, until all losses were eradicated and we would end up in a position exactly like Figure 9–9. EXERCISE: To test your understanding, draw the version of Figure 9–8 that corresponds to this case.

**THE COMPETITIVE FIRM AND THE COMPETITIVE INDUSTRY**

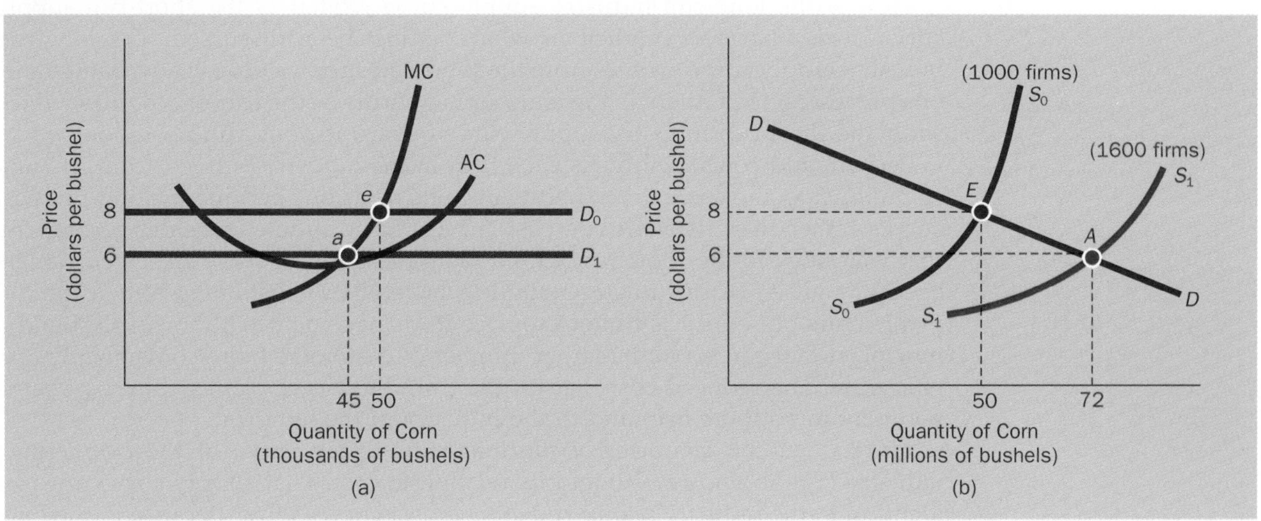


Here we show the interaction between developments at the industry level [in part (b)] and developments at the firm level [in part (a)]. An outward shift in the industry supply curve from $S_0S_0$ to $S_1S_1$ in part (b) lowers the market price from $8 to $6. In part (a), we see that a profit-maximizing competitive firm reacts to this decline in price by curtailing output. When the demand curve of the firm is $D_0$ (height = $8), it produces 50,000 bushels (point *e*). When the firm's demand curve falls to $D_1$ (height = $6), its output declines to 45,000 bushels (point *a*). However, there are now 1600 firms rather than 1000 so total industry output has expanded from 50 million bushels to 72 million bushels [part (b)]. Entry has reduced profits. But since *P* still exceeds AC at an output of 45,000 bushels per firm in part (a), some profits remain.

that for each firm $P = \text{MC}$. But free entry forces AC to be equal to *P* in the long run [point *M* in part (b) of the graph], for if *P* were not equal to AC, firms would either earn profits or suffer losses. That would mean, in turn, that firms would find it profitable to enter the industry or to leave it, which is incompatible with industry equilibrium. Thus:

When a perfectly competitive industry is in long-run equilibrium, firms maximize profits so that $P = \text{MC}$, and entry forces the price down until it is tangent to the long-run average cost curve ($P = \text{AC}$). As a result, in long-run competitive equilibrium it is always true that:

$$P = \text{MC} = \text{AC}.$$

Thus, even though every firm earns zero profit, profits are at the maximum that is attainable.[5]

## THE LONG-RUN INDUSTRY SUPPLY CURVE

We have now basically seen what lies behind the supply–demand analysis that was first introduced in Chapter 4. Only one thing remains to be explained. Figures 9–5 through 9–8 depicted short-run industry supply curves and short-run equilib-

[5]EXERCISE: Show what happens to the equilibrium of the firm and of the industry in Figure 9–9 if there is a rise in consumer income that leads to an outward shift in the industry demand curve.

rium. However, since Figure 9–9 describes long-run competitive equilibrium, its industry supply curve must also, obviously, pertain to the long run.

How is the long-run industry supply curve related to the short-run supply curve? The answer is implicit in what has just been discussed. The long-run industry supply curve evolves from the short-run supply curve via two simultaneous processes. First, there is the entry of new firms or the exit of old ones, which shifts the short-run industry supply curve toward its long-run position.

Second, and concurrently, as each firm in the industry is freed from its sunk commitments, the cost curves pertinent to its decisions become its long-run cost curves rather than its short-run cost curves. For example, consider a company that was stuck in the short run with a plant designed to serve 20,000 customers even though it was fortunate enough to have 25,000 customers. When the old plant wears out and it is time to replace it, management will obviously build a new plant that can serve the larger number of customers more conveniently and efficiently. The reduced cost that results from the larger plant is the cost that is pertinent to both the firm and to the industry in the long run.

Finally, we can characterize the long-run supply curve of the competitive industry ($S_2S_2$ in Figure 9–9) and its relation to cost. That supply curve must be identical to the industry's long-run *average* cost curve. Why? Because in the long run, as we have seen, economic profit must be zero. Thus, regardless of the quantity produced in equilibrium, the price the industry charges cannot exceed the long-run average cost (LRAC) of supplying that quantity. This must be so because any excess of price over LRAC would constitute a profit opportunity that would attract new firms. Similarly, price cannot be below LRAC because firms would then refuse to supply that output at this price. Therefore, for each possible long-run quantity supplied, the price must equal the industry's long-run average

**Figure 9–9 LONG-RUN EQUILIBRIUM OF THE COMPETITIVE FIRM AND INDUSTRY**

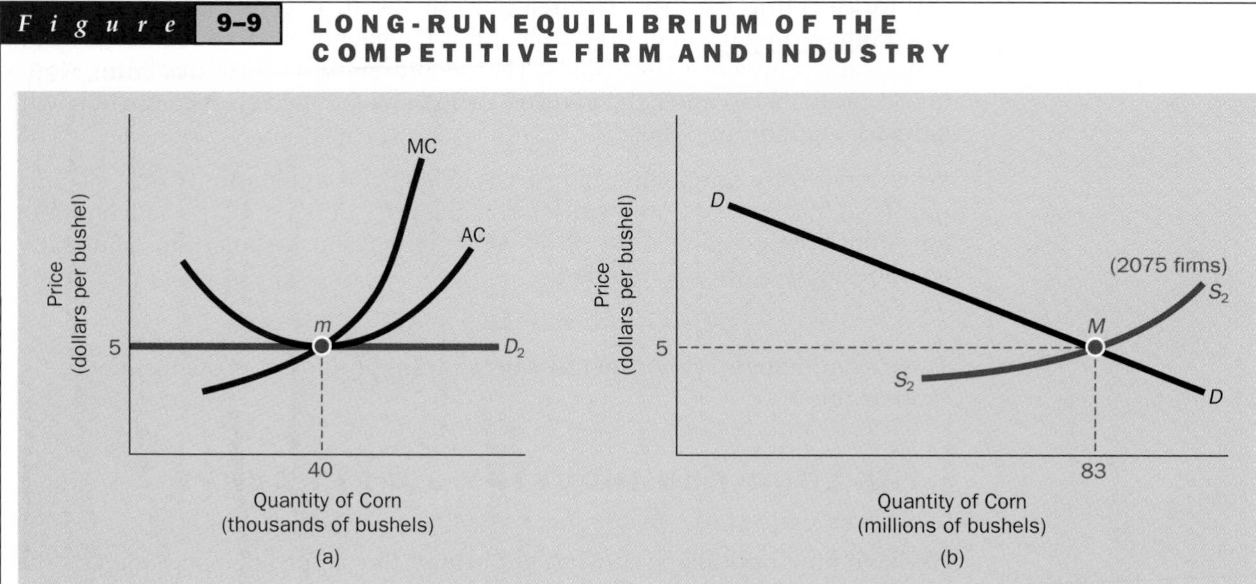


By the time 2075 firms have entered the industry, the industry supply curve is $S_2S_2$ and the market price is \$5 per bushel. At this price, the horizontal demand curve facing each firm is $D_2$ in part (a), so the profit-maximizing level of output is 40,000 bushels (point *m*). Here, since average cost and price are equal, there is *no* economic profit.

Figure 9–10 **SHORT-RUN INDUSTRY SUPPLY AND LONG-RUN INDUSTRY AVERAGE COST**

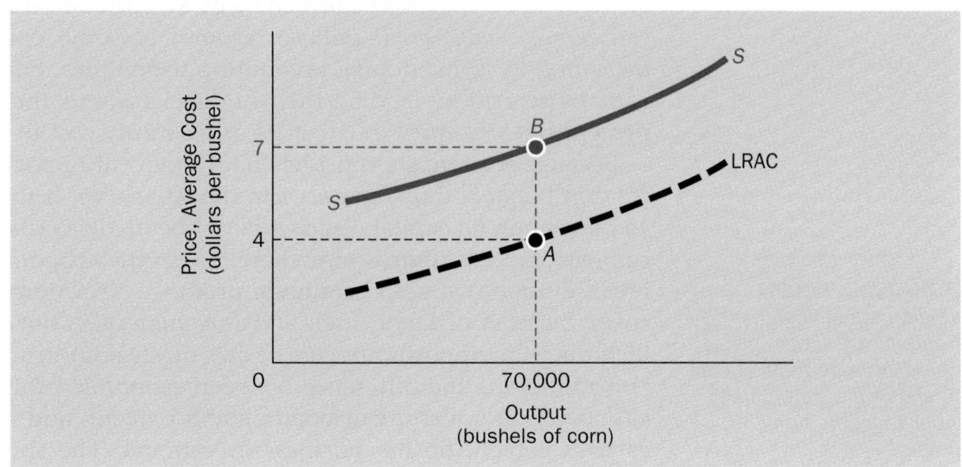


If the industry supply curve (*SS*) lies above and to the left of its long-run average cost curve (LRAC), the industry must earn economic profits (average economic profit = distance *AB*). That will induce entry, increase output at any given price, and shift the supply curve to the right until it coincides with the long-run average cost curve.

cost. It is this long-run industry supply curve that is relevant to the determination of long-run equilibrium price and quantity in a standard supply–demand diagram.

These points are illustrated in Figure 9–10, in which the short-run industry supply curve, SS, is above and to the left of the long-run average cost curve, LRAC. Consider any industry output, say 70 thousand bushels of corn per month. At that output, the long-run average cost is $4 per bushel (point A). But, if the price charged by farmers were given by the short-run supply curve for that output—that is, $7 per bushel (point B)— then the firms would earn $3 in economic profit on each and every bushel they sell.

Such economic profits would induce other firms to enter the industry, which would force prices downward as the industry supply curve shifted downward and to the right. So long as this shift does not take SS all the way down to LRAC, some economic profits will remain, and so entry will continue. Thus, SS must continue to fall until it reaches the position of the long run average cost curve. Then and only then entry will cease and long run equilibrium be attained.

The long-run supply curve of the competitive industry is also the industry's long-run average cost curve. The industry is driven to that supply curve by the entry or exit of firms and by the adjustment of firms already in the industry.

## ZERO ECONOMIC PROFIT: THE OPPORTUNITY COST OF CAPITAL

In our discussions of the long run, something may be troubling to you. Why would there be any firms in the industry *at all* if in the long run there were no profits to be made? What sense does it make to call a position of zero profit a "long-run equilibrium"? The answer is that the zero profit concept used in economics does not mean the same thing that it does in ordinary usage.

As has been noted repeatedly, when economists measure average cost, they include the cost of *all* the firm's inputs, *including the opportunity cost of the capital or any other inputs, such as labor, provided by the firm's owners.* Since the firm may not make explicit payments to some of those who provide it with capital, this element of cost may not be picked up by the firm's accountants. So what economists call *zero economic profit* will correspond to some positive amount of profit as measured by conventional accounting techniques. For example, if investors can earn 15 percent by lending their funds elsewhere, then the firm must earn a 15-percent rate of return to cover its opportunity cost of capital.

Because economists consider this 15-percent opportunity cost to be the *cost of the firm's capital,* they include it in the AC curve. If the firm cannot earn at least 15 percent on its capital, funds will not be made available to it, because investors can earn greater returns elsewhere. So, in the economist's language, in order to break even—earn zero **economic profit**—a firm must earn enough not only to cover the cost of labor, fuel, and raw materials, but also the cost of its funds, including the opportunity cost of any funds supplied by the owners of the firm.

**ECONOMIC PROFIT** equals net earnings, in the accountant's sense, minus the opportunity costs of capital and of any other inputs supplied by the firm's owners.

To illustrate the difference between economic profits and accounting profits, suppose U.S. government bonds pay 8 percent, and the owner of a small shop earns 6 percent on her business investment. The shopkeeper might say she is making a 6-percent profit, but an economist would say she is *losing* 2 percent on every dollar she has invested in her business. The reason is that by keeping her money tied up in the firm, she gives up the chance to buy government bonds and receive an 8-percent return. With this explanation of the meaning of economic profit, we can now understand the logic behind the zero-profit condition for the long-run industry equilibrium.

Zero profit in the economic sense simply means that firms are earning the normal economy-wide rate of profit in the accounting sense. This result is guaranteed, in the long run, under perfect competition by freedom of entry and exit.

Freedom of entry guarantees that those who invest in a competitive industry will receive a rate of return on their capital *no greater than* the return that capital could earn elsewhere in the economy. If economic profits were being earned in some industry, capital would be attracted into it. The new capital would shift the industry supply curve to the right, which would drive down prices and profits. This process would continue until the return on capital in this industry was reduced to the return that capital could earn elsewhere—its opportunity cost.

Similarly, freedom of exit of capital guarantees that in the long run, once capital has had a chance to move, no industry will provide a rate of return *lower than* the opportunity cost of capital. For if returns in one industry were particularly low, resources would flow out of it. Plant and equipment would not be replaced as it wore out. As a result, the industry supply curve would shift to the left, and prices and profits would rise toward their opportunity cost level.

## PERFECT COMPETITION AND ECONOMIC EFFICIENCY

Economists have long admired perfect competition as a thing of beauty, like one of King Tut's funerary masks (and just as rare!). Adam Smith's invisible hand produces results that are considered *efficient* in a variety of senses that we will examine carefully in the next chapter. But one aspect of the great efficiency of perfect competition follows immediately from the analysis we have just completed.

We have seen earlier that, when the firm is in long-run equilibrium, it must have $P = \text{MC} = \text{AC}$ (see Figure 9–9(a) on page 236). This implies that the long-run competitive equilibrium of the firm will occur at the lowest point on the firm's long-run AC curve, which is also where that curve is tangent to the firm's horizontal demand curve.

In long-run competitive equilibrium, every firm produces at the minimum point on its average cost curve. Thus the outputs of competitive industries are produced at the lowest possible cost to society.

Why is it always most efficient if each firm in a competitive industry produces at the point where AC is as small as possible? An example will bring out the point. Suppose the industry is producing 12 million bushels of corn. This amount can clearly be produced by 120 farms each producing 100,000 bushels, or by 100 farms each producing 120,000 bushels, or by 200 farms each producing 60,000 bushels. This is so since 120 × 100,000 = 100 × 120,000 = 60 × 200,000 = 12 million. (Of course the job can also be done instead by other numbers of farms, but for simplicity let us consider only these three possibilities.)

Suppose the AC figures for the firm are as shown in Table 9–3. Suppose, moreover, that an output of 100,000 bushels corresponds to the lowest point on the AC curve, with an AC of 70 cents per bushel. Which is the cheapest way for the industry to produce its 12 million bushel output? That is, what is the cost-minimizing number of firms for the job? Looking at the last column of Table 9–3, we see that the industry's total cost of producing the 12-million-bushel output is reduced to as low an amount as possible if it is done by 120 firms each producing the cost-minimizing output of 100,000 bushels.

Why is this so? The answer is not difficult to see. For any given industry output, $Q$, it is obvious that *total* industry cost = AC × $Q$ will be as small as possible if and only if AC for *each* firm is as small as possible, that is, if the number of firms doing the job is such that each is producing the output at which AC is as low as possible.

That this kind of cost efficiency characterizes perfect competition in the long run can be seen in Figures 9–8 and 9–9. Before full long-run equilibrium is reached (Figure 9–8), firms may not be producing in the least costly way. For example, the 50 million bushels being produced by 1000 firms at points *e* and *E* in Figures 9–8(a) and (b) could be produced more cheaply by more firms, each producing a smaller volume, because the point of minimum average cost lies to the left of point *e* in Figure 9–8(a). This problem is rectified, however, in the long run by entry of new firms seeking profit. We see in Figure 9–9 that after the entry process is complete, every firm is producing at its most efficient (lowest AC) level—40,000 bushels.

**Table 9–3 AVERAGE COST FOR THE FIRM AND TOTAL COST FOR THE INDUSTRY**

| FIRM'S OUTPUT (bushels) | FIRM'S AVERAGE COST (dollars) | NUMBER OF FIRMS | INDUSTRY OUTPUT (bushels) | TOTAL INDUSTRY COST (dollars) |
|---|---|---|---|---|
| 60,000 | 0.90 | 200 | 12,000,000 | $10,800,000 |
| 100,000 | 0.70 | 120 | 12,000,000 | 8,400,000 |
| 120,000 | 0.80 | 100 | 12,000,000 | 9,600,000 |

As Adam Smith might have put it, even though each farmer cares only about his own profits, the corn-farming industry as a whole is guided *by an invisible hand* to produce the amount of corn that society wants at the lowest possible cost.

## CUTTING POLLUTION: THE CARROT OR THE STICK?

We end the chapter by returning to the two puzzles with which it began, because we now have all the tools needed to resolve them. We begin with the two pollution-curbing proposals: Should polluters be taxed on their emissions, or should they, instead, be offered a subsidy to cut emissions? Such a subsidy would indeed induce firms to cut their emissions. Nevertheless, we stated early in the chapter that the paradoxical net result is likely to be an increase in total pollution. Let us see now why this is so.

In Figure 9–11 we depict the long-run average cost curve (LRAC) of the industry, curve *XX*. We now know that this must also be the industry's long-run supply curve, because if the supply curve lies above (to the left of) LRAC, economic profits would be earned and entry would drive the supply curve to the right. The opposite would occur if the supply was below and to the right of LRAC.

Now, a tax on business firms clearly raises the long-run average costs of the industry. Suppose it shifts the LRAC, and thus the long-run supply curve upward from *XX* to *TT* in the graph. This would move the equilibrium point to the northwest, from *E* to *B*. Similarly, a subsidy reduces average cost, and so it shifts the LRAC and the long-run supply curve downward and to the right (from *XX* to *SS*). This would move the equilibrium point to the southeast, from *E* to *A*.

Our paradoxical result follows from the presumption that the more a polluting industry produces the more it will emit. Under the tax on emissions, equilibrium

**Figure 9–11** TAXES VERSUS SUBSIDIES AS INCENTIVES TO CUT POLLUTION

Because a tax on emissions raises industry average cost, it will also raise the industry supply curve (the shift from *XX* to *TT*). This will move the equilibrium to point *B*, and reduce output from $Q_e$ to $Q_b$. The result is a cut in pollution. A subsidy for pollution reductions, however, cuts average cost and so shifts the industry supply curve downward to SS. The equilibrium point then moves to A and raises output to $Q_a$. Thus, the subsidy backfires by attracting so many additional polluting firms into the industry.

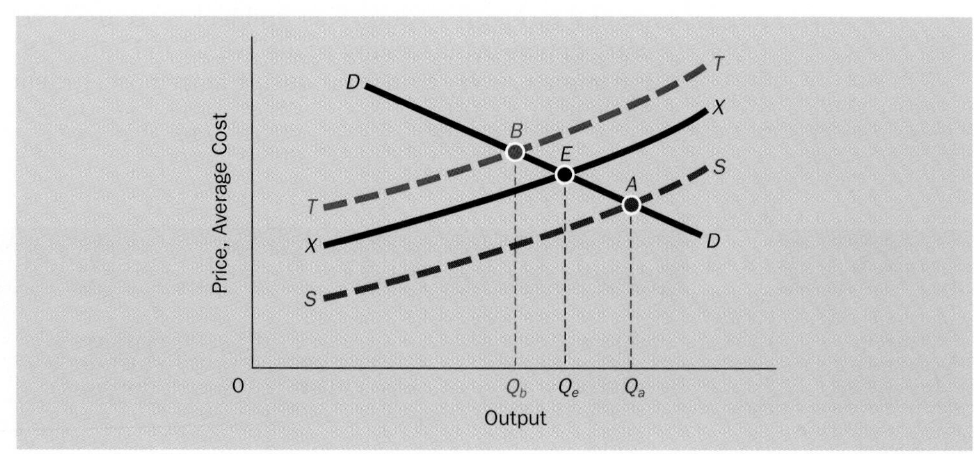

moves from *E* to *B*, and so output falls from $Q_e$ to $Q_b$. Thus emissions will fall—just as common sense leads us to expect. But, with the subsidy, industry output would *rise* from $Q_e$ to $Q_a$. Thus, contrary to intuition, and despite the fact that each firm emits less, the industry must pollute more!

What explains this paradox? The answer is *entry*. The subsidy will initially bring economic profits to the polluters, and that will attract even more polluters into the industry. In essence, a subsidy is a bribe for more polluters to open up for business. But our graph takes us one step beyond this simple observation. It is true that we end up with more polluting firms, but each will be polluting less than before. Thus we have one influence leading to increased pollution, and one pushing in the opposite direction. Which of these forces will win out? The graph tells us that if a rise in the polluting good's output always increases pollution, then when subsidy is the policy instrument used, increased pollution *must* be the victor.

## CAN FIRMS SHIFT A TAX TO THEIR CONSUMERS?

The second puzzle was why firms so strongly resist taxes on their products if they can simply raise prices and make consumers bear the costs. As we will see now, a tax of, say, \$3 per bushel of corn will generally raise the market price of corn by a smaller amount, say \$2. If that is so, then only \$2 of the \$3 tax will have been shifted to consumers. The remaining \$1 will somehow have to be borne by the suppliers. Let us see how.

The story is told in Figure 9–12. In the graph it is assumed that a \$3 tax is levied on every bushel of corn sold. This means that average cost must rise by exactly \$3 at every output level. For example, we see in the graph that if output is 70,000 bushels per week, then average cost rises from \$4 before the tax (point

**Figure 9–12** **CAN FIRMS SHIFT A TAX TO THEIR CONSUMERS?**

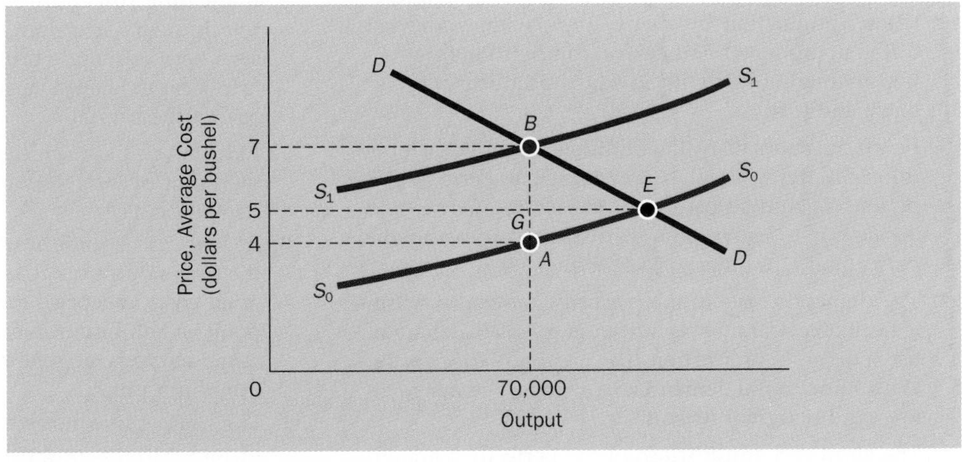


A \$3 tax per unit of output raises average cost by \$3, so the entire long-run supply curve shifts up by that amount (from $S_0S_0$ to $S_1S_1$). This moves the equilibrium point from *E* to *B* and raises price from \$5 to \$7 (from *G* to *B*). Thus, the price rise pays for only part of the \$3 tax (distance *AB*). Consumers do not bear the entire burden of the tax because of the decrease in quantity demanded in response to any rise in price—the negative slope of the demand curve.

*A*) to $7 after the tax is imposed (point *B*). Reasoning in this way, we see that the long-run industry supply curve must shift upward by exactly $3 at every output level. Thus, the industry supply curve shifts up from $S_0S_0$ to $S_1S_1$.

As a result, we see that the equilibrium point moves upward and to the left, from *E* to *B*, raising the equilibrium price from $5, to $7. This $2 price increase is only 2/3 of the $3 tax. In general terms, the price rise is shown by distance *GB*, while the tax is the larger distance, *AB*. The burden is therefore shared between consumers and producers.

How are consumers able to protect themselves from being stuck with the entire tax? The answer is simple. When price rises, they have a way of punishing suppliers: they simply purchase less. That is the meaning of the negative slope of the demand curve—the higher the price, the less consumers will buy. In fact, it can be shown that the flatter the demand curve, that is, the more elastic it is, the less of any given tax consumers will have to bear. (See Review Question 11 at the end of the chapter).

Does all this mean that profits will fall because of the tax? The surprising answer is no—at least not in the long run. Remember that long-run equilibrium profit is always zero under perfect competition, with or without the tax. So the tax cannot change the long-run profit rate. Then why does industry object to such a tax? Because, with a negatively sloped demand curve, a tax will cut into sales, cause short-term losses, and force some firms out of the industry. That is not a pleasant prospect for incumbent firms.

## *Summary*

1. **Markets** are classified into several types depending on the number of firms in the industry, the degree of similarity of their products, and the possibility of impediments to entry.
2. The four main market structures discussed by economists are **monopoly** (single-firm production), **oligopoly** (production by a few firms), **monopolistic competition** (production by many firms with somewhat different products), and **perfect competition** (production by many firms with identical products and free entry and exit).
3. Few industries satisfy the conditions of perfect competition exactly, although some come close. Perfect competition is studied because it is easy to analyze and because it is useful as a yardstick to measure the performance of other market forms.
4. The demand curve of the perfectly competitive firm is horizontal because its output is so small a share of the industry's production that it cannot affect price. With a **horizontal demand curve**, price, average revenue, and marginal revenue are all equal.
5. The **short-run equilibrium** of the perfectly competitive firm is at the level of output that maximizes profits; that is, where MC equals MR equals price. This equilibrium may involve either a profit or a loss.
6. The short-run **supply curve of the perfectly competitive firm** is the portion of its marginal cost curve that lies above its average variable cost curve.
7. The **industry's short-run supply curve** under perfect competition is the horizontal sum of the supply curves of all its firms.
8. In the **long-run equilibrium** of the perfectly competitive industry, freedom of entry forces each firm to earn zero economic profit; that is, no more than the firm's capital could earn elsewhere (the opportunity cost of the capital).
9. Industry equilibrium under perfect competition is at the point of intersection of the industry supply and demand curves.
10. In long-run equilibrium under perfect competition, the firm's output is chosen so that average cost, marginal cost, and price are all equal. Output is at the point of minimum average cost, and the firm's demand curve is tangent to its average cost curve at its minimum point.
11. The competitive industry's long-run supply curve coincides with its long-run average cost curve.
12. Both a tax on emission of pollutants and a subsidy payment for reduction in emissions induce firms to cut emissions. However, under perfect competition a

subsidy leads to the entry of more polluting firms and the likelihood of net increase of emissions by the industry.

13. A tax on a good generally leads to a rise in the price at which the taxed product is sold. However, the rise in price is generally less than the tax, so consumers usually pay less than the entire tax.

14. Consumers generally pay only part of a tax because the resulting rise in price leads them to buy less and the cut in the quantity they demand helps to keep price down. The more consumers cut their demands in response to a rise in price, that is, the more elastic their demand for the good, the smaller the share of a tax on the good that they will pay.

## Key Concepts and Terms

Market
Perfect competition
Pure monopoly
Monopolistic competition
Oligopoly

Price taker
Horizontal demand curve
Short-run equilibrium
Sunk cost
Variable cost

Supply curve of the firm
Supply curve of the industry
Long-run equilibrium
Opportunity cost
Economic profit

## Questions for Review

1. Explain why a perfectly competitive firm does not expand its sales without limit if its horizontal demand curve means that it can sell as much as it wants to at the current market price.
2. Explain why a demand curve is also a curve of average revenue. Recalling that when an average revenue curve is neither rising nor falling, marginal revenue must equal average revenue, explain why it is always true that $P$ = MR = AR for the perfectly competitive firm.
3. Under what circumstances might you expect the demand curve of the firm to be (a) vertical? (b) horizontal? (c) negatively sloping? (d) positively sloping?
4. Explain why in the short-run equilibrium of the perfectly competitive firm $P$ = MC, while in long-run equilibrium $P$ = MC = AC.

5a. Which of the four attributes of perfect competition (many small firms, freedom of entry, standardized product, perfect information) are primarily responsible for the fact that the demand curve of a perfectly competitive firm is horizontal?

5b. Which of the four attributes of perfect competition is primarily responsible for the firm's zero economic profits in long-run equilibrium?

6. It is indicated in the text (page 229) that the MC curve cuts the AVC curve at the *minimum* point of the latter. Explain why this must be so. (*Hint:* Since marginal costs are, by definition, entirely composed of variable costs, the MC curve can be considered the curve of *marginal variable costs*. Apply the general relationships between marginals and averages explained in Chapter 5.)
7. Explain why it is not sensible to close a business firm if it earns zero economic profits.
8. If the firm's lowest average cost is $24 and the corresponding average variable cost is $12, what does it pay a perfectly competitive firm to do if
   a. the market price is $22?
   b. the price is $15?
   c. the price is $4?
9. If the market price in a competitive industry is above its equilibrium level, what would you expect to happen?
10. Draw a long-run supply curve for a competitive industry. Assume that the government imposes a tax of $2 per unit of the product sold. What will happen to the supply curve? Why?
11. Draw two graphs like Figure 9–12. In one of them, make the demand curve fairly flat; in the other, make it fairly steep. Which of the demand curves is more elastic? In which of them is a larger share of the tax shifted to consumers? Why?
12. (More difficult) In this chapter we stated that the firm's MC curve goes through the lowest point of its AC curve and also through the lowest point of its AVC curve. Since the AVC curve lies below the AC curve, how can both of these statements be true? Why are they true? (*Hint*: see Figure 9–4).

Chapter 10

# THE PRICE SYSTEM AND THE CASE FOR LAISSEZ FAIRE

*If there existed the universal mind that . . . would register simultaneously all the processes of nature and of society, that could forecast the results of their inter-reactions, such a mind . . . could . . . draw up a faultless and an exhaustive economic plan. . . . In truth, the bureaucracy often conceives that just such a mind is at its disposal; that is why it so easily frees itself from the control of the market.*

**LEON TROTSKY (A LEADER OF THE RUSSIAN REVOLUTION)**

Our study of microeconomics is focussed on a crucial question: What does the market do well, and what does it do poorly? Our study of supply in Chapters 5 and 6 and of demand in Chapters 7 and 8 permits a fairly comprehensive answer to the first part of this question. This chapter will describe the tasks that the market carries out well—some, indeed, with spectacular effectiveness. ¶ We begin by recalling two important themes of Chapters 3 and 4: first, because all resources are scarce, it is critical to utilize them *efficiently*; second, an economy must have some way to *coordinate* the actions of many individual consumers and producers. Specifically, society must somehow choose *how much* of each good to produce, *what input quantities* to use in the production process, and *how to distribute* the resulting outputs among consumers. ¶ As suggested by the opening quotation (by an author who was in a position to know), these tasks are exceedingly difficult for central planners but are rather simple for a market system. This is why observers with philosophies as diverse as those of Adam Smith and Leon Trotsky have been admirers of the market, and why more and more of the formerly Marxist countries are now moving toward market economies. But the chapter should not be misinterpreted as a piece of salesmanship, for that is not its purpose.

Here we shall study an idealized price system in which every good is produced under the exacting conditions of perfect competition. While, as we have seen, a number of industries are reasonable approximations to perfect competition, other industries in our economy are as different from this idealized world as the physical world is from a frictionless vacuum tube. But just as the physicist uses the vacuum tube to study the laws of gravity, the economist uses the theoretical concept of a perfectly competitive economy to analyze the virtues of the market. There will be plenty of time in later chapters to study the vices.

## EFFICIENT RESOURCE ALLOCATION: THE CONCEPT

The fundamental fact of scarcity limits the volume of goods and services that any economic system can produce. In Chapter 3 we illustrated the concept of scarcity with a graphical device called a *production possibilities frontier*, which we repeat here for convenience as Figure 10–1. The frontier, curve *BC*, depicts all combinations of missiles and milk that this society can produce given the limited resources at its disposal. For example, if it decides to produce 300 missiles, it will have enough resources left over to produce *no more than* 500 billion quarts of milk (point *D*). Of course, it is always possible to produce fewer than 500 billion quarts of milk—at a point, such as *G*, below the production possibilities frontier. But if society

**Figure 10–1** **THE PRODUCTION POSSIBILITIES FRONTIER AND EFFICIENCY**

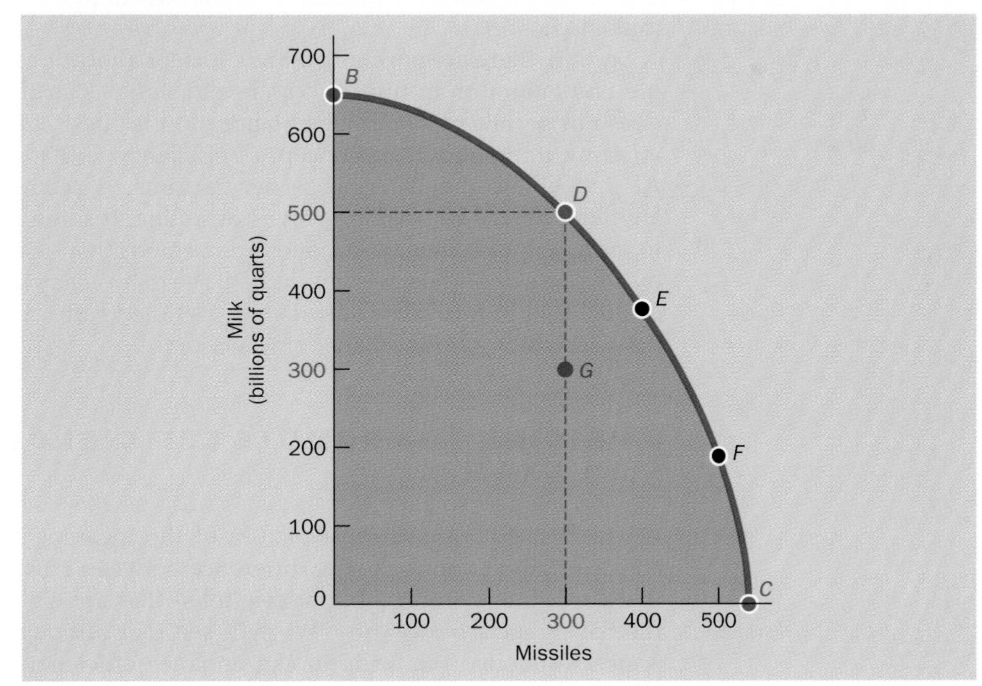


Every point on the production possibilities frontier, *BC*, represents an efficient allocation of resources because it is impossible to get more of one item without giving up some of the other. Any point below the frontier, like *G*, is inefficient, since it wastes the opportunity to obtain more of both goods.

does this, it is wasting some of its productive potential; that is, it is not operating *efficiently*.

In Chapter 3 we defined efficiency rather loosely as the absence of waste. Since the main subject of this chapter is how a competitive market economy allocates resources efficiently, we now need a more precise definition. It is easiest to define an **efficient allocation of resources** by saying what it is *not*. For example, suppose it were possible to rearrange our allocation of resources so that one group of people would get more of the things it wanted, while at the same time no one else would have to give up anything. Then, the failure to change the allocation of resources to take advantage of this opportunity would surely be wasteful—that is, *inefficient*. When society has taken advantage of every such opportunity for improvement through reallocation of resources, so that there remain no such possibilities for making some people better off without making anyone else worse off, we say that the allocation of resources is *efficient*.

An **EFFICIENT ALLOCATION OF RESOURCES** is one that takes advantage of every opportunity to make some individuals better off in their own estimation while not worsening the lot of anyone else.

Figure 10–1 illustrates the idea. Points below the frontier, like *G*, are inefficient because, if we start at *G*, we can make *both* milk lovers *and* missile lovers better off by moving to a point *on* the frontier, like *E*. Because *G* is below the frontier, there *must* be points like *E* on the frontier that lie above and to the right of *G*. This means that at *E* we get more of *both* outputs without any increase in input! Thus *no point below the frontier* can represent an efficient allocation of resources. By contrast, *every point on the frontier* is efficient because, no matter where on the frontier we start, it is impossible to get more of one good without giving up some of the other.

This example brings out two important features of the concept of efficiency. First, it is strictly a technical concept; there are no value judgments stated or implied, and tastes are not questioned. An economy is judged efficient if it is good at producing *whatever* people want. Thus the economy in the example can be as efficient when it produces only missiles at point *C* as when it produces only milk at point *B*.

Second, there are normally many efficient allocations of resources; in the example, *every* point on frontier *BC* can be efficient. As a rule, the concept of efficiency does not permit us to tell which allocation is "best" for society. In fact, the most amazing thing about the concept of efficiency is that it gets us anywhere at all. At first blush, the criterion seems vacuous. It seems to assert, in effect, that anything agreed to unanimously is desirable. If some people are made better off *in their own estimation*, and none are harmed, then society is certainly better off by anyone's definition. Yet, as we shall see in this chapter, the concept of efficiency can be used to formulate surprisingly detailed rules to steer us away from situations in which resources are being wasted.

## PRICING TO PROMOTE EFFICIENCY: AN EXAMPLE

Let us first give an intuitive picture of the meaning of efficiency and how the choice of prices can make the difference between efficiency and inefficiency. We use a real-life example—the prices (tolls) that are charged to use the bridges in the San Francisco Bay area. We will see that although proper pricing of these scarce resources (the bridges) can enhance efficiency, people nonetheless have often resisted the efficient solution and have adopted prices that prevent economic efficiency.

Figure 10–2 TOLL BRIDGES OF THE SAN FRANCISCO BAY AREA

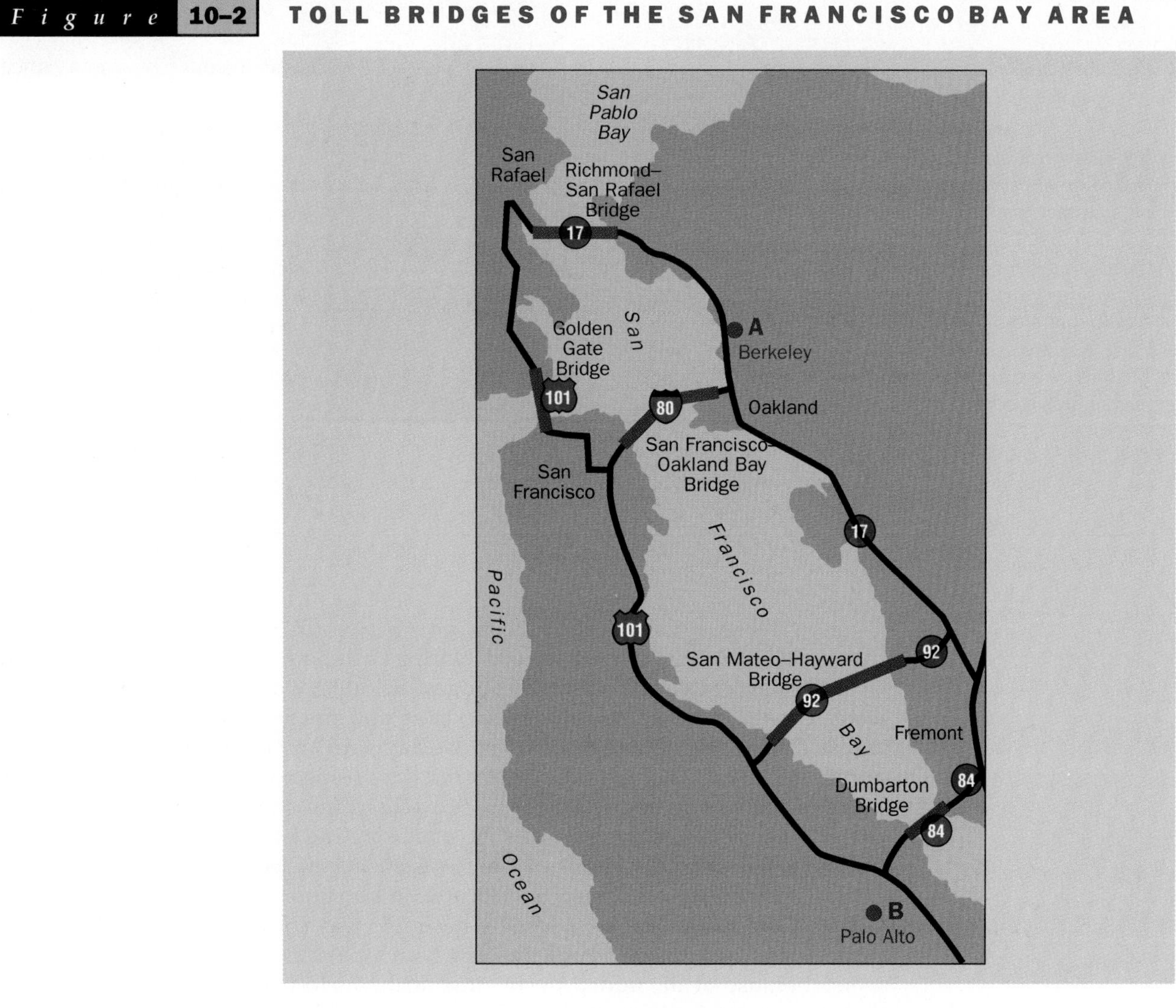


Figure 10–2 shows a map of the San Francisco Bay area, featuring the five bridges that serve the bulk of the traffic in and around the bay. A traveler going from north of Berkeley (point *A*) to Palo Alto (point *B*) has a choice of at least three routes:

1. Over the Richmond–San Rafael Bridge, across the Golden Gate Bridge, through San Francisco, and on southward.
2. Cross the bay on the San Francisco–Oakland Bay Bridge, and continue on southward as before.
3. Come down the eastern side of the bay, cross on the San Mateo–Hayward Bridge or the Dumbarton Bridge, and then head on to Palo Alto.

Let's consider which of these three choices utilizes society's resources most efficiently. The most crowded of the five bridges is the San Francisco–Oakland Bay Bridge, followed closely by the Golden Gate Bridge. The first carries 121,000

### *Earthquake, Bridge Congestion, and Route Substitution*

Bridge congestion and route substitution took on graphic proportions after the partial collapse of the San Francisco–Oakland Bay Bridge during the earthquake that shook the San Francisco area on October 17, 1989. According to one newspaper report:

The bridge closure forced commuters . . . [who] used it to cross the bay some other way. While many people stayed home the week after the disaster, they now appear to be rejoining the ranks of the daily rush. . . . The result has been major delay on alternative routes, such as the Golden Gate, San Mateo and San Rafael–Richmond bridges.*

**The Boston Globe*, October 31, 1989, page 15.

cars per day, and the second 120,000. During rush hours, delays are frequent and traffic barely crawls across these bridges. In other words, space is scarce, and every car that uses these bridges makes it that much harder for others to get across. On the other hand, the San Mateo–Hayward and Dumbarton bridges carry approximately 71,000 and 50,000 cars per day, respectively.[1] From the efficiency point of view, it is best if any driver to whom the choice between two of the routes makes little difference takes the one using the least crowded bridges. This will help reduce the amount of time wasted by the population as a whole in getting where they are going. Specifically, in our illustration, Route 1, using the Golden Gate Bridge, is not a socially desirable way for our driver to get to Palo Alto. Route 2, with its use of the San Francisco–Oakland Bay Bridge, is even worse because of the added delays it contributes to everyone else. Route 3, for drivers who are indifferent about these options, is the best choice from the viewpoint of the public interest. This is not meant to imply that it is socially efficient to equalize the traffic among the routes, but it certainly will help everyone's transportation speed if some of the traffic can be induced to leave the most crowded routes and to switch over to some less crowded ones.

It is here that prices can be used to promote efficiency in the utilization of bridges. Specifically, if we charge higher prices (very likely substantially higher prices) for the use of the most crowded bridges, on which space is a scarce resource, balanced by lower prices on the uncrowded bridges, we can induce more drivers to use the uncrowded bridges. This is just the same reasoning that leads economists to advocate low prices for abundant minerals and high prices for scarce ones.

[1]Source for data on average daily bridge traffic: Mr. Joseph Gallippi, California Department of Transportation, conversation of January 1993.

## CAN PRICE INCREASES EVER SERVE THE PUBLIC INTEREST?

This last discussion raises a point that people untrained in economics always find difficult to accept: *low prices may not always be in the public interest*. The reason is clear enough. If a price, such as the price of crossing a crowded bridge or the price of oil, is set "too low," then consumers will receive the "wrong" signals. They will be encouraged to crowd the bridge even more or to consume more oil, thereby squandering society's precious resources.

A historic illustration is perhaps the most striking way to bring out the point. In 1834, some ten years before the great potato famine caused unspeakable misery and death by starvation and brought so many people from Ireland to the United States, a professor of economics named Mountifort Longfield lectured at the University of Dublin about the price system. He offered the following remarkable illustration of his point:

> *Suppose the crop of potatoes in Ireland was to fall short in some year one-sixth of the usual consumption. If [there were no] increase of price, the whole . . . supply of the year would be exhausted in ten months, and for the remaining two months a scene of misery and famine beyond description would ensue. . . . But when prices [increase] the sufferers [often believe] that it is not caused by scarcity. . . . They suppose that there are provisions enough, but that the distress is caused by the insatiable rapacity of the possessors . . . [and] they have generally succeeded in obtaining laws against [the price increases] . . . which alone can prevent the provisions from being entirely consumed long before a new supply can be obtained.*[2]

Longfield's reasoning can usefully be rephrased. If the crop fails, potatoes become scarcer. If society is to use its very scarce resources efficiently, it must cut back on the consumption of potatoes—which is just what rising prices would do *automatically* if the market mechanism were left to its own devices. However, if the price is held artificially low, then consumers will be using society's resources inefficiently. In this case, the inefficiency shows up in the form of famine and suffering when the year's crop is consumed months before the next crop arrives.

It is not easy to accept the notion that higher prices can serve the public interest better than lower ones. Politicians who voice this view are put in the position of the proverbial father who, before spanking his child, announces, "This is going to hurt me much more than it hurts you!" Since advocacy of higher prices courts political disaster, the political system often rejects the market solution when resources suddenly become more scarce.

The pricing of landings at crowded airports offers a good example. The airports are particularly congested at the "peak hours," just before 9 A.M. and just after 5 P.M., and that is when passengers most often suffer long delays. But at many airports bargain landing fees continue to be charged throughout the day, even at those crowded hours. That makes it attractive even for small corporate jets or other planes carrying only a few passengers to arrive and take off at those hours, worsening the delays. Higher fees for peak-hour landings can be used to discourage such overuse. But they are politically unpopular, and many of the airports are run by local governments. So the ordinary passenger will probably continue to experience late arrivals as a normal feature of air travel.

---

[2]Mountifort Longfield, *Lectures on Political Economy* (Dublin, 1834), pages 53–56.

Prevention of a rise in prices where a rise is appropriate can have serious consequences indeed. We have seen from Longfield's example that it can contribute to famine. We know that it caused nationwide chaos in gasoline distribution after the sudden fall in Iranian oil exports in 1979. It has contributed to the surrender of cities under military siege when effective price ceilings discouraged the efforts of those who were taking the risk of smuggling food supplies through enemy lines. And it has discouraged the construction of housing in cities, when rent controls made building a losing proposition.

**INTERFERENCES WITH THE "LAW" OF SUPPLY AND DEMAND**

Recall from Chapter 4 that one of the **12 Ideas for Beyond the Final Exam** states that interfering with free markets by preventing price increases can sometimes serve the public very badly. In extreme cases it can even produce havoc—undermining production and causing extreme shortages of vitally needed products. The reason is that prohibiting price increases in situations of true scarcity prevents the market mechanism from reallocating resources to help cut down the shortage efficiently. The invisible hand is not permitted to do its work.

Of course there are cases in which it is appropriate to resist price increases—where unrestrained monopoly would otherwise succeed in gouging the public; where taxes are imposed on products capriciously and inappropriately; and where rising prices fall so heavily on the poor that rationing becomes the more acceptable option. But it is important to recognize that artificial restrictions on prices can produce serious and even tragic consequences—consequences that should be taken into account before a decision is made to tamper with the market mechanism.

## SCARCITY AND THE NEED TO COORDINATE ECONOMIC DECISIONS

Efficiency becomes a particularly critical issue for the general welfare when we concern ourselves with the workings of the economy as a whole rather than a narrower topic such as choice among several bridge routes or the output decision of a single firm. An economy may be thought of as a complex machine with literally millions of component parts. If this machine is to function efficiently, some way must be found to make the parts work in harmony.

A consumer in Peoria may decide to purchase two dozen eggs, and on the same day similar decisions are made by thousands of shoppers throughout the country. None of these purchasers knows or cares about the decisions of the others. Yet, scarcity requires that these demands must somehow be coordinated with the production process so that the total quantity of eggs demanded does not exceed the total quantity supplied. The supermarkets, wholesalers, shippers, and chicken farmers must somehow arrive at consistent decisions, for otherwise the economic process will deteriorate into chaos. And there are many other such decisions that must be coordinated. One cannot run machines that are completed except for a few parts that have not been delivered. Refrigerators and cars cannot be used unless there is an adequate supply of fuel.

## Economic Shock Therapy in Poland

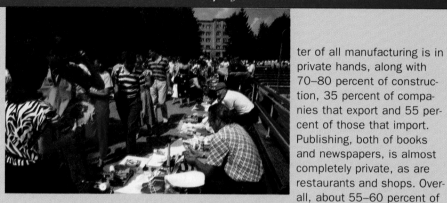

Since 1989 we all have witnessed the cataclysmic events in Eastern Europe, including the collapse of communist central planning and the embrace of the free market. Nowhere have these changes happened as quickly and dramatically as in Poland. The reforms in Poland have constituted no less than economic "shock therapy," and appear to have produced a thriving private sector, as these excerpts (and the accompanying table) from *The Economist* magazine show:

Instead of empty shops, Warsaw's streets are lined with bright kiosks selling everything from Polish magazines to American candy. After decades spent buying the same brands of toothpaste and washing powder, Poles now joke about the fierce soap wars conducted through television advertising. Across once-grey buildings billboards splash the names of Benetton and Levi Strauss. . . .

. . . private entrepreneurs [have] flourished. . . . The growth of this uncontrolled capitalist sector has already had a huge impact on the Polish economy. By now, there are 1.6 million non-agricultural private businesses, of which about 55,000 are incorporated (up from 15,000 two years ago); state companies number about 8,000. A quarter of all manufacturing is in private hands, along with 70–80 percent of construction, 35 percent of companies that export and 55 percent of those that import. Publishing, both of books and newspapers, is almost completely private, as are restaurants and shops. Overall, about 55–60 percent of Poles now work in the private sector, and it accounts for nearly half of GDP.

SOURCE: "Poland's Economic Reforms, If It Works, You've Fixed It," *The Economist*, January 23, 1993, pages 21–23. Source cited for table: Polish Central Statistical Office.

**ROLL OVER, KARL MARX**

| | **% Share of the Private Sector in:** | | |
|---|---|---|---|
| | **1989** | **1990** | **1991** |
| GDP | 29% | 31% | 42% |
| Employment, including private agriculture | 44 | 46 | 51 |
| Employment, excluding private agriculture | 22 | 23 | 27 |
| Exports | — | 5 | 22 |
| Imports | — | 14 | 50 |
| Investment | 35 | 42 | 41 |
| Industrial production | 16 | 18 | 24 |
| Construction | 33 | 32 | 55 |
| Commerce | 60 | 64 | 83 |
| Transport | 12 | 14 | 24 |

In an economy that is planned and centrally directed, it is easy to imagine how such coordination takes place—though the implementation turns out to be far more difficult than the idea. Central planners set production targets for firms and may even tell firms how to meet these targets. In extreme cases, consumers may even be told, rather than asked, what they want to consume.

In a market system, prices are used to coordinate economic activity instead. High prices discourage consumption of the resources that are most scarce, while low prices encourage consumption of the resources that are comparatively abundant. In this way, prices are the instrument used by Adam Smith's invisible hand to organize the economy's production.

The invisible hand has an astonishing capacity to handle a coordination problem of truly enormous proportions—one that will remain beyond the capabilities of electronic computers at least for the foreseeable future. It is true that like any mechanism this one has its imperfections, some of them rather serious. But it is all too easy to lose sight of the tremendously demanding task that the market constantly accomplishes—unnoticed, undirected, and at least in some respects, amazingly well. Let us, then, examine how the market goes about coordinating economic activity.

## THREE COORDINATION TASKS IN THE ECONOMY

We noted in Chapter 3 that any economic system, whether planned or unplanned, must find answers to three basic questions of resource allocation:

1. ***Output Selection*** How much of each commodity should be produced?
2. ***Production Planning*** What quantities of each of the available inputs should be used to produce each good?
3. ***Distribution*** How should the resulting products be divided among the consumers?

These coordination tasks may at first appear to be tailor-made for a regime of governmental planning like the one that used to be employed in the former Soviet Union. Yet most economists (even, nowadays, those in the formerly centrally planned economies) believe that it is in these tasks that central direction performs most poorly and, paradoxically, that the undisciplined free market performs best. To understand how the unguided market manages the miracle of creating order of what might otherwise be chaos, let us look at how each of these questions is answered by a system of free and unfettered markets—the method of economic organization that the eighteenth-century French economists named **laissez faire**. Under laissez faire, the government would prevent crime, enforce contracts, and build roads and other types of public works; but it would not set prices and would interfere as little as possible with the operation of free markets. How does such an unmanaged economy solve the three coordination problems?

**LAISSEZ FAIRE** refers to a program of minimal interference with the workings of the market system. The term means that people should be left alone in carrying out their economic affairs.

### OUTPUT SELECTION

A free-market system decides what should be produced via what we have called the "law" of supply and demand. Where there is a *shortage*—that is, where quantity demanded exceeds quantity supplied—the market mechanism pushes the price up, thereby encouraging more production and less consumption of the commodity in short supply. Where there is a *surplus*—that is, where quantity supplied exceeds quantity demanded—the same mechanism works in reverse: the price falls, which discourages production and stimulates consumption.

As an example, suppose millions of people wake up one morning with a craving for omelets. For the moment, the quantity of eggs demanded exceeds the quantity supplied. But within a few days the market mechanism swings into action to meet this sudden change in demand. The price of eggs rises, which stimulates the production of eggs. In the first instance, farmers simply bring more eggs to market by taking them out of storage. Over a somewhat longer period of time, chickens that otherwise would have been sold for meat are kept in the chicken coops laying eggs. Finally, if the high price of eggs persists, farmers begin to increase their flocks, build more cages, and so on. Thus, a shift in consumer demand leads to a shift in society's resources; more eggs are wanted, and so the market mechanism sees to it that more of society's resources are devoted to the production of eggs.

Similar reactions follow if a technological breakthrough reduces the input quantities needed to produce some item. Electronic calculators are a marvelous example. Just 20 years ago, calculators were so expensive that they could be found only in business firms and scientific laboratories. Then advances in science and engineering reduced their cost dramatically, and the market went to work. With costs sharply reduced, prices fell dramatically and the quantity demanded skyrocketed. Electronics firms flocked into the industry to meet this demand, which is to say that more of society's resources were devoted to producing the calculators that were suddenly in such great demand. These examples lead us to conclude that:

Under laissez faire, the allocation of society's resources among different products depends on two basic influences: consumer preferences and the relative difficulty of producing the goods, that is, their production costs. Prices vary so as to bring the quantity of each commodity produced into line with the quantity demanded.

Notice that no bureaucrat or central planner arranges the allocation of resources. Instead, allocation is guided by an unseen force—the lure of profits, which is the invisible hand that guides chicken farmers to increase their flocks when eggs are in greater demand and guides electronics firms to build new factories when the cost of electronic products falls.

## PRODUCTION PLANNING

Once the composition of output has been decided, the next coordination task is to determine just how those goods are going to be produced. The production-planning problem includes, among other things, the division of society's scarce inputs among enterprises. Which farm or factory will get how much of which materials? Such decisions can be crucial. If a factory runs short of an essential input, the entire production process may grind to a halt.

As a matter of fact, inputs and outputs cannot be selected separately. The inputs assigned to the growing of coffee rather than to bananas determine the quantities of coffee and bananas that can be obtained. However, it is simpler to think of these decisions as if they occurred one at a time.

Once again, under laissez faire it is the price system that apportions fuels and other raw materials among the different industries in accord with those industries' requirements. The firm that needs a piece of equipment most urgently will be the last to drop out of the market for that product when prices rise. If more grain is demanded by millers than is currently available, the price will rise and bring quantity demanded back into line with quantity supplied, always giving priority to those users who are willing to pay the most for grain. Thus:

In a free market, inputs are assigned to the firms that can make the most productive (most profitable) use of them. Firms that cannot make a sufficiently productive use of some input will be priced out of the market for that item.

This task, which sounds so simple, is actually almost unimaginably complex. It is also one on which many centrally planned systems have foundered. We will return to it shortly, as an illustration of how difficult it is to replace the market by a central planning bureau. But first let us consider the third of our three coordination problems.

### DISTRIBUTION OF PRODUCTS AMONG CONSUMERS

The third task of any economy is to decide which consumer gets each of the goods that has been produced. The objective is to distribute the available supplies so as to match the differing preferences of consumers as well as possible. Coffee lovers must not be flooded with tea while tea drinkers are showered with coffee.

The price mechanism solves this problem by assigning the highest prices to the goods in greatest demand and then letting individual consumers pursue their own self-interests. Consider our example of the rising price of eggs. As the price of eggs rises, those whose craving for omelets is not terribly strong will begin to buy fewer eggs. In effect, the price acts as a rationing device, which apportions the available eggs among the consumers who are willing to pay the most for them.

But the price mechanism has one important advantage over other rationing devices: it is able to pay attention to consumer preferences. If eggs are rationed by the most obvious and usual means (say, two to a person), everyone ends up with the same quantity—whether he thinks eggs the more unpleasant component of his breakfast or the ingredients of his evening's soufflé, for which he pangs all day long. The price system, on the other hand, permits each consumer to set his own priorities. If you just barely tolerate eggs, a rise in their price quickly induces you to get your protein from some other source. But the egg lover is not induced to switch so readily. Thus:

The price system carries out the distribution process by rationing goods on the basis of preferences *and relative incomes.*

Notice the last three words. This rationing process *does* favor the rich, and this is a problem that market economies must confront. However, we may still want to think twice before declaring ourselves opposed to the price system. If equality is our goal, might not a more reasonable solution be to use the tax system to equalize incomes, and *then* let the market mechanism distribute goods in accord with preferences?

We have just seen, in broad outline, how a laissez faire economy addresses the three basic issues of resource allocation: what to produce, how to produce it, and how to distribute the resulting products. Since it performs these tasks quietly, without central direction, and with no apparent concern for the public interest, many radical critics have predicted that such an unplanned system must degenerate into chaos. Yet that does not seem to be the way things work out. Unplanned the market may be, but its results are far from chaotic. In fact, quite ironically, it was the centrally planned economies that often found themselves in economic chaos. Perhaps the best way to appreciate the accomplishments of the market is to consider how a centrally planned system must cope with the coordination problems we have just outlined. We will examine just one of them: production planning.

## INPUT-OUTPUT ANALYSIS: THE NEAR IMPOSSIBILITY OF PERFECT CENTRAL PLANNING

Of the three coordination tasks of any economy, the assignment of inputs to specific industries and firms has claimed the most attention of central planners.

Why? Because the production processes of the various industries are interdependent. Industry X cannot operate without the output of industry Y, but Y, in turn, finds the product of X indispensable. So the whole economy can grind to a halt if the production planning problem is not solved satisfactorily.

Let's take a simple example. Unless planners allocate enough gasoline to trucking, products will not get to market. And unless they allocate enough trucks to haul the gasoline to gas stations, consumers will not be able to get the gasoline. Thus, trucking activity depends on gasoline production but gasoline production also depends on trucking activity. We seem to be caught in a circle. Though it turns out not to be a vicious circle, both truck and gasoline outputs must be decided together, not separately.

Because the output required from any one industry depends on the output desired from every other industry, planners can be sure that the production of the various outputs is sufficient to meet both consumer and industrial demands only by taking explicit account of the interdependencies among industries. If they change the output target for one industry, every other industry's output target also must be adjusted.

For example, if planners decide to provide consumers with more electricity, then more steel must be produced for more electric generators. But an increase in steel output requires more coal to be mined. More mining in turn means that still more electricity is needed to light the mines, to run the elevators, and perhaps even to run some of the trains that carry the coal, and so on and on. Any single change in production sets off a chain of adjustments throughout the economy that require still further adjustments.

To decide how much of each output an economy must produce, the planner must use statistics to form a set of equations, one equation for each product, and then solve those equations *simultaneously*. (The simultaneous solution process

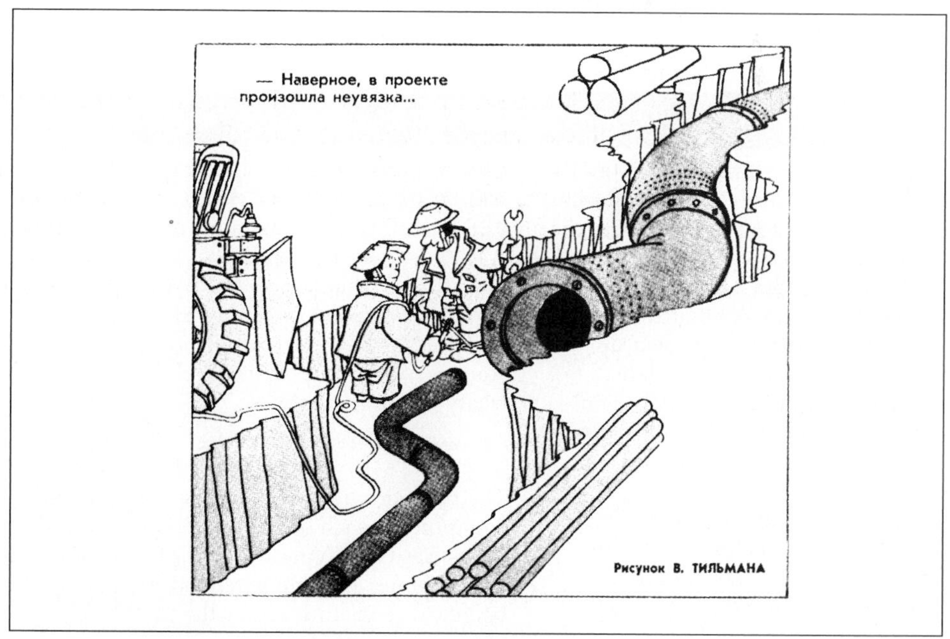


In this cartoon from a Soviet humor magazine, one construction worker comments to another, "A slight mistake in the plans, perhaps." It is interesting that there were many cartoons making fun of the inefficiencies of the Soviet economy in the humor magazines of the U.S.S.R. before the collapse of communism.

prevents the circularity of the analysis—electricity output depends on steel production, but steel output depends on electricity production—from becoming a vicious circle.) The technique used to solve these complicated equations—**input–output analysis**—was invented by economist Wassily Leontief, and it won him the Nobel Prize in 1973.

The equations of input–output analysis, which are illustrated in the boxed insert below, take account of the interdependence among industries by describing precisely how each industry's target output depends on every other industry's target. Only by solving these equations *simultaneously* for the required outputs of electricity, steel, coal, and so on, can one be sure of a consistent solution that produces the required amounts of each product—including the amount of each product needed to produce every other product.

The example of input-output analysis that appears in the box is not provided so that you can learn how to apply the technique yourself. Its real purpose is to illustrate the *very complicated* nature of the problem that faces a central planner. For the problem faced by a real planner, while analogous to the one in the box, is enormously more complex. In any real economy, the number of commodities is far greater than the three outputs in the example. In the United States, some large manufacturing companies individually deal in hundreds of thousands of items, and the armed forces keep several *million* different items in inventory. In planning, it is ultimately necessary to make calculations for each single item. It is not enough to plan the right number of bolts *in total;* we must make sure that the required number *of each size* is produced. (Try to put five million large bolts into five million small nuts.) So, to be sure our plans will really work, we need a separate equation for every size of bolt and one for every size and type of nut. But then, to replicate the analysis described in the boxed insert, we will have to solve simultaneously several *million* equations! This is a task that will strain the capability of the most powerful electronic computer, if it can do the job at all.

Worse still is the data problem. Each of our three equations requires *three* pieces of statistical information, making 3 × 3, or 9, numbers in total. This is because

## *Input–Output Equations: An Example*

Imagine an economy with only three outputs: electricity, steel, and coal; and let $E$, $S$, and $C$ represent the dollar value of their respective outputs. Suppose that for every dollar's worth of steel, $0.20 worth of electricity is used up, so that the total electricity demand of steel manufacturers is $0.2S$. Similarly, assume the coal manufacturers use up $0.30 of electricity in producing $1 worth of coal, or a total of $0.3C$ units of electricity. Since $E$ dollars of electricity are produced in total, the amount left over for consumers, after subtraction of industrial demands for fuel, will be $E$ (available electricity) − $0.2S$ (use in steel production) − $0.3C$ (use in coal production). Suppose further that the central planners have decided to supply $15 million worth of electricity to consumers. We end up with the electricity output equation

$$E - 0.2S - 0.3C = 15.$$

The planner will also need such an equation for each of the two other industries, specifying for each of them the net amounts intended to be left for consumers after the industrial uses of these products. The full set of equations might then be:

$$E - 0.2S - 0.3C = 15$$
$$S - 0.1E - 0.06C = 7$$
$$C - 0.15E - 0.4S = 10.$$

These are typical equations in an input–output analysis. Only, in practice, a typical analysis has dozens and sometimes hundreds of equations with similar numbers of unknowns. This, then, is the logic of input-output analysis.

the equation for electricity must indicate on the basis of statistical information how much electricity is needed in steel production, how much in coal production, and how much is demanded by consumers. Therefore, in a five-industry analysis, $5 \times 5$, or 25, pieces of data are needed, a 100-industry analysis requires $100^2$, or 10,000 numbers, and a million-item input–output study might need one *trillion* pieces of information. The data-gathering problems are therefore no easy task, to put it mildly. There are still other complications, but we have seen enough to conclude that:

A full, rigorous central-planning solution to the production problem is a tremendous task, requiring an overwhelming quantity of information and some incredibly difficult calculations. Yet this very difficult job is carried out automatically and unobtrusively by the price mechanism in a free-market economy.

## HOW PERFECT COMPETITION ACHIEVES EFFICIENCY: WHAT TO PRODUCE

We have now indicated how the market mechanism solves the three basic coordination problems of any economy—what to produce, how to produce, and how to distribute the goods to consumers. And we have suggested that these same tasks pose almost insurmountable difficulties for central planners. One critical question remains. Is the allocation of resources that the market mechanism selects *efficient*, according to the precise definition of efficiency presented at the start of this chapter? The answer is that, under the idealized circumstances of perfect competition, it is. Since a detailed proof of this assertion for all three coordination tasks would be long and time-consuming, we will present the proof only for the first of the three tasks—output selection. The corresponding analyses for the production planning and distribution problems are quite similar and are reserved for the appendix.

Our question is this: Given the output combination selected by the market mechanism, is it possible to improve matters by producing more of one good and less of another? Might it be "better," for example, if society produced more beef and less lamb? We shall answer this question in the negative, thus showing that, at least in theory, perfect competition does guarantee efficiency in production.

We will do this in two steps. First, we will derive a criterion for efficient output selection, that is, a test which tells us whether or not production is being carried out efficiently. Second, we will show that this test is *automatically* passed by the prices that emerge from the market mechanism under perfect competition.

### STEP 1: RULE FOR EFFICIENT OUTPUT SELECTION

We begin by stating the rule for efficient output selection:

Efficiency in the choice of output quantities requires that, for each of the economy's outputs, the marginal cost (MC) of the last unit produced be equal to the marginal utility (MU) of the last unit consumed.[3] In symbols:

$$MC = MU.$$

[3]It will be recalled from Chapter 7 that we measure marginal utility in money terms, that is, the amount of money that a consumer is willing to give up for an additional unit of the commodity. Economists usually call this the marginal rate of substitution between the commodity and money.

This rule is yet another example of the basic principle of marginal analysis that was derived in Chapter 5 (pages 109–25). The goal of the decision on output quantities is to maximize the total benefit (total utility) to society, − the cost to society of producing the output quantities that are chosen, that is, to maximize the surplus gained by society—total utility minus total cost. But, as was shown in Chapter 5, in order to maximize the difference between total utility and total cost, we must find the outputs that make the corresponding marginal figures, marginal utility, and marginal cost, equal to one another. That is what the preceding efficiency rule tells us.

Let us use an example to see explicitly why this rule *must* be satisfied for the allocation of resources to be efficient. Suppose the marginal utility of an additional pound of beef to consumers is $8, while its marginal cost is only $5. Then the value of the resources that would have to be used up to produce one more pound of beef (its MC) would be $3 less than the money value of that additional pound to consumers (its MU). By expanding the output of beef by one pound, society could get more (the MU) out of the economic production process than it was putting in (the MC). It follows that the output at which MU > MC cannot be optimal, since society would be made better off by an increase in that output level.

The opposite is true if the MC of beef exceeds the MU of beef. In that case, the last pound of beef must have used up more value (MC) than it produced (MU). It would therefore be better to have less beef and more of something else.

We have therefore shown that, if there is *any* product for which MU is not equal to MC, the economy must be wasting an opportunity to produce a net improvement in consumers' welfare. This is exactly what we mean by using resources *inefficiently*. Just as was true at point *G* in Figure 10–1, if MC ≠ MU for any commodity, it is possible to rearrange things so as to make some people better off while harming no one. It follows that efficiency in the choice of outputs is achieved only when MC = MU for *every* good.[4]

## STEP 2: THE CRITICAL ROLE OF THE PRICE SYSTEM

The next step in the argument is to show that under perfect competition the price system *automatically* leads buyers and sellers to behave in a way that makes MU and MC equal.

To see this, recall from the last chapter that under perfect competition it is most profitable for each beef-producing firm to produce the quantity of beef at which the marginal cost of the beef is equal to the price of beef:

$$\text{MC} = P.$$

This must be so because, if the marginal cost of beef were less than the price, the farmer could add to her profits by increasing the size of her herd (or the amount of grain that she feeds her animals); and the reverse would be true if the marginal cost of beef were greater than its price. Thus, under perfect competition, the lure of profits leads each producer of beef (and of every other product) to supply the quantity that makes MC = *P*.

[4]WARNING: As shown in Chapter 13, markets sometimes perform imperfectly because marginal cost to the decision maker is not the same as the marginal cost to society. This occurs when the individual who causes the cost gets someone else to bear the burden. Example: Firm X's production causes pollution emissions which increase the laundry bills of nearby households. In such a case, firm X will ignore the cost and produce inefficiently large outputs and emissions.

We also learned, in Chapter 7, that it is in the interest of each consumer to purchase the quantity of beef at which the marginal utility of beef in terms of money is equal to the price of beef:

$$\text{MU} = P.$$

If he did not do this, as we saw, either an increase or a decrease in his purchase of beef would leave him better off.

Putting these last two equations together, we see that the invisible hand enforces the following string of equalities:

$$\text{MC} = P = \text{MU}.$$

But if both the MC of beef and the MU of beef are equal to the same price, $P$, then they must surely be equal to each other. That is, it must be true that the quantity of beef produced and consumed in a perfectly competitive market satisfies the equation:

$$\text{MC} = \text{MU},$$

which is precisely our rule for efficient output selection. Since the same must be true of every other product supplied by a competitive industry:

Under perfect competition, the uncoordinated decisions of producers and consumers can be expected *automatically* and amazingly to tend to produce exactly the quantity of each good that satisfies the MC = MU rule for efficiency in deciding what to produce. That is, under the idealized conditions of perfect competition, the market mechanism, *without any government intervention*, and without anyone else directing it or planning for it to do so, is capable of allocating society's scarce resources efficiently.

## THE INVISIBLE HAND AT WORK

This is truly a remarkable result. How can the price mechanism automatically satisfy all the exacting requirements for efficiency (the marginal utility = marginal cost equation for each and every commodity)—requirements that no central planner can hope to handle because of the masses of statistics and the enormous calculations they entail? The conclusion seems analogous to the rabbit suddenly pulled from the magician's hat. But, as always, rabbits come out of hats only if they were hidden there in the first place. What really is the machinery by which our act of magic works? The secret is that the price system lets consumers and producers pursue their own best interests—something they are probably very good at doing. Prices are the dollar costs of commodities to consumers. So, in pursuing their own best interests, consumers will buy the commodities that give them the most satisfaction *per dollar*. As we learned in Chapter 7, this means that each consumer will continue to buy beef until the marginal utility of beef is equal to the market price. And since every consumer pays the same price in a perfectly competitive market, the market mechanism ensures that *every consumer's MU will be equal to this common price.*

Turning next to the producers, we know from Chapter 9 that competition equates prices with marginal costs. And, once again, since every producer faces the same market price, the forces of competition will bring the *MC of every producer into equality with this common price.* Since MC measures the resource cost (in every firm) of producing one more unit of the good and MU measures the money value (to every consumer) of consuming one more unit, then when MC = MU *the cost of the good to society is exactly equal to the value that consumers place on it*. Therefore:

When all prices are set equal to marginal costs, the price system is giving the correct cost signals to consumers. It has set prices at levels that induce consumers to use the resources of the society with the same care they devote to watching their own money, because the money cost of a good to the consumer has been set equal to the opportunity cost of the good to society.

This is the magic of the invisible hand. Unlike central planners, consumers need not know how difficult it is to manufacture a certain product, nor how scarce are the inputs required by the production process. Everything the consumer needs to know to make his or her decision is embodied in the market price, which, under perfect competition, accurately reflects marginal costs.

## OTHER ROLES OF PRICES: INCOME DISTRIBUTION AND FAIRNESS

So far we have stressed the role of prices most emphasized by economists: prices guide the allocation of resources. But a different role of prices often commands the spotlight in public discussions: prices influence the distribution of income between buyers and sellers. For example, high rents often make tenants poorer and landlords richer.

This rather obvious role of prices draws the most attention from the public, politicians, and regulators, and is one we should not lose sight of.[5] Markets only serve demands that are backed up by consumers' desire *and ability* to pay. Though the market system may do well in serving a poor family, giving that family more food and clothing than a less efficient economy would provide, it offers far more to the family of a millionaire. Many observers object that such an arrangement represents a great injustice, however efficient it may be.

Often, recommendations made by economists for improving the economy's efficiency are opposed on the grounds that they are unfair. For example, economists frequently advocate higher prices for transportation facilities at the time of day when they are most crowded. They propose a pricing arrangement called *peak, off-peak pricing* under which prices for public transportation are higher during rush hours than during other hours.

The rationale for this proposal should be clear from our discussion of efficiency. A seat on a train is a much scarcer resource during rush hours than during other times of the day when the trains run fairly empty. Thus, according to the principles of efficiency outlined in this chapter, seats should be more expensive during rush hours to discourage those consumers to whom the timing of travel makes little difference from using the trains during peak periods. The same notion applies to other services. Charges for nighttime long-distance telephone calls are lower than those in the daytime and, in some places, electricity is sold more cheaply at night, when demand does not strain the supplier's generating capacity.

Yet the proposal that higher fares should be charged for public transportation during peak hours—say, from 8:00 A.M. to 9:30 A.M., and from 4:30 P.M. to 6 P.M.—often runs into stiff opposition on the grounds that most of the burden will fall on lower-income working people who have no choice about the timing of their

---

[5]Income distribution is the subject of Part 4.

trips. For example, a survey in Great Britain of members of Parliament and of economists found that while high peak-period fares were favored by 88 percent of the economists, only 35 percent of the Conservative Party M.P.'s and just 19 percent of the Labor Party M.P.'s approved of this arrangement (see Table 10–1). We may surmise that the M.P.'s reflected the views of the public more accurately than did the economists. In this case, people simply find the efficient solution unfair, and so refuse to adopt it.

Our earlier example of bridges in the San Francisco area also raises issues of fairness. As will be recalled, we concluded from our analysis that efficient use of bridges requires higher tolls on the more crowded bridges such as the San Francisco–Oakland Bay and Golden Gate Bridges. Since this principle seems so clear and rational, it may be interesting to the reader to see at what levels the actual bridge tolls were set when this book was first written. Travel on the crowded Golden Gate Bridge required a $1.25 toll for a round trip. But the San Francisco–Oakland Bay, Dumbarton, and San Mateo–Hayward bridges each carried a 75-cent toll even though the Bay Bridge was far more crowded than the others. Even stranger, the Richmond–San Rafael Bridge, which was about as sparsely used as any, charged a $1 toll.

From the point of view of efficiency, this pattern of tolls obviously seems quite irrational. Some of the least crowded bridges were assigned the highest tolls! Yet some widely held notions of fairness explain why the authorities placed rather low tolls on some highly congested bridges.

Many people feel that it is fair for those who travel on a bridge to pay for its costs. In this view, it would be unjust for those who use the crowded San Francisco–Oakland Bay Bridge to pay for the less-crowded Richmond–San Rafael Bridge. Naturally, a bridge that is traveled heavily more quickly takes in the revenue necessary to recoup the cost of building, maintaining, and running it. That is why fairness is believed to dictate low tolls on crowded bridges. On the other hand, the relatively few users of a less-crowded bridge must pay higher tolls in order to make a fair contribution toward its costs.

*Table* **10–1** **REPLIES TO A QUESTIONNAIRE**

| QUESTION: In order to make the most efficient use of a city's resources, how should subway and bus fares vary during the day? | **ECONOMISTS (percent)** | **CONSERVATIVE PARTY M.P.'S (percent)** | **LABOR PARTY M.P.'S (percent)** |
|---|---|---|---|
| a. They should be relatively low during rush hour to transport as many people as possible at lower costs. | 1 | — | 40 |
| b. They should be the same at all times to avoid making travelers alter their schedules because of price differences. | 4 | 60 | 39 |
| c. They should be relatively high during rush hour to minimize the amount of equipment needed to transport the daily travelers. | 88 | 35 | 19 |
| d. Impossible to answer on the data and alternatives given. | 7 | 5 | 2 |

SOURCE: Adapted from Samuel Brittan, *Is There an Economic Consensus?*, page 93. Copyright Samuel Brittan, 1973. Reproduced by permission of Curtis Brown Ltd.

Of course, such a pattern of tolls slows traffic and lures even more drivers to the already overcrowded bridges, thereby contributing to inefficiency. But one cannot legitimately conclude that advocates of such prices are "stupid." Whether this pattern of tolls is or is not desirable must be decided, ultimately, on the basis of the public's sense of what constitutes fairness and justice in pricing and the amount it is willing to pay in terms of delays, inconvenience, and other inefficiencies in order to avoid apparent injustices.[6]

Economics alone cannot decide the appropriate trade-off between fairness and efficiency. It cannot even pretend to judge which pricing arrangements are fair and which are unfair. But it can and should indicate whether a particular pricing decision, proposed because it is considered fair, will impose heavy inefficiency costs upon the community. Economic analysis also can and should indicate how to evaluate these costs, so that the issues can be decided on the basis of an understanding of the facts.

## TOWARD ASSESSMENT OF THE PRICE MECHANISM

Our analysis of the case for laissez faire is not meant to imply that the free-enterprise system is an ideal of perfection, without flaw or room for improvement. In fact, it has a number of serious shortcomings that we will explore in subsequent chapters. But recognition of these imperfections should not conceal the enormous accomplishments of the price mechanism.

We have shown that, given the proper circumstances, it is capable of meeting the most exacting requirements of allocative efficiency, requirements that go well beyond the capacity of any central planning bureau. Even centrally planned economies used the price mechanism to carry out considerable portions of the task of allocation, most notably the distribution of goods among consumers. No one has invented an instrument for directing the economy that can replace the price mechanism, which no one ever designed or planned for, but that simply grew by itself, a child of the processes of history.

## ANOTHER LOOK AT THE MARKET'S ACHIEVEMENT: GROWTH VS. EFFICIENCY

This chapter has followed the standard approach by economists in evaluating the accomplishments of the market mechanism. Economists have stressed efficiency in resource allocation, and the role of the market in ensuring that resources are divided among alternative uses in a way that maximizes the net benefits to consumers.

However, that is not the accomplishment of the market which is likely to be emphasized by others. A very diverse group, including businesspersons, politicians, economic historians, leaders in the formerly communist economies, and even Marxists, admire the market primarily for a very different reason—the effectiveness with which it has led the outputs of the market economies to grow, and the historically unprecedented abundance that has resulted.

[6]Since this material was first published, the tolls have been changed, and it is interesting to note that their magnitudes now correspond more closely to the relative crowding of the bridges. This suggests that in public pricing policy, efficiency considerations do carry *some* weight.

Historians have estimated that before the arrival of the capitalistic market mechanism, output per person grew with glacial slowness. Indeed, it has been estimated that in the 1500 years between third century Rome and eighteenth century England, growth in output per person on the average was approximately zero! But in just the last century in the United States it has grown so rapidly that an average American today can afford seven or eight times the quantity of goods and services that an individual's income could have bought 100 years ago. Undoubtedly, it was the failure to achieve such growth and to bring such prosperity to its public (rather than allocative inefficiencies) that played a considerable part in the fall of communism in the countries of Eastern Europe. Even Karl Marx stressed this role of the market mechanism, and waxed lyrical in his description of its accomplishments. The following passage from his *Communist Manifesto* (1848) might have been penned by a publicist for the Chamber of Commerce:

> *[Capitalism] . . . has accomplished wonders far surpassing Egyptian pyramids, Roman aqueducts, and Gothic cathedrals. . . . The [capitalist] cannot exist without constantly revolutionizing the instruments of production. . . . [Capitalism], during its rule of scarce one hundred years, has created more massive and more colossal productive forces than have all preceding generations together.*[7]

It should be remembered that when Marx wrote, the capitalistic market mechanism was still very new and had only just begun to show what it can accomplish in terms of economic growth.

[7]Karl Marx, *Communist Manifesto, Collected Works*, Vol. 6 (New York: International Publishers, 1976), pages 487–89.

## Summary

1. An allocation of resources is considered *inefficient* if it wastes opportunities to change the use of the economy's resources in any way that makes consumers better off. Resource allocation is called *efficient* if there are no such wasted opportunities.
2. Under perfect competition, the free-market mechanism adjusts prices so that the resulting resource allocation is efficient. It induces firms to buy and use inputs in ways that yield the most valuable outputs per unit of input; it distributes products among consumers in ways that match individual preferences; and it produces commodities whose value to consumers exceeds the cost of producing them.
3. Resource allocation involves three basic **coordination tasks:** (a) How much of each good to produce, (b) What quantities of the available inputs to use in producing the different goods, and (c) How to distribute the goods among different consumers.
4. Efficient decisions about what goods to produce require that the marginal cost (MC) of producing each good be equated to its marginal utility (MU) to consumers. If the MC of any good differs from its MU, then society can improve resource allocation by changing the level of production.
5. Because the market system induces firms to set MC equal to price, and induces consumers to set MU equal to price, it automatically guarantees that the **MC = MU** condition is satisfied.
6. Sometimes improvements in efficiency require some prices to increase in order to stimulate supply or to prevent waste in consumption. This is why price increases can sometimes be beneficial to consumers.
7. In addition to allocating resources, prices also influence the distribution of income between buyers and sellers.
8. The workings of the price mechanism can be criticized on the grounds that it is unfair because of the preferential treatment it accords wealthy consumers.

## Key Concepts and Terms

Efficient allocation of resources
Coordination tasks: output selection, production planning, distribution of goods
Laissez faire
Input–output analysis
MC = $P$ requirement of perfect competition
MC = MU efficiency requirement

## Questions for Review

1. What are the possible social advantages of price rises in each of the two following cases?
   a. Charging higher prices for electrical power on very hot days when many people use air conditioners.
   b. Raising water prices in drought-stricken areas.
2. Discuss the fairness of the two preceding proposals.
3. Discuss the nature of the inefficiency in each of the following cases:
   a. An arrangement whereby relatively little coffee and much tea is made available to people who prefer coffee and that accomplishes the reverse for tea lovers.
   b. An arrangement in which skilled mechanics are assigned to ditchdigging and unskilled laborers to repairing cars.
   c. An arrangement that produces a large quantity of trucks and few cars, assuming both cost about the same to produce and to run but that most people in the community prefer cars to trucks.
4. In reality, which of the following circumstances might give rise to each of the preceding problem situations?
   a. Regulation of output quantities by a government.
   b. Rationing of commodities.
   c. Assignment of soldiers to different jobs in an army.
5. We have said that the economy's three coordination tasks are output selection, production planning, and product distribution. Which of these is done badly in the case described in question 3a? in 3b? in 3c?
6. In a free market, how will the price mechanism deal with each of the inefficiencies described in Question 3?
7. Suppose a given set of resources can be used to make either handbags or wallets, and the MC of a handbag is \$23 while the MC of a wallet is \$9. If the MU of a wallet is \$9 and the MU of a handbag is \$30, what can be done to improve resource allocation? What can you say about the gain to consumers?
8. In the early months after the end of communism in the countries of Eastern Europe, there seems to have been an almost superstitious belief that the free market can solve all problems. What sorts of problems do you think the leaders and the citizens of those countries had in mind? Which of those problems is there good reason to believe the market mechanism actually can deal with effectively? What disappointments and sources of disillusionment might have been expected?

# Appendix THE INVISIBLE HAND IN THE DISTRIBUTION OF GOODS AND IN PRODUCTION PLANNING

On pages 257–59 of this chapter, we offered a glimpse of the way economists analyze the workings of the invisible hand by showing how the market handles the problem of efficiency in one of the three tasks of resource allocation: the selection of outputs. We explained the MC = MU rule that must be followed for a set of outputs to be efficient, and showed how a free market can induce people to act in a way that satisfies that rule. In this appendix we complete the story, examining how the price mechanism handles the other two tasks of resource allocation: the distribution of goods among consumers and the planning of production.

## EFFICIENT DISTRIBUTION OF COMMODITIES: WHO GETS WHAT?

While decisions about distribution among consumers depend critically on value judgments, a surprising amount can be said purely on grounds of efficiency. For example, consumers' desires are not being served efficiently if large quantities of milk are given to someone whose preference is for apple cider, while gallons of cider are assigned to a milk lover. Deciding how much of which commodity goes to whom is a matter that requires delicate calculation. It causes great difficulties during wartime when planners must ration goods. The planners generally end up utilizing a crude egalitarianism: the same amount of butter to everyone, the same amount of bacon to everyone, and so on. This may be justified, to paraphrase the statement of a high official in another country, by an "unwillingness to pander to acquired tastes," but it is easy to see that such fixed rations are unlikely to produce an efficient result.

The analysis of the efficient distribution of the economy's different products among its many consumers turns out to be quite similar to our previous analysis of efficient output selection. Suppose there are two individuals, Mr. Steaker and Ms. Chop, and that Steaker wants lots of beef and little lamb, while the opposite is true of Chop. Suppose each is getting one pound of lamb and one pound of beef per week. It is then possible to make *both* people better off without increasing their total consumption of two pounds of beef and two pounds of lamb if Mr. Steaker trades some of his lamb to Ms. Chop in return for some beef. The initial distribution of goods was not efficient because it wasted opportunities for trades that yield *mutual* gains.

It is easy enough to think of allocations of commodities among consumers that are *inefficient*—simply assign to each person only what he does not like. But how does one recognize an allocation that *is* efficient? After all, there are many of us whose preferences have much in common. If two individuals both like beef and lamb, how should the available amounts of the two commodities be divided between them? We will now show that, as in the analysis of efficient output selection, there is a simple rule of marginal analysis that must be satisfied by *any* efficient distribution of products among consumers. Consider any two commodities in the economy, such as beef and lamb, and any two consumers, like Steaker and Chop, each of whom likes to eat some of each type of meat. Then:

The basic rules for the efficient distribution of beef and lamb between Steaker and Chop are that

Steaker's MU of beef = Chop's MU of beef

and

Steaker's MU of lamb = Chop's MU of lamb.

Analogous equations must be satisfied for every other pair of individuals, and for every other pair of products.

Why are these equalities required for efficiency? Recall that a distribution of commodities among consumers can be efficient only if it has taken advantage of every potential gain from trade. That is, if two people can trade in a way that makes them *both* better off, then the distribution cannot be efficient. We can show that if *either* of the previous equations is not satisfied, then such trades are possible.

Suppose, for example, that the following are the relevant marginal utilities:

Steaker's MU of beef = \$4

Chop's MU of beef = \$2

Steaker's MU of lamb = \$1

Chop's MU of lamb = \$1

In such a case a mutually beneficial exchange of beef and lamb can be arranged. For example, if Steaker gives Chop three pounds of lamb in return for one pound of beef, they will both be better off. Steaker loses three pounds of lamb, which are worth $3 to him, and gets a pound of beef, which is worth $4 to him. So he winds up $1 ahead. Similarly, Chop gives up one pound of beef, which is worth $2 to her, and gets in return three pounds of lamb, worth $3 to her. So she also gains $1.

Such a mutually beneficial exchange is possible here because the two consumers have different marginal utilities for beef. Each can benefit by giving up what he or she considers less valuable in exchange for something valued more highly. The initial position in which the two equations were not both satisfied was therefore not efficient because *without any increase in the total amounts of beef and lamb available to them, both could be made better off.* The lesson of this example is quite general:

Any time that two persons have unequal MU's for any commodity, the welfare of both parties can be increased by an exchange of commodities. Efficiency requires that any two individuals have the same MU's for any pair of goods.

The great virtue of the price system is that it induces people to carry out *voluntarily* all opportunities for mutually beneficial swaps. Without the price system, Steaker and Chop might not make the trade because they do not know each other. But the price system enables them to trade with each other by trading with the market. Remember from our discussion of consumer choice in Chapter 7 that it pays any consumer to buy any commodity up to the point where the good's money marginal utility is just equal to its price. In other words, in equilibrium:

$$\begin{aligned}\text{Mr. Steaker's MU of beef} &= \text{Price of beef}\\ &= \text{Ms. Chop's MU}\\ &\quad \text{of beef.}\end{aligned}$$

This is so because, if, say, Mr. Steaker's MU of beef were greater than the price of beef, he could improve his lot by exchanging more of his money for beef. And the reverse could be true if Steaker's MU of beef fell short of the price of beef. For the same reason, since the price of lamb is the same to both individuals, each will choose voluntarily to buy quantities of lamb at which:

$$\begin{aligned}\text{Mr. Steaker's MU of lamb} &= \text{Price of lamb}\\ &= \text{Ms. Chop's MU}\\ &\quad \text{of lamb.}\end{aligned}$$

Thus, we see that as long as both consumers face the same prices for lamb and beef, their independent decisions *must* satisfy our criterion for efficient distribution of beef and lamb between them:

$$\text{Steaker's MU of beef} = \text{Chop's MU of beef}$$

$$\text{Steaker's MU of lamb} = \text{Chop's MU of lamb.}$$

Given any prices for two commodities, each consumer, acting only in accord with his or her preferences and with no necessary consideration of the effects on the other person, will automatically make the purchases that efficiently serve the mutual interests of both purchasers.

This time, where have we sneaked the rabbit into our price system argument? The answer is that the market acts as a middleman between any pair of consumers. Given the prices offered by the market, each consumer will use his or her dollars in a way that exhausts all opportunities for gains from trade *with the market.* Mr. Steaker and Ms. Chop each take advantage of every such opportunity to gain by trading with the market, and in the process they automatically take advantage of every opportunity for advantageous trades between themselves.

## EFFICIENT PRODUCTION PLANNING: ALLOCATION OF INPUTS

Finally, we note briefly that a similar analysis shows how the price system leads to an efficient allocation of inputs among the different production processes—the third of our allocative issues. For precisely the same reasons as in the case of the distribution of products among consumers:

Efficient use of two inputs (say, labor and fertilizer) in the production of two goods (say, wheat and corn) requires that

$$\frac{MP_{\text{wheat, fertilizer}}}{MP_{\text{wheat, labor}}} = \frac{MP_{\text{corn, fertilizer}}}{MP_{\text{corn, labor}}}$$

where, for example, "$MP_{\text{wheat, fertilizer}}$" means "The marginal physical product of fertilizer when it is employed in wheat production."

By the same logic as before, it can be shown that if these equations do not hold, it is possible to produce more corn and more wheat using no more labor and fertilizer than before but merely by redistributing the quantities of the two inputs between the two crops.[8] But we learned in Chapter 6 that maximum profits require each wheat farmer to hire so much labor and so much fertilizer that the ratio of their marginal products equals the ratio of their prices. That is.

$$\frac{MP_{\text{wheat, fertilizer}}}{MP_{\text{wheat, labor}}} = \frac{= P_{\text{fertilizer}}}{P_{\text{labor}}}$$

(where, for example, "$P_{\text{fertilizer}}$" means "Price of fertilizer"). The same relationship must also hold true for every profit-maximizing corn producer:

$$\frac{MP_{\text{corn, fertilizer}}}{MP_{\text{corn, labor}}} = \frac{P_{\text{fertilizer}}}{P_{\text{labor}}}.$$

Since in a competitive industry such as agriculture, wheat farmers and corn farmers must pay the same prices for each of their inputs such as labor and fertilizer, it follows that the ratio of the marginal product of fertilizer and labor must be the same in wheat growing, corn growing, and in every other competitive industry that uses these two inputs, just as the formula for efficient production planning requires.

Thus, we conclude that by making the independent choices that maximize their own profits, and without necessarily considering the effects on anyone else, each farmer (firm) will *automatically* act in a way that satisfies the efficiency condition for the allocation of inputs among different products.

## *Summary*

1. The marginal analysis condition for efficient distribution of commodities among consumers is that every consumer have the same marginal utility (MU) for every product. If this condition is not met, then two consumers can arrange a swap that makes both of them better off.
2. In a free market, all consumers pay the same prices. So, if they pursue their own self-interest by setting $MU = P$, they automatically satisfy the condition for efficient distribution of commodities.
3. The condition for efficient allocation of inputs to the various production processes is that the ratio of the marginal products of any pair of inputs be the same in every industry.
4. Since all producers pay the same prices for inputs under perfect competition, if each firm pursues its own self-interest by setting the ratio of the marginal products of any two of its inputs equal to the ratio of the prices of these inputs, the condition for efficient production planning will be satisfied automatically.

## *Questions for Review*

1. Show that commodities are not being distributed efficiently if Mr. Olson's marginal utilities of a pound of tomatoes and a pound of potatoes are, respectively, 90 cents and 30 cents while Ms. Johnson's are, respectively, 60 cents and 50 cents.
2. Suppose the marginal revenue product of a gallon of petroleum in the trucking industry is $2.00 while the marginal revenue product of petroleum in the auto-racing industry is $1.50. Show that petroleum inputs are being allocated inefficiently. How would a market system tend to prevent this situation from occurring?

[8]See Question 2 at the end of this appendix.

Chapter 11

# MONOPOLY

*The price of monopoly is upon every occasion the highest which can be got.*

ADAM SMITH[1]

In Chapters 9 and 10 we described an idealized market system in which all industries are perfectly competitive, and we extolled the beauty of that system. In this chapter, we turn to one of the blemishes—the possibility that some industries may be monopolized—and to the consequences of such a blemish. ¶ We begin by defining *monopoly* and by investigating some of the reasons for its existence. Then, using the tools of Chapter 5, we consider the monopolist's choice of an optimal price–output combination. As we shall see, while it is possible to analyze how much a monopolist will choose to produce, a monopolist has no "supply curve" in the usual sense. This and other features of monopolized markets require basic modification of our supply–demand analysis of the market mechanism. That modification leads us to the central message of this chapter: that monopolized markets do not match the ideal performance of perfectly competitive ones. In the presence of monopoly, the market mechanism no longer allocates society's

[1]But Adam Smith's statement is incorrect! See Discussion Question 7 at the end of the chapter.

resources efficiently. This opens up the possibility that government actions to constrain monopoly might actually improve the workings of the market—a possibility we will study in detail in Chapters 18 and 19.

### APPLICATION: MONOPOLY AND POLLUTION CHARGES

As usual, we start with a real-life problem. Chapter 1 noted that most economists want to control pollution by charging polluters heavily, making them pay more money the more pollution they emit. Making it sufficiently expensive for firms to pollute, it is said, will force them to cut their emissions.[2] In Chapter 9 we found that this approach can be expected to work in a competitive industry. Even though in such an industry long-run profits are zero either with or without a pollution charge law, such a charge can be expected to reduce emissions.

A common objection to this proposal, however, is that it simply will not work when the polluter is a monopolist: "The monopolist can just raise the price of its product, pass the pollution charge on to its customers, and continue to emit filth as before, with total impunity." After all, if a firm is a monopoly, what is to stop it from raising its price when it is hit by a pollution charge?

Yet observation of the behavior of firms threatened with pollution charges suggests that there is something wrong with this objection. If the polluters could escape the penalty completely, we would expect them to acquiesce or to put up only token opposition. Yet wherever it has been proposed to levy a charge on the emission of pollutants, the outcries have been enormous, even among firms with no substantial rivals. Lobbyists are dispatched at once to do their best to stop the legislation. In fact, rather than agree to being charged for their emissions, firms usually indicate a preference for direct controls with detailed government rules that *force* them to adopt specific pollution-cutting processes—that is, the firms seem to prefer to have government tell them exactly what they must do!

In this chapter we will see how to analyze the issue, and why monopolies cannot make their customers pay the pollution charge—or at least not all of it, and why, in the long run, a pollution charge will actually hurt a polluting monopolist more than it does a polluting competitive firm.

## MONOPOLY DEFINED

A **PURE MONOPOLY** is an industry in which there is only one supplier of a product for which there are no close substitutes, and in which it is very hard or impossible for another firm to coexist.

The definition of **pure monopoly** (see Table 12–2 on page 306) is quite stringent. First, there must be only one firm in the industry—the monopolist must be "the only supplier in town." Second, there must be no close substitute for the monopolist's product. Thus, even the sole provider of natural gas in a city is not considered a pure monopoly, since other firms offer close substitutes like heating oil and electricity. Third, there must be some reason why survival of a potential competitor is extremely unlikely, for otherwise monopolistic behavior and its excessive profits could not persist.

These rigid requirements make pure monopoly a rarity in the real world. The local telephone company and the post office may be examples of one-firm industries that face little or no effective competition in some of their activities. But most firms face at least a degree of competition from substitute products. Even if only one railroad serves a particular town, it must compete with bus lines, trucking

[2]Details on this method of pollution control are provided in Chapter 21.

companies, and airlines. Similarly, the producer of a particular brand of beer may be the only supplier of that specific product but the firm is not a monopolist by our definition. Since many other beers are close substitutes for its product, the firm will lose much of its business if it tries to raise its price much above the prices of other brands.

And there is one further reason why the unrestrained pure monopoly of economic theory is rarely encountered in practice. We will learn in this chapter that pure monopoly can have a number of undesirable features. As a consequence, in markets where pure monopoly might otherwise prevail, the government has intervened to prevent monopolization or to limit the discretion of the monopolist to set its price.

If we do not study pure monopoly for its descriptive realism, why do we study it? Because, like perfect competition, pure monopoly is a market form that is easier to analyze than the more common market structures that we will consider in the next chapter. Thus, pure monopoly is a stepping stone toward models of greater reality. Also, the "evils of monopoly" stand out most clearly when we consider monopoly in its purest form, and this greater clarity will help us understand why governments have rarely allowed unfettered monopoly to exist.

## CAUSES OF MONOPOLY: BARRIERS TO ENTRY AND COST ADVANTAGES

The key element in preserving a monopoly is keeping potential rivals out of the market. One possibility is that some specific impediment prevents the establishment of a new firm in the industry. Economists call such impediments barriers to entry. Some examples are:

1. ***Legal restrictions.*** The U.S. Postal Service has a monopoly position because Congress has given it one. Private companies that might want to compete with the postal service directly are prohibited from doing so by law. Local monopolies of various kinds are sometimes established either because government grants some special privilege to a single firm (for example, the right to operate a food concession in a municipal stadium) or prevents other firms from entering the industry (for instance, by licensing only a single cable television supplier).
2. ***Patents.*** A special, but important, class of legal impediments to entry are patents. To encourage inventiveness, the government gives exclusive production rights for a period of time to the inventor of certain products. As long as the patent is in effect, the firm has a protected position and is a monopoly. For example, Xerox had for many years (but no longer has) a monopoly in plain paper copying.
3. ***Control of a scarce resource or input.*** If a certain commodity can be produced only by using a rare input, a company that gains control of the source of that input can establish a monopoly position for itself. Real examples are not easy to find.
4. ***Deliberately-erected entry barriers.*** A firm may deliberately attempt to make entry difficult for others. One way is to start costly lawsuits against new rivals, sometimes on trumped-up charges. Another is to spend exorbitant amounts on advertising, thus forcing any potential entrant to match that expenditure.

5. ***Large sunk costs.*** Entry into an industry will, obviously, be very risky if entry requires an investment of a large amount of money, and if that investment is sunk—meaning that one cannot hope to recoup the money for a considerable period of time. Thus, the need for large sunk investment serves to discourage entry into an industry, and many analysts therefore consider sunk costs to be the most important type of "naturally imposed" barrier to entry.

   Obviously, such barriers can keep rivals out and ensure that an industry is monopolized. But monopoly can also occur in the absence of barriers to entry if a single firm has important cost advantages over its potential rivals. Two examples of this are

6. ***Technical superiority.*** A firm whose technological expertise vastly exceeds that of potential competitors can, for a period of time, maintain a monopoly position. For example, IBM for many years had little competition in the computer business mainly because of its technological virtuosity. Eventually, however, competitors began to catch up.
7. ***Economies of scale.*** If mere size gives a large firm a cost advantage over a smaller rival, it is likely to be impossible for anyone to compete with the largest firm in the industry.

## NATURAL MONOPOLY

This last type of cost advantage is important enough to merit special attention. In some industries, economies of large-scale production or economies from simultaneous production of a large number of items (for example, car motors and bodies, truck parts, and so on) are so extreme that the industry's output can be produced at far lower cost by a single firm than by a number of smaller firms. In such cases, we say there is a **natural monopoly**, because once a firm gets large enough relative to the size of the market for its product, its natural cost advantage may well drive the competition out of business whether or not anyone in the relatively large firm has evil intentions.

A **NATURAL MONOPOLY** is an industry in which advantages of large-scale production make it possible for a single firm to produce the entire output of the market at lower average cost than a number of firms each producing a smaller quantity.

A monopoly need not be a large firm if the market is small enough. *What matters is the size of a single firm relative to the total market demand for the product.* Thus a small bank in a rural town or a gasoline station at a lightly traveled intersection may both be monopolies even though they are very small firms.

Figure 11–1 shows the sort of average cost (AC) curve that leads to natural monopoly. Suppose that any firm producing widgets would have this AC curve and that, initially, there are two firms in the industry. Suppose also that the larger firm is producing two million widgets at an average cost of $2.50, and the smaller firm is producing one million widgets at an average cost of $3. Clearly the larger firm can drive the smaller firm out of business if it offers its output for sale at a price below $3 (so the smaller firm can match the price only by running a loss) but above $2.50 (so it can still make a profit). Hence a monopoly may arise "naturally" even in the absence of barriers to entry. Once the monopoly is established (producing, say, 2.5 million widgets) the economies of scale act as a very effective deterrent to entry because no new entrant can hope to match the low average cost ($2) of the existing monopoly firm. Of course, the public interest may be well served if the natural monopolist uses its low cost to keep its prices low. The danger, however, is that the firm may raise its price once rivals have left the industry.

*Figure* 11–1 **NATURAL MONOPOLY**

When the average cost curve of a firm is declining, as depicted here, natural monopoly may result. A firm producing two million widgets will have average costs of $2.50, which are well below those of a smaller competitor producing one million widgets (average cost = $3). It can cut its price to a level (lower than $3) that its competitor cannot match and thereby drive the competitor out of business.

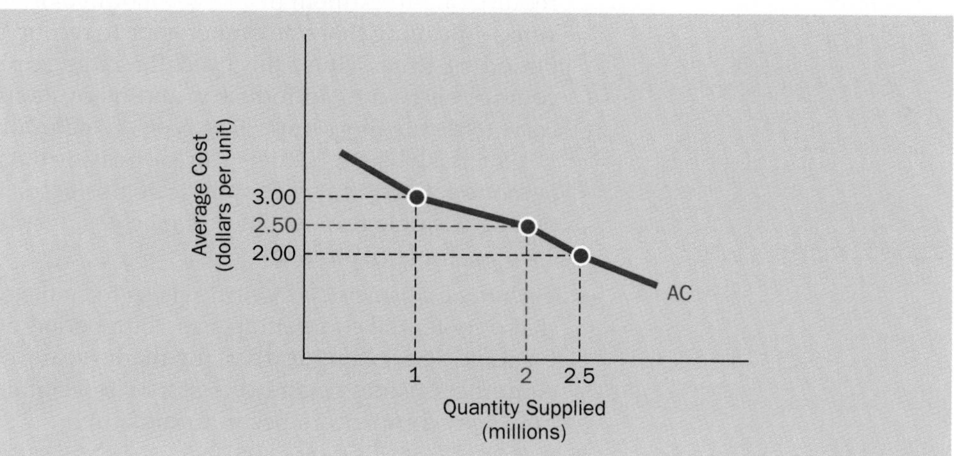


Many public utilities are permitted to operate as *regulated* monopoly suppliers for exactly this reason. It is believed that the technology of producing or distributing their output enables them to achieve substantial cost reductions when they produce large quantities. It is therefore often considered desirable to permit these firms to obtain the lower costs they achieve by having the entire market to themselves, and to subject them to regulatory supervision rather than break them up into a number of competing firms. The issue of regulating natural monopolies will be examined in detail in Chapter 18. To summarize this discussion:

There are two basic reasons why a monopoly may exist: barriers to entry, such as legal restrictions and patents, and cost advantages of large-scale operation that lead to natural monopoly. It is generally considered undesirable to break up a large firm whose costs are low because of scale economies, but barriers to entry are usually considered to be against the public interest except where, as in the case of patents, they are believed to offer offsetting advantages.

The rest of this chapter will analyze how a monopoly can be expected to behave if its freedom of action is not limited by the government.

## THE MONOPOLIST'S SUPPLY DECISION

A monopoly firm does not have a "supply curve," as we usually define the term; it does not just observe the market price of a product and then decide what quantity to produce. Unlike a perfect competitor, a monopoly is not at the mercy of the market; the firm does not have to take the market price as given and react to it. Instead, it has the power to set the price, or rather to select the price–quantity combination on the demand curve that suits its interests best.

Put differently, a monopolist is not a *price taker* who must simply adapt to whatever price the forces of supply and demand decree. Rather, a monopolist is a *price maker* who can, if so inclined, raise the product price. For any price that the monopolist might choose, the demand curve for the monopolist's product indicates how much consumers will buy. Thus, the standard supply–demand analysis described in Chapter 4 does not apply to the determination of price or output in a monopolized industry.

The demand curve of a monopoly, unlike that of a perfect competitor, is normally downward sloping, not horizontal. This means that a price rise will not cause the monopoly to lose *all* its customers. But any increase will cost it *some* business. The higher the price, the less the monopolist can expect to sell.

The market cannot impose a price on a monopolist as it imposes a price on the price-taking competitive firm. But the monopolist cannot select both price and the quantity it sells. In accord with the demand curve, the higher the price it sets, the less it can sell.

It is because of the downward-sloping demand curve that the sky is not the limit in pricing by a monopolist. Some price increases are not profitable. In deciding what price best serves the firm's interests, the monopolist must consider whether profits can be increased by raising or lowering the product's price.

In our analysis, we shall assume that the monopolist wants to maximize profits. That does not mean that a monopoly is guaranteed a positive profit. If the demand for its product is low or the firm is inefficient, it may lose money and may eventually be forced to go out of business. However, if a monopoly firm *does* earn a positive profit, it may be able to keep on doing so, even in the long run.

The methods of Chapter 5 can be used to determine which price the profit-maximizing monopolist will prefer. To maximize profits, the monopolist must compare marginal revenue (the addition to total revenue resulting from a one-unit rise in output) with marginal cost (the addition to total cost resulting from that additional unit). For this purpose, a marginal cost (MC) curve and a marginal revenue (MR) curve for a typical monopolist are drawn in Figure 11–2, which also contains the monopolist's demand curve (*DD*). Here it should be recalled that the firm's demand curve is always also its average revenue (AR) curve, because if a firm sells *Q* units of output, selling every unit of output at the price *P*, then the average revenue brought in by a unit of output must be the price, *P*. Since the demand curve gives the price at which any given output quantity can be sold, it also automatically indicates the AR ( = price) yielded by that output.

## THE MONOPOLIST'S PRICE AND MARGINAL REVENUE

Notice that the marginal revenue curve is always *below* the demand curve, meaning that MR is always less than price (*P*). This important fact is easy to explain. A monopoly normally must charge the same price to all of its customers. So, if the firm wants to increase sales by one unit, it must decrease the price somewhat to *all* of its customers. When the price is cut to attract new sales, all previous customers also benefit. Thus, the *additional* revenue that the monopolist takes in when sales increase by one unit (*marginal revenue*) is the price the firm collects from the new customer *minus the revenue it loses by cutting the price paid by all of its old customers*. This means that MR is necessarily *less than* price; graphically, it implies that the MR curve is *below* the demand curve, as in Figure 11–2.

Figure 11–3 illustrates the relationship between price and marginal revenue in a specific example. Suppose a monopoly is initially selling 15 units at a price of $2.10 per unit (point *A*), and the monopolist wishes to increase sales by one unit.

Figure 11–2 **PROFIT-MAXIMIZING EQUILIBRIUM FOR A MONOPOLIST**

This monopoly has the cost structure indicated by the black average cost (AC) curve and the blue marginal cost (MC) curve. Its demand curve is the black line labeled *DD*, and its marginal revenue curve is the brown line labeled MR. The monopoly maximizes profits by producing 150 units because at this level of production MC = MR (point *M*). The price it charges is $10 per unit (as given by point *P*, above *M*, on the demand curve). Since the average cost per unit ($4) is given by point *C* on the AC curve, the monopoly's total profit is indicated by the area of the shaded rectangle = profit per unit times quantity sold = ($10 − $4) × 150 = $900.

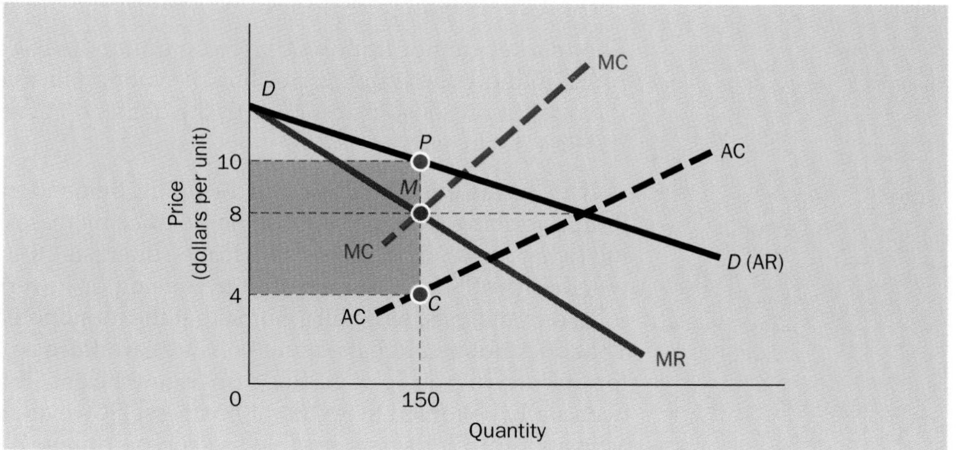


The demand curve indicates that in order to sell the 16th unit, the firm must reduce the price to $2 (point *B*). How much revenue will be gained from this increase in sales; that is, how large is the monopolist's marginal revenue?

As we know, *total revenue* at point *A* is the area of the rectangle whose upper right-hand corner is point *A*, or $2.10 × 15 = $31.50. Similarly, total revenue at point *B* is the area of the rectangle whose upper right-hand corner is point *B*, or $2 × 16 = $32. The *marginal revenue* of the 16th unit is, by definition, total revenue when 16 units are sold minus total revenue when 15 units are sold, or $32 − $31.50 = $0.50.

In Figure 11–3, marginal revenue appears as the area of the tall blue rectangle ($2) *minus* the area of the flat tan rectangle ($1.50). We can see that MR is less than price by observing that the price is shown in the diagram by the area of the blue rectangle.[3] Clearly, the price (area of the blue rectangle) must exceed the marginal revenue (area of the blue rectangle *minus* area of the tan rectangle), as was claimed.[4]

[3]Because the width of this rectangle is one unit, its area is height × width = ($2 per unit) × (1 unit) = $2.

[4]There is another way to arrive at this conclusion. Recall that the demand curve is the curve of *average revenue*. Since the average revenue is declining as we move to the right, it follows from one of the rules relating marginals and averages (see the appendix to Chapter 5) that the marginal revenue curve must always be below the average.

*Figure* **11–3** **THE RELATIONSHIP BETWEEN MARGINAL REVENUE AND PRICE**

Line *DD* is the demand curve of a monopoly. In order to raise sales from 15 to 16 units, the firm must cut its price from \$2.10 (point *A*) to \$2 (point *B*). If the monopolist does this, revenues increase by the \$2 price the monopolist charges to the buyer of the 16th unit (the area of the tall blue rectangle), but revenues decrease by the 10-cent price reduction the monopolist offers to previous customers (the area of the flat tan rectangle). The monopolist's marginal revenue, therefore, is the difference between these two areas. Since the price is the area of the blue rectangle, it follows that marginal revenue is less than price for a monopolist.

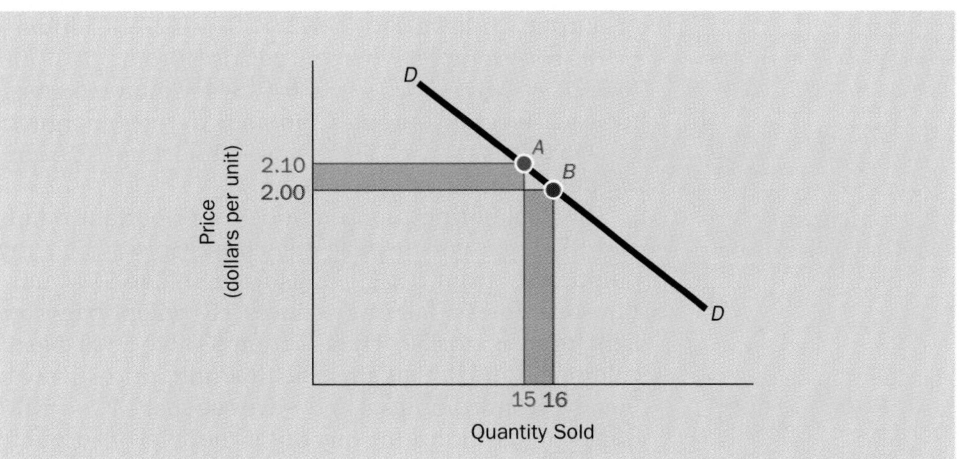


## DETERMINING THE PROFIT-MAXIMIZING OUTPUT

We return now to the supply decision of the monopolist depicted in Figure 11–2. Like any other firm, the monopoly maximizes its profits by setting marginal revenue (MR) equal to marginal cost (MC). It selects point *M* in the diagram, where output is 150 units. But point *M* does not tell us the monopoly price because, as we have just seen, price exceeds MR for a monopolist. To learn what price the monopolist charges, we must use the demand curve to find the price at which consumers are willing to purchase 150 units. The answer, we see, is given by point *P* directly above *M*. The monopoly price is \$10 per unit. Not surprisingly, it exceeds both MR and MC (which are equal at \$8).

The monopolist depicted in Figure 11–2 is earning a tidy profit. This profit is shown in the graph by the shaded rectangle whose height is the difference between price (point *P*) and average cost (point *C*) and whose width is the quantity produced (150 units). In the example, profits are \$6 per unit, or \$900.

To study the decisions of a profit-maximizing monopolist, we must

1. find the output at which MR = MC, to select the profit-maximizing output level;
2. find the height of the demand curve at that level of output, to determine the corresponding price;

3. compare the height of the demand curve with that of the AC curve at that output to see whether the net result is an economic profit or a loss.

A monopolist's profit-maximization calculation can also be shown numerically. In Table 11–1, the first two columns show the price and quantity figures that constitute the monopolist's demand curve. Column 3 shows total revenue (TR) for each output, which is the product of price and quantity. Thus, for three units of output we have TR = \$92 × 3 = \$276. Column 4 shows marginal revenue (MR). For example, when output rises from 3 to 4 units, TR increases from \$276 to \$320, so MR is \$320 − \$276 = \$44. Column 5 gives the monopolist's total cost for each level of output. Column 6 derives marginal cost (MC) from total cost (TC) in the usual way. Finally, by subtracting TC from TR for each level of output, we derive total profit in column 7.

This table brings out a number of important points. We note first (columns 2 and 3) that a cut in price sometimes raises total revenue. For example, when output rises from 1 to 2, *P* falls from \$140 to \$107 and TR rises from \$140 to \$214. But sometimes a fall in *P* reduces TR; when (between 5 and 6 units of output) *P* falls from \$66 to \$50, TR falls from \$330 to \$300. Next we observe, by comparing columns 2 and 4, that after the first unit, price always exceeds marginal revenue. Finally, from columns 4 and 6 we see that MC = MR = \$44 when *Q* is between 3 and 4 units, indicating that this is the level of output that maximizes the monopolist's total profit. That is confirmed in the last column of the table, which shows that at those outputs profit reaches its highest level, \$110, for any of the output quantities considered in the table.

## COMPARISON OF MONOPOLY AND PERFECT COMPETITION

This completes our analysis of the monopolist's price–output decision. At this point it is natural to wonder whether there is anything distinctive about the monopoly equilibrium. But, to find out, we need a standard of comparison. Perfect competition provides this standard because, as we learned in Chapters 9 and 10, it is a benchmark of ideal performance against which other market structures can be judged. By comparing the results of monopoly with those of perfect competi-

**Table 11–1 A PROFIT-MAXIMIZING MONOPOLIST S PRICE-OUTPUT DECISION**

| | | REVENUE | | COST | | TOTAL PROFIT |
|---|---|---|---|---|---|---|
| (1) Q | (2) P | (3) TR = P × Q | (4) MR | (5) TC | (6) MC | (7) TR — TC |
| 0 | — | \$ 0 | | \$ 10 | | \$−10 |
| | | | \$140 | | \$60 | |
| 1 | \$140 | 140 | | 70 | | 70 |
| | | | 74 | | 50 | |
| 2 | 107 | 214 | | 120 | | 94 |
| | | | 62 | | 46 | |
| 3 | 92 | 276 | | 166 | | 110 |
| | | | 44 | | 44 | |
| 4 | 80 | 320 | | 210 | | 110 |
| | | | 10 | | 43 | |
| 5 | 66 | 330 | | 253 | | 77 |
| | | | −30 | | 45 | |
| 6 | 50 | 300 | | 298 | | 2 |

tion, we will see why economists since Adam Smith have condemned monopoly as inefficient.

### A MONOPOLIST'S PROFIT PERSISTS

The first difference between competition and monopoly is a direct consequence of barriers to entry in the latter. Profits such as those shown in Figure 11–2 would be competed away by free entry in a perfectly competitive market. In the long run, a competitive firm must earn zero economic profit; that is, it can earn only enough to cover its costs, including the opportunity cost of the owner's capital and labor. But higher profits *can* persist under monopoly—if the monopoly is protected by barriers to entry. The fates can be kind to monopolists and allow them to grow wealthy at the expense of their consumers. Because people find such accumulations of wealth objectionable, monopoly is widely condemned. And, when monopolies are regulated by government, limitations are usually placed on the profits monopolists can earn.

### MONOPOLY RESTRICTS OUTPUT TO RAISE SHORT-RUN PRICE

Excess monopoly profits may be a problem, but the second difference between competition and monopoly is even more worrisome in the opinion of economists:

As compared with the perfectly competitive ideal, the monopolist restricts output and charges a higher price.

To see that this is so, let us conduct the following thought experiment. Imagine that a court order breaks up the monopoly firm depicted in Figure 11–2 (reproduced here as Figure 11–4) into a large number of perfectly competitive firms. Suppose further that the industry demand curve is unchanged by this event and that the MC curve in Figure 11–4 is also the (horizontal) sum of the MC curves of all the newly created competitive firms. These are unrealistic assumptions, as will soon be explained. However, they make it easy to compare the output–price

*Figure* **11–4** **COMPARISON OF A MONOPOLY AND A COMPETITIVE INDUSTRY**

The monopoly output is point *M* at which MC = MR. The long-run competitive output is greater than the monopoly's (point *B*) because it must be sufficiently large to yield zero profit (*P* = AR = AC).

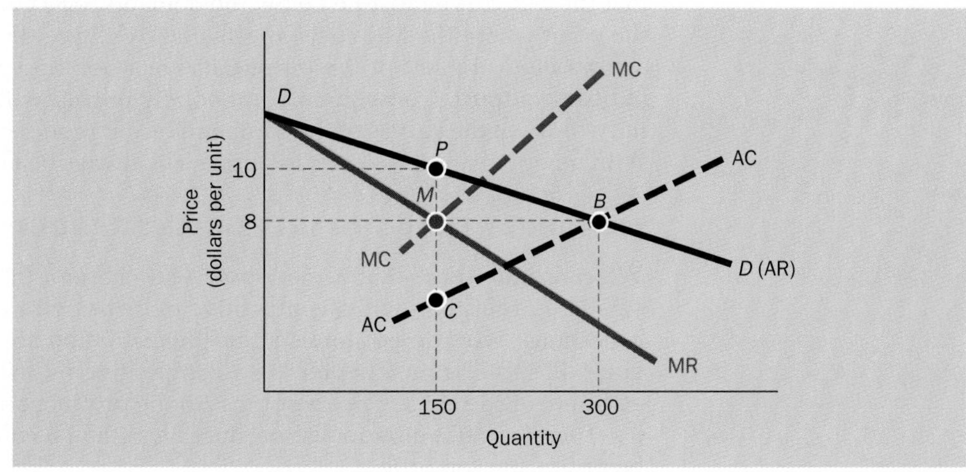

combinations that would emerge in the short run under monopoly and perfect competition.

Before making our comparison we must note that under monopoly the firm and the industry are exactly the same entity. But under perfect competition, any one firm is just a small portion of the industry. When we measure the output performance of monopoloy against that of perfect competition, then, should we compare the monopoly with an individual competitive firm or with the entire competitive industry? The answer is that we must do the latter. It is self-evident and not very interesting to observe that the output of the monopolist is virtually certain to be larger than that of a tiny competitive firm. The interesting issue, rather, is how much product gets into the hands of consumers under the two market forms? That is, how much output is produced by a monopoly as against the quantity that is provided by a comparable competitive industry? In the discussion that follows, therefore, we will always compare the monopoly's pricing and output with that of the competitive industry, and never with that of the lone competitive firm.

## MONOPOLY RESTRICTS OUTPUT TO RAISE LONG-RUN PRICE

As we have seen, monopoly output is determined by the profit maximization requirement that MC = MR (point *M*). But, in the long run, as we learned in Chapter 9, competitive equilibrium will occur at point *B*, where price and average cost are equal (and hence economic profits are zero).

By comparing point *B* with the monopolist's equilibrium (point *M*), we can see that the monopolist produces fewer units of output than would a competitive industry with the same demand and cost conditions. Since the demand curve slopes downward, producing less output means charging a higher price. The monopolist's price, indicated by point *P*, on the demand curve and directly above *M*, exceeds the price that would result from perfect competition at point *B*. This is the essence of the truth behind the popular view that monopolists "gouge the public."

We should note that matters will always turn out that way if the average cost curve has a positive slope between the monopoly and the competitive output levels. For we know, in this case, that the MC curve must lie above the AC curve (for review of the reason, see pages 110–20 of Chapter 5). We have also just seen that the MR curve must lie below the demand (AR) curve. We can see, then, that the point where the MR curve meets the MC curve (the monopoly output) must always lie to the left of the output at which AC and AR meet (the competitive industry output). Consequently, monopoly output will always be the smaller of the two when the curves of the competitive and monopoly industries are identical. With monopoly output lower, its price will always be higher, as was just asserted.

## MONOPOLY LEADS TO INEFFICIENT RESOURCE ALLOCATION

We conclude, then, that a monopoly will charge a higher price and produce a smaller output than will a competitive industry with the same demand and cost conditions. Why do economists find this situation so objectionable? Because, as you will recall from Chapter 10, a competitive industry devotes "just the right amount" of society's scarce resources to the production of its particular commodity. Therefore, if a monopolist produces less than a competitive industry, it must be producing too little.

Remember from Chapter 10 that efficiency in resource allocation requires that the marginal utility (MU) of each commodity be equal to its marginal cost, and that perfect competition guarantees that:

$$\text{MU} = P \text{ and MC} = P\text{, so MU} = \text{MC.}$$

Under monopoly, consumers continue to maximize their own welfare by setting MU equal to *P*. But the monopoly producer, we have just learned, sets MC equal to MR. Since MR is *below* the market price, *P*, we conclude that in a monopolized industry:

$$\text{MU} = P \text{ and MC} = \text{MR} < P \text{ so that MC} < \text{MU.}$$

Because MU exceeds MC, too small a share of society's resources is being used to produce the monopolized commodity. Adam Smith's invisible hand is sending out the wrong signals. Consumers are willing to pay an amount for an additional unit of the good (its MU) that exceeds what it costs to produce that unit (its MC). But the monopoly refuses to increase production, for if it raises output by one unit, the revenue it will collect (the MR) will be less than the price the consumer will pay for the additional unit (*P*). So the monopolist does not increase production, and resources are allocated inefficiently. To summarize this discussion of the consequences of monopoly:

Because it is protected from entry, a monopoly firm may earn profits in excess of the opportunity cost of capital. At the same time, monopoly breeds inefficiency in resource allocation by producing too little output and charging too high a price. For these reasons, some of the virtues of laissez faire evaporate if an industry becomes monopolized.

## CAN ANYTHING GOOD BE SAID ABOUT MONOPOLY?

Except for the case of natural monopoly—where a single firm offers important cost advantages—or the case of a monopoly obtained through an inventor's patent, which is designed to encourage innovation, it is not easy to find arguments in favor of monopoly. However, the preceding comparison of monopoly and perfect competition is very artificial. It assumes that all other things will remain the same, even though that is unlikely to happen in reality.

### MONOPOLY MAY SHIFT DEMAND

For one thing, we have assumed that the market demand curve is the same whether the industry is competitive or monopolized. But is this usually so? The demand curve will be the same if the monopoly firm does nothing to expand its market, but that is hardly plausible.

Under perfect competition, purchasers consider the products of all suppliers in an industry to be identical, and so no single supplier has any reason to advertise. Farmers who sell wheat through one of the major markets have absolutely no motivation to spend money on advertising because they can sell all the wheat they want to at the going price.

But if a monopoly takes over from a perfectly competitive industry, it may very well pay to advertise. If management believes that the touch of Madison Avenue can make consumers' hearts beat faster as they rush to the market to purchase the bread whose virtues have been extolled on television, then the firm will allocate a substantial sum of money to accomplish this feat. This should shift the demand curve outward; after all, that is the purpose of these expenditures. The monopoly's demand curve and that of the competitive industry will then no longer be the same. The higher demand curve for the monopoly's product will perhaps induce it to expand production and therefore reduce the difference between the competitive and the monopolistic output levels indicated in Figure 11–4. It may also, however, make it possible for the monopoly to charge even higher prices, so the increased output may not constitute a net gain for consumers.

## MONOPOLY MAY SHIFT THE COST CURVES

Similarly, the advent of a monopoly may produce shifts in the average and marginal cost curves. One reason for higher costs is the advertising we have just been discussing. Another is the sheer size of the monopolist's organization, which may lead to bureaucratic inefficiencies, coordination problems, and the like. On the other hand, a monopolist may be able to eliminate certain types of duplication that are unavoidable for a number of small independent firms: one purchasing agent may do the input-buying job where many buyers were needed before; and a few large machines may replace many small items of equipment in the hands of the competitive firms. In addition, the large scale of the monopoly firm's input purchases may permit it to take advantage of quantity discounts not available to small competitive firms.

If the unification achieved by monopoly does succeed in producing a downward shift in the marginal cost curve, monopoly output will thereby tend to move up closer to the competitive level, and the monopoly price will tend to move down closer to the competitive price.

## MONOPOLY MAY AID INNOVATION

In addition to this, some economists, most notably Joseph Schumpeter, have argued that it is potentially misleading to compare the cost curves of a monopoly and a competitive industry *at a single point in time*. Because it is protected from rivals, and therefore sure to capture the benefits from any cost savings it can devise, a monopoly has a particularly strong motivation to invest in research, these economists argue. If this research bears fruit, then the monopolist's costs will be lower than those of a competitive industry in the long run, even if they are higher in the short run. Monopoly, according to this view, may be the handmaiden of innovation. While the argument is an old one, it remains controversial. The statistical evidence is decidedly mixed.

## NATURAL MONOPOLY—WHERE SINGLE-FIRM PRODUCTION IS CHEAPEST

Finally, we must remember that the monopoly depicted in Figure 11–2 is not a natural monopoly. But some of the monopolies you find in the real world are. Where the monopoly is natural, costs of production would, by definition, be higher—and possibly much higher—if the single large firm were broken up into many smaller firms. (Refer back to Figure 11–1). In such cases, it may be in society's best interest to allow the monopoly to exist so that consumers can benefit from the economies of large-scale production. But then it may be appropriate to place legal limitations on the monopolist's ability to set a price; that is, to *regulate* the monopoly. Regulation of business is an issue that will occupy our attention in Chapter 18.

## MONOPOLY AND THE SHIFTING OF POLLUTION CHARGES

We conclude our discussion of monopoly by returning to the application that began this chapter—the effectiveness of pollution charges as a means to reduce emissions. Recall that the question is whether a monopoly can raise its price enough to cover any pollution fees, thus shifting these charges entirely to its customers and evading them altogether.

The answer is that any firm or industry can usually shift *part* of the pollution charge to its customers. Economists argue that this shifting is a proper part of a pollution-control program since it induces consumers to redirect their purchases from goods that are highly polluting to goods that are not. For example, a significant increase in taxes on leaded gasoline with, perhaps, a simultaneous decrease in the tax on unleaded gasoline will send more motorists to the unleaded-gas pumps, and that will reduce dangerous lead emissions into the atmosphere.

But more important for our discussion here is the other side of the matter. While some part of a pollution charge is usually paid by the consumer, *the seller will usually be stuck with some part of the charge, even if it is a monopolist*. Why? Because of the negative slope of the demand curve. If the monopoly raises its product's price, it will lose customers, and that will eat into its profits. The monopoly will therefore always do better by absorbing *some* of the charge itself rather than trying to pass all of it on to its customers.

This is illustrated in Figure 11–5. In part (a) we show the monopolist's demand, marginal revenue, and marginal cost curves. As in Figure 11–2, equilibrium output is 150 units—the point at which marginal revenue (MR) equals marginal cost (MC). And price is again \$10—the point on the demand curve corresponding to 150 units of output (point *A*).

Now, let a charge of \$5 per unit be put on the firm's polluting output, shifting the marginal cost curve up uniformly to the curve labeled "MC plus fee" in Figure 11–5 (b). Then the profit-maximizing output falls to 100 units (point *F*), for here MR = MC + pollution fee. The new output, 100 units, is lower than the precharge output, 150 units. Thus, the charge leads the monopoly to restrict its polluting output. The price of the product rises to \$12 (point *B*), the point on the demand curve corresponding to 100 units of output. But the rise in price from \$10 to \$12 is less than half the \$5 pollution charge per unit. Thus:

The pollution charge *does* hurt the polluter even if the polluter is a profit-maximizing monopolist, and the charge *does* force the monopolist to cut its polluting outputs.

No wonder the polluters' lobbyists fight so vehemently! Polluters realize that they often will be far better off with direct controls that impose a financial penalty *only* if they are caught in a violation, prosecuted, and convicted—and even then the fines are often negligible, as we will see in Chapter 21.

We may note, finally, that *any* rise in a monopoly's costs will hurt its profits. The reason is exactly the same as in the case of a pollution charge. Even though

Figure 11-5 MONOPOLY PRICE AND OUTPUT WITH AND WITHOUT A POLLUTION CHARGE

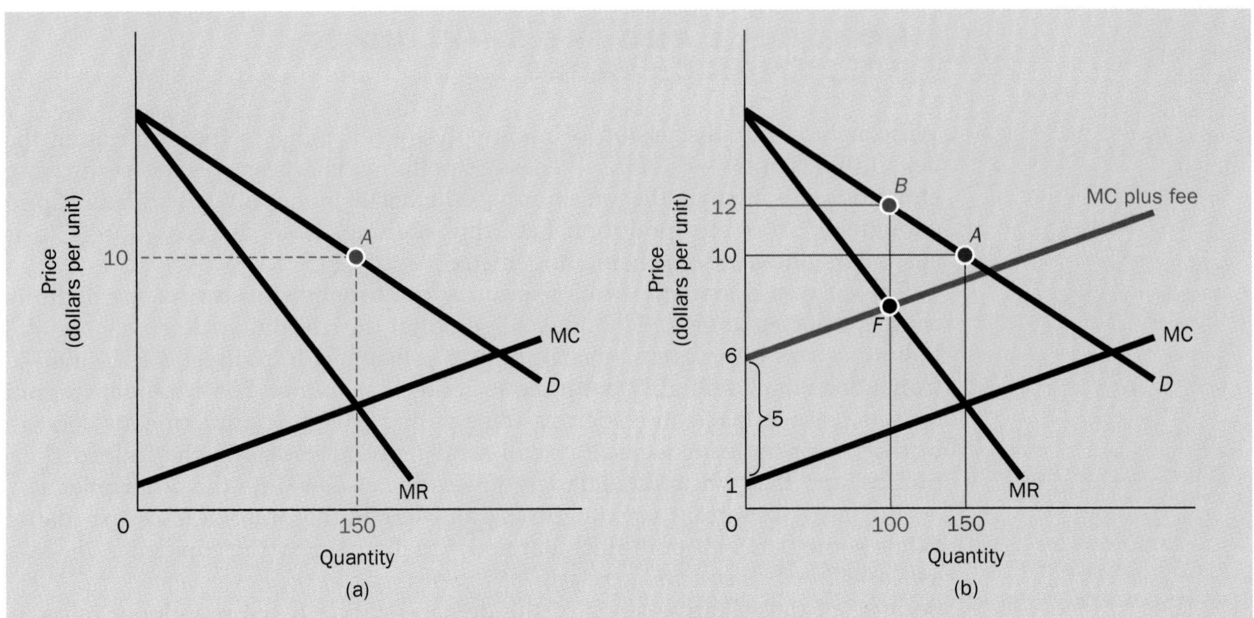


Part (a) shows the monopoly equilibrium without a pollution charge, with price equal to $10 and quantity equal to 150. In part (b) a $5 fee is levied on each unit of polluting output. This raises the marginal cost curve by the amount of the fee, from the black to the blue line. As a result, the output at which MC = MR falls from 150 to 100. Price rises from $10 to $12. Note that this $2 price rise is less than the $5 pollution fee, so the monopolist will be stuck with the remaining $3 of the charge.

the firm is a monopoly, it cannot simply raise its price and make up for any cost increase because consumers can and will respond by buying less of the monopolist's commodity. After all, that is what the negative slope of the demand curve means.

If a monopoly already charges the price that maximizes its profits, a rise in cost will always hurt because any attempt to offset it by a price rise must reduce sales. The monopolist cannot pass the entire burden of the cost increase to consumers.

There is a surprising consequence of all this. Contrary to general belief, in the long run a pollution charge is likely to hurt a monopoly firm more than it does a competitive firm that is able to bear the cost. For as we know, under competition the economic profits of a producing firm are always zero. Therefore, when a pollution charge is levied on a competitive industry, the exit of firms from the industry will always adjust the product price and the costs of the firms that remain in the industry so that those firms will earn exactly the amount of economic profit that they got before the pollution charge was imposed. That is, they will earn zero economic profit in both cases. But, in contrast, the monopolist, as we have just seen, can expect a loss in profit as a result of the pollution charge. And there simply is no reason for that profit loss to go away, even in the long run.

## Summary

1. A **pure monopoly** is a one-firm industry producing a product for which there are no close substitutes.
2. Monopoly can persist only if there are important cost advantages to single-firm operation or **barriers to free entry**. These barriers may be legal impediments (**patents**, licensing), or the special risks faced by a potential entrant resulting from the need to incur large sunk investments, or the result of "dirty tricks" designed to make things tough for an entrant.
3. One important case of cost advantages is **natural monopoly**: instances where only one firm can survive because of important economies of large-scale production.
4. A monopoly has no supply curve. It maximizes its profit by producing an output at which its marginal revenue equals its marginal cost. Its price is given by the point on its demand curve corresponding to that output.
5. In a monopolistic industry, if demand and cost curves are the same as those of a competitive industry, and if the demand curve has a negative slope and the supply curve a positive slope, then output will be lower and monopoly price will be higher than those of the competitive industry.
6. Economists consider the fact that monopoly output tends to be below the competitive level to constitute an (undesirable) inefficiency.
7. Advertising may enable a monopoly to shift its demand curve above that of a comparable competitive industry's, and through economies such as large-scale input purchases, a monopoly may be able to shift its cost curves below those of a competitive industry.
8. If a pollution charge is imposed on the product of a profit-maximizing monopoly, that monopoly will raise its price, but normally not by the full amount of the charge. That is, the monopolist will end up paying part of the pollution fee.
9. Any rise in costs generally hurts a monopolist. Because of the negatively sloping demand curve, a monopolist cannot simply pass cost increases entirely on to consumers.

## Key Concepts and Terms

Pure monopoly
Barriers to entry
Patents
Natural monopoly
Monopoly profits
Inefficiency of monopoly
Shifting of pollution charges

## Questions for Review

1. Which of the following industries are pure monopolies?
   a. The only supplier of heating fuel in an isolated town.
   b. The only supplier of Exxon gasoline in town.
   c. The only supplier of instant cameras.
   Explain your answers.
2. Suppose a monopoly industry produces less output than a similar competitive industry. Discuss why this may be considered "socially undesirable."
3. If a competitive firm earns zero economic profits, explain why anyone would invest money in it. (*Hint*: What is the role of the opportunity cost of capital in economic profit?)
4. The following are the demand and *total* cost schedules for Company Town Water Company, a local monopoly.

| OUTPUT (gallons) | PRICE (dollars per gallon) | TOTAL COST (dollars) |
|---|---|---|
| 50,000 | .28 | 6,000 |
| 100,000 | .26 | 13,000 |
| 150,000 | .22 | 22,000 |
| 200,000 | .20 | 32,000 |
| 250,000 | .16 | 46,000 |
| 300,000 | .12 | 64,000 |

How much output will Company Town Water produce, and what price will it charge? Will it earn a profit? How much? (*Hint*: You will first have to compute its MR and MC schedules.)

5. Show from the preceding table that for the water company, marginal revenue (per 50,000 gallon unit) is always less than price.

6. Suppose a tax of $12 is levied on each item sold by a monopolist, and as a result she decides to raise her price by exactly $12. Why may this decision be against her own best interest?

7. Use Figure 11–2 to show that Adam Smith was wrong when he claimed that a monopoly would always charge "the highest price which can be got."

8. MCI and Sprint have invested vast amounts of money in their fiber optics network, which is costly to construct but relatively cheap to operate. If both of them were to go bankrupt, why might this *not* result in a decrease in the competition facing AT&T? (*Hint*: At what price would the assets of the bankrupt companies be offered for sale?)

9. What does the answer to your preceding question tell you about ease or difficulty of entry into telecommunications?

Chapter 12

# BETWEEN COMPETITION AND MONOPOLY

*I was grateful to be able to answer promptly and I did. I said I didn't know.*

MARK TWAIN

Most productive activity in the United States, as in any advanced industrial society, can be found between the two theoretical poles considered so far: perfect competition and pure monopoly. Thus, if we want to understand the workings of the market mechanism in a real, modern economy, we must look between competition and monopoly, at the hybrid market structures first mentioned in Chapter 9: *monopolistic competition* and *oligopoly*. ¶ Monopolistic competition is a market structure characterized by many small firms selling somewhat different products. Here each firm's output is so small relative to the total output of closely related and, hence, rival products that it does not expect its rivals to respond to or even to notice any changes in its own behavior. Monopolistic competition or something close to it is widespread in retailing; shoe stores, restaurants, and gasoline stations are good examples. It may well be suspected that more firms in our economy should be classified as monopolistic competitors than those in any other of our categories. For even though small, such enterprises are abundant. ¶ We will begin the chapter by using the theory of the firm described in Chapter 5 to analyze the price–output decision of a monopolistically competitive firm, and then consider the role of entry and exit, as we did in Chapter 9. Then we turn to oligopoly, a market structure in which a few large firms dominate the market. Industries such as steel, automobiles, and airplane manufacture are good examples of oligopolies with few firms, despite the increasing number of strong foreign competitors. Probably the largest share of the output of the economy is produced by oligopolists, for while the number of these firms is not as great as the number of monopolistic competitors, many oligopoly firms are extremely large, with annual sales exceeding the total outputs of some of the smaller industrial countries of Europe. One critical feature distinguishing an oligopolist from either a monopolist or a perfect competitor is that the oligopolist cares very much about what other firms in the industry do. And the resulting *interdependence* of decisions, we will see, makes oligopoly very hard to analyze. Consequently, economic theory contains not one but many models of oligopoly (some of which will be reviewed in this chapter), and it is often hard to know which model to apply in any particular situation.

We will also see that the case for laissez-faire is certainly weakened where monopolistic competition or oligopoly occurs.

## SOME PUZZLING OBSERVATIONS

We need to study the hybrid market structures considered in this chapter because many things we observe cannot be explained by the theories of perfect competition or pure monopoly. Here are some examples:

1. *Why do oligopolists advertise more than "more-competitive" firms*? While some advertising is primarily informative (for example, help-wanted ads), much of the advertising that bombards us on TV and in magazines is part of a competitive struggle for our business. Many big companies use advertising as the principal weapon in their battle for customers, and advertising budgets can constitute a very large share of their expenditures. A number of such firms literally spend hundreds of millions of dollars per year on advertising. Yet oligopolistic industries containing only a few giant firms are often accused of being "uncompetitive," while farming, for example, is considered as close to perfect competition as any industry in our economy, even though most individual farmers spend nothing at all on advertising.[1] Why do the allegedly "uncompetitive" oligopolists make such heavy use of advertising while very competitive farmers do not?
2. *Why are there so many retailers*? You have all seen intersections with three or four gasoline stations in close proximity. Often, two or three of them have no cars waiting to be served and the attendants are unoccupied. There seem to be more gas stations than the available amount of traffic warrants, with a corresponding waste of labor, time, equipment, and other resources. Why do they all stay in business?
3. *Why do oligopoly prices seem to change so infrequently*? Many prices in the economy change from minute to minute. Every day the latest prices of such items as soybeans, pork bellies, and copper are published. But if you want to buy one of these at 11:45 A.M. some day, you cannot use yesterday's price because it has probably changed since then. Yet prices of other products,

[1]But farmers' *associations*, like Sunkist and various dairy groups, do spend money on advertising.

such as cars and refrigerators, generally change several times a year at most, even when inflation is proceeding at a fairly rapid pace. The firms that sell cars and refrigerators know that market conditions change all the time. Why don't they adjust their prices more often?

This chapter will offer some answers to each of these questions.

## MONOPOLISTIC COMPETITION

For years, economic theory told us little about market forms in between the two extreme cases: pure monopoly and perfect competition. This gap was partially filled, and the realism of economic theory increased, by the work of Edward Chamberlin of Harvard University and Joan Robinson of Cambridge University during the 1930s. The market structure they analyzed is called **monopolistic competition.**

**MONOPOLISTIC COMPETITION** refers to a market in which products are heterogenous but which is otherwise the same as a market that is perfectly competitive.

A market is said to operate under conditions of *monopolistic competition* if it satisfies four conditions, three of which are the same as those for perfect competition: (1) *Numerous participants*—that is, many buyers and sellers, all of whom are small; (2) *freedom of exit and entry*; (3) *perfect information*; and (4) *heterogeneity of products*—as far as the buyer is concerned, each seller's product is at least somewhat different from every other's.

Notice that monopolistic competition differs from perfect competition in only one respect (item 4 in the definition). While under perfect competition all products must be identical, under monopolistic competition products differ from seller to seller—in quality, in packaging, or in supplementary services offered (such as car window washing by a gas station). The factors that serve to differentiate products need not be "real" in any objective or directly measurable sense. For example, differences in packaging or in associated services can and do distinguish products that are otherwise identical. On the other hand, two products may perform quite differently in quality tests, but if consumers know nothing about this difference, it is irrelevant. In contrast to a perfect competitor, a monopolistic competitor's price will change when its quantity supplied varies. Each seller's product differs from everyone else's. So, in effect, each deals in a market that is slightly separated from the others and caters to a set of customers who vary in their "loyalty" to the particular product. If the firm raises its price somewhat, it will drive *some* of its customers into the arms of competitors. But those whose tastes make them like this firm's product very much will not switch. If one monopolistic competitor lowers its price, it may expect to attract some trade from rivals. But, since different products are imperfect substitutes, no one competitor will attract away *all* the business.

Thus, if Harriet's Hot Dog House reduces its price slightly, it will attract those customers of Sam's Sausage Shop who were nearly indifferent between the two. A bigger price cut by Harriet will bring in some customers who have a slightly greater preference for Sam's product. But even a big cut in Harriet's price will not bring her the hard-core sausage lovers who hate hot dogs. So the monopolistic competitor's demand curve is negatively sloped, like that of a monopolist, rather than horizontal, like that of a perfect competitor, who will lose all his business if he insists on a price at all higher than a rival's.

Since each product is distinguished from all others, a monopolistically competitive firm appears to have something akin to a small monopoly. Can we therefore expect it to earn more than zero economic profit? As with a perfect competitor, perhaps this is possible in the short run. But in the long run, high economic profits will attract new entrants into a monopolistically competitive market—not entrants with products *identical* to an existing firm's, but with products sufficiently similar to hurt.

If one ice-cream parlor's location enables it to do a thriving business, it can confidently expect another, selling a *different* brand, to open nearby. When one seller adopts a new, attractive package, rivals will soon follow suit, with slightly different designs and colors of their own. In this way, freedom of entry ensures that the monopolistically competitive firm earns no higher return on its capital in the long run than it could earn elsewhere. Just as under perfect competition, price will be driven to the level of average cost, including the opportunity cost of capital. In this sense, though its product is somewhat different from that of everyone else, the firm under monopolistic competition has no more monopoly *power* than one operating under perfect competition.

Let us now examine the process that ensures that economic profits will be driven to zero in the long run, even under monopolistic competition, and see to what prices and outputs it leads.

## PRICE AND OUTPUT DETERMINATION UNDER MONOPOLISTIC COMPETITION

The *short-run* equilibrium of the firm under monopolistic competition differs little from the case of monopoly. Since the firm faces a downward-sloping demand curve (labeled *D* in Figure 12–1), its marginal revenue (MR) curve will lie below its demand curve. Profits are maximized at the output level at which marginal revenue and marginal cost (MC) are equal. In Figure 12–1, the profit-maximizing output for a hypothetical gasoline station is 12,000 gallons per week, and it sells this output at a price of $1.00 per gallon (point *P* on the demand curve).

This analysis, you will note, is much like that of Figure 11–2 (page 274) for a monopoly. The main difference is that the demand curve of a monopolistic competitor is likely to be much flatter than the pure monopolist's because there are many close substitutes for the monopolistic competitor's product. If our gas station raises its price to $1.30 per gallon, most of its customers will go across the street. If it lowers its price to 70 cents, it will have long lines at its pumps.

The gas station depicted in Figure 12–1 is making economic profits. Since average cost at 12,000 gallons per week is only 90 cents per gallon (point *C*), the station is making a profit on gasoline sales of 10 cents per gallon, or $1200 per week in total (the shaded rectangle). Under monopoly, such profits can persist. But under monopolistic competition they cannot, because new firms will be attracted into the market. While the new stations will not offer the identical product, they will offer products that are close enough to take away some business from our firm (for example, they may sell Mobil or Shell gasoline instead of Exxon).

When more firms share the market, the demand curve facing any individual must fall. But how far? The answer is basically the same as it was under perfect competition: market entry will cease only when the most that the firm can earn is zero economic profit.

*Figure* **12–1** **SHORT-RUN EQUILIBRIUM OF THE FIRM UNDER MONOPOLISTIC COMPETITION**

Like any firm, a monopolistic competitor maximizes profits by equating marginal cost (MC) and marginal revenue (MR). In this example, the profit-maximizing output level is 12,000 gallons per week and the profit-maximizing price is $1.00 per gallon. The firm is making a profit of 10 cents per gallon, which is depicted by the vertical distance from *C* to *P*.

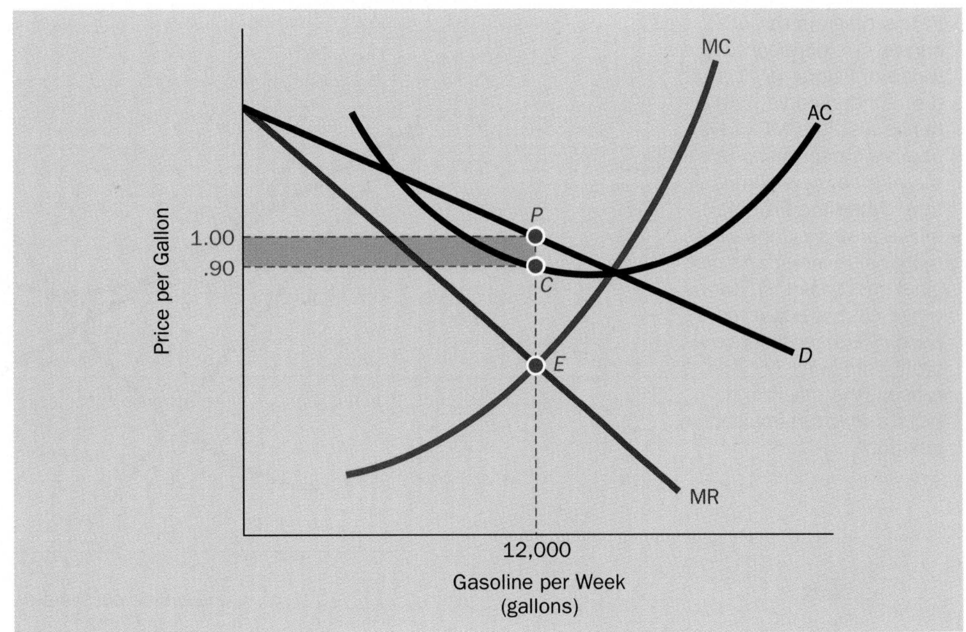


Figure 12–2 depicts the same monopolistically competitive firm as in Figure 12–1 *after* the adjustment to the long run is complete. The demand curve has been pushed down so far by the entry of new rivals that when the firm equates MC and MR in order to maximize profits (point *E*), it simultaneously equates price (*P*) and average cost (AC) so that profits are zero (point *P*). As compared to the short-run equilibrium depicted in Figure 12–1, price in long-run equilibrium is *lower* (95 cents per gallon versus $1.00), there are *more firms* in the industry, and each firm is producing a *smaller* output (10,000 gallons versus 12,000) at a *higher* average cost per gallon (95 cents versus 90 cents).[2] In general:

Long-run equilibrium under monopolistic competition requires that the firm's demand curve be tangent to its average cost curve.

Why? Because if the two curves intersected, there would be output levels at which price exceeded average cost, which means that economic profits could be earned and there would be an influx of new substitute products. Similarly, if the average cost curve failed to touch the demand curve altogether, the firm would be unable to obtain returns equal to those that its capital can get elsewhere, and firms would leave the industry.

This analysis of entry is quite similar to the perfectly competitive case. Moreover, the notion that firms under monopolistic competition earn exactly zero

[2]*Exercise*: Show that if the demand curve fell still further, the firm would incur a loss. What would then happen in the long run?

Figure 12–2 LONG-RUN EQUILIBRIUM OF THE FIRM UNDER MONOPOLISTIC COMPETITION

In this diagram the cost curves are identical to those of Figure 12–1, but the demand curve (and hence also the MR curve) has been depressed by the entry of new competitors. When the firm maximizes profits by equating marginal revenue and marginal cost (point *E*), its average cost is equal to its price ($.95), so economic profits are zero. For this reason, the diagram depicts a *long-run* equilibrium position.

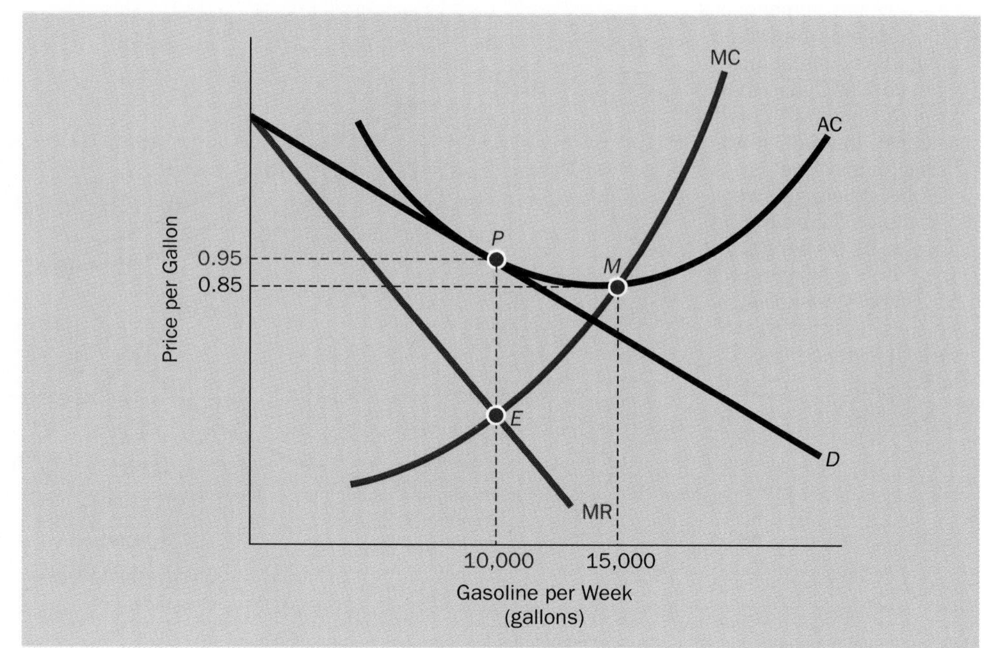


economic profits seems to correspond fairly well to what we see in the real world. Filling-station operators, whose market has the characteristics of monopolistic competition, do not earn notably higher profits than do small farmers, who operate under conditions closer to perfect competition.

## THE EXCESS CAPACITY THEOREM AND RESOURCE ALLOCATION

But there is one important difference between perfect and monopolistic competition. Look at Figure 12–2 again. The tangency point between the average cost and demand curves, point *P*, occurs along the *negatively sloping portion* of the average cost curve, since only there can the AC curve have the same (negative) slope as the demand curve. If the AC curve is U-shaped, the tangency point must therefore lie above and to the left of the *minimum point* on the average cost curve, point *M*. By contrast, under perfect competition the firm's demand curve is horizontal, so tangency must take place at the minimum point on the average cost curve, as is easily confirmed by referring back to Figure 9–9(a) on page 236. This observation leads to the following important conclusion:

Under monopolistic competition, the firm in the long run will tend to produce an output lower than that which minimizes its unit costs, and hence unit costs of the monopolistic competitor will be higher than is necessary. Since the level of output corresponding to minimum average cost is naturally considered to be the firm's optimal capacity, this result has been called the excess capacity theorem of monopolistic competition.

It follows that if every firm under monopolistic competition were to expand its output, cost per unit of output would be reduced. But we must be careful about jumping to policy conclusions from that observation. It does *not* follow that *every* monopolistically competitive firm *should* produce more. After all, such an overall increase in industry output means that a smaller portion of the economy's resources will be available for other uses; and from the information at hand we have no way of knowing whether that leaves us ahead or behind in terms of social benefits.

Yet the situation represented in Figure 12–2 can still be interpreted to represent a substantial *inefficiency*. While it is not clear that society would gain if *every* firm were to achieve lower costs by expanding its production, society *can* save resources if firms combine into a smaller number of larger companies that produce the same total output. For example, suppose that in the situation shown in Figure 12–2 there are 15 monopolistically competitive firms each selling 10,000 gallons of gas per week. The total cost of this output, according to the figures given in the diagram, would be

$$\begin{aligned}&(\text{Number of firms}) \times (\text{Output per firm}) \times (\text{Cost per unit})\\&= 15 \times 10{,}000 \times \$.95 = \$142{,}500.\end{aligned}$$

If, instead, the number of stations were cut to 10, and each sold 15,000 gallons, total production would be unchanged. But total costs would fall to 10 × 15,000 × $.85 = $127,500, a net saving of $15,000 *without any cut in total output*.

This result is not dependent on the particular numbers used in our illustration. It follows directly from the observation that lowering the cost per unit must always reduce the total cost of producing any *given* industry output. The economy must gain in the sense of getting the same total output as before but at a lower cost. After all, which do you prefer—a dozen bottles of soda for 50 cents each or a dozen bottles of soda at 35 cents each?

The excess capacity theorem explains one of the puzzles mentioned at the start of this chapter. The highway intersection with four filling stations, where two could serve the available customers with little increase in delays and at lower costs, is a practical example of excess capacity.

The excess capacity theorem seems to imply that there are too many sellers in monopolistically competitive markets and that society would benefit from a reduction in their numbers. However, such a conclusion may be a bit hasty. Even if a smaller number of larger firms could reduce costs, society may not benefit from the change because it would leave consumers a smaller range of choice. Since all products are at least slightly different under monopolistic competition, a reduction in the number of *firms* means that the number of different *products* falls as well. We achieve greater efficiency at the cost of greater standardization.

In some cases consumers may agree that this trade-off represents a net gain, particularly where the variety of products available was initially so great that it only served to confuse them. But for some products, most consumers would probably agree that the diversity of choice is worth the extra cost involved. After all, we would probably save money on clothing if every student were required to wear a uniform. But since the uniform is likely to be too hot for student A, too cool for student B, and aesthetically displeasing to everyone, would the cost saving really be a net benefit?

## OLIGOPOLY

An **OLIGOPOLY** is a market dominated by a few sellers at least several of which are large enough relative to the total market to be able to influence the market price.

An *oligopoly* is a market dominated by a few sellers at least several of which are large enough relative to the total market that they may well be able to influence the market price.

In highly developed economies, it is not monopoly, but oligopoly, that is virtually synonymous with "big business." Any oligopolistic industry includes a group of giant firms, each of which keeps a watchful eye on the actions of the others.[3] It is under oligopoly that rivalry among firms takes its most direct and active form. Here one encounters such actions and reactions as the frequent introduction of new products, free samples, and aggressive—if not downright nasty—advertising campaigns. A firm's price decision is likely to elicit cries of pain from its rivals, and the firms are often engaged in a continuing battle in which strategies are planned day by day and each major decision can be expected to induce a direct response.

Managers of large oligopolistic firms who have occasion to study economics are somewhat taken aback by the notion of perfect competition, because it is devoid of all harsh competitive activity as they know it. Remember that under perfect competition the managers of firms make no price decisions—they simply accept the price dictated by market forces and adjust their output accordingly. As we observed at the beginning of the chapter, a competitive firm does not advertise; it adopts no sales gimmicks; it does not even know who most of its competitors are. But since oligopolists are not as dependent on market forces, they do not enjoy such luxuries. They worry about prices, spend fortunes on advertising, and try to understand their rivals' behavior patterns.

The reasons for such divergent behavior should be clear. First, a perfectly competitive firm can sell all it wants at the current market price. So why should it waste money on advertising? By contrast, Ford and Chrysler cannot sell all the cars they want at the current price. Since their demand curves are negatively sloped, if they want to sell more they must either reduce prices or advertise more (to shift their demand curves outward).

Second, since the public believes that the products supplied by firms in a perfectly competitive industry are identical, if firm A advertises its product, the advertisement is just as likely to bring customers to firm B. Under oligopoly, however, consumer products are often not identical. Ford advertises to try to convince consumers that its automobiles are better than GM's or Toyota's. And if the advertising campaign succeeds, GM and Toyota will be hurt and probably will respond by more advertising of their own. Thus, it is the firm in an oligopoly with differentiated products that is forced to compete via advertising, while the perfectly competitive firm gains little or nothing by doing so.

### WHY OLIGOPOLISTIC BEHAVIOR IS SO HARD TO ANALYZE

The relative freedom of choice in pricing of at least the largest firms in an oligopolistic industry, and the necessity for them to take direct account of their rivals'

[3]Notice that nothing is said in the definition about the degree of product differentiation. Some oligopolies sell products that are essentially identical (such as steel plate from different steelmakers) while others sell products that are quite different in the eyes of consumers (for example, Chevrolets, Fords, and Plymouths). Some oligopoly industries also contain a considerable number of smaller firms (example: soft drink manufacture) but they are nevertheless considered oligopolies because the bulk of their business is carried out by a few large firms.

responses, can be troublesome. Producers who are able to influence the market price may find it expedient to adjust their outputs to secure more favorable prices. Just as in the case of monopoly, such actions are likely to be at the expense of the consumer and detrimental to the economy's efficient use of resources.

It is not easy to reach definite conclusions about resource allocation under oligopoly, however. The reason is that oligopoly is much more difficult to analyze than the other forms of economic organization. The difficulty arises from the interdependent nature of oligopolistic decisions. For example, Ford's management knows that its actions will probably lead to reactions by General Motors, which in turn may require a readjustment in Ford's plans, thereby producing a modification in GM's response, and so on. Where such a sequence of moves and countermoves may lead is difficult enough to ascertain. But the fact that Ford executives know all this in advance, and may try to take it into account in making their initial decision, makes even that first step difficult, if not impossible, to analyze and predict.

The truth is that almost anything can happen under oligopoly, and sometimes does. The early railroad kings went so far as to employ gangs of hoodlums who engaged in pitched battles to try to prevent the operation of a rival line. At the other extreme, overt or more subtle forms of collusion have been employed to avoid rivalry altogether—to transform an oligopolistic industry, at least temporarily, into a monopolistic one. Arrangements designed to make it possible for the firms to live and let live have also been utilized: price leadership (see page 295) is one example; an agreement allocating geographic areas among the different firms is another.

Because of this rich variety of behavior patterns, it is not surprising that economists have been unable to agree on a single, widely accepted model of oligopoly behavior. Nor should they. Since oligopolies in the real world are so diverse, oligopoly models in the theoretical world should also come in various shapes and sizes. The theory of oligopoly contains some really remarkable pieces of economic analysis, some of which we will review in the following sections.

## A SHOPPING LIST

An introductory course cannot hope to explain all the different models of oligopoly; nor would that serve any purpose but to confuse you. Since economists differ in their opinions about which approaches to oligopoly theory are the most interesting and promising, we offer in this section a quick catalogue of some models of oligopolistic behavior. Then, in the remainder of the chapter, we will describe in greater detail a few other models.

### IGNORE INTERDEPENDENCE

One simple approach to the problem of oligopolistic interdependence is to assume that the oligopolists themselves ignore it; that they behave as if their actions will not elicit reactions from their rivals. It *is* possible that an oligopolist, finding the "if they think that we think that they think . . . " chain of reasoning just too complex, will decide to ignore rivals' behavior. The firm may then just maximize profits on the assumption that its decisions will not affect those of its rivals. In this case, the analysis of oligopoly is identical to the analysis of monopoly in the previous chapter. Probably, no oligopolist totally ignores all the decisions of any of its major rivals, but many of them seem to do so in a number of their more routine decisions, many of which are nevertheless quite important.

## STRATEGIC INTERACTION

While it is possible that *some* oligopolies ignore interdependence *some* of the time, it is very unlikely that such models offer a general explanation for the behavior of *most* oligopoly behavior *most* of the time. The reason is quite simple. Because they operate in the same market, the price and output decisions of the makers of Brand X and Brand Y soap suds *really are* interdependent. Suppose, for example, that the management of Brand X, Inc., decides to cut its price to $1.05 on the assumption that Brand Y, Inc., will continue to charge $1.12 per box, to manufacture five million boxes per year, and to spend $1 million per year on advertising. It may find itself surprised when Brand Y, Inc., cuts its price to $1 per box, raises production to eight million boxes per year, and sponsors the Super Bowl. If so, Brand X's profits will suffer, and the company will wish it had not cut its price. Most important for our purposes, it will learn not to ignore interdependence in the future. For many oligopolies, then, competition may resemble military operations involving tactics, strategies, moves and countermoves. Thus it seems imperative to consider models that deal explicitly with oligopolistic interdependence. We will study several such models, probably the most notable of them being those provided by the theory of games.

## CARTELS

The opposite end of the spectrum from ignoring interdependence is for all the firms in an oligopoly to recognize their interdependence and agree to a peace treaty under which they collude overtly with one another, thereby transforming the industry into a giant monopoly—a **cartel**.

A **CARTEL** is a group of sellers of a product who have joined together to control its production, sale, and price in the hope of obtaining the advantages of monopoly.

A notable example of the formation of a cartel is the Organization of Petroleum Exporting Countries (OPEC), which first began to make decisions in unison in the 1970s. For a while, OPEC was one of the most spectacularly successful cartels in history. By restricting output, the member nations managed to quadruple the price of oil in 1973–1974. Then, unlike most cartels, which come apart in internal bickering or for other reasons, OPEC held together through two worldwide recessions and a variety of unsettling political events, and struck again with huge price increases in 1979–1980. Only in the mid-1980s did it run into trouble.

But the story of OPEC is not the norm. Cartels are not easy to organize and are even more difficult to preserve. Firms find it hard to agree on such things as the amount by which each will reduce its output in order to help push up the price. For a cartel to survive, each member must agree to produce no more than the level of output that has been assigned to it by the group. Yet once price is driven up and profitability is increased, it becomes tempting for each seller to offer secret discounts in order to lure some of the profitable business away from other members of the cartel. Indeed, some of this happened to OPEC in the 1980s. When this happens, or is even suspected by cartel members, it is often the beginning of the end of the collusive arrangement. Each member begins suspecting the others and is tempted to cut price first, before the others beat it to the punch.

Cartels, therefore, usually adopt elaborate policing arrangements, in effect spying on each member firm to make sure it does not sell more than it is supposed to or shave the price below that chosen by the cartel. This means that cartels are unlikely to succeed or to last very long if the firms sell many varied products whose prices are difficult to compare and whose outputs are difficult to keep track of. In addition, if prices are frequently negotiated on a customer-by-customer basis, and special discounts are common, a cartel may be almost impossible to arrange.

Many economists consider cartels to be one of the least desirable forms of market organization. If a cartel is successful, it may end up charging the monopoly price and obtaining monopoly profits. But because the firms do not actually combine their operations but continue to produce separately, the cartel offers the public no offsetting benefits in the form of economies of large-scale production. For these and other reasons, open collusion among firms is illegal in the United States, as we will see in Chapter 19, and outright cartel arrangements are rarely found. (However, in many other countries cartels are common.) There is only one major exception in the United States. The government has sometimes forced regulated industries such as telecommunications and gas pipeline transportation to behave as a cartel would, by prohibiting them from undercutting the prices set by the regulatory agency. This exception will be discussed in Chapter 18.

## PRICE LEADERSHIP AND TACIT COLLUSION

Although overt collusion—where firms meet together to decide on prices and outputs—is quite rare, some observers think that *tacit collusion*—where firms, without meeting together, do unto their competitors as they hope their competitors will do unto them—is quite common among oligopolists in our economy. Oligopolists who do not want to rock what amounts to a very profitable boat may seek to develop some indirect way of communicating with one another and signaling their intentions. Each tacitly colluding firm hopes that if it behaves in a way that does not make things too difficult for its competitors, then its rivals will return the favor. One common example of tacit collusion is **price leadership**, an arrangement in which one firm in the industry is, in effect, assigned the task of making pricing decisions for the entire group. It is expected that other firms will adopt the prices set by the price leader, even though there is no explicit agreement, only tacit consent. Often, the price leader will be the largest firm in the industry. But in some price-leadership arrangements the role of leader may rotate from one firm to another. For example, it was suggested that the steel industry for many years conformed to the price leadership model, with U.S. Steel and Bethlehem Steel assuming the role of leader at different times.

Under **PRICE LEADERSHIP,** one firm sets the price for the industry and the others follow.

Price leadership *does* overcome the problem of oligopolistic interdependence, although it is not the only possible way of doing so. If Brand X, Inc., is the price leader for the soap suds industry, it can predict how Brand Y, Inc., will react to any price increases it announces. (Brand Y will match the increases.) Similarly, Brand Z executives will be able to predict Brand Y's behavior as long as the price-leadership arrangement holds up.

But one problem besetting price leadership is that, while the oligopolists as a group may benefit by avoiding a damaging **price war,** the firms may not benefit equally. The firm that is the price leader may be in a better position to maximize its own profits than are any of the others in the group. But, if the price leader does not take into account its rivals' welfare when making its price decision, it may find itself dethroned! Like cartels, such arrangements can easily break down.

In a **PRICE WAR** each competing firm is determined to sell at a price that is lower than the prices of its rivals, usually regardless of whether that price covers the pertinent cost. Typically, in such a price war Firm A cuts its price below Firm B's; then B retaliates by undercutting A, and so on and on until one or more of the firms surrender and let themselves be undersold.

## SALES MAXIMIZATION[4]

Early in our analysis of the theory of the firm, we discussed the hypothesis that firms try to maximize profits and noted that other objectives are possible (see pages 107–108). Among these alternative goals, one that has achieved much attention is sales maximization.

Modern industrial firms are managed and owned by entirely different groups of people. The managers are paid executives who work for the company on a full-time basis and may grow to believe that whatever is good for themselves must be good for the company. The owners may be a large and diffuse group of stockholders, most of whom own only a tiny fraction of the outstanding stock, take little interest in the operations of the company, and do not feel that the company is "theirs" in any real sense. In such a situation, it is not entirely implausible that the company's decisions will be influenced more heavily by management's goals than by the goal of the owners (which is, presumably, to maximize profit).

There is some statistical evidence, for example, that management's compensation is often tied more directly to the company's *size*, as measured by its sales volume, than to its *profits*. The president of a large firm generally gets a much higher salary than the president of a tiny company. Therefore, the firm's managers may select a price–output combination that maximizes sales rather than profits. But does sales maximization lead to different decisions than does profit maximization? We shall see now that the answer is yes.

Figure 12–3 is a diagram that should be familiar by now. It shows the marginal cost (MC) and average cost (AC) curves for a firm—in this case Brand X, Inc.—along with its demand and marginal revenue (MR) curves. We have used such diagrams before and know that if the company wants to maximize profits, it will select point *A*, where MC = MR. This means that it will produce 2.5 million boxes of soap suds per year and sell them at a price of $1 each (point *E*). Since average cost at this level of output is only 80 cents per box, profit per unit is 20 cents. Total profits are therefore $.20 × 2,500,000 = $500,000 per year. This is the highest attainable profit level for Brand X, Inc.

Now what if Brand X wants to maximize sales revenue instead? In this case, it will want to keep producing until MR is depressed to *zero*; that is, it will select point *B*. Why? By definition, MR is the *additional* revenue obtained by raising output by one unit. If the firm wishes to maximize revenue, then any time it finds that MR is positive it will want to increase output further, and any time it finds that MR is negative it will want to decrease output. Only when MR = 0 can the maximum sales revenue have possibly been achieved.[5]

Thus if Brand X, Inc., is a sales maximizer, it will produce 3.75 million boxes of soap suds per year (point *B*), and charge 75 cents per box (point *F*). Since average costs at this level of production are only 69 cents per box, profit per unit is 6 cents and, with 3.75 million units sold, total profit is $225,000. Naturally, this level of profit is less than what the firm can achieve if it reduces output to the profit-maximizing level. But this is not the firm's goal. Its sales revenue at point *B* is 75 cents per unit times 3.75 million units, or $2,812,500, whereas at point *A*

[4]The three sections that follow may be read in any combination, and in any order, without loss of continuity.

[5]The logic here is exactly the same as the logic that led to the conclusion that a firm maximized *profits* by setting *marginal profit* equal to zero. If you need review, consult Chapter 5, especially pages 113–17.

**Figure 12–3** SALES-MAXIMIZATION EQUILIBRIUM

A firm that wishes to maximize sales revenue will expand output until marginal revenue (MR) is zero—point *B* in the diagram, where output is 3.75 million boxes per year. This is a greater output level than it would choose if it were interested in maximizing profits. In that case, it would select point *A*, where MC = MR, and produce only 2.5 million boxes. Since the demand curve is downward sloping, the price corresponding to point *B* (75 cents) must be less than the price corresponding to point *A* ($1).

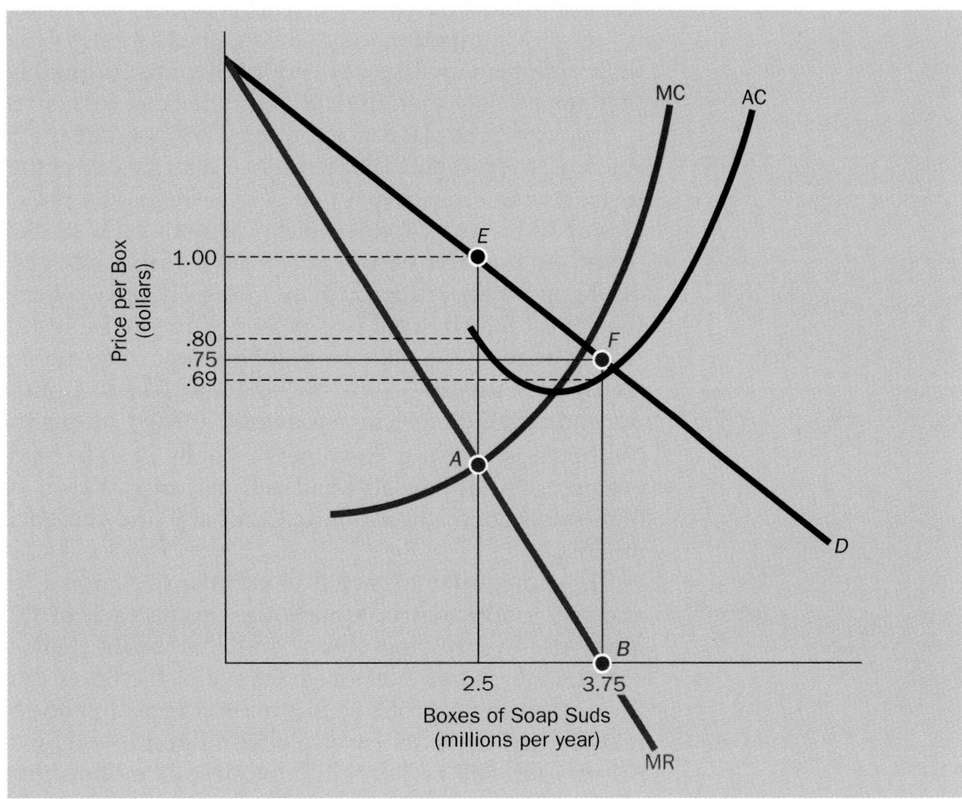


it was only $2,500,000 (2.5 million units at $1 each). What we conclude, then, is that:

If a firm is maximizing sales revenue, it will produce more output and charge a lower price than it would if it were maximizing profits.

We see clearly in Figure 12–3 that this result holds for Brand X, Inc. But does it always hold? The answer is yes. Look again at Figure 12–3, but ignore the numbers on the axes. At point *A*, where MR = MC, marginal revenue must be positive because it is equal to marginal cost (which, we may assume, is *always* positive). At point *B*, MR is equal to zero. Since the marginal revenue curve is negatively sloped, the point where it reaches zero (point *B*) must necessarily correspond to a higher level of output than the point where it cuts the marginal cost curve (point *A*). Thus, sales-maximizing firms always produce more than profit-maximizing firms and, to sell this greater volume of output, they must charge a lower price.

## THE GAME-THEORY APPROACH

Game theory, contributed in 1944 by mathematician John von Neumann (1903–1957) and economist Oskar Morgenstern (1902–1977), adopts a more imaginative approach than any other analysis of oligopoly. It attacks the issue of interdependence directly by assuming that each firm's managers proceed on the assumption *that their rivals are extremely ingenious decision makers*. In this model, each oligopolist is seen as a competing player in a game of strategy. Since managers act as though their opponents will always adopt the most profitable countermove to any move they make, they seek the optimal defensive response.

Two fundamental concepts of game theory are the *strategy* and the *payoff matrix*. A strategy represents an operational plan for one of the participants. In its simplest form, it may refer to just one of a participant's possible decisions. For example, "I will add to my product line a car with a TV set that the driver can watch," or "I will cut the price of my car to $9500." Since much of the game-theoretic analysis of oligopoly has focused on an oligopoly of two firms—a *duopoly*—we illustrate the payoff matrix for a two-person game in Table 12–1.

This matrix is a table of numbers reporting the profits that each of two rival firms, the Atlantic Company and the Pacific Company, can expect to earn—depending on the pricing strategy that each adopts (not knowing the secret price the other is offering customers). Table 12–1 is read like a mileage chart. For example, the upper left-hand cell indicates that, if both firms decide to charge high prices, both the Atlantic Company and the Pacific Company will earn $10 million.

The choice open to each firm is either to charge a "high price" or a "low price," and the payoff matrix reports the profits each of the firms can expect to earn, given its own pricing choice and that of its rival. We see that, if either firm succeeds in charging a low price when the other does not, the price cutter will actually raise its profit to $12 million (presumably by capturing enough of the market) and drive its rival to a $2 million loss. However, if *both* firms offer low prices, each will be left with a modest $3 million profit.

How does game theory analyze optimal strategy choice? We may envision the management of the Atlantic Company reasoning as follows: "If I choose a high-price strategy, the worst that can happen to me is that my competitor will select the low-price counterstrategy, which will cut my return to minus $2 million (the brown number in the first row of the payoff matrix). Similarly, if I select a low-price strategy, the worst outcome for which I must be prepared is $3 million (which is the brown minimum payoff in the second row of the matrix).

How can the management of Atlantic Company best protect itself from trouble in these circumstances? Game theory suggests that Atlantic should select among strategies on the basis of the *minimum* payoff to each, just as described above. It should pick the strategy whose minimum payoff is higher than that for any other strategy: the strategy that offers the highest of the brown numbers in the matrix.

**Table 12–1 A PAYOFF MATRIX**

| | | Pacific's Strategy | | | |
|---|---|---|---|---|---|
| | | High Price | | Low Price | |
| Atlantic's Strategy | High Price | A gets 10 | P gets 10 | A gets −2 | P gets 12 |
| | Low Price | A gets 12 | P gets −2 | A gets 3 | P gets 3 |

The **MAXIMIN CRITERION** means selecting the strategy that yields the maximum payoff, on the assumption that your opponent does as much damage to you as he or she can.

This is called the **maximin criterion**: one seeks the *max*imum of the *min*imum payoffs to the various available strategies. In this case, the maximin strategy for each firm is to offer a low price and earn a profit of $3 million.

Notice that, in this case, fear of what its rival will do virtually forces each firm to offer a low price and to forgo the high ($10 million) profit each could earn if it could trust the other to stick to a high price. This example illustrates why many observers conclude that, particularly where the number of firms is small, firms should not be permitted to confer or exchange information on prices. The same sort of analysis also helps to explain how competition limits profits and benefits consumers, and why price cartel arrangements are fragile.

A payoff matrix with a pattern like Table 12–1 has many other interesting applications. It is used, for example, to show how people get trapped into making each other (and themselves) worse off by driving polluting cars in the absence of laws requiring emission controls. Each does so because she does not trust other drivers to install emission controls voluntarily. (*Exercise*: Make up a payoff matrix that tells this story.)

There is still another interpretation, one which gave this matrix the name by which it is known to game theorists: "the prisoners' dilemma." Here, instead of a two-firm industry, the underlying scenario is that of two burglary suspects who are captured by the police and interrogated in separate rooms. Each suspect has two strategy options: to deny the charge or to confess. If both deny it, both go free, for the police have no other evidence. But if one confesses and the other does not, the silent prisoner can expect the key to his cell to be thrown away. The maximin solution, then, is for both to confess and receive the moderate sentence that this elicits.

There is, of course, a great deal more to game theory than we have been able to suggest in a few paragraphs. We have only sought to describe a little of its flavor. Game theory provides, for example, an illuminating analysis of coalitions, indicating, for cases involving more than two firms, which firms would do well to align themselves together against which others. The theory of games has also been used to analyze a variety of complicated problems outside the realm of oligopoly theory. It has been employed in management training programs and by a number of government agencies. It is used in political science and in formulating military strategy. It has been presented here to offer the reader a glimpse of the type of work that is taking place on the frontiers of economic analysis and to suggest how economists think about complex analytical problems. (For an example, see the box on page 300).

## THE KINKED DEMAND CURVE MODEL[6]

As our final example of oligopoly analysis, we describe a model designed to account for the alleged stickiness in oligopolistic pricing, meaning that prices in oligopolistic markets change far less frequently than do prices in competitive markets. It will be recalled that this is one of the puzzling phenomena with which

[6]Variants of this model were constructed by Hall and Hitch in England and by Sweezy in the United States. See R. L. Hall and C. J. Hitch, "Price Theory and Business Behavior," *Oxford Economic Papers*, No. 2, May 1939, and P. M. Sweezy, "Demand Under Conditions of Oligopoly," *Journal of Political Economy*, vol. 47, August 1939.

*At The* **FRONTIER**

## GAME THEORY AND ENTRY DETERRENCE

Game theory has moved toward domination of research on the theory of oligopoly. An example is the game theory model of strategic decisions by firms already inside an industry ("old firms") whose primary purpose is to prevent the entry of new rivals ("new firms"). One way in which this can be done is for the old firm to build a bigger factory than it would otherwise want, in the belief that the output of the excessive factory capacity will force prices down and thereby make entry unprofitable. By doing so, the old firm realizes that it gives up some potential profit—compared to what it could earn if no new firm even threatened to enter. However, the old firm hopes nevertheless that it will be better off than if entry occurs.

Some hypothetical numbers and a graph typical of those used in game theory will make the story clear. There are two options for the old firm: to build a small factory or a big one. There are also two options for the potential new firm: to open for business (that is, to enter) or not to enter. The accompanying figure shows the four resulting combinations of decisions that are possible and the corresponding profits or losses the two firms may expect in each case.

The graph shows that the best outcome for the old firm is when it builds a small factory and the new firm decides not to enter. In that case, the old firm will earn $6 million while the new firm (since it never starts up) will earn zero. However, if the old firm *does* decide to build a small factory, it can be pretty sure the new firm *will* open up for business, because then the new firm will earn $2 million (rather than zero). In the process, it will reduce the old firm's profits to $2 million.

On the other hand, if the old firm selects its other option and builds a big factory, the increased output will depress prices and profits. The old firm will now earn only $4 million if the new firm stays out while *each* firm will *lose* $2 million if the new firm enters. Obviously, if the old firm builds a big factory, the new firm will be better off staying out of the business rather than subjecting itself to a $2 million loss.

What size factory, then, will it be profitable for the old firm to build? When we consider the firms' interactions, it becomes clear that the old firm should build the large factory with its excessive capacity—for then it can expect the new firm to stay out, leaving the old firm a $4 million profit. In contrast, if a small factory is built, the new firm will open for business and reduce the old firm's profit to $2 million.

Thus, if we take the new firm's strategic choices into account, it is obvious that it would pay the old firm to build the oversized factory and take the $4 million in profits it would earn by deterring the other firm from entering. Moral: wasting money on excess capacity may not be wasteful in terms of the oligopolist's self-interest. This graph shows the possible choices of an old firm and the possible responses of a potential entrant. If the old firm builds a big factory, the entrant will avoid $2 million in losses by staying out of the business, leaving the old firm with $4 million in profit (asterisk lines). On the other hand, with a small factory the new firm will enter the business (dashed lines) so the old firm would be worse off, with only $2 million in profit.

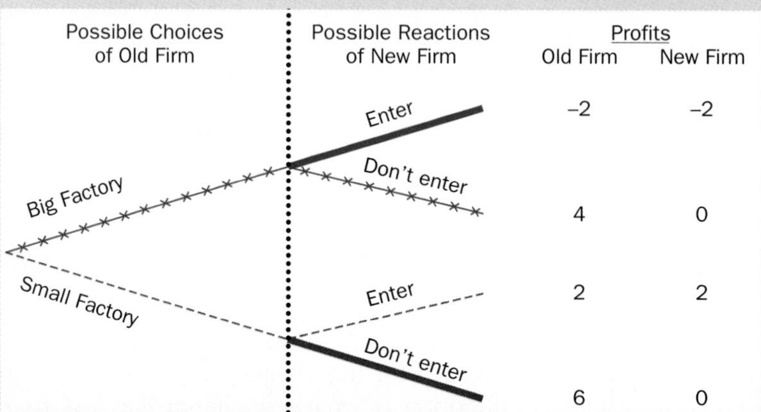


This graph shows the possible choices of an old firm and the possible responses of a potential entrant. If the old firm builds a big factory the entrant will avoid $2 million in losses by staying out of the business, leaving the old firm with $4 million in profit (asterisk lines). On the other hand, with a small factory the new firm will enter the business (dashed lines) so the old firm would be worse off, with only $2 million in profit.

we began this chapter. The prices of corn, soybeans, pork bellies, and silver, all of which are sold in markets with large numbers of buyers and sellers, change minute by minute. But prices of such items as cars, TV sets, and dishwashers, all of which are supplied by oligopolists, may change only every few months. These prices seem to resist frequent change even in periods of inflation.

One reason may be that, when an oligopolist cuts the product's price, it is never sure how its rivals will react. One extreme possibility is that Firm Y will ignore the price cut of Firm X, that is, Y's price will not change. Alternatively, Y may reduce its price, precisely matching that of Firm X. Accordingly, the model makes use of two different demand curves: one curve represents the quantities a given oligopolistic firm can sell at different prices *if competitors match its price moves*, and the other demand curve represents what happens when competitors stubbornly *stick to their initial price levels*.

Point *A* in Figure 12–4 represents the initial price and output of our firm: 1000 units at $10 each. Through that point pass two demand curves: *DD*, which represents our company's demand if competitors keep their prices fixed, and *dd*, the curve indicating what happens when competitors match our firm's price changes.

The *DD* curve is the more elastic (flatter) of the two, and a moment's thought indicates why this should be so. If our firm cuts its price from its initial level of $10 to, say, $8, and if competitors do not match this cut, we would expect our firm to get a large number of new customers—perhaps its quantity demanded will jump to 1400. However, if its competitors respond by also reducing their prices, its quantity demanded will rise by less—perhaps only to 1100. Conversely, when it raises its price, our firm may expect a larger loss of sales if its rivals fail

**Figure 12–4** **THE KINKED DEMAND CURVE**

It has been suggested that oligopolists are deterred from changing prices frequently because they fear the reactions of their rivals. If they raise prices they will lose many customers to competitors because the competitors will not match the price increase. (Elastic demand curve *DD* therefore applies to price increases.) But if they cut prices, competitors will be forced to match the price cut so that the price cut will not bring many new customers. (The inelastic demand curve *dd* applies to price cuts.) Thus, the demand curve facing the firm is the kinked, brown curve *DAd*.

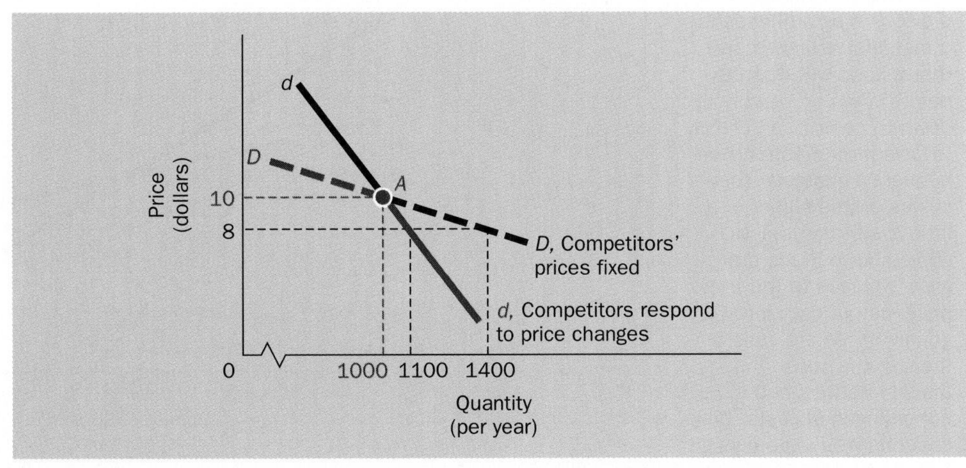

to match its increase, which the reader may readily verify by observing the relative flatness (elasticity) of the curve *DD* in Figure 12–4.

How does this relate to sticky oligopolistic prices? Here our firm's fears and expectations must be brought into the matter. The hypothesis of those who designed this model was that a typical oligopolistic firm has good reason to fear the worst. If it lowers its prices and its rivals do not, its sales will seriously cut into its competitor's volume, and so the rivals will *have* to match the price cut in order to protect themselves. The inelastic demand curve, *dd*, will therefore apply if our firm decides on a price reduction (points below and to the right of point *A*).

On the other hand, if our company chooses to *increase* its price, management will fear that its rivals will continue to sit at their old price levels, calmly collecting the customers that have been driven to them. Thus, the relevant demand curve for price increases (above *A*) will be *DD*.

In sum, our firm will figure that it will face a segment of the elastic demand curve *DD* if it raises its price and a segment of the inelastic demand curve *dd* if it decreases its price. Its true demand curve will then be given by the heavy brown line, *DAd*. For obvious reasons, this is called a kinked demand curve.

In these circumstances, it will pay management to vary its price only under extreme provocation, that is, only if there is an enormous change in costs. For the kinked demand curve represents a "heads you lose, tails you lose" proposition in terms of any potential price change. If it raises its price, the firm will lose many customers (demand is elastic); if it lowers its price, the increase in volume will be comparatively small (demand is inelastic).

Figure 12–5 illustrates this conclusion graphically. The two demand curves, *dd* and *DD*, are carried over precisely from the previous diagram. The dashed line, labeled MR, is the marginal revenue curve associated with *DD*, while the solid

**Figure 12–5 THE KINKED DEMAND CURVE AND STICKY PRICES**

The kinked demand curve *DAd* that we derived in the previous diagram leads to a marginal revenue curve that follows MR down to point *B* then drops directly down to point *C*, and finally follows mr thereafter. Consequently, marginal cost curves a little higher or a little lower than the MC curve shown in the diagram will lead to the same price–output decision. Oligopoly prices are "sticky," then, in the sense that they do not respond to minor changes in costs. Only cost changes large enough to push the MC curve out of the range *BC* will lead to a change in price.

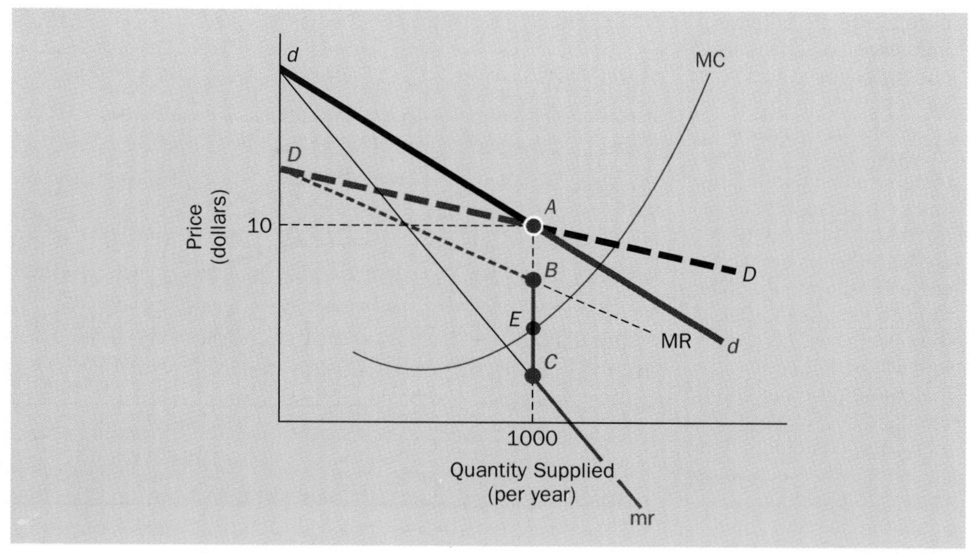

line, labeled mr, is the marginal revenue curve associated with *dd*. Since the marginal revenue curve relevant to the firm's decision making is MR for any output level *below* 1000 units but mr for any output level *above* 1000 units, the composite marginal revenue curve facing the firm is shown by the thin brown line *DBC*mr with two angles.

The marginal cost curve drawn in the diagram cuts this composite marginal revenue curve at point *E*, which indicates the profit-maximizing combination of output and price for this oligopolist. Specifically, the quantity supplied at point *E* is 1000 units, and the price is $10, which we read from demand curve *DAd*.

The unique aspect of this diagram is that the kinked demand curve leads to a marginal revenue curve that takes a sharp plunge between points *B* and *C*. Consequently, moderate upward or downward shifts of the MC curve will still leave it intersecting the marginal revenue curve somewhere between *B* and *C*, and thus will *not* lead the firm to change its output decision. Therefore, *the firm's price will remain unchanged*. (Try this for yourself in Figure 12–5.) This is the sense in which the kinked demand curve makes prices "sticky."

If this is in fact the way oligopolists feel about their competitors' behavior, it is easy to see why they may be reluctant to make frequent price changes. We can also understand why a system of price leadership might arise. The price leader can, in times of inflation for instance, raise prices when he or she thinks it appropriate, confident that the firm will not be left out on a limb (a kink?) by other firms' unwillingness to follow.

## MONOPOLISTIC COMPETITION, OLIGOPOLY, AND PUBLIC WELFARE

How good or bad, from the viewpoint of the general welfare, is the performance of firms that are monopolistically competitive or oligopolistic?

We have seen that their performance *can* leave much to be desired. For example, the excess capacity theorem showed us that monopolistic competition can lead to inefficiently high production costs. Similarly, because market forces may not be sufficiently powerful to restrain their behavior, oligopolists' prices and outputs may differ substantially from those that are socially optimal, particularly where the oligopoly organizes itself into a successful cartel. Moreover, there are those who believe that misleading advertising by corporate giants often distorts the judgments of consumers, leading them to buy things they do not need and would otherwise not want. It is said that such corporate giants wield political power, economic power, and power over the minds of consumers—and that all of these undermine the beneficent workings of Adam Smith's invisible hand.

But because oligopoly behavior is so varied, we cannot generalize with confidence. Because one oligopolist decides on price, output, and advertising in a manner very different from another, the implications for social welfare vary from case to case.

Yet, recent analysis has provided one theoretical case in which both the behavior and the quality of performance of an oligopolistic or monopolistically competitive firm can be predicted and judged unambiguously. This is the case in which entry into or exit from the market is costless and unimpeded. In such a case, called a **perfectly contestable market** (see the accompanying boxed insert), the constant threat of entry forces even the largest firm to behave well—to produce efficiently and never to overcharge. For if that firm is inefficient, or sets its prices too high,

A market is **PERFECTLY CONTESTABLE** if entry and exit are costless and unimpeded.

*At The* FRONTIER

## THE THEORY OF CONTESTABLE MARKETS

Perfect competition has long been used as a standard for the structure and behavior of an industry, although it is widely recognized to be unattainable in reality, except in a few activities such as agriculture. Recently, some economists have tried to supplement this concept with the aid of a generalized criterion, called a *perfectly contestable market.** Some markets that contain a few relatively large firms may be highly contestable, though they are certainly not perfectly competitive. Because perfect competition requires a large number of firms, all of them negligible in size relative to the size of the industry, no industry with economies of large-scale production can be perfectly competitive.

A market is defined as perfectly contestable if firms can enter it and, if they choose, exit without losing the money they invested. Note that the crucial issue is not the amount of capital that is required to enter the industry, but whether or not an entrant can withdraw the investment if he or she wishes—whether that expenditure is a *sunk* cost. For example, if entry involves investing in highly mobile capital—such as barges, airplanes,** or trucks—the entrant may be able to exit quickly and cheaply. If a barge operation decides to serve the lower Mississippi and finds business disappointing, it can easily transfer its boats to, say, the Ohio River.

A profitable market that is contestable is therefore attractive to *potential* entrants. Because of the absence of barriers to entry or exit, firms undertake little risk by

it will be threatened with replacement by an entrant who offers to serve customers more cheaply.

Of course, no industries are perfectly contestable and many are not even nearly so. But in those industries that are highly contestable—that is, in which entry and exit costs are negligible—market forces can do a good job of forcing business to behave in the manner that most effectively promotes the public interest. And where an industry is not very contestable, but there are ways to reduce entry and exit costs, the new theory of contestable markets suggests that this may sometimes be a more promising approach than any attempt by government to interfere with the behavior of the oligopolistic firms in order to improve their performance.

## A GLANCE BACKWARD: COMPARISON OF THE FOUR MARKET FORMS

This completes the set of chapters that has taken us through the four main forms of industrial organization which characterize the economy: perfect competition, going into such a market. If their entry turns out to have been a mistake, they can move to another market without loss.

## CONTESTABLE MARKETS' PERFORMANCE

The constant threat of entry elicits good performance by oligopolists, or even by monopolists, in a contestable market. In particular, perfectly contestable markets have at least two desirable characteristics.

First, profits exceeding the opportunity cost of capital are eliminated in the long run by freedom of entry, just as they are in a perfectly competitive market. If the current opportunity cost of capital is 12 percent while the firms in a contestable market are earning a return of 18 percent, new firms will enter the market, expand the industry's outputs, and drive down the prices of its products to the point where all excess profit has been removed. To avoid this outcome, established firms must expand output to a level that precludes excess profit.

Second, inefficient enterprises cannot survive in a perfectly contestable industry because cost inefficiencies invite replacement of the incumbents by entrants who can provide the same outputs at lower cost and lower prices. Only firms operating at the lowest possible cost, using the most efficient techniques, can survive.

In sum, firms in a perfectly contestable market will be forced to operate as efficiently as possible, and to charge as low prices as long-run financial survival permits. Soon after publication, these ideas were widely used by courts and government agencies concerned with the performance of business firms. They provide workable guidelines for improved or acceptable behavior in industries in which economies of scale mean that only a small number of firms can or should operate.

How many industries in reality approximate perfect contestability? There may, perhaps, be very few, just as is true of perfect competition. But no one knows yet, because only a few industries have so far been studied with this issue in mind. However, the analysis can be useful even for a market that is far from perfectly contestable. This is so because, if the government decides the industry needs regulation to prevent it from behaving like a monopoly, contestable markets provide a model of good behavior for regulation to try to achieve. These matters are discussed more fully in Chapter 18.

*See W.J. Baumol, J.C. Panzar, and R.D. Willig, *Contestable Markets and the Theory of Industry Structure*, San Diego: Harcourt Brace Jovanovich, revised edition, 1988.

**Earlier it was widely thought that air transportation is a highly contestable industry, but recent evidence suggests that while this judgment is not entirely incorrect, it requires considerable reservations.

monopoly, monopolistic competition, and oligopoly. You have probably absorbed a lot of information about the workings of these market forms as you have read through Chapters 9–12, but you may be confused by the profusion of details. To help you discern the main patterns that emerge, we provide Table 12–2 as an overview of the main attributes of each of the market forms. The material is presented in a way that permits ready comparison, and that may help you to pull the discussion together.

We will not review the entire table; however, it may be useful to mention some of the highlights:

1. Perfect competition and pure monopoly are concepts useful primarily for analytical purposes. Neither of these is found very often in reality. Monopolistically competitive firms occur in profusion, and oligopoly firms account for the largest share of the economy's output.
2. Profits are zero in long-run equilibrium under perfect competition and

**Table 12–2 ATTRIBUTES OF THE FOUR MARKET FORMS**

| Market Form | Number of Firms in the Market | Frequency in Reality | Entry Barriers | Public Interest Results | Long-Run Profit | Equilibrium Conditions |
|---|---|---|---|---|---|---|
| Perfect Competition | Very many | Rare (if any) | None | Good | Zero | MC = MR = AC = AR = *P* |
| Pure Monopoly | One | Rare | Likely to be high | Misallocates Resources | May be high | MR = MC |
| Monopolistic Competition | Many | Widespread | Minor | Inefficient | Zero | MR = MC<br>AR = AC |
| Oligopoly | Few | Produces large share of GDP | Varies | Varies | Varies | Vary |

monopolistic competition because entry is so easy, so that high profits attract new rivals into the market.

3. Consequently, AC = AR in long-run equilibrium under these two market forms. In equilibrium, MC = MR for the profit maximizing firm under any market form. However, under oligopoly, firms may adopt the strategies described by game theory or they may pursue goals other than profits; for example, they may be sales maximizers. Therefore, in the equilibrium of the oligopoly firm, MC may be unequal to MR.
4. The point is that the behavior of the perfectly competitive firm and industry theoretically leads to an efficient allocation of resources that maximizes the benefits to consumers given the resources available to consumers. The same is, incidentally, theoretically true for any market form if the market is perfectly contestable. But otherwise, monopoly misallocates resources by restricting its output in order to raise prices and profits. Under monopolistic competition, excess capacity and inefficiency are apt to result. Under oligopoly, almost anything can happen, so it is impossible to generalize about its vices or virtues.

## *Summary*

1. Under **monopolistic competition**, there are numerous small buyers and sellers; each firm's product is at least somewhat different from every other firm's product—that is, each firm has a partial "monopoly" of some product characteristics, and thus a downward-sloping demand curve; there is freedom of entry and exit; and there is perfect information.
2. In long-run equilibrium under monopolistic competition, free entry eliminates economic profits by forcing the firm's demand curve into a position of tangency with its average cost curve. Therefore, output will be below the point at which average cost is lowest. This is why monopolistic competitors are said to have "excess capacity."
3. An oligopolistic industry is composed of a few large firms selling similar products in the same market.
4. Under **oligopoly**, each firm carefully watches the major decisions of its rivals and will often plan

counterstrategies. As a result, rivalry is often vigorous and direct, and the outcome is difficult to predict.

5. One model of oligopoly behavior assumes that the oligopolists ignore interdependence and simply maximize profits or sales. Another assumes that they join together to form a **cartel** and thus act like a monopoly. A third possibility is **price leadership**, where one firm sets prices and the others follow suit. In a fourth model, each firm may assume that its rivals will adopt the optimal countermove to any move it makes.
6. A firm that maximizes sales will continue producing up to the point where marginal revenue is driven down to zero. Consequently, a sales maximizer will produce more than a profit maximizer and will charge a lower price.
7. **Game theory** provides new tools for the analysis of business strategies under conditions of oligopoly.
8. If a firm thinks that its rivals will match any price cut but fail to match any price increase, its demand curve becomes "kinked" and its price will be sticky—that is, it will be adjusted less frequently than would be the case under either perfect competition or pure monopoly.
9. Monopolistic competition and oligopoly can be harmful to the general welfare. But if the market is highly contestable, that is, if entry and exit are easy and costless, the threat of entry will lead toward optimal performance.

## *Key Concepts and Terms*

Monopolistic competition
Excess capacity theorem
Oligopoly
Oligopolistic interdependence
Cartel
Price leadership
Sales maximization
Game theory
Maximin criterion
Kinked demand curve
Sticky price
Perfectly contestable markets

## *Questions for Review*

1. How many real industries can you name that are oligopolies? How many that operate under monopolistic competition? Perfect competition? Which of these is hardest to find in reality? Why do you think this is so?
2. Consider some of the products that are widely advertised on TV. By what kind of firm is each produced—a perfectly competitive firm, an oligopolistic firm, or what? How many major products can you think of that are *not* advertised on TV?
3. In what ways may the small retail sellers of the following products differentiate their goods from those of their rivals to make themselves monopolistic competitors: hamburgers, radios, cosmetics?
4. Pricing of securities on the stock market is said to be done under conditions in many respects similar to perfect competition. The auto industry is an oligopoly. How often do you think the price of a share of Ford Motor Company's common stock changes? How about the price of a Ford Taurus? How would you explain the difference?
5. Suppose Chrysler hires a popular singer to advertise its compact automobiles. The campaign is very successful, and the company increases its share of the compact-car market substantially. What is Ford likely to do?
6. Using game theory, set up a payoff matrix similar to one Chrysler's management might employ in analyzing the problem presented in Question 5.
7. Question 4 at the end of Chapter 11 presented cost and demand data for a monopolist, and asked you to find the profit-maximizing solution. Use these same data to find the sales-maximizing solution. Are the answers different? Explain.
8. A new entrant, Bargain Airways, cuts air fares between Eastwich and Westwich by 20 percent. Biggie Airlines, which has been operating on this route, responds by cutting fares by 35 percent. What does Biggie hope to achieve?
9. If air transportation were perfectly contestable, why would Biggie fail to achieve the ultimate goal of its price cut?

10. Which of the following industries are most likely to be contestable?

    a. Aluminum production.
    b. Barge transportation.
    c. Automobile manufacturing.

    Explain your answers.

11. Since the recent deregulation of air transportation, a community served by a single airline is no longer protected by a regulatory agency from monopoly pricing. What market forces, if any, restrict the ability of the airline from raising prices as a pure monopolist would? How effective do you think those market forces are in keeping air fares down?

Chapter 13

# THE MARKET MECHANISM: SHORTCOMINGS AND REMEDIES

*When she was good*
*She was very, very good,*
*But when she was bad*
*She was horrid.*

HENRY WADSWORTH LONGFELLOW

What does the market do well, and what does it do poorly? This issue is the focus of our microeconomic analysis, and we are well on our way toward answers. Chapters 9 and 10 explained the workings of Adam Smith's invisible hand—the mechanism by which a perfectly competitive economy allocates resources efficiently without any guidance from government. While that model is just a theoretical ideal, observation of reality confirms the accomplishments of the market mechanism. Free-market economies have achieved levels of output, productive efficiency, variety in available consumer goods, and general prosperity that are unprecedented in history—and are now the envy of the formerly planned economies. Yet the market mechanism has its weaknesses. One of these—its vulnerability to exploitation by large and powerful business firms, which leads both to concentration of wealth and to misallocation of resources—was examined in Chapters 11 and 12. Now we take a more comprehensive view of the failures of the market and of some of the things that can be done to remedy them. ¶ This and other obvious examples make it clear that the market cannot do everything we want. Amid the outpouring of products, we find areas of appalling poverty, cities choked by traffic and pollution, and educational institutions and artistic organizations in serious financial trouble. Though our economy produces an overwhelming abundance of material wealth, it seems far less able to reduce social ills and environmental damage. We will examine the reasons for these failings and indicate why the price system *by itself* may not be able to deal with them.

Failure to recognize the shortcomings of the market mechanism and the fact that it cannot produce instantaneous miracles has already been a source of disillusionment in the countries of Eastern Europe, where early and unrealistic expectations seemed to anticipate immediate economic prosperity, with little or no social costs, as soon as the market mechanism was introduced.

However, recognition of the limitations of the market does not imply that the public interest calls for its abandonment. As we will see, many of the imperfections of this economic system seem to be amenable to treatment within the market environment, sometimes even making use of the market mechanism to cure its own deficiencies.

## WHAT DOES THE MARKET DO POORLY?

While an exhaustive list of its imperfections is not possible, we can list some major areas in which the market has been accused of failing:

1. Market economies suffer from severe business fluctuations.
2. The market distributes income rather unequally.
3. Where markets are monopolized, they allocate resources inefficiently.
4. The market deals poorly with the side effects of many economic activities.
5. The market cannot readily provide public goods, such as national defense.
6. The market may do a poor job of allocating resources between the present and the future.
7. The market mechanism makes public and personal services increasingly expensive, and often induces socially detrimental countermeasures by government.

The first three of these issues—business fluctuations, income inequality, and monopoly—have already been discussed in detail or will be later.

The remaining four items on our list are the subject of this chapter. To help us analyze these cases in which the market is not efficient, we offer a brief review of the concept of efficient resource allocation, which was discussed in detail in Chapter 10.

## EFFICIENT RESOURCE ALLOCATION: A REVIEW

The basic problem of resource allocation is deciding how much of each commodity should be produced by the economy. At first glance, it may seem that the solution is simple: the more the better; so we should produce as much of each good as we can. But careful thought tells us that this is not necessarily so.

Outputs are not created from thin air. They are produced from scarce supplies of labor, fuel, raw materials, and machinery. And if we use these resources to produce, say, more handkerchiefs, we must take them away from some other products, such as hospital linens. So, to decide whether increasing the production of handkerchiefs is a good idea, we must compare the utility of that increase with the loss of utility caused by having to produce less hospital linen. It is *efficient* to increase handkerchief output only if society considers the additional handkerchiefs more valuable than the forgone hospital linen.

**OPPORTUNITY COST AND RESOURCE ALLOCATION**

Here we recall the concept of *opportunity cost*, one of our **12 Ideas for Beyond the Final Exam**. The opportunity cost of an increase in the output of some product is the value of the other goods and services that must be forgone when inputs (resources) are taken away from their production in order to increase the output of the product in question. In our example, the opportunity cost of the increased handkerchief output is the decrease in output of hospital linen that results when resources are reallocated from the latter to the former. The general principle is that an increase in some output represents a *misallocation* of resources if the utility of that increased output is less than its opportunity cost.

To illustrate this idea, we repeat a graph encountered several times in earlier chapters—a *production possibilities frontier*—but we put it to a somewhat different use. Curve *ABC* in Figure 13–1 is a production possibilities frontier showing the alternative combinations of handkerchiefs and hospital linens the economy can produce by reallocating its resources between the production of the two goods. For example, point *A* amounts to allocation of all the resources to handkerchief production, so that 100 million of these items and no hospital linens are produced. Point *C* represents the reverse situation, with all resources allocated to hospital linens and none to handkerchiefs. Point *B* represents an intermediate allocation, resulting in the production of eight million yards of linen and 60 million handkerchiefs.

Suppose now that point *B* represents the *optimal* resource allocation: the only combination of outputs that best satisfies the wants of society among all the possibilities that are *attainable* (given the technology and resources as represented by the production frontier). Two questions are pertinent to our discussion of the price system:

1. What prices will get the economy to select point *B*; that is, what prices will yield an *efficient* allocation of resources?

2. How can the wrong set of prices lead to a misallocation of resources?

The first question was discussed extensively in Chapter 10. There we saw that:

An efficient allocation of resources requires that each product's price be equal to its marginal cost; that is:

$$P = \text{MC}.$$

The reasoning, in brief, is as follows. In a free market, the price of any good reflects the money value to consumers of an additional unit; that is, its *marginal utility* (MU). Similarly, if the market mechanism is working well, the *marginal cost*

**Figure 13-1** **THE ECONOMY'S PRODUCTION POSSIBILITIES FRONTIER FOR THE PRODUCTION OF TWO GOODS**

This graph shows combinations of outputs of the two goods that the economy can produce with the resources available to it. If $B$ is the most desired output combination among those that are possible, it will correspond to a market equilibrium in which each good's price is equal to its marginal cost. If the price of linen is above its marginal cost, or the price of a handkerchief is below its marginal cost, then linen output will be inefficiently small and handkerchief output inefficiently large (point $K$).

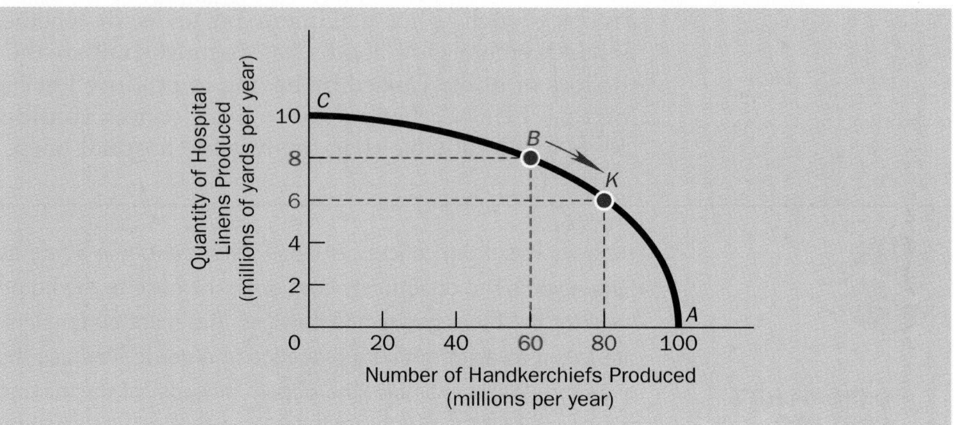


(MC) measures the value (the opportunity cost) of the resources needed to produce an additional unit of the good. Hence, if prices are set equal to marginal costs, then consumers, by using *their own money* in the most effective way to maximize *their own* satisfaction, will automatically be using *society's resources* in the most effective way. In other words, as long as it sets prices equal to marginal costs, the market mechanism automatically satisfies the MC = MU rule for efficient resource allocation that we studied in Chapter 10.[1] In terms of Figure 13–1, this means that if $P$ = MC for both goods, the economy will automatically gravitate to point $B$, which we assumed to be the optimal point.

This chapter is devoted mainly to the second question: How can the "wrong" prices cause a *mis*allocation of resources? The answer to this question is not too difficult, and we can use the case of monopoly as an illustration.

The "law" of demand tells us that a rise in the price of a commodity normally will reduce the quantity demanded. Suppose, now, that the linen industry is a monopoly, so the price of linens exceeds their marginal cost.[2] This will decrease the quantity of linens demanded below the eight million yards that we have assumed to be socially optimal (point $B$ in Figure 13–1). So the economy will move from point $B$ to a point such as $K$, where too few linens and too many handkerchiefs are being produced for maximal consumer satisfaction. By setting the "wrong" prices, then, the market prevents achievement of the most efficient use of the economy's resources.

If the price of a commodity is above its marginal cost, the economy will tend to produce less of that item than the amount necessary to maximize consumer benefits. The opposite will occur if an item's price is below its marginal cost.

---

[1]If you need review, consult pages 257–60.

[2]To review why price under monopoly may be expected to exceed marginal cost, you may want to reread pages 276–79.

In the remainder of this chapter, we will encounter several other instances in which the market mechanism may set the "wrong" prices.

## EXTERNALITIES

We come now to the fourth item on our list of market failures, the first studied in this chapter. It is one of the least obvious, yet one of the most consequential of the imperfections of the price system. Many economic activities provide incidental benefits to others for whom they are not specifically intended. For example, homeowners who plant beautiful gardens in front of their homes incidentally and unintentionally provide pleasure to their neighbors and to those who pass by—people from whom they receive no payment. We say then that their activity generates a **beneficial externality**.

An activity is said to generate a **BENEFICIAL OR DETRIMENTAL EXTERNALITY** if that activity causes incidental benefits or damages to others, and no corresponding compensation is provided to or paid by those who generate the externality.

Similarly, there are activities that indiscriminately impose costs on others. For example, the operators of a motorcycle repair shop, from which all sorts of noise besieges the neighborhood and for which they pay no compensation to others, is said to produce a **detrimental externality**. Pollution constitutes the classic illustration of a detrimental externality.

To see why the presence of externalities causes the price system to misallocate resources, we need only recall that the system achieves efficiency by rewarding producers who serve consumers well—that is, at as low a cost as possible. This argument breaks down, however, as soon as some of the costs and benefits of economic activities are left out of the profit calculation.

When a firm pollutes a river, it uses up some of society's resources just as surely as when it burns coal. However, if the firm pays for coal but not for the use of clean water, it is to be expected that management will be economical in its use of coal and wasteful in its use of water. Similarly, a firm that provides benefits to others for which it receives no payment is unlikely to be generous in allocating resources to the activity, no matter how socially desirable it may be.

In an important sense, the source of the market mechanism's difficulty here lies in society's rules about property rights. Coal mines are *private property*; their owners will not let anyone take coal without paying for it. Thus, coal is costly and so is not used wastefully. But waterways are not private property. Since they belong to everyone in general, they belong to no one in particular. They therefore can be used free of charge as dumping grounds for wastes by anyone who chooses to do so. Because no one pays for the use of the dissolved oxygen in a public waterway, that oxygen will be used wastefully. That is the source of detrimental externalities—the fact that waterways are exempted from the market's normal control procedures.

### EXTERNALITIES AND INEFFICIENCY

Using these concepts, we can see precisely why an externality has undesirable effects on the allocation of resources. In discussing externalities, it is crucial to distinguish between *social* and *private* marginal cost. We define **marginal social cost** (MSC) as the sum of two components: (1) **marginal private cost** (MPC), which is the share of marginal cost caused by an activity that is paid for by the persons who carry out the activity; and (2) *incidental cost*, which is the share borne by others.

The **MARGINAL SOCIAL COST** of an activity is the sum of **marginal private cost** plus the incidental cost (positive or negative) which is borne by others.

If increased output by a firm increases the smoke it emits, then, in addition to its direct private costs as recorded in the company accounts, expansion of its production imposes incidental costs on others in the form of increased laundry bills, medical expenditures, outlays for air conditioning and electricity, as well as the unpleasantness of living in a cloud of noxious fumes. These are all part of the activity's marginal *social* cost.

Where the firm's activities generate detrimental externalities, its marginal social cost will be greater than its marginal private cost. In symbols, MSC > MPC. Therefore, the firm's output must be too big. This must be so because, in equilibrium, the market will yield an output at which consumers' marginal utility (MU) is equal to the firm's marginal private cost (MU = MPC). It follows that the marginal utility is *smaller* than marginal social cost. Society would then necessarily benefit if output of that product were *reduced*. It would lose the marginal utility but save the marginal social cost. And, since MSC > MU means that the production of the marginal unit of the good entails a cost to society larger than the benefit contributed by that unit of the good, society would come out ahead. We conclude that:

Where the firm's activity causes detrimental externalities, free markets will leave us in a situation where marginal benefits are less than marginal social costs. Smaller outputs than those that maximize profits will be socially desirable.

We have already indicated why this is so. Private enterprise has no motivation to take into account costs that it causes to others but for which it does not have to pay. So goods that cause such externalities will be produced in undesirably large amounts by private firms. For precisely analogous reasons:

Where the firm's activity generates beneficial externalities, free markets will produce too little output. Society would be better off with larger output levels.

These principles can be illustrated with the aid of Figure 13–2. This diagram repeats the two basic curves needed for the analysis of the equilibrium of the firm: a marginal revenue curve and a marginal cost curve (see Chapter 5). These represent the *private* costs and revenues accruing to a particular firm (in this case, a paper mill). The mill's maximum profit is attained with 100,000 tons of output corresponding to the intersection between the marginal cost and marginal revenue curves (point *A*).

Now suppose that the factory's wastes pollute a nearby waterway, so that its production creates a detrimental externality whose cost the owners do not pay. Then marginal social cost must be higher than marginal private cost, as shown in the diagram; The output of paper, which is governed by private costs, will be 100,000 tons (point *A*)—an excessive amount from the viewpoint of the public interest, given its environmental consequences.

Notice that if instead of being able to impose the external costs on others the paper mill's owners were forced to pay them, then their private marginal cost curve would correspond to the higher of the two cost curves. Paper output would then fall to 70,000 tons, corresponding to point *B*, the intersection between the marginal revenue curve and the marginal *social* cost curve. But because the firm does not in fact pay for the pollution damage its output causes, it produces an output (100,000 tons) that is larger than the output it would produce if the cost imposed on the community were instead borne by the firm (70,000 tons).

The same sort of diagram can be used to show that the opposite relationship will hold when the firm's activity produces beneficial externalities. The firm will

Figure 13–2

## EQUILIBRIUM OF A FIRM WHOSE OUTPUT PRODUCES DETRIMENTAL EXTERNALITIES (POLLUTION)

The firm's profit-maximizing output, at which its marginal private cost and its marginal private revenue are equal, is 100,000 tons. But if the firm paid all the social costs of its output instead of shifting some of them to others, its marginal cost curve would be the curve labeled "marginal social cost." Then it would pay the firm to reduce its output to 70,000 tons, thereby reducing the pollution it causes.

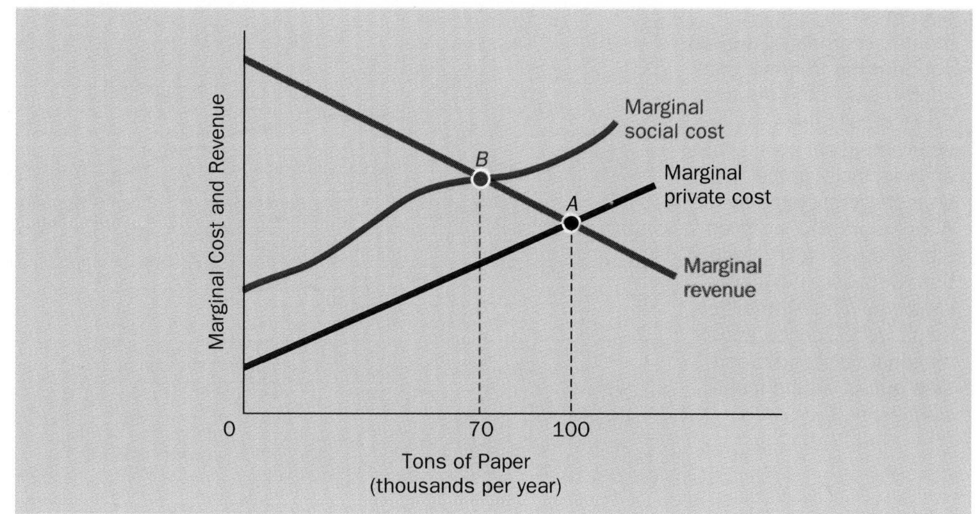


produce less of its beneficial output than it would if it were rewarded fully for the benefits that its activities yield. Beneficial externalities arise when the activities of firm A create incidental benefits for firm B or individual C (and perhaps for many others as well); or when A's activities *reduce* the costs of others' activity. For example, firm A's research laboratories, while making its own products better, may also incidentally discover new research techniques that reduce the research costs of other firms in the economy.

But these results can perhaps be seen more clearly with the help of a production possibilities frontier diagram similar to that in Figure 13–1. In Figure 13–3, we see the frontier for two industries: electricity generation, which causes air pollution (a detrimental externality), and tulip growing, which makes an area more attractive (a beneficial externality). We have just seen that detrimental externalities make marginal social cost greater than marginal private cost. Hence, if the electric company charges a price equal to its own marginal (private) cost, that price will be less than the true marginal social cost. Similarly, in tulip growing, a price equal to marginal private cost will be above the true marginal cost to society.

We saw earlier in the chapter that an industry that charges a price above marginal cost will reduce quantity demanded through this high price, and so it will produce an output too small for an efficient allocation of resources. The opposite will be true for an industry whose price is below marginal social cost. In terms of Figure 13–3, suppose point *B* again represents the efficient allocation of resources, involving the production of *E* kilowatt hours of electricity and *T* dozen tulips.

Because the polluting electric company charges a price below marginal social cost, it will sell more than *E* kilowatt hours of electricity. Similarly, because tulip growers generate external benefits, and so charge a price above marginal social cost, they will produce less than *T* dozen tulips. The economy will end up with the resource allocation represented by point *K* rather than that represented by point

Figure 13–3 **EXTERNALITIES, MARKET EQUILIBRIUM, AND EFFICIENT RESOURCE ALLOCATION**

Because electricity producers emit smoke (a detrimental externality), they do not bear the true marginal social cost of their output. So electricity price will be below marginal social cost, and electricity output will be inefficiently large (point *K*, not point *B*). The opposite is true of tulip production. Because they generate beneficial externalities, tulips will be priced above marginal social cost and tulip output will be inefficiently small.

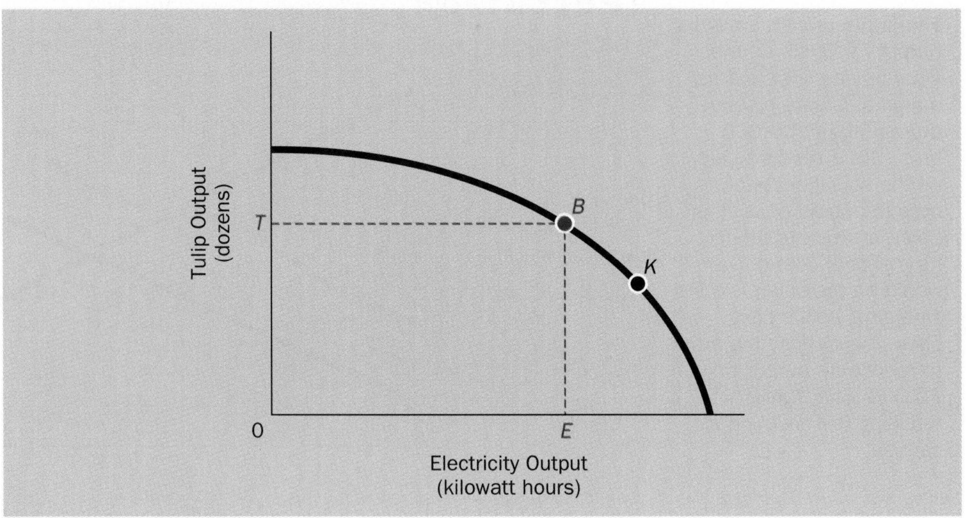


*B*. There will be too much smoky electricity production and too little attractive tulip growing. More generally:

An industry that generates detrimental externalities will have a marginal social cost higher than its marginal private cost. If its price is equal to its own marginal private cost, it will therefore be below the true marginal cost to society. The market mechanism thereby tends to encourage inefficiently large outputs of products that cause detrimental externalities. The opposite is true of products that cause beneficial externalities—private industry will provide inefficiently small quantities of these products.

## EXTERNALITIES ARE UNIVERSAL

Externalities occur throughout the economy. Many are beneficial. A factory that hires unskilled or semiskilled laborers gives them on-the-job training and provides the external benefit of better workers to future employers. Benefits to others are also generated when firms produce useful but unpatentable products, or even patentable products that can be imitated by others to some degree.

Detrimental externalities are also widespread. The emission of air and water pollutants by factories, cars, and airplanes is the source of some of our most pressing environmental problems. The abandonment of buildings causes the quality of a neighborhood to deteriorate and is the source of serious externalities for the city.

While it is entirely correct to conclude that the market mechanism, acting on its own, does nothing to cure externality problems, that is not the end of the story. It is true that market economies often have dirty air and rivers and suffer from toxic wastes improperly disposed of. But that does not mean that nonmarket economies do better. It was long known that the environmental record of the communist countries of Eastern Europe and the Soviet Union was nothing for them to be proud of. But when communism fell apart in those countries, the horrors of environmental degradation revealed were difficult to believe (see Chapter 21, pages 516–41 and, especially the box on page 520). It became abundantly clear that central planning is not a guaranteed cure for environmental difficulties.

Moreover, as we will see next, the market mechanism does offer us one way of dealing with such difficulties that is often extremely effective. In other words, while markets hardly can be claimed to protect the environment automatically, they do offer us a powerful tool for the purpose.

**EXTERNALITIES**

Externalities lie at the heart of some of society's most pressing problems: the problems of the cities, the environment, research policy, and a variety of other critical issues. For this reason, the concept of externalities is one of our **12 Ideas for Beyond the Final Exam**. It is a subject that will recur again and again in this book as we discuss some of these problems in greater detail.

## GOVERNMENT POLICY AND EXTERNALITIES

Because of the market's inability to cope with externalities, governments have found it appropriate to support activities that are believed to generate external benefits. Education is subsidized not only because it helps promote equal opportunity for all citizens, but also because it is believed to generate beneficial externalities. For example, educated people normally commit fewer crimes than uneducated people, so the more we educate people, the less, presumably, we will need to spend on crime prevention. Also, the academic research that has been provided partly as a byproduct of the educational system often benefits the entire population and has, indeed, been judged to be a major contributor to the nation's economic growth. We have consequently come to believe that, if education were offered only by profit-making institutions, the output of these beneficial services would be provided at less than the optimal level.

Similarly, governments have recently begun to impose fines on companies that contribute heavily to air and water pollution. This approach to policy is in fact suggested by the economist's standard analysis of the effects of externalities on resource allocation. The basic problem is that, in the presence of externalities, the price system fails to allocate resources efficiently in the way it usually does. Resources are used up without any price being charged for them, and benefits are supplied without financial compensation to the provider. As a result, the market will produce excessive quantities of polluting outputs and of other outputs that create detrimental externalities because they are, in effect, provided at a bargain price—a price that does not cover their entire marginal social cost. Consequently:

One effective way to deal with externalities may be to use taxes and subsidies, making polluters pay for the costs they impose on society and paying the generators of beneficial externalities for the incidental benefits of their activities (which can be considered as an offset or deduction from the social cost of the activity).

For example, firms that generate beneficial externalities should be given a *subsidy* per unit of their output equal to the difference between their marginal social costs and their marginal private costs. Similarly, those that generate detrimental externalities should be *taxed* so that the firm that creates such externalities will have to pay the entire marginal social cost. In terms of Figure 13–2, after paying the tax, the firm's marginal private cost curve will be shifted up until it coincides with its marginal social cost curve, and so the market price will be set in a manner consistent with an efficient resource allocation.

While there is much to be said for this approach in principle, it often is not easy to carry out. Social costs are rarely easy to estimate, partly because they are so widely diffused throughout the community (everyone in the area is affected by pollution) and partly because many of the costs and benefits (effects on health, unpleasantness of living in smog) are not readily assessed in monetary terms. The pros and cons of this approach and the alternative policies available for the control of externalities will be discussed in greater detail in Chapter 21 on environmental problems.

## PUBLIC GOODS

**A PUBLIC GOOD** is a commodity or service whose benefits are *not depleted* by an additional user and for which it is generally difficult or *impossible to exclude* people from its benefits, even if they are unwilling to pay for them. In contrast, a **private good** is characterized by both excludability and depletability.

A commodity is **DEPLETABLE** if it is used up when someone consumes it.

A commodity is **EXCLUDABLE** if someone who does not pay for it can be kept from enjoying it.

A second area in which the market fails to perform adequately is in the provision of what economists call **public goods**. These are commodities that are valuable socially but whose provision, for reasons we will now explain, cannot be financed by private enterprise, or at least not at socially desirable prices. Thus, government must pay for public goods if they are to be provided at all. Standard examples range from national defense to coastal lighthouses.

It is easiest to explain the nature of public goods by contrasting them with the sort of commodities called **private goods**, which are at the opposite end of the spectrum. *Private goods are characterized by two important attributes.* One can be called **depletability**. If you eat a steak or use a gallon of gasoline, there is that much less beef or fuel in the world available for others to use. Your consumption depletes the supply available for other people, either temporarily or permanently.

But a pure public good is like the legendary widow's jar of oil, which always remained full no matter how many people used it. Similarly, once the snow has been removed from a street, the improved driving conditions are available to every driver who uses that street, whether 10 or 1000 cars pass that way. One passing car does not make the road less snow-free for another. The same is true of the spraying of swamps near a town to kill disease-bearing mosquitoes. The cost of the spraying is the same whether the town contains 10,000 or 20,000 persons. A resident of the town who benefits from this service does not deplete its advantages to others.

The other property that characterizes private goods but not public goods is **excludability**, meaning that anyone who does not pay for the good can be excluded from enjoying its benefits. If you do not buy a ticket, you are excluded from the basketball game. If you do not pay for an electric guitar, the storekeeper will not give it to you.

But some goods or services are such that, if they are provided to anyone, they automatically become available to many other persons whom it is difficult, if not impossible, to exclude from the benefits. If a street is cleared of snow, everyone who uses the street benefits, regardless of who paid for the snowplow. If a country provides a strong military establishment, every citizen receives its protection, even persons who do not happen to want it.

A public good is defined as a good that lacks depletability. Very often, it also lacks excludability. Notice two important implications.

First, since nonpaying users usually cannot be excluded from enjoying a public good, suppliers of such goods will find it *difficult* or *impossible to collect fees* for the benefits they provide. This is the so-called "free rider" problem. How many people, for example, will *voluntarily* cough up $3500 a year to support our national defense establishment? Yet this is roughly what it costs per American household. Services such as national defense and public health, which are not depletable and where excludability is simply impossible, *cannot* be provided by private enterprise because people will not pay for what they can get free. Since private firms are not in the business of giving services away, the supply of public goods must be left to government authorities and nonprofit institutions.

The second implication we notice is that, since the supply of a public good is not depleted by an additional user, *the marginal (opportunity) cost of serving an additional user is zero.* With marginal cost equal to zero, the basic principle of optimal resource allocation (price equal to marginal cost) calls for provision of public goods and services to anyone who wants them *at no charge*. In a word, not only is it often *impossible* to charge a market price for a public good, it is often *undesirable* as well. Any nonzero price would discourage some users from enjoying the public good; but this would be inefficient, since one more person's enjoyment of the good costs society nothing. To summarize:

It is usually *not possible* to charge a price for a pure public good because people cannot be excluded from enjoying its benefits. It may also be *undesirable* to charge a price for it because that would discourage some people from benefiting from it even though using it does not deplete its supply. For both these reasons we find government supplying many public goods. Without government intervention, public goods simply would not be provided.

Referring back to our example in Figure 13–1, if hospital linens were a public good and their production were left to private enterprise, the economy would end up at point *A* on the graph, with zero production of hospital linens and far more output of handkerchiefs than is called for by efficient allocation (point *B*). Usually, communities have not been content to let that happen; and today a quite substantial proportion of government expenditure, indeed the bulk of municipal budgets, is devoted to the financing of public goods or to services believed to generate substantial external benefits. National defense, public health, police and fire protection, and research are among the services provided by governments because they offer beneficial externalities or because they are public goods.

## ALLOCATION OF RESOURCES BETWEEN PRESENT AND FUTURE

A third area in which the market seems to work imperfectly is in the division of its benefits between today and tomorrow. When a society invests, more resources are devoted to expanding its capacity to produce consumers' goods in the future. But the inputs that go into building new plants and equipment are unavailable for consumption now. Fuel used to make steel for a factory cannot be used to heat homes or drive cars. Thus, the allocation of inputs between current consumption and investment—their allocation between present and future—determines how fast the economy grows.

In principle, the market mechanism should be as efficient in allocating resources between present and future uses as it is in allocating resources among different outputs at any one time. If future demands for a particular commodity, say, personal computers, are expected to be higher than they are today, it will pay manufacturers to plan now to build the necessary plant and equipment so they will be ready to turn out the computers when the expanded market materializes. More resources are thereby allocated to future consumption.

The allocation of resources between present and future can be analyzed with the aid of a production possibilities frontier diagram, such as the one in Figure 13–1. Suppose the issue is how much labor and capital to devote to producing consumer goods and how much to devote to construction of factories to produce output in the future. Then, instead of handkerchiefs and linens, the graph will show consumer goods and number of factories on its axes, but otherwise it will be exactly the same as Figure 13–1. Figure 13–4 is such a graph.

The profit motive directs the flow of resources between one time period and another just as it handles resource allocation among different industries in a given period. The lure of profits directs resources to those products *and those time periods* in which high prices promise to make output most profitable. But at least one feature of the process of allocation of resources among different time periods distinguishes it from the process of allocation among industries. This is the special role that the *interest rate* plays in allocation among the periods.

If the receipt of a given amount of money is delayed until some time in the future, the recipient suffers an *opportunity cost*—the interest that the money could have earned if it had been received earlier and invested. For example, if the rate of interest is 9 percent and you can persuade someone who owes you money to make a $100 payment one year earlier than originally planned, you come out $9 ahead. Put the other way, if the rate of interest is 9 percent and the payment to you of $100 is postponed one year, you lose the opportunity to earn $9. Thus, the rate of interest determines the size of the opportunity cost to a recipient who gets money at some date in the future instead of now—the lower the interest rate, the lower the opportunity cost. For this reason, as we will see in greater detail in Chapter 8 of *Macroeconomics:*

*Figure* **13–4**

**PRODUCTION POSSIBILITIES FRONTIER BETWEEN PRESENT AND FUTURE**

With a given quantity of resources, the economy can produce one million cars for immediate use and build no factories for the future (point *A*). Alternatively, at the opposite extreme (point *B*), it can build 10 factories where products will become available in the future, while no cars are produced for current consumption. At points in between on the frontier, such as *C*, the economy will produce a combination of some cars for present consumption and some factories for future use.

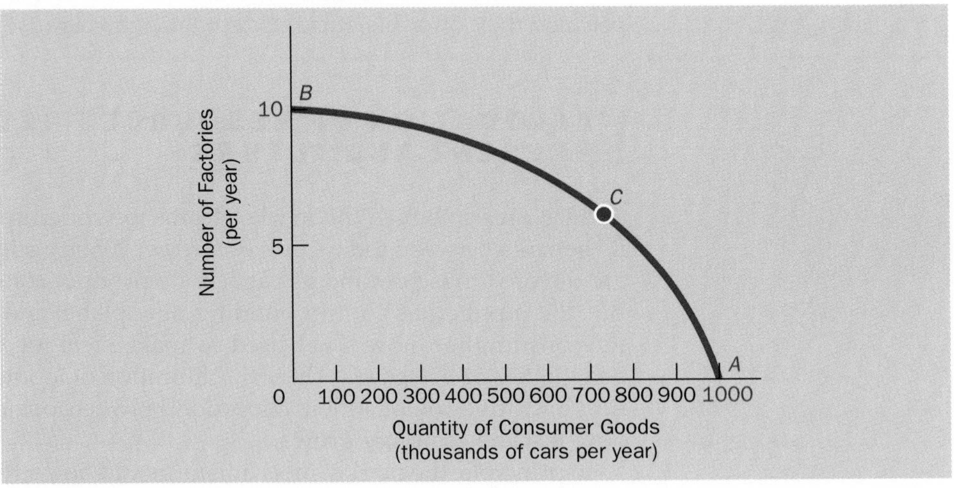

Low interest rates will persuade people to invest more now in long-lived factories and equipment, since such investments yield a large portion of their benefits in the future. Thus, more resources will be devoted to the future if interest rates are low. Similarly, high interest rates make durable investment, with its benefits in the future, less attractive. And so high interest rates will tend to increase the use of resources for current output at the expense of reduced future outputs.

On the surface, it seems that the price system can allocate resources among different time periods in the way consumers prefer. For the supply of and demand for loans (see Chapter 15), which determine the interest rate, reflects the public's preferences between present and future. Suppose, for example, that the public suddenly became more interested in future consumption (say, people wanted to save more for their old age). The supply of funds available for borrowing would increase and interest rates would tend to fall. This would stimulate investment and add to the future output of goods at the expense of current consumption.

But several questions have been raised about the effectiveness, in practice, with which the market mechanism allocates resources among different time periods.

One thing that makes economists uneasy is that the rate of interest, which is the price that controls allocation over time, is also used for a variety of other purposes. As we will see in Chapter 13 of *Macroeconomics*, the interest rate can be used to deal with business fluctuations. And, in Chapter 20 of *Macroeconomics* we will see that it plays an analogous role in international monetary relations. As a result, governments frequently manipulate interest rates deliberately. In so doing, policymakers seem to give little thought to the effects on the allocation of resources between present and future, and so we may well worry whether the resulting interest rates are the most appropriate ones.

Second, it has been suggested that even in the absence of government manipulation of the interest rate, the market may devote too large a proportion of the economy's resources to immediate consumption. One British economist, A.C. Pigou, argued simply that people suffer from "a defective telescopic faculty"—that they are too shortsighted to give adequate weight to the future. A "bird in hand" point of view leads people to care so much about the present that they sacrifice the legitimate interests of the future. On this view, too much goes into today's consumption and too little into investment for tomorrow.

A third reason why the free market may not invest enough for the future is that investment projects, like the construction of a new factory, are much greater risks to the investor than to the community. Even if a factory falls into someone else's hands through bankruptcy, it may well go on turning out goods. But the profits will not go to the investor or his or her heirs. Therefore, the loss to the individual investor will be far greater than the loss to society. For this reason, individual investment for the future may fall short of the amounts that are socially optimal. Investments too risky to be worthwhile to any group of private individuals may nevertheless be advantageous to society as a whole.

Fourth, our economy shortchanges the future when it despoils irreplaceable natural resources, exterminates whole species of plants and animals, floods canyons, "develops" attractive areas into acres of potential slums, and so on. Worst of all, industry, the military, and individuals bequeath a ticking time bomb to the future when they leave behind lethal and slow-acting residues, such as nuclear wastes, which may remain dangerous for hundreds or even thousands of years and whose disposal containers are likely to fall apart long before their contents lose their lethal qualities. Such actions are essentially *irreversible*. If a factory is not built this year, the deficiency in facilities provided for the future can be remedied by building it next year. But a canyon, once destroyed, can never be replaced. For this reason:

Many economists believe that **irreversible decisions** have a very special significance and must *not* be left entirely to the decisions of private firms and individuals, that is, to the market.

However, some writers have questioned the general conclusion that the free market will not tend to invest enough for the future. They have pointed out that the prosperity of our economy has grown fairly steadily from one decade to the next, and that there is reason to expect future generations to have real average incomes and an abundance of consumer goods far greater than our own. Pressures to increase investment for the future then may be like taking from the poor to give to the rich—a sort of backward Robin Hood redistribution of income.

## SOME OTHER SOURCES OF MARKET FAILURE

We have now completed our survey of the most important imperfections of the market mechanism. But that list is not complete, and it can never be. In this imperfect world nothing ever works out ideally, and by examining anything with a sufficiently powerful microscope one can always detect some more blemishes. However, some of the items we have omitted from our list are also important. Let us therefore conclude with a brief description of three of them.

### IMPERFECT INFORMATION

The analysis of the virtues of the market mechanism in Chapter 10 assumed that consumers and producers have all the information they need for their decisions. But in reality things are very different. When buying a house or a secondhand car, or selecting a doctor, consumers are vividly reminded of how little they know about what they are purchasing. The old motto "Let the buyer beware" applies. Obviously, if participants in the market are ill-informed, they will not always make the optimal decisions described in our theoretical models. (See the box opposite.)

Yet, not all economists agree that imperfect information is really a failure of the market mechanism. They point out that information, too, is a commodity that costs money to produce. Neither firms nor consumers have complete information because it would be irrational for them to spend the enormous amounts needed to get it. As always, the optimum is a compromise. One should, ideally, stop buying information at the point where the marginal utility of further information is no greater than its marginal cost. With this amount of information, the business executive or the consumer is able to make what have been referred to as "optimally imperfect" decisions.

### RENT SEEKING

An army of lawyers, expert witnesses, and business executives crowd our courtrooms and pile up enormous costs. Business firms seem to sue each other at the

At The FRONTIER

## ASYMMETRIC INFORMATION, LEMONS, AND AGENTS

Have you ever wondered why a six-month-old car sells for so much less than a new one? One explanation is offered by economists, who have recently intensified their study of the effects of imperfect information on markets. The problem is that some small proportion of automobiles are "lemons," plagued by mechanical troubles. The new-car dealer must sell *all* his cars, and, in any event, he probably knows no more than the buyer whether a particular car is a lemon. The information known to the two parties, therefore is said to be *symmetric*, and there is a low probability that a car purchased from a new-car dealer will turn out to be a lemon.

In the secondhand market, however, information is *asymmetric*. The seller knows whether the car is a lemon, but the buyer does not. Moreover, a seller who wants to get rid of a fairly new car is likely to be doing so only because it is a lemon. Potential buyers realize that. Hence, if some person is forced to sell a good new car because of an unexpected need for cash, she too will be stuck with a low price because she cannot *prove* that her car really works well. The moral is that asymmetric information also tends to harm the honest seller.

In addition, asymmetric information leads to what are called *principal-agent problems* whose analysis is a major concern of recent economic research. The issue arises because many critical tasks must be delegated to others. Stockholders in a corporation delegate the running of the firm to its management team;* U.S. citizens delegate lawmaking to Congress; union members delegate many decisions to the union leadership. In such cases the persons who give away part of their decision-making powers are called the *principals*, and those who exercise those powers are called the *agents*, who are, in effect, hired by the principals to do the jobs in question.

Asymmetric information is crucial here. The principals know only imperfectly whether their agents are serving their interests faithfully and efficiently or are instead neglecting or even acting against their interests to pursue selfish interests of their own. Misuse of principals' property, embezzlement, and political corruption are extreme examples of such dereliction of duty by agents and, unfortunately, they seem to occur often. Among other things, economic analysis studies ways of curing or at least alleviating such problems by arranging for types of compensation for agents that bring the agents' interests more closely into line with those of the principals. For example, if the salaries of corporate management depend heavily on company profits or on the market value of company shares, then by promoting the welfare of stockholders, managers will make themselves better off. Shareholders, even though they know only imperfectly what management is doing, can have a fair degree of confidence that management will try to serve their interests well.

*This has become an important issue in *takeover battles*, where some outside group tries to gain control of a corporation by buying up a large share of its stocks. Since the new owners are likely to fire the firm's current management, this latter group may fight hard to prevent the takeover even if it is in the interest of the company's stockholders. For more discussion of takeovers, see Chapter 14, pages 350–52.

slightest provocation, wasting vast resources and delaying business decisions. Why? Because it is possible to make money by such unproductive activities—by legal battles over profit-making opportunities.

For example, suppose a municipality awards a contract to produce its electricity to firm A, offering $20 million in profit. It may pay firm B to spend $5 million in a lawsuit against the municipality and firm A, hoping the courts will award it the contract (and thus the $20 million profit) instead.

**RENT SEEKING** refers to unproductive activity in the pursuit of economic profit—in other words, profit in excess of competitive earnings.

In general, any source of unusual profit, such as a monopoly, is a temptation for firms to waste economic resources in an effort to obtain control of that source of profits. This process, called **"rent seeking"** by economists (meaning that the firms hope to obtain earnings without contributing to production), has been judged by some observers to be a major source of inefficiency in our economy. (For more on rent seeking, see the box on page 376.)

## MORAL HAZARD

**MORAL HAZARD** refers to the tendency of insurance to discourage policyholders from protecting themselves from risk.

Another widely discussed problem for the market mechanism is associated with insurance. Insurance—the provision of protection against risk—is viewed by economists as a useful commodity, like shoes or the provision of information. But it also creates a problem by encouraging the very risks against which it provides protection. For example, if an individual has jewelry that is fully insured against theft, she has little motivation to take steps to protect it against burglars. She may, for example, fail to lock it up in a safe-deposit box, and this failure makes burglary a more attractive and lucrative profession. This problem—the tendency of insurance to encourage the source of risk—is called **moral hazard**, and it makes a free market in insurance hard to operate.

## MARKET FAILURE AND GOVERNMENT FAILURE

This chapter has pointed out some of the most noteworthy failures of the invisible hand. We seem forced to the conclusion that a market economy, if left entirely to itself, is likely to produce results that are, at least in some respects, far from ideal. In our discussion we have noted either directly or by implication some of the things government can do to correct these deficiencies. But the fact that government often *can* intervene in the operation of the economy in a constructive way does not always mean that it actually *will* succeed in doing so. The fact is that governments cannot be relied upon to behave ideally, any more than business firms can be expected to do so.

It is apparently hard to make this point in a way that is suitably balanced. Commentators too often stake out one extreme position or the other. Those who think the market mechanism is inherently unfair and biased by the greed of those who run its enterprises seem to think of government as the savior that can cure all economic ills. Those who deplore government intervention are prone to consider the public sector as the home of every sort of inefficiency, graft, and bureaucratic stultification. The truth, as usual, lies in between.

Governments are inherently imperfect, like the humans who compose them. The political process leads to compromises that sometimes bear little resemblance to rational decisions. For example, legislators' versions of the policies suggested by economic analysis are sometimes mere caricatures of the economists' ideas.

## *The Politics of Economic Policy*

In 1978, Alfred Kahn, a noted economist who served in the Carter administration, advocated reducing pollution by raising the tax on leaded gasoline and lowering the tax on unleaded gasoline. *The Washington Post*, in an editorial excerpted below, agreed that Kahn's idea was a sound one, but worried about what might emerge from Congress:

GROPPER, William. *The Senate.* (1935). Collection, The Museum of Modern Art, New York. Gift of A. Conger Goodyear.

If the administration adopts the Kahn plan, recent history offers a pretty clear view of the rest of the story. Mr. Kahn will draft a one-page bill to raise the tax on the one kind of gas and lower it on the other. But the White House political staff will immediately point out that his draft fails to address profound questions of social equity. What about the poor, who buy leaded gas because it's cheaper? What about young people driving old cars? What about the inhabitants of lower Louisiana, who need their outboard motors to get around the swamps and bayous? There will have to be a rebate formula. It will take into account each family's income, the number and ages of its various automobiles and the distance from its front doorstep to the bus stop. The legislative draftsmen at the Energy Department have had a lot of experience with that kind of formula and eventually the 53-page bill will be sent to Congress . . . .

The real fun will start when it arrives at the Senate Finance Committee. First the committee will add tuition tax credits for families with children in private schools. Then, warming to its work, it will vote import quotas on straw hats from Hong Kong, beef from

Argentina and automobiles from Japan. . . .[I]t will then add several obscure but pregnant provisions that seem to refer to the tax treatment of certain oil wells in the Gulf states. When the 268-page bill comes to the Senate floor, the administration will narrowly manage to defeat an amendment to improve business confidence by repealing the capital-gains tax and returning to the gold standard.

When the bill gets back to the Housé, liberal Democrats will denounce it as an outrage and declare all-out war. They will succeed in getting all references to gasoline taxes and the environment stricken—but not, fortunately, the import quotas or the obscure tax changes for the oil wells. By the time the staff of the Joint Committee on Taxation has straightened out a few technical difficulties, the bill will run to 417 pages and Ralph Nader will be calling on President Carter to veto it. But the feeling at the White House will be that Congress has worked so long and hard on the bill that he has no choice but to sign it. By the time the bill is finally enacted, Mr. Kahn might well wish he had chosen some other instrument of policy.

SOURCE: *The Washington Post*, December 26, 1978. Copyright *The Washington Post*.

(For a satirical editorial illustrating this point, see the box, above.) Yet often the problems engendered by an unfettered economy are too serious to be left to the free market. The problems of dealing with inflation, environmental decay, and the provision of public goods are cases in point. In such instances, government intervention is likely to yield substantial benefits to the general public. However, even when it is fairly clear that *some* government action is warranted, it may be difficult or impossible to calculate the *optimal* degree of governmental intervention. There is, then, the danger of intervention so excessive that the society might have been better off without it.

But in other areas the market mechanism is likely to work reasonably well, and the small imperfections that are present do not constitute adequate justification for intervention. In any event, *even where government intervention is appropriate, it is essential to consider market-like instruments as the means to correct the deficiencies in the workings of the market mechanism.* The tax incentives described in our discussion of externalities are an outstanding example of what we have in mind.

## THE COST DISEASE OF THE SERVICE SECTOR

The last problem to be considered in this chapter is *not* a failure of the market mechanism. But, in this case, the market's behavior creates that illusion and often leads to ill-advised *government* action which really does not serve the general welfare.

While private standards of living have increased and material possessions have grown, the community has simultaneously been forced to cope with deterioration in a variety of services, both public and private.

Throughout the world, streets and subways have grown increasingly dirty. Public safety has declined as crimes of violence have become more commonplace in almost every major city. Bus and train service has been reduced. In the middle of the nineteenth century in suburban London, there were twelve mail deliveries per day on weekdays and one on Sundays. We all know what has happened to postal services since then.

There have been parallel cutbacks in the quality of private services. Doctors have become increasingly reluctant to visit patients at home; in many areas the house call, which fifty years ago was a commonplace event, has now become something that occurs only in a life and death emergency, if even then. Another example, though undoubtedly a matter for less general concern, is what has happened to restaurants. Although they are reluctant to publicize the fact, a great number of restaurants, including some of the most elegant and expensive, serve preprepared, frozen, and reheated meals. They charge high prices for what amount to little more than TV dinners.

Perhaps even more distressing has been the persistent and dramatic rise in the cost of personal services such as health care and education. The readers of this book are likely to be all too painfully aware of the distressing rapidity with which college tuitions have been increasing. The cost of a stay at a hospital has been going up even more rapidly. The cost of health care has denied what is today considered to be adequate health services to a considerable portion of the population—the nation's poor, and even members of the middle class. These cost rises have made health care a prime subject of debate in political contests, not only in the United States but also in virtually every other industrialized country in the world.

There is no single explanation for all these matters. It would be naïve to offer any cut-and-dried hypothesis purporting to account for phenomena as diverse as the rise in crime and violence throughout Western society and the deterioration in postal services. Yet at least one common influence underlies all these problems of deterioration in service quality—an influence that is economic in character and that may be expected to grow more serious with the passage of time. The issue has been called the **cost disease of the personal services**.

Consider these facts. From 1948 to 1992, the Consumer Price Index increased at an average annual rate of about 4 percent per year compounded, whereas the price of a physician's services rose nearly 5.6 percent per annum. This difference may not seem large, but over those 44 years it increased the price of a visit to a physician more than 100 percent in dollars of constant purchasing power.

During this same period, the price of hospital care rose even faster: the average price of a hospital room increased at an annual rate of 8.8 percent compounded. This amounts to a 700 percent rise in constant dollars. The cost of education per pupil increased at a rate that was higher than doctor visits but lower than hospital costs: 7.6 percent per year. These are remarkable figures, particularly because the earnings of doctors barely kept up with the economy's overall rate of inflation during this period, while those of teachers fell behind. The cost disease of the personal services explains much of the persistent increase in these costs and the costs of other services, such as postal delivery, libraries, and theater tickets.[3]

One serious consequence of this phenomenon is that a terrible financial burden has been placed on municipal budgets by the soaring costs of education, health care, and police and fire protection. But what accounts for these ever-increasing costs? Are they attributable to inefficiencies in government management or to political corruption? Perhaps, in part, to both. But there is another reason—one that could not be avoided by any municipal administration no matter what its integrity and efficiency—and one that affects private industry just as severely as it does the public sector.

The problem stems from the basic nature of these personal services. Most such services require direct contact between those who consume the service and those who provide it. Doctors, teachers, and librarians are all engaged in activities that require direct person-to-person contact. Moreover, the quality of the service deteriorates if less time is provided by doctors, teachers, and librarians to each user of their services.

In contrast, the buyer of an automobile usually has no idea who worked on it, and could not care less how much labor time went into its production. A labor-saving innovation in auto production need not imply a reduction in product quality. As a result, it has proved far easier for technological change to save labor in manufacturing than in providing services. While output per hour of labor in manufacturing and agriculture went up in the period after World War II at an average rate of something like 2 percent a year, the number of teacher hours per pupil actually *increased* because classes became smaller.

These disparate performances in productivity have grave consequences for prices. When wages in manufacturing rise 2 percent, the cost of manufactured products is not affected because increased productivity makes up for the rise in wages. But the nature of services makes it very difficult to introduce labor-saving devices in the service sector. So a 2-percent rise in the wages of teachers or police officers is not offset by higher productivity and must lead to an equivalent rise in municipal budgets. Similarly, a 2-percent rise in the wages of hairdressers must lead beauty salons to raise their prices.

If services continue to grow ever more expensive in comparison to goods, the implications for life in the future are profound indeed. This analysis portends a world in which the typical home contains luxuries and furnishings that we can hardly imagine; but it is a home surrounded by garbage and perhaps by violence. It portends a future in which the services of doctors, teachers, and police officers

---

[3]These figures were derived from data provided by the U.S. Department of Labor, Bureau of Labor Statistics, March 1993; and U.S. Department of Education, *Digest of Education Statistics 1992*.

**THE COST DISEASE OF THE PERSONAL SERVICES**

In the long run, wages and salaries throughout the economy tend to go up and down together, for otherwise the activity whose wage rate falls seriously behind will tend to lose its labor force. Auto workers and police officers will see their wages rise at roughly the same rate in the long run. But if productivity on the assembly line advances while productivity in the patrol car does not, then police protection must grow ever more expensive as time goes on.

This phenomenon is another of our **12 Ideas for Beyond the Final Exam.** Because productivity improvements are very difficult for most services, their cost can be expected to rise faster, year in, year out, than the cost of manufactured goods. Over a period of several decades, this difference in the growth rate in costs of the two sectors can add up, making services enormously more expensive compared with manufactured goods.

are increasingly mass-produced and impersonal, and in which the arts and crafts are increasingly supplied only by amateurs because the cost of professional work in these fields is too high.

If this is the shape of the economy a hundred years from now, it will be significantly different from our own, and some persons will undoubtedly question whether the quality of life has increased commensurately with the increased material prosperity. Some may even ask whether it has increased at all.

Is this future inevitable? Is there anything that can be done to escape it? The answer is that it is by no means inevitable. To see why, we must first recognize that the source of the problem, paradoxically, is the growth in productivity of our economy—or rather, the *unevenness* of that growth. Trash removal costs go up not because garbage collectors become less efficient but because labor in car manufacturing becomes *more* efficient, thus enhancing the sanitation worker's potential value on the automotive assembly line. His wages must go up to keep him at his job of garbage removal.

But increasing productivity can never make a nation poorer. It can never make it unable to afford things it was able to afford in the past. Increasing productivity means that we can afford more of *all* things—medical care and education as well as TV sets and electric toothbrushes.

The role of services in our future depends on how we order our priorities. If we value services sufficiently, we can have more and better services—at *some* sacrifice in the rate of growth of manufactured goods. Whether that is a good choice for society is not for economists to say. But it is important to recognize that society *does* have a choice, and that if it fails to exercise it, matters are very likely to proceed relentlessly in the direction they are now headed—toward a world in which there is an enormous abundance of material goods and a great scarcity of many of the things that most people now consider primary requisites for a high quality of life.

How does the cost disease relate to the central topic of this chapter—the performance of the market and its implications for the economic role of government? Here the problem is that the market *does* give the appropriate price signals; but these signals are likely to be misunderstood by government and to lead to decisions that do not promote the public interest most effectively.

Health care is a good example. The cost disease itself is capable of causing the costs of health care (say, per hospital room) to rise faster than the economy's rate of inflation because medical care cannot be standardized enough to enjoy the productivity gains offered by automation and assembly lines. As a result, if standards of care in public hospitals are not to fall, it is not enough to allow health care budgets to grow at the rate of inflation. Those budgets must actually grow *faster* to prevent quality from declining. For example, when the inflation rate is 4 percent per year, it may be necessary to raise hospitals' budgets by 6 percent annually.

In these circumstances, something may seem amiss to a state legislature that increases the budget of its hospitals by only 5 percent per year. Responsible legislators will doubtless be disturbed by the fact that the budget is growing steadily, outpacing the rate of inflation, and yet standards of quality at public hospitals are constantly slipping. If the legislators do not realize that the cost disease is the cause of the problem, they will be expected to look for villains—greedy doctors or hospital administrators who are corrupt or inefficient, and so on. The net result, all too often, is a set of wasteful rules that hamper the freedom of action of hospitals and doctors inappropriately or that tighten hospital budgets below the level that demands and costs would require if they were determined by the market mechanism rather than by government.

In many cases price controls are proposed for sectors of the economy affected by the cost disease—for medical services, insurance services and the like. But as we know price controls can, at best, only eliminate the symptoms of the disease, and they often create problems—sometimes more serious than the disease itself.[4]

Politicians in the United States, desperate for a viable health-care policy, cite the varied health care systems of other countries as examples to be followed. But as part (a) of Figure 13–5 shows, in terms of the rise in health care costs the American record is not out of line. After correction for differences in the inflation rate in the various countries (the U.S. record looks even better if this correction is omitted), we see that our performance is somewhere in the middle—by no means the best, but far from the worst in this sample of 18 countries. (In part (b) we see that the same is true of increases in the cost of education—the U.S. growth rate over the 23-year period, 1965–88, falls in the middle of this group of six countries.) The conclusion is that, while a modification in our health care system may or may not be desirable for other reasons, it is hardly a promising cure for the cost disease. Congress can declare both cancer and the cost disease to be illegal, but that will do little to cure the disease, and such a law may well impede more effective approaches to the problem.

In sum, the cost disease is not a case where the market performs badly. But it is a case in which the market *appears* to misbehave by singling out certain sectors for particularly large cost increases. And because the market *seems* to be working badly there, it is likely to lead to reaction by governments, which can well be highly detrimental to the public interest.

## EVALUATIVE COMMENTS

This chapter, like Chapter 10, has offered a rather unbalanced assessment of the market mechanism. We spent Chapter 10 extolling the market's virtues and spent

[4]See Chapter 4, pages 75–76 and 91–97.

**Figure 13-5**

## GROWTH RATES OF REAL HEALTH CARE COSTS AND REAL EDUCATION COSTS, AN INTERNATIONAL COMPARISON

These two graphs show us how the United States compares with other countries in terms of the rising costs of health care and education.

Each nation's bar on the graphs represents its average yearly rate of increase in real (inflation-adjusted) health care costs between 1960 and 1990 [panel (a)], and real education costs between 1965 and 1988 [panel (b)]. The bars that are greater than zero represent percentage growth rates that exceeded the overall inflation rate during that time period in the respective economies, while bars that dip below zero mean that the growth rate was less than overall inflation.

For both of these personal services, the American record is not out of line with that of the other countries represented. The U.S. growth rate falls somewhere in the middle in both education and health care. Even more important, in most of the countries, health care and education costs rise considerably faster than the economy's average price level.

SOURCE: for part (a): Organization for Economic Cooperation and Development, *Health Data File*, unpublished data, 1993.
SOURCE: for part (b): UNESCO, *Statistical Yearbook*, various years.

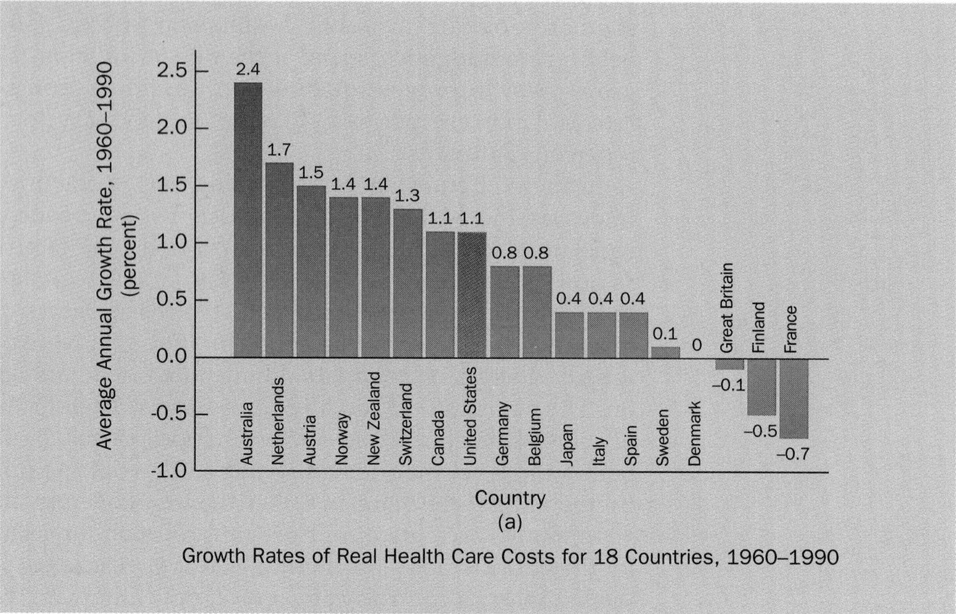

Growth Rates of Real Health Care Costs for 18 Countries, 1960–1990

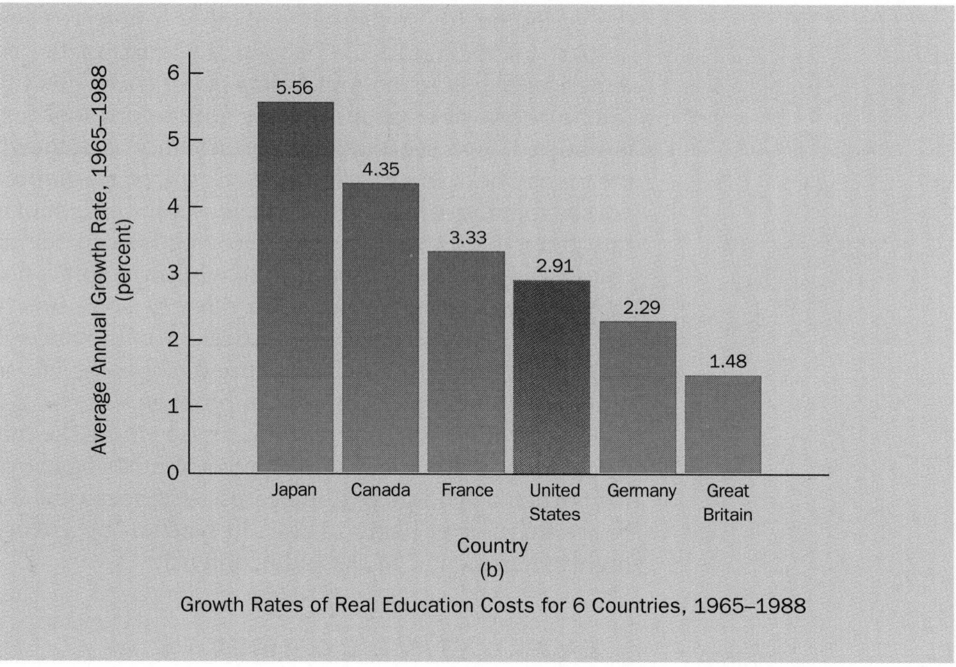

Growth Rates of Real Education Costs for 6 Countries, 1965–1988

this chapter cataloguing its vices. We come out, as in the nursery rhyme, concluding that the market is either very, very good or it is horrid.

There seems to be nothing moderate about the performance of a market system. As a means of achieving efficiency in the production of ordinary consumer goods and of responding to changes in consumer preferences, it is unparalleled. It is, in fact, difficult to overstate the accomplishments of the price system in these areas.

On the other hand, it has proven itself unable to cope with business fluctuations, income inequality, or the consequences of monopoly. It has proved to be a very poor allocator of resources among outputs that generate external costs and external benefits, and it has shown itself completely incapable of arranging for the provision of public goods. Some of the most urgent problems that plague our society—the deterioration of services in the cities, the despoliation of our atmosphere, the social unrest attributable to poverty—can be ascribed in part to one or another of these shortcomings of the market system.

Most economists conclude from these observations that while the market mechanism is virtually irreplaceable, the public interest nevertheless requires considerable modifications in the way it works. Proposals designed to deal directly with the problems of poverty, monopoly, and resource allocation over time abound in the economic literature. All of them call for the government to intervene in the economy, either by supplying directly those goods and services that, it is believed, private enterprise does not supply in adequate amounts, or by seeking to influence the workings of the economy more indirectly through regulation. Many of these programs have been discussed in earlier chapters; others will be encountered in chapters yet to come.

## EPILOGUE: THE UNFORGIVING MARKET, ITS GIFT OF ABUNDANCE, AND ITS DANGEROUS FRIENDS

As was said at the end of Chapter 10, the economists' analysis of the accomplishments of the market, while valid enough, may fail to emphasize its central contribution. The same can, perhaps with some justice, be said of their analysis of the market's shortcomings. The market's major contribution to the general welfare may well be its stimulation of the growth in productivity, which has yielded an abundance of consumers' goods, contributed to increases in human longevity, created new products, expanded education, and raised standards of living to levels undreamed of in earlier societies.

Perhaps the main shortcoming of the market, in the view of many observers, lies in the arena of justice and injustice, a subject that economists are no more competent to address than anyone else. The perception that markets are cruel and unjust springs from the very heart of the mechanism. The market mechanism has sometimes been described appropriately as the profit system, because it works by providing rich rewards to those who succeed in introducing very new products that are attractive to consumers, or in increasing efficiency sufficiently to permit sharp reductions in the prices of other items. At the same time, it is unforgiving in its treatment of those who fail, subjecting them to bankruptcy and perhaps to poverty. Both the wealth awarded to those who succeed, and the drastic treatment accorded those who fail are main sources of the productive power of markets. But they also generate disenchantment and opposition. For example, the new markets of the countries of Eastern Europe have predictably produced a number of successful entrepreneurs whose high incomes have led to widespread resentment and calls for restrictions on entrepreneurial earnings. But these critics do not seem to realize that a market without substantial rewards to entrepreneurs who do their job well is a market whose engine has been weakened if not altogether removed.

Indeed, markets that are effective and effectively competitive often elicit expressions of support from many groups who, at the same time, do their best to undermine that competition. For example, the politicians who seek to prevent telephone companies and carriers of cable television from competing with one another, and who, in other countries, arrange for the sale of government enterprises to private owners, only to constrain decision making by the new owners at every turn, are, in fact, doing their best to keep markets from working. When the general public demands price controls on interest rates, rents, and health care services, it is expressing its unwillingness to accept the decisions that emerge from the workings of the market. No less is done by the businesspersons who are tireless in expressing their support for the free-enterprise system and the free market, but who seek to acquire the monopoly power that can distort its activities. In short, the market has many professed supporters who genuinely believe in its virtues, but whose behavior poses a constant threat to its effectiveness.

One cannot take for granted the success of the newly introduced market mechanism in Eastern Europe, and even in the older free-enterprise economies, one cannot just assume that it will survive unscathed from the dangerous embrace of its most vocal supporters.

## *Summary*

1. There are at least seven major imperfections associated with the workings of the market mechanism: inequality of income distribution, fluctuations in economic activity (inflation and unemployment), monopolistic output restrictions, **beneficial and detrimental externalities**, inadequate provision of public goods, misallocation of resources between present and future, and, finally, deteriorating quality and rising costs of personal services.
2. Efficient resource allocation is basically a matter of balancing the benefits of producing more of one good against the benefits of devoting the required inputs to the production of some other good.
3. A detrimental externality occurs when an economic activity incidentally does harm to others; a beneficial externality occurs when an economic activity incidentally creates benefits for others.
4. When an activity causes a detrimental externality, the marginal social cost of the activity (including the harm it does to others) must be greater than the marginal private cost to those who carry on the activity. The opposite will be true when a beneficial externality occurs.
5. If manufacture of a product causes detrimental externalities, its price will generally not include all the **marginal social cost** it causes, since part of the cost will be borne by others. The opposite is true for beneficial externalities.
6. The market will therefore tend to overallocate resources to the production of goods that cause detrimental externalities and underallocate resources to the production of goods that create beneficial externalities. This is one of the **12 Ideas for Beyond the Final Exam.**
7. A **public good** is defined by economists as a commodity (like clean air) that is not depleted by additional users and from whose use it is often difficult to exclude anyone, even those who refuse to pay for it. A **private good**, in contrast, is characterized by both excludability and depletability.
8. Free-enterprise firms generally will not produce a public good even if it is extremely useful to the com-

munity, because they cannot charge money for the use of the good.

9. Many observers feel that the market often short-changes the future, particularly when it makes **irreversible decisions** that destroy natural resources.

10. Because personal services—such as education, medical care, and police protection—are not amenable to labor-saving innovations, they suffer from a cost disease whose symptom is that their costs tend to rise considerably faster than costs in the economy as a whole. The result can be a distortion in the supply of services by government because their rising cost is misinterpreted as mismanagement and waste. This **cost disease of the service sector** is another of our **12 Ideas for Beyond the Final Exam.**

## *Key Concepts and Terms*

Opportunity cost
Resource misallocation
Production possibilities frontier
Price above or below marginal cost
Externalities (detrimental and beneficial)
Marginal social cost and marginal private cost
Public goods
Private goods
Excludability
Depletability
Irreversible decisions
Asymmetric information
Principals
Agents
Rent seeking
Moral hazard
Cost disease of the personal services

## *Questions for Review*

1. Specifically, what is the opportunity cost to society of a kilowatt of electricity? Why may the price of that electricity not adequately represent that opportunity cost?
2. Suppose that because of a new disease that attacks coffee plants, far more labor and other inputs are required to raise a pound of coffee than before. How might that affect the efficient allocation of resources between tea and coffee? Why? How would the prices of coffee and tea react in a free market?
3. Give some examples of goods whose production causes detrimental externalities and some examples of goods that create beneficial externalities.
4. Compare cleaning an office building with cleaning the atmosphere of a city. Which is a public good and which is a private good? Why?
5. Give some other examples of public goods, and discuss in each case why additional users do not deplete them and why it is difficult to exclude people from using them.
6. Think about the goods and services that your local government provides. Which of these are "public goods" as economists use the term?
7. Explain why the services of a lighthouse are sometimes given as an example of a public good.
8. Explain why education is not a very satisfactory example of a public good.
9. In recent decades, college tuition costs have risen faster than the general price level even though the wages of college professors have failed to keep pace with the price level. Can you explain why?
10. A firm holds a patent that is estimated to be worth $20 million. The patent is repeatedly challenged in the courts by a large number of (rent seeking) firms, each hoping to grab away the patent. In what sense may the rent seekers be "competing perfectly" for the patent? If so, how much will end up being spent in the legal battles? (*Hint*: Under perfect competition should firms expect to earn any economic profit?)

Chapter 14

# REAL FIRMS AND THEIR FINANCING: STOCKS AND BONDS

*The action of the stock market must necessarily be puzzling at times since otherwise everyone who studies it only a little bit would be able to make money in it.*

**B. GRAHAM, D. L. DODD, AND S. COTTLE**

Earlier chapters have provided a theoretical analysis of the business firm's decisions. But a firm does more than select inputs, outputs, and prices. In this chapter, we look at some other salient features of real firms. We begin by describing the different types of firms that make up U.S. business—small firms operated by individual owners, partnerships, and corporations of all sizes. Then we describe the most important ways in which firms acquire resources for investment. This leads us to look at the stock and bond markets, to which many individuals bring money, hoping to make it grow. ¶ The stock market is something of an enigma. No other economic activity is reported in such detail in so many newspapers and followed with such concern by so many people; yet few activities have so successfully eluded prediction of their future. There is no shortage of well-paid "experts" prepared to forecast the future of the market, or of a particular stock. But there are real questions about what these experts deliver. For example, a widely noted study of leading analysts' predictions of company earnings (on which they based their stock-price forecasts) reports:

> *. . . we wrote to nineteen major Wall Street firms . . . among the most respected names in the investment business.*
>
> *We requested—and received—past earnings predictions on how these firms felt earnings for specific companies would behave over both a one-year and a five-year period. These estimates . . . were . . . compared with actual results to see how well the analysts forecast short-run and long-run earnings changes . . . .*
>
> *Bluntly stated, the careful estimates of security analysts (based on industry studies, plant visits, etc.) do very little better than those that would be obtained by simple extrapolation of past trends . . . .*
>
> *For example . . . the analysts' estimates were compared [with] the assumption that every company in the economy would enjoy a growth in earnings approximating the long-run rate of growth of the national income. It often turned out that . . . this naïve forecasting model . . . would make smaller errors in forecasting long-run earnings growth than . . . [did] the professional forecasts of the analysts . . . .*
>
> *When confronted with the poor record of their five-year growth estimates, the security analysts honestly, if sheepishly, admitted that five years ahead is really too far in advance to make reliable projections. They protested that while long-term projections are admittedly important, they really ought to be judged on their ability to project earnings changes one year ahead.*
>
> *Believe it or not, it turned out that their one-year forecasts were even worse than their five-year projections.*[1]

Later in this chapter we will suggest an explanation of this poor performance.

## FIRMS IN THE UNITED STATES

It is customary to divide firms into three groups: *corporations*, *partnerships*, and *individual proprietorships* (businesses having a single owner). The importance of corporations in the U.S. economy is indicated by the fact that they produce over half of the country's GDP. Almost all large American firms are corporations. General Motors by itself sold nearly $133 billion in 1992, and Exxon and Ford each sold over $100 billion. The combined sales of these three firms alone amount to considerably more than the GDP of Austria, Belgium, the Netherlands, Sweden, Switzerland, and many, many more countries.

But while a huge chunk of America's output comes from corporations, less than 20 percent of American business firms are incorporated. The reason is that most firms are small. Even corporations are often quite small—about 40 percent of them have business receipts of less than $100,000. But by far the greatest number of firms (counting all firms large and small, and including the corner grocery store and shoe repair shop) are proprietorships. For example, about 86 percent of family farms are proprietorships. Of the nearly 19 million business firms in the United States, about 14 million are proprietorships, 3.5 million are corporations, and 1.5 million are partnerships. Thus, as is true of the income of individuals:

A very small proportion of American firms accounts for a very large share of U.S. business. Obviously, business is not distributed equally among firms.

This result is brought out strikingly by *Fortune* magazine's annual listing of the largest American firms, their assets, and their volume of business. Taken together, in 1992 the 500 largest industrial corporations—that is, a negligible

---

[1]Burton G. Malkiel, *A Random Walk Down Wall Street* (New York: W. W. Norton & Company, Inc., 1990), pages 140–141.

proportion of America's almost 19 million firms—had more than two trillion dollars in sales, amounting to about 40 percent of the nation's GDP in that year. Most industries in which these giant firms are found are *oligopolies*, a market form we analyzed in Chapter 12. A few are *monopolies*, the market form discussed in Chapter 11.

At the other end of the spectrum, the nation's small business firms have a disproportionately small share of U.S. business. These small firms have earnings that are not only relatively low but also very risky—risky in the sense that the average new firm does not last very long (its average life is reported to be less than 7 years). When making economic decisions, the buyer is not the only one who must beware!

What are the basic forms of business organization, and what induces organizers of a firm to choose one form rather than another? Firms are divided into three types: proprietorships, partnerships, and corporations.

## PROPRIETORSHIPS

A **PROPRIETORSHIP** is a business firm owned by a single person.

Most small retail firms, farms, and many small factories are **proprietorships**. A proprietorship involves fewer legal complications than any other form of business organization. To start a proprietorship, an individual simply decides to go into business and to open a new firm or take over an existing one. Aside from special regulations, such as health requirements for a restaurant or zoning restrictions that limit business activity to particular geographical areas, the individual does not need anyone's permission to go into business. This is a major advantage of the proprietorship form of organization.

But its main attraction is probably that the owner can be his or her own boss and the firm's sole decision maker. No partners or stockholders have to be consulted when the proprietor wants to expand or change the company's product line or modify the firm's advertising policy. A proprietorship also has tax advantages, particularly compared with a corporation. A proprietor's income is taxed only once. If the same firm were to incorporate, its income would be taxed twice—once as the income of the firm (the corporate income tax) and again as the personal income of the owner.

**UNLIMITED LIABILITY** is a legal obligation of a firm's owner(s) to pay back company debts with whatever resources he or she owns.

On the other hand, a proprietorship has two basic disadvantages that make it almost impossible to organize large-scale enterprises as proprietorships. First, the owner has **unlimited liability** for the debts of the firm. If the company goes out of business leaving unpaid bills, the former owner can be forced to pay them out of personal savings. The owner can be made to sell the family home, private collections of stamps or paintings, or any other personal assets, no matter how unrelated to the business, so that the proceeds can be used to pay off the company's debts.

Often proprietors guard themselves against this danger by signing away their property to other members of their families or to others whom they feel they can trust. But such transfers are subject to federal and state gift taxes. In any event, there are many tragic tales that begin with the signing away of one's possessions—King Lear's betrayal by his daughters can serve as the classic warning to proprietors who are too trusting.

A second and equally basic shortcoming of the proprietorship is that it inhibits expansion of the firm by making it difficult to raise money. People outside the company are reluctant to put money into a firm over which they exercise no control. This means that the proprietorship's capital is usually no greater than the amount its owner is willing and able to put into it, plus the amount that banks or other commercial lenders are willing to provide.

SUMMARY

There are three main advantages of the individual proprietorship:

1. It leaves full control in the hands of the owner.
2. It involves little legal complication.
3. It generally reduces the taxes its owners must pay.

Its two main disadvantages are

1. The unlimited liability of the owner for the debts of the company.
2. The difficulty of raising substantial funds for the firm.

## PARTNERSHIPS

A **PARTNERSHIP** is a firm whose ownership is shared by a fixed number of proprietors.

Measured in terms of the amount of their capital, **partnerships** tend to be larger than proprietorships but smaller than corporations. However, the largest partnerships greatly exceed the smallest corporations in terms of both their financing and their influence. For example, some of the most prestigious law firms and investment banks are partnerships. When you call a law firm and are greeted by "Smith, Jones, Brown, and Pfafufnik; Good Morning," you are almost certainly being treated to a partial listing of the company's current or past senior partners (the partners who own the largest share of the firm or who founded the firm).

The advantage of the partnership over the proprietorship is that it brings together the funds and expertise of a number of people and permits them to be combined to form a company larger than any one of the owners could have financed or managed alone. If one cannot hope to run a particular type of firm with an inventory of less than $2 million, a person who is not rich may be unable to get into the business without the aid of a partner. A partnership may also bring together a variety of specialists, as often happens in a medical practice. The partnership also offers the advantage of freedom from double taxation, a benefit it shares with the proprietorship.

But the partnership has disadvantages, some of them substantial. Decision making in a partnership may be harder than in any other type of firm. The sole proprietor need consult no one before acting; the corporation appoints officers who are authorized to decide things for the company. But in a partnership it may be necessary for every partner to agree before any steps are taken by the firm, and this is the primary bane of this form of enterprise. A partnership has been compared to two people in a horse costume, each supplying two of the legs, each prepared to go in a different direction, and each unable to move without the other.

Furthermore, partners, like sole proprietors, have unlimited liability. They can conceivably be in danger of losing their personal possessions to pay off company debts. Finally, the partnership suffers from unique legal complications. A partnership agreement is like a marriage contract entered into solely for the financial advantage of the participants, and so there is likely to be considerable haggling about the terms. And under the law, if a partner dies, or decides to leave the firm, or the others decide to buy that person's share in the enterprise, the partnership may have to be dissolved and haggling about the contract may start all over again.

SUMMARY

The benefits of the partnership to the owners of the firm are

1. Access to larger quantities of capital.
2. Protection from double taxation.

Its disadvantages are

1. The need to obtain the agreement of many if not all partners to all major decisions.
2. Unlimited liability of the partners for the obligations of the company.
3. The legal complications, including automatic dissolution of the partnership when there is *any* change in ownership.

## CORPORATIONS

A **CORPORATION** is a firm that has the legal status of a fictional individual. This fictional individual is owned by a number of persons, called its stockholders, and is run by a set of elected officers (usually headed by a president) and a board of directors, whose chairman is often also in a powerful position.

**LIMITED LIABILITY** is a legal obligation of a firm's owners to pay back company debts only with the money they have already invested in the firm.

Most big firms are **corporations**, a form of business organization that has quite a different legal status from that of a proprietorship or a partnership. Though it seems strange, a corporation is an individual in the eyes of the law. So its earnings, like those of other individuals, are taxed. This leads to double taxation of the stockholders, who also pay tax on any dividends they receive from the firm.

But this disadvantage is counterbalanced by an important advantage: any debt of the corporation is regarded as an obligation of that fictitious individual, not as a liability of any stockholder. This means that the stockholders benefit from the protection of **limited liability**—they can lose no more than the money they have put into the firm. Creditors cannot force them to sell their personal possessions to help repay any outstanding debts incurred by the firm.

Limited liability is the main secret of the success of the corporate form of organization. Thanks to that provision, individuals from every part of the world are willing to put money into firms whose operations they do not understand and whose managements they do not know. A giant firm may produce computers, locomotives, and electrical generators; it may have, as subsidiaries, publishing houses and shoe factories. Few of its stockholders will know or care about all the firm's activities. Yet each investor knows that by providing money to the firm in return for a share of its ownership, no more is risked than the amount of money provided. This has permitted corporations to obtain financing from literally millions of shareholders, each of whom receives in return a claim on the firm's profits, and, at least in principle, a portion of the company's ownership.

As indicated, the profits of a corporation are subject to taxation. Smaller corporations get a tax break, but the larger firms, whose total profits are high, pay a federal tax rate of 34 percent on all *net* earnings over $100,000. In addition, most states levy corporate taxes of their own, pushing the total tax rate above 40 percent. This means that corporate investors are left with about 40 percent less out of each dollar of company earnings than investors in a partnership or a proprietorship. In other words, there is a *double taxation* of payments to the owners. That is, corporate earnings are taxed twice, once when they are earned by the company, and a second time when they go to the investors in the form of dividends and are subject to the ordinary income tax on the investor's income.

Corporations are directed by a hired group of managers: a chairman of the board of directors, a president, various vice-presidents, and so on. These executives are, legally, employees of the owners of the firm who, as we will see, are the stockholders of the corporation. This arrangement has great advantages. It prevents the quarrels and indecision that are often problems for partnerships. On the other hand, since the management is made up of hired personnel, it cannot always be trusted to do what is best for the owners. Managers are often accused of looking after their own interests first and, if necessary, sacrificing those of the stockholders (the owners). This is a problem that has recently received much attention in discussions of takeovers of corporations—that is, purchase of control of the firm by a group of outsiders—a subject examined later in this chapter.

Corporations escape one other problem that troubles partnerships. As we saw, if a partner wants to leave the firm, the entire enterprise may have to be reorganized. But in a corporation, any owner who wants to quit just sells her stocks on the stock market, while the corporation goes on exactly as before. In this way, at least in theory, a corporation can continue forever.

SUMMARY

Benefits of the corporate form to the owners:

1. Limited liability.
2. Access to large quantities of capital.
3. Ease of operation with the help of a hired management.
4. "Permanence": the firm is not dissolved or reorganized each time an owner leaves.

Its disadvantages are

1. Double taxation of payments to the owners.
2. The possibility that hired managers will act in their own interests rather than those of the owners.

## EFFECT OF DOUBLE TAXATION OF CORPORATE EARNINGS

Does an investor end up earning less by putting money in a corporation than by putting it in a company that is about equally risky but not subject to double taxation? Paradoxically, the answer is that investors, on the average, will *not* lose anything by choosing the corporation. The tax will not and cannot put those who make one type of investment at a disadvantage in comparison with those who choose any other.

How is this possible? How does the effect of the additional tax on corporate stocks disappear before it reaches the stockholder? There are two processes that achieve this act of magic.

First, corporations are forced to avoid some investment opportunities that partnerships and proprietorships can afford to take on. Suppose the market rate of return to people who provide money to firms is 9 percent, and a new product is invented that is expected to bring a 12 percent return to a firm that manufactures it. An individual proprietor can afford to produce the new item—borrowing the necessary funds at 9 percent and keeping the 3 percent additional return on the new item for herself. But a large corporation *cannot* afford to produce the new item. For, in order to compete for funds, it must also pay investors 9 percent, which means that it will have to earn about 15 percent on its investments since about 40 percent of that money will be siphoned off in corporate taxes.

Thus, double taxation keeps corporate business out of various economic activities that offer a real, but limited, earnings potential. This effect may be unfortunate from the viewpoint of the efficiency of the economy, because it means that many firms are induced to stay out of activities in which it might be useful for them to take part. For instance, corporations may find it too costly to open retail outlets in slum areas or to run trains to isolated rural areas—activities that might be profitable in the absence of the tax.

There is a second fail-safe mechanism that protects new investors in corporate stocks from earning a lower return on the average than they would on other securities of equal risk. Suppose two otherwise identical securities, A and B, each offer a return of $60 per year but A is subject to a 50 percent tax while B is not. *Question*: If the market price of security B is $1000, what will be the market price of A? *Answer*: The price of A will be only $500, exactly half the price of security B. Why? Because it will bring in only $30 per year after taxes, exactly half of what security A returns, investors will be willing to pay only half as much for it as they are willing to pay for the untaxed security. But at those prices, investors in either security will obviously earn the same rate of return after payment of taxes.

Double taxation of corporate earnings tends to restrict the activities of corporate firms, keeping them out of relatively low-profit operations. However, double taxation does not mean that the individual investor earns less by putting money into a corporation than by putting it into other businesses.

## FINANCING CORPORATE ACTIVITY

Our discussion of the earnings of an investor in corporate securities introduces a subject of interest to millions of Americans—*stocks* and *bonds*, the financial instruments that provide funds to the corporate sector of the economy. (Stocks and bonds will be defined later in the chapter.) In fact, as we will see, there are three principal ways in which corporations obtain money: by sale of stocks, by borrowing (which, we will note, includes the sale of bonds), and by "plowback"—keeping some part of company earnings to invest back into the company, rather than paying the money out as income to the firm's owners.

When a corporation needs money to add to its plant or equipment or to finance other types of real investment, it can get it by printing new stocks or new bonds and selling them to people who are looking for something in which to invest their money. What enables the firm to get money in exchange for printed paper? Doesn't the process seem a bit like counterfeiting? If done improperly, there are grounds for the suspicion. But, carried out appropriately, it is a perfectly rational economic process.

As long as the funds derived from a new issue of stocks and bonds are used effectively to increase the firm's capacity to produce and earn a profit, then these funds will automatically yield the means for any required repayment and for the payment of appropriate amounts of interest and dividends to the purchasers of the new bonds and stocks. But there have been times when this did not happen. It is alleged that one of the favorite practices of the more notorious nineteenth century manipulators of the market was "watering" of company stocks—the issue of stocks with little or nothing to back them up. The term is derived from the practice of some cattle dealers who would force their animals to drink large quantities of water just before bringing them to be weighed for sale.

**PLOWBACK** or **RETAINED EARNINGS** is the portion of a corporation's profits that management decides to keep and invest back into the firm's operations rather than to pay out directly to stockholders in the form of dividends.

Another major source of funds is **plowback** or **retained earnings**. For example, if a company earns $30 million after taxes and decides to pay out only $10 million in dividends and invest the remaining $20 million back into the firm, that $20 million is called "plowback."

When business is profitable so that management has the funds to reinvest in the company, it will often prefer plowback to other sources of funding. One reason for this preference is that it is usually less risky to management. This source of funds, unlike other sources, does not require prior scrutiny by the Securities and Exchange Commission (SEC), the government agency that regulates stocks.[2] Moreover, plowback does not depend on the availability of eager customers for new company stocks and bonds. An issue of new securities can be a disappointment if there is little public demand for them when they are offered. But plowback runs no such risk.

Above all, a plowback decision generally does not call attention to the degree of success of management's operations as a new stock issue does. In these instances, the SEC, potential buyers of the stock, and their professional advisers may all scrutinize the company carefully.

A second reason for the attractiveness of plowback is that issuing new stocks and bonds is usually an expensive and lengthy process. The company is required by the SEC to gather masses of data in its prospectus—a document describing the financial condition of the company—before the new issue is approved.

A final way for a company to obtain money is by borrowing it from banks, insurance companies, or other private firms with money to lend. It may also sometimes borrow from a U.S. government agency, either directly or with the agency's help (the agency serves as guarantor in this instance, promising to make sure the loan is repaid). For example, loans may be arranged with the help of the national defense agencies if they want a private firm to undertake the design and production of an expensive new weapons system. Small business firms, too, are eligible for various forms of assistance in borrowing.

Figure 14–1 (a bar chart) shows the relative importance of each of the different sources of funds to U.S. corporations. It indicates that plowback is by far the most important source of corporate financing, constituting about 83 percent of the total financing to the corporate sector of the economy in 1991. Issues of new bonds and other forms of borrowing supplied about 5 percent of the total, and sales of stock contributed about 4 percent.

A **COMMON STOCK** of a corporation is a piece of paper that gives the holder of the stock a share of the ownership of the company.

## THE FINANCING OF CORPORATE ACTIVITY: STOCKS AND BONDS

A **BOND** is simply an IOU by a corporation that promises to pay the holder of the piece of paper a fixed sum of money at the specified *maturity* date and some other fixed amount of money (the *coupon* or the *interest payment*) every year up to the date of maturity.

We return now to the other major sources of corporate financing besides plowback and direct borrowing—the corporate securities, like **common stocks** and **bonds**. Stocks represent ownership of part of the corporation. For example, if a company issues 100,000 shares, then a person who owns 1000 shares actually owns 1 percent

[2]The Securities and Exchange Commission, established in 1934, protects the interests of people who buy securities. It requires firms that issue stocks and other securities to provide information about their financial condition, and it regulates the issue and trading of securities.

Figure 14–1 SOURCES OF NEW FUNDS, U.S. CORPORATIONS, 1991

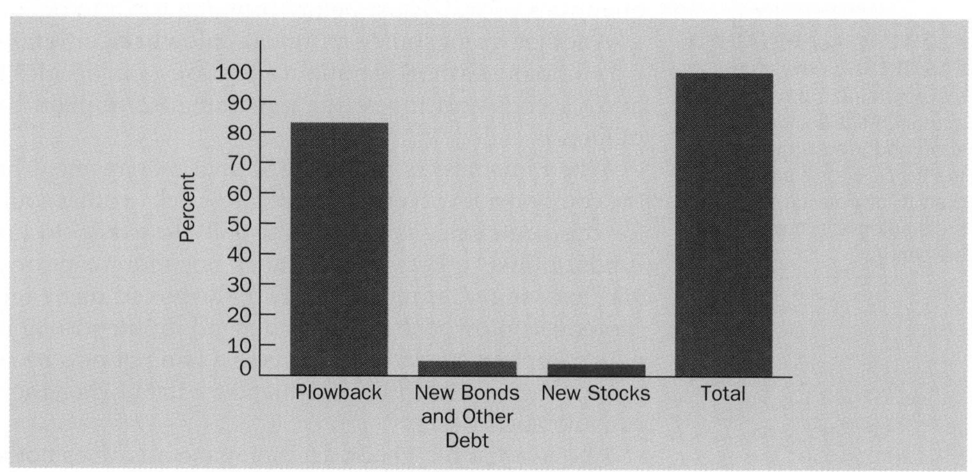


Corporations in the United States get about 83 percent of their reinvestment funds from plowback, which consists mostly of depreciation—funds accumulated for replacement of plant, equipment, and so on, as it wears out or becomes obsolete.

SOURCE: U.S. Bureau of the Census, *Statistical Abstract of the United States, 1992*, Washington, D.C.: U.S. Government Printing Office, 1992.

of the company and is entitled to 1 percent of the company's *dividends*, which are the corporation's annual payments to stockholders. The shareholder's vote counts for 1 percent of the total votes in an election of corporate officers or in a referendum on corporate policy.

Bonds differ from stocks in several ways. First, whereas the purchaser of a corporation's stock *buys* a share of its ownership and receives some control over its affairs, the purchaser of a bond simply *lends* money to the firm. Second, whereas stockholders have no idea how much they will receive for their stocks when they sell them, or how much they will receive in dividends each year while they own them, bondholders know with a high degree of certainty how much money they will be paid if they hold their bonds to maturity. For instance, a bond with a face value of $1000, with an $80 coupon that matures in 1998, will provide to its owner $80 per year every year until 1998, and in addition it will repay the $1000 to the bondholder in 1998. Unless the company goes bankrupt, there is no doubt about this repayment schedule. Third, bondholders have a *legally prior claim* on company earnings, which means that nothing can be paid by the company to its stockholders until interest payments to the company's bondholders have been met. For all these reasons, bonds are considered less risky to their buyers than stocks. An important exception are "junk bonds"—very risky bonds that became popular in the 1980s. They were used heavily by groups of persons trying to purchase enough stocks of some corporation to acquire control of that firm. More will be said later about such "takeover" activities and the use of junk bonds to finance them.

In reality, however, the differences between stocks and bonds are not as clear-cut as just described. Two relevant misconceptions are particularly worth noting. First, the ownership of the company represented by the holding of a few shares of its stock may be more apparent than real. A holder of 0.002 percent of the stocks of AT&T—which is a *very large* investment—exercises no real control over AT&T's operations.

In fact, many economists believe that the ownership of large corporations is so diffuse that stockholders or stockholder groups rarely have any effective control over management. In this view, the management of a corporation is a largely independent decision-making body; as long as it keeps enough cash flowing to stockholders to prevent discontent and organized rebellion, management can do anything it wants within the law. Looked at in another way, this last conclusion really says that stockholders are merely another class of persons who provide loans to the company. The only real difference between stockholders and bondholders, according to this interpretation, is that stockholders' loans are riskier and therefore entitled to higher payments.

Second, bonds *can* be quite risky to the bondholder. Persons who try to sell their bonds before maturity may find that the market price for bonds happens to be low, so that if they need to raise cash in a hurry, they may have to sell at a substantial loss. Also, bondholders may be exposed to losses from inflation. Whether the $1000 promised the bondholder at the 1998 maturity date represents substantial purchasing power or only a little depends on what happens to the general price level in the meantime. And no one can predict the price level this far in advance with any accuracy. Finally, a firm can issue bonds for which there is little backing; that is, the firm may own little valuable property that it can use as a guarantee of repayment to the lender—the bondholder. This has often been true of the junk bonds of the 1980s and it helps to explain their high riskiness.

## BOND PRICES AND INTEREST RATES

Why is investment in bonds risky; what makes their price go up and down? The main element in the answer is that changes in interest rates cause bond prices to change. There is a straightforward relationship between bond prices and interest rates: whenever one goes up, the other *must* go down.

For example, suppose that Sears, Roebuck had issued some 15-year bonds when interest rates were comparatively low, so that the company had to pay only 6 percent to sell bonds. People who invested $1000 in new Sears bonds then received in return a contract that promised them $60 per year for 15 years plus the return of their $1000 at the end of that period. Suppose now that interest rates in the economy rise, so that new 15-year bonds of companies of similar quality pay 12 percent. Now an investor with $1000 can buy a contract that offers $120 per year. Obviously, no longer will anyone pay $1000 for a bond that promises only $60 per year. Consequently, the market price of the old Sears bonds must fall.

This example is not hypothetical. Until a few years ago there were bonds in existence that had been issued much earlier at interest rates of 6 percent and even less. In the 1980s' markets, with interest rates well above 6 percent, such bonds sold for a price well below their original value.

When interest rates in the economy rise, there must be a fall in the prices of previously issued bonds with their lower interest earnings. For the same reason, when interest rates in the economy fall, the prices of previously issued bonds must rise.

It follows that as interest rates in the economy change because of changes in monetary policy or other reasons, bond prices fluctuate. That is one reason why investment in bonds can be risky.

## CORPORATE CHOICE BETWEEN STOCKS AND BONDS

We have seen why a corporation may prefer to finance its real investment, such as construction of factories and equipment, through plowback or retained earnings rather than through the issue of new stocks or bonds. But suppose it has decided to do the latter. How does it determine whether bonds or stocks suit its purposes better?

Two considerations are of prime importance. Although issuing bonds generally exposes the firm to more risk than issuing stocks, the corporation usually expects to pay more money to stockholders over the long run than to bondholders. In other words, to the firm that issues them, bonds are cheaper but riskier. The decision about which is better for the firm therefore involves a trade-off between the two considerations.

Why are bonds risky to the corporation? When it issues $20 million in new bonds at 10 percent, the company commits itself to pay out $2 million every year for the life of the bond. It is obligated to pay that amount each year, whether that year happens to be one in which business is booming or one in which the firm is losing money. That is a big risk. If the firm is unable to meet its obligation to bondholders in some year, it faces bankruptcy.

The issue of new stocks does not burden the company with any such risk since the company does not promise to pay the stockholders *any* fixed amount. Stockholders simply receive whatever is left of the company's net earnings after payments to bondholders. If nothing is left to pay the new stockholders in some years, legally speaking, that is just their bad luck.

Why, then, do stockholders normally obtain higher average expected payments from the company than bondholders? The answer is obtained by looking at the risk-return trade-off from the investor's point of view. In the case of bonds, the company assumes as much risk as possible by guaranteeing a specified payment to the bondholder. In the case of stocks, however, the company assumes little or no risk, leaving it all to the stockholder.

The situation is reversed for the individual who provides the money: bonds are safer than stocks. Since this is true, no investor will want to buy stocks rather than bonds unless she can expect a sufficiently higher return on the stocks to make up for the added risk. So, if a company offers both stocks and bonds, their prices and prospective returns must offer a higher (but riskier) average rate of return to stockholders than to bondholders.

To the firm that issues them, bonds are riskier than stocks because they commit the firm to make a fixed annual payment even in years when it is losing money. For the same reason, stocks are riskier than bonds to the buyers of securities. That is why stockholders expect to be paid more money than bondholders.

## BUYING STOCKS AND BONDS

Although stocks and bonds can be purchased through any brokerage firm, not all brokers charge the same fees. There are bargain brokerage houses that advertise in the financial pages of newspapers, offering investors very little service—no advice, no research, no other frills—other than merely buying or selling what the customer wants them to, at lower fees than those charged by higher-service brokerage firms.

Many investors are not aware of the various ways in which stocks can be purchased (or sold). The following are some of the possibilities: (a) *Round lot* purchases: purchases of 100 shares or 200 shares or any number of shares in multiples of 100. (b) *Odd lot* purchases: the purchase of some number of shares that is not a multiple of 100. The brokerage fee per dollar of investment is normally higher on an odd lot than on a round lot. (c) A *market order* purchase: this simply tells the broker to buy a specified quantity of stock (either a round lot or an odd lot) at the best price the market currently offers. (d) A *limit order*: an agreement to buy a given amount of stock when its price falls to a specified level. If the investor offers to buy at $18, then shares will be purchased by the broker if and when the market price falls to $18 per share or less.

There are many investment information services that supply subscribers with a variety of information on performance of stocks, bonds, and other securities. These firms offer analyses of particular companies, forecasts, and advice.

A recent survey of shareowners by the New York Stock Exchange (NYSE) estimated that 47 million individuals—about one in every four—owned stock in a publicly traded company or in a stock mutual fund. The NYSE estimates that an additional 100 million people also participate in the stock market indirectly through banks, pension funds, insurance companies and the like. Such "institutional investors" are estimated to own over half of all stocks traded on the NYSE.

## SELECTING A PORTFOLIO: DIVERSIFICATION

Rational planning by an individual of what stocks, bonds, and other financial investments to hold requires more than just careful examination of the merits and demerits of individual securities. It is important to select a combination of securities that meets one's needs effectively. Such a combination of holdings is called the individual's *portfolio* of investments. For example, an individual who is saving to send children to college in ten years does not need securities that pay money regularly in the meantime, whereas a retired person who depends on periodic payments wants securities that provide regular and convenient returns.

A far more important consideration in planning a portfolio is selecting combinations of securities with low risk. A portfolio may well be far less risky than any of the individual securities it contains. The secret is **diversification**, not putting all one's eggs in one basket.

**DIVERSIFICATION** means including a number and variety of stocks, bonds, and other such items in an individual's portfolio. If the individual owns airline stocks, for example, diversification requires the purchase of a stock or bond in a very different industry, such as a breakfast cereal producer.

If Joe Jones holds only stocks of company A and the company goes bankrupt, then all may be lost. However, if Jones divides his holdings among companies A, B, and C, then the portfolio may perform satisfactorily even if company A goes broke. Moreover, suppose company A specializes in producing luxury items, which do well in prosperous periods but very badly during recessions, while company B sells cheap clothing, whose cyclical demand pattern differs greatly from that of company A. If Jones holds stock in both companies, the overall risk is less than if he owned stock in only one of the companies. All other things being equal, a portfolio containing many different types of securities tends to be less risky than a portfolio with fewer types of securities.

Increasingly, institutional investors have adopted portfolios composed of a broad range of stocks typifying those offered by the entire stock market. By owning a representative basket of stocks, money managers can reduce the risks of owning individual stocks, and ensure that their portfolio is not significantly out-performed by the overall market.

Institutional money managers have been making increasing use of computers to decide on their portfolios and to buy or sell huge portfolios of stocks simultaneously and rapidly. And since 1982, some traders have allowed their computers to decide when to jump in and make massive sales or purchases. This is called *program trading*. During 1992, program trading accounted for 11.5 percent of total NYSE volume. Program trading is controversial, and some observers have argued that it has aggravated price fluctuations, especially during the stock market crash of October 1987.

## FOLLOWING A PORTFOLIO'S PERFORMANCE

Newspapers carry daily information on stock and bond prices. Figure 14–2 is an excerpt from a *Wall Street Journal* stock market report. In the first two columns, before the company name, the report gives the stock's highest and lowest price in the last year. In the highlighted example, the price of Boeing stock is reported to have ranged between \$45 3/8 and \$33 1/8. After the name of the stock and

**Figure 14–2** EXCERPT FROM A STOCK MARKET PAGE

This table from *The Wall Street Journal* gives the highest and lowest price in the current year; the name of the stock; the current dividend rate; the dividend yield; the ratio of stock price to company earnings (P/E ratio); the number of shares sold; the highest, lowest, and final price on the previous day; and the change in price from the day before.

SOURCE: *The Wall Street Journal*, June 7, 1993, p. C3.

| | 52 Weeks Hi | Lo | Stock | Sym | Div | Yld % | PE | Vol 100s | Hi | Lo | Close | Net Chg |
|---|---|---|---|---|---|---|---|---|---|---|---|---|
| | | | | -B-B-B- | | | | | | | | |
| | 15 | 11⅞ | BlackRockNoAm | BNA | 1.13 | 9.2 | ... | 536 | 12¼ | 12⅛ | 12¼ | ... |
| | 11 | 9⅜ | BlackRockStrat | BGT | .83 | 8.3 | ... | 852 | 10 | 9⅞ | 10 | + ⅛ |
| | 11⅛ | 9¾ | BlackRockTgt | BTT | .80 | 7.7 | ... | 1123 | 10⅜ | 10¼ | 10⅜ | + ⅛ |
| | 10¾ | 9½ | BlackRock1998 | BBT | .72 | 7.3 | ... | 1012 | 9⅞ | 9¾ | 9⅞ | ... |
| n | 10⅛ | 9⅜ | BlackRock1999 | BNN | .74 | 7.6 | ... | 455 | 9⅞ | 9⅝ | 9¾ | ... |
| n | 10⅛ | 8⅞ | BlackRock2001 | BLK | .72 | 7.6 | ... | 2202 | 9½ | 9⅜ | 9½ | + ⅛ |
| n | 20 | 17¾ | BlanchHldg | EWB | | ... | ... | 81 | 18⅞ | 18⅞ | 18⅞ | – ⅛ |
| x | 42¾ | 23⅛ | BlockHR | HRB | 1.00 | 2.8 | 24 | 1297 | 35¾ | 35⅛ | 35⅝ | + ¼ |
| | 20⅛ | 11⅛ | BlockbstrE | BV | .10f | .5 | 23 | 10388 | 19⅛ | 18½ | 19 | + ¼ |
| | 8½ | 7⅜ | BluChipValFd | BLU | .77e | 9.3 | ... | 163 | 8¼ | 8⅛ | 8¼ | + ⅛ |
| | 45⅜ | 33⅛ | Boeing | BA | 1.00 | 2.5 | 9 | 4526 | 39⅝ | 39⅛ | 39⅝ | ... |
| | 27½ | 16⅜ | BoiseCasc | BCC | .60 | 2.3 | dd | 894 | 26½ | 26⅛ | 26⅛ | – ½ |
| n | 26⅞ | 25¾ | BoiseCasc depF | | .43p | 1.6 | ... | 46 | 26⅞ | 26⅝ | 26⅝ | – ⅛ |
| | 27⅜ | 19¾ | BoiseCasc pf | | 1.79 | 6.7 | ... | 304 | 26⅞ | 26⅝ | 26¾ | ... |
| | 6¼ | 3⅝ | BoltBerNew | BBN | .06j | ... | dd | 1049 | 6 | 5½ | 6 | + ¼ |
| **s** | **53½** | **15** | **Bombay** | **BBA** | | **...** | **cc** | **2012** | **51½** | **47½** | **48⅝** | **–3** |
| | 19⅜ | 12⅜ | BordChm un | BCU | 1.44e | 10.8 | 33 | 880 | 13½ | 13⅛ | 13⅜ | – ⅛ |
| ▼ | 31⅞ | 19⅞ | BordenInc | BN | 1.20 | 6.1 | dd | 4534 | 19⅞ | 19⅝ | 19⅝ | – ⅜ |
| n | 22⅝ | 19⅝ | BorgWarner | BOR | | ... | ... | 41 | 20¾ | 20½ | 20½ | – ⅛ |
| | 23⅞ | 16¼ | BostCelts | BOS | 1.25e | 6.7 | 10 | 30 | 18¾ | 18½ | 18⅝ | – ⅜ |
| | 31⅛ | 24½ | BostEdsn | BSE | 1.70 | 5.8 | 14 | 782 | 29⅝ | 29⅜ | 29½ | ... |
| n | 27⅛ | 25 | BostEdsn pfA | | 2.06 | 7.8 | ... | 12 | 26½ | 26¼ | 26¼ | ... |
| n | 25⅜ | 25 | BostEdsn pfB | | | ... | ... | 42 | 25¼ | 25 | 25¼ | + ⅛ |
| | 23⅝ | 12¾ | BostonSci | BSX | | ... | 27 | 560 | 15¾ | 15⅜ | 15¾ | + ⅛ |
| x | 25⅝ | 17⅝ | Bowater | BOW | .60 | 2.8 | dd | 156 | 21¾ | 21½ | 21½ | – ½ |
| n | 20⅛ | 10⅝ | Bradlees | BLE | .60 | 3.5 | ... | 25 | 17⅜ | 17⅛ | 17⅜ | + ¼ |
| | 22 | 11 | BrazilFd | BZF | .53e | 3.1 | ... | 591 | 17⅜ | 17 | 17⅛ | – ⅛ |
| | 15⅛ | 7 | BrazEqtyFd | BZL | | ... | ... | 231 | 13 | 12¾ | 12⅞ | + ⅛ |
| n | 21¾ | 13¾ | BreedTech | BDT | | ... | ... | 275 | 17⅝ | 17½ | 17½ | ... |
| | 68⅝ | 42⅛ | BriggsStrat | BGG | 1.76f | 2.8 | 15 | 552 | 64 | 63 | 63¾ | – ¼ |
| n | 34¾ | 16¼ | BrillAuto | CBA | .02p | .1 | ... | 777 | 17 | 16½ | 16⅝ | – ⅛ |
| s | 37 | 20⅛ | BrinkerInt | EAT | | ... | 37 | 670 | 35⅞ | 35⅛ | 35⅛ | – ¼ |
| | 72⅜ | 52⅞ | BrisMyrsSqb | BMY | 2.88 | 4.9 | 14 | 10563 | 59⅞ | 59 | 59¼ | – ⅝ |
| | 54 | 37⅜ | BritAir | BAB | 2.18e | 4.8 | ... | 1560 | 45⅞ | 45¼ | 45¼ | – ¼ |
| n | 2⅞ | 1¾ | BritAir rt | | | ... | ... | 8694 | 2 | 1¾ | 1⅞ | + ⅛ |
| | 48¾ | 40⅛ | BritGas | BRG | 3.08e | 7.0 | ... | 47 | 44⅜ | 43¾ | 43¾ | –1 |
| | 61½ | 41⅛ | BritPetrol | BP | 2.14e | 3.8 | ... | 2270 | 57⅜ | 56⅝ | 56⅝ | –1¼ |

the stock symbol (BA), there appears the annual dividend per share ($1.00). Following that is the yield, or the dividend as a percent of the closing price (2.5 percent). The next column reports the *price earnings* (P/E) ratio (9 for Boeing). This latter figure is the price per share divided by the company's net earnings per share in the previous year, and it is usually taken as a basic measure indicating whether the current price of the stock overvalues or undervalues the company. However, no simple rule enables us to interpret the P/E figures—for example, a very risky firm or a slowly growing firm with a low P/E may be considered overvalued, while a safe, rapidly growing firm with a high P/E may still be a bargain. The next column indicates the number of shares that were traded on the previous day (452,600), an indication of whether that stock is actively traded. Finally, the last four figures indicate yesterday's highest price ($39 5/8), its lowest price ($39 1/8), the price at which the last transaction of the day took place ($39 5/8), and the change in that price from the previous day (no change).

Figure 14–3, also from *The Wall Street Journal*, gives similar information about bonds. The first thing to notice here is that a given company may have several different bonds—differing in maturity date and coupon (annual interest payment). For example, Citicorp offers four different bonds. The one that is highlighted is labeled Citicp $8\frac{1}{8}$07, meaning that these bonds pay an annual interest of 8 1/8 percent (the coupon) on their face value and that their maturity (redemption) date is 2007. Next, the current yield is reported as 8.0 percent. This is simply the

**Figure 14–3** **EXCERPT FROM A BOND PRICE TABLE**

This report from *The Wall Street Journal* shows the name of the bond; the annual payment; the year in which the bond will be redeemed (that is, the year in which the company will repay that debt); the yield (that is, the annual payment per dollar of current market price); and the previous day's closing price of the bond, as well as the change in price from the day before.

SOURCE: *The Wall Street Journal*, May 26, 1993, p. C15.

| Bonds | Cur Yld | Vol | Close | Net Chg |
|---|---|---|---|---|
| ChsCp 6½09t | 6.5 | 15 | 100¼ | ... |
| CPoM 7¼12 | 7.3 | 46 | 100 | + ⅛ |
| CPoV 8⅝09 | 8.3 | 6 | 103½ | − ⅛ |
| Chvrn 9⅜16 | 8.3 | 25 | 112¾ | + ⅝ |
| Chiquta 11⅞03 | 11.6 | 42 | 102⅛ | − ½ |
| Chiquta 10½04 | 10.6 | 92 | 98⅝ | + ¼ |
| Chiquta 10¼05 | 10.7 | 177 | 96 | − ¼ |
| ChckFul 7s12 | cv | 5 | 105 | + ½ |
| ChryF 9.30s94 | 9.1 | 84 | 102 | − ⅛ |
| ChryF 13¼99 | 10.2 | 80 | 130⅛ | − ⅞ |
| ChryF 12¾99 | 10.0 | 91 | 127½ | ... |
| ChryF 8⅜97 | 8.2 | 22 | 102⅜ | + ⅛ |
| ChryF 8⅛94 | 8.0 | 30 | 101½ | + 31/32 |
| ChryF 9½94 | 9.0 | 8 | 105½ | + 1½ |
| ChryF 9½99 | 8.5 | 29 | 112 | + ⅛ |
| Chryslr 13s97 | 11.8 | 148 | 110⅜ | ... |
| Chryslr 12s15 | 11.0 | 154 | 109½ | − ⅛ |
| Chryslr 9.6s94 | 9.1 | 21 | 105 | − ¼ |
| Chryslr 10.95s17 | 9.5 | 112 | 114⅞ | − ⅛ |
| Chryslr 10.4s99 | 9.3 | 75 | 112 | + ⅛ |
| Citicp 8.45s07 | 8.2 | 65 | 103½ | + ⅞ |
| Citicp 8⅛07 | 8.0 | 20 | 101⅝ | − ⅜ |
| Citicp 6.5s98t | 6.5 | 10 | 99¾ | + ½ |
| Citicp 6½04t | 6.5 | 6 | 99⅝ | ... |
| ClrkOil 9½04 | 9.3 | 45 | 102⅜ | + ⅜ |
| ClevEl 8⅜11 | 8.1 | 2 | 103¼ | + ½ |
| ClevEl 8⅜12 | 8.2 | 70 | 102¼ | ... |
| Coastl 11¼96 | 11.2 | 25 | 100 1/32 | ... |
| Coeur 7s02 | cv | 26 | 138 | ... |
| ColeWld zr13 | ... | 1245 | 24⅝ | + ⅛ |
| v\|ColG 9s94f | ... | 9 | 104 | + ½ |
| v\|ColuG 8¾s95f | ... | 25 | 102 | + ⅝ |
| v\|ColuG 9⅛s95f | ... | 10 | 105⅛ | + ¼ |
| v\|ColuG 8⅜s96f | ... | 19 | 103½ | − ½ |
| v\|ColuG 10⅛95f | ... | 1 | 106⅝ | − 1⅜ |
| v\|ColuG 9s93f | ... | 19 | 107¾ | − ⅛ |
| v\|ColuG 10¼11f | ... | 52 | 112¾ | + 2⅜ |
| v\|ColuG 10½12f | ... | 24 | 112½ | + 1½ |
| CmwE 7⅝03J | 7.5 | 3 | 101⅞ | + ¾ |
| CmwE 8s03 | 7.8 | 1 | 103⅛ | ... |
| CmwE 8⅛07J | 7.9 | 16 | 103 | + ¼ |
| CmwE 8¼07 | 8.0 | 13 | 102½ | + ½ |
| CmwE 9⅛08 | 8.7 | 8 | 104½ | ... |
| ConrPer 6¾01 | cv | 30 | 87 | + ¼ |
| ConrPer 6½02 | cv | 33 | 88¼ | + ¼ |
| Consec 8⅛03 | 8.0 | 20 | 101½ | ... |
| CnNG 7¾94 | 7.7 | 4 | 100¼ | − 1¾ |
| CnNG 8¼cld | ... | 4 | 101 | ... |
| CnNG 7⅝97 | 7.5 | 13 | 101⅝ | ... |
| ConNG 7¼15 | cv | 66 | 117¼ | − ¾ |
| CnPw 7⅝99 | 7.6 | 20 | 100⅜ | − 1⅝ |

coupon divided by the price. Since that yield, 8.0 percent, is lower than the coupon, the bond must be selling at a price above its face value, so that the return per dollar is correspondingly lower. The remaining information in the table means the same as that reported for stock prices.

## STOCK EXCHANGES AND THEIR FUNCTIONS

The *New York Stock Exchange*—the "Big Board"—is the most prestigious stock market. Located at the beginning of Wall Street in New York City, it is "*the* establishment" of the securities industry. Only the best known and most heavily traded securities are dealt with by the New York Stock Exchange, which handles over 2000 stocks. The leading brokerage firms hold "seats" on the Stock Exchange, which enable them to trade directly on the floor of the Exchange. Altogether, the Exchange has over 600 member organizations. Seats are traded on the open market; in February of 1993, for example, a seat on the New York Stock Exchange went for $575,000.

Someone who wants to buy a stock on the New York Stock Exchange must use a broker who will deal with a firm that has a seat on the Exchange. Suppose you live in Ohio and want to buy 200 shares of General Motors. The broker you approach may be employed by a firm that holds a seat on the Exchange, or she may work through another firm that holds one. The broker who is to fill your order contacts a person called a "specialist," who works on the floor of the Exchange and who handles GM stock.

The specialist usually owns some GM stock of his own that he will offer for sale to you if no other sellers are available at the moment. Usually, in addition, a number of investors have given to the specialist limit orders offering to sell specified quantities of GM stock at specified prices. There may, for example, be one offer to sell 5000 shares at any price above $55 and another offer to sell 1200 shares at any price above $60. Similarly, the specialist is likely to have a number of limit orders to buy at various specified prices.

Your order is brought by the floor broker to the specialist, who determines a price that, in his judgment, more or less balances supply and demand as indicated by his recent sales and purchases and the limit orders in his possession. At this price the specialist will fill your order from one of the limit orders to sell (he must do so whenever possible), or he will fill it from his personal inventory of General Motors stock. The price determination process that has just been described is sometimes called "the auction market" process.

The New York Stock Exchange expedites this "auction" by using an elaborate electronic system to link member firms directly to the appropriate specialists or floor brokers. This system handles approximately 75 percent of all NYSE orders.

The New York Stock Exchange is not the only exchange on which stocks are traded. While 85 percent of stock market transactions (in dollars) are handled by the Big Board, the *American Stock Exchange,* located a few blocks away, trades many stocks that are heavily demanded but that are not exchanged in quite as large a volume as those handled by the Big Board. About 2.5 percent of the dollar volume of stock trades occurs on the American Stock Exchange. There are also *regional exchanges*—such as the Midwest, Cincinnati, Pacific Coast, Philadelphia, and Boston exchanges—which deal in many of the same stocks that are handled on the New York Stock Exchange. A good portion of the business of regional exchanges, like that of the New York Stock Exchange, is serving large "institutional" customers such as banks, insurance companies, and mutual funds. Their volume amounts to about 12.5 percent of the total stock traded.

In addition to the trading on these organized exchanges, stocks are traded on the so-called *third market*. The third market is not a public market at all. It is not a place where many buyers and sellers meet to make exchanges simultaneously. Rather, the third market is run by a number of firms, each operating more or less independently of the others. When a buyer brings an order to such a firm, the broker simply shops around by telephone, seeking to find someone to match the purchase demand with a corresponding supply offer, or the broker may buy or sell for his own account the stocks supplied or demanded by the order. Thus, in dealing on the third market, each broker does the job that is done by a specialist on one of the exchanges. Obviously, trading on the third market is a much less structured and less organized affair than it is on the exchanges.

## REGULATION OF THE STOCK MARKET

The U.S. securities markets are regulated by both the government and the industry itself. At the base of the regulatory pyramid, brokerage firms maintain compliance departments to oversee their own operations. At the next level, the New York Stock Exchange, the American Stock Exchange, and the regional exchanges are responsible for monitoring the business practices, adequacy of funding, and the compliance and integrity of their member firms. They also utilize sophisticated computer surveillance systems to scrutinize trading activity. The Securities and Exchange Commission (SEC) is the federal government agency that oversees the market's self-regulation.

As an illustration of self-imposed rules, since the October 1987 market crash, the markets have undertaken a series of steps intended to cushion such price falls. For example, the NYSE and the Chicago Mercantile Exchange adopted a series of "coordinated circuit breakers" which halt all equities trading for one hour if the Dow Jones Industrial Average falls 250 points from the previous day's close. Trading would be halted for an additional two hours if the Dow were to fall another 150 points on the same day. However, no one is sure whether these and other similar measures will prove very effective in preventing sharp drops in stock prices.

## STOCK EXCHANGES AND CORPORATE CAPITAL NEEDS

While corporations often raise the funds they need by selling stocks, they do not normally do so through any of the stock exchanges. When new stocks are offered by a company, the new issue is usually handled by a special type of bank called an *investment bank*. In contrast, the stock markets trade almost exclusively in "secondhand securities"—stocks in the hands of individuals and others who had bought them earlier and who now wish to sell them.

Thus the stock market does not provide funds to corporations that need the financing to expand their productive activities. The markets only provide money to persons who already hold stocks previously issued by the corporations.

Yet stock exchanges have two functions that are of critical importance for the financing of corporations. First, by providing a secondhand market for stocks, they make it much less risky for an individual to invest in a company. Investors know that their money is not locked in—if they need the money, they can always sell their stocks to other investors or to the "specialist" at the price the market currently offers. This reduction in risk makes it far easier for corporations to issue new stocks.

Second, the stock market determines the current price of the company's stocks. That, in turn, determines whether it will be hard or easy for a corporation to raise money by selling new stocks. For example, suppose a company initially has one million shares and wants to raise $10 million. If the price is $40 per share, an issue of 250,000 shares can bring in the required funds, leaving the original stockholders with four-fifths of the company's ownership. But if the price of the stock is only $20, then 500,000 new shares will have to be issued, cutting the original stockholders back to two-thirds of the ownership of the company. This is a less attractive proposition.

Some people believe that the price of a company's stock is closely tied to the efficiency with which its productive activities are conducted, the effectiveness with which it matches its product to consumer demands, and the diligence with which it goes after profitable innovation. In this view, those firms that can make effective use of funds because of their efficiency are precisely the corporations whose stock prices will usually be comparatively high. In this way the stock market tends to channel the economy's investment funds to those firms that can make best use of the money. In sum:

If a firm has a promising future, its stock will tend to command a high price on the stock exchanges. The high price of its stock will make it easier for it to raise capital by permitting it to amass a large amount of money through the sale of a comparatively small number of new stocks. Thus, *the stock market helps to allocate the economy's resources to those firms that can make the best use of those resources.*

However, there are others who are skeptical about the claim that the price of a company's stock is closely tied to the company's efficiency. These observers believe that the demand for stock is disproportionately influenced by short-term developments in a company's profitability and that the market pays little attention to management decisions that promote the company's long-term earnings growth. These critics sometimes suggest that the stock market is close to a gambling casino in which hunch, rumor, and superstition have a critical influence on prices (more will be said about this later in the chapter).

## THE RECENT SURGE IN TAKEOVER BATTLES

The stock market is often used by small groups of individuals or by other enterprises to buy a number of stocks in a company sufficient to give the buyers control of the target. When the purchaser is another firm, the process is referred to as a "merger" or an "acquisition." Periodically, there have been bursts of such takeover activity, with a very large rise in the number of mergers and acquisitions. In the 1980s the stock market and the managements of a number of corporations were shaken by attempts by outsider corporate "raiders" to take over firms that they did not currently control. This boom in takeovers slackened during the recession of the early 1990s, but as this book was being written, there seemed to be signs of a new upturn.

A **TAKEOVER** is the acquisition by an outside group (the raiders) of a controlling proportion of the company's stock. When the old management opposes the takeover attempt, it is called a hostile takeover attempt.

A company is said to have undergone a **takeover** when a group of financiers not currently in control of the firm buys a sufficient amount of company stock to gain control. Often, the new controlling group will simply fire the current management and substitute a new chairman, president, and other top officers.

A company becomes a tempting target for a takeover attempt if the price of its stock is very low in comparison with the value of its plant, equipment, and other assets, or when a company's earnings seem very low compared to their potential level. This may be because the firm's current management is believed not to be very competent, or perhaps because the demand for a company's stocks is inordinately influenced by short-term developments, such as low profits, say, during the past three months, even if that profit level is the result of heavy investment in plant and equipment that is likely to raise profits a few years in the future.

An attempt to acquire the company by a group unfriendly to current management is called a "hostile takeover." Naturally, current management will try to fight it off since the officers of the corporation do not like to lose their high-paying jobs. They can fight back in many ways. For example, they can try to arrange instead for a "friendly takeover" by a group of investors whom the current management likes better. Or the current management may deliberately attempt to sabotage the company—often, by selling some of its most valuable parts in order to make what is left of the firm unattractive to the group attempting the takeover. Or management may seek to bribe the takeover group to go away by offering a very high price for the stocks that this group already has managed to acquire. Indeed, takeovers are often attempted in the hope that management will be forced to offer such a bribe to those who threaten to take the company over.

In the second half of the 1980s, when a large number of takeover battles broke out, the issue received a good deal of publicity and set off a heated debate over its pros and cons.

## The Colorful Vocabulary of Takeover Battles

Here are some curious terms you are likely to run across in newspaper discussions of takeovers: ***Corporate Raiders.*** People who specialize in seeking out corporations vulnerable to takeover threats. ***Golden Parachutes.*** Contracts with the members of current management giving them large payments and/or other privileges in case they are fired. ***Greenmail.*** The high price that current management pays the attempted takeover group for its shares, to bribe it to give up its attempt. ***Junk Bonds.*** Bonds (IOUs) that are highly risky, often because they have relatively little backing in comparison with the amount borrowed. Junk bonds are often issued by a corporate raider to get the money with which to buy enough stocks of the target corporation to achieve control. ***Poison Pill.*** New stocks printed by the company that go to the company's previous stockholders, but not to the people trying to take the company over. The object is to make it necessary for the raiders to buy more stocks in order to achieve control, in the hope that it will make the takeover too expensive for the raiders. Usually, a poison pill is set up to take effect automatically when, say, some group acquires 5 percent of the company's shares. ***White Knight.*** A group that undertakes to carry out a friendly takeover at the urging of current management, in order to head off a hostile takeover.

People who argue against strong legal restrictions on takeover activity point out that it is the most effective means to rid companies of incompetent managements, and so helps to keep the economy at peak efficiency. They also argue that this activity helps "create stockholder value," that is, drive the price of an undervalued company's stock up to its true economic value.

But advocates of stricter regulations or inhibition of takeovers argue that stockholders who are innocent bystanders can be badly hurt in the process, as when management pays a large bribe to the takeover group or sells off a valuable part of the company when it should not be sold. Moreover, those seeking to buy, say, 45 percent of the company's shares will try to do so as secretly as possible, hoping to obtain the stocks cheaply. Critics claim that in the process the raiders, in effect, cheat those who sold them the stocks.

Opponents of takeovers also point out that the time taken by bright, talented people in planning and carrying out the strategies and counter strategies uses up a valuable resource that could be better used elsewhere. On this view, takeover activity absorbs some of the nation's most capable individuals in financial manipulation rather than productive and innovative activity. These critics are wrong, however, when they argue that the billions of dollars that change hands in a takeover battle tie up the nation's capital wastefully or "use up" the economy's credit supply. Little or no *real* capital (machinery, factories, and the like) is tied up in a takeover process. And the money and credit that are used are simply transferred from one group of persons to another.

Often, takeovers have been financed by "junk bonds," that is, raiders issue bonds to raise the money which they need to acquire control of the target corporation. These bonds are frequently backed only by the profits that the raiders expect to grow out of their acquisition. Such profits may arise because the new owners bring in a more efficient management, or because they sell off at a high price a valuable portion of the corporation's activities (one of its successful products, for example) which they purchased cheaply because the corporation's stock price was low before the takeover.

Junk bonds backed only by such earnings prospects after the takeover are considered risky because of the danger that those promised profits may never materialize. A takeover financed in this way is called a "leveraged buyout" because the raider risks little of his or her own money in the process. Instead, the raider's limited resources are levered upward with the aid of other people's money—the money supplied by the junk bond purchasers. Critics of the process also note that it leaves the firm saddled with a heavy debt—its obligation to the junk bonds' purchasers.

## THE ISSUE OF SPECULATION

Individuals who engage in **SPECULATION** deliberately invest in risky assets, hoping to obtain a profit from the expected changes in the prices of these assets.

Dealings in securities are often viewed with hostility and suspicion because they are thought to be an instrument of **speculation** (see the discussion in *Macroeconomics*, Chapter 19). When something goes wrong in the market, say, when there is a sudden fall in prices, *speculators* are often blamed. The word "speculators" is used by editorial writers as a term of strong disapproval, implying that those who engage in the activity are parasites who produce no benefits for society and often do it considerable harm.

Economists disagree vehemently with this judgment. They say that speculators perform two vital economic functions:

1. They sell *protection from risk* to other people, much as a fire insurance policy sells protection from risk to a home owner.
2. They help to smooth out price fluctuations by purchasing items when they are abundant (and cheap) and holding them and reselling them when they are scarce (and expensive). In that way, they play a vital economic role in helping to alleviate and even prevent shortages.

Some examples from outside the securities markets will make the role of speculators clear. A ticket broker attends a preview of a new musical comedy and suspects that it is likely to be a hit. He decides to speculate by buying a large block of tickets for future performances. In that way he takes over part of the producer's risk, for the producer now has some hard cash and has reduced her inventory of risky tickets. If the show opens and is a flop, the broker will be stuck with the tickets. If it is a hit, he can sell them at a premium, if the law allows (and be denounced as a speculator or a "scalper").

Similarly, speculators enable farmers or producers of metals and other commodities whose future price is uncertain to get rid of their risk. A farmer who has planted a large crop but who fears its price may fall before harvest time can protect himself by signing a contract for future delivery at an agreed-upon price at which the speculator will purchase the crop when it comes in. In that case, if the price happens to fall, it is the speculator and not the farmer who will suffer the loss. Of course, if the price happens to rise, the speculator will reap the gain—that is the nature of risk bearing. The speculator who has agreed to buy the crop at the preset price, regardless of market conditions at the time the sale takes place, has, in effect, sold an insurance policy to the farmer. Surely this is a useful function.

The second role of speculators is perhaps even more important; in effect, they accumulate and store goods in periods of abundance and make goods available in periods of scarcity. Suppose the speculator has reason to suspect that next year's crop of a storable commodity will not be nearly as abundant as this year's. She will buy some now, when it is cheap, for resale when it becomes scarce and expensive. In the process, she will smooth out the swing in prices by adding her purchases to the total market demand in the period of low prices (which tends to bring the price up), and bringing in her supplies during the period of high prices (which tends to push the price down).[3]

Thus, the successful speculator will help to relieve matters during periods of extreme shortage. There are cases in which she literally helps to relieve famine by releasing the supplies she has deliberately hoarded for such an occasion. Of course, she is cursed for the high prices she charges on such occasions. But those who curse her do not understand that prices might have been even higher if the speculator's foresight and avid pursuit of profit had not provided for the emergency. On the securities market, famine and severe shortages are not an issue, but the fact remains that successful speculators tend to reduce price fluctuations by increasing demand for stocks when prices are low and contributing to supply when prices are high.

---

[3]For a diagrammatic analysis of this role of speculation, see Review Question 7 at the end of the chapter.

Far from aggravating instability and fluctuations, speculators work as hard as they can to iron out fluctuations by buying when prices are low and selling when prices are high, for that is how they make their profits.

## STOCK PRICES AS RANDOM WALKS

The beginning of this chapter cited evidence that the best professional securities analysts have a forecasting record so miserable that investors may do as well predicting earnings by hunch, superstition, or any purely random process as they would by following professional advice. (See the box, opposite). Similarly, it has been said that an investor is well advised to pick stocks by throwing darts at the stock market page—since it is far cheaper to buy a set of darts than to obtain the apparently useless advice of a professional analyst. Indeed, there have been at least two experiments, one by a U.S. senator and one by *Forbes* magazine, in which stocks picked by dart throwing actually outperformed the mutual funds, whose stocks are selected by the experts. Does this mean that analysts are incompetent people who do not know what they are doing? Not at all. Rather, there is fairly strong evidence that they have undertaken a task that is basically impossible.

How can this be so? The answer is that to make a good forecast of any variable—GDP, population, or fuel usage—there must be something in the past whose behavior is closely related to the future behavior of the variable whose path we wish to predict. If a 10 percent rise in this year's consumption always produces a 5 percent rise in next year's GDP, this fact can help us predict future GDP on the basis of current observations. But if we want to forecast the future of a variable whose behavior is completely unrelated to the behavior of *any* current or past variable, there is no objective evidence that can help us make that forecast. Throwing darts or gazing into a crystal ball is no less effective than analysts' calculations.

The time path of a variable such as the price of a stock is said to constitute a **RANDOM WALK** if its magnitude in one period (say, May 2, 1994) is equal to its value in the preceding period (May 1, 1994) plus a completely random number. That is: Price on May 2, 1994 = Price on May 1, 1994 + Random number where the random number (positive or negative) might be obtained by a roll of dice or some such procedure.

There is a mass of statistical evidence that the behavior of stock prices is largely unpredictable. In other words, the behavior of stock prices is essentially random; the paths they follow are what statisticians call **random walks**. A random walk is like the path followed by a drunk. All we know about his position after his next step is that it will be given by his current position plus whatever random direction his next haphazard step will carry him. The relevant feature of randomness, for our purposes, is that it is by nature unpredictable, which is just what the word *random* means.

If the evidence that stock prices approximate a random walk stands up to research in the future as it has so far, it is easy enough to understand why stock market predictions are as poor as they are. The analysts are trying to forecast behavior that is basically random; in effect, they are trying to predict the unpredictable.

Two questions remain. First, does the evidence that stock prices follow a random walk mean that investment in stocks is a pure gamble and never worthwhile? And, second, how does one explain the random behavior of stock prices?

To answer the first question, it is false to conclude that investment in stocks is generally not worthwhile. The statistical evidence is that, over the long run, stock prices *as a whole* have had a fairly marked upward trend, perhaps reflecting the long-term growth of the economy. Evidence *does* indicate that stock prices are likely to rise if one waits long enough. Thus, the random walk does not

## *Football and Financial Forecasting*

The following excerpt from a column in the business section of *The New York Times* suggests some of the gimmicks stock market analysts turn to in a desperate effort to predict stock prices.

The stock market verdict could yet change. But right now it looks as if Buffalo can confound the football forecasters and finally win the Super Bowl on its third try.

That prediction is based on a theory of forecasting football's biggest game by looking at the performance of the Dow Jones industrial average during the final weeks of the football season.

The indicator, first disclosed in this column four years ago, had correctly forecast 12 of the 14 previous Super Bowls up till then. Since then, it has been correct in three out of four years, raising its long-term record to 15 of the last 18 years—an 83 percent success rate.

The indicator predicts that if the Dow is higher at the time of the Super Bowl than it was at the end of November, then the team from the city whose name is later in the alphabet will win. This year, Dallas would be that team.

But the Dow ended November at 3,305.16, or 30.25 points higher than it closed yesterday, when it rose 3.79 points, to 3,274.91. Unless it rallies by the end of next week, Buffalo would seem likely to win the game, since a lower Dow indicates a victory by the team whose name appears first, alphabetically.*

Despite its impressive record, and perhaps because of its total implausibility, the theory does not seem to have developed many followers among those who bet on football games. That is in contrast to the other Super Bowl indicator, which uses the game's result to forecast the stock market for the next year.

This indicator, one of the most widely cited on Wall Street, has an even more impressive record, thanks in part to judicious changing of the rules when needed. It forecasts that if the Super Bowl is won by a team from the old American Football League, like Buffalo, the stock market will decline over the following year. But if the victor is a team that was part of the National Football League before the merger, then share prices will rise.

Last year's victory by the Washington Redskins, itself correctly forecast by a rising stock market coming into the game, was in turn interpreted as a sign of a rising stock market. It looks as if that indicator will work again, although it is not a sure thing. At the time of last year's Super Bowl, the Dow stood at 3,232.78, or 42.13 points below the current level. If the Dow stays above that level through the end of next week, the game will have correctly forecast the market every year except 1970, 1987, and 1990.

Some compilers of the Super Bowl theory dispute that 1987 was a failure. By using full-year numbers, they say, the Giants' victory forecast a rising year for the Dow, and it was indeed up for the year. The trouble with this interpretation is that all of the year's stock market gain came in January before the game was played. The minimum rule for any indicator is that it should forecast the future, not the past, which is why this column looks at market performance between Super Bowl games.

The other theory, using the stock market to forecast the game, has worked in each of the last 18 years except in 1982, 1986, and 1990. As it happens, each of those upset games was followed, in the next 12 months, by at least one quarter in which the economy did not grow. No other year since 1982 has had that unfortunate distinction.

Does this mean that the stock market, combined with the football game, can forecast the economy?

Or is all of this going far too far?

SOURCE: Floyd Norris, "Buffalo Fans Can Take Comfort from a Bearish Trend in Stocks" *Market Place, The New York Times,* January 19, 1993, p. D8.

*In fact, Dallas won. Forecasting is hazardous!

proceed in just any direction—rather, it represents a set of erratic movements *around a basic upward trend in stock prices.*

Moreover, it is not in the *overall* level of stock prices that the most pertinent random walk occurs, but in the performance of one company's stock compared with another's. For this reason professional advice may be able to predict that investment in the stock market is likely to be a good thing over the long haul. But, if the random walk evidence is valid, there is no way professionals can tell us which of the available stocks is most likely to go up—that is, which combination of stocks is best for the investor to buy.

The only appropriate answer to the second question is that no one is sure of the explanation. There are two widely offered hypotheses—each virtually the opposite of the other. The first asserts that stock prices are random because clever professional speculators are able to foresee almost perfectly every influence that is *not* random. For example, suppose a change occurs that makes the probable earnings of some company higher than had previously been expected. Then, according to this view, the professionals will instantly become aware of this change and immediately buy enough to raise the price of the stock accordingly. Then, the only thing for that stock price to do between this year and next is wander randomly, because the professionals cannot predict random movements, and hence cannot force current stock prices to anticipate them.

The other explanation of random behavior of stock prices is at the opposite pole from the view that all nonrandom movements are wiped out by supersmart professionals. This view holds that people who buy and sell stocks have learned that they cannot predict future stock prices. As a result they react to any signal, however irrational and irrelevant it appears. If the president catches cold, stock prices fall. If an astronaut's venture is successful, prices go up. For, according to this view, investors are, in the last analysis, trying to predict not the prospects of the economy or of the company whose shares they buy, but the supply and demand behavior of other investors, which will ultimately determine the course of stock prices. Since all investors are equally in the dark, their groping can only

result in the randomness that we observe. The classic statement of this view of stock market behavior was provided by Lord Keynes, a successful professional speculator himself:

> *Professional investment may be likened to those newspaper competitions in which the competitors have to pick out the six prettiest faces from a hundred photographs, the prize being awarded to the competitor whose choice most nearly corresponds to the average preferences of the competitors as a whole; so that each competitor has to pick not those faces which he himself finds prettiest, but those which he thinks likeliest to catch the fancy of the other competitors, all of whom are looking at the problem from the same point of view. It is not a case of choosing those which, to the best of one's judgment, are really the prettiest, nor even those which average opinion genuinely thinks the prettiest. We have reached the third degree where we devote our intelligences to anticipating what average opinion expects the average opinion to be. And there are some, I believe, who practice the fourth, fifth and higher degrees.*[4]

This may help to explain the impressive rise of the stock market from a Dow Jones index of 800 in 1982 to 2700 in 1987, its 700-point fall in two consecutive trading days in October 1987, and its several sharp ups and downs since then.

## Summary

1. The three basic types of firms are **corporations, partnerships**, and individual **proprietorships**. Most U.S. firms are individual proprietorships, but most U.S. manufactured goods are produced by corporations.
2. Individual proprietorships and partnerships have tax advantages over corporations. But corporate investors have greater protection from risk because they have ***limited liability***—they cannot be asked to pay more than they have invested in the firm.
3. Higher taxation of corporate earnings tends to limit the things in which corporations can invest and may lead to inefficiency in resource allocation.
4. Corporations finance their activities mostly by **plowback** (that is, by retaining part of their earnings and putting it back into the company) or by the sale of **stocks** and **bonds**.
5. A stock is a share in the ownership of the company. A bond is an IOU by a company for money lent to it by the bondholder. Many observers argue that the purchase of a stock also really amounts to a loan to the company—a loan that is riskier than the purchase of a bond.
6. If interest rates rise, bond prices will fall. In other words, if some bond amounts to a contract to pay 8 percent and the market interest rate goes up to 10 percent, people will no longer be willing to pay the old price for that bond.
7. If stock prices correctly reflect the future prospects of different companies, promising firms are helped to raise money because they are able to sell each stock they issue at favorable prices.
8. Bonds are relatively risky for the firms that issue them, but they are fairly safe for their buyers, because they are a commitment by the firm to pay a fixed annual amount to the bondholder whether or not the company made money that year. But stocks, which do not promise any fixed payment, are relatively safe for the company and risky for their owner.
9. A portfolio is a collection of stocks, bonds, and other assets of a single owner. The greater the number and variety of securities and other assets it contains, the less risky it is.
10. A corporation is said to be taken over when an outside group buys enough stocks to get control of the firm's decisions. **Takeovers** are a useful way to get rid of incompetent managements and to force other managements to be efficient. However the process is costly and leads to wasteful defensive and offensive activities.
11. **Speculation** affects stock market prices, but (contrary to what is widely assumed) there is reason to believe that speculation actually *reduces* the frequency and size of price fluctuations. Speculators are also useful to the economy because they undertake risks that others wish to avoid, thereby, in effect, providing others with insurance against risk.
12. Statistical evidence indicates that individual stock prices behave randomly.

[4]John Maynard Keynes, *The General Theory of Employment, Interest, and Money* (New York: Harcourt Brace Jovanovich, 1936), page 156.

## Key Concepts and Terms

Proprietorship
Unlimited liability
Partnership
Corporation
Limited liability
Double taxation
Limited partnership
Plowback or retained earnings
Common stock
Bond
Portfolio diversification
Stock exchanges
Takeovers
Speculation
Random walk

## Questions for Review

1. Why would it be difficult to run AT&T as a partnership or an individual proprietorship?
2. Do you think it is fair to tax a corporation more than a partnership doing the same amount of business? Why or why not?
3. If you hold shares in a corporation and management decides to plow back the company's earnings some year instead of paying dividends, what are the advantages and disadvantages to you?
4. Suppose interest rates are 8 percent in the economy and a safe bond promises to pay $4 a year in interest forever. What do you think the price of the bond will be? Why?
5. Suppose in the economy in the previous example, interest rates suddenly fall to 4 percent. What will happen to the price of the bond that pays $4 per year?
6. If you want to buy a stock, when might it be to your advantage to buy it using a market order? When will it pay to use a limit order?
7. Show in diagrams that if a speculator were to buy when price is high and sell when price is low he would increase price fluctuations. Why would it be in his best interest *not* to do so? (*Hint*: Draw two supply–demand diagrams, one for the high-price period and one for the low-price period. How would the speculator's activities affect these diagrams?)
8. If stock prices really are a random walk, can you nevertheless think of good reasons for getting professional advice before investing?
9. Hostile takeovers often end up in court when managements attempt to block them and raiders accuse management of selfishly sacrificing the interests of stockholders. The courts often look askance at "coercive" offers by raiders—an offer to buy, say, 20 percent of the company's stock by a certain date, from the first stockholders who offer to sell. By contrast, they take a more favorable attitude toward "noncoercive" offers to buy any and all stocks supplied to the raider at an announced price. Do you think the courts are right to reject "coercive offers" but prevent management from blocking "noncoercive" offers? Why?
10. In "program trading," computers decide when to buy or sell stocks on behalf of large institutional investors, and carry out those transactions with electronic speed. Critics claim that this is a major reason stock prices rose and fell sharply in the 1980s. Is this plausible? What other influences may have been important?

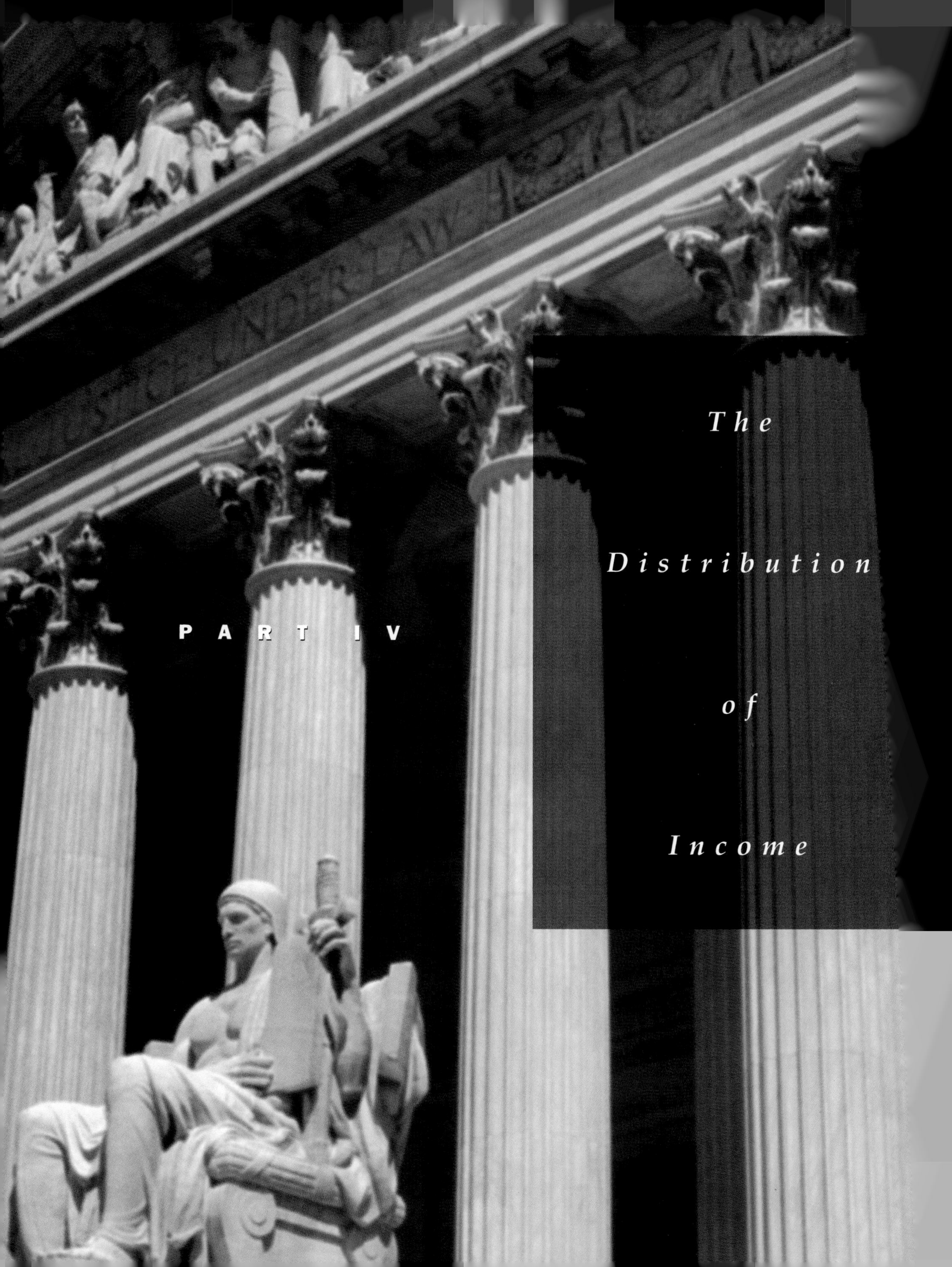

# PART IV

# The Distribution of Income

# PRICING THE FACTORS OF PRODUCTION

*Rent is that portion of the produce of the earth which is paid to the landlord for use of the original and indestructible powers of the soil.*

**DAVID RICARDO**

Chapter 13 mentioned that the market mechanism cannot be counted on to distribute income in accord with ethical notions of "fairness" or "justice," and listed this as one of the market's shortcomings. But there is much more to be said about how income is distributed in a market economy and about how governments interfere with this process. These are the subjects of Part 4. ¶ The broad outlines of how the market mechanism distributes income are familiar to all of us. Each person owns some **factors of production**—the inputs used in the production process. Many of us have only our own labor; but some of us also have funds that we can lend, land that we can rent, or natural resources that we can sell. These factors are sold on markets at prices determined by supply and demand. So the distribution of income in a market economy is determined by the level of employment of the factors of production and by their prices. For example, if wages are rather high and are fairly equal among workers, and if unemployment is low, then few people will be poor. But if wages are low and unequal and unemployment is high, then many people will be poor.

**ENTREPRENEURSHIP** is the act of starting new firms, introducing new products and technological innovations, and, in general, taking the risks that are necessary in seeking out business opportunities.

For purposes of discussion, the factors of production may be grouped into five broad categories: land, labor, capital, exhaustible natural resources, and a rather mysterious input called **entrepreneurship**. Labor is important enough to merit a full chapter (which follows this one), and exhaustible natural resources will be discussed in Chapter 21. Here we will study the payments made for the use of the other three factors: the interest paid to capital, the rent of land, and the profits earned by entrepreneurs.

This chapter focuses on the *theories* of interest, rents, and profits. But it is useful first to have a brief look at how much these factors earn in *reality* because the numbers are so very different from what the distribution of income among capitalists, landlords, and workers is commonly believed to be. According to U.S. data for 1989, interest payments accounted for about 10 percent of national income; land rents are minuscule, accounting for less than $\frac{1}{2}$ a percent; corporate profits for about 7 percent; and earnings of other proprietors for about 9 percent. In total, the returns to all the factors of production dealt with in this chapter amounted to about one-quarter of national income. Where did the rest of it go? The answer is that almost three-quarters of national income was composed of employee compensation—wages and salaries. The huge share of labor in national income is one of the reasons why the next chapter is devoted entirely to this subject.

The distribution of income is perhaps the one area in economics in which any one individual's interests almost inevitably conflict with someone else's. By definition, if a larger share of the total income is distributed to me, a smaller share will be left for you. It is also a topic about which emotions run high and the facts or the logic of the issues are often ignored. In this chapter we will encounter examples of serious misunderstandings about the facts: misapprehensions about the true magnitudes of interest rates and profits, people's unwillingness to face up to the consequences of rent controls, and so forth.

## THE PRINCIPLE OF MARGINAL PRODUCTIVITY

The **MARGINAL PHYSICAL PRODUCT** (MPP) of an input is the increase in output that results from a one-unit increase in the use of the input, holding the amounts of all other inputs constant.

The **MARGINAL REVENUE PRODUCT** (MRP) of an input is the money value of the additional sales that a firm obtains by selling the marginal physical product of that input.

By now it will not surprise you to learn that factor prices are analyzed in terms of supply and demand. The supply sides of the markets for the various factors differ enormously from one another, which is why each factor market must be considered separately. But one basic principle, the **principle of marginal productivity**, has been used to explain the *demand* for every input. Before restating the principle, it will be useful to recall two concepts that were introduced in Chapter 6: **marginal physical product** (MPP) and **marginal revenue product** (MRP).[1]

Table 15–1 helps us review these two concepts by recalling the example of Ivan and Ivana who had to decide how much corn to feed their chickens. The marginal *physical* product (MPP) column tells us how many additional kilos of chicken each additional bag of corn will yield. For example, according to the table, the fourth bag increases output by 17 kilos. The marginal *revenue* product (MRP) column tells us how many dollars this marginal physical product is worth. In the example in the table, chicken is assumed always to sell at $1.45 per kilo, so the marginal revenue product of the fourth bag of corn is $1.45 per kilo times 17 kilos, or $24.65 (last column of the table).

[1]To review these concepts see Chapter 6, pages 132–37.

Table 15–1 IVANA AND IVAN'S SCHEDULES FOR TOTAL PHYSICAL PRODUCT, MARGINAL PHYSICAL PRODUCT, AVERAGE PHYSICAL PRODUCT, AND MARGINAL REVENUE PRODUCT OF CORN

| INPUT (bags of corn) | TOTAL PHYSICAL PRODUCT (chicken output in kilos) | MARGINAL PHYSICAL PRODUCT (kilos per bag) | AVERAGE PHYSICAL PRODUCT (kilos per bag) | MARGINAL REVENUE PRODUCT (dollars per bag) |
|---|---|---|---|---|
| 0 | 0 | — | — | — |
| 1 | 7 | 7 | 7 | 10.15 |
| 2 | 18 | 11 | 9 | 15.95 |
| 3 | 33 | 15 | 11 | 21.75 |
| 4 | 50 | 17 | 12.5 | 24.65 |
| 5 | 65 | 15 | 13 | 21.75 |
| 6 | 78 | 13 | 13 | 18.85 |
| 7 | 87.5 | 9.5 | 12.5 | 13.78 |
| 8 | 92 | 4.5 | 11.5 | 6.53 |
| 9 | 92.7 | 0.7 | 10.3 | 1.02 |
| 10 | 90 | –2.7 | 9 | –3.92 |
| 11 | 82.5 | –7.5 | 7.5 | –10.88 |
| 12 | 72 | –10.5 | 6 | –15.23 |

The marginal productivity principle states that when factor markets are competitive it always pays a profit-maximizing firm to hire the quantity of any input that makes the marginal revenue product equal to the price of the input.

The basic logic behind the principle is both simple and powerful. If the input's marginal revenue product is, for example, greater than its price, it will pay the firm to hire more of it because an additional unit of input brings the firm an addition to revenue that exceeds its cost. Consequently, if MRP > input price, then the firm should expand the quantity of the input it purchases. It should increase the quantity purchased up to the amount at which diminishing returns reduce the MRP to the level of the input's price. By similar reasoning, if MRP is less than price, then the firm is using too much of the input. Let us use Table 15–1 to demonstrate how the marginal productivity principle works.

Suppose Ivan and Ivana were using four bags of corn at a cost of $10 per bag. Since the table tells us that a fifth bag has a marginal revenue product of 21.75, the firm could obviously add $11.75 to its profit by buying a fifth bag of corn. Only when the firm has used so much corn that (because of diminishing returns) the MRP of still another bag is less than $10 does it pay to stop expanding the use of corn. In this example, about seven bags is the optimal amount to use each week, because an eighth bag brings in a marginal revenue product of only $6.53, which is less that the $10 cost of buying the bag.

One corollary of the principle of marginal productivity is obvious: the quantity of the input demanded depends on its price. The lower the price of corn, the more it pays the farm to buy. In our example, it pays Ivana and Ivan to use between seven and eight bags when the price per bag is $10. But if corn were more expensive, say $20 per bag, that high price would exceed the value of the marginal product of either the sixth or seventh bag. It would, therefore, pay the firm to stop at five bags of corn. Thus, *marginal productivity analysis shows that the quantity demanded of an input normally declines as the price of the input rises*. The "law" of demand applies to inputs just as it applies to consumer goods.

## THE DERIVED DEMAND CURVE FOR AN INPUT

We can, in fact, be much more specific than this, for the marginal productivity principle tells us precisely how the demand curve for any input is derived from its marginal revenue product (MRP) curve.

Figure 15–1 presents graphically the MRP schedule from Table 15–1. Recall that, according to the marginal productivity principle, the quantity demanded of the input is determined by setting MRP equal to the input's price. Figure 15–1 considers three different possible prices for a bag of corn: $20, $15, and $10. At a price of $20 per bag, we see that the quantity demanded is about 5.6 bags of corn per week (point A) because at that point MRP = price. Similarly, if the price of corn drops to $15 per bag, quantity demanded rises to about 6.8 bags per week (point B). Finally, should the price fall all the way to $10 per bag, the quantity demanded would be about 7.5 bags per week (point C). Points A, B, and C are therefore three points on the demand curve for corn. By repeating this exercise for any other price, we learn that:

The demand curve for any input is the downward-sloping portion of its marginal revenue product curve.

Why is the demand curve restricted to only the *downward-sloping portion* of the MRP curve? The logic of the marginal productivity principle dictates this. For example, if the price of corn were $15 per bag, Figure 15–1 shows that there are two input quantities for which MRP = P: (approximately) two bags (point D) and 6.8 bags (point B). But point D cannot be the optimal stopping point because the MRP of a third bag ($21.75) is greater than the cost of the third bag ($15), so that the firm makes more money by expanding its input use beyond two bags per week. A similar profitable opportunity for expansion occurs any time the MRP curve slopes upward at the current price, since that means that an increase in the quantity of input used by the firm will raise MRP above the input's price.

*Figure* **15–1** **A MARGINAL REVENUE PRODUCT SCHEDULE**

This diagram depicts the data in Table 15–1, which show how the marginal revenue product (MRP) of corn first rises and then declines as more and more corn is used. Since the optimal purchase rule is to keep increasing the use of corn until its MRP is reduced to the price of corn, the downward sloping portion of the MRP curve is Ivana and Ivan's demand curve for corn.

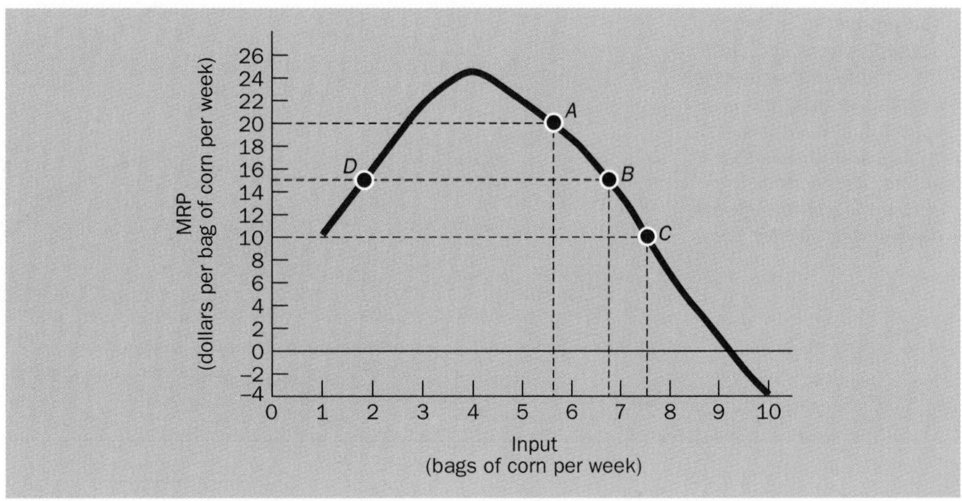

It follows that a profit-maximizing firm will always demand an input quantity that is in the range where MRP is diminishing.

The demand for corn or labor (or for any other input) is called a **derived demand** because it is derived from the underlying demand for the final product (chicken in this case). For example, suppose that a surge in demand drove the price of chicken to \$2.90 per kilo. Then, at each level of corn usage, the marginal revenue product would be twice as large as when chicken fetched only \$1.45 per kilo. This is shown in Figure 15–2 as an upward shift of the (derived) demand curve for corn, from $D_0D_0$ to $D_1D_1$.[2] We conclude that, in general:

An outward shift in the demand curve for any commodity causes an outward shift of the derived demand curve for all factors utilized in the production of that commodity.

Conversely, an inward shift in the demand curve for a commodity leads to inward shifts in the demand curves for factors used in producing that commodity.

This completes our discussion of the *demand* side of the analysis of input pricing. Perhaps the most noteworthy feature of the discussion is its reliance on the same marginal productivity principle as its foundation for the demand schedule for each and every type of input. In particular, as we will see in the next chapter, the marginal productivity principle serves us effectively as the basis for the determination of the demand for that crucial input—labor—the input whose financial reward plays so important a role in an economy's standard of living. On the demand side, apparently, one analysis fits all.

Things are very different when we turn to the supply side, however. Here we must deal with each of the main factors of production individually because each involves a somewhat different story. This must be done in order to see how their earnings are determined by the interaction of demand *and* supply. We begin with *interest payments*, the return on loans of money.

**Figure 15–2 A SHIFT IN THE DEMAND CURVE FOR CORN**

If the price of chicken goes up, the corn marginal *revenue* product curve shifts upward— from $D_0D_0$ to $D_1D_1$ in the diagram—even though the marginal *physical* product curve has not changed. In this sense *a greater demand for chicken leads to a greater derived demand for corn.*

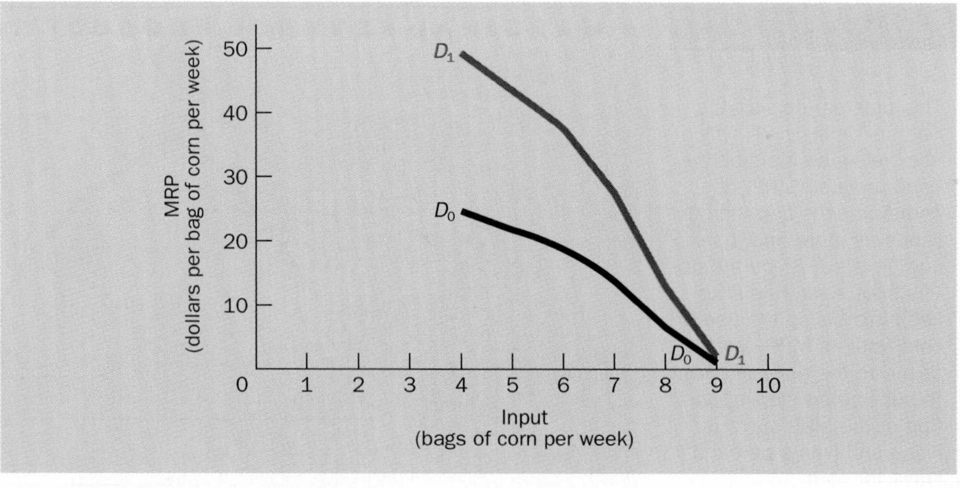


[2]To make the diagram easier to read, the (irrelevant) upward-sloping portion of each curve has been omitted.

## THE ISSUE OF USURY LAWS: ARE INTEREST RATES TOO HIGH?

The rate of interest is the price at which funds can be rented (borrowed). And, just like other factor prices, the rate of interest is determined by supply and demand. However, as is typical where distribution issues arise, people have often been dissatisfied with the workings of the market in the determination of interest rates. Fears that interest rates, if left unregulated, would climb to exorbitant levels have made usury laws quite popular in many times and places. In the middle ages the influence of the church led to total prohibition of interest payments in much of Europe, and attempts to control interest payments occurred far earlier than that. In some parts of the United States usury laws continued to govern maximum rates on consumer loans, home mortgages, and the like, at least until a few years ago.

However, usury laws are often evaded by unscrupulous lenders who charge interest rates even higher than the free market equilibrium rate—including a generous supplement to compensate them for the risk of being caught evading the law. Even when they are effective, usury laws interfere with the operation of supply and demand and, as will be demonstrated presently, they are often harmful to economic efficiency. That is not meant to say that concerns over high interest rates are always irrational. It may, for example, be appropriate to seek to combat homelessness by making financing of housing cheaper for poor people. But there is a difference between doing so by paying part of the necessary cost, for example, through government subsidies of interest on housing for the poor, and the alternative of declaring high costs illegal, thus pretending that those costs can simply be legislated away, which is what a usury ceiling tries to do.[3]

Whether a usury ceiling will or will not be effective depends on what the equilibrium rate of interest would have been in a free market. For example, a ceiling of 15 percent annual interest on consumer loans is quite irrelevant if the free-market equilibrium is 10 percent, but it can have important effects if the free-market rate is 20 percent. To see why this is so, we turn to the market determination of interest rates through the forces of supply and demand. But, first, it is necessary to define a few pertinent terms.

## INVESTMENT, CAPITAL, AND INTEREST

**INVESTMENT** is the *flow* of resources into the production of new capital. It is the labor, steel, and other inputs devoted to the *construction* of factories, warehouses, railroads, and other pieces of capital during some period of time.

**CAPITAL** refers to an inventory (*a stock*) of plant, equipment, and other productive resources held by a business firm, an individual, or some other organization.

There are many ways in which funds are loaned (that is, rented to users): home mortgages, corporation or government bonds, consumer credit, and so on. On the demand side of these credit markets are borrowers—people or institutions that, for one reason or another, wish to spend more than they currently have. In business, loans are used primarily to finance investment. To the business executive who "rents" (borrows) funds in order to finance an **investment** and pays interest in return, the funds really represent an intermediate step toward the acquisition of the machines, buildings, inventories, and other forms of physical **capital** that the firm will purchase.

[3] The law also sometimes concerns itself with discrimination in lending against women or members of ethnic minority groups. There is strong evidence suggesting sex and race discrimination in lending. For example, married women have been denied loans without the explicit permission of their husbands, even where the women had substantial independent incomes.

Though the words "investment" and "capital" are often used interchangeably in everyday parlance, it is important to keep the distinction in mind. The relation between investment and capital has an analogy in the filling of a bathtub: the accumulated water in the tub is analogous to the *stock* of capital, while the flow of water from the tap (which adds to the tub's water) is like the *flow* of investment. Just as the tap must be turned on in order for more water to accumulate, the capital stock increases only when there is investment. If investment ceases, the capital stock stops growing. Notice that when investment is *zero*, the capital stock *remains constant*; it does not fall to zero any more than a bathtub suddenly becomes empty when you shut the tap.

The process of building up capital by investing and then using this capital in production can be divided into five steps, which are listed below and summed up in Figure 15–3.

**Step 1.** The firm decides to enlarge its stock of capital.

**Step 2.** It raises the funds with which to finance its expansion either by getting the money from outside sources, such as banks, or by holding on to part of its earnings rather than paying them out to the owners of the company.

**Step 3.** It uses these funds to hire the inputs, which are put to work building factories, warehouses, and the like. This step is the act of *investment*.

**Step 4.** After the investment is completed, the firm ends up with a larger stock of *capital*.

**Step 5.** The capital is used (along with other inputs) either to expand production or to reduce costs. At this point, the firm starts earning *returns* on its investment.

Notice that what the investors put into the investment process is *money*, either their own or funds they borrow from others. The funds are then transformed, in a series of steps, into a physical input suitable for use in production. If the funds are borrowed, the investors will someday return them to the lender with some

**Figure 15–3 THE INVESTMENT PRODUCTION PROCESS**

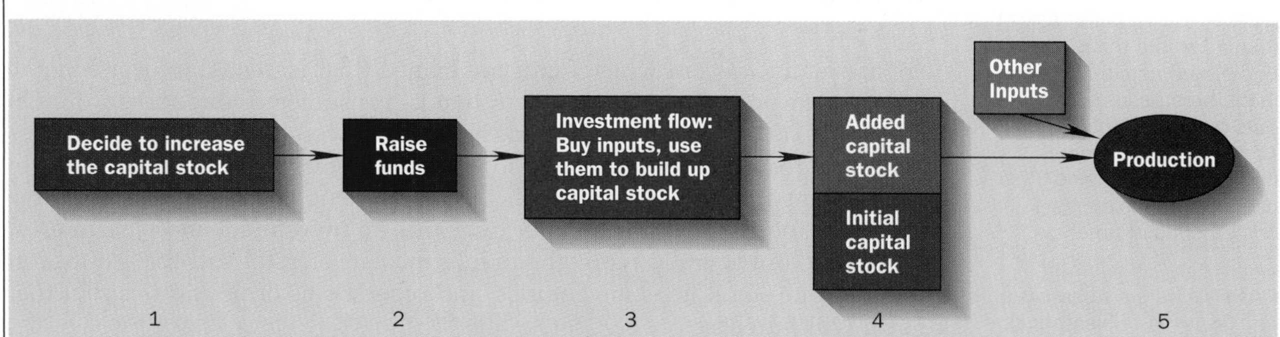


The investor (1) decides to increase the capital stock, (2) raises funds, (3) uses the funds to buy inputs that produce capital stock like machinery and factory buildings (this step is called *investment*): (4) now holds more capital than before, and (5) uses this capital and other inputs to produce goods and services.

**INTEREST** is the payment for the use of funds employed in the production of capital; it is measured as a percent per year of the value of the funds tied up in the capital.

payment for their use. This payment is called **interest**, and it is calculated as a percentage per year of the amount borrowed. For example, if the *interest rate* is 12 percent per year and $1000 is borrowed, the annual interest payment is $120.

The marginal productivity principle governs the quantity of funds demanded just as it governs the quantity of *corn* demanded for chicken feed. Specifically:

Firms will demand the quantity of borrowed funds that makes the marginal revenue product of the investment financed by the funds just equal to the interest payment charged for borrowing.

There is one noteworthy feature of capital that distinguishes it from other inputs, like corn, for example. When Ivana and Ivan feed corn to their chickens, it is used once and then it is gone. But a blast furnace, which is part of a steel company's capital, normally lasts many years. The furnace is a *durable* good; and because it is durable it contributes not only to today's production, but also to future production. This fact makes calculating the marginal revenue product more complex for a capital good than for other inputs.

To determine whether the MRP of a capital good is greater than the cost of financing it (that is, to decide whether an investment is profitable), we need a way to compare money values received at different times. To make such comparisons, economists and business people use a calculation procedure called **discounting**. Discounting is explained in detail in the appendix to this chapter, but it is not important that you master this technique in an introductory course. There are really only two important points to learn:

1. A sum of money received at a future date is worth less than the same sum of money received today.
2. This difference in values between money today and money in the future is greater when the rate of interest is higher.

It is not difficult to understand why this is so. Consider what you could do with a dollar that you received today rather than a year from today. If the annual rate of interest were 10 percent, you could lend it out (for example, by putting it in a bank account), and receive $1.10 in a year's time—your original $1 plus 10 cents interest. For this reason, money received today is worth more than the same number of dollars received later. Specifically, at a rate of interest of 10 percent per year, $1.10 to be received a year from today is equivalent to $1 of today's money. This illustrates the first of our two points.

Now suppose the annual rate of interest was 15 percent instead. In this case $1 invested today would grow to $1.15 (rather than $1.10) in a year's time, which means that $1.15 received a year from today would be equivalent to $1 received today, and so $1.10 one year in the future must now be worth less than $1 today. This illustrates the second point.

## THE MARKET DETERMINATION OF INTEREST RATES

Let us now return to the way in which interest rates are determined in the market. We are concerned about the rate of interest because it is a crucial determinant of the economy's level of investment, that is, in selecting the amount of current consumption that consumers will forgo in order to use the resources to build machines and factories that can increase the output of consumers' goods in the future. For that reason, the interest rate is crucial in determining the allocation of society's resources between present and future—an issue that we discussed in Chapter 13 (pages 319–22).

## THE DOWNWARD-SLOPING DEMAND CURVE FOR FUNDS

The two attributes of discounting discussed above are all we need to explain why the quantity of funds demanded declines when the interest rate rises, that is, why the demand curve for funds has a negative slope.

Remember that the demand for borrowed funds is a *derived demand*, derived from the desire to invest in capital goods. But part, and perhaps all, of the marginal revenue product of a machine or a factory is received in the future. Hence, the value of the MRP *in terms of today's money* shrinks as the rate of interest rises. Why? Because future returns must be *discounted more* when the rate of interest rises, for reasons just discussed. The consequence of this shrinkage is that a machine that appears to be a good investment when the rate of interest is 10 percent may look like a terrible investment when the rate of interest is 15 percent. That is, the higher the discount rate, the fewer machines a firm will demand. Thus, the demand curve for machines and other forms of capital will have a negative slope—the higher the interest rate, the smaller the quantity that firms will demand.

As the rate of interest on borrowing rises, more and more investments that previously looked profitable start to look unprofitable. The demand for borrowing for investment purposes, therefore, is lower at higher rates of interest.

It should be noted that while this analysis clearly applies to a firm's purchase of capital goods such as plant and equipment, it can also apply to the company's purchases of land and labor. Both of these are often financed by borrowed funds, and the marginal products of these inputs may accrue only months or even years after the inputs have been bought and put to work. (For example, it may take quite some time before newly-acquired agricultural land will yield a marketable crop.) For both reasons, then, a rise in the rate of interest will reduce the quantity demanded of investment goods like land and labor, just as it cuts the derived demand for investment in plant and equipment.

An example of a derived demand schedule for borrowing is given in Figure 15–4. Its negative slope illustrates the conclusion we have just stated:

The higher the interest rate, the less people and firms will want to borrow to finance their investments.

## THE SUPPLY OF FUNDS

Somewhat different relationships arise on the supply side of the market for funds—where the *lenders* are consumers, banks, and other types of business firms. Funds lent out are usually returned to the owner (with interest) only over a period of time. Loans will look better to lenders when they bear higher interest rates, so it is natural to think of the supply schedule for loans as being upward sloping—at higher rates of interest, lenders supply more funds. Such a supply schedule is shown by the curve *SS* in Figure 15–5, where we also reproduce the demand curve, *DD*, from Figure 15–4.

However, not all supply curves for funds slope uphill to the right like curve *SS*. Suppose, for example, that Melinda Martinez is saving to buy a $10,000 boat in three years, and that if she lends money out at interest in the interim, she must

**Figure 15–4** THE DERIVED DEMAND CURVE FOR LOANS

The rate of interest is the cost of a loan to the borrower. The lower the rate of interest, the more it will pay a business firm to borrow in order to finance new plant and equipment. That is why this demand curve has a negative slope.

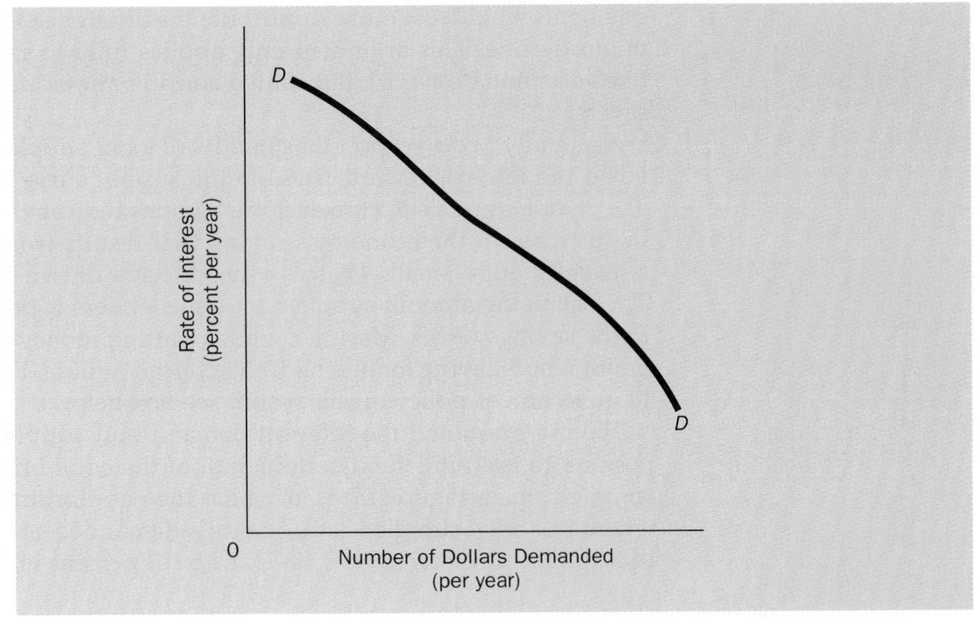


**Figure 15–5** EQUILIBRIUM IN THE MARKET FOR LOANS

Here the free-market interest rate is 12 percent. At this interest rate, the quantity of loans supplied is equal to the quantity demanded. However, if an interest-rate ceiling is imposed, say, at 8 percent, the quantity of funds supplied (point *A*) will be smaller than the quantity demanded (point *B*).

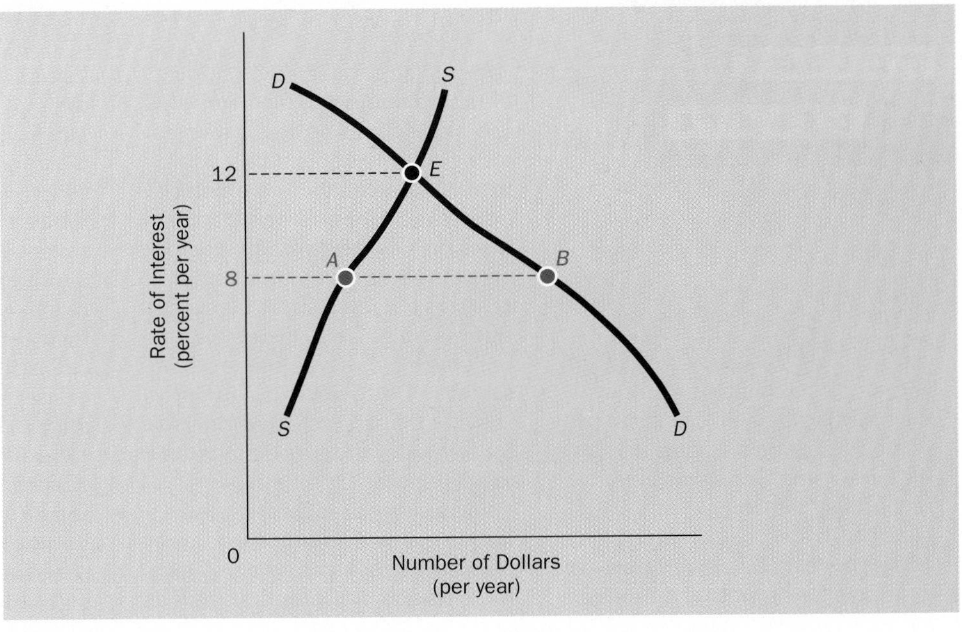

save $3000 a year to reach her goal. If interest rates were higher, she could save less than $3000 each year and still reach her $10,000 goal. (The higher interest payments would, of course, contribute the difference.) So her saving (and lending) might decline. This argument only applies fully to savers, like Martinez, with a fixed accumulation goal. But similar considerations affect the calculations of other savers.

Generally, we do expect the quantity of loans supplied to rise at least somewhat when the interest reward rises, so the supply curve will have a positive slope, like *SS* in Figure 15–5. However, for reasons indicated in the previous paragraph, the increase in the economy's saving that results from a rise in the interest rate is usually quite small. That is why we have drawn the supply curve so steep. The rise in the amount supplied by some lenders is partially offset by the decline in the savings of Ms. Martinez who is putting money away to buy a boat, or Mr. Smith who is saving for his children's college tuition. (For a noteworthy application to government policy of this result, see box below).

Having examined the relevant demand and supply curves, we are now in a position to examine the determination of the equilibrium rate of interest. This is summed up in Figure 15–5. in which the equilibrium is, as always, at point *E*, where quantity supplied and quantity demanded are equal. We conclude that the equilibrium interest rate on loans is 12 percent in the example in the graph.

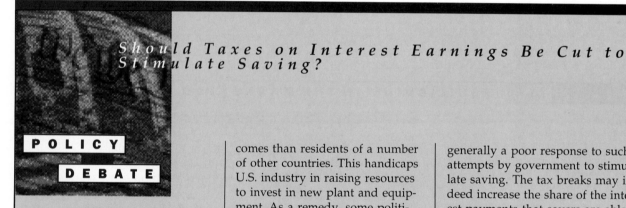

### *Should Taxes on Interest Earnings Be Cut to Stimulate Saving?*

The discussion in the text of the possibility that a rise in the interest rate will lead some people to reduce their savings has an important application for government policy. In recent years there has been widespread concern about the fact that Americans save a far smaller proportion of their incomes than residents of a number of other countries. This handicaps U.S. industry in raising resources to invest in new plant and equipment. As a remedy, some politicians have proposed reductions in taxes on interest earnings. Such a tax cut lets savers keep a larger share of the interest payments that their savings yield, thereby raising the effective interest rate on their savings. The idea behind the proposal is that an increased reward for savings will induce the public to save more.

A number of informed observers have, however, opposed this approach. As they point out, statistical evidence indicates that there is generally a poor response to such attempts by government to stimulate saving. The tax breaks may indeed increase the share of the interest payments that savers are able to keep. But that means that some savers, like Ms. Martinez and Mr. Smith, will not need to save as much as before in order to attain their future goals. So while the tax cuts will lead some people to increase their savings, they will induce a decline in the saving by some other persons. The net effect of such tax cuts may, perhaps, be some rise in the amounts saved. But the evidence indicates that this effect, at best, is usually disappointingly small.

## CEILINGS ON INTEREST RATES

Let us now assume that the preceding diagram refers to the supply of loans by banks to consumers. Consider what happens if there is a usury law that prohibits interest of more than 8 percent per annum on consumer loans. At this interest rate, the quantity supplied (point *A* in Figure 15–5) falls short of the quantity demanded (point *B*). This means that many applicants for consumer loans are being turned down even though the banks consider them to be credit-worthy.

Who generally gains and who loses from this usury law? The gainers are easiest to identify: those lucky consumers who are able to get loans at 8 percent even though they would have been willing to pay 12 percent. The law represents a windfall gain for them. The losers come on both the supply side and the demand side. First, there are the consumers who would have been willing and able to get credit at 12 percent but who are not lucky enough to get it at 8 percent. Then there are the banks (or, more accurately, bank stockholders) who could have made profitable loans at rates of up to 12 percent if there were no interest-rate ceiling.

This analysis helps explain the political popularity of usury laws. Few people sympathize with bank stockholders; indeed, it is the widespread feeling that banks are "gouging" their borrowers that provides much of the impetus for usury laws. The consumers who get loans at lower rates will, naturally, be quite pleased with the result of the law. The others, who would like to borrow at 8 percent but cannot because quantity supplied is less than quantity demanded, are quite likely to blame the bank for refusing to lend, rather than blaming the government for outlawing mutually beneficial transactions.

# THE DETERMINATION OF RENT: SIMPLE VERSION

The second main factor of production is land. Rent, the payment for the use of land, is another price which, when left to the market, often seems to settle at politically unpopular levels. In fact, rent controls are even more popular than usury ceilings. The effects of rent controls were discussed in Chapter 4 (pages 92–93), and a bit more will be said about them later in this chapter. But our main focus here is on the determination of rents in free markets.

The main special feature of the market for land occurs on the supply side. Land is one factor of production whose quantity supplied is (roughly) the same at every possible price. Indeed, the classical economists used this notion as the working definition of land. And the definition seems to fit, at least approximately. Although people may accumulate landfill, clear land, drain its swamps, fertilize it, build on it, or convert it from one use (a farm) to another (a housing development), it is difficult to change the total supply of land very much by human effort.

What does that fact tell us about the determination of land rents? Figure 15–6 helps to provide an answer. The vertical supply curve *SS* represents the fact that no matter what the level of rents, there are still 1000 acres of land in a small hamlet called Littletown. The demand curve *DD* is a typical marginal revenue product curve, predicated on the notion that the use of land, like everything else, is subject to diminishing returns. The free-market price is determined, as usual, by the intersection of the supply and demand curves. In this example, each acre of land in Littletown rents for $2000 per year. The interesting feature of this

Figure 15–6 **DETERMINATION OF LAND RENT IN LITTLETOWN**

The supply curve of land, *SS*, is vertical, meaning that 1000 acres are available in Littletown regardless of the level of rent. The demand curve for land slopes downward for the usual reasons. Equilibrium is established at point *E*, where the annual rental rate is $2000 per acre.

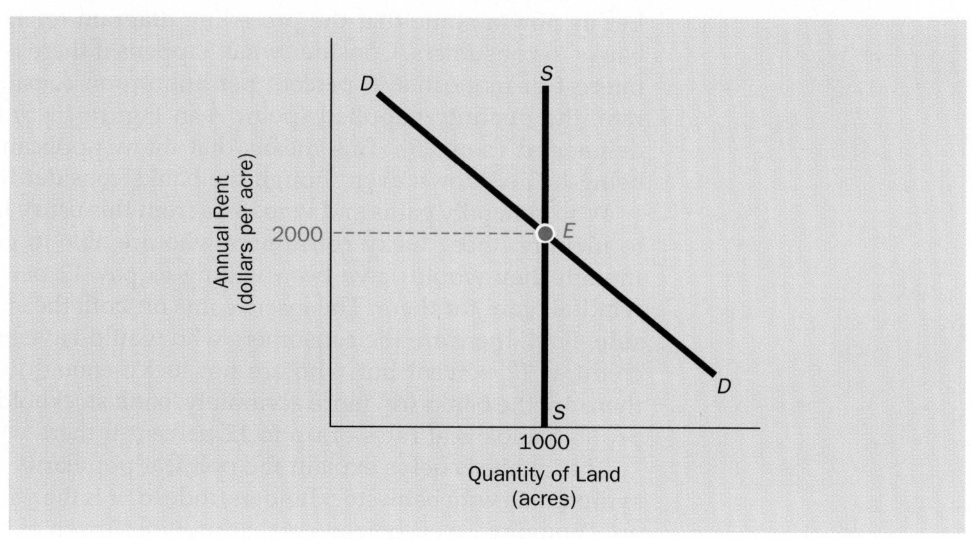


diagram is that, because quantity supplied is rigidly fixed at 1000 acres whatever the price:

The market level of rent is entirely determined by the demand side of the market.

If, for example, the relocation of a major university to Littletown attracts more people who want to live there, the *DD* curve will shift outward, as depicted in Figure 15–7. Equilibrium in the market will shift from point *E* to point *A*. There will still be only 1000 acres of land, but now each acre will command a rent of $2500 per acre. The landlords will collect more rent, though society gets no more land from the landlords in return for its additional payment.

The same process also works in reverse, however. Should the university shut its doors and the demand for land decline as a result, the landlords will suffer even though they in no way have contributed to the decline in the demand for land. (To see this, simply reverse the logic of Figure 15–7. The demand curve begins at $D_1D_1$ and shifts to $D_0D_0$.)

This discussion shows the special feature of rent that leads economists to distinguish it from payments to other factors of production: an **economic rent** is a payment for a factor of production (such as land) that does not change the amount of that factor that is supplied.

## THE RENT OF LAND: SOME COMPLICATIONS

If every parcel of land were of identical quality, this would be all there is to the theory of land rent. But, of course, plots of land do differ—in quality of soil, in topography, in access to sun and water, in proximity to marketplaces, and in other ways. The classical economists realized this, of course, and took it into account in their analysis of rent determination—a remarkable piece of economic logic formulated late in the eighteenth century and still considered valid today.

Figure 15–7

## A SHIFT IN DEMAND WITH A VERTICAL SUPPLY CURVE

Now imagine that something happens to increase the demand for land—that is, to shift the demand curve from $D_0D_0$ to $D_1D_1$. Quantity supplied cannot change, but the rental rate can, and does. In this example, the annual rental for an acre of land increases from $2000 to $2500.

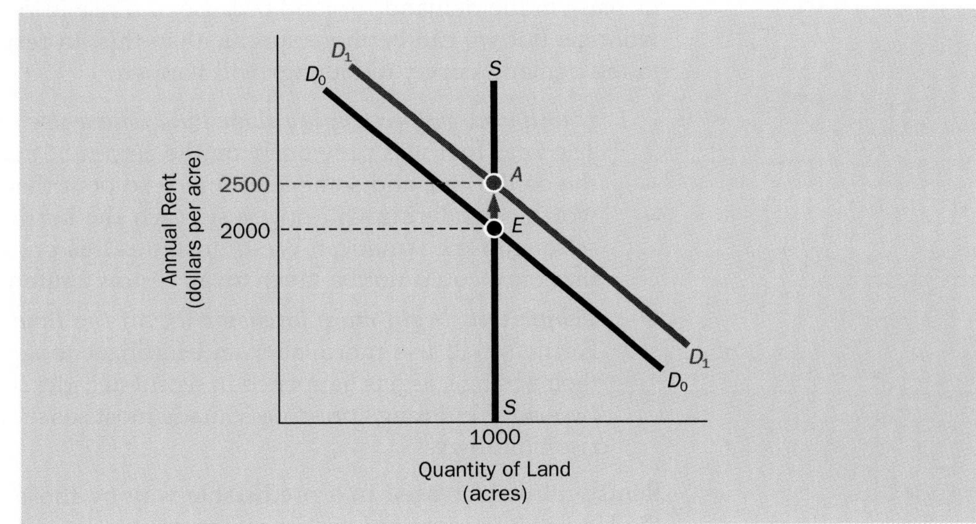


The basic notion is that capital invested on any piece of land must yield the same return as capital invested on any other piece that is actually used. Why? If it were not so, capitalists would bid against one another for the more profitable pieces of land until the rents of these parcels were driven up to a point where their advantages over other parcels had been eliminated.

Suppose that on one piece of land a given crop is produced for $160,000 per year in labor, fertilizer, fuel, and other non-land costs, while the same crop is produced for $120,000 on a second piece of land. The rent on the second parcel must be *exactly* $40,000 per year higher than the rent on the first, because otherwise production on one plot would be cheaper than on the other. If, for example, the rent difference were only $30,000 per year, it would be $10,000 cheaper to produce on the second plot of land. No one would want to rent the first plot and every grower would instead bid for the second plot. Obviously, rent on the first plot would be forced down by a lack of customers, and rent on the second would be driven up by eager bidders. These pressures would come to an end only when the rent difference reached $40,000, so that both plots became equally profitable.

Land that is just on the borderline of being used is called **MARGINAL LAND**.

At any given time, there are some pieces of land of such low quality that it does not pay to use them at all—remote deserts are a prime example. Any land that is exactly on the borderline between being used and not being used is called **marginal land**. By this definition, marginal land earns no rent because if any rent were charged for it, there would be no takers.

We now combine these two observations—that the difference between the costs of producing on any two pieces of land must equal the difference between their rents, and that zero rent is charged on marginal land—to conclude that:

Rent on any piece of land will equal the difference between the cost of producing the output on that land and the cost of producing it on marginal land.

That is, competition for the superior plots of land will permit the landlords to charge prices that capture the full advantages of their superior parcels.

A useful feature of this analysis is that it helps us to understand more completely the effects of an outward shift in the demand curve for land. Suppose there is an increase in the demand for land because of a rise in population. Naturally, rents will rise. But we can be more specific than this. In response to an outward shift in the demand curve, two things will happen:

1. ***It will now pay to employ some land whose use was formerly unprofitable.*** The land that was previously on the zero-rent margin will no longer be on the borderline, and some land that is so poor that it was formerly not even worth considering will now just reach the borderline of profitability. The settling of the American West illustrates this process quite forcefully. Land that once could not be given away is now quite valuable.
2. ***People will begin more intensive use of the land that was already in use.*** Farmers will use more labor and fertilizer to squeeze larger crops out of their acreage, as has happened in recent decades. Urban real estate on which two-story buildings previously made most sense will now be used for high-rise buildings.

Rents will be increased in a predictable way by those two developments. Since the land that is marginal *after* the change must be inferior to the land that was marginal previously, rents must rise by the difference in yields between the old and new marginal lands. Table 15–2 illustrates this point. We deal with three pieces of land: A, a very productive piece; B, a piece that was initially marginal; and C, a piece that is inferior to B but nevertheless becomes marginal when the upward shift in the demand curve for land occurs.

The crop costs $80,000 more when produced on B than on A, and $12,000 more when produced on C than on B. Suppose, initially, that demand for the crop is so low that C is unused and B is just on the margin between being used and left idle. Since B is marginal, it will yield no rent. We know that the rent on A will be equal to the $80,000 cost advantage of A over B. Now suppose demand for the crop increases enough so that plot C is just brought into use. Plot C is now marginal land, and B acquires a rent of $12,000, the cost advantage of B over C. Plot A's rent now must rise from $80,000 to $92,000, the size of its cost advantage over C, the new marginal land.

In addition to the differences in the quality of different pieces of land, there is a second factor pushing up land rents: the increased intensity of use of land that is already in cultivation. As farmers apply more fertilizer and labor to their land,

**Table 15–2 NONRENT COSTS AND RENT ON THREE PIECES OF LAND**

| TYPE OF LAND | NONLAND COST OF PRODUCING A GIVEN CROP | TOTAL RENT Before | TOTAL RENT After |
|---|---|---|---|
| A. A tract that was better than marginal before and after | $120,000 | $80,000 | $92,000 |
| B. A tract that was marginal before but is not anymore | 200,000 | 0 | 12,000 |
| C. A tract that was previously not worth using but is now marginal | 212,000 | 0 | 0 |

the marginal productivity of land increases just as factory workers become more productive when they are given better equipment. Once again, the landowner is able to capture this increase in productivity in the form of higher rents. (If you do not understand why, refer back to Figure 15–7 and remember that the demand curves are marginal revenue product curves—that is, they indicate the amount that capitalists are willing to pay landlords for the use of their land.) Thus, we can summarize the classical theory of rent as follows:

As the use of land increases, landlords receive higher payments from two sources:

1. Increased demand leads the community to employ land previously not good enough to use; the advantage of previously used land over the new marginal land increases, and rents go up correspondingly.
2. Land is used more intensively; the marginal revenue product of land rises, thus increasing the ability of the producer who uses the land to pay rent.

As late as the end of the nineteenth century, this analysis still exerted a powerful influence beyond technical economic writings. An American journalist, Henry George, was nearly elected mayor of New York in 1886, running on the platform that all government should be financed by "a single tax"—a tax on landlords who, he said, are the only ones who earn incomes while contributing nothing to the productive process and who reap the fruits of economic growth without contributing to economic progress. George's logic was based on the notion that landowners do not increase the supply of their factor of production—the quantity of land—when rents increase.

## GENERALIZATION: WHAT DETERMINES MICHAEL JORDAN'S SALARY?

Land is not the only scarce input whose supply is fixed, at least in the short run. Toward the beginning of this century some economists realized that the economic analysis of rent can be applied to inputs other than land (see the box on page 376 for some current research uses of the concept). As we will see, this extension yielded some noteworthy insights.

Consider as an example the earnings of Michael Jordan, the Chicago Bulls basketball star. Basketball players seem to have little in common with plots of land in downtown Boise. Yet, to an economist, the same analysis—the theory of rent—explains the incomes of these two factors of production. To understand why, we first note that there is only one Michael Jordan. That is, he is a scarce input whose supply is fixed just like the supply of land. Because he is in fixed supply, the price of his services must be determined in a way that is similar to the determination of land rents. Hence, economists have arrived at a more general definition of **economic rent** as *any payment made to a factor above the amount necessary to induce any of that factor to be supplied to its present employment.*

To understand the concept of economic rent, it is, then, useful to divide the payment for any input into two parts. The first part is simply the minimum payment needed to acquire the input: the cost of producing a ball bearing or the compensation for the unpleasantness, hard work, and loss of leisure involved in performing labor. Only this first part of the factor payment is essential to induce the owner to supply any of the input. If a worker, for example, is not paid at least this first part, he will not supply any of this labor.

*At The* **FRONTIER**

**RENT SEEKING**

Current research uses the rent concept to analyze such common phenomena as lobbying by industrial groups, lawsuits between rival firms, and battles over exclusive licenses (as for a TV station). Such interfirm battles can waste very valuable economic resources, for example, the time spent by executives, bureaucrats, judges, lawyers, and economists. Because this valuable time could have been used in production, such activities entail a large *opportunity cost*. The new analysis offers insights into the reasons for these battles, and provides a way to assess what *quantity* of resources is wasted.

What is the relevance of economic rent—a payment to a factor of production above and beyond the amount necessary to get the factor to make its contribution to production? Obviously, many people would like to get such a bonanza. Many rent-earning opportunities are available, and a number of individuals usually fight over them. The search for such opportunities and the battle for them is called "rent seeking," a concept introduced by Gordon Tullock, an economist who is also trained in legal matters.

An obvious source of such rents is a monopoly license, for example, to operate the only TV station in town, yielding enormous advertising profits. No wonder rent seekers swoop down when such a license becomes available. Similarly, the powerful lobby of U.S. producers of sweeteners pressures Congress to impede imports of cane sugar, since free importation would cut prices (and therefore rents) substantially.

How much of society's resources will be wasted in such a process? The theory of rent seeking gives us some idea. Thus, consider a race for a monopoly cable TV license which, once awarded, will keep competitors out. But nothing prevents anyone from entering the race to *grab* the license. Anyone can hire the lobbyists and lawyers or offer the bribes needed in the battle. Thus, while the cable business is itself not competitive, the process of fighting for the license is. But, we know from the analysis of long-run equilibrium under perfect competition (pages 233–37) that economic profit approximates zero—revenues just cover costs. So, if the cable license is expected to yield, over its life, say, \$900 million in rent, rent seekers are likely to waste something near that amount in the fight for the license.

Why? Suppose there are ten bidders, each with an equal chance at the prize. Then, to each bidder that chance should be worth about \$90 million. If the average bidder has so far spent, say, only \$70 million on the battle, there will still be an expected economic profit of \$90 − \$70 = \$20 million to the rent-seeking activity. This will tempt an eleventh bidder to enter and raise the ante, say, to \$80 million in lobbying fees, hoping to grab the rent. This process only stops when enough of the rent has been wasted on the rent-seeking process.

The second part of the payment is a bonus that does not go to every input, but only to those that are of particularly high quality. Payments to workers with exceptional natural skills are a good example. These bonuses are like the extra payment for a better piece of land, and so are called *economic rents*. Indeed, like the rent of land, an increase in the amount of economic rent paid to an input may not increase the quantity of that input supplied. This second part—the economic rent—is pure gravy. The skillful worker is happy to have it as an extra. But it is not a deciding consideration in the choice of whether or not to work.

A moment's thought shows how this general notion of rent applies both to land and to Michael Jordan. The total quantity of land available for use is the same whether rent is high, low, or zero; no payments to landlords are necessary to induce land to be supplied to the market. So, by definition, the payments to landholders for their land are entirely economic rent—payments that are not necessary to induce the provision of the land to the economy. Michael Jordan is (almost) similar to land in this respect. His athletic talents are somewhat unique and cannot be reproduced. What determines the income of such a factor? Since the quantity supplied of such a unique, nonreproducible factor is absolutely fixed, and therefore unresponsive to price, the analysis of rent determination summarized in Figure 15–6 applies. *The position of the demand curve determines the price.*

Figure 15–8 summarizes the "Michael Jordan market." The largely vertical supply curve *RS* represents the fact that no matter what wage he is paid there is only one Michael Jordan. Demand curve *DD* is a marginal productivity curve of sorts, but not quite the kind we encountered earlier in the chapter. Since the question, "What would be the value of a second unit of Michael Jordan?" is nonsensical, the demand curve is constructed by considering only the *portion* of his time demanded at various wage levels. The curve indicates that at an annual

*Figure* **15–8** **HYPOTHETICAL MARKET FOR MICHAEL JORDAN'S SERVICES**

At an annual wage of $8 million or more, no one is willing to bid for Jordan's time. At a lower wage, $6 million, two thirds of his time will be demanded (point *G*). Only at an annual wage no higher than $5 million will all of Jordan's available time be demanded (point *E*).

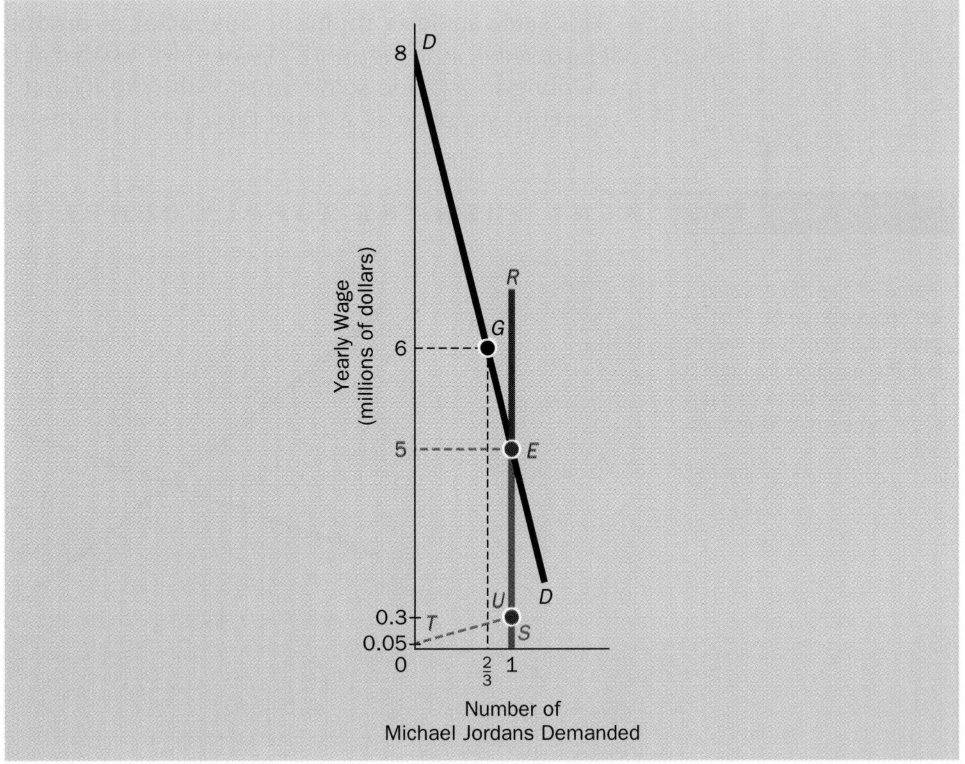

salary of $8 million no employer can afford even a little bit of Jordan. At a lower salary of, say, $6 million per year, however, there are enough profitable uses to absorb two-thirds of his time. At $5 million per year, Jordan's full time is demanded; and at lower wage rates, the demand for his time exceeds the amount of it that is for sale.

Equilibrium is at point *E* in the diagram, where the supply of and demand for his time are equal. His annual salary here is $5 million. Now we can ask: How much of Michael Jordan's salary is economic rent? According to the economic definition of rent, only part of his $5 million salary is rent. Because the supply schedule is only partly vertical, part of Jordan's financial reward is necessary to get him to supply his services, as is undoubtedly true in reality. Thus, it is not true that every penny he earns is rent.

This is why we said that top athletes like Michael Jordan are *almost* good examples of pure rent. For, in fact, if his salary were low enough, Jordan might well prefer to play golf rather than work. Suppose, for example, that $50,000 per year is the lowest salary at which Jordan will offer even one minute of his services, and that his labor supply then increases with his wage up to an annual salary of $300,000, at which point he is willing to work full time. Then, while his equilibrium salary will still be $5 million per year, not all of it will be rent, because some of it, at least $50,000, is required to get him to supply any services at all.

The portion of Michael Jordan's compensation that is not pure rent corresponds to the upward-sloping portion, *TU*, of his labor-supply curve. In Figure 15–8 that is why only part of the supply curve, *TUR*, is vertical—that portion above the $300,000 salary that will lead him to supply all his available time. And his equilibrium compensation level, *E*, will consist partly of rent (portion *UE*) and partly of a payment, *SU*, that is not rent.

This same analysis applies to any factor of production whose supply curve is not horizontal, as in Figure 15–9. There we see that at any price above $5, suppliers are willing to provide some units of the input; that is, at any price above point *S*, quantity supplied is greater than zero. Yet the supply–demand equilibrium

*Figure* **15–9** **RENT WHEN THE SUPPLY CURVE IS NOT VERTICAL**

Some of the input would be supplied (point *S*) at a price of $5 (or a bit more), but the equilibrium price is $7 so some units of input must be earning a rent of $2.

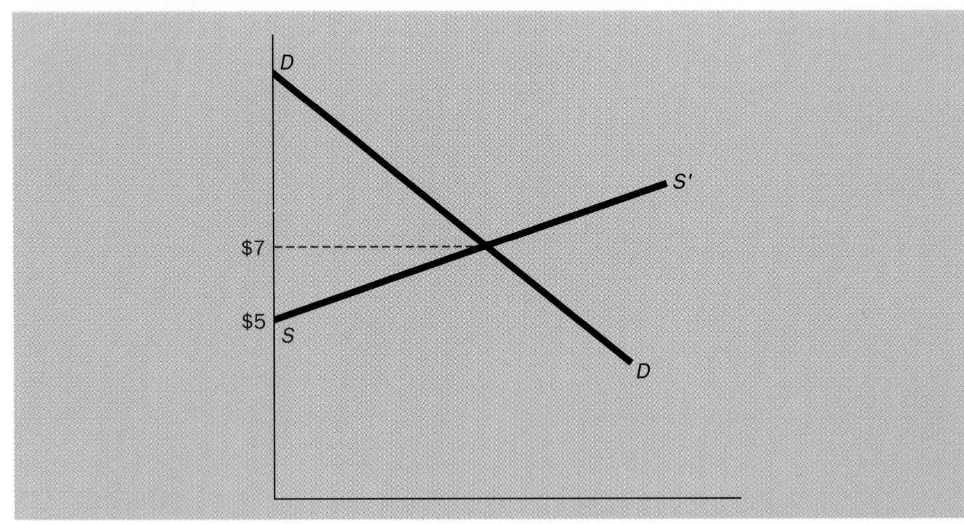

point yields a price of $7—well above the minimum price at which some input supply would be forthcoming. The difference must constitute a rent to the input suppliers, who get paid more than the minimum amount required to induce them to work.

Almost all employees earn some rent. What sorts of factors earn no rent? Those that can be exactly reproduced by a number of producers at constant cost. No supplier of ball bearings will ever receive any rent on a ball bearing, at least in the long run, because any desired number of them can be produced at (roughly) constant costs—say 50 cents each. If one supplier tried to charge a price above 50 cents, another manufacturer would undercut the first supplier and take its customers away. Hence the competitive price will include no rent.

## RENT CONTROLS: THE MISPLACED ANALOGY

Why is the analysis of economic rent important? Because only economic rent can be taxed away without reducing the quantity of the input supplied. And here common English gets in the way of sound reasoning. Many people feel that the *rent* that they pay to their landlord is economic rent. After all, their apartments will still be there if they pay $500 per month, or $300, or $100. This view, while true in the short run, is quite myopic.

**ECONOMIC RENT** is the portion of the earnings of a factor of production that exceeds the minimum amount necessary to induce any of that factor to be supplied.

Like the ball-bearing producer, the owner of a building cannot expect to earn *economic* rent because there are too many other potential owners whose costs of construction are roughly the same as her own. If the market price temporarily included some economic rent—that is, if price exceeded production costs plus the opportunity cost of the required capital—other builders would start new construction that would drive the price down. Thus, far from being in perfectly *inelastic* (vertical) supply, like raw land, buildings come rather close to being in perfectly *elastic* (horizontal) supply, like ball bearings. As we have learned from the theory of rent, this means that builders and owners of buildings cannot collect economic rent in the long run.

Since apartment owners collect very little economic rent, the payments that tenants make in a free market must be just enough to keep those apartments on the market. (This is the definition of zero economic rent.) If rent controls push these prices down, the apartments will start disappearing from the market.[4] Among other unfortunate results, we can therefore expect rent controls to contribute to the problem of homelessness—though it is, of course, not the only factor behind this distressing phenomenon.

## ISSUE: ARE PROFITS TOO HIGH OR TOO LOW?

This completes our analysis of rent. We turn next to business profits, a subject whose discussion seems to elicit more passion than logic. With the exception of

[4]None of this is meant to imply that temporary rent controls in certain locations cannot have salutary effects in the short run. In the short run, the supply of apartments and houses really is fixed, and large shifts in demand would hand windfall gains to landlords—gains that are true economic rents. Controls that eliminate such windfalls should not cause serious problems. But knowing when the "short run" fades into the "long run" can be a tricky matter. "Temporary" rent control laws have a way of becoming rather permanent.

some economists, almost no one thinks that the rate of profit is at about the right level. Critics on the left point accusingly at the billion-dollar profits of some giant corporations and argue that they are unconscionably high. They call for much stiffer profits taxes. On the other hand, the Chambers of Commerce, National Association of Manufacturers, and other business groups complain that regulations and "ruinous" competition keep profits too low, and they are constantly petitioning Congress for tax relief.

The public has many misconceptions about the nature of the U.S. economy, but probably none is more severe than the popular view of the amount of profit that American corporations earn. We suggest to you the following experiment. Ask five of your friends who have never had an economics course what fraction of the nation's income they imagine is accounted for by profits. While the correct answer varies from year to year, in 1990 about 6 percent of GDP (before-tax) was business profits. A comparable percent of the prices you pay represents before-tax profit. Most people think this figure is much, much higher—as we saw in the boxed insert on page 39.

As you have no doubt noticed by now, economists are reluctant to brand factor prices as "too low" or "too high" in some moral or ethical sense. Rather, they are likely to ask, first, What is the market equilibrium price? And then they will ask whether there are any good reasons to interfere with the market solution. This analysis, however, is not so easy to apply to the case of profits, since it is hard to use supply and demand analysis when you do not know what factor of production earns profit.

In both a bookkeeping and an economic sense, *profits are the residual*. They are what remains from the selling price after all other factors have been paid.

But what factor of production receives this reward? What factor's marginal productivity constitutes the profit rate?

## WHAT ACCOUNTS FOR PROFITS?

*Economic* profit, it will be recalled from Chapter 9, is the amount a firm earns *over and above* the payments for all other inputs, including the interest payments for the capital it uses and the opportunity cost of any capital provided by the owners of the firm. The profit rate and the interest rate are closely related. In an imaginary (and uninteresting) world in which everything was certain and unchanging, capitalists who invested money in firms would simply earn the market rate of interest on their funds. Profits beyond this level would be competed away. Profits below this level could not persist, because capitalists would withdraw their funds from the firms and deposit them in banks. Capitalists in such a world would be mere moneylenders.

But the real world is not at all like this. Some capitalists are much more than moneylenders, and the amounts they earn often exceed the interest rate by a considerable margin. These activist capitalists who seek out or even create earnings opportunities are called **entrepreneurs**. They are the ones who are responsible for the constant change that characterizes business firms and who prevent the operations of the firms from stagnating (see box on page 381). Since they are

## *Succeeding as an Entrepreneur: All You Need Is Love*

. . . Consider the advice of Paul Hawken, successful businessman, author, environmental activist and host of the PBS T.V. series "Growing a Business" . . . : "If you want to help people, don't join the Peace Corps; start a business."

Understanding a great paradox about entrepreneurial life reveals the essential motivation needed for entrepreneurial success. It is a "paradox of wealth." *Forbes* magazine every year publishes its list of the *Forbes* 400 richest Americans. Most of the people on the list are entrepreneurs. The heads of America's largest corporations are not rich enough to qualify—unless they founded their corporations. So if you crave great wealth, become an entrepreneur.

But know a second truth, and recognize the paradox. The entrepreneurs who make it to the top—even to the middle—of the wealth pyramid aren't primarily motivated by money. The paradox: Your only way to become very rich is to become an entrepreneur—but you probably won't succeed if wealth is your primary goal.

Sam Walton and the wife and children he endowed have dominated the top of the *Forbes* 400 for many years. Yet well after he was super-rich, Mr. Walton continued to work long hours and live simply, devoting himself entirely to opening more stores and improving his business—until he died in 1992. Making Wal-Mart the biggest and best retailer in the world was his overriding goal. . . .

Anita Roddick is arguably the most successful and visible female entrepreneur of the 1990s. . . . When her company [Body Shops, consisting of over 600 cosmetics stores in 38 countries] went public just 8 years after she opened her first modest shop, Ms. Roddick became very rich. Her reaction: "Wanting to be a millionaire seemed to be a positively obscene ambition. We had not gone into business to get rich; we have never even thought about getting rich.". . .

If money should not be the primary reason for starting a business, what should be? Love. The love of a challenge—of creating and building something; of scaling the mountain, not reaching the peak; of traveling the road, not resting at the inn at the end. Successful entrepreneurs are driven to express and prove themselves, be the best they can, beat the competition, break the rules, disprove the odds. And they love the game. Their biographies are full of phrases like, "My work was fun," "My business was my playground," and "I lived by the TGIM motto—thank goodness it's Monday, so I can go to work 5 to 9."

One last characteristic of successful entrepreneurs is critical. They are doggedly determined. H. Ross Perot, one of the great entrepreneurs of our era, loves to quote Winston Churchill when he is asked what it takes to succeed as an entrepreneur: "Never give up, never give up, never give up."

Excerpted from Robert Knapp, *The Margin*, Spring 1993, page 63.

always trying to do something new, it is difficult to provide a general description of their activities. However, we can list three primary ways in which entrepreneurs are able to drive profits above the level of interest rates.

### EXERCISE OF MONOPOLY POWER

If the entrepreneur can establish a monopoly over some or all of his products, even for a short while, he can use the monopoly power of his firm to earn monopoly profits. The nature of these monopoly earnings was analyzed in Chapter 11.

## RISK BEARING

The entrepreneur may engage in risky activities. For example, when a firm prospects for oil it will drill an exploratory shaft hoping to find a pool of petroleum at the bottom. But a high proportion of such attempts produces only dry holes, and the cost of the operation is wasted. Of course, if the investor is lucky and does find oil, she may be rewarded handsomely. The income she obtains is a payment for bearing risk.

Obviously, a few lucky individuals make out well in this process, while most suffer heavy losses. How well can we expect risk takers to do on the average? If, on the average, one exploratory drilling out of ten pays off, do we expect its return to be exactly ten times as high as the interest rate, so that the *average* firm will earn exactly the normal rate of interest? The answer is that the payoff will be *more* than ten times the interest rate if investors dislike gambling; that is, if they prefer to avoid risk. Why? Because investors who dislike risk will be unwilling to put their money into a business in which nine firms out of ten lose out unless there is some compensation for the financial peril to which they expose themselves.

In reality, however, there is no certainty that things always work out this way. Some people love to gamble, and these people tend to be overoptimistic about their chances of coming out ahead. They may plunge into projects to a degree unjustified by the odds. If there are enough such gamblers, the average payoff to risky undertakings may end up below the interest rate. The successful investor will still make a good profit, just like the lucky winner in Las Vegas. But the average participant will have to pay for the privilege of bearing risk.

## RETURNS TO INNOVATION

The third major source of profits is perhaps the most important of all from the point of view of social welfare. The entrepreneur who is first to market a desirable new product or employ a new cost-saving machine will receive a profit higher than that normally accruing to an uninnovative (but otherwise similar) business manager. **Innovation** is different from **invention**. Invention is the act of generating a new idea; innovation is the next step, the act of putting the new idea into practical use. Business people are rarely inventors, but they are often innovators.

**INVENTION** is the act of generating an idea for a new product or a new method for making an old product.

**INNOVATION**, the next step, is the act of putting the new idea into practical use.

When an entrepreneur innovates, even if her new product or new process is not protected by patents, she will be one step ahead of her competitors. She will be able to capture much of the market either by offering customers a better product or by supplying the product more cheaply. In either case she will temporarily find herself with some monopoly power left by the weakening of her competitors, and monopoly profit will be the reward for her initiative.

However, this monopoly profit, the reward for innovation, will only be temporary. As soon as the success of the idea has demonstrated itself to the world, other firms will find ways of imitating it. Even if they cannot turn out precisely the same product or use precisely the same process, they will have to find ways to supply close substitutes if they are to survive. In this way, new ideas are spread through the economy. And in the process the special profits of the innovator are brought to an end. The innovator can only resume earning special profits by finding still another promising idea.

Entrepreneurs are forced to keep searching for new ideas, to keep instituting innovations, and to keep imitating those ideas that they were not the first to put into operation. This process is at the heart of the growth of the capitalist system. It is one of the secrets of its extraordinary dynamism.

### THE ISSUE OF PROFITS TAXATION

So profits in excess of the market rate of interest can be considered as the return on entrepreneurial talent. But this is not really very helpful, since no one can say exactly what entrepreneurial talent is. Certainly we cannot measure it; nor can we teach it in a college course (though business schools try!). Therefore, we do not know how the observed profit rate relates to the minimum reward necessary to attract entrepreneurial talent into the market—a relationship that is crucial for the contentious issue of profits taxation.

Consider the windfall profits tax on oil companies as an example. If oil company profit rates are well above this minimum, they contain a large element of economic rent. In that case, we could tax away these excess profits (rents) without fear of reducing oil production. On the other hand, if the profits being earned by oil companies do not contain much economic rent, then the windfall profits tax might seriously curtail exploration and production of oil.

This example illustrates the general problem of deciding how heavily profits should be taxed. Critics of big business who call for high, if not confiscatory, profits taxes seem to believe that profits are mostly economic rent. But if they are wrong, if most of the observed profits are necessary to attract people into entrepreneurial roles, then a high profits tax can be dangerous. It can threaten the very lifeblood of the capitalist system. Business lobbying groups predictably claim that this is the case. Unfortunately, neither group has offered much evidence for its conclusion.

## CRITICISMS OF MARGINAL PRODUCTIVITY THEORY

The theory of factor pricing described in this chapter is another example of supply–demand analysis. Its special feature is its heavy reliance on the principle of marginal productivity to derive the shape and position of the demand curve. For this reason, the analysis is often rather misleadingly called *the marginal productivity theory of distribution*, when it is, at best, only a theory of the demand side of the pertinent market.

Over the years, this analysis has been subject to attack on many grounds. One frequent accusation, which is largely (but not entirely) groundless, is the assertion that marginal productivity theory is merely an attempt to justify the distribution of income that the capitalist system yields—that it is a piece of pro-capitalist propaganda. According to this argument, when marginal productivity theory claims that each factor is paid exactly its marginal revenue product, this is only a sneaky way of asserting that each factor is paid exactly what it deserves. These critics claim that the theory legitimizes the gross inequities of the systems—the poverty of many and the great wealth of the few.

The argument is straightforward but wrong. Payments are made not to *factors of production* but to the people who happen to own them. If an acre of land earns $2000 because that is its marginal revenue product, this does not mean, nor is it meant to imply that, the payment is *deserved* by the landlord, who may even have acquired the land by fraud.

Second, an input's marginal revenue product (MRP) does not depend only on "how hard it works" but also on how much of it happens to be employed—for, according to the "law" of diminishing returns, the more that is employed, the lower its MRP. Thus, that factor's MRP is not and cannot legitimately be interpreted as a measure of the intensity of its "productive effort." In any event, what an input deserves, in some moral sense, may depend on more than what it does in the factory. For example, workers who are sick or have many children may be more "deserving," even if they are no more productive.

On these and other grounds, no economist today claims that marginal productivity analysis shows that distribution under capitalism is either just or unjust. It is simply wrong to claim that marginal productivity theory is pro-capitalist propaganda. The marginal productivity principle is just as relevant to organizing production in a socialist society as it is in a capitalist one.

Others have attacked marginal productivity theory for using rather complicated reasoning to tell us very little about the really urgent problems of income distribution. In this view, it is all very well to say that everything depends on supply and demand and to express this in terms of many complicated equations (as is done in more advanced books and articles). But these equations do not tell us what to do about such serious distribution problems as malnutrition among Indians in Latin America or poverty among minority groups in the United States.

Though it does exaggerate somewhat, there is certainly truth to this criticism. We have seen in this chapter that the theory does provide some insights on real policy matters, though not as many as we would like. In Chapter 17 and in Chapter 21 of *Macroeconomics*, we will see that economists do have things to say about the problems of poverty and underdevelopment. But much of this does not flow from marginal productivity analysis.

Perhaps, in the end, what should be said for marginal productivity theory is that it is the best model we have at the moment, that it offers us *some* valuable insights into the way the economy works, and that until a more powerful model is found we are better off hanging on to what we have.

## *Summary*

1. A profit-maximizing firm purchases that quantity of any input at which the price of the input equals its marginal revenue product. Consequently, the firm's demand curve for an input is the downward-sloping portion of that input's curve.
2. Interest rates are determined by the supply of and demand for funds. The demand for funds is a derived demand, since these funds are used to finance business investment. Thus the demand for funds depends on the marginal productivity of capital.
3. A dollar obtainable sooner is worth more than a dollar obtainable later because of the interest that can be earned in the interim.
4. Increased demand for a good that needs land to produce it will drive up the prices of land either because inferior land will be brought into use or because land will be used more intensively.
5. Rent controls do not significantly affect the supply of land, but they do tend to reduce the supply of buildings.
6. Economic rent is any payment to the supplier of a factor of production that is greater than the minimum amount needed to induce the desired quantity of the factor to be supplied.
7. Factors of production that are unique in quality and difficult or impossible to reproduce will tend to be paid relatively high economic rents because of their scarcity.
8. Factors of production that are easy to produce at a constant cost and that are provided by many suppliers will earn little or no economic rent.
9. Economic profits over and above the cost of capital are earned (a) by exercise of monopoly power, (b) as a payment for bearing risk, and (c) as the earnings of successful innovation.
10. The desirability of increased taxation of profits depends on its effects on the supply of entrepreneurial talent. If most profits are economic rents, then higher profits taxes will have few detrimental effects. But if most profits are necessary to attract entrepreneurs into the market, then higher profits taxes can threaten the capitalist system.

## Key Concepts and Terms

Factors of production
Entrepreneurship
Marginal productivity principle
Marginal physical product
Marginal revenue product
Derived demand
Usury law
Investment
Capital
Interest
Discounting
Marginal land
Economic rent
Entrepreneurs
Risk bearing
Invention versus innovation

## Questions for Review

1. A profit-maximizing firm expands its purchase of any input up to the point where diminishing returns has reduced the marginal revenue product so that it equals the input price. Why does it not pay the firm to "quit while it is ahead," buying so small a quantity of the input that the input's MRP remains greater than its price?
2. Which of the following inputs do you think include a relatively large economic rent in their earnings?
   a. Nuts and bolts.
   b. Petroleum.
   c. A champion racehorse.

   Use supply–demand analysis to explain your answer.
3. Three machines are employed in an isolated area. They each produce 2000 units of output per month, the first requiring $17,000 in raw materials, the second $22,000, and the third $23,000. What would you expect to be the monthly charge for the first and second machines if the services of the third machine can be hired at a price of $9000 a month? What parts of the charges for the first two machines are economic rent?
4. Economists conclude that a tax on the revenues of firms will be shifted in part to consumers of the products of those firms, in the form of higher product prices. However, they believe that a tax on the rent of land usually cannot be shifted. What explains the difference?
5. Many economists argue that a tax on apartment houses is likely to reduce the supply of apartments, but that a tax on all land, including the land on which apartment houses stand, will not reduce the supply of apartments. Can you explain the difference? What is the relation of this answer to the answer to Question 4?
6. Distinguish between investment and capital.
7. If you have a contract under which you will be paid $10,000 two years from now, why do you become richer if the rate of interest falls?
8. What is the difference between interest and profit? Who earns interest, in return for what contribution to production? Who earns economic profit, in return for what contribution to production?
9. Do you know any entrepreneurs? How do they earn a living? How do they differ from managers?
10. Explain the difference between an invention and an innovation. Give an example of each.
11. "Marginal productivity does not determine how much a worker will earn—it only determines how many workers will be hired at a given wage. Therefore, marginal productivity analysis is a theory of demand for labor, not a theory of distribution." What, then, do you think determines wages? Does marginal productivity affect their level? If so, how?
12. (more difficult) American savings rates are among the lowest of any industrial country. This has caused concerns about our ability to finance new plant and equipment for United States industry. Some politicians and others have advocated lower taxes on saving as a remedy. Do you expect such a program to be very effective? Why?
13. If rent constitutes less than 1 percent of the incomes of Americans, why may the concept nevertheless be significant?
14. Litigation in which one company sues another often involves costs for lawyers and other court costs literally amounting to hundreds of millions of dollars per case. What does rent have to do with the matter?
15. (More difficult). In this chapter (pages 368–70), it was explained that a rise in interest rates will increase some peoples' savings (as one might expect), but will decrease other peoples' saving because it reduces the amount of saving they need to reach some target. Analyze the consequences of an increase in interest rate in terms of its income and substitution effects. (For review of these concepts see Chapter 7, pages 178–81).

## *Appendix* DISCOUNTING AND PRESENT VALUE[5]

Frequently, in business and economic problems, it is necessary to compare sums of money received (or paid) at different dates. Consider, for example, the purchase of a machine that costs $11,000 and will yield a marginal revenue product of $14,520 two years from today. If the machine can be financed by a two-year loan bearing 10 percent interest, it will cost the firm $1100 in interest at the end of each year, plus $11,000 in principal repayment at the end of the second year (see the table below). Is the machine a good investment?

**COSTS AND BENEFITS OF INVESTING IN A MACHINE**

| | End of Year 1 | End of Year 2 |
|---|---|---|
| Benefits | | |
| Marginal revenue product of the machine | 0 | $14,520 |
| Costs | | |
| Interest | $1100 | 1100 |
| Repayment of principal on loan | 0 | 11,000 |
| Total | 1100 | 12,100 |

The total costs of owning the machine over the two-year period ($1100 + $12,100 = $13,200) are less than the total benefits ($14,520). But this is clearly an invalid comparison, because the $14,520 in future benefits are not worth $14,520 in terms of today's money. Adding up dollars received (or paid) at different dates is a bit like adding apples and oranges. The process that has been invented for making these magnitudes comparable is called **discounting,** or **computing the present value** of a future sum of money.

To illustrate the concept of present value, let us ask how much $1 received a year from today is worth *in terms of today's money. If the rate of interest* is 10 percent, the answer is about 91 cents. Why? Because if we invest 91 cents today at 10 percent interest, it will grow to 91 cents plus 9.1 cents in interest = 100.1 cents in a year. Similar considerations apply to any rate of interest. In general:

If the rate of interest is $i$, the present value of $1 to be received in a year is:

$$\frac{\$1}{(1+i)}.$$

This is so, because in a year $\frac{\$1}{(1+i)}$ will grow to $\frac{\$1}{(1+i)}(1+i) = \$1.$

What about money to be received two years from today? Using the same reasoning, $1 invested today will grow to $\$1 \times (1.1) = \$1.10$ after one year and to $\$1 \times (1.1) \times (1.1) = \$1 \times (1.1)^2 = \$1.21$ after two years. Consequently, the present value of $1 to be received two years from today is

$$\frac{\$1}{(1.1)^2} = \frac{\$1}{1.21} = 82.64 \text{ cents}.$$

A similar analysis applies to money received three years from today, four years from today, and so on.

The general formula for the present value of $1 to be received $N$ years from today when the rate of interest is $i$ is

$$\frac{\$1}{(1+i)^N}.$$

The present value formula highlights the two variables that determine the present value of any future flow of money: the rate of interest ($i$) and how long you have to wait before you get it ($N$).

Let us now apply this analysis to our example. The present value of the revenue is easy to calculate since it all comes two years from today. Since the rate of interest is assumed to be 10 percent ($i = 0.1$) we have

$$\text{Present value of revenues} = \frac{\$14{,}520}{(1.1)^2} = \frac{\$14{,}520}{1.21} = \$12{,}000.$$

The present value of the costs is a bit trickier in this example since costs occur at two different dates.

The present value of the first interest payment is $\$1100/(1+i) = \$1100/1.1 = \$1000$. And the present value of the final payment of interest plus principal is

[5]The authors are grateful to Professor J. S. Hanson of Willamette University for correcting an error in an earlier edition.

$$\frac{\$12{,}100}{(1 + i)^2} = \frac{\$12{,}100}{(1.1)^2} = \frac{\$12{,}100}{1.21} = \$10{,}000.$$

Now that we have expressed each sum in terms of its present value, it is permissible to add them up. So the present value of all costs is

$$\begin{aligned}\text{Present value of costs} &= \$1000 + \$10{,}000\\ &= \$11{,}000.\end{aligned}$$

Comparison of this to the $12,000 present value of the revenues clearly shows that the machine is really a good investment. This same calculation procedure is applicable to all investment decisions.

## *Summary*

To determine whether a loss or a gain will result from a decision whose costs and returns will come at several different periods of time, the figures represented by these gains and losses must all be discounted to obtain their present value. For this, one uses the present value formula for X dollars receivable N years from now:

$$\text{Present value} = \frac{X}{(1 + i)^N}.$$

One then adds together the present values of all the returns and all the costs. If the sum of the present values of the returns is greater than the sum of the present values of the costs, then the decision to invest will promise a net gain.

## *Key Concepts and Terms*

Discounting

Present value

## *Questions for Review*

1. Compute the present value of $1000 to be received in three years if the rate of interest is 12 percent.
2. A government bond pays $100 in interest each year for three years and also returns the principal of $1000 in the third year. How much is it worth in terms of today's money if the rate of interest is 9 percent? If the rate of interest is 12 percent?

Chapter 16

# LABOR: THE HUMAN INPUT

*Masters are always and every where in a sort of tacit, but constant and uniform combination, not to raise the wages of labour . . .*

**ADAM SMITH**

Labor costs account, by far, for the largest share of GDP. As noted in the previous chapter, the earnings of labor amount to almost 75 percent of national income. Wages also represent the primary source of income to the vast majority of Americans and are related to a variety of important social and political issues. ¶ The chapter is divided into two main parts. In the first part we deal with the determination of wages and employment in *competitive labor markets*; that is, labor markets in which there are many buyers and many sellers, none of whom is large enough to have any appreciable influence on wages. We consider why some types of workers are paid far more than others and explore a number of important issues, including the effects of education on wages and of minimum wage legislation. ¶ In the second part of the chapter we consider labor markets that are monopolized on the selling side by trade unions. First, the development of the labor movement in America is summarized. Then we consider alternative goals for a union and how these goals might be pursued. Finally, we turn to situations in which a single seller of labor (a union) confronts a single buyer of labor (a monopsony firm), and examine some of the analytical and practical difficulties that arise under collective bargaining.

## ISSUE: THE MINIMUM WAGE AND UNEMPLOYMENT

Unemployment among teenagers is always higher than it is in the labor force as a whole, and among black teenagers it is much higher still. Figure 16–1 shows the record. It indicates that whenever unemployment rates went down in the economy as a whole, they almost always decreased for both black and white teenagers. However, young workers, and especially young black workers, have always suffered considerably more from unemployment than the average worker. When things are generally bad, things are much, much worse for them. Despite social and legislative pressures against race discrimination, efforts to improve the quality of education available to children in the inner cities, and many related programs, there has been no relative improvement in black teenage unemployment in recent years.

Many economists (but not all of them) feel less surprised than other concerned persons about the intractability of the problem. They maintain that despite all the legislation that has been adopted to improve the position of black people, there is a law on the books, which, although apparently designed to protect low-skilled workers, is suspected by these economists of being an impediment to improvement in job opportunities for blacks. As long as this law remains effective, the young, the inexperienced, and those with educational disadvantages will, according to this view, continue to find themselves handicapped on the job market, and attempts to eliminate their more serious unemployment problems will stand little chance of success.

What is the law? None other than the **minimum wage law**. Later in this chapter we will explain the grounds on which many observers believe that this law has

*Figure* **16–1** **THE TEENAGE UNEMPLOYMENT PROBLEM**

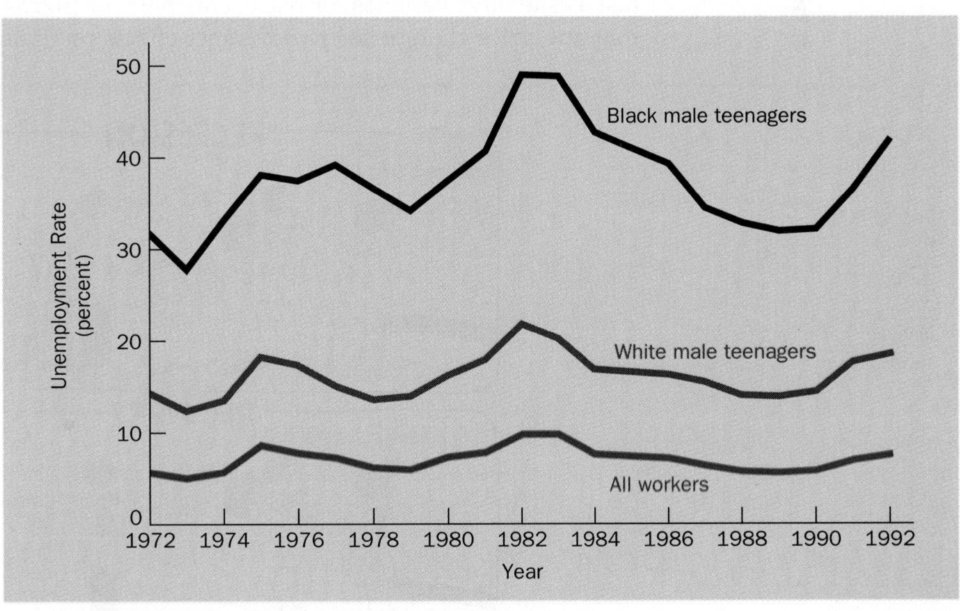


Teenage unemployment rates have consistently been much higher than the overall unemployment rate, and black teenagers have fared worse than white teenagers. For the most part the three employment rates have moved up and down together, as can be seen in this chart. NOTE: A teenager, here, is a person aged 16 to 19 years.

SOURCE: *Economic Report of the President*, Washington, D.C.: U.S. Government Printing Office, various years.

such pernicious—and presumably unintended—effects. (So we wrote in previous editions of this book, before some recent statistical studies suggested that these unintended effects are, in reality, neither very large nor very significant.)

## COMPETITIVE LABOR MARKETS

The minimum wage law interferes with the operation of a free labor market. But to understand how, we must first understand how the labor market would operate in its absence. We approach this in three steps. First we consider the determinants of the supply of labor, then the determinants of demand, and finally the market equilibrium, in which both wages and employment levels are established. As in the previous chapter, we will find that the demand for labor is determined, largely, like the demand for any other input, by labor's marginal revenue product. It is on the supply side that most of the special features of the labor market are found.

### THE SUPPLY OF LABOR

The economic analysis of labor supply is based on the following simple observation: given the fixed amount of time in a week, a person's decision to *supply labor* to firms is simultaneously a decision to *demand leisure* time for herself. Assuming that after necessary time for eating and sleeping is deducted a worker has 90 usable hours in a week, a decision to spend 40 of those hours working is simultaneously a decision to demand 50 of them for other purposes.

This suggests that we can analyze the *supply* of this particular input—labor—with the same tools we used in Chapter 8 to analyze the *demand* for commodities. In this case, the commodity is leisure. A consumer "buys" her own leisure time, just as she buys bananas, or back scratchers, or pizzas. In Chapter 8 we observed that any price change has two distinct effects on quantity demanded: an income

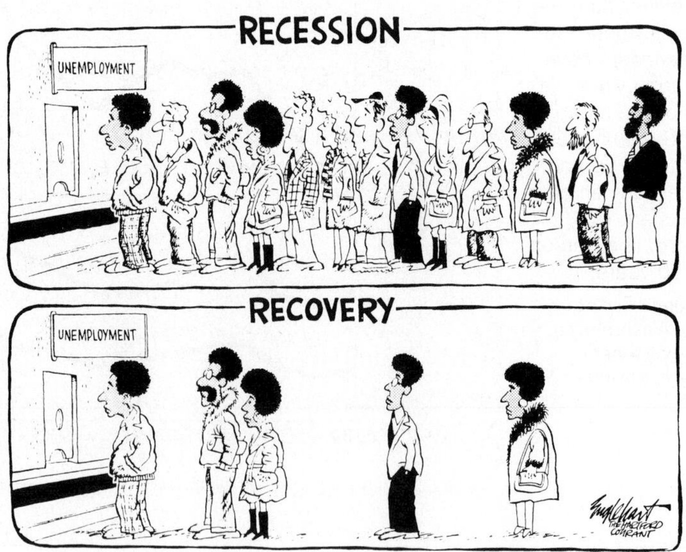

effect and a substitution effect. Let us review these two effects and see how they operate in the context of the demand for leisure (that is, the supply of labor). While in Chapter 8 these concepts did not provide very deep insights, we will see that they tell us a good deal about the labor market, as well as the markets for some other inputs (see question 15 at the end of the previous chapter).

1. ***Income effect.*** Higher wages make consumers richer. We expect this increased wealth to raise the demand for most goods, *leisure included.*

The income effect of higher wages probably leads most workers to want to work less.

2. ***Substitution effect.*** Consumers "purchase" their own leisure time by giving up their hourly wage, so the wage rate is the "price" (the opportunity cost) of leisure. When the wage rate rises, leisure becomes more expensive relative to other commodities that consumers might buy. Thus, we expect a wage increase to induce them to buy *less* leisure time and *more* goods.

The substitution effect of higher wages probably leads most workers to want to work more.

Putting these two effects together, we are led to conclude that some workers may react to an increase in their wage rate by working more, while others may react by working less. Still others will have little or no discretion over their hours of work. In terms of the market as a whole, therefore, higher wages can lead either to a larger or a smaller quantity of labor supplied.

Statistical studies of this issue in the United States have reached the conclusions that (a) the response of labor supply to wage changes is not very strong for most workers; (b) for low-wage workers the substitution effect seems clearly dominant, so they work more when wages rise; and (c) for high-wage workers the income effect just about offsets the substitution effect, so they do not work more when wages rise. Figure 16–2 depicts these approximate "facts." It shows labor supply rising (slightly) as wages rise up to point *A*. Thereafter, labor supply is roughly constant as wages rise.

It is even possible that when wages are raised sufficiently high, further increases in wages will lead workers to purchase more leisure and therefore to work less. The supply curve of labor is then said to be a **backward-bending supply curve**, as illustrated by the broken portion of the curve above point *B*.

Does the theory of labor supply apply to college students? A study of the hours of work performed by students at Princeton University found that it does.[1] Estimated substitution effects of higher wages on the labor supply of Princeton University students were positive and income effects were negative, just as the theory predicts. Apparently, substitution effects outweighed income effects by a slim margin, so that higher wages attracted a somewhat greater supply of labor. Specifically, a 10-percent rise in wages was estimated to increase the hours of work of the Princeton student body by about 3 percent.

## AN APPLICATION: THE LABOR SUPPLY PUZZLE

Income-substitution effect analysis plays an even more important role in explaining the striking historical trends in labor supply. Throughout the first three-

[1]Mary P. Hurley, "An Investigation of Employment among Princeton Undergraduates during the Academic Year," senior thesis submitted to the Department of Economics, May 1975.

Figure 16–2 A TYPICAL LABOR SUPPLY SCHEDULE

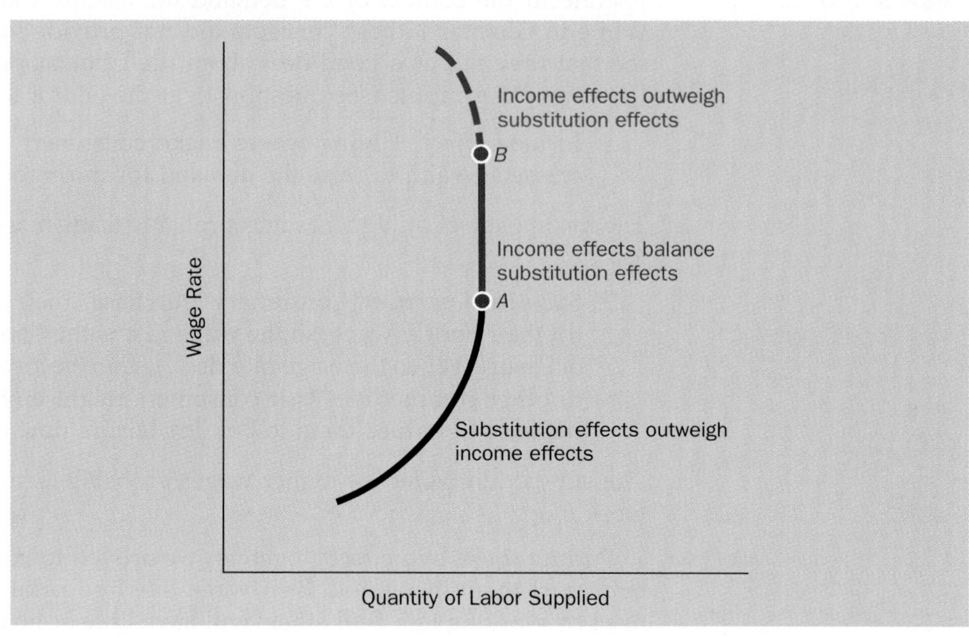


The labor supply schedule depicted here has a positive slope up to point *A*, as substitution effects outweigh income effects. At higher wages, however, income effects become just as important as substitution effects, and the curve becomes roughly vertical. At still higher wages (above point *B*), income effects might overwhelm substitution effects.

quarters of our century, wages rose, both in number of dollars paid per hour and in the quantity of goods those dollars could buy, as is clearly shown by the data depicted in Figure 16–3. Yet labor has asked for and received *reductions* in the length of the workday and workweek. At the beginning of the century, a workweek of $5\frac{1}{2}$ days and a workday of 10 or more hours (with virtually no vacations) were standard, making a workweek of 50 to 60 hours. Since then, labor hours have generally declined. Today the standard workweek is down to just about 35 hours. It has been estimated that since 1870 the number of hours an average American worker works per year has declined about 45 percent! Where has the commonsense view of the matter gone wrong? Why, as hourly wages have risen, have workers not sold more of the hours they have available instead of pressing for a shorter and shorter workweek?

Part of the answer becomes clear when one recalls that any wage increase sets in motion *both* a substitution effect *and* an income effect. If only the substitution effect operated, then rising wages would indeed cause people to work longer hours because the high price of leisure makes leisure less attractive. But this reasoning leaves out the income effect. As higher wages make workers richer, they will want to buy more of most commodities, including vacations and other leisure-time activities. Thus the income effect of increasing wages induces workers to work fewer hours.

It is the strong income effect of rising wages that may account for the fact that labor supply has responded in the "wrong" direction, with workers working evershorter hours despite their rising real wages. If so, the long-run supply curve of labor is indeed backward bending.

Figure 16–3 **TRENDS IN REAL WAGES AND HOURS WORKED**

This graph shows how real wages (measured in dollars of 1982–84 purchasing power) have, until recently, been rising throughout the twentieth century in the United States, while hours worked per week have been declining, despite the higher rewards for each hour of work. The sharp drop in hours during the 1930s reflects the high unemployment of the Great Depression, and the sharp rise in hours in the 1940s reflects the unusual circumstances of World War II. Note that real wages have actually fallen since about 1973.

SOURCE: Constructed by the authors from data in *Historical Statistics of the United States* and *Economic Report of the President*. Data on both weekly hours and hourly earnings pertain to the entire civilian economy for the period since 1947, but only to the manufacturing sector for earlier years because of the unavailability of economy-wide data.

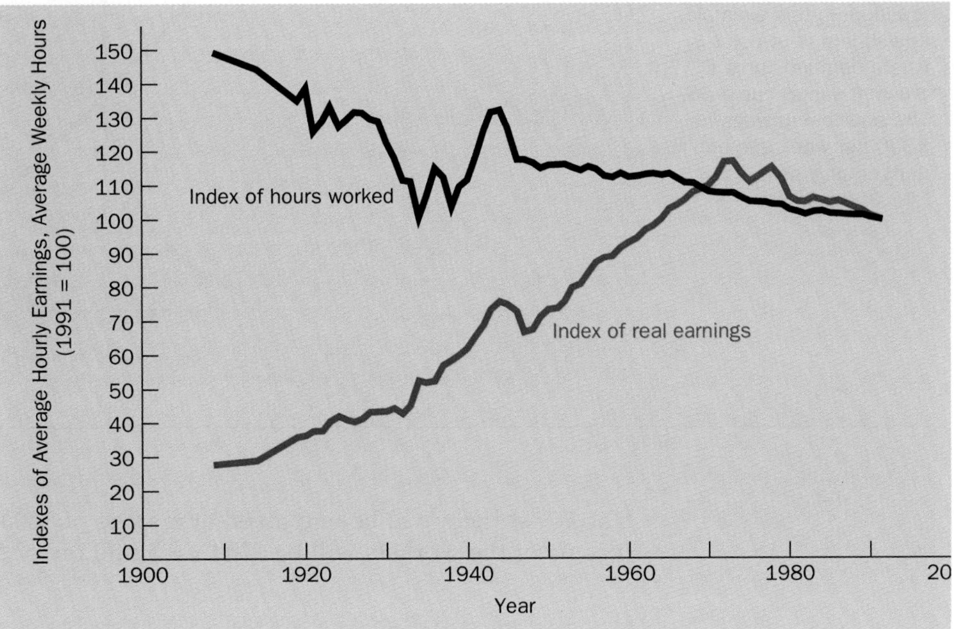


## THE DEMAND FOR LABOR AND THE DETERMINATION OF WAGES

There is not much to be said about the demand for labor that has not already been said about the demand for other inputs. As was shown in Chapter 15 for other factors of production, the derived demand and, consequently, the demand curve for labor are determined by labor's marginal revenue product. A profit-maximizing firm will want to hire that quantity of labor at which its marginal revenue product is equal to the market wage. Such a demand curve is shown in Figure 16–4 as curve *DD*. The figure also includes a supply curve, labeled *SS*, much like the one depicted in Figure 16–2.

If there are no interferences with the operation of a free market in labor (such as minimum wages or unions—which we will consider later), equilibrium will be at point *E*, where the supply and demand curves intersect. In this example,

Figure 16–4 **EQUILIBRIUM IN A COMPETITIVE LABOR MARKET**

In a competitive labor market, equilibrium will be established at the wage that equates the quantity supplied with the quantity demanded. In this example, equilibrium is at point *E*, where demand curve *DD* crosses supply curve *SS*. The equilibrium wage is $300 per week and equilibrium employment is 500,000 workers.

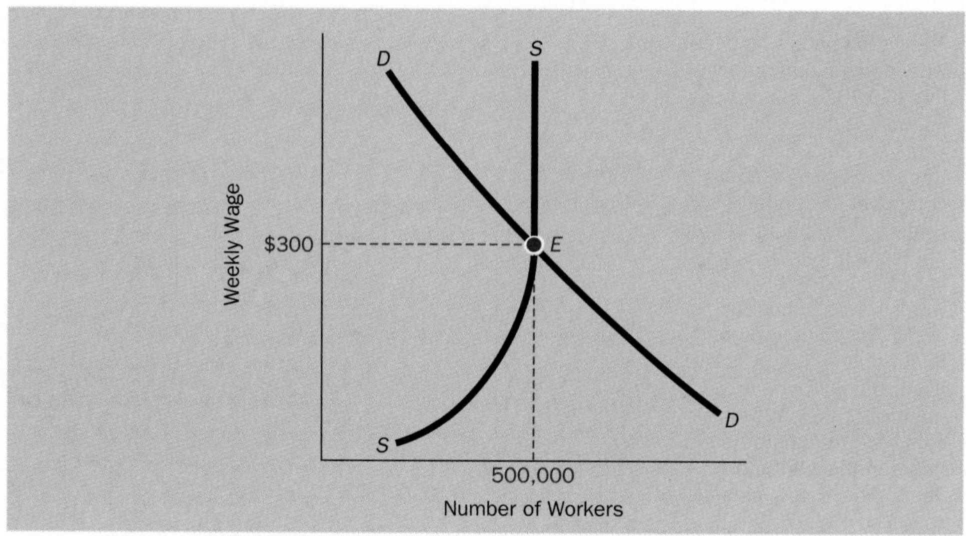


500,000 workers will be employed at a wage of $300 per week, so that the total income of the workers will be $300 x 0.5 million = $150 million.

## WHY WAGES DIFFER

However, of course, there is not one labor market but many—each with its own supply and demand curves and its own equilibrium wage. We all know that certain groups in our society (the young, the black, the uneducated) earn relatively low wages, and that some of our most severe social ills (poverty, crime, drug addiction) are related to this fact. But why are some wages so low while others are so high?

Supply-and-demand analysis at once tells us everything and nothing about this question. It implies that wages are relatively high in markets where demand is great and supply is small [see Figure 16–5(a)], while wages are comparatively low in markets where demand is weak and supply is high [see Figure 16–5(b)]. This can hardly be considered startling news. But to make the analysis useful, we need to breathe some life into the supply and demand curves.

We begin our discussion on the demand side. Why is the demand for labor greater in some markets than in others? The marginal productivity principle teaches us that there are two types of influences to be considered. Since the marginal revenue product of workers depends both on their *marginal physical product* and on the *price of the product* that they produce, variables that influence either of these will influence their wages.

The determinants of the prices of commodities were discussed at some length in earlier chapters, and there is no need to repeat the analysis here. It is sufficient to remember that because the demand for labor is a *derived demand*, anything that

Figure 16-5 **WAGE DIFFERENTIALS**

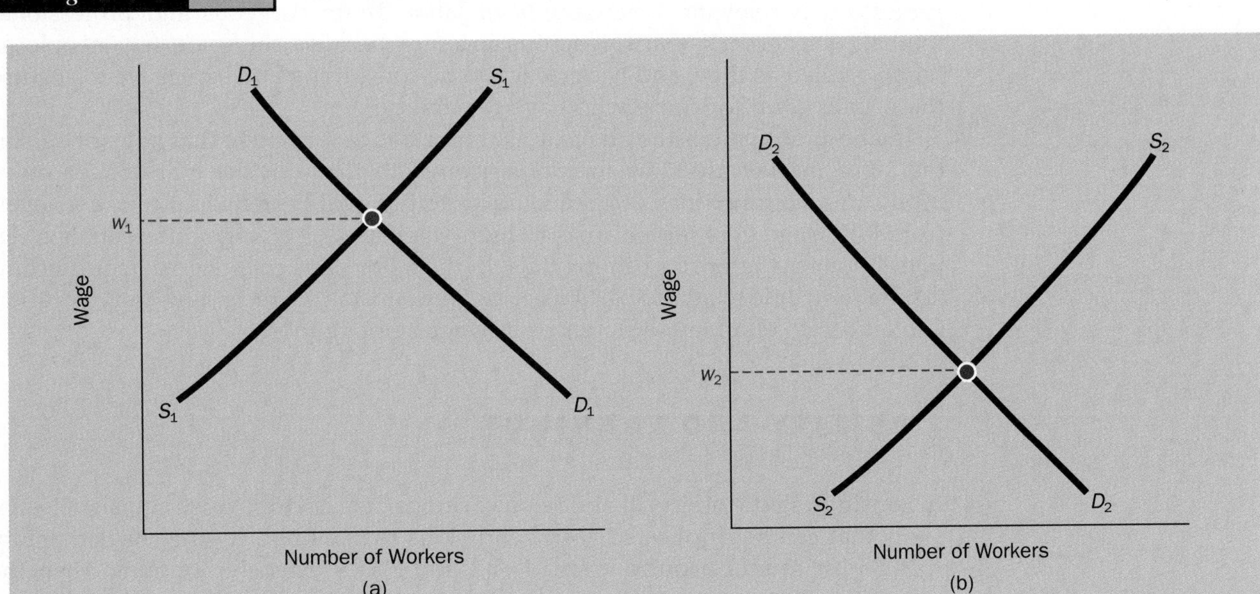


(a) The market depicted here has a high equilibrium wage, because demand is high relative to supply. This can occur if qualified workers are scarce, or if productivity on the job is high or if the demand for the product is great. (b) By contrast, the equilibrium wage $W_2$, is low here, where supply is high relative to demand. This can result from an abundant supply of qualified workers, or low productivity, or weak demand for the product.

raises or lowers the demand for a particular product will tend to raise or lower the wages of the workers that produce that product.

A worker's marginal physical product depends on several things, including of course, his own *abilities* and *degree of effort* on the job. But sometimes these characteristics are less important than the *other factors of production* that he has to work with. Workers in American industry are more productive than workers in many other countries because they have generous supplies of machinery, natural resources, and technical know-how to work with. As a consequence, they earn high wages.

Turning next to differences in the supply of labor to different areas, industries, or occupations, it is clear that the *size of the available working population* relative to the magnitude of industrial activity in a given area is of major importance. This helps explain why wages rose so high in sparsely populated Alaska when the Alaskan pipeline created many new jobs, and why wages have been and remain so low in Appalachia, where industry is dormant.

Second, it is clear that the *nonmonetary attractiveness* of any job will also influence the supply of workers to it. (The monetary attractiveness is the wage itself, which governs movements *along* the supply curve.) Jobs that people find pleasant and satisfying—such as teaching in suburban schools—will attract a large supply of labor, and will consequently pay a low wage. In contrast, a premium will have to be paid to attract workers to jobs that are onerous, disagreeable, or dangerous—such as washing the windows of skyscrapers.

Finally, the amount of ability and training needed to enter a particular job or profession is relevant to its supply of labor. Brain surgeons and professional football quarterbacks earn generous incomes because there are few people as highly skilled as they, and because it is time consuming and expensive to acquire these skills even for those who have the ability.

In addition to all of the above, it is important to recognize that adjustments in the labor market are slow in comparison with those in the markets for other inputs and commodities. Workers, for example, will be reluctant to move, even from low-wage geographic areas to high-wage areas; so wage differentials often persist longer than price differentials. In the labor markets, long-run equilibrium takes a long time to attain, particularly where substantial retraining and relocation is required to eliminate differences in wages among jobs.

## ABILITY AND EARNINGS

In considering the effects of ability on earnings, it is useful to distinguish between skills that can be duplicated easily and skills that cannot. If Jones has an ability that Smith cannot acquire, even if she undergoes extensive training, then the wages that Jones earns will contain an element of *economic rent*, just as in the case of basketball player Michael Jordan.[2]

Indeed, the salaries of professional athletes provide particularly clear examples of how economic rents can lead to huge wage differentials. Virtually anyone with moderate athletic ability can be taught to jump and toss a basketball at a hoop. But in most cases, no amount of training will teach the player to play basketball like Michael Jordan. Jordan's high salary is a reward for his unique ability.

But many of the abilities that the market rewards generously—such as the skills of doctors and lawyers—clearly are duplicable. Here the theory of rent does not apply, and we need a different explanation of the high wages that these skilled professionals earn. Once again, however, part of our analysis from Chapter 15 finds an immediate application because the acquisition of skills, through formal education and other forms of training has much in common with business investment decisions. Why? Because the decision to undertake more education in the hope of increasing future earnings involves a sacrifice of *current* income for the sake of *future* gain—precisely the hallmark of an investment decision.

## INVESTMENT IN HUMAN CAPITAL

That education is an investment is a concept familiar to most college students. You made a conscious decision to go to college rather than to enter the labor market, and you are probably acutely aware that this decision is now costing you money—lots of money. Your tuition payments may be only a minor part of the total cost of going to college. Think of a high school friend who chose not to go to college and is now working. The salary that he or she is earning could, perhaps, have been yours. You are deliberately giving up this possible income in order to acquire more education.

---

[2]See the previous chapter, pages 375–79.

In this sense, your education can be thought of as an *investment* in yourself—a *human investment*. Like a firm that devotes some of its money to building a plant that will yield profits at some future date, you are investing in your own future, hoping that your college education will help you earn more than your high school-educated friend or enable you to find a more pleasant or prestigious job when you graduate. Economists call activities such as going to college **investments in human capital** because such activities give the human being many of the attributes of a capital investment.

Doctors and lawyers earn such high salaries partly because of their many years of training. That is, part of their wages can be construed as a *return on their (educational) investments*, rather than as economic rent. Unlike the case of Michael Jordan, there are a number of people who conceivably *could* become surgeons if they found the job sufficiently attractive to endure the long years of training that are required. Few, however, are willing to make such a large investment of their own time, money, and energy. Consequently, the few who do become surgeons earn very generous incomes.

Economists have devoted quite a bit of attention to the acquisition of skills through human investment. There is an entire branch of economic theory—called **human capital theory**—that analyzes an individual's decisions about education, training, and so on in exactly the same way as we analyzed a firm's decision to buy a machine or build a factory in the previous chapter. Though educational decisions can be influenced by love of learning, desire for prestige, and a variety of other preferences and emotions, human capital theorists find it useful to analyze a schooling decision as if it were made purely as a business plan. The optimal length of education, from this point of view, is to stay in school until the marginal revenue (in the form of increased future income) of an additional year of schooling is exactly equal to the marginal cost.

One implication of human capital theory is that college graduates should earn enough more than high school graduates to compensate them for their extra investments in schooling. Do they? Will your college investment pay off? Many generations of college students have supposed that it would, and for years studies of the incomes earned by college students have indicated that they were right (the boxed insert on page 398 describes one of the more recent studies). These studies showed that the income differentials earned by college graduates provided a good "return" on the tuition payments and sacrificed earnings that they "invested" while in school.

Human capital theory stresses that jobs that require more education *must* pay higher wages if they are to attract enough workers, because people insist on a financial return on their human investments. But the theory does not address the other side of the question, What is it about more-educated people that makes firms willing to pay them higher wages? Put differently, the theory explains why the quantity of educated people *supplied* is limited but does not explain why the quantity *demanded* is substantial even at high wages.

Most human capital theorists complete their analyses by assuming that students in high schools and colleges acquire particular skills that are productive in the marketplace. In this view, educational institutions are factories that take less-productive workers as their raw materials, apply doses of training and produce more-productive workers as outputs. It is a view of what happens in schools that makes educators happy and accords well with common sense. However, a number of social scientists doubt that this is how schooling raises earning power.

## The Widening Wage Gap

Relative wages changed dramatically during the 1980s. The big winners were college-educated men and women. The big losers were young men with a high school education or less.

Two University of Michigan economists, John Bound and George Johnson, argue that the changes were the result of shifts in labor demand caused by technological change—particularly the increased use of computers in production.

The chart shows the ratios of wages for workers with a college education versus those with a high school education for men and women with various levels of work experience in 1979 and in 1988. In all cases the gap between wages for college-educated workers and high school-educated workers widened. The spread was particularly large for young workers. College-educated males with less than 10 years of experience, for example, earned 27 percent more than their high school-educated counterparts in 1979. By 1988, they earned 66 percent more.

The wider gap was a result both of wage gains for college-educated workers and of wage losses of workers with a high school education or less. The real wages of young high school-educated males fell 18 percent. Real wages for high school-educated women fell 10 percent.

. . . Women with less education lost less than did men, while women with college educations achieved greater gains than men. The result was that wages for all women rose by eight percent more than did wages for all men. That reduced the average wage gap between men and women from 30 percent in 1979 to 24 percent in 1988.

**Wages: High School vs. College**

1979
1988
Years of work experience
Men
0–9
10–19
20–29
30 or more
Women
0–9
10–19
20–29
30 or more
1
1.2
1.4
1.6
1.8
Wage of college-educated workers divided by wage of high school-educated workers, 1979 and 1988

SOURCE: Timothy Tregarthen, "Technological Change Boosts Wage Gap," *The Margin*, Spring 1993, pages 42–43, which is based on John Bound and George Johnson, "Changes in the Structure of Wages in the 1980s: An Evaluation of Alternative Explanations," *American Economic Review*, 82 (3), June 1992, pages 371–92.

## EDUCATION AND EARNINGS: DISSENTING VIEWS

Just why is it that jobs with stiffer educational requirements typically offer higher wages? The common-sense view that educating people makes them more productive is not universally accepted.

### EDUCATION AS A SORTING MECHANISM

One alternative view denies that the educational process teaches students anything directly relevant to their subsequent performance on jobs. On this view, people differ in ability when they enter the school system and differ in more or less the same way when they leave. What the educational system does, according to this theory, is to *sort* individuals by ability. Skills like intelligence and self-discipline that lead to success in schools, it is argued, are closely related to the skills that lead to success in jobs. As a result, more able individuals stay in school longer and perform better. Prospective employers know this, and consequently seek to hire those whom the school system has suggested will be the most productive workers.

## THE RADICAL VIEW OF EDUCATION

Many radical economists question whether the educational system really sorts people according to ability. The rich, they note, are better situated to buy the best education and to keep their children in school regardless of ability. Thus, education may be one of the instruments by which a more privileged family passes its economic position on to its heirs while making it appear that there is a legitimate reason for firms to give them higher earnings. As radicals see it, education sorts people according to their social class, not according to their ability.

Radicals also hold a different idea about what happens inside schools to make workers more "productive." In this view, instead of serving primarily as instruments for the acquisition of knowledge and improved ability to think, what schools do primarily is teach people discipline—how to show up five days a week at 9 A.M., how to speak in turn and respectfully, and so on. These characteristics, radicals claim, are what business firms prefer and what causes them to seek more educated workers. They also suggest that the schools teach docility and acceptance of the capitalist status quo, and that this, too, makes schooling attractive to business.

## THE DUAL LABOR MARKET THEORY

A third view of the linkages among education, ability, and earnings is part of a much broader theory of how the labor market operates—the theory of **dual labor markets**. Proponents of this theory suggest that there are two very different types of labor markets, with relatively little mobility between them.

The "primary labor market" is where most of the economy's "good jobs" are—jobs like computer programming, business management, and skilled crafts that are interesting and offer considerable possibilities for career advancement. The educational system helps decide which individuals get assigned to the primary labor market and, for those who make it, greater educational achievement does indeed offer financial rewards.

The privileged workers who wind up in the primary labor market are offered opportunities for additional training on the job; they augment their skills by experience and by learning from their fellow workers; and they progress in successive steps to more responsible, better paying positions. Where jobs in the primary labor market are concerned, dual labor market theorists agree with human capital theorists that education really is productive. But they agree with the radicals that admission to the primary labor market depends in part on social position, and that firms probably care more about steady work habits and punctuality than about reading, writing, and arithmetic.

Everything is quite different in the "secondary labor market"—where we find all the "bad jobs." Jobs like domestic service and fast-food service, which are often the only ones inner city residents can find, offer low rates of pay, few fringe benefits, and virtually no training to improve the workers' skills. They are dead-end jobs with little or no hope for promotion or advancement. As a result, lateness, absenteeism, and pilferage are expected as a matter of course, so that workers in the secondary labor market tend to develop the bad work habits that confirm the prejudices of those who assigned them to inferior jobs in the first place.

In the secondary labor market, increased education leads neither to higher wages nor to increased protection from unemployment—benefits that increased schooling generally offers elsewhere in the labor market. For this reason, workers in the secondary market have little incentive to invest in education.

In sum, we have a well-established fact—that people with more education generally earn higher wages—but very little agreement on the theory that accounts for this fact. Probably, there is some truth to all of the proposed explanations; each of which, consequently, has some relevance for the working of the labor market in reality.

## THE EFFECTS OF MINIMUM WAGE LEGISLATION

As we have observed, the "labor market" is really composed of many submarkets for labor of different types, each with its own supply and demand curves. To understand the possible effects of minimum wage legislation, the prime form of political intervention in the wage-determination process, it suffices to consider two such markets, which we call for convenience "skilled" and "unskilled" labor and portray in the two parts of Figure 16–6. Before proceeding, it should be noted that the following discussion is controversial and new evidence indicates that it

**Figure 16–6 POSSIBLE EFFECTS OF MINIMUM WAGE LEGISLATION**

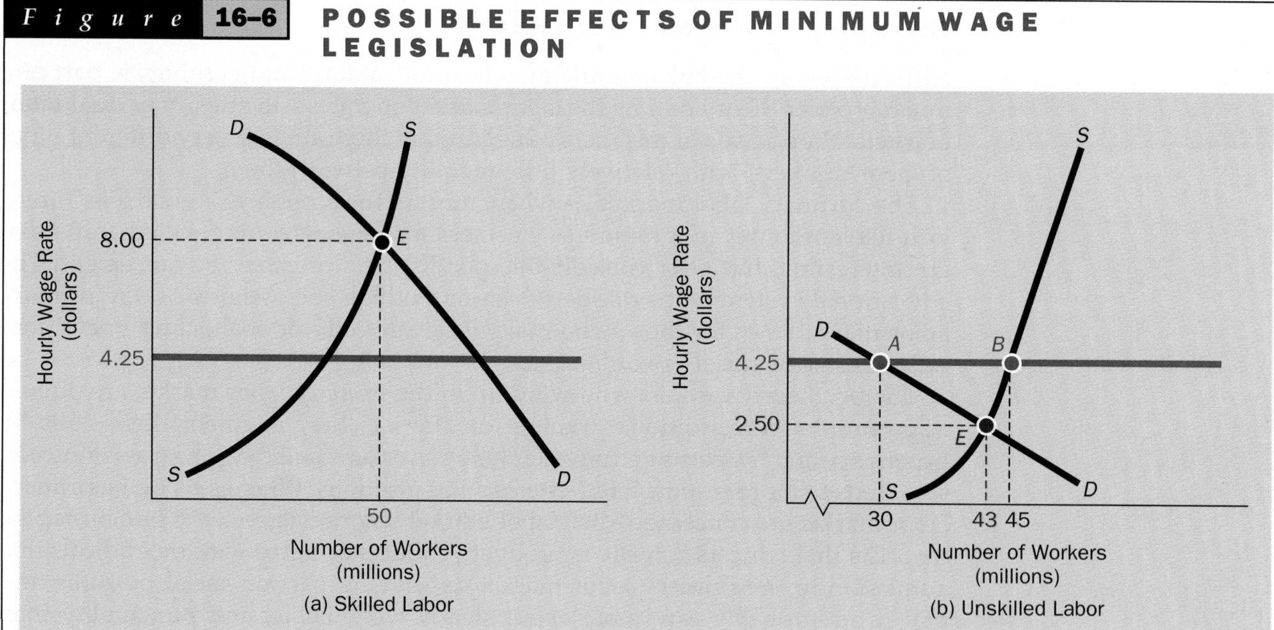


(a) Imposing a minimum wage of $4.25 per hour does not affect the market for skilled labor because the equilibrium wage there ($8 per hour) is well above the legal minimum. (b) However, the minimum-wage legislation does have important effects in the market for unskilled labor. There the equilibrium wage ($2.50 per hour) is below the minimum, so the minimum wage makes the quantity supplied (45 million workers) exceed the quantity demanded (30 million workers). The result is unemployment of unskilled labor.

exaggerates the matter, at the very least. As often happens in scientific study, research may force economists to change previous conclusions.

As drawn, the demand curve for skilled workers in the graph is higher than that for unskilled workers. The reason is obvious: skilled workers have higher productivity. We have also drawn the supply curve of skilled workers farther to the left than the supply curve of unskilled workers to reflect the greater scarcity of skilled workers. The consequence, as we can see in Figure 16–6, is that the equilibrium wage is much higher for skilled workers. In the example, the equilibrium wages are $8 per hour for skilled workers and $2.50 per hour for unskilled workers.

Now suppose the government, seeking to protect unskilled workers, imposes a legal minimum wage of $4.25 per hour (the blue line in both parts of Figure 16–6). Turning first to part (a), we see that the minimum wage has no effect in the markets for skilled workers like carpenters and electricians. Since their wages are well above $4.25 per hour, a law prohibiting the payment of wage rates below $4.25 cannot possibly matter.

But the effects of the minimum wage may be pronounced in the markets for unskilled labor—and possibly quite different from those that Congress intended. Figure 16–6(b) indicates that at the $4.25 minimum wage firms want to employ only 30 million unskilled workers (point *A*) whereas employment of unskilled workers would have been 43 million (point *E*) in a free market. Although the 30 million unskilled workers lucky enough to retain their jobs do indeed earn a higher wage ($4.25 instead of $2.50 per hour) in this hypothetical example, 13 million of their compatriots earn no wage at all because they have been laid off. The job losers will clearly be those workers with the lowest productivity, since the minimum wage effectively bans the employment of workers whose marginal revenue product is less than $4.25 per hour.

Although the minimum wage does lead to higher wages for those unskilled workers who retain their jobs, it also restricts employment opportunities for unskilled workers.

In addition, minimum wages may have particularly pernicious effects on those who are the victims of discrimination. Because of the minimum wage, as Figure 16–6(b) shows, employers of unskilled labor have more applicants than job openings. Consequently, they will be able to pick and choose among the available applicants and may, for example, discriminate against blacks who have been prevented by past discrimination from acquiring the skills required for admission to the higher-paid portion of the labor force.

For these reasons, many economists feel that the teenage unemployment problem, and especially the black teenage unemployment problem, will be very difficult to solve as long as the minimum wage remains effective. Obviously, the minimum wage is not the only culprit; the data strongly suggest that there is more to the story. Yet it is hard to dismiss the analytic conclusion that forced overpricing of unskilled labor contributes to unemployment. The question, of course, is how much? If minimum wage laws raise wages a good deal but restrict employment only to a negligible degree, one may well conclude that it is all worthwhile, even for the poorest and least skilled workers. Recent statistical studies suggest that this is in fact the case. If so, the undesirable effects of the minimum wage laws are far less serious than previously was widely believed by economists. It may even be reasonable to conclude that the laws are, on the whole, beneficial, despite their interference with the market mechanism.

## UNIONS AND COLLECTIVE BARGAINING

Our analysis of competitive labor markets has ignored one rather important fact: The supply of labor is not at all competitive in many labor markets; instead it is controlled by a labor monopoly, a union. This is a very distinctive feature of the supply side of the markets for labor.

While important, unions in America are not nearly so important as is popularly supposed. For example, most people who are not acquainted with the data are astonished to learn that just 16 percent of American workers belong to unions. This percentage is much higher than it was before the New Deal, when unions were quite unimportant in this country, but lower than it was in the heyday of unionism in the mid-1950s, when the figure was about 25 percent (see Figure 16–7). This percentage has been falling fairly steadily since then, and the decline has recently accelerated.

It seems to mean that the influence of unions on the American economy is eroding and that the use of nonunionized labor is becoming the norm rather than the exception. In part this trend has been attributed to the shift of the U.S. labor force (like that of every other industrial country) into services jobs and out of manufacturing where unions traditionally had their base. Deregulation, which freed firms such as airlines to compete intensively against one another, also influenced firms to move aggressively toward nonunion labor. However, there also seems to have been a shift in the preferences of the members of the United States labor force away from unionization and perhaps some decline in the power of the unions to improve the economic position of their members. The increasing

*Figure* **16–7** **UNIONIZATION IN THE UNITED STATES, 1930–1991**

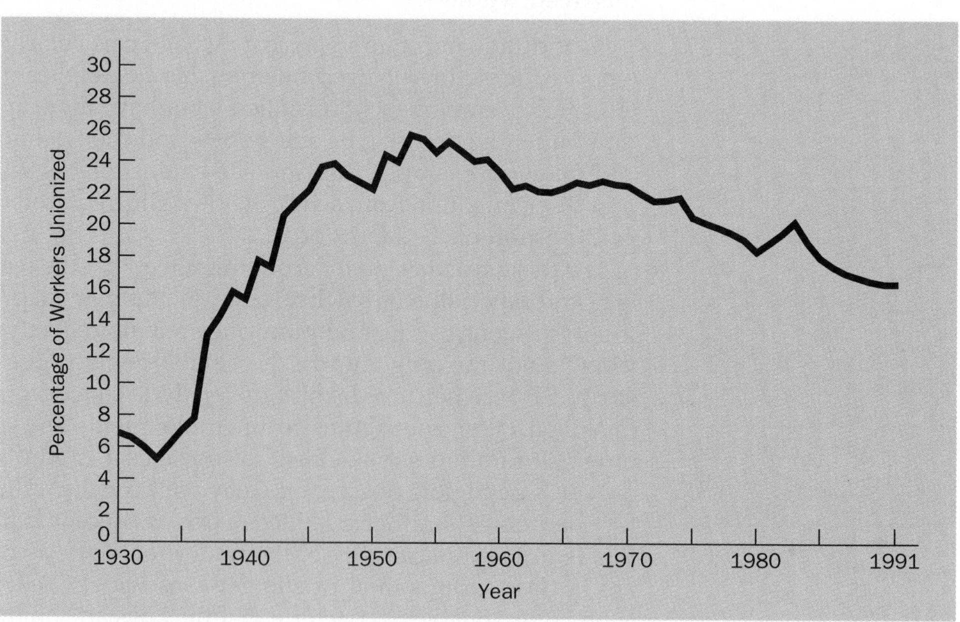


In 1930, unions had enrolled just under 7 percent of the U.S. labor force and by 1933 this figure had slipped to barely above 5 percent. Unionization took off with the New Deal, reaching almost 16 percent of the labor force by 1939. It then drifted irregularly upward to a peak of about 25 to 26 percent of all workers in the mid-1950s, from which it has since fallen more or less steadily back to 16 percent in 1991.

SOURCE: U.S. Department of Labor, Bureau of Labor Statistics, *Employment and Earnings*, January issues, various years.

share of women in the labor force—with women traditionally less prone to union membership—has also played a role. These, together with what seems to be a widespread change in attitudes toward unions, have led to the decline in unionization that has occurred in recent years.

Unionization is also much less prevalent in America than it is in most other industrialized countries. For example, 31 percent of western German workers and about 90 percent of Swedish workers belong to unions.[3] The differences are quite striking and doubtless have something to do with our tradition of "rugged individualism."

The main sector of the economy in which the unions are still fairly healthy is government employment. People who work for municipalities, the states, and the federal government are relatively unionized, perhaps because their job opportunities are controlled by political forces, and politicians find it far harder to resist the unions than private firms do.

## THE DEVELOPMENT OF UNIONISM IN AMERICA

Serious unionism in America is only about 100 years old. Large-scale unions in this country began with the Knights of Labor—a politically oriented organization quite different from the unions of today. Toward the end of the nineteenth century its membership approached 750,000 workers; but it failed to achieve higher wages or better working conditions, and the organization declined rapidly.

The current union structure began to take shape in 1881 with the founding of the American Federation of Labor (AFL) by Samuel Gompers, who headed the AFL for nearly 50 years and did more to shape the American labor movement than any other person. Working conditions then were incredibly bad by today's standards, and unscrupulous practices fostered the growth of unions (see the box on page 404).

Gompers believed strongly that unions should be nonpolitical organizations seeking to get their members more pay, better working conditions, longer vacations, and so on. He also believed that unions should be organized along craft lines—carpenters in one union, plumbers in another—rather than trying to include all types of workers in a given industry.

The AFL grew rather steadily from about 1900 until the 1920s, went into decline during the Roaring Twenties, but then grew rapidly thanks to the favorable legislation of the Roosevelt administration in the 1930s. The Norris-La Guardia Act of 1932 sharply limited the power of the federal courts to interfere in labor disputes. In 1938 the Fair Labor Standards Act abolished child labor, imposed a minimum wage on most activities in interstate commerce, and required extra pay for overtime work.

Even more important, the National Labor Relations Act (Wagner Act) in 1935 guaranteed workers the right to form unions and to choose the union to represent them in collective bargaining. It also set up the National Labor Relations Board (NLRB) to protect labor from "unfair labor practices" by employers. Today the NLRB oversees elections in firms to determine which union will represent the workers. It can also force employers to take back workers whom it considers to have been fired unjustly.

---

[3]Sources: For Germany: "Germany Labours On," *The Economist*, January 23, 1993, pages 63–64; for Sweden: R. Bean, *International Labour Statistics*, New York and London: Routledge, 1989.

## The Way It Was

The calamitous Triangle Shirtwaist Factory fire of 1911, in which 146 women and girls lost their lives, was a landmark in American labor history. It galvanized public opinion behind the movement to improve conditions, hours, and wages in the sweatshops. Pauline Newman went to work in the Triangle Shirtwaist Factory at the age of eight, shortly after coming to the Lower East Side. Many of her friends lost their lives in the fire. She went on to become an organizer and later an executive of the newly formed International Ladies Garment Workers' Union, and served as its educational director until she was almost 90 years of age.*

The Triangle Factory, now part of New York University.

We started work at seven-thirty in the morning, and during the busy season we worked until nine in the evening. They didn't pay you any overtime and they didn't give you anything for supper money. Sometimes they'd give you a little apple pie if you had to work very late. That was all. Very generous . . . .

We had a corner on the floor that resembled a kindergarten—we were given little scissors to cut the threads off. It wasn't heavy work, but it was monotonous.

Well, of course, there were laws on the books, but no one bothered to enforce them. The employers were always tipped off if there was going to be an inspection. "Quick," they'd say, "into the boxes!" And we children would climb into the big boxes the finished shirts were stored in. Then some shirts were piled on top of us, and when the inspector came—no children. The factory always got an okay from the inspector, and I suppose someone at City Hall got a little something, too.

The employers didn't recognize anyone working for them as a human being. You were not allowed to sing. . . . We weren't allowed to talk to each other. . . . If you went to the toilet and you were there longer than the floor lady thought you should be, you would be laid off for half a day and sent home. And, of course, that meant no pay. You were not allowed to have your lunch on the fire escape in the summertime. The door was locked to keep us in. That's why so many people were trapped when the fire broke out. . . .

The employers had a sign in the elevator that said: "If you don't come in on Sunday, don't come in on Monday." You were expected to work every day if they needed you and the pay was the same whether you worked extra or not.

Conditions were dreadful in those days. We didn't have anything. . . . There was no welfare, no pension, no unemployment insurance. There was nothing. . . . There was so much feeling against unions then. The judges, when one of our girls came before him, said to her: "You're not striking against your employer, you know, young lady. You're striking against God," and sentenced her to two weeks.

I wasn't at the Triangle Shirtwaist Factory when the fire broke out, but a lot of my friends were. . . . The thing that bothered me was the employers got a lawyer. How anyone could have *defended* them!—because I'm quite sure that the fire was planned for insurance purposes. And no one is going to convince me otherwise. And when they testified that the door to the fire escape was open, it was a lie! It was never open. Locked all the time. One hundred and forty-six people sacrificed, and the judge fined Blank and Harris seventy-five dollars!

*This introduction and the following narrative are excerpted from the book *American Mosaic: The Immigrant Experience in the Words of Those Who Lived It*, by Joan Morrison and Charlotte Fox Zabusky, copyright 1980 by Joan Morrison and Charlotte Fox Zabusky. Reprinted by permission of the publisher, E. P. Dutton, Inc.

An **INDUSTRIAL UNION** represents all types of workers in a single industry, such as auto manufacturing or coal mining.

A **CRAFT UNION** represents a particular type of skilled worker, such as newspaper typographers or electricians, regardless of what industry they work in.

A **CLOSED SHOP** is an arrangement that permits only union members to be hired.

A **UNION SHOP** is an arrangement under which nonunion workers may be hired, but then must join the union within a specified period of time.

By no coincidence, in the year of the Wagner Act, John L. Lewis founded the Congress of Industrial Organizations (CIO), a federation of many **industrial unions** that at first rivaled the AFL for leadership of the U.S. labor movement. It was felt by those who advocated industrial unions that many specialized **craft unions** (which often quarreled among themselves) were not likely to be very powerful in their dealings with large employers. Despite their differences, the AFL, with its craft unions, and the CIO, with its industrial unions, eventually merged in 1955.

The favorable public attitude toward unions soured somewhat after World War II, perhaps because of the rash of strikes that took place in 1946. One result of these strikes was the **Taft-Hartley Act** of 1947, which specified and outlawed certain "unfair labor practices" by unions and which sought to shift some of labor's power back to management. Specifically, the act:

1. Severely limited the extent of the **closed shop**, under which only union members can be hired.
2. Permitted state governments, at their discretion, to ban the **union shop**, an arrangement that *requires* employees to join the union. These so-called right-to-work laws have been adopted by several states.
3. Provided for court injunctions to delay strikes that threaten the national interest for an 80-day "cooling-off" period.

Today, the character of American unionism is still somewhat unsettled. Unions are struggling very hard to make inroads into labor markets that by tradition have not been unionized—such as the agricultural and white-collar office markets. Notable successes have been achieved in organizing teachers and many government employees. But at the same time union membership as a percent of the labor force is declining sharply.

U.S. labor unions are very different from those in Europe and Japan. Unlike Japanese unions, American unions and management often see themselves as adversaries. The century-long tradition of hostile labor-management relations in this country impedes current attempts to emulate the Japanese model of labor-management cooperation. It is reported that in several plants in the United States that are owned and run by Japanese companies, management has achieved an unprecedented degree of trust and support from the labor force. However, U.S. labor still seems to feel that employers in American firms are all too likely to adopt unfair practices unless they are restrained by powerful unions. Yet despite all this, U.S. unions are strongly committed to capitalism and rarely espouse socialism—unlike their Western European counterparts.

## UNIONS AS A LABOR MONOPOLY

Unions require that we alter our economic analysis of the labor market in much the same way that monopolies required us to alter our analysis of the goods market (see Chapter 11). You will recall that in a monopolized product market the firm selects the point on its demand curve that maximizes its profits. Much the same idea applies to unions, which are, after all, monopoly sellers of labor. They too face a demand curve—derived this time from the marginal productivity schedules of firms—and can choose the point on it that suits them best.

The problem for the economist trying to analyze union behavior—and perhaps also for the union leader trying to select a course of action—is how to decide which point on the demand curve is "best." Unlike the case of the business firm, there is no obvious goal analogous to profit-maximization that clearly delineates what the union should do. Instead there are a number of *alternative* goals that sound plausible. In part, the reason is that union members themselves differ in their objectives, particularly in the trade-off between higher wages and job security. If older workers are protected from being fired by **seniority rules**, which require those who have held jobs longest to be the last to be dismissed, these older workers may give greater priority to high wages than younger workers do. What policy union leaders will pursue may depend on the relative power of the different groups of members in a union's election of its leaders.

**SENIORITY RULES** are rules that give special job-related advantages to workers who have held their jobs longest. In particular this usually requires that workers most recently hired be the first to be fired when a firm cuts employment.

## ALTERNATIVE UNION GOALS

The different implications of alternative union goals can be illustrated with the aid of Figure 16–8, which depicts a demand curve for labor, labeled *DD*. The union leadership must decide which point on the curve is best. One possibility is to treat the size of the union as fixed and force employers to pay the highest wage they will pay and still employ all the union members. If, for example, the union has 4000 members, this would be point *A*, with a wage of $12 per hour. But this is a high-risk strategy for a union. Firms forced to pay such high wages will be at a competitive disadvantage compared with firms that have nonunion labor, and they may even be forced to shut down.

Alternatively, union leaders may be interested in increasing the size of their unions. As an extreme case of this, they might try to make employment as large as possible without pushing the wage below the competitive level. If the competitive wage were $6 per hour in the absence of the union, this strategy would

**Figure 16–8** ALTERNATIVE GOALS FOR A UNION

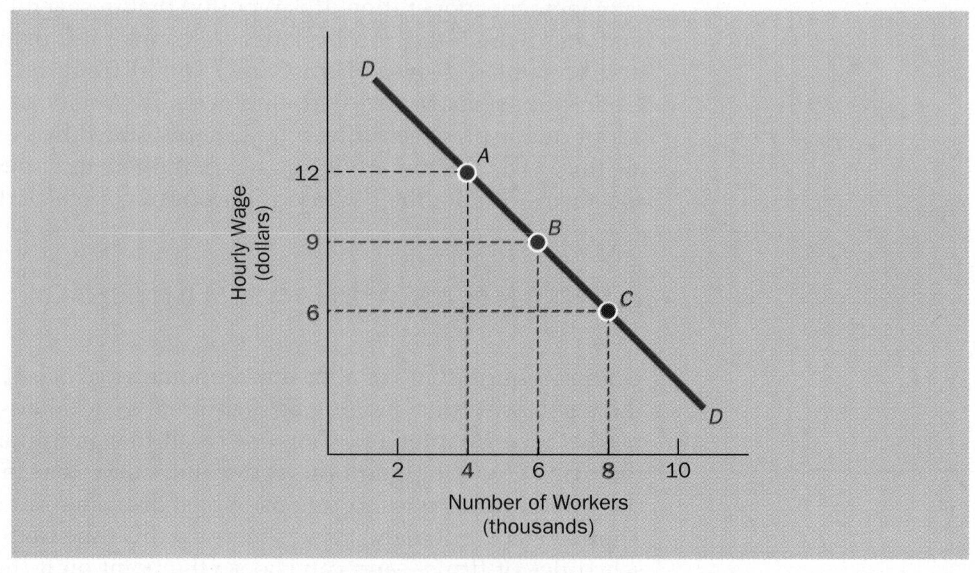


Line *DD* is the demand curve for labor in a market that becomes unionized. Point *C* is the equilibrium point before the union, when wages were $6 per hour. If the union wants to push wages higher, it normally will have to sacrifice some jobs. Points *A* and *B* show two of its many alternatives.

correspond to selecting point *C*, with employment for 8000 workers. In this case the existence of the union has no effect on wages or on employment.

An intermediate strategy that has often been suggested is that the union maximize the total income of all workers taken together. This would dictate choosing point *B*, with a wage of $9 per hour and jobs for 6000 workers. But it also means that employment will be lower than under the strategy of the previous paragraph. Presumably, with a wage that maximizes the total income of the workers as a group some way must be found to compensate any union members who become jobless as a result of this union policy. Other possible strategies can also be imagined, but these suffice to make the basic point clear.

Unions, as monopoly sellers of labor, have the power to push wages above the competitive levels. However, since the demand curve for labor is downward sloping, such increases in wages normally can be achieved only by reducing the number of jobs. Just as monopolists must limit their outputs to push up their prices, so the union must restrict employment to push up the wage.

This can be seen clearly by comparing points *B* and *A* with point *C* (the competitive solution). If it selects point *B*, the union raises wages by $3 per hour, but at the cost of 2000 jobs. If it goes all the way to point *A*, wages are raised to twice the competitive level, but employment is cut in half.

What do unions actually try to do? There are probably as many different choices as there are unions. Some seem to pursue a maximum-employment goal much like point *C*, raising wages very little. Others seem to push for the highest possible wages, much like point *A*. Most probably select an intermediate route. This implies, of course, that the effects of unionization on wage rates and employment will differ markedly among industries.

## ALTERNATIVE UNION STRATEGIES

How would a union that has decided to push wages above the competitive level accomplish this task? Two principal ways are illustrated in Figure 16–9, where we suppose that point *U* on demand curve *DD* is the union's choice, and point *C* is the competitive equilibrium.

In Figure 16–9(a), we suppose that the union pursues its goal by *restricting supply*. By keeping out some workers who would like to enter the industry or occupation, it shifts the supply curve of labor inward from $S_0S_0$ to $S_1S_1$. This sort of behavior is often encountered in craft unions, which may require a long period of apprenticeship. Such unions sometimes offer only a small number of new memberships each year, largely to replace members who have died or retired. Membership in such a union is very valuable and is sometimes offered primarily to children of current members.

Some unions have also sought to protect their members by excluding women and racial minority groups from membership or by putting severe impediments in their way. For example, when apprenticeships have been reserved for the children of current or past members of the union, if all or almost all of those members are and have been white, that is a roundabout but effective way to close the door to union membership and jobs to black workers and others.

In Figure 16–9(b), instead of restricting supply, the union simply *sets a high wage rate*, *W* in the example. In this case, it is the employers who will restrict entry into the job, because with wages so high they will not want to employ many workers. This second strategy is more typically employed by industrial unions

Figure 16–9 **TWO UNION STRATEGIES**

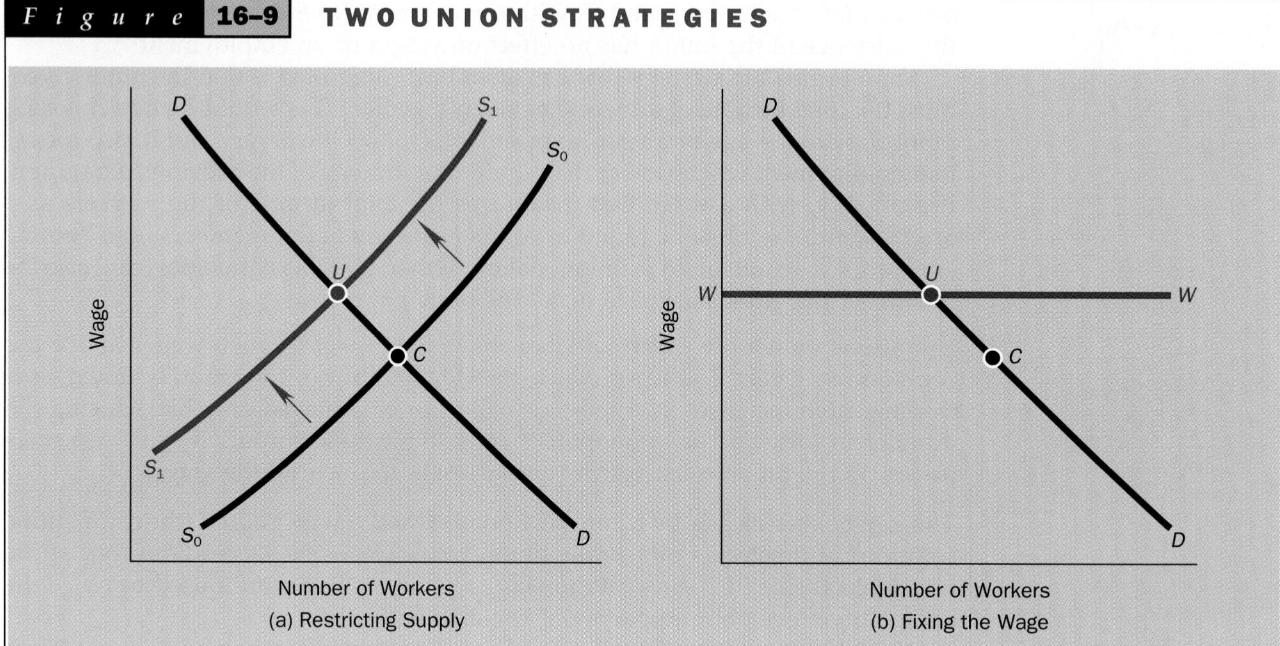


The two parts indicate two alternative ways for the union to move from point *C* to point *U*. In part (a), it keeps some workers out of the industry, thereby moving the supply curve to the left from $S_0S_0$ to $S_1S_1$. As a consequence, wages rise. In part (b), it fixes a high wage (*W*) and provides labor only at this wage. Therefore, firms reduce employment. The effects are the same under both strategies.

like the United Automobile Workers or the United Mine Workers. As the figure makes clear, the two wage-raising strategies achieve the same result (point *U* in either case) by what turns out to be the same means. Wages are raised only by reducing employment in either case.

In some exceptional cases, however, a union may be able to achieve wage gains without sacrificing employment. To do this, the union must be able to exercise effective control over the demand curve for labor. Figure 16–10 illustrates such a possibility. Union actions push the demand curve outward from $D_0D_0$ to $D_1D_1$, simultaneously raising both wages and employment. Typically, this is difficult to do. One way to do it is by *featherbedding*—forcing management to employ more workers than they really need.[4] Quite the opposite technique is to institute a campaign to raise worker productivity, which some unions seem to have been able to do. Alternatively, the union can try to raise the demand for the company's product either by flexing its political muscle (for example, by obtaining legislation to reduce foreign competition) or by appealing to the public to buy union products.

[4]The best-known example of featherbedding involved the railroad unions, which for years forced management to keep "firemen" in the cabs of diesel engines, in which there were no burning fires. Similarly, the musicians' union in New York City forces Broadway producers who use certain theaters to employ a minimum number of musicians—whether or not they actually play music. Of course, it is not only labor that has tried to create an artificial demand for its services. Lawyers, doctors, and business firms, among others, have sought ways to induce consumers to buy more of their products and services. EXERCISE: Can you think of ways in which they have done this?

Figure 16-10 **UNION CONTROL OVER THE DEMAND CURVE**

This diagram indicates yet a third way in which unions may affect the labor market—a pleasant alternative for workers in that wages can be raised while adding to employment. Strong unions may succeed in raising the demand curve from $D_0D_0$ to $D_1D_1$ by featherbedding, raising worker productivity, or using their influence to increase demand for the product. Equilibrium then shifts from point $E$ to point $A$.

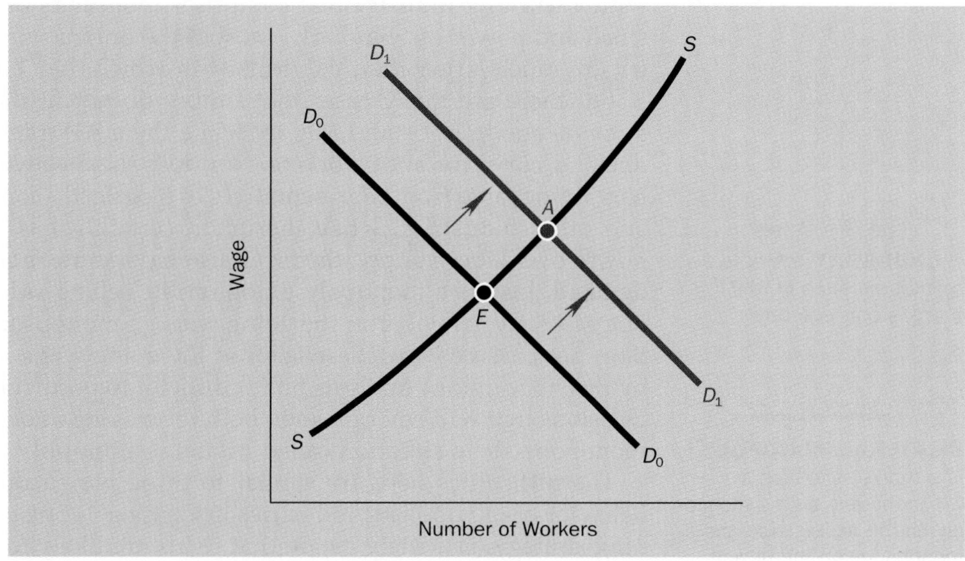


## HAVE UNIONS REALLY RAISED WAGES?

The theory of unions as monopoly sellers of labor certainly suggests that unions have some ability to raise wages, but it also shows that they may be hesitant to use this ability for fear of reducing employment. To what extent do union members actually earn higher wages than nonmembers?

The consensus that has emerged from economic research on this question would probably surprise most people. A study by H. Gregg Lewis[5] estimated that most union members earn wages about 15 percent above those of nonmembers who are otherwise identical (in skill, geographical location, and so on). While certainly not negligible, and while there are indications that this number has been going upward slightly, this can hardly be considered a huge differential.

This 15 percent differential does not mean, however, that unions have raised wages no more than 15 percent. Some observers believe that union activity has also raised wages of nonunion workers by forcing nonunion employers to compete harder for their workers. If so, the differential between union and nonunion workers will be less than the amount by which unions raised wages overall.

# MONOPSONY AND BILATERAL MONOPOLY

The analysis just presented oversimplifies matters in several important respects. For one thing, it envisions a market situation in which one powerful union is dealing with many powerless employers: the labor market is assumed to be

[5]H.G. Lewis, *Union Relative Wage Effects: A Survey*, Chicago: University of Chicago Press, 1986.

monopolized on the selling side but competitive on the buying side. There are industries that more or less fit this model. The giant Teamsters' union negotiates with a trucking industry that comprises thousands of firms, most of them quite small and powerless. Similarly, most of the unions within the construction industry are much larger than the firms with which they bargain.

But there are many cases that simply do not fit the model. The "Big Three" automakers do not stand idly by while the UAW picks its favorite point on the demand curve for auto workers. Nor does the Steelworkers' union sit across the bargaining table from representatives of a perfectly competitive industry. In these and other industries, while the union certainly has a good deal of monopoly power over labor supply, the firms also have some **monopsony** power over labor demand. Just as a monopoly union on the selling side of the labor market does not passively sell labor at the going wage, a monopsony firm on the buying side does not passively purchase labor at the going wage, nor at the wage suggested by the labor union. Analysts find it difficult to predict the wage and employment decisions that will emerge when both the buying and selling side of a market are monopolized—a situation called **bilateral monopoly**.

**MONOPSONY** refers to a market situation in which there is only one buyer.

**BILATERAL MONOPOLY** is a market situation in which there is both a monopoly on the selling side and a monopsony on the buying side.

The difficulties here are similar to those we encountered in considering the behavior of oligopolistic industries in Chapter 12. Just as one oligopolist, in planning strategy, is acutely aware that rivals are likely to react to anything the firm does, a union dealing with a monopsony employer knows that any move it makes will elicit a countermove by the firm. And this knowledge makes the first decision that much more complicated. In practice, the outcome of bilateral monopoly will depend partly on economic logic, partly on the relative power of the union and management, partly on the skill and preparation of the negotiators, and partly on luck.

Still, it is possible to say something a bit more concrete about the outcome of the wage determination process under bilateral monopoly. Where the demand for labor is highly competitive, we have seen that a union generally can achieve a higher wage rate only by paying the price—a reduction in employment. However, as shown in the appendix to this chapter, where the employer is a monopsonist, a union may be able to induce the firm both to raise wages and to increase employment. While the details of the analysis are left to the appendix, the underlying logic is simple enough to be explained here.

A monopsonist employer unrestrained by a union will use its market power to force wages down below the competitive level, just as a monopoly seller uses its market power to force prices higher. It accomplishes this by reducing its demand for labor below what would otherwise be the profit-maximizing amount, thereby cutting both wages and number of workers employed. However, a union may be in a position to prevent this from happening. It can deliberately set a floor on wages, pledging its members not to work at all at any wage level below this floor. If the union's threat is credible to the employer, the firm will lose the incentive to cut its demand for labor, since that attempt will no longer force down wages. Consequently, the presence of a union may force the monopsony employer to pay higher wages and, simultaneously, to hire more workers than he otherwise would.

Even though it is hard to think of industries that are pure monopsonists in their dealings with labor, these conclusions are of some importance for reality. For the fact is that large oligopolistic firms do often engage in one-on-one wage bargaining with the unions of their employees, and there is reason to believe that the resulting bargaining process resembles to a considerable degree the workings of the bilateral monopoly model that has just been described.

## COLLECTIVE BARGAINING AND STRIKES

The process by which unions and management settle upon the terms of a labor contract is called **collective bargaining**. Unfortunately, there is nothing as straightforward as a supply–demand diagram to tell us what wage level will emerge from a collective bargaining session. Furthermore, actual collective bargaining sessions range over many more issues than wages. For example, fringe benefits—such as pensions, health and life insurance, paid holidays, and the like—may be just as important as wages to both labor and management. Wage premiums for overtime work and seniority privileges will also be negotiated. Work conditions, such as the speed with which the assembly line should move, are often crucial issues. Many labor contracts specify in great detail the rights of labor and management to set work conditions—and also provide elaborate procedures for resolving grievances and disputes. This list could go on and on. The final contract that emerges from collective bargaining may well run to many pages of fine print.

With the issues so varied and complex, and with the stakes so high, it is no wonder that both labor and management employ skilled professionals who specialize in preparing for and carrying out these negotiations, and that each side enters a collective bargaining session armed with reams of evidence supporting its positions. The bargaining in these sessions is often heated, with outcomes riding as much on personalities and the skills of the negotiators as on cool-headed logic and economic facts. Negotiations may last well into the night, with each side seeming to try to wear the other out. Each side may threaten the other with grave consequences if it does not accept its own terms. Unions, for their part, generally threaten to strike or to carry out a work slow-down. Firms counter with the threat that they would rather face a strike than give in, or may even close the plant without a strike. (This is called a "lock-out.")

### MEDIATION AND ARBITRATION

Where the public interest is seriously affected, or when the union and firm reach an impasse, government agencies may well send in a **mediator**, whose job is to try to speed up the negotiation process. This impartial observer will sit down with both sides separately to discuss their problems, and will try to persuade each side to yield a bit to the other. At some stage, when an agreement looks possible, she may call them back together for another bargaining session in her presence.

Mediators, however, have no power to force a settlement. Their success hinges on their ability to smooth ruffled feathers and to find common ground for agreement. Sometimes, in cases where unions and firms simply cannot agree, and where neither wants a strike, differences are finally settled by **arbitration**—the appointment of an impartial individual empowered to settle the issues that negotiation could not resolve. This happens often, for example, in wage negotiations in baseball or for municipal jobs such as police and firefighters. In fact, in some vital sectors where a strike is too injurious to the public interest, the labor contract or the law may stipulate that there must be *compulsory arbitration* if the two parties cannot agree. However, both labor and management are normally reluctant to accept this procedure.

Recent studies have shown that professional arbitrators try to cultivate a reputation for fairness and that, as a result, when unions and management are asked to vote for an arbitrator from a preselected list of candidates, the choices of the two parties often overlap. Moreover, while the arbitrators usually make an effort to compromise between the claims of the two contending parties, this has not led labor or managements to systematic inflation of, say, the wage figure they claim is appropriate because, the evidence shows, arbitrators tend to give little weight to claims that are clearly excessive or inappropriately low.

## STRIKES

Most collective bargaining situations do not lead to strikes. But the right to strike, and to take a strike, remain fundamentally important for the bargaining process. Imagine, for example, a firm bargaining with a union that was prohibited from striking. It seems likely that the union's bargaining position would be quite weak. On the other hand, a firm that always capitulated rather than suffer a strike would be virtually at the mercy of the union. So strikes, or more precisely, the possibility of strikes, serve an important economic purpose.

Fortunately, however, the incidence of strikes is not nearly so common as many people believe. Figure 16–11 reports the percentage of worker-days of labor lost as a result of strikes in the United States from 1948 to 1991. Despite the headline-grabbing nature of major national strikes, the total amount of work time lost to strikes is truly trivial—far less, for example, than the time lost to coffee breaks! Compared with other nations, America suffers more from strikes than, say, Japan, but has many fewer strikes than such countries as Italy and Canada (see Figure 16–12).

**Figure 16–11** **WORK-TIME LOST IN THE UNITED STATES BECAUSE OF STRIKES, 1948–1991**

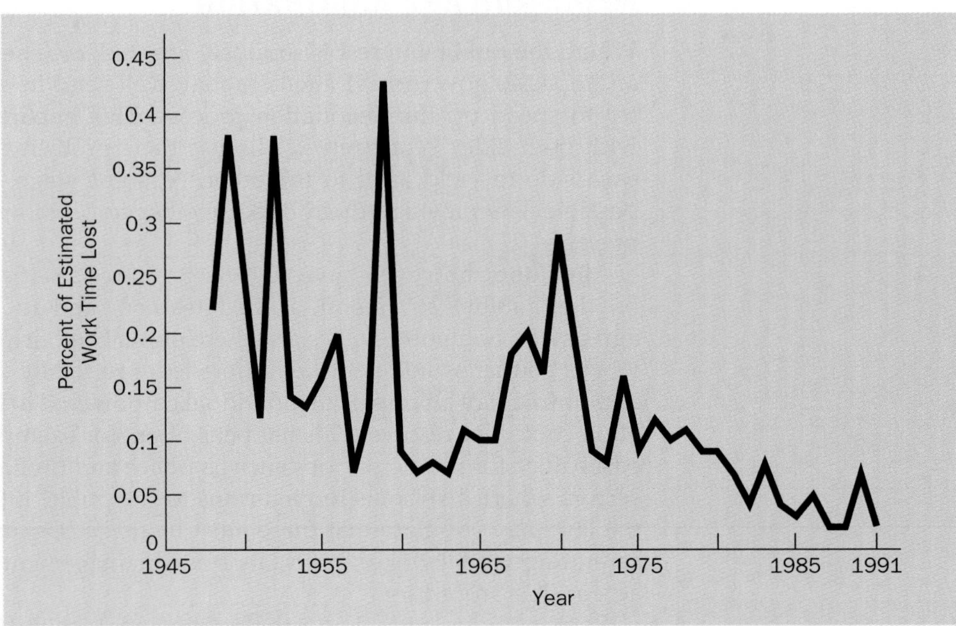


The fraction of total work time lost to work stoppages varies greatly from year to year, but is never very large. In most years, it is between one-tenth and one-quarter of 1 percent. The worst year for strikes was 1946, and it is probably no coincidence that the Taft-Hartley law was enacted in the following year.

SOURCE: U.S. Department of Labor, Bureau of Labor Statistics, *Monthly Labor Review*, various issues.

Figure 16–12 **THE INCIDENCE OF STRIKES IN EIGHT INDUSTRIAL COUNTRIES**

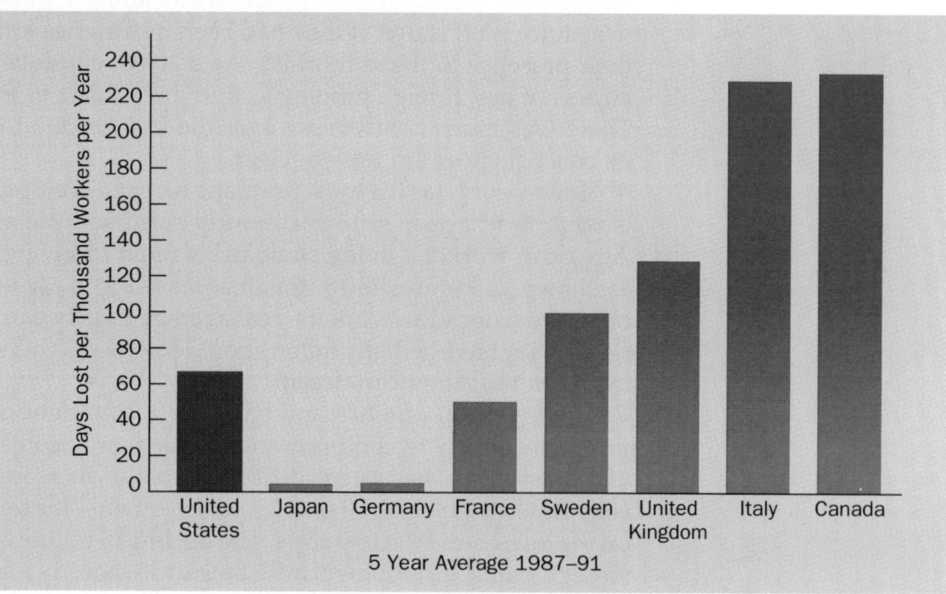


Although strikes in the United States are less common than they are in Italy or Canada, they are much more common here than in Japan. (*Note*: Data are averages for the five-year period 1987–1991.)

SOURCE: Personal communication from Mr. Todd M. Godbout, Office of Productivity and Technology, Bureau of Labor Statistics, U.S. Department of Labor, January 13, 1993.

## RECENT DEVELOPMENTS IN THE U.S. LABOR MARKET

The past decade has brought a number of noteworthy developments to the U.S. labor market. We have already discussed the decline in union membership and mentioned the increasing share of women in the labor force. The latter has given rise to a number of associated issues such as the extent to which employers or the government should be expected to provide for child care (for example, daycare centers needed to make it possible for the mothers to work and avoid deeply handicapping breaks in their careers). The growth in employment of women has also given urgency to issues related to fairness in pay. In a break from historical practice, it is now widely accepted that a woman who does the same job and is as competent as a man should receive the same wage. But what about cases where one type of job is handled almost exclusively by men, and another by women? Is there a "fair" pay ratio for the two occupations? The concept of "comparable worth" (see Chapter 17) is meant to connote that women should receive the same pay as men for performing "equally valuable" tasks. But the definition and measurement of the relative values of two very different jobs has proved to be far from easy, and the very attempt may aggravate disputes over equity rather than calming them.

The role of illegal aliens has also received a good deal of attention. Much of the relatively unskilled work in the United States is done by foreign workers, many of whom immigrated illegally. Crop picking in Florida and sewing in sweatshops in New York's Chinatown are two well-known examples; and many American enterprises fear what would happen if they were deprived of this labor force. But American workers are concerned about competition from this source. In search of a compromise, Congress passed the Immigration Reform and Control Act of 1986, permitting all illegal aliens already in the United States at the time to acquire legal status, if they had been in America long enough and had reported their presence to the authorities. As of 1988, employers are required to check the papers of any foreign employee, and are subject to fines for hiring illegal aliens. There was much controversy over the legislation at the time it was passed, and its consequences are not yet clear.

However, by far the most dramatic recent development in the U.S. labor market is what has happened to real hourly earnings. We are used to the idea that the American worker's living standard is fated to go ever onward and upward. But as shown in Figure 16–13, this has ceased to be true ever since about 1973. For nearly two decades, workers' real average hourly earnings have not only stopped rising, they have actually fallen about 15 percent. This surely seems a rude awakening from the American dream.

Moreover, no one has any basis for a confident opinion about how long the problem is likely to continue, and we have only conjectures about its causes. Part of the problem has been attributed to the increased share of the labor force constituted by blacks, Hispanics, and women—those who are traditionally found on the low-end of the pay scale. The decline in unionization and the accompanying strengthening of employer resistance to wage increases also probably played a role. The problem is often attributed to the slowing of the rate of growth in labor productivity that began in the late 1960s, since workers have usually been able to claim and get higher wages when their output per hour has gone up. However, this last explanation is not convincing. Even though productivity growth did *slow*

*Figure* **16–13** **TRENDS IN REAL WAGES PER HOUR, 1909–1992**

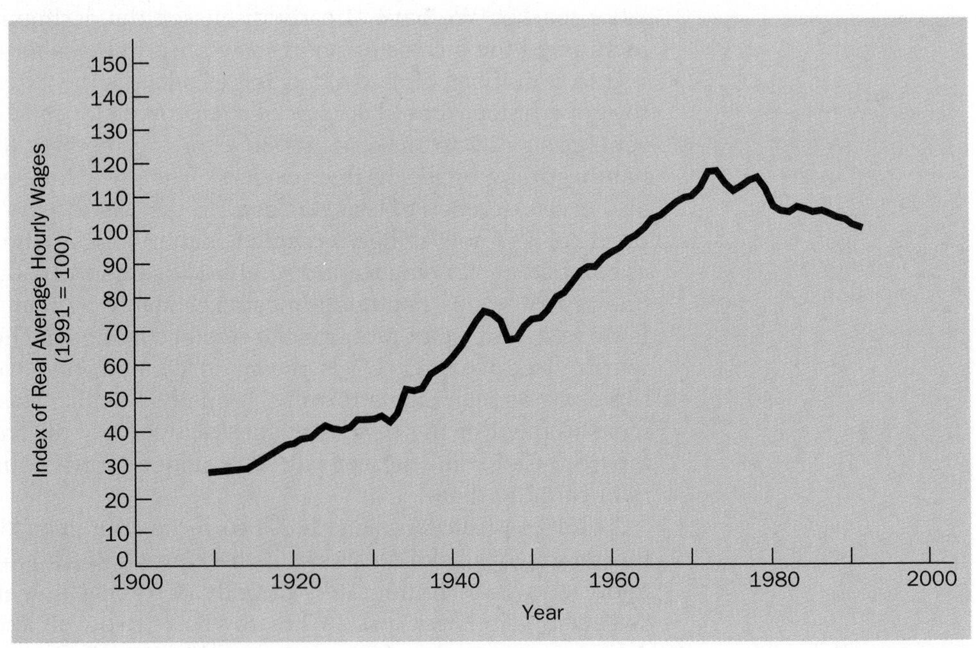


After correction for inflation, the average real earnings per hour of an American worker has actually been falling slightly for nearly 20 years. This is a sharp break with previous trends and a disappointing decrease from American expectations.

SOURCE: Constructed by the authors from data in *Historical Statistics of the United States* and *Economic Report of the President,* various years.

*down*, its *level* did continue to rise—and that rise even sped up somewhat during the 1980s. Nevertheless, real hourly earnings have failed to go up, and that is a matter for concern not only for workers, but for all Americans.

## Summary

1. The supply of labor is determined by free choices made by individuals. Because of conflicting **income and substitution effects**, the quantity of labor supplied may rise or fall as a result of an increase in wages.
2. Historical data show that hours of work per week have fallen as wages have risen, suggesting that income effects may be dominant.
3. The demand curve for labor, like the demand curve for any factor of production, is derived from the marginal revenue product curve. It slopes downward because of the "law" of diminishing marginal returns.
4. In a free market, the wage rate and the level of employment are determined by the interaction of supply and demand. Workers in great demand or short supply will command high wages and, conversely, low wages will be assigned to workers in abundant supply or with skills that are not in great demand.
5. Some valuable skills are virtually impossible to duplicate. People who possess such skills will earn **economic rents** as part of their wages.
6. But most skills can be acquired by means of "**investment in human capital**," such as education.
7. **Human capital theory** assumes that people make educational decisions in much the same way as businesses make investment decisions, and tacitly assumes that people learn things in schools that increase their productivity in jobs.
8. Other theories of the effects of education on earnings deny that schooling actually raises productivity. One view is that the educational system primarily sorts people according to their abilities. Another view holds that schools sort people according to their social class and teach them mainly discipline and obedience.
9. According to the theory of **dual labor markets**, there are two distinct types of labor markets, with very little mobility between them. The primary labor market contains the "good" jobs, where wages are high, prospects for advancement are good, and higher education pays off. The secondary labor market contains the "bad" jobs, with low wages, little opportunity for promotion, and little return to education.
10. One reason that teenagers, especially black teenagers, suffer from such high unemployment rates is, apparently, that minimum wage laws prevent the employment of low-productivity workers.
11. Sixteen percent of all American workers belong to **unions**, which can be thought of as monopoly sellers of labor. Compared with many other industrialized countries, unions in America are younger, less widespread, and less political.
12. Analysis of union behavior is complicated by the fact that a union can have many goals. For the most part, unions probably force wages to be higher and employment to be lower than they would be in a competitive labor market.
13. **Collective bargaining** agreements between labor and management are complex documents covering much more than employment and wage rates.
14. Strikes play an important role in collective bargaining as a way of dividing the fruits of economic activity between big business and big labor. Fortunately, strikes are not nearly so common as is often supposed.

## Key Concepts and Terms

Minimum wage law
Income and substitution effects
Backward-bending supply curve
Economic rent
Investment in human capital
Human capital theory
Dual labor markets
Union
Industrial and craft unions
Taft-Hartley Act (1947)
Closed shop
Union shop
Seniority rules
Monopsony
Bilateral monopoly
Collective bargaining
Mediator
Arbitration

## Questions for Review

1. Colleges are known to pay rather low wages for student labor. Can this be explained by the operation of supply and demand in the local labor markets? Is the concept of monopsony of any use? How might things differ if students formed a union?

2. College professors are highly skilled (or at least highly educated!) labor. Yet their wages are not very high. Is this a refutation of the marginal productivity theory?

3. The following table shows the number of pizzas that can be produced by a large pizza parlor employing various numbers of pizza chefs.

| NUMBER OF CHEFS | NUMBER OF PIZZAS PER DAY |
|---|---|
| 1 | 40 |
| 2 | 64 |
| 3 | 82 |
| 4 | 92 |
| 5 | 100 |
| 6 | 92 |

   a. Find the marginal physical product schedule of chefs.
   b. Assuming a price of $5 per pizza, find the marginal revenue product schedule.
   c. If chefs are paid $70 per day, how many chefs will this pizza parlor employ? How would your answer change if chefs' wages rose to $95 per day?
   d. Suppose the price of pizza rises from $5 to $6. Show what happens to the derived demand curve for chefs.

4. Discuss the concept of the financial rate of return to a college education. If this return is less than the return on a bank account, does that mean you should quit college? Why might you wish to stay in school anyway? Are there circumstances under which it might be rational not to go to college, even when the financial returns to college are very high?

5. It seems to be a well-established fact that workers with more years of education typically receive higher wages. What are some possible reasons for this?

6. Explain why many economists blame the minimum wage law for much of the employment problems of youth.

7. Approximately what fraction of the American labor force belongs to unions? (Try asking this question of a person who has never studied economics.) Why do you think this fraction is so low?

8. What are some reasonable goals for a union? Use the tools of supply and demand to explain how a union might pursue its goals, whatever they are. Consider a union that has been in the news recently. What was it trying to accomplish?

9. "Strikes are simply intolerable and should be outlawed." Comment.

10. In which of the following industries is wage determination most plausibly explained by the model of perfect competition? the model of pure monopoly? the model of bilateral monopoly? (a) Odd-job repairs in private homes; (b) Manufacture of low-priced clothing for women; (c) Steel manufacturing.

11. In a bitter strike battle between Eastern Airlines and several of its unions, it was clear from the beginning that the airline was in serious financial trouble, and the airline was, indeed, eventually forced to close down, at the cost of many jobs. Discuss what might nevertheless have led the unions to hold out so tenaciously.

12. Can you think of some types of workers whose marginal products probably were raised by computerization? Are there any whose marginal products were probably reduced? Can you characterize the difference between the two types of jobs in general terms?

13. The European labor unions have traditionally had a strong socialistic orientation. How would you guess this is likely to be affected by the movement of countries in Eastern Europe toward market economies?

14. Since about 1980 GDP per capita, that is, the average real income per person in the United States, has risen fairly substantially. Yet real wages have failed to rise. What do you think may explain this?

# Appendix THE EFFECTS OF UNIONS AND MINIMUM WAGES UNDER MONOPSONY

We have shown in this chapter that if a union or a minimum wage law raises wages, it will usually reduce employment. But we also noted a possible exception to this rule; this appendix analyzes that exception.

When there is a monopsony on the buying side of the labor market, a union or a minimum wage law may succeed in raising wages without reducing employment. It may even be able to increase employment.

## THE HIRING DECISIONS OF A MONOPSONIST

To establish these results, we begin by considering the hiring decision of a single firm operating in a labor market that is competitive on the supply side. (Later we will bring unions into the picture.) In such a market structure, there is a competitive supply curve for labor as usual, but there is a rather different sort of *demand* curve. In Figure 16–14, the supply curve is labeled *SS* and the firm's marginal revenue product (MRP) schedule is labeled *RR*. In the monopsony context, however, the MRP schedule is *not* the demand curve. The diagram has one additional curve, which will be explained presently.

How many workers will the monopsonist wish to hire? Table 16–1 helps us answer this question by displaying the monopsonist's cost and revenue calculations. What does he gain by hiring an additional worker? He gains that worker's marginal revenue product, which is given in column 5 of the table.

What does he lose? Not just the wage he pays to the new worker. Because he is the only employer, and because the labor supply schedule is upward-sloping, he can attract an additional worker only by *raising the wage rate*. And this higher wage must be paid to *all his employees*, not just the new one. For this reason, the cost of hiring an additional worker—what we call **marginal labor costs**—exceeds the wage rate. By how much? Table 16–1 provides the answer. The first two columns are just the labor supply schedule, curve *SS* of Figure 16–14. By multiplying the wage rate by the number of workers, we can compute the *total labor cost*, which is shown in

**Figure 16–14 LABOR MARKET EQUILIBRIUM UNDER MONOPSONY**

Under monopsony, labor market equilibrium occurs at the employment level that equates marginal labor cost (curve MLC in the diagram) to the marginal revenue product (curve *RR*). In this case, equilibrium is at point *E*, where six workers are employed. The corresponding wage is $225 per week. By contrast, if this were a competitive market, equilibrium would be at point *C*, with a wage of $275 and employment of eight workers.

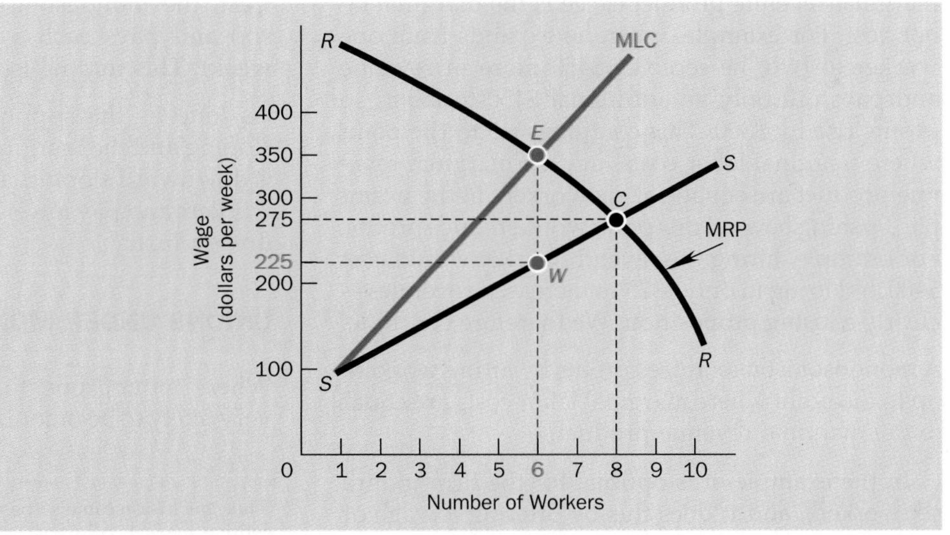

**Table 16–1 LABOR COSTS AND MARGINAL REVENUE PRODUCT OF A MONOPSONIST**

| (1) NUMBER OF WORKERS | (2) WAGE RATE | (3) TOTAL LABOR COST | (4) MARGINAL LABOR COST | (5) MARGINAL REVENUE PRODUCT |
|---|---|---|---|---|
| 1 | $100 | $100 | $100 | $475 |
| 2 | 125 | 250 | 150 | 450 |
| 3 | 150 | 450 | 200 | 425 |
| 4 | 175 | 700 | 250 | 400 |
| 5 | 200 | 1000 | 300 | 375 |
| 6 | 225 | 1350 | 350 | 350 |
| 7 | 250 | 1750 | 400 | 325 |
| 8 | 275 | 2200 | 450 | 275 |
| 9 | 300 | 2700 | 500 | 225 |
| 10 | 325 | 3250 | 550 | 150 |

column 3. For example, the total labor cost of hiring five workers is five times the weekly wage of $200, or $1000. From these data, *marginal labor costs* are computed in the usual way—as the changes in successive total labor costs—and the results are displayed in column 4. This is the information the monopsonist wants, for it tells him that the first worker costs him $100, the next $150, and so on. The numbers in column 4 are displayed on the graph by the blue curve labeled MLC (marginal labor cost).

What employment level maximizes the monopsonist's profits? The usual marginal analysis applies. As he hires more workers, his profits rise if the marginal revenue product exceeds the marginal labor cost. For example, when he expands from one worker to two, he receives $450 more in revenue and pays out only an additional $150 to labor; so profits rise by $300. This continues up to the point where marginal labor costs and the marginal revenue product are equal—at six workers in the example. Pushing beyond this point would reduce profits. For example, hiring the seventh worker would cost $400 and bring in only $325 in increased revenues—clearly a losing proposition. We therefore conclude:

A monopsonist maximizes profits by hiring workers up to the point where marginal labor costs are equal to the marginal revenue product.

In the example, it is optimal for the firm to hire six workers, and it does this by offering a wage of $225 per week. This solution is shown in Figure 16–14 by points *E* and *W*. Point *E* is the equilibrium of the firm, where marginal labor costs and marginal revenue product are equal. To find the corresponding wage rate, we move vertically downward from *E* until we reach the supply curve at point *W*.

Let us compare this result with what would have emerged in a competitive labor market. As we know, equilibrium would be established where the supply curve of labor intersects the marginal revenue product curve, *RR*, because the marginal revenue product curve *is* the demand curve of a competitive industry. Figure 16–14 shows that this competitive equilibrium (point *C*) would have been at a wage of $275 and employment of eight workers.[6] In contrast, the monopsonist hires fewer workers (only six) and pays each a lower wage (only $225 per week). This finding is quite a general result:

As long as the supply curve of labor is upward sloping and the marginal revenue product schedule is downward sloping, a monopsonist will hire fewer workers and pay lower wages than would a competitive industry.

## UNIONS UNDER MONOPSONY

Where monopsony firms exist, their workers are very likely to be unionized. Let us therefore consider

[6]This conclusion can also be seen in Table 16–1 where, in a competitive market, columns 1 and 2 give the supply curve, while columns 1 and 5 give the demand curve. Quantity supplied equals quantity demanded when the wage is $275.

**Table 16–2 LABOR COSTS AND MARGINAL REVUE PRODUCT OF A MONOPSONIST FACING A UNION**

| (1) NUMBER OF WORKERS | (2) WAGE RATE | (3) TOTAL LABOR COST | (4) MARGINAL LABOR COST | (5) MARGINAL REVENUE PRODUCT |
|---|---|---|---|---|
| 1 | $250 | $250 | $250 | $475 |
| 2 | 250 | 500 | 250 | 450 |
| 3 | 250 | 750 | 250 | 425 |
| 4 | 250 | 1000 | 250 | 400 |
| 5 | 250 | 1250 | 250 | 375 |
| 6 | 250 | 1500 | 250 | 350 |
| 7 | 250 | 1750 | 250 | 325 |
| 8 | 275 | 2200 | 450 | 275 |
| 9 | 300 | 2700 | 500 | 225 |
| 10 | 325 | 3250 | 550 | 150 |

what would happen if the workers organized into a union and demanded a wage of no less than $250 per week. This action would change the supply curve, and hence the MLC curve, that the monopsonist faces in a straightforward way. No labor could be hired at wages below $250 per week. At that wage, the monopsonist could attract up to seven workers (see column 2 of Table 16–1). At higher wages, he could attract still more labor according to the supply curve. Thus, his new effective supply curve would be *horizontal* at the wage of $250 up to the employment level of seven workers, and then would follow the old supply curve. This is given numerically in column 2 of Table 16–2 and is shown graphically by the kinked supply curve *SWS* in Figure 16–15.

**Figure 16–15 THE EFFECTS OF A UNION UNDER MONOPSONY**

A union can change the character of the MLC schedule facing a monopsonist. In this example, MLC is horizontal up to seven workers, and then jumps as indicated by the heavy blue line. Consequently, equilibrium employment is determined by point *E*, where seven workers are employed at a wage of $250. Comparing this with Figure 16–14, we see that the union can raise both wages and employment.

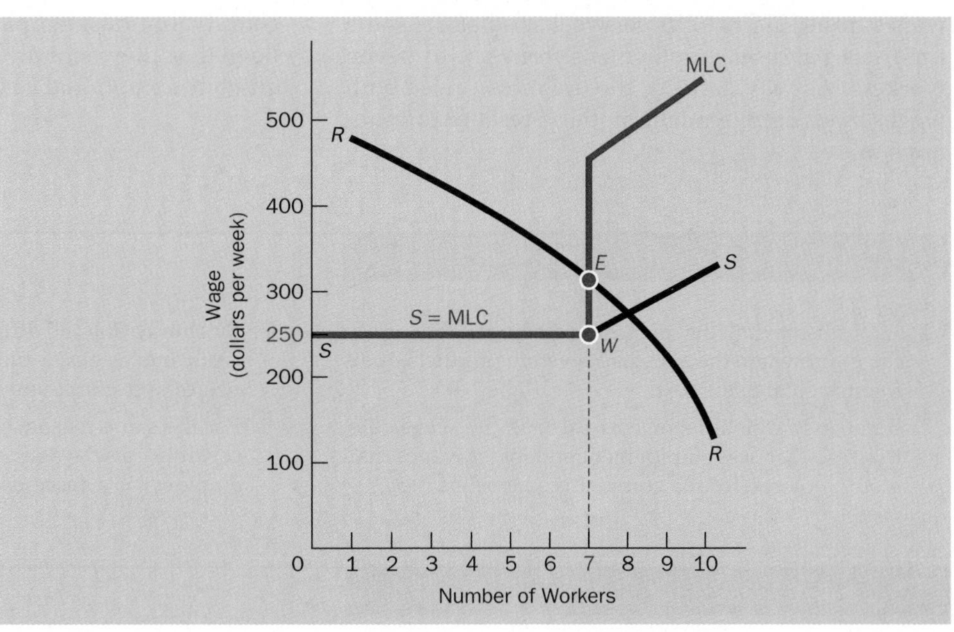

From this information, we can compute the revised marginal labor cost (MLC) schedule just as we did before. Column 3 in Table 16–2 gives us total labor costs at each employment level, and column 4 shows the corresponding marginal cost. The heavy blue curve labeled MLC in Figure 16–15 depicts this information graphically. Notice that the marginal labor cost schedule has become *horizontal* up to the point where seven workers are hired. This is a result of the union's behavior, which tells the monopsonist that he must pay the *same* wage per worker whether he hires one or seven employees. Beyond seven workers, the schedule returns to its previous level since the union minimum is irrelevant.

The condition for profit maximization is unchanged, so the monopsonist seeks the employment level at which marginal labor costs and marginal revenue product are equal. Since MLC jumps abruptly from $250 for the seventh worker to $450 for the eighth, this cannot be achieved exactly. But Table 16–2 makes it quite clear that it is now profitable to employ the seventh worker (marginal labor cost equals $250, marginal revenue product equals $325), but unprofitable to employ the eighth (marginal labor cost equals $450, marginal revenue product equals $275). Points *E* and *W* in Figure 16–15 show, once again, the monopsonist's equilibrium point and the wage he must pay.

Comparing Figures 16–14 and 16–15 (or Tables 16–1 and 16–2), we see that the union has raised wages from $225 to $250 per week, and at the same time has *increased* employment from six to seven workers. As was claimed, the union can raise both wages and employment in the presence of monopsony.

## MINIMUM WAGE LAWS UNDER MONOPSONY

Virtually the same kind of result as the one just discussed *can* be achieved by a minimum wage law under monopsony. That is, *if* the government selects the right minimum wage, it might succeed in raising both wages and employment.

Refer back to Figure 16–14, in which we depicted the equilibrium wage ($225 per week) and employment level (six workers) in a monopsonized labor market with no minimum wage. Just like our union, a minimum wage law creates a horizontal supply curve at the minimum wage. The effects will be just the same as the effects of the union. In both cases, the differences between wages and marginal labor costs are eliminated. As an exercise, use Figure 16–14 to convince yourself that a minimum wage can succeed in raising *both* wages *and* employment by imposing a horizontal supply curve of labor at a wage between $225 and $350 per week. (*Hint*: What will be the monopsonist's MLC under the minimum wage?)

We caution you against reading strong policy conclusions into this finding, however. Examples of actual monopsony (one buyer) in labor markets are quite hard to find. Certainly the types of service establishments that tend to hire the lowest-paid workers—restaurants and snack bars, amusement parks, car washes, and so on—have no monopsony power whatever. While minimum wage laws *can* conceivably raise employment, few economists believe that they actually have this pleasant effect in any but exceptional cases.

## *Summary*

1. A profit-maximizing monopsonist hires labor up to the point where the marginal revenue product equals the marginal labor cost.
2. Because marginal labor cost exceeds the wage rate, this results in less employment and lower wages than would emerge from a competitive labor market.
3. By eliminating the difference between marginal labor costs and wages, a union can conceivably raise both wages and employment under monopsony.
4. For the same reason, a minimum wage law can conceivably raise wages without sacrificing jobs if the employer is a monopsonist.

## *Key Concepts and Terms*

Marginal labor costs

## Questions for Review

1. Consider the pizza chef example of Question 3 on page 416 and suppose that pizzas sell for $5 each. Let the supply curve of chefs be as follows:

| NUMBER OF CHEFS | WAGE PER DAY |
|---|---|
| 1 | 30 |
| 2 | 35 |
| 3 | 40 |
| 4 | 50 |
| 5 | 60 |
| 6 | 70 |

   a. How many chefs will be employed, and at what wage, if the market is competitive?
   b. How many chefs will be employed, and at what wage, if the market has a monopsony pizza parlor? (*Hint*: First figure out the schedule of marginal labor cost.)
   c. Compare your answers to a and b. What do you conclude?
   d. Now suppose that a union is organized to fight the monopsonist. If it insists on a wage of $45 per day, what will the monopsonist do?

2. Given what you have learned about minimum wage laws in the chapter and in the appendix, do you think they are a good or a bad idea?

# POVERTY, INEQUALITY, AND DISCRIMINATION

*The white man knows how to make everything, but he does not know how to distribute it.*

SITTING BULL

The last two chapters analyzed the principles by which factor prices—wages, rents, and interest rates—are determined in a market economy. One reason for concern with this issue is that these payments determine the *incomes* of the people to whom the factors belong. The study of factor pricing is, therefore, an indirect way to learn about the *distribution of income* among individuals. ¶ In this chapter we turn to the problem of income distribution directly. Specifically, we seek answers to the following questions: How much income inequality is there in the United States, and why? How can society decide rationally on how much equality it wants? And, once this decision is made, what policies are available to pursue this goal? In trying to answer these questions, we must necessarily consider the related problems of poverty and discrimination, and so these issues, too, receive attention in this chapter. ¶ We will also offer a full explanation of one of the **12 Ideas for Beyond the Final Exam:** *the fundamental trade-off between economic equality and economic efficiency.* Taking it for granted that equality and efficiency are both important social goals, we shall learn why policies that promote greater income equality may interfere with economic efficiency. In this chapter we explain *why* this is so and *what* can be done about it.

## THE POLITICS AND ECONOMICS OF INEQUALITY

The trade-off between equality and efficiency is not well understood by the public at large. Social reformers often argue that society should adopt even the most outlandish programs to reduce discrimination, increase income equality, or eradicate poverty—regardless of the potential side effects these policies might have. Defenders of the status quo, for their part, often seem so obsessed with these undesirable side effects—whether real or imagined—that they ignore the benefits of redistribution or of antidiscrimination programs.

The national debate over supply-side economics in the 1980s is a good illustration.[1] Many of the tax incentives advocated by supply siders, such as reducing or eliminating taxes on interest, dividends, and capital gains, clearly were of greatest benefit to the wealthy. The poor, after all, do not own much corporate stock. On the other hand, these measures were designed to increase the incentives to save and invest; and, if they had been successful, the whole nation would have benefited from the resulting increases in investment and productivity. Zealous advocates of supply-side initiatives trumpeted the hoped-for gains in productivity and showed little appreciation of the harmful effects on income equality. Some of their opponents vocally decried the widening of income differentials and showed little concern for increasing the nation's productivity. Each side claimed to have a monopoly on virtue. Neither side had one.

Economists try not to phrase the issue so starkly. They prefer to think in terms of trade-offs: To reap gains on one front, you often must make sacrifices on another. A policy is not necessarily ill conceived simply because it has an undesirable effect on income inequality, *if* it makes an important enough contribution to productivity. On the other hand, policies with very bad distributive consequences may deserve to be rejected, even if they would raise the GDP.

Admitting that there is a trade-off between equality and efficiency—that while supply-side tax cuts may contribute to productivity, they may also increase inequality—may not be the best way to win votes. But it does face the facts. And in that way it helps us make the inherently political decisions about what should be done. If we are to understand these complex issues, a good place to start is, as always, with the facts.

## THE FACTS: POVERTY

In 1962, Michael Harrington published a little book called *The Other America*, which was to have a profound effect on American society. The "other Americans" of whom Harrington wrote were the poor who lived in the land of plenty. Ill clothed in the richest country on earth, inadequately nourished in a nation where obesity was a problem, infirm in a country with some of the world's highest

[1]This debate will be considered in greater detail in *Macroeconomics* Chapter 11.

health standards, these people lived an almost unknown existence in their dilapidated hovels, according to Harrington. And, to make matters worse, their inadequate nutrition, lack of education, and generally demoralized state often condemned the children of the "other Americans" to repeat the lives of their parents. There was, Harrington argued, a "cycle of poverty" that could be broken only by government action.

The work of Harrington and others touched the hearts of many Americans who, it seemed, really had no idea of the abominable living conditions of some of their countrymen. Within a few years, the growing outrage over the plight of the poor had crystallized into a "War on Poverty," which was declared by President Lyndon Johnson in 1964. An official definition of poverty was adopted: the poor were those families with an income below $3000 in 1964.

The **POVERTY LINE** is an amount of income below which a family is considered "poor."

This dividing line between the poor and nonpoor was called the **poverty line**, and a goal was established: to get all Americans above the poverty line by the nation's bicentennial in 1976. (The goal was not met.) The poverty line was subsequently modified to account for differences in family size and other considerations, and it is now also adjusted each year to reflect changes in the cost of living. In 1993, the poverty line for a family of four was $14,350 and about 14 percent of all Americans remained in poverty by official definitions.

Who are the poor? Relative to their proportions in the overall population, they are more likely to be black than white, young than old, and female than male. They are less educated and in worse health than the population as a whole; and they tend to live in bigger families. Indeed, nearly 40 percent of the poor are children.

Substantial progress toward eliminating poverty was made in the decade from 1963 to 1973; the percentage of people living below the poverty line dropped from 20 percent to 11 percent (see Figure 17–1). But thereafter a series of recessions and a slowdown in the growth of social welfare programs reversed the trend. By 1983, the poverty rate was back to what it had been in the 1960s. Since then, the poverty rate has crept down and then crept back up again in the 1990–91 recession. But it is still well above its 1970s low.

The rise in poverty since the 1970s worries many people, especially since poverty nowadays seems often to be associated with homelessness, illegitimacy, drug dependency, and ill health—all symptoms of a growing underclass whose lives are no better, and in many respects worse, than the people Harrington wrote about in 1962. (See boxed insert on page 426.)

However, other critics argue that the official data badly overstate the poverty population; some even go so far as to claim that poverty would be considered a thing of the past if the official definition (based on cash income) were amended to include the many goods that the poor are given in kind: public education, public housing, health care, food, and the like.

These criticisms prompted the Census Bureau to develop several experimental measures of poverty which include the value of goods given in kind. If these new measures are accepted as valid, fewer people are classified as poor, but the basic trend in recent years is the same: poverty rose sharply from 1979 to 1983, fell through 1988, and has risen since. (See again Figure 17–1.)

This debate raises a fundamental question, How do we define "the poor?" Continuing economic growth will eventually pull almost everyone above any arbitrarily established poverty line. Does this event mark the end of poverty? Some would say, "Yes." But others would insist that the biblical injunction is right: "The poor ye have always with you."

Figure 17-1 PROGRESS IN THE WAR ON POVERTY


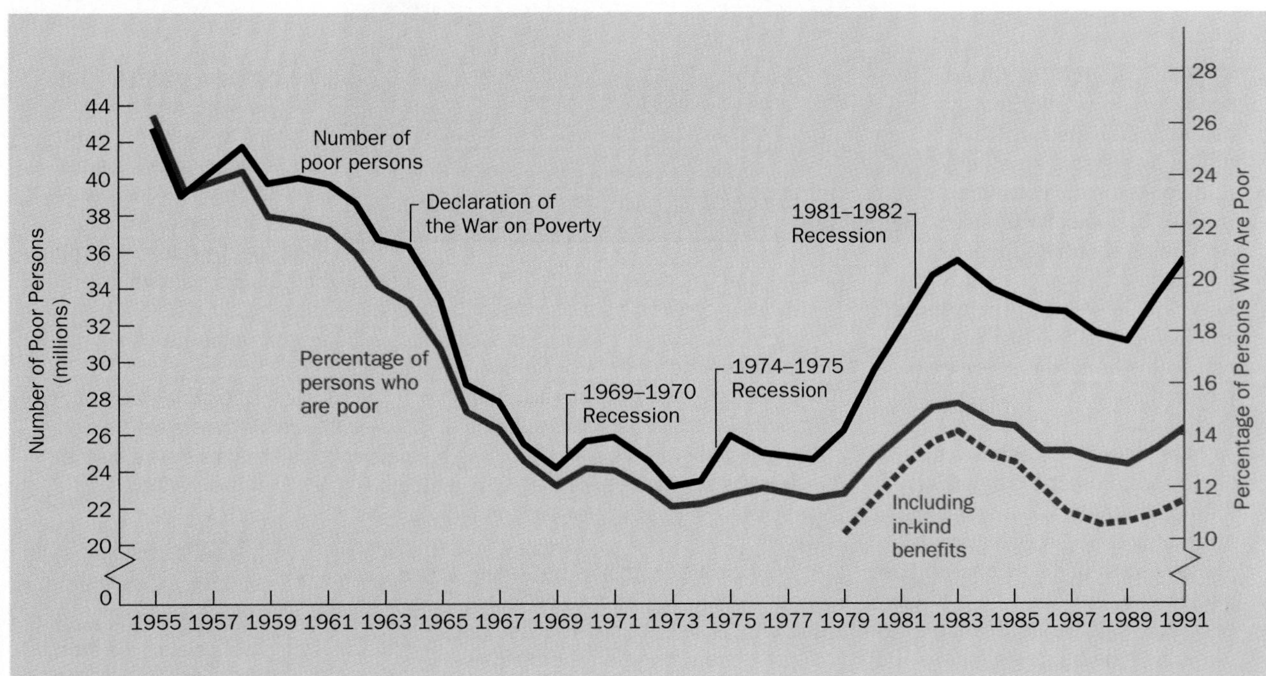


This figure charts the number and percentage of Americans classified as "poor" by official definitions. While substantial progress has been made in the War on Poverty, about 14 percent of Americans remain below the poverty line. The broken line shows one of the experimental measures of poverty that includes noncash benefits.

SOURCE: For 1959–1992, U.S. Bureau of the Census. For 1955–1958, estimates kindly provided by Gordon M. Fisher.

There are two ways to define poverty. The more optimistic definition uses an *absolute concept of poverty*: if you fall short of a certain minimum standard of living, you are poor; once you pass this standard, you are no longer poor. The second definition is based on a *relative concept of poverty*: the poor are those who fall too far behind the average income.

Each definition has its pros and cons. The basic problem with the absolute poverty concept is that it is arbitrary. Who sets the line? Most of the people of Bangladesh would be delighted to live a bit below the U.S. poverty line and would consider themselves quite prosperous. Similarly, the standard of living that we now call "poor" would probably not have been considered so in America in 1780, and certainly not in Europe during the Middle Ages. Different times and different places apparently call for different poverty lines.

The fact that the concept of poverty is culturally, not physiologically, determined suggests that it must be a relative concept. For example, one suggestion is to define the poverty line as one-half of the national average income. In this way, the poverty line would automatically rise as the nation grows richer.

Once we start moving away from an absolute concept of poverty toward a relative concept, the sharp distinction between the poor and the nonpoor starts to evaporate. Instead, we begin to think of a parade of people from the poorest

## *Life and Death in Harlem and Bangladesh*

Many thoughtful Americans were shocked by a study published in 1990, which found that residents of New York's Harlem community had shorter life expectancies than residents of Bangladesh. Since the study pertained to 1979–1980—before crack and before AIDS—there is every reason to think things are even worse there now.

. . . For Harlem males at birth, the likelihood of reaching age 65 is lower than that for males in the state of Matlab, in Bangladesh. Matlab is not quite as bad as Bangladesh as a whole, where life expectancy is 49 years; Matlab's figure is 57, the same as India's. But in that part of the world, low life expectancy is caused mainly by very high infant mortality—a statistic that has improved even in Harlem.

So if you look at life expectancy *after* childhood, *that* is better in Bangladesh than in Harlem, regardless of sex. Male or female, if you are an adult, your chances of dying in any given year between age 15 and 65 are higher in Harlem than in Matlab.

Well, you say, this is not really about health. It's about homicide and drug abuse, things that the people of Harlem bring on themselves. But you would be wrong. . . . True, homicide rates were 14 times the national average; but killings were still few enough to account for only 15 percent of the excess deaths; cancer caused almost as high a proportion. Drug death rates were hundreds of times the national average; yet this highly visible killer caused only 7 percent of the excess.

All in all, the leading cause of extra deaths in Harlem was plain, dull cardiovascular disease—also the leading killer in the nation. . . .

SOURCE: Melvin Konner, "Still Invisible, and Dying, in Harlem," *The New York Times*, February 24, 1990. 

soul to the richest billionaire. The "poverty problem," then, seems to be that disparities in income are "too large" in some sense. At least in part, the poor are so poor because the rich are so rich. If we follow this line of thought far enough, we are led away from the narrow problem of *poverty* toward the broader problem of *inequality of incomes.*

## THE FACTS: INEQUALITY

Nothing in the market mechanism guarantees income equality. On the contrary, the market tends to breed inequality, for the basic source of its great efficiency is its system of rewards and penalties. The market is generous to those who are successful in operating efficient enterprises that are responsive to consumer demands, and it is ruthless in penalizing those who are unable or unwilling to satisfy consumer demands efficiently.

Its financial punishment of those who try and fail can be particularly severe. At times it even brings down the great and powerful. Robert Morris, once perhaps the wealthiest resident of the American colonies, ended up in debtors' prison. In more recent years, the newspapers have carried periodic stories about the financial travails of the Hunt brothers of Texas and Donald Trump of New York, once among America's richest people.

Most people have a pretty good idea that the income distribution is quite spread out—that the gulf between the rich and the poor is wide. But few have any concept of where they stand in the distribution. In the next paragraph, you will find some statistics on the 1991 income distribution in the United States. But before looking at these, try the following experiment. First, write down what you think your family's income before tax was in 1991. (If you do not know, take a guess.) Next, try to guess what percentage of American families had incomes *lower* than this. Finally, if we divide America into three broad income classes—rich, middle class, and poor—to which group do you think your family belongs?

Now that you have written down answers to these three questions, look at the income distribution data for 1991 in Table 17–1. If you are like most college students, these figures will contain a few surprises for you. First, if we adopt the tentative definition that the lowest 20 percent are the "poor," the highest 20 percent are the "rich," and the middle 60 percent are the "middle class," many fewer of you belong to the celebrated "middle class" than thought so. In fact, the cut-off point that defined membership in the "rich" class in 1991 was only about $63,000 before taxes, an income level exceeded by the parents of many college students. (Your parents may be shocked to learn that they are rich!)

Next, use Table 17–1 to estimate the fraction of U.S. families that have incomes lower than your family's. (The caption to Table 17–1 has instructions to help you do this.) Most students who come from households of moderate prosperity have an instinctive feeling that they stand somewhere near the middle of the income distribution; so they estimate about half, or perhaps a little more. In fact, the median income among American families in 1991 was only $36,000.

This exercise has perhaps brought us down to earth. America is not nearly as rich as Madison Avenue would like us to believe. Let us now look past the average level of income and see how the pie is divided. Table 17–2 shows the shares of income accruing to each fifth of the population in 1991 and several earlier years.

**Table 17–1 DISTRIBUTION OF FAMILY INCOME IN THE UNITED STATES IN 1991**

| INCOME RANGE (dollars) | PERCENTAGE OF ALL FAMILIES IN THIS RANGE | PERCENTAGE OF FAMILIES IN THIS AND LOWER RANGES |
|---|---|---|
| Under 5000 | 3.6 | 3.6 |
| 5000 to 9999 | 6.1 | 9.7 |
| 10,000 to 14,999 | 7.2 | 16.9 |
| 15,000 to 24,999 | 16.0 | 32.9 |
| 25,000 to 34,999 | 15.6 | 48.5 |
| 35,000 to 49,999 | 19.5 | 68.0 |
| 50,000 to 74,999 | 18.9 | 86.9 |
| 75,000 to 99,999 | 7.5 | 94.4 |
| 100,000 and over | 5.6 | 100.0 |

SOURCE: U.S. Bureau of the Census.

If your family's income falls close to one of the end points of the ranges indicated here, you can approximate the fraction of families with income *lower* than yours by just looking at the last column.

If your family's income falls within one of the ranges, you can interpolate the answer. *Example*: Your family's income was $45,000. This is two-thirds of the way from $35,000 to $50,000, so your family was richer than roughly ($\frac{2}{3}$) × 19.5 percent = 13.0 percent of the families in this class. Adding this to the percentage of families in lower classes (48.5 percent in this case) gives the answer—about 61.5 percent of all families earned less than yours.

**Table 17–2** INCOME SHARES IN SELECTED YEARS

| INCOME GROUP | 1991 | 1980 | 1970 | 1960 | 1950 |
|---|---|---|---|---|---|
| Lowest fifth | 4.5 | 5.1 | 5.5 | 4.9 | 4.5 |
| Second fifth | 10.7 | 11.6 | 12.0 | 12.0 | 12.0 |
| Middle fifth | 16.6 | 17.5 | 17.4 | 17.6 | 17.4 |
| Fourth fifth | 24.1 | 24.3 | 23.5 | 23.6 | 23.5 |
| Highest fifth | 44.2 | 41.6 | 41.6 | 42.0 | 43.6 |

SOURCE: U.S. Bureau of the Census.

In a perfectly equal society, all the numbers in this table would be "20 percent" since each fifth of the population would receive one-fifth of the income. In fact, as the table shows, this is far from true. In 1991, for example, the poorest fifth of all families had less than 5 percent of the total income, while the richest fifth had more than 44 percent—almost ten times as much.

## DEPICTING INCOME DISTRIBUTIONS: THE LORENZ CURVE

Statisticians and economists use a convenient tool to portray data like these graphically. The device, called a **Lorenz curve**, is shown in Figure 17–2. To construct a Lorenz curve, we first draw a square whose vertical and horizontal dimensions both represent 100 percent. Then we record the percentage of families (or persons) on the horizontal axis and the percentage of income that these families (or persons) receive on the vertical axis, using all the data that we have. For example, point *C* in Figure 17–2 depicts the fact (known from Table 17–2) that the bottom 60 percent (the three lowest fifths) of American families in 1991 received 31.8 percent of the total income. Similarly, points *A*, *B*, and *D* represent the other information contained in Table 17–2. We can list four important properties of a Lorenz curve.

1. It begins at the origin because zero families naturally have zero income.
2. It always ends at the upper-right corner of the square, since 100 percent of the nation's families must receive all the nation's income.
3. If income were distributed equally, the Lorenz curve would be a straight line connecting these two points (the thin solid line in Figure 17–2). This is because, with everybody equal, the bottom 20 percent of the families would receive 20 percent of the income, the bottom 40 percent would receive 40 percent, and so on.
4. In a real economy, with significant income differences, the Lorenz curve will "sag" downward from this line of perfect equality. It is easy to see why this is so. If there is any inequality at all, the poorest 20 percent of families must get less than 20 percent of the income. This corresponds to a point below the equality line, such as point *A*. Similarly, the bottom 40 percent of families must receive less than 40 percent of the income (point *B*), and so on.

**Figure 17–2** **A LORENZ CURVE FOR THE UNITED STATES**

This Lorenz curve for the United States is based on the 1991 distribution of income given in Table 17–2. The percentage of families is measured along the horizontal axis, and the percentage of income that these families receive is measured along the vertical axis. Thus, for example, point *C* indicates that the bottom 60 percent of American families received 31.8 percent of the total income in 1991.

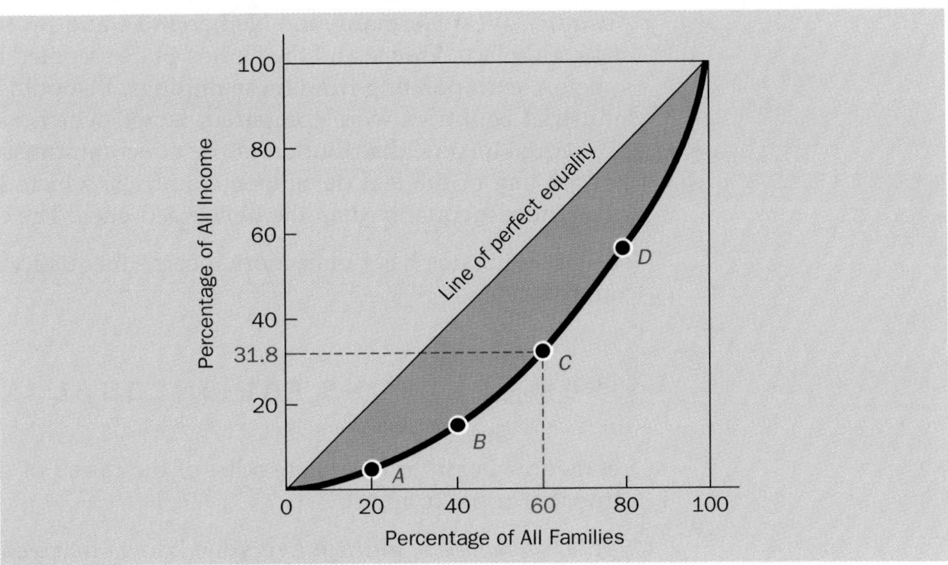


In fact, the size of the area between the line of perfect equality and the Lorenz curve (the shaded area in Figure 17–2) is often used as a handy measure of inequality. The larger this area, the more unequal is the income distribution. For U.S. family incomes, this so-called area of inequality usually fills about 40 percent of the total area underneath the equality line.

By itself, the Lorenz curve tells us little. To interpret it, we must know what it looked like in earlier years or what it looks like in other countries.

The historical data in Table 17–2 show that *the U.S. Lorenz curve has not moved much in the last 40 years*. To some, this remarkable stability in the income distribution is deplorable. To others, it suggests some immutable law of the capitalist system. In fact, neither view is correct. The apparent long-run stability in the income distribution is the result of a standoff between certain demographic forces that were pushing inequality up, such as more young and old people and more families headed by women, and other forces that were pulling inequality down, such as government antipoverty programs.

Notice, however, that the distribution of income grew substantially more unequal after 1980. The share of the poorest fifth is now at the lowest point, and the share of the richest fifth is now near the highest point they have reached since the government began collecting data in 1947.

The distribution of income in the United States grew slightly more equal from the 1950s to the 1970s, but grew slightly more unequal during the 1980s.

Comparing the United States with other countries is much harder, since no two countries use precisely the same definition of income distribution. More than a decade ago, the Organization for Economic Cooperation and Development (OECD) made a heroic effort to standardize the income distribution data of its member countries so they could be compared.[2] In this analysis, Japan stood out as the industrialized country with the most equal income distribution, with Australia, West Germany, the Netherlands, and Sweden bunched rather closely in second place. France and the United States seemed to have the most inequality.

Before extrapolating from these findings, it should be pointed out that only 12 industrial countries were compared. Israel, which is often thought to have the most equal income distribution in the noncommunist world, is not in the OECD. Nor are any of the less developed countries, which are generally found to have much more inequality than the developed ones. The conclusion seems to be that:

The United States has rather more income inequality than most other developed countries.

## SOME REASONS FOR UNEQUAL INCOMES

Let us now begin to formulate a list of the *causes* of income inequality. Here are some that come to mind.

1. ***Differences in ability***. Everyone knows that people have different capabilities. Some can run faster, ski better, do calculations more quickly, type more accurately, and so on. Hence it should not be surprising that some people are more adept at earning income. Precisely what sort of ability is relevant to earning income is a matter of intense debate among economists, sociologists, and psychologists. The talents that make for success in school seem to have some effect, but hardly an overwhelming one. The same is true of innate intelligence ("IQ"). It is clear that some types of inventiveness are richly rewarded by the market, as is that elusive characteristic called "entrepreneurial ability." Also, it is obvious that poor health often impairs earning ability.
2. ***Differences in intensity of work***. Some people work longer hours than others, or labor more intensely when they are on the job. This results in certain income differences that are largely voluntary.
3. ***Risk taking***. Most people who have acquired large sums of money have done so by taking risks—by investing their money in some uncertain venture. Those who gamble and succeed become wealthy. Those who try and fail go broke. Most others prefer not to take such chances and wind up somewhere in between. This is another way in which income differences arise voluntarily.
4. ***Compensating wage differentials***. Some jobs are more arduous than others, or more dangerous, or more unpleasant for other reasons. To induce people to take these jobs, some sort of financial incentive normally must be offered. For example, factory workers who work the night shift normally receive higher wages than those who work during the day.
5. ***Schooling and other types of training***. In Chapter 16 we spoke of schooling and other types of training as "investments in human capital." The term refers to the idea that workers can sacrifice *current* income in order to improve

[2]Malcolm Sawyer, "Income Distribution in OECD Countries," *OECD Occasional Studies*, July 1976, pages 3–36.

their skills so that their *future* incomes will be higher. When this is done, income differentials naturally rise. Consider a high school friend who did not go on to college. Even if you are working at a part-time job, your annual earnings are probably much below his or hers. Once you graduate from college, however, the statistics suggest that your earnings will quickly overtake your friend's earnings.

It is generally agreed that differences in schooling are an important cause of income differentials. This particular cause has both voluntary and involuntary aspects. Young men or women who *choose* not to go to college have made voluntary decisions that affect their incomes. But many never get the choice: their parents simply cannot afford to send them. For them, the resulting income differential is not voluntary.

6. ***Work experience***. It is well known to most people and well documented by scholarly research that more experienced workers earn higher wages.
7. ***Inherited wealth***. Not all income is derived from work. Some is the return on invested wealth, and part of this wealth is inherited. While this cause of inequality applies to few people, many of America's super-rich got that way through inheritance.

   And financial wealth is not the only type of capital that can be inherited; so can human capital. In part this happens naturally through genetics: high-ability parents tend to have high-ability children, although the link is an imperfect one. But it also happens partly for economic reasons: well-to-do parents send their children to the best schools, thereby transforming their own *financial* wealth into *human* wealth for their children. This type of inheritance may be much more important than the financial type.
8. ***Luck***. No observer of our society can fail to notice the role of chance. Some of the rich and some of the poor got there largely by good or bad fortune. A farmer digging for water discovers oil instead. An investor strikes it rich on the stock market. A student trains herself for a high-paying occupation only to find that the opportunity has disappeared while she was in college. A construction worker is unemployed for a whole year because of a recession that he had no part in creating. The list could go on and on. Many large income differentials arise purely by chance.

## THE FACTS: DISCRIMINATION

Some of the factors we have just listed lead to income differentials that are widely accepted as "just." For example, most people believe it is fair for people who work harder to receive higher incomes. Other factors on our list ignite heated debates. For example, some people view income differentials that arise purely by chance as perfectly acceptable. Others find these same differentials intolerable. However, almost no one is willing to condone income inequalities that arise from discrimination.

**ECONOMIC DISCRIMINATION** occurs when equivalent factors of production receive different payments for equal contributions to output.

The facts about discrimination are not easy to come by. **Economic discrimination** is defined to occur when equivalent factors of production receive different payments for equal contributions to output. But this definition is hard to apply in practice because we cannot always tell when two factors of production are "equivalent."

**Table 17–3 MEDIAN INCOMES IN 1991**

| POPULATION GROUP* | MEDIAN INCOME | PERCENTAGE OF WHITE MALE INCOME |
|---|---|---|
| White males | $21,395 | 100 |
| Black males | 12,962 | 60 |
| White females | 10,721 | 50 |
| Black females | 8,816 | 41 |

*Persons 15 years old and over.
SOURCE: U.S. Bureau of the Census.

Probably no one would call it "discrimination" if a woman with only a high school diploma receives a lower salary than a man with a college degree. Even if a man and a woman have the same education, the man may have 10 more years of work experience than the woman. If they receive different wages for this reason, are we to call that "discrimination"?

Ideally, we would compare men and women whose *productivities* are equal. In this case, if women receive lower wages than men, we would clearly call it discrimination. But discrimination normally takes much more subtle forms than paying unequal wages for equal work. For instance, employers can simply relegate women to inferior jobs, thus justifying the lower salaries they pay them.

One clearly *incorrect* way to measure discrimination is to compare the typical incomes of different groups. Table 17–3 displays such data for white men, white women, black men, and black women in 1991. Virtually everyone agrees that the amount of discrimination is less than these differentials suggest, but far greater than zero. Precisely how much is a topic of continuing economic research. Several studies suggest that about half of the observed wage differential between black and white men, and at least half of the differential between white women and white men, is caused by discrimination in the labor market (though more might be due to discrimination in education, and so on). Other studies have reached somewhat different conclusions. While no one denies the existence of discrimination, its quantitative importance is a matter of ongoing controversy and research.

## THE ECONOMIC THEORY OF DISCRIMINATION[3]

Let us see what economic theory tells us about discrimination. In particular, consider the following two questions:

1. Must *prejudice*, which we define as arising when one group dislikes associating with another group, lead to *discrimination* (unequal pay for equal work)?
2. Are there "natural" economic forces that tend either to erode or to exacerbate discrimination over time?

As we shall see now, the analysis we have provided in previous chapters sheds light on both these issues.

[3]This section may be omitted in shorter courses.

## DISCRIMINATION BY EMPLOYERS

Most attention seems to focus on discrimination by employers, so let us start there. What happens if, for example, some firms refuse to hire blacks? Figure 17–3 will help us find the answer. Part (a) pertains to firms that discriminate; part (b) pertains to firms that do not. There are supply and demand curves for labor in each market, based on the analysis of Chapter 16. We suppose the two demand curves to be identical. However, the supply curve in market (b) must be farther to the right than the supply curve in market (a) because whites *and* blacks can work in market (b) whereas only whites can work in market (a). The result is that wages will be lower in market (b) than in market (a). Since all the blacks are forced into market (b), we conclude that they are discriminated against.

But now consider the situation from the point of view of the *employers*. Firms in market (a) of Figure 17–3 are paying more for labor; they are paying for the privilege of discriminating against blacks. The nondiscriminatory firms in market (b) have a cost advantage. As we learned in earlier chapters, if there is effective competition, these nondiscriminatory firms will tend to capture more and more customers. The discriminators will gradually be driven out of business. If, on the other hand, many of the firms in market (a) have protected monopolies, they will be able to remain in business. But they will pay for the privilege of discriminating by earning lower monopoly profits than they otherwise could (because they pay higher wages than they have to).

## DISCRIMINATION BY FELLOW WORKERS

Thus competitive forces will tend to reduce discrimination over time *if* employers are the source of discrimination. Such optimistic conclusions cannot necessarily be reached, however, if it is workers who are prejudiced. Consider what happens if, for example, men do not like to have women as their supervisors. If men do not give their full cooperation, female supervisors will be less effective than

**Figure 17–3** WAGE DISCRIMINATION

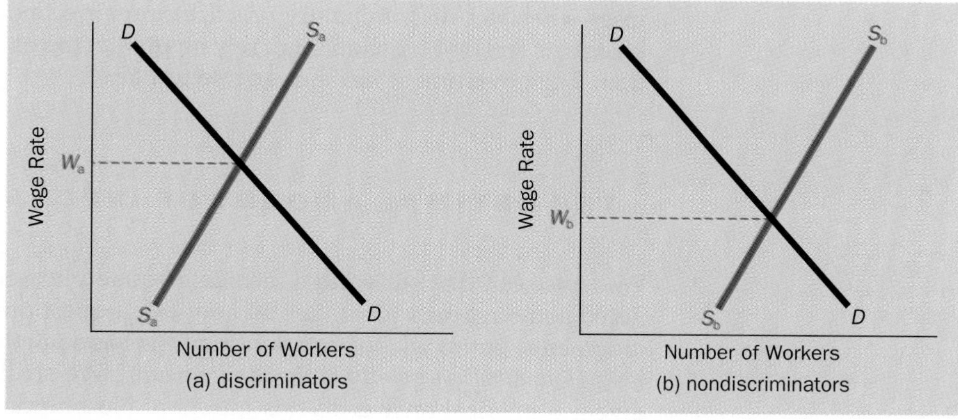


Part (a) depicts supply and demand curves for labor among discriminatory firms; part (b) shows the same for nondiscriminatory firms. Since only whites can work in market (a), while both races can work in market (b), the supply curve in market (b) is farther to the right than the supply curve in market (a). Consequently, the wage rate in market (b), $W_b$, winds up below the wage rate in market (a), $W_a$. Workers in market (b) are discriminated against.

male supervisors and hence will earn lower wages. Here prejudice does lead to discrimination. Furthermore, in this case, firms that put women into supervisory positions will be at a competitive disadvantage relative to firms that do not. So market forces will not erode discrimination.

### STATISTICAL DISCRIMINATION

**STATISTICAL DISCRIMINATION** is said to occur when the productivity of a particular worker is estimated to be low just because that worker belongs to a particular group (such as women).

A final type of discrimination, called **statistical discrimination**, may be the most stubborn of all and can exist even when there is no prejudice. Here is an important example. It is, of course, a fact that only women can have babies. It is also a fact that many, though certainly not all, working women who have babies quit their jobs (at least for a while) to care for their newborns. Employers know this. What they cannot know, however, is *which* women of child-bearing age are likely to drop out of the labor force for this reason.

Suppose three candidates apply for a job that requires a long-term commitment. Susan plans to quit after a few years to raise a family. Jane does not plan to have any children. Jack is a man. If he knew all the facts, the employer might prefer either Jane or Jack to Susan, but would be indifferent between Jane and Jack. But the employer cannot tell Susan and Jane apart. He therefore presumes that both Jane and Susan, being young women, are more likely than Jack to quit to raise a family; so he hires Jack, even though Jane is just as good a prospect. Jane is discriminated against.

Lest it be thought that this example actually justifies discrimination against women on economic grounds, it should be pointed out that women typically have less absenteeism and job turnover for nonpregnancy health reasons than men do. The accompanying boxed insert argues that employers often fail to take account of these other sex-related differences, and thus mistakenly favor men.

### THE ROLES OF THE MARKET AND THE GOVERNMENT

In terms of the two questions with which we begin this section, we conclude that different types of *discrimination* lead to different answers. Prejudice often, but not always, leads to economic discrimination. And discrimination may occur even in the absence of prejudice. Finally, the forces of competition tend to erode some, but not all, of the inequities caused by discrimination.

However, the victims of discrimination are not the only losers. Society also loses whenever discriminatory practices impair economic efficiency. Hence most observers feel that we should not rely on market forces *alone* to combat discrimination. The government has a clear role to play.

## THE OPTIMAL AMOUNT OF INEQUALITY

We have seen that substantial income inequality exists in America, and we have noted some reasons for it. Let us now ask a question that is loaded with value judgments, but to which economic analysis has something to contribute nonetheless: *How much inequality is the ideal amount*? We shall not, of course, be able to give a numerical answer to this question. No one can do that. Our objective is rather to see the type of analysis that is relevant to answering the question. We begin in a simple setting in which the answer is easily obtained. Then we shall see how the real world differs from this simple model.

## Do Women Make Better Workers?

In this 1989 op-ed piece, economist Audrey Freedman argues that female employees can be a better bargain than male employees, even though only women request pregnancy leaves, and it is mainly women who miss workdays for child-care reasons.

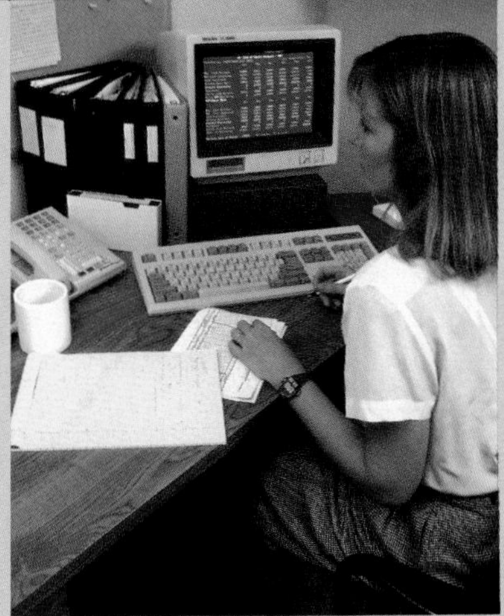

It is undeniable . . . that women, not men, take pregnancy leaves. It is also undeniable that women are the primary nurturers in a family. They are the most likely to be responsible for the care and support of children, as well as their elderly parents. If we stop there, . . . women in business are more costly than men.

But the built-in bias of that analysis is the failure to account for far more costly drains on corporate productivity from behavior that is more characteristic of men than of women.

For example, men are more likely to be heavy users of alcohol. . . . This gender-related habit causes businesses to suffer excessive medical costs, serious performance losses and productivity drains. Yet the male-dominated corporate hierarchy most often chooses to ignore these "good old boy" habits . . . .

Drug abuse among the fast-movers of Wall Street seems to be understood as a normal response to the pressures of taking risks with other people's money. The consequences in loss of judgment are tolerated. They are not calculated as a male-related cost of business.

Apart from performance problems at high levels, alcohol and drug abuse causes costly accidents. We never think of them, however, as a risk primarily associated with male employees. . . .

In our culture, lawlessness and violence are found far more often among men than women. The statistics on criminals and prison population are obvious; yet we seem to be unable to recognize this as primarily male behavior. . . .

A top executive of a major airline once commented to me that his company's greatest problem is machismo in the cockpit—pilots and copilots fighting over the controls. There is an obvious solution: Hire pilots from that half of the population that is less susceptible to the attacks of rage that afflict macho males.

SOURCE: Audrey Freedman, "Those Costly 'Good Old Boys,'" *The New York Times*, July 12, 1989, page A23. 

Consider a society in which two people, Smith and Jones, are to divide \$100 between them. The objective is to maximize *total utility*. Suppose Smith and Jones are alike in their ability to enjoy money; technically, we say that their *marginal utility* schedules are identical.[4] This identical marginal utility schedule is depicted in Figure 17–4. We can prove the following result: *the optimal distribution of income is to give \$50 to Smith and \$50 to Jones*, which is point $E$ in Figure 17–4.

We prove it by showing that, if the income distribution is unequal, we can improve things by moving closer to equality. So suppose that Smith has \$75 (point $S$ in the figure) and Jones has \$25 (point $J$). Then, as we can see, Smith's *marginal utility* (which is $s$) must be *less* than Jones's (which is $j$). This is a simple consequence of the law of diminishing marginal utility.

If we take \$1 away from Smith, Smith *loses* the low marginal utility, $s$, of a dollar to him. Then, when we give it to Jones, Jones *gains* the high marginal utility, $j$, that a dollar gives him. On balance, society's total utility rises by $j - s$ because

[4]If you need to refresh your memory about marginal utility, see Chapter 8, especially pages 191–94.

*Figure* **17–4** **THE OPTIMAL DISTRIBUTION OF INCOME**

If Smith and Jones have the identical marginal utility schedule (curve *MU*), then the optimal way to distribute \$100 between them is to give \$50 to each (point *E*). If income is not distributed this way, then their marginal utilities will be unequal, so that a redistribution of income can make society better off. This is illustrated by points *J* and *S*, representing an income distribution in which Jones gets \$25 (and hence has marginal utility *j*) while Smith gets \$75 (and hence has marginal utility *s*).

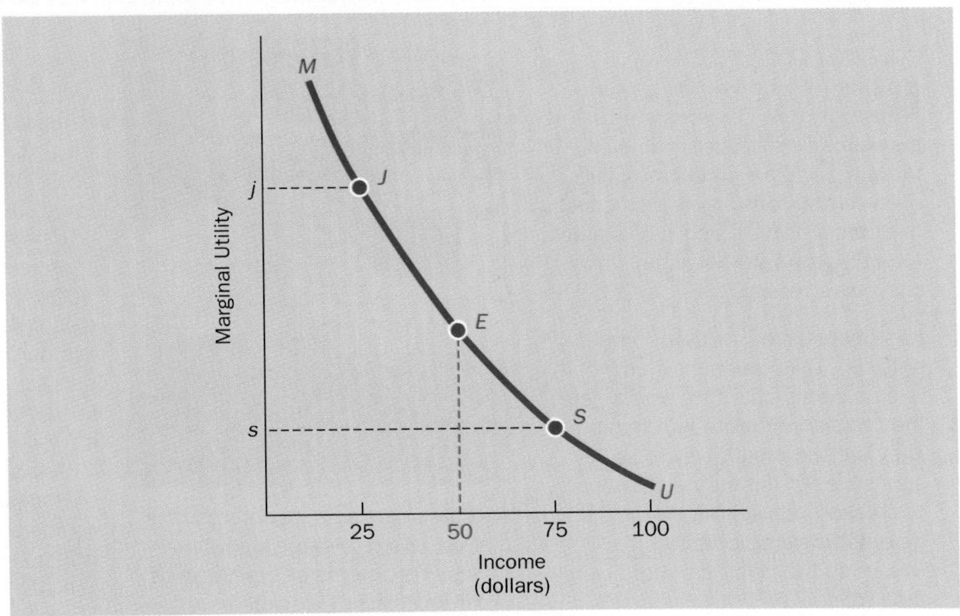


Jones's gain exceeds Smith's loss. Therefore, a distribution with Smith getting only \$74 is better than one in which he gets \$75. Since the same argument can be used to show that a \$73/\$27 distribution is better than \$74/\$26, and so on, we have established our result that a \$50/\$50 distribution—point *E*—is best.

Now in this argument there is nothing special about the fact that we assumed only two people or that exactly \$100 was available. Any number of people and dollars would do as well. What really *is* crucial is our assumption that the same amount of money would be available no matter how we chose to distribute it. Thus we have proved the following general result:

To maximize total utility, the best way to distribute any *fixed* amount of money among people with identical marginal utility schedules is to divide it equally.

## THE TRADE-OFF BETWEEN EQUALITY AND EFFICIENCY

If we seek to apply this analysis to the real world, two major difficulties arise. First, people are different and have different marginal utility schedules. Thus *some* inequality can probably be justified.[5] The second problem is much more formidable.

The total amount of income in society is *not* independent of how we try to distribute it.

[5]It can be shown that if we know that people differ, but cannot tell who has the higher marginal utility schedule, then the best way to distribute income is still in equal shares.

To see this in an extreme form, ask yourself the following question, What would happen if we tried to achieve perfect equality by putting a 100 percent income tax on all workers and then dividing the tax receipts equally among the population? No one would have any incentive to work, to invest, to take risks, or to do anything else to earn money, because the rewards for all such activities would disappear. The gross domestic product (GDP) would fall drastically. While the example is extreme, the same principle applies to more moderate policies to equalize incomes; indeed, it is the basic idea behind supply-side economics.

**THE TRADE-OFF BETWEEN EQUALITY AND EFFICIENCY**

Policies that redistribute income reduce the rewards of high-income earners while raising the rewards of low-income earners. Hence, they reduce the incentive to earn high income. This gives rise to a trade-off that is one of the most fundamental in all of economics, and one of our **12 Ideas for Beyond the Final Exam.** ¶ Measures taken to increase the amount of economic equality will often reduce economic efficiency—that is, lower the gross domestic product. In trying to divide the pie more equally, we may inadvertently reduce its size.

Because of this trade-off, equal incomes are not optimal in practice. On the contrary:

The optimal distribution of income will always involve *some* inequality.

But this does not mean that attempts to reduce inequality are misguided. What we should learn from this analysis are two things:

1. There are better and worse ways to promote equality. In pursuing further income equality (or fighting poverty), we should seek policies that do the least possible harm to incentives.
2. Equality is bought at a price. Thus, like any commodity, we must decide rationally how much to purchase. We will probably want to spend some of our potential income on equality, but not all of it.

Figure 17–5 illustrates both of these lessons. The curve *abcde* represents possible combinations of GDP and income equality that are obtainable under the present system of taxes and transfers. If, for example, point *c* is the current position of the economy, raising taxes on the rich to finance more transfers to the poor might move us downward to the right, toward point *d*. Equality increases, but GDP falls as the rich react to higher marginal tax rates by producing less. Similarly, reducing both taxes and social welfare programs might move us upward to the left, toward point *b*. Notice that, to the left of point *b*, GDP falls as inequality rises. Here there is no trade-off—perhaps because very poorly paid workers are less productive due to inadequate investment in human capital, poor nutrition, or just a general sense of disaffection.

The curve *ABCDE* represents possible combinations of GDP and equality under some new, more efficient, redistributive policy. It is more efficient in the sense that, for any desired level of equality, we can get more GDP with the policy represented by *ABCDE* than with the policy represented by *abcde*.

The first lesson is obvious: we should stick to the higher of the two curves. If we find ourselves at any point on curve *abcde*, we can always improve things by

*Figure* **17–5** **THE TRADE-OFF BETWEEN EQUALITY AND EFFICIENCY**

This diagram portrays the fundamental trade-off between equality and efficiency. If the economy is initially at point *c*, then movements toward greater equality (to the right) normally can be achieved only by reducing economic efficiency, and thus reducing the gross domestic product. The movements from points *C* and *c* toward points *D* and *d* represent two alternative policies for equalizing the income distribution. The policy that leads to *D* is preferred since it is more efficient.

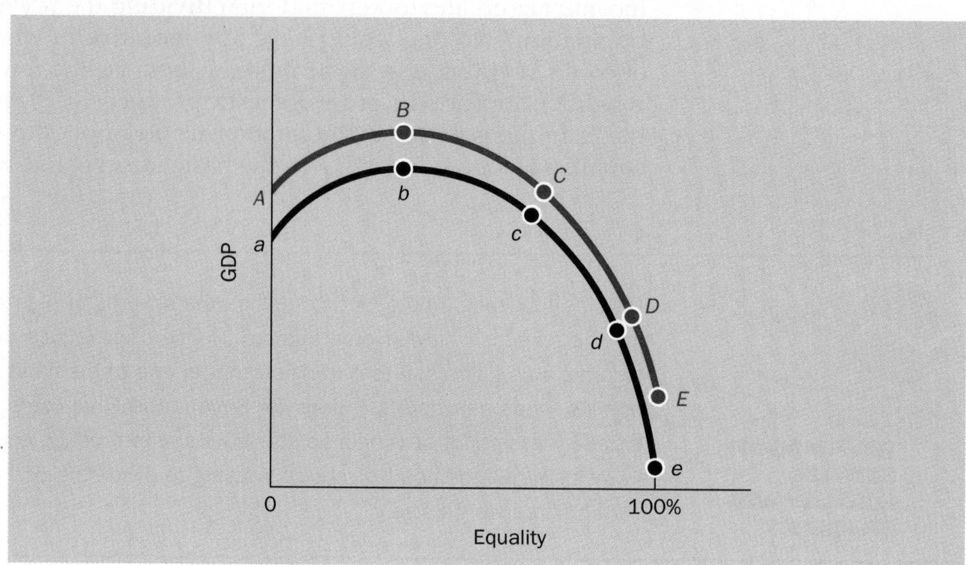


moving up to the corresponding point on curve *ABCDE,* that is, by changing policies. By picking the most efficient redistributive policy, we can have more equality *and* more GDP. In the rest of this chapter, we discuss alternative policies and try to indicate which ones do the least harm to incentives.

The second lesson is that neither point *B* nor point *E* would normally be society's optimal choice. At point *B* we are seeking the highest possible GDP with utter disregard for whatever inequality might accompany it. At point *E* we are forcing complete equality, even if work incentives vanish and a minuscule GDP is the result.

It is astonishing how much confusion is caused by a failure to understand these two lessons. Proponents of measures that further economic equality often feel obliged to deny that their programs will have any harmful effects on incentives. At times these vehement denials are so patently unrealistic that they undermine the very case that the egalitarians are trying to defend. Conservatives who oppose these policies also undercut the strength of their case by making outlandish claims about the efficiency losses from redistribution.

Neither side, it seems, is willing to acknowledge the fundamental trade-off between equality and efficiency depicted in Figure 17–5. And so the debate generates more heat than light. Since these debates are sure to continue for the next 10 or 20 years, and probably for the rest of your lives, we hope that some understanding of this trade-off stays with you well **Beyond the Final Exam.**

But just understanding the terms of the trade-off will not tell you what to do. By looking at Figure 17–5, we know that the optimal amount of equality lies between points *B* and *E*, but we do not know what it actually is. Is it something like point *D*, with more equality and less GDP than we now have? Or is it a movement back toward point *B*? Everyone will have a different answer to this question, because it is basically one of value judgments. Just how much is more equality worth to you?

The late Arthur Okun, once chairman of the Council of Economic Advisers, put the issue graphically. Imagine that money is liquid, and that you have a bucket that you can use to transport money from the rich to the poor. But the bucket is leaky. As you move the money, some gets lost. Will you use the bucket if only 1 cent is lost for each $1 you move? Probably everyone would say yes. But what if each $1 taken from the rich results in only 10 cents for the poor? Only the most extreme egalitarians will still say yes. Now try the hard questions. What if 20 to 40 cents is lost for each $1 that you move? If you can answer questions like these, you can decide how far down the hill from point *B* you think society should travel, for you will have expressed your value judgments in quantitative terms.

## POLICIES TO COMBAT POVERTY

Let us take it for granted that the nation has a commitment to reduce poverty. What are some policies that can promote this goal? Which of these does the least harm to incentives, and hence is most efficient?

Education is often thought of as one of the principal ways to escape from poverty. There is no doubt that many people have used this route successfully, and still do.[6] However, delivering quality education to the children of the poor is no simple matter. Many of them, especially in the inner cities, come to school ill-equipped to learn and attend schools that are ill-equipped to teach. Dropout rates are staggering. An astonishing number of youths leave the public school system without even acquiring basic literacy. All of these problems are familiar; none is easy to solve.

In truth, our educational system is designed to serve many goals; and the alleviation of poverty is not the major one. If it were, we would almost certainly be spending more on, for example, pre-school and remedial education, and less on college education. Furthermore, education is not a particularly effective way to lift *adults* out of poverty. Its effects take a generation or more to be realized.

By contrast, a variety of programs collectively known as *public assistance* are specifically designed to alleviate poverty, are meant to help adults as well as children, and are intended to have quick effects. The best known, and most controversial, of these is **Aid to Families with Dependent Children (AFDC)**. This program provides direct cash grants to families in which there are children but no breadwinner, perhaps because there is no father and the children are too young to permit the mother to work. In 1991, about 12.5 million people received benefits from AFDC, and the average monthly grant was about $135 per person. In total, some $20 billion was spent.

AFDC has been attacked as a classic example of an inefficient redistributive program. Why? One reason is that it provides no incentive for the mother to earn income. Once monthly earnings pass a few hundred dollars, welfare payments are reduced by $1 for each $1 that the family earns as wages. Thus, if a member

[6]The role of education as a determinant of income was considered at length in the previous chapter.

of the family gets a job, the family is subjected to a 100 percent marginal tax rate. It is little wonder that many welfare recipients do not look very hard for work.

A second criticism is that AFDC provided an incentive for families to break up. As originally conceived, welfare was not to be paid to a family with a father who could work, even if he was unemployed. So if this father earned very little, or if he had no job, the children would get more income if he left them. Some fathers did. All the states have now started a special AFDC-UP program (the "UP" stands for unemployed parent) so that benefits can be paid to families with an unemployed father.

A third problem is geographical disparities in benefits. It is widely thought (though not conclusively proven) that many poor families migrated from the South to northern cities because of the more generous welfare benefits available there. This placed an enormous financial burden on these cities. Finally, the tedious case-by-case approach of AFDC, with its cumbersome bureaucracy and mountains of detailed regulations, seems to frustrate all parties concerned.

Another welfare program that burgeoned in the 1970s and was cut back in the 1980s is **Food Stamps**, under which poor families are sold stamps which they can exchange for food. The dollar amount of the stamps they receive, and how much they pay for them, depends on the family's income. The more income the family earns, the more it must pay for the stamps. Headlines were made in March 1993 when it was reported that a stunning 10 percent of all Americans were receiving Food Stamps. The program now costs the federal government about $18 billion per year.

In addition, many of the poor are provided with a number of important goods and services, either at no charge or at prices that are well below market levels. Medical care under the Medicaid (as opposed to Medicare) program[7] and subsidized public housing are two notable examples. These programs significantly enhance the living standards of the poor. However, most of them offer benefits that decline as family income rises. Taken as a whole, all the antipoverty programs may actually put a poor family in a position where it is *worse* off if its earnings *rise*—an effective marginal tax rate of over 100 percent. When this occurs, there is a powerful incentive not to work.

These and other problems have contributed to the "welfare mess" and have led to frequent calls to scrap the whole system. The latest of these came from President Clinton during the 1992 presidential campaign, when he promised a reform of the system that would "end welfare as we know it."

## THE NEGATIVE INCOME TAX

Different reformers have somewhat different goals in mind for welfare reform. But many seek a simple structure that would get income into the hands of the poor without destroying their incentives to work. The solution suggested most frequently by economists is called the **negative income tax (NIT)**.

Table 17–4 illustrates how the NIT might work. A particular NIT plan is defined by picking two numbers: a minimum income level below which no family is allowed to fall (the "guarantee"), and a rate at which benefits are "taxed away"

[7]The *Medicaid* program pays for the health care of low-income people, whereas *Medicare* is available to all elderly people, regardless of income.

Table 17–4 ILLUSTRATION OF A NEGATIVE INCOME TAX PLAN

| EARNINGS | BENEFITS PAID | TOTAL INCOME |
|---|---|---|
| $ 0 | $6000 | $6000 |
| 2000 | 5000 | 7000 |
| 4000 | 4000 | 8000 |
| 6000 | 3000 | 9000 |
| 8000 | 2000 | 10000 |
| 10000 | 1000 | 11000 |
| 12000 | 0 | 12000 |

as income rises. The table considers a plan with a $6000 guaranteed income (for a family of four) and a 50 percent tax rate. Thus, a family with no earnings (top row) would receive a $6000 payment (a "negative tax") from the government. A family earning $2000 (second row) would have the basic benefit reduced by 50 percent of its earnings. Thus, since half its earnings is $1000, it would receive $5000 from the government plus the $2000 earned income for a total income of $7000.

Notice in Table 17–4 that, with a 50 percent tax rate, the increase in total income as earnings rise is always half of the increase in earnings. Thus, there is *always some* incentive to work. Notice also that there is a level of income at which benefits cease—$12,000 in this example. This "break-even" level of income is not a third number that policymakers can select in the way they select the guarantee and the tax rate. Rather, it is dictated by the other two choices. In our example, $6000 is the maximum possible benefit, and benefits are reduced by 50 cents for each $1 of earnings. Hence benefits will be reduced to zero when 50 percent of earnings is equal to $6000—which occurs when earnings are $12,000. The general relation is

$$\text{Guarantee} = \text{Tax rate} \times \text{Break-even level.}$$

The fact that the break-even level is completely determined by the guarantee and the tax rate creates a vexing problem. To make a real dent in the poverty problem, the guarantee will have to come fairly close to the poverty line. But then, any moderate tax rate will push the break-even level way above the poverty line. This means that families who are not considered "poor" (though they are certainly not rich) will also receive benefits. For example, a low tax rate of $33\frac{1}{3}$ percent means that some benefits are paid to families whose income is as high as three times the guarantee level.

But if we raise the tax rate to bring the guarantee and the break-even level closer together, the incentive to work shrinks, and with it the principal rationale for the NIT in the first place. So the NIT is no magic cure-all. Difficult choices must still be made.

## THE NEGATIVE INCOME TAX AND WORK INCENTIVES

For people now covered by welfare programs, the NIT would increase work incentives substantially. However, we have just seen that it is virtually inevitable that a number of families who are now too well-off to collect welfare would become eligible for NIT payments. For these people, the NIT imposes work disincentives, both because it provides them with more income and because it subjects them to the relatively high NIT tax rate, which reduces their aftertax wage rate.[8]

These possible disincentive effects worried social reformers and legislators so much that the government conducted a series of social experiments in the 1960s to estimate the effect of the NIT on the supply of labor. Families were offered negative income tax payments in return for allowing researchers to monitor their behavior. A matched set of "control" families, who were not given NIT payments, was also observed. The idea was to measure how the behavior of the families receiving NIT payments differed from that of the families that did not receive them. The experiments lasted about a decade and showed clearly that the net effects of the NIT on labor supply were small—but certainly not zero. Members of families receiving benefits did work less than the others, but only slightly.

Economists believe that it is more efficient to redistribute income through an NIT than through the existing welfare system because the NIT provides better work incentives. In terms of Figure 17–5, the NIT is curve *ABCDE*, while the present system is curve *abcde*. If this view is correct, then replacing the current welfare system with NIT would lead to both more equality *and* more efficiency. But this does not mean that equalization would become costless. The curve *ABCDE* still slopes downward—by increasing equality, we still diminish the GDP.

Actually, however, adopting an NIT would not be as great a change in social policy as some people imagine. The reason is simple: We already have one (or two)! Specifically, the Food Stamp program functions very much like an NIT because Food Stamps are used like cash in many neighborhoods. Similarly, a feature of the income tax code called the Earned Income Tax Credit resembles an NIT for the working poor and near-poor.

## THE PERSONAL INCOME TAX

If we take the broader view that society's objective is not just to eliminate poverty but to reduce income disparities, then the fact that many nonpoor families would receive benefits from the NIT is perhaps not a serious drawback. After all, unless the plan is outlandishly generous, these families will still be well below the average income. Still, in popular discussions the NIT is largely thought of as an antipoverty program, not as a tool for general income equalization.

By contrast, the federal personal income tax *is* thought to be a means of promoting equality. Indeed, it is probably given more credit for this than it actually deserves. The reason is that the income tax is widely known to be *progressive*.[9] The fact that the tax is progressive means that incomes *after* tax are distributed more equally than incomes *before* tax because the rich turn over a larger share of their incomes to the tax collector. This is illustrated by the two Lorenz curves in Figure 17–6. These curves, however, are not drawn accurately to scale. If they were, they would lie almost on top of each other because research suggests that the degree of equalization attributable to the tax is rather modest.

---

[8]For a review of income and substitution effects in labor supply analysis, refer to Chapter 16, pages 390–91.

[9]For definitions of progressive, proportional, and regressive taxes, see Chapter 20, pages 496–97.

*Figure* **17-6** **THE EFFECT OF PROGRESSIVE INCOME TAXATION ON THE LORENZ CURVE**

Since a progressive income tax takes proportionately more income from the rich than from the poor, it reduces income inequality. Graphically, this means that society's Lorenz curve shifts in the manner shown here. The magnitude of the shift however, is exaggerated to make the graph more readable. In reality, the income tax has only a small effect on the Lorenz curve.

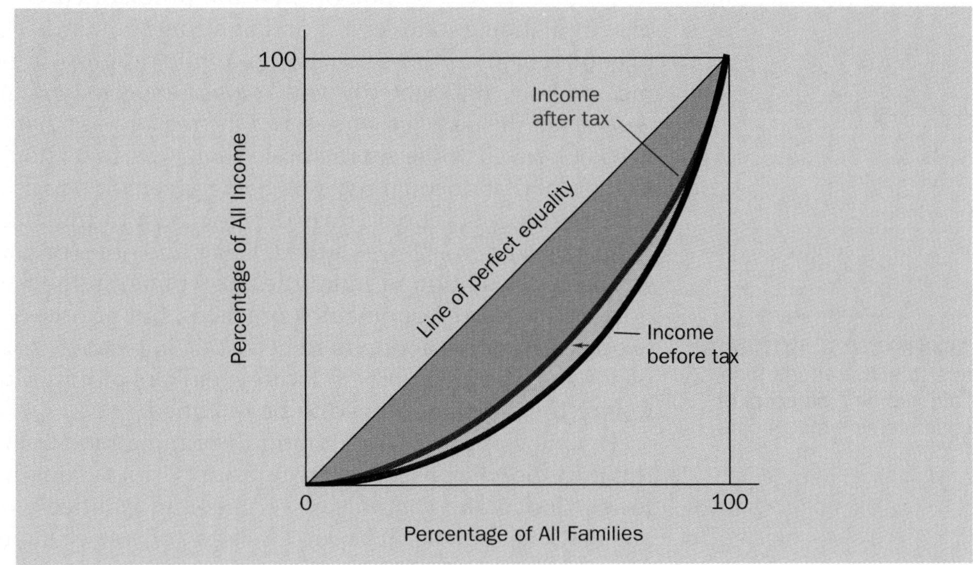


## DEATH DUTIES AND OTHER TAXES

Taxes on inheritances and estates levied by both the state and the federal governments are another equalizing feature of our tax system. And in this case they seem clearly aimed at limiting the incomes of the rich, or at least at limiting their ability to transfer this largesse from one generation to the next. But the amount of money involved is too small to make much difference to the overall distribution of income. Total receipts from estate and gift taxes by all levels of government are well under 1 percent of total tax revenues.

There are many other taxes in the U.S. system, and most experts agree that the remaining taxes as a group—including sales taxes, payroll taxes, and property taxes—are decidedly regressive. On balance, the evidence seems to suggest that:

The U.S. tax system as a whole is only slightly progressive.

## POLICIES TO COMBAT DISCRIMINATION

The policies we have just considered are all based on taxes and transfer payments—on moving dollars from one set of hands to another. This has not been the approach used to fight discrimination. Instead, governments have decided to make it *illegal* to discriminate.

Perhaps the major milestone in the war against discrimination was the **Civil Rights Act of 1964**, which outlawed many forms of discrimination and established the **Equal Employment Opportunities Commission (EEOC)**. When you read a want ad in which a company asserts it is "an equal opportunity employer," the firm is proclaiming its compliance with this and related legislation.

Originally, it was thought that the problem could be attacked by outlawing discrimination in rates of pay and in hiring standards—and by devoting resources to enforcement of these provisions. While progress in reducing discrimination by race and sex undoubtedly was made between 1964 and the early 1970s, many people felt the pace was too slow. One reason was that discrimination in the labor market proved to be more subtle than was first thought. Officials rarely could find proof that unequal pay was being given for equal work, because determining when work was "equal" turned out to be a formidable task.

So a new approach was added. Firms and other organizations with suspiciously small representation of minorities or women in their work forces were required not just to end discriminatory practices, but also to demonstrate that they were taking **affirmative action** to remedy this imbalance. That is, they had to *prove* that they were making efforts to locate members of minority groups and females and to hire them if they proved to be qualified.

**AFFIRMATIVE ACTION** refers to active efforts to locate and hire members of underrepresented groups.

This new approach to fighting discrimination remains highly controversial to this day. (See the boxed insert opposite.) Critics claim that affirmative action really means quotas and compulsory hiring of unqualified workers simply because they are black or female. If so, it exacts a toll on economic efficiency. Proponents counter that without affirmative action, discriminatory employers would simply claim they could not find qualified minority or female employees.

The difficulty revolves around the impossibility of deciding on *purely objective criteria* who is "qualified" and who is not. What one person sees as government coercion to hire an unqualified applicant to fill a quota, another sees as a discriminatory employer being forced to mend his or her ways. Nothing in this book—or anywhere else—will teach you which view is correct in any particular instance.

Lately, some people have concluded that affirmative action will never put appreciable numbers of women into "men's jobs" and have sought to combat sex discrimination by setting wage rates according to some standard of **comparable worth**. The argument, which has sparked acrimonious debate, runs as follows. Women are frequently discriminated against by relegating them to low-paying occupations while men get the better-paid jobs. To remedy the resulting wage disparities, the government should use job evaluations to decide which men's and women's jobs are "comparable," and then insist that employers pay equal wages to jobs judged to be of comparable worth. Canada's province of Ontario is doing that right now. (See the boxed insert on page 446.)

**COMPARABLE WORTH** refers to pay standards that assign equal wages to jobs judged "comparable."

Critics of comparable worth scoff at the idea that the government can decide the relative values of different jobs. The forces of supply and demand described in Chapter 16, they argue, are the only sensible way to set relative wages. The wages that emerge from the marketplace reflect both the marginal revenue products in the various occupations and the availability of labor to each. Any other wages invite shortages in some occupations while others are beseiged by a surplus of applicants.

The controversies over affirmative action and comparable worth are excellent examples of the trade-off between equality and efficiency. There is no doubt that giving more high-paying jobs to members of minority groups and to women would make the distribution of income more equal. Supporters of affirmative action and comparable worth ardently seek this result. But if affirmative action disrupts industry and requires firms to replace "qualified" white males by other "less qualified" workers, the nation's productivity may fall. And if comparable

## The Supreme Court on Affirmative Action

The legal issues surrounding affirmative action programs are many and complex. Although several landmark cases have been decided by the Supreme Court, the current situation is murkier than ever. Indeed, the Court's actions suggest that the issue is as much political as legal.

The earliest decisions were generally favorable to affirmative action. For example, although *Regents of the University of California* v. *Bakke* (1978) held that the affirmative action plan at a California medical school illegally discriminated against whites, the Court explicitly noted that better conceived admissions plans favoring blacks might be legal. A year later, the Court clarified its views in *United Steelworkers* v. *Weber* by approving a quota plan that gave blacks preference for admission to a special training program. *Fullilove* v. *Klutznick* (1980) extended this concept beyond the workplace by upholding a federal law that set aside 10 percent of public-works funds for minority businesses.

Since the mid 1980s, an increasingly conservative Court has been retreating from its earlier stance. In *Firefighters Local* v. *Stotts* (1984), for example, the Court ruled that layoffs of firefighters must follow seniority rules unless particular black employees were victims of racial bias.

But two important verdicts in 1986—*Firefighters* v. *City of Cleveland* and *Local 28* v. *Equal Employment Opportunity Commission*—nonetheless upheld affirmative action as a remedy for past job discrimination, even when particular victims could not be identified. More recently, a series of cases in 1989—the most famous of which was *City of Richmond* v. *Croson*—tossed out a minority set-aside program in construction and made it easier for white males to bring reverse discrimination suits.

In the 1990s, advocates of affirmative action have worried that a more conservative Supreme Court would curtail affirmative action. But, so far, that has not happened.

worth creates chronic surpluses in some occupations and shortages in others, economic efficiency may suffer. Opponents of affirmative action and comparable worth are greatly troubled by these potential losses. How far should these programs be pushed? A good question, but one without a good answer.

## POSTSCRIPT ON THE DISTRIBUTION OF INCOME

Now that we have completed our analysis of the distribution of income, it may be useful to see how it all relates to our central theme, **What does the market do well, and what does it do poorly**?

We have learned that a market economy uses the marginal productivity principle to assign an income to each individual. In so doing, the market attaches high prices to scarce factors and low prices to abundant ones, and therefore guides firms to make *efficient* use of society's resources. This is one of the market's great strengths.

However, by attaching high prices to some factors and low prices to others, the market mechanism often creates a distribution of income that is quite unequal. Some people wind up fabulously rich while others wind up miserably poor. For this reason, the market has been widely criticized for centuries for doing a rather

## Ontario's Experiment with Comparable Worth

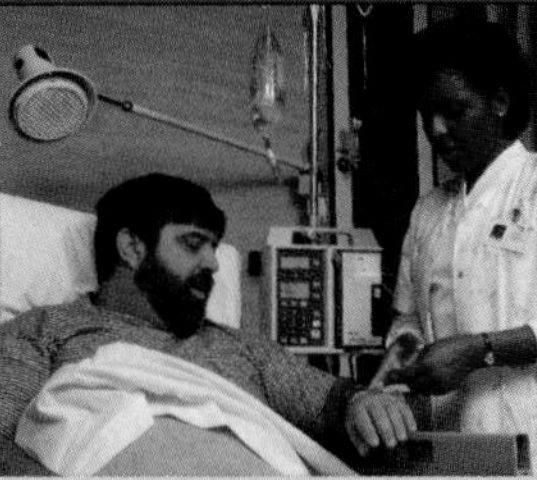

The Canadian province of Ontario was the first major jurisdiction to require employers to devise and implement standards of comparable worth. As the following excerpt from *The Economist* suggests, the task is not easy.

The Canadian province of Ontario is discovering that paying women the same wages as men is less simple than it sounds. This month Ontario extended the world's toughest pay-equity law to include all of the 8,000 firms and government agencies in the province which employ more than 100 workers. Employers covered by the law must draw up plans for paying the same wages to men and women for work of comparable value.

Employers must also set aside at least 1% of their total payroll each year to close the sex gap. Advertisements on Toronto buses and subway trains encourage workers to complain to the pay-equity commission if their employers fail to meet the deadlines.

The law has already brought handsome benefits to thousands of women. Hospitals and schools have made the biggest adjustments. Individual pay increases of 30-50% are common.

In a less tangible sense, the law has created a greater awareness of the value of many jobs done by women. Brigid O'Reilly, the province's pay-equity commissioner, notes that "it has brought home to people that the decisions which clerical, administrative and secretarial staff make are often quite complex." She points to a school which raised its secretary's salary by about C$300 a month after determining that her job had the same value as that of the audio-visual technician. But pay-equity has also soured relations between some employers and their workers, and even opened rifts among workers themselves.

A feature of the Ontario system is that it requires a job-by-job comparison between men and women. Companies must grade all jobs according to four criteria: skill, effort, responsibility and working conditions. Those where women predominate are then compared with jobs of equal value held by men, and wages for the two groups must be brought into line.

Job-by-job comparison has bred much discontent. The women who stick labels on bottles at a Seagram's distillery have complained that they deserve better than being compared with male labourers who move packing cases around the factory floor. One hospital's nursing assistants received no extra pay because their salaries already matched that of the apprentice electrician whose job was deemed to be of equal value. But the assistants at another hospital just ten miles away received increases of more than C$200 a month to bring them into line with a male laboratory technician.

In a particularly strange case, one city has had to pay a copy typist more than a mid-level secretary because the male-dominated jobs given the same score as the typist happen to be on a higher pay scale than the secretary.

The heart of the problem is the difficulty of identifying suitable "male comparators". Many of the biggest employers of women—such as hospitals, day-care centres, libraries and the clothing industry—do not have a big enough range of male-dominated occupations against which to measure their female staff.

In its most celebrated case so far, the pay-equity tribunal decided that 50 nurses in south-west Ontario could compare their pay to that of policemen, because the two groups' employers are financed by the same local authority.

SOURCE: "Papering over the Sex Gap," *The Economist*, January 12, 1991, pages 62–63.

poor job of distributing income in accord with commonly held notions of *fairness* and *equity*.

On balance, most observers feel that the criticism is justified: the market mechanism is extraordinarily good at promoting efficiency but not very good at promoting equality. As we said at the outset, the market has both virtues and vices.

## Summary

1. The War on Poverty was declared in 1964, and within a decade the fraction of families below the official **poverty line** had dropped substantially. However, the poverty population has risen since the late 1970s.
2. The difficulty in agreeing on a sharp dividing line between the poor and the nonpoor leads one to broaden the problem of poverty into the problem of inequality in incomes.
3. In the United States today, the richest 20 percent of families receive over 44 percent of the income, while the poorest 20 percent of families receive under 5 percent. These numbers have changed little over the past 40 years, although inequality increased in the 1980s. The U.S. income distribution appears to be somewhat more unequal than those of many other industrial nations.
4. Individual incomes differ for many reasons. Discrimination and differences in native ability, in the desire to work hard and to take risks, in schooling and experience, and in inherited wealth all account for income disparities. All of these factors, however, explain only part of the inequality that we observe. A portion of the rest is due simply to good or bad luck, and the balance is unexplained.
5. Prejudice against a minority group may lead to **discrimination** in rates of pay, or to segregation in the workplace, or to both. However, discrimination may also arise even when there is no prejudice (this is called **statistical discrimination**).
6. There is a **trade-off between the goals of reducing inequality and enhancing economic efficiency**: policies that help on the equality front normally harm efficiency, and vice versa. This is one of the **12 Ideas for Beyond the Final Exam**.
7. Because of this trade-off, there is an **optimal degree of inequality** for any society. Society finds this optimum in the same way that a consumer decides how much to buy of different commodities: the trade-off tells us how costly it is to "purchase" more equality, and preferences then determine how much should be "bought." However, since people differ in their value judgments about the importance of equality, there is disagreement over the ideal amount of equality.
8. Whatever goal for equality is selected, society can gain by using more efficient redistributive policies because these policies let us buy any given amount of equality at a lower price in terms of lost output. Economists claim, for example, that a **negative income tax** is preferable to our current welfare system on these grounds.
9. But the negative income tax is no panacea. Its primary virtue lies in the way it preserves incentives to work. But if this is done by keeping the tax rate low, then either the minimum guaranteed level of income will have to be low or many nonpoor families will become eligible to receive benefits.
10. The goal of income equality is also pursued through the tax system, especially through the progressive federal income tax and death duties. But other taxes are typically regressive, so the tax system as a whole is only slightly progressive.
11. Economic discrimination has been attacked by making it illegal, not through the tax and transfer system. But simply declaring discrimination to be illegal is much easier than actually ending discrimination. The trade-off between equality and efficiency applies once again: strict enforcement of **affirmative action** or standards of **comparable worth** will certainly reduce discrimination and increase income equality, but it may do so at a cost in terms of economic efficiency.

## Key Concepts and Terms

Poverty line
Absolute and relative concepts of poverty
Lorenz curve
Economic discrimination
Statistical discrimination
Optimal amount of inequality
Trade-off between equality and efficiency
Aid to Families with Dependent Children (AFDC)
Food stamps
Negative income tax (NIT)
Civil Rights Act
Equal Employment Opportunities Commission (EEOC)
Affirmative action
Comparable worth

## *Questions for Review*

1. Discuss the "leaky bucket" analogy (page 439) with your classmates. What maximum amount of income would you personally allow to leak from the bucket in transferring money from the rich to the poor? Explain why people differ in their answers to this question.
2. Continuing the leaky bucket example, explain why economists believe that replacing the present welfare system with a negative income tax would help reduce the leak.
3. Suppose you were to design a negative income tax system for the United States. Pick a guaranteed income level and a tax rate that seem reasonable to you. What break-even level of income is implied by these choices? Construct a version of Table 17–4 (page 441) for the plan you have just devised.
4. Following is a complete list of the distribution of income in Disneyland. From these data, construct a Lorenz curve for Disneyland.

| NAME | INCOME |
|---|---|
| Donald Duck | $100,000 |
| Mickey Mouse | 172,000 |
| Minnie Mouse | 68,000 |
| Pluto | 44,000 |
| Ticket taker | 16,000 |

How different is this from the Lorenz curve for the United States (Figure 17–2 on page 429)?

5. Suppose the War on Poverty were starting anew and you were part of a presidential commission assigned the task of defining the poor. Would you choose an absolute or a relative concept of poverty? Why? What would be your specific definition of poverty?
6. Discuss the concept of the "optimal amount of inequality." What are some of the practical problems in determining how much inequality really is optimal?
7. Why do you think the distribution of income grew more unequal during the 1980s?
8. One of the reasons offered by President Clinton for raising the taxes of upper-income people was that the distribution of income had grown much more unequal in the 1980s. Does the evidence support that view? Is it a decisive argument in favor of redistributive taxation? How is the trade-off between equality and efficiency involved here?

# PART V

# The Government and the Economy

Chapter 18

# LIMITING MARKET POWER: REGULATION OF INDUSTRY

*[There probably exists some rational] boundary between regulated and unregulated portions of an industry.*

ELIZABETH E. BAILEY AND ANN F. FRIEDLAENDER[1]

Because the market system may not function ideally in monopolistic or oligopolistic industries, governments have frequently intervened. In the United States, such intervention has followed two basic patterns. Antitrust laws, which will be studied in detail in the next chapter, have sought to prohibit the acquisition of monopoly power and to ban certain monopolistic practices. In addition, some firms have been subjected to **regulation**, which constrains their pricing policies and other decisions. ¶ Yet, despite the good intentions of its designers, the regulatory mechanism, particularly in the form it took before the 1980s, was criticized for costing the consuming public dearly rather than protecting its interests. This chapter will explain the nature of the problems and the steps, many of them suggested by simple economic theory, taken since the late 1970s to remedy them. ¶ In evaluating these changes, we should constantly keep in mind that the purpose of regulation is, in essence, to prevent the market mechanism from working as

[1] "Market Structure of Multiproduct Industries," *Journal of Economic Literature* 20(3), September 1982, p. 1044.

**REGULATION OF INDUSTRY** is a process established by law which restricts or controls some specified decisions made by the affected firms. Regulation is usually carried out by a special government agency assigned the task of administering and interpreting the law. That agency also acts as a court in enforcing the regulatory laws.

it would if it were left unhampered. We saw in Chapter 13 that there are various consequences of the operations of the market that can reasonably be taken to merit improvement. But many observers feel that once regulators are given the power to intervene, they cannot be counted upon to stop where the logic of Chapter 13 indicates they should. Rather, some observers believe, government regulators are all too likely to interfere with the market mechanism in places where it is at its best. Despite deregulation, there are signs that in a number of areas regulators continue to do so, as we shall see.

Much of the chapter will deal with restrictions on *pricing* by the firm under regulatory control. Regulators oversee a variety of economic activities other than pricing, as will be noted. But price-setting rules and their consequences for economic welfare are most easily analyzed with the help of the tools studied in previous chapters of this book, and pricing issues pervade many of the other activities of the regulator.

## MONOPOLY, REGULATION, AND NATIONALIZATION

Throughout the Western economies, a number of industries are traditionally run as monopolies. These include postal services, electricity generation, transportation, and gas supply. Since there may be little competition to protect the interests of consumers from monopolistic exploitation in these cases, it is generally agreed that some substitute form of protection from excessive prices and restricted outputs should be found.

Most of Western Europe has adopted **nationalization** as its solution, which means that the state owns and operates certain monopolistic industries. Much of the world has had second thoughts about this approach. The last decade has witnessed an outburst of privatization, from Eastern Europe to Latin America, and in much of the British Commonwealth. **Privatization** refers to the sale to private owners of government-owned firms that produce a variety of services and goods. This is a process that is still going on, and it has proved far less straightforward than had been expected. In the United States, we are more reluctant to have government involved in the running of businesses. Yet even here it has happened to some degree. Most cities now run their own public transport systems; the post office and much of the passenger railroad system in the United States are run by public corporations; and the Tennessee Valley Authority is a major experiment in electricity supply by a public agency.

In the United States, however, the main instrument of control of privately owned public utilities has been the regulatory agency. Both the federal and the state governments have created a large number of agencies that regulate prices, standards of service, provisions for safety, and a variety of other aspects of the operations of telephone companies, radio and television stations, electric utilities, airlines, trucking companies, and firms in many other industries—all of which remain in private ownership. Many of these industries are not pure monopolies, but include firms that nevertheless are believed to possess so much market power that their regulation is considered to be in the public interest. In some other countries, nationalized firms that have undergone privatization have immediately been subjected to the oversight of a regulatory agency that operates in much the same way as its U.S. counterpart.

### PUZZLE: INDUSTRY OPPOSITION TO DEREGULATION

An observer who knew nothing about regulated industries might expect that deregulation would be welcomed by the firms affected. After all, regulations curb their freedom of decision making in many ways.

Yet many airlines, trucking companies, and bus lines—and their unions—have bitterly fought deregulation. Later, we will discuss some reasons for this opposition. But already we may surmise from this observation that regulation may, inadvertently or deliberately, have been serving the interests of some of the regulated firms rather than making life harder for them.

### PUZZLE: WHY DO REGULATORS SOMETIMES WORRY MORE ABOUT PRICES BEING TOO LOW THAN BEING TOO HIGH?

In a famous passage in *The Wealth of Nations*, Adam Smith tells us:

> *It always is and must be the interest of the great body of the people to buy whatever they want of those who sell it cheapest. The proposition is so very manifest, that it seems ridiculous to take any pains to prove it; nor could it ever have been called into question had not the interested sophistry of merchants and manufacturers confounded the common sense of mankind.*[2]

Since regulation of industry has presumably been instituted to protect "the interest of the great body of the people," it is quite natural to surmise that the time of the regulatory agencies would have been spent mostly on price reductions. One would think that the typical complaint before a regulatory agency would be that a firm with monopoly power was charging excessively high prices, and that a typical decision of the agency would require prices to be reduced.

In fact, this seems to be virtually the reverse of what has happened. The bulk of cases devoted to price regulation have dealt with complaints that prices charged by the regulated firm are *too low*! Often regulators have then required the firms to raise their prices higher than they wanted to. For example, because the cost of additional shipments via railroad is sometimes lower than the cost of shipping via barges, regulators have been known to require the low-priced suppliers (railroads) to raise their fees to match the prices charged by their high-cost competitors (barges).

What reason is there for this curious pattern—for a regulatory agency to devote itself primarily to the imposition of *price floors* rather than *price ceilings*? Later in this chapter, we will be able to indicate just how and why this has happened.

## WHAT IS REGULATED? BY WHOM?

The regulatory agencies in the United States can be divided, roughly, into two classes: those that limit the market power of regulated firms and those devoted to consumer and worker protection and safety. In a recent count, at least 14 regulatory agencies were concerned with restraining market power and about 30 were involved in issues such as environmental protection and product safety. A primary example of an agency working toward the latter goal is the Food and Drug Administration (FDA), whose tasks are protecting the public from the sale of harmful, impure, infected, or adulterated foods, drugs, and cosmetics, and

---

[2]*The Wealth of Nations* (New York: Modern Library, Random House, Inc., 1937), page 461.

preventing the mislabeling or bad packaging of any of these products. Similarly, since 1906 the U.S. Department of Agriculture has supervised the packing and grading of meats and poultry going into interstate commerce.

The federal government also regulates the safety of automobiles and mines and the use of such substances as dangerous pesticides. An enormous proportion of the nation's economic activity is affected by these sorts of regulations. For instance, the drug industry, agriculture, auto manufacturing, and the chemical and power industries are just some of the businesses affected by health and safety regulation. And virtually every manufacturing industry is affected by environmental regulations.

Regulations designed to limit market power affect industries that together provide perhaps 10 percent of the GDP of the United States. Among the principal industries still regulated in this way are telecommunications, railroads, electric utilities, and oil pipelines.

## A BRIEF HISTORY OF REGULATION

Regulation of industry in the United States first began when indignation over abuse of market power by the nation's railroads led to the establishment of the Interstate Commerce Commission (ICC) in 1887. In particular, there was a public outcry over the support the railroads gave John D. Rockefeller, Sr., in the battle of his Standard Oil Company against its rivals. This, along with other abuses by the railroads, invited government intervention. But for several decades afterward there was little attempt to expand regulation to other industries. Then the Federal Power Commission (FPC) was established in 1920 and the Federal Communications Commission (FCC) in 1934; a substantial proportion of the remaining regulatory agencies were also formed during the 1930s as part of Roosevelt's New Deal.

Today, the principal regulatory agencies of the federal government that control prices include the ICC, which regulates railroads, barges, pipelines, and some categories of trucking; the FCC, which regulates broadcasting and telecommunications; the Federal Energy Regulatory Commission (FERC), which regulates interstate transmission of electric power and sales of natural gas; the Securities and Exchange Commission (SEC), which regulates the sale of securities (stocks); and several agencies led by the Federal Reserve System, which control banking operations. The work of these agencies is complemented by a variety of state agencies, which regulate activities that do not enter into interstate commerce.

Economists have long questioned the effectiveness and desirability of regulation. But not until the mid-1970s did such questions begin to be raised seriously outside of academia. Several laws were enacted by Congress that limit the powers of regulatory agencies. Several industries were "deregulated"—that is, most of the powers of the regulatory agencies were eliminated. In other industries, such as railroads and telecommunications, the rules have been changed to give regulated firms considerably more freedom in their decision making. This process is still under way.

In the 1970s and 1980s Presidents Ford, Carter, Reagan, and Bush all concluded that the economy was overregulated and that this imposed unnecessary costs on consumers. Deregulation began in earnest in the last few years of the Carter administration. In 1978, an act ending regulation of passenger air transportation was passed by Congress, with the regulatory agency going out of existence in

1984. In the period since 1978, regulatory control over truck transportation rates and entry into or exit from the field have been curtailed sharply. Rail transportation activities that are judged to be adequately competitive have been freed from regulatory constraints, while the remaining rail activities have been placed under a less restrictive regulatory regime consistent with ideas emerging from economic analysis.

In telecommunications, AT&T's monopoly was ended, and the firm itself broken up under the terms of settlement of an antitrust case. AT&T continues to be regulated quite closely, though these regulatory rules have recently been modified in accord with the recommendations of economists. AT&T's competitors are now largely free of regulation and the remaining constraints upon AT&T are being re-examined as this is written. In sum, substantial deregulation has occurred during the past 15 years.

## WHY REGULATION?

Economists recognize a number of reasons that sometimes justify the regulation of an industry.

### ECONOMIES OF SCALE AND SCOPE

As we learned in Chapter 11, one main reason for regulation of industry is the phenomenon of **natural monopoly**. In some industries it is apparently far cheaper to have production carried out by one firm rather than by a number of different firms. One reason why this may occur is because of economies of large-scale production. An example of such **economies of scale** is a railroad track, which can carry 100 trains a day with total cost hardly higher than when it carries one. Here is a case in which savings are made possible by expanding the volume of an activity—a case of economies of scale. As we saw in Chapter 6, scale economies lead to an average cost curve that goes downhill as output increases (see Figure 18–1). This means that a firm with a large output can cover its costs at a price lower than a firm whose output is smaller. In Figure 18–1 point *A* represents the larger firm whose AC is $5 while *B* is the smaller firm with AC = $7.

**ECONOMIES OF SCALE** are savings that are acquired through increases in quantities produced.

Another reason why a single large firm may have a cost advantage over a group of small firms is that it is sometimes cheaper to produce *a number of different commodities together* rather than turn them out separately, each by a different firm. The saving made possible by the simultaneous production of many different products is called **economies of scope**. An example of economies of scope is the manufacture of both cars and trucks by the same producer. The techniques employed in producing both commodities are sufficiently similar to make specialized production by different firms impractical.

**ECONOMIES OF SCOPE** are savings that are acquired through simultaneous production of many different products.

In industries where there are great economies of scale *and* scope, society will obviously incur a significant cost penalty if it insists on maintaining a large number of firms. Supply by a number of smaller competing firms will be far more costly and use up far larger quantities of resources than it would if the goods were supplied by a monopoly. Moreover, in the presence of strong economies of scale and economies of scope, society *will not be able to preserve free competition, even if it wants to*. The large, multiproduct firm will have so great a cost advantage over its rivals that the small firms simply will be unable to survive. We say in such a case that free competition is *not sustainable*.

*Figure* **18-1** **MARGINAL COST PRICING UNDER ECONOMIES OF SCALE**

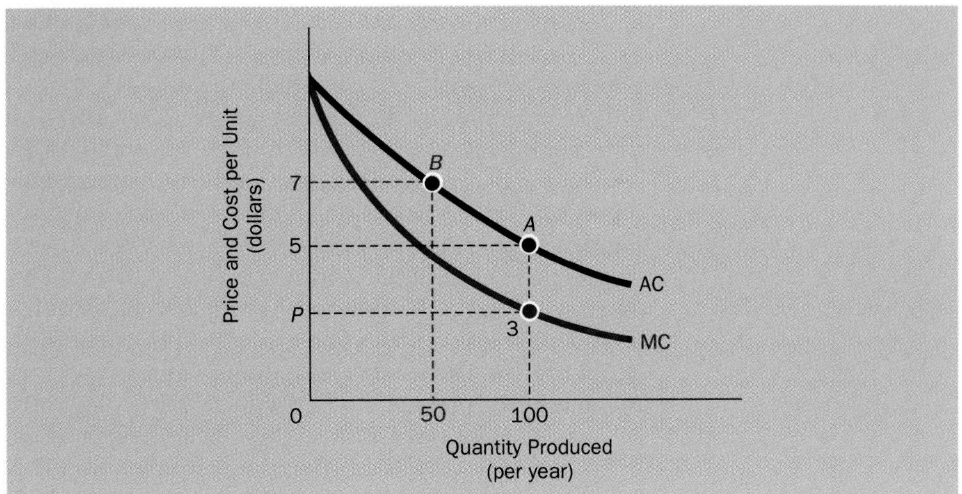


Economies of scale imply that the average cost (AC) curve is declining, and therefore that the marginal cost (MC) curve is below the average cost curve. If, for example, the regulator forces the firm to produce 100 units and charge a price equal to its marginal cost ($3 per unit), then the firm will take in $300 in revenues. But, since its average cost at 100 units is $5 per unit, its total cost will be $500, and the firm will lose money.

Where monopoly production is cheapest, and where free competition is not sustainable, the industry is a natural monopoly. Because monopoly is cheaper, society may not want to have competition; and if free competition is not sustainable, it will not even have a choice in the matter.

But even if society reconciles itself to monopoly, it will generally not want to let the monopoly firm do whatever it wants to with its market power. Therefore, it will consider either regulation of the company's decisions on matters such as prices or nationalization of monopoly firms.

### "UNIVERSAL SERVICE" AND RATE AVERAGING

A second reason for regulation is the desire for "universal service," that is, the availability of service at "reasonable prices" even to small communities where the small scale of operation may make costs extremely high. In such cases, regulators have sometimes encouraged a public utility to supply services to some consumers at a financial loss. But a loss on some sales is financially feasible only when the firm is permitted to make up for it by obtaining higher profits on its other sales.

This so-called "rate averaging" of gains and losses, also referred to as **cross-subsidization**, is possible only if the firm is protected from price competition and free entry of new competitors in its more profitable markets. If no such protection is provided by a regulatory agency, potential competitors will sniff out the profit opportunities in the markets where service is supplied at a price well above cost. Many new firms will enter the business and cause prices to be driven down in those markets. This practice is referred to as "cream skimming." The entrants choose to enter only into the profitable markets and skim away the cream of the profits for themselves, leaving the unprofitable markets (the skimmed milk) to the supplier who had attempted to provide universal service. This phenomenon is one reason why regulatory rules, until recently, made it very difficult or impossible for new firms to enter when and where they saw fit.

Airlines and telecommunications are two industries in which these issues have arisen. In both cases, fears have been expressed that without regulation of entry and rates, or the granting of special subsidies, less populous communities would effectively be isolated, losing their airline services and obtaining telephone service only at cripplingly high rates. Many economists question the validity of this argument for regulation, which, they say, calls for hidden subsidy of rural consumers by all other consumers. The airline deregulation act provided for government subsidies to help small communities attract airline service. In fact, what has happened is that this market has been taken over to a considerable extent by specialized "commuter" airlines flying much smaller aircraft than the major airlines, which have withdrawn from many such routes.

A similar issue affects the U.S. Postal Service, which charges the same price to deliver a letter anywhere within the United States, regardless of the distance or the special difficulties and costs of a particular route. To maintain this pricing scheme, the law must protect the Postal Service from direct competition in many of its activities; otherwise, its extreme form of uniform pricing would soon deprive it of its most profitable routes.

We conclude that the goal of "universal service" leads to regulatory control of entry and exit, and not just to control of prices.

## "DESTRUCTIVE COMPETITION"

A third reason for regulation is to help prevent **self-destructive competition**, which, for example, economies of scale make possible. In an industry such as railroading, equipment—including roadbeds, tracks, switching facilities, locomotives, and cars—is extremely expensive. Suppose that two railroads, having been built and equipped, are competing for some limited business that happens to be insufficient to use their total facilities to anything near capacity. That is, to meet this level of consumer demand, each railroad may only have to run 40 percent as many trains over the track as can conveniently be scheduled over that route.

The management of each road will feel that, with its unused capacity, any business will be worthwhile, provided that it covers more than its short-run marginal costs—fuel, labor, and expenses other than plant and equipment. If the short-run marginal cost of shipping an additional ton of, say, coal is $5, then either railroad will be happy to lure coal-shipping customers away from the other at a price of, say, $7 per ton, even though that price may not cover the entire cost of track and equipment. Each ton of business that pays $7 when marginal cost is $5 will put the railroad $2 ahead of where it would have been without the business. The new business does not add much to the cost of the tracks or locomotives or other equipment, which must be paid for whether that business is acquired or not. Thus, even if the new business only pays for its own marginal cost and a little more, it seems financially desirable.

But the temptation to accept business on such terms will drive both firms' prices down toward their marginal costs, and, in the process, both railroads are likely to go broke. If no customer pays for the track, the roadbed, and the equipment, the railroad simply will be unable to go on. Thus there are those who believe that regulation of rates can be sensible, even in industries subject to competitive pressures, simply to protect the industries from themselves. Without this regulation, self-destructive competition could end up sinking those industries financially, and the public would thereby be deprived of vital services. There are those who believe that this problem now besets the major U.S. airlines, most of which have been sustaining losses, some of them huge, for a considerable number of years.

### PROTECTION AGAINST MISINFORMATION

A final reason for regulation is the danger that consumers will be misinformed or cheated, that the consumers or employees of the firm or the environment will be threatened by unscrupulous sellers, or that even conscientious sellers will be forced to keep up with the questionable practices of less scrupulous rivals. This sort of protection is the province of the second type of regulatory agency described earlier.

SUMMARY
There are four basic reasons for the activities of regulatory agencies:

1. Prevention of excessive prices and other undesirable monopolistic practices in an industry that is considered to be a natural monopoly.
2. The desire for universal service—that is, the desire to provide service at relatively low rates to customers whom it is particularly expensive to serve, and to do so without government subsidy.
3. The desire to prevent self-destructive price competition in multifirm industries with large capital costs and low marginal costs.
4. The desire to protect customers, employees, and the environment from damage resulting from inappropriate behavior by firms.

## WHY REGULATORS SOMETIMES RAISE PRICES

It has been suggested that regulation sometimes results in prices to consumers higher than they would pay in its absence. One of the most widely publicized examples illustrating the tendency of regulation to push rates upward was the difference in airplane fares between San Francisco and Los Angeles and those between Washington, D.C., and New York City before the airlines were deregulated. The former fare was never regulated by the federal government (since the flight is entirely within the state of California), whereas it did control the interstate flight between New York and Washington, D.C. The distance of the California trip is nearly twice as great as the East Coast trip, and neither is sparsely traveled nor beset by any other noteworthy features that would make for substantial differences in cost per passenger mile. Yet at the time of deregulation, fares were a little over $40 for the long California trip and a little over $50 for the short Washington to New York trip.

Why should regulators ever push for higher prices? (This is the second puzzle with which this chapter began.) The answer is that they typically do so when they want to prevent the demise of existing firms in an industry. We saw earlier that strong economies of scale and scope may make it impossible for a number of firms to survive. The largest firm in an industry will have such cost advantages over its competitors that it will be able to drive them out of the market while still operating at prices that are profitable. Most observers applaud low prices and price cuts that reflect such cost advantages. However, a firm that wants the market for itself may conceivably engage in price cutting even when such cuts are not justifiable in terms of cost.

Setting price below the pertinent cost may not reduce the overall profits of a regulated firm because regulation often imposes an upper limit on the amount of profit a firm is permitted to earn. To see the connection, consider a regulated firm that produces two commodities, A and B, and that is forced to set each price below its profit-maximizing level in order to limit profits to the allowable ceiling. The firm may be able, without loss of profit, to cut the price of A even below its marginal cost, and make up for any resulting decrease in profit by a sufficient rise in the price of B. In this case, we say that the firm has instituted a **cross subsidy** from the consumers of product B to the consumers of product A. That is, consumers of B pay an excessive amount for their purchases to make up for the deficit in the sale of product A.

**CROSS-SUBSIDIZATION** means selling one product at a loss, which is balanced by higher profits on another product.

Why would any firm want to do this? Suppose A is threatened by competition while product B has no competitors on the horizon. Then a cross subsidy from B to A may permit a cut in price of A sufficient to prevent the entry of the potential competitors of A or even to drive some current competitors out of the field. The fear by the Department of Justice of such cross subsidy of telephone equipment by the monopoly local telephone companies, which formerly were subsidiaries of AT&T, was one of the elements underlying the decision to break up the single-firm telephone system. After all, one way to prevent a cross subsidy from product B to product A is to require B and A to be produced by two different firms.

But regulation sometimes goes beyond the prevention of cross subsidy. Firms that feel they are hurt by competitive pressures will complain to regulatory commissions that the prices charged by their rivals are "unfairly low." The commission, afraid that unrestrained pricing will reduce the number of firms in the industry, then attempts to "equalize" matters by imposing price floors that permit all the firms in the industry to operate profitably, even those that operate inefficiently and incur costs far higher than those of their competitors. This has been one of the main criticisms economists have raised on regulatory performance. The ICC once described itself as a "giant handicapper" whose task was presumably to make sure that no firm within its jurisdiction got too far ahead of the others. It did not seem to show a similar concern with whether consumers were winning or losing—with the high prices they had to pay to enable inefficient supplier firms to survive.

This attitude has produced many strange patterns of resource utilization. For example, there is evidence that for distances of more than, say, 200 miles, railroads have a clear-cut cost advantage over trucks. Yet ICC influence over railroad rates had forced those rates upward sufficiently to make it possible for trucks to "compete" from coast to coast. The resulting waste of resources was probably enormous. Many economists maintain that this approach to pricing is a perversion of the idea of competition. The virtue of competition is that, where it occurs, firms force one another to supply consumers with products of high quality at *low* prices. Any firm that cannot do this is driven out of business by the market forces. If competition does not do this, it loses its purpose, because to the economist it is a means to an end, not an end in itself. An arrangement under which firms are enabled to coexist only by *preventing* them from competing with one another preserves the appearance of competition but destroys its substance.

## MARGINAL VERSUS FULL-COST RATE FLOORS

Price floors are used by regulators to prevent "excessive" price reduction, for reasons just discussed. Debate over the proper levels of such floors has raged over hundreds of thousands of pages of records of regulatory hearings and has involved literally hundreds of millions of dollars of expenditures in fees for lawyers, expert witnesses, and research in preparation of the cases. The question has been not whether all floors on the prices of regulated utilities are improper, for virtually everyone agrees that some sort of lower boundary on prices is required in order to prevent cross subsidies, but rather what constitutes the proper formula to set the rate floors. Two alternative criteria have been most widely proposed to determine appropriate floors for prices.

*CRITERION 1.* The price of a commodity should never be less than its *marginal cost.*

*CRITERION 2.* The price should not be less than that commodity's *fully distributed cost*—that is, its "fair share" of the firm's total cost as determined by some accounting calculation.

To calculate the **fully distributed costs** of the various products of the firm, one simply takes the firm's total costs and divides them up in some way among its various products. First, one allocates to each product the costs for which it is obviously directly responsible. For example, a railroad allocates to coal transportation the cost of hauling all cars that were devoted exclusively to carrying coal, plus the cost of operating locomotives on runs in which they carried only coal cars, and so on.

Then, one takes all costs that are incurred *in common* for several or all of the outputs of the company (such as the cost of constructing the roadbed and tracks) and divides them on the basis of some rule of thumb (generally conceded to be arbitrary) among the firm's various products. Usually, the basis of this allocation is some measure of the relative use of the common facilities by the different products. But even "relative use" is an ambiguous term. How does one divide up the cost of the track of a railroad among its shipments of lead, lumber, and gold? If relative use is defined by the weight of the shipments, then the accountants will assign a high proportion of the cost to lead shipments. If prices are then required to exceed full cost, under this definition of "relative use" the railroad will be placed at a disadvantage in competing for lead traffic. If, instead, relative use is defined in terms of bulk, the railroad's lumber business will be harmed; if relative use is defined in terms of market value, it will lose out in competing for gold shipments.

Those who advocate the use of *marginal cost* rather than fully distributed cost as the appropriate basis for any floor on prices argue that **marginal cost** is the relevant measure of the cost that any shipment actually incurs—for, by definition, marginal cost is the difference that an additional shipment makes to the firm's total cost. It is the difference between the cost to the firm if that shipment takes place and the cost to the firm if the shipment is carried by some other means of transportation. The advocates of marginal cost criteria argue that customers of *every* product of the supplier may benefit if the company is permitted to charge a price based on marginal cost, particularly if, as until recently was usual under regulation, there is a legal ceiling on the firm's total profits.

Suppose that a railroad considers taking on some new business whose marginal cost is $7 and whose fully distributed cost is figured at $12. Suppose also that at any price over $10 the railroad will lose the business to truckers. If the railroad charges $9 and gets the business, the price does not cover the fully distributed cost, but it still adds $2 to the company's net earnings for every unit it sells to the new customers. If it was already earning as much profit as the law allows, the company would normally have to reduce its price on other products. Thus every group of customers can gain—the new customers because they get the product more cheaply than it can be supplied by competitors, and the old customers because the prices on their products must be cut in order to satisfy the firm's profit ceiling. Everyone gains except the company's competitors, who will, of course, complain that the price is unfair because it does not cover fully distributed cost. (For an example of an opinion by a regulator defending the use of marginal cost analysis against fully distributed cost, see the boxed insert, opposite.)

## A PROBLEM OF MARGINAL COST PRICING

Setting price equal to marginal cost is a solution generally favored by most economists, *where it is feasible*. However, a serious problem prevents the use of the principle of marginal cost pricing in many industries and consequently marginal cost pricing in regulated industries is not very common in practice. The problem is easily stated:

In many regulated industries, the firms would go bankrupt if all prices were set equal to marginal costs.

This seems a startling conclusion, but its explanation is really quite simple. The conclusion follows inescapably from three simple facts:

***FACT 1: IN MANY REGULATED INDUSTRIES, THERE ARE SIGNIFICANT ECONOMIES OF LARGE-SCALE PRODUCTION.*** As we pointed out earlier, economies of scale are one of the main reasons why certain industries were regulated in the first place.

***FACT 2: IN AN INDUSTRY WITH ECONOMIES OF SCALE, THE LONG-RUN AVERAGE COST CURVE IS DOWNWARD SLOPING.*** This means that long-run average cost falls as the quantity produced rises, as illustrated by the AC curve in Figure 18–1 on page 455. Fact 2 is something we learned back in Chapter 6 (pages 143–45, 154–55). The reason, to review briefly, is that total costs must double if all input quantities are doubled. But, where there are economies of scale, output will *more* than double if all input quantities are doubled. Since average cost (AC) is simply total cost (TC) divided by quantity ($Q$), AC $=$ TC$/Q$ must decline when all input quantities are doubled.

***FACT 3: IF AVERAGE COST IS DECLINING, THEN MARGINAL COST MUST BE BELOW AVERAGE COST.*** This fact follows directly from one of the general rules relating marginal and average data that were explained in the appendix to Chapter 6. Once again, the logic is simple enough to review briefly. If, for example, your average quiz score is 90 percent but the next quiz pulls your average down to 87 percent, then the grade on this most recent test (the marginal grade) must

## Marginal versus Fully Distributed Cost in Rate Regulation

In the following dissenting opinion, Commissioner Benjamin Hooks of the FCC (who later headed the National Association for the Advancement of Colored People—the NAACP) argues that a fully distributed cost floor is illogical. He says that a marginal (incremental) cost test may cause more work for the regulator, but points out that it is the public interest, not an easy job for regulators, that is important. The rest of the commission disagreed and voted for a fully distributed cost criterion. Since that time, many regulatory commissions, including the FCC, have moved the other way.

The Commission here, over all dictates of common sense, views of Congressional experts, the practices of other regulatory agencies, and the protestations of state regulatory agencies, has adopted a Fully Distributed Cost accounting method that is all but unyielding and defies every proven rule of economic logic. Virtually every economist-observer cited in this proceeding concedes that incremental cost methods are the closest approximation to a free market environment and the courts have ratified the use of marginal cost pricing in the utility field. I concede that there are imperfections inherent in monitoring marginal costing structures in terms of regulatory administration not present with a simplistic, Fully Distributed Cost basis. However, governmental decisions should not be predicated disproportionately on convenience to the government, but on the broader public interest. What was clearly called for out of this Docket was a system which allows flexibility . . . . Instead we have ordered rigor mortis.

SOURCE: FCC Docket 18128, *FCC Reports*, second series, October 1, 1976.

be below both the old and the new average quiz scores. That is, it takes a marginal grade (or cost) that is below the average to pull the average down.

Putting these three facts together, we conclude that in many regulated industries marginal cost (MC) will be below average cost, as depicted in Figure 18–1. Now suppose regulators set the price at the level of marginal cost. Since $P$ = MC, $P$ must be below AC and the firm must lose money. So $P$ = MC is simply not an acceptable option. What, then, should be done? One possibility is to nationalize the industry, set price equal to marginal cost, and make up for the deficit out of public funds. Nationalization, however, is not very popular in the United States or, nowadays, in most other countries. (More is said about nationalization at the end of the chapter.)

A second option, which is quite popular among regulators, is to (try to) set price equal to *average cost*. In practice, this principle leads to pricing at *fully distributed cost*. But, as explained in the previous section, this method of pricing is neither desirable nor possible to carry out except on the basis of arbitrary decisions.

The problem is that almost no firm produces only a single commodity. Almost every company produces a number of different varieties and qualities of some product, and often they produce thousands of different products, each with its own price. Even General Motors, a fairly specialized firm, produces many makes and sizes of cars and trucks in addition to refrigerators, washing machines, and quite a few other things. In a multiproduct firm we cannot even define AC = TC/$Q$, since to calculate $Q$ (total output) we would have to add up all the apples and oranges (and all the other different items) the firm produces. But we know that one cannot add up apples and oranges. So, since we cannot calculate AC for a multiproduct firm, it is hardly possible for the regulator to require $P$ = AC for each of the firm's products, though regulators sometimes think they can do so.

### THE RAMSEY PRICING RULE

In recent years, economists have been attracted to an imaginative third approach to the problem of pricing in regulated industries that produce a multiplicity of products. This approach derives its name from its discoverer, Frank Ramsey, a brilliant English mathematician who died in 1930 at the age of 26 after making several enduring contributions to both mathematics and economics.

The basic idea of Ramsey's pricing principle can be explained in a fairly straightforward manner. We know that prices must be set *above* marginal costs if a firm with increasing returns to scale is to break even. But how much above? In effect, Ramsey argued as follows: the reason we do not like prices to be above marginal costs is that such high prices distort the choices made by consumers, leading them to buy "too little" of the goods whose prices are set way above MC. Yet, it is necessary to set prices somewhat above marginal costs to allow the firm to survive. Therefore it makes sense to raise prices *most* above marginal cost where consumers will respond the *least* to such a price increase; that is, where the *elasticity of demand* is the lowest so that price rises will create the least distortion of demand. This line of argument led Ramsey to formulate the following rule:

**Ramsey Pricing Rule**: In a multiproduct, regulated firm in which prices must exceed marginal cost in order to permit that firm to break even, the ratios of $P$ to MC should be largest for those of the firm's products whose elasticities of demand are the smallest.

Economists accept this pricing rule as the correct conclusion on theoretical grounds. It has even been proposed for postal and telephone pricing, and the Interstate Commerce Commission has explicitly decided to adopt the Ramsey principle as its general guide for the regulation of railroad rates.

## MODIFIED RAIL REGULATION POLICY AND STAND-ALONE COST CEILINGS

In the regulation of railroads, the Interstate Commerce Commission (ICC) has recently adopted a new approach to regulation explicitly derived from the theory of contestability that we mentioned in Chapter 12 (see pages 303–305). In its decision, the ICC recognized the value of the Ramsey pricing rule as a general guideline for policy. (Excerpts from this ICC decision are quoted in the box, opposite.) But the commissioners felt it was not practical to calculate statistically and update constantly all the demand elasticity numbers and marginal cost figures that use of the Ramsey rule requires. Instead the ICC decided to adopt a four-part rule. Its intent is to compel railroads to set the prices they would have set if all of their activities were contestable; that is, as if entry into freight transportation were everywhere sufficiently easy to subject the railroads to a perpetual and constant threat of new competition. The four parts of the new rule are:

## Economic Theory in an ICC Decision

Here are excerpts from the ICC decision described in the text as an embodiment of materials taken directly from economic analysis. Stand-alone cost (SAC) is the ceiling imposed on a railroad's prices because no higher prices could be charged in an unregulated competitive market.

. . . [the] stand-alone cost (SAC) test . . . is used to compute the rate a competitor in the marketplace would need to charge in serving a captive shipper or a group of shippers who benefit from sharing joint and common costs. A rate level calculated by the SAC methodology represents the theoretical maximum rate that a railroad could levy on shippers without substantial diversion of traffic to a hypothetical competing service. It is, in other words, a simulated competitive price. . . .

The theory behind SAC is best explained by the concept of contestable markets. This recently developed economic theory augments the classical economic model of pure competition with a model which focuses on the entry and exit from an industry as a measure of economic efficiency. . . . The underlying premise is that a monopolist or oligopolist will behave efficiently and competitively where there is a threat of losing some or all of its markets to a new entrant. In other words, contestable markets have competitive characteristics which preclude monopoly pricing.

The applicability of the principles in this decision to rates on other types of freight was reconfirmed in 1993 by the U.S. Court of Appeals (Case No. 88-1114, decided February 9, 1993).

SOURCE: Interstate Commerce Commission, "Coal Rate Guidelines, Nationwide," Ex Parte No. 347 (Sub-No. 1), Aug. 3, 1985, p. 10.

1. For those types of freight and routes where competition happens to be substantial and effective, the railroads should be deregulated; that is, let market forces do the job of policing the railroads' behavior.
2. Where competition is inadequate, a floor and a ceiling should be set for each and every railroad price and leave the railroads free to select any level of price they wish within those bounds.
3. The price floor should be the lowest level to which price could fall in the long run under perfectly competitive conditions. This provision, in effect, prohibits the railroad from adopting any price below marginal cost. It is designed to provide adequate and defensible protection to any railroad's rivals against any attempt by the railroad at unfair competitive price cutting.
4. The price ceiling should be the cost that a *hypothetical* (that is, imaginary) efficient entrant would have to bear to supply each specific service. In other words, in activities where entry is difficult or impossible, the idea is to prohibit the railroads from charging more than they could get away with if entry were instead easy and cheap. The hypothetical cost figure for the efficient entrant is called the **stand-alone cost** of the service. It is the cost that would be required if an efficient entrant were to supply just the service or group of services in question. This provision is intended to protect the interests of railroad customers, guaranteeing them prices no higher than those that might be charged if the markets were effectively contestable.

Most economists who have studied the issue seem to approve of this new approach to rate regulation, although there are still some disputes about details of its operation.

## REGULATION OF PROFIT AND INCENTIVES FOR EFFICIENCY

Many opponents of regulation maintain that it seriously impairs the efficiency of American industry. Government regulation, these critics argue, interferes with the operation of Adam Smith's invisible hand. One source of inefficiency—the seemingly endless paperwork and complex legal proceedings that impede the firm's ability to respond quickly to changing market conditions—is obvious enough. (Though what to do about this administrative problem is far from obvious.)

In addition, economists believe that regulatory interference in pricing decisions adds to economic inefficiency. By forcing prices to be either lower or higher than those that would prevail on a free competitive market, regulations give consumers the wrong signals and induce them to demand a quantity of the regulated product that is inconsistent with maximization of consumer benefits from the quantity of resources available to the economy. (This resource misallocation issue was discussed in Chapter 13, pages 310–13.

But there is a third source of inefficiency that may be even more important. It stems from the problem regulators have of trying to prevent the regulated firm from earning excessive profits, while at the same time (a) offering it financial incentives for maximum efficiency of operation, and (b) allowing it enough profit to attract the capital it needs when growing markets justify expansion. From this point of view, it would be ideal if the regulator would just permit the firm to take in that amount of revenue that covers its costs, including the cost of its capital. That is, the firm should earn exactly enough to pay for its ordinary costs plus the normal profit that potential investors could get elsewhere for the same money (the opportunity cost of the money). Thus, if the prevailing rate of return is 10 percent, the regulated firm should recover its expenditures plus 10 percent on its investment and not a penny more or less.

The trouble with such an arrangement is that it removes all incentive for efficiency, responsiveness to consumer demand, and innovation—for such an arrangement eliminates the profit motive for efficiency and good service to consumers, in effect *guaranteeing* just *one standard rate* of profit to the firm, no more and no less. This is so whether its management is totally incompetent or extremely talented and hard working.

Competitive markets do *not* work in this way. While under perfect competition the *average* firm will earn just the opportunity cost of capital, a firm with an especially ingenious and efficient management will do better, and a firm with an incompetent management is likely to go broke. It is the possibility of great rewards and harsh punishments that gives the market mechanism its power to cause firms to strive for high efficiency and productivity growth.

We have strong evidence that where firms are guaranteed a fixed return, no matter how well or how poorly they perform, gross inefficiencies are likely to result. For example, many contracts for purchases of military equipment have offered prices calculated on a *cost-plus* basis, meaning that the supplier was guaranteed that its costs would be covered and that, in addition, it would receive some prespecified amount as a contribution to profit. Studies of the resulting performance of cost-plus arrangements have confirmed that the suppliers' inefficiencies have been enormous.

A regulatory arrangement that in effect guarantees a regulated firm its cost plus a "fair rate of return" on its investment obviously has a good deal in common with a cost-plus contract of an unregulated firm. Fortunately, there are also substantial differences between the two cases, and so regulatory profit ceilings need not always have serious effects on the firm's incentives for efficiency.

For one thing, when a regulated industry is in financial trouble, as is true of the railroads, there is nothing the regulator can do to guarantee a "fair rate of return." If the current return on capital is 10 percent, but market demand for railroading is only sufficient to give it 3 percent at most, the regulatory agency cannot help matters by any act of magic. Even if it grants higher prices to the railroad (or forces the railroad to raise its prices) the result will be to drive even more business away and therefore cause the firm to earn still lower profits. Thus, the regulated firm will sometimes have to struggle hard to earn even the rate of profit that regulation permits. The regulated firm is not promised any minimum profit rate, unlike the case of an unregulated firm with a cost-plus contract.

There is a second reason why profit regulation does not work in the same way as does a cost-plus arrangement. Curiously, this is a result of the much-criticized delays that characterize many regulatory procedures. In a number of regulated industries, a proposed change in rates is likely to take a minimum of several months before it gets through the regulatory machinery. Where it is bitterly contested, the resulting hearings before the regulatory commission, the appeals to the courts, and so on are likely to last for years. Rate cases lasting ten years are not unknown. This was true, for example, in the case before the ICC referred to in the boxed insert on page 463. This phenomenon, known as **regulatory lag**, is perhaps the main reason that profit regulation has not eliminated all rewards for efficiency and all penalties for inefficiency.

Suppose, for example, the regulatory commission approves a set of prices calculated to yield exactly the "fair rate of return" to the company, say, 10 percent. If management then invests successfully in new processes, which reduce its costs sharply, the rate of return under the old prices may rise to, say, 12 percent. If it takes two years for the regulators to review the prices they previously approved and adjust them to the new cost levels, the company will earn a 2 percent bonus reward for its efficiency during the two years of regulatory lag. Similarly, if management makes a series of bad decisions, which reduces the company's return to 7 percent, the firm may well apply to the regulator for some adjustments in prices to permit it to recoup its losses. If the regulator takes 18 months to act, the firm suffers a penalty for its inefficiency. It may be added that where mismanagement is *clearly* the cause of losses, regulators will be reluctant to permit the regulated firm to make up for such losses by rate adjustments. But in most cases it is difficult to pinpoint responsibility for a firm's losses.

All in all, those who have studied regulated industries have come away deeply concerned about the effects of regulation upon economic efficiency. Although some regulated firms seem to operate very efficiently, others seem to behave in quite the opposite way.

While regulatory lag does permit some penalty for inefficiency and some reward for superior performance by the regulated firm, the arrangement only works in a rough and ready manner. It still leaves the provision of incentives for efficiency as one of the fundamental problems of regulation. How can one prevent regulated firms from earning excessive profits, but also permit them to earn enough to attract the capital they need while still allowing rewards for superior performance and penalties for poor performance?

## MODIFIED REGULATION WITH INCENTIVES FOR EFFICIENCY

The problems of regulation just mentioned, along with some other criticisms, have in recent years produced a number of proposals for changes in the regulatory process. Three such proposals are discussed below.

### DEREGULATION PLUS INCREASED COMPETITION

One of the most widely advocated proposals is for regulators to get out of the business of regulating, leaving much more (if not all) of the task of looking after consumer interests to the natural forces of competition. This approach is promising in areas of the economy in which competition can be expected to survive without government intervention—for example, in freight transportation, airlines, and pipelines. As a consequence, a number of economists representing a broad range of political views have been advocating at least some deregulation in these industries. And, as we have seen, deregulation of air travel and freight transportation by truck and rail has largely been completed.

Of course, deregulation will not work in industries where competitors can survive only if government protects them from real competition. The experience of the airlines after deregulation is not entirely reassuring on this subject. While considerable competition continues to prevail, many of the new airlines established since the end of regulation have gone bankrupt or have been purchased by the older firms. On many routes the number of rivals has decreased sharply. This has given rise to concerns about the ability of competition to continue to protect consumer interests, at least on some of the routes. In other industries, competition is considered sufficiently weak that many think some continued regulation is indispensable. So there remains the question, Just which regulatory controls will not destroy all incentives for efficiency?

### PERFORMANCE CRITERIA FOR PERMITTED RATE OF RETURN

Some observers have advocated that the legally permitted rate of return not be set at a fixed number, say 10 percent, but that it be varied from firm to firm depending on the firm's record of efficiency and performance. That is, if some measure of quality of performance can be agreed upon (a measure that should take account of cost efficiency as well as product and service quality), then the better the performance score of the regulated firm the more it would be permitted to earn. A firm that performed well in a given year might be permitted 12 percent profits for that year, whereas a firm that did badly might be allowed only 8 percent, and a firm that performed abominably might be permitted only 4 percent.

Such incentives sometimes can be successfully built into the rules that control the operations of the firm. For example, in 1974 such a program was designed for Amtrak, the public corporation that, in effect, then rented passenger transportation service from U.S. railroads (Amtrak now runs its own trains). Under this program, the amount Amtrak paid the railroads depended upon such features as promptness of arrival of trains, infrequency of breakdowns of locomotives, and so on. Thus, the more frequently its trains were on time, the more Amtrak paid to that railroad. The results were dramatic. While over the period 1973 to 1975 the percentage of trains arriving on time increased for railroads as a whole by about 17.5 percentage points from its miserable 60 percent figure in 1973, the railroads that signed incentive contracts increased their on-time arrivals by about 29.5 percentage points from their initial (1973) average of 61 percent.

However, financial incentives cannot easily be built into rate of return formulas that contain no good objective criteria of performance (such as number of minutes behind schedule for a railroad train). Moreover, it is difficult to balance incentives for different aspects of performance. For example, if the formula assigns too high a weight to product quality and too low a weight to low cost, the firm will be encouraged to incur costs that are unjustifiably high from the point of view of public welfare in order to turn out products of slightly higher quality.

### INSTITUTIONALIZED REGULATORY LAG (YOU READ IT HERE FIRST!)

A third alternative is now in use in Great Britain for airport services and in the United States for telephone rates. The basic idea is for regulation consciously to take advantage of the incentive for efficiency provided by regulatory lag. Under this program, the regulators assign ceilings (*price caps*) for the product prices of the firms they oversee.

However, the price caps—measured in inflation-adjusted *real* terms—are reduced each year at a rate based on the rate of cost reduction (productivity growth) previously achieved by the regulated firm. Thus, if in the future the regulated firm can manage to achieve cost savings (by innovation or other means) greater than those it obtained in the past, the firm's real costs will fall faster than its real prices, and it will be permitted to keep the resulting profits as its reward for its effective cost-reduction program. Of course, for the regulated firm there is a catch. If the firm proves able to reduce its costs by, say, 2 percent per year in real terms but on the basis of its past record its regulatory price cap is cut 3 percent per year, the firm will lose profits, though consumers will continue to benefit from the cuts in real prices.

Thus, in order to earn economic profits, management is constantly forced to look for ever more economical ways of doing things.

This approach clearly gives up any attempt to limit the profit of the regulated firm. But it protects the consumer nonetheless by controlling the firm's prices. Indeed, it makes those prices lower and lower, in real terms.

## SOME EFFECTS OF DEREGULATION

The effects of deregulation are still being hotly debated. Yet, several conclusions are becoming clear.

1. ***Effects on Prices***. There seems little doubt that deregulation has generally led to lower prices. Airline fares, railroad freight rates, and telephone rates all declined on the average (at least in real terms), though, at least in the case of the airlines, the rate of decline slowed abruptly toward the end of the 1980s. Still, observers conclude that most of these prices are well below the levels that would have prevailed under regulation.
2. ***Effects on Local Service***. During the debates on deregulation, it was widely feared, even by supporters of deregulation, that smaller and more isolated communities would be deprived of service because the small number of

customers would make service unprofitable. It was said that airlines, railroads, and telephone companies would withdraw from such communities once they were no longer forced to stay there by the regulators. These worries have largely proved groundless. True, the larger airlines have left the smaller communities, as predicted. But they have usually been replaced by smaller commuter airlines that have provided, on the average, more frequent service than their regulated predecessors. A few communities have been left without service or with service of poorer quality, but other locations have benefited considerably.

3. ***Effects on Entry***. As a result of deregulation, older airlines invaded one another's routes and a number of new airlines sprang up. Altogether some 14 new airlines and about 10,000 new truck operators entered the markets since deregulation. Almost all of the new airlines ran into trouble and were sold to the older airlines. But since 1990 about a half-dozen airlines were launched.
4. ***Effects on the Unions***. Deregulation has badly hurt unions such as the Teamsters (of the trucking industry) and the Airline Pilots Association. In the new competitive climate, firms have been forced to make sharp cuts in their work forces and to resist wage increases and other costly changes in working conditions. Indeed, there has been strong pressure for retrenchment on all these fronts. It should not be surprising, then, that some of the affected unions have undertaken efforts to get Congress to reimpose regulation.
5. ***Concentration and Mergers***. Particularly in aviation and rail freight transportation, deregulation was followed by a wave of mergers in which two firms agreed to join together or in which one firm agreed to be bought out by another. This has led to an expansion of the size of the largest companies in the affected industries.

That this has happened should not be surprising since, as we saw earlier in the chapter, industries with important economies of scale are the most likely targets for regulation. Once freed from regulatory constraints, it was to be expected that firms in such industries would try to take advantage of the opportunity to achieve cost reductions through rapid expansion or by mergers.

Evaluations of the merger movement have differed sharply. Some have concluded that mergers threaten to increase monopoly power and exploit the public. Others have argued that indirect competitive pressures (for example, barges and trucks are rivals of large railroads) remain strong, and that economies of scale resulting from the mergers will be passed on to the consuming public.

## CONSEQUENCES OF DEREGULATION: GENERAL COMMENTS

The preceding list of the effects of deregulation helps us to solve the first puzzle with which this chapter started out. That is, we can see now why many airlines, trucking firms, and bus lines, as well as their unions, strongly opposed deregulation even though it offered them more freedom. They realized that regulation protected them from entry and competition. Rather than serving as an instrument to foster competition, regulation had become a means to forestall it. Of course, there were other reasons why regulated firms were unhappy about the offer of increased freedom provided by deregulation, but fear of competition was surely a major reason.

The general consequences of deregulation brought few surprises to economists. Reduced prices, reduced costs, increased pressures upon unions, and some rise in mergers were all expected. What *did* come as a surprise was the magnitude of these changes. No one seems to have expected that wages and working hours of pilots employed by the new airlines would differ so sharply from those traditional in the industry. No one seems to have expected that merger activity would be quite so extensive.

The general public seems to have been unpleasantly surprised in another respect. It was to have been anticipated that increased price competition would bring with it some reduction in "frills." To cut costs in order to reduce prices, airlines have had to make meals less elaborate and less costly. They have had to limit the number of flights to avoid empty seats, and increased crowding of planes is the clear consequence. To fill planes more, many airlines have turned to a "hub and spoke" system (see Figure 18–2). Instead of running a flight directly from a low-demand airport, A, to another low-demand airport, B, the airline flies all passengers from A to the airline's "hub airport," H, where all passengers bound for destination airport B are asked to board the same airplane. This clearly saves money and gives passengers more options as the number of flights between hubs and spokes increases. But it is not as convenient for air passengers as a direct flight from origin to destination. Critics of deregulation have placed a good deal of emphasis on the reductions of passenger comfort, but economists argue that competition would not bring such results unless passengers as a group prefer the reduction in fares to the greater standards of luxury that preceded them.

In addition, some observers have been concerned about the safety effects of deregulation. In 1985, when there was an unusually large number of air accidents, critics even implied that this might be attributable to deregulation as airlines cut expenditures on safety to keep prices low. However, in the following year U.S. commercial airlines achieved an all-time record in terms of passenger safety. Deregulation seems not to have produced any break in the trend toward increased safety in air transportation, as Figure 18–3 shows. Still, deregulation may require special vigilance to guard against neglect of safety as a cost-cutting measure, and the expense of additional governmental inspection can be considered a required cost of deregulation.

*Figure* **18–2** **A "HUB AND SPOKE" AIRLINE ROUTING PATTERN**

Passengers do not fly directly along the sparsely traveled route from airport A to airport B. Instead, passengers from A are flown to hub airport H and then redistributed to an airplane flying to airport B. Deregulation greatly increased use of this procedure.

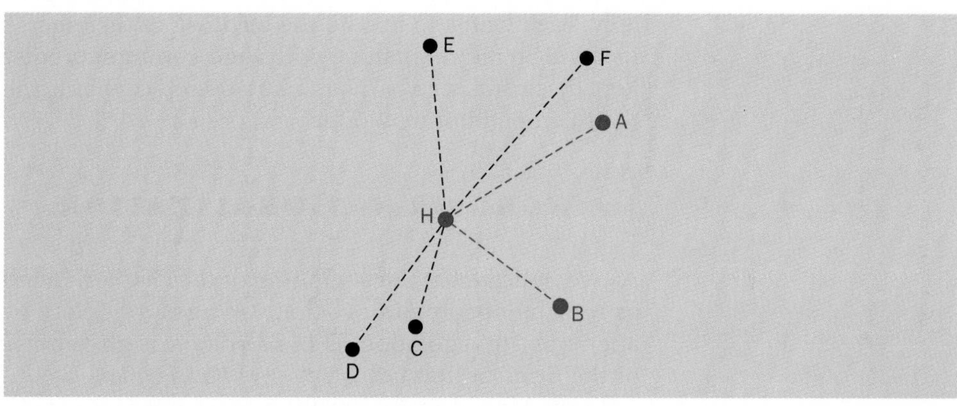

*Figure* **18–3** **AIRCRAFT ACCIDENTS PER MILLION DEPARTURES, U.S. SCHEDULED AIRLINERS, 1955–1990**

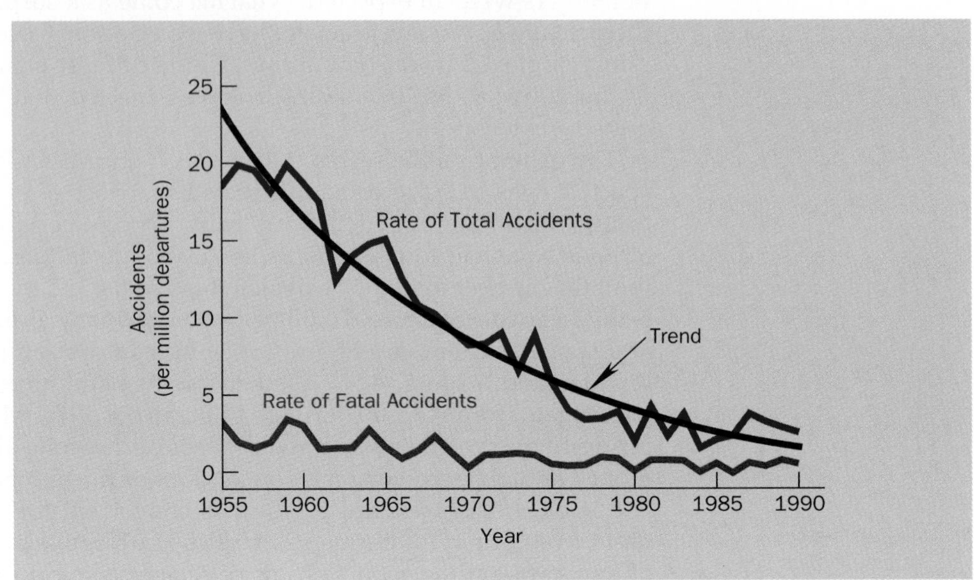


Although accident rates vary widely from year to year, both total and fatal accidents per million departures declined substantially during this period, both before and after deregulation.

SOURCE: Nancy L. Rose, "Fear of Flying? Economic Analysis of Airline Safety," *Journal of Economic Perspectives*, Vol. 6, No. 2, Spring 1992, pages 75–94.

The general conclusion is that deregulation has, in general, worked out well, and has served to promote the welfare of consumers. But the battle for deregulation is far from over. Even if those who wish for a return to the good old days of regulation (and there are many) do not succeed, there are many areas in which regulation of the old-time variety still continues its grip. For example, many state regulatory commissions continue to rely on fully distributed costs to constrain price setting. Moreover, there is an ongoing battle between the local telephone companies and the cable television firms, each of which wants to invade the other's territory, but are restrained from doing so by the regulators. Because they have wires that enter so many homes, the cable television carriers are virtually the only prospective rivals with the power to create effective competition for the phone companies that supply local service to households and businesses. But similar facts make the telephone firms a real competitive threat to cable. Predictably, each wants to invade the territory of the other, but to keep the other out of its own. So far, regulators, with their common predisposition against entry, have kept these prospective rivals apart, thereby denying the public of whatever benefits their competition may offer.

## A WORD ON NATIONALIZATION

As we indicated at the beginning of the chapter, in industries in which monopoly or near monopoly offer cost advantages to society over competition, there is an alternative to regulation. This alternative is government ownership and operation of the firms in that industry, or *nationalization*.

In the United States, tradition does not favor such government operation, but the exceptions have grown in number. For example, we have government supply of electricity by the TVA; the U.S. Postal Service; and, more recently, the operation of railroads by the publicly owned agencies Amtrak and Conrail, which may be regarded as an intermediate step in the direction of nationalization, although Conrail was returned to private operation in 1986. A number of cities operate their own public transport facilities, collect their own garbage, and offer other services that elsewhere are provided by private enterprise.

It is almost an instinctive reaction by people in the United States to consider such public enterprises as being prone to extreme mismanagement and waste. And the near-legendary problems of the Post Office do seem to support this supposition. However, here, too, one should be careful not to jump to conclusions. In recent decades, when railroads were entirely in private hands, that industry had difficulties no less serious than those of the Post Office. It is true that visitors find the nationalized French telephone system a model of chaos and mismanagement. But at the same time, the Swedish telephone system, which is also nationalized, is smooth-working and efficient. And the French government-supplied electricity system has set world standards in its use of the most modern analytic techniques of economics and engineering, and it has adopted innovative pricing policies that promote efficiency.

Despite these accomplishments, nationalized industries continue to be beset by weak incentives for efficiency. First, governments virtually never permit a nationalized firm to go bankrupt, and, as a result, management is deprived of one of the most powerful motivations for minimization of their costs. Second, no one has yet found a systematic incentive mechanism for efficiency that can do for nationalized industries what the profit motive does for private enterprise. Where the market is unsparing in its rewards for accomplishments and in its penalties for poor performance, one can be quite sure that a firm's inefficiency will not readily be tolerated. But nationalized industries have no such automatic mechanism handing out rewards and penalties dependably and impartially. We have seen, however, that there are analogous problems under regulation; where profits are controlled by the regulator, the rewards for efficiency are also far from automatic. Hence, the relative efficiency of nationalized and regulated private firms is far from clear. (The boxed insert on page 472 offers some illustrative evidence.)

By now there have been several dozen studies comparing the efficiency of private unregulated, private regulated, and nationalized firms.[3] While a majority conclude that the costs of unregulated private firms are the lowest, they find considerably more variation in the relative performance of nationalized and private regulated firms. Results seem to vary by type of industry, by country, and by size of enterprise. In sum, it is by no means clear that the regulatory approach always serves the public better than nationalization. In both cases, much seems to depend on the rules employed by the pertinent government agency.

Still, in a number of countries, trends have moved sharply away from nationalization. Among free-market economies, Great Britain is the prime example. The conservative government of Margaret Thatcher, by one estimate, "privatised" no less than 40 percent of the industries that were nationalized between 1945 and 1979.[4] The list includes telecommunications, oil and gas production, airports and

---

[3]For a good survey of these studies see Yair Aharoni, *The Evolution and Management of State-Owned Enterprises*, Ballinger Publishing Company, Cambridge, Mass., 1986, pp. 197–204.

[4]Martin Holmes, *Thatcherism*, London: Macmillan, 1989; Dennis Swann, *The Retreat of the State: Deregulation and Privatisation in the UK and US*, New York: Harvester-Wheatsheaf, 1988; and Christopher Johnson, *The Economy Under Mrs. Thatcher*, London: Penguin Books, 1992.

## *Evidence of Inefficiency and Efficiency in Public Enterprise*

**EVIDENCE OF INEFFICIENCY IN PUBLIC ENTERPRISE**

Since residential garbage collection is a relatively homogeneous task and is carried out both by government and private firms, this service is particularly well suited to comparing the costs of competition, private monopoly, and government monopoly. A study of the relative costs of private and public collection of garbage in about 300 municipalities in the United States found that collection costs were about the same whether the job was done by government or by a group of competing firms.* Competition was expensive because each firm served only scattered customers, and there was much duplication of routes. On the other hand, the costs of both government collection and competitive private collection were some 34 percent higher than the costs of service by a private monopoly collector working under contract to the municipal government. The government services typically had significantly larger crews, higher rates of employee absenteeism, smaller trucks, and less frequent use of incentive systems than did the private collectors.

**EVIDENCE OF EFFICIENCY IN PUBLIC ENTERPRISE**

A recent study compared the costs of 33 private electric utilities with 23 public ones in the United States.** On the basis of a rather sophisticated statistical analysis, the authors concluded that publicly owned electric utilities perform better than their privately owned regulated counterparts. The costs of the government-owned firms were 24 to 33 percent lower than those of the private firms, a difference similar to that found in other studies of the issue. Thus, at least for the electric utilities they studied, the authors judged that public ownership is a better choice than production by regulated private firms.

*E. S. Savas, "Evaluating the Organization of Service Delivery: Solid Waste Collection and Disposal; A Summary." Center for Government Studies, Graduate School of Business, Columbia University, April 1976. **See D. R. Pescatrice and J. M. Trapani III, "The Performance and Objectives of Public and Private Utilities Operating in the United States," *Journal of Public Economics*, vol. 13, 1980, pages 259–76.

airlines, trucking, rail hotels, seaports, ship building, and the aerospace, automobile, and semiconductor industries. Under "Thatcherism," bus routes were also deregulated, local governments began to contract out services to private contractors, private pensions, health care and education grew, and over a million public housing units were sold to tenants. Television broadcasting, formerly the exclusive province of the BBC, a government-owned corporation, is going increasingly into private hands. The movement has spread to many other geographic areas. For example, privatization of telecommunications has occurred or is contemplated in places as diverse as New Zealand, Venezuela, and Puerto Rico.

Privatization in the free-market economies has not proved to be as easy or as trouble-free as some had expected. Many of the government firms that were candidates for sale to the public were such money losers that no one could be found to buy them. In some cases, firms were sold with what amounted to a guarantee that they would receive a governmentally enforced monopoly, presumably in order to increase the price that the government could extract from the sale. In other cases, the firms sold seemed to be natural monopolies, so that in neither case could the firm's decision making be entrusted to the market mechanism. Consequently, some such companies, British Telecom for example, found themselves enmeshed in regulatory constraints that severely inhibited their decisions. Other such firms, such as New Zealand Telecom, were sold on condition that cross subsidies (called the "Kiwi share" in New Zealand) and other peculiarities of government operation be continued under private ownership. Such costly restrictions predictably lead to expensive litigation between the privatized firms and their rivals, on the proper consequences of the obligations adopted as part of the sale for pricing rules that give neither firm an indefensible competitive advantage.

However, it is in the formerly centrally planned economies of Eastern Europe that proposed moves away from nationalization sound like a stampede. Proposals to transform the economies of Poland, Hungary, Czechoslovakia, East Germany, and Lithuania into free-market systems imply extreme disillusionment with the performance of government-owned industry. As this is being written, there is too much turmoil to permit any sensible guesses about the future of this movement. But, already, the attempts to put the general notion of privatization into practice has run into a number of daunting difficulties. To whom does one sell the inefficient and unprofitable dinosaur firms that emerged from the Communist regime? How does one prevent ownership and control of the firms from falling into a few private hands, most of them those of foreigners? If the firms are democratized by giving every citizen a tiny share, who among these new stockholders, if anyone, will have the clout to prevent managements from exploiting the enterprises for their own ends? All of these matters and many more will have to be dealt with if privatization in Eastern Europe is to proceed in a rational way. (For a bit more on the subject see the box on page 121).

## *Summary*

1. **Regulation** has two primary purposes: to put brakes on the decisions of industries with monopoly power, and to contribute to public health and safety.

2. Railroads, trucking, telecommunications, and gas and electricity supply are among the industries that are regulated in the United States. In Europe the firms that provide these services are usually owned by the government (they are nationalized).

3. In recent years there has been a major push toward reduction of regulation. So far, air, truck, and rail transportation have been deregulated in whole or in part.

4. Among the major reasons given for regulation are: (a) economies of scale and scope, which make industries into natural monopolies; (b) the danger of self-destructive competition in industries with low (short-run) marginal costs; (c) the desire to provide service to isolated areas where supply is expensive and unprofitable; and (d) the protection of consumers, employees, and the environment.

5. Regulators often reject proposals by regulated firms to cut their prices, and sometimes the regulators even force firms to raise their prices. The purpose of such action is to prevent "unfair competition," and to protect customers of some of the firm's products from being forced to **cross-subsidize** customers of other products. Many economists disagree with such actions and argue that the result is usually to stifle competition and make all customers pay more than they otherwise would.

6. Economists generally argue that a firm should be permitted to cut its price as long as it covers its **marginal cost**. However, others (usually noneconomists) argue that fully distributed cost is a better criterion. A fully distributed cost criterion, in this sense, usually means that price will be higher than it will be if marginal cost is used as the standard.

7. Regulation is often criticized for providing little or no incentive for efficiency, for tending to push prices upward, and for forcing the regulated parties to engage in an expensive and time-consuming adversary process.

8. Several regulatory agencies, including the FCC and the ICC, have recently adopted new methods of regulation intended, among other things, to provide incentives for efficiency analogous to those supplied by the free market.
9. Deregulation so far has clearly reduced costs and prices. However, it has also reduced "frills" in service to customers and has been followed by a substantial number of mergers.
10. Nationalized (government-run) industries are frequently suspected of being wasteful and inefficient, but the evidence is not uniform and there are cases in which nationalized firms seem more efficient than similar regulated firms.
11. There has recently been a worldwide movement for **privatization** of nationalized firms, that is, for their sale to private owners. However, this has proved more difficult than might have been expected.

## *Key Concepts and Terms*

Regulation
Nationalization
Privatization
Price floor
Price ceiling
Natural monopoly
Economies of scale
Economies of scope
Cross-subsidization
Self-destructive competition
Fully distributed cost
Marginal cost pricing
Ramsey pricing rule
Stand-alone cost
Regulatory lag
Price caps

## *Questions for Review*

1. Why is an electric company in a city usually considered to be a natural monopoly? What would happen if two competing electric companies were established? How about telephone companies?
2. Suppose a 20 percent cut in the price of freight transportation brings in so much new business that it permits a railroad to cut its passenger fares by 2 percent. In your opinion, is this equitable? Is it a good idea or a bad one?
3. In some regulated industries, prices are prevented from falling by the regulatory agency, and as a result many firms open up business in that industry. In your opinion, is this competitive or anticompetitive? Is it a good idea or a bad one?
4. What industries in the United States can be considered nationalized or partly nationalized? What do you think of the quality of their services? Why might this criterion be inadequate as evidence on which to base a judgment of the idea of nationalization?
5. List some industries with regulated rates whose services you have bought. What do you think of the quality of their service?
6. In which if any of the regulated industries mentioned in your previous answer is there competitive rivalry? Why is regulation appropriate in these cases? (Or is it inappropriate in your opinion, and if so, why?)
7. Regulators are much concerned about the prevention of "predatory pricing"—pricing policies designed to destroy competition. The U.S. Court of Appeals has, however, noted that "the term probably does not have a well-defined meaning, but it certainly bears a sinister connotation." How might one go about distinguishing "predatory" from "nonpredatory" pricing? What would you do about it? (Note that no one has yet come up with a final answer to this problem.)
8. Do you think it is fair or unfair for rural users of telephone service to be cross-subsidized by other telephone users ?
9. Can you think of a way in which a new rural telephone subscriber contributes a beneficial externality? If so, does it make sense to provide a subsidy to rural subscribers, and who should pay the subsidy?
10. A regulated industry is prohibited from earning profits higher than it now is getting. It begins to sell a new product at a price above its long-run marginal cost. Explain why the prices of other company products will, very likely, have to be reduced.
11. To provide incentives for increased efficiency, several regulatory agencies have eliminated ceilings on the profits of the regulated firm but instead put caps on their prices. Suppose a regulated firm manages to cut its prices in half but in the process doubles its profits. Should rational consumers consider this to be a good or a bad development? Why?
12. Why do you think Great Britain has privatized some of its nationalized industries? How about Poland? Where is it more urgent?

Chapter 19

# LIMITING MARKET POWER: ANTITRUST POLICY

*We demand that big business give the people a square deal.*

**THEODORE ROOSEVELT**

The preceding chapter described the process of regulation, one of the two main instruments used by the U.S. government to offset the undesirable effects of unrestrained monopoly and oligopoly. This chapter analyzes the second of these instruments, *antitrust policy*. **Antitrust policy** refers to programs to preclude the deliberate creation of monopoly and to prevent powerful firms from engaging in related "undesirable practices." Firms accused of violating the antitrust laws are likely to be sued in court by the federal government, or by other private firms, seeking a ruling that prevents the practice from recurring, provides compensation to the victims, and punishes the offender by fines or even a prison term. ¶ Antitrust suits are likely to be well-publicized affairs because the accused firms are often the giants of industry. The more spectacular cases in the history of antitrust policy involve such names as Standard Oil, U.S. Steel, the Aluminum Company of America (Alcoa), General Electric, International Business Machines (IBM), and American Telephone and Telegraph (AT&T). More recently, the enterprises accused of antitrust violations have included some of the nation's most prestigious colleges and universities, which were said to have engaged in a pricing conspiracy (see box, page 492).

The magnitude of an antitrust suit is difficult to envision. After the charges have been filed, it is not unusual for more than five years to elapse before the case even comes up for trial. The parties spend this period preparing their cases: assembling witnesses, gathering evidence, and drawing up numerous documents. With the permission of the courts, the parties may undertake massive searches of one another's files, each side collecting many millions of pages from those files. Dozens of lawyers, scores of witnesses, and hundreds of researchers are likely to participate in the process of preparation. The trial itself is likely to run for years, with each day's proceedings producing a fat volume of transcript. A major case can pour forth literally several thousand volumes of material, and the total cost to the defendant can easily run to *several hundred million* dollars.

Thus, the ability of the government or of another firm to haul a company into court, accusing it of an antitrust violation, is an awesome power. For, win or lose, or even if the case is flimsy and is thrown out of court before it comes to trial, it is likely to constitute a heavy burden on the accused firm, draining its funds, taking the time and attention of its management, and delaying its decisions until the outcome of the legal proceedings.

What justifies the investment of so much power in a government agency such as the Department of Justice or the Federal Trade Commission? What are the purposes of the antitrust laws? And how well has the program succeeded? In fact, there is much dispute about whether antitrust laws have done much to increase competition, and some observers have even argued that they are often abused and twisted into an anticompetitive tool. (See the box, opposite.) These are the main concerns of this chapter.

Today, a primary issue for antitrust policy is whether its rules, which are generally much more severe than those in other countries, seriously handicap U.S. companies in their efforts to compete in world markets. And if so, are the benefits of the antitrust laws sufficient to offset that cost to society? This chapter will provide pertinent evidence. But, since the issue is a matter of controversy, we will not attempt categorical answers. Rather, we will leave you to judge the issue for yourself.

## THE PUBLIC IMAGE OF BUSINESS WHEN THE ANTITRUST LAWS WERE BORN

The Sherman Act, the forerunner of all modern antitrust legislation, was passed in 1890. To understand what led Congress to attempt to interfere with freedom of business enterprise, we must glance briefly at the character of the most publicized business practices in the United States during the half century following the Civil War. There were, no doubt, many businessmen at that time whose mode of operation was beyond reproach. But these were not the businessmen who made the headlines and who amassed the most spectacular fortunes. The adventures of the more daring breed of entrepreneurs, those who have been described as "the robber barons," compete in lurid detail with the tales of their contemporaries in the Wild West.

One of the most widely publicized cases was that of John D. Rockefeller, Sr., and his Standard Oil Company. About five years after starting in the oil-refining business with an investment of $4000, Rockefeller and his partners created the

## Issue: Can Antitrust Be Used to Prevent Competition?

Many observers are concerned that the antitrust laws are often used by inefficient firms to protect themselves from the competition of more-efficient rivals. When they are unable to win out in the marketplace, the argument goes, they simply start a lawsuit against their competitors, claiming that those rivals have achieved success by means that violate the antitrust laws. Not only do they seek the protection of the courts against what they describe as "unfair competition" or "predatory practices," but they often sue for compensation which, under the law, can sometimes be three times as large as the damages they have suffered. Moreover, even if the defendant is found to be innocent, it must normally pay the very high costs of the litigation itself. Aside from the enormous waste that such suits entail, observers worry that this is a perversion of the antitrust laws, which were, after all, designed to *promote* competition, *not* to *prevent* it. Three examples, one very old and two recent, illustrate the nature of such litigation.* These three cases also show that the courts are often sufficiently wise to throw out such attempts to use the antitrust laws to prevent competition.

The Schoolmaster Case. In 1410, two Gloucester schoolmasters brought suit charging a third schoolmaster with trespass, on the ground that the latter had entered into business in competition against themselves in the same town, and in the process offered a per-pupil fee some 70 percent lower than their own. The claim was rejected by the court, and one of the judges commented " . . . though another equally competent with the plaintiffs comes to teach the children, this is a virtuous and charitable thing, and an ease to the people, for which he cannot be punished by our law." (Court of Common Pleas [1410]).

*AMI versus IBM.* Allen-Myland Inc. (AMI) is a small firm specializing in the upgrading of computers, in which it had obtained handsome profits, in a period when expansion of a computer's capacity was very laborious. However, technological progress by IBM had reduced a labor-intensive task to the simple installation of a small and highly reliable part that took several minutes of essentially unskilled labor, thus rendering obsolete many of the services offered by AMI. AMI sued IBM, seeking to persuade the court to impose an artificial and expensive market niche for upgrading services, with AMI permanently protected from competitive pressures. The court's decision completely rejected AMI's position (Eastern District of Pennsylvania [1988]). The decision is now under appeal.

*Sewell Plastics versus Coca-Cola, Southeastern Container et al.* The Sewell Plastics Company had a preponderant share in the manufacture of plastic soft-drink bottles in the United States. At one time, it sold two-liter bottles at a price somewhat above 30 cents per bottle. A group of Coca-Cola bottlers in the Southeast considered the price too high, and formed a cooperative firm, "Southeastern Container," to manufacture plastic bottles for themselves. Within five years Southeastern had reduced its cost below 14 cents per bottle, and real retail prices of soft drinks also fell. Despite rising national sales and profits, Sewell decided to sue Southeastern, explicitly admitting that it was seeking to persuade the court to force a sale of Southeastern to itself or, as a possible alternative, to force Southeastern's customers to sign exclusive purchasing contracts with Sewell. In the spring of 1989 the judge dismissed Sewell's claims, holding that there was no need for a trial (U.S. District Court, Western District, North Carolina [April, 1989]).

*One of the authors of this book was involved as an expert witness in both of the recent cases.

Standard Oil Company in 1870. Under its leadership, a number of refineries and other shippers formed a cooperative powerful enough to force the railroads not only to provide discounts to members of the group *and not to its competitors*, but even to give the group "drawbacks"—that is, payments on every shipment of oil refined by a *rival* firm. In 1872 the organization controlled only about 10 percent of the country's refining capacity. Yet only seven years later Standard Oil and its associated companies were producing some 90 percent of the nation's refined oil and had control of all its pipeline capacity.

Then, in 1882, lacking confidence in the trustworthiness of the alliance, and because of legal obstacles to its interstate operations, the group formed the Standard Oil Trust (from which the word "antitrust" was derived). This involved the appointment of a group of nine trustees into whose hands the 40 associated firms placed enough of their stock to give irrevocable control to the trustees. The trust closed down "excessive" and inefficient refinery operations, involving more than half its plants, in an effort to limit output and keep prices at levels that yielded monopoly profits.

While the oil trust was the first to be established in the United States, others soon followed. Successful trusts were formed in sugar, whiskey, lead, cottonseed oil, and linseed oil. In 1892 the Supreme Court of Ohio ordered the dissolution of the Standard Oil Trust, which nevertheless managed to survive as a cooperating set of firms by arranging for the directors of the major refining companies to serve on one another's boards.

Other, more lurid tales of business practices in this period are easy to find: how J.P. Morgan hired an army of toughs to engage literally in pitched battle for a contested section of railroad outside Binghamton, New York; how Philip Armour and his confederates obtained control of meat processing by an understanding with their rivals that each day a different one of them would offer a low bid for the morning shipment of cattle and no one else would ever enter a higher bid. It is easy to go on and on with such stories. But the point is clear:

There was good reason in 1890 for popular distrust of free-swinging business activity. Business practices in the preceding decades had been ridden by scandal.

Business leaders repeatedly indicated their contempt for the public interest. J.P. Morgan announced, "I owe the public nothing," and people long remembered W.H. Vanderbilt's phrase "the public be damned." The population was warned by advocates of control measures that it faced a country "in which the citizen was born to drink the milk furnished by the milk trust, eat the beef of the beef trust, illuminate his home by grace of the oil trust and die and be carried off by the coffin trust."[1] The circumstances were clearly propitious for some legislative action.

## THE ANTITRUST LAWS

Five acts of Congress constitute the basis of the federal government's antitrust policy. Major provisions of these acts are summarized in Table 19–1. The **Sherman Act**, the first of the U.S. antitrust laws, was passed in 1890, soon after the trust-

[1]Matthew Josephson, *The Robber Barons, The Great American Capitalists 1861–1901* (New York: Harcourt Brace Jovanovich, 1934), page 358.

Table 19-1 BASIC ANTITRUST LAWS

| NAME | DATE | MAJOR PROVISIONS |
|---|---|---|
| Sherman Act | 1890 | Prohibits "all contracts, combinations and conspiracies in restraint of trade" (Section 1), and monopolization in interstate and foreign trade (Section 2). |
| Clayton Act | 1914 | Prohibits price discrimination; contracts in which the seller prevents buyers from purchasing goods from the seller's competitors (tying contracts); and acquisition by one corporation of another's shares if these acts are likely to reduce competition or tend to create monopoly: also prohibits directors of one company from sitting on the board of a competitor's company. |
| Federal Trade Commission Act | 1914 | Establishes the FTC as an independent agency with authority to prosecute unfair competition and to prevent false and misleading advertising. |
| Robinson-Patman Act | 1936 | Prohibits special discounts and other discriminatory concessions to large purchasers unless based on differences in cost or "offered in good faith to meet an equally low price of a competitor." |
| Celler-Kefauver Antimerger Act | 1950 | Prohibits any corporation from acquiring the assets of another where the effect is to reduce competition substantially or to tend to create a monopoly. |

creating activity reached its peak. The act is brief and very general, containing two main provisions: a prohibition of all contracts, combinations, and conspiracies in restraint of trade (Section 1), and a prohibition of any acts of, or attempts at, monopolization of trade (Section 2). However, the Sherman Act provided no definition of its terms and no special agency to oversee its enforcement. Thirteen years elapsed after its passage before the antitrust division of the Department of Justice was established under the energetic antitrust proclivities of Theodore Roosevelt.

It was believed by many during Woodrow Wilson's administration that the Sherman Act did not provide adequate protection to the public against restrictive business practices. Consequently, in 1914 Congress passed two supplemental laws, the Clayton Act and the Federal Trade Commission Act.

**PRICE DISCRIMINATION** occurs when different prices, relative to costs, are charged to different buyers of the same product.

The **Clayton Act** deals with certain specific practices thought to be conducive to encroachment of monopoly. It took two steps toward protecting smaller firms from what was considered unfair competition by larger rivals. First, it prohibited **price discrimination**, which it defined as the act, by a seller, of charging different prices to different buyers of the same product. This provision would, for example, have prohibited the railroad rebates that Rockefeller had used to squeeze out his rivals. Second, the Clayton Act prohibited *tying contracts*—arrangements under which a customer who wants to buy some product from a given seller is required as part of the price to agree to buy some other product or products exclusively from that same seller. In addition, the Clayton Act prohibited one firm from purchasing the stock of another if that acquisition tended to reduce competition. While this provision was intended to prevent a firm from buying out its rivals, business found it possible to circumvent the intent of the law by buying a rival's stocks and then merging assets. When this practice was recognized, a new law—

the **Celler-Kefauver Antimerger Act** of 1950—was enacted to prohibit it. Finally, the Clayton Act prohibited *interlocking directorates* between competitors, arrangements under which two companies have in common some of the members of their boards of directors.

The **Federal Trade Commission Act** created a commission to investigate "unfair" and "predatory" competitive practices and declared illegal all "unfair methods of competition and commerce." But since no definition of "unfairness" was provided by the law, and since, in any event, the Commission's powers were substantially restricted by the courts, the FTC was a rather ineffective agency for the first quarter-century of its existence. In 1938, however, it was given the task of preventing false and deceptive advertising, a task to which it has subsequently devoted a substantial portion of its energies.

In 1936, Congress passed the **Robinson-Patman Act**, which was designed to protect independent sellers—both wholesalers and retailers (primarily in groceries and drugs)—from the "unfair competition" of chain stores and mass distributors. The Robinson-Patman Act was not a natural step in the succession of antitrust laws, since it sought to *restrain* competition by protecting small firms from the competition of larger ones. It was felt that large firms were powerful enough to wrest special financial terms from their suppliers, which gave them an unfair competitive edge over their rivals. Accordingly, the Act prohibited several types of discriminatory arrangements, such as:

1. Special concessions, like promotional allowances by sellers to any favored set of buyers; any such allowances being legal only if available to all buyers on essentially equal terms;
2. Special discounts to favored buyers who purchase the same goods in the same quantities as other buyers who do not get the discount;
3. Lower prices in one geographic area than in another, or prices that are "unreasonably low," if the objective is to eliminate competition;
4. Payment of brokerage fees to a buyer who does not actually use a middleman broker;
5. Discounts for larger purchases, or any other form of discrimination that tends to *reduce* competition or encourage monopoly. This was perhaps the most important provision of the Act, although it did continue to permit price discrimination if it could be justified either by differences in costs or by the necessity of meeting the price charged by a competitor.

## THE COURTS AND THE SHERMAN ACT

From the earliest days of the Sherman Act, the courts have been rather consistent in their use of Section 1—the part of the Act that prohibits all contracts, combinations, and conspiracies in restraint of trade. Section 1 has been invoked primarily against price-fixing agreements—that is, agreements under which several ostensibly competing firms coordinate their pricing decisions. The courts have held that such agreements are illegal *per se*; that is, they have held that no excuses or exonerating circumstances can render a price-fixing agreement acceptable to the law.

In the Addyston Pipe case of 1899, six manufacturers of cast-iron pipe argued that the prices they had agreed upon were reasonable and that, had there been no agreement, prices would have been driven to ruinous levels. But Justice William Howard Taft rejected the argument, affirming that *any* price-setting agreement was illegal. This doctrine has been confirmed many times, most notably in the G.E.-Westinghouse case, which was decided in 1961. General Electric, Westinghouse, and several dozen other producers of electrical equipment had gotten together to divide the market up among themselves and to agree on prices. The firms were found guilty of a conspiracy to fix prices and were fined several million dollars. Even more remarkable, officers of the major companies were sentenced to (brief) prison terms.

Cases in which there are no *explicit* price agreements, but in which there are grounds for suspicion that more subtle means have been used to attain the same goals, have proven more difficult for the courts to deal with. For example, a large firm may publish a price list so that all its competitors know in advance what prices it is going to charge. If it also announces in advance that it will reduce its price to equal that of any competitor who attempts to undercut it, this may discourage rivals from undercutting the published prices. A variety of such types of behavior have been held to facilitate coordination of prices; and some, though not all, of them have been held to be illegal.

Section 2 of the Sherman Act deals with persons "who shall monopolize or attempt to monopolize . . . any part of the trade or commerce among the several states, or with foreign nations." That is, Section 2 deals with a single decision maker, rather than a group of conspirators, and focuses on attempts to create a monopoly. At first the courts proceeded very timidly in dealing with industrial cases under Section 2. For example, in the E. C. Knight case of 1895, the court held that a monopoly of sugar manufacturing was legal on the grounds that manufacturing was not commerce! But the Supreme Court's position toughened markedly in 1911, when it decided to require both the American Tobacco Company and the Standard Oil Company to give up substantial shares of their holdings in other firms. Many of today's leading gasoline suppliers—including Standard Oil of California, Exxon, and Sohio—are offspring of the original Standard Oil Company, spawned by the Court's decision.

At the same time, however, the Court also formulated the troublesome **rule of reason**, which held that monopolizing trade restraints are not *necessarily* illegal per se. According to this rule, a restraint is against the law only if it is "unreasonable." On that basis, U.S. Steel was exonerated in 1920 even though, when it was formed, it controlled 80 to 95 percent of U.S. output of some steel products. The Court held (and many economists agree) that mere size does not constitute an offense—that a firm must commit objectionable overt acts before it can be found guilty of violating Section 2 of the Sherman Act. Eastman Kodak and International Harvester, each with very large market shares, were found not guilty on similar grounds. Thus, while the courts held that there were *no* excusable cases of price fixing under Section 1, they ruled that there *were* excusable monopolies under Section 2.

However, a profound departure from this doctrine was enunciated in the decision on the Department of Justice's case against Alcoa. Launched in 1937, the case was settled only eight years later. The Court ruled that Alcoa was guilty *because it controlled some 90 percent of the market*, even though it had not used means to gain this control that would previously have been declared "unreasonable." Thus, the Court's decision took the position that a firm's monopoly power, if sufficiently great, was illegal when *consciously maintained*, even if the firm had done nothing illegal to acquire that power. In other words the Court decided that the legality of the organization of an industry could be determined at least in part from its observable *structure*, for example, from the market share of the largest firm as well as from the *conduct* of any firm in that industry. This feature of the Alcoa decision has so far not been used widely as a precedent for other cases, and some commentators claim it was just an aberration. Others, though, feel that the conclusion about the illegality of monopoly, however acquired, heralded a new phase in the history of antitrust policy.

## ON MERGER POLICY

A **MERGER** occurs when two previously independent firms are combined under a single owner or group of owners. A **horizontal merger** is the merger of two firms producing similar products, as when one toothpaste manufacturing firm purchases another. A **vertical merger** involves the joining of two firms, one of which supplies an ingredient of the other's product, as when an auto maker acquires a tire manufacturing firm. A **conglomerate merger** is the union of two unrelated firms, as when a defense industry firm joins a firm that produces video tapes.

**Mergers** have long been a subject of suspicion by the antitrust authorities. Particularly when a merger is **horizontal**—meaning that the merging firms supply products that are identical or very similar, thus competing directly with one another—it is often feared that because the number of firms in the industry is reduced (that is, concentration is increased), competition will decline.

The Department of Justice and the Federal Trade Commission are both concerned with mergers. They do not wish to impede mergers that seem likely to increase efficiency by improving the coordination of production activities, permitting economies of scale, getting one of the firms out of financial difficulties, or facilitating operations in a variety of other ways. But the antitrust agencies do want to prevent mergers that threaten to reduce competition.

To help firms decide whether a proposed merger will get them into trouble, and for other reasons as well, the Department of Justice issues guidelines that indicate when the Department is (or is not) likely to try to block a merger. For example, the guidelines indicate that the Department generally will not oppose mergers in industries that are very unconcentrated or into which entry is very easy. However, in highly concentrated industries where entry is difficult, the merger of two large firms will usually be opposed. In 1982, 1984, and 1991, the Department issued new, more permissive guidelines.

One result of the loosening of the anti-merger rules and the Reagan administration's view that mergers were generally good for the economy was a much-publicized rise in merger activity. In the entire decade 1972–1982, companies are reported to have spent about $340 billion (in dollars of 1989 purchasing power) buying other firms. In 1988, the total spent on "dealmaking" activity (including mergers, acquisitions, and leveraged buyouts) topped $250 billion. It fell somewhat in 1989 but still was more than $200 billion. In total, about $1.5 trillion was spent during the decade of the 1980s.[2]

This rash of mergers has given rise to a good deal of controversy; some observers conclude that it has increased the likelihood of monopoly power, while others believe it has served largely to make the merged firms more efficient. In any event, defenders of the mergers argue that they have not increased the share of big business in the United States (see the discussion of concentration in the next section). For example, in 1989 the percentage of the nation's assets held by the top 500 U.S. corporations (44 percent) was about the same as its level in 1970,

[2]*Businessweek*, January 15, 1990, pp. 52–53, which cites M & A Data Base, *Mergers and Acquisitions*. These figures are all expressed in 1989 dollars of purchasing power.

and the share of the labor force employed by those corporations in 1989 was about 10 percent, compared with about 17 percent in 1970.[3]

Though by no means unanimous on the subject, most economists agree that mergers *sometimes* reduce competition, particularly in a market that is not contestable,[4] so that threats of entry do not prevent the merged firm from raising prices above competitive levels. This danger is particularly acute if the number of firms is sufficiently small to make collusion a real possibility.

On the other hand, where there is reason to believe that the merger will not reduce competition, many economists oppose impediments to merger. They believe that mergers that are not undertaken to reduce competition can have only one purpose—to achieve greater efficiency. For example, the larger firm that results from the merger may enjoy substantial economies of scale not available to smaller firms. Or the two merging companies may learn special skills from one another. Or they may offset one another's risks.

Mergers have sometimes proved disappointing and brought little cost saving; a number have subsequently been dissolved. But economists who defend freedom to merge when there is no demonstrated threat to competition pose a challenging question: Who can judge better than the firms involved whether their marriage is likely to make their activities more efficient? Indeed, a recent study of roughly 22,000 large manufacturing establishments, of which 1100 had been purchased and merged ("taken over") between 1981 and 1986, found that the merged manufacturing plants subsequently had rates of productivity growth some 14 percent higher than the others in the same industry.[5]

## ISSUES IN CONCENTRATION OF INDUSTRY

Having reviewed the antitrust laws and their interpretation by the courts, the next logical question is, Do they work? One very rough way to measure the success of antitrust legislation is to look at what has happened to the share of American business in the hands of the largest firms. Some observers, particularly the Marxists, have predicted that one of the basic tendencies of capitalism is **concentration of industry**, because small firms are increasingly driven out of business, especially during economic crises, and large firms consequently acquire ever-larger shares of the market. One can therefore investigate whether such a tendency has been observed in the United States. If, in fact, concentration has *not* increased, someone who holds these views might be led to surmise that the antitrust program has had a hand in preventing the growth of monopoly. But first we should consider what might have been expected to happen to concentration in the United States in the absence of any countermeasures by government. Is there good reason to expect an inexorable trend toward bigness, as the Marxists suggest?

---

[3]Fortune 500 issues of *Fortune*, May 1971 and April 23, 1990; and *Economic Report of the President, 1990*. The first calculation is percentage of U.S. GNP represented by the combined assets held by the Fortune 500 companies.

[4]See Chapter 12, pages 303–305 for a definition and discussion of this concept.

[5]Frank Lichtenberg and David Siegel, *The Effects of Leveraged Buyouts on Productivity and Related Aspects of Firm Behavior*, NBER Working Paper No. 3022, 1989.

There are two basic reasons why the larger firms in an industry may triumph over the small. First, larger firms may obtain monopoly power, which they can use to their advantage. They can force sellers of equipment, raw materials, and other inputs to give them better terms than are available to small competitors; and they can also force retailers to give preferences to their products. These are, of course, the sorts of advantages to bigness that the antitrust laws were designed to eliminate.

The second reason why an industry's output may tend to be divided among fewer and larger firms with the passage of time has to do with technology. In some industries, fairly small firms can produce as cheaply or more cheaply than large ones, while in other industries only rather large firms can achieve maximal economy. By and large, the difference in number of firms from one industry to another has tended to correspond to the size of the firm that is least costly. Automobile and airplane manufacturing are industries in which tiny companies cannot hope to produce economically and, indeed, these are industries made up of a relatively few large firms. In clothing production and farming, matters go quite the other way.

Frequently, innovation seems to have increased the plant size that minimizes costs. Such examples as automated processes or assembly lines suggest that new techniques always call for gigantic equipment; but this is not always true. For example, the invention of truck transportation took much of the freight-shipping market away from the giant railroads and gave it to much smaller trucking firms. Technological change also seems to have favored the establishment of small electronics firms. Similarly, the continued development of cheaper and smaller computers is likely to provide a competitive advantage to smaller firms in many other industries. Furthermore:

If innovation provides increased cost advantages to larger firms, the growth of firms will be stimulated. But a fall in the number of firms in the industry need not inevitably result. If demand for the industry's output grows faster than the optimal size of firms, we may end up with a larger number of firms, each of them bigger than before, but each having a smaller share of an expanded market.

For example, suppose in some industry a new process is invented that requires a far larger scale of operation than currently is typical. Specifically, suppose that the least costly plant size becomes twice as large. If demand for the industry's product increases only a little, we can expect a decrease in the number of firms. But if, because the new process reduces costs or improves the product significantly, the quantity of the industry's product demanded triples at the same time, then the optimal number of firms will in fact increase to one and a half times the original number—each firm will be twice as big as before—so that together they serve three times the volume. In such a case, each firm's share of industry output will in fact have declined.

In the nineteenth century, technological developments do seem to have called, predominantly, for larger firms that can take advantage of the resulting economies. If the same has been true in the current century, and if this has somewhat outstripped even the rate of growth in output—that is, the growth of GDP, we should expect some fall in the number of firms in a typical industry, somewhat as many Marxists expect. However, as was just noted, not all technological change has worked in this direction. For example, many firms in the electronics industry are relatively small, and there are observers who argue that new techniques will permit smaller firms to supply some telecommunications services without incurring high costs. We must turn to the evidence to judge whether or not American industry has grown more concentrated.

## EVIDENCE ON CONCENTRATION IN INDUSTRY

A **CONCENTRATION RATIO** is the percentage of an industry's output produced by its *four* largest firms. It is intended to measure the degree to which the industry is dominated by large firms.

There have been many statistical studies of concentration in American industry. One common way of measuring concentration is to calculate the share of the industry's output produced by the four largest firms in an industry, the so-called **concentration ratio**. Of course, there is no reason why the three or five or ten largest firms should not be used for the purpose, but conventionally four firms are the standard.

Table 19–2 shows concentration ratios in a number of industries in the United States. We see that concentration varies greatly from industry to industry: automobiles, electric lamps, bulbs and tubes, and breakfast cereals are produced by highly concentrated industries, while the jewelry, clothing, and soft drink industries show very little concentration.

In the United States there seems to have been little trend in concentration ratios, at least since the beginning of this century. The evidence is that, on the average during this period, concentration ratios remained remarkably constant. It has been estimated that, at the turn of the century, 32.9 percent of manufactured goods were produced by industries in which the concentration ratio was 50 percent or more (meaning that at least 50 percent of industry output was produced by the four largest firms). By 1963 the figure had risen only to 33.1 percent. And by 1970 it actually fell to 26.3 percent, although it has risen slightly since then. These figures and those for other years are shown in Table 19–3.

*Table* **19–2** **1987 CONCENTRATION RATIOS FOR REPRESENTATIVE INDUSTRIES**

| INDUSTRY | 4-FIRM RATIO | INDUSTRY | 4-FIRM RATIO |
|---|---|---|---|
| Hard surface floor coverage | 82 | Ship building and repairing | 49 |
| Motor vehicles and car bodies | 90 | Musical instruments | 31 |
| Electric lamps, bulbs, and tubes | 91 | Pharmaceutical preparations | 22 |
| Cereal breakfast foods | 87 | Apparel: mens' and boys' suits and coats | 34 |
| Rubber tires and inner tubes | 69 | Aircraft | 72 |
| Brooms and brushes | 19 | Primary aluminum | 74 |
| Fluid milk | 21 | Precorded records and recorded tapes | 63 |
| Jewelry, precious metal | 12 | Boat building and repairing | 33 |
| Fabricated metal cans | 54 | Bottled and canned soft drinks | 30 |
| Fasteners, buttons, needles, and pins | 33 | Bolts, nuts, rivets and washers | 16 |
| Dolls and stuffed toys | 34 | Apparel: women's and misses' and juniors' dresses | 6 |
| Motors and generators | 36 | | |

SOURCE: U.S. Bureau of the Census, "Concentration Ratios in Manufacturing," *1987 Census of Manufactures*, MC87-S-6, February, 1992.

Table 19–3 THE TREND IN CONCENTRATION IN MANUFACTURING INDUSTRIES (1901–1987)

| | (around) 1901 | 1947 | 1954 | 1958 | 1963 | 1966 | 1970 | 1972 | 1982 | 1987 |
|---|---|---|---|---|---|---|---|---|---|---|
| Percent of value-added in industries with 4-firm concentration ratios over 50 percent | 32.9 | 24.4 | 29.9 | 30.2 | 33.1 | 28.6 | 26.3 | 29.0 | 25.2 | 27.9 |

SOURCES: P.W. McCracken and T.G. Moore, "Competition and Market Concentration in the American Economy," Subcommittees on Antitrust and Monopoly, U.S. Senate, March 29, 1973, and F.M. Scherer, *Industrial Market Structure and Economic Performance* (Boston: Houghton Mifflin, 1980), page 68; F.M. Scherer and David Ross, *Industrial Market Structure and Economic Performance, 3rd edition* (Boston: Houghton Mifflin, 1990), page 84; and personal communication with Professor F.M. Scherer, March 10, 1993.

More recent data show the share of total manufacturing value-added (that is, roughly speaking, the total investments) that are owned by the 200 largest manufacturing corporations. Table 19–4 does suggest that concentration has increased from 37 percent to 43 percent during the 33 years from 1954 to 1987. But, as the previous table indicates, we have had comparable rises (and comparable falls) in concentration before.

In a frequently quoted statement, M. A. Adelman, a noted authority on the subject, concluded, "Any tendency either way, if it does exist, must be at the pace of a glacial drift."[6] Or, as a more recent report puts it, "Almost all observers of the industrial scene . . . agree that . . . the evidence fails to support a claim that competition has declined. While concentration has increased in some areas, decreases have occurred elsewhere, leaving the overall structure unaffected."[7]

Over the course of the twentieth century, *concentration in individual U.S. industries has shown no tendency to increase.*

Since concentration is intended as a measure of the "bigness" of the firms in an industry, from such information one can perhaps surmise that the antitrust program has been effective to some degree in inhibiting whatever trend toward bigness may in fact exist. But even this very cautious conclusion has been questioned by some observers. In fact, some economists and other observers have expressed the view that these laws have made virtually no difference in the size and the behavior of American business. Whether it is desirable for the antitrust program or for some other program to inhibit concentration or big size of firms is the issue to which we turn next.

## THE PROS AND CONS OF BIGNESS

Why has antitrust become so accepted a part of government policy? Are the effects of bigness or monopoly always undesirable? We *do* know that monopoly power

[6]M.A. Adelman, "The Measurement of Industrial Concentration," *Review of Economics and Statistics*, vol. 33, November 1951, pages 295–96.

[7]P.W. McCracken and T.G. Moore, "Competition and Market Concentration in the American Economy," Subcommittee on Antitrust and Monopoly, U.S. Senate, March 29, 1973.

**Table 19-4 THE TREND IN CONCENTRATION IN MANUFACTURING VALUE-ADDED (1954–1987)**

| | 1954 | 1958 | 1962 | 1963 | 1966 | 1967 | 1970 | 1972 | 1976 | 1977 | 1982 | 1987 |
|---|---|---|---|---|---|---|---|---|---|---|---|---|
| Share of value-added accounted for by the 200 largest manufacturing companies (percent) | 37 | 38 | 40 | 41 | 42 | 42 | 43 | 43 | 44 | 44 | 43 | 43 |

SOURCE: U.S. Department of Commerce, Economics and Statistics Administration, Bureau of the Census, *1987 Census of Manufactures, Concentration Ratios in Manufacturing*, Subject Series MC87-S-6, February 1992, page 6-3.

can be abused; the history of the Rockefellers, the Armours, and the Morgans described at the beginning of this chapter confirms that adequately. But even when the giants of business are not so swashbuckling in their operations, unrestrained monopoly and bigness give rise to a number of problems:

1. ***Distribution of income.*** The flow of wealth to firms with market power—and thus to those which are able to influence prices in their favor—is widely considered to be unfair and socially unacceptable.
2. ***Restriction of output.*** We learned in Chapter 11 that if an unrestrained monopoly is to maximize its profits, it must restrict its output below the amount that would be provided by an equivalent competitive industry. This means that unregulated, monopolized industries are likely to produce smaller outputs than the quantities that serve society's interests best.
3. ***Lack of inducement for innovation.*** It is sometimes argued that firms in industries with little or no competition are under less pressure to introduce new production methods and new products than are firms in industries in which each is constantly trying to beat out the others. Without competition, the management of a firm may choose the quiet life, taking no chances on risky investments in research and development. But a firm that operates in constant fear that its rivals will come up with a better idea, and come up with it first, can afford no such luxury.

So far we have presented only one side of the picture. In fact, bigness in industry need not be advantageous only to the firm. It can also, at least *sometimes*, work to the advantage of the general public. Again, there are several reasons:

1. ***Economies of large size.*** Probably the most important advantage of bigness is to be found in those industries in which technology dictates that small-scale operation is inefficient. One can hardly imagine the costs if automobiles were produced in little workshops rather than giant factories. The notion of a small firm operating a long-distance railroad does not even make sense, and a multiplicity of firms replicating the same railroad service would clearly be incredibly wasteful.

   On these grounds, most policymakers have never even considered an attempt to eliminate bigness. Their objective, rather, is to curb its potential abuses and to try at the same time to help the public benefit from its advantages. Of course, it does not follow that every industry in which firms happen to be big is one in which big firms are best. There are observers who argue that many firms in fact exceed the size required for cost minimization.

2. ***Required scale for innovation.*** Some economists have argued that only large firms have the resources and the motivation for really significant innovation. While many inventions are still contributed by individuals, to put a new invention into commercial production is often an expensive, complex venture that can only be carried out on a large scale. And only large firms can afford the funds and bear the risks that such an effort demands. In addition, according to this view, only large firms have the motivation to lay out the funds required for the innovation process, because only large firms will get to keep a considerable share of the benefits. A small company, on the other hand, will find that its innovative idea is soon likely to be followed by close imitations, which enable competitors to profit from its research outlays.

There have been many studies of the relationship between firm size, competitiveness of the industry, and the level of expenditure on research and development (R and D). While the evidence is far from conclusive, it does indicate that highly competitive industries comprising very small firms tend not to spend a great deal on research. Up to a point, R and D outlays and innovation seem to increase with size of firm and concentration of industry. However, some of the most significant innovations introduced in the twentieth century have been contributed by smaller firms. Examples include the electric light, alternating current electricity, the photocopier, FM radio, and the electronic calculator.

## OTHER GOVERNMENT PROGRAMS RELATED TO BIGNESS

Because the issues raised by bigness and concentration are complex, they would appear to call for a variety of policy measures. Certainly, antitrust programs alone cannot do everything that the public interest requires. For example, in cases where large firms are far more efficient than small ones, it does not seem reasonable to break up industrial giants. In fact, it is often considered most desirable, on grounds of economy, to permit a market to be served by only a single firm—such as a supplier of electricity, local transportation, or local telecommunications services.

Where one firm offers considerable savings in comparison to a multiplicity of suppliers—that is, where the industry is a *natural monopoly*—it is usually agreed that it would not serve the public interest to subdivide the supplying firm into a number of rival companies. Instead, one of two policies is usually adopted. Either the monopoly firm is *nationalized* and run as a government enterprise (telephone service in Sweden and electricity generation in France are good examples). Or, as is typical in the United States, the natural monopoly is left as a private firm but its operations are *regulated* in one of the ways described in the previous chapter.

A **PATENT** is a temporary grant of monopoly rights over an innovation.

The possibility of inhibition of innovation by competition is another important issue, which, as we have seen, affects policy toward bigness and concentration. The main instrument government has employed in this area is the **patent** system, which rewards the innovator by the grant of a temporary monopoly. The patent restricts imitation and is designed to offer small-firm innovators the same advantages from their research activities as are enjoyed by innovators in industries that contain no competitors ready to erode profits by imitation. Thus, somewhat ironically, while government prohibits monopolization, it also guarantees monopoly power to protect innovative firms in competitive industries. Of course, sometimes the protected firms themselves grow big with the help of the protection.

Once-small firms like Polaroid and Xerox grew into industrial giants with the help of government protection through the patent laws.

Questions have been raised about the effectiveness of patents in inducing expenditure on R and D, and the evidence certainly does not provide overwhelming support for the view that patents constitute a strong stimulus for innovation. Questions have also been raised about the desirability of granting an innovator an unrestricted monopoly for 17 years, as the patent program now does in the United States. Similar issues have been raised about copyright laws, which restrict reproduction of written works.

Finally, government has provided special help to small business in a variety of ways. For example, there are programs designed to make it easier for small firms to raise capital; and special government agencies, such as the Small Business Administration, have been set up for the purpose. There is also some degree of *progressivity* in business taxation, meaning that smaller firms are subject to taxes lower than those paid by larger firms. And special legislation, such as the "fair trade" laws—which, though since repealed, permitted manufacturers to designate and enforce "fair" retail prices for products—are intended, in part, to protect small retailers from the competition of larger rivals.

## ISSUES IN ANTITRUST POLICY

In recent years there has been a searching reexamination of government policy toward business. For example, there have been calls for a decrease in the overall power of the regulatory agencies; and the antitrust program is unlikely to be ignored in such a review. Some voices call for abolition of the antitrust laws altogether, while others advocate their strengthening and expansion. But even if one grants the desirability of an antitrust program with teeth in it, there still remain questions about whom or what to bite.

### STRUCTURE VERSUS CONDUCT

A major issue is the relative weights that should be assigned to *structure* and *conduct* in deciding which firms it is in the social interest to prosecute. Most people accept the basic notion that socially damaging conduct, such as price fixing or threats of physical violence, should be discouraged; though there is often disagreement over what types of conduct are undesirable.

But many more questions are raised about the use of structural criteria in antitrust policy. Is bigness always undesirable per se? What if the large firm is more efficient and has engaged in no practices that can reasonably be considered to constitute predatory competition? Many economists have reservations about the prosecution of such a firm, fearing that it will only serve to grant protection to inefficient competitors and do so at the expense of consumers. They also point out the danger that successful firms will be singled out for attention under the antitrust laws simply because their success makes them noticeable and their efficiency enables them to outstrip their competitors. The fear is that such an orientation will discourage efficiency and entrepreneurship and reduce competition.

### CONCENTRATION AND MARKET POWER

In this chapter, as in many other discussions of antitrust issues, much was said about concentration. Why should anyone care about concentration ratios? One

**MARKET POWER** is the ability of a firm to raise its price significantly above the competitive price level and to maintain this high price profitably for a considerable period.

should care about them if they are a good measure of **market power**. Market power is usually defined as the ability of a firm to raise its price significantly above the competitive price level and to maintain this high price profitably for a considerable period. The question, then, is this, If an industry becomes more concentrated, will the firms necessarily increase their ability to institute a profitable rise in price above the competitive level?

Many economists have concluded that this does not necessarily happen. Specifically, the following three conclusions are now widely accepted:

1. If, after an increase in concentration, an industry still has a very low concentration ratio, then its firms are very unlikely to have any market power either before or after the rise in concentration.
2. If circumstances in the industry are in other respects favorable for successful price collusion (tacit or explicit agreement on price), a rise in concentration will facilitate market power. It will do so by reducing the number of firms that need to be consulted in arriving at an agreement and by decreasing the number of firms that have to be watched to make sure they do not betray the collusive agreement.
3. Where entry into and exit from the industry are easy and quite costless, that is, where the market is highly *contestable*, then even when concentration increases, market power will not be enhanced because an excessive price will attract new entrants who will soon force the price down.

## PRICE DISCRIMINATION

An example of lack of agreement between economists and lawmakers about the sorts of conduct that the law should proscribe concerns the issue of *price discrimination*, which, we learned earlier in the chapter, the law defines as the sale of the same item to two different customers at different prices. To economists, this legal definition is misleading. Suppose, for instance, that one person lives on a mountain top far from the place where a good is produced, and another customer is located in an area that enjoys easy access to the good in question. Economists would say that it is not discriminatory to charge each a different price for products delivered to the home. *On the contrary, economists hold that in such cases it is discriminatory to charge both customers the same price, because it does not cover the substantial difference in the two delivery costs.*

Even more important than this definitional argument, though, is the issue of the desirability or undesirability of discrimination. The word *discrimination* is what has been called a "persuasive term"—in this case, a word that automatically implies gross misconduct. *But, in fact, price discrimination can sometimes be beneficial to all parties to a transaction.*

Suppose, for example, a commodity is available to the poor only if it is sold at a relatively low price, though one that still more than covers the good's marginal cost (the cost incurred in expanding into the lower-income market). In this case, the contribution from the lower-income market may permit *some* reduction in price to the rich, even though the firm might not be able to cover its total cost if it were to charge the rich the *same* low price necessary for entry into the low-income market. The result is that everyone—the poor, the wealthy, and the selling firm—will benefit from this discriminatory pricing.

An example is pricing by doctors, who often charge higher fees to their wealthy patients than to their poor ones. If the reduced fees permit more patients to visit them, the doctors may be able to earn an even better income than they could by charging a uniformly high fee to everyone. Even the fee to the rich may go down in the process because of the doctors' increased earnings from their enlarged pool of poor patients. If this is so, and discrimination leads to lower fees for everyone, again, all parties are made better off—the wealthy patients, the poor ones, and the doctors.

Regulated firms whose overall earnings are restrained by a regulatory profit ceiling have often argued that lower fees to some classes of buyers can permit them to cover their costs in markets that they could not otherwise afford to serve. In such cases, it is asserted, the regulatory profit ceiling forces the firm to charge lower fees than it would have otherwise—to all its customers. Are such acts of discrimination unjust?

See the box on page 492 for a recent example of price fixing allegations directed toward noncommercial institutions—colleges and universities.

## COOPERATION IN RESEARCH BY COMPETING FIRMS

Innovation, and the research that must underlie it, has grown increasingly expensive. Firms are therefore frequently inclined to work cooperatively with other companies in the same industry in financing, planning, and conducting research activities, with all of the participants sharing in the end product. America's antitrust laws pose a threat to such cooperative activity by competing firms. In no other country is such cooperative activity subject to as great a danger from the law.

The American antitrust authorities have stated repeatedly that they do not want to interfere in research and development; and they have in fact largely avoided any steps that discourage it. Still, the threat is there, and it may well have inhibited some of the cooperative research activity that U.S. firms might otherwise have undertaken. Thus, there is good reason to consider whether explicit amendment of the U.S. antitrust laws—so far as they relate to cooperation in research—might not contribute to productivity growth in American industry and to its ability to compete effectively on the international marketplace.

## USE OF ANTITRUST TO PREVENT COMPETITION

Finally, let us turn to an important issue that was mentioned at the beginning of the chapter: the misuse of the antitrust laws to prevent competition. There is no doubt that many firms that have been unable to compete effectively on their own merits have turned to the courts to seek protection from successful competitors. And they have sometimes succeeded. Those who try to protect themselves in this way always claim that their rivals have not achieved success through superior ability but, rather, by means that are described as "monopolization." Sometimes the evidence is clear-cut, and the courts can readily discern whether the accused firms have violated the antitrust laws or whether they have simply been too efficient and innovative for the complaining competitors' tastes. In other cases, however, the issues are complicated, and only a long and painstaking legal proceeding offers any prospect of resolving them.

There are those who point out that this sort of litigation is almost unheard of in Japan, and suggest that this freedom from the burden of litigation offers a great advantage to Japanese firms in the international marketplace. Various steps have been suggested to deal with the issue. For example, it has been proposed that if the courts decide that a firm has been falsely accused by another of violating

## Universities: A New Target for the Antitrust Authorities

The year 1992 witnessed the culmination of an effort by the U.S. Department of Justice to extend the antitrust laws to noncommercial institutions—the nation's colleges and universities. The Justice Department claimed that by coordinating their scholarship and fellowship awards to students these institutions were engaging in price fixing, which under the Sherman Act is illegal *per se*. Only the Massachusetts Institute of Technology chose to fight it out in the courts. MIT argued that it was not a commercial organization so that the antitrust laws do not apply to its actions. It pointed out that in granting a scholarship, the institution gives money away rather than charging it to a customer, as a set of conspiring firms would do. MIT also argued that prohibition of coordination of scholarship decisions would raise awards to star applicants, severely cutting the amounts available to others. The judge in the case agreed with the Justice Department, as the following news story reports:

A federal judge ruled that Massachusetts Institute of Technology violated antitrust laws by colluding with Ivy League colleges to illegally fix the amount of financial aid given to some needy students . . . .

The ruling, in a civil antitrust case filed by the Justice Department, involves the so-called Ivy Overlap Group that shared financial information on students who applied to more than one school. Schools in the group used the data to limit price competition by setting aid awards so the net tuition cost to these students would be the same at different schools.

Judge Bechtle stated in his ruling that the collusion "denied students the ability to compare prices when choosing" among colleges in the group. MIT said it will appeal the decision.

The eight Ivy League colleges in the overlap group earlier agreed to settle similar antitrust charges filed by the Justice Department by agreeing not to collude in the future, but MIT had declined to join the settlement. The group, which had met for 35 years, stopped meeting in 1991 after an investigation of its practices began . . .

In ruling against MIT . . . Judge Bechtle rejected the . . . argument that the overlap group wasn't subject to antitrust laws. MIT contended that the group's activities involved charitable acts by non-profit institutions, and thus didn't involve commerce. The judge said this reasoning was "pure sophistry." He stated, "The court can conceive of few aspects of higher education that are more commercial than the price charged students."

MIT also argued that the overlap activities were good for needy students as a whole, not bad as the Justice Department claimed. Each college has a limited amount of aid to offer. By agreeing on the level of aid a student deserves—based on what his family can afford to pay—instead of competing by offering more aid for individual students, schools in the overlap group were able to spread out aid to more students.

SOURCE: *The Wall Street Journal*, September 3, 1992.

the antitrust laws, then (as is done in other countries) the latter should be required to pay the costs the former incurred in order to defend itself. It has also been proposed that such suits require prescreening by a government agency, as is done in Japan. Still, the issue is hardly open and shut, since anything that restricts anticompetitive, private antitrust suits will almost certainly also inhibit legitimate attempts by individual firms to defend themselves from genuine acts of monopolization by rival enterprises.

## Summary

1. **Antitrust policy** refers to programs designed to control the growth of monopoly and to prevent big business from engaging in "undesirable" practices.
2. The **Sherman Act** is the oldest U.S. antitrust law. It prohibits contracts, combinations, and conspiracies in restraint of trade and also prohibits monopolization.
3. The **Clayton Act** prohibits **price discrimination** that tends to reduce competition or create monopoly; it also prohibits competing firms from sharing directors.
4. There are several other important antitrust laws, including the **Federal Trade Commission Act**, which sets the commission up as an independent antitrust agency, and the **Robinson-Patman Act**, which generally prohibits discriminatory price discounts.
5. In early cases, the courts generally held that a large share of market by a single firm was illegal only if the firm had acquired its relatively large share by illegal means; but in the early postwar period the courts seemed to take the view that bigness *per se* was presumed to be illegal unless such bigness was "thrust upon the firm" by economies of scale, unusual efficiency, or other similar influences.
6. The evidence indicates that there has been no significant increase in the concentration of individual American industries into fewer, relatively larger firms during the twentieth century. Evidence as to whether antitrust laws have been effective in preventing monopoly is inconclusive, and observers disagree on the subject.
7. Unregulated monopoly is apt to distribute income unfairly, produce undesirably small quantities of output, and provide inadequate motivation for innovation.
8. However, sometimes only large firms may have funds sufficient for effective research, development, and innovation; and where economies of scale are available, large firms can serve customers more cheaply than can small ones.
9. Contrary to popular thinking, price discrimination is not necessarily undesirable *per se*. Discriminatory pricing in some instances can be beneficial to all parties to a transaction.

## Key Concepts and Terms

Antitrust policy
Sherman Act
Clayton Act
Price discrimination
Celler-Kefauver Antimerger Act
Federal Trade Commission Act
Robinson-Patman Act
Rule of reason
Structure versus conduct
Horizontal merger
Vertical merger
Conglomerate merger
Concentration of industry
Concentration ratio
Patent
Market power

## Questions for Review

1. Suppose Sam lives in the central city while Fran's home is far away, so that it requires much more gas to deliver newspapers to Fran than to Sam. Yet the newspaper charges them exactly the same amount. Would the courts consider this to be price discrimination? Would an economist? Would you? Why?
2. A shopkeeper sells his store and signs a contract that restrains him from opening another store in competition with the new owner. The courts have decided that this contract is a *reasonable* restraint of trade. Can you think of any other types of restraint of trade that seem reasonable? Any that seem unreasonable?
3. Which of the following industries do you expect to have high concentration ratios? Automobiles, aircraft manufacture, hardware production, railroads, production of expensive jewelry. Compare your answers with Table 19–2.
4. Why do you think the industries you selected in Question 3 are highly concentrated?

5. Do you think structure or conduct is the more reasonable basis for antitrust regulation? Give reasons for your answer.
6. Do you think it is in the public interest to launch an antitrust suit that costs a billion dollars? What leads you to your conclusion?
7. In Japan and a number of European countries, the antitrust laws are much less severe than those in the United States. Do you think this helps or harms American industry in its efforts to compete with foreign producers? Why?
8. Can you think of some legal rules that can discourage the use of antitrust to prevent competition while at the same time not interfering with legitimate antitrust actions?
9. Do you think the antitrust authorities should interfere more than they do now in corporate takeover activities? What are some pros and cons?
10. a. If the oil industry were perfectly competitive, would gasoline prices have risen after oil supplies from Iraq and Kuwait were cut off in the aftermath of the 1990 invasion by Iraq?
    b. Draw the pertinent supply–demand diagram.
11. During the 1970s oil crisis, the long lines at gas stations disappeared soon after price controls were removed and gas prices were permitted to rise. Should this be interpreted as evidence that the oil companies have monopoly power? Why or why not?

Chapter 20

# TAXATION AND RESOURCE ALLOCATION

*The taxing power of the government must be used to provide revenues for legitimate government purposes. It must not be used to regulate the economy or bring about social change.*

**RONALD REAGAN (1981)**

To reduce the yawning federal budget deficit, President Bill Clinton had to do what no politician likes to do: raise taxes. Just four weeks into his term of office, the new president's proposals to raise a variety of taxes on individuals and businesses, and to institute an entirely new tax on energy, set in motion a national debate over both the level and structure of taxation in America. ¶ Taxes have never been very popular in this country, which was born in part out of a tax protest. But they are inevitable in any modern mixed economy, as we noted in Chapter 2. While the vast majority of economic activities in the United States is left to the private sector, some—such as provision of national defense and highways—are reserved for the government. And any such government spending necessitates taxes to pay the bills. In addition, the government sometimes deliberately interferes with the workings of the market in order to promote some social goal. Often, these interferences involve levying taxes. For example, we will see in the next chapter that taxes may be useful in correcting misallocations of resources caused by externalities. ¶ This chapter discusses the types of taxes that are used to raise the necessary revenue, the effects of taxation on the allocation of resources and the distribution of income, and the principles that distinguish "good" from "bad" taxes.

## THE LEVEL OF TAXATION

It is widely believed that taxes have been gobbling up an ever-increasing share of the U.S. economy. Figure 20–1, however, shows that this has not been true in recent decades by charting the behavior of both federal and state and local taxes *as a percentage of GDP* since 1929. The figure shows that the share of federal taxes in GDP has been rather steady since the early 1950s. It climbed from less than 4 percent in 1929 to 20 percent during World War II, fell back to 15 percent in the immediate postwar period, and has fluctuated in the 18 to 20 percent range ever since. (It is now about 20 percent.) The share of GDP taken by state and local taxes climbed substantially from World War II until the early 1970s. But since then it, too, has been remarkably stable—at about 12 percent.

The shares of GDP taken in taxes by both the federal and state and local government have been approximately constant for about 20 years.

A **PROGRESSIVE TAX** is one in which the average tax rate paid by an individual rises as income rises.

### PROGRESSIVE, PROPORTIONAL, AND REGRESSIVE TAXES

Economists classify taxes as *progressive, proportional,* or *regressive.* Under a **progressive tax**, the fraction of income paid in taxes *rises* as a person's income increases.

**Figure 20–1** TAXES AS A PERCENTAGE OF GROSS DOMESTIC PRODUCT

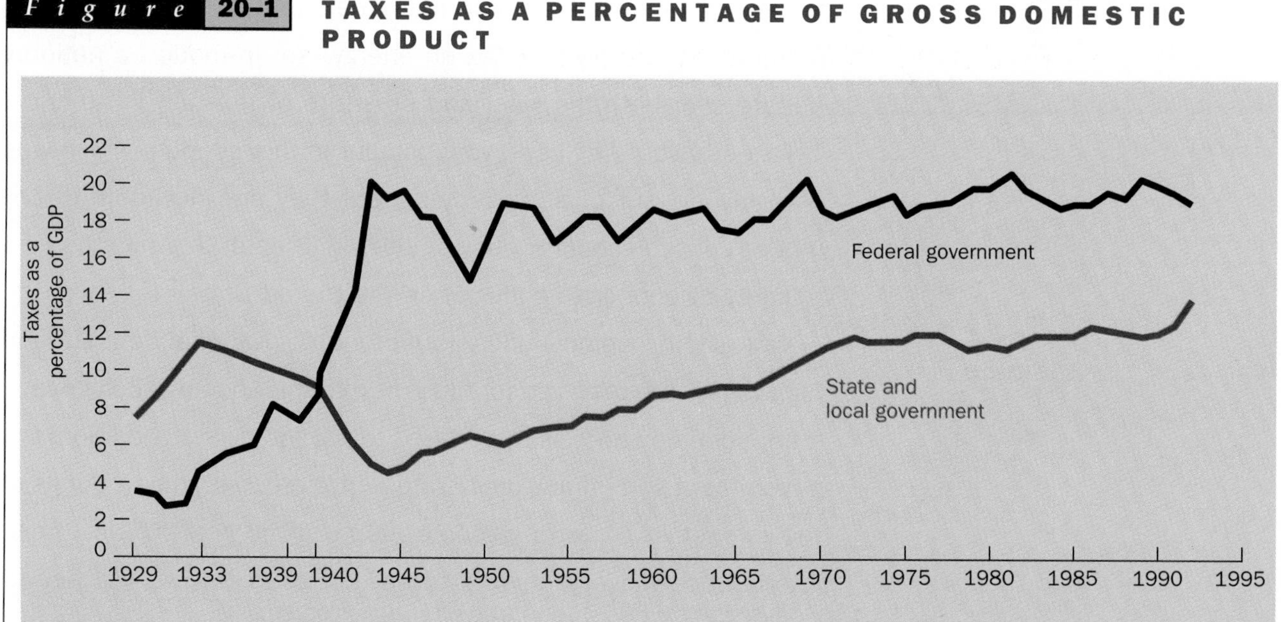


Federal taxes have accounted for a fairly constant fraction of GDP since the 1950s. State and local taxes absorbed an ever-increasing portion from the 1940s until the early 1970s but since then have been a constant share.

SOURCE: Economic Report of the President, 1993.

A **PROPORTIONAL TAX** is one in which the average tax rate is the same at all income levels.

A **REGRESSIVE TAX** is one in which the average tax rate falls as income rises.

The **AVERAGE TAX RATE** is the ratio of taxes to income.

The **MARGINAL TAX RATE** is the fraction of each *additional* dollar of income that is paid in taxes.

**DIRECT TAXES** are taxes levied directly on people.

**INDIRECT TAXES** are taxes levied on specific economic activities.

Under a **proportional tax**, this fraction is constant. And under a **regressive tax**, the fraction of income paid to the tax collector *declines* as income rises. Since the fraction of income paid in taxes is called the **average tax rate**, these definitions can be reformulated as in the margin.

Often, however, the *average* tax rate is less interesting than the **marginal tax rate**, which is the fraction of each *additional* dollar that is paid to the tax collector. The reason, as we will see, is that the *marginal* tax rate, not the *average* tax rate, most directly affects economic incentives.

### DIRECT VERSUS INDIRECT TAXES

Another way to classify taxes is to divide them into **direct taxes** and **indirect taxes**. Direct taxes are levied directly on *people*. Primary examples are *income taxes* and *inheritance taxes*, though the notoriously regressive *head tax*—which charges every person the same amount—is also a direct tax.[1] In contrast, indirect taxes are levied on particular activities, such as buying gasoline, using the telephone, or owning a home.

It is only a slight distortion of the facts to say that the federal government raises revenues by direct taxes, while the states and localities raise funds via indirect taxes. *Sales taxes* and *property taxes* are the most important indirect taxes in the United States, although many other countries rely heavily on the *value-added tax*—a tax that has often been discussed, but never been adopted, in the United States.[2] In fact, as a broad generalization, the U.S. government relies more heavily on direct taxes than do the governments of most other countries.

## THE FEDERAL TAX SYSTEM

The **personal income tax** is the biggest source of revenue to the federal government. Many people do not realize that the **payroll tax**—a tax levied on wages and salaries up to a certain limit—is the next biggest source. Furthermore, payroll taxes have been growing more rapidly than income taxes for decades. In 1963, payroll tax collections were just 42 percent of personal income tax collections; by 1983 this figure had reached 72 percent. And by 1993, after a series of large income tax reductions and payroll tax increases in the 1980s, payroll taxes amounted to 83 percent of personal income-tax collections.

The rest of the federal government's revenues come mostly from the **corporate income tax** and from various excise (sales) taxes. Figure 2–14 on page 46 showed the breakdown of federal revenues anticipated for the fiscal year 1994 budget. Let us now look at these taxes in more detail.

### THE FEDERAL PERSONAL INCOME TAX

The tax on individual incomes traces its origins to the Sixteenth Amendment to the Constitution in 1913, but it was inconsequential until the beginning of World War II. Then the tax was raised substantially to finance the war, and it has been the major source of federal revenue ever since. The personal income tax has been

[1]In 1990, Prime Minister Margaret Thatcher caused riots in Great Britain by instituting a head tax.

[2]The concept of *value added* was defined and explained in an appendix to *Macroeconomics* Chapter 7. The value-added tax simply taxes each firm on the basis of its value added.

at the top of the news since 1980. In 1981, President Reagan made phased reductions in personal tax rates the cornerstone of his economic policy. In 1986, the tax code was thoroughly rewritten. President Bush was elected in 1988 on a pledge not to raise taxes. And President Clinton proposed higher income taxes on upper-income groups shortly after taking office in 1993.

Many taxpayers have little or no tax to pay when the annual April 15th day of reckoning comes around, because income taxes are *withheld* from payrolls by employers and forwarded to the U.S. Treasury. In fact, many taxpayers are, "overwithheld" during the year and receive a refund check from Uncle Sam. Nevertheless, most taxpayers dread the arrival of their Form 1040 because of its legendary complexity.

The personal income tax is **progressive**. That fact is evident in Table 20–1 because average tax rates rise as income rises. Ignoring a few complications, the current tax law has five basic marginal rates, each of which applies within a specific tax bracket rate. As income rises above certain points, the marginal tax rate increases from 15 percent to 28 percent to 31 percent, and then finally to 36 percent and 39.6 percent on very high incomes (over $140,000 for a married couple). These last two brackets were added to the tax code by President Clinton in 1993 as a way to raise revenue and to restore progressivity at the high end. The Tax Reform Act of 1986 had pushed the marginal rate in the top bracket down to 28 percent. This was possible because that same act closed numerous **tax loopholes**.

A **TAX LOOPHOLE** is a special provision in the tax code that reduces taxation below normal rates (perhaps to zero) if certain conditions are met.

However, some loopholes remain open and a few new ones have been added since 1986. Let us see what a few major ones are.

A particular source of income is **TAX EXEMPT** if income from that source is not taxable.

***Tax exempt status of municipal bonds.*** As a way of helping state and local governments and certain public authorities raise funds, Congress has made interest on their bonds exempt from federal income tax. Whether or not this was the intent of Congress, this provision has turned out to be one of the biggest loopholes for the very rich, who invest much of their wealth in tax-free municipal bonds. It has long been the principal reason why some millionaires pay virtually no income tax.

*Table* **20–1** **FEDERAL PERSONAL INCOME TAX RATES IN 1993***

| INCOME | TAX | AVERAGE TAX RATE (percent) | MARGINAL TAX RATE (percent) |
|---|---|---|---|
| $ 5,000 | 0 | 0 | 0 |
| 10,000 | 0 | 0 | 0 |
| 25,000 | 1,400 | 5.6 | 15 |
| 50,000 | 5,150 | 10.3 | 28 |
| 100,000 | 18,800 | 18.8 | 31 |
| 250,000 | 70,000 | 28.0 | 36 |
| 1,000,000 | 366,300 | 36.6 | 39.6 |

*For a married couple with two children filing jointly and claiming the standard deduction. In fact, families with very high incomes rarely used the standard deduction; so their tax would be lower than shown.

NOTE: These numbers are approximate. Congress was debating the 1993 tax rates when this book went to press.

A **TAX DEDUCTION** is a sum of money that may be subtracted before the taxpayer computes his or her taxable income.

***Tax benefits for homeowners.*** Among the sacred cows of our income tax system is the deductibility of payments that homeowners make for mortgage interest and property taxes. These **tax deductions** substantially reduce homeowners' tax bills and give them preferential treatment compared to renters. The plain intent of Congress is to encourage homeownership. However, since homeowners are, on the average, richer than renters, this loophole also erodes the progressivity of the income tax.

But why call this a "loophole" when other interest expenses and taxes (such as those paid by shopkeepers, for example) are considered to be legitimate deductions? The answer is that it is a loophole because—unlike shopkeepers—homeowners do not have to declare the income they earn by incurring these expenses. This is because the "income" from owning a home accrues not in cash, but in the form of living without paying rent.

An example will illustrate the point. Jack and Jill are neighbors. Each earns $30,000 a year and lives in a $100,000 house. The difference is that Jack owns his home while Jill rents. Most observers would agree that Jack and Jill *should* pay the same income tax. Will they? Suppose Jack pays $2000 a year in local property taxes and has an $80,000 mortgage at a 10 percent interest rate, which costs him about $8000 a year in interest. Both of these payments are tax deductible, so he gets to deduct $10,000 in housing expenses. But Jill, who may pay $10,000 a year in rent, does not. Thus Jill's tax burden is higher than Jack's.

This inequity can be rectified in several ways. One is to allow renters to deduct their rent bills. Another is to disallow the interest and tax deductions of homeowners. Still a third alternative is to force homeowners to add their "imputed rent" ($10,000 a year in this example) to their income. All of these give Jack and Jill the same taxable income.

We could go on listing more tax loopholes, but enough has been said to illustrate the main point:

Every tax loophole encourages particular patterns of behavior and favors particular types of people. But since most loopholes are mainly beneficial to the rich, they erode the progressivity of the income tax.

This problem was much more serious in the United States before the 1986 tax reform, but it has by no means disappeared

## THE PAYROLL TAX

The second most important tax in the United States is the payroll tax, whose proceeds are earmarked to be paid into various "trust funds." These funds, in turn, are used to pay social security benefits, unemployment compensation, and other social insurance dividends. The payroll tax is levied at a fixed percentage rate (now about 16 percent) that is divided between employees and employers, each paying roughly half the amount. This means that a firm paying an employee a gross monthly wage of, say, $2000 will deduct $160 (8 percent of $2000) from that worker's check, add an additional $160 of its own funds, and send the $320 to the government.

On the face of it, this seems like a *proportional* tax, but it is actually highly *regressive* for two reasons. First, only wages and salaries are subject to the tax. Income from interest and dividends is not taxed. Second, because there are upper limits on social security benefits, earnings above a certain level (which changes each year) are exempted from the tax. In 1993, this level was $57,600 per year. Above this limit, the *marginal tax rate* on earnings is zero.[3]

### THE CORPORATE INCOME TAX

The tax on corporate profits is also considered a "direct" tax, because corporations are fictitious "people" in the eyes of the law.[4] The basic marginal tax rate is now 35 percent, and this rate is paid by all large corporations (firms with smaller profits pay a lower rate). Since the tax applies to *profits*, not to income, all wages, rents, and interest paid by corporations are deducted before the tax is applied. Since World War II, corporate income tax collections have accounted for a declining share of federal revenue—now just 9 percent.

### EXCISE TAXES

An excise tax is a sales tax on the purchase of a particular good or service. While sales taxes are mainly reserved for state and local governments in the United States, the federal government does levy excise taxes on a hodgepodge of miscellaneous goods and services, including cigarettes, alcoholic beverages, gasoline, and tires. While these taxes constitute a minor source of federal government revenue, raising revenue is not their only goal. Some of them are designed to discourage consumption of a good by raising its price. For example, conservation is among the goals of the gasoline tax.

## THE PAYROLL TAX AND THE SOCIAL SECURITY SYSTEM

In government statistical documents, the payroll tax is euphemistically referred to as "contributions for social insurance," although these "contributions" are far from voluntary. The term signifies the fact that, unlike other taxes, the proceeds from this particular tax are set aside in "trust funds" for use in paying benefits to social security recipients and others.

But the standard notion of a trust fund does not apply. Some private pension plans *are* trust funds. You pay in money while you are working, it is invested for you, and you withdraw it bit by bit in your retirement years. But the social security system does not function that way. For most of its history, the system has simply taken the payroll tax payments of the current working generations and handed them over to the current retired generation. The benefit checks that your grandparents receive each month are not, in any real sense, the dividends on the investments they made while they worked. Instead they are the payroll taxes that you or your parents pay each month.

For many years, this "pay as you go" system managed to give every retired generation more in benefits than it contributed in payroll taxes. Social security "contributions" were indeed a good investment! How was this miracle achieved? It relied heavily on growth: both population growth and economic growth. As

[3]This is not quite true. The portion of the payroll tax that goes to pay for Medicare is applied to all earnings, without limit.

[4]For a discussion of corporations and other forms of business organization, see Chapter 14.

long as population growth continues, there are always more and more young people to tax in order to pay the retirement benefits of senior citizens. Similarly, as long as wages keep increasing, the same payroll tax *rates* permit the government to pay benefits to each generation that exceeds that generation's contributions. Ten percent of today's average wage is, after all, a good deal more money than 10 percent of the wage your grandfather earned 50 years ago.

Unfortunately, the growth magic stopped working in the 1970s. First, the growth in real wages slowed dramatically; by some measures, it actually ceased. But social security benefits continued to grow rapidly nonetheless, and in 1975 they became fully protected from inflation by *indexing*, whereas wages are not.[5] So the burden of financing social security grew.

Second, population growth has slowed significantly in the United States. Birthrates in this country were very high from the close of World War II until about 1958 (the "postwar baby boom") and have generally been falling since. As a result, the fraction of the U.S. population that is over 65 has climbed from only 7.5 percent in 1945 to 12.7 percent today, and is certain to go much higher in the next century. Thus each retired person will have fewer working people to support her.

By the early 1980s, it was clear that social security needed an infusion of funds. It was also clear that pay-as-you-go financing could be maintained only by either much higher payroll taxes or much lower benefits in the 21st century. In 1983, a bipartisan presidential commission headed by Alan Greenspan, then a private economist and now chairman of the Federal Reserve System, recommended remedies for both problems, and Congress speedily enacted them. First, benefits were trimmed and payroll taxes were increased. Second, and most significantly, social security abandoned its tradition of pay-as-you-go financing. It was decided, instead, to start accumulating funds with which to pay the retirement benefits of the baby boom generation.

Since then, the trust fund has been taking in more money than it has been paying out. The annual social security surplus is now running at about $50–$60 billion. If current projections of population, real wages, and retirement behavior prove reasonably accurate, these annual surpluses will cumulate into a huge trust fund by the second decade of the next century, when it will start to be drawn down.

The social security surplus has proven to be quite controversial. Some people object to the fact that it makes the government budget deficit look smaller than it "really" is. Others think it wrong to force current working people to shoulder the burden for future social security benefits.

## THE STATE AND LOCAL TAX SYSTEM

Indirect taxes are the backbone of state and local government revenues, although income taxes are becoming increasingly popular. Sales taxes are the principal source of revenue to the states, while cities and towns rely heavily on property taxes. Figure 2–14 (page 46) showed the breakdown of state and local government receipts for 1991.

[5]For a full discussion of indexing, see *Macroeconomics* Chapter 16.

## SALES AND EXCISE TAXES

These days, the majority of states and large cities levy a broad-based sales tax on the purchase of most goods and services, with certain specific exemptions. For example, food is exempted from sales tax in many states. Overall sales tax rates are typically in the 5 to 7 percent range. In addition, there are special excise taxes in most states on such things as tobacco products, liquor, gasoline, and luxury items.

## PROPERTY TAXES

Municipalities raise revenue by taxing the values of properties, such as houses and office buildings, again with certain exemptions such as educational institutions and churches. The procedure is generally to assign to each taxable property an *assessed value*, which is an estimate of its market value, and then to place a tax rate on the community's total assessed value that yields enough revenue to cover expenditures on local services.

Because properties are *reassessed* much less frequently than market values change, certain inequities arise. For example, one person's house may be assessed at almost 100 percent of its true market value while another's may be assessed at less than 50 percent. Property taxes generally run between 1 and 4 percent of true market value.

Is the property tax progressive or regressive? Some economists view it as a tax on a particular type of wealth—real estate. On this view, since families with higher incomes generally own much more real estate than do families with low incomes, the property tax is *progressive* relative to income. However, other economists view the property tax as an excise tax on rents. And since expenditures on rent generally account for a larger fraction of the incomes of the poor than of the rich, this makes the property tax seem *regressive*.

There is also political controversy over the property tax. Because local property taxes are the main source of financing for public schools, wealthy communities with expensive real estate have been able to afford higher-quality schools than have poor communities. The reason is made clear with a simple arithmetical example. Suppose that real estate holdings in Richtown average $150,000 per family, while real estate holdings in Poortown average only $50,000 per family. If both towns levy a 2 percent property tax to pay for their schools, Richtown will generate $3000 per family in tax receipts, while Poortown will generate only $1000. Glaring inequalities like this have led courts in many states to declare unconstitutional the financing of public schools by local property taxes because it deprives children in poorer districts of an equal opportunity to receive a good education.

## STATE AND LOCAL INCOME TAXES

Although some states and localities have been taxing individual and corporate incomes for decades, taxes on individual incomes began to account for a substantial share of state and local revenue only recently. Between 1938 and 1960, only one state enacted a personal income tax. But many more have joined the club since the 1960s, and by now 41 states have income taxes. Experts in public finance generally applaud this trend because, for reasons we will explain at the end of this chapter, they view the personal income tax as among the best ways to raise revenue.

### FISCAL FEDERALISM

**FISCAL FEDERALISM** refers to the system of grants from one level of government to the next.

Figure 2–14 pointed out that grants from the federal government are a major source of revenue to state and local governments. In addition, grants from the states are vital to local governments. This system of transfers from one level of government to the next is referred to as **fiscal federalism** and has a long history.

Aid from this source has come traditionally in the form of *restricted grants*, that is, money given from one level of government to the next on the condition that it be spent for a specific purpose. For example, the U.S. government may grant funds to a state *if* that state will use the money to build highways. Or a state government may give money to a school district to spend on a specified program or facility.

## THE CONCEPT OF EQUITY IN TAXATION

Taxes are judged on two criteria: *equity* (Is the tax fair?) and *efficiency* (Does the tax interfere unduly with the workings of the market economy?). While economists have been mostly concerned with the latter, public discussions about tax proposals focus almost exclusively on the former. Let us, therefore, begin our discussion by investigating the concept of equitable taxation.

### HORIZONTAL EQUITY

**HORIZONTAL EQUITY** is the notion that equally situated individuals should be taxed equally.

There are three distinct concepts of tax equity. The first is **horizontal equity**, which simply asserts that equally situated individuals should be taxed equally. Few would quarrel with that principle, but it is often difficult to apply in practice. So violations of horizontal equity can be found throughout the tax code.

Consider, for example, the personal income tax. Horizontal equity calls for two families with the same income to pay the same tax. But what if one family has eight children and the other has one child? Well, you answer, we must define "equally situated" to include equal family sizes, so only families with the same number of children can be compared on grounds of horizontal equity. But what if one family has unusually high medical expenses, while the other has none? Are they still "equally situated"? By now the point should be clear: determining when two families are "equally situated" is no simple task. In fact, the U.S. tax code lists dozens of requirements that must be met before two families are construed to be "equal."

### VERTICAL EQUITY

**VERTICAL EQUITY** refers to the notion that differently situated individuals should be taxed differently in a way that society deems to be fair.

The **ABILITY-TO-PAY PRINCIPLE** refers to the idea that people with greater ability to pay taxes should pay

The second concept of fair taxation seems to flow naturally from the first. If equals are to be treated equally, it appears that unequals should be treated unequally. This precept is known as **vertical equity**.

Just saying this, however, does not get us very far, for vertical equity is a slippery concept. Often it is translated into the **ability-to-pay-principle**, according to which those most able to pay should pay the highest taxes. But this still leaves a definitional problem similar to the problem of defining "equally situated": How do we measure ability to pay? The nature of each tax often provides a straightforward answer. In income taxation, we measure ability to pay by income; in property taxation, we measure it by property value; and so on.

A thornier problem arises when we try to translate the notion into concrete terms. Consider the three alternative income-tax plans listed in Table 20–2. Under

*Table* **20–2** **THREE ALTERNATIVE INCOME-TAX PLANS**

| | PLAN 1 | | PLAN 2 | | PLAN 3 | |
|---|---|---|---|---|---|---|
| INCOME | TAX | AVERAGE TAX RATE | TAX | AVERAGE TAX RATE | TAX | AVERAGE TAX RATE |
| $ 10,000 | $ 300 | 3% | $1,000 | 10% | $1,000 | 10% |
| $ 50,000 | 8,000 | 16% | 5,000 | 10% | 3,000 | 6% |
| $250,000 | 70,000 | 28% | 25,000 | 10% | 7,500 | 3% |

all three plans, families with higher incomes pay higher taxes. So all three plans can be said to follow the ability-to-pay principle. Yet the three have very different distributive consequences. Plan 1 is a progressive tax, like the individual income tax in the United States: the average tax rate is higher for richer families. Plan 2 is a proportional tax: every family pays 10 percent of its income. Plan 3 is regressive: since tax payments rise more slowly than income, the average tax rate for richer families is lower than that for poorer families.

Which plan comes closest to the ideal notion of vertical equity? Many people find that Plan 3 offends their sense of "fairness," for it makes the distribution of income *after taxes* more unequal than the distribution *before taxes*. But there is much less agreement over the relative merits of Plan 1 (progressive taxation) and Plan 2 (proportional taxation). Often, in fact, the notion of vertical equity is taken to be synonymous with progressivity. Other things being equal, progressive taxes are seen as "good" taxes in some ethical sense while regressive taxes are seen as "bad." On these grounds, advocates of greater equality of incomes support progressive income taxes and oppose sales taxes.

### THE BENEFITS PRINCIPLE

Whereas the principles of horizontal and vertical equity, for all their ambiguities and practical problems, at least do not conflict with one another, the final principle of fair taxation often violates commonly accepted notions of vertical equity. According to the **benefits principle of taxation**, those who reap the benefits from government services should pay the taxes.

The **BENEFITS PRINCIPLE OF TAXATION** holds that people who derive the benefits from the service should pay the taxes that finance it.

The benefits principle is often applied by earmarking the proceeds from certain taxes for specific public services. For example, receipts from gasoline taxes typically go to finance maintenance and construction of roads. Thus those who use the roads pay the tax roughly in proportion to their usage. Most people seem to find this system fair. But in other contexts—such as public schools, hospitals, and libraries—the body politic has been loath to apply the benefits principle because it clashes so dramatically with common notions of fairness. So these services are normally financed out of general tax revenues rather than by direct charges for their use.

## THE CONCEPT OF EFFICIENCY IN TAXATION

The concept of **economic efficiency** is among the most central notions of economics. The economy is said to be *efficient* if it has used every available opportunity to make someone better off without making someone else worse off. In this sense, taxes almost always introduce *inefficiencies*. That is, if the tax were removed, some people could be made better off without anyone being harmed.

However, a comparison of a world with taxes to a world without taxes is not terribly pertinent. The government does, after all, levy taxes for a reason: to pay for the services it provides. And these public services yield benefits to their beneficiaries. So when economists discuss the notion of "efficient" taxation, they are usually looking for the taxes that cause the *least* amount of inefficiency.

The **BURDEN OF A TAX** to an individual is the amount he would have to be given to make him just as well off with the tax as he was without it.

To explain the concept of efficient taxation, we need to introduce one new term. Economists define the **burden of a tax** as the amount the taxpayer would have to be given to be just as well off in the presence of the tax as is in its absence. An example will clarify this notion and also make clear why:

The burden of a tax normally exceeds the revenues raised by the tax.

Suppose the government, in the interest of energy conservation, levies a high tax on the biggest gas-guzzling cars, with progressively lower taxes on smaller cars.[6] For example, a simple tax schedule might be the following:

| CAR TYPE | TAX |
|---|---|
| Cadillac | $1000 |
| Chrysler | 500 |
| Ford | 0 |

Harry has a taste for big cars and has always bought Cadillacs. (Harry is clearly no pauper.) Once the new tax takes effect, he has three options. He can still buy a Cadillac and pay $1000 in tax; he can switch to a Chrysler and avoid half the tax; or he can switch to a Ford and avoid the entire tax.

If Harry chooses the first option, we have a case in which the burden of the tax is exactly equal to the amount of tax the person pays. Why? Because if someone gave Harry $1000, he would be exactly as well off as he was before the tax was enacted. In general:

When a tax induces no change in economic behavior, the burden of the tax can be measured accurately by the revenue collected.

However, this is not what we normally expect to happen. And it is certainly not what the government intends by levying a tax on big cars.

Normally, we expect taxes to induce some people to alter their behavior in ways that reduce or avoid tax payments.

So let us look into Harry's other two options.

If he decides to purchase a Chrysler, Harry pays only $500 in tax. But this does not measure his full burden because Harry is greatly chagrined by the fact that he no longer drives a Cadillac. How much money would it take to make Harry just as well off as he was before the tax? Only Harry knows for sure. But we do know that it is more than the $500 tax that he pays. Why? Because, even if someone gave Harry the $500 needed to pay his tax bill, he would still be less happy than he was before the tax was introduced, owing to his switch from a Cadillac to a Chrysler. Whatever the (unknown) burden of the tax is, the amount by which it exceeds the $500 tax bill is called the **excess burden** of the tax.

The **EXCESS BURDEN** of a tax to an individual is the amount by which the burden of the tax exceeds the tax that is paid.

[6]A tax like this has been in effect since 1984.

## *Excess Burden and Mr. Figg*

Humorist Russell Baker discussed the problem of excess burden in the newspaper column reproduced below. It seems that every time his mythical Mr. Figg took a step to avoid paying taxes and to satisfy the tax man, he became less and less happy.

New York—The tax man was very cross about Figg. Figg's way of life did not conform to the way of life several governments wanted Figg to pursue. Nothing inflamed the tax man more than insolent and capricious disdain for governmental desires. He summoned Figg to the temple of taxation.

"What's the idea of living in a rental apartment over a delicatessen in the city, Figg?" he inquired. Figg explained that he liked urban life. In that case, said the tax man, he was raising Figg's city sales and income taxes. "If you want them cut, you'll have to move out to the suburbs," he said.

To satisfy his local government, Figg gave up the city and rented a suburban house. The tax man summoned him back to the temple.

"Figg" he said, "you have made me sore wroth with your way of life. Therefore, I am going to soak you for more federal income taxes." And he squeezed Figg until beads of blood popped out along the seams of Figg's wallet.

"Mercy, good tax man" Figg gasped. "Tell me how to live so that I may please my government, and I shall obey."

The tax man told Figg to quit renting and buy a house. The government wanted everyone to accept large mortgage loans from bankers. If Figg complied, it would cut his taxes.

Figg bought a house, which he did not want, in a suburb where he did not want to live, and he invited his friends and relatives to attend a party celebrating his surrender to a way of life that pleased his government.

The tax man was so furious that he showed up at the party with blood-shot eyes. "I have had enough of this, Figg" he declared, "Your government doesn't want you entertaining friends and relatives. This will cost you plenty."

Figg immediately threw out all his friends and relatives, then asked the tax man what sort of people his government wished him to entertain. "Business associates," said the tax man. "Entertain plenty of business associates, and I shall cut your taxes."

To make the tax man and his government happy, Figg began entertaining people he didn't like in the house he didn't want in the suburb where he didn't want to live.

Then was the tax man enraged indeed. "Figg," he thundered, "I will not cut your taxes for entertaining straw bosses, truck drivers and pothole fillers."

"Why not?" said Figg. "These are the people I associate with in my business."

"Which is what?" asked the tax man.

"Earning my pay by the sweat of my brow," said Figg.

"Your government is not going to bribe you for performing salaried labor," said the tax man. "Don't you know, you imbecile, that tax rates on salaried income are higher than on any other kind?"

And he taxed the sweat of Figg's brow at a rate that drew exquisite shrieks of agony from Figg and little cries of joy from Washington, which already had more sweated brows than it needed to sustain the federally approved way of life.

"Get into business, or minerals, or international oil," warned the tax man "or I shall make your taxes as the taxes of 10."

Figg went into business, which he hated, and entertained people he didn't like in the house he didn't want in the suburb where he did not want to live.

At length the tax man summoned Figg for an angry lecture. He demanded to know why Figg had not bought a new plastic factory to replace his old metal and wooden plant. "I hate plastic," said Figg. "Your government is sick and tired of metal, wood and everything else that smacks of the real stuff, Figg," roared the tax man, seizing Figg's purse. "Your depreciation is all used up."

There was nothing for Figg to do but go to plastic and the tax man rewarded him with a brand new depreciation schedule plus an investment credit deduction from the bottom line.

SOURCE: *International Herald Tribune,* April 13, 1977, page 14. 

Harry's final option makes the importance of understanding excess burden even more clear. If he switches to buying a Ford, Harry will pay no tax. Are we therefore to say he has suffered no burden? Clearly not, for he longs for the Cadillac that he no longer has. The general principle is

Whenever a tax induces people to change their behavior—that is, whenever it "distorts" their choices—the tax has an *excess burden*. This means that the revenue collected systematically understates the true burden of the tax.

The excess burdens that arise from tax-induced changes in economic behavior are precisely the inefficiencies we referred to at the outset of this discussion. And the basic precept of efficient taxation is to try to devise a tax system that *minimizes* these inefficiencies. In particular:

In comparing two taxes that raise the same total revenue, the one that produces less excess burden is the more efficient.

Notice the proviso that the two taxes being compared must yield the *same* revenue. We are really interested in the *total* burden of each tax. Since

$$\text{Total burden} = \text{Tax collections} + \text{Excess burden},$$

we can unambiguously state that the tax with less *excess* burden is more efficient only when tax collections are equal. Excess burdens arise when consumers and firms alter their behavior on account of taxation. So this precept of sound tax policy can be restated in a way that sounds consistent with President Reagan's statement at the beginning of this chapter:

In devising a tax system to raise revenue, try to raise any given amount of revenue through taxes that induce the smallest changes in behavior.[7]

## SHIFTING THE BURDEN OF TAXATION: TAX INCIDENCE

The **INCIDENCE OF A TAX** is an allocation of the burden of the tax to specific individuals or groups.

The **FLYPAPER THEORY OF INCIDENCE** holds that the burden of a tax always sticks where the government puts it.

When economists speak of the **incidence of a tax**, they are referring to who actually bears the burden of the tax. In discussing the tax on gas-guzzling autos, we have adhered so far to what has been called the **flypaper theory of tax incidence**: that the burden of any tax sticks where the government puts it. In this case, the theory holds that the burden stays on Harry. But often things do not work out this way.

Consider, for example, what will happen if the government levies a $1000 tax on luxury cars like Cadillacs. Figure 20–2 shows this tax as a $1000 vertical shift of the supply curve. If the demand curve does not shift, the market equilibrium moves from point *A* to point *B*. The quantity of luxury cars declines as Harrys all over America react to the higher price by buying fewer luxury cars. Notice that the price rises from $20,000 to $20,500, an increase of $500. So people who continue buying luxury cars bear a burden of only $500—just half the tax that they pay!

Does this mean that the tax imposes a *negative* excess burden? Certainly not. What it means is that consumers who refrained from buying the taxed commodity

[7]Sometimes, in contrast to President Reagan's statement, a tax is levied not primarily as a revenue-raiser, but as a way of inducing individuals or firms to alter their behavior. This possibility will be discussed later.

Figure 20–2 **THE INCIDENCE OF AN EXCISE TAX**

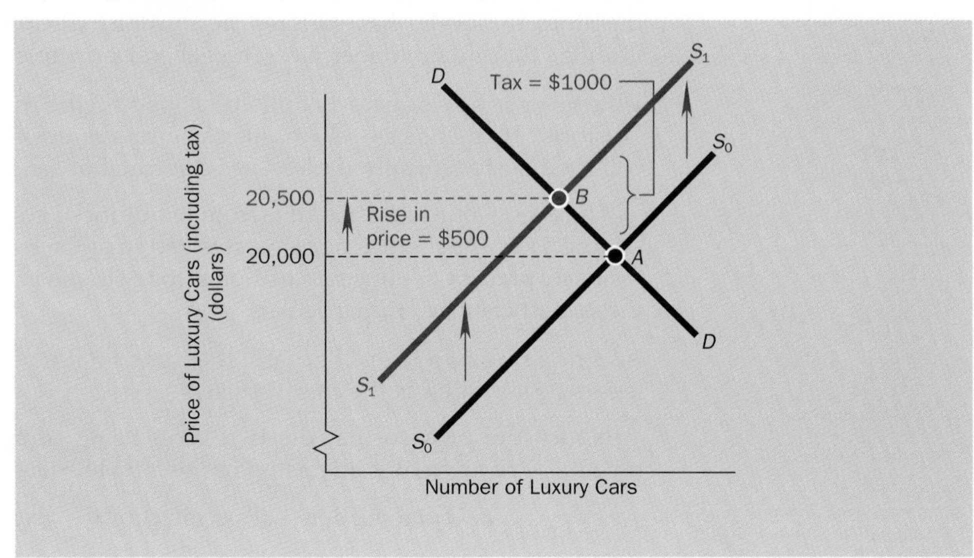


When the government imposes a $1000 tax on luxury cars, the supply curve relating quantity supplied to the price *inclusive of tax* shifts upward from $S_0S_0$ to $S_1S_1$. The equilibrium price in this example rises from $20,000 to $20,500, so the burden of the tax is shared equally between car sellers (who receive $500 less) and car buyers (who pay $500 more, including the tax). In general, how the burden is shared depends on the elasticities of demand and supply.

**TAX SHIFTING** occurs when the economic reactions to a tax cause prices and outputs in the economy to change, thereby shifting part of the burden of the tax onto others.

managed to *shift* part of the burden of the tax away from consumers as a whole, including those who continue to buy luxury cars. Who are the victims of this **tax shifting**? In our example, there are two main candidates. First are the automakers or, more precisely, their stockholders. Stockholders bear the burden to the extent that the tax cuts into their profits by reducing auto sales. The other principal candidates are auto workers. To the extent that reduced production leads to layoffs or lower wages, the automobile workers bear part of the burden of the tax.

People who have never studied economics almost always believe in the flypaper theory of incidence, which holds that sales taxes are borne by consumers, property taxes are borne by homeowners, and taxes on corporations are borne by stockholders. Perhaps the most important lesson of this chapter is that:

The flypaper theory of incidence is often wrong.

Failure to grasp this basic point has led to all sorts of misguided tax legislation in which Congress or state legislatures, *thinking* they were placing a tax burden on one group of people, inadvertently placed it squarely on another. Of course, there are cases where the flypaper theory of incidence is roughly correct. So let us consider some specific examples of tax incidence.

## THE INCIDENCE OF EXCISE TAXES

Excise taxes have already been covered by our automobile example, because Figure 20–2 could represent any commodity that is taxed. The basic finding is that *part* of the burden will fall on consumers of the taxed commodity (including those who stop buying it because of the tax), and part will be shifted to the firms and the workers who produce the commodity.

The amount that is shifted depends on the slopes of the demand and supply curves. We can see intuitively how this works. If consumers are very loyal to the taxed commodity, so that they will continue to buy almost the same quantity no matter what the price, then they will be stuck with most of the tax bill because they leave themselves vulnerable to it. Thus we would expect that:

The more inelastic the demand for the product, the larger is the share of the tax that consumers will pay.

Similarly, if suppliers are determined to supply the same amount of the product no matter how low the price, then most of the tax will be borne by suppliers. That is

The more inelastic the supply curve, the larger is the share of the tax that suppliers will pay.

One extreme case arises when no one stops buying luxury cars when their prices rise. The demand curve becomes vertical, like the demand curve *DD* in Figure 20–3. Then there can be no tax shifting. The price of a luxury car (inclusive of tax) rises by the full amount of the tax—from $20,000 to $21,000. So consumers bear the entire burden.

The other extreme case arises when the supply curve is totally inelastic (see Figure 20–4). Since the number of luxury cars supplied is the same at any price, the supply curve will not shift when a tax is imposed. Consequently, automakers must bear the full burden of any tax that is placed on their product. Figure 20–4 shows that the tax does not change the market price (including tax), which, of course, means that the price received by sellers must fall by the full amount of the tax.

**Figure 20–3** **AN EXTREME CASE OF TAX INCIDENCE**

If the quantity demanded is totally insensitive to price (completely *inelastic*), then the demand curve will be vertical. As the diagram shows, the price inclusive of tax rises to $21,000, so buyers bear the entire burden. Since price exclusive of tax remains at $20,000, none of the burden falls on the sellers.

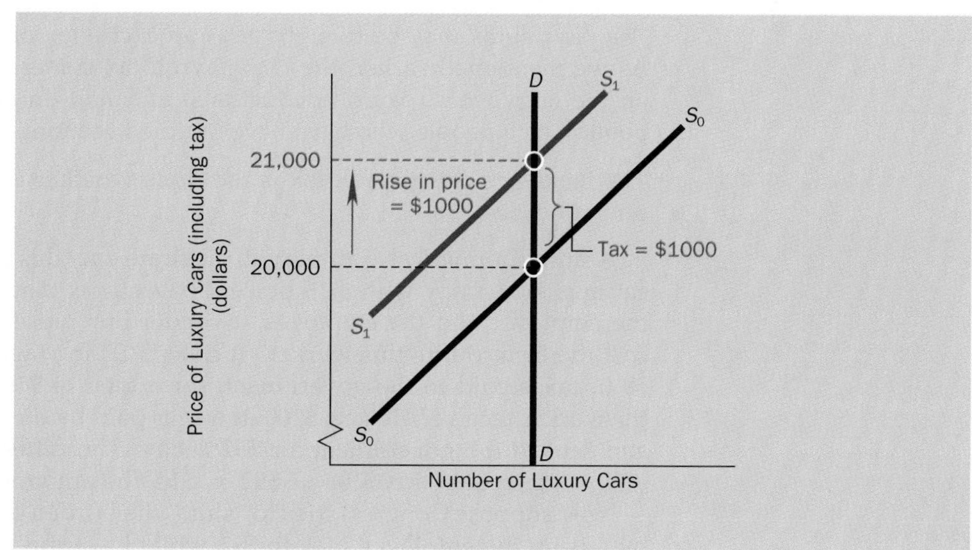

*Figure* **20–4** **ANOTHER EXTREME CASE OF TAX INCIDENCE**

If the quantity supplied is totally insensitive to price, then the supply curve *SS* will be vertical and will not shift when a tax is imposed. The seller will bear the entire burden because the price he receives ($19,000) will fall by the full amount of the tax.

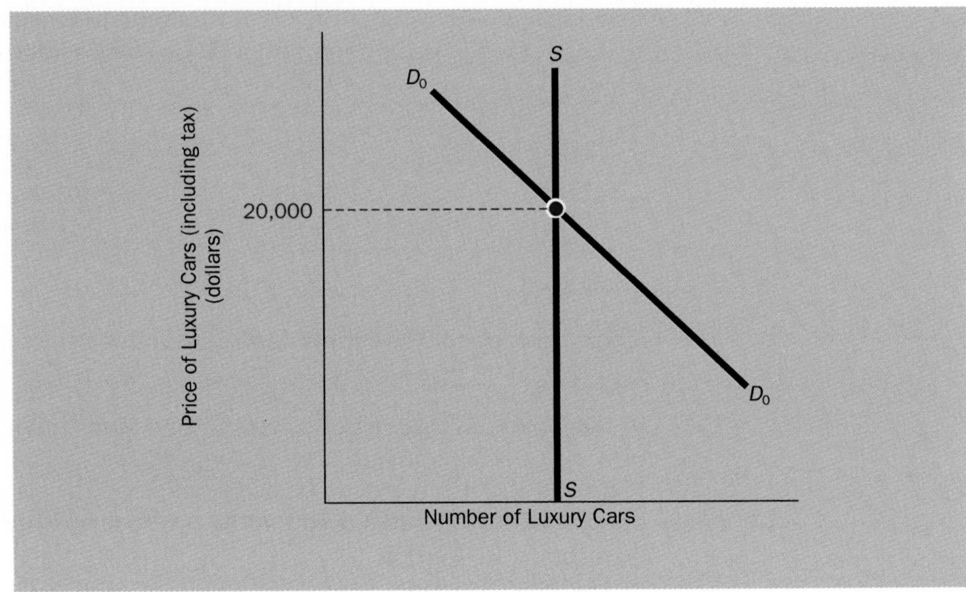


Demand and supply schedules for most goods and services are not as extreme as those depicted in Figures 20–3 and 20–4, so the burden is shared. Precisely how it is shared depends on the elasticities of the supply and demand curves.

## THE INCIDENCE OF THE PAYROLL TAX

The payroll tax may be thought of as an excise tax on the employment of labor. As we mentioned earlier, the U.S. payroll tax comes in two parts: half is levied on the employees (payroll deductions) and half on employers. A fundamental point, which people who have never studied economics often fail to grasp is that:

The incidence of a payroll tax is the same whether it is levied on employers or on employees.

A simple numerical example will illustrate why this is so. Consider an employee earning $100 a day with a 16 percent payroll tax that is shared equally between the employer and the employee, as under our present law. How much does it cost the firm to hire this worker? It costs $100 in wages paid to the worker plus $8 in taxes paid to the government, for a total of $108 a day. How much does the worker receive? He gets $100 in wages paid by the employer less $8 deducted and sent to the government, or $92 a day. The difference between wages paid and wages received is $108 − $92 = $16, the amount of the tax.

Now suppose Congress tries to "shift" the burden of the tax entirely onto firms by raising the employer's tax to $16 while lowering the employee's tax to zero. At first, the daily wage is fixed at $100, so firms' total labor costs (including tax) rise to $116 per day and workers' net income rises to $100 per day. Congress seems to have achieved its goal.

But the achievement is fleeting, for this is not an equilibrium situation. With the daily cost of labor at $116 for firms, the quantity of labor *demanded* will be *less* than when labor cost only $108 per day. Similarly, with take-home pay up to $100 for workers, the quantity of labor *supplied* will be *more* than when the after-tax wage was only $92. There will therefore be a *surplus of labor* on the market (an excess of quantity supplied over quantity demanded), and this surplus will put downward pressure on wages.

How far will wages have to fall? It is easy to see that an after-tax wage of $92 will restore equilibrium. If daily take-home pay is $92, labor will cost firms $108 per day, just as it did before the tax change. So they will demand the same quantity as they did when the payroll tax was shared. Similarly, workers will receive the same $92 net wage as they did previously; so quantity supplied will be the same as it was before the tax change. Thus, in the end, the market will completely frustrate the intent of Congress.

The payroll tax is an excellent example of a case in which Congress, misled by the flypaper theory of incidence, thinks it is "taxing firms" when it raises the employer's share and "taxing workers" when it raises the employee's share. In truth, who really pays in the long run depends on the incidence of the tax. But no lasting difference results from a change in the employee's and the employer's shares.

Who, then, really bears the burden of the payroll tax? Like any excise tax, the incidence of the payroll tax depends on the elasticities of the supply and demand schedules. In the case of labor supply, there is a large body of empirical evidence pointing to the conclusion that the quantity of labor supplied is not very responsive to price for most population groups. The supply curve is almost vertical, like that shown in Figure 20–4. The result is that workers as a group are able to shift little of the burden of the payroll tax.

But employers *can* shift it in most cases. Firms view their share of the payroll tax as an additional cost of using labor. So when payroll taxes go up, firms try to substitute cheaper factors of production (capital) for labor wherever they can. This reduces the quantity of labor demanded, lowering the wage received by workers. And this is how market forces shift part of the tax burden from firms to workers.

To the extent that the supply curve of labor has some positive slope, the quantity of labor supplied will fall when the wage goes down, and in this way workers can shift some of the burden back onto firms. But the firms, in turn, can shift that burden onto consumers by raising their prices. As we know from Part 3, prices in competitive markets generally rise when costs (like labor costs) increase. It is doubtful, therefore, that firms bear much of the burden of the payroll tax. Here, the flypaper theory of incidence could not be further from the truth. Even though the tax is collected by the firm, it is really borne by workers and consumers.

## WHEN TAXATION CAN IMPROVE EFFICIENCY

We have spent much of this chapter discussing the kinds of inefficiencies and excess burdens that arise from taxation. But, before we finish this discussion, two things must be pointed out.

First, economic efficiency is not society's only goal. For example, a tax on energy causes inefficiencies if it changes people's behavior patterns. But this, presumably, is exactly what the government intends. The government wants to conserve energy and is willing to tolerate some economic inefficiency to accomplish this goal. We can, of course, argue whether that is a good idea—whether the conservation achieved is worth the efficiency loss. But the general point is that:

Some taxes that introduce economic inefficiencies are nonetheless good social policy because they help achieve some other goal.

A second, and more fundamental, point is that:

Some taxes that change economic behavior may lead to efficiency gains, rather than to efficiency *losses*.

As you might guess, this can happen only when there is an inefficiency in the system prior to the tax. Then an appropriate tax may help set things right. One important example of this phenomenon came up in Chapter 13 and will occupy much of the next chapter. Because firms and individuals who despoil clean air and water often do so without paying any price, these precious resources are used inefficiently. A corrective tax on pollution can remedy this problem.

## EQUITY, EFFICIENCY, AND THE OPTIMAL TAX

In a perfect world, the ideal tax would raise the revenues the government needs, reflect society's views on equity in taxation, and induce no changes in economic behavior—and so have no excess burden. Unfortunately, there is no such tax.

Sometimes, in fact, the taxes with the smallest excess burdens are the most regressive. For instance, a head tax, which charges every person the same number of dollars, is incredibly regressive. But it is also quite efficient. Since no change in economic behavior will enable anyone to avoid it, there is no reason for anyone to change his or her behavior. As we have noted, the regressive payroll tax also seems to have small excess burdens.

Fortunately, however, there is a tax that, while not ideal, still scores highly on both the equity and efficiency criteria: a comprehensive personal income tax with few loopholes.

While it is true that income taxes can be avoided by earning less income, we have already observed that in reality the supply of labor is changed little by taxation. Investing in relatively safe assets (like government bonds) rather than risky ones (like common stocks) is another possible step people can take to reduce their tax bills, since less risky assets pay lower rates of return. But it is not clear that the income tax actually induces such behavior because, while it taxes away some of the profits when investments turn out well, it also offers a tax deduction when investments turn sour. Finally, because an income tax reduces the return on saving, many economists have worried that it would discourage saving and thus retard economic growth.[8] But the empirical evidence does not suggest that this has happened to any great extent.

[8]For this reason, some economists prefer a tax on consumption to a tax on income.

On balance then, while there are still unresolved questions and research is continuing:

Most of the studies that have been conducted to date suggest that a comprehensive personal income tax with no loopholes induces few of the behavioral reactions that would reduce consumer well-being, and thus has a rather small excess burden.

On the equity criterion, we know that personal income taxes can be made as progressive as society deems desirable, though if marginal tax rates on rich people get extremely high, some of the potential efficiency losses might get more serious than they now seem to be. On both grounds, then, many economists—including both liberals and conservatives—view a comprehensive personal income tax as one of the best ways for a government to raise revenue.

## THE REAL VERSUS THE IDEAL

That seems to be a cheerful conclusion because the federal personal income tax, the biggest tax in the U.S. revenue system, was thoroughly reformed in 1986—bringing it closer to the ideal, comprehensive income tax. However, many loopholes remained and several more have been added since then.

We have emphasized in this chapter that loopholes make the income tax less progressive than it seems to be. They also make it far less *efficient* than it could be. The reason follows directly from our analysis of the incidence of taxation.

When different income-earning activities are taxed at different marginal rates, economic choices are distorted by tax considerations; and this impairs economic efficiency.

Thus a major objective of the Tax Reform Act of 1986 was to enhance both the equity and efficiency of the personal income tax by closing loopholes and lowering tax rates. To a remarkable extent, the effort succeeded. By roughly doubling the personal exemption, the law removed about six million households from the tax rolls. For most of the rest of the population, tax progressivity—as measured by average tax rates—was left about the same as under the old law. But marginal tax rates were reduced sharply. Most Americans today are in the 15 percent tax bracket, meaning that their taxes rise by only 15 cents for each dollar they earn. Most of the rest are in the 28 percent tax bracket, although wealthly Americans nowadays pay marginal income tax rates that can rise as high as 43 percent.

These low tax rates were achieved by shifting some of the tax burden onto corporations and by closing many important tax loopholes. Tax rates on different sources of income were equalized. Many deductions and exemptions were reduced or eliminated. Abusive tax shelters were a particular target of tax reformers, though the details are best left to more advanced courses on taxation. The United States personal income tax code still falls a good distance short of the economist's ideal. But it is a giant step closer than it was prior to 1986.

## *Summary*

1. Taxes in the United States have been quite constant as a percentage of gross domestic product since 1972.

2. The federal government raises most of its revenue by **direct taxes**, such as the personal and corporate

**income taxes** and the payroll tax. Of these, the payroll tax is increasing most rapidly.

3. The social security system relied successfully on pay-as-you-go financing for decades. In recent years, however, it has been accumulating a large trust fund to be used to pay benefits to the baby boom generation when it retires.
4. State and local governments raise most of their tax revenues by **indirect taxes**. States rely mainly on sales taxes, while localities are dependent upon property taxes.
5. There is controversy over whether the property tax is **progressive** or **regressive**, and even more controversy over whether local property taxes are an equitable way to finance public education.
6. In our multilevel system of government, the federal government makes various sorts of grants to state and local governments, and states in turn make grants to municipalities and school districts. This system of intergovernmental transfers is called **fiscal federalism**.
7. There are three concepts of fair, or "equitable," taxation that occasionally conflict. **Horizontal equity** simply calls for equals to be treated equally. **Vertical equity**, which calls for unequals to be treated unequally, has often been translated into the **ability-to-pay principle**—that people who are better able to pay taxes should be taxed more heavily. The **benefits principle of tax equity** ignores ability to pay and seeks to tax people according to the benefits they receive.
8. The **burden of a tax** is the amount of money an individual would have to be given to make her as well off with the tax as she was without it. This burden normally exceeds the taxes that are paid, and the difference between the two is called the **excess burden** of the tax.
9. Excess burden arises when a tax induces some people or firms to change their behavior. Because excess burdens signal **economic inefficiencies**, the basic principle of efficient taxation is to utilize taxes that have small excess burdens.
10. When people change their behavior on account of a tax, they often shift the burden of the tax onto someone else. This is why the "**flypaper theory of incidence**"—the belief that the burden of any tax sticks where Congress puts it—is often incorrect.
11. The burden of a sales or **excise tax** normally is shared between the suppliers and the consumers. The manner in which it is shared depends on the elasticities of supply and demand.
12. The **payroll tax** is like an excise tax on labor services. Since the supply of labor is much less elastic than the demand for labor, workers bear most of the burden of the payroll tax. This includes both the employer's and the employee's share of the tax.
13. Sometimes, "inefficient" taxes—that is, taxes that cause a good deal of excess burden—are nonetheless desirable because the changes in behavior they induce further some other social goal.
14. When there are inefficiencies in the system for reasons other than the tax system (for example, externalities), taxation can conceivably improve efficiency.
15. The Tax Reform Act of 1986 moved the U.S. income-tax system closer to the ideal by closing loopholes and lowering tax rates.

## Key Concepts and Terms

Progressive, proportional, and regressive taxes
Average and marginal tax rates
Direct and indirect taxes
Personal income tax
Payroll tax
Corporate income tax
Excise tax
Tax loopholes
Tax Reform Act of 1986
Social security system
Property tax
Fiscal federalism
Horizontal and vertical equity
Ability-to-pay principle
Benefits principle of taxation
Economic efficiency
Burden of a tax
Excess burden
Incidence of a tax
Flypaper theory of incidence
Tax shifting

## Questions for Review

1. "If the federal government continues to raise taxes as it has been doing, it will ruin the country." Comment.
2. Soon after taking office, President Clinton proposed a package of tax increases. Critics argued that these

taxes would do harm to the economy. Why did they say this?

3. Using the hypothetical income tax table just below, compute the marginal and average tax rates. Is the tax progressive, proportional, or regressive?

| INCOME | TAX |
|---|---|
| $20,000 | $0 |
| 30,000 | 2,500 |
| 40,000 | 5,000 |
| 50,000 | 7,500 |

4. Which concept of tax equity, if any, seems to be served by each of the following:
   a. The progressive income tax.
   b. The excise tax on cigarettes.
   c. The property tax.
5. Use the example of Mr. Figg (see the boxed insert on page 503) to explain the concepts of efficient taxes and excess burden.
6. Think of some tax that you personally pay. What steps have you taken or could you take to reduce your tax payments? Is there an excess burden on you? Why or why not?
7. Suppose the supply and demand schedules for cigarettes are as follows:

| PRICE PER CARTON (dollars) | QUANTITY DEMANDED (millions of cartons per year) | QUANTITY SUPPLIED (millions of cartons per year) |
|---|---|---|
| 3.00 | 360 | 160 |
| 3.25 | 330 | 180 |
| 3.50 | 300 | 200 |
| 3.75 | 270 | 220 |
| 4.00 | 240 | 240 |
| 4.25 | 210 | 260 |
| 4.50 | 180 | 280 |
| 4.75 | 150 | 300 |
| 5.00 | 120 | 320 |

   a. What is the equilibrium price and equilibrium quantity?
   b. Now the government levies a $1.25 per carton excise tax on cigarettes. What is the equilibrium price paid by consumers, the price received by producers, and the quantity now?
   c. Explain why it makes no difference whether Congress levies the $1.25 tax on the consumer or the producer. (Relate your answer to the discussion of the payroll tax on pages 510–11 of the text.)
   d. Suppose the tax is levied on the producers. How much of the tax are producers able to shift onto consumers? Explain how they manage to do this.
   e. Will there be any excess burden from this tax? Why? Who bears this excess burden?
   f. By how much has cigarette consumption declined on account of the tax? Why might the government be happy about this outcome, despite the excess burden?
8. The country of Taxmania produces only two commodities: rice and caviar. The poor spend all their income on rice, while the rich purchase both goods. Both demand for and supply of rice are quite inelastic. In the caviar market, both supply and demand are quite elastic. Which good would be heavily taxed if Taxmanians cared mostly about efficiency? What if they cared mostly about vertical equity?
9. Discuss President Reagan's statement on taxes quoted on the first page of the chapter. Do you agree with the president?
10. Use the criteria of equity and efficiency in taxation to evaluate the proposal to tax capital gains at a lower rate than other sources of income.

Chapter 21

# ENVIRONMENTAL PROTECTION AND RESOURCE CONSERVATION

*"Since Fuel is become so expensive, and will of course grow scarcer and dearer; any new Proposal for saving the [fuel] . . . may at least be thought worth Consideration."*

**BENJAMIN FRANKLIN (1744)**

We learned in Chapter 13 that *externalities*

(the incidental benefits or damages imposed upon people not directly involved in an economic activity) can cause the market mechanism to malfunction. The first half of this chapter studies a particularly important application—externalities as explanation of the problems of the environment. The second half addresses a closely related subject—natural resource depletion.

## THE ECONOMICS OF ENVIRONMENTAL PROTECTION

Environmental problems are not new. What *is* new and different is the attention the community now gives them. Much of this increased interest can be attributed to rising incomes, which have reduced concerns about food, clothing, and shelter, and have allowed the luxury of concentrating on the next target—the *quality* of life.

Economic thought on the environment preceded the outburst of public concern over the subject by nearly half a century. In 1911, a noted British economist, A. C. Pigou, wrote a remarkable book called *The Economics of Welfare*, which offered an explanation of the market economy's poor environmental performance and outlined an approach to environmental policy that is still favored by most economists and that is beginning to win over lawmakers and bureaucrats. Pigou's analysis suggested that a system of charges on emissions can be an effective means to control pollution. In this way, the price mechanism can remedy one of its own shortcomings!

### THE FACTS: IS EVERYTHING REALLY GETTING STEADILY WORSE?

First, let us see what the facts really are. Much of the discussion in the press gives the impression that environmental problems have been growing steadily worse, and that *all* pollution is attributable to modern industrialization and the profit system. But in fact pollution is nothing new. Medieval cities were pestholes; the streets and rivers were littered with garbage and the air stank of rotting wastes—a level of filth that was accepted as normal. And early in the twentieth century, the automobile was hailed as a source of major improvement in the cleanliness of city streets, which until then had fought a losing battle against the proliferation of horse dung.

"The picture's pretty bleak, gentlemen . . . The world's climates are changing, the mammals are taking over, and we all have a brain about the size of a walnut."[1]

[1]See page 579 for a brief discussion of the "greenhouse effect" and global warming.

Since World War II, there has been marked progress in solving a number of pollution problems. The quality of the air has improved in most U.S. cities. In New York City, for example, the concentration of suspended particulates, or soot, in the air has fallen dramatically since World War II. In fact, national pollution standards for suspended particulates, sulfur dioxide, lead, and nitrogen dioxide have now been achieved for most of the United States (the Los Angeles basin is the notable exception). Concentration of most air pollutants is still declining. Figure 21–1 portrays the generally encouraging trends in national air pollution levels. Rapid declines in automobile pollution have played a large role in this improvement, along with decreases in emissions from power plants.

There have also been some spectacular gains in water quality. In the Great Lakes region, where the Cuyahoga River once caught fire because of its toxic load and where Lake Erie was pronounced dead, tough pollution controls have gradually effected a recovery. There has also been progress in Europe. For example, the infamous, killing fogs of London, once the staple backdrop of British mystery fiction, are a thing of the past because of the improvement in air quality since 1950. In short, pollution problems are not a uniquely modern phenomenon, nor is every part of the environment deteriorating relentlessly.

Environmental problems do not occur exclusively in capitalist economies. For example, in the People's Republic of China, coal soot from factory smokestacks

Figure 21-1 **U.S. NATIONAL AIR QUALITY TRENDS, 1975–1991 (AMBIENT CONCENTRATIONS OF SIX POLLUTANTS)**

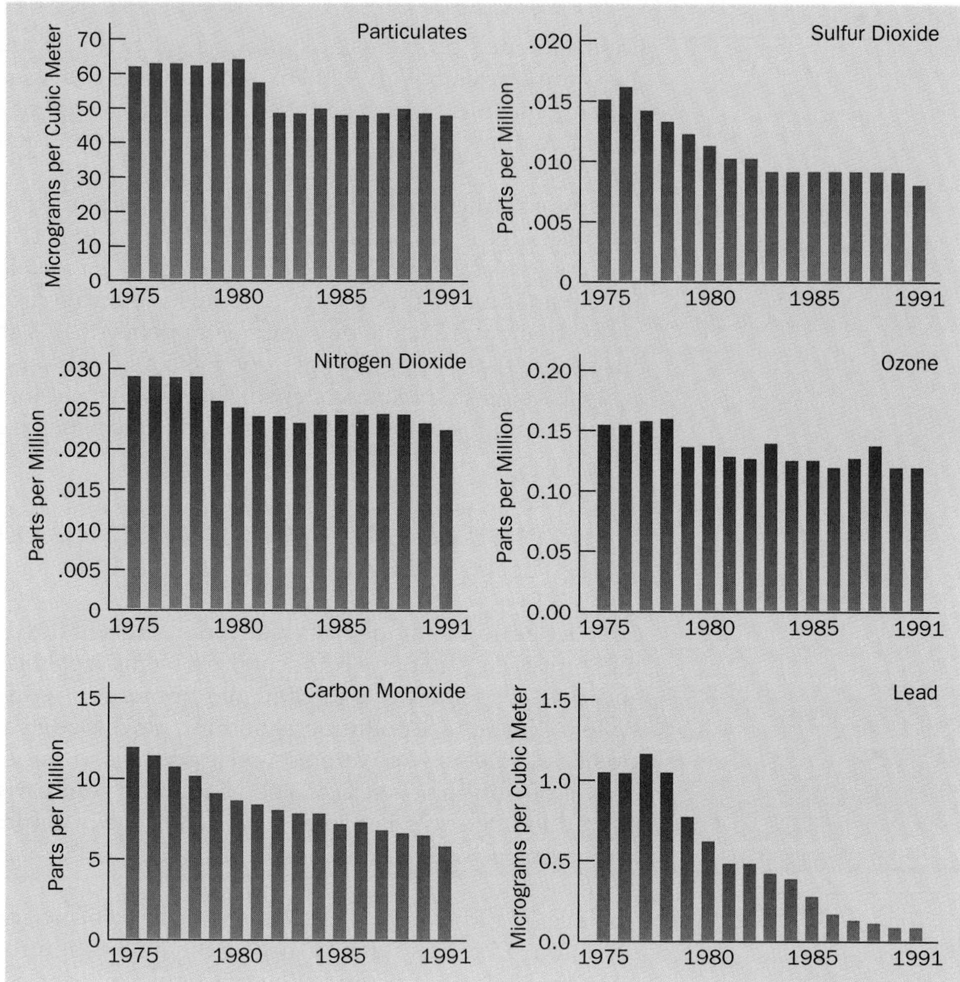


Taken as a whole, the trends are encouraging. During the 1980s the United States made substantial progress in improving air quality. The most dramatic success story was an 89 percent reduction in lead levels in the air. Carbon monoxide also decreased by 30 percent, nitrogen oxides by 6 percent, ozone by 8 percent, and sulfur dioxide by 20 percent. Levels of particulate matter have dropped by 10 percent since 1987. With the exception of ozone, average concentrations were well below the National Ambient Air Quality Standards.

SOURCE: Council on Environmental Quality, *Environmental Quality 1992*, Washington, D.C.: U.S. Government Printing Office, January 1993.

in Beijing envelops the city in a thick haze reminiscent of Pittsburgh in the old days of unbridled industrial activity. In many of China's cities, particularly in the north, air pollution exceeds, five to six times over, the standards set by the World Health Organization—that is about seven to eight times worse than the air quality in New York City.[2]

Grave environmental problems plague Eastern Europe and the former Soviet Union. Smoke from brown coal furnaces pollutes the air almost everywhere in the former East bloc countries. The Polish government had to declare Bogomice and four other towns "unfit for human habitation," because of heavy metals in the air and deposits in the soil by emissions from nearby copper-smelting plants; and it has been estimated that a third of Poland's citizens live in areas of "ecological

[2]Sheryl Wu Dunn, "Chinese Suffer from Rising Pollution as Byproduct of the Industrial Boom," *The New York Times*, February 28, 1993.

disaster." The collapse of communism in the former Soviet Union revealed a staggering array of environmental horrors in that land, including the massive poisoning of air, ground, and water in the vicinity of industrial plants, which has resulted in terrible human suffering and countless premature deaths; and some truly monumental ecological disasters, such as the desiccation of the Aral Sea, once the fourth largest inland sea in the world, and now reduced to less than half of its original volume.[3]

The preceding discussion is meant to put matters into perspective, but we certainly are not suggesting that all is well with our own environment, nor that there is nothing more it is appropriate to do. Despite improvements, many U.S. urban areas still have severe air quality problems. According to the U.S. Council on Environmental Quality, 86 million Americans live in counties where pollution levels in 1991 still exceeded at least one national air quality standard. Urban smog continues to be the most widespread problem, while carbon monoxide and particulate pollution exceed federal limits in some areas. Formerly pristine wilderness areas also are threatened by air pollution.

Our world is subjected to new pollutants, some far more dangerous than those we have reduced, although less visible and less malodorous. Highly toxic substances—such as PCBs (polychlorinated biphenyls), chlorinated hydrocarbons, dioxins, heavy metals, and radioactive materials—have been dumped carelessly and have been found to cause cancer and threaten life and health in other ways. The threat from some of these can persist for thousands of years, causing damage that is all but irreversible. Ironically, although successful cleanup of conventional water pollutants has returned fish life to some previously "dead" waterways, those fish are sometimes inedible since they are so contaminated by toxic substances. This is true of the Great Lakes, where vast quantities of toxic pesticides and other chemicals remain trapped in bottom sediments. New York State warns residents to eat only one meal per week of fish caught anywhere in the state, and New Jersey advises pregnant women not to consume any fish caught there.[4]

Even these problems pale when compared to an environmental threat that may hang over our future—the long-term warming of the earth's atmosphere attributable to the buildup of "greenhouse gases," particularly carbon dioxide (primarily from the burning of fossil fuels such as oil, natural gas, and coal). There is fear among many climatologists that, if the concentration of $CO_2$ in the atmosphere continues to increase, then a significant rise in global temperatures will occur and may already have begun to occur. The impending dramatic climate changes could shift world rain patterns, disrupt agriculture, threaten coastal cities with inundation, and expand deserts.

While environmental problems are neither new nor confined to capitalist, industrialized economies, we continue to inflict damage on ourselves and our surroundings.

---

[3]Lester R. Brown, *et al.*, *State of the World, 1989*, A Worldwatch Institute Report, New York: W.W. Norton & Company, 1989, p. 68; Marlise Simons, "Rising Iron Curtain Exposes Haunting Veil of Polluted Air," *The New York Times*, April 8, 1990, pages 1 and 14; and "Rubishing of a Superpower," *The Economist*, April 25, 1992, pages 99–100, a review of Murray Feshbach and Alfred Friendly, *Ecocide in the USSR*, New York: Basic Books, 1992.

[4]William Drayton, *America's Toxic Protection Gap* (Washington, D.C.: Environmental Safety, July 1984), p. 38; he cites U.S. Environmental Protection Agency, "Summary of the 1983 Regional Environmental Management Reports," August 23, 1983, SW11.

## *Washed Up*

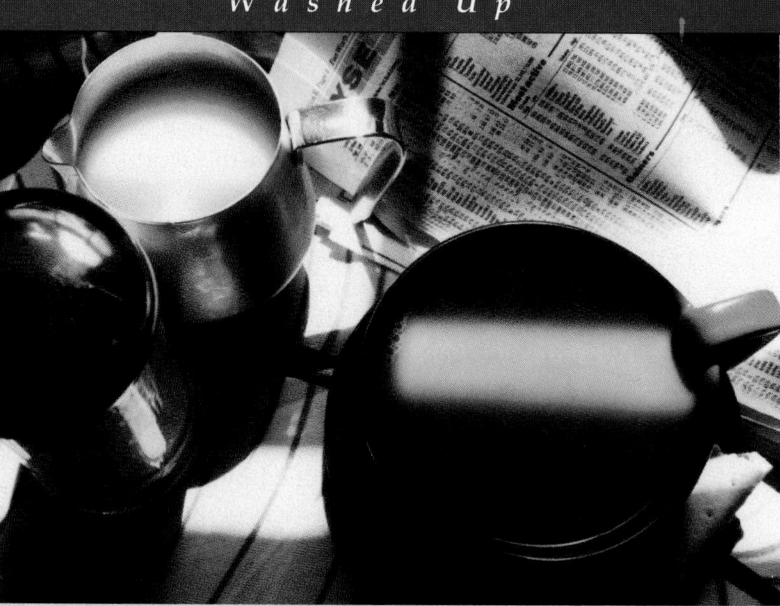

Trust the Dutch to do it. With admirable thoroughness, Holland's environment ministry has settled a venerable and vital question in a 123-page report, complete with appendices, charts, tables and chemical equations. The question was this: which are more environmentally friendly, china coffee-cups and saucers, polystyrene (styrofoam) mugs, or paper mugs? The answer, inevitably: it depends.

The report looks at the life-cycle of the cup from cradle to grave: from the extraction and processing of raw materials through production and use to final disposal. It takes account of the consumption of raw materials, the use of energy (for processing, transport and cleaning), the output of hazardous substances into the air and water, and the volume of rubbish created (assuming 40% is incinerated). It ignores some other environmental effects that are more locally varied, such as noise, smell and harm to the landscape.

China cups and saucers start with one big handicap: they need to be washed. "To wash a porcelain cup and saucer once, in an average dishwasher," avers the report, "has a greater impact on the water than the entire life cycle of a disposable cup." The surfactants in detergents, which clean off the grease, see to that. In their impact on air, energy consumption and volume of rubbish, china cups may do less harm in the end than their disposable rivals. But each time a china cup and saucer are put through a dishwasher, they use energy, cause nasty gases to be released into the air and create a bit more solid rubbish.

Whether it is greener to drink coffee from a china cup and saucer or a plastic or paper one depends on two things: how many times the china cup and saucer are used, and how frequently they are washed. Have only one cuppa between washes, and the cup and saucer need to be used 1,800 times before they have less impact on the air during their lifetime than a polystyrene mug. That still gives china the edge: Dutch caterers reckon to use a china cup and saucer 3,000 times. But ask for a refill, and the china crockery need be used only 114 times before it beats polystyrene on energy use, and only 86 times before it does less damage to the air. Paper cups do more harm than polystyrene on every count except their impact on water.

The answer, says the report, is to pay more attention to the amount of energy used by dishwashers and the pollution caused by detergents. Most office-workers have another answer: allow a fine patina of old coffee to develop around the inside of the mug. It may not be hygienic, but it is good for the planet.

SOURCE: *The Economist*, August 1, 1992, page 68.

### So now you know

Number of times you must use each china cup and saucer to be a greener citizen than your neighbour who uses a polystyrene or paper cup, assuming you wash the china cup and saucer after every second drink.

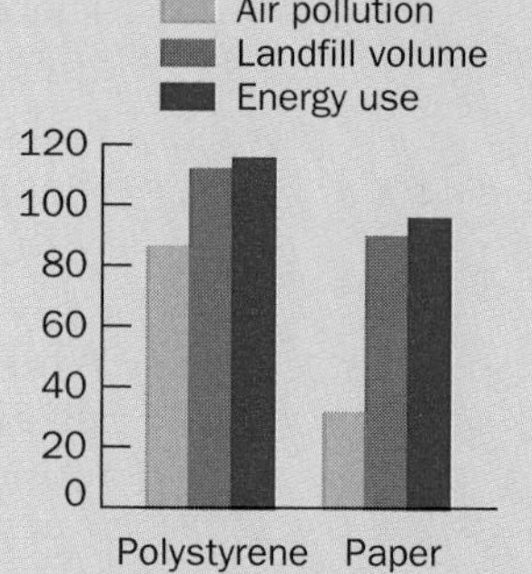


Source: *The Economist*, August 1, 1992, page 58.

## THE LAW OF CONSERVATION OF MATTER AND ENERGY

The physical law of conservation of matter and energy tells us that objects cannot disappear—at most they can be changed into something else. Oil, for instance, can be transformed into heat (and smoke) or into plastic—but it will never vanish. This means that after a raw material has been used, either it must be used again (recycled) or it becomes a waste product that requires disposal.

If it is not recycled, any input used in production must ultimately become a waste product. It may end up in some municipal dump, or it may literally go up in smoke, contributing to atmospheric pollution, or it may be transformed into heat, warming up adjacent waterways and killing aquatic life. But the laws of physics tell us nothing can be done to make used inputs disappear altogether.

Recycling rates for such commonly used materials as aluminum, paper, and glass are rising in many industrial countries. In the United States the Environmental Protection Agency estimates that the rate at which materials in the municipal solid waste stream were recycled rose from 7 percent in 1960 (6 million tons) to 17 percent (33 million tons) in 1990. Figure 21–2 shows that rates of recycling in a number of industrial countries generally exceed the rates in the United States. In recent years, however, recycling in America has been helped by a number of local and state ordinances that require garbage removal to be priced on a fee-per-container basis—thus giving residents a financial incentive to reduce the amount of garbage they produce and increasing the proportion of garbage that is recycled. In New Jersey, for instance, state plans call for fully half of all garbage to be recycled by 1995; a number of municipal "per bag" pricing schemes in the state have already reduced the tide of trash by as much as 25 percent. (But see the box, opposite, for a reminder that "environmentally correct" solutions to solid waste problems may not always be obvious.)

*Figure* **21–2**

### RECYCLING RATES (PERCENTAGE) IN SEVEN INDUSTRIAL COUNTRIES

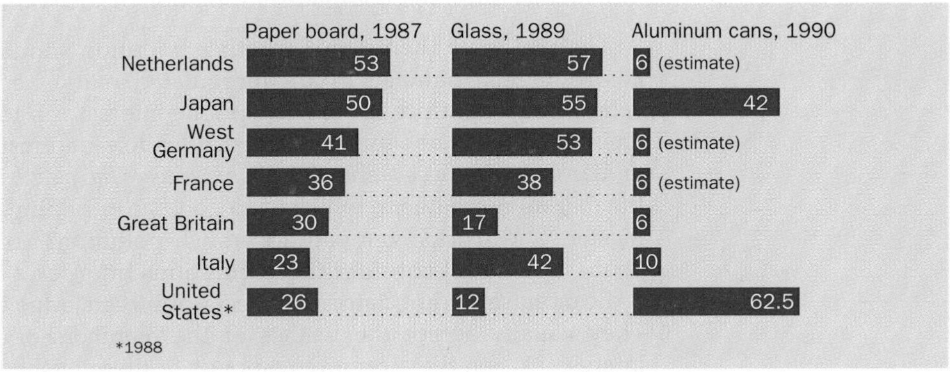

| | Paper board, 1987 | Glass, 1989 | Aluminum cans, 1990 |
|---|---|---|---|
| Netherlands | 53 | 57 | 6 (estimate) |
| Japan | 50 | 55 | 42 |
| West Germany | 41 | 53 | 6 (estimate) |
| France | 36 | 38 | 6 (estimate) |
| Great Britain | 30 | 17 | 6 |
| Italy | 23 | 42 | 10 |
| United States* | 26 | 12 | 62.5 |

*1988

The United States lags behind in the recycling of paper and glass, but recovers more than half of the aluminum cans it produces. Recycling rates in all these countries are sharply up in the last decade.

SOURCES: U.S. Department of Commerce, *Statistical Abstract of the United States, 1992*, Washington, DC: U.S. Government Printing Office, 1992; Council on Environmental Quality, *Environmental Quality 1992*, Washington, DC: U.S. Government Printing Office, 1993; "Recycling in Germany: A Wall of Waste," *The Economist*, November 30, 1991, page 73, which cites the Organization for Economic Cooperation and Development; "Recycling: How to Throw Things Away," *The Economist*, April 13, 1991, page 18; and World Resources Institute, *1992 Information Please Environmental Almanac*, New York: Houghton Mifflin, 1992, page 123.

## GOVERNMENTS AND INDIVIDUALS AS DAMAGERS OF THE ENVIRONMENT

Many people think of industry as the primary villain in environmental damage. But:

While firms have done their share in harming the environment, private individuals and government have also been prime contributors.

Cars driven by individuals are a critical air pollution problem for most major cities; wood-burning stoves are a source of particulate pollution, and wastes from flush toilets and residential washing machines also cause significant harm.

Governments, too, add to the problem. The wastes of municipal treatment plants are a major source of water pollution. Military aircraft create exhaust and make much noise. Obsolete atomic materials and byproducts associated with chemical and nuclear weapons are among the most dangerous of all wastes, and their disposal is an unsolved problem.

Governments also construct giant dams and reservoirs that flood farmlands and destroy canyons, often rendering surrounding soil unusable by seepage of salt into the earth, and changing the level of water underground. Drainage of swamps has altered local ecology irrevocably; canal-building has diverted the flow of rivers. The U.S. Army Corps of Engineers has been accused of acting on the basis of this so-called *edifice complex.* But that complex reached its greatest heights in the communist states under Stalin, whose pride in enormous hydroelectric installations and huge canals was well publicized in the Soviet press.

## ENVIRONMENTAL DAMAGE AS AN EXTERNALITY

Our very existence makes some environmental damage inevitable. Products of the earth are used up, and wastes must be generated as people eat and protect themselves from the elements.

There is no question of reducing environmental damage to zero. As long as the human race survives, complete elimination of such damage is literally impossible.

The real issue then is not whether pollution should exist at all, but whether environmental damage in an unregulated market economy tends to be more serious and widespread than the public interest can tolerate. This issue immediately raises three key questions. First, why do economists believe that environmental damage is unacceptably severe *in terms of the public interest*? Second, why does the market mechanism, which is so good at providing about the right number of toasters and trucks, generate too much pollution? And, third, what can we do about it? We will consider these questions in order.

Economists do not claim any special ability to judge what is good for the public. They usually accept the wishes of the members of the public as "the public interest." When the economy responds to these wishes as closely as the available resources and technology permit, economists conclude it is working effectively. When it operates in a way that frustrates the desires of the people, they conclude that the economy is functioning improperly. In such terms, why do economists believe the market generates "too much" pollution?

In Chapter 13 we discussed externalities as a primary source of failure of the market mechanism. An *externality*, it will be recalled, is an incidental consequence of some economic activity that can be either beneficial or detrimental to someone who neither controls the activity nor is intentionally served by it. The emission of pollutants constitutes one of the most clear-cut examples. The smoke from a chemical plant affects persons other than the employees of the plant or its customers. Because the incidental damage done by the smoke does not enter the financial accounts of the firm that produces the emissions, the owners of the firm have no financial incentive to restrain them, particularly since emission control costs money. Instead, they will find it profitable to emit their smoke as though it caused no external damage to the community.

This is a *failure of the pricing system*—the smoke-generating business firm is able to use up some of the community's clean air without paying for the privilege. Just as the firm would undoubtedly use oil and electricity wastefully if they were obtainable at no charge, the firm will use "free" air wastefully, despoiling it with smoke far beyond the level that the public interest can justify. Rather than being at the (low) socially desirable level, the quantity of smoke will be at whatever (usually high) level is necessary to save as much money as possible for the firm that emits it, because the external damage caused by the smoke costs the firm nothing.

**EXTERNALITIES**

Externalities play a crucial role affecting the quality of life. They show why the market mechanism, which is so efficient in supplying consumers' goods, has a much poorer record in terms of its effects on the environment. The problem of pollution illustrates the importance of externalities for public policy and indicates why their analysis is one of our **12 Ideas for Beyond the Final Exam.**

## SUPPLY–DEMAND ANALYSIS OF ENVIRONMENTAL EXTERNALITIES

Basic supply–demand analysis can be used to explain both how externalities lead to environmental problems and how these problems can be cured. As an illustration, consider the damage that massive generation of garbage does to our environment.

Figure 21–3 shows a demand curve, *DE*, for garbage removal. As usual, this curve has a negative slope, meaning that if the price of garbage removal is raised, people will order less garbage removal. They may bring more waste to recycling centers, they may repair broken items rather than throwing them out, and so on.

The graph also shows the supply curve, *SS*, of an ideal market for garbage removal. As we saw in our analysis of competitive industries (Chapter 9), the position of the market's supply curve depends on the marginal cost of garbage removal. If suppliers had to pay the full costs of garbage removal—including the cost of the pollution caused when the garbage is burned at the dump—the supply curve would be comparably high (as drawn in the graph). For the community

Figure 21-3 **FREE DUMPING OF POLLUTANTS AS AN INDUCEMENT TO ENVIRONMENTAL DAMAGE**

Whether wastes are solid, liquid, or gaseous, they impose costs upon the community. If the emitter is not charged for the damage, it is as though the resulting wastes were removed with zero charges to the polluter (brown removal supply curve *TT*). The polluter is then induced to pollute a great deal (25 million tons in the figure). If the charges to the polluter reflect the true cost to the community (supply curve *SS* of waste removal), it would pay to emit a much smaller amount (10 million tons in the figure).

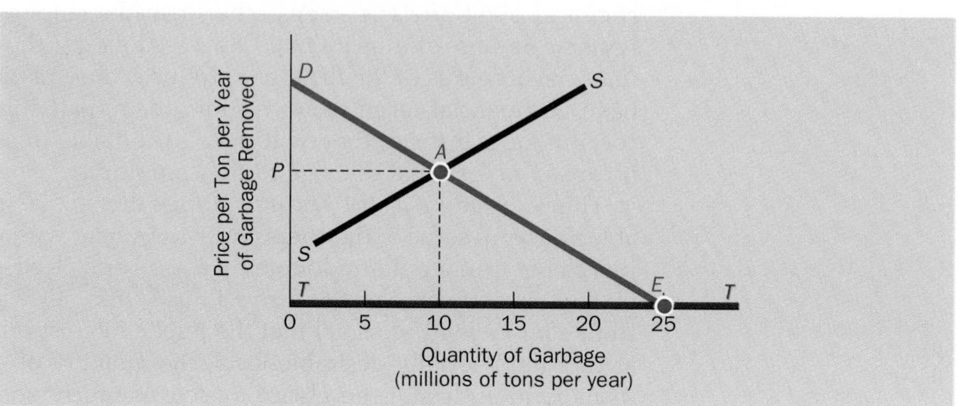


depicted in the graph, the price of garbage removal will be *P* dollars per ton, and 10 million tons will be generated (point *A*).

But what if the community's government decides to remove garbage "free"? Of course, the consumer still really pays through taxes, but not in a way that makes each person pay for the quantity of garbage that he or she produces. The result is that the supply curve is no longer *SS*. Rather it becomes the brown line *TT*, which lies along the horizontal axis, because any household can increase the garbage it throws away at no cost to itself. Now the intersection of the supply and demand curve is no longer point *A*. Rather it is point *E*, at which the price is zero, and the quantity of garbage generated is 25 million tons—a substantially greater amount.

Similar problems occur if the community offers the dissolved oxygen in its waterways and the purity of its atmosphere without charge. The amount that will be wasted and otherwise used up is likely to be enormously greater than it would be if users had to pay for the cost of their actions to society. That is a key reason for the severity of our environmental problems.

The magnitude of our pollution problem is attributable in large part to the fact that the market lets individuals, firms, and government agencies deplete such resources as oxygen in the water and pure air without charging them any money for using those resources.

It follows that one way of dealing with pollution problems is to charge those who emit pollution, and who despoil the environment in other ways, a price commensurate with the costs they impose on society.

## BASIC APPROACHES TO ENVIRONMENTAL POLICY

In broad terms, three general methods have been proposed for the control of activities that damage the environment.

1. **Voluntary programs**, such as nonmandatory investment in pollution control equipment by firms motivated by social responsibility, or voluntary recycling of solid wastes by consumers.
2. **Direct controls**, which either (a) impose legal ceilings on the amount any polluter is permitted to emit or (b) specify how particular activities must be carried on—for example, they may prohibit backyard incinerators, or the use of high-sulfur coal, or require smokestack "scrubbers" to capture emissions of electric-generating installations.
3. **Taxes on emissions**, or the use of other monetary incentives or penalties to make it unattractive financially for emitters of pollutants to continue to pollute as usual.

Each of these methods has a useful role. Let us consider each of them in turn.

### VOLUNTARISM

Voluntarism often has proved weak and unreliable. Voluntary programs for recycling of garbage have rarely managed to keep more than a small fraction of a community's wastes from the garbage dump. Some firms have shown good intentions and have made sincere attempts to adopt environmentally beneficial practices. Yet competition has usually prevented them from spending more than token amounts for this purpose. No business, whatever its virtues, can long afford to spend so much on good works that rivals can easily underprice them. As a result, voluntary business programs sometimes have been more helpful to the companies' public relations activities than to the environment. Firms with a real interest in environmental protection have called for legislation that *requires* all firms, including competitors, to undertake the same measures, thereby subjecting all firms in the industry to similar cost handicaps.

Yet voluntary measures do have their place. They are appropriate where surveillance and, consequently, enforcement is impractical, as in the prevention of littering by campers in isolated areas, where there is no alternative to an appeal to people's consciences. And in brief but serious emergencies, in which there is no time to plan and enact a systematic program, there also may be no good substitute for voluntary compliance. Several major cities have, for example, experienced episodes of temporary but dangerous concentrations of pollutants, forcing the authorities to appeal to the public to cut emissions drastically. The public response to appeals requiring cooperation for short periods often has been enthusiastic and gratifying, particularly when civic pride was a factor: for example, during the 1984 Summer Olympic Games, Los Angeles city officials asked motorists to carpool, businesses to stagger workhours, and truckers to restrict themselves to essential deliveries and to avoid rush hours. The result was an extraordinary decrease in traffic and smog, sufficient to enable the 6000-foot San Gabriel Mountains suddenly to become visible behind the city. To summarize:

Voluntary programs are not dependable ways to protect the environment. However, in brief, unexpected emergencies or where effective surveillance is impossible, the policymaker may have no other choice.

### DIRECT CONTROLS

Direct controls have been the chief instrument of environmental policy in the United States (the so-called "command and control" approach). The federal government, through the Environmental Protection Agency (EPA), formulates standards for air and water quality and requires state and local governments to adopt rules that will ensure achievement of those goals. Probably the best known of these are the standards for automobile emissions. New automobiles are required to pass tests showing that their emissions do not exceed specified amounts.

As another example, localities sometimes prohibit the use of particularly "dirty" fuels by industry or require the adoption of processes to "cleanse" those fuels. Typical of these programs are local ordinances regulating the type and sulfur content of the fuels used by power plants, factories, and other stationary sources of sulfur dioxide pollution.

### TAXES ON EMISSIONS

Most economists agree that a nearly exclusive reliance on direct controls is a mistake and that, in most cases, financial penalties on polluters can do the same job more dependably, effectively, and economically.

The most common suggestion is that firms be permitted to pollute all they want but be forced to pay a tax for the privilege, in order to make them *want* to pollute less. Under such a plan, the quantity of the polluter's emissions would be metered just like the use of electricity. At the end of the month the government would automatically send the polluter a bill charging a stipulated amount for each gallon of emissions (the amount would also vary with the quality of the emissions—a higher tax rate being imposed on emissions that were more dangerous or unpleasant). Thus, the more environmental damage done, the more the polluter would have to pay.

Such taxes are deliberately designed to *encourage* the use of a glaring tax loophole—the polluter *can* reduce the tax owed by polluting less. In terms of Figure 21–3, if the tax is used to increase the payment for waste emissions from zero (brown supply line *TT*) and instead forces the polluter to pay its true cost to society, emissions will automatically be reduced from 25 to 10 million tons.

Businesses do respond to such taxes. One widely publicized example is the Ruhr River basin in Germany, where emissions taxes have been used for more than three decades. Though the Ruhr is one of the world's most concentrated industrial centers, those of its rivers that are protected by taxes are sufficiently clean to be usable for fishing and other recreational purposes. Firms have also found it profitable to avoid taxes by extracting pollutants from their liquid discharges and recycling them. Almost 70 percent of the industrial acids used in the Ruhr have been recovered in this way.

## EMISSIONS TAXES VERSUS DIRECT CONTROLS

It is important to see why taxes on emissions may prove more effective and reliable than direct controls. Direct controls essentially rely on the enforcement mechanism of the criminal justice system. But the polluter who violates the rules must first be caught. Then the regulatory agency must decide whether it has enough evidence to prosecute. Next, it must win its case in court. And, finally, the court must impose a penalty strong enough to matter. If any *one* of these does not occur, the polluter gets away with the environmentally damaging activities.

## ENFORCEMENT ISSUES

The enforcement of direct controls requires vigilance and enthusiasm by the regulatory agency, which must assign the resources and persons needed to carry out the task of enforcement. In many cases the resources devoted to enforcement are pitifully small. Under the Reagan administration, environmental outlays were, indeed, cut severely, and the progress that was made in the 1970s nearly came to a standstill in the 1980s. The Bush administration produced a major new regulatory program in the form of the 1990 Clean Air Act Amendments, which require significant reductions in emissions that contribute to air pollution. The box on page 530 describes two components of the Amendments, which utilize various market incentives to induce polluters to cut their emissions. The administration of President Clinton came into office with the promise of much more attention to environmental matters and plans to devote considerably greater resources and human power to this area.

The effectiveness of direct controls also depends upon the speed and rigor of the courts. Yet the courts are often slow and lenient. An example is the notorious case of the Reserve Mining Company. More than a decade of litigation was required to stop this company from pouring its wastes (which contain asbestos-like fibers believed to cause cancer) into Lake Superior, the source of drinking water of a number of communities.

Finally, direct controls can work only if the legal system imposes significant penalties on violators. In a few cases, sizable penalties have been levied. For instance, in 1988 Ocean Spray Cranberries, Inc., was ordered to pay a $400,000 fine for water pollution violations, plus $100,000 for sewage equipment for the town of Middleboro, Massachusetts. But there are many more cases in which large firms have been convicted of polluting and fined less than $5000—an amount beneath the notice of even a relatively small corporation.

In contrast to all this, pollution taxes are automatic and certain. No one need be caught, prosecuted, convicted, and punished. The tax bills are just sent out automatically by the untiring tax collector. The only sure way for the polluter to avoid paying pollution charges is to pollute less.

## EFFICIENCY IN CLEAN UP

A second important difference between direct controls and taxes on emissions is the ability of the latter to do the job at a lower cost. Statistical estimates for several pollution control programs suggest that the cost of doing the job through direct controls can easily be twice as high as under the tax alternative. Why should there be such a difference? The answer is that under direct controls the job of cutting back emissions is usually *not* apportioned among the various polluters on the basis of ability to do it cheaply and efficiently.

Suppose it costs firm A only 3 cents a gallon to reduce emissions while firm B must spend 20 cents a gallon to do the same job. If both firms spew out 2000 gallons of pollution a day, a 50 percent reduction in pollution can be achieved by ordering both firms to limit emissions to 1000 gallons a day. This may or may not be fair, but it is certainly not efficient. The social cost will be 1000 times 3 cents, or \$30, to firm A and 1000 times 20 cents, or \$200, to firm B, a total of \$230. If, instead, a tax of 10 cents a gallon had been imposed, all the work would have been done by firm A—which can do it more cheaply. Firm A would have cut its emissions out altogether, paying the 3 cents a gallon this requires, to avoid the 10 cents a gallon tax. Firm B would go on polluting as before, because it is cheaper to pay the tax than the 20 cents a gallon it costs to control its pollution. In this way, under the tax, *total daily emissions will still be cut by 2000 gallons a day*. But the total daily cost of the program will therefore be \$60 (3 cents × 2000 gallons) instead of the \$230 it would cost under direct controls.

The secret of the efficiency induced by a tax on pollution is straightforward. Only polluters who can reduce emissions cheaply and efficiently can afford to take advantage of the built-in loophole—the opportunity to save on taxes by reducing emissions. The tax approach simply assigns the job to those who can do it most effectively—and rewards them by letting them escape the tax.

### ADVANTAGES AND DISADVANTAGES

Given all these advantages of the tax approach, why would anyone want to use direct controls?

There are three general and important situations in which direct controls have a clear advantage:

1. *Where an emission is so dangerous that it is decided to prohibit it altogether.*
2. *Where a sudden change in circumstances—for example, a dangerous air quality crisis—calls for prompt and substantial changes in conduct, such as temporary reductions in use of cars or incinerators.* It is difficult and clumsy to change tax rules, and direct controls will usually do a better job here. The mayor of a city threatened by a dangerous air-quality crisis can, for example, forbid the use of private passenger cars until the crisis passes.
3. *Where effective and dependable metering devices have not been invented or are prohibitively costly to install and operate.* In such cases there is no way to operate an effective tax program because the amount of wastes the polluter has emitted cannot be determined and so the tax bill cannot be calculated. In that case the only effective option may be a *requirement* to use "clean" fuel, or install emissions-purification equipment.

## OTHER FINANCIAL DEVICES TO PROTECT THE ENVIRONMENT: EMISSIONS PERMITS

The basic idea underlying the emissions-tax approach to environmental protection is that it provides financial incentives that induce polluters to reduce the damage they do to the environment. But emissions taxes are not the only form of financial inducement that has been proposed. There is at least one other that deserves consideration: the requirement of *emissions permits* for polluters, each permit authorizing the emission of a specified quantity of pollutant. Such permits would be offered for sale in limited quantities fixed by the authorities at prices set by demand and supply.

Under this arrangement, the environmental agency decides what quantity of emissions per unit of time (say, per month) is tolerable and then issues a batch of permits authorizing (altogether) just that amount of pollution. The permits are offered for sale to the highest bidders. Their price is therefore determined by demand and supply. It will be high if the number of permits offered for sale is small and there is a large amount of industrial activity that must use the permits. Similarly, the price of a permit will be low if many permits are issued but the quantity of pollution for which they are demanded is small.

The emissions permit in many ways works like a tax—it simply makes it too expensive for polluters to continue emitting as much as before. However, the permit approach has some advantages over taxes. For example, it reduces uncertainty about the quantity of pollution that will be emitted. Under a tax, we cannot be sure about this in advance, since that depends on the extent to which polluters respond to the tax rate that is selected. In the case of permits, a ceiling on emissions is simply decided in advance by the environmental authorities, who then issue permits authorizing just that quantity of emissions.

Many people react indignantly to the notion of "licenses to pollute." Yet the EPA has introduced some compromise measures that seem palatable politically and that can be regarded as approximations to a market in emissions permits (see the boxed insert on page 530).

## TWO CHEERS FOR THE MARKET

We have seen in the first part of this chapter that protecting the environment is one task that cannot be left to the free market: because of the important externalities involved, the market will systematically allocate too few resources to the job. However, this market failure does not imply that the price mechanism must be discarded. On the contrary, we have seen that a legislated market solution based on pollution charges may well be the best way to protect the environment. At least in this case, the power of the market mechanism can be harnessed to correct its own failings.

We turn now, in the second half of the chapter, to the case of natural resources, where the market mechanism also plays a crucial role.

# THE ECONOMICS OF ENERGY AND NATURAL RESOURCES

The "energy crisis" of the 1970s and early 1980s, during which prices of oil leaped dramatically, had profound effects throughout the world—one of which was a marked change in our attitudes about unlimited stocks of natural resources simply ours for the taking. Indeed, at that time there was near-panic about the prospect of running out of a number of commodities—from coffee and paper products to oil itself. One headline in a leading magazine asked, "Are we running out of *everything*?"

Natural resources have always been scarce, and they undoubtedly have been used wastefully. Nevertheless, we are *not* about to run out of the most vital

## Putting Ivory-Tower Theory to the Test in America: Market-Based Incentives to Protect the Environment

Economists have long advocated using the power of the free market to discipline polluters. Back in 1976, the U.S. Environmental Protection Agency gingerly stuck its toe into these uncharted waters when it began to experiment with a program of air pollution emissions trading. In the years since then the agency has, in a piecemeal fashion, incorporated into U.S. environmental policy a number of ideas from the economist's bag of tricks. Market-based programs have included:

- *netting*, which allows a company to create a new source of air pollution in its factory if it reduces emissions from another source within the same factory, thus effecting an internal trade of emissions;
- *offsets*, which allow new factories or other new sources of air pollution to be constructed in areas where pollution standards have not been met, so long as their emissions are more than offset by reductions in pollution from elsewhere (for example, firm A can open for business if it can induce firm B to adopt pollution controls that cut down B's emissions by an amount at least equal to A's proposed emissions);
- the *bubble* program, which is similar to the offsets program but applies to firms already in operation rather than to newly established plants or firms. Under the bubble concept, all operations of a firm are considered to be encased in an imaginary bubble with a single discharge point; the firm is permitted to satisfy the air pollution ceiling for its "bubble" in any way it finds most economical;
- *banking*, which permits firms whose total emissions fall below the required limits to sell the unused emission rights to other firms whose "bubbles" are not performing so well, or to store these extra rights in an emission reduction "bank" for future use or trade.

These elements of EPA's emissions trading program clearly did not amount to a true market in pollution trading. Very few of the pollution trades that have occurred have been between different firms (the vast majority were internal swaps within one firm), but the program has been an improvement on the strict command-and-control approach, and (according to one expert) ". . . afforded many firms flexibility in meeting emission limits . . . this flexibility has resulted in significant aggregate costs savings—in the billions of dollars."*

With the recent passage of the 1990 Amendments to the Clean Air Act we may finally see the real thing—a national market in pollution permits. The Amendments set out a tradable emissions permit system for achieving the stiff task of cutting sulfur dioxide emissions—the principal cause of acid rain—from electric power plants by 50 percent by 2000. Every power plant receives a number of tradable "allowances," each of which confers the right to release one ton of sulfur dioxide into the atmosphere. Each plant is then free to use, sell or buy allowances. Some may find an inexpensive way to reduce their $SO_2$ output below their allowances (freeing up some to sell to other firms, or to bank for the future), and others may find it cheaper to buy up allowances from other plants. This flexibility in the market for $SO_2$ allowances is reckoned to be able to save up to a third of the $5 billion that the command and control approach would cost each year.**

Another market-based innovation of the Clean Air Act Amendments, which may be particularly dear to the hearts of young drivers, is the proposed "Cash for Clunkers" program. Under this scheme a company which finds that a planned expansion in its industrial plant will increase its pollutant emissions over an existing EPA standard will be able to offset the increase by buying up "clunkers"—pre-1980 automobiles—in the same region and "putting them out to pasture." According to the EPA, these vehicles cause 53 percent of hydrocarbon and 61 percent of carbon monoxide emissions, even though they represent only 29 percent of registered vehicles.

*Robert W. Hahn, "Economic Prescriptions for Environmental Problems: How the Patient Followed the Doctor's Orders," *Journal of Economic Perspectives*, Vol. 3, No. 2, Spring 1989, page 101.** "Unshackling the Invisible Hand," *The Economist*, January 4, 1992, page 66.

resources. There is reason to be optimistic about the availability of substitutes, and many of the shortages of the 1970s can with some justice be ascribed as much to the folly of government programs as to imminent exhaustion of petroleum and other natural resources.

### A PUZZLE: THOSE RESILIENT RESOURCE SUPPLIES

It is a plain fact that the earth is endowed with only finite quantities of such vital resources as oil, copper, lead, and coal. This has elicited a parade of doomsday forecasts about the imminent exhaustion of one resource or another. The boxed insert on page 532 lists a number of bleak prophecies about oil production in the United States, all of which have proved far off the mark. And Table 21–1 depicts some equally mysterious estimates of known reserves of four important nonfuel minerals—aluminum, copper, iron, and lead. Reading this table, we see that the supplies of each of these minerals actually *grew* between 1950 and 1980, even though in the interim humankind had used up most of the reserves reported for 1950. Economic principles, as we will see at the end of this chapter, help a great deal in clearing up these mysteries.

## THE FREE MARKET AND PRICING OF DEPLETABLE RESOURCES

If figures on known reserves behave as peculiarly as those we have just seen, one begins to doubt their ability to measure whether we are really running out of certain natural resources. Is there another indicator that is more reliable? Most economists agree that there is—*the price of the resource.*

As a resource becomes scarcer, we expect its price to rise for several reasons. One is that for most resources the process of depletion is not simply a matter of gradually using up the supply of a homogeneous product, every unit of which is equally available. Rather, the most accessible and highest quality deposits of the resource are generally used up first, then industry turns to less accessible supplies that are more costly to get at and/or deposits of lower purity or quality. Oil is a clear example. First, Americans relied primarily on the most easily found domestic oil. Then they turned to imports from the Middle East with their higher

**Table 21–1** WORLD RESERVES OF ALUMINUM, COPPER, IRON, AND LEAD: 1950 AND 1980 (millions of metric tons of metal content)

| MINERAL | 1950 RESERVES | CONSUMPTION 1950–1980 | 1980 RESERVES |
|---|---|---|---|
| Aluminum | 1,400 | 1,346 | 5,200 |
| Copper | 100 | 156 | 494 |
| Iron | 19,000 | 11,040 | 93,466 |
| Lead | 40 | 85 | 127 |

SOURCE: Robert Repetto, "Population, Resources, Environment: An Uncertain Future," *Population Bureau*, Vol. 42, No. 2, Washington, D.C.: Population Reference Bureau, Inc., July 1987, p. 23, who cites William Vogeley, "Nonfuel Minerals and the World Economy," in Repetto, Robert, Ed., *The Global Possible: Resources, Development, and the New Century*, New Haven: Yale University Press, 1985.

## The Permanent Fuel Crisis

Humanity has a long history of panicking about the imminent exhaustion of natural resources. In the thirteenth century a large part of Europe's forests was cut down, primarily for use in metal-working (much of it for armor). Wood prices rose, and there was a good deal of talk about depletion of fuel stocks. People have been doing it ever since, as the following cases illustrate.

**PAST PETROLEUM PROPHECIES (and Realities)**

| DATE | U.S. OIL PRODUCTION RATE (billion barrels/year) | PROPHECY | REALITY |
|---|---|---|---|
| 1866 | 0.005 | Synthetics available if oil production should end (U.S. Revenue Commission). | In next 82 years, the U.S. produced 37 billion barrels with no need for synthetics. |
| 1891 | 0.05 | Little or no chance for oil in Kansas or Texas (U.S. Geological Survey). | 14 billion barrels produced in these two states since 1891. |
| 1914 | 0.27 | Total future production only 5.7 billion barrels. (Official of U.S. Bureau of Mines). | 34 billion barrels produced since 1914 or six times this prediction. |
| 1920 | 0.45 | U.S. needs foreign oil and synthetics: peak domestic production almost reached (Director of U.S. Geological Survey) | 1948 U.S. production in excess of U.S. consumption and more than four times 1920 output. |
| 1939 | 1.3 | U.S. oil supplies will last only 13 years (Radio Broadcasts by Interior Department). | New oil found since 1939 exceeds the 13 years' supply known at that time. |
| 1947 | 1.9 | Sufficient oil cannot be found in United States (Chief of Petroleum Division, State Department). | 4.3 billion barrels found in 1948, the largest volume in history and twice our consumption. |
| 1949 | 2.0 | End of U.S. oil supply almost in sight (Secretary of the Interior). | Recent industry shows ability to increase U.S. production by more than a million barrels daily in the next 5 years. |

SOURCE: William M. Brown, "The Outlook for Future Petroleum Supplies," in Julian L. Simon and Herman Kahn, eds., *The Resourceful Earth: A Response to Global 2000* (Oxford, England: Basil Blackwell Publishers Ltd., 1984), p. 362, who cites Presidential Energy Program, Hearings Before the Subcommittee on Energy and Power of the Committee on Interstate and Foreign Commerce, House of Representatives. First session on the implication of the President's proposals in the Energy Independence Act of 1975, Serial No. 94–20, p. 643. 17, 18, 20, and 21 February, 1975.

transport costs. At that point it was not yet profitable to embark on the dangerous and extremely costly process of bringing up oil from the floor of the North Sea. We know that the United States still possesses tremendous stocks of petroleum embedded in shale (rock), but so far this has been too difficult and, therefore, too costly to get at.

Increasing scarcity of a resource such as oil is not usually a matter of imminent and total disappearance. Rather, it takes the form of exhaustion of the most accessible and cheapest sources so that new supplies become more costly.

Growing scarcity also raises resource prices for the usual supply-demand reason. As we know, goods in short supply tend to become more expensive. To see just how this works out for natural resources, imagine a mythical mineral, Zipthon, all of identical quality, which can be extracted and delivered to market with negligible extraction and transportation costs. How quickly will the reserves of Zipthon be used up, and what will happen to its price with the passage of time?

If the market for Zipthon is perfectly competitive, we can provide remarkably concrete answers, discovered by the American economist Harold Hotelling. They tell us that as long as the supply of Zipthon lasts, its price must rise at a rate equal to the prevailing rate of interest. That is, if in 1989 the price of Zipthon is $100 per ounce and the interest rate is 10 percent, then its price in 1990 must be $110.

Under perfect competition, the price of a depletable resource whose costs of transportation and extraction are negligible must rise at the rate of interest. If the rate of interest is 10 percent, the price of the resource must rise 10 percent every year.

Why is this so? The answer is simple. People who are considering tying up money in inventories of Zipthon must earn exactly as much per dollar of investment as they would by putting their money into, say, a government bond. For suppose instead that $100 invested in bonds would next year rise in value to $112, while $100 in Zipthon would grow only to $110, and suppose the two were equally risky. What would happen? Investors would obviously find it unprofitable to buy the Zipthon and would put their money into bonds instead.

But because Zipthon resources lack people willing to invest in them, its *current* price will fall. Now the Zipthon that will be worth $110 in one year will cost less than $100 today. This fall in current price will continue until the return on a dollar invested in Zipthon will equal the return per dollar invested in bonds—the interest rate.

The same process, working in reverse, would apply if Zipthon prices were rising faster than the rate of interest. Investors would switch from bonds to Zipthon, and current prices of Zipthon would rise.

This fundamental principle tells us what will happen to the price of $100 worth of Zipthon over, say, four years:

| INITIAL DATE | ONE YEAR LATER | TWO YEARS LATER | THREE YEARS LATER | FOUR YEARS LATER |
|---|---|---|---|---|
| $100 | $110 | $121 | $133.10 | $146.41 |

These prices follow from the fact that $110 is 10 percent higher than $100, $121 is 10 percent higher than $110, and so on. Note that, because of compounding, the dollar price grows greater each year. Zipthon price rises $10 in the first year, $11 in the second year, $12.10 in the third, $13.31 in the fourth, and so on indefinitely.

The basic law of pricing of a depletable resource tells us that as its stocks are used up, its price in a perfectly competitive market will rise every year by greater and greater dollar amounts.

*Figure* **21–4** **CONSUMPTION OVER TIME OF A DEPLETABLE RESOURCE**

The price of the resource must rise year after year (from $100 to $110 to $121, and so on). If the demand curve does not shift [part (a)], quantity demanded will be reduced every year. Even if the demand curve does shift outward [as in part (b)], the increasing price will keep any rise in quantity demanded lower than it would otherwise have been.

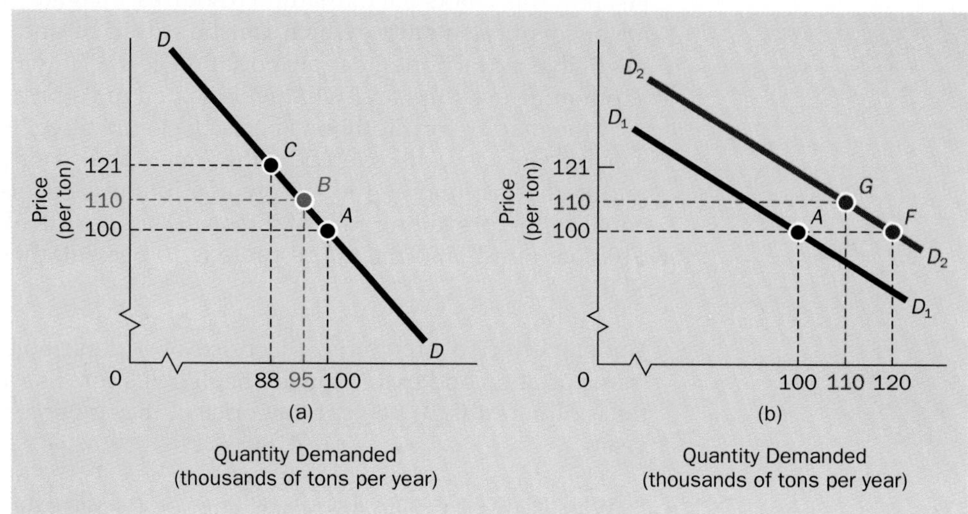


Notice that we can make these predictions about the price of Zipthon without any knowledge about the supply of Zipthon or consumer demand for it. This is really remarkable. But if we want to determine what will happen to the consumption of Zipthon—the rate at which it will be used up—we do need to know something about supply and demand.

Figure 21–4(a) is a demand curve for Zipthon, *DD*, which shows the amount people want to use up *per year* at various price levels. On the vertical axis, we show how the price must rise from year to year in the pattern we have just calculated—from $100 per ton in the initial year to $110 in the next year, and so on. Because of the negative slope of the demand curve, it follows that each year consumption of Zipthon will fall. That is, *if there is no shift in the demand curve*, consumption will fall from 100,000 tons initially to 95,000 tons in the next year, and so on.

But in reality such demand curves rarely stay still. As the economy grows and population and incomes increase, demand curves shift outward, and this has probably been true for most scarce resources. Such shifts in the demand curve will offset at least part of the reduction in quantity demanded that results from rising prices. Nevertheless, it remains true that rising prices do cut consumption growth relative to what it would have been if price had remained constant. In Figure 21–4(b) we depict an outward shift in demand from curve $D_1D_1$ in the initial period to curve $D_2D_2$ a year later. If price had remained constant at the initial value, $100 per ton, quantity consumed per year would have risen from 100,000 tons to 120,000 tons. But since, in accord with the basic principle, price must rise to $110, quantity demanded will only increase to 110,000 tons—which is smaller than 120,000 tons. Thus, whether or not the demand curve shifts, we conclude:

The ever-rising prices that accompany increasing scarcity of a depletable resource discourage consumption (encourage conservation). Even if quantity demanded is growing, it will grow less rapidly than if prices were not rising.

## RESOURCE PRICES IN THE TWENTIETH CENTURY

How do the facts match up with this theoretical analysis? As we will see now, their correspondence is very poor indeed. Figure 21–5 shows the behavior of the prices of three critical metals—lead, zinc, and tin—since the beginning of the twentieth century. These figures are all expressed in real terms—in dollars of constant purchasing power—to eliminate the effects of inflation or deflation.

What we find is that instead of rising steadily, as the theory might have led us to expect, two of them actually remained amazingly constant. Between 1900 and 1940 lead and zinc prices actually rose more slowly than the general price level, while tin prices just about kept pace with general inflation between 1900 and 1945. During the 1960s and 1970s the price of tin went up substantially faster than other prices, but by 1990 had returned to its level of the early 1960s. But even during the 1970s and 1980s, zinc and lead prices rose only slightly faster than prices in general.

Figure 21–6 shows the relative real price of crude oil in the United States since 1949. It gives price at the wellhead, that is, at the point of production, with no transportation cost included. The data show that in 1973 the price of oil was actually about 25 percent lower, relative to other prices, than it was in 1949. Only from 1973 to 1981 did it rise faster than prices in general; by the mid-1980s, the price of oil had fallen most of the way back to its real price in 1973.

How does one explain this strange behavior of the prices of finite resources, which surely are being used up, even if only gradually? While many things can

**Figure 21–5** PRICES OF LEAD, ZINC, AND TIN, 1900–1990, IN 1967 CENTS*

Note that these real prices have not been rising steadily even though all three minerals are gradually being used up.

SOURCE: *Historical Statistics of the U.S., Metal Statistics,* 1981 (American Metal Market, Fairchild Publications), and U.S. Bureau of the Census, *Statistical Abstract of the United States,* various issues.

*As deflated by the producer price index (all commodities).

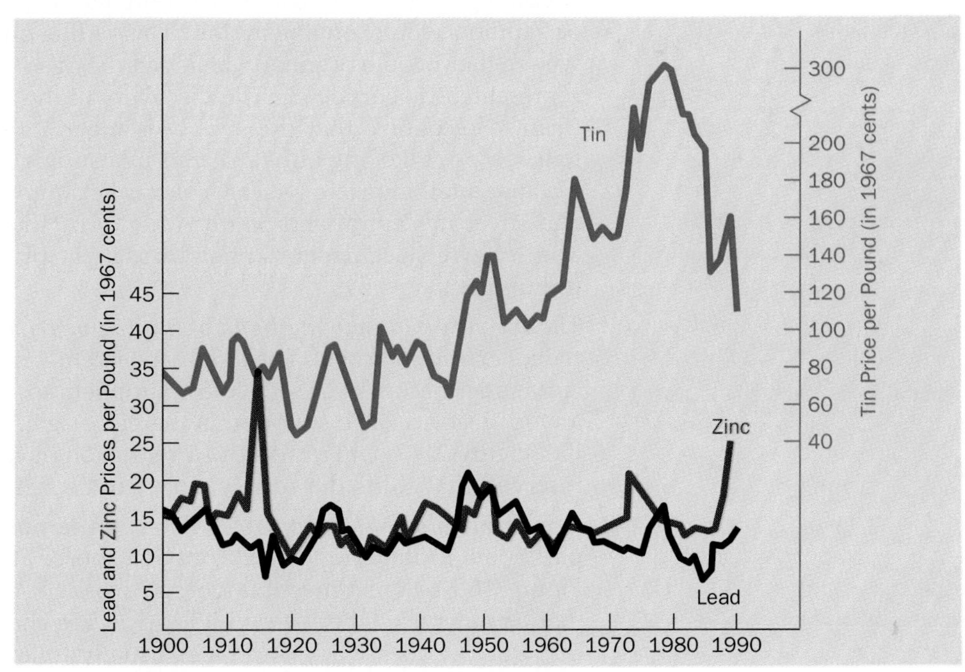

Figure 21-6 **PRICE OF DOMESTIC OIL AT THE WELLHEAD, 1949–1992, IN 1982 DOLLARS***

Note the long period of near constancy in real oil prices.

SOURCE: U.S. Department of Energy, Energy Information Administration, *Annual Energy Review*, various years and *Monthly Energy Review*, various issues.

*As deflated with implicit GNP price deflators.

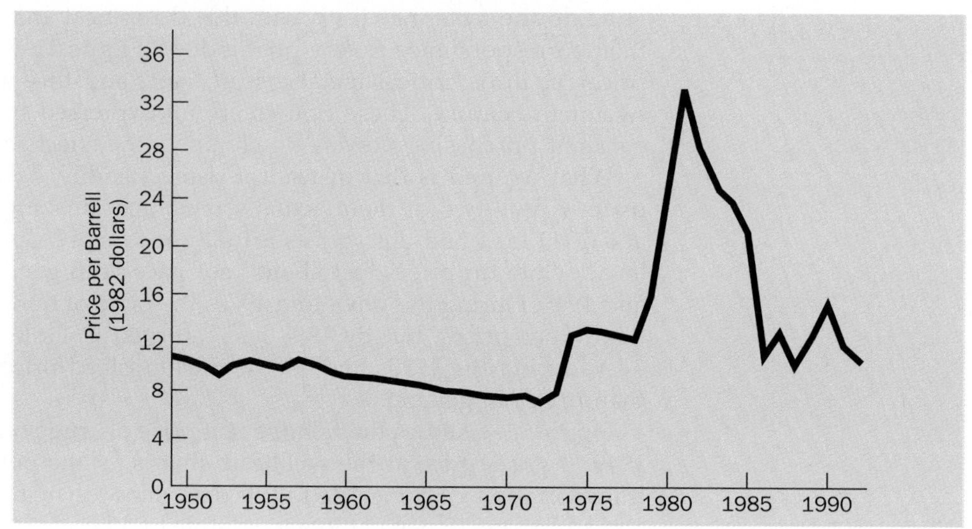


interfere with the price patterns that the theory leads us to expect, we will mention only three:

1. ***Unexpected discoveries of reserves whose existence was previously not suspected.*** If we were to stumble upon a huge and easily accessible reserve of Zipthon, which would come as a complete surprise to the market, the price of Zipthon would obviously fall. This is illustrated in Figure 21–7, where we see that people originally believed the available supply curve to be that represented by curve $S_1S_1$. The discovery of the new Zipthon reserves leads them to recognize that the supply is much larger than they had thought (curve $S_2S_2$). Like any outward shift in a supply curve, this can be expected to cause a fall in price. A clear historical example was the discovery of gold and silver in Central and South America by the Spaniards in the sixteenth century, which led to substantial drops in the prices of these precious metals in Europe.
2. ***The invention of new methods of mining or refining that may significantly reduce extraction costs.*** This, too, can lead to a rightward shift in the supply curve as it becomes profitable for suppliers to deliver a larger quantity at any given price. The situation is therefore again represented by a diagram like Figure 21–7. Only it is now a reduction in cost, not a new discovery of reserves, that shifts the supply curve to the right.
3. ***Price controls that hold prices down or decrease them.*** A legislature can pass a law prohibiting the sale of the resource at a price higher than $P^*$ (see Figure 21–8). Sometimes this doesn't work; in many cases an illegal black market emerges, where very high prices are charged more or less secretly. But when it does work, shortages usually follow. Since the objective is to make the legal ceiling price, $P^*$, lower than the market equilibrium price, $P$, at price $P^*$ quantity demanded (five million tons in the figure) will be higher

Figure 21-7 **PRICE EFFECTS OF A DISCOVERY OF ADDITIONAL RESERVES**

A discovery causes a rightward shift in the supply curve of the resource. That is so because the cost to suppliers of any given quantity of the resource is reduced by the discovery, so it will pay them to supply a larger quantity at any given price. This must lead to a price fall (from $P_1$ to $P_2$).

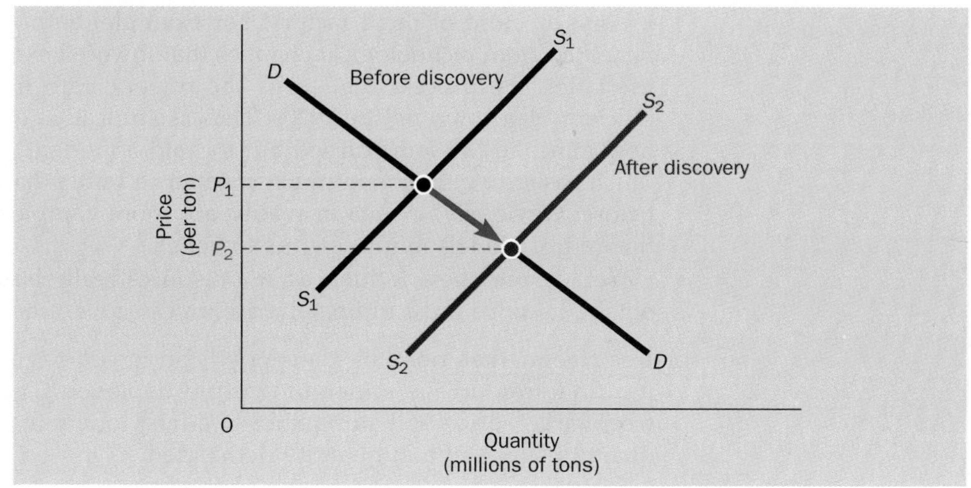


than the free-market level (four million tons). Similarly, we may expect quantity supplied (two million tons in the figure) to be less than its free-market level. Thus, as always happens in these cases, quantity supplied is less than quantity demanded—a shortage.

Many economists believe that this is exactly what happened after 1971 when President Nixon decided to experiment with price controls. It was then that the economy experienced a plague of shortages, and we seemed to be "running out

Figure 21-8 **CONTROLS ON THE PRICE OF A RESOURCE**

By law, price is kept to $P^*$, which is below the equilibrium price, $P$. This reduces quantity supplied from four to two million tons and raises quantity demanded from four to five million tons. A shortage measured by length AB, or three million tons, is the result.

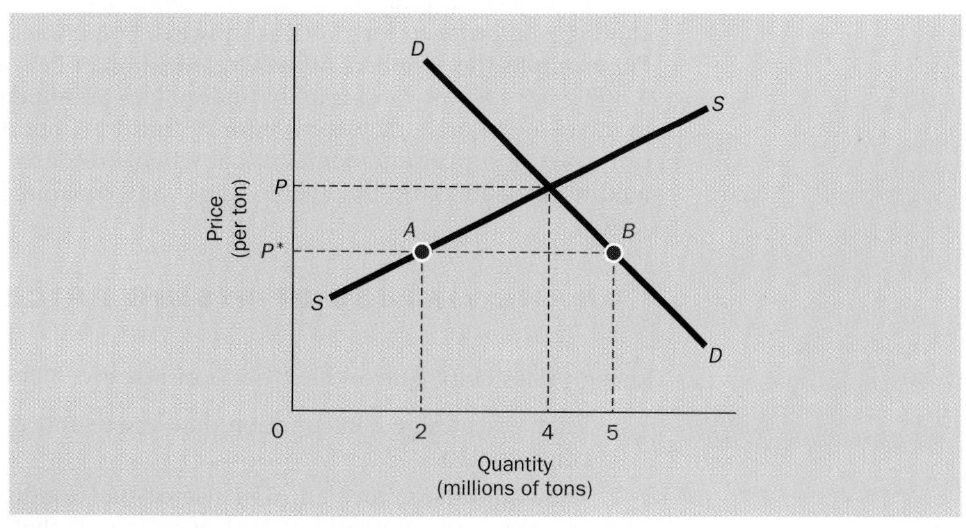

of nearly everything." And after price controls ended in 1974, most of the shortages disappeared.

Each of the examples of minerals whose prices did not rise can be explained by one or more of these factors. For example, both zinc and magnesium have benefited from technological changes that lowered extraction costs. In the case of the latter, the process that turns the mineral into ingots has grown far more efficient than it was in the 1920s. The case of lead is quite different. There, some new mines in Missouri turned out to hold abundant quantities of ore that were much easier to extract and much cheaper to refine than what had been available before. Obviously, events in reality are more complex than a naïve reading of theoretical models might lead us to believe.

Yet, despite these influences, if a resource really becomes scarce and costly to obtain, its price must ultimately rise unless government interferes. Moreover:

In a free market, quantity demanded can never exceed quantity supplied, even if a finite resource is undergoing rapid depletion. The reason is simple: in any free market, price will automatically adjust to eliminate any difference between quantity supplied and quantity demanded.

In theory, any shortage—any excess of quantity demanded over quantity supplied—must be artificial, ascribable to a decision to prevent the price mechanism from doing its job.

To say that the cause is artificial, of course, does not settle the basic issue—whether freedom of price adjustments is desirable when resources are scarce, or whether interference with the pricing process is justified.

There are many economists who believe that this is another of those cases in which the disease—shortages and the resulting dislocations in the economy—is far worse than the cure—deregulation of prices. They hold that the general public is misguided in its clamor against the rising prices that must ultimately accompany depletion of a resource, and that people are mistaken in regarding these price rises as the problem, when in fact they are part of the (rather painful) cure.

It is, of course, easy to understand why no consumer loves a price rise. And it is also easy to understand why many consumers ascribe any such price rise to a plot—to a conspiracy by greedy suppliers who somehow deliberately arrange shortages in order to force prices upward. Sometimes, this view is even correct. For example, the members of the Organization of Petroleum Exporting Countries (OPEC) have openly and frankly undertaken to influence the flow of oil in order to increase the price they receive for it. But it is important to recognize from the principles of supply and demand that when a resource grows scarce its price will tend to rise automatically, even without any conspiracies or plots.

## ON THE VIRTUES OF RISING PRICES

Rising prices help control the process of resource depletion in three basic ways:

1. They discourage consumption and waste and provide an inducement for conservation.
2. They stimulate more efficient use of the resource by industry, providing incentives for the employment of processes that are more sparing in their use of the resource or that use substitute resources.

3. They encourage innovation—the discovery of other, more abundant resources that can do the job and of new techniques that permit these other resources to be used economically.

Let us examine each of these a bit more carefully.

It used to be said that consumer demand for oil was highly *inelastic*—that prices would never make a significant dent in consumption of petroleum—but events proved otherwise. In response to the sharply rising fuel prices of the 1970s, people began to insulate their homes, keep home temperatures lower, take fewer shopping trips, and buy smaller automobiles. All of this had striking results: between 1960 and 1973, U.S. demand for oil increased by over 75 percent, but between 1973 and 1985, demand actually declined by about 10 percent.[5] Strong economic growth and stable oil prices during the last part of the 1980s pushed demand back up, but the galloping increases in energy use that characterized the pre-energy crisis era have not recurred.

The second way in which a price increase helps to conserve a scarce resource is by inducing the firm to economize on its use of a resource. It can use more fuel-efficient means of transportation and more insulation. It can locate its new plants in ways that reduce the need for transportation. And it can substitute labor and other inputs for scarce resources. Pick and shovel methods employ more labor to save the fuel that might have been used by a bulldozer.

Finally, rising prices help to slow the disappearance of a resource by stimulating the production of substitutes and even by inducing more production of the resource itself. The last statement is paradoxical: If a resource is finite, how can more be produced? Of course, it cannot. But rising prices will make it feasible to use repositories of the resource that otherwise would have been considered too inaccessible and simply not worth the effort. In times of high oil prices it has proved profitable, for example, to reopen abandoned oil wells and to use expensive procedures to force out substantial amounts of petroleum that will not flow out unaided.

And higher prices of the vanishing resource also stimulate research and development that yields substitute products. Only high oil prices may be able to transform solar power, wind, and biomass into viable sources of energy.

Freedom of pricing of a dwindling resource induces conservation by consumers and by industry, and it encourages the introduction of substitute products.

## GROWING RESERVES OF EXHAUSTIBLE RESOURCES: OUR PUZZLE REVISITED

In Table 21–1, page 531) we saw, strangely enough, that between 1950 and 1980 the reserves of aluminum, copper, iron, and lead actually increased! This paradox has a straightforward economic explanation: rising reserves are a tribute to the success of exploration activity that took place in the meantime. Minerals are not discovered by accident. It entails costly work requiring geologists and engineers and expensive machinery. Industry does not find it worth spending this money when reserves are high and when mineral prices are low.

Over the course of the twentieth century every time some mineral's known reserves fell and its price tended to rise, exploration increased until the decline

[5]Dermot Gateley, "Lessons from the 1986 Oil Price Collapse," *Brookings Papers on Economic Activity* 2: 1986, pp. 269–70.

was offset. The law of supply and demand worked. In the 1970s, for example, the rising price of oil led to very substantial increases in oil exploration, which helped to build up reserves. While, to protect ourselves from OPEC, it may not be wise for us to *consume* more oil from American sources, it certainly does seem prudent for us to increase our reserves through exploration. Increased profitability of exploration is perhaps the most effective way to get that done.

## *Summary*

1. Pollution is as old as human history; and contrary to some popular notions, some forms of pollution were actually decreasing even before government programs were initiated to protect the environment.
2. Both planned and market economies suffer from substantial environmental problems.
3. The production of commodities *must* cause waste disposal problems unless everything is recycled, but even recycling processes cause pollution (and use up energy).
4. Industrial activity causes environmental damage, but so does the activity of private individuals (as when they drive cars that emit pollutants). Government agencies also damage the environment (as when military airplanes emit noise and exhaust, or a hydroelectric project floods large areas).
5. Pollution is an **externality**—when a factory emits smoke, it dirties laundry and may damage the health of persons who neither work for the smoking factory nor buy its products. Hence, pollution control cannot be left to the free market. This is another of our **12 Ideas for Beyond the Final Exam**.
6. Pollution can be controlled by voluntary programs, **direct controls**, **taxes on emissions**, or other monetary incentives for the reduction of emissions.
7. Most economists believe that the monetary incentives approach is the most efficient and effective way to control detrimental externalities.
8. The quantity demanded of a scarce resource can exceed the quantity supplied only if something prevents the market mechanism from operating freely.
9. As a resource grows scarce on a free market, its price will rise, inducing increased conservation by consumers, increased exploration for new reserves, and increased substitution of other items that can serve the same purpose.
10. In fact, in the twentieth century the relative prices of many resources have remained roughly constant, largely because of the discovery of new reserves and because of cost-saving innovations.
11. The price mechanism and **rationing** are the only known alternatives to chaos in the allocation of scarce resources.
12. In the 1970s, **OPEC** succeeded in raising the relative price of petroleum, but the rise in price led to a substantial decline in world demand as well as to an increase in production in countries outside OPEC.
13. **Known reserves** of depletable scarce resources have not tended to fall with the passage of time because, as the price of the resource rises with increasing scarcity, increased exploration for new reserves becomes profitable.

## *Key Concepts and Terms*

Externality
Direct controls
Pollution charges (taxes on emissions)
Subsidies for reduced emissions
Emissions permits
Known reserves
Organization of Petroleum Exporting Countries (OPEC)
Rationing
Paradox of growing reserves of finite resources

## *Questions for Review*

1. What sorts of pollution problems would you expect in a small African village? In a city in India? In communist China? In New York City?
2. Suppose you are assigned the task of drafting a law to impose a tax on the emission of smoke. What provisions would you put into the law?
   a. How would you decide the size of the tax?
   b. What would you do about smoke emitted by a municipal electricity plant?
   c. Would you use the same tax rate in densely and sparsely settled areas?

   What information will you need to collect before determining what you would do about each of the preceding provisions?
3. Production of commodity X creates 10 pounds of emissions for every unit of X produced. The demand and supply curves for X are described by the following table:

| **PRICE (DOLLARS)** | **10** | **9** | **8** | **7** | **6** | **5** |
|---|---|---|---|---|---|---|
| Quantity demanded | 80 | 85 | 90 | 95 | 100 | 105 |
| Quantity supplied | 100 | 95 | 90 | 85 | 80 | 75 |

   What is the equilibrium price and quantity, and how much pollution will be emitted?
4. If the price of X to consumers is $9, and the government imposes a tax of $2 per unit, show that because suppliers get only $7, they will produce only 85 units of output, not the 95 units of output they would produce if they received the full $9 per unit.
5. Show that, with this tax, the equilibrium price is $9, and the equilibrium quantity demanded is 85. How much pollution will now be emitted?
6. Compare your answers to Questions 3 and 5 and show how large a reduction in pollution emissions occurs because of the $2 tax on the polluting output.
7. Discuss some valid and some invalid objections against letting rising prices eliminate shortages of supplies of scarce resources.
8. Describe what must be done by a government agency that is given the job of rationing a scarce resource.
9. Some observers believe that a program of rationing may work fairly satisfactorily for a few months or for one or two years, particularly during an emergency period when patriotic spirit is strong. However, they believe that over longer periods and when there is no upsurge of patriotism it is likely to prove far less satisfactory. Do you agree or disagree? Why?
10. Why may a rise in the price of fuel lead to more conservation after several years have passed than it does in the months following the price increase? What does your answer imply about the relative size of the long-run elasticity of demand for fuel and its short-run elasticity?

# PART VI

# The Macro-Economy: Aggregate Supply and Demand

Chapter 22

# THE REALM OF MACROECONOMICS

*Where the telescope ends, the microscope begins. Which of the two has the grander view?*

VICTOR HUGO

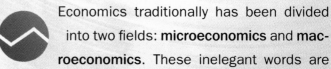

Economics traditionally has been divided into two fields: **microeconomics** and **macroeconomics**. These inelegant words are derived from the Greek, where "micro" means something small and "macro" means something large. This chapter introduces you to macroeconomics. ¶ We begin the chapter by exploring the dividing line between microeconomics and macroeconomics: How do the two branches of the discipline differ and why? Next, we stress that while the *questions* studied by macroeconomists differ from those addressed by microeconomists, the underlying *tools* each group uses are almost the same. Supply and demand provide the basic organizing framework for constructing macroeconomic models, just as they do for microeconomic models. Third, we define some important macroeconomic concepts, such as recession, inflation, and gross domestic product. Fourth, we look briefly at the broad sweep of American economic history to get some idea of the prevalence and seriousness of the macroeconomic problems of recession and inflation. And, finally, we preview what is to come in subsequent chapters by introducing the notion of government management of the economy.

# DRAWING A LINE BETWEEN MACROECONOMICS AND MICROECONOMICS

In microeconomics *we study the behavior of individual decision-making units.* The chicken farmers and other businesses of Parts 2–5 were all individual decision-making units; so were the consumers who purchased chicken and other commodities. How do they decide what courses of action are in their own best interests? How are these millions of decisions coordinated by the market mechanism, and with what consequences? Questions like these are the substance of microeconomics and were taken up in Parts 2 through 5.

Although Plato and Aristotle might wince at the abuse of their language, microeconomics applies to the decisions of some astonishingly large units. Exxon and the American Telephone and Telegraph Company, for instance, have annual sales that exceed the total production of many nations. Yet someone who studies the pricing policies of AT&T is a microeconomist, whereas someone who studies inflation in Trinidad–Tobago is a macroeconomist. So the micro versus macro distinction in economics is certainly not based solely on size. What, then, is the basis for this time-honored distinction? Whereas microeconomics focuses on the decisions of individual units (no matter how large), *macroeconomics concentrates on the behavior of entire economies* (no matter how small). Rather than looking at the price and output decisions of a single company, macroeconomists study the overall price level, unemployment rate, and other things that we call *economic aggregates.*

## AGGREGATION AND MACROECONOMICS

An "economic aggregate" is nothing but an *abstraction* that people find convenient in describing some salient feature of economic life. For example, while we observe the prices of butter, telephone calls, and movie tickets every day, we never observe "the price level." Yet many people (not just economists) find it both meaningful and natural to speak of "the cost of living"—so natural, in fact, that the government's monthly attempts at measuring it are widely publicized by the news media.

Among the most important of these abstract notions is the concept of *domestic product*, which represents the total production of a nation's economy. The process by which real objects like hairpins, baseballs, and theater tickets get combined into an abstraction called total domestic product is called **aggregation**, and it is one of the foundations of macroeconomics. We can illustrate it by a simple example.

**AGGREGATION** means combining many individual markets into one overall market.

Imagine a nation called Agraria, whose economy is far simpler than the U.S. economy: Business firms in Agraria produce nothing but foodstuffs to sell to consumers. Rather than deal separately with all the markets for pizzas, candy bars, hamburgers, and so on, macroeconomists group them all into a single abstract "market for output." Thus, when macroeconomists in Agraria announce that output in Agraria rose 10 percent this year, are they referring to more potatoes or hot dogs, more soybeans or green peppers? The answer is: They do not care. In the aggregate measures of macroeconomics, output is output, no matter what form it takes.

Amalgamating many markets into one means that distinctions among different products are ignored. Can we really believe that no one cares whether the national output of Agraria consists of $800,000 worth of pickles and $200,000 worth of ravioli rather than $500,000 each of lettuce and tomatoes? Surely this is too much to swallow! Macroeconomists certainly do not believe that no one cares; instead, they rest the case for aggregation on two foundations.

1. While the *composition* of demand and supply in the various markets may be terribly interesting and important for *some* purposes (such as how income is distributed and what kinds of diets the citizens enjoy or endure), it may be of little consequence for the economy-wide issues of inflation and unemployment—the issues that concern macroeconomists.
2. During economic fluctuations, markets tend to move in unison. When demand in the economy rises, there is more demand for potatoes *and* tomatoes, more demand for artichokes *and* pickles, more demand for ravioli *and* hot dogs.

Though there are exceptions to these two principles, both seem serviceable enough as approximations. In fact, if they were not, there would be no discipline called macroeconomics, and this book would be only half as long as it is. Lest this cause you a twinge of regret, bear in mind that many people feel that unemployment and inflation would be far more difficult to control without macroeconomics—which would be even more regrettable.

## THE LINE OF DEMARCATION REVISITED

These two principles—that markets normally move together and that the composition of demand and supply may be unimportant for some purposes—enable us to draw a different kind of dividing line between the territories of microeconomics and macroeconomics.

In macroeconomics, we typically assume that most details of resource allocation and income distribution are of secondary importance to the study of the overall rates of inflation and unemployment.

In microeconomics, we typically ignore inflation and unemployment and focus instead on how individual markets allocate resources and distribute income.

To use a well-worn metaphor, the macroeconomist analyzes the determination of the size of the economic "pie," paying scant attention to what is inside it or to how it gets divided among the dinner guests. A microeconomist, on the other hand, assumes that the pie is of the right size and shape, and frets over its ingredients and its division. If you have ever baked or eaten a pie, you will realize that either approach alone is a trifle myopic.

In some chapters of this book (especially in Parts 6 and 7), macroeconomic issues are discussed as if they could be divorced from questions of resource allocation and income distribution. In other chapters (especially those in Parts 2 through 5), microeconomic problems are investigated with scarcely a word about overall inflation and unemployment. Only in certain sections of the book (especially Parts 8 and 9) are the two modes of analysis brought to bear simultaneously on the same social problems. This is done solely for the sake of pedagogical clarity. In reality, the crucial interconnection between macroeconomics and microeconomics is with us all the time. There is, after all, only one economy.

## SUPPLY AND DEMAND IN MACROECONOMICS

Some students reading this book will be taking a course that concentrates on macroeconomics while others will be studying microeconomics. The discussion of supply and demand in Chapter 4 serves as an invaluable introduction to both fields because the basic apparatus of supply and demand is just as fundamental to macroeconomics as it is to microeconomics.

Figure 22–1 shows two diagrams that should look familiar from Chapter 4. In Figure 22–1(a), there is a downward-sloping demand curve, labeled *DD*, and an upward-sloping supply curve, labeled *SS*. The axes labeled "Price" and "Quantity" do not specify what commodity they refer to because this is a multipurpose diagram. To start on familiar terrain, first imagine that this is a picture of the market for milk, so the price axis measures the price of milk while the quantity axis measures the quantity of milk demanded and supplied. As we know, if there are no interferences with the operation of a free market, equilibrium will be at point *E* with a price $P_0$ and a quantity of output $Q_0$.

Next, suppose something happens to shift the demand curve outward. For example, we learned in Chapter 4 that an increase in consumer incomes might have this effect. Figure 22–1(b) shows this shift as a rightward movement of the demand curve from $D_0D_0$ to $D_1D_1$. Equilibrium shifts from *E* to *A*, so both price and output rise.

**Figure 22–1 TWO INTERPRETATIONS OF A SHIFT IN THE DEMAND CURVE**

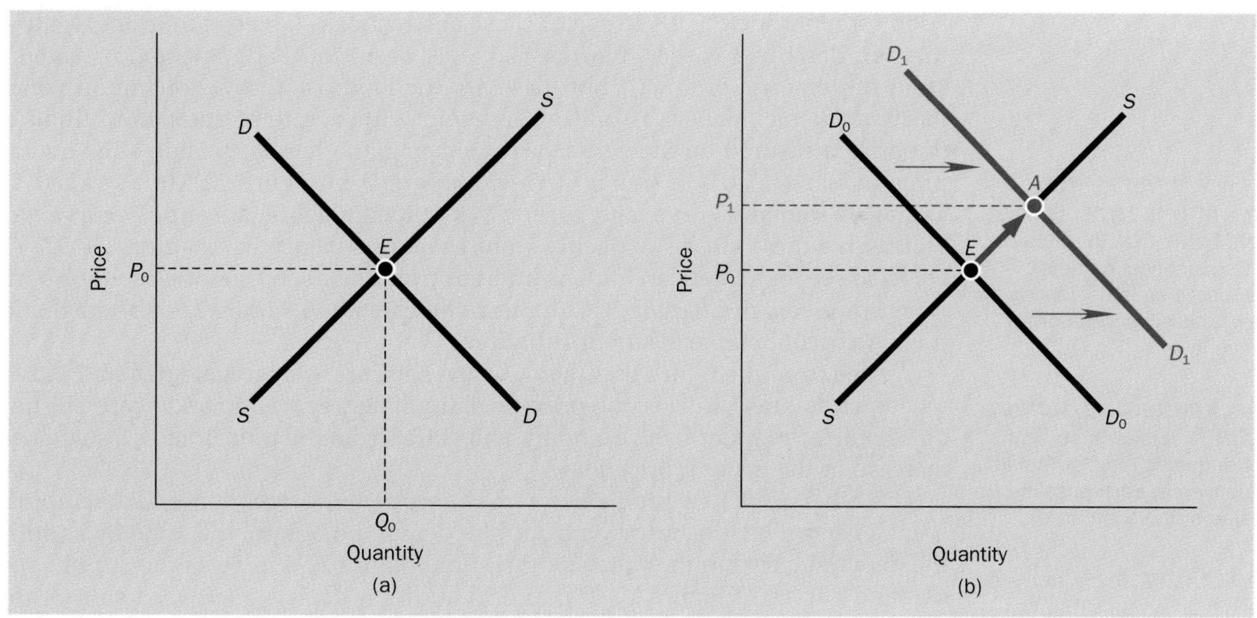


Part (a) shows an equilibrium at point *E*, where demand curve *DD* intersects supply curve *SS*. Part (b) shows how this equilibrium moves from point *E* to point *A* if the demand curve moves outward. If this graph represents the market for milk, as it did in Chapter 4, then it shows an increase in the price of milk. But if the graph represents the aggregate market for "domestic product," then it shows inflation—a rise in the general price level.

Figure 22–2 **AN ECONOMY SLIPPING INTO A RECESSION**

In this aggregate supply–demand diagram, there is an initial equilibrium at point $E$, where demand curve $D_0D_0$ intersects supply curve $SS$. When the demand curve shifts inward from $D_0D_0$ to $D_2D_2$, equilibrium moves to point $B$, and output falls from $Q_0$ to $Q_2$.

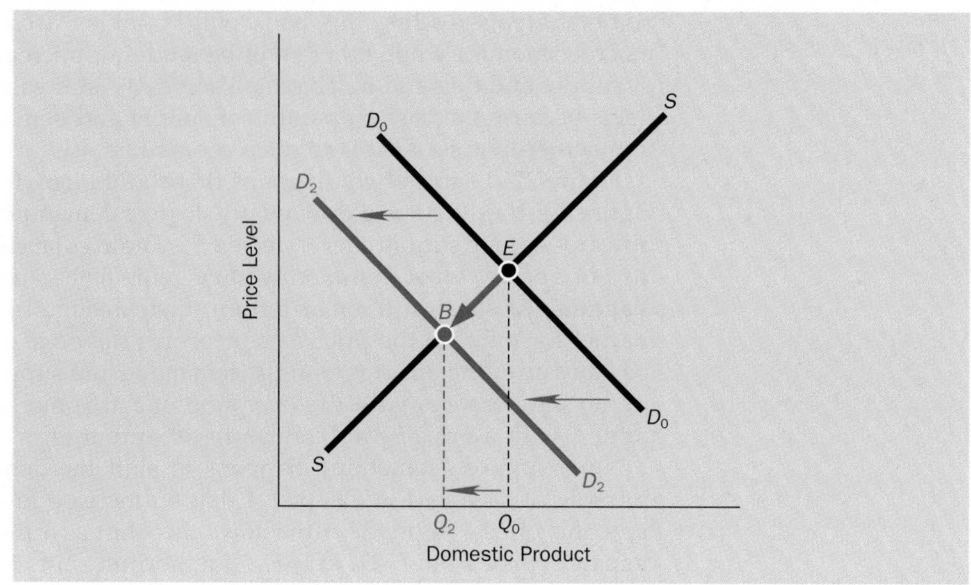


Now let us reinterpret Figure 22–1 as representing an abstract market for "domestic product." This is one of those abstractions—an economic aggregate—that we described earlier. No one has ever seen, touched, smelled, or eaten a "unit of domestic product," but these are the kinds of abstractions upon which macroeconomic analysis is built. Consistent with this reinterpretation, think of the price measured on the vertical axis as being another abstraction—the overall price index, or "cost of living."[1] Then curve *DD* in Figure 22–1(a) is called an **aggregate demand curve**, and curve *SS* is called an **aggregate supply curve**. We will derive these curves explicitly from economic theory in Chapters 24–27. As we shall see there, they are rather different from the microeconomic counterparts we encountered in Chapter 4. With this reinterpretation, Figure 22–1(b) can depict the macroeconomic problem of **inflation**.

The **AGGREGATE DEMAND CURVE** shows the quantity of domestic product that is demanded at each possible value of the price level.

The **AGGREGATE SUPPLY CURVE** shows the quantity of **domestic** product that is supplied at each possible value of the price level.

**INFLATION** refers to a sustained increase in the general price level.

A **RECESSION** is a period of time during which the total output of the economy declines.

We see from the figure that the outward shift of the aggregate demand curve, whatever its cause, pushes the price level up. If aggregate demand keeps shifting out month after month, the economy will suffer from inflation, that is, a sustained increase in the general price level.

The other principal problems of macroeconomics, recession and unemployment, also can be illustrated on a supply–demand diagram, this time by shifting the demand curve in the opposite direction. Figure 22–2 repeats the supply and demand curves of Figure 22–1(a) and in addition depicts a leftward shift of the aggregate demand curve from $D_0D_0$ to $D_2D_2$. Equilibrium now moves from point *E* to point *B* so that domestic product (total output) declines. This is what we normally mean by a **recession**.

[1]The appendix to Chapter 23 explains how such price indexes are calculated.

## GROSS DOMESTIC PRODUCT

**GROSS DOMESTIC PRODUCT (GDP)** is the sum of the money values of all final goods and services produced in the domestic economy during a specified period of time, usually one year.

The economy's total output, we have just seen, is one of the major variables of concern to macroeconomists. While there are several ways to measure it, the most popular choice undoubtedly is the **gross domestic product**, a term you have probably encountered in the news media. The gross domestic product, or "GDP" for short, is the most comprehensive measure of the output of all the factories, offices, and shops in the U.S. economy. Specifically, it is the sum of the money values of all final goods and services produced *in the domestic economy* within the year.

Several features of this definition need to be underscored.[2] First, you will notice that:

We add up the *money values* of things.

The GDP consists of a bewildering variety of goods and services: mousetraps and computers, tanks and textbooks, ballet performances and rock concerts. How are we to combine all of these into a single number? To an economist, the natural way to do this is first to convert every good and service into *money* terms. If we want to add 10 apples and 20 oranges, we first ask: How much *money* does each cost? If apples cost 20¢ and oranges cost 25¢, then the apples count for $2 and the oranges for $5, so the sum is $7 worth of "output." The market *price* of each good or service is used as an indicator of its *value* to society for a simple reason: *someone* is willing to pay that much money for it.

This decision raises the question of what prices to use in valuing the different outputs. The official data offer two choices. First, we can value each good and service at the price at which it was actually sold during the year. If we do this, the resulting measure is called **nominal GDP**, or *money GDP*, or *GDP in current dollars*. This seems like a perfectly sensible choice. But as a measure of output, it has one serious drawback: nominal GDP rises when prices rise, even if there is no increase in actual production. For example, if hamburgers cost $2.00 this year but cost only $1.50 last year, then 100 hamburgers will contribute $200 to this year's nominal GDP but only $150 to last year's. But 100 hamburgers are still 100 hamburgers—output has not grown.

**NOMINAL GDP** is calculated by valuing all outputs at current prices.

For this reason, government statisticians have devised an alternative measure that corrects for inflation by valuing all goods and services at some fixed set of prices. (Currently, the prices of 1987 are used.) For example, if the hamburgers were valued at $1.50 each in both years, $150 worth of hamburger output would be included in GDP in each year. When we treat every output in this way, we obtain **real GDP** or *GDP in constant dollars*. The news media often refer to it as "GDP corrected for inflation." Throughout most of this book, and certainly when we are discussing the nation's output, it is real GDP that we shall be concerned with. The distinction between nominal and real GDP leads us to a working definition of a *recession* as a period in which *real* GDP declines. For example, between 1990 and 1991, nominal GDP rose from $5546 billion to $5723 billion; but real GDP *fell* from $4897 billion to $4861 billion.

**REAL GDP** is calculated by valuing all outputs at the prices that prevailed in some agreed-upon year (currently 1987). Therefore, real GDP is a far better measure of changes in total production.

[2]Certain exceptions to the definition are dealt with in Appendix B of Chapter 24, especially on page 612. Some instructors may prefer to take up that material here.

The next important aspect of the definition of GDP is that:

The GDP for a particular year includes only goods and services produced during that year. Sales of items produced in previous years are explicitly excluded.

For example, suppose you buy a perfectly beautiful 1979 Dodge next week and are overjoyed by your purchase. The national income statistician will not share your glee because she already counted your car in the GDP in 1979 when it was first produced and sold; the car will never be counted again. The same holds true of houses. Old houses (unlike old cars) often sell for more than their original purchasers paid; yet the resale values of houses do not count in GDP since they were already counted in the years they were built. For the same reason, exchanges of other existing assets are not included in GDP.

**FINAL GOODS AND SERVICES** are those that are purchased by their ultimate users.

An **INTERMEDIATE GOOD** is a good purchased for resale or for use in producing another good.

Third, you will note the use of the phrase **final goods and services** in the definition. The adjective "final" is the key word here. For example, when a supermarket buys milk from a farmer, the transaction is not included in the GDP because the supermarket does not want the milk for itself. It buys milk only for resale to consumers. Only when the milk is sold to consumers is it considered a final product. When the supermarket buys it, economists consider it an **intermediate good**. The GDP does not include sales of intermediate goods or services.[3]

Fourth, the adjective "domestic" directs attention to production within the geographic boundaries of the United States. Some Americans work abroad, and many American companies have offices or factories in foreign countries. All these people and businesses produce valuable outputs, but none of this is counted in the GDP of the United States. (It is counted, instead, in the GDPs of the foreign countries.) On the other hand, quite a number of foreigners and foreign companies produce goods and services in the U.S. All this activity does count in our GDP.[4]

Finally, although the definition does not state this explicitly:

For the most part, only goods and services that pass through organized markets count in the GDP.

This, of course, excludes many economic activities. For example, illegal activities are not included in the GDP. Thus, gambling services in Chicago are not in the GDP, but gambling services in Atlantic City are. The definition reflects the statisticians' confession that they could not hope to measure the value of many of the economy's most important activities, such as housework, do-it-yourself repairs, and leisure time. While these are certainly economic activities that result in currently produced goods or services, they all lack that important measuring rod—a market price.

This omission results in certain oddities. For example, suppose that each of two neighboring families hires the other to clean house, generously paying $1000 a week for the services. Each family can easily afford such generosity since it collects an identical salary from its neighbor. Nothing real changes, but GDP goes up by $104,000 a year. This example is not fanciful. The accompanying boxed insert shows that including the value of housework would have a profound effect on the measurement of GDP.

---

[3]Actually, there is another way to add up the GDP by counting a portion of each intermediate transaction. This is explained in Appendix B of Chapter 24, especially pages 616–17.

[4]There is another concept, called gross *national* product, which counts the goods and services produced by all Americans, regardless of where they work. For consistency, the outputs produced by foreigners working in the United States are not included in GNP. In practice, the two measures—GDP and GNP—are very close.

### Housework and GDP

How large is a country's economic output? Certainly much bigger than its gross domestic product (GDP), which excludes big chunks of activity . . . [performed] within the home, such as cleaning, caring for children and decorating. This has the bizarre result that, if a man marries his cleaner, turning a paid employee into an unpaid housewife, then GDP falls instantly even though much the same work gets done. A recent study by the OECD confirms what every household drudge has always claimed—working at home is more valuable than it is believed to be by those who spend their time making the wheels of commerce and industry turn.

But how to put a value on it? There are two main methods. The first is to value the time spent doing housework using the person's wage in the formal economy, ie, the opportunity cost of his—or more likely her—time. The snag with this, however, is that it produces the ludicrous result that washing-up done by an investment banker is worth more than washing-up done by a nurse. The second method is to value that time at the wage rate of a maid. Doing this, the [study] concludes that the value of housework would add between one-third to one-half to the GDP of the five large countries which it studied. [See table] . . .

The hours spent doing housework have fallen over the years as more women have taken paid jobs. But the value of housework has not necessarily dropped because productivity has been increased by blenders, dishwashers and the like. When unemployment rises, people spend more time doing up their homes. If governments included this in GDP, there would be fewer recessions.

SOURCE: *The Economist*, July 4, 1992, p. 58.

Percentage Increase in GDP if Unpaid Housework Was Valued at Market Prices

| | |
|---|---|
| Australia | 49% |
| France | 46% |
| United States | 44% |
| Canada | 41% |
| Germany | 32% |

SOURCE: Ann Chadeau, "What Is Households' Non-market Production Worth?," OECD Economic Studies No. 18.

## LIMITATIONS OF THE GDP: WHAT GDP IS NOT

Having seen in some detail what the GDP *is*, it is worth pausing to expand upon what it *is not*. In particular:

Gross domestic product is not a measure of the nation's economic well-being.

The GDP is not intended to measure economic well-being, and does not do so for several reasons.

1. *Only market activity is included in GDP.* As we have just seen, a great deal of work done in the home contributes to the nation's well-being, but it is not measured in the GDP because it has no price tag. One important implication of this exclusion arises when we try to compare the GDPs of developed and less-developed countries. Americans are always incredulous to learn that the per capita GDP of the poorest African countries is less than $250 a year. Surely, no one could survive in America on $5 a week. How can Africans do it? Part of the answer, of course, is that these people are incredibly

poor. We shall study their plight in Chapter 38. But another part of the answer is that:

International GDP comparisons are vastly misleading when the two countries differ greatly in the fraction of economic activity that each conducts in organized markets.

This fraction is relatively large in the United States and relatively small in the less-developed countries, so when we compare their respective measured GDPs we are not comparing the same economic activities at all. Many things that get counted in the U.S. GDP are not counted in the GDPs of less-developed nations. So it is ludicrous to think that these people, poor as they are, survive on what to Americans would amount to $5 a week.

A second implication is that GDP statistics take no account of the so-called "underground economy." This includes not just criminal activities, but a great deal of legitimate business activity that is conducted in cash (or by barter) to escape the tax collector. Naturally, we have no good data on the size of the underground economy; but some observers think it may amount to 10 percent or more of U.S. GDP. In some foreign countries, it is surely a much bigger share than this.

2. *GDP places no value on leisure*. As a country gets richer, one of the things that happens is that its citizens take more and more leisure time. The steady decrease in the length of the typical workweek in the United States is clear evidence for this. As a result, the gap is steadily widening between official GDP and some truer measure of national well-being that would include the value of leisure time. For this reason, growth in GDP systematically *underestimates* the growth in national well-being. But there are also reasons why the GDP *overstates* how well-off we are. For example:

3. *"Bads" as well as "goods" get counted in GDP*. Suppose there is a natural disaster—such as Hurricane Andrew, which devastated parts of Florida and Louisiana in September 1992. Surely the well-being of the United States was diminished by this catastrophe. Scores of people were killed; many homes and businesses were destroyed. Yet the disaster probably raised U.S. GDP. Consumers spent more to clean up and replace lost homes and possessions. Businesses spent more to rebuild and repair damaged stores and plants. The government spent more for disaster relief and cleanup. Yet no one would think America was better off for its higher GDP.

   Wars represent an extreme example. Mobilization for outright war always causes a country's GDP to rise rapidly. But men and women serving in the army could be producing civilian output. Factories assigned to produce armaments could instead be making cars, washing machines, and televisions. A country at war is surely worse off than a country at peace, but this fact will not be reflected in its GDP.

4. *Ecological costs are not netted out of the GDP*. Many of the activities in a modern industrial economy that produce goods and services also have undesirable side effects on the environment. Automobiles provide enjoyment and a means of transportation, but they also despoil the atmosphere. Factories pollute rivers and lakes while manufacturing valuable commodities. Almost everything seems to produce garbage, which creates a serious disposal problem. None of these ecological costs are deducted from the GDP in an effort to give us a truer measure of the *net* increase in economic welfare that our

economy produces. Is this foolishness? Not if we remember the job that national income statisticians are trying to do: they are measuring the economic activity conducted through organized markets, not national welfare.

## THE ECONOMY ON A ROLLER COASTER

Having defined several of the basic concepts of macroeconomics, let us breathe some life into them by perusing the economic history of the United States. Figures 22–3 and 22–4 provide a capsule summary of this history since the Civil War.

Figure 22–3 charts the behavior of the growth rate of real GDP. The fact that the growth rate is almost always positive indicates that the main feature has been *economic growth*. In fact, the average annual growth rate over this period has been about 3.3 percent. But the figure also shows that recessions—periods of falling real GDP—have been a persistent feature of America's economic performance. Especially before the Korean War, the graph gives the impression of an economy on a roller coaster. The ups and downs that are apparent in Figure 22–3 are called *economic fluctuations*, or sometimes *business cycles*.

**DEFLATION** refers to a sustained *decrease* in the general price level.

The history of the inflation rate displayed in Figure 22–4 also shows more positive numbers than negative ones—more inflation than **deflation**. Although the price level rose about 13-fold since 1869, the upward trend is of rather recent

**Figure 22–3** THE GROWTH RATE OF REAL GROSS DOMESTIC PRODUCT OF THE UNITED STATES, 1870–1993

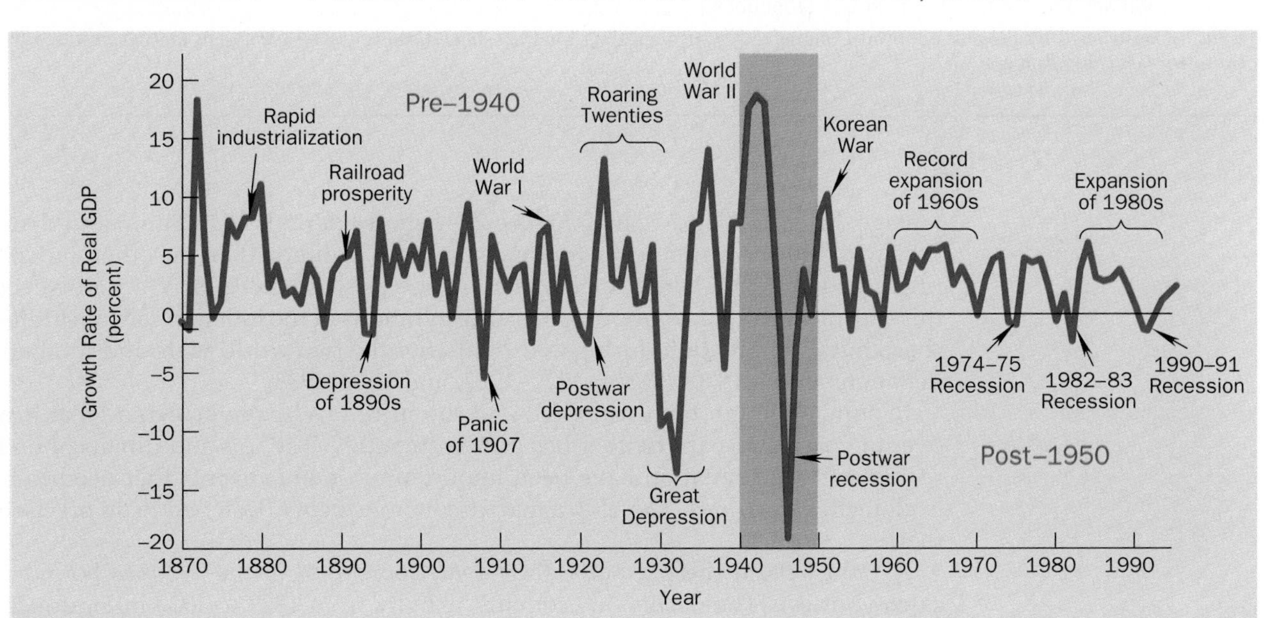


This time series chart displays the growth rate of real gross domestic product in the United States from 1870 to 1993. (Here real GDP is measured in 1987 prices.) The Great Depression (1929–1939) stands out vividly. The years during and just after World War II are shaded. Does the growth rate look smoother to the right of this shaded area?

SOURCE: Constructed by the authors from Commerce Department data for 1929–1993. Data for 1869–1928 are based on research by Professor Christina Romer.

Figure 22–4 **THE INFLATION RATE IN THE UNITED STATES, 1870–1993**

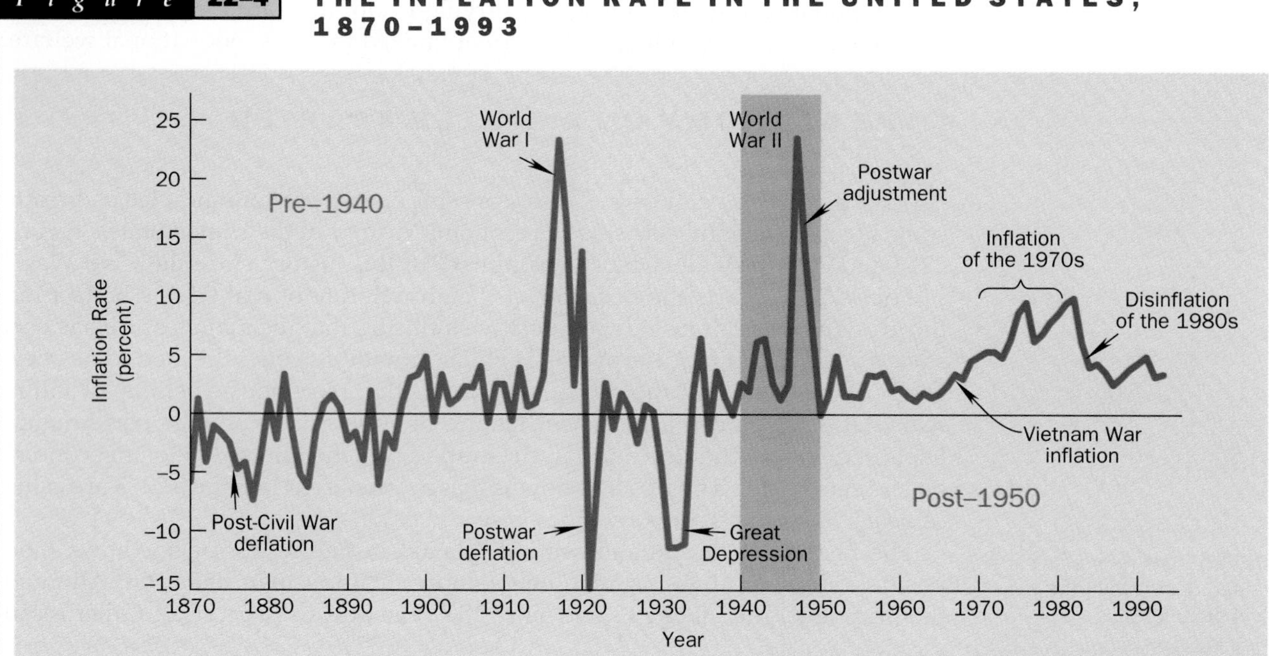


This time series chart portrays the behavior of the U.S. inflation rate from 1870 to 1993. (The specific price index used is called the GDP deflator, and it is defined as the ratio of nominal GDP divided by real GDP.) The difference between the 1870–1940 period and the 1950–1993 period is pronounced.

SOURCE: Constructed by the authors from Commerce Department data for 1929–1993. Data for 1869–1928 were kindly provided by Professor Christina Romer.

vintage. Prior to World War II, Figure 22–4 shows periods of inflation and deflation, with little or no tendency for one to be more common than the other. Indeed, prices in 1940 were barely higher than at the close of the Civil War. However, this capsule history does show some large gyrations in the inflation rate, including sharp bursts of inflation during and right after the two world wars and dramatic deflations in the 1870s, 1880s, 1921–1922, and 1929–1933.

In sum, although both real GDP and the price level have grown a great deal over the past 123 years, neither has grown smoothly. The ups and downs of both real growth and inflation have been important economic events that need to be explained. Parts 6 and 7 develop a macroeconomic theory designed to do precisely that.

As you look at these graphs, the Great Depression of the 1930s is bound to catch your eye. The decline in economic activity from 1929 to 1933 in Figure 22–3 was the most severe in our nation's history, and the rapid deflation in Figure 22–4 was most unusual. The Depression is but a dim memory now, but those who lived through it will never forget it.

While statistics usually conceal the true drama of economic events, this is not so of the Great Depression—instead they stand as bitter testimony to its severity. The production of goods and services dropped 30 percent, business investment almost ceased entirely, and the unemployment rate rose ominously from about

## *Life in "Hooverville"*

During the worst years of the Great Depression, unemployed workers often congregated in shantytowns on the outskirts of many major cities. Conditions in these slums were deplorable. With a heavy dose of irony, these communities were known as "Hoovervilles," in honor of the president of the United States who preached rugged individualism. A contemporary observer described a Hooverville in New York City as follows:

It was a fairly popular "development" made up of a hundred or so dwellings, each the size of a dog house or chickencoop, often constructed with much ingenuity out of wooden boxes, metal cans, strips of cardboard or old tar paper. Here human beings lived on the margin of civilization by foraging for garbage, junk, and waste lumber. I found some splitting or sawing wood with dull tools to make fires; others were picking through heaps of rubbish they had gathered before their doorways or cooking over open fires or battered oilstoves. Still others spent their days improving their rent-free homes, making them sometimes fairly solid and weather-proof. . . . Most of them, according to the police, lived by begging or trading in junk; when all else failed they ate at the soup kitchens or public canteens. They were of all sorts, young and old, some of them rough-looking and suspicious of strangers. They lived in fear of being forcibly removed by the authorities, though the neighborhood people in many cases helped them and the police tolerated them for the time being.

SOURCE: Mathew Josephson, *Infidel in the Temple* (New York: Knopf, 1967), pages 82–83.

3 percent in 1929 to 25 percent in 1933. One person in four was jobless. From the data alone, you can conjure up pictures of soup lines, beggars on street corners, closed factories, and homeless families. (See the boxed insert above.)

The Great Depression was a worldwide event. No country was spared its ravages, which literally changed the history of many nations. In Germany, it facilitated the ascendancy of Nazism. In the United States, it enabled Franklin Roosevelt's Democratic party to engineer one of the most dramatic political realignments in history and to push through a host of political and economic reforms.

The worldwide depression also caused a much-needed revolution in the thinking of economists. Up until the 1930s, the prevailing economic theory held that a capitalist economy, while it occasionally misbehaved, had a natural tendency to cure recessions or inflations by itself. The roller coaster bounced around but did not normally run off the tracks.

This optimistic view was not confined to academia. It characterized the views of most politicians (including President Herbert Hoover) and business leaders as well. As the great American humorist Will Rogers remarked with characteristic sarcasm:

> *It's almost been worth this depression to find out how little our big men knew. Mayby [sic] this depression is just "normalcy" and we don't know it. It's made a dumb guy as smart as a smart one. . . . Depression used to be a state of mind, Now it's a state of coma, now it's permanent. Last year we said, "Things can't go on like this," and they didn't, they got worse.*[5]

---

[5]From *Sanity Is Where You Find It* by Will Rogers, edited by Donald Day; copyright © 1955 by Rogers Company; reprinted by permission of Houghton Mifflin Company; pages 120–21.

The stubbornness of the Great Depression shook almost everyone's faith in the ability of the economy to right itself. In Cambridge, England, this questioning attitude led John Maynard Keynes, one of the world's most respected economists, to write *The General Theory of Employment, Interest, and Money* (1936). Probably the most important book in economics of the twentieth century, it carried a rather revolutionary message. Keynes discarded the notion that the economy always gravitated toward high levels of employment, replacing it with the assertion that—if a pessimistic outlook led business firms and consumers to curtail their spending plans—the economy might be condemned to years of stagnation.

While this doleful prognosis sounded all too realistic at the time, Keynes closed his book on a hopeful note. For he showed how government actions might prod the economy out of its depressed state. The lessons he taught the world then are the lessons we will be learning in Parts 6 and 7. They show how governments can manage their economies so that recessions will not turn into depressions and depressions will not last as long as the Great Depression. While Keynes was working on *The General Theory*, he wrote his friend George Bernard Shaw that, "I believe myself to be writing a book on economic theory which will largely revolutionize . . . the way the world thinks about economic problems." In many ways he was right, though parts of the Keynesian message remain controversial to this day.

## FROM WORLD WAR II TO 1973

The Great Depression finally ended when the country mobilized for war in the early 1940s. With government spending at extraordinarily high levels, the economy boomed and the unemployment rate fell as low as 1.2 percent during the war.

Wartime spending of this magnitude usually leads to inflation, but much of the potential inflation during World War II was contained by price controls. With prices held below the levels at which quantity supplied equaled quantity demanded, many goods had to be rationed, and shortages of consumer goods were common. All of this ended with a burst of inflation when controls were lifted after the war.

The period from the end of the war until the early 1960s was marked by several short recessions. Moderate but persistent inflation also became a fact of life. When the economy emerged from recession in 1961, it entered a period of unprecedented—and noninflationary—growth which was credited widely to the success of what came to be called "The New Economics," a term the media created for the economic policies prescribed by Keynes in the 1930s. For a while it looked as if we could avoid both unemployment and inflation. But the optimistic verdicts were premature in both cases.

Inflation came first, beginning about 1966. Its major cause, as it had been so many times in the past, was high levels of wartime spending—this time for the Vietnam War. Unemployment followed when the economy ground to a halt in 1969. Despite a short and mild recession, inflation continued at 5 to 6 percent a year.

Faced with persistent inflation, President Richard Nixon stunned the nation by instituting wage and price controls in 1971, the first time this had ever been done in peacetime. The controls program, which will be discussed in Chapter 33,

*Biographical Note*

JOHN MAYNARD KEYNES (1883–1946)

John Maynard Keynes was something of a child prodigy. After an outstanding scholastic career at Eton and Cambridge, Keynes took the civil service examination. Ironically, his second-place score was not good enough to land him the position he wanted—in the Treasury. Some years later, reflecting on the fact that his lowest score on the exam was in the economics section, he suggested with characteristic immodesty that, "The examiners presumably knew less than I did." He was probably right.

During World War I, Keynes was called to the Treasury to assist in planning the financial aspects of the war. There his unique combination of daring and intellect quickly established him as a dominant figure. At the war's end, he represented the British Treasury at the peace conference in Versailles. The conference was a turning point in Keynes's life, though it was one of his few failures. He sought unsuccessfully to persuade the Allies to take a less punitive attitude toward the vanquished Germans, and then stormed out of the conference to write his *Economic Consequences of the Peace* (1919), which created a furor. In it Keynes argued that the Germans could never meet the harsh economic terms of the treaty, and that its viciousness posed the threat of continued instability and perhaps another war in Europe.

No longer welcome in government, Keynes returned to Cambridge and to his circle of literary and artistic friends in London's Bloomsbury district—a remarkable group that included Virginia Woolf, Lytton Strachey, and E. M. Forster. In 1925 he married the beautiful ballerina Lydia Lopokova, who gave up her stage career for him (though she later acted in a theater that Keynes himself established).

Between the wars, Keynes devoted himself to making money, to economic theory, and to political economy. He managed to make both himself and King's College rich by speculating in international currencies and commodities—allegedly by studying the newspapers while still in bed each morning! In 1936, he published his masterpiece, *The General Theory of Employment, Interest, and Money*, on which much of modern macroeconomics is based.

A heart attack in 1937 reduced Keynes's activities, but he returned to the Treasury during World War II to conduct several delicate financial negotiations with the Americans. Then, as the capstone to a truly remarkable career, he represented Great Britain—and by all accounts dominated the proceedings—at the 1944 conference in Bretton Woods, New Hampshire, that established an international financial system that served the Western world for 27 years. (See Chapter 36.)

He died at home of a heart attack as Lord Keynes, Baron of Tilton, a man who had achieved almost everything that he sought, and who had only one regret: he wished he had drunk more champagne.

held inflation in check for a while. But inflation worsened dramatically in 1973, mainly because of an explosion in food prices caused by poor harvests around the world.

## THE GREAT STAGFLATION, 1973–1980

Then things began to get much worse, not only for the United States, but for all oil-importing nations. A 1973 war between Israel and the Arab nations led to a quadrupling of the price of oil by the Organization of Petroleum Exporting Countries (OPEC). At the same time, continued poor harvests in many parts of the globe pushed world food prices higher. Prices of other raw materials also skyrocketed. Naturally, higher costs of fuel and other materials soon were reflected in the prices of manufactured goods.

By unhappy coincidence, these events coincided with the lifting of wage and price controls. Just as had happened after World War II, the elimination of controls led to a temporary acceleration of inflation as prices that had been held artificially below equilibrium levels were allowed to rise. For all these reasons, the inflation rate in the United States soared to above 12 percent during 1974.

Meanwhile, the U.S. economy was slipping into what was, up to then, its longest and most severe recession since the 1930s. Real GDP fell between late 1973 and early 1975, and the unemployment rate rose to nearly 9 percent. With both inflation and unemployment unusually virulent in 1974 and 1975, a new term—**stagflation**—was coined to refer to the simultaneous occurrence of economic *stag*nation and rapid in*flation*.

**STAGFLATION** is inflation that occurs while the economy is growing slowly ("stagnating") or having a recession.

Thanks partly to government actions, but mostly to natural economic forces, a sustained recovery from recession began in 1975. Inflation tumbled rapidly as the adjustment to the end of price controls ended and food and energy prices stopped soaring. The severity of the recession also put a brake on inflation, just as it had in the past. In total, the inflation rate tumbled from over 12 percent back down to the 5–7 percent range.

But the price of oil soared again in 1979 following a revolution in Iran, bringing stagflation back. This time, inflation hit the astonishing rate of 16 percent during the first half of 1980 and credit controls were clamped on. Output fell at an extraordinarily rapid pace, but only for a few months. By late 1980, recovery was underway.

## REAGANOMICS AND ITS AFTERMATH

When President Ronald Reagan assumed office in January 1981, the economy was showing signs of reviving, but the inflation rate seemed stuck near 10 percent. The new president promised to change things with a package of policies called "supply-side economics."[6]

At first, things did change dramatically—but not in the way President Reagan wanted. While inflation fell remarkably to only about 4 percent in 1982, the lowest rate in a decade, the economy slumped into its worst recession since the Great Depression. When the 1981–1982 recession hit bottom, the unemployment rate was approaching 11 percent, the financial markets were in disarray, and the word "depression" had reentered the American vocabulary.

However, the recovery that began in the winter of 1982–1983 proved to be one of the most vigorous and long-lasting in our history. Unemployment fell more or less steadily for about six years, eventually dropping below 5½ percent. Meanwhile, inflation remained tame. All this provided an ideal economic platform on which President George Bush ran to succeed Reagan—and to continue his policies.

Unfortunately for President Bush, the good times did not continue to roll. Shortly after he took office, the economy began to sputter. Then, in 1990–1991, the U.S. experienced another recession—precipitated, according to some observers, by yet another spike in oil prices before the Persian Gulf War. While the 1990–1991 recession was below average in size, the economy had failed to recover by the

[6]Supply-side economics is discussed further in Chapter 28.

time of the 1992 election. In fact, the growth rate during George Bush's presidency was the weakest for any four-year period since World War II. This fact was not lost on candidate Bill Clinton, who hammered away at the lackluster economic performance of 1989–1992. Most observers believe that the weak economy was the main factor behind George Bush's electoral rout.

## THE PROBLEM OF MACROECONOMIC STABILIZATION: A SNEAK PREVIEW

This brief look at the historical record shows that our economy has not generally produced steady growth without inflation. Rather, it has been buffeted by periodic bouts of unemployment or inflation, and sometimes has been plagued by both. There was also a hint that government policies may have had something to do with this performance. Let us now expand upon this hint.

**STABILIZATION POLICY** is the name given to government programs designed to prevent or shorten recessions and to counteract inflation (that is, to *stabilize* prices).

We can provide a preliminary analysis of **stabilization policy**, the name given to government programs designed to prevent or shorten recessions and to counteract inflation, by using the basic tools of aggregate supply and aggregate demand analysis. To facilitate this, we have reproduced as Figures 22–5 and 22–6 two of the diagrams found earlier in this chapter (Figures 22–1[b] and 22–2), but we now give them slightly different interpretations.

Figure 22–5 offers a simplified view of government policy to fight unemployment. Suppose that, in the absence of government intervention, the economy would reach an equilibrium at point *E*, where demand curve $D_0D_0$ crosses supply curve *SS*. Now if the output corresponding to point *E* is so low that many workers are unemployed, *the government can reduce unemployment by increasing aggregate demand*. Chapter 28 will consider in detail how the government might do this. In

*Figure* **22–5** **STABILIZATION POLICY TO FIGHT UNEMPLOYMENT**

This diagram duplicates Figure 22–1(b), but here we assume that Point *E*—the intersection of demand curve $D_0D_0$ and supply curve *SS*—corresponds to high unemployment. With the kind of policy tools that we will study in later chapters, the government can shift the aggregate demand curve outward to $D_1D_1$. This would raise output and lower unemployment.

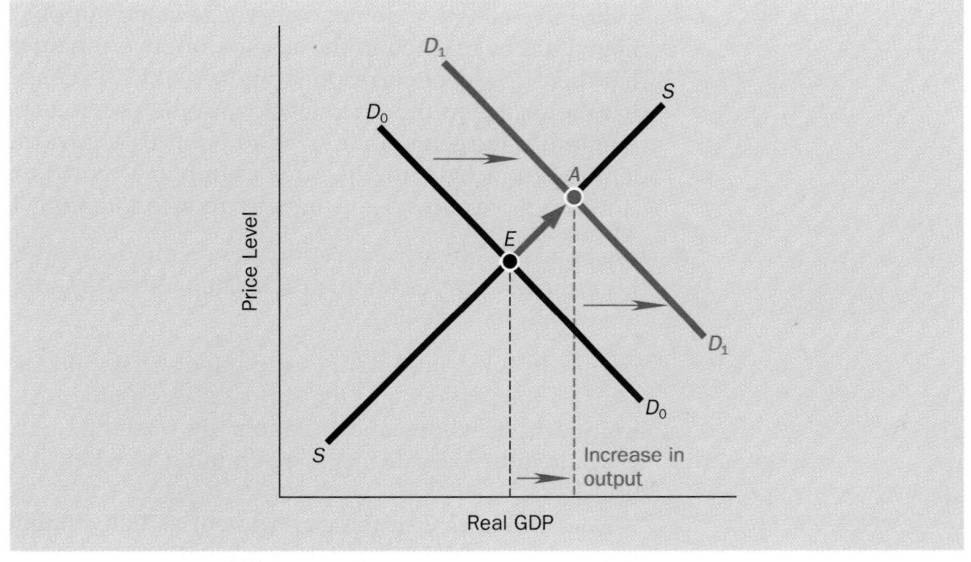

**Figure 22-6** STABILIZATION POLICY TO FIGHT INFLATION

This diagram duplicates Figure 22–2, but here we assume that point *E*—the equilibrium the economy would attain without government intervention—represents high inflation (that is, the price level corresponding to point *E* is far above last year's price level). By using its policy instruments to shift the aggregate demand curve inward to $D_2D_2$, the government can keep this year's price level lower than it would otherwise have been; in other words, the government can reduce inflation.

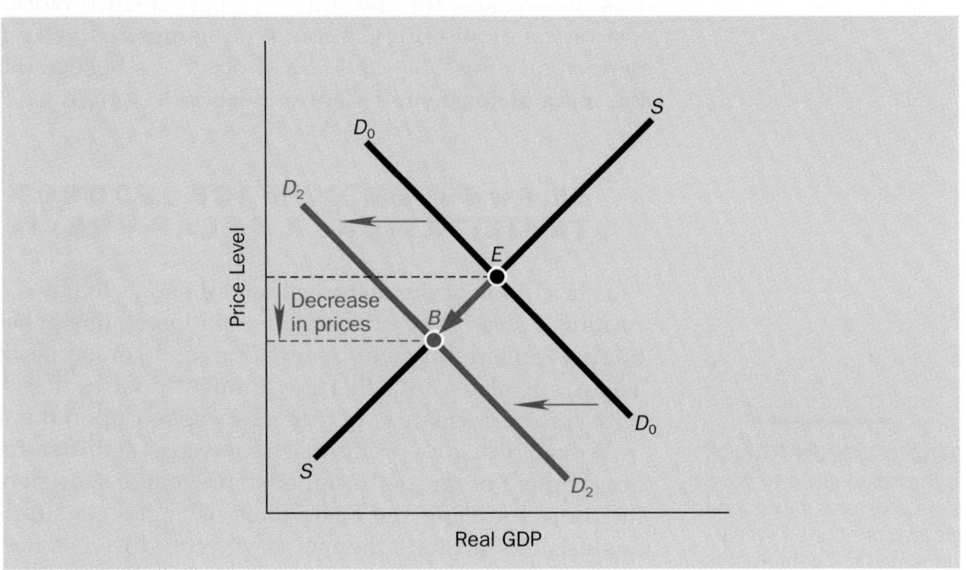


the diagram, such an action would shift the demand curve to $D_1D_1$, causing equilibrium to move to point *A*. In general:

Recessions and unemployment are often caused by insufficient aggregate demand. When this is so, government policies that successfully augment demand—such as increases in government spending—can be an effective way to increase output and reduce unemployment.

The opposite type of demand management is called for when inflation is the main macroeconomic problem. Figure 22–6 illustrates this case. Here again, point *E*, the intersection of demand curve $D_0D_0$ and supply curve *SS*, is the equilibrium that would be reached in the absence of government policy. But now we suppose that the price level corresponding to point *E* is considered "too high," meaning that the *change* in the price level from the previous period to this one would be too rapid if the economy moved to point *E*. A government program that reduces demand from $D_0D_0$ to $D_2D_2$ (for example, a reduction in government spending) can keep prices down and thereby reduce inflation. Thus:

Inflation is frequently caused by aggregate demand racing ahead too fast. When this is the case, government policies that reduce aggregate demand can be effective anti-inflationary devices.

This, in brief, summarizes the intent of stabilization policy. When aggregate demand fluctuations are the source of economic instability, the government can limit both recessions and inflations by pushing aggregate demand ahead when it would otherwise lag, and restraining it when it would otherwise grow too quickly.

Does it work? Can the government actually stabilize the economy? That is a matter of some debate, a debate we will be examining in Part 7. But a look back at Figures 22–3 and 22–4 may be enlightening right now. First, cover the portions of Figures 22–3 and 22–4 that deal with the period beginning in 1941, the portions from the shaded area rightward in each figure. The picture that emerges for the 1870–1940 period is of an economy whose gyrations were frequent and sometimes quite pronounced.

Now do the reverse. Cover the data before 1950 and look only at the postwar period. There is, indeed, a difference. Instances of negative real GDP growth are less common and business fluctuations look less severe. While perfection has not been achieved, things do look much better. When we turn to inflation, however, things look rather worse. Gone are the periods of deflation and price stability that occurred before World War II. Prices now seem only to rise.

This quick tour through the data suggests that something has changed. The U.S. economy behaved differently in 1950–1993 than it did in 1870–1940. Although there is controversy on this point, many economists attribute this shift in the economy's behavior to lessons the government has learned about managing the economy—lessons we will be learning in Part 7.

When you look at the pre-1940 data, you are looking at an unmanaged economy that went through booms and recessions for "natural" economic reasons. The government did little about either. When you examine the post-1950 data, on the other hand, you are looking at an economy that has been increasingly managed by government policy—sometimes successfully and sometimes unsuccessfully. While the recessions are less severe, a cost seems to have been exacted: the economy appears to be more inflation-prone than it was in the more distant past. These two changes in our economy may be connected. But, to understand why, we will have to provide some relevant economic theory.

## *Summary*

1. **Microeconomics** studies the decisions of individuals and firms, how these decisions interact, and how they influence the allocation of society's resources and the distribution of income. **Macroeconomics** looks at the behavior of entire economies and studies the pressing social problems of inflation and unemployment.

2. While their respective subject matters differ greatly, the basic tools of microeconomics and macroeconomics are virtually identical. Both rely on the supply and demand analysis introduced in Chapter 4.

3. Macroeconomic models use abstract concepts like "the price level" and "domestic product" that are derived by amalgamating many different markets into one. This process is known as **aggregation**; it should not be taken literally but should be viewed as a useful approximation.

4. The best specific measure of the abstract concept "domestic product" is **gross domestic product (GDP)**, which is obtained by adding up the money values of all **final goods and services** produced in a given year. These outputs can be evaluated at current market prices (to get **nominal GDP**) or at the prices of some previous year (to get **real GDP**). Neither **intermediate goods** nor transactions that take place outside organized markets are included in GDP.

5. The GDP is meant to be a measure of the *production* of the economy, not of the increase in its *well-being*. For example, the GDP places no value on housework and other do-it-yourself activities, nor on leisure time. On the other hand, even commodities that might be considered as "bads" rather than "goods" are counted in the GDP (for example, activities that harm the environment).

6. America's economic history is one of growth punctuated by periodic **recessions**; that is, periods in which real GDP declined. While the distant past included some periods of falling prices (**deflation**), more recent history shows only rising prices (**inflation**).

7. The Great Depression of the 1930s was the worst in our country's history. It had profound effects both on our nation and on countries throughout the world and led also to a revolution in economic thinking, thanks to the work of John Maynard Keynes.

8. From World War II to the early 1970s, the American economy exhibited much steadier growth than it had in the past. Many observers attributed this to the implementation of the economic policies that Keynes suggested. At the same time, however, the price level seems only to rise, never to fall, in the modern economy. The economy seems to have become more "inflation prone."
9. Since 1973, the U.S. economy has suffered through several serious recessions. Between 1973 and about 1981, inflation was also unusually virulent. This unhappy combination of economic stagnation with rapid inflation was nicknamed "**stagflation**." Since 1982, however, inflation has been low and mostly steady.
10. One major cause of inflation is that **aggregate demand** may grow more quickly than **aggregate supply**. In such a case, a government policy that reduces aggregate demand may be able to check the inflation.
11. Similarly, recessions often occur because aggregate demand grows too slowly. In this case, a government policy that stimulates demand may be an effective way to fight the recession.

## *Key Concepts and Terms*

Microeconomics
Macroeconomics
Domestic product
Aggregation
Aggregate demand and aggregate supply curves
Inflation
Deflation
Recession
Gross domestic product (GDP)
Nominal versus real GDP
Final goods and services
Intermediate goods
Stagflation
Stabilization policy

## *Questions for Review*

1. Which of the following problems are likely to be studied by a microeconomist and which by a macroeconomist?
   a. The allocation of a university budget.
   b. Why the economy took so long to recover from the 1990–1991 recession.
   c. Why Japan's economy grows faster than the United States' economy, while Britain's grows slower.
   d. Why "clone" computers have gained market share from IBM.
2. You probably use "aggregates" frequently in everyday discussions. Try to think of some examples. (Here is one: Have you ever said, "The students at this college generally think . . ."? What, precisely, did you mean?)
3. Use an aggregate supply and demand diagram to study what would happen to an economy in which the aggregate demand curve never moved while the aggregate supply curve shifted outward year after year.
4. Try asking a friend who has not studied economics in which year he or she thinks prices were higher: 1870 or 1900? 1920 or 1940? (In both cases, prices were higher in the earlier year.) Most people your age think that prices have always risen. Why do you think they have this opinion?
5. Which of the following transactions are included in gross domestic product, and by how much does each raise GDP?
   a. Smith pays a carpenter $10,000 to build a garage.
   b. Smith purchases $3000 worth of materials and builds himself a garage, which is worth $10,000.
   c. Smith goes to the woods, cuts down a tree, and uses the wood to build himself a garage that is worth $10,000.
   d. The Jones family sells its old house to the Reynolds family for $130,000. The Joneses then buy a newly constructed house from a builder for $175,000.
   e. You purchase a used computer from a friend for $250.
   f. Your university purchases a new mainframe computer from IBM, paying $250,000.
   g. You win $100 in an Atlantic City casino.
   h. You make $100 in the stock market.
   i. You sell a used economics textbook to your college bookstore for $25.
   j. You buy a new economics textbook from your college bookstore for $50.
6. Give some reasons why gross domestic product is not a suitable measure of the well-being of the nation. (Have you noticed newspaper accounts in which journalists seem to use GDP for this purpose?)

# Chapter 23

# UNEMPLOYMENT AND INFLATION: THE TWIN EVILS OF MACROECONOMICS

*When men are employed, they are best contented.*

BENJAMIN FRANKLIN

*Inflation is repudiation.*

CALVIN COOLIDGE

Among the many trials faced by Odysseus, the hero of Homer's *Odyssey*, one of the most difficult was to steer his fragile boat through a narrow strait. On one side lay the rock of the monster Scylla, which threatened to break his craft into pieces, and on the other was the menacing whirlpool of Charybdis. The makers of national economic policy face a similarly difficult task in trying to chart a middle course between the Scylla of unemployment and the Charybdis of inflation. If they steer the economy far from the rocks of unemployment, they run the risk of being swept up in the swift currents of inflation. But if they maintain a safe distance from inflation, they may smash against the rocks of unemployment. ¶In Parts 6 and 7 we will explain how economic planners attempt to strike a balance between high employment and low inflation, why these goals cannot be attained with machinelike precision, and why improvement on one front generally spells deterioration on the other. A great deal of attention will be paid to the *causes* of inflation and unemployment. ¶ But before getting involved in such weighty issues of theory and policy, we pause in this chapter to take a close look at the twin evils themselves: Why does a rise in unemployment cause such social distress? Why is inflation so loudly deplored? Can we measure the costs of unemployment and inflation? The answers to some of these questions may seem obvious at first. But we will see that there is more to them than meets the eye.

The chapter is divided into two parts. The first deals with unemployment. After discussing the human and economic costs of high unemployment, we explain how government statisticians measure unemployment. Then we consider how the elusive concept of "full employment" can be defined. We conclude by investigating our country's system of unemployment insurance.

The second part of the chapter is devoted to inflation. We begin by exploding some persistent myths about inflation. But the costs of inflation are not all mythical. For example, inflation capriciously redistributes income and wealth from one group of people to another, and certain laws make inflation impose heavy economic costs that could be avoided if the laws were written differently. This last cost stems from failure to understand one of the **12 Ideas for Beyond the Final Exam**: the effect of inflation on interest rates. Finally, we define and analyze the difference between creeping and galloping inflation and explode another myth about inflation: that creeping inflation always leads to galloping inflation.

An appendix explains how inflation is measured.

## THE COSTS OF UNEMPLOYMENT

The human costs of unemployment are probably sufficiently obvious. Years ago, loss of a job meant not only enforced idleness and a catastrophic drop in income, it often led to hunger, cold, ill health—even death. This is the way one unemployed worker during the Great Depression described his family's plight in a mournful letter to the governor of Pennsylvania:

> *I have six little children to take care of. I have been out of work for over a year and a half. Am back almost thirteen months and the landlord says if I don't pay up before the 1 of 1932 out I must go, and where am I to go in the cold winter with my children? If you can help me please for God's sake and the children's sakes and like please do what you can and send me some help, will you, I cannot find any work. I am willing to take any kind of work if I could get it now. Thanksgiving dinner was black coffee and bread and was very glad to get it. My wife is in the hospital now. We have no shoes to were [sic]; no clothes hardly. Oh what will I do I sure will thank you.*[1]

Nowadays, unemployment does not have such dire consequences for most families, although it still holds these terrors for some. Part of the sting has been taken out of unemployment by our system of unemployment insurance (discussed below), and there are other social welfare programs to support the incomes of the poor (see Chapter 17). Yet most families still suffer a painful loss of income when a breadwinner becomes unemployed.

[1]From *Brother, Can You Spare a Dime? The Great Depression 1929–1933*, by Milton Meltzer, page 103. Copyright © 1969 by Milton Meltzer. Reprinted by permission of Alfred A. Knopf, Inc.

**Figure 23-1** **UNEMPLOYMENT RATES FOR SELECTED GROUPS, 1992**

This figure shows that, in 1992, unemployment rates for specific demographic groups varied widely. Similar patterns hold in most years.

SOURCE: Bureau of Labor Statistics

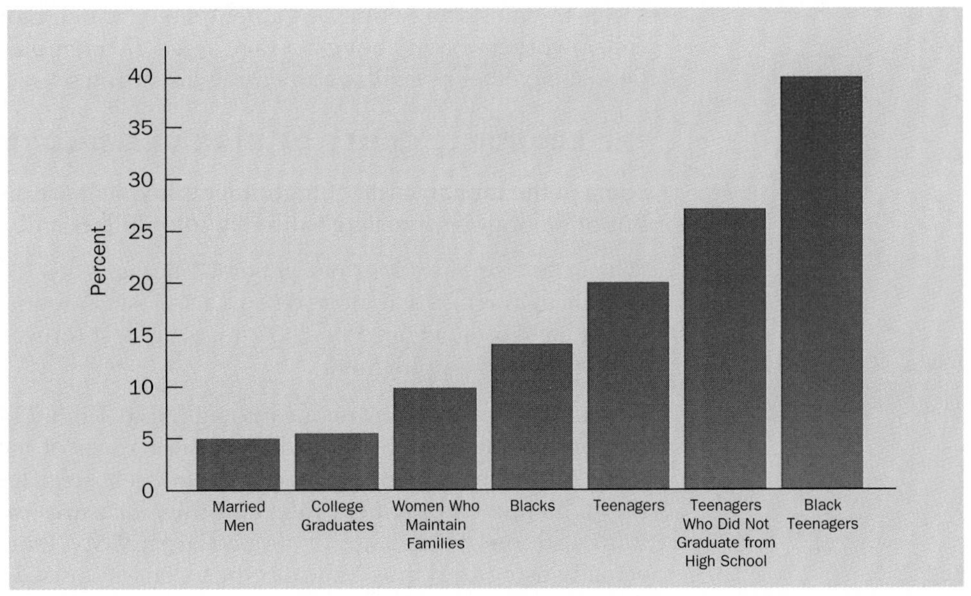


Even families that are well protected by unemployment compensation suffer when joblessness strikes. Ours is a work-oriented society. A man's place has always been in the office or shop, and lately this has become true for many women as well. A worker forced into idleness by a recession endures a psychological cost that is no less real for our inability to measure it. Martin Luther King put it graphically: "In our society, it is murder, psychologically, to deprive a man of a job . . . You are in substance saying to that man that he has no right to exist."[2] High unemployment has been linked to higher incidence of certain types of crimes, psychological disorders, divorces—even suicides.

Nor are the costs only psychological. Accumulated work experience is a valuable asset. When forced into idleness, workers not only cease accumulating experience, but lengthy periods of unemployment may make them "rusty," and thus less productive when they are reemployed. Short periods of unemployment exact different kinds of costs. A record of steady employment is important in applying for a new job. And a worker who has frequently been laid off will lack this record of reliability.

The **UNEMPLOYMENT RATE** is the number of unemployed people, expressed as a percentage of the **labor force.**

It is important to realize that these costs, whether large or small in total, are distributed most unevenly across the population. In 1992, for example, the **unemployment rate** among all workers averaged 7.5 percent. But, as Figure 23–1 shows, 14.1 percent of black workers were unemployed, as were 9.9 percent of women who maintained families. For teenagers, the situation was worse still, with unemployment at 20 percent, and that of black teenagers about 40 percent.

[2] Quoted in Coretta Scott King (ed.), *The Words of Martin Luther King* (New York: Newmarket Press, 1983), page 45.

men had the lowest rate—about 5 percent. These relationships among unemployment rates are typical:

In good times and bad, married men suffer the least unemployment and teenagers suffer the most; nonwhites are unemployed much more often than whites; blue-collar workers have above-average rates of unemployment; and well-educated people have below-average unemployment rates.

### THE ECONOMIC COSTS OF HIGH UNEMPLOYMENT

Some of the human costs of high unemployment are, as we just noted, intangible. But others can be translated directly into dollars and cents because:

When the economy does not generate enough jobs to employ all those who are willing to work, a valuable resource is lost. Potential goods and services that might have been enjoyed by consumers are lost forever. This is the real economic cost of high unemployment.

And these costs are by no means negligible. Table 23–1 summarizes the idleness of workers and machines, and the resulting loss of national output, for some of the years of lowest economic activity in recent decades. The second column lists the civilian unemployment rate, and thus measures unused labor resources. The third lists the percentage of industrial capacity that U.S. manufacturers were actually using, and thus indicates the extent of unused plant and equipment. And the fourth column is an estimate of how much more output (real GDP) could have been produced if these labor and capital resources had been fully employed. For comparison, the bottom line shows the situation in 1990, a year of approximately full utilization of resources.

While Table 23–1 shows extreme examples, inability to utilize all of the nation's available resources has been a recurrent problem for our economy, especially in the 1980s. The blue line in Figure 23–2 shows actual real GDP in the United States from 1952 to 1992, while the black line shows the real GDP we *could have* produced if "full-employment" had been maintained. This last statement defines a concept called **potential GDP**.

**POTENTIAL GROSS DOMESTIC PRODUCT** is the real GDP the economy would produce if its labor and other resources were fully employed.

It *is* possible to push employment beyond its normal full employment level. This occurs whenever the unemployment rate dips below the "full-employment

**Table 23–1 THE ECONOMIC COSTS OF HIGH UNEMPLOYMENT**

| YEAR | CIVILIAN UNEMPLOYMENT RATE (percent) | CAPACITY UTILIZATION RATE (percent) | PERCENTAGE OF REAL GDP LOST DUE TO IDLE RESOURCES |
|---|---|---|---|
| 1958 | 6.8 | 75.0 | 4.4 |
| 1961 | 6.7 | 77.3 | 3.3 |
| 1975 | 8.5 | 72.3 | 4.6 |
| 1982 | 9.7 | 70.3 | 7.4 |
| 1992 | 7.5 | 78.6 | 2.3 |
| 1990 | 5.5 | 83.0 | 0 |

SOURCES: Bureau of Labor Statistics; Federal Reserve System; and Robert J. Gordon, Macroeconomics, Sixth Edition (Boston: Little, Brown, 1993).

**Figure 23-2 ACTUAL AND POTENTIAL GDP IN THE UNITED STATES, 1952–1992**

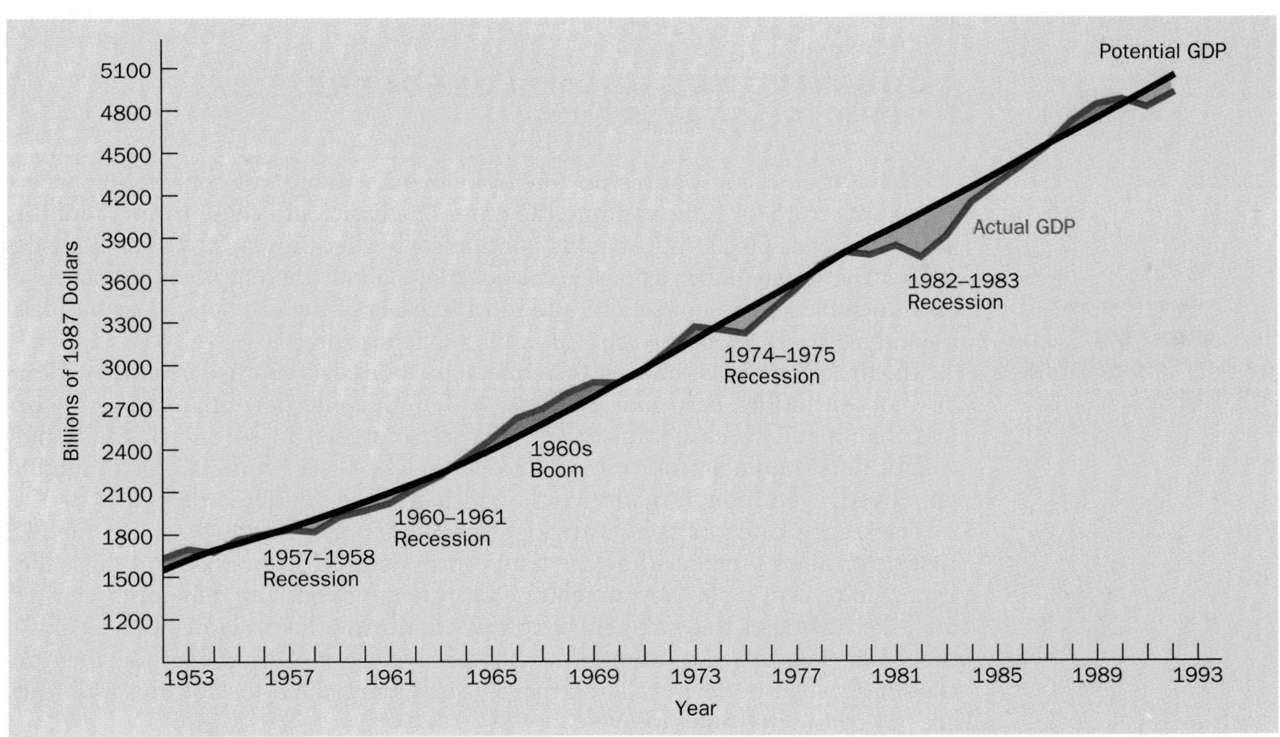


This chart compares the growth of actual GDP (blue line) with that of potential GDP (black line). There have been two lengthy periods during which real GDP remained below its potential (1957–1963 and 1974–1987), but only one lengthy period during which GDP remained above potential (1965–1970). The large short-fall of GDP from potential in the 1980s stand out.

SOURCES: U.S. Department of Commerce and Robert J. Gordon, *Macroeconomics*, Sixth edition (Boston: Little, Brown, 1993). Professor Gordon's estimates of potential GDP are generally considered quite conservative; other estimates of the GDP gap are therefore higher.

unemployment rate." Consequently, it *is* possible for actual GDP to exceed potential GDP. Figure 23–2 shows several instances where this happened, shaded in blue. But it also shows, quite dramatically, that actual GDP has fallen short of potential GDP often since 1974—sometimes by huge amounts. In fact:

A conservative estimate of the cumulative gap between actual and potential GDP over the years 1974–1992 (all evaluated in 1987 prices) is approximately $1300 billion. At 1993 levels, this loss in output as a result of unemployment would be about 3 months' worth of production. And there is no way to redeem these losses. The labor wasted in 1991 cannot be utilized in 1994.

Those who argue that unemployment is nothing to worry about today because of unemployment insurance, or because unemployment is concentrated among certain kinds of workers (such as teenagers), or because many unemployed workers become reemployed within a few weeks, should ponder Figure 23–2. Is the loss of this much output really no cause for worry? Would these optimists react the same way if the government collected a fraction of the output of every factory in America and dumped it into the sea? Waste is waste no matter who ultimately pays the cost.

## COUNTING THE UNEMPLOYED: THE OFFICIAL STATISTICS

We have been using figures on unemployment without yet considering where they come from, or how accurate they are. The basic data come from a monthly survey of over 50,000 households conducted by the Bureau of Labor Statistics (BLS). The census-taker asks several questions about the employment status of each member of the household and, on the basis of the answers, classifies each person as *employed, unemployed*, or *not in the* **labor force**.

The **LABOR FORCE** is the number of people holding or seeking jobs.

The first category is simplest to define. It includes everybody currently working at a job, including part-time workers. Although some part-time workers work less than a full week because they choose to, others do so only because they cannot find a suitable full-time job. Nevertheless, these workers are counted as employed, even though many would consider them "underemployed."

The second category is a bit trickier. For those not currently working, the BLS first determines whether they are temporarily laid off from a job to which they expect to return. If so, they are counted as unemployed. The remaining workers are asked whether they actively sought work during the previous four weeks. If they did, they are also counted as unemployed. But if they did not, they are classified as *out of the labor force*; that is, since they failed to look for a job they are not considered unemployed.

This seems a reasonable way to draw the distinction—after all, we do not want to count college students who work during the summer months as unemployed between September and May. Yet, there is a problem: research has shown that many unemployed workers give up looking for jobs after a time. These so-called **discouraged workers** are victims of poor job prospects, just like the officially unemployed. Ironically, when they give up hope, the official unemployment statistics decline! Some critics have therefore argued that an estimate should be made of the number of discouraged workers and that these people should be added to the roles of the unemployed. In 1992 the BLS estimated that about 1.1 million workers fell into this category.

A **DISCOURAGED WORKER** is an unemployed person who gives up looking for work and is therefore no longer counted as part of the labor force.

Involuntary part-time work, loss of overtime or shortened work hours, and discouraged workers are all examples of "hidden" or "disguised" unemployment. Those who are concerned about these phenomena argue that we should include them in the official unemployment rate because, if we do not, the magnitude of the problem will be underestimated. Others, however, argue that measured unemployment overestimates the problem because, to count as unemployed, a person need only *claim* to be looking for a job, even if he or she is not really interested in finding one.

## TYPES OF UNEMPLOYMENT

Providing jobs for those willing to work is one principal goal of macroeconomic policy. How are we to define this goal? One clearly *incorrect* answer would be "a zero measured unemployment rate." Ours is a dynamic, highly mobile economy.

Households move from one state to another. Individuals quit jobs to seek better positions or retool for more attractive occupations. These and other phenomena produce some minimal amount of unemployment—people who literally are *between* jobs. Economists call this the level of **frictional unemployment**.

**FRICTIONAL UNEMPLOYMENT** is unemployment that is due to normal turnover in the labor market. It includes people who are temporarily between jobs because they are moving or changing occupations, or for similar reasons.

The critical distinguishing feature of frictional unemployment is that it is short-lived. A frictionally unemployed person has every reason to expect to find a new job soon. People tend to think of frictional unemployment as irreducible, but that is not true. During World War II, for example, unemployment in this country fell below 2 percent—substantially below the frictional level.

Frictional unemployment is irreducible only in the sense that—under normal circumstances—it is socially undesirable to do so. Geographical and occupational mobility play important roles in our market economy—enabling people to search for better jobs. Similarly, waste is avoided by allowing inefficient firms, or firms producing items no longer in demand, to be replaced by new firms. Inhibition of either of these phenomena must hamper the workings of the market economy. But, if these adjustment mechanisms are allowed to operate, there will always be some temporarily unemployed workers looking for jobs; and there will always be some firms with unfilled positions looking for workers. This is the genesis of frictional unemployment.

A second type of unemployment is often difficult to distinguish from frictional unemployment, but it has very different implications. **Structural unemployment** arises when jobs are eliminated by changes in the structure of the economy, such as automation or permanent changes in demand. The crucial difference between frictional and structural unemployment is that, unlike frictionally unemployed workers, structurally unemployed workers cannot realistically be considered "between jobs." Instead, they may find their skills and experience unwanted in the changing economy in which they live. They are thus faced with either a prolonged period of unemployment or the necessity of making a major change in their occupation. For older workers, learning a new occupation may be nearly impossible.

**STRUCTURAL UNEMPLOYMENT** refers to workers who have lost their jobs because they have been displaced by automation, because their skills are no longer in demand, or for similar reasons.

The remaining type of unemployment, **cyclical unemployment**, will occupy most of our attention. Cyclical unemployment arises when the level of economic activity declines, that is, in a recession. Thus when economists speak of maintaining "full employment," they do not mean achieving zero measured unemployment, but rather limiting unemployment to its frictional and structural components. A key question, therefore, is: How much measured unemployment is that?

**CYCLICAL UNEMPLOYMENT** is the portion of unemployment that is attributable to a decline in the economy's total production. Cyclical unemployment rises during recessions and falls as prosperity is restored.

## HOW MUCH EMPLOYMENT IS "FULL EMPLOYMENT"?

President John F. Kennedy, in 1961, was the first to commit the federal government to a specific numerical goal. Looking at experience in the prosperous early 1950s, he picked a 4 percent unemployment target. But during the 1970s, the 4 percent goal was rejected as outmoded, and no new numerical target was put in its place. There were two major reasons for rejecting 4 percent.

First, some economists argued that the 4 percent target had to be adjusted upward because the composition of the labor force had changed. In particular, there were many more young workers in the 1970s than in the 1950s, and teenagers always have higher rates of unemployment than adults. Second, they suggested, the increased generosity of unemployment compensation (which is discussed just below) had reduced the incentive to get off the unemployment rolls. Why work, if unemployment benefits and other programs provide an income nearly as large as the salary one could earn on the job?

In the 1980s, there was considerable debate over exactly how much measured unemployment corresponded to **full employment**. Some observers argued that full employment came at a measured unemployment rate above 6 percent. Others pointed out that the main factors that had raised the full-employment unemployment rate in the 1970s were reversed in the 1980s: the teenage labor force dwindled, and unemployment benefits went to a smaller percentage of the unemployed.

As is so often the case, actual events helped settle the argument. Measured unemployment fell below 6 percent late in the 1980s and remained there until the end of 1990. This persuaded many economists that full employment came at an unemployment rate around $5\frac{1}{2}$ percent. But some felt it might be lower, and others thought it was higher. The definition of "full employment" remains controversial.

## UNEMPLOYMENT INSURANCE: THE INVALUABLE CUSHION

One surprising feature of the 1980s was the equanimity with which the electorates of the United States and other industrial countries tolerated high unemployment rates. One major reason was **unemployment insurance**.

One of the most valuable pieces of legislation to emerge from the trauma of the Great Depression was the Social Security Act of 1935. Among other things, it established an unemployment insurance system that is now administered by each of the 50 states under federal guidelines. Thanks to this system, many—but not all—American workers can never experience the complete loss of income that devastated so many during the 1930s.

While the precise amounts vary substantially, the average weekly benefit check to unemployed workers in 1992 was about $180. This amounted to about 45 percent of average earnings. Though a 55 percent drop in earnings still poses serious problems, the importance of this 45 percent income cushion can scarcely be exaggerated, especially since it may be supplemented by funds from other welfare programs. Families that are covered by unemployment insurance simply do not have to go hungry when they lose their jobs, and they are only rarely dispossessed from their homes.

Who is eligible to receive these benefits? Precise qualifications vary from state to state, but some stipulations apply quite generally. Only experienced workers qualify; so persons just joining the labor force (such as recent graduates of high schools and colleges) or reentering after a prolonged absence (such as women resuming work after years of child rearing) cannot collect benefits. Neither can those who have quit their jobs, except under unusual circumstances. And benefits end after a stipulated period of time. For all these reasons, less than one-third of the almost 10 million people who were unemployed during 1992 actually received benefits.

The importance of unemployment insurance to the unemployed is obvious. But there are also significant benefits to citizens who never become unemployed. During recession years, many billions of dollars are paid out in unemployment benefits, and since recipients probably spend most of their benefits, unemployment insurance limits the severity of recessions by providing additional purchasing power when and where it is most needed.

The unemployment insurance system is one of several "cushions" that have been built into our economy since 1933 to prevent the possibility of another Great Depression. By giving money to those who become unemployed, the system helps prop up aggregate demand during recessions.

While the U.S. economy is now probably "depression proof," this should not be a cause for too much rejoicing, for the long-lasting recession of the early 1990s amply demonstrated that we are far from "recession proof."

### UNEMPLOYMENT INSURANCE AND THE COSTS OF UNEMPLOYMENT

The fact that unemployment insurance and other social welfare programs replace a significant fraction of lost income has led some skeptics to claim that unemployment is no longer a serious problem. But the fact is that:

Unemployment insurance is just what the name says—an *insurance* program. And insurance can never prevent a catastrophe from occurring; it can only *spread the costs* of a catastrophe among many people instead of letting them all fall on the shoulders of those few unfortunate souls whom it affects directly.

Fire insurance is an example. If your family is covered by fire insurance and your house burns down, you will probably suffer only a small financial loss because the insurance company will pay most of the expenses. Where does it get the money? It cannot create it out of thin air. Rather, it must have collected the funds from the many other families who purchased insurance but did not suffer any fire damages. Thus, one family's loss of perhaps $100,000 is covered by the insurance payments of 500 families each paying $200 a year. In this way, the costs of the catastrophe are spread among hundreds of families, and in the process, made much more bearable.

But despite the insurance, the family whose house is destroyed by fire suffers anguish and inconvenience. No insurance policy can eliminate this. Furthermore, society loses a valuable resource—a house. It will take much wood, cement, nails, paint, and labor to replace the burnt-out home. *An insurance policy cannot insure society against losses of real resources.*

The case is precisely the same with insurance against unemployment. All workers and employers pay for the insurance policy by a tax that the government levies on wages and salaries. With the funds so collected, the government compensates the victims of unemployment. Thus, instead of letting the costs of unemployment fall entirely on the minority of workers who lose their jobs:

Our system of payroll taxes and unemployment benefits *spreads* the costs of unemployment over the entire population. But it does not eliminate the basic economic cost.

## THE COSTS OF INFLATION

Both the human and economic costs of inflation are less obvious than the costs of unemployment. But this does not necessarily make them any less real, for if one thing is crystal clear about inflation, it is that people do not like it.

Public opinion polls consistently show that inflation ranks high on people's list of major national problems, generally even ahead of unemployment. Surveys also find that inflation, like unemployment, causes a deterioration in consumers' sense of well-being—it makes people unhappy. Finally, studies of elections suggest that voters penalize the party that occupies the White House when inflation is high.

The fact is beyond dispute: People consider inflation to be something bad. The question is: Why?

## INFLATION: THE MYTH AND THE REALITY

At first, the question may seem ridiculous. During times of inflation, people keep paying higher prices for the same quantities of goods and services they had before. So more and more income is needed just to maintain the same standard of living. Is it not obvious that this erosion of **purchasing power**—that is, the decline in what money will buy—makes everyone worse off?

The **PURCHASING POWER** of a given sum of money is the volume of goods and services it will buy.

This would indeed be the case were it not for one very significant fact. The wages people earn are also prices—prices for labor services. During a period of inflation, wages also rise and, in fact, the average wage typically rises more or less in step with prices. Thus, contrary to popular myth, workers as a group are not usually victimized by inflation.

The **REAL WAGE RATE** is the wage rate adjusted for inflation. It indicates the volume of goods and services that money wages will buy.

The purchasing power of wages—what is called the **real wage**—is not systematically eroded by inflation. Sometimes wages rise faster than prices, and sometimes prices rise faster than wages. The fact is that in the long run wages tend to outstrip prices as new capital equipment and innovation increase output per worker.

Figure 23–3 illustrates this simple fact. The blue line shows the annual rate of increase of consumer prices in the United States for each year since 1948, while the black line shows the annual rate of wage increase. The difference between the two indicates the rate of growth of *real* wages. Generally, wages rise faster than prices, reflecting the steady advance of technology and of labor productivity; so real wages rise.

The feature of Figure 23–3 that virtually jumps off the page is the way the two lines dance together. Wages normally rise rapidly when prices rise rapidly, and rise slowly when prices rise slowly. But you should not draw any hasty conclusions from this association. We cannot, for example, learn from this figure whether rising prices cause rising wages or whether rising wages cause rising prices. Remember the warnings given in Chapter 1 about trying to infer causation just by looking at data. But analyzing cause and effect is not our purpose right now. We merely want to explode the myth that inflation inevitably erodes real wages.

Why is this myth so widespread? Imagine a world without inflation in which wages are rising 2 percent a year because of the increasing productivity of labor. Now imagine that, all of a sudden, inflation sets in and prices start rising 4 percent a year but that nothing else changes. Figure 23–3 suggests that, with perhaps a small delay, wage increases will accelerate to 2 percent plus 4 percent, or 6 percent a year.

Will workers view this change with equanimity? Probably not. To each worker, the 6 percent wage increase will be seen as something he earned by the sweat of his brow. In his view, he *deserves* every penny of his 6 percent raise. And, in a sense, he is right because "the sweat of his brow" earned him a 2 percent increment

**Figure 23-3** **RATES OF CHANGE OF WAGES AND PRICES IN THE UNITED STATES, 1948–1992**

This chart compares the rate of price inflation (blue line) with the rate of growth of nominal wages (black line) in the postwar period. The patterns are clearly quite similar, with wages and prices normally accelerating or decelerating together. Notice that wage increases generally outstrip price increases; that is, *real* wages normally rise from year to year.

SOURCE: Bureau of Labor Statistics.

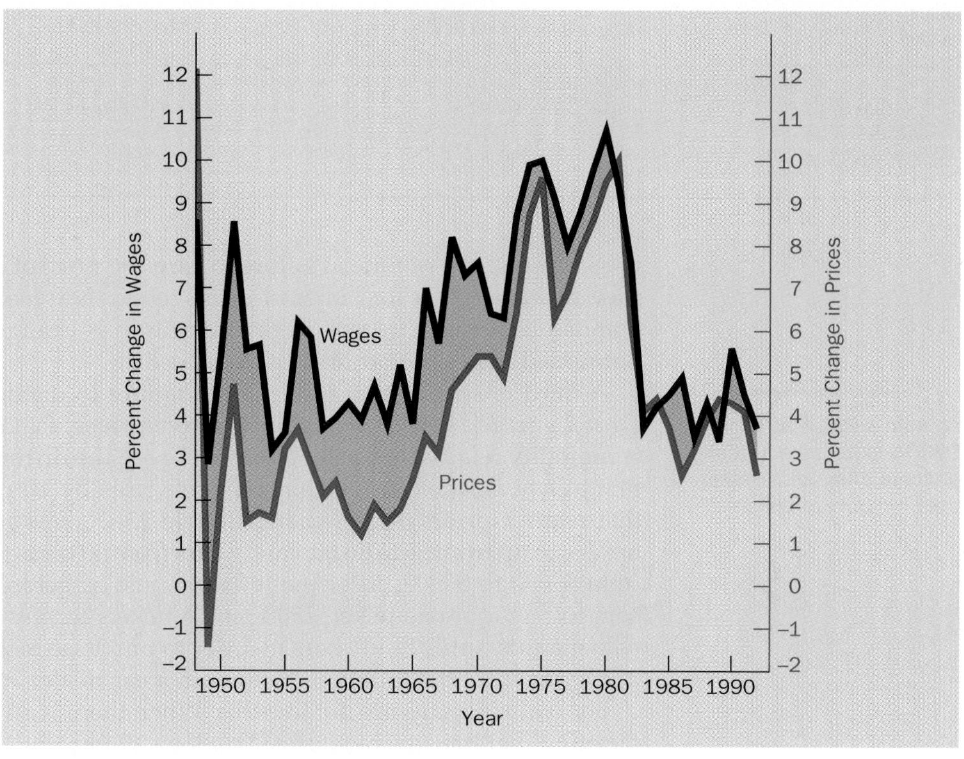


in real wages that, when the inflation rate is 4 percent, can only be achieved by increasing his money wages by a total of 6 percent. An economist would divide the wage increase in the following way:

| REASON FOR WAGE INCREASE | AMOUNT |
|---|---|
| Higher productivity | 2% |
| Compensation for higher prices | 4% |
| Total | 6% |

"Sure, you're raising my allowance. But am I actually gaining any purchasing power?"

But the worker will probably keep score differently. Feeling that he earned the entire 6 percent by his own merits, he will view inflation as having "robbed" him of 4 percent of his just deserts. The higher the rate of inflation, the more of his raise the worker will feel has been stolen from him.

Of course, nothing could be further from the truth. Basically, the economic system is rewarding the worker with *the same 2 percent real wage increment for higher productivity regardless of the rate of inflation*. The "evils of inflation" are often exaggerated because of a failure to understand this mechanism.

A second reason for misunderstanding the effects of inflation is that people are in the habit of thinking in terms of the number of dollars it takes to buy something rather than in terms of the *purchasing power* of these dollars. For example, if inflation doubles both prices and wages, workers will have to labor exactly

*Table* **23–2**

| ITEM | LAST YEAR'S PRICE | THIS YEAR'S PRICE | PERCENT INCREASE |
|---|---|---|---|
| Candy bar | $0.50 | $0.55 | 10 |
| Movie ticket | 6.00 | 6.60 | 10 |
| Automobile | 9000 | 9900 | 10 |

the same amount of time as before to earn the price of a loaf of bread. But because they now pay $1 a loaf instead of 50 cents, they feel that the price of bread is scandalously high. In fact, nothing really has changed; but people cling to an outmoded idea of what bread *should* cost.

An item's **RELATIVE PRICE** is its price in terms of some other item, rather than in terms of dollars.

A third misperception results from failure to distinguish between a *rise in the general price level* and a change in **relative prices**, that is, a rise in the price of one commodity relative to that of another. To see the distinction most clearly, imagine first a *pure inflation* in which *every* price rises by 10 percent during the year, so that relative prices do not change. Table 23–2 gives an example in which movie tickets go up from $6 to $6.60, candy bars from 50 cents to 55 cents, and automobiles from $9000 to $9900. After the inflation, just as before, it will still take 12 candy bars to buy a movie ticket, 1500 movie tickets to buy a car, and so on. A person who manufactures candy bars in order to purchase movie tickets is neither helped nor harmed by the inflation. Neither is a car dealer with a sweet tooth.

But real inflations are not like this. When there is 10 percent general inflation—meaning that the "average price" rises by 10 percent[3]—some prices may jump 20 percent or more while others actually fall. Suppose that, instead of the price increases shown in Table 23–2, prices rise as shown in Table 23–3. Movie prices go up by 25 percent, but candy prices do not change. Surely, candy manufacturers who love movies will be disgruntled because it now costs 15 candy bars instead of 12 to get into the theater. They will blame inflation for raising the price of movie tickets, even though their real problem stems from the *increase in the price of movies relative to candy*. (They would have been hurt as much if movie tickets had remained at $6 while the price of candy fell to 40 cents.)

Since car prices have risen by only 5 percent, theater owners in need of new cars will be delighted by the fact that an auto now costs only 1260 movie admissions—just as they would have cheered if car prices had fallen to $7560 while movie tickets remained at $6. However, they are unlikely to attribute their good fortune to inflation—as indeed they should not. What has actually happened is that *cars became cheaper relative to movies*.

Because real-world inflations proceed at *uneven* rates, relative prices are constantly changing. There are gainers and losers, just as some would gain and others lose if relative prices changed without any general inflation. Inflation, however, gets a bad name because losers often blame inflation for their misfortune while gainers rarely credit inflation for their good luck. Alas, nobody loves inflation.

These three kinds of misconceptions may go a long way toward explaining why respondents to public opinion polls consistently list inflation as a major

[3]The way statisticians figure out "average" price increases is discussed in the appendix to this chapter.

**Table 23-3**

| ITEM | LAST YEAR'S PRICE | THIS YEAR'S PRICE | PERCENT INCREASE |
|---|---|---|---|
| Candy bar | $0.50 | $0.50 | 0 |
| Movie ticket | 6.00 | 7.50 | 25 |
| Automobile | 9000 | 9450 | 5 |

national issue, why higher inflation rates depress consumers, and why voters express their ire at the polls when inflation is high.

Inflation does not systematically erode the purchasing power of wages. Nor does it lead to "unfair" prices. Nor is it usually to blame when some goods become more expensive relative to others.

But not all of the costs of inflation are mythical. Let us now turn to some of the real costs.

## INFLATION AS A REDISTRIBUTOR OF INCOME AND WEALTH

We have just seen that the *average* person is neither helped nor harmed by inflation. But almost no one is exactly average! Some persons gain from inflation and others lose. It is hard to say anything more systematic than this about the effects of inflation on particular prices and wages.

But inflation does have systematic effects on the distribution of income and wealth. Senior citizens trying to scrape by on pensions or other fixed incomes suffer badly from inflation. Since they earn no wages, it is little solace to them that wages keep pace with prices. Their pension incomes do not.[4]

This example actually illustrates a much more general problem. We can think of pensioners as people who "lend" money to an organization (the pension fund) when they are young in order to be "paid back" with interest when they are old. Because of the rise in the price level during the intervening years, the unfortunate pensioners get paid back in less valuable dollars than those they originally loaned. In general:

Those who lend money are usually victimized by rising inflation.

While lenders lose heavily, borrowers do quite well. For example, homeowners who borrowed money from banks in the form of mortgages back in the 1950s, when interest rates were 3 or 4 percent, gained enormously from the surprisingly virulent inflation of the late 1960s and 1970s. They paid back dollars of much lower value than those that they borrowed. And the same is true of other borrowers.

Borrowers usually gain from rising inflation.

---

[4]This is not, however, true of social security benefits, which are automatically increased to compensate recipients for changes in the price level. For further discussion of the social security system, see Chapter 20.

Since the redistribution caused by inflation generally benefits borrowers at the expense of lenders, and since both lenders and borrowers can be found at every income level, we must conclude that:

Inflation does not always steal from the rich to aid the poor, nor does it always do the reverse.

Why, then, is the redistribution caused by inflation so widely condemned? Because its victims are selected capriciously. Nobody legislates this redistribution. Nobody enters into it voluntarily. The gainers do not earn their spoils, and the losers do not deserve their fate. Moreover, there are particular classes of people whom inflation has systematically robbed of purchasing power year after year—people living on private pensions, families who save money and "loan" it to banks, and workers on long-term contracts or whose wages and salaries do not adjust easily for some other reason. Even if people "on the average" suffer no damage from inflation, that offers little consolation to those who are hurt by it persistently and systematically. This is the fundamental indictment of inflation.

Inflation redistributes income in an arbitrary way. The actual income distribution should reflect the interplay of the operation of free markets and the purposeful efforts of government to alter the distribution. Inflation interferes with and distorts this process.

## REAL VERSUS NOMINAL INTEREST RATES

But wait. Must inflation always rob lenders to bestow gifts upon borrowers? If both parties see inflation coming, won't lenders demand that borrowers pay a higher interest rate as compensation for the coming inflation? Indeed they will. For this reason, economists draw a sharp distinction between inflation that is *expected* and inflation that comes as a *surprise*.

What happens when inflation is fully expected by both parties? Suppose Diamond Jim wants to borrow $1000 from Scrooge, and both agree that, in the absence of inflation which erodes the purchasing power of money, a fair rate of interest would be 3 percent on a one-year loan. This means that Diamond Jim would pay back $1030 at the end of the year for the privilege of having $1000 now.

If both expect prices to increase by 6 percent, Scrooge may reason as follows, "If Diamond Jim pays me back $1030 a year from today, that money will buy less than what $1000 buys today. Thus I'll really be *paying him* to borrow from me! I'm no philanthropist. Why don't I charge him 9 percent instead? Then he'll pay back $1090 at the end of the year. With prices 6 percent higher, this will buy roughly what $1030 is worth today. So I'll get the same 3 percent increase in purchasing power that we would have agreed on in the absence of inflation, and won't be any worse off. That's the least I'll accept."

Diamond Jim may follow a similar chain of logic. "With no inflation, I was willing to pay $1030 a year from now for the privilege of having $1000 today, and Scrooge was willing to lend it. He'd be crazy to do the same with a 6 percent inflation. He'll want to charge me more. How much should I pay? If I offer him $1090 a year from now, that will have roughly the same purchasing power as $1030 today, so I won't be any worse off. That's the most I'll pay."

This kind of thinking will lead Scrooge and Diamond Jim to write a contract with a 9 percent interest rate—3 percent as the increase in purchasing power that

Diamond Jim pays to Scrooge and 6 percent as compensation for expected inflation. Then, if the expected 6 percent inflation actually materializes, neither party will have been made better or worse off than was expected at the time the contract was signed.

This example illustrates a general principle. The 3 percent increase in purchasing power that Diamond Jim agrees to hand over to Scrooge is called the **real rate of interest**. And the 9 percent contractual interest charge that Diamond Jim and Scrooge write into the loan agreement is called the **nominal rate of interest**. The nominal rate of interest is arrived at by adding the **expected rate of inflation** to the real rate of interest. Expected inflation is added to compensate the lender for the loss of purchasing power that he is expected to suffer as a result of inflation. Because of this:

The **REAL RATE OF INTEREST** is the percentage increase in purchasing power that the borrower pays to the lender for the privilege of borrowing. It indicates the increased ability to purchase goods and services that the lender earns.

The **NOMINAL RATE OF INTEREST** is the percentage by which the money the borrower pays back exceeds the money that he borrowed, making no adjustment for any fall in the purchasing power of this money that results from inflation.

Inflation that is accurately predicted need not redistribute income between borrowers and lenders. If the *expected* rate of inflation that is embodied in the nominal interest rate closely approximates the *actual* rate of inflation, no one gains and no one loses. However, to the extent that expectations prove incorrect, inflation will still redistribute income.[5]

It need hardly be pointed out that errors in predicting the rate of inflation are the norm, not the exception. Published forecasts bear witness to the fact that economists have great difficulty in predicting the rate of inflation. The task is no easier for businesses, consumers, and banks. This is one reason why inflation is so widely condemned as unfair and undesirable. It sets up a guessing game that no one likes.

## INFLATION AND THE TAX SYSTEM

So inflation imposes costs on society because it is hard to predict. But other costs arise from inflation even when it is predicted accurately. These costs stem from the fact that the laws and regulations that govern our financial system were designed for an inflation-free economy; and these laws may malfunction when inflation is high.

The tax system is probably the most important example. The law does not recognize the distinction between nominal and real interest rates; it simply taxes nominal interest regardless of how much real interest it represents. As a result, strange things happen when there is high inflation. Our example of Scrooge's loan to Diamond Jim will illustrate the problem.

The top line of Table 23–4 shows how taxation affects the loan agreement when there is no inflation and the nominal and real interest rates are both 3 percent. Scrooge earns $30 in nominal interest income (column 3). Since there is no inflation, this also represents $30 in real interest income (column 5). If Scrooge pays one-third of his income in taxes, his tax bill rises by $10 (column 6), leaving him with $20 after tax (column 7). This $20 amounts to 2 percent of the $1000 originally loaned (column 8). Because his $10 tax payment is one-third of his $30 in real interest income, Scrooge's effective tax rate is $33\frac{1}{3}$ percent (column 9), just as Congress intended.

[5]EXERCISE: Who gains and who loses if the inflation turns out to be only 4 percent instead of the 6 percent that Scrooge and Diamond Jim expected? What if the inflation rate is 8 percent?

**Table 23–4 INFLATION AND THE TAXATION OF INTEREST INCOME**

| (1) INFLATION RATE (percent) | (2) NOMINAL INTEREST RATE (percent) | (3) INTEREST INCOME (dollars) | (4) LOSS OF PURCHASING POWER DUE TO INFLATION (dollars) | (5) REAL INTEREST INCOME (dollars) | (6) TAXES PAID (dollars) | (7) REAL INCOME AFTER TAX (dollars) | (8) REAL INCOME AFTER TAX (as a percentage of $1000 loan) | (9) EFFECTIVE RATE OF TAXATION (percent) |
|---|---|---|---|---|---|---|---|---|
| 0 | 3 | 30 | 0 | 30 | 10 | 20 | 2% | $33\frac{1}{3}$ |
| 6 | 9 | 90 | 60 | 30 | 30 | 0 | 0% | 100 |

Now let's consider the same transaction when the inflation rate is 6 percent and Scrooge and Diamond Jim settle on a 9 percent nominal interest rate. Scrooge collects $90 in interest (column 3). But, with 6 percent inflation, the purchasing power of the $1000 he lends declines by $60 (column 4). Thus his real interest income is again $30 (column 5). However, the tax collector taxes the $90 *nominal* interest income, not the $30 real interest income, so Scrooge must pay $30 (one-third of $90) in taxes (column 6). As we can see in column 7, his after-tax real income on the loan is zero since the tax collector takes all his real income. Thus the effective tax rate on Scrooge's real interest income is 100 percent (column 9), far larger than the $33\frac{1}{3}$ percent rate intended by Congress.

So a tax system that works well at zero inflation misfires at 6 percent inflation because it taxes nominal, rather than real, interest. This little example illustrates a general, and very serious, problem:

Because it fails to recognize the distinction between nominal and real interest rates, our tax system levies high, and presumably unintended, tax rates on interest income when there is high inflation. And similar problems arise in the taxation of capital gains, corporate profits, and other items. Many economists feel that these high tax rates discourage saving, lending, and investing, and that high inflation therefore retards economic growth.

A **CAPITAL GAIN** is the difference between the price at which an asset is sold and the price at which it was bought.

A particularly acute version of this problem arises in the taxation of **capital gains**—the difference between the price at which an investor sells an asset and the price she paid for it. An example will bring out the point. Between 1979 and 1993 the price level doubled, approximately. Consider some stock that was purchased for $5000 in 1979 and sold for $7500 in 1993. The investor actually *lost* purchasing power in the transaction because $7500 in 1993 purchased less than $5000 in 1979. Yet, since the law levies taxes on nominal capital gains, with no correction for inflation, the investor will be taxed on the $2500 nominal capital gain as though there had been a profit rather than a loss.

Many economists have proposed that this, presumably unintended, feature of the law be changed by taxing only capital gains that exceed inflation. But, up to now, Congress has not adopted this suggestion.

A **USURY LAW** sets down a maximum permissible interest rate for a particular type of loan. Loans at rates above the usury ceiling are illegal.

## USURY LAWS, INTEREST RATE CEILINGS, AND OTHER IMPEDIMENTS

Another example of laws that malfunction under inflation is **usury laws**, which set *maximum* permissible interest rates on particular types of loans. Usury laws date back to biblical days and command widespread popular support. The problem is that, when they place ceilings on *nominal* interest rates rather than on *real* interest rates, they can have perverse effects in an inflationary environment.

In our previous example of Scrooge and Diamond Jim, suppose that a usury law sets a maximum rate of 8 percent on consumer loans. Diamond Jim is willing to pay a 9 percent nominal interest rate and Scrooge is willing to lend at this rate. But the law intervenes: "Thou shalt not charge usurious interest." The deal cannot be completed, and both Diamond Jim and Scrooge go away disappointed.

The problem is that usury ceilings were set in periods of fairly steady prices, when there was no great difference between nominal and real interest rates. If, for example, the usury law set the legal maximum at an 8 percent *real* rate of interest, it would not prevent Scrooge from lending to Diamond Jim. As it is, however, a loan carrying a 3 percent real interest rate is perfectly legal at zero inflation but illegal at 6 percent inflation!

Usury laws set in nominal terms created so much havoc during the period of double-digit inflation in 1979–1980 that Congress took drastic action to curtail them. Consequently, usury ceilings on interest rates are far less prevalent today than they were a decade ago, and are set at higher levels in states that still have them.

Usury laws and problems with the tax system are just two examples of a general phenomenon:

Many of the laws that govern our financial system become extremely counterproductive in an inflationary environment, causing problems that were never intended by the legislators.

And it is important to note that *these costs of inflation are not purely redistributive.* Society as a whole loses when mutually beneficial transactions are prohibited by obsolete legislation, when saving and investing are discouraged, and when loans are not provided to those who need them.

Why do such laws stay on the books so long? One reason is a general lack of understanding of the difference between real and nominal interest rates. People fail to understand that it is normally the *real* rate of interest that matters in an economic transaction because only that rate reveals how much borrowers pay and lenders receive *in terms of the goods and services that money can buy.* They focus on the high nominal interest rates caused by inflation, even when these rates correspond to low real interest rates. Here are some other examples that may help you appreciate how widespread and important this interest rate illusion is.

***REGULATION OF PUBLIC UTILITIES*** During 1980, when the rate of inflation rose above 12 percent, there was a public uproar when regulated utilities asked the regulatory agencies to permit them to earn a rate of return closer to 11 percent—a *negative* real rate of return! They frequently found that their requests were considered exorbitant by the commissions and by the general public. The consequence was that many utilities could not afford to borrow the money needed to serve expanding public demand.

***RECORD PROFIT RATES*** Amazingly, even business managers were subject to the same form of illusion. Often they were taken aback by the notion that their investors actually lost out (earned a negative *real* rate of return) when the company was earning a 10 percent profit. The managers noted that 10 percent was the company's highest earnings rate in recent history. But with inflation at 12 percent, it turned out that in real terms it was in fact the firm's lowest.

Thus, failure to understand that high *nominal* interest rates can signify low *real* interest rates has been known to impoverish savers during a period of inflation. It has made profits appear high when they were really low. It has sometimes made it impossible for public utilities to raise the capital they need to serve rising consumer demands, and power shortages and failures have been the predictable results.

**THE ILLUSION OF HIGH INTEREST RATES**

The difference between real and nominal interest (and profit) rates, and the fact that the real rate matters economically while the nominal rate is politically significant, are matters that are of the utmost importance and yet are understood by very few people, including many persons who make public policy decisions in these areas.

This concept is one of the **12 Ideas for Beyond the Final Exam**, and if you remember it ten years from now, you will truly have gotten a great deal out of studying economics.

## OTHER COSTS OF INFLATION

Another cost of inflation is that rapidly changing prices make it risky to enter into long-term contracts. In an extremely severe inflation, the "long term" may be only a few days. But even moderate inflations can have remarkable effects on long-term loans. Suppose a corporation wants to borrow $1 million to finance the purchase of some new equipment and needs the loan for 20 years. If inflation averages 4 percent over this period, the $1 million it repays at the end of 20 years will be worth $456,387 in today's purchasing power. If inflation averages 8 percent instead, it will be worth only $214,548. Lending or borrowing for this long a period is obviously a big gamble. With the stakes this high, the outcome may be that neither lenders nor borrowers want to get involved in long-term contracts. But without long-term loans, business investment becomes impossible. The economy stagnates.

Inflation also makes life difficult for the shopper. You probably have a group of stores that you habitually patronize because they carry the items you want to buy at (roughly) the prices you want to pay. This knowledge saves you a great deal of time and energy. But when prices are changing rapidly, your list quickly becomes obsolete. You return to your favorite clothing store to find that the price of jeans has risen drastically. Should you buy? Should you shop around at other stores? Will they have also raised their prices? Business firms have precisely the same problem with their suppliers. Rising prices force them to shop around more, which imposes costs on the firms and, more generally, reduces the efficiency of the whole economy.

Shopping costs may sound frivolous and unimportant, but they are not. Arthur Okun, who chaired the Council of Economic Advisers under President Johnson, suggested an ingenious mental exercise that illustrates the importance of shopping costs. Ask yourself the following question: How much would you have to be paid to promise never again to buy anything from any of the stores you have patronized in the past? When you ponder this for a while, you realize the great value of having normal places to shop. Inflation takes some of this value away.

## CREEPING VERSUS GALLOPING INFLATION

The preceding litany of costs of inflation alerts us to one very important fact: *predictable inflation is far less burdensome than unpredictable inflation*. When is inflation most predictable? When it proceeds year after year at more or less the same rate. Thus the *variability of the inflation rate* is a crucial factor. Inflation of 4 percent a year for three consecutive years will exact lower social costs than inflation that is 2 percent in the first year, zero in the second, and 10 percent in the third. In general:

Steady inflation is more predictable than variable inflation and therefore has smaller social and economic costs.

But the *average level of the inflation rate* is also important. Partly because of the interest rate illusions mentioned above and partly because of the more rapid breakdown in normal customer relationships that we have just mentioned, a steady inflation of 6 percent a year does more damage than a steady inflation of 3 percent a year.

**CREEPING INFLATION** refers to an inflation that proceeds for a long time at a moderate and fairly steady pace.

**GALLOPING INFLATION** refers to an inflation that proceeds at an exceptionally high rate, perhaps for only a relatively brief period. Galloping inflations are generally characterized by accelerating rates of inflation so that the rate of inflation is higher this month than it was last month.

Economists distinguish between **creeping inflations** and **galloping inflations** partly on their average level and partly on their variability. Under creeping inflation, prices rise for a long time at a moderate and fairly steady rate. From 1982 to 1992 in the United States, for example, prices climbed a total of 44 percent, for an average annual inflation rate of 3.7 percent. And the pace of inflation was remarkably steady, never dropping below 2.6 percent nor rising above 4.4 percent.

Galloping inflation refers to an inflation that proceeds at an exceptionally high rate, perhaps for only a brief period. In recent decades, for example, quite a few Latin countries have experienced inflation rates exceeding 100 percent, and sometimes 1000 percent, per year. (See the accompanying boxed insert on Nicaragua.) Russia is suffering a similar fate at this writing.

The German hyperinflation after World War I is perhaps the most famous episode of galloping inflation. Between December 1922 and November 1923, when a hard-nosed reform finally broke the spiral, wholesale prices in Germany increased by almost 100 million percent! But even this experience was dwarfed by the great Hungarian inflation of 1945–1946, the greatest inflation of them all. For a period of one year, the *monthly* rate of inflation averaged about 20,000 percent. And in the final month, the price level skyrocketed 42 quadrillion percent!

While the distinction between creeping and galloping inflation is a quantitative one, we refrained from putting any specific numbers into the definitions. This is because different societies at different points in time hold very different conceptions of what rate constitutes creeping inflation and what rate constitutes galloping inflation. For example, in the United States today, annual rates of inflation in the 2 to 4 percent range are generally considered to be "creeping," while rates in the 25 to 30 percent range would surely be construed as "galloping." In many Latin American countries, however, inflation consistently in the 25 to 30 percent range is viewed as "creeping." And in the United States of the 1950s, a 4 percent annual inflation might have been branded "galloping."

## *Hyperinflation and the Piggy Bank*

While mild inflations are barely noticeable in everyday life, hyperinflation makes all sorts of normal economic activities more difficult and transforms a society in strange and unexpected ways. This article, excerpted from *The New York Times,* illustrates some of the problems that hyperinflation created for Nicaraguans in 1989.

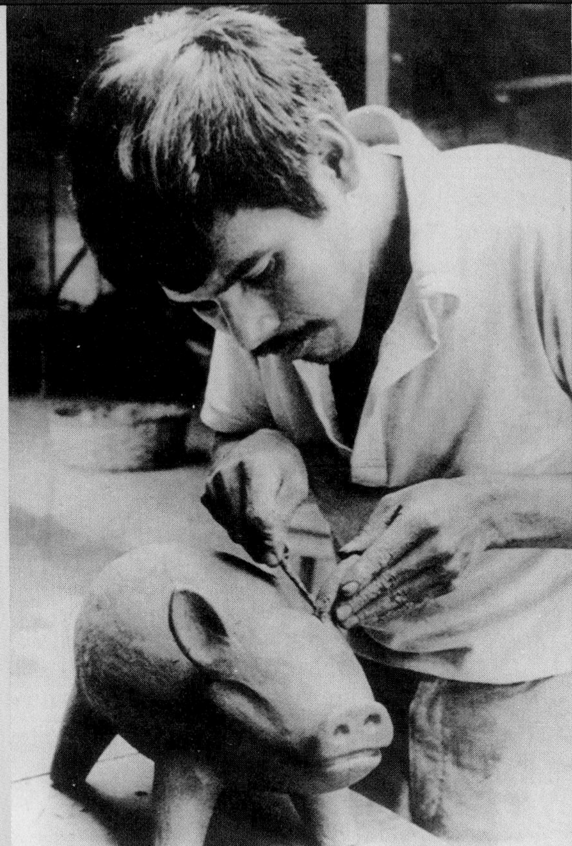

For generations, Nicaraguans have guarded their savings in piggy banks . . . But no longer. In a country where inflation recently reached 161 percent for a two-week period, a penny saved is a penny spent. "No one wants a bank now," said a potter who has given over his kilns to making beer mugs. "We've given up even making them."

The demise of the piggy bank is only the least of the complications that have vexed the public as inflation and Government efforts to combat it have sent the value of the Nicaraguan córdoba fluctuating wildly.

After inflation became unbearable, the Government replaced all of its currency in February 1988 at a new rate of 10 córdobas to a dollar. But by December, the new money had reached 4,500 to the dollar, and despite months of harsh austerity measures, it has now surged upward again, reaching 26,250 to the dollar.

That kind of uncertainty has left the banking system in shambles, despite savings accounts that offer up to 70 percent interest a month. . . . And it has left a legacy of quirks that now extends throughout the country's daily life . . . .

In many parts of the country, enterprising mechanics have converted the nation's once-precious stock of coins into something more valuable: metal washers to fit the nuts and bolts of rapidly deteriorating machinery . . . .

In Managua, it is still necessary to deposit a copper-colored one-córdoba coin to make a pay phone call. But . . . not everybody even remembers what a one-córdoba coin looks like, and fewer still actually own one. That is probably just as well for the phone system, because if anyone bothered to carry the coins, they could make about 26,250 phone calls for a dollar . . . .

Beating the exchange rates is particularly trying for restaurant owners who must have any price increases approved by the Government Institute of Tourism. Since that process consumes precious amounts of time, restaurant owners must aim high with their requests in the anticipation that new inflation will make their prices competitive, but still profitable, at some future date.

When exchange rates are changing, therefore, prices at a given restaurant can shoot far out of sight, emptying it of patrons for days or weeks. Then, as has happened recently, a new devaluation can make the same prices absurdly low in dollar terms. A steak dinner for two at one of Managua's leading restaurants on a recent weekend cost a little over $3, if you could get a table.

SOURCE: Mark A. Uhlig, "Is Nicaraguan Piggy Bank an Endangered Species?" *The New York Times,* June 24, 1989.

## THE COSTS OF CREEPING VERSUS GALLOPING INFLATION

If you review the costs of inflation that have been discussed in this chapter, you will see why the distinction beween creeping and galloping inflation is so fundamental. Many economists think we can live very nicely in an environment of creeping inflation. No one believes we can survive very well under galloping inflation.

Under creeping inflation, the rate at which prices rise is relatively easy to predict and to take into account in setting interest rates (as long as the law allows). Under galloping inflation, where prices are rising at ever-increasing rates, this is extremely difficult, and perhaps impossible, to accomplish. The potential redistributions become monumental, and as a result, lending and borrowing may cease entirely.

Any inflation makes it difficult to write long-term contracts. With creeping inflation, the "long term" may be 20 years, or 10 years, or 5. But with galloping inflation, the "long term" may be measured in weeks or even hours. Restaurant prices may change before you finish your dessert. Railroad fares may go up while you are in the middle of your journey. When it is impossible to enter into contracts of any duration longer than a few hours, economic activity becomes paralyzed. We conclude that:

The horrors of galloping inflation either are absent in creeping inflation or are present in such muted forms that they can scarcely be considered horrors.

## CREEPING INFLATION DOES NOT NECESSARILY LEAD TO GALLOPING INFLATION

We noted earlier that inflation is surrounded by a mythology that bears precious little relation to reality. It seems appropriate to conclude this chapter by disposing of one particularly persistent myth: that creeping inflation invariably leads to galloping inflation.

There is neither statistical evidence nor theoretical support for the myth that creeping inflation inevitably leads to galloping inflation. To be sure, creeping inflations sometimes accelerate. But at other times they slow down.

While creeping inflations have many causes, galloping inflations have occurred only when the government has printed incredible amounts of money, usually to finance wartime expenditures.

These children in Germany during the hyperinflation of the 1920s are building a pyramid with cash, worth no more than the sand or sticks used by children elsewhere.

In the German inflation of 1923, the government finally found that its printing presses could not produce enough paper money to keep pace with the exploding prices. Not that it did not try. By the end of the inflation, the *daily* output of currency was over 400 quadrillion marks! The Hungarian authorities in 1945–1946 tried even harder. The average growth rate of the money supply was more than 12,000 percent *per month*. Needless to say, these are not the kind of inflation problems that are likely to face the United States in the foreseeable future.

But this should not be interpreted to imply there is nothing wrong with creeping inflation. Much of this chapter has been spent analyzing the very real costs of any inflation, no matter how slow. A case against even moderate inflation can indeed be built, but it does not help this case to shout foolish slogans like "Creeping inflation always leads to galloping inflation." Fortunately, it is simply not true.

## *Summary*

1. Unemployment exacts heavy financial and psychological costs from those who are its victims, costs that are borne quite unevenly by different groups in the population.
2. In recent decades, the U.S. economy often has produced less output than it could have were it operating at full employment. This shortfall between actual and **potential GDP** was particularly large in the 1980s.
3. The **unemployment rate** is measured by a government survey that some critics claim understates the unemployment problem. Others, however, contend that the survey methods overstate the problem.
4. **Frictional unemployment** arises when people are between jobs for normal reasons. Thus, most frictional unemployment is desirable.
5. **Structural unemployment** is due to shifts in the pattern of demand or to technological change that makes certain skills obsolete.
6. **Cyclical unemployment** is the portion of unemployment that rises in recessions and falls when the economy booms.
7. President Kennedy first enunciated the goal of 4 percent unemployment in 1961. But few economists think this is a realistic target for the 1990s. Most now think that **"full employment"** comes at an unemployment rate between 5 and 6 percent.
8. **Unemployment insurance** replaces nearly one-half the lost income of unemployed persons who are insured. But less than one-third of the unemployed collect benefits, and no insurance program can bring back the lost output that could have been produced had these people been working.
9. People have many misconceptions about inflation. For example, many people believe that inflation systematically erodes **real wages**, are appalled by rising prices even when wages are rising just as fast, and blame inflation for any unfavorable changes in **relative prices**. All of these are myths.
10. Other costs of inflation are real, however. For example, inflation often redistributes income from lenders to borrowers.
11. This redistribution can be eliminated by adding the **expected rate of inflation** to the interest rate. But legal limitations sometimes prevent this, and expectations often prove to be inaccurate.
12. The **real rate of interest** is the **nominal rate of interest** minus the expected rate of inflation.
13. Since the real rate of interest indicates the command over real resources that the borrower surrenders to the lender, it is of primary economic importance.
14. Yet public attention often is riveted on nominal rates of interest, and this confusion can lead to costly policy mistakes when high inflation converts high nominal interest rates into very low real interest rates. This is one of the **12 Ideas for Beyond the Final Exam**.
15. Because nominal, not real, interest is taxed, our tax system levies heavy taxes on interest income when inflation is high.
16. **Creeping inflation**, which proceeds at moderate and fairly predictable rates year after year, carries far lower social costs than **galloping inflation**, which proceeds at high and variable rates.
17. The notion that creeping inflation inevitably leads to galloping inflation is a myth with no foundation in economic theory and no basis in historical fact.

## *Key Concepts and Terms*

Unemployment rate
Potential GDP
Labor force
Discouraged workers
Frictional unemployment
Structural unemployment
Cyclical unemployment

Full employment
Unemployment insurance
Purchasing power
Real wage
Relative prices
Redistribution by inflation

Real rate of interest
Nominal rate of interest
Expected rate of inflation
Inflation and the tax system
Usury laws
Creeping inflation
Galloping inflation

## Questions for Review

1. Why is it not as terrible to become unemployed nowadays as it was during the Great Depression?
2. "Unemployment is no longer a social problem because unemployed workers receive unemployment benefits and other benefits that make up for most of their lost wages." Comment.
3. Using what you learned about aggregate demand and aggregate supply in Chapter 22, try to explain why the U.S. economy has failed so frequently to produce up to its potential. (You will learn more about this question in later chapters, so don't worry if you find the question difficult now.)
4. Why is it so difficult to define "full employment"? What unemployment rate should the government be shooting for today?
5. Show why each of the following complaints is based on a misunderstanding about inflation:
   a. "Inflation must be stopped because it robs workers of their purchasing power."
   b. "Inflation is a terrible social disease. It leads to unconscionably high prices for basic necessities."
   c. "Inflation makes it impossible for working people to afford many of the things they were hoping to buy."
   d. "Inflation must be stopped today, for if we do not stop it, it will surely accelerate to ruinously high rates and lead to disaster."
6. What is the *real interest rate* paid on a credit-card loan bearing 18 percent nominal interest per year, if the rate of inflation is
   a. zero
   b. 3 percent
   c. 6 percent
   d. 18 percent
   e. 24 percent.
7. Suppose you agree to lend money to your friend on the day you both enter college, at what you both expect to be a zero *real* rate of interest. Payment is to be made at graduation, with interest at a fixed *nominal* rate. If inflation proves to be *lower* during your four years in college than what you both had expected, who will gain and who will lose?
8. You have lived with inflation all your life. Think about the costs that inflation has imposed on you personally. How do these costs relate to the material in this chapter?
9. Add a third line to Table 23–4 showing what would happen if the inflation rate went to 12 percent and the real interest rate remained 3 percent.

# *Appendix* HOW STATISTICIANS MEASURE INFLATION

## INDEX NUMBERS FOR INFLATION

Inflation is generally measured by the change in some index of the general price level. For example, between 1973 and 1992, the Consumer Price Index (CPI) rose from 44.4 to 140.3, an increase of 216 percent. The meaning of the *change* is clear enough. But what is the meaning of the 44.4 figure for 1973 and the 140.3 figure for 1992?

These numbers are **index numbers**, each expresses the cost of a market basket of goods *relative to its cost in some "base" period*. Since the CPI currently uses 1982–1984 as its base period, the CPI of 140.3 for 1992 means that it cost $140.30 to purchase the same basket of goods and services that cost $100 in 1982–1984.

Now, the particular basket of consumer goods and services under scrutiny really did not cost $100 in 1982–1984. When constructing index numbers, it is conventional to set the index at 100 in the base period. How is this conventional figure used in obtaining index numbers of other years? Very simply. Suppose the budget needed to buy the roughly 250 items included in the CPI was $2200 per month in 1982–1984 and $3087 per month in 1992. Then the index is defined by the following rule:

$$\frac{\text{CPI in 1992}}{\text{CPI in 1982–1984}} =$$

$$\frac{\text{Cost of the 250-item market basket in 1992}}{\text{Cost of the 250-item market basket in 1982–1984}}.$$

Since the CPI in 1982–1984 is set at 100:

$$\frac{\text{CPI in 1992}}{100} = \frac{\$3087}{\$2200} = 1.403$$

or

$$\text{CPI in 1992} = 140.3.$$

Exactly the same sort of equation enables us to calculate the CPI in any other year. We have the rule:

$$\text{CPI in given year} =$$

$$\frac{\text{Cost of market basket in given year}}{\text{Cost of market basket in base year}} \times 100.$$

Of course, not every combination of consumer goods that cost $2200 in 1982–1984 rose to $3087 by 1992. For example, a color TV set that cost $400 in 1982 might still have cost $400 in 1992, but a $400 hospital bill in 1982 might have ballooned to $1200. Since no two families buy precisely the same bundle of goods and services, no two families suffer precisely the same increase in their cost of living unless all prices rise at the same rate. Economists refer to this phenomenon as the **index number problem**.

When relative prices are changing, there is no such thing as a "perfect price index" that is correct for every consumer. Any statistical index will understate the increase in the cost of living for some families and overstate it for others. At best, the index can represent the situation of an "average" family.

## THE CONSUMER PRICE INDEX

The most closely watched price index is surely the **Consumer Price Index**, which is calculated and announced each month by the Bureau of Labor Statistics (BLS). When you read in the newspaper or see on television that the "cost of living rose by 0.3 percent last month," chances are the reporter is referring to the CPI.

The CPI is measured by pricing the items on a list representative of a typical urban household budget. To know what items to include and in what amounts, the BLS conducts an extensive survey of spending habits roughly once every decade (the last one was in 1982–1984). This means that the *same* bundle of goods and services is used as a standard for 10 years or so, whether or not spending habits change.[6] Of course, spending habits do change; and this introduces a small error into the CPI's measurement of inflation.

A simple example will help us understand how the CPI is constructed. Imagine that college students purchase only three items—hamburgers, jeans, and movie tickets—and that we want to devise a cost-of-living index (call it SPI, for "student price index") for them. First we would conduct a survey of spending habits in the base year (suppose it is 1983). Table 23–5 represents the hypothetical results. You will

[6]Economists call this a *base-period weight index* because the relative importance it attaches to the price of each item depends on how much money consumers actually chose to spend on the item during the base period.

**Table 23–5 RESULTS OF STUDENT EXPENDITURE SURVEY, 1983**

| ITEM | AVERAGE PRICE | AVERAGE QUANTITY PURCHASED PER MONTH | AVERAGE EXPENDITURE PER MONTH |
|---|---|---|---|
| Hamburger | $0.80 | 70 | $56 |
| Jeans | $24.00 | 1 | $24 |
| Movie ticket | $5.00 | 4 | $20 |
| | | | Total $100 |

note that the frugal students of that day spent only $100 per month: $56 on hamburgers, $24 on jeans, and $20 on movies.

Table 23–6 presents hypothetical prices of these same three items in 1994. Each price has risen by a different amount, ranging from 25 percent for jeans up to 50 percent for hamburgers. By how much has the SPI risen? Pricing the 1983 student budget at 1994 prices, we find that what once cost $100 now costs $142, as the calculation in Table 23–7 shows. Thus the SPI, based on 1983 = 100, is

$$\text{SPI} = \frac{\text{Cost of budget in 1994}}{\text{Cost of budget in 1983}} \text{ x } 100$$

$$= \frac{\$142}{\$100} \text{ x } 100 = 142.$$

So the SPI in 1994 stands at 142, meaning that students' cost of living has increased 42 percent over the 11 years.

## HOW TO USE A PRICE INDEX TO "DEFLATE" MONETARY FIGURES

One of the most common uses of price indexes is in the comparison of monetary figures relating to two different points in time. The problem is that, if there has been inflation, the dollar is not a good measuring rod because it is worth less now than it was in the past.

Here is a simple example. Suppose that the average student spent $100 per month in 1983 but $130 per month in 1994. If there was an outcry that students had become spendthrifts, how would you answer the charge?

The obvious answer is that a dollar in 1994 does not buy what it did in 1983. Specifically, our SPI shows us that it takes $1.42 in 1994 to purchase what $1 would purchase in 1983. To compare the spending habits of students in the two years, we must divide the 1994 spending figure by 1.42. Specifically, *real* spending per student in 1994 (where "real" is defined by 1983 dollars) is,

$$\text{Real spending in 1994} = \frac{\text{Nominal spending in 1994}}{\text{Price index of 1994}}.$$

Thus,

$$\text{Real spending in 1994} = \frac{\$130}{1.42} = \$91.55.$$

This calculation shows that, despite appearances to the contrary, the change in nominal spending from

**Table 23–6 PRICES IN 1994**

| ITEM | PRICE | PERCENTAGE INCREASE OVER 1983 |
|---|---|---|
| Hamburger | $1.20 | 50% |
| Jeans | $30.00 | 25% |
| Movie ticket | $7.00 | 40% |

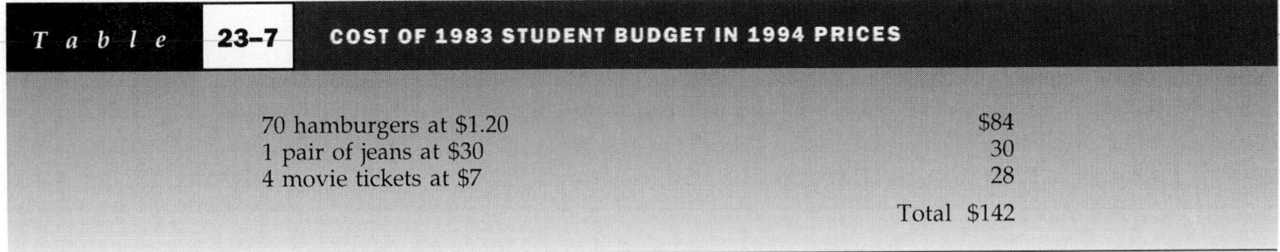

Table 23-7 COST OF 1983 STUDENT BUDGET IN 1994 PRICES

| | |
|---|---|
| 70 hamburgers at \$1.20 | \$84 |
| 1 pair of jeans at \$30 | 30 |
| 4 movie tickets at \$7 | 28 |
| Total | \$142 |

\$100 to \$130 actually represented a *decrease* in real spending.

This calculation procedure is called **deflating by a price index**, and it serves to translate noncomparable monetary figures into more directly comparable real figures.

**Deflating** is the process of finding the real value of some monetary magnitude by dividing by some appropriate price index.

A good practical illustration is the real wage, a concept we have discussed in this chapter. Average hourly earnings in the U.S. economy were \$8.02 in 1983 and \$10.59 in 1992. Since the CPI in 1992 was 140.3 (with 1982–1984 as the base period), the real wage in 1992 (expressed in 1982–84 dollars) was:

$$\text{Real wage in 1992} = \frac{\text{money wage in 1992}}{\text{price index of 1992}} = \frac{\$10.59}{140.3} \times 100 = \$7.55.$$

Thus, by this measure, the real wage fell 5.9 percent over the nine years.

## THE GDP DEFLATOR

In macroeconomics, one of the most important of the monetary magnitudes that we have to deflate is the nominal gross domestic product (GDP). The price index used to do this is called the **GDP deflator**. Our general principle for deflating a nominal magnitude tells us precisely how to go from nominal GDP to real GDP:

$$\text{Real GDP} = \frac{\text{Nominal GDP}}{\text{GDP deflator}} \times 100.$$

As with the CPI, the 100 simply serves to establish the base of the index as 100, rather than 1.00.

Economists often consider the GDP deflator to be a better measure of overall inflation in the economy than the Consumer Price Index. The main reason for this is that the two price indexes are based on different market baskets. As already mentioned, the CPI is based on the budget of a typical urban family. By contrast, the GDP deflator is constructed from a market basket that includes *every* item in the GDP—that is, every final good and service produced by the economy. Thus, in addition to prices of consumer goods, the GDP deflator includes the prices of airplanes, lathes, and other goods purchased by business. It also includes government services. For this reason, the measures of inflation that these two indexes give are rarely the same. Usually their disagreements are minor. But sometimes they can be substantial, as in 1980 when the CPI recorded a 13.5 percent inflation rate over 1979 while the GDP deflator recorded only 9.5 percent.

## Summary

1. Inflation is measured by the percentage increase in an **index number** of prices, which shows how the cost of some basket of goods has changed over a period of time.
2. Since relative prices are changing all the time, and since different families purchase different items, no price index can represent precisely the change in the cost of living for every family.
3. The **Consumer Price Index (CPI)** tries to measure the cost of living for an "average" urban household by pricing a "typical" market basket every month.
4. Price indexes like the CPI can be used to **deflate** monetary figures to make them more comparable. This amounts to dividing the monetary magnitude by the appropriate price index.
5. The **GDP deflator** is a better measure of economy-wide inflation than is the CPI because it includes the prices of all goods and services in the economy.

## Key Concepts and Terms

Index number
Index number problem
Consumer Price Index
Deflating by a price index
GDP deflator

## Questions for Review

1. On the next page, you will find the yearly average value of the Dow Jones Industrial Average, the most popular index of stock market prices, for four different years. The Consumer Price Index for each year (on a base of 1982–1984 = 100) can be found on the inside back cover of this book. Use these numbers to deflate all four stock market values. In which year were stocks really worth the most?

| YEAR | 1964 | 1972 | 1987 | 1992 |
|---|---|---|---|---|
| DOW JONES AVERAGE | 834 | 951 | 2276 | 3284 |

2. Just below you will find nominal GDP and the GDP deflator for 1971, 1981, and 1991.
   a. Compute real GDP for each year.
   b. Compute the percentage change in nominal and real GDP from 1971 to 1981, and from 1981 to 1991.
   c. Compute the percentage change in the GDP deflator over these two periods.

**GDP STATISTICS**

| | 1971 | 1981 | 1991 |
|---|---|---|---|
| Nominal GDP (billions of dollars) | 1097 | 3031 | 5723 |
| GDP deflator | 37.0 | 78.9 | 117.7 |

3. Fill in the blanks in the following table of GDP statistics.

| YEAR | 1990 | 1991 | 1992 |
|---|---|---|---|
| Nominal GDP | 5546.1 | | 6038.5 |
| Real GDP | 4897.3 | 4861.4 | |
| GDP deflator | | 117.7 | 121.1 |

4. Use the following data to compute the College Price Index for 1994 using the base 1972 = 100.

| ITEM | PRICE IN 1972 | QUANTITY PER MONTH IN 1972 | PRICE IN 1994 |
|---|---|---|---|
| Button-down shirts | $10 | 1 | $25 |
| Loafers | 25 | 1 | 55 |
| Sneakers | 10 | 3 | 35 |
| Textbooks | 12 | 12 | 40 |
| Jeans | 12 | 3 | 30 |
| Restaurant meals | 5 | 11 | 14 |

5. Average hourly earnings in the U.S. economy during several past years were as follows:

| 1961 | 1971 | 1981 | 1991 |
|---|---|---|---|
| $2.14 | $3.45 | $7.25 | $10.33 |

Use the CPI numbers provided on the inside back cover to calculate the real wage (in 1982–1984 dollars) for each of these years. Which decade had the fastest growth of money wages? Which had the fastest growth of real wages?

6. The example in the appendix showed that the Student Price Index (SPI) rose by 42 percent from 1983 to 1994. You can understand the meaning of this better if you:
   a. Use Table 23–5 to compute the fraction of total spending accounted for by each of the three items in 1983. Call these the "expenditure weights."
   b. Compute the weighted average of the percentage increases of the three prices shown in Table 23–6, using the expenditure weights you have just computed.
   c. You should get 42 percent as your answer. This shows that "inflation," as measured by the SPI, is a weighted average of the percentage price increases of all the items that are included in the index.

Chapter 24

# INCOME AND SPENDING: THE POWERFUL CONSUMER

*Men are disposed, as a rule and on the average, to increase their consumption as their income increases, but not by as much as the increase in their income.*

JOHN MAYNARD KEYNES

In Chapter 22 we saw how the strength of aggregate demand influences the performance of the economy. When aggregate demand is growing briskly, the economy is likely to be booming, though it may also be having trouble with inflation. When aggregate demand stagnates, a recession is likely to follow. ¶ This chapter begins our detailed study of the theory of income determination, the tool economists use to analyze issues like these. The theory is based on the concepts of aggregate demand and supply. In this and the next two chapters, we construct a simplified model of aggregate demand and learn why the *aggregate demand curve* of Chapter 22 has a negative slope. Then Chapter 27 completes the model by adding the *aggregate supply curve.* ¶ This first model of the macroeconomy can teach us much about the causes of unemployment and inflation. But it is too simple to deal with policy issues because the government and the financial system are largely ignored. These omissions are remedied in Part 7, where government spending, taxation, and interest rates are given appropriately prominent roles. The influence of the exchange rate between the U.S. dollar and foreign currencies is considered in Part 8.

We build our model in steps, starting with aggregate demand. Since consumer spending accounts for the lion's share of total demand, it is natural to begin the analysis there. First, we need some definitions of alternative concepts of economic activity—distinguishing carefully among total *spending* (aggregate demand), total *output*, and total *income*. Next, we turn to the interactions among these three concepts, using a convenient pictorial device that shows how they are all interrelated. Then we note that government attempts to influence consumer spending have sometimes succeeded and sometimes failed, and we pose the question: Why?

The bulk of the chapter is devoted to answering this question. We describe the important relationship between consumer income and consumer spending, and then use it to show how government policies have worked when they have been successful. Then we discuss some complications that arise from the fact that consumer income, though crucial, is not the only factor governing consumer spending. One of these complications holds the clue to why government policies have sometimes failed to influence consumer spending as expected.

## AGGREGATE DEMAND, DOMESTIC PRODUCT, AND NATIONAL INCOME

**AGGREGATE DEMAND** is the total amount that all consumers, business firms, and government agencies are willing to spend on final goods and services.

**CONSUMER EXPENDITURE**, symbolized by the letter **C**, is the total amount spent by consumers on newly produced goods and services (excluding purchases of new homes, which are considered investment goods).

**INVESTMENT SPENDING**, symbolized by the letter **I**, is the sum of the expenditures of business firms on new plant and equipment and households on new homes. Financial "investments" are not included, nor are resales of existing physical assets.

**GOVERNMENT PURCHASES**, symbolized by the letter **G**, refers to the goods (such as airplanes and paper clips) and services (such as school teaching and police protection) purchased by all levels of government.

We have already introduced the concept of **gross domestic product** as the standard measure of the economy's total output.[1] For the most part, goods are produced in a market economy only if firms think they can sell them. **Aggregate demand**, another concept encountered in Chapter 22, is the total amount that all consumers, business firms, government agencies, and foreigners wish to spend on all U.S. final goods and services.

The downward-sloping aggregate demand curve of Chapter 22 alerted us to the fact that aggregate demand is a *schedule*, not a fixed number. The actual numerical value of aggregate demand will depend on the price level, and several reasons for this dependence will emerge in coming chapters.

But the level of aggregate demand also depends on a variety of other factors like consumer incomes, various government policies, and events in foreign countries. We can understand the nature of aggregate demand best if we break it up into its major components.

**Consumer expenditure** (*"consumption"* for short) is simply the total demand for all consumer goods and services. This is the focus of the current chapter, and we shall represent it by the letter **C**.

**Investment spending**, which we represent by the letter **I**, is the amount that firms spend on factories, machinery, and the like plus the amount that families spend on new houses. Notice that this usage of the word "investment" differs from common parlance. Most people speak of "investing" in the stock market or in a bank account. This kind of "investment" merely swaps one form of financial asset (such as money) for another form (such as a share of stock). When economists speak of "investment," they mean instead the purchase of some *new physical* asset, like a drill press or an oil rig or a house. It is only these kinds of investments that lead directly to additional demand for newly produced goods in the economy and, subsequently, to greater productive capacity.

The third major component of aggregate demand is **government purchases** of goods and services; that is, items like paper, typewriters, airplanes, ships, and

[1]See Chapter 22, pages 549–53.

labor that are bought by all levels of government—federal, state, and local. We use the shorthand symbol **G** to denote this variable.

**NET EXPORTS** symbolized by (**X** − **IM**), is the difference between U.S. exports and U.S. imports. It indicates the difference between what we sell to foreigners and what we buy from them.

The final component of aggregate demand is **net exports**, which are simply defined as U.S. exports minus U.S. imports. The reasoning here is simple. Part of the demand for American goods and services originates beyond our borders—as when foreigners buy our wheat, our computers, and our banking services. So this must be added to domestic demand. Similarly, some items included in $C$ and $I$ are not American made—think, for example, of German beer, Japanese cars, and Korean textiles. So these must be subtracted, if we want to measure total spending on U.S. products. The inclusion of exports, which we represent by the symbol **X**, and the subtraction of imports, **IM**, leads us to the following shorthand definition of aggregate demand:

Aggregate demand is the sum $C + I + G + (X - IM)$.

The relative sizes of these four components of aggregate demand are indicated in the bar chart in Figure 24–10 (page 618). Consumer spending, the focus of this chapter, is the biggest by far.

The last concept we need for our vocabulary is a way to measure the total *income* of all the individuals in the economy. There are two versions of this: one for before-tax incomes, called **national income**, and one for after-tax incomes, called **disposable income**.[2] The term "disposable income" is meant to be descriptive: it tells us how many dollars consumers actually have available to spend or to save. Because it plays such a prominent role in this chapter, we shall need an abbreviation for it as well; we call it **DI**.

**NATIONAL INCOME** is the sum of the incomes of all the individuals in the economy earned in the forms of wages, interest, rents, and profits. It excludes transfer payments and is calculated before any deductions are taken for income taxes.

**DISPOSABLE INCOME** is the sum of the incomes of all the individuals in the economy after all taxes have been deducted and all transfer payments have been added.

## THE CIRCULAR FLOW OF SPENDING, PRODUCTION, AND INCOME

Enough definitions. How do these three concepts—domestic product, total expenditure, and national income—interact in a market economy? We can answer this best with a rather elaborate diagram (Figure 24–1). For obvious reasons, Figure 24–1 is called a **circular flow diagram**. It depicts a large circular tube in which a fluid is circulating in a clockwise direction. There are several breaks in the tube where either some of the fluid leaks out or additional fluid is injected in.

Let us examine this system, beginning on the far left. At point 1 on the circle, we find consumers. Disposable income (*DI*) is flowing into them, and two things are flowing out: consumption (*C*), which stays in the circular flow, and saving (*S*), which "leaks out." This just says that consumers normally spend less than they earn and save the balance. The "leakage" to savings, of course, does not disappear, but flows into the financial system. We postpone consideration of what happens there until Chapter 29.

The upper loop of the circular flow represents expenditures, and as we move clockwise to point 2, we encounter the first "injection" into the flow: investment spending (*I*). The diagram shows this as coming from "investors"—a group that includes both business firms and consumers who buy new homes.[3] As the circular flow moves past point 2, it is bigger than it was before. Total spending has increased from $C$ to $C + I$.

[2]More detailed information on these and other concepts is provided in Appendix B to this chapter.

[3]You are reminded of the specific definition of investment on page 591.

*Figure* **24–1** **THE CIRCULAR FLOW OF EXPENDITURE AND INCOME**

The upper part of this circular flow diagram depicts the flow of expenditures on goods and services that comes from consumers (point 1), investors (point 2), government (point 3), and foreigners (point 4), and goes to the firms that produce the output (point 5). The lower part of the diagram indicates how the income paid out by firms (point 5) flows to consumers (point 1), after some is siphoned off by the government in the form of taxes and part of this is replaced by transfer payments (point 6).

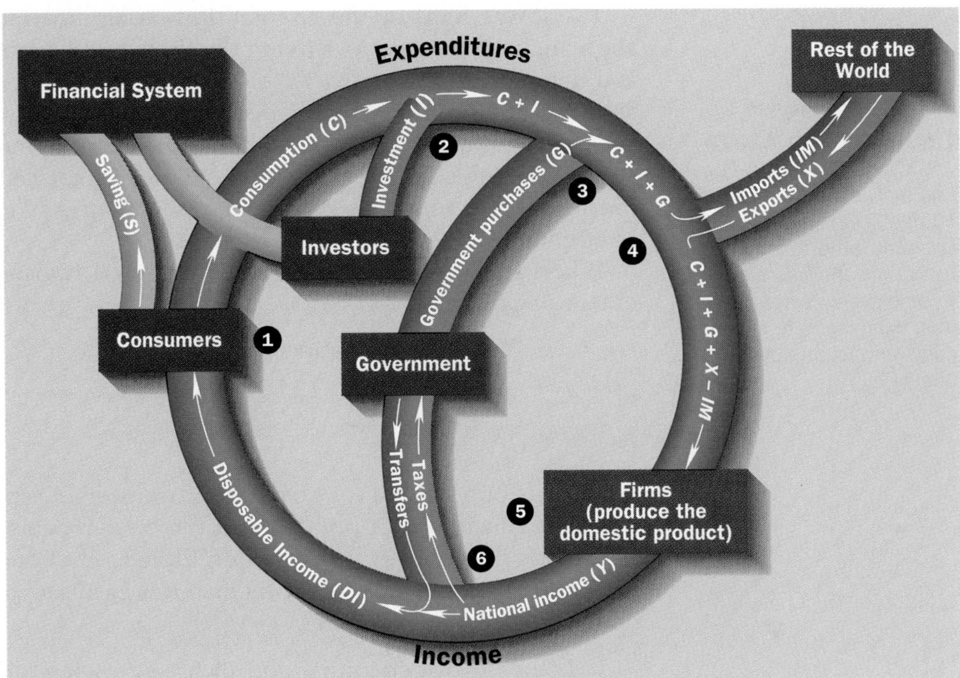


At point 3 there is yet another injection. The government adds its demand for goods and services ($G$) to those of consumers and investors ($C + I$). Now aggregate demand is up to $C + I + G$.

The final leakage and injection comes at point 4. Here we see export spending entering the circular flow from abroad and import spending leaking out. The net effect of these two forces, net exports, may increase or decrease the circular flow. In either case, by the time we pass point 4 we have accumulated the full amount of aggregate demand, $C + I + G + (X - IM)$.

The circular flow diagram shows this aggregate demand for goods and services arriving at the business firms, which are located at point 5 at the southeast portion of the diagram. Responding to this demand, firms produce the domestic product. As the circular flow emerges from the firms, however, we have renamed it *national income*. Why? The reason is that, except for some complications explained in the appendix:

National income and domestic product must be equal.

Why is this the case? When a firm produces and sells \$100 worth of output, it pays most of the proceeds to its workers, to people who have lent it money, and to the landlord who owns the property on which it is located. All of these payments are *income* to some individuals. But what about the rest? Suppose, for example, that the wages, interest, and rent that the firm pays add up to \$90, while its output is \$100. What happens to the remaining \$10? The answer is that the owners of the firm receive it as *profits*. But these owners are also citizens of the country, so their incomes count in national income, too.[4] Thus, when we add up all the wages, interest, rents, *and profits* in the economy to obtain the national *income*, we must arrive at the *value of output*.

The lower loop of the circular flow diagram traces the flow of income by showing national income leaving the firms and heading for consumers. But there is a detour along the way. At point 6, the government does two things. First, it siphons off a portion of the national income in the form of taxes. Second, it adds back government **transfer payments**, like unemployment compensation and social security benefits, which are sums of money that certain individuals receive as outright *grants* from the government rather than as payments for services rendered to employers.

**TRANSFER PAYMENTS** are sums of money that certain individuals receive as outright *grants* from the government rather than as payments for services rendered to employers. Some common examples are social security and unemployment benefits.

When taxes are subtracted from GDP, and transfer payments are added, we obtain disposable income.[5]

$$DI = \text{GDP} - \text{Taxes} + \text{Transfer Payments},$$

or

$$DI = \text{GDP} - \text{T},$$

where T is our symbol for taxes net of transfers. Disposable income flows unimpeded to consumers at point 1, and the cycle repeats.

This diagram raises several complicated questions. Although we pose them here, we will not try to answer them at this early stage. The answers will be made clear in subsequent chapters.

1. Is the flow of spending and income growing larger or smaller as we move clockwise around the circle, and why?
2. Is the output that the firms produce at point 5 (the GDP) equal to aggregate demand? If so, what makes these two quantities equal? If not, what happens?

Chapter 25 provides the answers to these two questions.

3. Are the government's accounts in balance, so that what flows in at point 6 (taxes minus transfers) is equal to what flows out at point 3 (government purchases)? What happens if they are not?

This important question is first addressed in Chapter 28 and then recurs many times, especially in Chapter 32, which is devoted to discussing budget deficits.

4. Is our international trade balanced, so that exports equal imports? More generally, what factors determine net exports and what are the consequences of trade deficits or surpluses?

These questions are taken up briefly in Chapters 25 and 26, and then considered fully in Part 8, which is devoted to international economic issues.

However, we cannot discuss any of these issues profitably until we first understand what goes on at point 1, where consumers make decisions, and point 2, where investors make decisions. We turn next, therefore, to the determinants of consumer spending.

---

[4]Some of the income paid out by American companies goes to non-citizens. Similarly, some Americans earn income from foreign firms. This complication is dealt with in Appendix B.

[5]This definition omits a few minor details, which are explained in Appendix B to this chapter.

## DEMAND MANAGEMENT AND THE POWERFUL CONSUMER

As we suggested in Chapter 22, the government sometimes wants to shift the aggregate demand curve. There are a number of ways in which it can try to do so. One direct approach is to alter its own spending (*G*), becoming extravagant when private demand is weak and miserly when private demand is strong. But the government can also take a more indirect route by using taxes and other policy tools to influence *private* spending decisions.

A government desiring to change private spending can concentrate its energies on consumer spending (*C*), on investment spending (*I*), or on net exports ($X - IM$). At various times in our history, the U.S. government has endeavored to change each. Since consumer expenditures constitute about two-thirds of gross national product, *C* presents the most tempting target.

While there are many things it can do to alter consumer spending, the government's principal weapon is the personal income tax. Many of you already have encountered Form 1040, the unwelcome New Year's greeting that every taxpayer receives from the federal government each January. Many more of you probably have been on a payroll and have seen a share of your wages deducted and sent to the Internal Revenue Service. It should be no mystery, then, how changes in personal taxes affect consumer spending. Any reduction in personal taxes leaves consumers with more disposable income to spend. Any increase in taxes leaves less.

The linkage from taxes to disposable income to consumer spending seems direct and unmistakable, and, in a certain sense, it is. But a look at the history of some major tax changes aimed at altering *C* is sobering. The varying degrees of success both of the measures themselves and of the predictions of their effects explain why economic research into the relationship between taxes and consumption continues.

### CASE 1: THE 1964 TAX REDUCTION

The year 1964 was a good one for economists. For years they had been proclaiming that a cut in personal taxes would be an excellent way to stimulate a stagnating economy. But the plea fell on deaf ears until President John F. Kennedy was persuaded of the basic logic of the argument and his successor, Lyndon Johnson, pushed the legislation through Congress. The 1964 tax cut was designed to spur consumer spending, and it succeeded admirably. Consumers reacted just about as the textbooks of the day predicted, the economy improved rapidly and markedly, and economists smiled knowingly.

### CASE 2: THE 1975 TAX REDUCTION

The next major attempt to stimulate the economy by cutting taxes met with much less success. In the spring of 1975, as the economy hit the bottom of a recession, President Gerald Ford and Congress agreed on a temporary tax cut to spur consumer spending: They returned to each taxpayer part of the taxes paid in 1974 and reduced income tax rates for the balance of 1975. However, consumers confounded the wishes of the president and Congress by saving a good deal of their rebates rather than spending them.

### CASE 3: THE 1981–1984 TAX CUTS

A series of reductions in personal income tax rates was a major campaign promise of Ronald Reagan, one which was promptly redeemed. Tax rates fell by about 23 percent between 1981 and 1984, and consumer spending increased by more or less the amounts that economists predicted, thereby contributing to the long economic expansion of the 1980s.

Thus tax policy did more or less what it was expected to do in 1964 and 1981–1984 but seemed to be less effective in 1975. Why? This chapter will attempt to provide some answers. We begin by exploring the important relationship between consumer income and consumer spending, more or less retracing the chain of logic that led government economists to the right conclusion in 1964. Once this is accomplished, we turn to some of the complications that made things go awry in 1975.

## CONSUMER SPENDING AND INCOME: THE IMPORTANT RELATIONSHIP

An economist interested in predicting how consumer spending will respond to a change in personal income tax payments must first ask how $C$ is related to disposable income; for an increase in taxes is a decrease in after-tax income, and a reduction in taxes is an increase in after-tax income. This section, therefore, will examine what we know about the response of consumer spending to a change in disposable income.

Figure 24–2 depicts the historical paths of $C$ and $DI$ for the United States since 1929. The association is obviously rather close and certainly suggests that consumption will rise whenever disposable income does, and fall whenever income falls. The difference between the two lines is personal saving. Notice how little saving consumers did during the Great Depression of the 1930s, where the two lines are very close together, and how much they did during World War II, when many consumer goods were either unavailable or rationed so there was little on which to spend money.

Of course, knowing that consumer expenditures, $C$, will move in the same direction as disposable income, $DI$, is not enough for policy planners. They need to know *how much* one will go up when the other rises a given amount. Figure 24–3 presents the same data as in Figure 24–2, but in a way designed to help answer the "how much" question.

A **SCATTER DIAGRAM** is a graph showing the relationship between two variables (such as consumption and disposable income). Each year is represented by a point in the diagram. The coordinates of each year's point show the value of the two variables in that year.

Economists call such pictures **scatter diagrams**, and they are very useful in predicting how one economic variable (in this case, consumer spending) will change in response to a change in another economic variable (in this case, disposable income). Each dot in the diagram represents the data on $C$ and $DI$ corresponding to a particular year. For example, the point labeled "1976" shows that real consumer expenditures in 1976 were $2207 billion (which we read off the vertical axis), while real disposable incomes amounted to $2441 billion (which we read off the horizontal axis). Similarly, each year from 1929 to 1992 is represented by its own dot in Figure 24–3.

How can such a diagram assist the fiscal policy planner? Imagine that this is 1963 and you must decide whether to recommend to Congress a tax cut of $5 billion, $10 billion, or $15 billion. You have forecasts of what consumer expenditures are expected to be if taxes are not reduced. This, plus other forecasts of

Figure 24–2 **CONSUMER SPENDING AND DISPOSABLE INCOME IN THE UNITED STATES SINCE 1929**

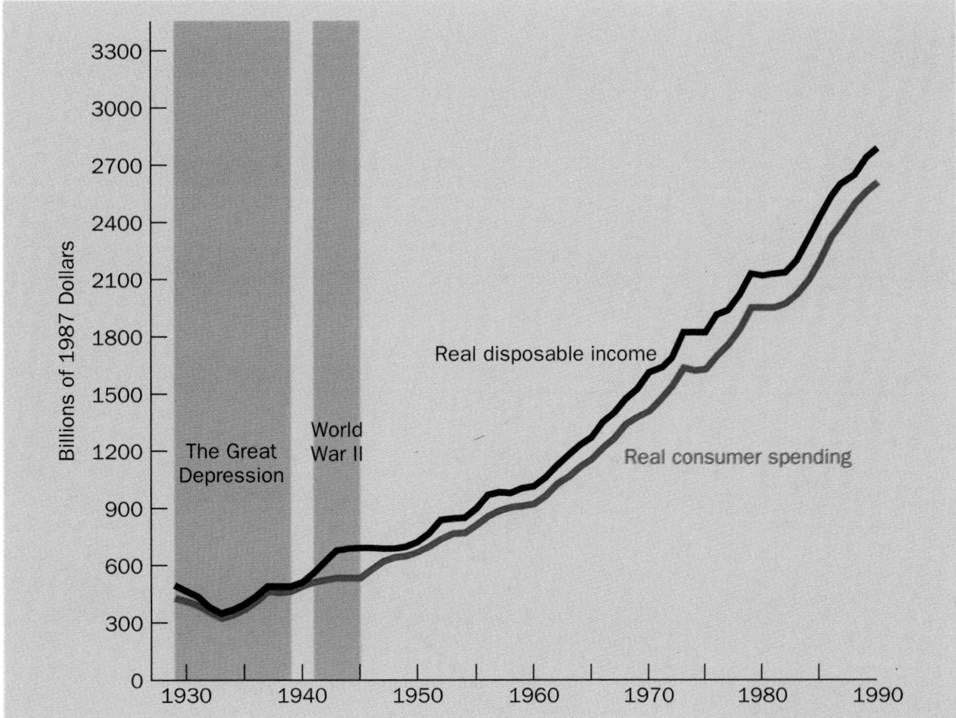


This time series chart shows the behavior of consumer spending and disposable income in the United States since 1929. Except for the World War II years, the correspondence between the two variables is remarkably close. The distance between the two lines represents consumer saving, which was obviously quite small during the Great Depression of the 1930s and quite large during World War II.

SOURCE: U.S. Department of Commerce.

investment, government spending, and net exports has led you to conclude that aggregate demand in 1964 will be insufficient if taxes are not reduced.

To assist your imagination, another scatter diagram is given in Figure 24–4. This one removes the points for 1964 through 1992, which appear in Figure 24–3; after all, these were not known in 1963. Years prior to 1947 have also been removed because both the Great Depression and wartime rationing seriously disturbed the normal relationship between *DI* and *C*. With no more training in economics than you have right now, what would you do?

One rough-and-ready approach is to get a ruler, set it down on Figure 24–4, and sketch a straight line that comes as close as possible to hitting all the points. Try that now. You will not be able to hit each point exactly, but you will find that you can come remarkably close. The line you have just drawn summarizes, in a very rough way, the consumption-income relationship that is the focus of this chapter. We see at once that it confirms something we might have guessed—that a rise in income is associated with a rise in consumer spending. The slope of the line is certainly positive.

The slope of your line is very important.[6] That line has been drawn into Figure 24–5, and we note that its slope is

$$\text{Slope} = \frac{\text{Vertical change}}{\text{Horizontal change}} = \frac{\$90 \text{ billion}}{\$100 \text{ billion}} = 0.90.$$

[6]To review the concept of *slope*, turn back to page 20.

Figure 24–3 **SCATTER DIAGRAM OF CONSUMER SPENDING AND DISPOSABLE INCOME IN THE UNITED STATES SINCE 1929**

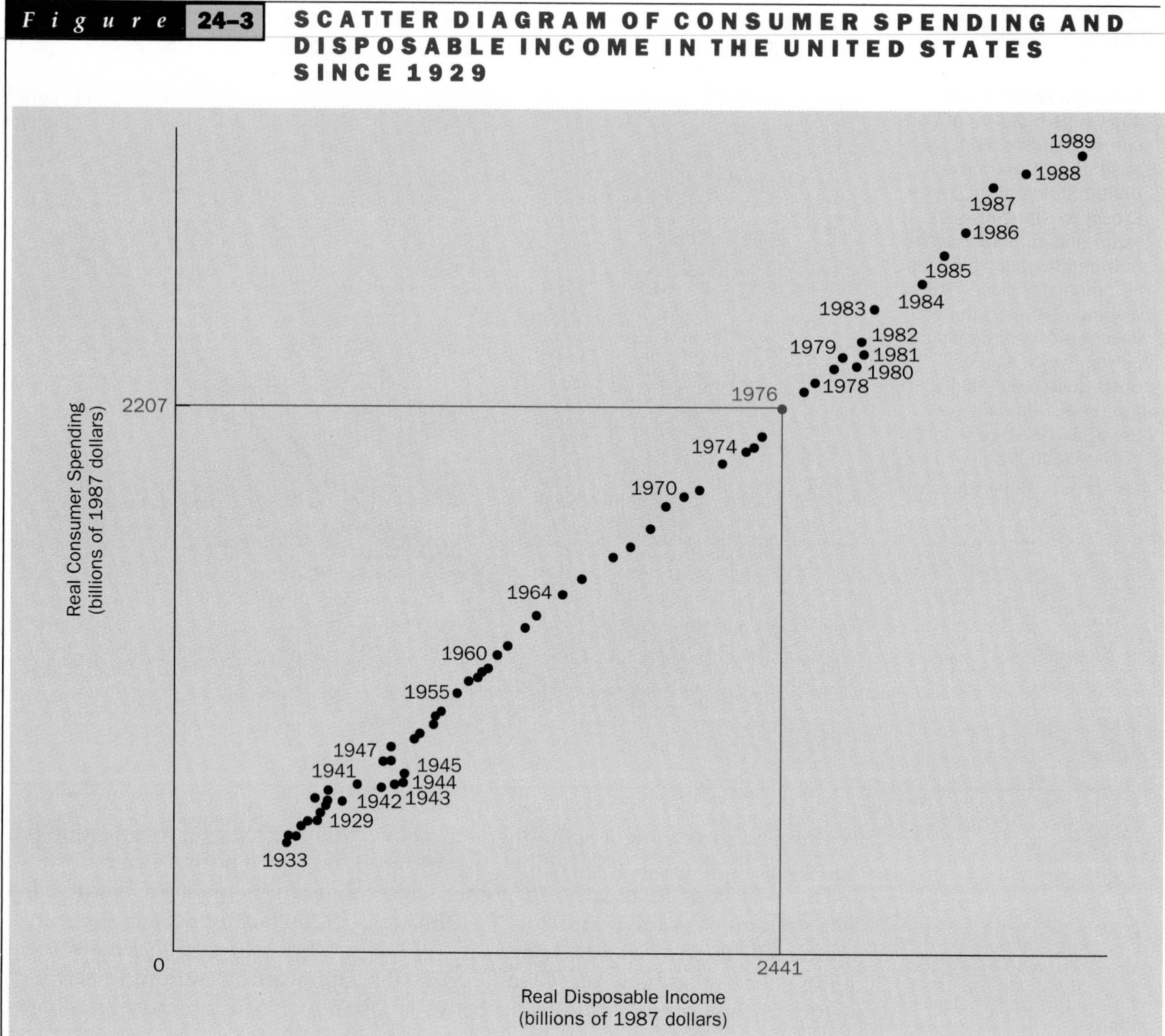


This diagram shows the same data as depicted in Figure 24–2 but in a different manner. Each point on the diagram represents the data for both consumer spending and disposable income during a particular year. For example, the point labeled "1976" indicates that in that year consumer spending was $2207 billion while disposable income was $2441 billion. Diagrams like this one are called "scatter diagrams."

Since the horizontal change involved in the move from *A* to *B* represents a rise in disposable income of $100 billion (from $1000 billion to $1100 billion), and the corresponding vertical change represents the associated $90 billion rise in consumer spending (from $900 to $990 billion), the slope of the line indicates how spending responds to changes in disposable income. In this case, we see that each additional $1 of income leads to 90 cents of additional spending.

**Figure 24–4**

## SCATTER DIAGRAM OF CONSUMER SPENDING AND DISPOSABLE INCOME IN THE UNITED STATES, 1947–1963

This scatter diagram omits some of the data found in Figure 24–3 and indicates the information that policy planners might have used in deciding upon the size of the 1964 income tax cut.

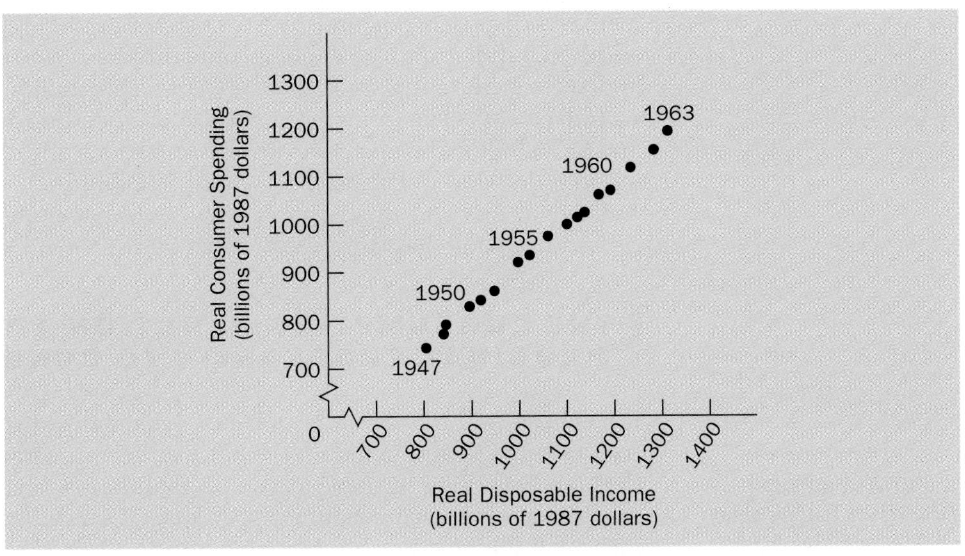


**Figure 24–5**

## SCATTER DIAGRAM OF CONSUMER SPENDING AND DISPOSABLE INCOME IN THE UNITED STATES, 1947–1963

This diagram is the same as Figure 24–4 except for the addition of a straight line that comes about as close as possible to fitting all the data points.

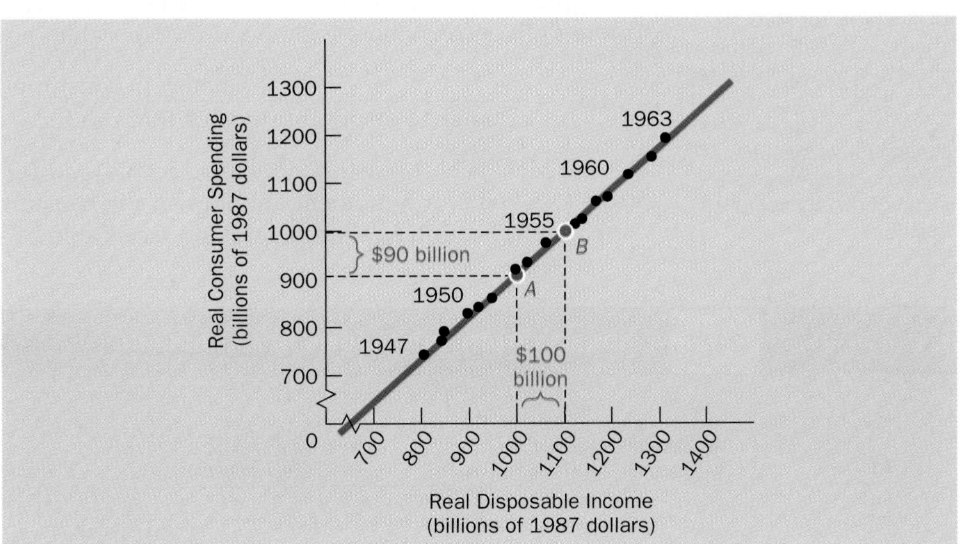

In terms of the policy issue of 1964, this line can therefore help provide an answer to the question, How much more consumer spending will be induced by tax cuts of $5 billion, $10 billion, or $15 billion, if the effects are similar to those observed in the past? First, we need to keep in mind that each dollar of tax cut increases disposable income by $1. Then we apply Figure 24–5's finding that each additional dollar of disposable income increases consumer spending by 90 cents, and we conclude that proposed tax cuts of $5 billion, $10 billion, or $15 billion would be expected to increase consumer spending by $4.5 billion, $9.0 billion, and $13.5 billion, respectively. Similar questions addressed by economists in 1964 led to a decision to cut taxes by about $9 billion.

Later in this and other chapters, we will encounter several reasons why this procedure, while basically valid, must be used with great caution.

## THE CONSUMPTION FUNCTION AND THE MARGINAL PROPENSITY TO CONSUME

The **CONSUMPTION FUNCTION** is the relationship between total consumer expenditure and total disposable income in the economy, holding all other determinants of consumer spending constant.

The **MARGINAL PROPENSITY TO CONSUME** (or **MPC** for short) is the ratio of the change in consumption to the change in disposable income that produces the change in consumption. On a graph, it appears as the slope of the consumption function.

It has been said that economics is just systematized common sense. Let us, then, try to organize and generalize what has been a completely intuitive discussion thus far. One thing we have learned is that there is a close and apparently reliable relationship between consumer spending, *C*, and disposable income, *DI*. Economists call this relationship the **consumption function**.

A second fact we have picked up from these figures is that the *slope* of the consumption function is fairly constant. We infer this from the fact that the straight line in Figure 24–5 comes close to touching every point. If the slope of the consumption function had changed a lot, it would not be possible to do so well with a single straight line. Because of its importance in such applications as the tax-cut example, economists have given a special name to this slope—the **marginal propensity to consume**, or **MPC** for short. The *MPC* tells us how many more dollars consumers will spend if disposable income rises by $1 billion.

$$\text{MPC} = \frac{\text{Change in consumption}}{\text{Change in disposable income that produces the change in consumption}}$$

The MPC is best illustrated by an example, and for this purpose we turn away from U.S. data for a moment and look at the consumption and income data of a hypothetical country called Macroland (see Table 24–1). The data for Macroland

**Table 24–1 CONSUMPTION AND INCOME IN MACROLAND**

| YEAR | (1) CONSUMPTION, *C* (billions of dollars) | (2) DISPOSABLE INCOME, *DI* (billions of dollars) | (3) MARGINAL PROPENSITY TO CONSUME, MPC |
|---|---|---|---|
| 1989 | 2700 | 3200 | |
| | | | 0.75 |
| 1990 | 3000 | 3600 | |
| | | | 0.75 |
| 1991 | 3300 | 4000 | |
| | | | 0.75 |
| 1992 | 3600 | 4400 | |
| | | | 0.75 |
| 1993 | 3900 | 4800 | |
| | | | 0.75 |
| 1994 | 4200 | 5200 | |

Figure 24–6 THE CONSUMPTION FUNCTION OF MACROLAND

This diagram is similar to Figure 24–5, except that it applies to a hypothetical (and blissfully simple!) economy called Macroland. As can be seen, a straight-line consumption function passes through every point exactly. The slope of this line is 0.75, which is the marginal propensity to consume in Macroland.

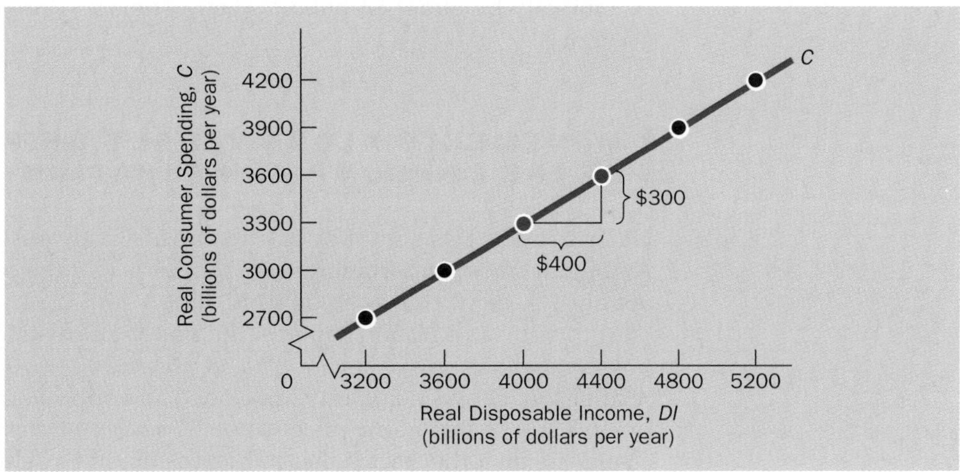


resemble those for the United States, except that in Macroland, *C* and *DI* figures happen to be nice round numbers, which facilitates computation.

Columns 1 and 2 of Table 24–1 show annual consumer expenditure and disposable income from 1989 to 1994. These two columns constitute Macroland's consumption function and are plotted in Figure 24–6. Column 3 in the table shows the marginal propensity to consume (MPC), which is the slope of the line in Figure 24–6; it is derived from the first two columns. We can see that between 1991 and 1992, *DI* rose by $400 billion (from $4000 to $4400) while *C* rose by $300 billion (from $3300 to $3600). Thus the MPC was

$$\frac{\text{Change in consumption}}{\text{Change in disposable income}} = \frac{\$300}{\$400} = 0.75.$$

As you can easily verify, the MPC between any other pair of years in Macroland is also 0.75. This explains why the slope of the line in Figure 24–5 was so crucial in estimating the effect of a tax cut. This slope, which we found to be 0.90, is nothing but the MPC for the United States. And it is the MPC that tells us how much *additional* spending will be induced by each dollar *change* in disposable income. For each $1 of tax cut, economists expect consumption to rise by $1 times the marginal propensity to consume.

To estimate the *initial* effect of a tax cut on consumer spending, economists must first estimate the MPC and then multiply the amount of the tax cut by the estimated MPC. But since they never know the true MPC with certainty, this prediction is always subject to some margin of error.[7]

[7]The word "initial" in the first sentence is an important one. Later chapters explain why the effects discussed in this chapter are only the beginning of the story.

In 1963, for example, economists multiplied the anticipated $9 billion tax cut by the estimated MPC of 0.90 and concluded that consumer spending would rise initially by about $8 billion. Their estimate seems to have been remarkably accurate.

## MOVEMENTS ALONG VERSUS SHIFTS OF THE CONSUMPTION FUNCTION

Unfortunately, this sort of calculation does not always yield such precise results. Among the most important reasons for this is that the consumption function does not always stand still; sometimes it shifts.

You will recall from Chapter 4 the important distinction between a *movement along* a demand curve and a *shift* of the curve. A demand curve depicts the relationship between quantity demanded and only *one* of its many determinants—price. Thus, a change in price causes a *movement along the demand curve,* but a change in any other factor that influences quantity demanded causes a *shift of the entire demand curve.*

Because consumer spending is influenced by factors other than disposable income, a similar distinction is vital to understanding real-world consumption functions. Look back at the definition of the consumption function in the margin of page 600. A change in disposable income leads to a **movement along the consumption function** precisely because the consumption function depicts the relationship between *C* and *DI*. (See the red arrow in Figure 24–7.) This is what we have been considering so far. But consumption also has other determinants, and a change in any of these "other determinants" will **shift the entire consumption function**—as indicated by the blue lines in Figure 24–7. These shifts account for many of the errors in forecasting consumption. To summarize:

Any change in disposable income moves us *along* a given consumption function. But a change in any of the other variables that influence consumption *shifts* the entire consumption schedule (see Figure 24–7).

Let us now list some of these "other variables" that can shift the consumption function.

## OTHER DETERMINANTS OF CONSUMER SPENDING

### WEALTH

One factor affecting consumption is consumers' *wealth,* which is a source of purchasing power in addition to income. Wealth and income are different things. For example, a wealthy person who does not work, but has a healthy bank account, may have little current *income*. Similarly, a high-income individual who spends all she earns will not accumulate wealth. To appreciate the importance of the distinction, consider two consumers, both earning $35,000 this year. One of them has $100,000 in the bank, while the other has no assets at all. Who do you think will spend more this year? Presumably the one with the big bank account.

Figure 24–7 **SHIFTS OF THE CONSUMPTION FUNCTION**

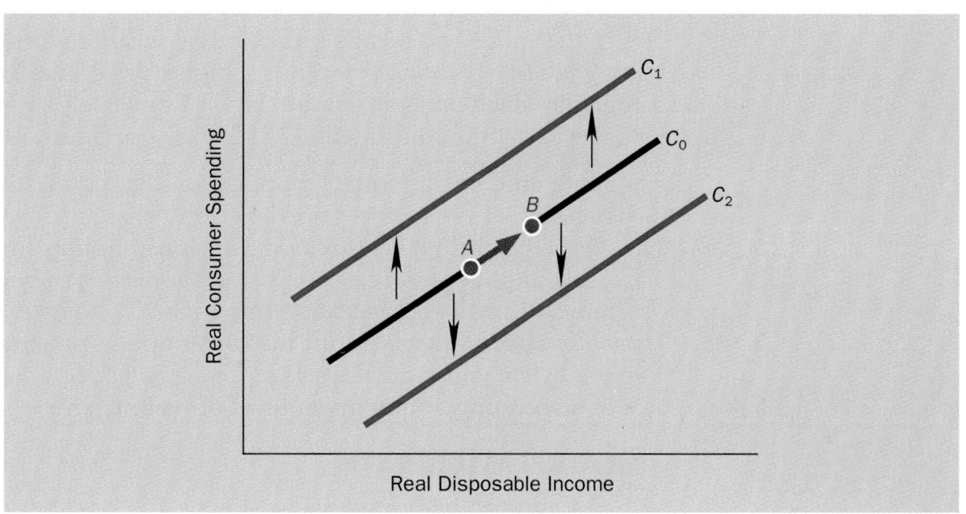


An increase in disposable income causes a movement along a fixed consumption function, such as the movement from point *A* to point *B* on consumption function $C_0$ (see the red arrow). But a change in any other determinant of consumer spending will cause the whole consumption function to shift upward (consumption function $C_1$) or downward (consumption function $C_2$).

The general point is that current income is not the only source of funds that households have; they can also finance spending by withdrawals from their bank accounts or by cashing in other forms of wealth. A stock market boom may therefore raise the consumption function (see the shift from $C_0$ to $C_1$ in Figure 24–7), while a collapse of stock prices may lower it (see the shift from $C_0$ to $C_2$).

## THE PRICE LEVEL

A **MONEY FIXED ASSET** is an asset with a face value fixed in terms of dollars, such as money itself, government bonds, and corporate bonds.

A good deal of consumer wealth is held in forms whose values are fixed in money terms. Money itself is the most obvious example of this, but government bonds, savings accounts, and corporate bonds are all assets with fixed face values in money terms. The purchasing power of any **money fixed asset** obviously declines whenever the price level rises, which means that the asset can buy less. For example, if the price level rises by 10 percent, a $1000 government bond will buy about 10 percent less than it could when prices were lower. Consequently:

Higher prices decrease the demand for goods and services by eroding the purchasing power of consumer wealth.

This is no trivial matter. It has been estimated that consumers in the United States hold money fixed assets worth over $3 *trillion*, so that each 1 percent rise in the price level reduces the purchasing power of consumer wealth by over $30 billion, a tidy sum. The process, of course, operates equally well in reverse. Since a decline in the price level increases the purchasing power of money fixed assets:

Lower prices increase the demand for goods and services by enhancing the purchasing power of consumer wealth.

For these reasons, a change in the price level will shift the entire consumption function. Specifically:

A higher price level leads to lower real wealth and therefore to less spending *at any given level of real income*. Thus, a higher price level leads to a lower consumption function (such as $C_2$ in Figure 24–7). Conversely, a lower price level leads to a higher consumption function (such as $C_1$ in Figure 24–7).

Since students are often confused on this point, it is worth repeating that the depressing effect of the price level on consumer spending works through real *wealth*, not through real *income*. The consumption function is a relationship between *real consumer income* and *real consumer spending*. Thus any decline in real income, regardless of its cause, moves the economy *leftward along a fixed consumption function*; it does not shift the consumption function.[8] By contrast, any decline in *real wealth* will *shift the whole consumption function downward*, meaning that there is less spending at any given level of real income.

## THE INFLATION RATE

Prices may be high and rising slowly, or they may be low but rising rapidly. Therefore, the depressing effect of a high *price level* on real consumer spending must be distinguished from any effect on spending of the *rate of inflation* (that is, the rate at which prices are rising).

If there is any effect of inflation on consumer spending, it must be small. Economists are not even sure whether inflation stimulates or depresses spending. It used to be thought that high rates of inflation lead consumers to spend more now to "beat" the higher prices that loom on the horizon. But behavior during the inflationary 1970s belied this idea. Consumers actually spent a *lower* fraction of their disposable incomes in the 1970s than they did in the 1980s.

Because there is no strong evidence that the rate of inflation shifts the consumption function systematically in one direction or the other, we shall assume that the position of the consumption function is influenced by the *price level*, but not by the *inflation rate*.

## THE RATE OF INTEREST

A higher rate of interest raises the rewards for saving. For this reason, many people believe it is "obvious" that higher interest rates encourage saving, and therefore discourage spending. Statistical studies of this relationship suggest otherwise, however. With very few exceptions, they show that interest rates have virtually no effect on consumption decisions in the United States. Hence, in developing our model of the economy, we will assume that changes in interest rates do not shift the consumption function.

## EXPECTATIONS OF FUTURE INCOMES

It is hardly earth shattering to suggest that consumers' expectations about future income may affect how much they spend today. This final determinant of consumer spending turns out to hold the key to understanding why tax policy succeeded so well in 1964 and the early 1980s, but failed to alter consumer spending much in 1975.

[8]This is true even if a rise in the price level lies behind the decline in real income. However, wages and prices normally move together, so there is no reason to expect real wages to fall when the price level rises.

## WHY TAX POLICY FAILED IN 1975

To understand how expectations of future incomes affect current consumer expenditures, consider the abbreviated life histories of three consumers given in Table 24–2. The reason for giving our three imaginary individuals such odd names will be apparent shortly.

The consumer named "No Change" earned $100 in each of the four years considered in the table. The consumer named "Temporary Rise" earned $100 in three of the four years, but had a good year in 1975. The consumer named "Permanent Rise" enjoyed a permanent increase in income in 1975 and was clearly the richest.

Now let us use our common sense to figure out how much each of these consumers might have spent in 1975. "Temporary Rise" and "Permanent Rise" had the same income that year. Do you think they spent the same amount? Not if they had some ability to foresee their future income, because "Permanent Rise" was richer in the long run.

Now compare "No Change" and "Temporary Rise." Temporary Rise had 20 percent higher income in 1975 ($120 versus $100) but only 5 percent more over the entire four-year period ($420 versus $400). Do you think his spending in 1975 was closer to 20 percent above No Change's or closer to 5 percent above it? Most people guess the latter.

The point of this example is that it is reasonable for consumers to decide on their *current* consumption spending by looking at their *long-run* income prospects. This should come as no surprise to a college student. Are you spending only what you earn this year? Probably not. But that does not make you a foolish spendthrift. On the contrary, you know that your college education gives you a reasonable expectation of much higher income in the future, and you are spending with that in mind.

Now let us see what all this has to do with the failure of the 1975 income tax rebate. For this purpose, imagine that the three rows in Table 24–2 now represent the entire economy under three different government policies. Recall that 1975 was the year of the rebate. The first row ("No Change") shows the unchanged path of disposable income if no tax cut was enacted. The second ("Temporary Rise") shows an increase in disposable income attributable to a tax cut *for one year only*. The bottom row ("Permanent Rise") shows a policy that increases *DI* in *every future year* by cutting taxes permanently in 1975. Which of the two lower rows do you imagine would have generated more consumer spending in 1975?

**Table 24–2 INCOMES OF THREE CONSUMERS**

| | INCOMES IN EACH YEAR | | | | |
|---|---|---|---|---|---|
| CONSUMER | 1974 | 1975 | 1976 | 1977 | TOTAL INCOME |
| No change | 100 | 100 | 100 | 100 | 400 |
| Temporary Rise | 100 | 120 | 100 | 100 | 420 |
| Permanent Rise | 100 | 120 | 120 | 120 | 460 |

The bottom row ("Permanent Rise"), of course. What we have concluded, then, is this:

Permanent cuts in income taxes cause greater increases in consumer spending than do temporary cuts of equal magnitude.

The application of this analysis to the case of the 1975 tax cut is immediate. The rebates were clearly one-time increases in income like that experienced by "Temporary Rise" in Table 24–2. No future income was affected, and so consumers did not curtail their spending as much as government officials had hoped. The general lesson is

A permanent increase in income taxes provides a greater deterrent to consumer spending than does a temporary increase of equal magnitude.

We have, then, what appears to be a general principle, backed up both by historical evidence and common sense. Permanent changes in income taxes have a more significant impact on consumer spending than do temporary changes. Though it may now seem obvious, this is not a lesson you would have learned from the introductory textbooks of 20 years ago. It is one that we learned the hard way, through bitter experience.

## THE PREDICTABILITY OF CONSUMER BEHAVIOR

We have now learned enough to see why the economist's problem in predicting how consumers will react to an increase or decrease in taxes is not nearly as simple as suggested earlier in this chapter.

The principal problem seems to be anticipating how taxpayers will view any changes in the income tax law. If the government *says* that a tax cut is permanent, will consumers *believe* it and increase their spending accordingly? Perhaps not, if the government has a history of raising taxes after promising to keep them low. Similarly, when (as in 1975) the government explicitly announces that a tax cut is temporary, will consumers always believe this? Or might they greet such an announcement with a hefty dose of skepticism? This is quite possible if there is a long history of "temporary" tax changes that stayed on the books indefinitely.

Thus the effectiveness of any *future* tax policy move may well depend on the government's *past* track record. A government that repeatedly uses a succession of so-called "permanent" tax cuts and tax increases for short-run stabilization purposes may find consumers beginning to ignore the tax changes entirely. The story of the boy who cried wolf should probably be required reading for fiscal policy planners.

Nor is this the only problem. Consumer spending may be influenced by large and rapid accumulations of wealth (as happened immediately after World War II) or of sizable losses of wealth (such as the drastic decline in the stock market in 1987). Poor forecasts of future prices may lead consumption forecasts astray. And there are further hazards that we have not even mentioned here. Economic predictions are inexact, and predictions of consumption illustrate this well.

There is much more that could be said about the determinants of consumption, but it is best to leave the rest to more advanced courses. For we are now ready to apply our knowledge of the consumption function to the construction of the first model of the whole economy. While it is true that income determines consumption, the consumption function in turn helps to determine the level of income. If that sounds like circular reasoning, read the next chapter!

## *Summary*

1. **Aggregate demand** is the total volume of goods and services purchased by consumers, businesses, government units, and foreigners. It can be expressed as the sum $C + I + G + (X - IM)$, where $C$ is **consumer spending**, $I$ is **investment spending**, $G$ is **government purchases**, $X$ is exports, and $IM$ is imports.
2. Aggregate demand is a schedule: the aggregate quantity demanded depends (among other things) on the price level. But, for a given price level, aggregate demand is a number.
3. Economists reserve the term "investment" to refer to purchases of newly produced factories, machinery, and houses.
4. Domestic product is the total volume of final goods and services produced in the country. It is most commonly measured by the gross domestic product.
5. **National income** is the sum of the *before-tax* wages, interest, rents, and profits earned by all individuals in the economy. By necessity, it must be approximately equal to domestic product.
6. **Disposable income** is the sum of the incomes of all individuals in the economy *after taxes and transfers*, and is the chief determinant of consumer expenditure.
7. All of these concepts, and others, can be depicted in a **circular flow diagram** that shows expenditures on all four sources flowing into business firms and national income flowing out.
8. The government often has tried to manipulate aggregate demand by influencing private consumption decisions, usually through the personal income tax. Although this policy seemed to work well in 1964 and 1981, it did not work well in 1975.
9. The close relationship between consumer spending, $C$, and disposable income, $DI$, is called the **consumption function**. Its slope, which is used to predict the change in consumption that will be caused by a change in income taxes, is called the **marginal propensity to consume** (MPC).
10. Changes in disposable income move us **along a given consumption function**. Changes in any of the other variables that affect $C$ **shift the entire consumption function**. Among the most important of these other variables are total consumer wealth, the price level, and expected future incomes.
11. Because consumers hold so many **money fixed assets**, they lose out when prices rise, which leads them to reduce their spending.
12. Future income prospects help explain why tax policy did not affect consumption as much as was hoped in 1975. This is because the 1975 tax cut was temporary, and therefore left future incomes unaffected. By contrast, the 1964 and 1981–1984 tax cuts were permanent, and affected future as well as current incomes. It is no surprise, then, that the 1964 and 1981 actions had stronger effects on spending than did the 1975 action.

## *Key Concepts and Terms*

Aggregate demand
Consumer expenditure ($C$)
Investment spending ($I$)
Government purchases ($G$)
Net exports ($X - IM$)
$C + I + G + (X - IM)$
National income
Disposable income ($DI$)
Circular flow diagram
Transfer payments
Scatter diagram
Consumption function
Marginal propensity to consume (MPC)
Movements along versus shifts of the consumption function
Money fixed assets
Temporary versus permanent tax changes

## Questions for Review

1. What are the four components of aggregate demand? Which of these is the largest? Which is the smallest?
2. What is the difference between "investment" as the term is used by most people and "investment" as defined by an economist? Which of the following acts constitute "investment" according to the economist's definition?
   a. IBM opens a new factory to assemble personal computers.
   b. You buy 100 shares of IBM stock.
   c. A small computer company goes bankrupt, and IBM purchases its factory and equipment.
   d. Your family buys a newly constructed home from a developer.
   e. Your family buys an older home from another family. (*Hint*: Are any *new* products demanded by this action?)
3. What would the circular flow diagram (Figure 24–1, page 593) look like in an economy with no government? Draw one for yourself.
4. The marginal propensity to consume (MPC) for the nation as a whole is roughly 0.90. Explain in words what this means. What is your personal MPC?
5. Look at the scatter diagram in Figure 24–3 (page 598). What does it tell you about what was going on in this country in the years 1942–1945?
6. What is a "consumption function," and why is it a useful device for government economists planning a tax cut?
7. On a piece of graph paper, construct the consumption function for Simpleland from the data given below and determine the MPC.

| YEAR | CONSUMER SPENDING | DISPOSABLE INCOME |
|---|---|---|
| 1989 | 1800 | 2000 |
| 1990 | 2250 | 2500 |
| 1991 | 2700 | 3000 |
| 1992 | 3150 | 3500 |
| 1993 | 3600 | 4000 |

8. In which direction will the consumption function for Simpleland shift if the price level rises? Show this on your graph.
9. Explain why permanent tax cuts are likely to lead to bigger increases in consumer spending than are temporary tax cuts.
10. (More difficult) Between 1990 and 1991, real disposable income (in 1987 dollars) rose only from $3525 billion to $3529 billion, owing to a recession. Use the data on real consumption expenditures given on the inside front cover of this book to compare the change in *C* to the change in *DI*. Explain why dividing the two does *not* give a good estimate of the marginal propensity to consume.
11. For several years now, various members of Congress have been recommending the establishment of tax-favored accounts for savers. How would such accounts be expected to shift the consumption function?

# Appendix A THE SAVING FUNCTION AND THE MARGINAL PROPENSITY TO SAVE

There is an alternative way of looking at the relationships we have discussed in this chapter. Disposable income that is not spent must be saved. Therefore, we can examine the effect of income on *saving* as well as its effect on consumer *spending*.

To see how saving appears on the consumption function diagram, we have repeated the consumption function of Macroland (see Figure 24–6) in Figure 24–8 and added a 45° line. You will recall that a 45° line marks those points where the distances along the horizontal and vertical axes are equal. (If you wish to review, see page 22.) Since the consumption schedule is below the 45° line, the figure shows that consumer spending is less than income, so some is being *saved*.

To find the amount of saving at each level of income, we need only read the vertical distance from the consumption function up to the 45° line. For example, when income is $4400 billion, saving is the distance *AB*, or $800 billion.

There is also a more direct way to find saving. Table 24–3 repeats the consumption and disposable income data for Macroland from Table 24–1 (page 601). Then, in column 3, we compute the difference between disposable income and consumption, which gives us **aggregate saving**.

**Aggregate saving** is the difference between disposable income and consumer expenditure. In symbols, $S = DI - C$.

This subtraction is exactly what we showed graphically in Figure 24–8. Columns 2 and 3 of Table 24–3 constitute what economists call the **saving function**.

The **saving function** is the relationship between total consumer saving and total disposable income in the economy, holding other determinants of saving constant.

The data of Table 24–3 are portrayed in Figure 24–9, which could equally well have been constructed as the difference between the 45° line and the *C* line in Figure 24–8. (Because saving is so much less than consumption, we have stretched the scale of the vertical axis a bit.) Points *A* and *B* correspond to the same points in Figure 24–8. When the consumption function is a straight line, and thus has a constant slope, the same will be true of the saving function. In Figure 24–9, we show this slope as the ratio of distance *EB* to distance *DE* or $200/$800 = 0.25. Economists call this slope the **marginal propensity to save**.

## Figure 24–8 THE CONSUMPTION FUNCTION OF MACROLAND

The consumption function of Macroland, which we encountered in Figure 24–6 (page 601), is repeated here, and a 45° line is added for convenience. Since consumption and saving must always add up to disposable income, the vertical distance between the two lines represents saving. For example, points *A* and *B* indicate that when disposable income is $4400 billion, saving is $800 billion.

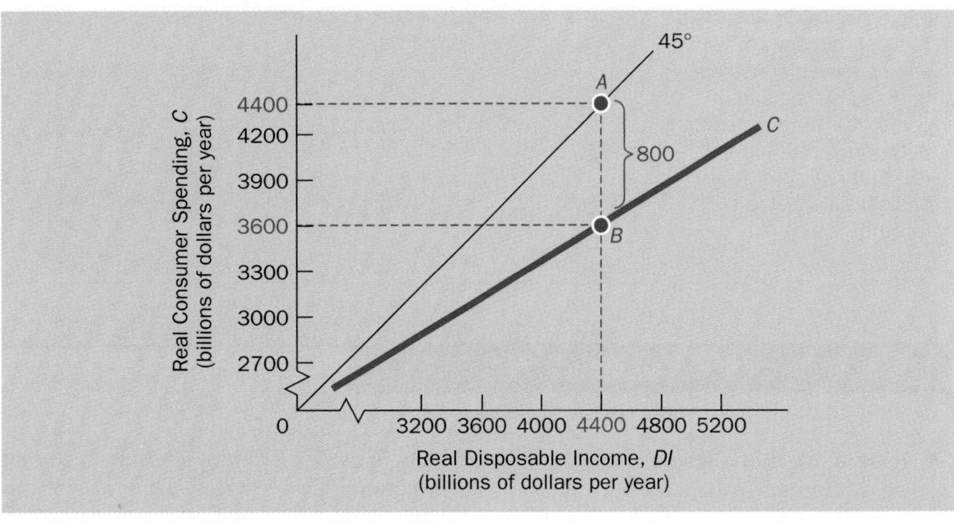

**Table 24–3 SAVING IN MACROLAND**

| YEAR | CONSUMPTION, *C* (billions of dollars) | DISPOSABLE INCOME, *DI* (billions of dollars) | SAVINGS, *S* (billions of dollars) | MARGINAL PROPENSITY TO SAVE, MPS |
|---|---|---|---|---|
| 1989 | 2700 | 3200 | 500 | |
| | | | | 0.25 |
| 1990 | 3000 | 3600 | 600 | |
| | | | | 0.25 |
| 1991 | 3300 | 4000 | 700 | |
| | | | | 0.25 |
| 1992 | 3600 | 4400 | 800 | |
| | | | | 0.25 |
| 1993 | 3900 | 4800 | 900 | |
| | | | | 0.25 |
| 1994 | 4200 | 5200 | 1000 | |

The **marginal propensity to save** (or **MPS**) is the slope of the saving function. It tells us how much more consumers will save if disposable income rises by $1 billion.

You may have noticed that the MPS is 0.25 while the MPC for Macroland is 0.75. They add up to 1, and not by accident. Since the portion of each additional dollar of disposable income that is not spent must be saved, the MPC and the MPS always add up to 1. It is a simple fact of accounting.

The MPC and the MPS always add up to 1, meaning that an additional dollar of income must be divided between consumption and saving. In symbols:

$$\text{MPC} + \text{MPS} = 1.$$

This enables us to compute either one of them from the other.

**Figure 24–9 THE SAVING FUNCTION OF MACROLAND**

The saving function of Macroland, depicted here, can be constructed either from the data in Table 24–3 or from Figure 24–8. This is because when we plot saving against disposable income (as we do here), we are also plotting the difference between consumption and disposable income (the vertical distance between line *C* and the 45° line in Figure 24–8) against disposable income.

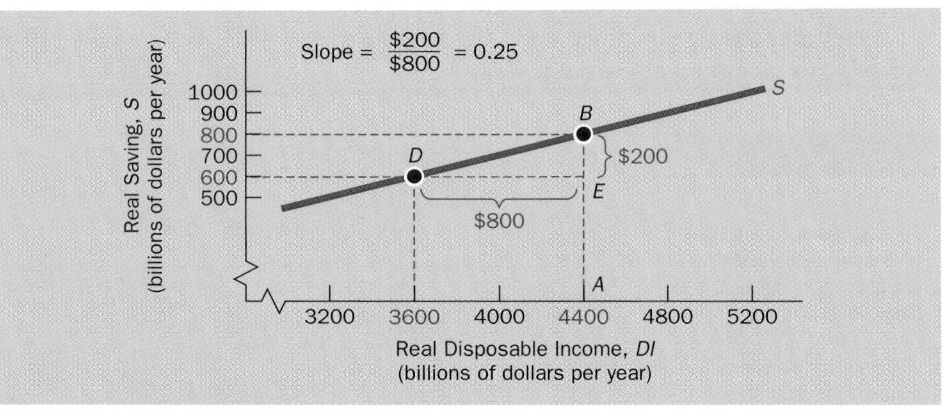


## Summary

1. Instead of studying the consumption function, it is possible to study the same data by looking at the **saving function**, which is defined as the relationship between disposable income and consumer saving.

2. Since consumer saving is merely the difference between disposable income and consumer expenditure, everything we have learned about the consumption function applies to the saving function.

3. The amount of additional saving caused by a $1 increase in disposable income is called the **marginal propensity to save**, or MPS.
4. Since each additional $1 of disposable income is either spent or saved, the MPC and the MPS must always add up to 1. Thus, knowledge of one implies knowledge of the other.

## Key Concepts and Terms

Aggregate saving

Saving function

Marginal propensity to save

## Questions for Review

1. Look at the circular flow diagram in Figure 24–1 (page 593). Where does the saving function enter the picture?
2. If the MPC in the U.S. economy is about 0.90, how large is the MPS?
3. Take the data from Simpleland in Question 7 on page 608 and use them to construct a saving function for Simpleland on a piece of graph paper.
4. (More difficult) If taxes are cut *temporarily* and consumer spending does not increase much, what must happen to consumer saving? Ask your instructor what happened to consumer saving immediately after the 1975 tax cuts.

# *Appendix B* NATIONAL INCOME ACCOUNTING

The type of macroeconomic analysis presented in this book dates from the publication of John Maynard Keynes's *The General Theory of Employment, Interest, and Money* in 1936. But at that time there was really no way to test Keynes's theories because the necessary data did not exist. It took some years for the theoretical notions used by Keynes to find concrete expression in real-world data. The system of measurement devised for this purpose is called **national income accounting**.

The development of this system of accounts ranks as a great achievement in applied economics, perhaps as important in its own right as Keynes's theoretical work. For without it the practical value of Keynesian analysis would be severely limited. Many men and women spent long hours wrestling with the numerous difficult conceptual questions that arose in translating the theory into numbers, but they had one acknowledged leader: the late Professor Simon Kuznets, who was awarded the Nobel Prize in economics for his contributions to economic measurement techniques. Along the way some more-or-less arbitrary decisions and conventions had to be made. You may not agree with all of them, but the accounting framework that was devised is eminently serviceable, though, inevitably, it has some limitations that must be understood.

## DEFINING GDP: EXCEPTIONS TO THE RULES

We first encountered the concept of **gross domestic product (GDP)** in Chapter 2.

**Gross domestic product (GDP)** is the sum of the money values of all final goods and services produced during a specified period of time, usually one year.

However, the definition of GDP has certain exceptions we have not yet noted.

First, the treatment of government output involves a minor departure from the principle of using market prices. Outputs of private industries are sold on markets, so their prices are observed. But "outputs" of government offices are not sold; indeed, it is sometimes even difficult to define what those outputs are. Lacking prices for outputs, national income accountants fall back on the only prices they have: prices for the inputs from which the outputs are produced. Thus:

Government outputs are valued at the cost of the inputs needed to produce them.

This means, for example, that if a clerk at the Department of Motor Vehicles earns $10 an hour and spends one-half hour torturing you with explanations of why you cannot get a driver's license, that particular government "service" is considered as being worth $5, and will increase GDP by that amount.

Second, some goods that are not actually sold on markets during the year are nonetheless counted in that year's GDP. These are the goods that are produced during the year but not sold; that is, goods that firms stockpile as *inventories*. Goods that are added to inventories count in GDP even though they do not pass through markets.

National income statisticians treat inventories as if they were "bought" by the firms that produced them, even though this "purchase" never takes place.

Finally, the treatment of investment goods runs slightly counter to the rule that only final goods are to be counted. In a broad sense, factories, generators, machine tools, and the like might be considered as intermediate goods. After all, their owners want them only for use in producing other goods, not for any innate value that they possess. But this would present a real problem, for factories and machines normally are never sold to consumers. So when would we count them in GDP? National income statisticians avoid this problem by defining investment goods as final products demanded by the firms that buy them.

Now that we have a more complete definition of what the GDP is, let us turn to the problem of actually measuring it. National income accountants have devised three ways to perform this task, and we consider each in turn.

## GDP AS THE SUM OF FINAL GOODS AND SERVICES

The first way to measure GDP seems to be the most natural, since it follows so directly from the circular flow diagram in this chapter. It also turns out to be the most useful definition for macroeconomic analysis. We simply add up the final demands of all consumers, business firms, government, and foreigners. Using the symbols $C$, $I$, $G$, and $(X - IM)$ just as we did in the text, we have:

$$\text{GDP} = C + I + G + (X - IM).$$

The $I$ that appears in the actual U.S. national accounts is called **gross private domestic investment**. The word "gross" will be explained presently. "Private" indicates that government investment is considered part of $G$, and "domestic" just means that machinery sold by American firms to foreign companies is included in exports rather than in $I$. Gross private domestic investment in the United States has three components: business investment in plant and equipment, residential construction (home building), and inventory investment. We repeat again that *only* these three things are **investment** in national income accounting terminology.

As defined in the national income accounts, **investment** includes only newly produced capital goods, such as machinery, factories, and new homes. It does not include exchanges of existing assets.

In common parlance, all sorts of activities that are not part of the GDP are often called "investment." People are said to "invest" in the stock market when they purchase shares. Or wealthy individuals "invest" in works of art. But since transactions like these merely exchange one type of asset (money) for another (stock or art works), they are not included in the GDP.

The symbol $G$, for government purchases, represents the *volume of current goods and services purchased by all levels of government*. Thus anything the government pays to its employees is counted in $G$, as are its purchases of paper, pencils, airplanes, bombs, typewriters, and so forth.

Few citizens realize that *most of what the federal government spends its money on is not for purchases of goods and services*. Instead, it is on **transfer payments**—literally, giving away money—either to individuals or to other levels of government.

The importance of the conceptual distinction lies in the fact that $G$ represents the part of the national product that government uses up for its own purposes—to pay for armies, bureaucrats, paper, and ink—whereas transfer payments merely represent shuffling of purchasing power from one group of citizens to another group. Except for the administrators needed to run the programs, real economic resources are not used up in this process.

In adding up the nation's total output as the sum of $C + I + G + (X - IM)$, we are summing the shares of GDP that are used up by consumers, investors, government, and foreigners, respectively. Since transfer payments merely give someone the capability to spend on $C$, it is logical to exclude them from our definition of $G$, including in $C$ only the portion of these transfer payments that is spent. If we included them in $G$, the same spending would get counted twice: once in $G$ and then again in $C$.

The final component of GDP is net exports, which are simply exports of goods and services minus imports of goods and services. Notice that both goods *and services* count, though the news media devote most attention to the monthly data on trade in goods ("merchandise trade").

Table 24–4 shows GDP for 1992, in both nominal and real terms, computed as the sum of $C + I + G + (X - IM)$. You will note that the numbers for net exports in the table are actually negative. We will have much to say about America's trade deficit in Part 8.

## GDP AS THE SUM OF ALL FACTOR PAYMENTS

There is another way to count up the GDP—by *adding up all the incomes in the economy*. Let's see how this method handles some typical transactions. Suppose General Electric builds a generator and sells it to General Motors for \$1 million. The first method of calculating GDP simply counts the \$1 million as part of $I$. The second method asks: What incomes resulted from the production of this generator? The answer might be something like this:

| | |
|---|---|
| Wages of G.E. employees | \$400,000 |
| Interest to bondholders | \$ 50,000 |
| Rentals of buildings | \$ 50,000 |
| Profits of G.E. stockholders | \$100,000 |

The total is \$600,000. The remaining \$400,000 is accounted for by inputs that G.E. purchased from other companies: steel, circuitry, tubing, rubber, and so on.

But if we traced this \$400,000 back further, we would find that it is accounted for by the wages,

**Table 24–4 GROSS DOMESTIC PRODUCT IN 1992 AS THE SUM OF THE FINAL DEMANDS**

| ITEM | AMOUNT (billions of current dollars) | AMOUNT (billions of 1987 dollars) |
|---|---|---|
| Personal consumption expenditures (C) | 4139.9 | 3341.8 |
| Gross private domestic investment(*I*) | 796.5 | 732.8 |
| Government purchases of goods and services (G) | 1131.8 | 945.2 |
| Net exports (*X* – *IM*) | –29.6 | –33.6 |
| Exports (*X*) | 640.5 | 57.0 |
| Imports (*IM*) | 670.1 | 611.0 |
| Gross domestic product (*Y*) | 6038.5 | 4986.3 |

SOURCE U.S. Department of Commerce. Totals do not add up precisely due to rounding.

interest, and rentals paid by these other companies, *plus* their profits, *plus* their purchases from other firms. In fact, for *every* firm in the economy, there is an accounting identity that says:

$$\text{Revenues from sales} = \begin{array}{l}\text{Wages paid } + \\ \text{Interest paid } + \\ \text{Rentals paid } + \\ \text{Profits earned } + \\ \text{Purchases from} \\ \text{other firms.}\end{array}$$

Why must this always be true? Because profits are the balancing item; they are what is *left over* after the firm has made all its other payments. In fact, this accounting identity is really just the definition of profits: sales revenue less all costs of production.

Now apply this accounting identity to *all the firms in the economy*. Total purchases from other firms are precisely what we call *intermediate goods*. What, then, do we get if we subtract these intermediate transactions from both sides of the equation?

$$\begin{array}{c}\text{Revenues from sales} \\ \textit{minus} \\ \text{Purchases from} \\ \text{other firms}\end{array} = \begin{array}{l}\text{Wages paid } + \\ \text{Interest paid } + \\ \text{Rentals paid } + \\ \text{Profits earned.}\end{array}$$

On the right-hand side, we have the sum of all factor incomes: payments to labor, land, and capital. On the left-hand side, we have total sales minus sales of intermediate goods. This means that we have only sales of *final* goods, which is precisely our definition of GDP. Thus, the accounting identity for the entire economy can be rewritten as:

$$\text{GDP} = \text{Wages} + \text{Interest} + \text{Rents} + \text{Profits},$$

and this gives national income accountants another way to measure the GDP.

Table 24–5 shows 1992's GDP measured by the sum of all incomes. Once again, a few details have been omitted in our discussion. The sum of wages, interest, rents, and profits actually adds up to only $4837 billion (whereas GDP is $6039 billion). We call this sum **national income** because it is the sum of all factor payments. But the actual selling prices of goods include another category of income that we have ignored so far: sales taxes, excise taxes, and the like. National income statisticians call these *indirect business taxes*, and when we add these to national income we obtain the **net national product (NNP).**

Notice here the use of the adjective "national" rather than "domestic." When we add up all the wages, interest, rents, and profits received by Americans, we will inevitably include some payments derived from production in other countries. Similarly, some of the factor payments made by American businesses go to citizens of other countries. If we subtract the former and add back the latter, we change net national product into net domestic product.

Now we are almost at the GDP. The only difference between GDP and NDP is **depreciation** of the nation's capital stock.

**Depreciation** is the value of the portion of the nation's capital equipment that is used up within the year. It tells us how much output is needed just to keep the economy's capital stock intact.

The difference between "gross" and "net" simply refers to whether depreciation is included or ex-

**Table 24-5 GROSS DOMESTIC PRODUCT IN 1992 AS THE SUM OF INCOMES**

| ITEM | AMOUNT (billions of dollars) | |
|---|---|---|
| Compensation of employees (wages) | 3582.0 | |
| plus | | |
| Net interest | 442.0 | |
| plus | | |
| Rental income | –8.9 | |
| plus | | |
| Profits | 821.5 | |
| Corporate profits | | |
| Proprietors' income | | 407.2 |
| equals | | 414.3 |
| National income | | |
| plus | 4836.6 | |
| Indirect business taxes and | | |
| miscellaneous items | 551.3 | |
| equals | | |
| National net product | 5387.9 | |
| minus | | |
| income received | 129.2 | |
| from other countries | | |
| plus | | |
| income paid | | |
| to other countries | 121.9 | |
| equals | 5380.6 | |
| Net domestic product | | |
| plus | 657.9 | |
| Depreciation | | |
| equals | | |
| Gross domestic product | 6038.5 | |

SOURCE: U.S. Department of Commerce. Totals do not add up precisely due to rounding.

cluded. We add depreciation to NDP to get GDP. Thus, GDP is a measure of all final output, taking no account of the capital used up in the process (and therefore in need of replacement). NDP deducts the required replacements to arrive at a *net* production figure.

From a conceptual point of view, most economists feel that NDP is a more meaningful indicator of the economy's output than GDP. After all, the depreciation component of GDP represents the output that is needed just to repair and replace worn out factories and machines; it is not available for anybody to consume.[9] So NDP seems to be a better measure of well-being than GDP. But, alas, GDP is much easier to measure because depreciation is a particularly tricky item. What fraction of his tractor did Farmer Jones "use up" last year? How much did the Empire State Building depreciate during 1993? If you ask yourself these difficult questions, you will understand why most economists feel that GDP is measured more accurately than is NDP. For this reason, most economic models are based on GDP.

In Table 24–5 you can hardly help noticing the preponderant share of employee compensation in total national income—about 74 percent. Labor is by far the most important factor of production. The return on land is negligible; and interest accounts for about 9 percent. Profits account for the remaining 17 percent, though the size of corporate profits (less than 9 percent of GDP) is much less than the public

[9]If the capital stock is used for consumption, it will decline, and the nation will wind up poorer than before.

thinks. If, by some magic stroke, we could eliminate all corporate profits without upsetting the performance of the economy, the average worker would get a raise of about 11 percent!

## GDP AS THE SUM OF VALUES ADDED

It may strike you as strange that national income accountants include only *final* goods and services in GDP. Aren't *intermediate* goods part of the nation's product? They are, of course. The problem is that, if all intermediate goods were included in GDP, we would wind up double and triple counting things and therefore get an exaggerated impression of the amount of economic activity that is actually going on.

To explain why, and to show how national income accountants cope with this difficulty, we must introduce a new concept, called **value added.**

**The value added** by a firm is its revenue from selling a product minus the amount paid for goods and services purchased from other firms.

The intuitive sense of the concept is clear: if a firm buys some inputs from other firms, does something to them, and sells the resulting product for a price higher than it paid for the inputs, we say that the firm has "added value" to the product. If we sum up the values added in this way by all the firms in the economy, we must get the total value of all final products. Thus:

GDP can be measured as the sum of the values added by all firms.

To verify that this is so, look back at the second accounting identity on page 614. The left-hand side of this equation, sales revenue minus purchases from other firms, is precisely the firm's value added. Thus:

$$\text{Value added} = \text{Wages} + \text{Interest} + \text{Rents} + \text{Profits}.$$

Since the second method we gave for measuring GDP is to add up wages, interest, rents, and profits, we see that the value-added approach must also yield the same answer.

The value-added concept is useful in avoiding double counting. Often it is hard to distinguish intermediate goods from final goods. Paint bought by a painter, for example, is an intermediate good. But paint bought by a do-it-yourselfer is a final good. What happens, then, if the professional painter has some paint left over and uses it to refurbish his own garage? The intermediate good becomes a final good. You can see that the line between intermediate goods and final goods is a fuzzy one in practice.

If we measure GDP by the sum of values added, however, it is not necessary to make such subtle distinctions. In this method, *every* purchase of a new good or service counts, but we do not count the entire selling price, only the portion that represents value added.

To illustrate this idea, consider the data in Table 24–6 and how they would affect GDP as the sum of final products. Our example begins when a farmer who grows soybeans sells them to a mill for $3 a bushel. This transaction does *not* count in the GDP, because the miller does not purchase the soybeans for his own use. The miller then grinds up the soybeans and sells the resulting bag of soy meal to a factory that produces soy sauce. The miller receives $4, but GDP still has not increased because the ground beans are also an intermediate product.

**Table 24–6 AN ILLUSTRATION OF FINAL AND INTERMEDIATE GOODS**

| ITEM | SELLER | BUYER | PRICE |
|---|---|---|---|
| Bushel of soybeans | Farmer | Miller | $ 3 |
| Bag of soy meal | Miller | Factory | 4 |
| Gallon of soy sauce | Factory | Restaurant | 8 |
| Gallon of soy sauce used as seasoning | Restaurant | Consumers | $10 |
| | | | Total: $25 |

**Addendum: Contribution to GDP: $10**

**Table 24–7 AN ILLUSTRATION OF VALUE ADDED**

| ITEM | SELLER | BUYER | PRICE | VALUE ADDED |
|---|---|---|---|---|
| Bushel of soybeans | Farmer | Miller | $ 3 | $ 3 |
| Bag of soy meal | Miller | Factory | 4 | 1 |
| Gallon of soy sauce | Factory | Restaurant | 8 | 4 |
| Gallon of soy sauce used as seasoning | Restaurant | Consumers | 10 | 2 |
| | | | Total: $25 | $10 |

**Addendum: Contribution to GDP**
Final products ........................................ $10
Sum of values added ................................ $10

Next, the factory turns the beans into soy sauce, which it sells to your favorite Chinese restaurant for $8. Still no effect on GDP.

But then the big moment arrives: The restaurant sells the sauce to you and other customers as a part of your meals, and you eat it. At this point, the $10 worth of soy sauce becomes a final product and is included in the GDP. Notice that if we had also counted the three intermediate transactions (farmer to miller, miller to factory, factory to restaurant), we would have come up with $25—two and one-half times too much.

Why is it too much? The reason is straightforward. Neither the miller nor the factory owner nor the restaurateur value the product we have been considering *for its own sake*. Only the customers who eat the final product (the soy sauce) have had an increase in their material well-being. So only this last transaction counts in the GDP. However, as we shall now see, value-added calculations enable us to come up with the right answer ($10) by counting only *part* of each transaction. The basic idea is to count at each step only the contribution to the value of the ultimate final product that is made at that step, excluding the values of items produced at earlier steps.

Ignoring the minor items (such as fertilizer) that the farmer purchases from others, the entire $3 selling price of the bushel of soybeans is new output produced by the farmer; that is, the whole $3 is value added. The miller then grinds the beans and sells them for $4. He has added $4 − $3 = $1 to the value of the beans. When the factory turns this soy meal into soy sauce and sells it for $8, it has added $8 − $4 = $4 more in value. And finally, when the restaurant sells it to hungry customers for $10, a further $2 of value is added.

Table 24–7 shows this chain of creation of value added by appending another column to Table 24–6. We see that the total value added by all four firms is $10, exactly the same as the restaurant's selling price. This is as it must be, for only the restaurant sells the soybeans as a final product.

## ALTERNATIVE MEASURES OF THE INCOME OF THE NATION

Economists use the term *national income* in two different ways. The most common usage is as a general term indicating the size of the income of the nation as a whole, without being specific about exactly how this income is to be measured. This is the sense in which the term "national income" is used in this book. The second, and much more precise, use of the term refers to a particular concept in national income accounting which we encountered in Table 24–5 on page 615: the sum of wages, interest, rents, and profits.

Aside from this formal definition of national income, what other accounting concept might be used to measure the total income of the nation? The first and most obvious candidate is the GDP itself. GDP, however, is intended to be a measure of *production*, and so has several drawbacks as a measure of *income*.

First, it includes some output that represents income to no one—output that simply replaces worn-out machinery and buildings (depreciation). When we deduct this depreciation, we obtain the net domestic product (NDP), as shown in Figure 24–10.

Figure 24–10 ALTERNATIVE MEASURES OF THE INCOME OF THE NATION

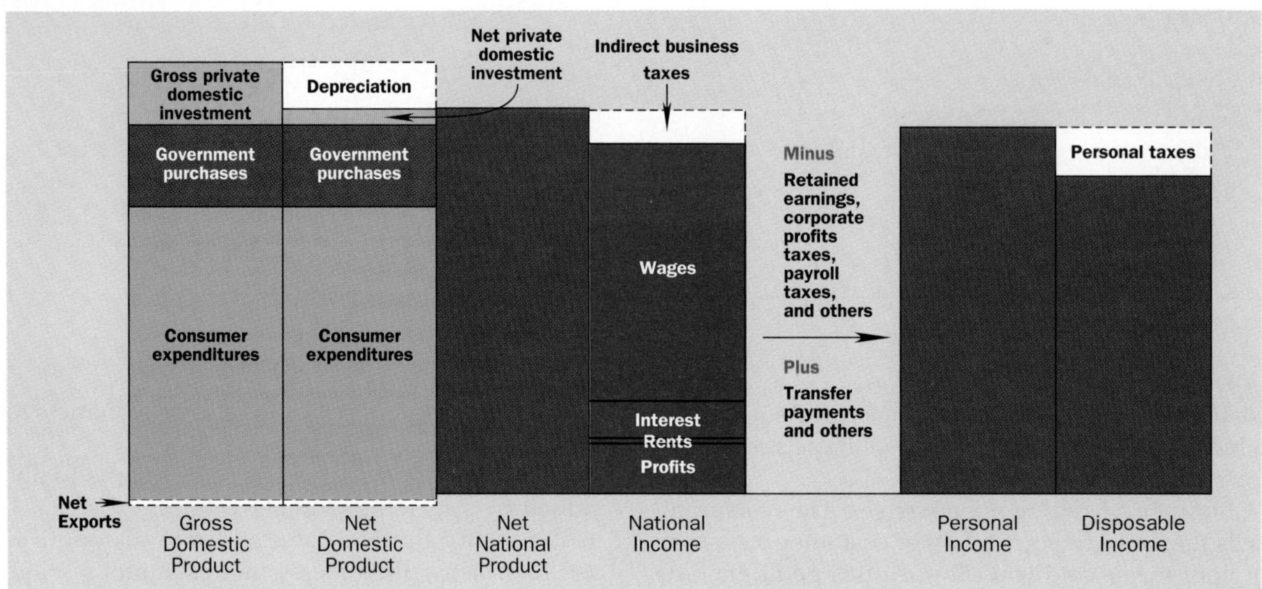


This bar chart indicates the relationships among six alternative measures of the total income of the nation, starting with the largest and most comprehensive measure (GDP) and ranging down to the measure that most closely approximates the spendable income of consumers (disposable income).

Second, we learned earlier that some of the income included in NDP is paid to foreigners, rather than to Americans; and, similarly, some of the income receipts of Americans derive from business activities abroad. Making these two corrections gives us a better measure of American incomes, and turns NDP into net *national* product, NNP—the next bar shown in the figure. As you can see, NNP hardly differs from NDP.

Third, because of sales taxes and related items (indirect business taxes), part of the price paid for each good and service does not represent income to any individual. When we deduct these indirect business taxes from NNP, we arrive again at the formal definition of national income (refer to Figure 24–10).

There are, however, two other measures of income. **Personal income** is meant to be a better measure of the income that actually accrues to individuals. It is obtained from national income by *subtracting* corporate profits taxes, retained earnings, and payroll taxes (because these items are never received by individuals), and then *adding in* transfer payments (because these sources of income are not part of the wages, interest, rents, or profits that constitute the national income). As Figure 24–10 suggests, this adding and subtracting normally results in a number slightly larger than national income. Finally, if we subtract personal income taxes from personal income, we obtain **disposable income**.

Among all the concepts of the nation's income depicted in Figure 24–10, only two are used frequently in the construction of models of the economy: gross domestic product (GDP) and disposable income (*DI*). Since the models presented in this book ignore depreciation and indirect business taxes, GDP is basically identical to national income (see Figure 24–10). Similarly, if we ignore retained earnings, GDP and *DI* differ only by the amounts of taxes and transfers (again, see Figure 24–10).

## Summary

1. **Gross domestic product** (GDP) is the sum of the money values of all final goods and services produced during a year and sold on organized markets. There are, however, certain exceptions to this definition.
2. One way to measure the GDP is to add up the final demands of consumers, investors, government, and foreigners: GDP $= C + I + G + (X - IM)$.
3. A second way to measure the GDP is to start with all the factor payments—wages, interest, rents, and profits—that constitute the **national income**, and then add indirect business taxes and **depreciation**.
4. A third way to measure the GDP is to sum up the **values added** by every firm in the economy (and then once again add indirect business taxes and depreciation).
5. Except for possible bookkeeping and statistical errors, all three methods must give the same answer.

## Key Concepts and Terms

National income accounting
Gross National Product (GNP)
Gross Domestic Product (GDP)
Gross Private Domestic Investment
Government purchases
Transfer payments
Net exports
National Income
Net Domestic Product (NDP)
Net National Product (NNP)
Depreciation
Value added
Personal Income
Disposable Income (*DI*)

## Questions for Review

1. Which of the following transactions are included in the gross domestic product, and by how much does each raise GDP?
   a. You buy a new car, paying $11,000.
   b. You buy a used car, paying $3000.
   c. Apple builds a $100 million factory to make computers.
   d. Your grandmother receives a government social security check for $1000.
   e. Chrysler manufacturers 2000 automobiles at a cost of $12,000 each. Unable to sell them, it holds them as inventories.
   f. Mr. Black and Mr. Blue, each out for a Sunday drive, have a collision in which their cars are destroyed. Black and Blue each hire a lawyer to sue the other, paying the lawyers $2000 each for services rendered. The judge throws the case out of court.
   g. You sell a poster to your roommate for $20.
2. Explain the difference between final goods and intermediate goods. Why is it sometimes difficult to apply this distinction in practice? In this regard, why is the concept of value added useful?
3. Explain the difference between government spending and government purchases of goods and services (*G*). Which is larger?
4. Explain why national income and gross domestic product would be essentially equal if there were no depreciation and no indirect business taxes.
5. The following is a complete description of all economic activity in Trivialand for 1993. Draw up versions of Tables 24–4 and 24–5 for Trivialand showing GDP computed in two different ways.
   a. There are thousands of farmers but only two big business firms in Trivialand: Specific Motors (an auto company) and Super Duper (a chain of food markets). There is no government and no depreciation.
   b. Specific Motors produced 1000 small cars, which they sold at $6000 each, and 100 trucks, which they sold at $8000 each. Consumers bought 800 of the

cars, and the remaining 200 cars were exported to the United States. Super Duper bought all the trucks.

c. Sales at Super Duper markets amounted to $14 million, all of it sold to consumers.
d. All the farmers in Trivialand are self-employed and sell all their wares to Super Duper.
e. The costs incurred by all the businesses were as follows:

| | SPECIFIC MOTORS | SUPER DUPER | FARMERS |
|---|---|---|---|
| Wages | $3,800,000 | $4,500,000 | $ 0 |
| Interest | 100,000 | 200,000 | 700,000 |
| Rent | 200,000 | 1,000,000 | 2,000,000 |
| Purchases of food | 0 | 7,000,000 | 0 |

6. (More difficult) Now complicate Trivialand in the following ways and answer the same questions. In addition, calculate national income, personal income, and disposable income.
   a. The government bought 50 cars, leaving only 150 cars for export. In addition, the government spent $800,000 on wages for soldiers and made $1,200,000 in transfer payments.
   b. Depreciation for the year amounted to $600,000 for Specific Motors and $200,000 for Super Duper. (The farmers had no depreciation.)
   c. The government levied sales taxes amounting to $500,000 on Specific Motors and $200,000 on Super Duper (none on farmers). In addition, the government levied a 10 percent income tax on all wages, interest, and rental income.
   d. In addition to the food and cars mentioned in Question 5, consumers in Trivialand imported 500 computers from the United States at $2,000 each.

# DEMAND-SIDE EQUILIBRIUM: UNEMPLOYMENT OR INFLATION?

*Investment . . . is a flighty bird, which needs to be controlled.*

J.R. HICKS

We learned in Chapter 22 that the interaction of aggregate demand and aggregate supply determines whether the economy will stagnate or prosper, whether our labor and capital resources will be fully employed or unemployed. And we learned in Chapter 24 that aggregate demand has four components: consumer expenditure ($C$), investment ($I$), government purchases ($G$), and net exports ($X - IM$). It is now time to start building a theory that fits all the pieces together. ¶ Our approach is sequential. Since it is necessary to walk before you can to run, we imagine in this chapter that the price level, the rate of interest, and the international value of the dollar are all constant. None of these assumptions are true, of course, and each will be eliminated later in the book. But these three unrealistic assumptions enable us to construct a simple but useful model of how the state of aggregate demand influences the level of gross domestic product (GDP). In this simple model, only $C$ is variable; the other three components of spending—$I$, $G$, and $X - IM$—are all assumed to be fixed. ¶ Subsequent chapters will drop the three unrealistic assumptions in turn. In Chapter 27, we bring in the supply side of the economy, which enables us to treat the price level as variable rather than constant. In Chapter 30, we will see how interest rates—and hence investment—are determined. Finally, Chapters 36–37 bring the exchange rate into the picture and study the determination of net exports.

But first things first. This chapter begins by examining the most volatile component of aggregate demand: investment. What factors determine investment spending, and why is it so variable and hard to predict?[1] Then we add net exports and government purchases to the model. Treating *I*, *G*, and $X - IM$ as constants, we next see how equilibrium is established on the demand side of the economy. Finally, we consider a question of great importance to policymakers: Can the economy be expected to achieve full employment of its resources if the government does not intervene?

## THE EXTREME VARIABILITY OF INVESTMENT

The first thing to be said about investment spending is that it is extraordinarily variable.

Unlike consumer spending, which follows movements in disposable income with great (though not perfect) reliability, investment spending swings from high to low levels with annoying speed. During recessions, for example, the decline in investment generally constitutes the bulk of the drop in real GDP, even though investment is only a small portion of GDP—about 17 percent in the postwar United States. What accounts for these movements of investment demand?

### BUSINESS CONFIDENCE AND EXPECTATIONS ABOUT THE FUTURE

While many factors influence business people's desires to invest, Keynes himself laid great stress on the *state of business confidence*, which in turn depends on *expectations about the future*.

While tricky to measure, it does seem obvious that businesses will build more factories and purchase more new machines when they are optimistic. Conversely, their investment plans will be very cautious if the economic outlook appears bleak. Keynes pointed out that psychological perceptions like these are subject to abrupt shifts, so that fluctuations in investment can be a major cause of instability in aggregate demand. Hence, Hicks's analogy to a "flighty bird" in the chapter's opening quotation.

Unfortunately, neither economists nor, for that matter, psychologists have many good ideas about how to *measure*—much less *control*—business confidence. Therefore, economists usually focus on several more objective determinants of investment—determinants that are easier to quantify and, perhaps even more important, are more easily influenced by government policy.

### THE LEVEL AND GROWTH OF DEMAND

Firms have a strong incentive to invest when demand is pushing against capacity. Under these circumstances, business executives are likely to feel that new factories

[1]We repeat the warning given in the previous chapter about the meaning of the word *investment*. It *includes* spending by businesses and individuals on *newly produced* factories, machinery, and houses. But it *excludes* sales of used industrial plants, equipment, and homes, and it *also excludes* purely financial transactions, such as the purchase of stocks and bonds.

and machinery can be employed profitably. By contrast, if there is a great deal of unused machinery, empty factories, and the like, managers may not find investment opportunities very attractive.

Because it takes a substantial amount of time to order machinery or to build a factory, investment plans are made with an eye on the future. Even when pressures on current capacity are not particularly severe, a firm that is expecting rapid growth in sales may start investing now in order to have adequate capacity for the future. Furthermore, briskly growing sales are likely to make business people more optimistic. Conversely, slow growth of output will discourage investment. We can summarize this discussion by saying that:

High levels of sales relative to current capacity and expectations of rapid economic growth create an atmosphere favorable to investment. Low levels of sales and slow anticipated growth are likely to discourage investment.

Government stabilization policy thus has a handle on investment spending, for by stimulating aggregate demand it can induce business firms to invest more, though the precise amount may be hard to predict.

## TECHNICAL CHANGE AND PRODUCT INNOVATION

Some investments are driven by technology. When a new product like the VCR is invented, or when a technological breakthrough makes an existing product much cheaper or better, as happened with microcomputers, new investment opportunities suddenly appear. In our capitalist market system, entrepreneurs seize these opportunities quickly—building new factories, stores, and offices. These new investments need not be "high tech." The VCR, for example, spawned an entire service industry of video rental shops that now dot the American landscape. Two decades ago, such stores did not even exist.

## THE RATE OF INTEREST

The rate of interest is the determinant of investment that will play a pivotal role in later chapters. A good deal of business investment is financed by borrowing, and the interest rate indicates how much firms pay for that privilege. Some investment projects that look profitable at an interest rate of 7 percent will look disastrous if the firm has to pay 12 percent.

The amount that businesses will want to invest depends on the real interest rate they must pay on their borrowings. The lower the real rate of interest, the more investment spending there will be.

In Chapter 30, we will study in some detail how the government can influence the rate of interest. Since interest rates affect investment, policymakers have another handle on aggregate demand—a handle they do not hesitate to use. The point is that, unlike business confidence, expectations, and technology, interest rates are visible and manipulable. Therefore, even if investment responds much more dramatically to changes in confidence than to changes in interest rates, interest rates are nonetheless a more important instrument of government policy. But this is a topic for later in the book.

## TAX PROVISIONS

The government has still another important way to influence investment spending—by altering various provisions of the tax law. For example, one of the first things President Clinton proposed after his inauguration was a temporary *investment tax credit*, a subsidy for certain types of capital spending.[2] Under a 10% investment tax credit, for example, a company that spends $100,000 on eligible equipment has its tax bill reduced by $10,000. This obviously reduces the effective cost of investing in machinery. In addition, there is a *tax on corporate profits*, and the government can reduce the statutory tax rate as a way to spur investment—as it did in 1986. There are other, more complicated, tax provisions as well. To summarize:

The tax law gives the government several ways to influence business spending on investment goods. But influence is far from control. Investment remains a "flighty bird."

## THE DETERMINANTS OF NET EXPORTS

Another highly variable source of demand for U.S. products is foreign purchases of U.S. goods—our *exports*. However, as we learned in Chapter 24, to obtain the net contribution of foreigners to aggregate demand in the United States we must subtract *imports*, which is the portion of domestic demand that is satisfied by foreign producers.

### NATIONAL INCOMES

While both exports and imports depend on many factors, the predominant one is *national income*. Some of the additional consumption and investment spending that American consumers and firms do as their spending rises is on foreign goods. So:

Our imports rise when our GDP rises and fall when our GDP falls.

Similarly, our *exports* are the *imports* of other countries, so it is natural to assume that our exports depend on *their* GDPs, not on our own. Thus:

Our exports are relatively insensitive to our own GDP, but are quite sensitive to the GDPs of other countries.

### RELATIVE PRICES OF EXPORTS AND IMPORTS

While GDP levels at home and abroad are important influences on a country's net exports, they are not the only relevant factor. International price differences matter, too. To make things concrete, let us focus on trade between the United States and Japan. Suppose the prices of American goods rise while Japanese prices are constant. This makes U.S. products more expensive *relative to Japanese goods* than was true previously. If American consumers react to the new relative prices by buying more Japanese goods, our *imports rise*. If Japanese consumers react to the same relative price changes by buying fewer American products, our *exports fall*. Both reactions reduce America's net exports.

[2]But Congress did not enact the proposal.

Naturally, the effects of a decline in American prices are precisely the opposite: Exports are stimulated and imports are discouraged, so net exports rise. Thus:

A rise in the prices of a country's goods will lead to a reduction in that country's net exports. Analogously, a fall in the prices of a country's goods will raise that country's net exports.

Since trade patterns are governed by the prices of one country's goods *relative to* those of other countries, precisely the same logic applies to changes in Japanese prices. If Japanese prices fall while U.S. prices remain constant, Americans will import more and export less. So $(X - IM)$ will decline. By similar reasoning, rising Japanese prices increase U.S. net exports. Thus:

Price increases abroad raise a country's net exports while price decreases abroad have the opposite effect.

This simple idea holds the key to understanding how rates of exchange among the world's currencies influence exports and imports—a topic we will consider in depth in Chapters 36 and 37. The reason is that exchange rates translate foreign prices into terms customers are familiar with—their own currencies. Consider, for example, Americans interested in buying British sweaters that cost £30. If the British pound is worth $1.50, the sweaters cost potential American buyers $45 each. But, if the pound is worth $2.00, those same sweaters cost Americans $60, and they are likely to buy fewer.

## THE MEANING OF EQUILIBRIUM GDP

The fourth component of total spending, government purchases of goods and services ($G$), is determined in the political arena by our elected representatives. Let us now put the four pieces together and see how they interact, using as our organizing framework the circular flow diagram introduced in the last chapter.

In doing so, we will at first ignore the possibility—raised in Chapter 22—that the government might vary its taxes ($T$) and spending ($G$) to steer the economy in some desired direction. Aside from pedagogical simplicity, there is an important reason for doing this. One of the crucial questions surrounding government stabilization policy is whether the economy would *automatically* gravitate toward full employment if the government simply left it alone. John Maynard Keynes, contradicting the teachings of generations of economists before him, claimed that it would not. But Keynes' views remain controversial to this day. We can study this issue best by imagining an economy in which the government never tried to manipulate aggregate demand. This is just what we do in this chapter.

Look now at Figure 25–1, which repeats Figure 24–1 of the last chapter. We can use this circular flow diagram to begin the construction of a simple model of the determination of national income. But first we must understand what we mean by "equilibrium income."

As was explained in the last chapter, total *product*ion and total *income* must, of necessity, be equal. But the same need not be true of total *spending*. Imagine that, for some reason, the total expenditures, $C+I+G+(X - IM)$, being made after point 4 in the figure are greater than the value of the output being produced by the business firms at point 5.

*Figure* **25–1** **THE CIRCULAR FLOW DIAGRAM**

Here we repeat the circular flow of income and expenditures that we introduced in Chapter 24. Equilibrium occurs when $C + I + G + (X - IM)$ is equal to $Y$.

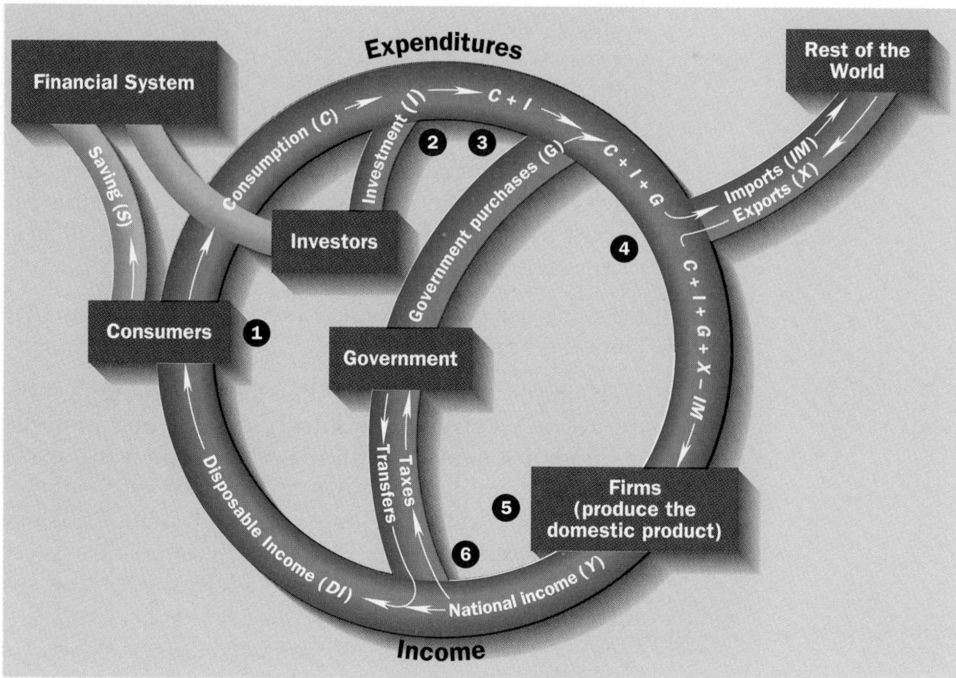


Two things may happen in such a situation. Since consumers, business firms, government, and foreigners together are buying more than firms are producing, businesses are being forced to take goods out of their warehouses to meet customer demands. Thus, inventory stocks must be falling. These inventory reductions are a signal to retailers of a need to increase their orders, and to manufacturers of a need to step up their production. Consequently, production is likely to rise. At some later date, if there is evidence that the high level of spending is not just a temporary aberration, either manufacturers or retailers (or both) may also respond to the buoyant sales performances by raising their prices. Economists therefore say that neither output nor the price level is in **equilibrium** when total spending exceeds the value of current production.

**EQUILIBRIUM** refers to a situation in which neither consumers nor firms have any incentive to change their behavior. They are content to continue with things as they are.

It is clear from the definition of equilibrium that the economy cannot be in equilibrium when total spending exceeds production, for the falling inventories demonstrate to firms that their production and pricing decisions were not quite appropriate.[3] Thus, since we normally use GDP to measure output:

The equilibrium level of GDP cannot be one at which total spending exceeds the value of output because firms will notice that inventory stocks are being depleted. They may first decide to increase production sufficiently to meet the higher demand. Later they may decide to raise prices as well.

[3]All the models in this book assume, strictly for simplicity, that firms want constant inventories. Deliberate changes in inventories are treated in more advanced courses.

Now imagine the other case, in which the flow of spending reaching firms falls short of current production. Some output cannot be sold and winds up as additions to inventories. The inventory pile-up acts as a signal to firms that at least one of their decisions was wrong. Once again, they will probably react first by cutting back on production, causing GDP to fall. If the imbalance persists, they may also lower prices to stimulate sales. But they certainly will not be happy with things as they are. Thus:

The equilibrium level of GDP cannot be one at which total spending is less than the value of output, because firms will not allow inventories to continue to pile up. They may decide to decrease production, or they may decide to cut prices in order to stimulate demand. Normally, firms are reluctant to cut prices until they are certain that the low level of demand is not a temporary phenomenon. So they rely more heavily on reductions in output.

## EQUILIBRIUM ON THE DEMAND SIDE OF THE ECONOMY

We have now determined, through a process of elimination, the level of output that is consistent with peoples' desires to spend. We have reasoned that GDP will rise whenever it is below total spending, $C + I + G + (X - IM)$, and that GDP will fall whenever it is above $C + I + G + (X - IM)$. Equilibrium can only occur, then, when there is just enough spending to absorb the current level of production. Under such circumstances, producers conclude that their price and output decisions are correct, and have no incentive to change them. We conclude that:

The **equilibrium level of GDP on the demand side** is the one at which total spending equals production. In such a situation, firms find their inventories remaining at desired levels; so there is no incentive to change output or prices.

Thus the circular flow diagram has helped us to understand the concept of equilibrium GDP on the demand side. It has also shown us how the economy is driven toward this equilibrium. It leaves unanswered, however, three important questions:

1. How large is the equilibrium level of GDP?
2. Will the economy suffer from unemployment, inflation, or both?
3. Is the equilibrium level of GDP on the demand side also consistent with firms' desires to produce? That is, is it also an equilibrium on the *supply* side?

The first two questions will occupy our attention in this chapter; the third question is reserved until Chapter 27.

## CONSTRUCTING THE EXPENDITURE SCHEDULE

Our first objective is to determine precisely the equilibrium level of GDP and to see what factors it depends upon. To make the analysis more concrete, we turn to a numerical example. Specifically, we examine the relationship between total spending and GDP in Macroland, the hypothetical economy that was introduced in the last chapter.

Columns 1 and 2 of Table 25–1 repeat the consumption function of Macroland that we first encountered in Table 24–1. They show how consumer spending, *C*, depends on national income, which we now begin to symbolize by the letter *Y*. Columns 3–5 provide the other three components of total spending, *I*, *G*, and *X* – *IM*, through the simplifying assumptions that each is just a fixed number regardless of the level of GDP. Specifically, we assume that investment spending is $900 billion, government purchases are $1300 billion, and net exports are –$100 billion—meaning that in Macroland, as in the United States at present, imports exceed exports.

By adding together columns 2 through 5, we calculate *C* + *I* + *G* + (*X* – *IM*), or total expenditure, which is displayed in column 6. Columns 1 and 6 are shaded and show how total expenditure depends on income in Macroland. We call this the **expenditure schedule**.

An **EXPENDITURE SCHEDULE** shows the relationship between national income (GDP) and total spending.

Figure 25–2 shows the construction of the expenditure schedule graphically. The black line labeled *C* is the consumption function of Macroland and simply duplicates Figure 24–6 of the last chapter. It plots on a graph the numbers given in columns 1 and 2 of Table 25–1.

The blue line, labeled *C* + *I*, displays our assumption that investment is fixed at $900 billion, regardless of the level of GDP. It lies a fixed distance (corresponding to $900 billion) above the *C* line. If investment were not always $900 billion, the two lines would either move closer together (at income levels at which investment was below $900 billion) or grow farther apart (at income levels at which investment was above $900 billion). For example, our list of determinants of investment spending suggested that *I* might be larger at higher levels of GDP. Because of this added investment—which is called **induced investment**—the resulting *C* + *I* schedule would have a steeper slope than the *C* schedule.

**INDUCED INVESTMENT** is the part of investment spending that rises when GDP rises and falls when GDP falls.

The brown line, labeled *C* + *I* + *G* adds in government purchases. Since they are assumed to be $1300 billion regardless of the size of GDP, the brown line is parallel to the blue line and $1300 billion higher.

Finally, the red line labeled *C* + *I* + *G* + (*X* – *IM*) adds in net exports. It is parallel to the brown line and $100 billion below, reflecting our assumption that net exports in Macroland are always –$100 billion. Once again, if imports depend on GDP, as our previous discussion suggested, the *C* + *I* + *G* and *C* + *I* + *G* + (*X* – *IM*) lines would not be parallel.

*Table* **25–1** **TOTAL EXPENDITURE IN MACROLAND (billions of dollars)**

| (1) INCOME (*Y*) | (2) CONSUMPTION (*C*) | (3) INVESTMENT (*I*) | (4) GOVERNMENT PURCHASES (*G*) | (5) NET EXPORTS (*X* – *IM*) | (6) TOTAL EXPENDITURE |
|---|---|---|---|---|---|
| 4800 | 3000 | 900 | 1300 | –100 | 5100 |
| 5200 | 3300 | 900 | 1300 | –100 | 5400 |
| 5600 | 3600 | 900 | 1300 | –100 | 5700 |
| 6000 | 3900 | 900 | 1300 | –100 | 6000 |
| 6400 | 4200 | 900 | 1300 | –100 | 6300 |
| 6800 | 4500 | 900 | 1300 | –100 | 6600 |
| 7200 | 4800 | 900 | 1300 | –100 | 6900 |

**Figure 25–2 CONSTRUCTION OF THE EXPENDITURE SCHEDULE**

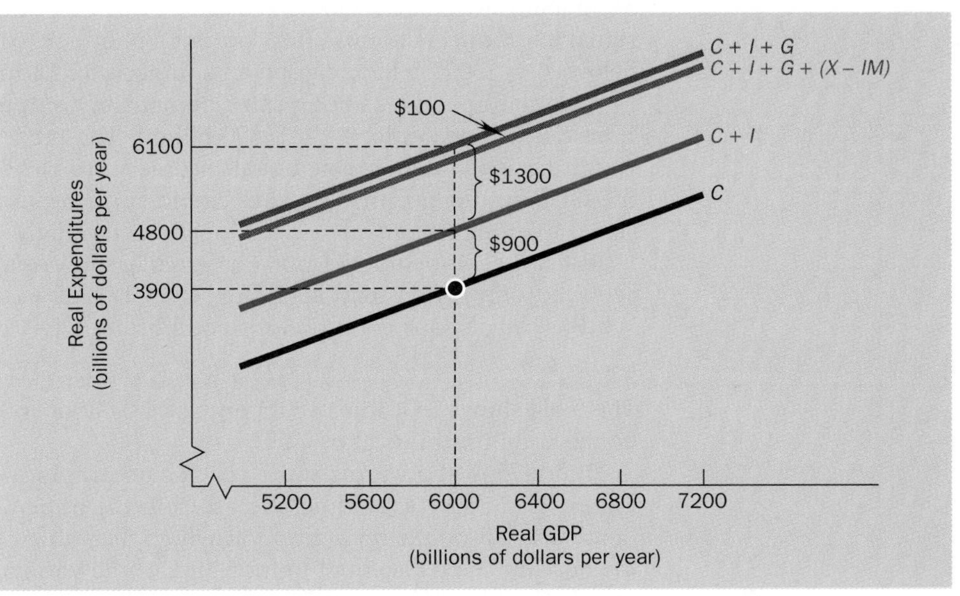


This figure shows in a diagram what Table 25-1 showed numerically—the construction of a total expenditure schedule from its components. Line *C* is the consumption function that we first encountered in Figure 24-6. Line *C* + *I* adds investment (assumed always to be $900 billion in this example), and line *C* + *I* + *G* adds government purchases (which are $1300 billion). Line *C* + *I* + *G* + (*X* – *IM*) is the expenditure schedule and is obtained by adding net exports to *C* + *I* + *G*. For example, when GDP is $6000, *C* is $3900, *I* is $900, *G* is $1300, and (*X* – *IM*) is – $100, for a total of $6000.

## THE MECHANICS OF INCOME DETERMINATION

We are now ready to determine demand-side equilibrium in Macroland. Look first at Table 25–2, which presents the logic of our circular flow argument in tabular form. The first two columns of this table reproduce the expenditure schedule that was constructed in Table 25–1. The other columns explain the process by which equilibrium is approached. Let us see why a GDP of $6000 billion must be the equilibrium level.

**Table 25–2 THE DETERMINATION OF EQUILIBRIUM OUTPUT**

| (1) OUTPUT (*Y*) (billions of dollars) | (2) TOTAL SPENDING (*C* + *I* + *G* + *X* – *IM*) (billions of dollars) | (3) BALANCE OF SPENDING AND OUTPUT | (4) INVENTORIES ARE: | (5) PRODUCERS WILL RESPOND BY: |
|---|---|---|---|---|
| 4800 | 5100 | Spending exceeds output | Falling | Producing more |
| 5200 | 5400 | Spending exceeds output | Falling | Producing more |
| 5600 | 5700 | Spending exceeds output | Falling | Producing more |
| 6000 | 6000 | Spending = output | Constant | Not changing production |
| 6400 | 6300 | Output exceeds spending | Rising | Producing less |
| 6800 | 6600 | Output exceeds spending | Rising | Producing less |
| 7200 | 6900 | Output exceeds spending | Rising | Producing less |

Consider first any output level below \$6000 billion. For example, at output level $Y$ = \$5200 billion, total expenditure is \$5400 billion (column 2), which is \$200 billion more than production. With spending greater than output (column 3), inventories will be falling (column 4). As the table suggests, this will be a signal to producers to raise their output (column 5). Clearly, then, no output level below $Y$ = \$6000 billion can be an equilibrium. Output is too low.

A similar line of reasoning can eliminate any output level above \$6000 billion. Consider, for example, $Y$ = \$6800 billion. The table shows that total spending would be \$6600 billion if national income were \$6800 billion. So \$200 billion of the GDP would go unsold. This would raise producers' inventory stocks and signal them that their rate of production is too high.

Just as we concluded from our circular flow diagram, equilibrium will be achieved only when total spending, $C + I + G + (X - IM)$, is equal to GDP ($Y$). In symbols, our condition for equilibrium GDP is:

$$Y = C + I + G + (X - IM).$$

The table shows that this occurs only at a GDP of \$6000 billion. This, then, must be the equilibrium level of GDP.

Figure 25–3 shows this same conclusion graphically, by adding a 45° line to Figure 25–2. Why a 45° line? Recall from the appendix to Chapter 1 that a 45° line marks all points on a graph at which the value of the variable measured on the horizontal axis is equal to the value of the variable measured on the vertical axis. In this convenient graph of the expenditure schedule, gross domestic product ($Y$) is measured on the horizontal axis and total expenditure, $C + I + G + (X - IM)$, is measured on the vertical axis. So the 45° line shows all the points

**Figure 25–3** **INCOME-EXPENDITURE DIAGRAM**

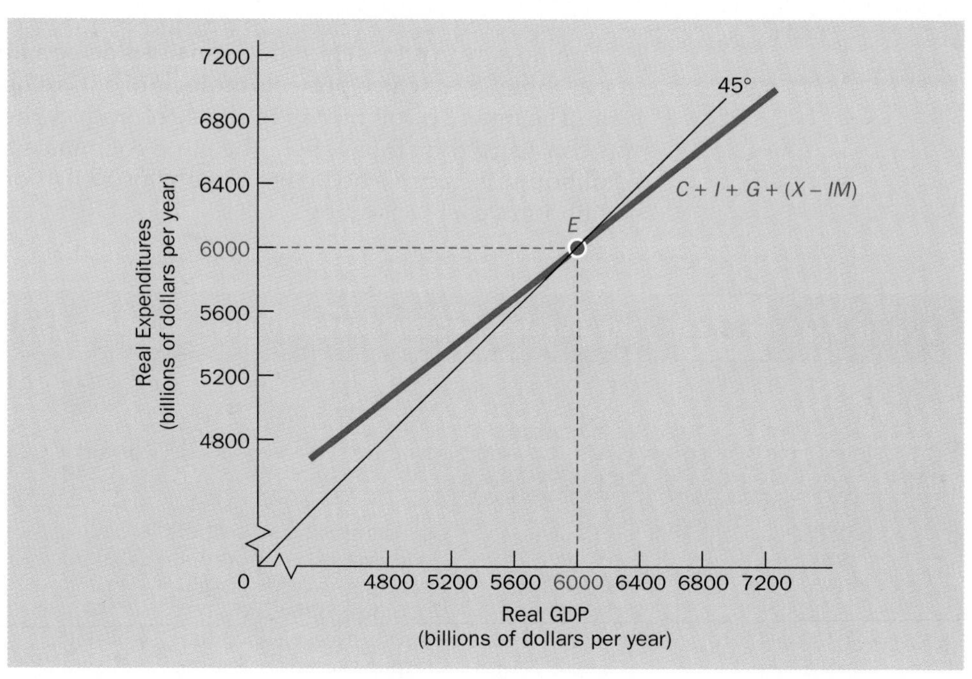


This figure adds a 45° line—which marks off points where expenditure and output are equal—to Figure 25–2. Since the condition for equilibrium GDP is that expenditure and output must be equal, this line can be used to determine the equilibrium level of GDP. In this example, equilibrium is at point *E*, where GDP is \$6000 billion—precisely as we found in Table 25–2.

at which output and spending are equal; that is, where $Y = C + I + G + (X - IM)$. The 45° line therefore displays all the points at which the economy *can possibly* be at equilibrium, for if total spending is not equal to production, firms will not be content with current output levels.

Now we must compare these *potential* equilibrium points with the *actual* combinations of spending and output that the economy can attain, given the behavior of consumers and investors. That behavior, as we have seen, is described by the $C + I + G + (X - IM)$ line in Figure 25–3, which shows how total expenditure varies as income changes. Thus, the economy will *always* be on the expenditure line because only points on the $C + I + G + (X - IM)$ line are consistent with the spending plans of consumers and investors. Similarly, *if* the economy is in equilibrium, it *must* be on the 45° line. As Figure 25–3 shows, these two requirements together imply that the only viable equilibrium is at point $E$, where the $C + I + G + (X - IM)$ line intersects the 45° line. Only this point is consistent both with equilibrium and with the actual desires to consume and invest.

Notice that to the left of the equilibrium point, $E$, the expenditure line lies above the 45° line. This means that total spending exceeds total output, as we have already noted in words and with numbers. Hence inventories will be falling and firms will conclude that they should increase production. Thus production will rise toward the equilibrium point, $E$. The opposite is true to the right of point $E$. Here spending falls short of output, inventories are rising, and firms will cut back production—thereby moving closer to $E$.

An **INCOME-EXPENDITURE DIAGRAM**, also called a **45° LINE DIAGRAM**, plots total real expenditure (on the vertical axis) against real income (on the horizontal axis). The 45° line marks off points where income and expenditure are equal.

In other words, whenever production is above the equilibrium level, market forces will drive output down. And whenever production is below equilibrium, market forces will drive output up. Thus, in either case, deviations from equilibrium will be eliminated.

Diagrams like this one will recur so frequently in this and the next several chapters that it will be convenient to have a name for them. Let us therefore call them **income-expenditure diagrams** since they show how expenditures vary with income. Sometimes we shall also refer to them simply as **45° line diagrams**.

## THE AGGREGATE DEMAND CURVE

Chapter 22 sketched a framework for macroeconomic analysis by introducing aggregate demand and aggregate supply curves which relate aggregate quantities demanded and supplied to the price level. The expenditure schedule graphed in Figure 25–3 is not the aggregate demand curve. How could it be, for we have yet to bring the price level into our discussion? It is now time to remedy this omission and derive the aggregate demand curve, for only then will we be able to analyze inflation.

Fortunately, no further mechanical apparatus is required. The price level can be brought into our income-expenditure analysis by recalling something we learned in the last chapter: At any given level of real income, higher prices lead to lower real consumer spending. The reason, you will recall, is that consumers own many assets whose values are fixed in money terms, and which therefore lose purchasing power when prices rise.[4] With real wealth lower, consumers

[4]The money in your bank account is a prime example. If prices rise, it will buy less.

spend less. Therefore total spending in the economy falls *even with no change in real income.*

In terms of our 45° line diagram, then, a rise in the price level will pull down the consumption function depicted in Figure 25–2 and, hence, will pull down the total expenditure schedule as well. Conversely, a fall in the price level will raise both the $C$ and $C + I + G + (X - IM)$ schedules in the diagram. The two parts of Figure 25–4 illustrate both these sorts of shifts.

What, then, do changes in the price level do to the equilibrium level of real GDP on the demand side? Common sense says that, with lower spending, equilibrium GDP should fall. And Figure 25–4 shows that this conclusion is correct. Part (a) shows that a rise in the price level, by shifting the expenditure schedule downward from $C_0 + I + G + (X - IM)$ to $C_1 + I + G + (X - IM)$ leads to a reduction in the equilibrium quantity of real GDP demanded from $Y_0$ to $Y_1$. Part (b) shows that a fall in the price level, by shifting the expenditure schedule upward from $C_0 + I + G + (X - IM)$ to $C_2 + I + G + (X - IM)$, leads to a rise in the equilibrium quantity of real GDP demanded from $Y_0$ to $Y_2$. In summary:

A rise in the price level leads to a lower equilibrium level of real aggregate quantity demanded. This relationship between the price level and the equilibrium quantity of real GDP demanded is depicted in Figure 25–5 and is precisely what

**Figure 25–4** **THE EFFECT OF THE PRICE LEVEL ON EQUILIBRIUM AGGREGATE QUANTITY DEMANDED**

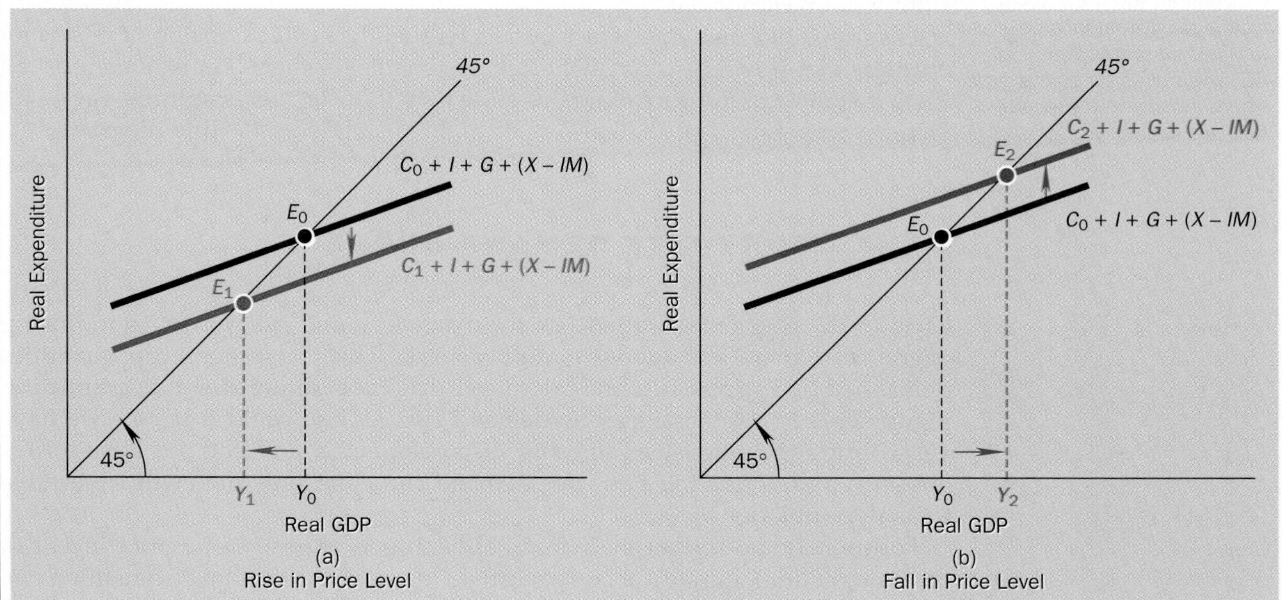


Because a change in the price level causes the expenditure schedule to shift, it changes the equilibrium quantity of real GDP demanded. Part (a) shows what happens when the price level rises, causing the expenditure schedule to shift downward from $C_0 + I + G + (X - IM)$ to $C_1 + I + G + (X - IM)$. Equilibrium quantity demanded falls from $Y_0$ to $Y_1$. Part (b) shows what happens when the price level falls, causing the expenditure schedule to shift upward from $C_0 + I + G + (X - IM)$ to $C_2 + I + G + (X - IM)$. Equilibrium quantity demanded rises from $Y_0$ to $Y_2$.

**Figure 25–5** **THE AGGREGATE DEMAND CURVE**

The graphic analysis in Figure 25–4 showed that higher prices lead to lower aggregate quantity demanded. This relationship is called the aggregate demand curve and is shown in this figure.

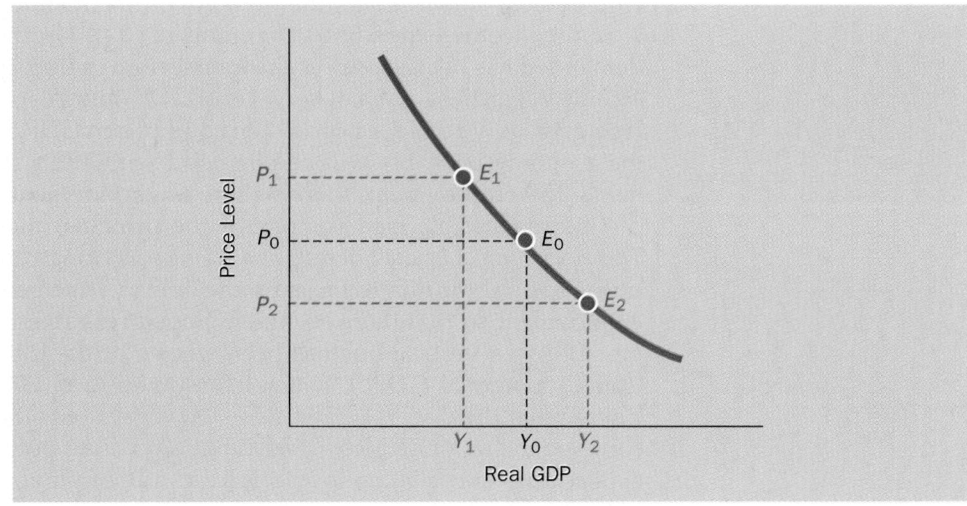


we called the **aggregate demand curve** in earlier chapters. It comes directly from the 45° line diagrams in Figure 25–4. Thus, points $E_0$, $E_1$, and $E_2$ in Figure 25–5 correspond precisely to the points bearing the same labels in Figure 25–4.

The effect of higher prices on consumer wealth is just one of several reasons why the aggregate demand curve relating the price level to real GDP demanded slopes downward. Another reason comes from international trade. In our discussion of the determinants of net exports (see page 624–25), we pointed out that higher U.S. prices will depress exports ($X$) and stimulate imports ($IM$), provided that foreign prices are held constant. That means that, other things equal, a higher U.S. price level will reduce the $(X - IM)$ component of total expenditure, thereby shifting the $C + I + G + (X - IM)$ line downward and lowering real GDP as depicted in Figure 25–4(a).

Later in the book, after we have studied interest rates and exchange rates, we will encounter still more reasons for a downward-sloping aggregate demand curve. All of them imply that:

An income-expenditure diagram like Figure 25–3 can be drawn up only for a *specific* price level. At different price levels, the $C + I + G + (X - IM)$ schedule will be different and, hence, the equilibrium quantity of GDP demanded will be different.

As we shall now see, this finding is critical to understanding the genesis of unemployment and inflation.

## DEMAND-SIDE EQUILIBRIUM AND FULL EMPLOYMENT

We now turn to the second major question of this chapter: Will the economy achieve an equilibrium at full employment without inflation, or will there be unemployment, inflation, or both? This is one of the crucial questions surrounding government stabilization policy, for if the economy always gravitates toward full employment *automatically*, then the government should simply leave it alone.

In the income-expenditure diagrams used so far, the equilibrium level of GDP demanded has been shown as the intersection of the expenditure schedule and the 45° line, regardless of whatever level of GDP might correspond to full employment. However, as we will see now, when equilibrium GDP falls above full employment, the economy probably will be plagued by inflation. And when equilibrium falls below full employment, there will be unemployment and recession.

This remarkable fact was one of the principal messages of Keynes's *General Theory of Employment, Interest, and Money*. Writing during the Great Depression, it was natural for him to focus on the case in which equilibrium falls short of full employment so that there are unemployed resources. Figure 25–6 illustrates this possibility. A vertical line has been erected at the full-employment level of GDP (called "potential GDP"), which is assumed to be $7000 billion in the example. We see that the $C + I + G + (X - IM)$ curve cuts the 45° line at point $E$, which corresponds to a GDP ($Y = \$6000$ billion) below potential GDP. In this case, the expenditure curve is too low to lead to full employment.

Such a situation might arise because either consumers or investors are unwilling to spend at normal rates, because government spending is low, because foreign demand is weak, or because the price level is "too high." Any of these would depress the $C + I + G + (X - IM)$ curve. Unemployment must then occur because not enough output is demanded to keep the entire labor force busy.

The **RECESSIONARY GAP** is the amount by which the equilibrium level of real GDP falls short of potential GDP.

The distance between the *equilibrium* level of output demanded and the *full-employment* level of output (that is, potential GDP) is called the **recessionary gap**—

*Figure* **25–6** **A RECESSIONARY GAP**

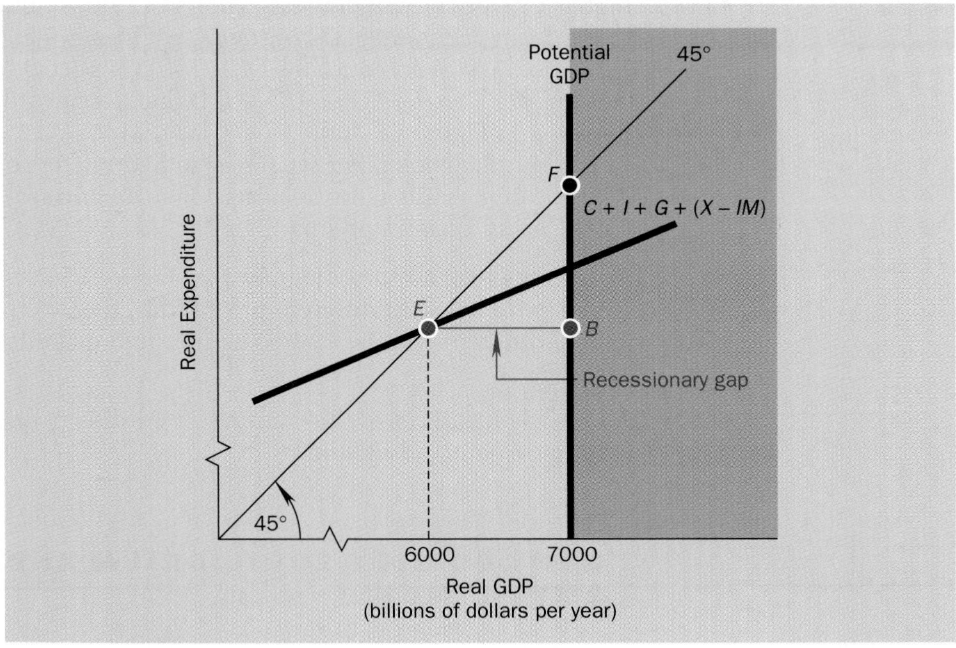


Sometimes equilibrium GDP may fall below potential GDP, so that some workers are unemployed. This diagram illustrates such a case. The horizontal distance *EB* between equilibrium GDP and potential GDP is called the recessionary gap.

**Figure 25–7** AN INFLATIONARY GAP

Sometimes equilibrium GDP may lie above potential GDP, meaning that there are more jobs than required for full employment. This diagram illustrates such a case. The horizontal distance BE between potential GDP and equilibrium GDP is called the inflationary gap. It is gradually eliminated by rising prices, which pull the $C + I + (X - IM)$ schedule down until it passes through point $F$.

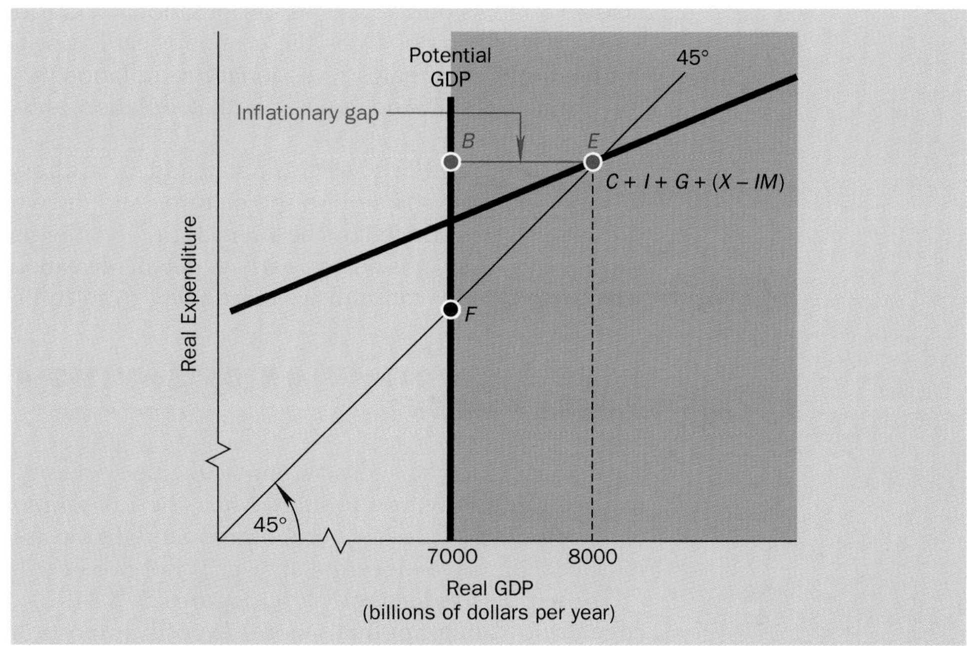


and is shown by the horizontal distance from $E$ to $B$. While Figure 25–6 is entirely hypothetical, real-world gaps of precisely this sort were shown shaded brown in Figure 23–2 (page 627). They are a pervasive feature of recent U.S. economic history.

It is clear from Figure 25–6 that full employment can be reached only by raising the total spending schedule to eliminate the recessionary gap. Specifically, the $C + I + G + (X - IM)$ schedule must move upward until it cuts the 45° line at point $F$. Can this happen without government intervention? We know that a sufficiently large drop in the price level can do the job. But is that a realistic prospect? We shall return to this question after we bring the supply side into the picture. But first let us consider the other case, in which equilibrium GDP exceeds full employment.

Figure 25–7 illustrates this possibility. Now the expenditure schedule intersects the 45° line at point $E$, where GDP is $8000 billion. But this exceeds the full employment level, $Y$ = $7000 billion. A case like this can arise when consumer or investment spending is unusually buoyant, when foreign demand is unusually strong, when the government spends too much, or when a "low" price level pushes the $C + I + G + (X - IM)$ curve upward.

The **INFLATIONARY GAP** is the amount by which equilibrium real GDP exceeds the full-employment level of GDP.

To reach an equilibrium at full employment, the price level would have to rise enough to drive the expenditure schedule *down* until it passed through point $F$. The horizontal distance $BE$—which indicates the amount by which the quantity of GDP demanded exceeds potential GDP—is called the **inflationary gap**. If there is an inflationary gap, a higher price level or some other means of reducing total expenditure is necessary to reach an equilibrium at full employment. Real-world inflationary gaps were shown shaded blue in Figure 23–2.

In sum, only if the price level and spending plans are "just right" will the expenditure curve intersect the 45° line precisely at full employment, so that neither a recessionary gap nor an inflationary gap occurs. Are there reasons to expect this outcome? Does the economy have a self-correcting mechanism that automatically eliminates recessionary or inflationary gaps and propels it toward full employment? And how is it that inflation and unemployment sometimes occur together?

These are questions we are not ready to address because we have not yet brought *aggregate supply* into the picture. And, as we learned in Chapter 22, the price level is determined by the interaction of *both* aggregate demand *and* aggregate supply. However, it is not too early to get an idea about why things can go wrong, why the economy can find itself far away from full employment.

## THE COORDINATION OF SAVING AND INVESTMENT

To understand what goes wrong with the economy in a recession, it is useful to pose the following question: Must the full-employment level of GDP be an equilibrium? Decades ago, economists thought the answer was yes. Since Keynes, most economists believe the answer is not necessarily.

To help us understand why, Figure 25–8 offers a simplified version of the circular flow diagram that ignores exports, imports, and the government. In this

**Figure 25–8** A SIMPLIFIED CIRCULAR FLOW

Here we show a simplified version of the circular flow of income and expenditures shown in Figure 25–1. The simplification amounts to shutting off the pipes leading into and out of the government, and into and out of the rest of the world. Thus, this circular flow represents an economy with no government and no foreign trade.

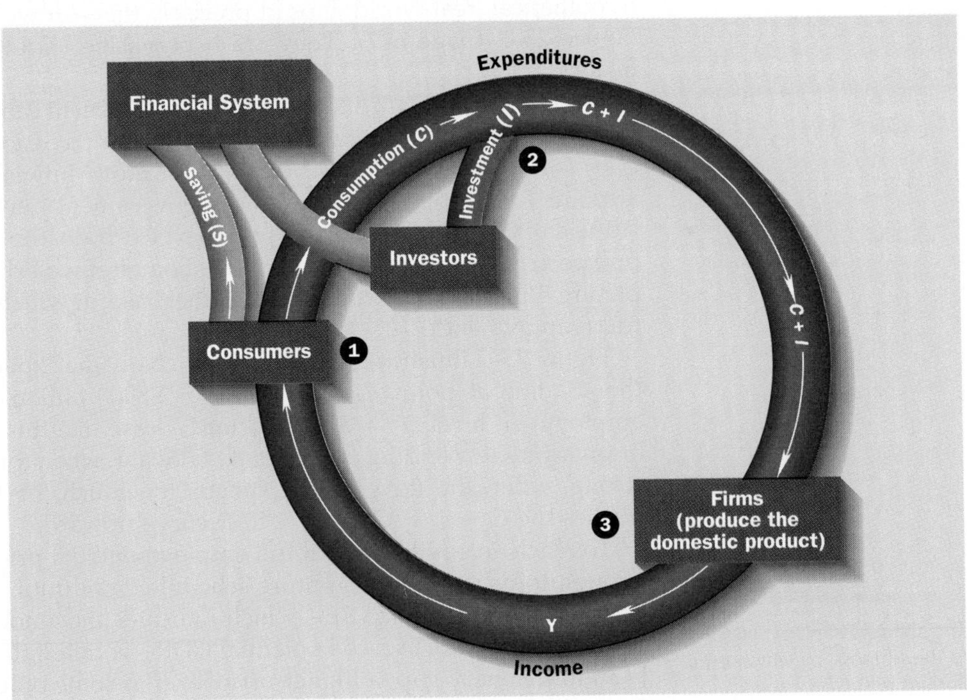

version, there is just one place for income to "leak out" of the circular flow: at point 1, where consumers save some of their income. Similarly, there is just one place for this lost spending to be replaced: at point 2, where investment enters the circular flow.

What happens if firms produce exactly the full-employment level of GDP at point 3 in the diagram? Will this income level be maintained as we move around the circle? Or will it shrink or grow? The answer is that full-employment income will be maintained only if the spending by investors at point 2 exactly balances the saving done by consumers at point 1. In other words:

The economy will reach an equilibrium at full employment only if the amount that consumers wish to save out of full-employment incomes happens to be equal to the amount that investors want to invest. If these two magnitudes are unequal, then full employment will not be an equilibrium for the economy.

Specifically, we can see from the circular flow diagram that if saving exceeds investment at full employment, then the total demand arriving at the firms (point 3) will fall short of total output because the added investment spending is not enough to replace the leakage to saving. With demand inadequate to support production at full employment, we know that the GDP must fall below potential. There will be a recessionary gap. Conversely, if investment exceeds saving when the economy is at full employment, then total demand will exceed potential GDP and production will rise above the full-employment level. There will be an inflationary gap.

Now this discussion does nothing but restate what we already know in different words.[5] But these words hold the key to understanding why the economy can find itself stuck below full employment (or above it, for that matter), for *the people who do the investing are not the same people who do the saving*. In a modern capitalist economy, investing is done by one group of individuals (primarily corporate executives and home buyers) while saving is done by another group.[6] It is easy to imagine that their plans may not be well coordinated. If they are not, we have just seen how either unemployment or inflation can arise.

Notice that these problems would never arise if the acts of saving and investing were not separated in time or space. Imagine a primitive economy of farmers, each of whom invests only in his own farm. There is no borrowing or lending, and no financial system. In this world, any farmer wanting to buy a new plow or tractor (that is, wanting to *invest*) would have to refrain from consuming part of his income (that is, would have to *save*). Therefore, the amount that all farmers together planned to save out of full-employment income would have to be equal to the amount of planned investment. Total spending and production would always have to be equal at full employment.

Almost the same holds true in a centrally planned economy. There the state decides how much will be invested and has a great deal of leverage over how much saving people do. If the planners do their calculations correctly, they can

---

[5]In symbols, our equilibrium condition without government or foreign trade is $Y = C + I$. If we note that $Y$ is also the sum of consumption plus saving, $Y = C + S$, it follows that $C + S = C + I$, or $S = I$, is a restatement of the equilibrium condition. A more complicated version of the saving = investment approach is described in Appendix A.

[6]In a modern economy, it is not only households that save. Businesses save also, in the form of retained earnings. Nonetheless, households are the ultimate source of the saving needed to finance investment.

At The FRONTIER

### UNEMPLOYMENT AND INFLATION AS COORDINATION FAILURES

The idea that recessions are times when the market system fails to perform properly is a very old one, predating Keynes. As we have seen in this chapter, Keynes attributed this failure to a *lack of coordination* between the decisions of savers and those of investors. If savers want to save more out of full-employment income than investors want to invest, full employment cannot be an equilibrium for the economy. GDP must be lower and unemployment must be higher.

In recent years, economic theorists have begun to formalize Keynes's common sense notion that coordination failures may be the root cause of recessions and unemployment. Although normally couched in mathematical terms, replete with symbols and complicated diagrams, the basic idea is elementary and is well illustrated by the parable of the football game.

Picture a crowd watching a football game. Now something exciting happens and the fans rise from their seats. The people in the front rows begin standing first, and those seated behind them are forced to stand if they want to see the game. Soon everyone in the stadium is on their feet.

But with everyone standing,

force saving to be equal to investment at full employment. Consequently, business fluctuations were not historically major problems for the former Soviet and Chinese economies. (They had plenty of others!) However, as these two countries liberalized their economies, they found that they had to deal with the inflation and unemployment problems that have long plagued the West.

Keynes observed that modern market economies differ from either primitive societies or centrally planned societies in this fundamental way, and that this flaw in the market mechanism leaves them vulnerable to recessions. However, one should not conclude that in order to avoid unemployment and recession the U.S. economy should revert to either a primitive form of capitalism or to rigid central planning. These "remedies" are far worse than the disease. Fortunately, there are policies the government can follow in an advanced capitalist economy to ease the pain of unemployment and recession—policies that we shall be studying in the following chapters.

no one can see any better than when everyone was sitting. And the fans are enduring the further discomfort of being on their feet. (Never mind that stadium seats are uncomfortable!) So everyone in the stadium would be better off if everyone would sit down. But coordinating the decisions of tens of thousands of fans is virtually impossible. So everyone stands.

In the terminology of economics, the football stadium has *two equilibria*—a superior one with everyone sitting, and an inferior one with everyone standing. In practice, we all know what happens. The crowd rises to its feet on every exciting play, sits during lulls in the action, and then rises again at the slightest hint of excitement. Thus it vacillates between the good equilibrium and the bad equilibrium.

Now, what does all this have to do with unemployment? Recall Keynes's idea that unemployment arises because the decisions of savers and investors are not coordinated. If left to their own devices, individuals acting in their own best interests might choose actions that lead to the inferior equilibrium with high unemployment (analogous to standing at the football game) even though there is a superior equilibrium with low unemployment (like sitting at the game). Although people prefer the equilibrium with low unemployment, they may be unable to coordinate their decisions in order to produce it.

If high unemployment does in fact arise from *coordination failures* like this, the government might be able to do something to cure it. Keynes certainly thought so. However, the football analogy reminds us that a central authority may not find it easy to solve the coordination problem.

The coordination failure idea may also help to explain why it is so hard to stop inflation.

Everyone prefers stable prices to rising prices. But stopping inflation is a bit like watching a football game.

Think of yourself as the seller of a product. If everyone else in the economy would hold their prices steady, you would happily hold yours steady, too. Hence, zero inflation is an equilibrium for the economy, just as sitting at the football game is an equilibrium for the football stadium. But, if you believe that others will continue to raise their prices at, say, 5 percent per year, you may find it dangerous not to increase yours apace. Hence, 5 percent inflation may also be an equilibrium, like standing at a football game. Everyone in society may agree that the equilibrium with no inflation is better than the equilibrium with 5 percent inflation. But society may nonetheless get stuck with 5 percent inflation, just as football fans must frequently stand at ball games.

## *Summary*

1. Investment is the most volatile component of aggregate demand, largely because it is tied so closely to the state of business confidence and to expectations about the future performance of the economy.

2. Government policy cannot influence business confidence in any reliable way, so policies designed to alter investment spending are aimed at more objective, though possibly less important, determinants of investment. Among these are interest rates, the overall state of aggregate demand, and tax incentives.

3. Net exports depend on GDPs and relative prices both here and abroad.

4. The **equilibrium** level of national income on the demand side is the level at which total spending just equals the value of production (GDP). Since total spending is the sum of consumption, investment, government purchases, and net exports, the condition for equilibrium is $Y = C + I + G + (X - IM)$.

5. Income levels below equilibrium are bound to rise because, when spending exceeds output, firms will see their inventory stocks being depleted and will react by stepping up production.

6. Income levels above equilibrium are bound to fall because, when total spending is insufficient to absorb

total output, inventories will pile up and firms will react by curtailing production.

7. The determination of the equilibrium level of GDP on the demand side can be portrayed on a convenient **income-expenditure diagram** as the point at which the **expenditure schedule**—defined as the sum of $C + I + G + (X - IM)$—crosses the 45° line. The 45° line is significant because it marks off points at which spending and output are equal—that is, at which $Y = C + I + G + (X - IM)$—and this is the basic condition for equilibrium.

8. An income-expenditure diagram can only be drawn up for a specific price level, however. Thus the equilibrium GDP so determined depends on the price level.

9. Because higher prices reduce the purchasing power of consumers' wealth and hence reduce their spending, equilibrium real GDP demanded is lower when prices are higher. This downward-sloping relationship is known as the **aggregate demand curve**.

10. Equilibrium GDP can be above or below **potential GDP**, which is defined as the GDP that would be produced if the labor force were fully employed.

11. If equilibrium GDP exceeds potential GDP, the difference is called an **inflationary gap**. If equilibrium GDP falls short of potential GDP, the resulting difference is called a **recessionary gap**.

12. Such gaps can occur because the saving that consumers want to do at full-employment income levels may differ from the investing that investors want to do. This problem is not likely to arise in a planned economy or in a primitive economy.

## *Key Concepts and Terms*

Equilibrium level of GDP
Expenditure schedule
Induced investment
$Y = C + I + G + (X - IM)$
Income-expenditure (or 45° line) diagram
Aggregate demand curve
Full-employment level of GDP (or potential GDP)
Recessionary gap
Inflationary gap
Coordination of saving and investment

## *Questions for Review*

1. For the last several years, imports have exceeded exports in the United States economy. This is often considered a major problem. Does this chapter give you any hints about why? (You may want to discuss this issue with your instructor, and you will certainly learn more about it in later chapters.)

2. Why is not any arbitrary level of GDP an equilibrium for the economy? (Do not give a mechanical answer to this question, but explain the economic mechanism involved.)

3. From the following data, construct an expenditure schedule on a piece of graph paper. Then use the income-expenditure (45° line) diagram to determine the equilibrium level of GDP.

| INCOME | CONSUMPTION | INVESTMENT | GOVERNMENT PURCHASES | NET EXPORTS |
|---|---|---|---|---|
| 1800 | 1610 | 120 | 60 | 20 |
| 1850 | 1655 | 120 | 60 | 20 |
| 1900 | 1700 | 120 | 60 | 20 |
| 1950 | 1745 | 120 | 60 | 20 |
| 2000 | 1790 | 120 | 60 | 20 |

4. From the following data, construct an expenditure schedule on a piece of graph paper. Then use the income-expenditure (45° line) diagram to determine the equilibrium level of GDP. Compare your answer with your answer to Question 3.

| INCOME | CONSUMPTION | INVESTMENT | GOVERNMENT PURCHASES | NET EXPORTS |
|---|---|---|---|---|
| 1800 | 1640 | 90 | 60 | 20 |
| 1850 | 1670 | 105 | 60 | 20 |
| 1900 | 1700 | 120 | 60 | 20 |
| 1950 | 1730 | 135 | 60 | 20 |
| 2000 | 1760 | 150 | 60 | 20 |

5. Suppose investment spending was always \$250, government purchases were \$100, net exports were always −\$50, and consumer spending depended on the price level in the following way:

| PRICE LEVEL | CONSUMER SPENDING |
|---|---|
| 80 | 740 |
| 90 | 720 |
| 100 | 700 |
| 110 | 680 |
| 120 | 660 |

On a piece of graph paper, use these data to construct an aggregate demand curve. Why do you think this example supposes that consumption declines as the price level rises?

6. Does the economy this year seem to have an inflationary gap or a recessionary gap? (If you do not know the answer from reading the newspaper, ask your instructor.)
7. Why were there no recessions in the former Soviet Union?
8. (More difficult)[7] Consider an economy in which the consumption function takes the following simple algebraic form:

$$C = 300 + 0.75\text{DI}$$

and in which investment ($I$) is always 900 and net exports are always $-100$. Government purchases are fixed at 1300 and taxes are fixed at 1200. Find the equilibrium level of GDP and compare your answer to Table 25–2 and Figure 25–3. (HINT: Remember that in this case disposable income is GDP minus taxes: $\text{DI} = Y - T = Y - 1200$.)

9. (More difficult) An economy has a consumption function:

$$C = 200 + 0.8\text{ DI}.$$

The government budget is balanced with government purchases and taxes both fixed at 1000. Net exports are 100. Investment is 600. Find equilibrium GDP.

[7]The answer to this question is provided in Appendix B.

## Appendix A THE "LEAKAGES" AND "INJECTIONS" APPROACH

There is another way of looking at the determination of the equilibrium level of GDP on the demand side. In the text, we studied the condition that total expenditure, $C + I + G + (X - IM)$, is equal to the value of production ($Y$). As an alternative, we can study the condition that the three "leakages" from the circular flow diagram (Figure 25–1 on page 626)—saving ($S$), taxes ($T$), and imports ($IM$)—just balance the three "injections"—investment ($I$), government purchases ($G$), and exports ($X$)—so that the amount of money going around the circle is maintained; that is:

$$\begin{aligned} &\text{Leakages} &&= \text{Injections} \\ &S + T + IM &&= I + G + X. \end{aligned}$$

It must be emphasized at the outset that this is not a *new* approach. It is merely another way of looking at precisely the same phenomenon. The reason is that income ($Y$) must be either spent on consumer goods ($C$), saved ($S$), or paid to the government in taxes ($T$). Since $Y = C + S + T$ *always*, and since $Y = C + I + G + (X - IM)$ when $Y$ is at its equilibrium value, we can describe equilibrium by the condition that:

$$C + S + T = C + I + G + (X - IM).$$

After cancelling $C$ on both sides, this equation is equivalent to the previous one.

### GRAPHICAL ANALYSIS

This way of looking at equilibrium has a different graphic representation. It does not use the 45° line diagram, but it contains precisely the same information.

Recall that in an appendix to Chapter 24 we constructed the saving schedule, which we repeat here as Figure 25–9. Since the equilibrium condition now under scrutiny is $S + T + IM = I + G + X$, we need to add $T$ and $IM$ to this line. In our numerical example of Macroland, $T = 1200$ and $IM = 750$, so the "leakages schedule" (the sum of $S + T + IM$) shown in Figure 25–10 is parallel to the saving schedule in Figure 25–9, but \$1950 billion higher.

To complete the story, we add to Figure 25–10 a horizontal line at a height equal to the sum of investment plus government purchases plus exports, which is \$900 + \$1300 + \$650 = \$2850 billion in our example. Call this the "injections schedule." Point $E$ then shows the equilibrium level of GDP, which is at an income level of \$6000 billion. As must be the case, this is the same answer we obtained with the 45° line diagram.

You will notice that at income levels below \$6000 billion, injections ($I + G + X$) exceed leakages ($S + T + IM$), just as $C + I + G + (X - IM)$ exceeded output in the 45° line diagram. Similarly, at income

**Figure 25–9** THE SAVING SCHEDULE

This diagram shows the relationship between saving and income in Macroland and duplicates Figure 24–9 (page 610).

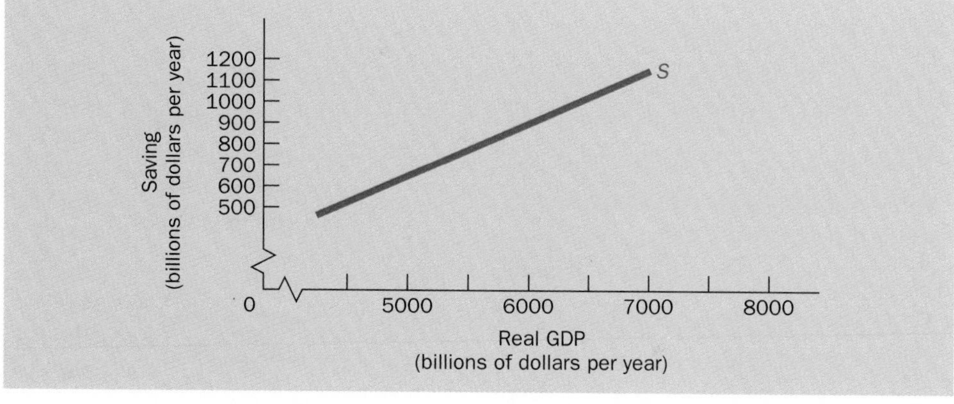

**Figure 25-10** DETERMINATION OF EQUILIBRIUM GDP BY LEAKAGES = INJECTIONS

This diagram depicts the equilibrium of the economy at point *E*, where the sum of saving plus taxes plus imports ($S + T + IM$) equals the sum of investment plus government purchases plus exports ($I + G + X$). The equilibrium is at a real GDP of $6000 billion, which, as must be the case, is the same conclusion that we reached with the aid of the 45° line diagram (Figure 25–3 on page 630).

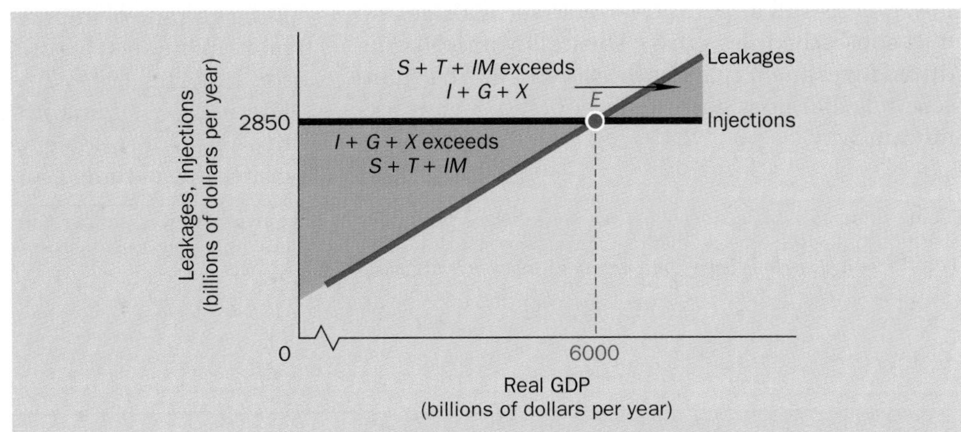


levels above $6000 billion, leakages exceed injections. (In the 45° line diagram, $Y$ exceeded $C + I + G + (X - IM)$ in this range.) This must be the case since the two graphs are alternative depictions of the same phenomena. The economic analyses behind them are precisely the same.

## INDUCED INVESTMENT

In the chapter we mentioned the possibility of *induced investment*, that is, that investment rises as GDP rises. But we did not examine this possibility in our graphs. (However, this case did arise in Review Question 4.) The reason is that what matters in the 45° line diagram is the slope of the *combined* $C + I + G + (X - IM)$ schedule, not the *individual* slopes of the $C$, $I$, and $(X - IM)$ schedules. So an upward-sloping investment schedule makes little difference to the analysis.

When using the leakages = injections approach, however, the slope of the investment schedule becomes more apparent, though not really more important. So Figure 25–11 illustrates the case of

**Figure 25-11** INCOME DETERMINATION WITH INDUCED INVESTMENT

When investment rises with GDP ("induced investment"), the investment schedule, and hence the $I + G + X$ line, acquires a positive slope. Apart from this, the determination of equilibrium output is precisely as it was before. Point *E*, where the leakages and injections schedules cross, is the equilibrium.

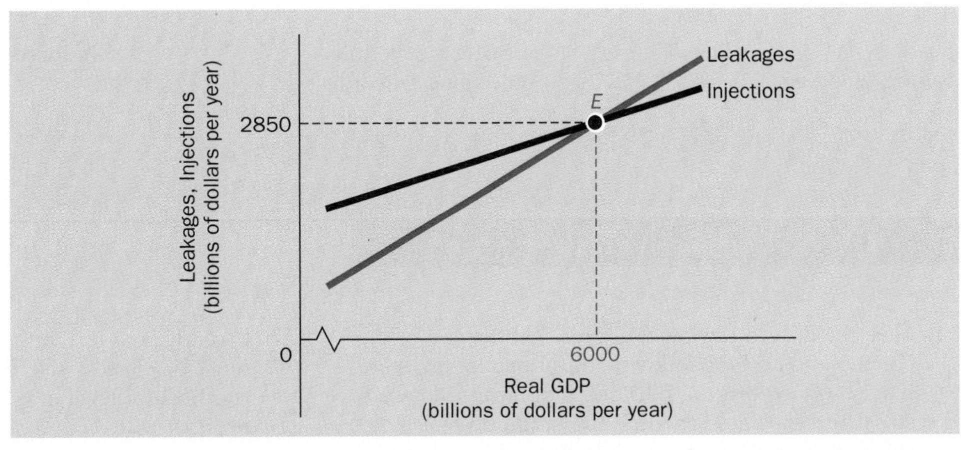

induced investment. In this diagram, the investment schedule is upward sloping, and so the schedule of total leakages ($I + G + X$) is, too. Equilibrium, however, is still at point $E$—where the leakage and injections schedules cross. Thus allowance for induced investment changes the slope of the injections schedule, but does not alter our analysis in any significant way.[8]

## VARIABLE IMPORTS

A similar amendment to the analysis must be made if the volume of imports depends on GDP—a possibility mentioned early in the chapter. Consider again the leakages ($S + T + IM$) schedule depicted in Figure 25–11. If imports are increasing as GDP rises, this line will be steeper than indicated in the diagram. But nothing else changes.

[8]Some students may wonder what happens if the slope of the injections schedule exceeds that of the leakages schedule. This is a difficult question that is best reserved for more advanced courses. Suffice it to say here that the simple model of income determination constructed in this chapter will not work in such a case.

## *Summary*

1. The condition for equilibrium GDP—which we gave in the chapter as the equation of total spending with output, $Y = C + I + G + (X - IM)$—can be restated as the requirement that saving plus taxes plus imports be equal to the sum of investment plus government purchases plus exports: $S + T + IM = I + G + X$. In shorthand, total **leakages** equal total **injections**. This does not change anything, but simply says the same thing in different words.
2. These different words lead to a different graphical presentation, in which we look for equilibrium at the point where the upward-sloping leakages schedule crosses the horizontal line depicting injections.
3. **Induced investment**—that is, investment that rises as the GDP rises—would give the injections schedule a positive slope, but require no other change in the analysis.
4. If imports grow with GDP, the slope of the leakages schedule in the diagram increases, but nothing else changes.

## *Key Concepts and Terms*

$S + T + IM = I + G + X$
Saving schedule
Leakages schedule
Injections schedule
Induced investment

## *Questions for Review*

1. Take the data in Review Question 3 at the end of the chapter and add the following information: taxes are fixed at 60, exports are 200, and imports are 180. Construct the leakages schedule that adds up $S + T + IM$ and the injections schedule that adds up $I + G + X$ on a piece of graph paper. (In doing so, remember that any income that is not consumed or paid in taxes must be saved.) Use these constructions to find the equilibrium level of GDP.
2. Do the same thing with the data in Review Question 4 at the end of the chapter.

## Appendix B THE SIMPLE ALGEBRA OF INCOME DETERMINATION

The model of demand-side equilibrium that the chapter presented graphically and in tabular form can also be handled with some simple algebra.

Written as an equation, the consumption function in our example is:

$$C = 300 + 0.75\text{DI}$$
$$= 300 + 0.75(Y - T),$$

since, by definition DI $= Y - T$. This is simply the equation of a straight line with a slope of 0.75 and an intercept of $300 - 0.75T$. Since $T = 1200$ in our example, the intercept is $-600$ and the equation can be written more simply as:

$$C = -600 + 0.75Y.$$

Investment in the example was assumed to be 900, regardless of the level of income, government purchases were 1300, and net exports were $-100$. So the sum $C + I + G + (X - IM)$ is:

$$C + I + G + (X - IM)$$
$$= -600 + 0.75Y + 900 + 1300 - 100$$
$$= 1500 + 0.75Y,$$

which describes the expenditure curve in Figure 25–3. Since the equilibrium quantity of GDP demanded is defined by:

$$Y = C + I + G + (X - IM),$$

we can solve for the equilibrium value of $Y$ by substituting $1500 + 0.75Y$ for $C + I + G + (X - IM)$ to get:

$$Y = C + I + G + (X - IM) = 1500 + 0.75Y.$$

To solve this equation for $Y$, first subtract $0.75Y$ from both sides to get:

$$0.25Y = 1500.$$

Then divide both sides by 0.25 to obtain the answer:

$$Y = 6000.$$

This, of course, is precisely the solution we found by graphical and tabular methods in the chapter.

The method of solution is easily generalized to deal with any set of numbers in our equations. Suppose the consumption function is:

$$C = a + b\text{DI} = a + b(Y - T).$$

(In the example, $a = 300$, T $= 1200$, and $b = 0.75$.) Then the equilibrium condition that $Y = C + I + G + (X - IM)$ implies:

$$Y = a + b\text{DI} + I + G + (X - IM)$$
$$= a - bT + bY + I + G + (X - IM).$$

Subtracting $bY$ from both sides leads to:

$$(1 - b)Y = a - bT + I + G + (X - IM),$$

and dividing through by $1 - b$ gives:

$$Y = \frac{a - bT + I + G + (X - IM)}{+ 1 - b}.$$

This formula, which is certainly *not* to be memorized, is valid for any numerical values of $a$, $b$, $T$, $G$, $I$, and $(X - IM)$ (so long as $b$ is between zero and one.)

## Questions for Review

1. Find the equilibrium level of GDP demanded in an economy in which investment is always \$300, net exports are always $-\$50$, the government budget is balanced with purchases and taxes both equal to \$400, and the consumption function is described by the following algebraic equation:

$$C = 150 + 0.75\text{DI}.$$

*Hint:* Do not forget that DI $= Y - T$.

2. Do the same for an economy in which investment is \$250, net exports are zero, government purchases and taxes are both \$400, and the consumption function is:

$$C = 250 + 0.5\text{DI}.$$

3. In each of the above cases, how much saving is there in equilibrium? (*Hint:* Income not consumed must be saved.) Is saving equal to investment?

4. Imagine an economy in which consumer expenditure is represented by the following equation:

$$C = 50 + .75DI.$$

Imagine also that investors want to spend 500 at every level of income ($I = 500$), net exports are zero ($X - IM = 0$), government purchases are 300 and taxes are 200.

a. What is the equilibrium level of income?
b. If the full employment level of income is 3000, is there a recessionary or inflationary gap? If so, how much?
c. What will happen to the equilibrium level of income if investors become optimistic about the country's future and raise their investment to 600?
d. Is there a recessionary or inflationary gap now? How much?

5. Ivyland has the following consumption function:

$$C = 100 + .8DI.$$

Firms in Ivyland always invest $700 and net exports are zero, initially. The government budget is balanced with spending and taxes both equal to $500.

a. Find the equilibrium level of GDP.
b. How much is saved? Is saving equal to investment?
c. Now suppose an export-promotion drive succeeds in raising net exports to $100. Answer (a) and (b) under these new circumstances.

# Chapter 26

# CHANGES ON THE DEMAND SIDE: MULTIPLIER ANALYSIS

*A definite ratio, to be called the* Multiplier, *can be established between income and investment.*

JOHN MAYNARD KEYNES

In the last chapter we derived the economy's *aggregate demand curve*, which shows how the equilibrium quantity of real GDP demanded depends on the price level—holding all other factors constant. But often these "other factors" do not remain constant and, as a consequence, the entire aggregate demand curve shifts. This chapter is the first of several that are devoted to enumerating these "other factors" and explaining how and why they make the aggregate demand curve shift. ¶ The central concept of this short chapter is the *multiplier*—the idea that an increase in spending will bring about an *even larger* increase in equilibrium GDP. We approach this idea from three different perspectives, each of which provides different insights into the multiplier process. First, the multiplier is illustrated graphically using the income-expenditure diagram from Chapter 25. Next, we reach the same conclusion through the use of a numerical example, and finally, we offer an algebraic statement. Each of these is an expression of the remarkable multiplier result. ¶ Near the end of the chapter, we use multiplier analysis to explain how economic developments abroad affect the U.S. economy and why a drive to increase national saving might not succeed.

## THE MAGIC OF THE MULTIPLIER

Because it is subject to such abrupt swings, investment spending is often the cause of business fluctuations in the United States and elsewhere. Let us, therefore, ask what would happen to equilibrium income in our fictitious country, Macroland, if firms there suddenly decided to spend more on investment goods. As we shall see, such a decision would have a *multiplied* effect on GDP in Macroland; that is, each $1 of additional investment spending would add more than $1 to GDP. The same would be true in the U.S. economy.

For simplicity, we continue to assume that the price level is fixed—an assumption we will drop in the very next chapter. Refer first to Table 26–1, which looks very much like Table 25–1 (page 628). The only difference is that we assume here that, for some reason, firms in Macroland now want to invest $200 billion more than they previously did—for a total of $1100 billion. The **multiplier** principle says that Macroland's GDP will rise by more than the $200 billion increase in investment. Specifically, the multiplier is defined as the ratio of the change in equilibrium GDP ($Y$) divided by the original change in spending that causes the change in GDP. In shorthand, when we deal with the multiplier for investment ($I$), the formula is

The **MULTIPLIER** is the ratio of the change in equilibrium GDP ($Y$) divided by the original change in spending that causes the change in GDP.

$$\text{Multiplier} = \frac{\text{Change in } Y}{\text{Change in } I}.$$

Let us verify that the multiplier is indeed greater than 1. Table 26–1 shows how to derive a new expenditure schedule by adding up $C$, $I$, $G$, and $(X - IM)$ at each level of $Y$, just as we did in Chapter 25. If you compare the last column of Table 26–1 with that of Table 25–1, you will see that the new expenditure schedule lies uniformly above the old one by $200 billion.

Figure 26–1 illustrates this diagrammatically. The schedule marked $C + I_0 + G + (X - IM)$ is derived from the last column of Table 25–1, while the higher

**Table 26–1 TOTAL EXPENDITURE AFTER A $200 BILLION RISE IN INVESTMENT SPENDING (billions of dollars)**

| (1) INCOME (*Y*) | (2) CONSUMPTION (*C*) | (3) INVESTMENT (*I*) | (4) GOVERNMENT PURCHASES (*G*) | (5) NET EXPORTS (*X* − *IM*) | (6) TOTAL EXPENDITURE |
|---|---|---|---|---|---|
| 4800 | 3000 | 1100 | 1300 | −100 | 5300 |
| 5200 | 3300 | 1100 | 1300 | −100 | 5600 |
| 5600 | 3600 | 1100 | 1300 | −100 | 5900 |
| 6000 | 3900 | 1100 | 1300 | −100 | 6200 |
| 6400 | 4200 | 1100 | 1300 | −100 | 6500 |
| 6800 | 4500 | 1100 | 1300 | −100 | 6800 |
| 7200 | 4800 | 1100 | 1300 | −100 | 7100 |

This table shows the construction of a total expenditure schedule for Macroland after investment has risen to $1100 billion. As indicated by the shaded numbers, only income level $Y$ = $6800 billion is an equilibrium on the demand side of the economy because only at this level is total spending ($C + I + G + X - IM$) equal to production ($Y$).

Figure 26-1 **ILLUSTRATION OF THE MULTIPLIER**

This figure depicts the multiplier effect of a rise in investment spending of \$200 billion. The expenditure schedule shifts upward from $C + I_0 + G + (X - IM)$ to $C + I_1 + G + (X - IM)$, thus moving equilibrium from point $E_0$ to point $E_1$. The rise in income is \$800 billion, so the multiplier is \$800/\$200 = 4.

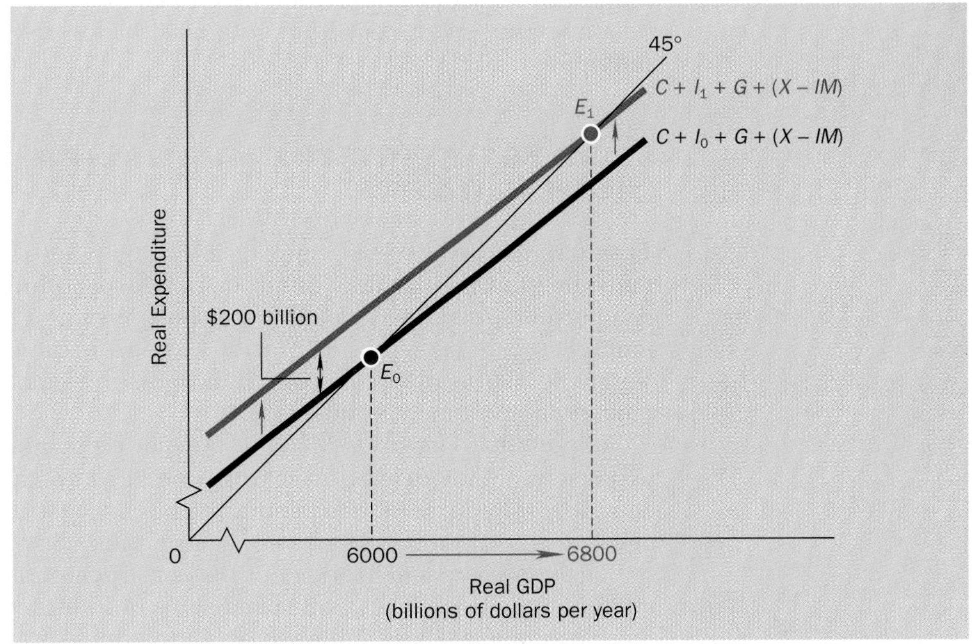


schedule marked $C + I_1 + G + (X - IM)$ is derived from the last column of Table 26–1. The two expenditure lines are parallel and \$200 billion apart.

So far no act of magic has occurred—things look just as you might expect. But one more step will bring the multiplier rabbit out of the hat. Let us see what the upward shift of the expenditure line does to equilibrium income. In Figure 26–1, equilibrium moves outward from point $E_0$ to point $E_1$; that is, from \$6000 billion to to \$6800 billion. The difference is an increase in national income of \$800 billion. All this from a \$200 billion stimulus to investment? That is the magic of the multiplier.

Because the change in $I$ is \$200 billion and the change in equilibrium $Y$ is \$800 billion, by applying our definition, the multiplier is

$$\text{Multiplier} = \frac{\text{Change in } Y}{\text{Change in } I} = \frac{\$800}{\$200} = 4.$$

This tells us that, in our example, every additional dollar of investment demand will add \$4 to the equilibrium GDP!

This does indeed seem mysterious. Can something be created from nothing? Let us, therefore, check to be sure that the graph has not deceived us. The first and last columns of Table 26–1 show in numbers what Figure 26–1 shows in a picture. Notice that, at any income level below \$6800 billion, spending, $C + I + G + (X - IM)$, exceeds output ($Y$). As we know, this cannot be an equilibrium situation because inventories would be disappearing. On the other hand, at any income level above \$6800 billion inventories would be piling up, since $C + I + G + (X - IM)$ is less than $Y$.

Only at $Y$ = \$6800 billion are spending and production in balance, as Table 26–1 shows. This is \$800 billion higher than the \$6000 billion equilibrium GDP found in the last chapter, when investment was only \$900 billion. Thus a \$200 billion rise in investment leads to a \$800 billion rise in equilibrium GDP. The multiplier really is 4.

## DEMYSTIFYING THE MULTIPLIER: HOW IT WORKS

The multiplier result seems implausible at first, but it loses its mystery once we remember the circular flow of income and expenditure, and the simple fact that one person's spending is another person's income. To illustrate the logic of the multiplier, and see why it is exactly 4 in our model economy, let us look more closely at what actually happens if businesses decide to spend an additional \$1 million on investment goods.

Suppose that Generous Motors—a major corporation in Macroland—decides to spend \$1 million to retool a factory to manufacture cars powered by compressed natural gas. Its \$1 million expenditure goes to construction workers and owners of construction companies as wages and profits. That is, it becomes their *income*.

But the owners and workers of the construction firms will not keep their \$1 million in the bank. They will spend some of it. If they are "typical" consumers, their spending will be \$1 million times the marginal propensity to consume (MPC). In our example, the MPC is 0.75. So let us assume that they spend \$750,000 and save the rest. *This \$750,000 expenditure is a net addition to the nation's demand for goods and services exactly as Generous Motors' original \$1 million expenditure was.* So, at this stage, the \$1 million investment has already pushed GDP up some \$1.75 million.

But the process by no means stops here. Shopkeepers receive the \$750,000 spent by construction workers, and these shopkeepers in turn also spend 75 percent of their new income. This accounts for \$562,500 (75 percent of \$750,000) in additional consumer spending in the "third round." Next follows a fourth round in which the recipients of the \$562,500, in their turn, spend 75 percent of this amount, or \$421,875, and so on. At each stage in the spending chain, people spend 75 percent of the additional income they receive, and the process continues. Consumption grows in each round.

Where does it all end? Does it all end? The answer is that it does, indeed, eventually end—with GDP a total of \$4 million higher than it was before Generous Motors spent the original \$1 million. The multiplier, is, indeed, 4.

Table 26–2 displays the basis for this conclusion. In the table, "round 1" represents Generous Motors' initial investment, which creates \$1 million in income for construction workers; "round 2" represents the construction workers' spending which creates \$750,000 in income for shopkeepers. The rest of the table proceeds accordingly. Each entry in column 2 is 75 percent of the previous entry, and column 3 tabulates the running sum of column 2.

We see that after 10 rounds of spending, the initial \$1 million investment has mushroomed to \$3.77 million, and the sum is still growing. After 20 rounds, the total increase in GDP is over \$3.98 million—near its eventual value of \$4 million. While it takes quite a few rounds of spending before the multiplier chain is near 4, we see from the table that it hits 3 rather quickly. If each income recipient in

**Table 26–2 THE MULTIPLIER SPENDING CHAIN**

| (1) ROUND NUMBER | (2) SPENDING IN THIS ROUND | (3) CUMULATIVE TOTAL |
|---|---|---|
| 1 | $1,000,000 | $1,000,000 |
| 2 | 750,000 | 1,750,000 |
| 3 | 562,500 | 2,312,500 |
| 4 | 421,875 | 2,734,375 |
| 5 | 316,406 | 3,050,781 |
| 6 | 237,305 | 3,288,086 |
| 7 | 177,979 | 3,466,065 |
| 8 | 133,484 | 3,599,549 |
| 9 | 100,113 | 3,699,662 |
| 10 | 75,085 | 3,774,747 |
| ⋮ | ⋮ | ⋮ |
| 20 | 4,228 | 3,987,317 |
| ⋮ | ⋮ | ⋮ |
| "Infinity" | 0 | 4,000,000 |

This table shows how the multiplier unfolds through time. Round 1 is Generous Motors' initial spending, which leads to $1 million in additional income to construction workers. Round 2 shows the construction workers spending 75 percent of this amount, since the marginal propensity to consume is 0.75. The other rounds proceed accordingly, with spending in each successive round equal to 75 percent of that in the previous round. Technically, the full multiplier of 4 is reached only after an "infinite" number of rounds. But, as can be seen, we are very close to the full amount after 20 rounds.

the chain waits, say, two months before spending his new income, the multiplier will reach 3 in only about 10 months.

Figure 26–2 provides a graphical presentation of the numbers in the last column of Table 26–2. Notice how the multiplier builds up rapidly at first and then tapers off to approach its ultimate value (4 in this example) gradually.

## ALGEBRAIC STATEMENT OF THE MULTIPLIER

Figure 26–2 and Table 26–2 probably make a persuasive case for the fact that the multiplier eventually reaches 4. But for the remaining skeptics we offer a simple algebraic proof.[1] Most of you learned about something called an "infinite geometric progression" in high school. This term refers to an infinite series of numbers, each one of which is a fixed fraction of the previous one. The fraction is called the "common ratio." A geometric progression beginning with 1 and having a common ratio of 0.75 would look like this:

$$1 + 0.75 + (0.75)^2 + (0.75)^3 + \ldots.$$

More generally, a geometric progression beginning with 1 and having a common ratio $R$ would be

$$1 + R + R^2 + R^3 \ldots.$$

[1]Students who blanch at the sight of algebra should not be put off. Anyone who can balance a checkbook (even many who cannot!) will be able to follow the argument.

**Figure 26–2** HOW THE MULTIPLIER BUILDS

This diagram portrays the numbers from Table 26–2 and shows how the multiplier builds through time. Notice how the effect grows quickly at first and how the full effect is almost reached after 20 rounds.

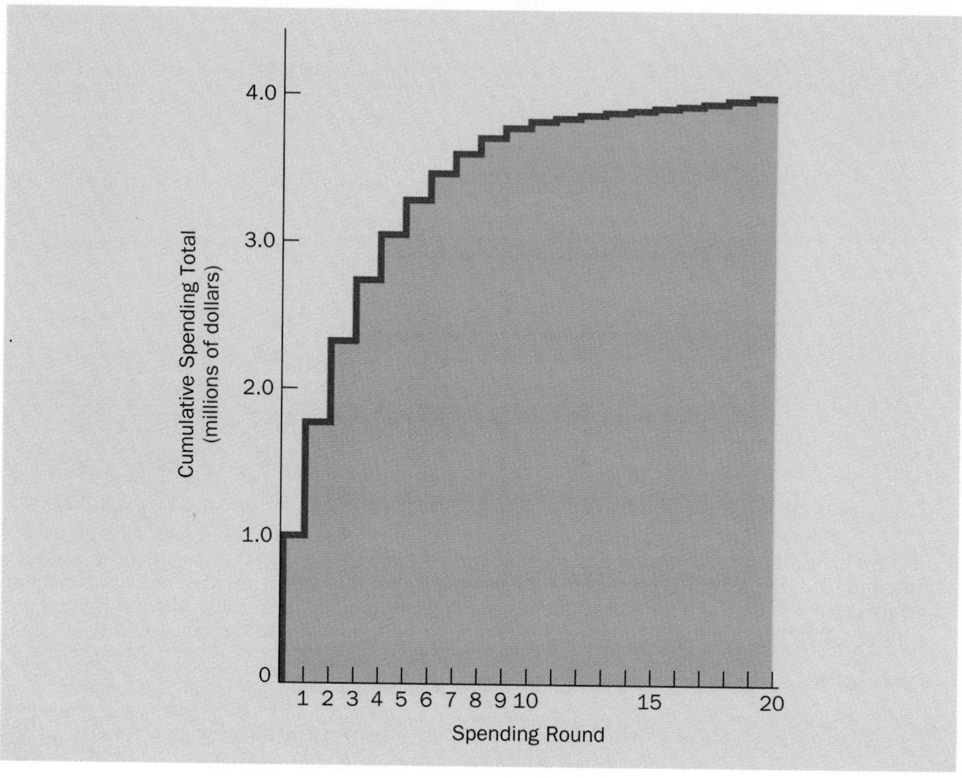


A simple formula enables us to sum such a progression as long as $R$ is less than 1.[2] The formula is[3]

$$\text{Sum of infinite geometric progression} = \frac{1}{1 - R}.$$

Now we can recognize that the multiplier chain in Table 26–2 is just an infinite geometric progression with 0.75 as its common ratio. That is, each \$1 spent by Generous Motors leads to a $(0.75) \times \$1$ expenditure by construction workers, which in turn leads to a $(0.75) \times (0.75 \times \$1) = (0.75)^2 \times \$1$ expenditure by the

[2]If $R$ exceeds 1, nobody can possibly sum it—not even with the aid of a modern computer—because the sum is not a finite number.

[3]The proof of the formula is simple. Let the symbol $S$ stand for the (unknown) sum of the series:

$$S = 1 + R + R^2 + R^3 + \ldots.$$

Then, multiplying by $R$,

$$RS = R + R^2 + R^3 + R^4 + \ldots.$$

By subtracting $RS$ from $S$, we obtain:

$$S - RS = 1$$

or

$$S = \frac{1}{1 - R}.$$

shopkeepers, and so on. Thus, for each initial dollar of investment spending, the progression is

$$1 + 0.75 + (0.75)^2 + (0.75)^3 + (0.75)^4 + \ldots.$$

Applying the formula for the sum of such a series, we find that:

$$\text{Multiplier} = \frac{1}{1 - 0.75} = \frac{1}{0.25} = 4.$$

Notice how this result can be generalized. If we did not have a specific number for the marginal propensity to consume, but simply called it "MPC," the geometric progression in Table 26–2 would have been

$$1 + \text{MPC} + (\text{MPC})^2 + (\text{MPC})^3 + \ldots,$$

which has the MPC as its common ratio. Applying the same formula for summing a geometric progression to this more general case gives us the following general result:

OVERSIMPLIFIED FORMULA FOR THE MULTIPLIER

$$\text{Multiplier} = \frac{1}{1 - \text{MPC}}.$$

We call this formula "oversimplified" because it ignores many factors that are important in the real world. One of them is international trade—in particular, the fact that a country's imports depend on its GDP. This complication is dealt with in Appendix B. A second factor is *inflation*, a complication we will address in the next chapter. A third is *income taxation*, a point we will elaborate in Chapter 28. The last important influence arises from the *financial system* and, after we discuss money and banking in Chapters 29 and 30, we will explain it in Chapter 31. As it turns out, each of these factors *reduces* the size of the multiplier.

We can begin to appreciate just how unrealistic the "oversimplified" formula is by considering some real numbers for the U.S. economy. The marginal propensity to consume (MPC) has been estimated many times and is about 0.9. From our oversimplified formula, then, it would seem that the multiplier should be about

$$\text{Multiplier} = \frac{1}{1 - 0.9} = \frac{1}{0.1} = 10.$$

In fact, the actual multiplier for the U.S. economy is believed to be less than 2. This is quite a discrepancy! But it does not mean that anything we have said about the multiplier so far is incorrect. Our story is simply incomplete. As we progress through this and subsequent chapters, you will learn why the multiplier is below 2 even though the MPC is close to 0.9. For now, we simply point out that:

While the multiplier is larger than 1 in the real world, it cannot be calculated with any degree of accuracy from the oversimplified formula. The actual multiplier is *much lower* than the formula suggests.

## THE MULTIPLIER EFFECT OF CONSUMER SPENDING

Business firms that invest are not the only ones that can work the magic of the multiplier; so can consumers. To see how the multiplier works when the process is initiated by an upsurge in consumer spending, we must distinguish between two types of change in consumer spending.

An **INDUCED INCREASE IN CONSUMPTION** is an increase in consumer spending that stems from an increase in consumer incomes. It is represented on a graph as a movement along a fixed consumption function.

An **AUTONOMOUS INCREASE IN CONSUMPTION** is an increase in consumer spending without any increase in incomes. It is represented on a graph as a shift of the entire consumption function.

When $C$ rises because income rises—that is, when consumers move outward *along a fixed consumption function*—we call the increase in $C$ an **induced increase in consumption**. However, if instead $C$ rises because the entire consumption function *shifts up*, we call this an **autonomous increase in consumption**. The name indicates that consumption changes independently of income, and Chapter 24's discussion pointed out that a number of events, such as a change in the price level or in the value of the stock market, can initiate such a shift.

Let us suppose that, for some reason, consumer spending rises autonomously by $200 billion. In this case, our table of aggregate demand would have to be revised to look like Table 26–3. Comparing this to Table 26–1 on page 648, we note that each entry in column 2 is $200 billion *higher* than the corresponding entry in Table 26–1 (because consumption is higher), and each entry in column 3 is $200 billion *lower* (because investment is lower).

The equilibrium level of income is clearly $Y = \$6800$ billion once again. Indeed, the entire expenditure schedule (column 6) is the same as it was in Table 26–1. The initial rise of $200 billion in spending leads to an ultimate rise of $800 billion in GDP, just as occurred in the case of higher investment spending. In fact, Figure 26–1 applies directly to this case once we note that the upward shift is now caused by an autonomous change in $C$ rather than in $I$. The multiplier for autonomous changes in consumer spending, then, is also 4 ( = $800/$200).

The reason is straightforward. It does not matter who injects an additional dollar of spending into the economy, whether it is business investors or consumers. Wherever it comes from, 75 percent of it will be respent if the MPC is 0.75, and the recipients of this second round will, in turn, spend 75 percent of their additional income, and so on and on. And that is what constitutes the multiplier process.

## THE MULTIPLIER EFFECT OF GOVERNMENT PURCHASES

What about the third component of total spending, government purchases ($G$)? Table 26–4, which can usefully be compared to earlier tables, shows that $G$ has

**Table 26–3 TOTAL EXPENDITURE AFTER CONSUMERS DECIDE TO SPEND $200 BILLION MORE (billions of dollars)**

| (1) INCOME ($Y$) | (2) CONSUMPTION ($C$) | (3) INVESTMENT ($I$) | (4) GOVERNMENT PURCHASES ($G$) | (5) NET EXPORTS ($X - IM$) | (6) TOTAL EXPENDITURE |
|---|---|---|---|---|---|
| 4800 | 3200 | 900 | 1300 | −100 | 5300 |
| 5200 | 3500 | 900 | 1300 | −100 | 5600 |
| 5600 | 3800 | 900 | 1300 | −100 | 5900 |
| 6000 | 4100 | 900 | 1300 | −100 | 6200 |
| 6400 | 4400 | 900 | 1300 | −100 | 6500 |
| 6800 | 4700 | 900 | 1300 | −100 | 6800 |
| 7200 | 5000 | 900 | 1300 | −100 | 7100 |

This table shows the construction of the total expenditure schedule for Macroland following an autonomous increase of $200 billion in consumption rather than in investment. Notice that columns 2 and 3 differ from the corresponding columns in Table 26–1, but column 6 is the same in both tables. Thus the expenditure schedule in the 45° line diagram is the same as in the earlier example.

**Table 26–4 TOTAL EXPENDITURE AFTER THE GOVERNMENT SPENDS $200 BILLION MORE ON GOODS AND SERVICES (billions of dollars)**

| (1) INCOME ($Y$) | (2) CONSUMPTION ($C$) | (3) INVESTMENT ($I$) | (4) GOVERNMENT PURCHASES ($G$) | (5) NET EXPORTS ($X - IM$) | (6) TOTAL EXPENDITURE |
|---|---|---|---|---|---|
| 4800 | 3000 | 900 | 1500 | −100 | 5300 |
| 5200 | 3300 | 900 | 1500 | −100 | 5600 |
| 5600 | 3600 | 900 | 1500 | −100 | 5900 |
| 6000 | 3900 | 900 | 1500 | −100 | 6200 |
| 6400 | 4200 | 900 | 1500 | −100 | 6500 |
| 6800 | 4500 | 900 | 1500 | −100 | 6800 |
| 7200 | 4800 | 900 | 1500 | −100 | 7100 |

This table shows the total expenditure schedule for Macroland after government purchases have risen to $1500 billion. Once again, only income level $Y$ = $6800 billion is an equilibrium on the demand side of the economy.

the very same multiplier as *I* and *C*. The consumption, investment, and net export columns in Table 26–4 are the same as in Chapter 25. The only change appears in column 4, where we have raised government purchases from $1300 billion to $1500 billion.

Summing the four components as usual gives us our new total expenditure schedule in columns 1 and 6. Clearly, this is the same total expenditure column as in Tables 26–1 and 26–3. So the equilibrium level of GDP must also be the same: $6800 billion, or $800 billion more than we found in the previous chapter. The multiplier is, once again, 4.

Figure 26–1 can again be used to illustrate the conclusion graphically—just think of the upward shift as being caused by a change in *G* this time.

The multipliers are identical because the logic behind them is identical. The multiplier spending chain set in motion when Generous Motors spent $1 million to build a factory could equally well have been kicked off by the federal government buying $1 million worth of new cars from Generous Motors. Thereafter, each recipient of additional income would spend 75 percent of it (the assumed marginal propensity to consume), until $4 million in new income had eventually been created.

The idea that changes in *G* have multiplier effects on GDP will play a central role in the discussion of government stabilization policy that begins in Chapter 28. So it is worth noting here that:

Changes in the volume of government purchases of goods and services will change the equilibrium level of GDP in the same direction, and by a multiplied amount.

## THE MULTIPLIER EFFECT OF NET EXPORTS

At this point, it will not surprise you to learn that a change in net exports has precisely the same multiplier effect on equilibrium GDP as a change in any of the other components of spending. Let us quickly verify that this is so by turning to Table 26–5.

Here net exports are assumed to have risen from −$100 billion (their value in Chapter 25) to +$100 billion—an increase of $200 billion. Table 26–5, which looks

Table 26–5 **TOTAL EXPENDITURE AFTER NET EXPORTS RISE BY $200 BILLION (billions of dollars)**

| (1) INCOME ($Y$) | (2) CONSUMPTION ($C$) | (3) INVESTMENT ($I$) | (4) GOVERNMENT PURCHASES ($G$) | (5) NET EXPORTS ($X - IM$) | (6) TOTAL EXPENDITURE |
|---|---|---|---|---|---|
| 4800 | 3000 | 900 | 1300 | 100 | 5300 |
| 5200 | 3300 | 900 | 1300 | 100 | 5600 |
| 5600 | 3600 | 900 | 1300 | 100 | 5900 |
| 6000 | 3900 | 900 | 1300 | 100 | 6200 |
| 6400 | 4200 | 900 | 1300 | 100 | 6500 |
| 6800 | 4500 | 900 | 1300 | 100 | 6800 |
| 7200 | 4800 | 900 | 1300 | 100 | 7100 |

This table shows the construction of the total expenditure schedule for Macroland following an increase of $200 billion in net exports rather than in consumption or investment. Notice that columns 3 and 5 differ from the corresponding columns in Table 26–1, but column 6 is the same in both tables. Thus the expenditure schedule in the 45° line diagram is the same as in the earlier example.

just like the previous tables, shows us that equilibrium once again occurs at a GDP of $Y = \$6800$ billion.

The reason is hardly mysterious. When foreigners buy U.S. products, they put income into the hands of Americans, just as domestic investment does. As this income is spent and respent, a multiplier process is set in motion, raising GDP. Specifically, in this example an increase of $200 billion in net exports leads to an increase of $800 billion in GDP (from $6000 billion to $6800 billion). So the multiplier is 4. Once again, Figure 26–1 applies.

Although we will have much more to learn about how the U.S. economy is linked to the economies of other countries in Part 8, this simple analysis of the multiplier effect of foreign trade already teaches us an important lesson: *Booms and recessions tend to be transmitted across national borders.*

Why is that? Suppose a boom abroad raises aggregate demand and GDP in foreign countries. With rising incomes, foreigners will buy more American goods—which means that U.S. exports will rise. But a rise in our exports will, via the multiplier, raise GDP in the United States. By this mechanism, rapid economic growth abroad contributes to rapid economic growth here.

Of course, the same mechanism also operates in the downward direction. Suppose some of the countries that trade with us slip into recession. As their GDPs decline, so do their *imports*. But this means that the United States will experience a decline in *exports* which, through the multiplier, will pull down GDP here. Hence a recession abroad can contribute to recessionary conditions in the United States.

Naturally, what foreign countries do to us, we also do to them. Thus rapid economic growth in the United States tends to produce boom conditions in the countries from which we buy, and recessions here tend quickly to spill beyond our borders. In summary:

The GDPs of the major economies are linked by trade. A boom in one country tends to raise its imports and hence push up exports and GDP in other countries. Similarly, a recession in one country tends to pull GDP down in other countries.

## THE MULTIPLIER IN REVERSE

A good way to check your understanding of the multiplier process is to run it in reverse: What happens if, for example, consumers autonomously decide to spend less? For example, suppose a wave of thriftiness comes over the people of Macroland so that, no matter what their total income, they now want to spend $200 billion *less* than they did previously rather than the $200 billion *more* assumed in Table 26–1.

A decision to spend $200 billion less out of any given level of income is, by definition, a *downward* shift of the total expenditure schedule by $200 billion. This is shown in Figure 26–3, where the $C + I + G + (X - IM)$ schedule falls from $C_0 + I + G + (X - IM)$ to $C_1 + I + G + (X - IM)$. The horizontal distance between these two parallel lines is the $200 billion drop in spending.

There are two ways of calculating the multiplier. First, our oversimplified multiplier formula tells us that the multiplier is

$$\frac{1}{1 - \text{MPC}} = \frac{1}{1 - 0.75} = \frac{1}{0.25} = 4.$$

So a $200 billion drop in spending will lead to a multiplier effect of $800 billion. Alternatively, we can read this conclusion from Figure 26–3. Here the economy's equilibrium point moves down the 45° line from point $E_0$ to $E_1$; income drops from $6000 billion to $5200 billion—a decline of $800 billion.

**Figure 26–3** THE MULTIPLIER IN REVERSE

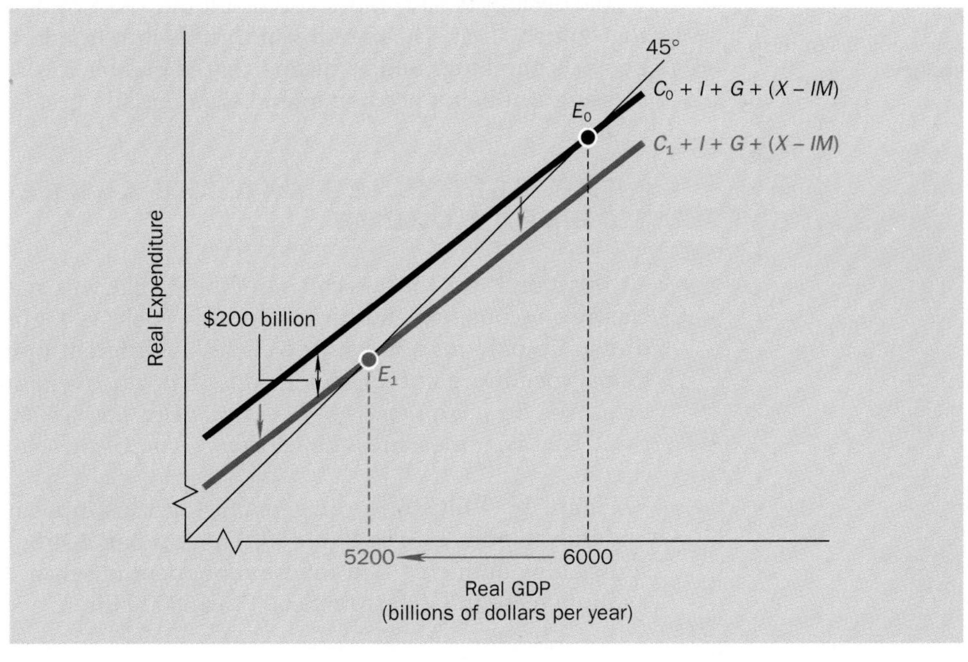


This diagram shows the multiplier effect of an autonomous decline in consumer spending of $200 billion. The decline appears as a downward shift of $200 billion in the expenditure schedule, which falls from $C_0 + I + G + (X - IM)$ to $C_1 + I + G + (X - IM)$. Equilibrium, which is always at the intersection of the expenditure schedule and the 45° line, moves from point $E_0$ to point $E_1$, and income falls from $6000 billion to $5200 billion.

Now compare the analysis of a decline in spending summarized in Figure 26–3 with the previous analysis of an increase in spending shown in Figure 26–1 on page 649. You will see that everything is simply turned in the opposite direction. The multiplier works in both directions.

## THE PARADOX OF THRIFT

This last example of multiplier analysis teaches us an important lesson: it shows that an increase in the desire to save will lead to a cumulative fall in GDP. And, *because saving depends on income*, the resulting decline in national income will pull saving down. In consequence, saving may fail to rise despite an increase in the public's desire to save.

Let us be a bit more specific about this remarkable result. Before the upsurge in saving, consumers were spending \$3900 billion out of a total national income of \$6000 billion, as we can see in Table 25–1 on page 628. How much was being saved? Since taxes in Macroland are assumed to be fixed at \$1200 billion, disposable income was DI $= Y - T =$ \$6000 $-$ \$1200 $=$ \$4800. Hence saving was \$900 billion ( $=$ \$4800 $-$ \$3900).

In Figure 26–3, GDP falls to \$5200 billion, so disposable income drops to \$4000. Since investment, government purchases, and net exports are all unchanged, the entire \$800 billion drop in GDP must come out of consumption, which therefore falls by \$800 billion (to \$3100 billion). Thus DI is down to \$4000 billion and $C$ is down to \$3100 billion, leaving total saving still \$900 billion. The effort to save more has been totally frustrated by the decline in GDP.[4]

The **PARADOX OF THRIFT** is the fact that an effort by a nation to save more may simply reduce national income and fail to raise total saving.

This remarkable result is called the **paradox of thrift**, because it shows that, while saving may pave the road to riches for an individual, if the nation as a whole decides to save more, the result may be a recession and the falling incomes that come with it. The paradox of thrift is important because it is contrary to most people's thinking, and it means that a greater desire to save may be a mixed blessing if it is not accompanied by an equally greater desire to invest.

## THE MULTIPLIER AND THE AGGREGATE DEMAND CURVE

At this point, we must recall something that was mentioned at the start of the chapter: income-expenditure diagrams such as Figures 26–1 and 26–3 can be drawn up only for a given price level. A different price level leads to a different total expenditure curve. This means that our oversimplified multiplier formula measures *the increase in real GDP demanded that would occur if the price level were fixed*. That is, it measures the *horizontal shift* of the economy's aggregate demand curve.

Figure 26–4 illustrates this conclusion by supposing that the price level that underlies Figure 26–1 is $P = 100$. The top panel simply repeats Figure 26–1 and shows how an increase in investment spending from \$900 to \$1100 billion leads to an increase in GDP from \$6000 to \$6800 billion.

[4]It is even possible to devise examples in which total saving goes *down* when people attempt to save more. This will happen, for example, if there is *induced investment*.

*Figure* **26–4** **TWO VIEWS OF THE MULTIPLIER**

The top panel repeats Figure 26–1. The bottom panel shows two aggregate demand curves. Curve $D_0D_0$, which applies when investment is $900 billion, shows that equilibrium GDP on the demand side comes at $Y$ = $6000 billion when $P$ = 100 (point $E_0$). Curve $D_1D_1$, which applies when investment is $1100 billion, shows that equilibrium GDP on the demand side comes at $Y$ = $6800 billion when $P$ = 100 (point $E_1$). The horizontal distance between points $E_0$ and $E_1$ in the bottom panel indicates the oversimplified multiplier effect.

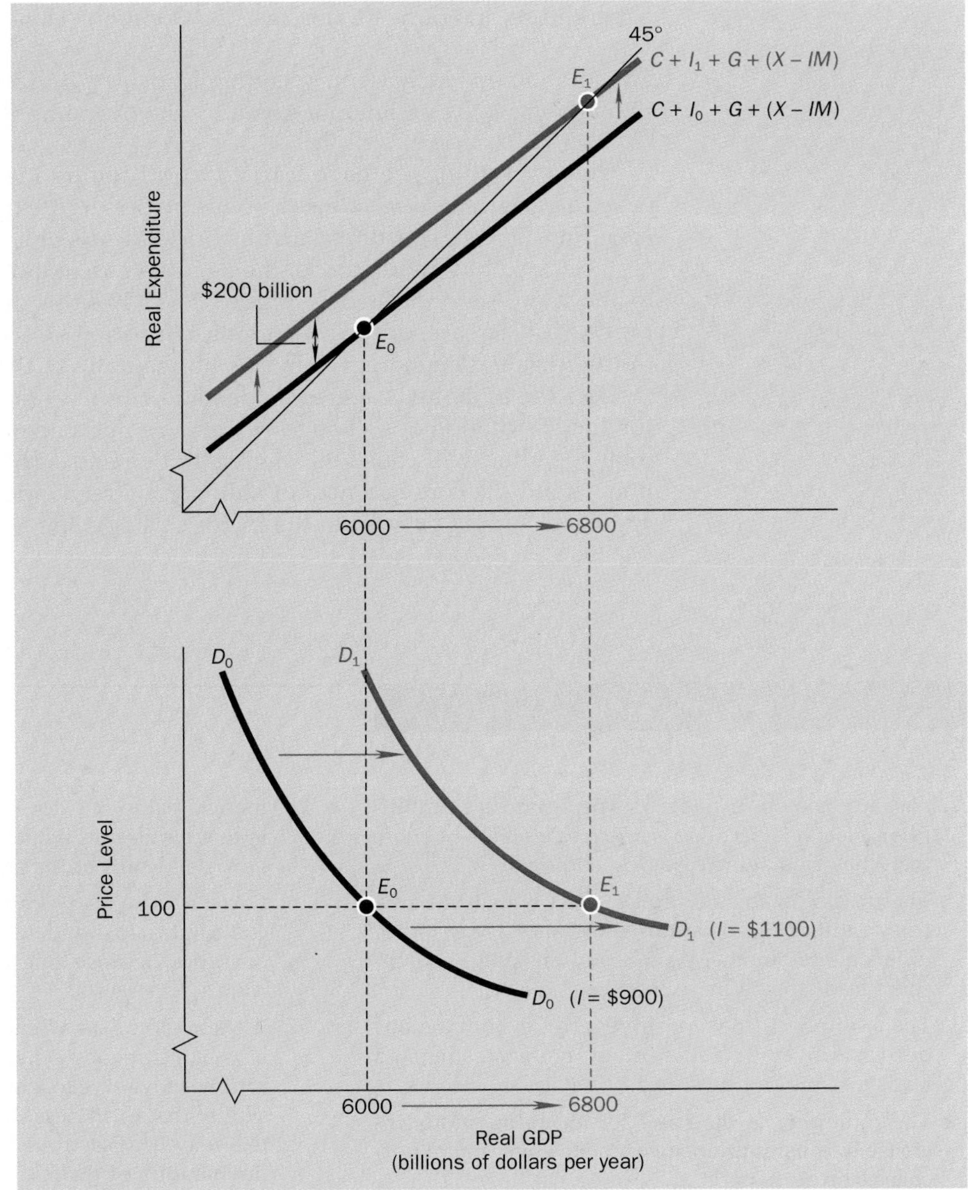


The bottom panel shows two downward-sloping aggregate demand curves. The first, labeled $D_0D_0$, depicts the situation when investment is $900 billion. Point $E_0$ on this curve indicates that, at the given price level ($P$ = 100), the equilibrium quantity of GDP demanded is $6000 billion. It corresponds exactly to point $E_0$ in the top panel. The second aggregate demand curve, $D_1D_1$, depicts the situation after investment has risen to $1100 billion. Point $E_1$ on this curve indicates that the equilibrium quantity of GDP demanded when $P$ = 100 has risen to $6800 billion, which corresponds exactly to point $E_1$ in the top panel.

As Figure 26–4 shows, the horizontal distance between the two aggregate demand curves is exactly equal to the increase in real GDP shown in the income-expenditure diagram—in this case, $800 billion. Thus:

An autonomous increase in spending leads to a horizontal shift of the aggregate demand curve by an amount given by the oversimplified multiplier formula.

Thus everything we have learned about the multiplier applies to *shifts of the economy's aggregate demand curve.* If businesses decide to increase their investment spending, or if the consumption function shifts up, or if the government or foreigners decide to buy more goods, the aggregate demand curve moves horizontally to the right—as indicated in Figure 26–4. If either investment or government purchases decrease, or the consumption function shifts down, or net exports fall, the aggregate demand curve moves horizontally to the left.

Thus the economy's aggregate demand curve cannot be expected to stand still for long. Autonomous changes in one or another of the four components of total spending will cause the aggregate demand curve to move around. But to understand the consequences of shifts of aggregate demand, we must bring the aggregate supply curve into the picture. That is the task of the next chapter.

## Summary

1. Any autonomous increase in expenditure has a **multiplier** effect on GDP; that is, it increases GDP by more than the original increase in spending.
2. The reason for this multiplier effect is that one person's additional expenditure constitutes a new source of income for another person, and this additional income leads to still more spending, and so on.
3. The multiplier also works in reverse: an autonomous decrease in any component of aggregate demand leads to a multiplied decrease in national income.
4. The multiplier is the same for an **autonomous increase in consumption**, investment, government purchases, or net exports.
5. A simple formula for the multiplier says that its numerical value is 1/(1 − MPC). This formula, which is too simple to give accurate results, measures the horizontal shift of the aggregate demand curve.
6. Rapid (or sluggish) economic growth in one country contributes to rapid (or sluggish) growth in other countries because one country's imports are other countries' exports.
7. If the nation as a whole decides to save more, that is, to consume less, the resulting decline in national income may serve to make everyone poorer. This possibility that thriftiness, while a virtue for the individual, may be disastrous for an entire nation, is called the **paradox of thrift**.

## Key Concepts and Terms

The multiplier
Induced increase in consumption
Autonomous increase in consumption
Paradox of thrift

## *Questions for Review*

1. Try to remember where you last spent a dollar. Explain how this dollar will lead to a multiplier chain of increased income and spending. (Who received the dollar? What will he or she do with it?)
2. Use both numerical and graphical methods to find the multiplier effect of the following shift in the consumption function in an economy in which investment is always $110, government purchases are always 50 and net exports are always −20.

| INCOME | CONSUMPTION BEFORE SHIFT | CONSUMPTION AFTER SHIFT |
|---|---|---|
| 540 | 440 | 460 |
| 570 | 460 | 480 |
| 600 | 480 | 500 |
| 630 | 500 | 520 |
| 660 | 520 | 540 |
| 690 | 540 | 560 |
| 720 | 560 | 580 |
| 750 | 580 | 600 |

(*Hint*: What is the marginal propensity to consume?)

3. Turn back to Review Question 3 in Chapter 25 (page 640). Suppose investment spending rises to $130, and the price level is fixed. By how much will the equilibrium GDP increase? Derive the answer both numerically and graphically.
4. Explain the paradox of thrift. Why do you think it is called a paradox?
5. (More difficult) Suppose the consumption function is as given in Review Question 8 of Chapter 25 (page 641)

$$C = 300 + 0.75DI$$

and investment ($I$) rises to 1100 while net exports ($X - IM$) remain at − 100, government purchases remain at 1300, and taxes remain at 1200. Use the equilibrium condition $Y = C + I + G + (X - IM)$ to find the equilibrium level of GDP. (In working out the answer, assume the price level is fixed.) Compare your answer to Table 26–1 and Figure 26–1. Now compare your answer to the answer to Review Question 8 of Chapter 25. What do you learn about the multiplier?
6. (More difficult) Look back at Review Question 9 of Chapter 25 (page 641). What is the multiplier for this economy? If $G$ rises by 100, what happens to Y? What happens to $Y$ if both $G$ and $T$ rise by 100 at the same time?

## Appendix A THE SIMPLE ALGEBRA OF THE MULTIPLIER

Appendix B to Chapter 25 presented a general expression for the equilibrium level of GDP when the price level is fixed, investment ($I$), government purchases ($G$), taxes ($T$), and net exports ($X - IM$) are all constant, and the consumption function is

$$C = a + b\text{DI} = a + b(Y - T).$$

The answer obtained there (which can be found on page 645) was

$$Y = \frac{a - bT + I + (X - IM)}{1 - b}.$$

From this formula, it is easy to derive the oversimplified multiplier formula algebraically and to show that it applies equally well to a change in investment, autonomous consumer spending, government purchases, or net exports. To do so , suppose that any of the symbols in the numerator of the multiplier formula increases by 1 unit. In any of these cases, GDP would rise from the previous formula to

$$Y = \frac{a - bT + I + (X - IM) + 1}{1 - b}.$$

By comparing this with the previous expression for $Y$, we see that a 1 unit change in any component of spending changes equilibrium GDP by

$$\text{change in } Y = \frac{a - bT + I + (X - IM) + 1}{1 - b} - \frac{a - bT + I + (X - IM)}{1 - b}$$

or

$$\text{change in } Y = \frac{1}{1 - b}.$$

Recalling that $b$ is the marginal propensity to consume, we see that this is precisely the oversimplified multiplier formula.

# Appendix B THE MULTIPLIER IN THE PRESENCE OF FOREIGN TRADE

In Chapters 25 and 26, we assumed that net exports were a fixed number. But in fact a nation's imports depend on its GDP. The reason is simple: higher GDP leads to higher incomes, some of which is spent on foreign goods. Thus:

Our imports rise as our GDP rises and fall as our GDP falls.

Similarly, our *exports* are the *imports* of other countries, so it is natural to assume that our exports depend on *their* GDPs, not on our own. Thus:

Our exports are relatively insensitive to our own GDP, but are quite sensitive to the GDPs of other countries.

This appendix derives the implications of these rather elementary observations. In particular, it shows that:

International trade lowers the value of the multiplier.

To see why, we begin with Table 26–6, which adapts the concrete example of Macroland from Chapter 25 to allow imports to depend on GDP. Columns 2–4 are the same as in Table 25–1 on page 628; they show *C*, *I*, and *G* at alternative levels of GDP. Columns 5 and 6 record revised assumptions about the behavior of exports and imports. Exports are fixed at $650 billion regardless of (our) GDP. But imports are assumed to rise by $60 billion for every $400 billion rise in GDP, which is a simple numerical example of the idea that imports depend on GDP. Column 7 subtracts imports from exports to get net exports, $(X - IM)$, and column 8 adds up the four components of total expenditure, $C + I + G + (X - IM)$.

The equilibrium, you can see, occurs at $Y = \$6000$ billion, just as it did in Chapter 25.

Figures 26–5 and 26–6 display the same conclusion graphically. The upper panel of Figure 26–5 shows that exports are fixed at $650 billion regardless of GDP while imports increase as GDP rises, just as in Table 26–6. The difference between exports and imports, or net exports, is positive until GDP reaches around $5300 billion and negative once GDP surpasses that amount. The bottom panel of Figure 26–5 shows the subtraction explicitly and makes it clear that:

Net exports decline as GDP rises.

Figure 26–6 carries this analysis over to the 45° line diagram. We begin with the familiar $C + I + G + (X - IM)$ line of Chapters 25 and 26, in black. There we simply assumed that net exports were fixed at − $100 billion regardless of GDP. Now that we have amended our model to note that net exports decline with GDP, the sum $C + I + G + (X - IM)$ rises more slowly than we previously assumed. This

**Table 26–6 EQUILIBRIUM INCOME WITH VARIABLE IMPORTS**

| (1) GROSS DOMESTIC PRODUCT (*Y*) (billions) | (2) CONSUMER EXPENDITURES (*C*) (billions) | (3) INVESTMENT (*I*) (billions) | (4) GOVERNMENT PURCHASES (*G*) (billions) | (5) EXPORTS (*X*) (billions) | (6) IMPORTS (*IM*) (billions) | (7) NET EXPORTS (*X* − *IM*) (billions) | (8) TOTAL EXPENDITURE [*C* + *I* + *G* + (*X* − *IM*)] (billions) |
|---|---|---|---|---|---|---|---|
| 4800 | 3000 | 900 | 1300 | 650 | 570 | +80 | 5280 |
| 5200 | 3300 | 900 | 1300 | 650 | 630 | +20 | 5520 |
| 5600 | 3600 | 900 | 1300 | 650 | 690 | −40 | 5760 |
| 6000 | 3900 | 900 | 1300 | 650 | 750 | −100 | 6000 |
| 6400 | 4200 | 900 | 1300 | 650 | 810 | −160 | 6240 |
| 6800 | 4500 | 900 | 1300 | 650 | 870 | −220 | 6480 |
| 7200 | 4800 | 900 | 1300 | 650 | 930 | −280 | 6720 |

**Figure 26–5** THE DEPENDENCE OF NET EXPORTS ON GDP

This graph displays the data on exports, imports, and net exports found in Table 26–6. Exports, *X*, are independent of GDP while imports, *IM*, rise as GDP rises (top panel). As a result, net exports, (*X* − *IM*), decline as GDP rises (bottom panel).

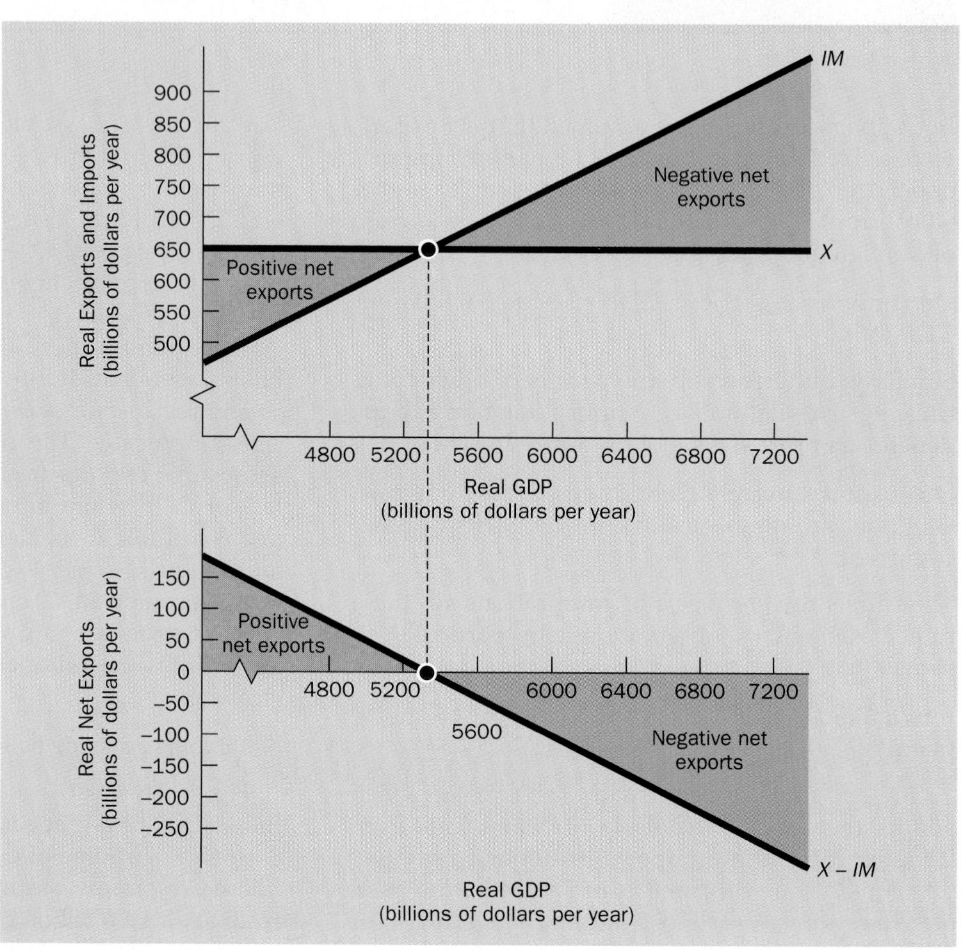


**Figure 26–6** EQUILIBRIUM GDP WITH FOREIGN TRADE

In the presence of variable imports, equilibrium GDP occurs where the blue *C* + *I* + *G* + (*X* − *IM*) line, rather than the black one, crosses the 45° line. In the graph, equilibrium is at point *E*, where GDP is $6000 billion. This matches the equilibrium we found in Chapter 25 (Figure 25–3 on page 630) with fixed imports because we have rigged the example to come out that way.

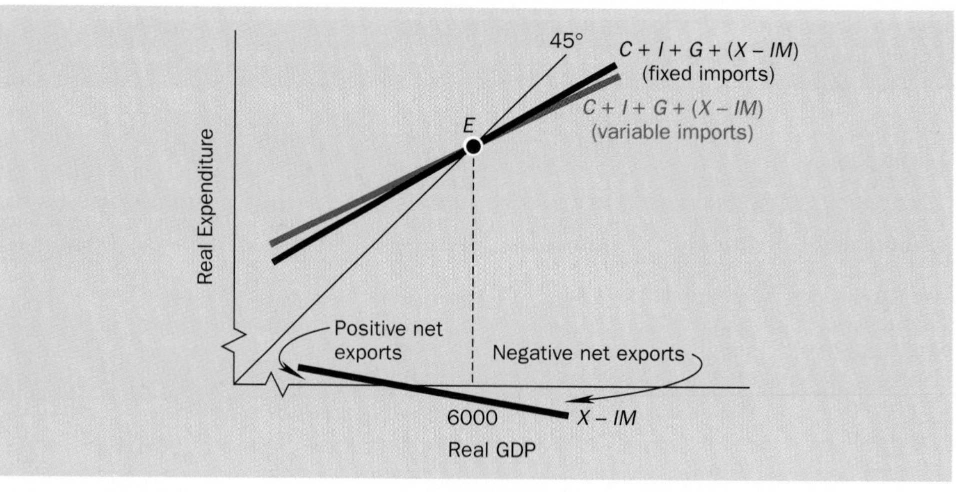

**Table 26–7 EQUILIBRIUM INCOME AFTER A $160 BILLION RISE IN EXPORTS**

| (1) GROSS DOMESTIC PRODUCT (Y) (billions) | (2) CONSUMER EXPENDITURES (C) (billions) | (3) INVESTMENT (I) (billions) | (4) GOVERNMENT PURCHASES (G) (billions) | (5) EXPORTS (X) (billions) | (6) IMPORTS (IM) (billions) | (7) NET EXPORTS (X − IM) (billions) | (8) TOTAL EXPENDITURE [C + I + G + (X − IM)] (billions) |
|---|---|---|---|---|---|---|---|
| 4800 | 3000 | 900 | 1300 | 810 | 570 | +240 | 5440 |
| 5200 | 3300 | 900 | 1300 | 810 | 630 | +180 | 5680 |
| 5600 | 3600 | 900 | 1300 | 810 | 690 | +120 | 5920 |
| 6000 | 3900 | 900 | 1300 | 810 | 750 | +60 | 6160 |
| 6400 | 4200 | 900 | 1300 | 810 | 810 | 0 | 6400 |
| 6800 | 4500 | 900 | 1300 | 810 | 870 | −60 | 6640 |
| 7200 | 4800 | 900 | 1300 | 810 | 930 | −120 | 6880 |

is shown by the blue line. Note that it is less steep than the black line.

Let us now consider what happens if exports rise by $160 billion while imports remain as in Table 26–6. Table 26–7 shows us that equilibrium now occurs at a GDP of $Y = \$6400$ billion. Naturally, higher exports have raised domestic GDP. But consider the magnitude. A $160 billion increase in exports (from $650 billion to $810 billion) leads to an increase of $400 billion in GDP (from $6000 billion to $6400 billion). So the multiplier is 2.5 ( = $400/$160).[5]

This same conclusion is shown graphically in Figure 26–7, where the line $C + I + G + (X_0 - IM)$ represents the original expenditure schedule and the line $C + I + G + (X_1 - IM)$ represents the expenditure schedule after the rise in exports. Equilibrium shifts from point $E$ to point $A$, and GDP rises by $400 billion.

Notice that the multiplier in this example is 2.5, whereas in the chapter, with net exports taken to be a fixed number, it was 4. This simple example illustrates a general result: *international trade lowers the numerical value of the multiplier.* Why is this so? Because, in an open economy, any autonomous increase in spending is partly dissipated in purchases of foreign goods, which creates additional income for foreigners rather than for domestic citizens.

[5]EXERCISE: Construct a version of Table 26–6 to show what would happen if imports rose by $160 billion at every level of GDP while exports remained at $650 billion. You should be able to show that the new equilibrium would be $Y = \$5600$.

**Figure 26–7 THE MULTIPLIER WITH FOREIGN TRADE**

This diagram shows a $160 billion increase in exports as a vertical shift of the total expenditure schedule from $C + I + G + (X_0 - IM)$, to $C + I + G + (X_1 - IM)$. As a result, equilibrium shifts from point $E$ to point $A$, and GDP rises from $6000 billion to $6400 billion. The multiplier is therefore 2.5 ( = $400/$160).

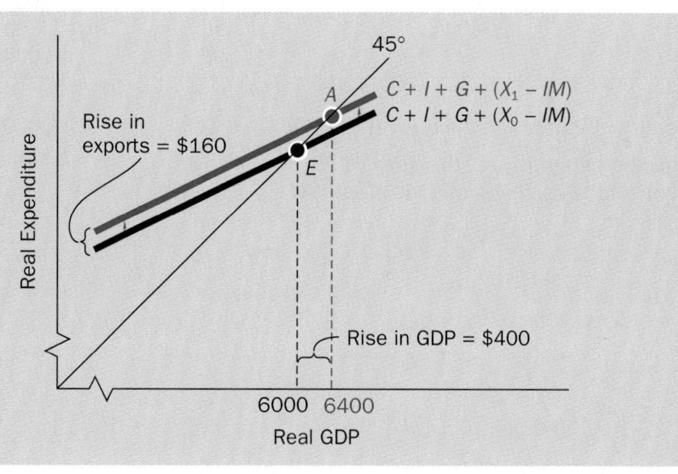

Figure 26–6 shows this same conclusion graphically. Because net exports decline as GDP rises, the total expenditure line is *flatter* in the presence of variable imports [blue $C + I + G + (X - IM)$ line] than it would be with fixed imports (black line). As we know from earlier chapters, the *size* of the multiplier depends on the *slope* of the expenditure schedule—steeper expenditure schedules lead to larger multipliers. Since variable imports flatten the expenditure schedule, they lower the multiplier.[6]

Thus international trade gives us the first of what will eventually be several reasons why the oversimplified multiplier formula overstates the true value of the multiplier.

[6]For those who like formulas, we can amend the oversimplified multiplier formula to allow for international trade. That formula was: multiplier $= 1/(1 - b)$ where $b$ is the marginal propensity to consume. If we define the *marginal propensity to import* as the rise in imports per dollar of GDP (the marginal propensity to import is 0.15 in our example) and symbolize it by the letter $m$, the formula for the multiplier with foreign trade is: multiplier $= 1/(1 - b + m)$. This formula clearly shows that a higher value of $m$ leads to a lower multiplier.

## *Summary*

1. Because imports rise as GDP rises while exports are insensitive to (domestic) GDP, net exports decline as GDP rises.
2. International trade reduces the value of the multiplier.

## *Questions for Review*

1. Suppose exports and imports of a country are given by

| GDP | EXPORTS | IMPORTS |
|---|---|---|
| $2500 | $400 | $250 |
| 3000 | 400 | 300 |
| 3500 | 400 | 350 |
| 4000 | 400 | 400 |
| 4500 | 400 | 450 |
| 5000 | 400 | 500 |

   Calculate net exports at each level of GDP.

2. If domestic expenditure (the sum of $C + I + G$) in the economy described in Question 1 is as shown below, construct a 45°-line diagram and locate the equilibrium level of GDP.

| GDP | DOMESTIC EXPENDITURES |
|---|---|
| $2500 | $3100 |
| 3000 | 3400 |
| 3500 | 3700 |
| 4000 | 4000 |
| 4500 | 4300 |
| 5000 | 4600 |

3. Now raise exports to $650 and find the equilibrium again. How large is the multiplier?

Chapter 27

# SUPPLY-SIDE EQUILIBRIUM: UNEMPLOYMENT *and* INFLATION?

*We might as well reasonably dispute whether it is the upper or the under blade of a pair of scissors that cuts a piece of paper, as whether value is governed by [demand] or [supply].*

ALFRED MARSHALL

In Chapter 25 we learned that the level of prices, in conjunction with the economy's total expenditure schedule, governs whether the economy will experience a recessionary or an inflationary gap. If the $C + I + G + (X - IM)$ schedule is "too low," a *recessionary gap* will arise, while a $C + I + G + (X - IM)$ schedule that is "too high" leads to an *inflationary gap*. Which sort of gap actually occurs is of considerable importance because a recessionary gap normally spells unemployment while an inflationary gap leads to inflation. ¶ The tools provided in Chapter 25, however, are not sufficient to determine which sort of gap will arise because, as we know, the position of the expenditure schedule depends on the price level. And the price level is determined by *both aggregate demand and aggregate supply*. Thus, the task of the present chapter is to bring the supply side of the economy into the picture. ¶ We begin by explaining how the *aggregate supply curve* is derived from business costs. Next we consider the interaction of aggregate supply and aggregate demand, and the joint determination of output and the price level. With this apparatus in hand, we return to recessionary and inflationary gaps and study how the economy adjusts to each. Doing this puts us in a position to deal with the crucial question raised in earlier chapters: Does the economy have an efficient self-correcting mechanism? We shall see that the answer is "yes, but." Yes, but it works slowly. Finally, we use aggregate supply-aggregate demand analysis to explain the vexing problem of *stagflation*—the simultaneous occurrence of high unemployment *and* high inflation—that plagued the economy in the 1980s.

### TWO SIDES TO THE SUPPLY SIDE

In 1981, President Ronald Reagan brought to Washington a doctrine called "supply-side economics"—a new theory advertised as a replacement for the Keynesian theory we studied in the last three chapters. Reaganite supply-side economics, which was controversial from the start and remains so, emphasized tax incentives that allegedly would increase saving and investment—and thus augment the supply of capital.

Twelve years later, the American voters repudiated Reaganomics and voted in President Bill Clinton who, ironically, also ran on what might be called a "supply-side" platform. Clintonomics, with its emphasis on upgrading the skills of the American workforce through education and training, was starkly different from Reaganomics. But the two programs share one idea in common: that what happens on the supply side of the economy matters a great deal for inflation, unemployment, and economic growth.

It is therefore time for us to consider the origins of the aggregate supply curve and the factors that can make it shift. Only when we have done so will we be ready to analyze the *joint* determination of output *and* the price level—with its consequences for inflationary and recessionary gaps.

## THE AGGREGATE SUPPLY CURVE

In earlier chapters we noted that aggregate demand is a schedule, not a fixed number. The quantity of real GDP that will be demanded depends on the price level, as summarized in the economy's *aggregate demand curve*.

Analogously, the concept of *aggregate supply* does not refer to a fixed number, but rather to a schedule (a *supply curve*). The volume of goods and services that will be provided by profit-seeking enterprises depends on the prices they obtain for their outputs, on wages and other production costs, on the state of technology, and on other things. The relationship between the price level and the quantity of real GDP supplied, *holding all other determinants of quantity supplied constant*, is called the economy's **aggregate supply curve**.

The **AGGREGATE SUPPLY CURVE** shows, for each possible price level, the quantity of goods and services that all the nation's businesses are willing to produce during a specified period of time, holding all other determinants of aggregate quantity supplied constant.

A typical aggregate supply curve is drawn in Figure 27–1. It slopes upward, meaning that as prices rise more output is produced, *other things held constant*. It is not difficult to understand why. Producers in the U.S. economy are motivated mainly by profit. The profit made by producing a unit of output is simply the difference between the price at which it is sold and the unit cost of production:

$$\text{profit per unit} = \text{price} - \text{cost per unit}.$$

So the response of output to a rising price level—which is what the slope of the aggregate supply curve shows—depends on the response of costs.

**Figure 27–1** **AN AGGREGATE SUPPLY CURVE**

This graph shows a typical aggregate supply curve. It has a positive slope (that is, it rises as we move to the right), meaning that the quantity of output supplied rises as the price level rises.

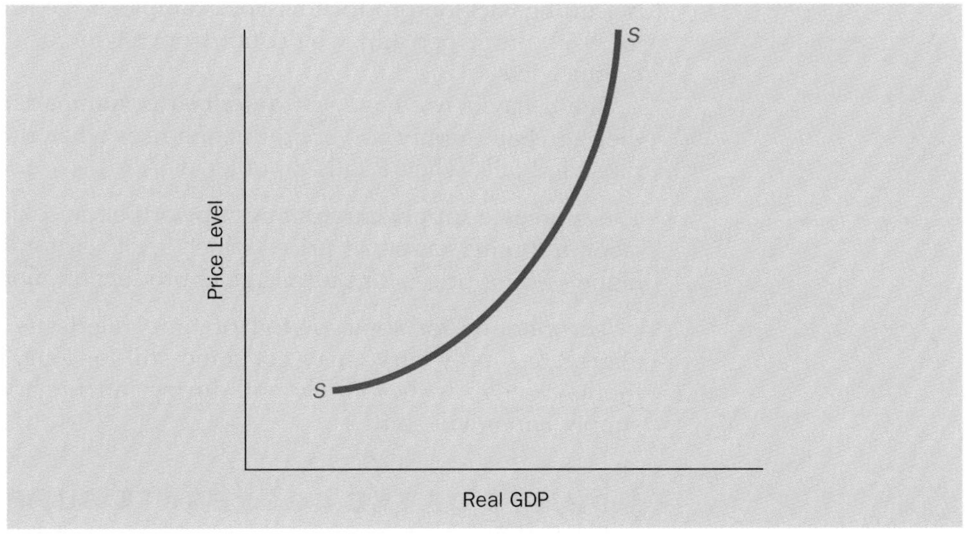


One critical fact affecting this response is that labor and other inputs used by firms normally are available at relatively fixed prices for some period of time—though certainly not forever. There are many reasons for this. Some workers and firms enter into long-term labor contracts that set money wages up to three years in advance. Even where there are no explicit contracts, employees typically have their wages increased only once per year. During the interim period, money wages are fixed. Much the same is true of other factors of production. Many firms get deliveries of raw materials under long-term contracts at prearranged prices. None of these contracts lasts forever, of course, but many of them last long enough to matter.

Why is it significant that firms often purchase inputs at prices that stay fixed for considerable periods? Because firms decide how much to produce by comparing their selling prices with their costs of production; and production costs depend, among other things, on input prices. If the selling prices of the firm's products rise while wages and other factor costs are fixed, production becomes more profitable, and so firms will increase output.

A simple example will illustrate the idea. Suppose a firm uses one hour of labor to manufacture a gadget that sells for \$9. If workers earn \$8 per hour, and the firm has no other production costs, its profit per unit is

$$\begin{aligned}\text{profit per unit} &= \text{price} - \text{cost per unit}\\ &= \$9 - \$8 = \$1.\end{aligned}$$

Now what happens if the price of a gadget rises to \$10, but wage rates remain constant? The firm's profit per unit becomes

$$\begin{aligned}\text{profit per unit} &= \text{price} - \text{cost per unit}\\ &= \$10 - \$8 = \$2.\end{aligned}$$

With production more profitable, it is likely that the firm will supply more gadgets.

The same process operates in reverse. Suppose selling prices fall while input costs are relatively fixed. Since this squeezes their profit margins, firms may react by cutting back on production. For example, if the price of a gadget fell from $9 to $8.50, profit per unit would fall from $1 to 50¢, and firms would probably produce less.

The behavior we have just described is summarized by the upward slope of the aggregate supply curve: production rises when the price level (henceforth, *P*) rises, and falls when *P* falls. In other words:

The aggregate supply curve slopes upward because firms normally can purchase labor and other inputs at prices which are fixed for some period of time. Thus, higher selling prices for output make production more attractive.[1]

The phrase "for some period of time" alerts us to the possibility that the aggregate supply curve may not stand still for long. If wages or prices of other inputs change, as they surely will during inflationary times, then the aggregate supply curve will shift.

## SHIFTS OF THE AGGREGATE SUPPLY CURVE

We have concluded so far that, for given levels of wages and other input prices, there will be an upward-sloping aggregate supply curve relating the price level to aggregate quantity supplied. But what factors determine the *position* of this curve? What things can make it shift?

### THE MONEY WAGE RATE

Our discussion suggests the most obvious determinant of the position of the aggregate supply curve: the money wage rate. Wages are the major element of cost in the economy, accounting for more than 70 percent of all inputs. Since higher wage rates mean higher costs, they spell lower profits at any given prices.

Let us return to our example and consider what would happen to a gadget producer if the money wage rose to $8.75 per hour while the price of a gadget remained $9. Profit per unit would decline from

$$\$9 - \$8 = \$1$$

to

$$\$9 - \$8.75 = \$0.25.$$

With profits squeezed, the firm would probably cut back on production.

This is the way firms in our economy typically react to a rise in wages. Therefore, a wage increase leads to a decrease in aggregate quantity supplied at current prices. Graphically, the aggregate supply curve shifts to the left (or inward), as shown in Figure 27–2. In this diagram, when wages are low, firms are willing to supply $6000 billion in goods and services at a price level of 100 (point *A*). After wages increase, however, these same firms are willing to supply only $5500 billion

[1]There are both differences and similarities between the *aggregate* supply curve and the *microeconomic* supply curves studied in Parts 2–4. Both are based on the idea that quantity supplied depends on how output prices move relative to input prices. But the aggregate supply curve pertains to the behavior of the overall price level, whereas a microeconomic supply curve pertains to the price of some particular commodity.

Figure 27–2 A SHIFT OF THE AGGREGATE SUPPLY CURVE

This diagram shows what happens to the economy's aggregate supply curve when money wages rise. Higher wages shift the supply curve inward from $S_0S_0$ to $S_1S_1$, leading, for example, to an output level of \$5500 billion (point *B*), rather than \$6000 (point *A*), when the price level is 100. The aggregate supply curve will shift inward in the same manner if the price of any other input (such as energy) increases.

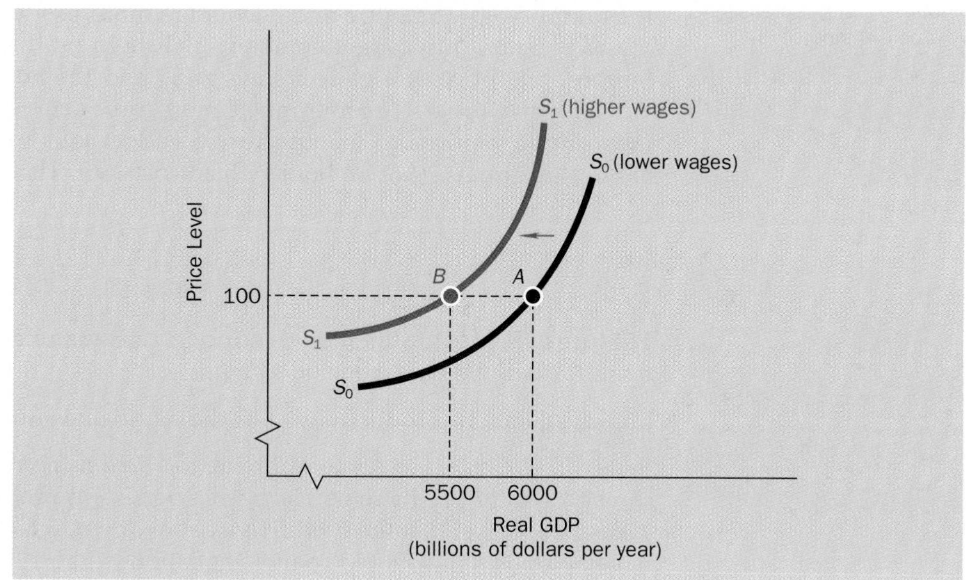


at this price level (point *B*). By similar reasoning, the aggregate supply curve will shift to the right (or outward) if wages fall. Thus:

A rise in the money wage rate causes the aggregate supply curve to *shift inward*, meaning that the quantity supplied at any price level *declines*. A fall in the money wage rate causes the aggregate supply curve to *shift outward*, meaning that the quantity supplied at any price level *increases*.

## PRICES OF OTHER INPUTS

In this regard, there is nothing special about wages. An increase in the price of *any* input that firms buy will shift the aggregate supply curve in the same way. That is

The aggregate supply curve is shifted inward by an increase in the price of any input to the production process, and it is shifted *outward* by any decrease.

While there are many inputs other than labor, the one that has attracted the most attention in recent years is energy. We have much to say about energy in this book, including further discussion in this chapter and in Chapter 21. But for present purposes the important thing to realize is that increases in the price of energy, such as those that took place in the early 1980s and again during the 1990 Gulf War, push the aggregate supply curve inward more or less as shown in Figure 27–2. By the same token, a rise in the price of *any* input we import from abroad would have the effect shown in the figure.

## TECHNOLOGY AND PRODUCTIVITY

Another factor that determines the position of the aggregate supply curve is the state of technology. Suppose, for example, that a technological breakthrough

**PRODUCTIVITY** is the amount of output produced by a unit of input.

increases the **productivity** of labor, that is, output per hour of work. If wages do not change, such an improvement in productivity will *decrease* business costs and thus improve profitability and encourage more production.

Once again, our gadget company will help us understand how this works. Suppose the price of a gadget stays at $9 and the hourly wage rate stays at $8, but gadget workers become much more productive. Specifically, suppose the labor input required to manufacture a gadget falls from one hour (which costs $8) to three-quarters of an hour (which costs $6). Then profit per unit rises from

$$\$9 - \$8 = \$1$$

to

$$\$9 - \$6 = \$3.$$

The lure of higher profits should induce gadget manufacturers to increase production. In brief, we have concluded that:

Improvements in productivity shift the aggregate supply curve outward.

Figure 27–2 can be viewed as applying to a *decline* in productivity. Since the 1970s, slow growth of productivity has been a persistent problem for the U.S. economy. Many people feel that the productivity slowdown, which we will discuss at length in Chapter 34, contributed to the stagflation of the 1970s.

### AVAILABLE SUPPLIES OF LABOR AND CAPITAL

The last determinant of the position of the aggregate supply curve is obvious, but we list it anyway for the sake of completeness. The bigger the economy—as measured by its available supplies of labor and capital—the more it is capable of producing. So:

As the labor force grows or improves in quality, and as the capital stock is increased by investment, the aggregate supply curve shifts *outward* to the right, meaning that more output can be produced at any given price level.

These, then, are the major "other things" that we hold constant when drawing up an aggregate supply curve: wage rates, prices of other inputs (such as energy), technology, labor force, and capital stock. While a change in the price level moves the economy *along a given supply curve*, a change in any of the other determinants of aggregate quantity supplied *shifts the entire supply schedule.*

## THE SHAPE OF THE AGGREGATE SUPPLY CURVE

One other feature of the aggregate supply curve depicted in Figure 27–1 merits comment. We have drawn our supply curve with a characteristic curvature: it is relatively flat at low levels of output and gets steeper at high levels of output (as we move to the right). There is a reason for this.

When economic activity is weak, product demand slack, and capacity utilization low, firms are likely to respond to an upsurge in demand by bringing their unused capital and labor resources back into production. They will find, therefore, that costs of production do not rise much as output expands. As a result, they will find it neither necessary nor advisable to raise prices much. Rapidly rising output with relatively unchanged prices means an aggregate supply curve that is relatively flat.

By contrast, if the economy is booming, demand is buoyant, and production is straining capacity, firms will be able to increase output only by hiring more workers, acquiring more capital, or putting workers on overtime. Whatever they do, unit costs of production rise—even with wages and other input prices constant. Price increases will thus be encouraged by cost developments and, incidentally, will not be resisted forcefully on the demand side. So any rise in output will be accompanied by a significant rise in prices. The aggregate supply curve will be steep. Thus:

The slope of the aggregate supply curve, which tells us the price increase that is associated with a unit increase in quantity supplied, generally rises as the degree of resource utilization rises.

## EQUILIBRIUM OF AGGREGATE DEMAND AND SUPPLY

In Chapter 25 we learned that the price level is a crucial determinant of whether equilibrium GDP is below full employment (a "recessionary gap"), precisely at full employment, or above full employment (an "inflationary gap"). We are now in a position to analyze which type of gap, if any, will actually occur in any particular case by combining the analysis of aggregate supply just completed with the analysis of aggregate demand from the last two chapters to determine *simultaneously* the equilibrium level of real GDP ($Y$) and the equilibrium price level ($P$).

Figure 27–3 displays the mechanics. The aggregate demand curve *DD* and the aggregate supply curve *SS* intersect at point *E*, where real GDP is $6000 billion and the price level is 100. As can be seen in the graph, at any higher price

*Figure* **27–3** **EQUILIBRIUM OF REAL GDP AND THE PRICE LEVEL**

This diagram shows how the equilibrium levels of real GDP and the price level are simultaneously determined by the intersection of the aggregate demand curve (*DD*) and the aggregate supply curve (*SS*). In this example, equilibrium occurs at point *E*, with a real GDP of $6000 billion and a price level of 100.

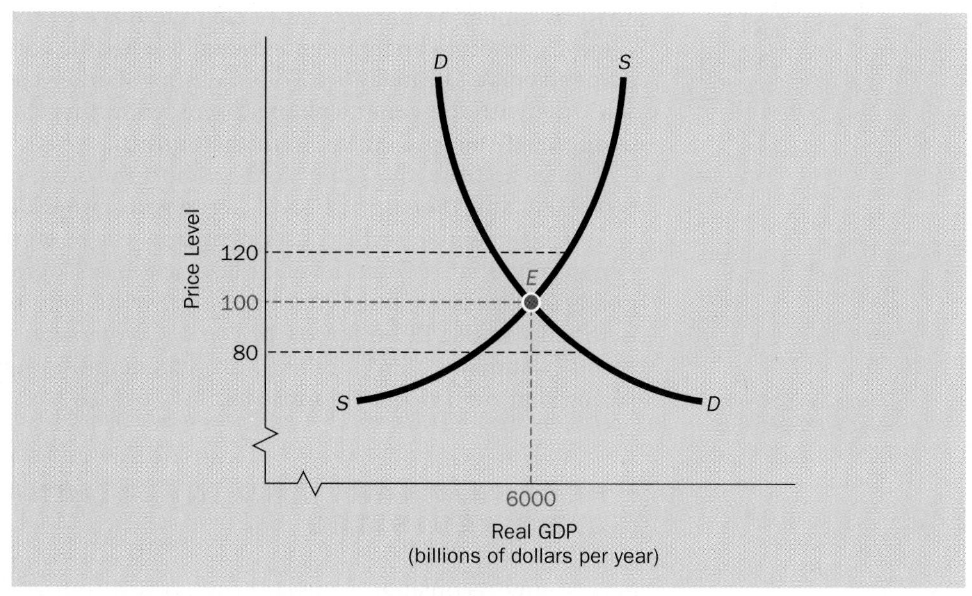

**Table 27–1 THE DETERMINATION OF THE EQUILIBRIUM PRICE LEVEL**

| (1) PRICE LEVEL | (2) AGGREGATE QUANTITY DEMANDED (billions of dollars) | (3) AGGREGATE QUANTITY SUPPLIED (billions of dollars) | (4) BALANCE OF SUPPLY AND DEMAND | (5) PRICES WILL |
|---|---|---|---|---|
| 75 | 6400 | 5600 | Quantity demanded exceeds quantity supplied | Rise |
| 80 | 6300 | 5700 | Quantity demanded exceeds quantity supplied | Rise |
| 100 | 6000 | 6000 | Quantity demanded equals quantity supplied | Remain the same |
| 120 | 5800 | 6200 | Quantity supplied exceeds quantity demanded | Fall |
| 150 | 5600 | 6400 | Quantity supplied exceeds quantity demanded | Fall |

level, such as 120, aggregate quantity supplied would exceed aggregate quantity demanded. There would be a glut on the market as firms found themselves unable to sell all their output. As inventories piled up, firms would compete more vigorously for the available customers, thereby forcing prices down. The price level would fall, as would production.

At any price level lower than 100, such as 80, quantity demanded would exceed quantity supplied. There would be a shortage of goods on the market. With inventories disappearing and customers knocking on their doors, firms would be encouraged to raise prices. The price level would rise, and so would output.

Only when the price level is 100 are the quantities of real GDP demanded and supplied equal. Hence, only the combination $P = 100$, $Y = \$6000$ is an equilibrium.

Table 27–1 illustrates the same conclusion in another way, using a tabular analysis similar to that of Chapter 25 (refer back to Table 25–2 page 629). Columns 1 and 2 constitute an aggregate demand schedule corresponding to the aggregate demand curve *DD* in Figure 27–3. Columns 1 and 3 constitute an aggregate supply schedule with the general shape discussed in this chapter. It corresponds exactly to aggregate supply curve *SS* in the figure.

It is clear from the table that equilibrium occurs only at $P = 100$ and $Y = \$6000$. At any other price level, aggregate quantities supplied and demanded would be unequal, with consequent upward or downward pressure on prices. For example, at a price level of 80, customers demand \$6300 billion worth of goods and services, but firms wish to provide only \$5700 billion. The price level is too low and will be forced upward. Conversely, at a price level of, say, 120, quantity supplied (\$6200 billion) exceeds quantity demanded (\$5800 billion), implying that the price level must fall.

## RECESSIONARY AND INFLATIONARY GAPS REVISITED

Let us now reconsider a question we posed, but could not answer, in Chapter 25: Will equilibrium occur at, below, or beyond full employment?

We could not give a complete answer to this question in Chapter 25 because we had no way to determine the equilibrium price level, and therefore no way to tell which type of gap, if any, would arise. The aggregate supply and demand analysis summarized in Figure 27–3 gives us the information we need to determine the price level. But we find that our answer is nonetheless the same as it was in Chapter 25: anything can happen.

The reason is that nothing in Figure 27–3 tells us where full employment is; it could be above the $6000 billion equilibrium level or below it. Depending on the locations of the aggregate demand and aggregate supply curves, then, we can reach equilibrium above full employment (an inflationary gap), at full employment, or below full employment (a recessionary gap). In the short run, with wages and other input costs fixed, that is all there is to it.

All three possibilities are illustrated in Figure 27–4. The three upper panels are familiar from Chapter 25. As we move from left to right, the expenditure schedule rises from $C + I_0 + G + (X - IM)$ to $C + I_1 + G + (X - IM)$ to $C + I_2 + G + (X - IM)$, leading respectively to a recessionary gap, an equilibrium at full employment, and an inflationary gap. In fact, the upper left-hand diagram looks just like Figure 25–6 (page 634), and the upper right-hand diagram duplicates Figure 25–7 (page 635). We stressed in Chapter 25 that any one of the three cases is possible, depending on the price level and the expenditure schedule.

In the three lower panels, the equilibrium price level is determined at point *E* by the intersection of the aggregate supply curve (*SS*) and the aggregate demand curve (*DD*). But the same three possibilities emerge nonetheless.

In the lower left-hand panel, aggregate demand is too small to provide jobs for the entire labor force, so there is a recessionary gap equal to distance *EB*, or $1000 billion. This corresponds precisely to the situation depicted on the income–expenditure diagram immediately above it.

In the lower right-hand panel, aggregate demand is so high that the economy reaches an equilibrium well beyond full employment. There is an inflationary gap equal to *BE*, or $1000 billion, just as in the diagram immediately above it.

In the lower middle panel, the aggregate demand curve $D_1D_1$ is at just the right level to produce an equilibrium at full employment. There is neither an inflationary nor a recessionary gap, as in the diagram just above it.

It may seem, therefore, that we have done nothing but restate our previous conclusions. But, in fact, we have done much more. Because now that we have studied the determination of the equilibrium price level, we are able to examine how the economy adjusts to either a recessionary gap or an inflationary gap. Specifically, since wages are fixed in the short run, any one of the three cases depicted in Figure 27–4 can obtain. But, in the long run, wages will adjust to labor market conditions. It is to that adjustment process that we now turn.

## ADJUSTING TO AN INFLATIONARY GAP: INFLATION

Suppose the economy starts with an inflationary gap, as in the lower right-hand panel of Figure 27–4. As we shall see now, the tight labor market produces an inflation that eventually eliminates the gap, though perhaps in a slow and painful way. Let us see how this works.

If equilibrium GDP is above potential, jobs are plentiful and labor is in great demand. Although some workers are unemployed, this minimal unemployment

**Figure 27–4 RECESSIONARY AND INFLATIONARY GAPS REVISITED**

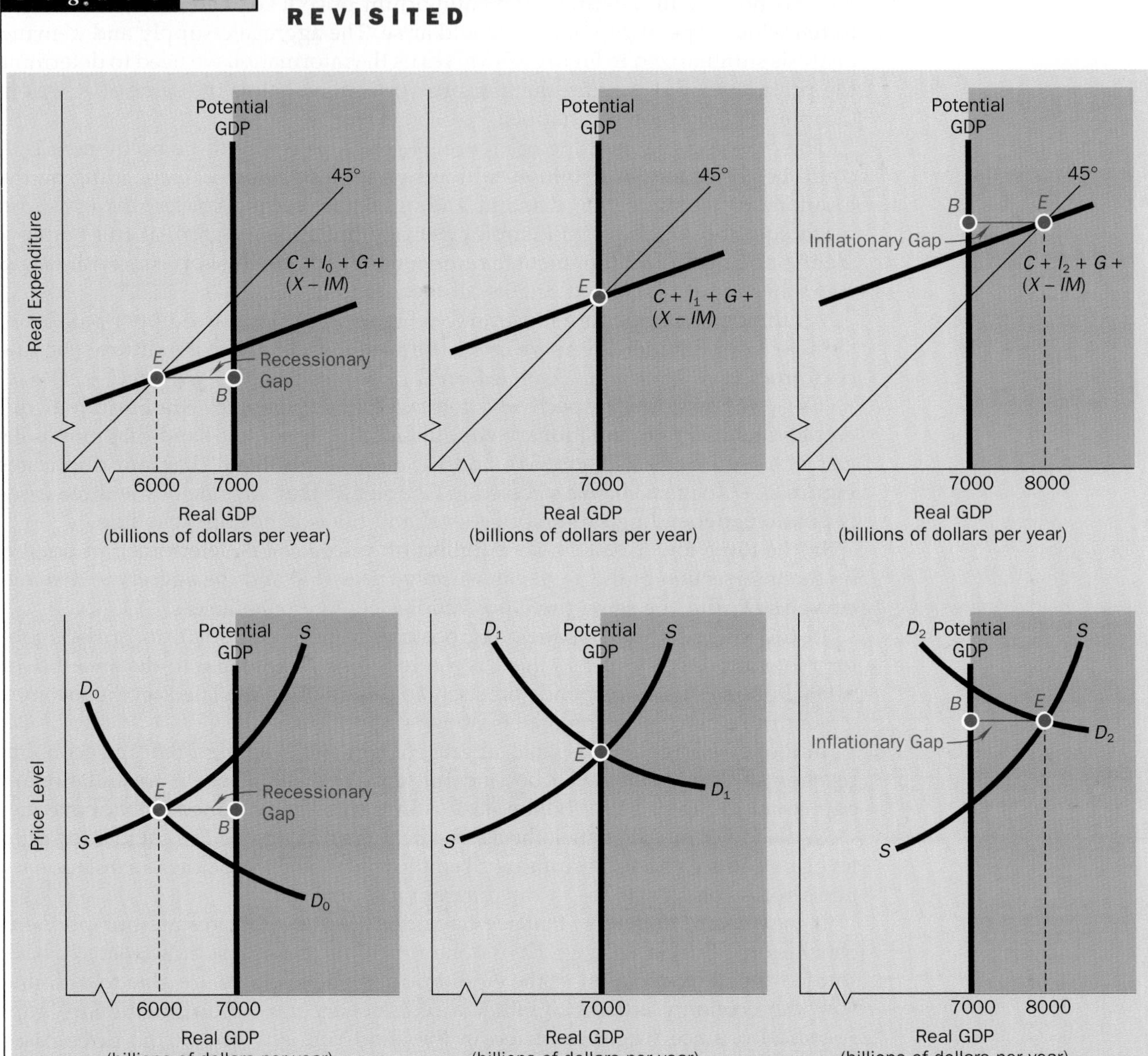


This diagram shows three possible types of equilibrium on two different diagrams. In the top row, income-expenditure diagrams from Chapter 25 are used to depict a recessionary gap, an equilibrium at full employment, and an inflationary gap. In the bottom row, these same three situations are shown on aggregate supply and demand diagrams. In each case, the aggregate supply curve is the same (*SS*), equilibrium occurs at point *E*, and full-employment GDP is \$7000 billion. In part (a), the aggregate demand curve $D_0D_0$ is relatively low, so that equilibrium falls below full employment. There is a recessionary gap measured by the distance *EB*, or \$1000 billion. In part (b), the aggregate demand curve $D_1D_1$ is higher, and equilibrium occurs precisely at full employment. There is no gap of either kind. In part (c), the aggregate demand curve $D_2D_2$ is so high that equilibrium occurs beyond full employment. There is an inflationary gap measured by the distance *BE*, or \$1000 billion.

is less than the frictional level—that is, less than the number we usually expect to be jobless because of moving, changing occupations, and so on. Many firms, on the other hand, are having trouble finding workers. They may even be having trouble hanging on to their current employees, as other firms try to lure them away with higher wages.

Such a situation is bound to lead to rising money wages, and rising wages add to business costs, thus shifting the aggregate supply curve inward. (Remember, an aggregate supply curve is drawn for a *given* money wage.) But as the aggregate supply curve shifts inward—eventually moving from $S_0S_0$ to $S_1S_1$ in Figure 27–5, for example—the size of the inflationary gap steadily declines. This is the process by which inflation erodes the inflationary gap, eventually leading the economy to an equilibrium at full employment (point *F* in Figure 27–5).

There is a straightforward way of looking at the economics that underlies the self-correcting process. The inflation problem arises because buyers are demanding more output than the economy is capable of producing at normal operating rates. To paraphrase an old cliché, there is too much demand chasing too little supply. Naturally, such an environment encourages price hikes. Rising prices eat away at the purchasing power of consumers' wealth, forcing them to cut back on consumption, as explained in Chapter 24. In addition, exports fall and imports rise, as explained in Chapter 25. Eventually, aggregate quantity demanded is scaled down to the economy's capacity to produce; and, at this point, the self-correcting process stops. That, in essence, is the unhappy process by which the economy cures itself of the problem of excessive aggregate demand.

One caveat should be mentioned. The conclusion that an inflationary gap sows the seeds of its own destruction holds *only in the absence of additional forces propelling the aggregate demand curve outward*. But in Chapter 26 we have already encountered

**Figure 27–5** **THE ELIMINATION OF AN INFLATIONARY GAP**

When the aggregate supply curve is $S_0S_0$ and the aggregate demand curve is *DD*, the economy will initially reach equilibrium (point *E*) with an inflationary gap. The resulting inflation of wages will push the supply curve inward until it has shifted to the position indicated by curve $S_1S_1$. Here, with equilibrium at point *F*, the economy is at normal full employment. But, during the adjustment period from *E* to *F*, there will have been inflation.

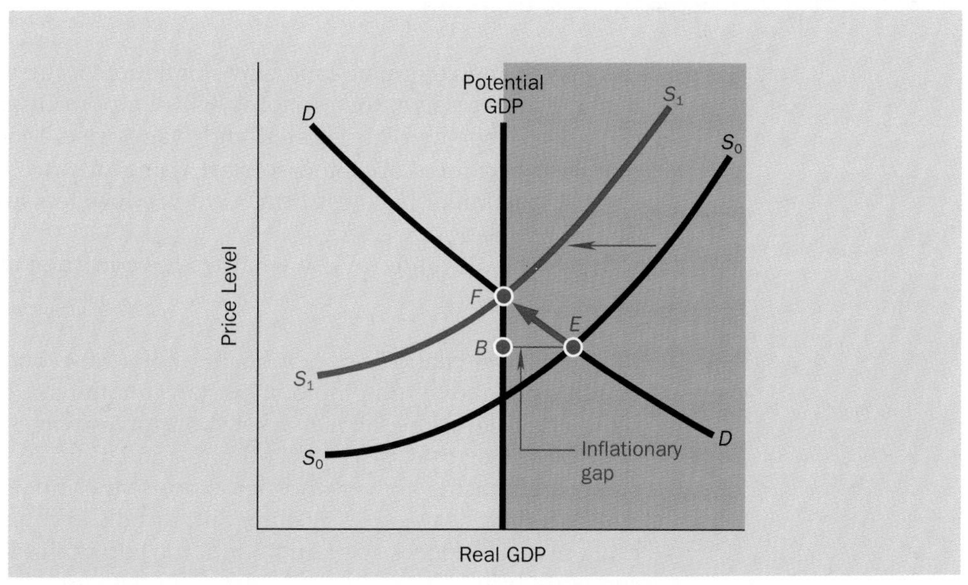

several forces that might shift the aggregate demand curve outward. As you can see by manipulating the aggregate demand–aggregate supply diagram, if aggregate demand is shifting out at the same time that aggregate supply is shifting in, there will certainly be inflation, but the inflationary gap may not shrink. (Try this as an exercise, to make sure you understand how to use the apparatus.) So not all inflations come to a natural end.

## DEMAND INFLATION AND STAGFLATION

Simple as it is, this adjustment model teaches us a number of important lessons about inflation in the real world. First of all, Figure 27–5 reminds us that the real culprit in this particular inflation is excessive aggregate demand—relative to potential GDP. The aggregate demand curve is initially so high that it intersects the aggregate supply curve well beyond full employment. The resulting intense demand for workers pushes wages higher; and higher wages lead to higher prices. While aggregate demand in excess of potential GDP is not the only possible cause of inflation in the real world, it certainly is the cause in our example.

However, business managers and journalists may blame inflation on rising wages. In a superficial sense, of course, they are right, because higher wages do indeed lead firms to raise their prices. But in a deeper sense they are wrong. Both rising wages and rising prices are symptoms of an underlying malady: too much aggregate demand. Blaming labor for inflation in such a case is a bit like blaming high doctor bills for making you ill.

Second, we see that output falls while prices rise as the economy adjusts from point *E* to point *F* in Figure 27–5. This process thus provides our first (but not our last!) explanation of the phenomenon of **stagflation**. We see that:

**STAGFLATION** is inflation that occurs while the economy is growing slowly or having a recession.

A period of stagflation is part of the normal aftermath of a period of excessive aggregate demand.

It is easy enough to understand why stagflation occurs in this case. When aggregate demand is excessive, the economy will temporarily produce beyond its normal capacity. Labor markets tighten and wages rise. Machinery and raw materials may also become scarce and so start rising in price. Faced by higher costs, the natural reaction of business firms is to produce less and to charge a higher price. That is stagflation.

It may be useful to review what we have learned about inflationary gaps thus far.

If aggregate demand is exceptionally high, the economy may reach a short-run equilibrium above full employment (an inflationary gap). When this occurs, the tight situation in the labor market soon forces wages to rise. Since rising wages raise business costs, prices rise; there is inflation. As higher prices cut into consumer purchasing power and net exports, the inflationary gap begins to close. As the inflationary gap is closing, output falls and prices continue to rise; so the economy experiences stagflation until the gap is eliminated. At this point, a long-run equilibrium is established with a higher price level and with GDP equal to potential GDP.

## AN EXAMPLE FROM RECENT HISTORY: 1988 TO 1990

The stagflation that follows a period of excessive aggregate demand is, you will note, a rather benign form of the dreaded disease. After all, while output is falling, it nonetheless remains above potential GDP; and unemployment is low. Some observers think the U.S. economy experienced such a period between 1988 and 1990, when the unemployment rate dropped below many people's estimate of the full-employment rate and, indeed, inflation accelerated.

The long economic expansion that began at the very end of 1982 brought the unemployment rate down to 5.5 percent by mid 1988 and (briefly) to a 15-year low of 5 percent by March 1989. Most economists believe that 5 percent is below the full-employment unemployment rate, that is, that the U.S. economy had an inflationary gap in 1989. As the theory suggests, inflation began to accelerate—from 4.4 percent in 1988 to 4.6 percent in 1989 and 6.1 percent in 1990.

In the meantime, the economy was stagnating. Real GDP growth fell from 3.3 percent during 1988 to 1.6 percent in 1989 and −0.5 percent in 1990. Inflation was eating away at the inflationary gap, which was virtually gone by mid-1990, when the recession started. Yet inflation remained high through the early months of the recession. The U.S. economy was in the stagflation phase. In sum, the economy behaved more or less as our simple model suggests.

## ADJUSTING TO A RECESSIONARY GAP: DEFLATION OR UNEMPLOYMENT?

Let us now consider what can happen when the economy finds itself in equilibrium *below* full employment—that is, when there is a *recessionary* gap. This might be caused, for example, by inadequate consumer spending or by anemic investment spending. Figure 27–6 illustrates such a case and gives an impression of the economic situation inherited by President Clinton when he took office in January 1993.

You might expect that we could just run our previous analysis in reverse: High unemployment leads to falling wages; falling wages reduce business costs and shift the aggregate supply curve outward, so firms cut prices; falling wages and prices eliminate the recessionary gap by propping up aggregate quantity demanded; and full employment is restored. The economy moves smoothly from point *E* to point *F* in Figure 27–6. Very simple. But somewhat misleading in our modern economy.

Why is it misleading? Our brief review of the historical record in Chapter 22 showed that, while the economy may have operated like this long ago, it certainly does not work this way now. The history of the United States shows several examples of deflation before World War II but none since then. Not even the severe recession of 1981–1982, during which unemployment climbed above 10 percent, was able to force average prices and wages down—though it certainly slowed their rates of increase. Similarly, the recession of the early 1990s reduced inflation, but certainly did not bring deflation.

Exactly why wages and prices rarely fall in our modern economy has been a subject of intense and continuing controversy among economists for years.

Some economists emphasize institutional factors like minimum wage laws, union contracts, and a variety of government regulations that place legal floors

*Figure* 27–6 **THE ELIMINATION OF A RECESSIONARY GAP**

At point *E* there is a recessionary gap because the aggregate demand curve *DD* crosses the aggregate supply curve $S_0S_0$ below the level of potential GDP. If wages fall, the aggregate supply curve gradually shifts outward until it reaches the position indicated by supply curve $S_1S_1$. Here the economy has attained a full-employment equilibrium at point *F*. But if wages fall very slowly, the economy gets stuck with a recessionary gap and high unemployment for a long time.

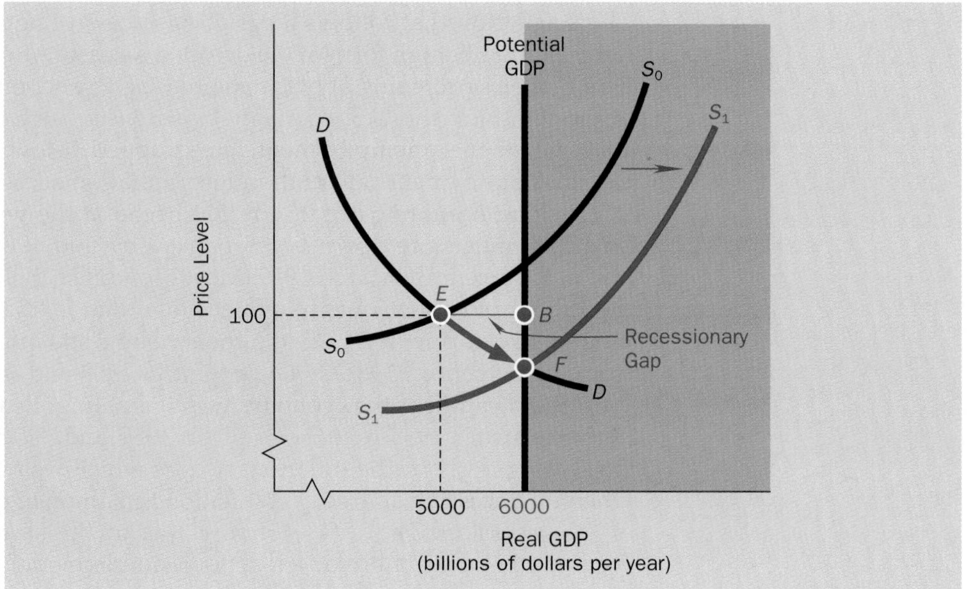


under particular wages and prices. Because most of these institutions are of relatively recent vintage, this theory successfully explains why wages and prices fall less frequently now than they did before World War II. However, only a small minority of the U.S. economy is subject to legal restraints on wage and price cutting. So it seems doubtful that legal restrictions can provide a complete explanation.

Other observers subscribe to the theory that workers have a profound psychological resistance to accepting a wage reduction. This theory certainly has the ring of truth. Think how you would react if your boss announced she was cutting your hourly wage rate. You might quit, or you might devote less care and attention to your job. If the boss suspects you will react this way, she may be reluctant to cut your wage. Nowadays, genuine wage reductions are rare enough to be newsworthy.

While no one doubts that wage cuts are bad for morale, the psychological theory has one major drawback. It fails to explain why the psychological resistance to wage cuts apparently started only after World War II. Until a satisfactory answer to this question is provided, many economists will remain skeptical.

A third explanation is based on a fact we emphasized in Chapter 22—that business cycles were less severe in the postwar period than they were in the prewar period. Because workers and firms came to believe that recessions would not turn into depressions, the argument goes, they may have decided to wait out the bad times rather than accept wage or price reductions that they would later regret.

Yet another theory is based on the old adage, "you get what you pay for." The idea is that workers differ in productivity, but that productivities of individual employees are hard to identify. Firms therefore worry that a general wage reduction will result in the loss of their best workers—since these are the ones who have the best opportunities elsewhere in the economy. Rather than take this chance, the argument goes, firms prefer to maintain high wages even in recessions.

There are other theories as well, none of which commands a clear majority of professional opinion. But, regardless of the cause, we may as well accept the fact that, in our modern economy, prices and wages generally fall only sluggishly when demand is weak.

The implications of this rigidity are quite serious, for a recessionary gap cannot cure itself without some deflation. And if wages and prices will not fall, recessionary gaps like EB in Figure 27–6 will linger for a long time. That is:

When aggregate demand is low, the economy may get stuck with a recessionary gap for a long time. If wages and prices fall very slowly, the economy will endure a prolonged period of production below potential GDP.

## DOES THE ECONOMY HAVE A SELF-CORRECTING MECHANISM?

Now a situation like this would, presumably, not last forever. As the recession lengthened, and perhaps deepened, more and more workers would be unable to find jobs at the prevailing high wages. Eventually their resistance to wage cuts, whatever the cause, would be worn down by their need to be employed.

Firms, too, would become increasingly willing to cut prices as the period of weak demand lasted longer and managers became convinced that the slump was not merely a temporary aberration. Prices and wages did, in fact, fall during the Great Depression of the 1930s. And they might fall again if a sufficiently drastic depression were allowed to occur. They certainly slowed markedly in the weak markets of the early 1990s.

However, nowadays political leaders of both parties believe it is folly to wait for falling wages and prices to eliminate a recessionary gap. They agree that *some* government action is both necessary and appropriate under recessionary conditions. But there is still vocal—and highly partisan!—debate over how much and what kind of intervention is warranted. One reason for the disagreement is that the **self-correcting mechanism** does operate—if only weakly—to cure recessionary gaps.

Consider recent history as an example. Even the weak, and long-delayed, recovery from the 1990–1991 recession was, after all, a recovery. After peaking at 7.8 percent in June 1992, the unemployment rate began a slow descent which brought it to 6.7 percent by the time this book went to press (September 1993). Meanwhile the inflation rate was falling from 6.1 percent in 1990 to 3.1 percent in 1991, 2.9% in 1992, and 2.8% in the first 8 months of 1993. Qualitatively, this is just the sort of behavior the theoretical model predicts. But it sure took a long time! Hence the practical policy question is: How long can we afford to wait?

Our overall conclusion about the economy's ability to right itself, then, seems to run something like this:

The economy does indeed have a self-correcting mechanism that tends to eliminate either unemployment or inflation. However, this mechanism works slowly and unevenly. In addition, its beneficial effects on either inflation or unemployment are sometimes swamped by strong forces (such as rapid increases or decreases in aggregate demand) pushing in the opposite direction. Thus the self-correcting mechanism cannot always be relied upon.

*At The* **FRONTIER**

## DOES GDP RETURN TO POTENTIAL?

The theory of aggregate supply and demand described in this chapter treats **potential GDP** as a fixed number at any point in time. Potential GDP may grow over time as the economy acquires more labor and capital. But it is not supposed to be affected by changes in *aggregate demand*. Thus, when a spurt in aggregate demand temporarily drives real GDP above its potential level, we expect actual GDP to gravitate back toward potential, as shown in Figure 27–5. Similarly, when a decline in aggregate demand pulls real GDP below potential, we expect a subsequent period of rapid growth to bring GDP back toward potential (see Figure 27–6).

This is the theory of the **self-correcting mechanism** to which most economists ascribe. However, some controversial recent research has cast doubt not only on this conventional view, but also on the entire concept of potential GDP. Since the debate is basically statistical, considerable technical sophistication is required to understand it. But the central issue is easily explained.

If there really is a self-correcting mechanism, we should see its imprint in actual data for the United States and other countries. Specifically, we should see that real GDP typically grows rapidly when it is below potential and slowly when it is above potential. For many years, this is in fact what economists thought they saw. After all, neither booms nor recessions last forever; they are both just memories in the end.

Or are they? It is precisely this "finding" that new research calls into question. When the statistical details are stripped away, the debate boils down to the following simple question: If real GDP spurts this year, should we raise our forecast of what real GDP is likely to be ten years from now?

The conventional view is that we should not. Because the self-correcting mechanism eventually returns real GDP to its potential level, the best guess we can make about GDP far in the future is always that it will be near potential. Transitory ups and downs in real GDP growth should not change the long-run forecast because they do not change the economy's long-run potential GDP.

The maverick view, which began to appear in scholarly journals in the late 1980s, is that today's growth rate leaves a lasting imprint on output. Proponents argue that a 1 percent rise in this year's real GDP should lead us to raise our forecast of real GDP ten years from now by *more than* 1 percent! For this to be true, a boom must raise potential GDP and a slump must lower it. But, if there is no tendency for the economy to return to any fixed level of potential GDP, the theory of the self-correcting mechanism goes out the window.

Which view is correct? The issue may seem easy to resolve. Just look to see whether real GDP does in fact return to its previous path. Economists are trying to do precisely that, but the statistical problem is harder than it seems. To learn about the consequences of *current* events for events ten years into the future, you need data covering a very long span of time. There are data on U.S. GDP dating back to about the Civil War; but they are much less accurate than modern data. Besides, very old data are relevant to the present only if the economy's self-correcting mechanism has not changed much over time. But no one really believes that is so.

So the controversy continues in the pages of scientific journals and in unpublished papers circulated by mail. However, one thing *has* changed already at the research frontier. Complacent acceptance of the old theory is gone. Research economists are now asking two fundamental questions. Are the new statistical findings correct? And, if they are, what theory will explain them?

## STAGFLATION FROM SUPPLY SHIFTS

We have so far encountered one type of stagflation in this chapter—the stagflation that follows in the aftermath of an inflationary boom. However, that is not what happened in the more serious stagflationary episodes of the 1970s and early 1980s. What was going on during those years that caused so much unemployment and inflation at the same time? What were the causes of this more virulent type of stagflation? Several things, but the principal villain was the rising price of energy.

In 1973 the Organization of Petroleum Exporting Countries (OPEC) reached a collusive agreement that quadrupled the price of crude oil. American consumers found the prices of gasoline and home heating fuels increasing sharply. American businesses found that one important input to the production process—energy—rose drastically in price, thus increasing the costs of doing business. OPEC struck again in 1979–1980, this time doubling the price of oil. Then the same thing happened a third time, albeit on a smaller scale, when Iraq invaded Kuwait in 1990.

Higher energy prices, we observed earlier, make the economy's aggregate supply curve shift inward in the manner shown in Figure 27–2 (page 671). If the aggregate supply curve shifts inward, as it surely did in 1973–1974, 1979–1980, and 1990, production will be reduced. And in order to reduce demand to the available supply, prices will have to rise. The result is the worst of both worlds: falling production and rising prices.

This conclusion is shown graphically in Figure 27–7, which superimposes an aggregate demand curve, *DD*, on the two aggregate supply curves of Figure 27–2.

**Figure 27–7** **STAGFLATION FROM AN ADVERSE SHIFT IN AGGREGATE SUPPLY**

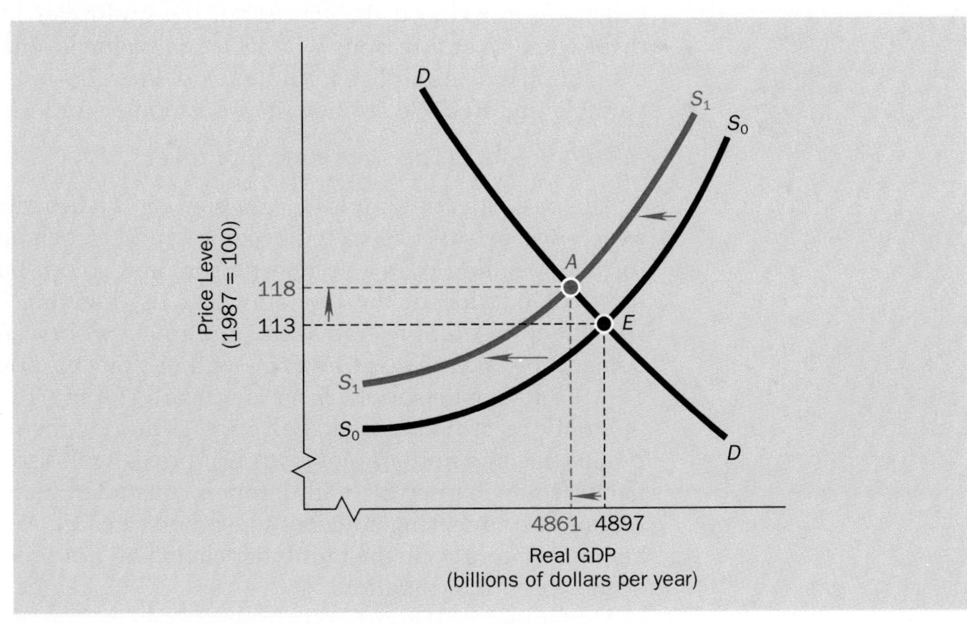


This diagram illustrates how stagflation arises if the aggregate supply curve shifts inward to the left (from $S_0S_0$ to $S_1S_1$). If the aggregate demand curve does not change, equilibrium moves from point *E* to point *A*. Output falls as prices rise, which is what we mean by stagflation. The diagram indicates roughly what happened in the United States during 1990–1991, when higher energy prices caused stagflation around the time of the Persian Gulf War.

The economy's equilibrium shifts upward to the left, from point $E$ to point $A$. Thus, output falls while prices rise. In brief:

Stagflation is the typical result of adverse supply shifts.

The numbers used in Figure 27–7 are roughly indicative of what happened in the United States between 1990 (represented by supply curve $S_0S_0$ and point $E$) and 1991 (represented by supply curve $S_1S_1$ and point $A$). Real GDP, in 1987 prices, fell by $36 billion, while the price level rose about 4 percent.

The stories of the 1973–1975 and 1979–1980 periods were similar, but much more severe. After each "energy shock," inflation soared and the economy weakened. Thus the general lesson to be learned from the U.S. experience with supply shocks is both clear and important:

The typical results of an adverse supply shock are a fall in output and an acceleration in inflation. This is one reason why the world economy was plagued by stagflation in the mid-1970s and early 1980s. And it can happen again if another series of supply-reducing events takes place.

Of course, supply shifts can work in the other direction as well. The world oil market weakened markedly in 1986, and oil prices plummeted. Just after the Persian Gulf War, the price of oil tumbled by about 50 percent. Both of these favorable supply shocks stimulated U.S. economic growth somewhat and curbed inflation. In 1986, the Consumer Price Index actually fell for a few months! The aggregate supply curve was shifting outward.

Favorable supply shocks tend to push output up and reduce inflation.

## INFLATION AND THE MULTIPLIER

When we introduced the concept of the multiplier in Chapter 26, we said that there were several reasons why its actual value is smaller than suggested by the oversimplified multiplier formula. One emerged in an appendix to Chapter 26: variable imports. We are now in a position to understand the second:

Inflation reduces the size of the multiplier.

The basic idea is simple. In Chapter 26, we described a multiplier process in which one person's spending becomes another person's income, which leads to further spending by the second person, and so on. But this story is confined to the demand side of the economy. Let us therefore consider what is likely to happen on the supply side as the multiplier process unfolds. Will the additional demand be taken care of by firms without raising prices?

If the aggregate supply curve is upward sloping, the answer is no; more goods will only be provided at higher prices. Thus, as the multiplier chain progresses, pulling income and employment up, prices will also be rising. And this, as we know from Chapter 24, will dampen consumer spending because rising prices reduce the purchasing power of consumers' wealth. And it will also reduce exports and raise imports. So the multiplier chain will not proceed as far as it would have in the absence of inflation.

How much inflation results from the rise in demand? How much of the multiplier chain is cut off by inflation? The answers depend on the slope of the economy's aggregate supply curve.

For a concrete example of the analysis, let us return to the $200 billion increase in investment spending used in Chapter 26. As we learned there (see especially page 659), $200 billion in additional investment spending eventually leads—through the multiplier process—to *a horizontal shift of $800 billion in the aggregate demand curve*. But to know the actual quantity that will ultimately be produced, and the actual price level, we must bring the aggregate supply curve into the picture.

Figure 27–8 does this. Here we show the $800 billion horizontal shift of the aggregate demand curve, from $D_0D_0$ to $D_1D_1$, that is derived from the oversimplified multiplier formula (which ignores rising prices). The aggregate supply curve, *SS*, then tells us how this expansion of demand is apportioned between higher output and higher prices. We see that as the economy's equilibrium moves from point $E_0$ to point $E_1$, real GDP does not rise by $800 billion. Instead, prices rise, which, as we know, tends to cancel out part of the rise in quantity demanded. So output increases only from $6000 billion to $6600 billion—an increase of $600 billion. Thus, in our example, inflation reduces the multiplier from $800/$200 = 4 to $600/$200 = 3. In general:

As long as the aggregate supply curve is upward sloping, any increase in aggregate demand will push up the price level. This, in turn, will drain off some of the higher real demand by eroding the purchasing power of consumer wealth and by reducing net exports. Thus, inflation reduces the value of the multiplier below that suggested by the oversimplified formula.

**Figure 27–8** **INFLATION AND THE MULTIPLIER**

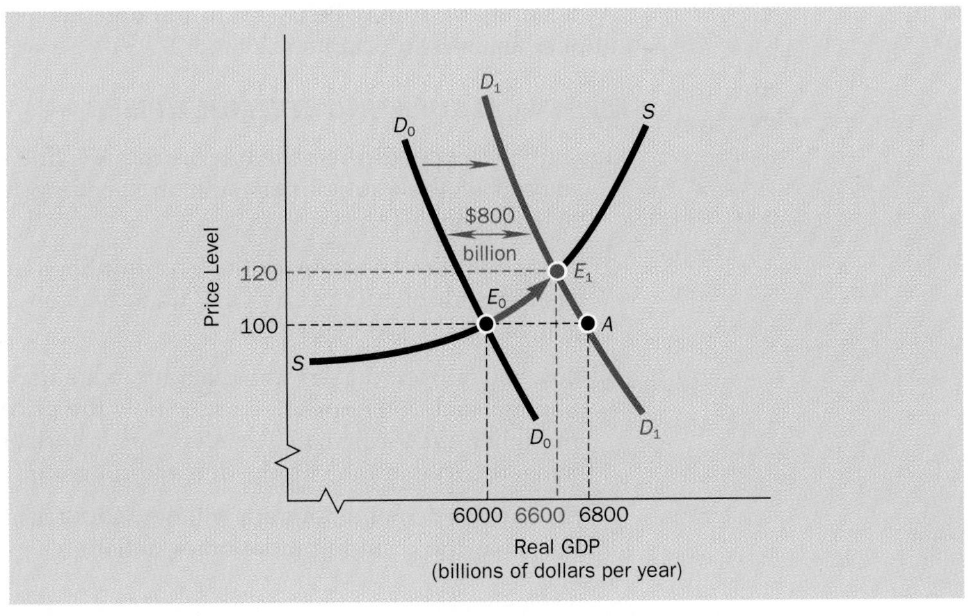


This figure illustrates the complete analysis of the multiplier, including the effect of inflation. The simple multiplier of Chapter 26, which ignored changes in the price level, appears here as a *horizontal* shift of $800 billion in the aggregate demand curve, meaning that the multiplier would be $800/$200 = 4 if prices did not rise. However, when aggregate demand shifts from $D_0D_0$ to $D_1D_1$, prices rise. In the diagram, the price level increases from 100 to 120 or by 20 percent. Consequently, equilibrium real income increases from $6000 billion to only $6600 billion—for a rise of $600 billion, or a multiplier of $600/$200 = 3.

Notice also that the price level in this example has been pushed up (from 100 to 120, or 20 percent) by the rise in investment demand. This, too, is a general result:

As long as the aggregate supply curve is upward sloping, any outward shift of the aggregate demand curve will cause some rise in prices.

The economic behavior behind these results certainly cannot be considered surprising. Firms faced with large increases in quantity demanded at their original prices respond to these changed circumstances in two natural ways: they raise production (so GDP rises), and they raise prices (so the price level rises). But this rise in the price level reduces the purchasing power of the bank accounts and bonds held by consumers, and they too react in the natural way: they cut down on their spending. Such a reaction amounts to a movement *along* aggregate demand curve $D_1D_1$ in Figure 27–8 from point $A$ to point $E_1$.

Higher prices thus play their usual dual role in a market economy: they encourage suppliers to produce more, and they encourage demanders to consume less. In this way, equilibrium is reestablished at higher levels of output and higher prices through the process of inflation.

Figure 27–8 also shows us exactly where the oversimplified multiplier formula goes wrong. By ignoring the effects of the higher price level, the oversimplified formula erroneously supposes that the economy moves horizontally from point $E_0$ to point $A$. As the diagram clearly shows, output does not actually rise this much. Output *would* rise this much only if the aggregate supply curve were horizontal, meaning that output can rise indefinitely without any increase in price. (Verify this for yourself by penciling in an imaginary horizontal aggregate supply curve through points $E_0$ and $A$ in Figure 27–8.) That is, the oversimplified multiplier formula tacitly assumes that the aggregate supply curve is horizontal. Normally, this is an unrealistic assumption, which is one reason why the oversimplified formula exaggerates the size of the multiplier.

As a summary, it may be useful to put together what we have learned about multiplier analysis in Chapters 26 and 27.

### *STEPS IN CALCULATING THE MULTIPLIER*

1. Shift the expenditure schedule in the 45° line diagram vertically by the amount of the autonomous shift in spending (as, for example, in Figure 26–1 on page 649).

2. Use the 45° line diagram, or the oversimplified multiplier formula, to calculate the multiplier effect on GDP that *would* occur *if* the price level did not change (again, see Figure 26–1).

3. Now move from the 45° line diagram to an aggregate supply and demand diagram such as Figure 27–8 to see how the price level will react. Enter the multiplier effect calculated in step 2 as a horizontal shift of the aggregate demand curve in the supply–demand diagram.

4. The supply–demand diagram will now show the actual effect on real output as well as the resulting inflation or deflation.[2]

[2]The change in the price level reacts back on the 45° diagram. See Review Question 11 at the end of the chapter.

## A ROLE FOR STABILIZATION POLICY

Chapter 25 emphasized the volatility of investment spending, and Chapter 26 noted that changes in investment have multiplier effects on aggregate demand. This chapter took the next step by showing how shifts in the aggregate demand curve cause fluctuations in both real GDP growth and inflation—fluctuations that are widely decried as undesirable. It also suggested that the economy's self-correcting mechanism works, but slowly, thereby leaving room for government stabilization policy to improve the workings of the free market. Can the government really do this? If so, how? These are the questions for Part 7.

## *Summary*

1. The economy's **aggregate supply curve** relates the quantity of goods and services that will be supplied to the price level. It normally slopes upward to the right because the costs of labor and other inputs are relatively fixed in the short run, meaning that higher selling prices make input costs relatively "cheaper" and therefore encourage greater production.
2. The position of the aggregate supply curve can be shifted by changes in money wage rates, prices of other inputs, technology, or quantities or qualities of labor and capital.
3. The aggregate supply curve normally gets steeper as output increases. This means that, as output and capacity utilization rise, any given increase in aggregate demand leads to more inflation and less growth of real output.
4. The **equilibrium price level** and the **equilibrium level of real GDP** are jointly determined by the intersection of the economy's aggregate supply and aggregate demand schedules. This intersection may come at full employment, below full employment (a recessionary gap), or above full employment (an inflationary gap).
5. If there is an **inflationary gap**, the economy has a mechanism that erodes the gap through a process of inflation. Specifically, unusually strong job prospects push wages up, which shifts the aggregate supply curve to the left and reduces the inflationary gap.
6. One consequence of this **self-correcting mechanism** is that, if a surge in aggregate demand opens up an inflationary gap, part of the economy's natural adjustment to this event will be a period of stagflation; that is, a period in which prices are rising while output is falling.
7. The economy also has a self-correcting mechanism that erodes a **recessionary gap**. This mechanism works in much the same way as the inflationary-gap mechanism: a weak labor market reduces wages, thereby shifting the aggregate supply curve outward. But this happens only slowly.
8. An inward shift of the aggregate supply curve will cause output to fall while prices rise; that is, it will cause **stagflation**. Among the events that have caused such a shift are abrupt increases in the price of foreign oil.
9. Adverse supply shifts like this plagued our economy when oil prices skyrocketed in 1973–1974, 1979–1980, and again in 1990, leading to stagflation each time.
10. Among the reasons why the oversimplified multiplier formula is wrong is the fact that it ignores any inflation that may be caused by an increase in aggregate demand. Such **inflation decreases the multiplier** by reducing both consumer spending and net exports.

## *Key Concepts and Terms*

Aggregate supply curve
Productivity
Equilibrium of real GDP and the price level
Inflationary gap
Self-correcting mechanism
Stagflation
Recessionary gap
Inflation and the multiplier

## *Questions for Review*

1. In an economy with the following aggregate demand and aggregate supply schedules, find the equilibrium levels of real output and the price level. Graph your solution. If full employment comes at $2800 billion, is there an inflationary or a recessionary gap?

| AGGREGATE QUANTITY DEMANDED (in billions) | PRICE LEVEL | AGGREGATE QUANTITY SUPPLIED (in billions) |
|---|---|---|
| 3200 | 85 | 2600 |
| 3150 | 90 | 2650 |
| 3000 | 95 | 2800 |
| 2900 | 110 | 2900 |
| 2800 | 130 | 3000 |

2. Suppose a worker receives a wage of $15 per hour. Compute the real wage (money wage deflated by the price index) corresponding to each of the following possible price levels: 85, 95, 100, 110, 120. What do you notice about the relationship between the real wage and the price level? Relate this to the slope of the aggregate supply curve.

3. In 1989, capacity utilization averaged 84 percent. In 1992, it averaged 80 percent. In which year do you think the economy found itself on a steeper portion of its aggregate supply curve? Explain why.

4. Explain why a decrease in the price of foreign oil shifts the aggregate supply curve outward to the right. What are the consequences of such a shift?

5. Comment on the following statement: "Inflationary and recessionary gaps are nothing to worry about because the economy has a built-in mechanism that cures either type of gap automatically."

6. Give *two* different explanations of how the economy can suffer from stagflation.

7. Why do you think wages tend to be rigid in the downward direction?

8. Add the following aggregate supply and demand schedules to the example in Question 3 of Chapter 25 (page 640) to see how inflation affects the multiplier.

| (1) PRICE LEVEL | (2) AGGREGATE DEMAND (when investment is $120) | (3) AGGREGATE DEMAND (when investment is $130) | (4) AGGREGATE SUPPLY |
|---|---|---|---|
| 90 | $1930 | $2030 | $1830 |
| 95 | 1915 | 2015 | 1865 |
| 100 | 1900 | 2000 | 1900 |
| 105 | 1885 | 1985 | 1935 |
| 110 | 1870 | 1970 | 1970 |
| 115 | 1855 | 1955 | 2005 |

Draw these schedules on a piece of graph paper. Then:

a. Notice that the difference between columns 2 and 3 (the aggregate demand schedule at two different levels of investment) is always $100. Discuss how this relates to your answer in the previous chapter.

b. Find the equilibrium GDP and the equilibrium price level both before and after the increase in investment. What is the value of the multiplier?

9. Explain in words why rising prices reduce the multiplier effect of an autonomous increase in aggregate demand.

10. Use an aggregate supply and demand diagram to show that multiplier effects are smaller when the aggregate supply curve is steeper. Which case gives rise to more inflation—the steep aggregate supply curve or the flat one? What happens to the multiplier if the aggregate supply curve is vertical?

11. (More difficult) Assume that investment spending rises. Draw a set of graphs illustrating the Steps in Calculating the Multiplier listed on page 686. Your aggregate supply and demand diagram from steps 3 and 4 will show a change in the price level. How would this change in the price level react back on the 45° line diagram you used in step 1? In view of this, use the 45° line diagram to show that inflation reduces the multiplier.

# PART VII

# Fiscal and Monetary Policy

*Chapter* 28

# MANAGING AGGREGATE DEMAND: FISCAL POLICY

*Next, let us turn to the problems of our fiscal policy. Here the myths are legion and the truth hard to find.*

**JOHN F. KENNEDY**

In the model of the economy constructed in Part 6, the government played an entirely passive role. It did a fixed amount of spending and collected a fixed amount of taxes, and that was it. We concluded from this analysis that such an economy has a very weak tendency to move toward high employment with low inflation. Furthermore, we hinted in Chapter 22 that well-designed government policies might improve the economy's performance. It is now time to pick up that hint—and to learn about some of the difficulties the government must overcome if it is to conduct a successful stabilization policy. ¶ Traditionally, the government has used its taxing and spending powers to influence the demand side of the economy. So this chapter begins there, in the domain of conventional **fiscal policy**. The next two chapters take up the government's other main tool for managing aggregate demand: *monetary policy*. ¶ We start by allowing taxes to depend on income—as they do in the real world—and then considering the multipliers for tax policy. As we shall see, none of this requires any fundamental change in the way we analyze the determination of GDP and the price level. However, it does reduce the size of the multiplier.

As Presidents Reagan, Bush, and Clinton have all realized, the effects of tax policy are not limited to aggregate *demand*. Taxes also affect aggregate *supply*. So the last parts of the chapter examine both the Reagan-Bush and Clinton versions of "supply-side economics."

The government's **FISCAL POLICY** is its plan for spending and taxation. It is designed to steer aggregate demand in some desired direction.

## ISSUE: SHOULD FISCAL POLICY BE USED TO STIMULATE THE ECONOMY?

It is widely believed that the weak economy cost President George Bush the 1992 election. That very same weakness posed a dilemma for the incoming Clinton administration. Should it try to stimulate economic activity by using the tools of fiscal policy, that is, by raising government spending or cutting taxes? Or should it instead try to reduce the large government budget deficit, which everyone acknowledged to be a problem? The two objectives are in conflict because government policy stimulates the economy by raising spending or cutting taxes but reduces the deficit by raising taxes or cutting spending.

The Clinton administration's answer gave primacy to deficit reduction. This chapter begins by describing the principles that policymakers should—and sometimes do!—use to answer such questions. But we will have much more to say about the budget deficit in Chapter 32.

# INCOME TAXES AND THE CONSUMPTION SCHEDULE

**FIXED TAXES** are tax taxes that do not vary with the level of GDP.

**VARIABLE TAXES** are taxes that do vary with the level of GDP.

Before attempting to address such difficult policy questions, we must think a little harder about how to integrate taxes into our model of income determination. We do this in stages. First, we contrast **fixed taxes**, which are the only kind we have considered so far, with **variable taxes**, which are much more important in practice. Then we will see how each type of tax affects income determination and the multiplier.

Most of the taxes collected by the federal, state, and local governments vary with the level of GDP. In some cases, the reason is obvious: *personal* and *corporate income tax* collections, for example, depend on how much income there is to be taxed. But even *sales tax* receipts depend indirectly on GDP because consumer spending is higher when GDP is higher. On the other hand, there are some taxes—such as property taxes levied by local governments—that do not vary with GDP. Therefore, we will call the first kind of tax *variable taxes* and the second kind *fixed taxes*.

Why is this distinction important? Remember that gross domestic product (GDP) is the difference between disposable income ($DI$) and taxes ($T$):

$$Y = DI - T.$$

Thus when taxes are increased, disposable income falls—and hence so does consumption—*even if GDP is unchanged*. As a result:

An increase in taxes shifts the consumption schedule in our 45° line diagram downward. Similarly, a reduction in taxes shifts the consumption schedule upward.

But precisely how the consumption schedule shifts depends on the nature of the tax change. If a fixed tax is increased, the resulting decrease in disposable income is the *same* regardless of the level of GDP; hence the decline in consumer spending is the same. In a word, the *C* schedule shifts downward in a parallel manner, as shown in Figure 28–1(a).

But more often than not tax policy changes disposable income by amounts that depend on the level of income, normally being larger at high income levels than at low ones. This is true, for example, whenever Congress varies the bracket rates in the personal income tax code, as it did in 1993. Since an increase in tax rates decreases disposable income more when GDP is higher, the downward shift of the *C* schedule is sharper at high income levels than at low ones. Figure 28–1(b) illustrates how this type of tax policy shifts the consumption schedule.

The two parts of Figure 28–1, then, explain the first reason why the distinction between fixed and variable taxes is important. Figure 28–2 illustrates the second. Here we show two consumption lines, $C_1$ and $C_2$. $C_1$ is the consumption schedule used in previous chapters; it is constructed on the assumption that taxes are fixed at $1200 billion regardless of GDP. $C_2$ depicts a more realistic case in which tax collections are 20% percent of GDP. You will notice that $C_2$ is flatter than $C_1$. This is no accident. In fact:

Variable taxes such as the income tax flatten the consumption schedule in a 45° line diagram.

It is easy to understand why, and Table 28–1 helps us do so. It shows in column 1 alternative values of GDP ranging from $4.5 trillion to $7.5 trillion. Column 2 then indicates that taxes are always one-fifth of this amount. Column 3 subtracts column 2 from column 1 to arrive at disposable income (*DI*). Column 4 then gives the amount of consumer spending corresponding to each level of *DI*. The consumption schedule we need for our 45° line is therefore found in columns 1 and 4.

Notice that for each $500 billion increase in GDP (say, from $5500 billion to $6000 billion), consumer spending rises by $300 billion (from $3600 billion to $3900 billion). Thus the slope of line $C_2$ in Figure 28–2 is $300/$500 = 0.6. But, if you look back at any of the tables in Chapter 26, you will find that consumption

**Figure 28–1** **HOW TAX POLICY SHIFTS THE CONSUMPTION SCHEDULE**

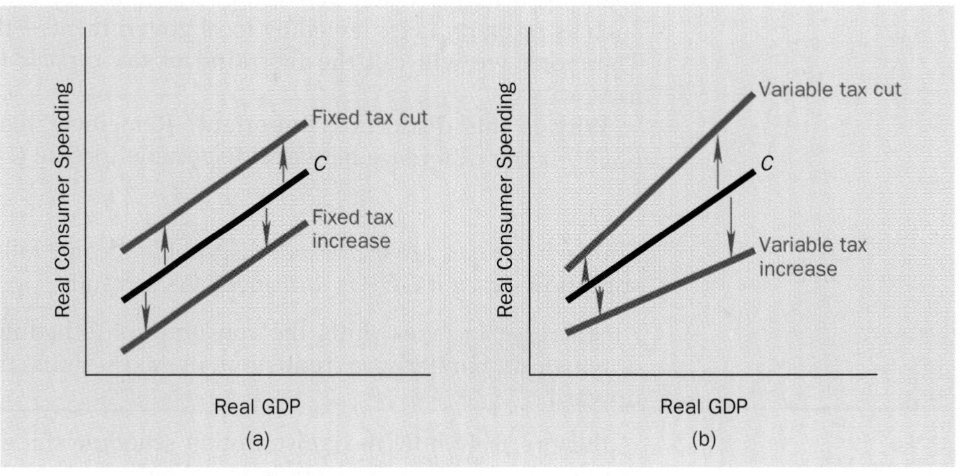


Because consumption depends on disposable income, not GDP, any change in taxes will shift the consumption schedule relating consumption to GDP. Part (a) shows how the curve shifts for changes in fixed taxes. Part (b) shows how the *C* curve shifts if the tax cut (or tax increase) is larger at high incomes than at low incomes.

Figure 28–2 **THE CONSUMPTION SCHEDULE WITH FIXED AND VARIABLE TAXES**

Line $C_1$ is the consumption schedule used in earlier chapters, when taxes were taken to be fixed. If, instead, tax receipts rise with GDP, the consumption schedule is flatter—see line $C_2$.

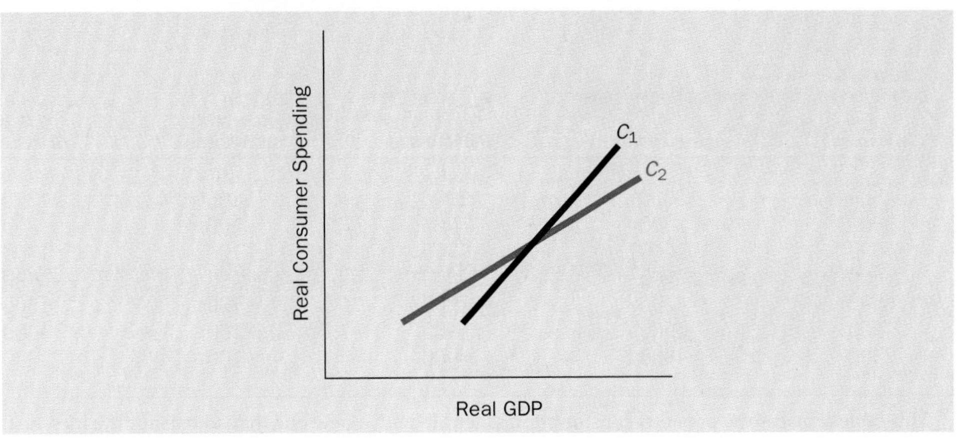


there rose by \$300 billion each time GDP increased \$400 billion—making the slope \$300/\$400 = 0.75. (See the steeper line $C_1$ in Figure 28–2.)

All this sounds terribly mechanical, but the economic reasoning behind it is straightforward. When taxes are fixed, as in schedule $C_1$, each additional dollar of GDP raises disposable income (*DI*) by \$1. Consumer spending then rises by \$1 times the marginal propensity to consume (MPC), which is 0.75 in our example. Hence each additional dollar of GDP leads to 75¢ more spending. But when taxes vary with income, each additional dollar of GDP raises *DI* by less than \$1 because the government takes a share in taxes. In our example, taxes are 20 percent of GDP, so each additional \$1 of GDP leads to 80¢ more disposable income. With an MPC of 0.75, that means that spending rises 60¢ (75 percent of 80¢) each time GDP rises by \$1. That is why the slope of the line $C_2$ in Figure 28–2 is only 0.6, instead of 0.75.

Table 28–1 **THE EFFECTS OF AN INCOME TAX ON THE CONSUMPTION SCHEDULE**

| (1) GROSS DOMESTIC PRODUCT (billions) | (2) TAXES (billions) | (3) DISPOSABLE INCOME (GDP minus taxes) (billions) | (4) CONSUMPTION (billions) |
|---|---|---|---|
| \$4500 | \$900 | \$3600 | \$3000 |
| 5000 | 1000 | 4000 | 3300 |
| 5500 | 1100 | 4400 | 3600 |
| 6000 | 1200 | 4800 | 3900 |
| 6500 | 1300 | 5200 | 4200 |
| 7000 | 1400 | 5600 | 4500 |
| 7500 | 1500 | 6000 | 4800 |

This table shows how an income tax lowers the slope of the consumption schedule (column 4) in a concrete example. For every \$500 billion increase in GDP, consumption rises by \$300 billion in this example (compare columns 1 and 4). So the slope of the $C_2$ line in Figure 28–2 is \$300/\$500 = 0.6. In earlier chapters, the slope of the consumption schedule (line $C_1$ in Figure 28–2) was \$300/\$400 = 0.75.

**Table 28–2 TOTAL EXPENDITURE SCHEDULE WITH A 20 PERCENT INCOME TAX**

| (1) GROSS DOMESTIC $Y$ (billions) | (2) CONSUMPTION $C$ (billions) | (3) INVESTMENT $I$ (billions) | (4) NET EXPORTS $(X - IM)$ (billions) | (5) GOVERNMENT PURCHASES $G$ (billions) | (6) TOTAL EXPENDITURE $C + I + G + (X - IM)$ (billions) |
|---|---|---|---|---|---|
| $4500 | $3000 | $900 | −$100 | $1300 | $5100 |
| 5000 | 3300 | 900 | −100 | 1300 | 5400 |
| 5500 | 3600 | 900 | −100 | 1300 | 5700 |
| 6000 | 3900 | 900 | −100 | 1300 | 6000 |
| 6500 | 4200 | 900 | −100 | 1300 | 6300 |
| 7000 | 4500 | 900 | −100 | 1300 | 6600 |
| 7500 | 4800 | 900 | −100 | 1300 | 6900 |

This table replaces the previous consumption schedule with a new one that adjusts for the income tax (as shown in Table 28–1) and shows that the equilibrium level of income is still $6000 billion.

Table 28–2 and Figure 28–3 take the next step by replacing the old consumption schedule with this new one in both the tabular presentation of income determination and the 45° line diagram. We see immediately that the equilibrium level of GDP is at point *E*. Here, gross domestic product is $6000 billion, consumption is $3900 billion, investment is $900 billion, net exports are −$100 billion, and government purchases are $1300 billion. As we know, full employment may occur above or below $Y = \$6000$ billion. If below, there is an inflationary gap. Prices probably will start to rise, pulling the expenditure schedule down and reducing equilibrium GDP. If above, there is a recessionary gap, and history suggests that prices will fall only slowly. In the interim, there will be a period of high unemployment.

In short, once we adjust the expenditure schedule to include the effects of variable taxes, the determination of national income proceeds exactly as before. The effects of government spending and taxation, therefore, are fairly straightforward and can be summarized as follows:

Government purchases of goods and services add to total spending directly through the $G$ component of $C + I + G + (X - IM)$. Taxes indirectly reduce total spending by lowering disposable income and thus reduce the $C$ component of $C + I + G + (X - IM)$. On balance, then, the government's actions may raise or lower the equilibrium level of GDP, depending on how much spending and taxing it does.

However, there is more to the story. As we will see now:

The multiplier is smaller in the presence of an income tax.

Let us see why.

## THE MULTIPLIER REVISITED

We learned in Chapter 26 that the multiplier works through a chain of spending and respending, as one person's expenditure becomes another's income. But, when there is an income tax, some of the additional income leaks out of the circular flow at each stage. Specifically, if the income tax rate is 20 percent, when Generous Motors spends \$1 million on salaries, workers actually receive only \$800,000 in *after-tax* (that is, disposable) income. If workers spend 75 percent of this amount (because the MPC is 0.75), spending in the next round will be only \$600,000. Notice that this is only *60 percent* of the original expenditure, not *75 percent* as in our earlier example—just as we observed in the last section.

Thus the multiplier chain for each original dollar of spending shrinks from

$$1 + 0.75 + (0.75)^2 + (0.75)^3 + \ldots = \frac{1}{1 - 0.75} = \frac{1}{0.25} = 4$$

to

$$1 + 0.6 + (0.6)^2 + (0.6)^3 + \ldots = \frac{1}{1 - 0.6} = \frac{1}{0.4} = 2\tfrac{1}{2}.$$

This is clearly a large reduction in the multiplier. We thus have a third reason why the oversimplified multiplier formula of Chapter 26 gives an exaggerated impression of the size of the multiplier:

*REASONS WHY THE OVERSIMPLIFIED MULTIPLIER FORMULA IS WRONG*

1. It ignores variable imports, which serve to reduce the size of the multiplier.
2. It ignores price-level changes, which also reduce the multiplier.
3. It ignores income taxes, which serve to reduce the size of the multiplier.

The last of these three reasons is very important in practice.

Figure 28–3 **INCOME DETERMINATION WITH A VARIABLE INCOME TAX**

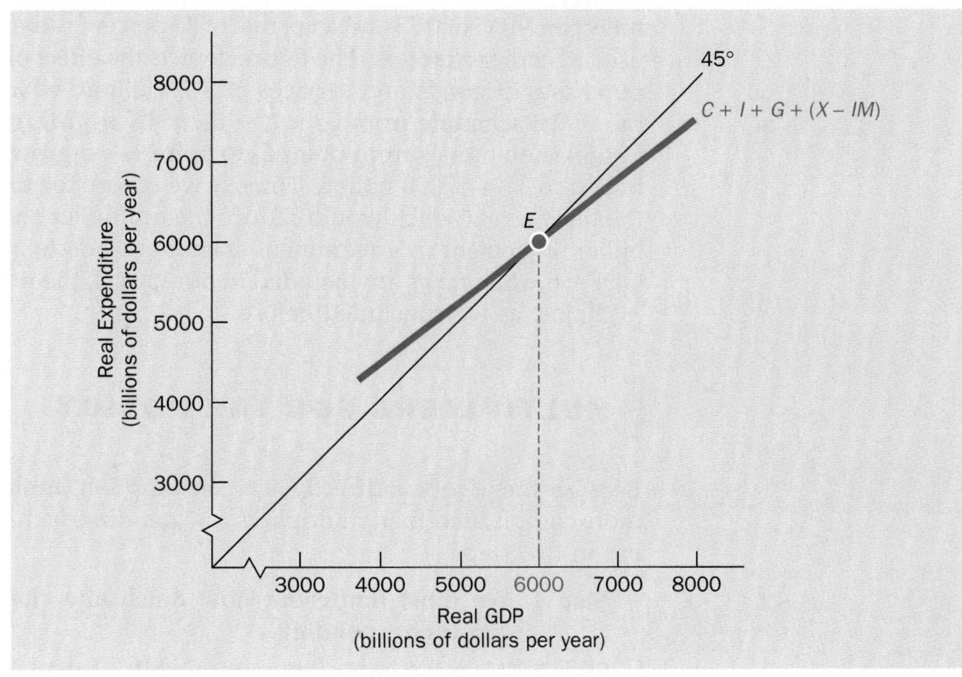


This diagram adds a 20 percent income tax to the model economy portrayed in earlier chapters. Because of this, the $C + I + G + (X - IM)$ schedule is flatter. But otherwise things look just as before. In particular, equilibrium is at point $E$, where the $C + I + G + (X - IM)$ schedule crosses the 45° line. Thus equilibrium GDP is \$6000 billion.

Figure 28–4 **THE MULTIPLIER IN THE PRESENCE OF AN INCOME TAX**

This diagram illustrates that an economy with an income tax (in this case a 20 percent income tax) has a lower multiplier than an economy without one. Specifically, the $C + I + G + (X - IM)$ curve is shifted upward by a \$400 billion increase in $G$, and the diagram shows that equilibrium GDP rises by \$1000 billion—from \$6000 billion to \$7000 billion. The multiplier is therefore \$1000/\$400 = $2\frac{1}{2}$, whereas without an income tax it was 4.

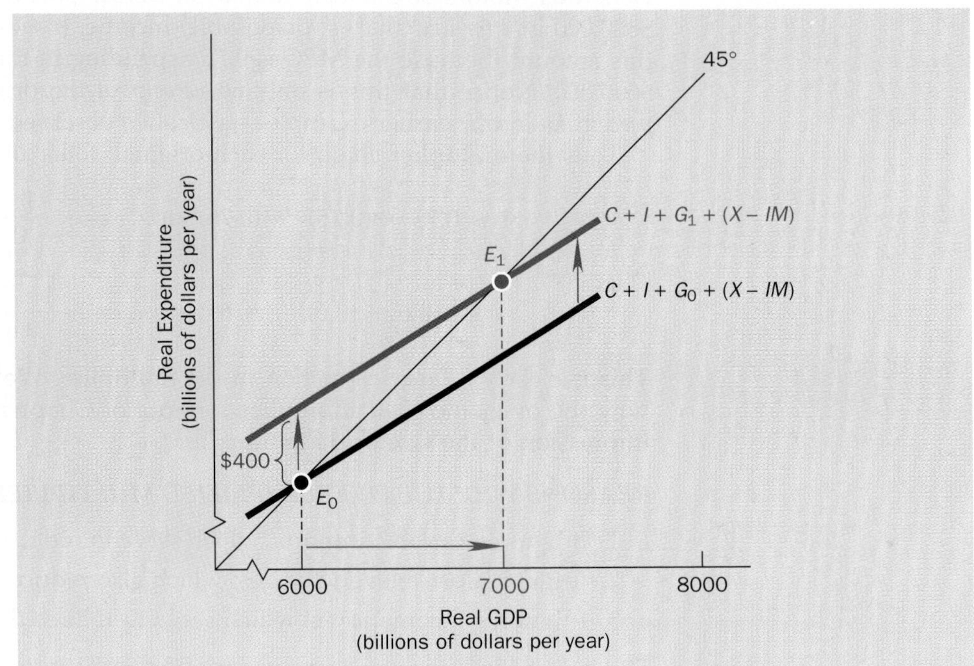


This conclusion about the multiplier is shown graphically in Figure 28–4, where we have drawn our $C + I + G + (X - IM)$ schedules with a slope of 0.6 to reflect an MPC of 0.75 and a tax rate of 20 percent rather than the 0.75 slope that we used in earlier chapters. The figure depicts the effect of an increase in government purchases of goods and services of \$400 billion, which shifts the $C + I + G + (X - IM)$ schedule from $C + I + G_0 + (X - IM)$ to $C + I + G_1 + (X - IM)$. Equilibrium moves from point $E_0$ to point $E_1$—a growth in GDP from $Y$ = \$6000 billion to $Y$ = \$7000 billion. Thus, if we ignore for the moment any increases in the price level (which would reduce the multiplier shown in Figure 28–4), a \$400 billion increment in government spending leads to a \$1000 billion increment in GDP. So when taxes are included in our model, the multiplier is only \$1000/\$400 = $2\frac{1}{2}$, just as we concluded before.

## MULTIPLIERS FOR TAX POLICY

Because they work indirectly via consumption, multipliers for tax changes are more complicated than multipliers for spending such as $G$. They must be worked out in two steps.

**Step 1.** We must figure out how much any change in the tax law affects consumer spending.

**Step 2.** We must enter this vertical shift of the consumption schedule in the 45° line diagram and see how it affects output.

A reduction in income taxes provides a convenient example of this two-step procedure because we have already done Step 1 in an earlier chapter. Specifically, in Chapter 24 we studied how consumer spending would respond to a cut in income taxes. We concluded that, if the tax reduction were viewed as permanent, consumers would increase their spending by an amount equal to the tax cut times the marginal propensity to consume. (If you need review, turn back to pages 596–601.)

To create a simple and familiar numerical example, let us suppose that income taxes fall from $0.2Y$ (that is, 20 percent of GDP) to $0.2Y - \$400$ billion—meaning that tax receipts decline by $400 billion at each level of GDP. Step 1 instructs us to multiply the $400 billion tax cut by the marginal propensity to consume (MPC), which is 0.75, to get $300 billion as the vertical shift of the consumption schedule.

Step 2 then amounts to multiplying this $300 billion increase in consumption by the multiplier—which is 2.5 in our example—giving $750 billion as the rise in GDP. Figure 28–5 verifies that this is so by entering a $300 billion vertical shift of the consumption function into the 45° line diagram and noting that GDP does indeed rise by $750 billion as a result.

Notice something interesting here. The $400 billion tax cut raises GDP by $750 billion. Thus the multiplier is $700/$400 = 1.875. But the multiplier for the $400 government purchases that we worked out on page 695 and depicted in Figure 28–4 was 2.5. What's going on here? Apparently:

The multiplier for changes in taxes is smaller than the multiplier for changes in government purchases.

The reason is not mysterious. While $G$ is a direct component of total expenditure, taxes are not. Taxes work indirectly, first by changing disposable income and then by changing $C$. Since some of the change in disposable income affects *saving* rather than *spending*, a one-dollar tax cut does not pack as much punch as a dollar

**Figure 28–5** **THE MULTIPLIER FOR A REDUCTION IN FIXED TAXES**

In this example, the $C + I + G + (X - IM)$ schedule is shifted vertically upward by $300 billion, from $C_0 + I + G + (X - IM)$ to $C_1 + I + G + (X - IM)$, by a $400 billion tax cut. Equilibrium GDP therefore increases from $6000 billion to $6750 billion. So the multiplier is $750/$400 = 1.875.

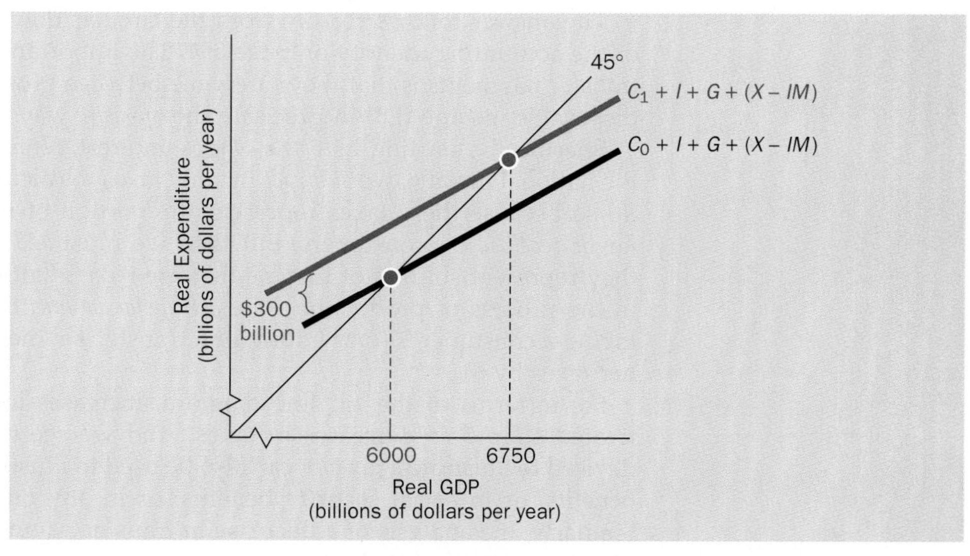

of $G$. That is why we had to multiply the \$400 billion change in taxes by 0.75 to get the \$300 billion shift of the $C$ schedule shown in Figure 28–5.

The fact that the multiplier for taxes is smaller than the multiplier for $G$ has a surprising implication:

If government purchases ($G$) and taxes ($T$) rise by equal amounts, the government seems to be giving to the public with one hand and taking away an equal amount with the other. But the effects do not cancel out. Instead, the equilibrium level of GDP on the demand side rises. Similarly, if $G$ and $T$ fall by equal amounts, the equilibrium level of GDP on the demand side falls.

For example, we have seen that a \$400 billion increase in $G$ raises GDP by \$1000, while a \$400 billion cut in $T$ lowers GDP by just \$750 billion. Thus if *both G and T* were raised by \$400 billion, GDP would go up by \$250 billion.

The intuitive explanation is that every dollar of government spending adds \$1 to total expenditure in the economy while every dollar collected in taxes reduces consumer spending by less than \$1. The rest comes out of saving. (In our example, consumers take one quarter of any tax hike out of saving and three-quarters out of spending.)

The moral of the story is that fiscal policies that keep the deficit the same do not necessarily keep aggregate demand the same. A cut in government spending balanced by an equal cut in tax revenues can be expected to reduce $Y$—a lesson that politicians frequently forget.

## GOVERNMENT TRANSFER PAYMENTS

Finally, we should mention the last major tool of fiscal policy: **government transfer payments**. A transfer, you will remember, is a payment by government to an individual that is not compensation for work done or for any other direct contribution to production. How are transfers treated in our models of income determination—like purchases of goods and services ($G$) or like taxes ($T$)?

The answer follows readily from the circular flow diagram back on page 626 or the accounting identity on page 594. The important thing to understand about transfer payments is that they intervene between gross domestic product ($Y$) and disposable income (DI) in precisely the *opposite* way from income taxes.

Specifically, starting with the wages, interest, rents, and profits that constitute the national income, we *subtract* income taxes to calculate disposable income. We do so because these taxes represent the portion of incomes that are *earned* but never *received* by consumers. But then we must *add* transfer payments because they represent sources of income that are *received* although they were not *earned* in the process of production. Thus, *transfer payments are basically negative taxes;* giving a consumer \$1 in the form of a transfer payment is equivalent to reducing her taxes by \$1.

So, in terms of the 45° line diagram, increases in transfer payments can be treated simply as decreases in taxes. And we see that Figure 28–5, which we devised to illustrate a tax cut, can also be used to illustrate a rise in unemployment benefits, or in social security benefits, or in any other such transfer payment. Similarly, the analysis of a decrease in transfer payments would proceed exactly like the analysis of an increase in taxes.

## PLANNING EXPANSIVE FISCAL POLICY

Now, at last, you are ready to pretend that you were in President Clinton's shoes in January 1993, trying to decide whether to use fiscal policy to stimulate the economy—and, if so, by how much. Suppose that the economy would have a GDP of \$6000 billion if last year's budget were simply repeated. Suppose further that your goal is to achieve a fully employed labor force and that staff economists tell you this would require a GDP of approximately \$7000 billion. Finally, just to keep the calculations manageable, imagine that the price level is fixed. What sort of budget should you recommend to Congress?

This chapter has taught us that the government has three ways to raise GDP by \$1000 billion. Congress can raise government purchases, reduce taxes, or increase transfer payments by enough to close the recessionary gap between actual and potential GDP.

Figure 28–6 illustrates the problem, and its cure through higher government spending, on our 45° line diagram. Figure 28–6(a) shows the equilibrium of the economy if no changes are made in the budget. Except for the full-employment line at $Y = \$7000$ and the corresponding recessionary gap, it looks just like Figure 28–3. With an expenditure multiplier of $2\frac{1}{2}$, you can figure out that an additional \$400 billion of government spending will be needed to push the GDP up \$1000 billion and eliminate this gap ($\$1000 \div 2\frac{1}{2} = \$400$).

So you might vote to raise $G$ from $G_0 = \$1300$ billion to $G_1 = \$1700$ billion, hoping to move the $C + I + G + (X - IM)$ line in Figure 28–6(a) out to the position indicated in Figure 28–6(b), thereby achieving full employment. Of course, you might prefer to achieve this fiscal stimulus by lowering income taxes rather than by increasing expenditures. Or you might prefer to rely on more generous transfer

**Figure 28–6**

**FISCAL POLICY TO ELIMINATE A RECESSIONARY GAP**

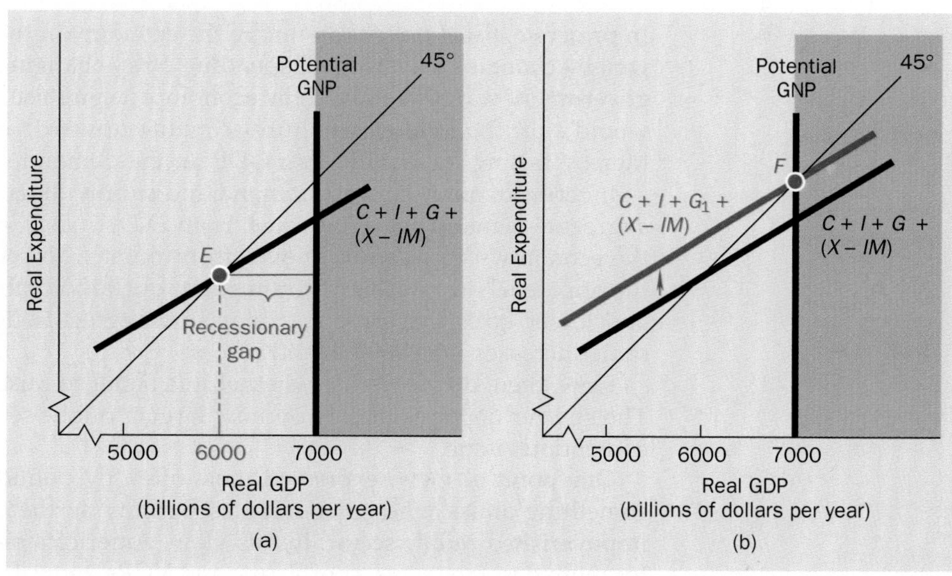


This diagram shows, with more precision than can actually be achieved in practice, how fiscal policy can eliminate a recessionary gap. Part (a) shows the gap: Equilibrium GDP (\$6000 billion) falls short of potential GDP (\$7000 billion). Part (b) shows how fiscal policy—by moving the $C + I + G + (X - IM)$ curve up just enough—can wipe out this gap and restore full employment. With a multiplier of $2\frac{1}{2}$, a rise in $G$ of \$400 billion or a cut in taxes large enough to shift $C$ up by \$400 billion would do the trick.

payments. The point is that there are a variety of budgets capable of pushing the economy up to full employment by increasing GDP by $1000 billion. Figure 28–6 applies equally well to any of them.

## PLANNING RESTRICTIVE FISCAL POLICY

The preceding example assumed that the basic problem of fiscal policy is to overcome a deficiency of aggregate demand, as was the case at the start of the Clinton administration. Often this is so. But early in the Bush administration in 1989 many people believed that the problem was the opposite: aggregate demand exceeded the economy's capacity to produce and inflation was on the rise. In such a case, fiscal policy should assume a restrictive stance in order to reduce inflation.

It does not take much imagination to run our previous analysis in reverse. If, under a continuation of current budget policies, there would be an inflationary gap, contractionary fiscal policy tools can eliminate it. Either by cutting spending programs out of the budget, or by raising taxes, or by some combination of these policies, the government can pull the $C + I + G + (X - IM)$ schedule down to a noninflationary position and achieve an equilibrium at full employment.

Notice the difference between this way of eliminating an inflationary gap and the natural self-correcting mechanism of the economy that we discussed in Chapter 27. There we observed that, if the economy were left to its own devices, a cumulative but self-limiting process of inflation eventually would eliminate the inflationary gap and return the economy to full employment. Here we see that it is not necessary to put the economy through the inflationary wringer. Instead, a restrictive fiscal policy can limit aggregate demand to the level that the economy can produce at full employment.

## THE CHOICE BETWEEN SPENDING POLICY AND TAX POLICY

In principle, fiscal policy can nudge the economy in the desired direction equally well by changing government spending or by changing taxes. For example, if the government wants to expand the economy, it can raise $G$ or lower $T$. Either policy would shift the total expenditure schedule upward, as depicted in Figure 28–6, thereby raising the equilibrium GDP on the demand side.

In terms of our aggregate demand and supply diagram, either policy shifts the aggregate demand curve outward, from $D_0D_0$ to $D_1D_1$ in Figure 28–7. As a result, the economy's equilibrium moves from point $E$ to point $A$. Both real GDP and the price level rise. As this diagram points out, any combination of higher spending and lower taxes that produces the same aggregate demand curve leads to the same increases in real GDP and prices.

How, then, do we decide whether it is better to raise spending or to cut taxes? The answer depends mainly on how large a public sector we want, and this is a contentious issue.

One point of view, expressed most often by political liberals, is that there is something amiss when a country as wealthy as the United States has such an impoverished public sector. In this view, America's most pressing needs are not for more designer jeans, sports cars, and VCRs, but rather for better schools, more efficient public transportation systems, and cleaner and safer city streets. People

Figure 28-7 **EXPANSIONARY FISCAL POLICY**

Any of a variety of expansionary fiscal policies will push the aggregate demand curve outward to the right as depicted by the shift from $D_0D_0$ to $D_1D_1$ in this aggregate supply and demand diagram. The economy's equilibrium moves upward to the right along aggregate supply curve *SS*, from point *E* to point *A*. Comparing *A* with *E*, we note that output is higher but prices are also higher. The expansionary policy has caused some inflation.

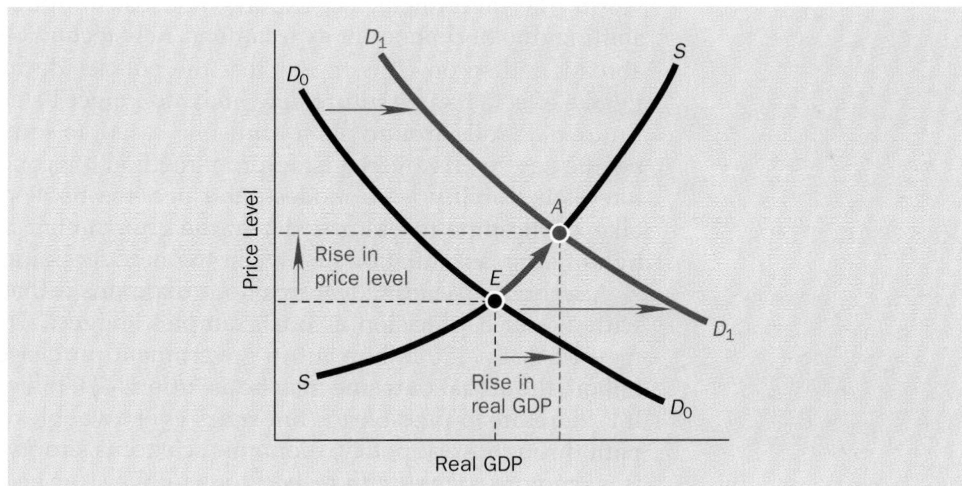


on this side of the debate believe that we should *increase* spending when the economy needs stimulus, and pay for these improved public services by *increasing taxes* when the economy needs to be reined in.

An opposing opinion, advocated forcefully by both Presidents Reagan and Bush, was ascendant in the 1980s. In this view, the government sector is already too large; we are foolish to rely on government to do things that private individuals and businesses could do better on their own; and the growth of government interferes too much in our everyday lives, and in so doing circumscribes our freedom. Those who hold this view argue for *tax cuts* when macroeconomic considerations call for expansionary fiscal policy, and for *reductions in public spending* when restrictive policy is required.

Too often the use of fiscal policy for economic stabilization is erroneously associated with a large and growing public sector—that is, with "big government." This need not be the case. Individuals favoring a smaller public sector can advocate an active fiscal policy just as well as those who favor a larger public sector. Advocates of big government budgets should seek to expand demand (when appropriate) through higher government spending and contract demand (when appropriate) through tax increases. By contrast, advocates of small public budgets should seek to expand demand by cutting taxes and reduce demand by cutting expenditures.

## SOME HARSH REALITIES

The mechanics outlined so far in this chapter make the fiscal policy planner's job look rather simple. The elementary diagrams suggest, rather misleadingly, that the authorities can drive GDP to any level they please simply by manipulating spending and tax programs. It seems as though they should be able to hit the full-employment bull's eye every time.

But, in fact, a better analogy is to shooting through dense fog at an erratically moving target with an inaccurate gun. The target is moving because, in the real world, the investment, net exports, and consumption schedules are constantly shifting due to changes in expectations, new technological breakthroughs, events abroad, and so on. This means that the policies decided upon today, which are to take effect at some future date, may no longer be appropriate by the time that future date rolls around. Policy must be based, to some extent, on *forecasting*, and no one has yet discovered a foolproof method of economic forecasting.[1] Since our forecasting ability is so modest, and because fiscal policy decisions sometimes take a long time to be carried out, the government may occasionally find itself fighting the last inflation just when the new recession gets under way.

A second misleading feature of our diagrams is that multipliers are not known with as much precision as our examples suggest. Thus while the "best guess" may be that a $20 billion cut in government purchases will reduce GDP by $40 billion, the actual outcome may be as little as $20 billion or as much as $60 billion. It is therefore impossible to "fine tune" every wobble out of the economy's growth path through fiscal policy; economic science is simply not that precise. The point is even more cogent with respect to tax policy, for here we get involved in trying to guess whether consumers will view tax changes as permanent or temporary.

A third complication is that our target—full-employment GDP—may be only dimly visible, as if through a fog. The present time is a good example of this since economists are now debating what measured unemployment rate corresponds to full employment.

Finally, in trying to decide whether to push the unemployment rate lower, legislators would like to know how large the inflation cost is likely to be. As we know, an expansionary fiscal policy that reduces a recessionary gap by increasing aggregate demand will lower unemployment. But it also tends to be inflationary. This undesirable side effect may make the government hesitant to use fiscal policy to combat recessions.

Is there a way out of this dilemma? Can we carry on the battle against unemployment without aggravating inflation? During the late 1970s, a small but influential minority of economists, journalists, and politicians argued that we could. They called their approach "supply-side economics." The idea helped sweep Ronald Reagan into office in 1980. But by 1992 Bill Clinton won the presidency by running against it. Popular opinion had certainly changed! Just what is supply-side economics?

## THE IDEA BEHIND SUPPLY-SIDE TAX CUTS

The central idea of supply-side economics is that certain types of tax cuts can be expected to increase aggregate supply. For example, taxes can be cut in ways that raise the rewards for working, saving, and investing. *If people actually respond to these incentives*, such tax cuts would increase the total supplies of labor and capital in the economy, thereby increasing aggregate supply.

Figure 28–8 illustrates the idea on an aggregate supply and demand diagram. If policy measures can shift the economy's aggregate supply to position $S_1S_1$, then prices will be lower and output higher than if the aggregate supply curve were

[1]Some problems and techniques of economic forecasting are considered in Chapter 31.

Figure 28–8 **THE IDEA BEHIND SUPPLY-SIDE TAX CUTS**

The basic idea of supply-side tax cuts is that, if they achieve their desired objective, they shift the economy's aggregate supply curve outward to the right. For example the aggregate supply curve might be $S_1S_1$ under a program of supply-side tax cuts, whereas it would only be $S_0S_0$ without such tax cuts. If aggregate demand is the same in either case, the supply-side tax cuts would lead to the equilibrium point *B* instead of the equilibrium point *A*. Comparing *B* with *A*, we see that the program reduces prices and raises output.

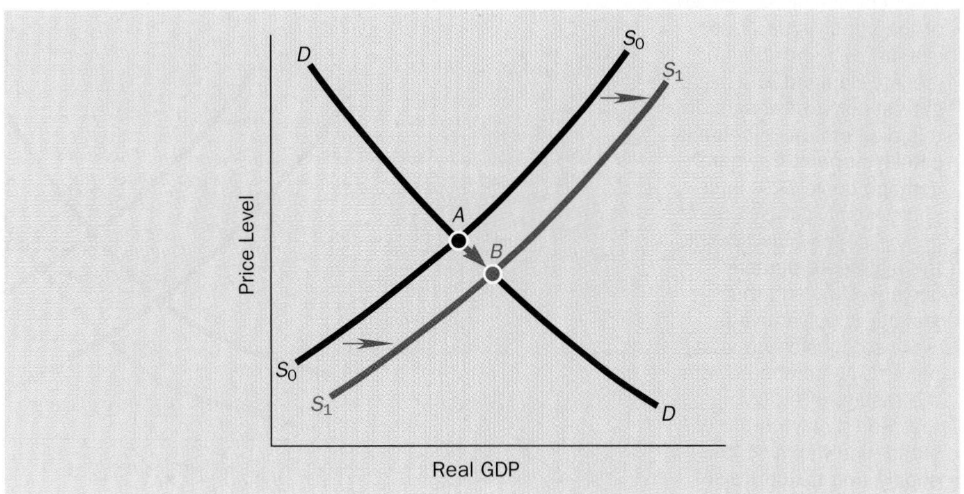


$S_0S_0$. Policymakers will have succeeded in reducing inflation and raising real output (lowering unemployment) at the same time. The trade-off between inflation and unemployment will have been defeated. This is the goal of supply-side economics.

What sorts of policies do supply siders advocate? Here is a small sample of their long list of recommended tax cuts:

1. ***Lower Personal Income Tax Rates.*** Sharp cuts in personal taxes were the cornerstone of President Reagan's economic strategy. Tax rates on individuals were reduced in stages between 1981 and 1984 and then again in 1986. By 1987, the richest Americans were in the 28 percent tax bracket, and most taxpayers were in the 15 percent bracket. Such low tax rates, supply siders argued, augment the supplies of both labor and capital.
2. ***Reduce Taxes on Income from Savings.*** One extreme form of this proposal would simply exempt from taxation all income from interest and dividends. Since income must be either consumed or saved, this would, in effect, change our present personal income tax into a tax on consumer spending.
3. ***Reduce the Corporation Income Tax.*** By reducing the tax burden on corporations, it is argued, the government can provide both greater investment incentives (by raising the profitability of investment) and more investable funds (by letting companies keep more of their earnings). This advice was followed in 1981 by making depreciation allowances more generous[2] and in 1986 by lowering the corporate tax rate.

[2]A company investing in a machine or factory may not deduct the entire cost of that asset as a business expense in the year it is purchased. Instead, it must spread the cost over the lifetime of the asset in a series of tax deductions called *depreciation allowances*. Naturally, firms prefer to get these allowances sooner rather than later, because higher depreciation in the early years of an investment means an immediate cut in tax burdens.

**Figure 28–9** **A SUCCESSFUL SUPPLY-SIDE TAX REDUCTION**

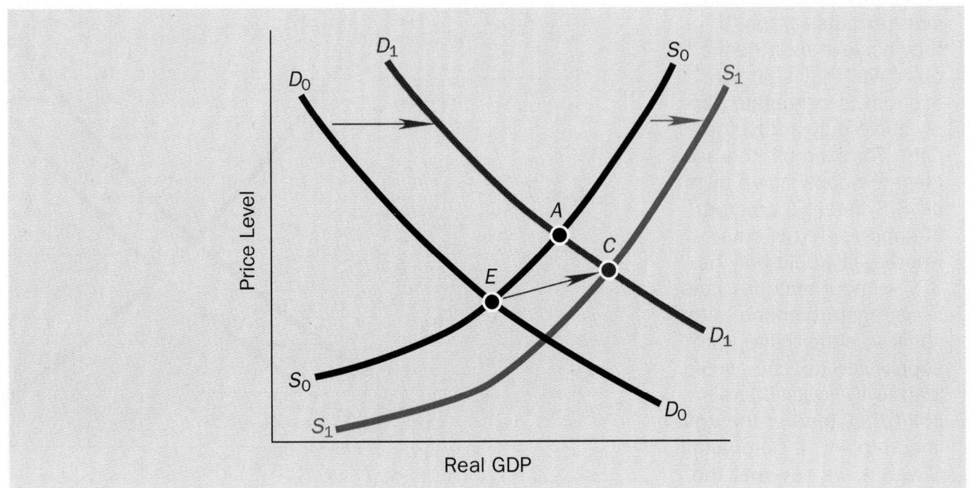


A tax cut specifically aimed at the supply side, if successful, will shift *both* aggregate demand *and* aggregate supply to the right. In this diagram, equilibrium is initially at point *E*, where demand curve $D_0D_0$ intersects supply curve $S_0S_0$. After the supply-side tax cut, the aggregate demand curve is $D_1D_1$ and the aggregate supply curve is $S_1S_1$, so equilibrium is at point *C*. As compared with the results of a tax cut that works only on the demand side (point *A*), the supply-side tax cut raises output more and prices less.

4. ***Provide Tax Credits for Research and Development.*** To encourage companies to spend money on research and development, Congress allows special tax reductions for firms that do so. The hope is obvious: more R & D should lead to improvements in technology.

Let us suppose, for the moment, that a successful supply-side tax cut is enacted to help close a recessionary gap. Since *both* aggregate demand *and* aggregate supply increase simultaneously, the economy may be able to avoid the painful inflationary consequences of an expansionary fiscal policy that were shown in Figure 28–7.

Figure 28–9 illustrates this conclusion. The two aggregate demand curves and the initial aggregate supply curve $S_0S_0$ are carried over directly from Figure 28–7. But we have introduced an additional supply curve, $S_1S_1$, to reflect the successful supply-side tax cut depicted in Figure 28–8. The equilibrium of the economy moves from *E* to *C*, whereas with a conventional demand-side tax cut it would have moved from *E* to *A*. As compared with point *A*, output is higher and prices are lower at point *C*.

A good deal, you say! Indeed it is. The supply-side argument is extremely attractive in principle. The question is: Does it work in practice? Can we actually do what is depicted in Figure 28–9? Let us consider some difficulties.

## SOME FLIES IN THE OINTMENT

Supply-side economics was, and remains, controversial. Critics rarely question the goals of supply-side economics or the basic idea that lower taxes improve incentives. They argue, instead, that supply siders exaggerate the beneficial effects of tax cuts and ignore some undesirable side effects. Here is a brief rundown of some of the main objections to supply-side tax cuts:

1. ***Small Magnitude of Supply-Side Effects.*** The first objection is that supply siders are simply too optimistic: we really do not know how to do what Figure 28–8 shows. While it is easy, for example, to design tax cuts that make working more *attractive* financially, people may not actually behave this way. Instead, they may find themselves able to afford the goods and services they want with fewer hours of labor, and react by working *less.* Most of the statistical evidence suggests that we should expect tax reductions to lead to very small increases in either labor supply or household savings. As economist Charles Schultze once quipped: "There's nothing wrong with supply-side economics that division by ten couldn't cure."
2. ***Demand-Side Effects.*** The second objection is that supply siders underestimate the effects of tax cuts on aggregate demand. If you cut personal taxes, individuals *may possibly* work more, but they *will certainly* spend more. If you reduce business taxes and thereby encourage expansion of industrial capacity, business firms will demand more investment goods.

   The combined implications of these two objections are depicted in Figure 28–10. Here we depict a small outward shift in the aggregate supply curve (which reflects the first objection) and a large outward shift of the aggregate demand curve (which reflects the second). The result is that the economy's equilibrium moves from point $A$ (the intersection of $S_0S_0$ and $D_0D_0$) to point $E$ (the intersection of $S_1S_1$ and $D_1D_1$). Prices rise as output expands. The outcome differs only a little from the straight "demand-side" fiscal stimulus depicted in Figure 28–7 (page 701).
3. ***Problems in Timing.*** The most promising types of supply-side tax cuts seek to encourage greater business investment or R&D. But the benefits from

*Figure* **28–10** **A MORE PESSIMISTIC VIEW OF SUPPLY-SIDE TAX CUTS**

If the effect of supply-side tax initatives on the aggregate supply curve is actually much smaller than suggested by Figure 28–8, the anti-inflationary impact will be correspondingly smaller. As you can see in this diagram, it is possible that a large shift in the aggregate demand curve could overwhelm the favorable effects of the tax cuts on the price level.

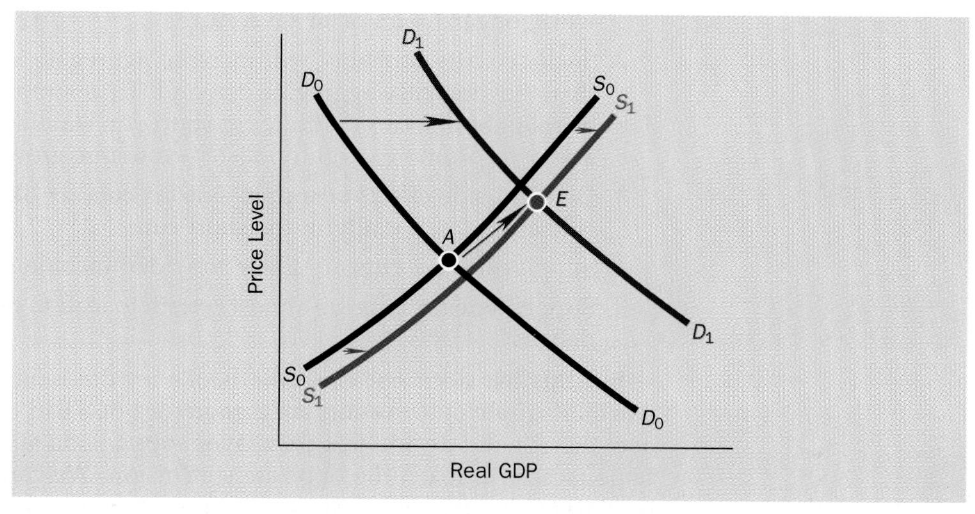

such activities do not arrive overnight. It may, in fact, take years before we see any substantial increases in industrial capacity. Thus it seems certain that the *expenditures* on investment goods come before the *expansion of capacity*. In a word, supply-side tax cuts will have their primary effects on aggregate demand in the short run. Effects on aggregate supply come later.

4. ***Effect on the Distribution of Income.*** The preceding objections all pertain to the likely effects of supply-side policies on aggregate supply and demand. But there is a different problem that bears mention: most supply-side initiatives increase income inequality. While raising the incomes of the wealthiest members of our society may not be their primary aim, most supply-side cuts cannot help but concentrate their benefits on the rich simply because it is the rich who own most of the capital.

   Indeed, this tilt toward the rich is almost an inescapable corollary of supply-side logic. The basic aim of supply-side economics is to increase the incentives for working and investing, that is, to increase the gap between the rewards of those who succeed in the economic game (by working hard, investing well, or by just plain luck) and those who fail. It can hardly be surprising, therefore, that supply-side policies tend to increase economic inequality.

5. ***Losses of Tax Revenue.*** You can hardly help noticing that most of the policies suggested by supply siders involve cutting one tax or another. Thus, unless some other tax is raised or spending is cut, supply-side tax cuts are bound to raise the government budget deficit—as they certainly did in the 1980s.

## TOWARD ASSESSMENT OF SUPPLY-SIDE ECONOMICS

On balance, most economists have reached the following conclusions about supply-side tax initiatives:

1. The likely effectiveness of supply-side tax cuts depends on what kinds of taxes are cut. Tax reductions aimed at stimulating business investment are likely to pack more punch than tax reductions aimed at getting people to work longer hours or to save more.
2. Such tax cuts probably will increase aggregate supply much more slowly than they increase aggregate demand. Thus supply-side policies should not be thought of as a substitute for short-run stabilization policy, but rather as a way to promote (slightly) faster economic growth in the long run.
3. Demand-side effects of supply-side tax cuts are likely to overwhelm supply-side effects, especially in the short run.
4. Supply-side tax cuts are likely to widen income inequalities.
5. Supply-side tax cuts are almost certain to lead to bigger, not smaller, budget deficits.

But this list does not close the books on the issue. It does not even tell us whether supply-side tax cuts are a good idea or a bad one. Some people will look over this list and decide that they favor supply-side tax cuts; others, perusing the same facts, will reach the opposite conclusion. We cannot say that either group is "wrong" because, like almost every economic policy, supply-side economics has its pros and cons.

## Clintonomics: A New Brand of Supply-Side Economics

President Bill Clinton advertised his economic program as a reversal of Reagonomics. In many ways, it is. But there are also similarities in that both Clintonomics and Reagonomics focus on aggregate supply rather than on aggregate demand. The following excerpt from the Clinton administration's first economic report puts the emphasis squarely on investment and on increases in the economy's capacity to produce.

In recent years, our leaders . . . embraced trickle-down policies that benefitted the wealthy at the expense of the middle class and the working poor. We have deluded ourselves that somehow economic growth and fairness are at odds, when in fact they go hand in hand. While the privileged few have prospered, millions of Americans who worked hard and played by the rules have been left behind. . . . Debt has soared as individuals, businesses, and governments have lived beyond their means. Our commitment to invest in the future and to bequeath a promising future to our children has somehow fallen by the wayside.

To reverse the legacy of failure and move toward our vision of the future, drastic changes in Federal policy are needed.

The over-arching theme of the Clinton Administration's economic plan is *increasing public and private investment* in the broadest sense. To ensure more productive, higher-wage jobs and greater economic opportunities for ourselves and our children, we need to devote a larger share of our current resources to modernizing factories and equipment, developing skills, and accelerating the advance of technology. We must increase the share of the Government's budget devoted to investment in future growth and must create incentives for the private sector to shift from consumption to investment. The need to increase investment motivates all three elements of the Clinton economic plan: stimulus, investment, and deficit reduction.

The *stimulus* package* is designed to ensure that recovery from recession is strong and durable. What we call stimulus in this plan, however, is not a conventional prescription for adding to consumer demand by cutting taxes or creating make-work jobs. Instead, it is a down payment on longer-run investment.

The *investment* package proposes major additions to ongoing activities that expand America's capacity to produce . . . It is designed to help fill the investment deficit by increasing spending for highways and other infrastructure, to enhance the opportunities and skills of future workers, to accelerate the development and use of science and technology, to improve the delivery of health care for underserved groups, and to increase incentives and opportunities for productive employment.

The *deficit reduction* plan makes a vital contribution to increasing investment and raising standards of living by gradually reducing the structural deficit in the Federal budget. Cutting the deficit will reduce the Federal Government's drain on national savings, lower long-term interest rates, and encourage productive private investment.

*The stimulus package was blocked in the Senate by a Republican filibuster and never became law.

SOURCE: *A Vision of Change for America*, White House report, February 17, 1993, pages 1, 21–22.

Why, then, did so many economists and politicians react so negatively to supply-side economics in the early 1980s? The main reason seems to be that the claims made by the most ardent supply siders were clearly excessive. Naturally, these claims were proven wrong. But showing that wild claims are wild does not dispose of the kernel of truth in supply-side economics: reductions in marginal tax rates do improve economic incentives. Any specific supply-side tax cut must be judged on its individual merits.

## CLINTONOMICS AS SUPPLY-SIDE ECONOMICS

During the 1992 presidential campaign, Bill Clinton attacked the Reagan-Bush brand of supply-side economics as "trickle-down economics," and argued that it had failed. He emphasized, in particular, the last two items in our assessment: the effects on income inequality and the budget deficit. The voters apparently agreed.

Ironically, however, candidate Clinton also ran on an avowedly supply-side platform—though it was quite different from Reaganomics. President Clinton's emphasis was and is on building up the nation's resources of labor, capital, and technology so that our capacity to produce will be higher in the long run. This, of course, is precisely the goal of supply-side economics: to push the aggregate supply curve outward.

But, unlike Presidents Reagan and Bush, President Clinton did not propose to accomplish this mainly by cutting taxes. While some tax cuts were included in the Clinton plan, especially tax credits for investment and R&D, there were also tax increases. The real emphasis of Clintonomics is on improving the quality of the American workforce through more and better education and training. It is a program plainly focused on the long run. Only time will tell how well it works.

## *Summary*

1. The government's **fiscal policy** is its plan for managing aggregate demand through its spending and taxing programs. It is made jointly by the president and Congress.
2. The net effect of the government on aggregate demand—and hence on equilibrium output and prices—depends on whether the expansionary effects of its spending are greater or smaller than the contractionary effects of its taxes.
3. Since consumer spending (*C*) depends on disposable income (*DI*), and DI is GDP minus taxes, any change in taxes will shift the consumption schedule on a 45° line diagram. The nature of this shift depends on whether it is **fixed taxes** or **variable taxes** that are changed.
4. Such shifts in the consumption function caused by tax policy are subject to the same multiplier as autonomous shifts in $G$, $I$, or $X - IM$.
5. An income tax reduces the size of this common multiplier.
6. The multiplier for changes in taxes is smaller than the multiplier for changes in government purchases.
7. **Government transfer payments** are treated like negative taxes, not like government purchases of goods and services, because they influence total spending only indirectly through their effect on consumption.
8. If the multipliers were known precisely, it would be possible to plan any of a variety of fiscal policies to eliminate either a recessionary or an inflationary gap. Recessionary gaps can be cured by raising $G$, cutting taxes, or increasing transfers. Inflationary gaps can be cured by cutting $G$, raising taxes, or reducing transfers.
9. Active stabilization policy can be carried out either by means that tend to expand the size of government (by raising either $G$ or $T$ when appropriate) or by means that hold back the size of government (by reducing either $G$ or $T$ when appropriate).
10. Expansionary fiscal policy can cure recessions, but it normally exacts a cost in terms of higher inflation. This dilemma has led to a great deal of interest in **"supply-side" tax cuts** designed to stimulate aggregate supply.
11. Supply-side tax cuts aim to push the economy's aggregate supply curve outward to the right. If successful, they can expand the economy and reduce inflation at the same time—a highly desirable outcome.
12. But critics point out at least five serious problems with supply-side tax cuts: they also stimulate aggregate demand; the beneficial effects on aggregate supply may be small; the demand-side effects occur before the supply-side effects; they make the income distribution more unequal; and large tax cuts lead to large budget deficits.

## *Key Concepts and Terms*

Fiscal policy
Fixed taxes
Variable taxes
Government transfer payments
Effect of income taxes on the multiplier
Supply-side tax cuts

## *Questions for Review*

1. America is beginning to reap a "peace dividend" from the end of the Cold War, that is, a reduction in military expenditures. How would GDP in the United States be affected if the peace dividend were
   a. used to reduce the budget deficit, so that government purchases fell?
   b. used for other public purposes, so that government purchases remained the same?
2. Consider an economy in which tax collections are always $400 and in which the four components of aggregate demand are as follows:

| GDP | TAXES | *DI* | *C* | *I* | *G* | (*X* − *IM*) |
|---|---|---|---|---|---|---|
| $680 | $400 | $280 | $210 | $100 | $400 | $15 |
| 740 | 400 | 340 | 255 | 100 | 400 | 15 |
| 800 | 400 | 400 | 300 | 100 | 400 | 15 |
| 860 | 400 | 460 | 345 | 100 | 400 | 15 |
| 920 | 400 | 520 | 390 | 100 | 400 | 15 |

   Find the equilibrium of this economy graphically. What is the marginal propensity to consume? What is the multiplier? What would happen to equilibrium GDP if government purchases were reduced by $30 and the price level were unchanged?
3. Now consider a related economy in which investment is also $100, government purchases are also $400, net exports are also $15, and the price level is also fixed. But taxes now vary with income, and as a result the consumption schedule looks like the following:

| GDP | TAXES | *DI* | *C* |
|---|---|---|---|
| $680 | $360 | $320 | $255 |
| 740 | 380 | 360 | 285 |
| 800 | 400 | 400 | 315 |
| 860 | 420 | 440 | 345 |
| 920 | 440 | 480 | 375 |

   Find the equilibrium graphically. What is the marginal propensity to consume? What is the tax rate? Use your diagram to show the effect of a decrease of $30 in government purchases. What is the multiplier? Compare this answer to your answer to Question 2 above. What do you conclude?
4. Explain why *G* has the same multiplier as *I*, but taxes have a different multiplier.
5. Return to the hypothetical economy in Question 2 and suppose that *both* taxes and government purchases are increased by $60. Find the new equilibrium under the assumption that consumer spending continues to be exactly three-quarters of disposable income (as it is in Question 2).
6. If the government today decides that aggregate demand is excessive and is causing inflation, what options are open to it? What if it decides that aggregate demand is too weak instead?
7. Suppose that you are in charge of the fiscal policy of the economy in Question 2. There is an inflationary gap and you want to reduce income by $60. What specific actions can you take to achieve this goal?
8. Now put yourself in charge of the economy in Question 3, and suppose that full employment comes at a GDP of $920. How can you push income up to that level?
9. Which of the proposed supply-side tax cuts appeals to you most? Draw up a list of arguments for and against enacting such a cut right now.
10. (more difficult) Advocates of an investment tax credit (see Chapter 25, page 624) argue that it will raise aggregate supply by spurring investment. But, of course, any increase in investment spending will also raise aggregate demand. Compare the effects on aggregate supply and demand of three different types of investment tax credit:
    a. The credit is applied to *all* investments.
    b. The credit is applied only to purchases of certain types of assets, such as industrial equipment.
    c. The credit is applied only once investment exceeds some base level.

    Which of the three seems more desirable. Why?

# *Appendix* ALGEBRAIC TREATMENT OF FISCAL POLICY AND AGGREGATE DEMAND

In this appendix we explain the simple algebra behind the fiscal policy multipliers discussed in the chapter. In so doing, we deal only with a simplified case in which prices do not change. While it is possible to work out the corresponding algebra for the more realistic aggregate demand-aggregate supply analysis with variable prices, the analysis is rather complicated and is best left to more advanced courses.

We start with the example used in the chapter (especially on pages 694 and 696). The government spends \$1300 billion on goods and services ($G = 1300$) and levies an income tax equal to 20 percent of GDP. So, if the symbol $T$ denotes tax receipts:

$$T = .20\,Y.$$

Since the consumption function we have been working with is

$$C = 300 + 0.75\,DI,$$

where $DI$ is disposable income, and since disposable income and GDP are related by the accounting identity

$$DI = Y - T,$$

it follows that the $C$ schedule used in the 45° line diagram is described by the algebraic equation:

$$\begin{aligned} C &= 300 + 0.75(Y - T) \\ &= 300 + 0.75(Y - .2Y) \\ &= 300 + 0.75(.8Y) \\ &= 300 + 0.6\,Y. \end{aligned}$$

We can now apply the equilibrium condition

$$Y = C + I + G + (X - IM).$$

Since investment in this example is $I = 900$ and net exports are $-100$, substituting for $C$, $I$, $G$, and $(X - IM)$ into this equation gives

$$\begin{aligned} Y &= 300 + 0.6\,Y + 900 + 1300 - 100 \\ 0.4Y &= 2400 \\ Y &= 6000. \end{aligned}$$

This is all there is to finding equilibrium GDP in an economy with a government.

To find the multiplier for government spending, increase $G$ by 1 and resolve the problem:

$$\begin{aligned} Y &= C + I + G + (X - IM) \\ Y &= 300 + 0.6Y + 900 + 1301 - 100 \\ 0.4Y &= 2401 \\ Y &= 6002.5 \end{aligned}$$

So the multiplier is $6002.5 - 6000 = 2.5$, as stated in the text.

To find the multiplier for an increase in fixed taxes, change the tax schedule to

$$T = .2Y + 1.$$

Disposable income is then

$$\begin{aligned} DI = Y - T &= Y - (.2Y + 1) \\ &= .8Y - 1, \end{aligned}$$

so the consumption function is

$$\begin{aligned} C &= 300 + 0.75DI \\ &= 300 + 0.75(.8Y - 1) \\ &= 299.25 + 0.6Y. \end{aligned}$$

Solving for equilibrium GDP as usual gives

$$\begin{aligned} Y &= C + I + G + (X - IM) \\ Y &= 299.25 + 0.6Y + 900 + 1300 - 100 \\ 0.4Y &= 2399.25 \\ Y &= 5998.125 \end{aligned}$$

So a \$1 increase in fixed taxes lowers Y by \$1.875. The tax multiplier is $-1.875$.

Now let us proceed to a more general solution, using symbols rather than specific numbers. The equations of the model are as follows

$$Y = C + I + G + (X - IM) \qquad (1)$$

is the usual equilibrium condition;

$$C = a + bDI \qquad (2)$$

is the same consumption function we have used in the appendixes of Chapters 25 and 26;

$$DI = Y - T \qquad (3)$$

is the accounting identity relating disposable income to GDP;

$$T = T_0 + tY \qquad (4)$$

is the tax function, where $T_0$ represents fixed taxes (which are zero in our numerical example) and $t$ represents the tax rate (which is 0.2 in the example). Finally, $I$, $G$, and $(X - IM)$ are just fixed numbers.

We begin the solution by substituting (3) and (4) into (2) to derive the consumption schedule relating $C$ to $Y$:

$$\begin{aligned} C &= a + b\,DI \\ C &= a + b(Y - T) \\ C &= a + b(Y - T_0 - tY) \\ C &= a - bT_0 + b(1 - t)Y. \end{aligned} \qquad (5)$$

You will notice that a change in fixed taxes ($T_0$) shifts the *intercept* of the $C$ schedule while a change in the tax rate ($t$) changes its *slope*, as explained in the text (pages 691–93).

Next substitute (5) into (1) to find equilibrium GDP:

$$\begin{aligned} Y &= C + I + G + (X - IM) \\ Y &= a - b\,T_0 + b(1 - t)Y + I + G + (X - IM) \\ [1 - b(1 - t)]Y &= a - bT_0 + I + G + (X - IM) \end{aligned}$$

or

$$Y = \frac{a - bT_0 + I + G + (X - IM)}{1 - b(1 - t)}. \qquad (6)$$

Equation (6) shows us that the multiplier for $G$, $I$, $a$, or $(X - IM)$ is

$$\text{Multiplier} = \frac{1}{1 - b(1 - t)}.$$

To see that this is in fact the multiplier, raise any of $G$, $I$, $a$, or $(X - IM)$ by 1 unit. In each case, equation (6) would be changed to read:

$$Y = \frac{a - bT_0 + I + G + (X - IM) + 1}{1 - b(1 - t)}.$$

Subtracting equation (6) from this expression gives the change in $Y$ stemming from a one-unit change in $G$ or $I$ or $a$:

$$\text{Change in Y} = \frac{1}{1 - b(1 - t)}.$$

We noted in Chapter 26 (page 653) that if there were no income tax ($t = 0$), a realistic value for $b$ (the marginal propensity to consume) would yield a multiplier of 10, which is much bigger than the true multiplier. Now that we have added taxes to the model, our multiplier formula produces much more realistic numbers. Approximate values for the parameters for the U.S. economy are $b = \frac{9}{10}$ and $t = \frac{1}{3}$. The multiplier formula then gives:

$$\begin{aligned} \text{Multiplier} &= \frac{1}{1 - \frac{9}{10}(1 - \frac{1}{3})} \\ &= \frac{1}{1 - \frac{3}{5}} = \frac{1}{\frac{2}{5}} \\ &= 2.5 \end{aligned}$$

which is not far from its actual estimated value, nearly 2.

Finally, we can see from equation (6) that the multiplier for a change in fixed taxes ($T_0$) is

$$\text{Tax multiplier} = \frac{-b}{1 - b(1 - t)}.$$

For the example considered in the text and earlier in this appendix, $b = 0.75$ and $t = 0.2$, so the formula gives:

$$\frac{-.75}{1 - .75(1 - .2)} = \frac{-.75}{1 - .75(.8)}$$

$$\frac{-.75}{1 - .6} = \frac{-.75}{.4} = -1.875.$$

According to these figures, each \$1 *increase* in $T_0$ *reduces* $Y$ by \$1.875.

## Questions for Review

1. In an economy described by the following set of equations:

$$\begin{aligned} C &= 20 + .8DI \\ I &= 220 \\ G &= 380 \\ (X - IM) &= 20 \\ T &= 100 + .25Y, \end{aligned}$$

find the equilibrium level of GDP. Then find the multipliers for government purchases and for fixed taxes. If full employment comes at $Y = 1300$, what are some policies that would get GDP there?

2. This is a variant of the previous problem that approaches things the way a fiscal policy planner might. In an economy whose consumption function and tax

function are as given in Question 1, with investment fixed at 220 and net exports fixed at 20, find the value of $G$ that would make GDP equal to 1300.

3. You are given the following information about an economy.

$$C = 10 + .9\,\text{DI}$$
$$I = 140$$
$$G = 540$$
$$(X - IM) = -90$$
$$T = (1/3)Y$$

   a. Find equilibrium GDP and the budget deficit.
   b. Suppose the government, unhappy with the budget deficit, decides to cut government spending by precisely the amount of the deficit you found in (a). What actually happens to GDP and the budget deficit, and why?

4. (More difficult) In the economy considered in Question 3, suppose the government, seeing that it has not wiped out the deficit, keeps cutting $G$ until it succeeds in balancing the budget. What levels of GDP will then prevail?

Chapter 29

# MONEY AND THE BANKING SYSTEM

*[Money] is a machine for doing quickly and commodiously what would be done, though less quickly and commodiously, without it.*

JOHN STUART MILL

The circular flow diagrams that were used in earlier chapters to explain equilibrium GDP had a "financial system" in their upper left-hand corners. Savings flowed into this system and investment flowed out. Something obviously goes on inside the financial system to channel the savings into investment, and it is time we learned just what this something is. ¶ There is another, equally important, reason for studying the financial system. *Fiscal policy* is not the only lever the government has on the economy's aggregate demand curve; it also exercises significant control over aggregate demand by manipulating *monetary policy*. If we are to understand monetary policy (the subject of Chapters 30 and 31), we must first acquire some understanding of the financial system. ¶ The present chapter has three major objectives. It first seeks to explain the nature of money: what it is, what purposes it serves, and how it is measured. Once this is done, we turn our attention to the banking system, explaining its historical origins, the nature of banking as a business, and why this industry is so heavily regulated. Finally, we learn how banks create money—a subject that is of great importance because you cannot hope to understand monetary policy until you first understand how money is created.

At the end of the chapter, we will see why government authorities must exercise control over the supply of money in a modern economy. This leads naturally into next chapter's discussion of *central banking*, that is, the techniques used to implement monetary policy.

## POLICY ISSUE: SHOULD WE DEREGULATE OR REREGULATE THE BANKS?

As this is written, bank regulation stands at a crossroads. Some observers think the United States went too far in deregulating its banking and financial system in the 1980s and needs to take a step or two back in the opposite direction. Such people fear that deregulation has made our financial system more fragile and harder to control. The massive wave of bankruptcies in the savings and loan industry in the 1980s and the much smaller outbreak of bank failures in the early 1990s seemed to support those who claimed that deregulation had gone too far. And, indeed, both banks and, especially, S&Ls were subjected to some new regulations.

Others, however, argue that we should push further down the path of deregulation. True, legal limitations on interest rates have been abolished, and financial institutions can now engage in a much wider spectrum of activities than was true a decade ago. But banking across state lines is still heavily restricted, and banks can neither own nor be owned by industrial companies. Furthermore, these people argue, heavy-handed banking regulators made the 1990–1991 recession worse than need be by discouraging lending. More deregulation, it is claimed, would continue to make our financial system more fluid and our economy more efficient.

To make an informed judgment on the relative merits of deregulation and reregulation, we must first ask a more basic question, Why were banks so heavily regulated in the first place?

Banking is certainly not heavily monopolized. While there are financial giants such as Citibank (New York) and Bank of America (California), the industry is populated by literally thousands of small banks located in cities and towns throughout the country. There are more than 12,000 commercial banks and over 3000 savings institutions nationwide. So why did government regulations formerly tell banks, to some degree, how much they could accept in deposits, how much interest they could pay on these deposits, what types of investments they could make, and so on?

A first reason is that the major "output" of the banking industry—the nation's supply of money—is an important determinant of aggregate demand, as we will see in Chapter 30. Bank managers presumably do what is best for their stockholders. That, at any rate, is their job. But as we shall see, what is best for bank stockholders may not be best for the whole economy. For this reason, the government does not allow bankers to determine the level of the nation's money supply by profit considerations alone.

A second reason for the extensive regulation of banks is concern for the safety of depositors. In a free-enterprise system, new businesses are born and die every day; and no one other than those people immediately involved takes much notice of these goings-on. When a firm goes bankrupt, stockholders lose money and employees may lose their jobs. (The latter may not even happen if new management takes over the assets of the bankrupt firm.) But, except for the case of very large firms, that is about it.

But banking is different. If banks were treated like other firms, depositors would lose money whenever one went bankrupt. That is bad enough by itself, but the real danger comes in the case of a **run on a bank**. When depositors get jittery about the security of their money, they may all rush in at once to cash in their accounts. For reasons we will learn in this chapter, most banks could not survive a "run" like this and would be forced into insolvency. Worse yet, this disease is highly contagious. If Mr. Smith hears that his neighbor has just lost her life savings because the Main Street National Bank went broke, he is quite likely to rush to his own bank to make a hefty withdrawal. In fact, that is precisely what happened to a number of savings banks in the 1980s.

A **RUN ON A BANK** occurs when many depositors withdraw cash from their accounts all at once.

Without modern forms of bank regulation, therefore, one bank failure might lead to another. Indeed, bank failures were common throughout most of American history and have become distressingly common again in recent years. (See Figure 29–1.) But recent bank failures generally have not been precipitated by runs because the government has taken steps to ensure that such an infectious disease, if it occurs, will not spread. It has done this in several ways that will be mentioned in this chapter.

## BARTER VERSUS MONETARY EXCHANGE

Money is so much a part of our day-to-day existence that we are likely to take it for granted, failing to appreciate all that it accomplishes. But it is important to realize that money is very much a social contrivance. Like the wheel, it had to be invented. The most obvious way to trade commodities is not by using money, but by **barter**—a system in which people exchange one good directly for another. And the best way to appreciate what monetary exchange accomplishes is to imagine a world without it.

**BARTER** is a system of exchange in which people directly trade one good for another, without using money as an intermediate step.

Under a system of direct barter, if Farmer Jones grows corn and has a craving for peanuts, he has to find a peanut farmer, say, Farmer Smith, with a taste for corn. If he finds such a person (this was called the *double coincidence of wants* by the classical economists), they make the trade. If this sounds easy, try to imagine how busy Farmer Jones would be if he had to repeat the sequence for every commodity he consumed in a week. For the most part, the desired double coincidences of wants are more likely to turn out to be double wants of coincidence, where Jones gets no peanuts and Smith gets no corn. Worse yet, with so much time spent looking for trading partners, Jones would have far less time to grow corn. Thus:

Money greases the wheels of exchange, and thus makes the whole economy more productive.

Under a monetary system, Farmer Jones gives up his corn for money. He does so not because he wants the money per se, but because of what that money can buy. Money makes his shopping tasks much easier, for it allows him simply to locate a peanut farmer who wants money. And what peanut farmer does not? For these reasons, monetary exchange replaced barter at a very early stage of human civilization, and only extreme circumstances, like massive wars and runaway inflations, have been able to bring barter (temporarily) back.

Figure 29-1 BANK FAILURES IN THE UNITED STATES, 1915–1991

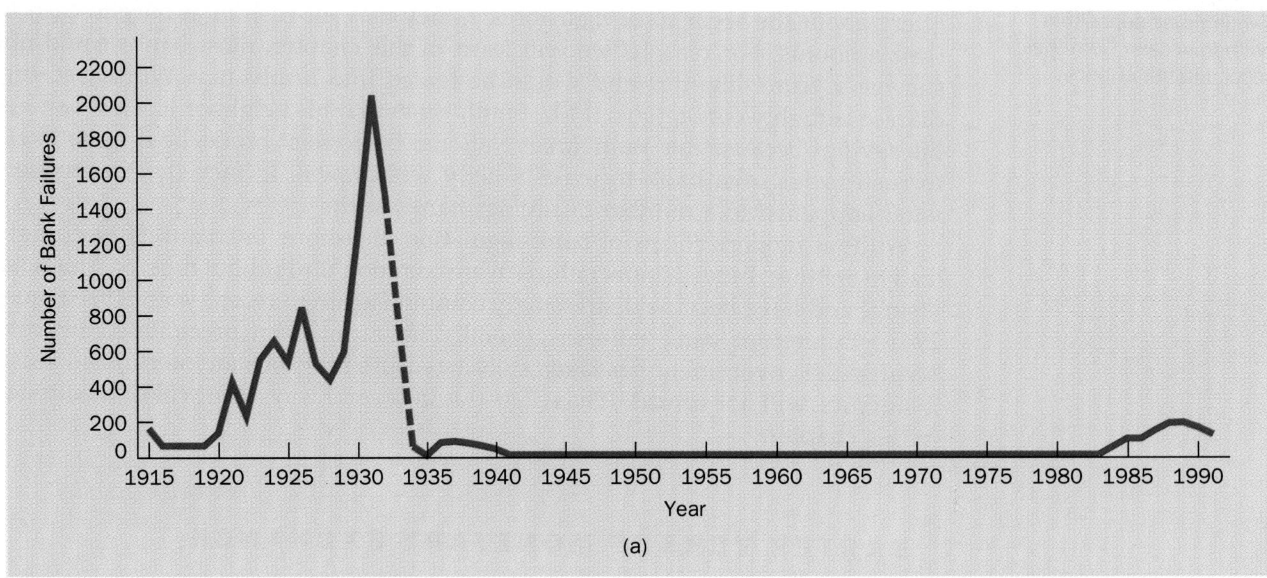

(a)

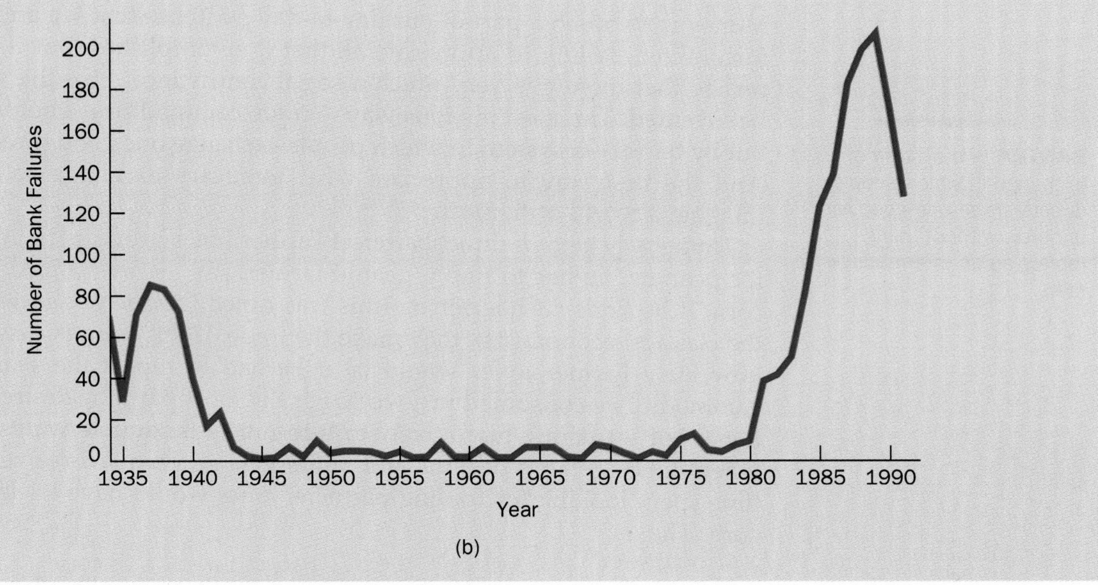

(b)

This chart shows the number of commercial banks that failed each year from 1915 through 1991. Notice the sharp drop in the number of failures from 1932 to 1934 and the steep rise in recent years. Failures clearly are much less common in the postwar period than they were in earlier years. But they have become much more frequent since the 1980s than they were between World War II and 1980.

SOURCE: Federal Deposit Insurance Corporation.

## THE CONCEPTUAL DEFINITION OF MONEY

**MONEY** is the standard object used in exchanging goods and services. In short, money is the **MEDIUM OF EXCHANGE**.

The **UNIT OF ACCOUNT** is the standard unit for quoting prices.

A **STORE OF VALUE** is an item used to store wealth from one point in time to another.

Monetary exchange is the alternative to barter. In a system of monetary exchange, people trade **money** for goods when they purchase something and trade goods for money when they sell something; but they do not trade goods directly for other goods. This defines money's principal role as the **medium of exchange**. But once it has become accepted as the medium of exchange, whatever object is serving as money is bound to take on other functions as well. For one, it will inevitably become the **unit of account**, that is, the standard unit for quoting prices. Thus, if inhabitants of an idyllic tropical island used coconuts as money, they would be foolish to quote prices in terms of sea shells.

Money may also come to be used as a **store of value**. If Farmer Jones temporarily produces and sells corn of more value than he wants to consume, he may find it convenient to store the difference in the form of money until he wants to use it. This is because he knows that money can be "sold" easily for goods and services at a later date, whereas land, gold, and other stores of value might not be. Of course, if money pays no interest and inflation is substantial, he may decide to forgo the convenience of money and store his wealth in some other form rather than see its purchasing power rapidly eroded. So this role of money is far from inevitable.

Since money may not always serve as a store of value, and since there are many stores of value other than money, it is best not to include the store-of-value function as part of our conceptual definition of money. Instead, we simply label as "money" whatever serves as the medium of exchange.

## WHAT SERVES AS MONEY?

Anthropologists and historians will testify that a bewildering variety of things have served as money in different times and places. Cattle, stones, candy bars, cigarettes, woodpecker scalps, porpoise teeth, and giraffe tails are a few of the more colorful examples.

A **COMMODITY MONEY** is an object in use as a medium of exchange, but which also has a substantial value in alternative (nonmonetary) uses.

In primitive or less organized societies, the commodities that served as money generally had value in themselves. If not used as money, cattle could be slaughtered for food, cigarettes could be smoked, and so on. But such **commodity money** generally runs into several severe difficulties. To be useful as a medium of exchange, the commodity must be divisible. This makes cattle a poor choice. It must also be of uniform, or at least readily identifiable, quality so that inferior substitutes are easy to recognize. This may be why woodpecker scalps never achieved great popularity. The medium of exchange must also be storable and durable, which presents a serious problem for candy-bar money. Finally, because commodity money needs to be carried and stored, it is helpful if the item is compact, that is, has high value per unit of volume and weight. (See the boxed insert on page 719).

All of these traits make it sensible that gold and silver have circulated as money since the first coins were struck about 2500 years ago. As they have high value in nonmonetary uses, a lot of purchasing power can be carried without too much weight. Pieces of gold are also storable, divisible (with a little trouble), and of identifiable quality (with a little more trouble).

The same characteristics suggest that paper would make an ideal money. Since we can print any number on it that we please, we can make paper money as divisible as we like and also make it possible to carry a large value in a lightweight and compact form. Paper is easy to store and, with a little cleverness, we can make counterfeiting hard (though never impossible). The Chinese originated paper money in the eleventh century, and Marco Polo brought word of this invention to Europe.

**FIAT MONEY** is money that is decreed as such by the government. It is of little value as a commodity, but it maintains its value as a medium of exchange because people have faith that the issuer will stand behind the pieces of printed paper and limit their production.

Paper cannot, however, serve as a commodity money because its value per square inch in alternative uses is so small. A paper currency that is repudiated by its issuer can, perhaps, be used as wallpaper or to wrap fish, but these uses will surely represent only a small fraction of the paper's value as money.[1] Contrary to the popular expression, such a currency literally *is* worth the paper it is printed on, which is to say that it is not worth much. Thus paper money is always **fiat money**.

Money in the contemporary United States is almost entirely fiat money. Look at a dollar bill. Next to George Washington's picture it states: "This note is legal tender for all debts public and private." Nowhere on the certificate is there a promise, stated or implied, that the U.S. government will exchange it for anything else. A dollar bill is convertible into 4 quarters, 10 dimes, 20 nickels, or any other similar combination, but not into gold, chocolate, or any other commodity.

Why do people hold these pieces of paper? Only because they know that others are willing to accept them for things of intrinsic value—food, rent, shoes, and so on. If this confidence ever evaporated, these dollar bills would cease serving as a medium of exchange and, given that they make ugly wallpaper, would become virtually worthless.

But don't panic. This is not likely to occur. Our current monetary system has evolved over hundreds of years during which *commodity* money was first replaced by *full-bodied paper money*—paper certificates that were backed by gold or silver of equal value held in the issuer's vaults. Then the full-bodied paper money was replaced by certificates that were only partially backed by gold and silver. Finally,

[1]The first paper money issued by the federal government, the Continental dollar, was essentially repudiated. (Actually, the new government of the United States redeemed the Continentals for 1 cent on the dollar in the 1790s.) This gave rise to the derisive expression, "It's not worth a Continental."

## *Dealing by Wheeling on Yap*

Primitive forms of money still exist in some remote places, as this extract from a newspaper article shows.

YAP, Micronesia—On this tiny South Pacific Island . . . the currency is as solid as a rock. In fact, it is rock. Limestone to be precise.

For nearly 2,000 years the Yapese have used large stone wheels to pay for major purchases, such as land, canoes and permission to marry. Yap is a U.S. trust territory, and the dollar is used in grocery stores and gas stations. But reliance on stone money . . . continues.

Buying property with stones is "much easier than buying it with U.S. dollars," says John Chodad, who recently purchased a building lot with a 30-inch stone wheel. "We don't know the value of the U.S. dollar."

Stone wheels don't make good pocket money, so for small transactions, Yapese use other forms of currency, such as beer. . . .

Besides stone wheels and beer, the Yapese sometimes spend *gaw*, consisting of necklaces of stone beads strung together around a whale's tooth. They also can buy things with *yar*, a currency made from large sea shells. But these are small change.

The people of Yap have been using stone money ever since a Yapese warrior named Anagumang first brought the huge stones over-from limestone caverns on neighboring Palau, some 1,500 to 2,000 years ago. Inspired by the moon, he fashioned the stone into large circles. The rest is history . . . .

By custom, the stones are worthless when broken. You never hear people on Yap musing about wanting a piece of the rock. . . .

Stone wheel money from Yap.

SOURCE: Adapted from Art Pine, "Hard Assets, or Why a Loan in Yap Is Hard to Roll Over," *The Wall Street Journal*, March 29, 1984, page 1.

we arrived at our present system, in which paper money has no "backing" whatsoever. Like a hesitant swimmer who first dips her toes, then her legs, then her whole body into a cold swimming pool, we have "tested the water" at each step of the way—and found it to our liking. It is unlikely that we will ever take a step back in the other direction.

## HOW THE QUANTITY OF MONEY IS MEASURED

Since the amount of money in circulation is of profound importance for the determination of national product and the price level, it is important for the government to know how much money there is, that is, to devise some *measure* of the money supply.

Our conceptual definition of money describes it as the medium of exchange. But this raises difficult questions about just what items to include and exclude when we count up the money supply—questions that have long made the statistical definition of money a subject of dispute. In fact, the U.S. government has several official definitions of the money supply, two of which we will meet in this section.

Some components are obvious. All of our coins and paper money, the small change of our economic system, clearly should count as money. But we cannot stop there if we want to include the main vehicle for making payments in our society, for the lion's share of our nation's payments are made neither in metal nor in paper money, but by check.

Checking deposits are actually no more than bookkeeping entries in bank ledgers. Many people think of checks simply as a convenient way to give coins or dollar bills to someone else. But that is not so. In fact, the volume of money held in the form of checking deposits far exceeds the volume of currency. For example, when you pay the grocer $50 by check, dollar bills rarely change hands. Instead, that check normally travels back to your bank, where $50 is deducted from the bookkeeping entry that records your account and added to the bookkeeping entry for your grocer's account. (If you and the grocer hold accounts at different banks, more books get involved; but still no coins or bills are likely to be moved.)

Since so many transactions are made by check, it seems imperative that checking deposits be included in any useful definition of the money supply. Unfortunately, this is not an easy task nowadays because of the bewildering variety of ways to transfer money by check. Traditional checking accounts in commercial banks are the most familiar. But many people can also write checks on their savings accounts, on their deposits at credit unions, on their mutual funds, their accounts with stockbrokers, and so on.

The narrowly defined money supply, usually abbreviated **M1**, is the sum of all coins and paper money in circulation, plus certain checkable deposit balances at banks and savings institutions.[2]

One popular definition of the money supply draws the line early and includes only coins, paper money, travelers' checks, and certain checkable balances held in banks and savings institutions. In the official U.S. statistics, this narrowly defined concept of money is called **M1**. The left-hand side of Figure 29–2 shows the composition of M1 as of March 1993.

But there are other types of accounts that allow withdrawals by check and which therefore are candidates for inclusion in the money supply. Most notably, *money market deposit accounts* allow only a few checks per month but pay market-determined interest rates. Consumers have found these accounts extremely attractive vehicles for short-term investment, and balances in them now exceed all the checkable deposits included in M1.

In addition, many mutual fund organizations and brokerage houses offer *money market mutual funds*. These funds sell shares and use the proceeds to purchase a variety of short-term securities. But the important point, for our purposes, is that owners of shares in money market mutual funds can withdraw their funds simply by writing a check. So depositors can—and do—use their holdings of fund shares just like checking accounts.

The broadly defined money supply, usually abbreviated **M2**, is the sum of all coins and paper money in circulation, plus all types of checking account balances, plus most forms of savings account balances, plus shares in money market mutual funds, and a few other minor items.

Finally, although you cannot write a check on a *savings account*, many economists feel that modern banking procedures have blurred the distinction between checking balances and savings balances. For example, most banks these days offer convenient electronic transfers of funds from one account to another, either by telephone or by pushing a button on an automated teller. Consequently, savings balances can become checkable almost instantly. For this reason, savings accounts are included—along with money market deposit accounts, money market mutual fund shares, and a few other small items—in the broader definition of the money supply known as **M2**.

[2]This includes travelers' checks and NOW (negotiable order of withdrawal) accounts.

Figure 29–2 **TWO DEFINITIONS OF THE MONEY SUPPLY**

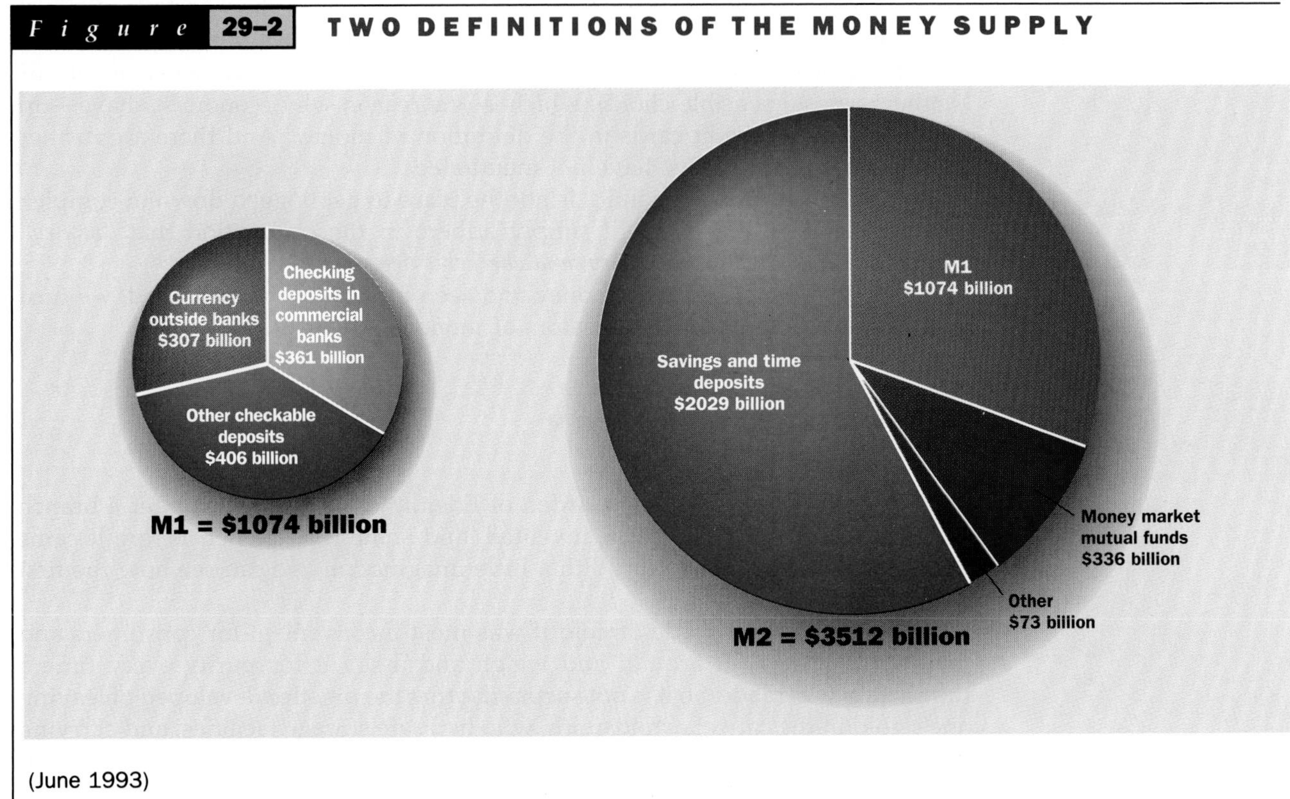


(June 1993)
SOURCE: Federal Reserve.

The composition of M2 as of March 1993 is shown on the right-hand side of Figure 29–2. You can see that savings deposits predominate, dwarfing everything that is included in M1. Figure 29–2 illustrates two points that are worth remembering. First, our money supply comes not only from banks, but also from savings institutions, brokerage houses, and mutual fund organizations. Second, however, banks still play a predominant role.

Some economists do not want to stop counting at M2; they prefer still broader definitions of money (M3, and so on) which include more types of bank deposits and other closely related assets. The problem with this approach is that there is no obvious place to stop, no clear line of demarcation between those assets that *are* money and those that are merely *close substitutes* for money—so called **near moneys**.

**NEAR MONEYS** are liquid assets that are close substitutes for money.

An asset's **LIQUIDITY** refers to the ease with which it can be converted into cash.

If we define an asset's **liquidity** as the ease with which it can be converted into cash, there is a range of assets of varying degrees of liquidity. Everything in M1 is completely "liquid"; the money market fund shares and passbook savings accounts included in M2 are a bit less so; and so on, until we encounter such things as short-term government bonds, which, while still quite liquid, would not normally be included in the money supply. Any number of different "Ms" can be defined—and have been—by drawing the line in different places.

And there are still more complexities. For example, credit cards clearly serve as a medium of exchange. So should they be included in the money supply? Yes, you say. But how would we do this? How much money does your credit card represent? Is it the amount you currently owe on the card, which may well be zero? Or is it your entire line of credit, even though you may never use it all? Neither seems a sensible choice, which is one reason why economists have—up to now—ignored credit cards in the definition of money. And there are further definitional issues that we have not mentioned.

But a first course in economics is not the place to get bogged down in complex definitional issues. So we will simply adhere to the convention that *"money" consists only of coins, paper money, and checkable deposits.*

Now that we have defined money and seen how it can be measured, we turn our attention to the principal creators of money—the banks.

## HOW BANKING BEGAN

When Adam and Eve left the Garden of Eden, they did not encounter a branch of Citibank. Banking had to be invented, and some time passed before it came to be practiced as it is today. With a little imagination, we can see how the first banks must have begun.

When money was made of gold it was most inconvenient for consumers and merchants to carry it around and weigh and assay it for purity every time a transaction was made. So it is not surprising that the practice developed of leaving one's gold in the care of a goldsmith, who had safe storage facilities, and carrying in its place a receipt from the goldsmith stating that John Doe did indeed own five ounces of gold of a certain purity. When people began trading goods and services for the goldsmiths' receipts, rather than for the gold itself, the receipts became an early form of paper money.

At this stage, paper money was fully backed by gold. But gradually the goldsmiths began to notice that the amount of gold they were actually required to pay out in a day was but a small fraction of the total gold they had stored in their warehouses. Then one day some enterprising goldsmith hit upon a momentous idea that must have made him fabulously wealthy.

His thinking probably ran something like this. "I have 2000 ounces of gold stored away in my vault, for which I collect storage fees from my customers. If I get much more, I'll need an expensive new vault. But in the last year, I was never called upon to pay out more than 100 ounces on a single day. What harm could it do if I lent out, say, half the gold I now have? I'll still have more than enough to pay off any depositors that come in for a withdrawal, so no one will ever know the difference. And I could earn 30 additional ounces of gold each year in interest on the loans I make (at 3 percent interest on 1000 ounces). With this profit, I could lower my service charges to depositors and so attract still more deposits. I think I'll do it."

**FRACTIONAL RESERVE BANKING** is a system under which bankers keep as reserves only a fraction of the funds they hold on deposit.

With this resolution, the modern system of **fractional reserve banking** was born. This system has three important features—features that are crucially important to this chapter.

1. *Bank profitability.* By getting deposits at zero interest and lending some of them out at positive interest rates, goldsmiths made a profit. The history of banking as a profit-making industry was begun and has continued to this date. *Banks, like other enterprises, are in business to earn profits.*

2. *Bank discretion over the money supply.* When goldsmiths decided that they could get along by keeping only a fraction of their total deposits on reserve in their vaults and lending out the balance, they acquired the ability to *create money*. As long as they kept 100 percent reserves, each gold certificate represented exactly one ounce of gold. So whether people decided to carry their gold or leave it with their goldsmith did not affect the money supply, which was set by the volume of gold.

   With the advent of fractional reserve banking, however, new paper certificates were added whenever goldsmiths lent out some of the gold they held on deposit. The loans, in effect, created new money. In this way, the total amount of money came to depend on the amount of gold that each goldsmith felt compelled to maintain as reserves in his vault. For any given volume of gold on deposit, the lower the reserves the goldsmiths kept, the more loans they could make, and therefore the more money there would be. While we no longer use gold to back our money, this principle remains true today. *Bankers' business decisions influence the supply of money.*

3. *Exposure to runs.* A goldsmith who kept 100 percent reserves never had to worry about a run on his vault. Even if all his depositors showed up at the door at once, he always had enough gold to return their deposits. But as soon as the first goldsmith decided to get by with only fractional reserves, the possibility of a run on the vault became a real concern. If that first goldsmith who lent out half his gold had found 51 percent of his customers at his door one unlucky day, he would have had a lot of explaining to do. Similar problems have worried bankers for centuries. *The danger of a run on the bank has induced bankers to keep prudent reserves and to lend out money carefully.*

## PRINCIPLES OF BANK MANAGEMENT: PROFITS VERSUS SAFETY

Bankers have a reputation, probably deserved, for conservatism in politics, dress, and business affairs. From what has been said so far, the economic rationale for this conservatism should be clear. Checking deposits are pure fiat money. Years ago, these deposits were "backed" by nothing more than the bank's promise to convert them into currency on demand. If people lost trust in a bank, the bank was doomed.

Thus, it has always been imperative for bankers to acquire a reputation for prudence. This they did in two principal ways. First, they had to maintain a sufficiently generous level of reserves to minimize their vulnerability to runs. Second, they had to be somewhat cautious in making loans and investments, since any large losses on their loans would undermine the confidence of depositors.

It is important to realize that banking under a system of fractional reserves is an inherently risky business that is rendered relatively safe only by cautious and prudent management. America's continuing history of bank failures bears sober testimony to the fact that many bankers have been neither cautious nor prudent. Why? Because this is not a recipe for high profits. Bank profits are maximized by keeping reserves as low as possible, by making at least some risky investments, and by giving loans to borrowers of questionable credit standing (because these borrowers will pay the highest interest rates).

The art of bank management is to strike the appropriate balance between the lure of profits and the need for safety. When a banker errs by being too stodgy, his bank will earn inadequate profits. When he errs by taking unwarranted risks, his bank may not survive at all. Many banks have perished in the latter way in recent years, especially in the savings and loan industry. (See the boxed insert on the following page.)

## BANK REGULATION

The public authorities have decided that the balance between profits and safety likely to be preferred by profit-minded bankers often will not be at the place where society wants it struck. So government has thrown up a web of regulations designed to insure the safety of depositors and to control the supply of money.

**DEPOSIT INSURANCE** is a system that guarantees that depositors will not lose money even if their bank goes bankrupt.

The principal innovation guaranteeing the safety of bank deposits is **deposit insurance**. Today most bank deposits are insured against loss by the **Federal Deposit Insurance Corporation (FDIC)**—an agency of the U.S. government. If your bank belongs to the FDIC (and most do), your checking account is insured for up to $100,000 regardless of what happens to the bank. Thus, while bank failures may spell disaster for the bank's stockholders, they do not give many depositors cause for concern. Deposit insurance eliminates the motive for customers to rush to their bank just because they hear some bad news about the bank's finances. Many observers give this innovation much of the credit for the pronounced decline in bank failures after 1933, the year in which the FDIC was established. (Refer back to Figure 29–1 on page 716.)

Until 1989, there was a separate government agency that insured the deposits of thrift institutions. However, so many S&Ls and savings banks went bankrupt in the 1980s that the deposit insurance fund was overwhelmed—which is what forced Congress to restructure the industry. (See the accompanying boxed insert.) Unfortunately, the recent rash of bank failures has not been confined to thrift institutions. As Figure 29–1 shows, an alarming number of ordinary commercial banks also failed in the late 1980s and early 1990s. These failures strained the finances of the FDIC, and Congress responded by raising premiums for deposit insurance several times.[3]

In addition to insuring depositors against loss, the government takes steps to see that banks do not get into financial trouble. For one thing, various regulatory authorities conduct periodic *bank examinations and audits* in order to keep tabs on the financial condition and business practices of the banks under their purview. Bank supervision was tightened in 1992 by legislation which permits the authorities to intervene in the affairs of financially troubled banks. There are also laws and regulations that *limit the kinds and quantities of assets in which banks may invest*. For example, most banks are prohibited from purchasing common stock. Both these forms of regulation are clearly aimed at maintaining bank safety.

A final type of regulation also has some bearing on safety but is motivated primarily by the government's desire to control the money supply. We have seen that the amount of money any bank will issue depends on the amount of reserves

[3]Banks pay premiums for deposit insurance just as individuals pay premiums for fire, automobile, and life insurance.

## America's Savings and Loan Industry: Cleaning Up the Mess

After years of procrastination, Congress finally passed legislation in 1989 to clean up the debris left by the collapse of the savings and loan industry. The process is going on right now, and the ultimate bill to the nation's taxpayers may go as high as $150 billion.* How did such a highly regulated industry ever get into such trouble?

The savings and loan business used to be a very simple one: S&Ls accepted saving deposits and lent out money in the form of home mortgages. A web of regulations protected them from competition from commercial banks, so S&L executives led the quiet life. But seeds of disaster were sown when interest rates skyrocketed in the 1970s. S&Ls found themselves losing money because the interest rates they had to pay for new deposits rose far above the rates they were earning on old mortgages. Many thrift institutions were mortally wounded at that time, but staggered on.

Then came financial deregulation in the 1980s. S&Ls were exposed to greater competition and given freedom to expand their lending beyond their traditional domain of home mortgages. Pressure to earn higher rates of return tempted many S&Ls into making risky loans—secured by oil fields, unbuilt shopping centers, and sometimes by nothing at all. The industry began to be populated by financial cowboys instead of stodgy bankers.

Unfortunately, in its zeal to deregulate, the U.S. government forgot that an unregulated savings and loan industry requires more supervision than a regulated one. It was a costly error. Too much imprudent risk-taking and mismanagement was tolerated, and the industry was beset by an outrageous amount of fraud. Then a recession in 1981–1982 and the collapse of oil prices in the mid-1980s piled yet more losses on beleaguered S&Ls—especially in Texas.

Many executives concluded that their only hope was to "bet the bank" on risky investments which, if they paid off, might put them back in the black. Since their banks were going under anyway, they had little to lose if the bets went bad. So gambling S&Ls began to offer above-market interest rates to attract new deposits and wagered the money on speculative ventures, many of which turned sour. Taxpayers were being set up for a crash landing because federal deposit insurance obligated the government to pay off the depositors (up to $100,000 per account) of any thrift institution that went bankrupt. This, many people believed, was the essence of the problem: S&L operators were allowed to gamble with the taxpayers' money.

Although this was well understood by the mid-1980s, Congress and the Reagan administration did nothing about it. Why? Because closing down insolvent S&Ls would entail current expenses that would enlarge the budget deficit. An example will show why. Suppose a bankrupt S&L has $500 million in insured deposits, but its assets are worth only $400 million. If the government takes it over, sells all the assets at market value, and pays off the depositors, it takes in $400 million and pays out $500 million—leaving it $100 million short.

Since neither Congress nor President Reagan wanted to face up to the bill, the problem worsened. The government only got serious about closing down the thrifts early in the Bush administration. But even then the agency created to clean up the mess—the Resolution Trust Corporation (RTC)—was persistently underfunded. So the job dragged on, and on, and on.

Today, the RTC is still in the process of taking over, and eventually trying to sell, hundreds of ailing financial institutions. Tighter regulations, stiffer penalties for fraud, and higher premiums for deposit insurance were also imposed on the industry to make sure the thrift debacle would not be repeated. It has been an expensive lesson for the U.S. government and its taxpayers.

One final point: The cleanup operation is often misleadingly called a "bailout"—a term which suggests that government funds are being used to save ailing firms. Except in a few isolated instances, that is not the case. It is the depositors who are being "bailed out," not the managers and stockholders of the S&Ls, who generally lose their jobs and their investments, respectively.

*In the popular press, cost estimates much higher than $150 billion are sometimes reported. These inflated figures result from misleadingly treating $1 to be paid in the distant future as equivalent to $1 paid today. As the appendix to Chapter 15 explained, a dollar payable, say, 10 years in the future is worth considerably less than a dollar payable today.

**REQUIRED RESERVES** are the minimum amount of reserves (in cash or the equivalent) required by law. Normally, required reserves are proportional to the volume of deposits.

it elects to keep. For this reason, most banks are subject by law to minimum **required reserves**. While banks may (and sometimes do) keep reserves in excess of these legal minimums, they may not keep less. It is this regulation that places an upper limit on the money supply. The rest of this chapter is concerned with the details of this mechanism.

## HOW BANKERS KEEP BOOKS

Before we can fully understand the mechanics of modern banking and the process by which money is "created," we must acquire at least a nodding acquaintance with the way in which bankers keep their books. The first thing to know is how to distinguish assets from liabilities.

An **ASSET** of an individual or business firm is an item of value that the individual or firm owns.

A **LIABILITY** of an individual or business firm is an item of value that the individual or firm owes. Many liabilities are known as "debts."

An **asset** of a bank is something of value that the bank *owns*. This "thing" may be a physical object, such as the bank building, a computer, or a vault, or it may be just a piece of paper, such as an IOU of a customer to whom the bank has made a loan. A **liability** of a bank is something of value that the bank *owes*. Most bank liabilities take the form of bookkeeping entries. For example, if you have a checking account in the Main Street Bank, your bank balance is a liability of the bank. (It is, of course, an asset to you.)

There is an easy test to see whether some piece of paper or bookkeeping entry is a bank's *asset* or *liability*. Ask yourself whether, if this paper were converted into cash, the bank would receive the cash (if so, it is an asset) or pay it out (if so, it is a liability). This test makes it clear that loans to customers are bank assets (when loans are repaid, the bank collects), while customers' deposits are bank liabilities (when deposits are cashed in, the bank must pay). Of course, things are just the opposite to the bank's customers: the loans are liabilities and the deposits are assets.

A **BALANCE SHEET** is an accounting statement listing the values of all the assets on the left-hand side and the values of all the liabilities and **net worth** on the right-hand side.

**NET WORTH** is the value of all assets minus the value of all liabilities.

When accountants draw up a complete list of all the bank's assets and liabilities, the resulting document is called the bank's **balance sheet**. Typically, the value of all the bank's assets exceeds the value of all its liabilities. (On the rare occasions when this is not so, the bank is in serious trouble.) In what sense, then, do balance sheets "balance"?

They balance because accountants have invented the concept of **net worth** to balance the books. Specifically, they define the net worth of a bank to be the difference between the value of all its assets and the value of all its liabilities. Thus, by definition, when accountants add net worth to liabilities, the sum they get must be the same as the value of the bank's assets. In short:

$$\text{Assets} = \text{Liabilities} + \text{Net Worth}.$$

Table 29–1 illustrates this with the balance sheet of a fictitious bank, Bank-a-mythica, whose finances are extremely simple. On December 31, 1993, it had only two kinds of assets (listed on the left-hand side of the balance sheet)—\$1 million in cash, which it held as reserves, and \$4,500,000 in outstanding loans to its customers, that is, in customers' IOUs. And it had only one type of liability (listed on the right-hand side)—\$5 million in checking deposits. The difference between total assets (\$5.5 million) and total liabilities (\$5 million) was the bank's net worth (\$500,000), shown on the right-hand side of the balance sheet.

*Table* **29–1** **BALANCE SHEET OF BANK-A-MYTHICA, DECEMBER 31, 1993**

| ASSETS | | LIABILITIES AND NET WORTH | |
|---|---|---|---|
| **Assets** | | **Liabilities** | |
| Reserves | $1,000,000 | Checking deposits | $5,000,000 |
| Loans outstanding | 4,500,000 | | |
| Total | $5,500,000 | **Net Worth** | |
| **Addendum: Bank Reserves** | | Stockholders' equity | 500,000 |
| Actual reserves | $1,000,000 | | |
| Required reserves | 1,000,000 | | |
| Excess reserves | 0 | | |
| | | Total | $5,500,000 |

## THE LIMITS TO MONEY CREATION BY A SINGLE BANK

Let us now turn to the process of deposit creation. Many bankers will deny that they have any ability to "create" money. The phrase itself has a suspiciously hocus-pocus sound to it. But they are not quite right. For although any individual bank's ability to create money is severely limited in a system with many banks, the banking system as a whole can achieve much more than the sum of its parts. Through the modern alchemy of **deposit creation**, it can turn one dollar into many dollars. But to understand this important process, we had better proceed in steps, beginning with the case of a single bank, our hypothetical Bank-a-mythica.

According to the balance sheet in Table 29–1, Bank-a-mythica is holding cash reserves that are equal to 20 percent of its deposits ($1 million in cash is equal to 20 percent of the $5 million in deposits). Let us assume that this is the minimum reserve ratio prescribed by law and that the bank strives to keep its reserves down to the legal minimum; that is, it strives to keep its **excess reserves** down to zero.

**EXCESS RESERVES** are any reserves held in excess of the legal minimum.

Now let us suppose that on January 2, 1994, an eccentric widower comes into Bank-a-mythica and deposits $100,000 in cash in his checking account. The bank now has acquired $100,000 more in cash reserves, and $100,000 more in checking deposits. But since deposits are up by $100,000, *required* reserves are up only by 20 percent of this amount, or $20,000, leaving $80,000 in *excess* reserves. Table 29–2 illustrates the effects of this transaction on Bank-a-mythica's balance sheet. It is tables such as this, which show *changes* in balance sheets rather than the balance sheets themselves, that will help us follow the money-creation process.[4]

If Bank-a-mythica does not want to hold excess reserves, it will be unhappy with the situation illustrated in Table 29–2, for it is holding $80,000 in excess reserves on which it earns no interest. So as soon as possible it will lend out the extra $80,000—let us say to Hard-Pressed Construction Company. This loan leads to the balance sheet changes shown in Table 29–3: Bank-a-mythica's loans rise by $80,000 while its holdings of cash reserves fall by $80,000.

[4]Notice that in all such tables, which are called "T accounts," the two sides of the ledger must balance. This is because changes in assets and changes in liabilities must be equal if the balance sheet is to balance both before and after the transaction.

**Table 29–2 CHANGES IN BANK-A-MYTHICA'S BALANCE SHEET, JANUARY 2, 1994**

| ASSETS | | LIABILITIES | |
|---|---|---|---|
| Reserves | +$100,000 | Checking deposits | +$100,000 |
| **Addendum: Bank Reserve** | | | |
| Actual reserves | +$100,000 | | |
| Required reserves | + 20,000 | | |
| Excess reserves | + $80,000 | | |

Bank-a-Mythica receives $100,000 cash deposit. It now holds excess reserves of $80,000, since required reserves rise by only $20,000 (20 percent of $100,000).

By combining Tables 29–2 and 29–3, we arrive at Table 29–4, which summarizes all the bank's transactions for the week. Reserves are up $20,000, loans are up $80,000 and, now that the bank has had a chance to adjust to the inflow of deposits, it no longer holds excess reserves.

Looking at Table 29–4 and keeping in mind our specific definition of money, it appears at first that the chairman of Bank-a-mythica is right when he claims not to have engaged in the nefarious practice of "money creation." All that happened was that, in exchange for the $100,000 in cash it received, the bank issued the widower a checking balance of $100,000. This does not change M1; it merely converts one form of money into another.

But wait. What happened to the $100,000 in cash that the eccentric man brought to the bank? The table shows that $20,000 was retained by Bank-a-mythica in its vault. Since this currency is no longer in circulation, it no longer counts in the official money supply. (Notice that Figure 29–2 included only "currency outside banks.") But the other $80,000, which the bank lent out, is still in circulation. It is held by Hard-Pressed Construction, which probably will redeposit it in some other bank. But even before this happens, the original $100,000 in cash has supported a rise in the money supply: there is now $100,000 in checking deposits and $80,000 in cash in circulation, making a total of $180,000. The money-creation process has begun.

**Table 29–3 CHANGES IN BANK-A-MYTHICA'S BALANCE SHEET, JANUARY 3–6, 1994**

| ASSETS | | LIABILITIES |
|---|---|---|
| Loans outstanding | +$80,000 | No change |
| Reserves | − 80,000 | |
| **Addendum: Changes in Reserves** | | |
| Actual reserves | −$80,000 | |
| Required reserves | No change | |
| Excess reserves | −$80,000 | |

Bank-a-Mythica gets rid of its excess reserves by making a loan of $80,000 to Hard-Pressed Construction Company.

**Table 29–4 CHANGES IN BANK-A-MYTHICA'S BALANCE SHEET, JANUARY 2–6, 1994**

| ASSETS | | LIABILITIES | |
|---|---|---|---|
| Reserves | +$20,000 | Checking deposits | +$100,000 |
| Loans outstanding | +$80,000 | | |
| **Addendum: Changes in Reserves** | | | |
| Actual reserves | +$20,000 | | |
| Required reserves | +$20,000 | | |
| Excess reserves | No change | | |

When it receives $100,000 in cash deposits, Bank-A-Mythica keeps only the required $20,000 in reserves and lends out the remaining $80,000 to Hard-Pressed Construction Company. Its excess reserves return to zero.

## MULTIPLE MONEY CREATION BY A SERIES OF BANKS

Let us now trace the $80,000 in cash and see how the process of money creation gathers momentum. Suppose that Hard-Pressed Construction Company, which banks across town at the First National Bank, deposits the $80,000 into its bank account. First National's reserves increase by $80,000. But because deposits are up by $80,000, *required* reserves rise by only 20 percent of this amount or $16,000. If the management of First National Bank behaves like that of Bank-a-mythica, the $64,000 of excess reserves will be lent out.

Table 29–5 shows the effects of these events on First National Bank's balance sheet. (The preliminary steps corresponding to Tables 29–2 and 29–3 are not shown separately.) At this stage in the chain, the original $100,000 in cash has led to $180,000 in deposits—$100,000 at Bank-a-mythica and $80,000 at First National Bank—and $64,000 in cash, which is still in circulation (in the hands of the recipient of First National's loan—Al's Auto Shop). Thus, from the original $100,000, a total of $244,000 has been added to the money supply ($180,000 in checking deposits plus $64,000 in cash).

**Table 29–5 CHANGES IN FIRST NATIONAL BANK'S BALANCE SHEET**

| ASSETS | | LIABILITIES | |
|---|---|---|---|
| Reserves | +$16,000 | Checking deposits | +$80,000 |
| Loans outstanding | + 64,000 | | |
| **Addendum: Changes in Reserves** | | | |
| Actual reserves | +$16,000 | | |
| Required reserves | +$16,000 | | |
| Excess reserves | No change | | |

Hard-Pressed deposits its $80,000 in First National Bank, which sets aside the required $16,000 in reserves (20 percent of $80,000) and lends $64,000 to Al's Auto Shop.

But, to coin a phrase, the bucks do not stop here. Al's Auto Shop will presumably deposit the proceeds from its loan into its own account at Second National Bank, leading eventually to the balance sheet adjustments shown in Table 29–6 when Second National makes an additional loan rather than hold on to excess reserves. You can see how the money-creation process continues.

Figure 29–3 is a graphical summary of the balance-sheet changes of the first five banks in the chain (from Bank-a-mythica through the Fourth National Bank) on the assumptions that each bank holds exactly the 20 percent required reserves (no excess reserves), and that each loan recipient redeposits the proceeds in the next bank. But the chain does not end there. The Main Street Movie Theatre, which received the $32,768 loan from the Fourth National Bank, then deposits these funds into the Fifth National Bank. Fifth National has to keep only 20 percent of this deposit, or $6,553.60, on reserve and will lend out the balance. And so the chain continues.

Where does it all end? The running sums in Figure 29–3 show what eventually happens to the entire banking system. The initial deposit of $100,000 in cash is ultimately absorbed in bank reserves (column 1), leading to a total of $500,000 in new deposits (column 2) and $400,000 in new loans (column 3). The money supply rises by $400,000 because the nonbank public eventually holds $100,000 *less* in currency and $500,000 *more* in checking deposits.

So there really is some hocus-pocus. Somehow, an initial deposit of $100,000 leads to $500,000 in new bank deposits—a multiple expansion of $5 for every original dollar—and a net increase of $400,000 in the money supply. We had better understand why this is so. But first let us verify that the calculations in Figure 29–3 are correct.

If you look carefully at the numbers, you will see that each column forms a *geometric progression*; specifically, each entry is equal to exactly 80 percent of the entry that preceded it. Recall that in our discussion of the multiplier in Chapter 26 we learned how to sum an infinite geometric progression, which is just what each of these chains eventually will be. In particular, if the common ratio is $R$, the sum of an infinite geometric progression is

$$1 + R + R^2 + R^3 + \ldots = \frac{1}{1 - R}.$$

**Table 29–6 CHANGES IN SECOND NATIONAL BANK'S BALANCE SHEET**

| ASSETS | | LIABILITIES | |
|---|---|---|---|
| Reserves | +$12,800 | Checking deposits | +$64,000 |
| Loans outstanding | + 51,200 | | |
| **Addendum: Changes in Reserves** | | | |
| Actual reserves | +$12,800 | | |
| Required reserves | +$12,800 | | |
| Excess reserves | No change | | |

When Al deposits his $64,000 in Second National Bank, that bank retains $12,800 as required reserves (20 percent of $64,000 and lends out the remaining $51,200.

**Figure 29–3** THE CHAIN OF MULTIPLE DEPOSIT CREATION

This diagram indicates how the deposit creation process spreads through the banking system. Each bank that receives a deposit keeps 20 percent of the deposit as reserves and lends out the other 80 percent—which becomes a deposit to the next bank in the chain. And so the chain continues. The numbers on the right-hand side of the diagram indicate the running sums of reserves, deposits, and loans caused by the initial $100,000 deposit.

NOTE: This schematic diagram was suggested to us by Dr. Ivan K. Cohen, whom we thank.

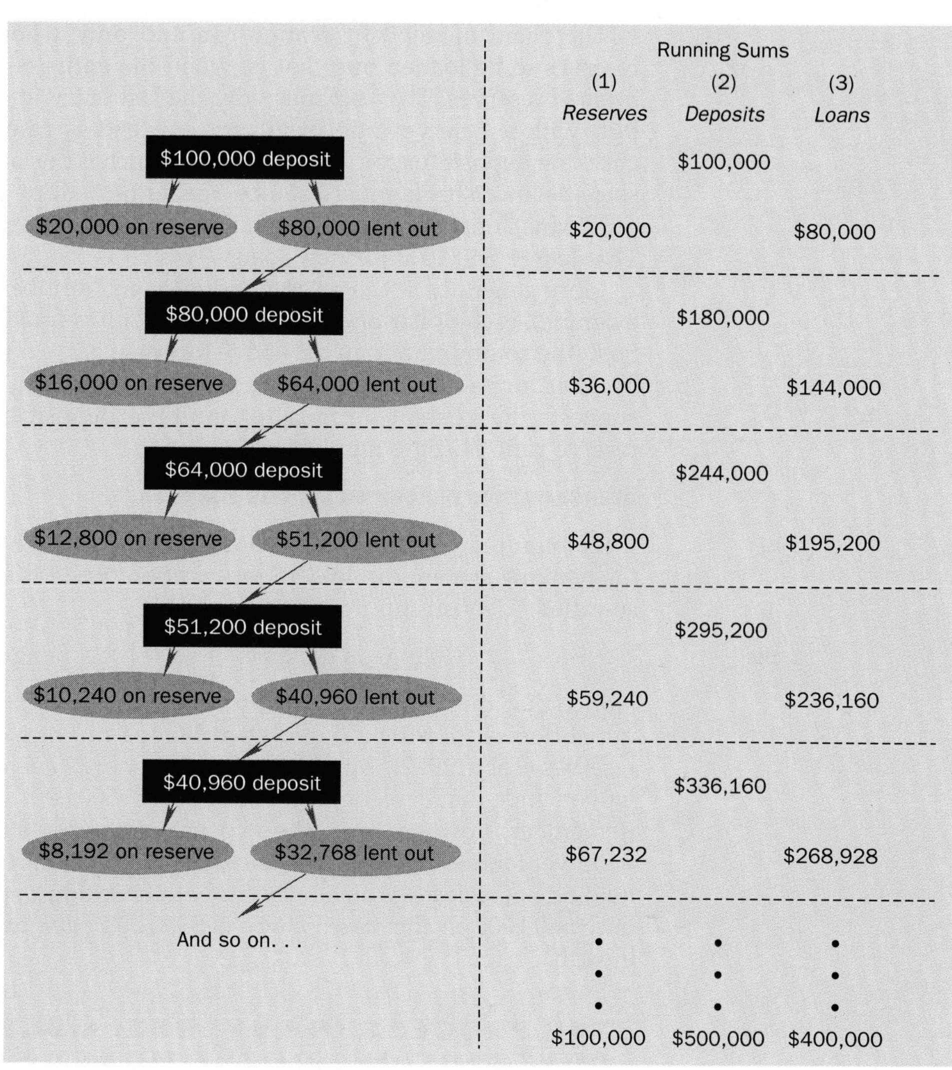


By applying this formula to the chain of checking deposits in Figure 29–3, we get:

$$
\begin{aligned}
&\$100{,}000 + \$80{,}000 + \$64{,}000 + \$51{,}200 + \ldots \\
&= \$100{,}000 \times (1 + 0.8 + 0.64 + 0.512 + \ldots) \\
&= \$100{,}000 \times (1 + 0.8 + 0.8^2 + 0.8^3 + \ldots) \\
&= \$100{,}000 \times \frac{1}{1 - 0.8} = \frac{\$100{,}000}{0.2} = \$500{,}000.
\end{aligned}
$$

Proceeding similarly, we can verify that the new loans sum to $400,000 and that the new required reserves sum to $100,000. (Check these as exercises.) So the numbers in Figure 29–3 are correct. Let us, therefore, think through the logic behind them.

The chain of deposit creation can end only when there are no more *excess* reserves to be loaned out; that is, when the entire $100,000 in cash is tied up in *required* reserves. That explains why the last entry in column 1 must be $100,000. But, with a reserve ratio of 20 percent, excess reserves disappear only when checking deposits expand by $500,000—which is the last entry in column 2. Finally, since balance sheets must balance, the sum of all newly created assets (reserves plus loans) must equal the sum of all newly created liabilities ($500,000 in deposits). That leaves $400,000 for new loans—which is the last entry in column 3.

More generally, if the reserve ratio is some number $m$ (rather than the $\frac{1}{5}$ in our example), each dollar of deposits requires only a fraction $m$ of a dollar in reserves. So $R$, the common ratio in the above formula, is $1 - m$, and deposits must expand by $1/m$ for each dollar of new reserves that are injected into the system. This suggests the general formula for multiple deposit creation when the required reserve ratio is some number $m$:

**OVERSIMPLIFIED DEPOSIT MULTIPLIER FORMULA**

If the required reserve ratio is some fraction, $m$, each $1 of reserves injected into the banking system can lead to the creation of $\$1/m$ in new deposits. That is, the so-called "deposit multiplier" is given by:

$$\text{Change in deposits} = (1/m) \times \text{Change in reserves.}$$

Notice that this formula correctly describes what happens in our example. The initial deposit of $100,000 in cash at Bank-a-mythica constitutes $100,000 in new reserves (Table 29–2). Applying a multiplier of $\$1/m = 1/0.2 = 5$ to this $100,000, we conclude that bank deposits will rise by $500,000—which is just what happens. Remember, however, that the expansion process started when some eccentric widower took $100,000 in cash and deposited it in his bank account. So the public's holdings of *money*—which includes both checking deposits *and cash*—increase by only $400,000 in this case: There is $500,000 *more* in deposits, but $100,000 *less* in cash.

## THE PROCESS IN REVERSE: MULTIPLE CONTRACTIONS OF THE MONEY SUPPLY

Let us now briefly consider how this deposit-creation mechanism operates in reverse—as a system of deposit *destruction*. In particular, suppose that our eccentric widower came back to Bank-a-mythica to withdraw $100,000 from his checking account and return it to his mattress, where it rightfully belongs. Bank-a-mythica's *required* reserves would fall by $20,000 as a result of this transaction (20 percent of $100,000), but its *actual* reserves would fall by $100,000. The bank would be $80,000 short, as indicated in Table 29–7(a).

How does it react to this discrepancy? As some of its outstanding loans are routinely paid off, the bank will cease granting new ones until it has accumulated the necessary $80,000 in required reserves. The data for Bank-a-mythica's contraction are shown in Table 29–7(b), assuming that borrowers pay off their loans in cash.[5]

---

[5]In reality, they would probably pay with checks drawn on other banks. Bank-a-mythica would then cash these checks to acquire the reserves.

**Table 29–7 CHANGES IN THE BALANCE SHEET OF BANK-A-MYTHICA**

| (a) ASSETS | | (a) LIABILITIES | | (b) ASSETS | | (b) LIABILITIES |
|---|---|---|---|---|---|---|
| Reserves | –$100,000 | Checking deposits | –$100,000 | Reserves | +$80,000 | No change |
| | | | | Loans outstanding | – 80,000 | |
| **Addendum: Changes in Reserves** | | | | **Addendum: Changes in Reserves** | | |
| Actual reserves | –$100,000 | | | Actual reserves | +$80,000 | |
| Required reserves | – 20,000 | | | Required reserves | No change | |
| Excess reserves | – 80,000 | | | Excess reserves | +$80,000 | |

When Bank-a-Mythica loses a $100,000 deposit, it must reduce its loans by $80,000 to replenish its reserves.

But where did the borrowers get this money? Probably by making withdrawals from other banks. In this case, let us assume it all came from First National Bank, which loses an $80,000 deposit and $80,000 in reserves. It finds itself short some $64,000 in reserves (see Table 29–8[a]) and therefore must reduce its loan commitments by $64,000 (see Table 29–8[b]). This, of course, causes some other bank to suffer a loss of reserves and deposits of $64,000, and the whole process repeats just as it did in the case of deposit expansion.

After the entire banking system had become involved, the picture would be just as shown in Figure 29–3, except that all the numbers would have *minus* signs in front of them. Deposits would shrink by $500,000, loans would fall by $400,000, bank reserves would be reduced by $100,000, and the money supply would fall by $400,000. As suggested by our deposit multiplier formula with $m = 0.2$, the decline in the bank deposits is $1/0.2 = 5$ times as large as the decline in excess reserves.

**Table 29–8 CHANGES IN THE BALANCE SHEET OF THE FIRST NATIONAL BANK**

| (a) ASSETS | | (a) LIABILITIES | | (b) ASSETS | | (b) LIABILITIES |
|---|---|---|---|---|---|---|
| Reserves | –$80,000 | Checking deposits | –$80,000 | Reserves | +$64,000 | No change |
| | | | | Loans outstanding | – 64,000 | |
| **Addendum: Changes in Reserves** | | | | **Addendum: Changes in Reserves** | | |
| Actual reserves | –$80,000 | | | Actual reserves | +$64,000 | |
| Required reserves | – 16,000 | | | Required reserves | No change | |
| Excess reserves | – 64,000 | | | Excess reserves | +$64,000 | |

First National Bank's loss of $80,000 deposit forces it to cut back its loans by $64,000.

One of the authors of this book was a student in Cambridge, Massachusetts, during the height of the radical student movement of the late 1960s. One day a circular appeared urging citizens to withdraw all funds from their checking accounts on a prescribed date, hold them in cash for one week, and then redeposit them. This act, the circular argued, would surely wreak havoc upon the capitalist system. Obviously, some of these radicals were well-schooled in modern money mechanics, for the argument was basically correct. The tremendous multiple contraction of the banking system and consequent multiple expansion that a successful campaign of this sort could have caused might have seriously disrupted the local financial system. But history records that the appeal met with little success. Checking-account withdrawals are not the stuff of which revolutions are made.

## WHY THE DEPOSIT CREATION FORMULA IS OVERSIMPLIFIED

So far, our discussion of the process of money creation has made it all seem rather mechanical. If all proceeds according to formula, each $1 in new excess reserves will lead to a $\$1/m$ increase in new deposits. But in reality things are not this simple. Just as we did in the case of the expenditure multiplier, we must stress that the oversimplified formula for deposit creation is accurate only under very particular circumstances. These circumstances require that:

1. Every recipient of cash must redeposit the cash into another bank rather than hold it.
2. Every bank must hold reserves no larger than the legal minimum.

The "chain" diagram in Figure 29–3 shows clearly what happens if either of these assumptions is violated.

Suppose first that the business firms and individuals who receive bank loans decide to redeposit only a fraction of the proceeds into their bank accounts. Then, for example, the first $80,000 loan would lead to a deposit of less than $80,000—and similarly down the chain. The whole chain of deposit creation would therefore be reduced. Thus:

If individuals and business firms decide to hold more cash, the multiple expansion of bank deposits will be curtailed because fewer dollars of cash will be available to be used as reserves to support new checking deposits. Consequently, the money supply will be smaller.

The basic idea here is simple. Each $1 of cash held by a bank can support several dollars (specifically, $\$1/m$) of money. But $1 of cash held by an individual is exactly one dollar of money; it supports no bank deposits. Hence, any time cash leaves the banking system, the money supply will decline. And any time cash enters the banking system, the money supply will rise.

Next, suppose that bank managers become more conservative, or that the outlook for loan repayments worsens because of a recession. Then banks might decide to keep more reserves than the legal requirement and lend out less than the amounts assumed in Figure 29–3. If this happens, banks further down the chain receive smaller deposits and, once again, the chain of deposit creation is curtailed. Thus:

If banks wish to keep excess reserves, the multiple expansion of bank deposits will be restricted. A given amount of cash will support a smaller supply of money than would be the case if banks held no excess reserves.

## THE NEED FOR MONETARY CONTROL

If we pursue this point a bit further, we will see why government regulation of the money supply is so important for economic stability. We have just suggested that banks will wish to keep excess reserves when they do not foresee profitable and secure opportunities to make loans. This is most likely to happen during the downswing and around the bottom of a business contraction. At such times, the propensity of banks to hold excess reserves will turn the deposit creation process into one of deposit destruction. Thus:

During a recession, profit-oriented banks would be prone to reduce the money supply by increasing their excess reserves—if the monetary authorities did not intervene. As we will learn in subsequent chapters, the money supply is an important influence on aggregate demand, so such a contraction of the money supply would aggravate the recession.

On the other hand, banks will want to squeeze the maximum possible money supply out of any given amount of cash reserves by keeping their reserves at the bare minimum when the demand for bank loans is buoyant, profits are high, and secure investment opportunities abound. This reduced incentive to hold excess reserves in prosperous times means that:

During an economic boom, the behavior of profit-oriented banks is likely to make the money supply expand, adding undesirable momentum to the booming economy and paving the way for a burst of inflation. The authorities must intervene to prevent this.

Regulation of the money supply, then, is necessary because profit-oriented bankers might otherwise provide the economy with a gyrating money supply that dances to the tune of the business cycle. Precisely how the authorities keep the money supply under control is the subject of the next chapter.

## *Summary*

1. It is more efficient to exchange goods and services by using money as a **medium of exchange** than by **bartering** them directly.
2. In addition to being the medium of exchange, whatever serves as money is likely to become the standard **unit of account** and a popular **store of value**.
3. Throughout history, all sorts of things have served as money. **Commodity money** gave way to fullbodied paper money (certificates backed 100 percent by some commodity, like gold), which in turn gave way to partially backed paper money. Nowadays our paper money has no commodity backing whatsoever; it is pure **fiat money**.
4. The most widely used definition of the U.S. money supply is **M1**, which includes coins, paper money, and several types of checking deposits. However, many economists prefer the **M2** definition, which adds to M1 other types of checkable accounts and most savings deposits. Much of M2 is held outside of banks.
5. Under our modern system of **fractional reserve banking,** banks keep cash reserves equal to only a fraction

of their total deposit liabilities. This is the key to their profitability, since the remaining funds can be loaned out at interest. But it also leaves them potentially vulnerable to **runs**.

6. Because of this vulnerability, bank managers are generally conservative in their investment strategy. They also keep a prudent level of reserves. Even so, the government keeps a watchful eye over banking practices.
7. Before 1933, bank failures were common; but they declined sharply when **deposit insurance** was instituted. Nonetheless, recent years have witnessed an upsurge of bank failures and a virtual collapse of the savings and loan industry.
8. Because it holds only fractional reserves, even a single bank can create money. But its ability to do so is severely limited because the funds it lends out probably will be deposited in another bank.
9. As a whole, the banking system can create several dollars of deposits for each dollar of reserves it receives. Under certain assumptions, the ratio of new deposits to new reserves will be $1/m$, where m is the required reserve ratio.
10. The same process works in reverse, as a system of money destruction, when cash is withdrawn from the banking system.
11. Because banks and individuals may want to hold more cash when the economy is shaky, the money supply would probably contract under such circumstances if the monetary authorities did not intervene. Similarly, the money supply would probably expand rapidly in boom times if it were unregulated.

## *Key Concepts and Terms*

Run on a bank
Barter
Unit of account
Money
Medium of exchange
Store of value
Commodity money
Fiat money
M1 versus M2
Near moneys
Liquidity
Fractional reserve banking
Deposit insurance
Federal Deposit Insurance Corporation (FDIC)
Required reserves
Asset
Liability
Balance sheet
Net worth
Deposit creation
Excess reserves

## *Questions for Review*

1. If ours were a barter economy, how would you pay your tuition bill? What if your college did not want the goods or services you offered in payment?
2. How is "money" defined, both conceptually and in practice? Does the U.S. money supply consist of commodity money, full-bodied paper money, or fiat money?
3. What is fractional reserve banking, and why is it the key to bank profits? (*Hint*: What opportunities to make profits would banks have if reserve requirements were 100 percent?) Why does fractional reserve banking give bankers discretion over how large the money supply will be? Why does it make banks potentially vulnerable to runs?
4. Explain why the many bank failures of the 1990s have not led to runs on banks.
5. Suppose that no banks keep excess reserves and no individuals or firms hold on to cash. If someone suddenly discovers $7.5 million in buried treasure, explain what will happen to the money supply if the required reserve ratio is 10 percent.
6. How would your answer to Question 5 differ if the reserve ratio were 25 percent? If the reserve ratio were 100 percent?
7. Each year during Christmas shopping season, consumers and stores wish to increase their holdings of cash. Explain how this could lead to a multiple contraction of the money supply. (As a matter of fact, the authorities prevent this contraction from occurring by methods explained in the next chapter.)
8. Excess reserves make a bank less vulnerable to runs. Why, then, don't bankers like to hold excess reserves?

What circumstances might persuade them that it would be advisable to hold excess reserves?

9. Use tables such as Tables 29–2 and 29–3 to illustrate what happens to bank balance sheets when each of the following transactions occurs:
   a. You withdraw $300 from your checking account to buy Christmas presents.
   b. Sam finds a $50 bill on the sidewalk and deposits it into his checking account.
   c. Mary Q. Contrary withdraws $900 in cash from her account at Hometown Bank, carries it to the city, and deposits it into her account at Big City Bank.
10. For each of the transactions listed in Question 9, what will be the ultimate effect on the money supply if the required reserve ratio is 10 percent? (Assume that the oversimplified deposit multiplier formula applies.)
11. If the government takes over a bankrupt thrift institution with liabilities (mostly deposits) of $2 billion, pays off the depositors, and sells the assets for $1.5 billion, where does the missing $500 million come from? Why?

Chapter 30

# MONETARY POLICY AND THE NATIONAL ECONOMY

*Victorians heard with grave attention that the Bank Rate had been raised. They did not know what it meant. But they knew that it was an act of extreme wisdom.*

J. K. GALBRAITH

Now that we understand the rudiments of the banking system, we are ready to bring money and interest rates into our model of income determination and the price level. In earlier chapters, we took investment ($I$) to be a fixed number. But this is a poor assumption. Not only is investment highly variable, but it also depends on interest rates. And interest rates are, in turn, heavily influenced by *monetary policy*. The main task of this chapter is to explain how monetary policy affects interest rates and investment and, thereby, aggregate demand. ¶ We begin by learning about the operations of America's *central bank*, the *Federal Reserve System*. The "Fed," as it is often called, is a very special kind of bank. Its customers are banks rather than individuals, and it performs some of the same services for them as your bank performs for you. Although it turns out to be an effective profit maker, its actions are not guided by the profit motive. Instead, the Fed tries to manage the money supply in what it perceives to be the national interest. Just how the Fed does its job, and why its performance has fallen short of perfection, are the first subjects of this chapter.

Next we integrate money into the Keynesian model. The mechanisms through which monetary policy affects aggregate demand are spelled out and analyzed in detail, and we learn an additional reason why the aggregate demand curve slopes downward. By the end of the chapter, we will have constructed a complete macroeconomic model, which we then use in the remaining chapters of Part 7 to investigate a variety of important policy issues.

## MONEY AND INCOME: THE IMPORTANT DIFFERENCE

But first we must get some terminology straight. The words "money" and "income" are used almost interchangeably in common parlance. This is a pitfall we must learn to avoid.

**Money** is a snapshot concept. It is the answer to questions like: "How much money do you have right now?" or "How much money did you have at 3:32 p.m. on Friday, November 5th?" To answer questions like these, you would add up the cash you are (or were) carrying and whatever checking balances you have (or had), and answer something like: "I have $126.33," or "On Friday, November 5th, at 3:32 p.m., I had $31.43."

**Income**, by contrast, is more like a motion picture; it comes to you only over a period of time. If you are asked "What is your income?" you must respond by saying "$200 *per week*," or "$800 *per month*," or "$10,000 *per year*," or something like that. Notice that there is a unit of time attached to each of these responses. If you just say "My income is $452," without indicating whether it is per week or per month or per year, no one will understand what you mean.

That the two concepts are very different is easy to see. A typical American family has an *income* of perhaps $35,000 per year, but its holdings of *money* at any point in time (using the M1 definition) are more like $2000. Similarly, at the national level, nominal GDP in 1992 was almost $6000 billion, while the money stock (M1) in the middle of the year was only about $950 billion.

While money and income are very different, they are certainly related. This chapter is precisely about that relationship. Specifically, we will look at how the stock of *money* in existence at any moment of time influences the rate at which people will be earning *income*, that is, how money affects the GDP.

## THE FEDERAL RESERVE SYSTEM: ORIGINS AND STRUCTURE

When the **Federal Reserve System** was established in 1914, the United States joined the company of most of the other advanced industrial nations. Up until then, the United States, distrustful of centralization of economic power, was almost the only important nation without a **central bank**. Britain's central bank, the Bank of England, for example, dates from 1694.

A **CENTRAL BANK** is a bank for banks. America's central bank is the **Federal Reserve System.**

The impetus for the establishment of a central bank in the United States came not from the power of economic logic but from some painful experiences with economic reality. Four severe banking panics between 1873 and 1907 convinced legislators and bankers alike that a central bank that would regulate credit conditions was not a luxury but a necessity. After the 1907 crisis, the National Monetary Commission was established to find out what was wrong with America's banking system. Its report in 1912 led directly to the establishment of the Federal Reserve System.

Figure 30–1 **THE TWELVE FEDERAL RESERVE DISTRICTS**

This map shows the boundaries of the 12 Federal Reserve districts and the locations of the 12 Federal Reserve banks. In which Federal Reserve district do you live?

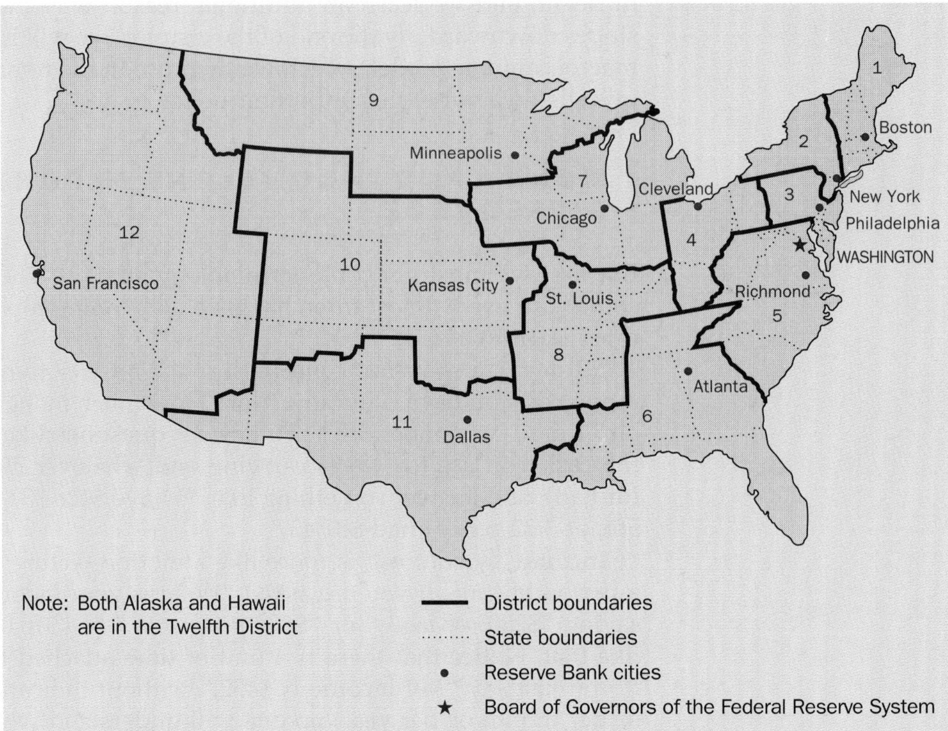


Although the basic idea of central banking came from Europe, some changes were made when it was imported, making the Federal Reserve System a uniquely American institution. Owing to the vastness of our country, the extraordinarily large number of commercial banks, and our tradition of dual state-federal regulations, it was decided that the United States should have not one central bank but 12. The boundaries of the 12 Federal Reserve districts and the location of each of the 12 district banks are shown in Figure 30–1.

Technically, each of the Federal Reserve banks is a corporation; its stockholders are the banks that belong to it. But your bank, if it is a member of the System, does not enjoy the privileges normally accorded to stockholders: it receives only a token share of the Federal Reserve's immense profits (the bulk is donated to the U.S. Treasury), and it has no say in the decisions of the corporation. The private banks are more like customers of the Fed than like owners.

Who, then, controls the Fed? Most of the power resides in the seven-member Board of Governors of the Federal Reserve System, headquartered in Washington, and especially in its chairman, who is now Alan Greenspan, an economist. Members of the board are appointed by the president of the United States, with the advice and consent of the Senate, for 14-year terms. The president also designates one of the members to serve a four-year term as chairman of the board, and thus to be the most powerful central banker in the world; for the United States differs from many other countries in that the Federal Reserve Board, once appointed by the president, is *independent* of the rest of the government. So long as it stays within the statutory authority delineated by Congress, it alone has responsibility for determining the nation's monetary policy. The power of appointment, however, gives the president considerable long-run influence over Federal Reserve policy.

Closely allied with the Board of Governors is the powerful **Federal Open Market Committee (FOMC)**, which meets periodically in Washington. For reasons to be explained shortly, the decisions of the FOMC largely determine the size of the U.S. money supply. This 12-member committee consists of the seven governors of the Federal Reserve System and the presidents of five of the district banks.

## THE INDEPENDENCE OF THE FED

The institutional independence of the Federal Reserve System is looked upon as a source of pride by some and as an antidemocratic embarrassment by others. The proponents of Federal Reserve independence argue that it enables monetary policy decisions to be made on objective, technical criteria and keeps monetary control out of the "political thicket." Without this independence, it is argued, there would be a tendency for politicians to force the Fed to expand the money supply too rapidly, thereby contributing to chronic inflation and undermining faith in America's financial system.

Opponents of this view counter that there is something profoundly undemocratic about having a group of unelected bankers and economists make decisions that affect the well-being of 260 million Americans. Monetary policy, they argue, should be formulated by the elected representatives of the people, just like fiscal policy. Those who argue for executive or congressional control over the Fed can point to historical instances in which monetary and fiscal policy have been at loggerheads—with the Fed undoing or even overwhelming the effects of fiscal policy decisions.

There is plenty of middle ground between the two extremes. One far less drastic proposal would put the Secretary of the Treasury on the Federal Reserve Board and/or shift the term of its chairman to make it coincide with that of the president of the United States. As things stand today, a newly elected president must retain the Fed chairman that his predecessor appointed whether or not he agrees with his policies.

Another suggested reform would require the Fed to announce its ultimate targets for unemployment and inflation and explain how it expects its monetary policy actions to promote these goals. An extreme version of this proposal would force the Fed to adopt the goals of the administration or Congress. But a more moderate version would simply make the Fed announce its own goals and subject them to public scrutiny. A yet weaker proposal in the same vein would force the Fed to announce its policy decisions as soon as they are made. At present, it normally waits about six weeks after each FOMC meeting before announcing its decisions.

How people react to these and other reform proposals that would affect the Fed's independence depends on how they perceive the office. Are governors of the Federal Reserve System akin to judges and therefore, at least in principle, best thought of as nonpartisan and independent technocrats? The 14-year term of office certainly suggests an analogy to the judiciary, but the board's role is most assuredly one that involves policy making, not just "impartial" interpretation of the law. Or are the governors more like members of the Cabinet, that is, policy-making officials who should properly serve only at the pleasure of the president? Since neither analogy fits precisely, the issue is a vexing one.

## CONTROLLING THE MONEY SUPPLY: OPEN-MARKET OPERATIONS

**OPEN-MARKET OPERATIONS** refer to the Fed's purchase or sale of government securities through transactions in the open market.

Partly for historical reasons, the Fed normally relies on what are called **open-market operations** to manipulate the money supply. Open-market operations have the effect of giving the banks more reserves or taking reserves away from them, thereby triggering a multiple expansion or contraction of the money supply as described in Chapter 29.

How does this work? Suppose the Federal Open Market Committee decides that the money supply is too low. It can issue instructions that the money supply be expanded through operations in the open market. Specifically, this means that the Federal Reserve System *purchases* U.S. government securities (generally short-term securities called "Treasury bills") from any individual or bank that wishes to sell, thus putting more reserves in the hands of the banks.

An example will illustrate the mechanics of open-market operations. Suppose the order is to purchase $100 million worth of securities and that commercial banks are the sellers. *The Fed makes payment by giving the banks $100 million in new reserves.* So, if they held only the required amount of reserves initially, the banks now have $100 million in excess reserves, as shown in Table 30–1.

When the Fed buys $100 million worth of securities from the banks, it adds this amount to the bookkeeping entries that represent the banks' accounts at the Fed (called "bank reserves"). Since deposits have not increased at all, required reserves are unchanged by this transaction. But actual reserves are increased by $100 million, so there are $100 million in excess reserves. This will trigger a multiple expansion of the banking system.

Where does the Fed get the money that it gives to the banks in return for the securities? It could pay in cash, but normally does not. Instead, it manufactures the funds out of thin air or, more literally, by punching the keyboard of a computer terminal. Specifically, the Fed pays the banks for the securities by adding the

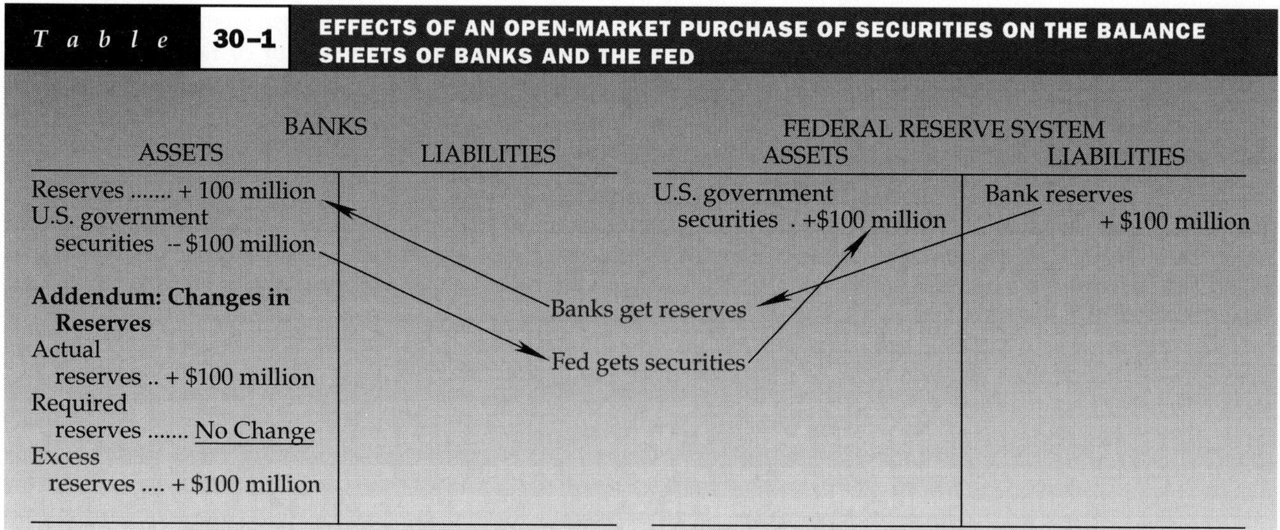

**Table 30–1 EFFECTS OF AN OPEN-MARKET PURCHASE OF SECURITIES ON THE BALANCE SHEETS OF BANKS AND THE FED**

| BANKS: ASSETS | BANKS: LIABILITIES | FEDERAL RESERVE SYSTEM: ASSETS | FEDERAL RESERVE SYSTEM: LIABILITIES |
|---|---|---|---|
| Reserves ....... + 100 million<br>U.S. government securities -- $100 million | | U.S. government securities . +$100 million | Bank reserves + $100 million |
| **Addendum: Changes in Reserves**<br>Actual reserves .. + $100 million<br>Required reserves ....... No Change<br>Excess reserves .... + $100 million | | | |



When the Fed buys $100 million worth of securities from the banks, it adds this amount to the bookkeeping entries that represent the banks' accounts at the Fed (called "bank reserves"). Since deposits have not increased at all, required reserves are unchanged by this transaction. But actual reserves are increased by $100 million, so there are $100 million in excess reserves. This will trigger a multiple expansion of the banking system.

appropriate sums to the accounts that the banks maintain at the Fed. Balances held in these accounts constitute bank reserves, just like cash in bank vaults.

While this process of creating bookkeeping entries at the Federal Reserve is commonly referred to as "printing money," the Fed does not literally run the printing presses. Instead, it simply exchanges its IOUs for an existing asset (a government security). But unlike your IOUs, the Fed's IOUs constitute legal bank reserves, and thus can support a multiple expansion of the money supply in the same way that cash does. The banks, not the Fed, actually increase the money supply; but the Fed's actions give the banks the wherewithal to do it.

Once excess reserves are created, multiple expansion of the banking system proceeds in the usual way. It is not hard for the Fed to estimate the ultimate increase in the money supply that will result from its actions. As we saw in the last chapter, each dollar of excess reserves can support $1/m$ dollars of checking deposits, if $m$ is the required reserve ratio. In our example, $m = 0.20$; so \$100 million in new reserves can support \$100/0.2 = \$500 million in new money.

But *estimating* the ultimate monetary expansion is a far cry from *knowing it* with certainty. As we know from Chapter 29, the simple money multiplier formula is predicated on the assumptions that people will want to hold no more cash, and that banks will want to hold no more excess reserves, as the monetary expansion proceeds. In practice, these assumptions are unlikely to be literally true. So, if the Fed is to predict the eventual effect of its action on the money supply correctly, it must estimate both the amount that firms and individuals will want to add to their currency holdings and the amount that banks will want to add to their excess reserves. Neither of these can be estimated with utter precision. In summary:

When the Federal Reserve System wants to increase the money supply, it purchases U.S. government securities in the open market. It pays for these securities by creating new bank reserves, and these additional reserves lead to a multiple expansion of the money supply. However, because of fluctuations in people's desires to hold cash and banks' desires to hold excess reserves, the Fed cannot predict the consequences of these actions with perfect accuracy. Thus, over short periods, control over the money supply must of necessity be imperfect.

The procedures followed when the FOMC wants to *contract* the money supply are just the opposite of those we have just explained. In brief, it orders a *sale* of government securities in the open market. This takes reserves *away* from banks, since banks pay for the securities by drawing down their deposits at the Fed. A multiple *contraction* of the banking system ensues. The principles are exactly the same as when the process operates in reverse—and so are the uncertainties.

## OPEN-MARKET OPERATIONS, BOND PRICES, AND INTEREST RATES

When it offers more government bonds for sale on the open market, the Federal Reserve normally depresses the price of bonds. This is illustrated by Figure 30–2, which shows a rightward shift of the (vertical) supply curve of bonds—from $S_0S_0$ to $S_1S_1$—with an unchanged demand curve, $DD$. The price of bonds falls from $P_0$ to $P_1$ as equilibrium in the bond market shifts from point $A$ to point $B$.

Falling bond prices translate directly into rising interest rates. Why is that? Most bonds pay a fixed number of dollars of interest per year. For concreteness,

Figure 30–2 **OPEN-MARKET SALES AND BOND PRICES**

If the Fed offers bonds for sale in the open market, the supply curve of bonds shifts rightward from $S_0S_0$ to $S_1S_1$. In consequence, equilibrium in the bond market shifts from point *A* to point *B*. The price of bonds declines from $P_0$ to $P_1$. By the same reasoning, an open-market purchase drives bond prices up.

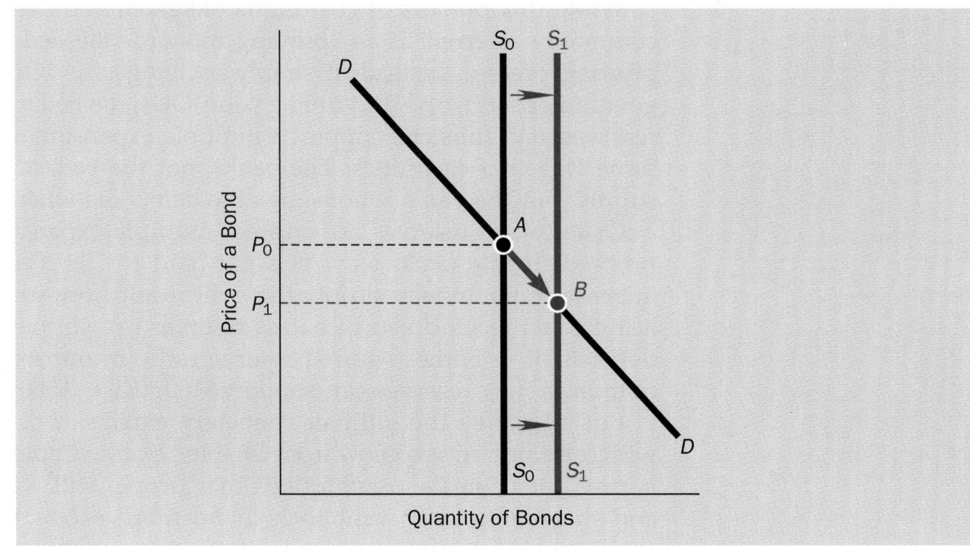


consider a bond that pays $90 each year. If the bond sells for $1000, bondholders earn a 9 percent return on their investment since $90 is 9 percent of $1000. We say that *the interest rate on the bond is 9 percent*. Now suppose the price of the bond falls to $900. The annual interest payment is still $90, so bondholders now earn 10 percent on their money ($90 is 10 percent of $900). *The effective interest rate on the bond has risen to 10 percent*. This relationship between bond prices and interest rates is completely general:

When bond prices fall, interest rates must rise because the purchaser of a bond spends less money than before to earn a given number of dollars of interest per year. Similarly, when bond prices rise, interest rates must fall.

In fact, the relationship amounts to nothing more than two ways of saying the same thing. Higher interest rates *mean* lower bond prices; lower interest rates *mean* higher bond prices.

We thus see that the Fed, through its open-market operations, exercises direct influence over interest rates. Specifically:

An open-market purchase of bonds by the Fed not only raises the money supply but also drives up bond prices and pushes interest rates down. Conversely, an open-market sale of bonds, which reduces the money supply, lowers bond prices and raises interest rates.

## CONTROLLING THE MONEY SUPPLY: RESERVE REQUIREMENTS

The Fed also has another way to control the money supply: by varying the minimum required reserve ratio. To see how this works, consider the balance

**Table 30–2 BALANCE SHEET OF MIDDLE AMERICAN BANK, OCTOBER 25, 1993**

| ASSETS | | LIABILITIES AND NET WORTH | |
|---|---|---|---|
| Reserves | $ 200,000 | Checking deposits | $1,000,000 |
| Loans outstanding | 1,000,000 | Net worth | 200,000 |
| Total assets | $1,200,000 | Total liabilities plus net worth | $1,200,000 |

If the required reserve ratio is 20 percent, Middle American Bank holds exactly its required reserves on October 25, 1993—no more and no less. However, if the reserve ratio falls to 15 percent, its required reserves will fall to only $150,000 (15 percent of $1 million), and it will have $50,000 in excess reserves.

sheet of a hypothetical bank shown in Table 30–2. If the minimum required reserve ratio is 20 percent, and the bank wishes to hold only the legal minimum in reserves, Middle American Bank is in equilibrium on October 25, 1993. Its $1 million in checking deposits mean that its required reserves amount to $200,000, which just matches its actual reserves. Excess reserves are zero.

Now suppose that the Federal Reserve Board decides that the money supply needs to be increased. One action it can take is to lower the required reserve ratio. As an exaggerated example, suppose it reduces reserve requirements to 15 percent of deposits.

Middle American Bank's balance sheet is unaffected by this action, but the bank's managers are sure to react to it. For now required reserves are only $150,000 (15 percent of $1 million), so the bank is holding $50,000 in excess reserves—funds that are earning no interest for the bank. The effect is the same as if a new depositor had brought in cash: the bank now has more money to lend. Once it lends out this $50,000, its balance sheet will be as shown in Table 30–3; it now holds $50,000 less in reserves and $50,000 more in loans.

Although no new deposits are created by this transaction, we know from the previous chapter that the wheels of a multiple expansion of the banking system have been set in motion. For the recipient of the loan will deposit the proceeds in his own bank, giving that bank excess reserves and, therefore, the ability to grant more loans, and so on.

Once again, while the Fed's control over banks' excess reserves may be quite precise, its control over the money supply is a good deal looser. It can and will rely on its past experience to *estimate* the ultimate effect of any change in reserve requirements on the money supply. In normal times, these estimates are quite accurate. That, presumably, is the definition of "normal times." But at other times

**Table 30–3 BALANCE SHEET OF MIDDLE AMERICAN BANK, OCTOBER 26, 1993**

| ASSETS | | LIABILITIES | |
|---|---|---|---|
| Reserves | $ 150,000 | Checking deposits | $1,000,000 |
| Loans outstanding | 1,050,000 | Net worth | 200,000 |
| Total assets | $1,200,000 | Total liabilities plus net worth | $1,200,000 |

If Middle American Bank does not wish to hold excess reserves, its balance sheet will look like this after it loans out the extra $50,000 in excess reserves. At this point, it once again has no excess reserves.

banks may surprise the Fed by holding larger or smaller excess reserves than anticipated, or businesses and consumers may surprise it by holding more or less currency. In such cases, the Fed will not get the money supply it was shooting for and will have to adjust its policies.

It does not take much imagination to see what the Fed must do to reserve requirements when it wants to engineer a *contraction* of the money supply. If banks are not holding excess reserves, an increase in the required reserve ratio will force them to contract their loans and deposits until their reserve deficiencies are corrected. Of course, if banks do have sufficient excess reserves, they can flout the Fed's wishes. But the Fed normally will be trying to rein in the money supply when the economy is booming, and these are precisely the times when banks will not want to hold more idle reserves than necessary.

In fact, the Fed has not relied much on the reserve ratio as a weapon of monetary control. Current legislation provides for a basic reserve ratio of 12 percent against checking deposits, which changes very infrequently.

## CONTROLLING THE MONEY SUPPLY: LENDING TO BANKS

When the Federal Reserve System was first established, its founders did not intend it to pursue an active monetary policy to stabilize the economy. Indeed, the basic ideas of stabilization policy were foreign at the time. Instead, the Fed's founders viewed it as a means of preventing the supplies of money and credit from drying up during economic contractions, as had happened so often in the pre-1914 period.

One of the principal ways in which the Fed was to provide such insurance against financial panics was to act as a "lender of last resort." That is, when risky business prospects made commercial banks hesitant to extend new loans, or when banks were in trouble, the Fed would step in by lending money to the banks, thus inducing the banks to lend more money to their customers. The Fed last performed this role in dramatic fashion in October 1987, when the stock market crash stunned the financial community. Its prompt actions helped avert a financial panic.

When the Fed extends borrowing privileges to a bank in need of reserves, that bank receives a credit in its deposit account at the Fed (see Table 30–4). This addition to bank reserves may lead to an expansion of the money supply; or it may eliminate a reserve deficiency and thereby prevent a multiple contraction of the banking system. In either case, the Fed makes monetary conditions more expansive by making borrowing easier.

The **DISCOUNT RATE** is the interest rate the Fed charges on loans it makes to banks.

Federal Reserve officials can influence the volume of member bank borrowing by setting the *rate of interest charged on these loans*. For historical reasons, this is called the **discount rate** in the United States. In most foreign countries, it is known as the "bank rate." If the Fed wants to give banks more reserves, it can reduce the interest rate that it charges, thereby tempting banks to borrow more. Alternatively, it can soak up reserves by raising its rate and persuading the banks to reduce their borrowings.

While this type of *active* manipulation of the discount rate is practiced widely in foreign countries, where the bank rate is often the centerpiece of monetary policy, it is much less common in the United States, where the Fed usually relies on open market operations in conducting its monetary policy. More often the Fed adjusts the discount rate *passively* to keep it in line with market interest rates.

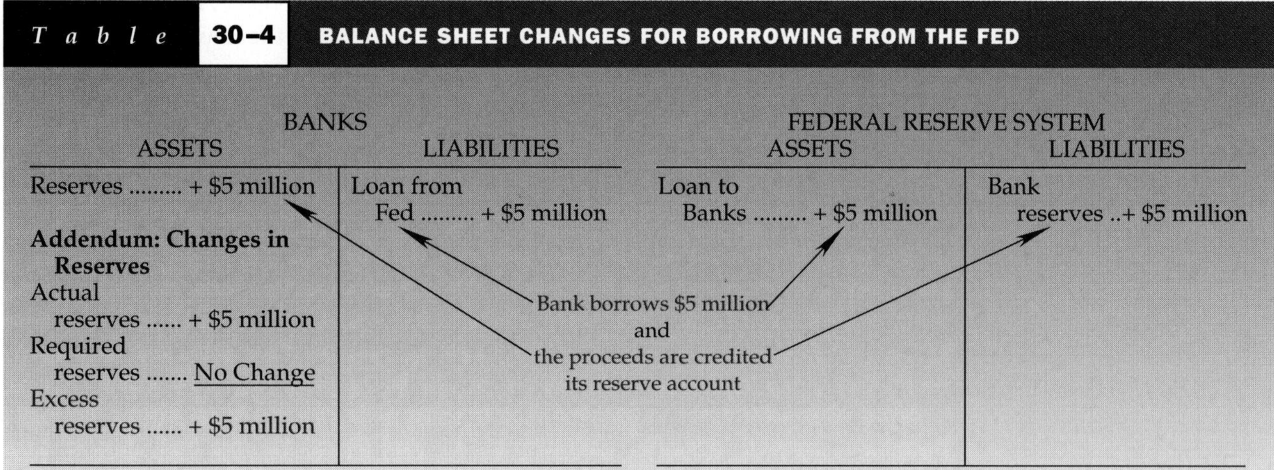

**Table 30-4 BALANCE SHEET CHANGES FOR BORROWING FROM THE FED**

| BANKS | | FEDERAL RESERVE SYSTEM | |
|---|---|---|---|
| ASSETS | LIABILITIES | ASSETS | LIABILITIES |
| Reserves ......... + \$5 million | Loan from Fed ......... + \$5 million | Loan to Banks ......... + \$5 million | Bank reserves ..+ \$5 million |
| **Addendum: Changes in Reserves** | | | |
| Actual reserves ...... + \$5 million | | | |
| Required reserves ....... No Change | | | |
| Excess reserves ...... + \$5 million | | | |



When the Fed lends \$5 million to a bank, it simply adds this amount to the bookkeeping entry that represents that bank's account at the Fed. Once again, actual reserves increase while required reserves do not change (because bank deposits do not change). Hence this loan would be expected to initiate a multiple expansion of the banking system.

Nonetheless, changes in the discount rate have important psychological effects on financial markets, where they are widely interpreted as signals of the Fed's attitude toward interest rates.

As in the case of changes in reserve requirements and open market operations, the Fed cannot know for sure how banks will react to changes in the discount rate. Sometimes they may respond vigorously to a cut in the rate, borrowing a great deal from the Fed and lending a correspondingly large amount to their customers. At other times they may essentially ignore the Fed's actions. The link between the lending rate and the money supply is a loose one.

**MORAL SUASION** refers to informal requests and warnings designed to persuade banks to limit their borrowings from the Fed.

Often, though, the Fed tries to tighten this link by using a more direct way of controlling the volume of bank borrowing—**moral suasion**. This phrase refers to some not-so-subtle methods that the Fed has for letting banks know when it thinks they are borrowing too much. Since banks are anxious to maintain the good will of the Fed, they often respond to warnings that they have overused their borrowing privileges—especially when such warnings are accompanied by a veiled threat that these privileges might be suspended if the offending bank does not mend its ways. As the Fed often reminds the banks, borrowing is "a privilege, not a right."

## PROPOSALS FOR TIGHTENING MONETARY CONTROL

The fact that each of the Federal Reserve's principal instruments of monetary control is somewhat imperfect has led to a number of suggestions designed to improve the System's ability to regulate the supply of money.

Because banks' discretion over the amount of reserves they hold (subject only to the legal minimums) makes the link between changes in Federal Reserve policy and changes in the money supply rather slippery at times, some economists would like to see a return to a system of 100 percent reserve requirements. Under such a rule, no bank could add to or subtract from its excess reserves because there would never be any excess reserves. Each dollar of bank reserves would support exactly one dollar of deposits, no more and no less; so there would be no such thing as a multiple expansion or contraction of the banking system. The Fed can now control bank reserves with great precision; and under a system of 100 percent reserve requirements, its control over the money supply would be equally precise.

While such a change in banking regulations undoubtedly would make the Fed's job easier, it would also change the face of banking in dramatic and possibly unpredictable ways. It will be recalled from Chapter 29 that banking as we know it today evolved from that first goldsmith's momentous discovery that he could get along with only fractional reserves. This discovery has been the mainspring of bank profits ever since. Abolition of fractional reserve banking should therefore be viewed as a major overhaul of the financial system. This does not necessarily mean that it is a bad idea, only that it should be approached with some caution.

Some observers have suggested that lending to banks, far from aiding the Fed's monetary control, actually undermines it, and therefore the Fed should stop lending except in emergency cases. Their reasoning is as follows: when the Fed tries to force a contraction of the banking system, some banks may resist this desire by borrowing the reserves they need. Similarly, some banks may relinquish reserves to pay back loans just when the Fed wants the money supply to expand.

No doubt this occasionally happens. But there are also times when Federal Reserve lending is a valuable supplement to open market policy. Since it is by no means clear that monetary control would be tighter if lending were abolished, the Fed is understandably reluctant to give up one of its major traditional weapons.

## THE MONEY SUPPLY MECHANISM

This completes our discussion of the Fed's methods of controlling the money supply and the limitations of these methods. One point, however, merits further emphasis. We have noted several times that the Fed's control of the money supply is imperfect because banks can and do vary their holdings of excess reserves. Since reserves earn no interest, banks will hold substantial *excess* reserves only when they feel that funds cannot be put to profitable uses. This may happen if shaky business conditions make loans to customers look unusually risky or if interest rates are very low. Conversely, banks will work hard to hold reserves to the legal minimum when loans to customers look safe and when interest rates are high. Thus:

As interest rates rise, banks normally find it more profitable to expand their volume of loans and deposits, thus increasing the supply of money. However, the Fed can shift the relationship between the money supply and interest rates by employing any of its principal weapons of monetary control: open market operations, changes in reserve requirements, or changes in lending policy to banks.

These ideas are depicted graphically in Figure 30–3. Figure 30–3(a) shows a typical money supply schedule labeled *MS*, illustrating the fact that bank behavior makes the money stock rise as interest rates rise.[1] Notice that the sensitivity of the money supply to interest rates is rather weak in the diagram—a large rise in

[1]There are many interest rates in the economy. However, they all tend to move up and down together. Hence, for present purposes, we can speak of "the" rate of interest.

Figure 30–3 **THE SUPPLY SCHEDULE FOR MONEY**

Part (a) shows a typical supply schedule for money. It is rising as we move toward the right, meaning that banks will supply more money when interest rates are higher. Part (b) illustrates what happens to the money supply schedule when the Fed purchases securities in the open market, or lowers required reserves, or provides banks with more loans. The supply schedule shifts outward. Part (c) depicts the effect of using these same policy instruments in the opposite (contractionary) direction. The supply schedule shifts inward.

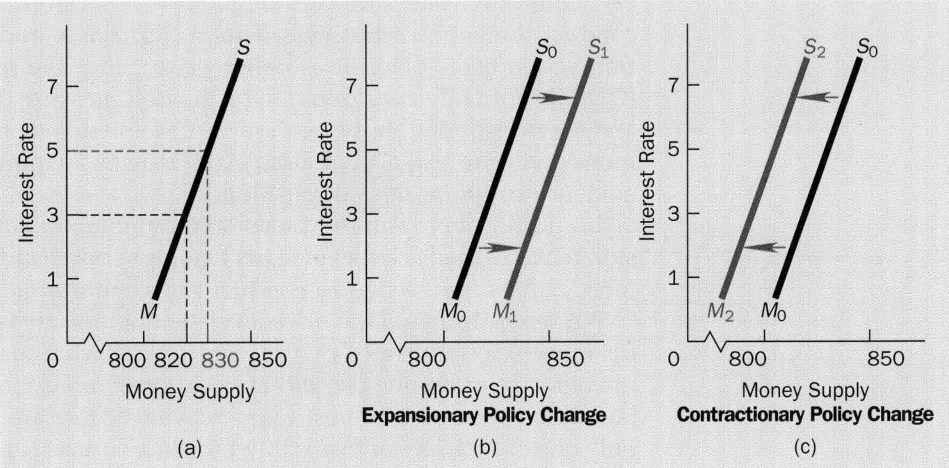


the rate of interest (from 3 percent to 5 percent) induces only a small increase in the supply of money (from $820 billion to $830 billion). The drawing is deliberately constructed that way because that is what the statistical evidence shows.

The curve in Figure 30–3(a) shows the money supply schedule corresponding to some specific monetary policy. Figure 30–3(b) portrays how the money supply schedule responds to an *expansionary change in monetary policy*, such as an open market purchase of government bonds, a reduction in reserve requirements, or a drop in the Fed's lending rate. The money supply schedule shifts outward from $M_0S_0$ to $M_1S_1$, as indicated by the arrows. After banks have adjusted to the change, there is more money at any given interest rate.

Figure 30–3(c) shows what happens in the reverse case—a *contractionary monetary policy*, such as an open market sale of securities, an increase in reserve requirements, or a rise in the lending rate. The money supply shifts inward from $M_0S_0$ to $M_2S_2$.

As we have emphasized, the diagrams make things look rather more precise than they actually are. Since the Fed's control over the money supply schedule is imperfect in the short run, the actual *MS* schedule is obscured by a bit of fog. In what follows, we portray all the graphs as clean straight lines only for pedagogical simplicity. The Fed wishes things were so simple in the real world!

## THE DEMAND FOR MONEY

Just as we must know something about both the supply of and the demand for wheat before we can predict how much will be sold and at what price, it is necessary to know something about the **demand for money** if we are to understand the amount of money actually in existence and the prevailing interest rate.

The definition of money given in Chapter 29 suggests the most important reason why people hold money balances: the medium of exchange is needed to carry out purchases and sales of goods and services. More dollars are needed to conduct the nation's business if more purchases and sales are made or if each transaction takes place at a higher price. Since the real gross domestic product (GDP) is normally considered to be the best measure of the total volume of goods and services traded in the economy, it seems safe to assume that the demand for money will rise as real GDP rises. And, indeed, an impressive amount of statistical evidence supports this supposition.

In addition, both common sense and mountains of evidence point to the conclusion that a higher price level leads to a higher demand for money simply because more dollars are needed to conduct the same transactions.

But real output and the price level are not the only factors affecting the demand for money; interest rates matter, too. At first, that may seem surprising because many forms of money pay either no interest or an interest rate which is fixed by law. Why, then, are interest rates relevant? They are relevant because money is only one of a variety of forms in which individuals can hold their wealth. Holders of money *give up* the opportunity to hold one of these other assets, such as government bonds, in order to gain the convenience of money. In so doing, they *give up* the interest that they could have earned on one of these alternative assets.

This is another example of the concept of **opportunity cost.**[2] On the surface, it seems virtually costless to hold money. But, *compared with the next best alternative,* this action is not costless at all. For example, if the best alternative to holding $100 in cash is to put those funds into a government bond that pays 8 percent interest, then the opportunity cost of holding that money is $8 per year (8 percent of $100).

How, then, should the rate of interest influence the quantity of money that people demand? People hold money because it facilitates making transactions. But this benefit comes at a cost: the potential interest that could have been earned by investing the funds in, say, government bonds. It is natural, therefore, to assume that when interest rates are high people make more strenuous efforts to economize on their holdings of money balances than they do when interest rates are low. In a word, rational behavior of consumers and business firms should make the demand to hold money *decline* as the interest rate *rises.* And, once again, careful analysis of the data shows this to be true. To summarize:

People and business firms hold money primarily to finance their transactions. Therefore, the quantity of money demanded increases as real output rises or as prices rise. However, the quantity of money demanded decreases as the rate of interest rises because the rate of interest is the opportunity cost of holding money balances.

It is possible to portray the demand for money by a graphical device, as shown in the three panels of Figure 30–4. In panel (a) we show a downward-sloping demand schedule for money (the curve labeled *MD*)—the quantity of money demanded decreases as the rate of interest rises. But since the quantity of money demanded also depends on real output and the price level, we must hold both real output and the price level constant in drawing up such a curve. Changes in either

---

[2]If you need to review this concept, see Chapter 3.

Figure 30–4 THE DEMAND SCHEDULE FOR MONEY

The downward-sloping line *MD* in part (a) is a typical demand curve for money. It slopes down because money is a less-attractive asset when interest rates on alternative assets are higher. However, such a curve can be drawn up only for particular levels of output and prices. A rise in either real output or the price level will shift the money-demand curve outward, as shown in part (b). Conversely, a fall in either real output or the price level will shift the curve inward, as in part (c).

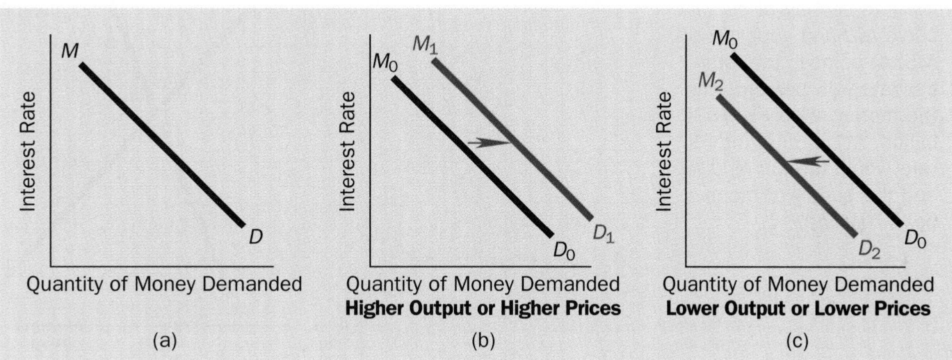


of these variables will shift the *MD* curve in the manner indicated in the other two panels because at higher levels of real GDP and higher prices, demand for money is greater; and at lower levels of real GDP and lower prices, demand for money is smaller.

## EQUILIBRIUM IN THE MONEY MARKET

As is usual in supply and demand analysis, it is useful to put both sides of the market together on a single graph. Figure 30–5 combines the money supply schedule of Figure 30–3(a) (labeled *MS*) with the money demand schedule of Figure 30–4(a) (labeled *MD*). Point *E* is the equilibrium of the money market. The diagram thus shows that *given* real output and the price level (which locates the *MD* curve) and *given* the Federal Reserve's monetary policy (which locates the *MS* curve), the money market is in equilibrium at an interest rate of 5 percent and a money stock of $830 billion. At any interest rate above 5 percent, the quantity of money supplied would exceed the quantity demanded and the interest rate—which is the price for renting money—would therefore decline. At any interest rate below 5 percent, more money would be demanded than supplied, and so the interest rate would rise. This is familiar ground.

**MONETARY POLICY** refers to actions that the Federal Reserve System takes in order to change the equilibrium of the money market; that is, to alter the money supply, move interest rates, or both.

Since the Fed can shift the *MS* curve, it can alter this equilibrium through its **monetary policy**. Expansionary monetary policy actions include purchasing government securities in the open market, reducing reserve requirements, and encouraging banks to borrow. Any of these actions will provide additional excess reserves to the banking system, thus encouraging banks to increase their loans and deposits. As money becomes more plentiful, interest rates drop.

Our supply–demand analysis of the money market shows this in Figure 30–6(a). By shifting the money supply schedule outward from $M_0S_0$ to $M_1S_1$, the Fed

Figure 30–5 EQUILIBRIUM IN THE MONEY MARKET

Equilibrium in the market for money is determined by the intersection of demand curve *MD* and supply curve *MS*. At point *E*, the interest rate is 5 percent, and the money supply is $830 billion. At no other interest rate would the demand for and the supply of money be in balance.

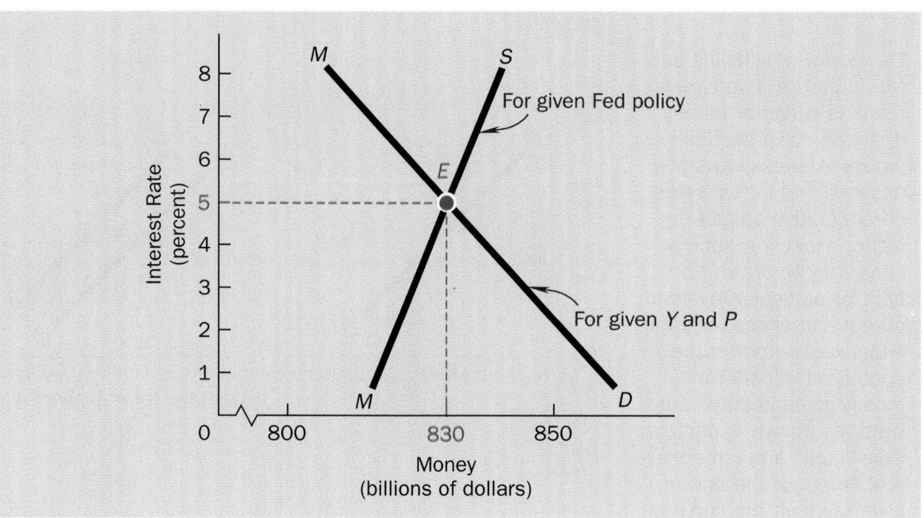


moves the market equilibrium from point *E* to point *A*—thus forcing the interest rate down. Contractionary monetary policy actions, such as selling securities in the open market, raising reserve requirements, and discouraging borrowing, have the opposite effect. They push interest rates up, as Figure 30–6(b) shows. Thus:

Monetary policies that expand the money supply normally lower interest rates. Monetary policies that reduce the money supply normally raise interest rates.

## INTEREST RATES AND TOTAL EXPENDITURE

We are now ready to see precisely how the Federal Reserve's monetary policy decisions affect unemployment, inflation, and the overall state of the economy. To begin, we go back to the analysis of Chapters 24–28, where we learned that aggregate demand is the sum of consumption spending (*C*), investment spending (*I*), government purchases of goods and services (*G*), and net exports (*X* – *IM*). We know that *fiscal policy* controls *G* directly and exerts influence over both *C* and *I* through the tax laws. We now want to find out how *monetary policy* affects total spending.

Most economists agree that, of the four components of aggregate demand, investment and net exports are the most sensitive to monetary policy. The effects of monetary and fiscal policy on net exports will be studied in detail in Chapter 37, after we have learned about international exchange rates. The rest of this chapter focuses on investment (*I*).

*Business investment* in new factories and machinery is sensitive to interest rates for reasons that have been explained in earlier chapters.[3] Since the rate of interest that must be paid on borrowings is one element of the cost of making an invest-

[3]See, for example, Chapter 25, page 623.

ment, business executives will find investment prospects less attractive as interest rates rise. Therefore, they will spend less. For similar reasons, *investment in housing* by individuals may also be deterred by high interest rates. Since the interest cost of a home mortgage is the major component of the total cost of owning a home, fewer families will want to buy a new home when interest rates are high than when interest rates are low. We conclude that:

Higher interest rates lead to lower investment spending. But investment ($I$) is a component of total spending, $C + I + G + (X - IM)$. Therefore, when interest rates rise, total spending falls. In terms of the 45° line diagram of previous chapters, a higher interest rate leads to a lower expenditure schedule. Conversely, a lower interest rate leads to a higher expenditure schedule. (See Figure 30–7.)

## MONETARY POLICY AND AGGREGATE DEMAND IN THE KEYNESIAN MODEL

The effect of interest rates on spending provides a mechanism through which monetary policy affects aggregate demand in the Keynesian model. We know from our analysis of the money market that monetary policy can have a profound effect on the rate of interest. Let us, therefore, outline how monetary policy works.

Suppose the Federal Reserve, seeing the economy stuck with unemployment and a recessionary gap, raises the money supply. It would normally do this by purchasing government securities in the open market, but the specific weapon that the Fed uses is not terribly important for present purposes. What matters is that the money supply ($M$) expands.

With the demand schedule for money (temporarily) fixed, such an increase in the supply of money has the effect that an increase in supply always has in a free market—it lowers the price. (See Figure 30–8.) In this case, the price of renting money is the rate of interest, $r$; so $r$ falls.

**Figure 30–6** THE EFFECTS OF MONETARY POLICY ON THE MONEY MARKET

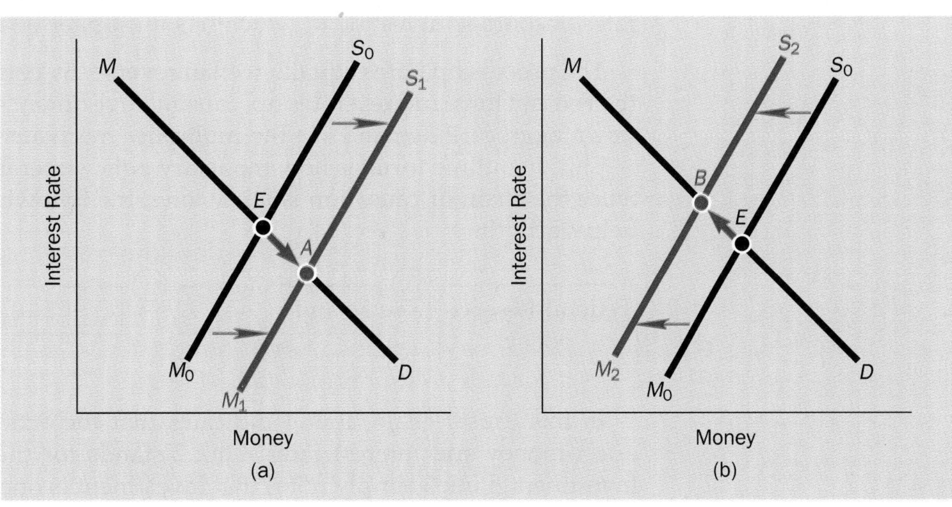


The two parts of this figure show the effects of monetary policy on the money supply ($M$) and the rate of interest ($r$). In part (a), expansionary monetary policies shift the supply schedule from $M_0S_0$ to $M_1S_1$ and push the equilibrium from point $E$ to point $A$; $M$ rises while $r$ falls. In part (b), contractionary policies pull the supply schedule in from $M_0S_0$ to $M_2S_2$ causing equilibrium to move up from point $E$ to point $B$; $M$ falls as $r$ rises.

Figure 30–7 **THE EFFECT OF INTEREST RATES ON AGGREGATE DEMAND**

Because interest rates are an important determinant of investment spending, $I$, the $C + I + G + (X - IM)$ schedule shifts whenever the rate of interest changes. Specifically, as shown here, lower interest rates shift the curve upward and higher interest rates shift it downward.

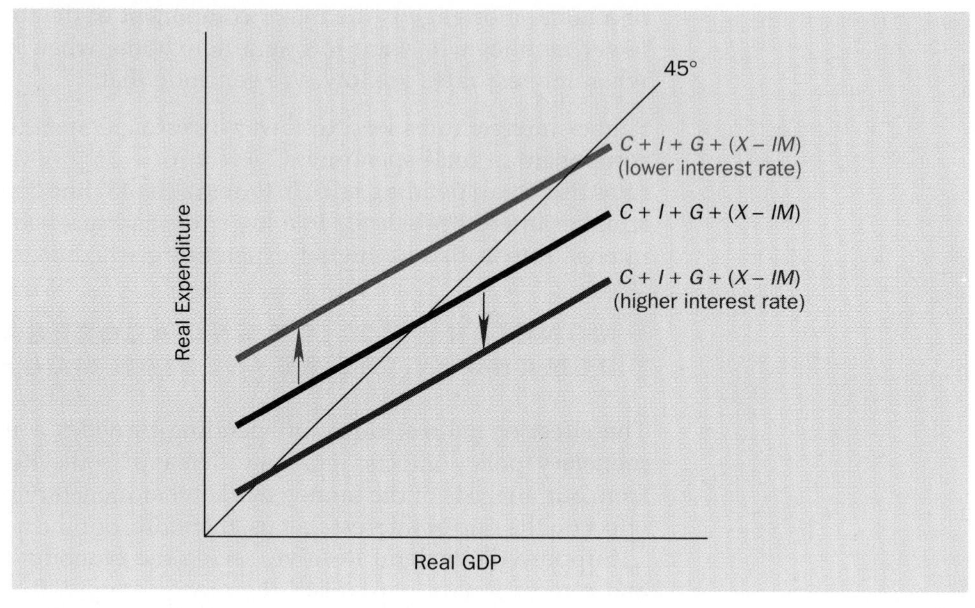


Next, for reasons we have just outlined, investment spending ($I$) rises in response to the lower interest rates. But, as we learned in Chapter 26, such an autonomous rise in investment kicks off a multiplier chain of increases in output and employment. Thus, finally, we have completed the links from the money supply to the level of aggregate demand. In brief, monetary policy works as follows:

A higher money supply leads to lower interest rates, and these lower interest rates encourage investment, which has multiplier effects on aggregate demand.

The process operates equally well in reverse. By contracting the money supply, the Fed can force interest rates up, causing investment spending to fall and pulling down aggregate demand via the multiplier mechanism.

This, in outline form, is how monetary policy operates in the Keynesian model. Since the chain of causation is fairly long, the following schematic diagram may help clarify it.

[Federal Reserve policy] →(1) [$M$ and $r$] →(2) [$I$] →(3) [$C + I + G + (X + IM)$] →(4) [GDP]

In this causal chain, link 1 indicates that the actions of the Federal Reserve affect money and interest rates. Link 2 stands for the effect of interest rates on investment. Link 3 simply notes that investment is one component of total spending. And link 4 is the multiplier, relating an autonomous change in investment to the ultimate change in aggregate demand.

Let us next review what we know about each of these links and fill in some illustrative numbers. In the process, we will see what economists must study if they are to estimate the effects of monetary policy.

Link 1 is the subject of this chapter and of Figure 30–8. Given the initial level of real GDP and prices, the demand schedule for money is shown by curve *MD*. The Fed's expansionary action shifts the supply schedule out from $M_0S_0$ to $M_1S_1$, resulting in an increase in the money stock from \$830 billion to \$880 billion in this example, and a decline in the interest rate from 5 percent to 3 percent. Thus the first thing an economist must know is how sensitive interest rates are to changes in the supply of money.

Link 2 translates the drop in the interest rate into an increase in investment spending (*I*), which we take to be \$200 billion in this example. To estimate this effect in practice, economists must study the sensitivity of investment to interest rates.

Link 3 instructs us to enter this \$200 billion rise in *I* as an autonomous shift in the $C + I + G + (X - IM)$ schedule of a 45° line diagram. Figure 30–9 carries out this step. The expenditure schedule rises from $C + I_0 + G + (X - IM)$ to $C + I_1 + G + (X - IM)$.

Finally, link 4 applies multiplier analysis to this vertical shift in the expenditure schedule in order to predict the eventual increase in real GDP demanded. In our examples, we have been using a multiplier of 2.5, so multiplying \$200 billion by 2.5 gives the final effect on aggregate demand—a rise of \$500 billion. This is shown in Figure 30–9 as a shift in equilibrium from $E_0$ (where GDP is \$6000 billion) to $E_1$ (where GDP is \$6500 billion). Of course, the size of the multiplier itself must also be estimated. To summarize:

The effect of monetary policy on aggregate demand depends on the sensitivity of interest rates to the money supply, on the responsiveness of investment spending to the rate of interest, and on the size of the multiplier.

**Figure 30–8** THE EFFECT OF EXPANSIONARY MONETARY POLICY ON THE MONEY SUPPLY AND RATE OF INTEREST

An expansionary monetary policy pushes the money supply schedule outward from $M_0S_0$ to $M_1S_1$, causing equilibrium in the money market to shift from point $E_0$ to point $E_1$. The money supply rises from \$830 billion to \$880 billion, while the interest rate falls from 5 percent to 3 percent.

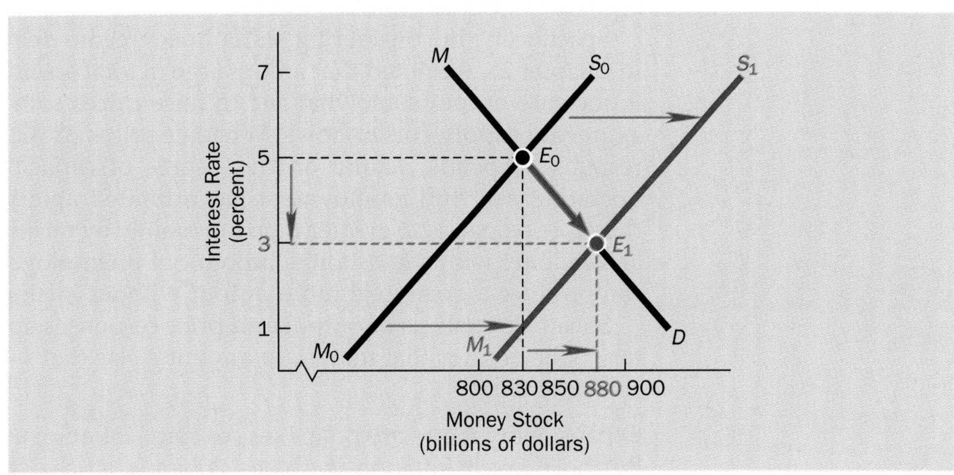

Figure 30-9 THE EFFECT OF EXPANSIONARY MONETARY POLICY ON AGGREGATE DEMAND

Expansionary monetary policies, which lower the rate of interest, will cause the $C + I + G + (X - IM)$ schedule to shift upward from $C + I_0 + G + (X - IM)$ to $C + I_1 + G + (X - IM)$, as shown here. In this example, since the multiplier is 2.5, a \$200 billion rise in investment leads, via the multiplier process, to a \$500 billion rise in GDP.

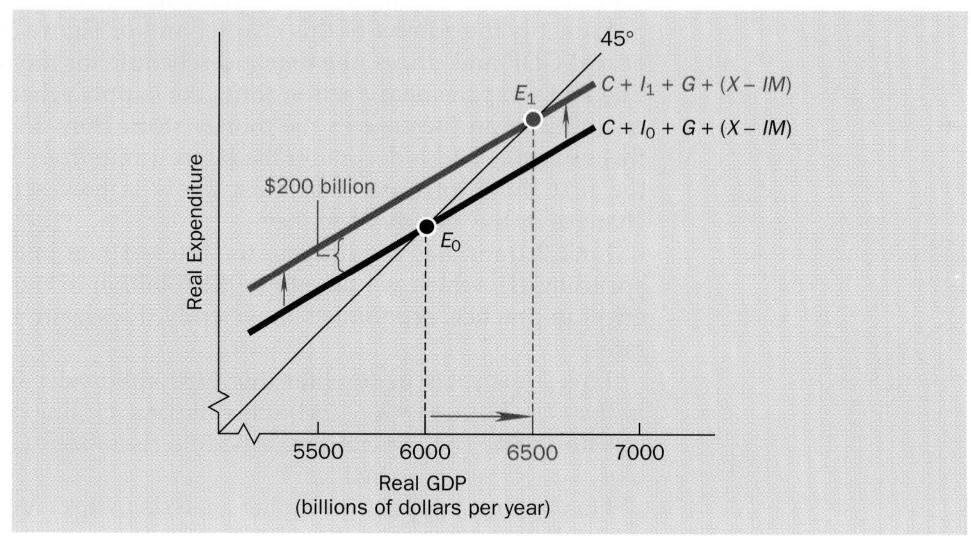


## MONEY AND THE PRICE LEVEL IN THE KEYNESIAN MODEL

The analysis up to this point leaves one important question unanswered: What happens to the price level? To find the answer, we must simply remember once again that prices and output are determined jointly by aggregate demand *and* aggregate supply. The analysis of monetary policy that we have completed so far has shown us how an increase in the money supply shifts the aggregate demand curve, that is, increases the *aggregate quantity demanded at any given price level*. But to learn what happens to the price level and to real output, we must consider *aggregate supply* as well.

Specifically, in considering shifts in aggregate demand caused by *fiscal* policy in Chapter 28, we noted that an upsurge in total spending normally induces firms to increase output somewhat *and* to raise prices somewhat. This is just what an aggregate supply curve shows. Whether prices or real output exhibit the greater response depends mainly on the degree of capacity utilization. An economy operating near full employment has a limited ability to increase production; it therefore responds to greater demand mainly by raising prices. On the other hand, an economy with a substantial amount of unemployed labor and unused capital can produce a great deal more output without raising prices.

Since this analysis of output and price responses applies equally well to monetary policy or, for that matter, to anything else that raises aggregate demand, we conclude that:

Expansionary monetary policy causes some inflation under normal circumstances. But how much inflation it causes depends on the state of the economy. If the money supply is expanded when unemployment is high and there is much unused industrial capacity, then the result may be little or no inflation. If, however, increases in the money supply occur when the economy is fully employed, then the main result is likely to be inflation.

The effect of a rise in the money supply on the price level is depicted graphically on an aggregate supply and demand diagram in Figure 30–10. The curved shape of aggregate supply curve *SS* reflects the assumptions that output rises with little inflation when the economy is depressed, while prices rise with little gain in output when the economy is near full employment.

In the example we have been using, the Fed's actions raise the money supply by $50 billion, and this increases aggregate demand (through the multiplier) by $500 billion. We enter this in Figure 30–10 as a horizontal shift of $500 billion in the aggregate demand curve, from $D_0D_0$ to $D_1D_1$. The diagram shows that this expansionary monetary policy raises the economy's equilibrium from point *E* to point *B*—the price level therefore rises from 100 to 103, or 3 percent. The diagram also shows that real GDP rises by only $400 billion, which is less than the $500 billion stimulus to aggregate demand. The reason, as we know from earlier chapters, is that rising prices stifle demand.

By taking account of the effect of an increase in the money supply on the price level, we have completed our story about the role of monetary policy in the Keynesian model. We can thus expand our schematic diagram of monetary policy as follows:

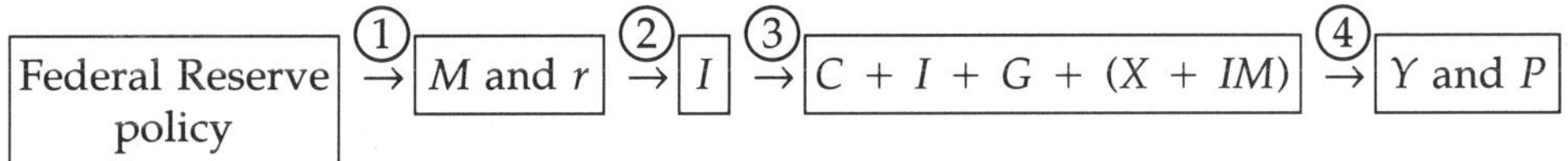


**Figure 30–10** **THE INFLATIONARY EFFECTS OF EXPANSIONARY MONETARY POLICY**

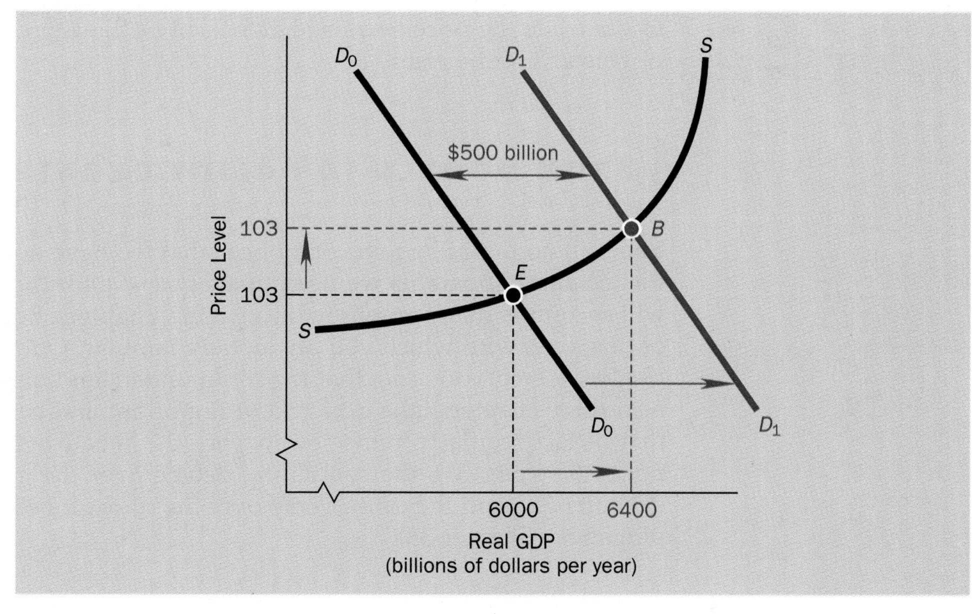


Raising the money supply normally causes inflation. When expansionary monetary policy causes the aggregate demand curve to shift outward from $D_0D_0$ to $D_1D_1$, the economy's equilibrium shifts from point *E* to point *B*. Real output expands (in this case by $400 billion), but prices also rise (in this case by 3 percent).

The last link now recognizes that *both* output *and* prices normally are affected by changes in the money supply.

### APPLICATION: WHY THE AGGREGATE DEMAND CURVE SLOPES DOWNWARD

This analysis of the effect of money on the price level puts us in a better position to understand why higher prices reduce aggregate quantity demanded; that is, why the aggregate demand curve slopes downward. In earlier chapters, we explained this phenomenon in two ways. First, we observed that rising prices reduce the purchasing power of certain assets held by consumers, especially money and government bonds, and that this in turn retards consumption spending. Second, we noted that higher domestic prices depress exports and stimulate imports.

There is nothing wrong with this analysis. But higher prices have an important effect on aggregate demand through another channel that we are now in a position to understand.

Money is demanded primarily to conduct transactions and, as we have noted in this chapter, a rise in the *average money cost* of each transaction—as a result of a rise in the price level—will increase the quantity of money demanded. This means that when expansionary policy of any kind pushes the price level up, more money will be demanded at any given interest rate.

But, if the supply of money is *not* increased, an increase in the quantity of money demanded at any given interest rate must force the cost of borrowing money—the rate of interest—to rise. As we know, increases in interest rates reduce investment and, hence, reduce aggregate demand. This, then, is the main reason why the economy's aggregate demand curve has a negative slope, meaning that aggregate quantity demanded is lower when prices are higher. In sum:

At higher price levels, the quantity of money demanded is greater. Given a fixed supply schedule, therefore, a higher price level must lead to a higher interest rate. Since high interest rates discourage investment, aggregate quantity demanded is lower when the price level is higher. That is, the aggregate demand curve slopes downward to the right.

## FROM MODELS TO POLICY DEBATES

You will no doubt be relieved to hear that we have now provided just about all the technical apparatus we need to analyze stabilization policy. To be sure, you will encounter many graphs in the next few chapters. But most of them are repeats of diagrams with which you are already familiar. Our attention now turns from *building* a theory to *using* that theory to understand important policy issues. The next three chapters take up a trio of important and controversial policy debates that surface regularly in the newspapers: the debate over the efficacy of monetary policy (Chapter 31), the continuing debate over the government budget deficit (Chapter 32), and the controversy over the tradeoff between inflation and unemployment (Chapter 33).

## *Summary*

1. A **central bank** is a bank for banks.
2. The **Federal Reserve System** is America's central bank. There are 12 Federal Reserve banks, but most of the power is held by the Board of Governors in Washington and by the **Federal Open Market Committee.**
3. The Federal Reserve is independent of the rest of the government. There is controversy over whether this **independence** is a good idea, and a number of reforms have been suggested over the years that would make the Fed more accountable to the president or to Congress.
4. The Fed has three major weapons for control of the money supply: **open-market operations, reserve requirements**, and its **lending policy** to the banks.
5. By lowering or raising reserve requirements, the Fed makes it possible for each dollar of reserves to support more or fewer dollars of deposits. Thus, lowering or raising the reserve ratio is one way to increase or decrease the money supply.
6. But the Fed does not do this very often. More typically, it raises the money supply by purchasing government securities in the open market. The Fed's payments to the banks for such purchases provide banks with new reserves and, hence, lead to a larger money supply. Conversely, open market sales of securities take reserves from the banks and lead to a smaller money supply.
7. When the Fed buys bonds, bond prices rise and interest rates fall. When the Fed sells bonds, bond prices fall and interest rates rise.
8. The Fed can also increase the money supply by allowing banks to borrow more reserves, perhaps by reducing the interest rate it charges on such loans. Alternatively, by discouraging borrowing, it can make the money supply contract.
9. None of these weapons, however, gives the Fed perfect control over the money supply in the short run, because it cannot predict perfectly how far the process of deposit creation or destruction will go.
10. The **money supply schedule** shows that more money is supplied at higher interest rates because, as interest rates rise, banks find it more profitable to expand their loans and deposits. This schedule can be shifted by Federal Reserve policy.
11. The **money demand schedule** shows that less money is demanded at higher interest rates because interest is the opportunity cost of holding money. This schedule shifts when output or the price level changes.
12. The **equilibrium** money stock ($M$) and the equilibrium rate of interest ($r$) are determined by the intersection of the money supply and money demand schedules.
13. Federal Reserve policy can shift this equilibrium. Expansionary policies cause $M$ to rise and $r$ to fall. Contractionary policies reduce $M$ and increase $r$.
14. Investment spending ($I$), including business investment and investment in new homes, is sensitive to interest rates ($r$). Specifically, $I$ is lower when $r$ is higher.
15. This fact explains how **monetary policy** works in the Keynesian model. Raising the money supply ($M$) leads to lower $r$; the lower interest rates stimulate more investment spending; and this investment stimulus, via the multiplier, then raises aggregate demand.
16. However, prices are likely to rise as output rises. The amount of inflation caused by increasing the money supply depends on the levels of unemployment and of capacity utilization. There will be much inflation when the economy is near full employment, but little inflation when there is a great deal of slack.
17. The main reason **why the aggregate demand curve slopes downward** is that higher prices increase the demand to hold money in order to finance transactions. Given the money supply, this pushes interest rates up; and this, in turn, discourages investment.

## *Key Concepts and Terms*

Central bank
Federal Reserve System
Federal Open Market Committee (FOMC)
Independence of the Fed
Reserve requirements
Open-market operations
Bond prices and interest rates
Contraction and expansion of the money supply
Federal Reserve lending to banks
Moral suasion
Supply of money
Demand for money
Opportunity cost
Equilibrium in the money market
Monetary policy
Why the aggregate demand curve slopes downward

## *Questions for Review*

1. Why does a modern industrial economy need a central bank?
2. A few years ago, Congressman Lee Hamilton proposed legislation that would have reduced much of the secrecy about the Fed's operations, put the secretary of the treasury on the Federal Reserve Board, and made the term of the Fed chairman coincide with that of the president. Which, if any, of these provisions would you favor? Explain your reasons.
3. Suppose there is $100 billion of cash in existence, and that half of it is held in bank vaults as *required* reserves (that is, banks hold no *excess* reserves). How large will the money supply be if the required reserve ratio is $16\frac{2}{3}$ percent? 20 percent? 25 percent?
4. Show the balance sheet changes that would take place if the Federal Reserve Bank of San Francisco purchased an office building from the Bank of America for a price of $100 million. Compare this to the effect of an open-market purchase of securities shown in Table 30–1. What do you conclude?
5. Suppose that the Fed purchases $6 million worth of government bonds from Donald Trump, who banks at Citibank in New York. Show the effects on the balance sheets of the Fed, Citibank, and Donald Trump. (*Hint*: What will Trump do with the $6 million check he receives from the Fed?) Does it make any difference if the Fed buys bonds from a bank or from an individual?
6. Why would the Fed's control over the money supply be tighter under a system of 100 percent reserves?
7. Explain why the quantity of money supplied normally is higher and the quantity of money demanded normally is lower at higher interest rates.
8. Starting sometime in the spring of 1989, the Fed decided that interest rates were too high and took steps to drive them down—a process it continued for more than three years. How could the Fed push interest rates down? Illustrate on a diagram.
9. Explain why both business investments and purchases of new homes are expected to decline when interest rates rise.
10. Explain what a $50 billion increase in the money supply will do to real GDP under the following assumptions:
    a. Each $10 billion increase in the money supply reduces the rate of interest by 0.5 percentage point.
    b. Each 1 percentage point decline in interest rates stimulates $30 billion of new investment spending.
    c. The expenditure multiplier is 2.
    d. There is so much unemployment that prices do not rise noticeably when demand increases.
11. Explain how your answer to Question 10 would differ if each of the assumptions were changed. Specifically, what sorts of changes in the assumptions would make monetary policy very weak?
12. Use graphs like Figures 30–5 and 30–7 to explain why the aggregate demand curve has a negative slope.
13. For years now, the federal government has been trying to lower its budget deficit by reducing spending or raising taxes. If the Federal Reserve wants to maintain the same level of aggregate demand in the face of a deficit reduction, what should it do? What would you expect to happen to interest rates?
14. (More difficult) Consider an economy in which government purchases, taxes, and net exports are all zero, the consumption function is:

$$C = 300 + 0.75\,Y,$$

and investment spending ($I$) depends on the rate of interest ($r$) in the following way:

$$I = 1000 - 100\,r.$$

Find the equilibrium GDP if the Fed makes the rate of interest (a) 2 percent ($r = 0.02$), (b) 5 percent, (c) 10 percent.

Chapter 31

# THE DEBATE OVER MONETARY POLICY

*The love of money is the root of all evil.*

**THE NEW TESTAMENT**

*Lack of money is the root of all evil.*

**GEORGE BERNARD SHAW**

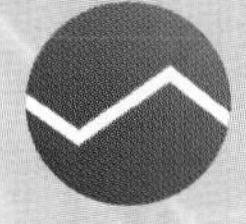

Up to now our discussion of stabilization policy has been almost entirely objective and technical. In seeking to understand how the national economy works and how government policies affect it, we have mostly ignored the intense economic and political controversies that surround the actual conduct of stabilization policy. Chapters 31 through 33 are about precisely these issues. ¶ We begin the chapter by explaining an alternative theory of how money affects the economy, known as *monetarism*. Although the monetarist and Keynesian views seem to contradict one another, we will see that the conflict is more apparent than real. In fact, the disagreement is akin to hearing a Briton say, "Yes," and a Frenchman say, "Oui." The uninitiated hear two different languages, but knowledgeable listeners understand that they mean the same thing. ¶ However, while monetarist and Keynesian *theories* are not very different, there *are* significant differences among economists over the appropriate design and execution of monetary *policy*. These differences occupy the rest of the chapter. We will learn about the continuing debates over the nature of aggregate supply, over the relative importance of monetary and fiscal policy, and over whether the Federal Reserve should try to control the money stock or interest rates. As we shall see, the resolution of these issues is crucial for the proper conduct of monetary policy and, indeed, to the decision of whether the government should try to conduct any stabilization policy at all. Finally, since economists' abilities to forecast the future are critical for the success or failure of stabilization efforts, some time is devoted to the techniques and accuracy of economic forecasting.

## VELOCITY AND THE QUANTITY THEORY OF MONEY

We saw in the last chapter how money influences real output and the price level in the Keynesian model. But there is another way to look at these matters, using a model that is much older than the Keynesian model. This model is known as the **quantity theory of money**, and it is easy to understand once we have introduced one new concept—*velocity*.

We learned in Chapter 29 that because barter is so cumbersome, virtually all economic transactions in advanced economies are conducted by the use of money. This means that if there are, say, \$4500 billion worth of transactions in the economy during a particular year, and there is an average money stock of \$900 billion during that year, then each dollar of money must get used an average of five times during the year (since $5 \times \$900$ billion $=$ \$4500 billion).

**VELOCITY** indicates the number of times per year that an "average dollar" is spent on goods and services. It is the ratio of nominal GDP to the number of dollars in the money stock. That is:

$$\text{Velocity} = \frac{\text{Nominal GDP}}{\text{Money stock}}$$

The number 5 in this example is called the **velocity of circulation**, or just **velocity** for short, because it indicates the speed at which money circulates. For example, a particular dollar bill might be used to buy a haircut in January; the barber might use it to buy a sweater in March; the storekeeper might then use it to pay for gasoline in May; the gas station owner could pay it out to the painter who paints his house in October; and the painter might spend it on a Christmas present in December. This would mean that the dollar was used five times during the year. If it were used only four times during the year, its velocity would be only 4, and so on. Similarly, a \$20 bill circulating with a velocity of 8 would be the monetary instrument used to finance \$160 worth of transactions in that year.

No one has data on all the transactions in the economy. To make velocity an operational concept, economists must settle on a precise definition of transactions that they can actually measure. The most popular choice is gross domestic product in current dollars (nominal GDP), even though it ignores many transactions that use money—such as sales of existing assets. If we accept nominal GDP as a measure of the money value of transactions, we are led to a concrete definition of velocity as the ratio of nominal GDP to the number of dollars in the money stock. Since nominal GDP is the product of real GDP times the price level, we can write this definition in symbols as:

$$\text{Velocity} = \frac{\text{Value of transactions}}{\text{Money Stock}} = \frac{\text{Nominal GDP}}{M} = \frac{P \times Y}{M}.$$

The **EQUATION OF EXCHANGE** states that the money value of GDP transactions must be equal to the product of the average stock of money times velocity. That is:

$$M \times V = P \times Y.$$

By multiplying both sides of the equation by $M$, we arrive at an identity called the **equation of exchange** that relates the money supply and nominal GDP:

$$\text{Money supply} \times \text{Velocity} = \text{Nominal GDP}.$$

Alternatively, stated in symbols, we have:

$$M \times V = P \times Y.$$

Here we have an obvious link between the stock of money, $M$, and the nominal value of the nation's output. But it is only a matter of arithmetic, not of economics. For example, it does not imply that the Fed can raise nominal GDP by increasing $M$. Why not? Because $V$ might simultaneously fall by enough to prevent $M \times V$ from rising. In words, if there were more dollar bills in circulation than before, but each bill changed hands more slowly, total spending might not rise. Thus:

The quantity theory of money transforms the equation of exchange from an accounting identity into an economic model by assuming that changes in velocity are so minor that velocity can be taken to be virtually constant.

You can see that if $V$ never changed, the equation of exchange would be a marvelously simple model of the determination of nominal GDP—far simpler than the Keynesian model. To see this, we need only to turn the equation of exchange around to read,

$$P \times Y = V \times M.$$

This equation says, for example, that if the Federal Reserve wants to increase nominal GDP by 12.7 percent, it need only raise the money supply by 12.7 percent. In such a simple world, economists could use the equation of exchange to *predict* nominal GDP simply by predicting the quantity of money. And policymakers could *control* nominal GDP simply by controlling the money supply.

In the real world things are not so simple because velocity is not a fixed number. But this does not necessarily destroy the usefulness of the quantity theory. We explained in Chapter 1 why all economic models make assumptions that are at least mildly unrealistic—without such assumptions they would not be models at all, just tedious descriptions of reality. The question is really whether the assumption of constant velocity is a useful abstraction from annoying detail or a gross distortion of facts.

Figure 31–1 sheds some light on this question by showing the behavior of velocity since 1929. You will note that there are two different measures of velocity, labeled $V1$ and $V2$. Why? Recall from Chapter 29 that there are several ways to measure money, the most popular of which are $M1$ and $M2$. Since velocity ($V$) is simply nominal GDP divided by the money stock ($M$), we get a different measure of $V$ for each measure of $M$. Figure 31–1 shows the velocities of both $M1$ and $M2$.

Several features are apparent. You will undoubtedly notice the difference in the behavior of $V1$ versus $V2$. There is a clear downward trend in $V1$ from 1929 until 1946, a pronounced upward trend until 1981, and quite erratic behavior in recent years. Clearly, *the velocity of M1 is not constant over long periods of time.* However, *the velocity of M2 is much more constant* and shows little if any trend since 1929. Closer examination of monthly or quarterly data on either $V1$ or $V2$ reveals some rather substantial fluctuations of velocity. Such fluctuations have led most economists to conclude that *velocity is not constant in the short run.* And predictions of nominal GDP based on the product of $V$ times $M$ have not fared very well, regardless of how $M$ is measured. It seems, then, that the strict quantity theory of money is not an adequate model of aggregate demand.

## THE DETERMINANTS OF VELOCITY

Since it is abundantly clear that velocity is a variable, not a constant, we can use the equation of exchange as a model of GDP determination only by examining

Figure 31-1 VELOCITY OF CIRCULATION, 1929–1992

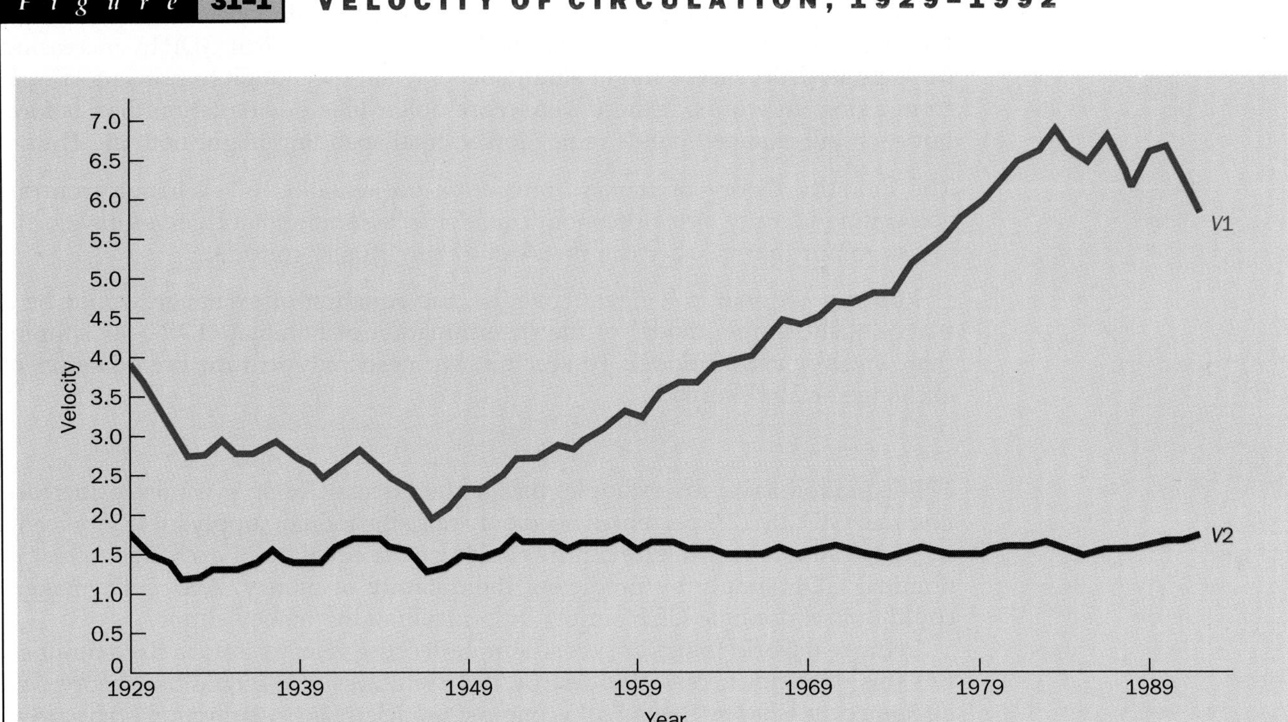


During a period of American history of almost 65 years, the velocity of *M*1 fell from about 3.5 in 1930 to 2 in 1946, and then rose to almost 7 in 1981 before falling again. Clearly, it has not been constant over long periods of time. The velocity of *M*2, however, looks much more stable.

SOURCE: Constructed by the authors; data from Bureau of Economic Analysis, Federal Reserve Board, and Professor Robert Rasche.

the determinants of velocity. What factors decide whether *V*1 or *V*2 will be 4 or 5 or 6; that is, whether a dollar will be used to buy goods and services four or five or six times a year?

Perhaps the principal factor is the *frequency with which paychecks are received.* This can best be explained through a numerical example. Consider a worker who earns $24,000 a year, paid to her in 12 monthly paychecks of $2000 each. Suppose that she spends the whole $2000 over the course of each month and maintains a minimum balance in the checking account of $500. Each payday her bank balance will shoot up to $2500 and then be gradually whittled down as she makes withdrawals to purchase goods and services. Finally, on the day before her next paycheck arrives, her checking balance will be just $500. Over the course of a typical month, then, her average checking account balance will be $1500 (halfway between $2500 and $500).

Now suppose her employer switches to a twice-a-month payroll. Her paychecks come twice as often, but are reduced to $1000 each. There is no reason for her rate of spending to change, but her *cash balances* will change. For now her checking balance will rise only to $1500 on payday (the $500 minimum balance plus the $1000 paycheck), and it will still be drawn down gradually to $500. Her average cash balance will therefore decline to $1000 (halfway between $1500 and $500).

Why is this so? Because, with the next paycheck coming sooner than before, it is not necessary to keep as much cash in the bank in order to carry out a given quantity of transactions.

But what does this have to do with velocity? Notice that when she was on a monthly payroll, this worker's personal velocity was:

$$V = \frac{\text{Annual income}}{\text{Average cash balance}} = \frac{\$24{,}000}{\$1500} = 16.$$

When she switched to a semimonthly payroll, velocity rose to:

$$V = \frac{\text{Annual income}}{\text{Average cash balance}} = \frac{\$24{,}000}{\$1000} = 24.$$

The general lesson to be learned is that:

More frequent wage payments mean that people can conduct their transactions with lower average cash balances. Since they will want to hold less cash, money will circulate faster. In other words, velocity will rise.

A second factor influencing velocity is the *efficiency of the payments mechanism*, including how quickly checks clear banks, the use of credit cards, and other methods of transferring funds. It is easy to see how this works.

The example in the previous paragraph assumed that our worker holds her entire paycheck in the form of money until she uses it to make a purchase. But, given that many forms of money pay little or no interest, this method may not be the most rational behavior. If it is possible to convert interest-bearing assets into money on short notice and at low cost, a rational individual might use her paycheck to purchase such assets and then use credit cards for most purchases, making periodic transfers to her checking account as necessary. For the same amount of total transactions, then, she would require lower money balances. This means that money would circulate faster: velocity would rise.

The incentive to limit cash holdings depends on the ease and speed with which it is possible to exchange money for other assets. This is what we mean by the "efficiency of the payments mechanism." As computerization has speeded up the bookkeeping procedures of banks, as financial innovations have made it possible to transfer funds rapidly between checking accounts and other assets, and as credit cards have come to be used instead of cash, the need to hold money balances has declined. By definition, then, velocity has risen.

Fortunately such basic changes in the payments mechanism usually take place only gradually, and thus often are easy to predict. But this is not always so. For example, a host of financial innovations in the 1970s and 1980s—some of which were mentioned in Chapter 29's discussion of the definitions of money—gave analysts fits in predicting velocity and led many to question the usefulness of the concept.

A third determinant of velocity is the *rate of interest*. The basic motive for economizing on money holdings is that most money (at least $M1$) pays little or no interest, while many alternative stores of value pay higher rates. The higher these alternative rates of interest, the greater the incentive to economize on holding money. Therefore, as interest rates rise, people want to hold less money. So the existing stock of money circulates faster, and velocity rises.

It is this factor that most directly undercuts the usefulness of the quantity theory of money as a guide for monetary policy. For in the last chapter we learned that expansionary monetary policy, which increases $M$, normally also decreases the interest rate. But if interest rates fall, other things being equal, velocity ($V$) will also fall. Thus, *when the Fed raises the money supply (M), the product $M \times V$ may go up by a smaller percentage than does M itself.*

One component of the interest rate is worth singling out for special attention: *the expected rate of inflation*. We explained in Chapter 23 why an "inflation premium" equal to the expected inflation rate often gets built into market interest rates.[1] Thus, in many instances, high inflation is the principal cause of high nominal interest rates. High rates of inflation, which erode the purchasing power of money, therefore lead both individuals and businesses to hold as little money as they can get by on—actions that increase velocity. To summarize this discussion of the determinants of velocity:

Velocity is not a strict constant but depends on such things as the frequency of payments, the efficiency of the financial system, the rate of interest, and the rate of inflation. Only by studying these determinants of velocity can we hope to predict the level of nominal GDP from knowledge of the money supply.

## MONETARISM: THE QUANTITY THEORY MODERNIZED

The foregoing does not mean, however, that the equation of exchange cannot be a useful framework within which to organize macroeconomic analysis. Under the right circumstances, it can be. And during the past 30 years or so a group of economists called *monetarists* has convincingly demonstrated that this is so.

Monetarists recognize that velocity is not literally constant. But they stress that it is fairly *predictable*—certainly in the long run and probably also in the short run. This leads them to the conclusion that the best way to study economic activity is to start with the *equation of exchange:* $M \times V = P \times Y$. From here, careful study of the determinants of $M$ (which we provided in the previous two chapters) and of $V$ (which we just completed) can be used to *predict* the behavior of nominal GDP. Similarly, given an understanding of movements in $V$, control over the money supply gives the Fed *control* over nominal GDP.

**MONETARISM** is a mode of analysis that uses the equation of exchange to organize and analyze macroeconomic data.

These are the central tenets of **monetarism**. When something happens in the economy, monetarists ask two questions:

1. What does this event do to the stock of money?
2. What does this event do to velocity?

From the answers, they assert that they can predict the path of nominal GDP.

By comparing the monetarist approach with the Keynesian approach that we described in the previous chapter, we can put both theories into perspective and understand the limitations of each. As we mentioned earlier, they differ more in style than in substance. Keynesians divide economic knowledge into four neat compartments—marked "*C*," "*I*," "*G*," and "($X - IM$)"—and unite them all with the equilibrium condition that $Y = C + I + G + (X - IM)$. In Keynesian analysis, money affects the economy by first affecting interest rates.

[1]If you need review, turn back to pages 576–77.

Monetarists, on the other hand, organize their knowledge into two alternative boxes—labeled "$M$" and "$V$"—and then use a simple identity that says $M \times V = P \times Y$ to bring this knowledge to bear in predicting aggregate demand. In the monetarist model, the role of money in the national economy is not necessarily limited to working through interest rates.

The bit of arithmetic that multiplies $M$ and $V$ to get $P \times Y$ is neither more nor less profound than the one that adds up $C$, $I$, $G$ and $(X - IM)$ to get $Y$. And certainly both are correct. The only substantive difference is that the monetarist equation leads to a prediction of *nominal* GDP, that is, the demand for goods and services measured in money terms, while the Keynesian equation leads to a prediction of *real* GDP, that is, the demand for goods and services measured in dollars of constant purchasing power.

Why, then, do we not simply mesh the two theories—using the monetarist approach to study nominal GDP and the Keynesian approach to study real GDP? It seems that by doing so we could use the separate analyses of real and nominal GDP to obtain a prediction of the future behavior of the price level, which, of course, is the ratio of nominal GDP to real GDP.

The reason that this appealing procedure will not work helps point out the major limitation of each theory. *Taken by itself, either theory is incomplete.* Each gives us a picture of the *demand* side of the economy without saying anything about the *supply* side. To try to predict both the price level and real output solely from these demand-oriented models would be like trying to predict the price of peanuts by studying only the behavior of consumers and ignoring that of farmers. It just will not work. In terms of our earlier aggregate supply and demand analysis:

Both the monetarist and Keynesian analyses are ways of studying the aggregate demand curve. In neither case is it possible to learn anything about both output and the price level without also studying the *aggregate supply curve.*

Economists thus are forced to choose between two alternative ways of predicting aggregate demand. Those who choose the monetarist route will use velocity and the money supply to study the demand for *nominal* GDP, that is, they view money as the key determinant of aggregate demand in nominal terms. But then they must turn to the supply side to estimate how any predicted change in nominal demand gets apportioned between changes in production and changes in prices. The schematic diagram on page 757, with its emphasis on interest rates, plays little role in the monetarist analysis of the transmission mechanism for monetary policy.

On the other hand, an economist working with the Keynesian approach will start by using the schematic diagram on page 757 to predict how monetary policy affects the demand for *real* GDP, that is, aggregate demand in real terms. But then he will have to turn to the aggregate supply curve to estimate the inflationary consequences of this real demand.

Which approach works better? There is no generally correct answer for all economies in all periods of time. Therefore, it is not surprising that some economists prefer one approach while others favor the alternative. When velocity behaved predictably in the 1960s and early 1970s, monetarism won many converts—in the United States and around the world. But then velocity behaved erratically and inexplicably here and in other countries during the 1980s, and most economists abandoned monetarism.

## FISCAL POLICY, INTEREST RATES, AND VELOCITY

We have now almost reconciled the Keynesian and monetarist views of how the economy operates. Keynesian analysis lends itself naturally to the study of fiscal policy, since $G$ is a part of $C + I + G + (X - IM)$. But we learned in the previous chapter that Keynesian economics also provides a powerful and important role for monetary policy: an increase in the money supply reduces interest rates, which, in turn, stimulates the demand for investment.

Monetarist analysis provides an obvious and direct route by which monetary policy influences both output and prices. But can the monetarist approach also handle fiscal policy? It can, because fiscal policy has an important effect on the rate of interest. And it is not hard to understand how this effect operates.

Let's see what happens to real output and the price level following, say, a rise in government purchases of goods and services. We learned in Chapter 28 that both real GDP ($Y$) and the price level ($P$) rise. But Chapter 30's analysis of the demand for money taught us that rising $Y$ and $P$ push the demand curve for money outward to the right. With no change in the supply curve for money, the rate of interest must rise. So *expansionary fiscal policy raises interest rates.*

If the government uses its spending and taxing weapons in the opposite direction, the same process works in reverse. Falling output and (possibly) falling prices shift the demand curve for money inward to the left. With a fixed supply curve for money, equilibrium in the money market leads to a lower interest rate. Thus:

Monetary policy is not the only type of policy that affects interest rates. Fiscal policy also affects interest rates. Specifically, increases in government spending or tax cuts normally push interest rates up, whereas restrictive fiscal policies normally pull interest rates down.

The fact that fiscal policy affects interest rates gives it a role in the monetarist model despite the fact that the equation of exchange, $M \times V = P \times Y$, does not include either government spending or taxation among its variables. Any fiscal policy that a Keynesian would call expansionary—higher spending, lower taxes, and so on—pushes up the rate of interest. And rising interest rates push up velocity because people want to hold less money when the interest they can earn on alternative assets increases. So it is through the $V$ term in $M \times V$ that fiscal policy does its work in the monetarist framework. The equation of exchange, $M \times V = P \times Y$, then implies that nominal GDP must rise when, say, government spending increases—even if $M$ is fixed—because velocity is higher.

Conversely, restrictive fiscal policies like tax increases and expenditure cuts reduce the quantity of money demanded and lower interest rates. The consequent drop in velocity reduces income through the equation of exchange, because the money supply circulates more slowly.

The translation, then, is complete. The Keynesian story about how fiscal policy works can be phrased in the monetarist dialect. And the monetarist tale about monetary policy can be told with a Keynesian accent. Furthermore, both modes of analysis help only to explain the mysteries of aggregate *demand* and must be supplemented by an analysis of aggregate *supply* to be complete. We must conclude, then, that:

The differences between Keynesians and monetarists have been grossly exaggerated by the news media. Indeed, when it comes to matters of basic economic theory, there are hardly any differences at all.

### APPLICATION: THE MULTIPLIER FORMULA ONCE AGAIN

The fact that expansionary fiscal policy pushes up interest rates has one other important consequence that we should mention. Recall that higher interest rates deter private investment spending. This means that when the government raises the $G$ component of $C + I + G + (X - IM)$, one of the side effects of its action will be to reduce the $I$ component (by raising interest rates). Consequently, total spending will rise by less than simple multiplier analysis might suggest. The fact that a surge in government demand ($G$) discourages some private demand ($I$) provides another reason why the oversimplified multiplier formula, $1/(1 - \text{MPC})$, exaggerates the size of the multiplier:

Because a rise in G (or, for that matter, an autonomous rise in any component of total expenditure) pushes interest rates higher, and hence deters some investment spending, the increase in the sum $C + I + G + (X - IM)$ is smaller than what the oversimplified multiplier formula predicts.

Combining this observation with our previous analysis of the multiplier, we now have the following complete list of:

#### REASONS WHY THE OVERSIMPLIFIED MULTIPLIER FORMULA IS WRONG

1. It ignores variable imports, which reduce the size of the multiplier.
2. It ignores price-level changes, which reduce the size of the multiplier.
3. It ignores the income tax, which reduces the size of the multiplier.
4. It ignores the rising interest rates that accompany any autonomous increase in spending, which also reduce the size of the multiplier.

Notice that all four of these adjustments point in the same direction—toward a smaller multiplier. No wonder the actual multiplier (estimated to be below 2 for the U.S. economy) is so much less than the oversimplified formula suggests.

## DEBATE: SHOULD STABILIZATION POLICY RELY ON FISCAL OR MONETARY POLICY?

We have seen that the Keynesian and monetarist approaches are more like two different languages than two different theories. However, it is well known that language can influence attitudes in many subtle ways. For example, even though English prose can be translated into French, the British and the French do not always see eye-to-eye.

In a similar vein, the Keynesian language biases things subtly toward thinking first about fiscal policy simply because fiscal actions influence aggregate demand so directly. $G$ is, after all, a part of $C + I + G + (X - IM)$. Monetarists, on the other hand, see a more indirect channel that works through interest rates and velocity, and they wonder if something might not go wrong along the way.

The roles are reversed in the analysis of monetary policy. To monetarists, the equation of exchange—$M \times V = P \times Y$—makes the effect of money on aggregate demand clear and direct. While monetary policy also affects aggregate demand in the Keynesian model, the mechanisms are complex, and there is obviously room for a slip-up. Monetary expansion might not affect the interest rate much, or a fall in the interest rate might not induce much additional investment. Thus, some Keynesians have had their doubts when monetarists attributed great powers to monetary policy.

Years ago, Keynesians and monetarists conducted a spirited and well publicized debate in which extreme monetarists claimed that fiscal policy was futile, while extreme Keynesians argued that monetary policy was useless. But accumulating evidence made each extreme view seem less and less tenable, and this is not a major issue today. Instead:

Most economists today agree that both fiscal and monetary policy have significant effects on aggregate demand. Nonetheless, Keynesians tend to look more toward fiscal policy while monetarists tend to rely more on monetary policy.

More important than the issue of which type of policy is more *powerful* is the question of which type of medicine—fiscal or monetary—cures the patient more *quickly*. Up to now, we have ignored questions of timing and pretended that the authorities instantly noticed the need for stabilization policy, decided upon a course of action, and administered the appropriate medicine. In reality, each of these steps takes time.

First, delays in data collection mean that the latest macroeconomic data pertain to the economy of a few months ago. Second, one of the prices of democracy is that the government often takes a distressingly long time to decide what should be done, to muster the necessary political support, and to put its decisions into effect. Finally, our $6 trillion economy is a bit like a sleeping elephant that reacts rather sluggishly to moderate fiscal and monetary prods. As it turns out, these **lags in stabilization policy**, as they are called, play a pivotal role in the choice between fiscal and monetary policy. Here's why.

The main policy tool for manipulating consumer spending (*C*) is the personal income tax, and Chapter 24 documented why the fiscal policy planner can feel fairly sure that each $1 of tax reduction will lead to about 90 to 95 cents of additional spending *eventually*. But not all of this will happen at once.

First, consumers must learn about the tax change. Then they may need to be convinced that the change is permanent. Finally, there is the simple force of habit: households need time to adjust their spending habits when circumstances change. For all these reasons, consumers may increase their spending by only 30 to 50 cents for each $1 of additional income within the first few months after a tax cut. Only gradually, will they raise their spending up to about 90 to 95 cents for each additional dollar of income.

Lags are much longer for investment (*I*), which provides the main vehicle by which monetary policy affects aggregate demand. Planning for capacity expansion in a large corporation is a long, drawn-out process. Ideas must be submitted and approved, plans must be drawn up, funding acquired, orders for machinery or contracts for new construction placed. And most of this occurs *before* any apprecia-ble amount of money is spent. Economists have found that much of the response of investment to changes in interest rates or tax provisions is delayed for several *years*.

The fact that *C* responds more quickly than *I* has important implications for the choice among alternative stabilization policies. The reason is that the most common varieties of fiscal policy affect aggregate demand either directly—*G* is a component of $C + I + G + (X - IM)$—or work through consumption with a relatively short lag, while monetary policy has its major effects on investment. Therefore:

Conventional types of fiscal policy actions, such as changes in *G* or in personal taxes, probably affect aggregate demand much more promptly than do monetary policy actions.

Notice that the statement says nothing about which instrument is more *powerful*. It simply asserts that the fiscal weapon acts more *quickly*. This important fact has been used to build a case that fiscal policy should bear the major burden of economic stabilization. But before you jump to such a conclusion, you should realize that the lags we have just described are not the only ones affecting the timing of stabilization policy.

Apart from these lags in expenditure, which are beyond the control of policymakers, there are further lags that are due to the behavior of the policymakers themselves! We are referring here to the delays that occur while the policymakers are studying the state of the economy, contemplating what steps they should take, and putting their decisions into effect. And here most observers believe that monetary policy has an important edge; that is:

Policy lags are normally much shorter for monetary policy than for fiscal policy.

The reasons are apparent. The Federal Open Market Committee (FOMC) meets about eight times a year—and more often if necessary. So monetary policy decisions are made frequently. And once the Fed decides on a course of action, it normally can be executed almost instantly by buying or selling bonds on the open market.

In contrast, Federal budgeting procedures operate on an annual budget cycle. Except in rare circumstances, *major* fiscal policy initiatives can occur only at the time of the annual budget. Tax laws can be changed at any time, but the wheels of Congress grind slowly and it may take many months before Congress acts on a tax change. In sum, one has to be very optimistic to suppose that important fiscal policy actions can be taken on short notice. Even President Clinton's first budget, which passed through Congress in record time in 1993, took almost six months from introduction to enactment.

So where does the combined effect of expenditure lags and policy lags leave us? With nothing conclusive, we are afraid. As the late Arthur Okun put it, the debate over whether the nation should rely only on monetary policy or only on fiscal policy is a bit like arguing whether a safe car is one with good headlights or one with good brakes. It is unwise to drive at night unless you have both.

## DEBATE: SHOULD THE FED CONTROL THE MONEY SUPPLY OR CONTROL INTEREST RATES?

Once we recognize that monetary policy is an important tool of stabilization policy, other questions arise. In several cases, the answers are the subject of intense dispute.

One major controversy is over how the Federal Reserve should conduct monetary policy. Some economists argue that the Fed should use open-market operations and its other tools to control the rate of interest ($r$) while others, especially monetarists, insist that the Fed should concentrate on controlling the money supply ($M$). To understand the nature of this debate, we must first understand why the Fed cannot control both $M$ and $r$ at the same time.

Figure 31–2 will help us see why. It shows an initial equilibrium in the money market at point $E$, where money demand curve $M_0D_0$ crosses money supply curve $MS$. Here the interest rate is $r = 5$ percent and the money stock is $M = \$830$ billion. Let us assume that these are the Fed's targets for $M$ and $r$; it wants to keep the money supply and interest rates just where they are.

Figure 31–2 THE FEDERAL RESERVE'S POLICY DILEMMA

This diagram illustrates the dilemma facing the Fed when the demand schedule for money shifts. In this case, we suppose that it increases from $M_0D_0$ to $M_1D_1$. If the equilibrium at point *E* satisfied its goals both for the money supply ($830 billion) and for the rate of interest (5 percent), either one or both of these goals will have to be abandoned after the demand schedule shifts. Points *W*, *A*, and *Z* illustrate three of the many choices. At *W*, the Fed is keeping the money supply at $830 billion through contractionary policies, but at a cost of skyrocketing interest rates. At *Z*, the Fed is holding interest rates at 5 percent, but the required expansionary monetary policies raise the money supply to $850 billion. At *A*, the Fed is not adjusting its policy and is accepting an increase in both the money supply and the rate of interest.

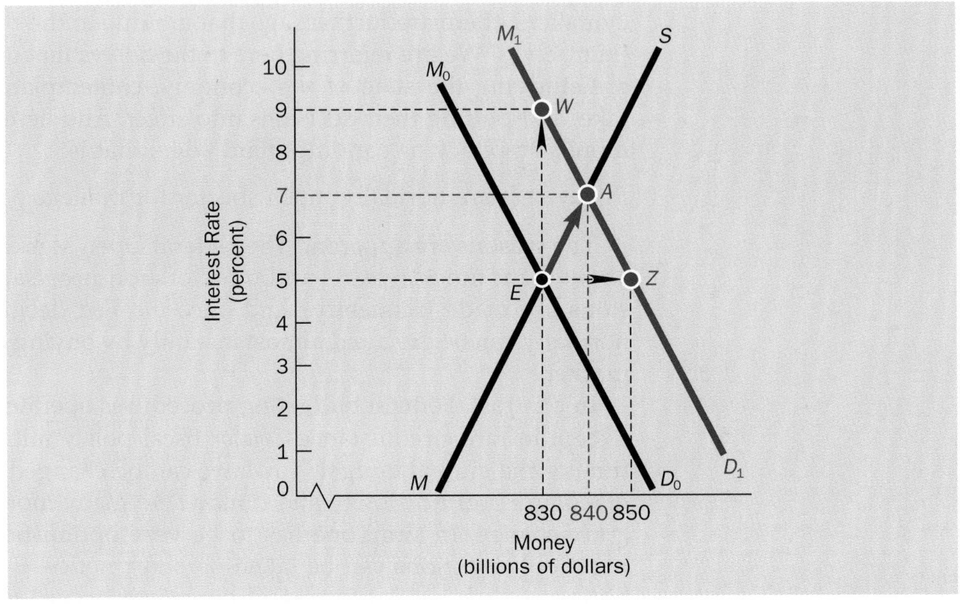


If the demand curve for money holds still, this is possible. But suppose the demand for money is not so obliging. Suppose, instead, that the demand curve shifts outward to the position indicated by $M_1D_1$ in Figure 31–2. As we learned in the last chapter (see, especially, Figure 30–4 on page 751), this might happen because output increases or because prices rise. Or it might happen simply because people decide to hold more money. Whatever the reason, the Fed can no longer achieve both of its previous targets.

If the Fed takes no action, the outward shift in the demand curve will push up both the quantity of money (*M*) and the rate of interest (*r*). Figure 31–2 shows this graphically. If the demand curve for money shifts outward from $M_0D_0$ to $M_1D_1$ and there is no change in monetary policy (so that supply schedule *MS* does not move), equilibrium moves from point *E* to point *A*. The money stock rises to $840 billion and the interest rate rises to 7 percent.

However, the supply of money is one of the major determinants of aggregate demand. Consequently, if the economy is already operating near full employment, the Fed might be unwilling to let *M* rise. In that case, it can use any of its contractionary weapons to prevent *M* from rising. But, if it does this, it will push *r* up even higher because, with no increase in the money supply, an even higher interest rate is necessary to keep quantity supplied and quantity demanded equal.

This is also shown in Figure 31–2. After the demand curve for money shifts, point *E* is unattainable. The Fed must choose from among the points on $M_1D_1$, and point *W* is the point on this curve that keeps the money supply at $830 billion. If the supply curve is pushed inward so that it passes through point *W*, *M* will remain at $830 billion. However, the interest rate will skyrocket to 9 percent.

Alternatively, if the economy is operating at low levels of resource utilization, the Fed might decide that a rise in *M* is permissible, but that a rise in *r* is to be avoided. Why? Because, as we know, investment spending normally declines when interest rates rise. In this case, the Fed would be forced to engage in expansionary monetary policy to prevent the outward shift of the demand curve for money from pushing up *r*. In terms of Figure 31–2, the interest rate can be held at 5 percent by shifting the supply curve outward to pass through point *Z*. But to do this, the Fed will have to push the money supply up to $850 billion. To summarize this discussion:

When the demand curve for money shifts outward, the Fed must tolerate a rise in interest rates, a rise in the money stock, or both. It simply does not have the weapons to control *both* the supply of money *and* the interest rate. If it tries to keep *M* steady, then *r* will rise sharply. Conversely, if it tries to stabilize *r*, then *M* will shoot up.

This explains why the Fed often finds it impossible to control both the money supply and the rate of interest. A shift in the demand schedule for money supply may make previously selected targets for *M* and *r* unattainable.

## TWO IMPERFECT ALTERNATIVES

For years, economists have debated what the Fed should do about this dilemma. Should it adhere rigidly to its target growth path for the money supply, regardless of the consequences for interest rates? Should it hold interest rates steady even if that causes wild gyrations in the money stock? Or is some middle ground more appropriate? Let us explore the issues before considering what has actually been done.

The main problem with rigid targets for the *supply* of money is that the *demand* for money does not cooperate by growing smoothly and predictably from month to month; instead it dances about quite a bit in the short run. This confronts the recommendation to control the money supply with two problems:

1. It is almost impossible to achieve. Since the volume of money in existence depends on *both* the demand *and* supply schedules, it would require exceptional dexterity on the part of the Fed to keep *M* on target in the face of significant fluctuations in demand for money.
2. For reasons that were just explained, rigid adherence to money-stock targets might lead to wide fluctuations in interest rates, which could create an unsettled atmosphere for business decisions.

By the same token, even more powerful objections can be raised against exclusive concentration on interest rate movements. Since increases in nominal GDP shift the demand schedule for money outward (as Figure 31–2 shows), a central bank determined to keep interest rates from rising would have to expand the money supply in response. Conversely, when GDP sagged, it would have to contract the money supply to keep rates from falling. Thus, interest rate *pegging* would make the money supply expand in boom times and contract in recessions—with potentially grave consequences for the stability of the economy. Ironically, this is precisely the sort of monetary behavior the Federal Reserve System was designed to prevent. Hence, if the Fed is to control interest rates, it had better formulate flexible targets, not fixed ones.

### WHAT HAS THE FED DONE?

In the early part of the postwar period, the predominant Keynesian view held that the interest rate target was much the more important of the two. The rationale for this view was that gyrating interest rates would cause abrupt and unsettling changes in investment spending, and this in turn would make the whole economy fluctuate. Stabilization of interest rates was believed to be the best way to stabilize GDP. If fluctuations in the money supply were required to keep interest rates on a steady course, that would be nothing to worry about. Consequently, the Fed looked mostly at interest rates.

In the 1960s, this prevailing view came under increasing attack by Professor Milton Friedman and other monetarists. They argued that the Fed's obsession with stabilization of interest rates actually *destabilized* the economy because it led to undue fluctuations in the money supply. The monetarist prescription was simple. The Fed should stop worrying about fluctuations in interest rates and make the money supply grow at a constant rate from month to month and year to year.

Monetarism made important inroads at the Fed during the inflationary 1970s. Early in the decade, the central bank began to keep much closer tabs on the money stock than it previously had. More important, a major change in the conduct of monetary policy was announced by then-Chairman Paul Volcker in October 1979. Henceforth, he asserted, the Fed would stick more closely to its target for money stock growth regardless of the implications for interest rates. Interest rates would go wherever the law of supply and demand took them.

According to our analysis, this change in policy should have led to wider fluctuations in interest rates. And it did. Unfortunately, the Fed ran into some bad luck. The ensuing three years were marked by unusually severe gyrations in the demand for money, so the ups and downs of interest rates were far more extreme than anyone had expected. Figure 31–3 gives an indication of just how volatile interest rates were between late 1979 and late 1982. Naturally, this erratic performance led to some heavy criticism of the Fed.

Then, in October 1982, Chairman Volcker announced that the Fed was temporarily abandoning its attempts to stick to a target growth path for the money supply. Although he did not say so, his announcement presumably meant that the Fed started once again to pay more attention to interest rate targets. As you can see in Figure 31–3, interest rates were much more stable after the change in policy. Most observers think this was no coincidence.

Since late 1982, the Fed has distanced itself more and more from the position that the money supply should grow at a constant rate. In 1993, Chairman Alan Greenspan went so far as to state that the Fed was no longer using the various *M*s to guide policy. He strongly hinted that the Fed was targeting interest rates, especially *real* interest rates. In truth, it had little choice. The demand curve for money behaved so erratically and so unpredictably in the 1980s and early 1990s that stabilizing the money stock was probably impossible and certainly undesirable. Whether this situation will continue is anyone's guess.

**Figure 31-3** THE BEHAVIOR OF INTEREST RATES, 1979–1985

This chart traces interest rate movements from 1979 through 1985. Notice the extreme volatility of rates during the period from late 1979 to mid-1982—the period in which the Fed was concentrating more on stabilizing the money supply. After mid-1982, interest rates became much less volatile.

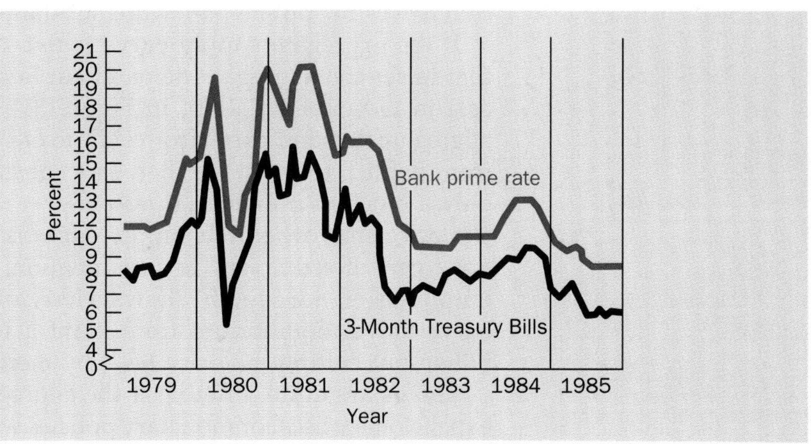


## DEBATE: THE SHAPE OF THE AGGREGATE SUPPLY CURVE

Another lively debate over stabilization policy revolves around the shape of the economy's aggregate supply curve. Many economists, including most Keynesians, think of the aggregate supply curve as quite flat in the short run, as in Figure 31–4(a), so that large increases in output can be achieved with little inflation.

**Figure 31-4** ALTERNATIVE VIEWS OF THE AGGREGATE SUPPLY CURVE

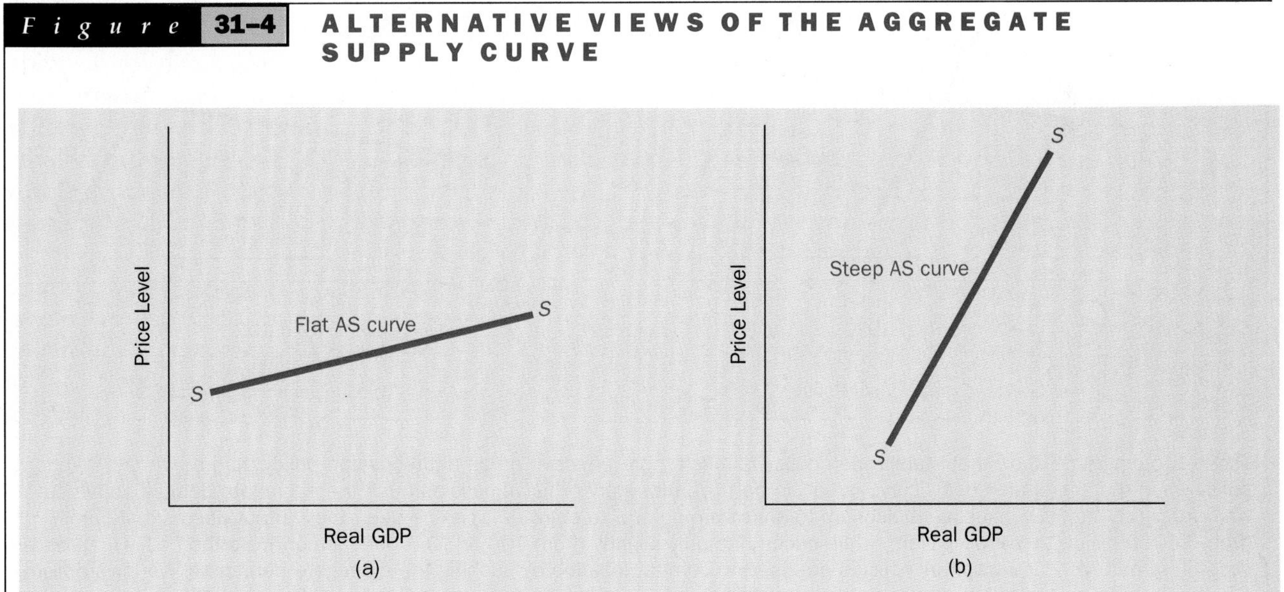


Some economists, especially Keynesians, think of the economy's aggregate supply schedule as very flat, as in part (a). Others, especially monetarists, think of it as quite steep, as in part (b).

Other economists, including most monetarists, envision the supply curve as steep, as in Figure 31–4(b), so that prices are very responsive to changes in output. The differences for public policy are substantial.

If the aggregate supply curve is flat, expansionary fiscal or monetary policy that raises the aggregate demand curve can buy large gains in real GDP at low cost in terms of inflation. In Figure 31–5(a), stimulation of demand raises the aggregate demand curve from $D_0D_0$ to $D_1D_1$ and moves the economy's equilibrium from point *E* to point *A*. There is a substantial rise in output ($400 billion) with only a pinch of inflation (1 percent).

Conversely, when the supply curve is flat, a restrictive stabilization policy is not a very effective way to cure inflation; instead, it serves mainly to reduce real output, as Figure 31–5(b) shows. Here, a leftward shift of the aggregate demand curve moves equilibrium from point *E* to point *B*, lowering real GDP by $400 billion but cutting the price level by merely 1 percent.

Things are quite different if the aggregate supply curve is steep. In that case, expansionary fiscal or monetary policies will cause a good deal of inflation without adding much to real GDP. (See Figure 31–6(a), where expansionary policies shift

**Figure 31–5** **STABILIZATION POLICY WITH A FLAT AGGREGATE SUPPLY CURVE**

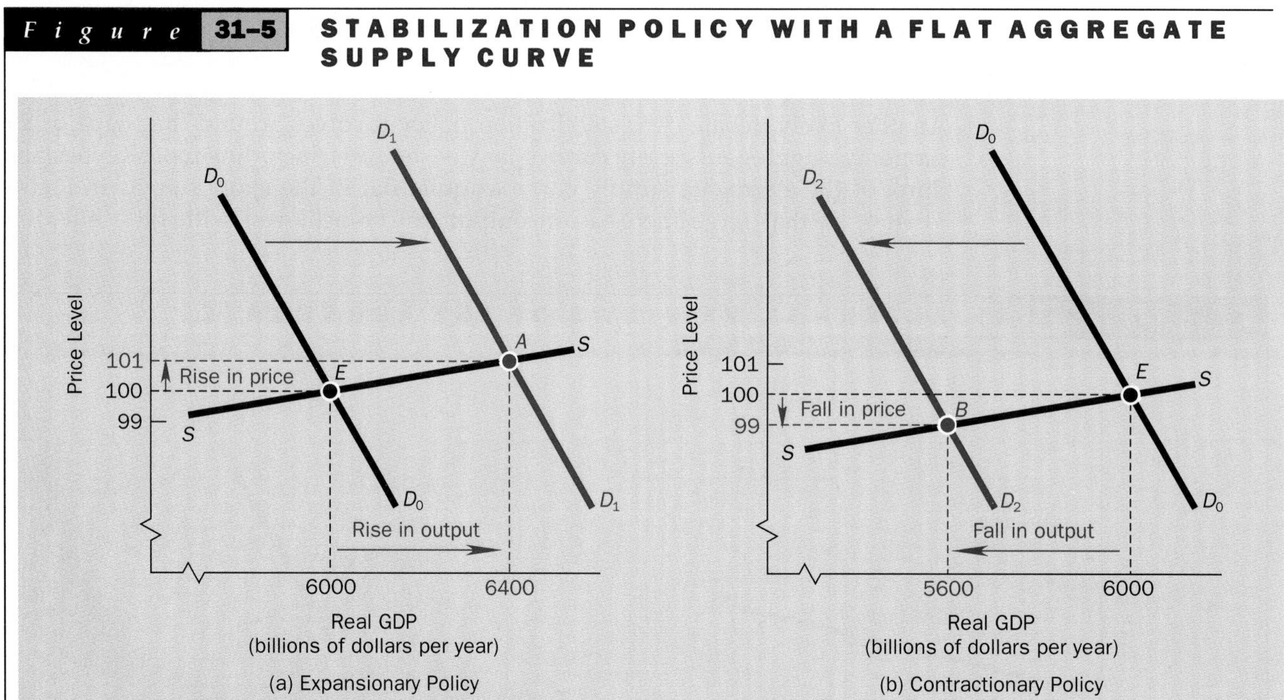


These two diagrams show that stabilization policy is much more effective as an antirecession policy than as an anti-inflation policy when the aggregate supply curve is flat. In part (a), monetary or fiscal policies push the aggregate demand curve outward from $D_0D_0$ to $D_1D_1$, causing equilibrium to shift from point *E* to point *A*. It can be seen that output rises substantially (from $6000 billion to $6400 billion), while prices rise only slightly (from 100 to 101, or 1 percent). So the policy is quite successful. In part (b), contractionary policies are used to combat inflation by pushing the aggregate demand curve inward from $D_0D_0$ to $D_2D_2$. Prices do fall slightly (from 100 to 99) as equilibrium shifts from point *E* to point *B*, but real output falls much more dramatically (from $6000 billion to $5600 billion); so the policy has had little success.

Figure 31–6 **STABILIZATION POLICY WITH A STEEP AGGREGATE SUPPLY CURVE**

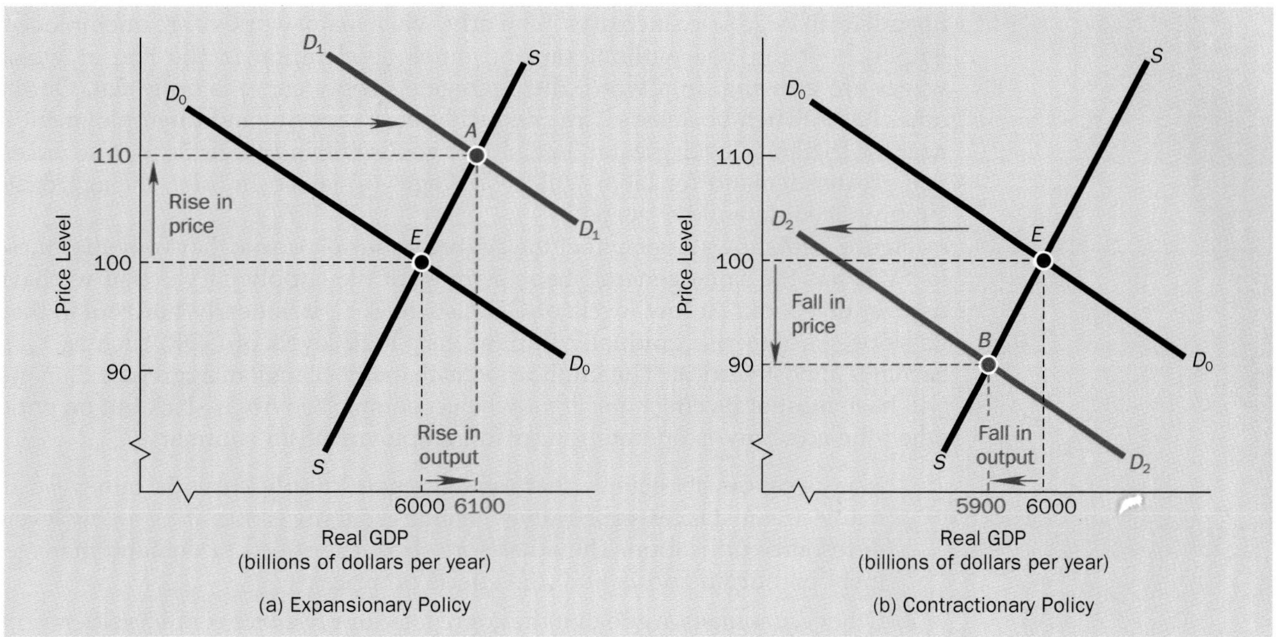


These two diagrams show that stabilization policy is much more effective at fighting inflation than at fighting recession when the aggregate supply curve is steep. In part (a), expansionary policies that push aggregate demand outward from $D_0D_0$ to $D_1D_1$ raise output by only $100 billion but push up prices by 10 percent as equilibrium moves from point *E* to point *A*. So demand management is not a good way to end a recession. In part (b), contractionary policies that pull aggregate demand inward to $D_2D_2$ are successful in that they lower prices markedly (from 100 to 90, or about 10 percent) but reduce output only slightly (from $6000 billion to $5900 billion).

equilibrium from *E* to *A*.) Similarly, contractionary policies are effective ways of bringing down the price level without much sacrifice of output, as shown by the shift from *E* to *B* in Figure 31–6(b).

The resolution of this debate is of fundamental importance for the proper conduct of stabilization policy. If the supply curve is flat, stabilization policy is much more effective at combating recession than inflation. If the supply curve is steep, precisely the reverse is true.

But why does the argument persist? Why cannot economists determine the shape of the aggregate supply curve and stop arguing? The answer is that supply conditions in the real world are far more complicated than our simple diagrams suggest. Some industries may have flat supply curves while others have steep ones. For reasons explained in Chapter 27, supply curves shift over time. And, unlike many laboratory scientists, economists cannot perform the controlled experiments that would reveal the shape of the aggregate supply curve directly. Instead, they must use statistical inference to make educated guesses.

Although empirical research is proceeding, our understanding of aggregate supply remains much less settled than our understanding of aggregate demand.

Nevertheless, many economists believe that the dim outline of a consensus view has emerged. This view stresses that the steepness of the aggregate supply schedule depends on the degree of slack in the economy.

If industry has a great deal of spare capacity, then increases in demand will not call forth large price increases. Similarly, when many workers are unemployed, employment can rise without causing much acceleration in the rate at which wages are growing. In a word, the aggregate supply curve is quite flat. On the other hand, when businesses are producing near capacity and unemployment is near the frictional level, greater demand for goods will induce firms to raise prices; and greater demand for labor will push wages up faster. In brief, the aggregate supply schedule will be steep.

Figure 31–7 shows a version of the aggregate supply curve that embodies these ideas. It has the same general shape as most of the supply curves that we have used in this book. At low levels of GDP, such as $Y_1$, it is nearly horizontal; then its slope starts to rise gradually until at very high levels of GDP, such as $Y_2$, it becomes almost vertical. The implication is that any change in aggregate demand will have most of its effect on *output* when economic activity is slack but on *prices* when the economy is operating near full employment. In summary:

1. Many economists believe that the aggregate supply curve is rather *flat* in many circumstances, especially when the economy is operating at low levels of resource utilization. They therefore stress the effects of demand management on output and belittle the effects on prices.
2. Other economists argue that the aggregate supply curve is often rather *steep*, especially when the economy has little slack. They therefore emphasize the

*Figure* **31–7**

**AN AGGREGATE SUPPLY CURVE WITH BOTH STEEP AND FLAT REGIONS**

The view that the aggregate supply curve is flat is most likely to be accurate when there is much unemployment and unused capacity. The alternative view, that the supply curve is steep, is likely to be more accurate when there is full employment and high capacity utilization.

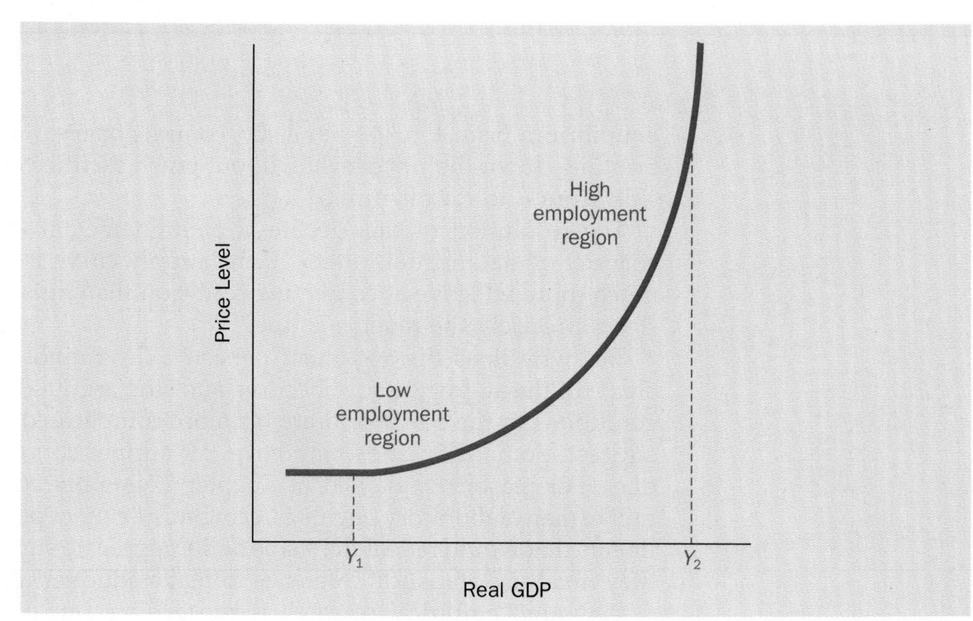

effects of demand management on prices and belittle the effects on real output.

3. A middle-of-the-road view would hold that the aggregate supply curve is probably flat when there is a great deal of unemployment, but steep when the economy is near full employment. Not all economists accept this middle-of-the-road view, but many do.

## DEBATE: SHOULD THE GOVERNMENT INTERVENE?

We have yet to consider what may be the most fundamental and controversial issue of all: Is it likely that the government can conduct a successful stabilization policy? Or are its well-intentioned efforts likely to be harmful, so that it would be better to adhere to fixed rules?

This controversy has raged for several decades with no end in sight. It is in part a political or philosophical debate because economists, like other people, come with both liberal and conservative stripes. Liberal economists tend to be more intervention-minded and hence look more favorably on discretionary stabilization policy. Conservative economists are more inclined to keep the government's hands off the economy and hence are more attracted to fixed rules. Such political differences are not surprising. But more than ideology propels the debate. We need to understand the economic issues.

Critics of stabilization policy point to the lags and uncertainties that surround the operation of both fiscal and monetary policies—lags and uncertainties that we have stressed repeatedly in this and earlier chapters. Will the Fed's actions have the desired effects on the money supply? What will these actions do to interest rates and spending? Can fiscal policy actions be taken promptly? How large is the expenditure multiplier? The list could go on and on.

They look at this formidable catalogue of difficulties, add a dash of skepticism about our ability to forecast the future state of the economy (see pages 782–87), and worry that stabilization policy may do more harm than good. These skeptics advise both the fiscal and monetary authorities to pursue a passive policy rather than an active one—adhering to fixed rules that, while incapable of ironing out every bump in the economy's growth path, will at least keep it roughly on track in the long run.

Advocates of activist stabilization policy admit that perfection is unattainable. But they are much *more optimistic* about the prospects for success. And they are much *less optimistic* about how smoothly the economy would function in the absence of demand management. They therefore advocate discretionary increases in government spending (or decreases in taxes) and more rapid growth of the money supply when the economy has a recessionary gap. By this policy mix, they believe, government can keep the economy closer to its full-employment growth path.

Naturally, each side can point to evidence that buttresses its own view. Activists look back with pride at the tax cut of 1964 and the sustained period of economic growth that it helped usher in. They also point to the tax cut of 1975, which was enacted at just about the trough of a severe recession, the Federal Reserve's switch to easy money in 1982, and the Fed's expert steering of the economy in the late 1980s. Advocates of rules remind us of the government's refusal to curb what was obviously a situation of runaway demand during the 1966–1968 Vietnam buildup, its over-expansion of the economy in 1972, the monetary overkill that helped bring on the sharp recession of 1981–1982, and and the absence of antirecession policy in the early 1990s.

The historical record of fiscal and monetary policy is far from glorious. It shows that while there were many instances in which appropriate stabilization policy *could have been* helpful, the authorities instead either took inappropriate steps or did nothing at all. The question of whether the government should adopt passive rules or attempt an activist stabilization policy therefore merits a closer look. As we shall see, the lags in the effects of policy that we discussed earlier in this chapter play a pivotal role in the debate.

## LAGS AND THE RULES-VERSUS-DISCRETION DEBATE

The reason that lags lead to a fundamental difficulty for stabilization policy—a difficulty so formidable that it has led many economists to conclude that attempts to stabilize economic activity are likely to do more harm than good—can be explained best by reference to Figure 31–8. Here we chart the behavior of both actual and potential GDP over the course of a business cycle in a hypothetical economy with no stabilization policy. At point *A*, the economy begins to slip into a recession and does not recover to full employment until point *D*. Then, between points *D* and *E*, it overshoots and is in an inflationary boom.

The case for stabilization policy runs like this. The recession is recognized to be a serious problem at point *B*, and appropriate actions are taken. These actions have their major effects around point *C* and therefore curb both the depth and the length of the recession.

But suppose the lags are really much longer than this. Suppose, for example, that delays in taking action postpone policy initiatives until point *C* and that stimulative policies do not have their major effects until after point *D*. Then

**Figure 31–8** **A TYPICAL BUSINESS CYCLE**

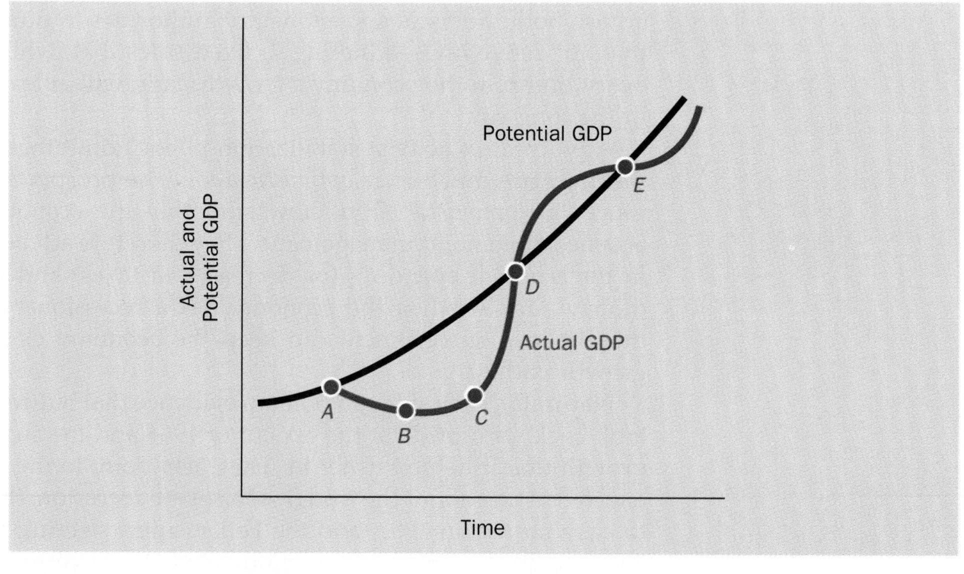


This is a stylized representation of the relationship between actual and potential GDP during a typical business cycle. The imaginary economy slips into a recession at point *A*, bottoms out around point *B*, and is in a recovery period until point *D*. After point *D*, it enters an inflationary boom that lasts until point *E*.

policy will be of little help during the recession and will actually do harm by overstimulating the economy during the ensuing boom. Thus:

In the presence of long lags, attempts at stabilizing the economy can actually succeed in destabilizing it.

Because of this, some economists argue that we are better off letting the economy alone and relying on its natural self-corrective forces to cure recessions and inflations. Instead of embarking on periodic programs of monetary and fiscal stimulus or restraint, they advise policymakers to stick to fixed rules; that is, to rigid formulas that ignore current economic events.

### AUTOMATIC STABILIZERS

The rule generally associated with monetarism has been mentioned already: the Fed should keep the money supply growing at a constant rate. For fiscal policy, proponents of rules often recommend that the government resist temptations to manage aggregate demand actively and rely instead on **automatic stabilizers**—features of the economy that reduce its sensitivity to shocks.

An **AUTOMATIC STABILIZER** is any arrangement that automatically serves to support aggregate demand when it would otherwise sag and to hold down aggregate demand when it would otherwise surge ahead. In this way, an automatic stabilizer reduces the sensitivity of the economy to shifts in demand.

Examples of automatic stabilizers are not hard to find in the federal budget. The personal income tax is the most obvious example. The tax acts as a shock absorber because it makes disposable income, and thus consumer spending, less sensitive to fluctuations in GDP. When GDP rises, disposable income (*DI*) rises also, but by less than the rise in GDP because part of the income is siphoned off by the U.S. Treasury. This helps limit the upward fluctuation in consumption spending. And when GDP falls, *DI* falls less sharply because part of the loss is absorbed by the Treasury rather than by consumers. So consumption does not drop as much as it otherwise might. Thus, as we noted in Chapter 28, income taxes lower the value of the multiplier. In truth, the unloved personal income tax is one of several modern institutions that help ensure us against a repeat performance of the Great Depression.

There are many other automatic stabilizers in our economy. For example, in Chapter 23 we studied the U.S. system of unemployment insurance. This serves as an automatic stabilizer in a similar way. When GDP begins to fall and people lose their jobs, unemployment benefits prevent the disposable incomes of the jobless from falling as much as their earnings. As a result, unemployed workers can maintain their spending, and consumption need not fluctuate as dramatically as employment.

And the list could continue. The basic principle is the same: each of these automatic stabilizers, in one way or another, serves as a shock absorber, thereby lowering the multiplier. And each does so without the need for any decisionmaker to take action. In a word, they work *automatically*.

## DEBATE: RULES OR DISCRETION?

Believers in fixed rules assert that we should forget about discretionary policy and put the economy on automatic pilot—relying on automatic stabilizers and the economy's natural, self-correcting mechanisms. Are they right? As usual, the answer depends on many factors.

### HOW FAST DOES THE ECONOMY'S SELF-CORRECTING MECHANISM WORK?

We emphasized in Chapter 27 that the economy does have a self-correcting mechanism. If the economy can cure recessions and inflations quickly by itself, then the case for intervention is weak. For if such problems typically last only a short time, then lags in discretionary stabilization policy mean that the medicine will often have its major effects only after the disease is over. (In terms of Figure 31–8, this would be a case where point *D* comes very close to point *A*.)

While extreme advocates of rules argue that this is what indeed happens, most economists agree that the economy's self-correcting mechanism is slow and not terribly reliable, even when supplemented by the automatic stabilizers. On this count, then, a point is scored for discretionary policy.

### HOW LONG ARE THE LAGS IN STABILIZATION POLICY?

As we explained earlier, if there are long lags before stabilization measures are adopted or take effect, it is unlikely that policy can do much good. Short lags point in the opposite direction. Thus, advocates of fixed rules emphasize the length of lags while proponents of discretion discount them.

Who is right? It all depends on the circumstances. Sometimes fiscal policy actions are taken promptly, and the economy feels much of the stimulus from expansionary policy within a year after slipping into a recession. While far from an instant cure, such timely actions certainly would be felt soon enough to do some good. But, as we have seen, very slow fiscal responses may actually be destabilizing. Since history offers examples of each type, no general conclusion can be drawn.

### HOW ACCURATE ARE ECONOMIC FORECASTS?

One way to cut down the policy-making lag enormously is to have good economic forecasts. If we could see a recession coming a full year ahead of time (which we certainly *cannot* do), even a rather sluggish policy response would still be timely. (In terms of Figure 31–8, this would be a case where the recession is predicted well before point *A*.)

It therefore behooves us to take a look at the techniques that economists in universities, government agencies, and private businesses have developed over the years to assist them in predicting what the economy will do. There are a variety of techniques, none of them foolproof.

## TECHNIQUES OF ECONOMIC FORECASTING

### THE USE OF ECONOMETRIC MODELS

An **ECONOMETRIC MODEL** is a set of mathematical equations that embody the economist's model of the economy.

Among the most widely publicized forecasts are those generated by the use of **econometric models** of the economy. Put simply, an econometric model is merely a mathematical version of the models of macroeconomic activity that we have described in Parts 6 and 7. The difference is that the basic notions are cast in the form of mathematical equations rather than in diagrams. For example, our consumption function could have been expressed by the formula:

$$C = a + bDI,$$

where $C$ is consumer spending and $DI$ is disposable income, instead of by a graph.[2]

The builder of an econometric model takes equations like these and uses actual data to estimate the sizes of $a$ and $b$. For example, statistical analysis may lead a forecaster to the conclusion that the correct magnitude of $a$ in the previous formula is approximately 300 and that the most reasonable value of $b$ is 0.75. Then the consumption function formula is:

$$C = 300 + 0.75\,DI.$$

This formula shows us that consumer spending is $300 (billion) plus 75 percent of disposable income. The economist can complete the model by adding a definition of disposable income as GDP minus tax receipts:

$$\text{DI} = Y - T,$$

and appending the fact that GDP is the sum of $C$, $I$, $G$ and $(X - IM)$:

$$Y = C + I + G + (X - IM).$$

In this simple model, then, we have a total of three equations. If we hypothesize that government purchases, tax receipts, net exports, and investment are all unaffected by the relationships in the model, then these three equations are just enough to determine the values of the three remaining variables: $C$, $DI$, and $Y$. These last three variables are called the model's *endogenous variables*, meaning that their values are determined *inside* the model. The remaining variables—$G$, $T$, $I$ and $(X - IM)$—are called the model's *exogenous variables* because they must be provided from *outside* the model. With this nomenclature, it is easy to describe how the user of an econometric model forecasts the state of the economy:

An econometric forecaster uses a model to transform forecasts of the exogenous variables into corresponding forecasts of the endogenous variables.

Models actually used to forecast the behavior of the U.S. economy have hundreds of variables and equations. Because of their complexity, the only practical way to solve them for forecasts of all the endogenous variables is to use a high-speed computer. But making the forecasts accurate is another thing entirely because of the "garbage in, garbage out" problem: If you feed junk into a computer, that's exactly what comes out at the end. In the forecasting context, this "junk" can be either bad predictions of the exogenous variables or inaccurate equations. This is why model builders are constantly seeking to improve their equations. But they have yet to achieve perfection.

And, even if they did, their forecasts would still not be infallible because there is a certain amount of unavoidable randomness in macroeconomic behavior. After all, we are dealing with the behavior of literally millions of individuals and business firms, and events essentially outside our control can sometimes exert a profound influence on our economy. (Example: The near-collapse of OPEC in 1986 made inflation lower than forecasters expected.) So forecasts of the exogenous variables are bound to be wide of the mark at times. Furthermore, econometric models are basically complicated statistical summaries of the past. No one can really be sure that the future will be like the past. But this is what we assume whenever we use an econometric model for forecasting. (See the accompanying boxed insert.)

---

[2]This is nothing but the formula for a straight line with a slope of $b$ and an intercept of $a$.

*At The* **FRONTIER**

## ARE ECONOMETRIC MODELS USEFUL FOR POLICY ANALYSIS?

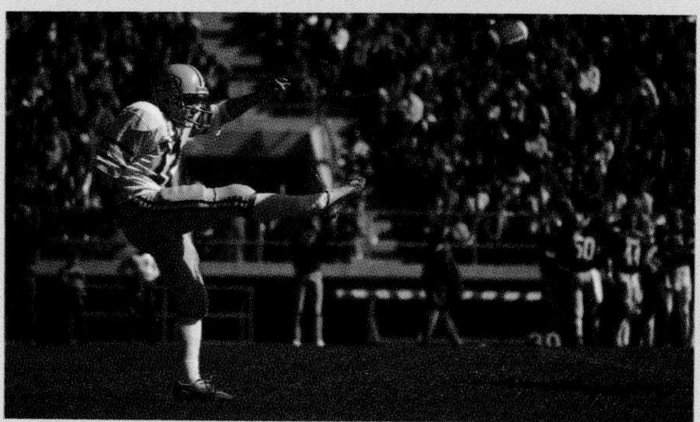

Econometric models of the U.S. economy are used routinely in Washington, D.C., and elsewhere to produce numerical estimates of the effects of government policies. Some economists are highly critical of this procedure, however, arguing that the models give misleading answers. Newer and more complicated methods, they maintain, are necessary to evaluate the effects of policy.

One major shortcoming of standard econometric models was first pointed out by Professor Robert E. Lucas, Jr., of the University of Chicago. He argued that changes in economic policy often alter people's behavior, thereby making the future different from the past.* An econometric model is nothing but a complicated summary of the statistical patterns found in historical data. Therefore, when we use such a model to assess the likely effects of policy, we tacitly assume that the future will be like the past. If this proves to be untrue, the conclusions we reach may be quite wrong.

But why should a change in policy upset historical behavior patterns? A noneconomic example may help explain why.** If you watch football, you know that teams almost always punt on fourth down when they have three or more yards to go. Now suppose the rules were changed to allow a team five downs rather than four. Someone who knew nothing about football, but simply extrapolated past behavior, would continue to expect teams to punt on fourth down. But, in fact, the rule change would probably make punting on fourth down a rare event.

Professor Lucas argued that many government policy changes are like rule changes in football: they may induce people, acting in their own best interests, to alter their behavior. We encountered one example of this in Chapter 24, when we discussed why consumers will react less strongly to a *temporary* drop in income than to a *permanent* one (see pages 604–606). Suppose economists have estimated the marginal propensity to consume, and hence the multiplier. Now suppose stabilization policy improves, making recessions shorter and shallower. Consumers who understand this will assume that any income loss from a recession is now more transitory than it used to be. In consequence, they will cut their spending by less. So the marginal propensity to consume should decline, making our previous econometric estimate (based on past behavior) a bad one.

Virtually all economists concede that Lucas is correct *in principle*. However, they continue to debate how important his criticism is *in practice*. Some ignore the problem and continue to use econometric models for policy analysis. Others are working on complex new methods that use economic theory and statistical analysis to deduce people's *objectives* from their observed *behavior*. The idea is that, even if observed behavior (punting on fourth down) changes when the rules change, underlying objectives (winning football games) do not. Unfortunately, the new methods, which are far too complicated to explain here, are quite difficult to apply. Because of this, no one has yet been able to use them to build a complete model of the economy.

*Robert E. Lucas, Jr., "Econometric Policy Evaluation: A Critique," in K. Brunner and A.H. Meltzer (eds.), *The Phillips Curve and Labor Markets*, Carnegie-Rochester Conference Series, No. 1 (Amsterdam: North-Holland), 1976.

**This example is from Thomas J. Sargent, *Rational Expectations and Inflation* (New York: Harper & Row), 1986, pages 1–2.

## LEADING INDICATORS

A **LEADING INDICATOR** is a variable that, experience has shown, normally turns down before recessions start and turns up before expansions begin.

A second forecasting method, pioneered at the National Bureau of Economic Research, exploits observed historical timing relationships through the use of certain **leading indicators** that have in the past given advance warning of economic events.

For example, the stock market is a leading indicator because stock market downturns normally begin several months before downturns in industrial production. *Why* does this happen? Does the decline in the stock market cause economic downturns by reducing consumer spending? Or are both the stock market and industrial production just reacting to some other influence, with the stock market's reaction coming sooner? Certainly these are fascinating questions. But the answers may not be crucial to a forecaster *if* the stock market continues to be as good a leading indicator of industrial production in the future as it has been in the past. In that event, we will be able to make use of the observed relationship between stock prices and industrial production for forecasting even if we do not entirely understand its origins.

As it turns out, however, excessive reliance on any single leading indicator produces an unimpressive forecasting record. An obvious solution is to look at many indicators. But once we start to do this, we will often receive conflicting signals. If one indicator is rising rapidly while another is falling, what are we to do?

One way to resolve this conflict is to form an average of several leading indicators. For example, every month the news media report the latest reading on the Commerce Department's composite index, which is a weighted average of 11 of their leading indicators. (See the boxed insert on page 787.) Figure 31–9 compares the behavior of this index with movements in real GDP. As you can see, the agreement is usually quite good. The leading indicators occasionally call for a recession that never comes (as in 1966), and occasionally they give clear early warning signals of a downturn (as in 1979). But often movements of the leading indicators are followed so closely by movements in real gross domestic product that the advance warning they provide comes too late to be of much use to policymakers.

## SURVEY DATA

A third method of forecasting utilizes periodic surveys of the intentions of business and consumers. The Bureau of Economic Analysis of the Commerce Department and the Securities and Exchange Commission regularly ask firms how much money they plan to invest in factories and machinery over the next 3 to 12 months. These data are published in the financial press and are widely used by economists in industry, government, and academia. The Survey Research Center of the University of Michigan and the Conference Board (a business organization) regularly conduct surveys of how consumers feel about both their personal finances and the general state of the economy. Some economists have found that this information is useful in forecasting consumer spending.

## JUDGMENTAL FORECASTS

This term is used to describe the forecasts of those desperate (and probably prudent!) forecasters who refuse to rely on any one method, but look instead at every available scrap of evidence. They study the outputs of the econometric models; they watch the leading indicators; and they scrutinize the findings of

Figure 31-9 **REAL GDP AND THE LEADING INDICATORS, 1950–1993**

This diagram compares the path of the leading indicators (in blue) with that of real GDP (in black). The scales have been adjusted to make the two series comparable. It can be seen that the leading indicators sometimes give advance warning of a turning point in economic activity (for example, in 1979) but often give false signals of turning points that never occur (for example, 1984).

SOURCE: *Business Conditions Digest* and *Survey of Current Business*.

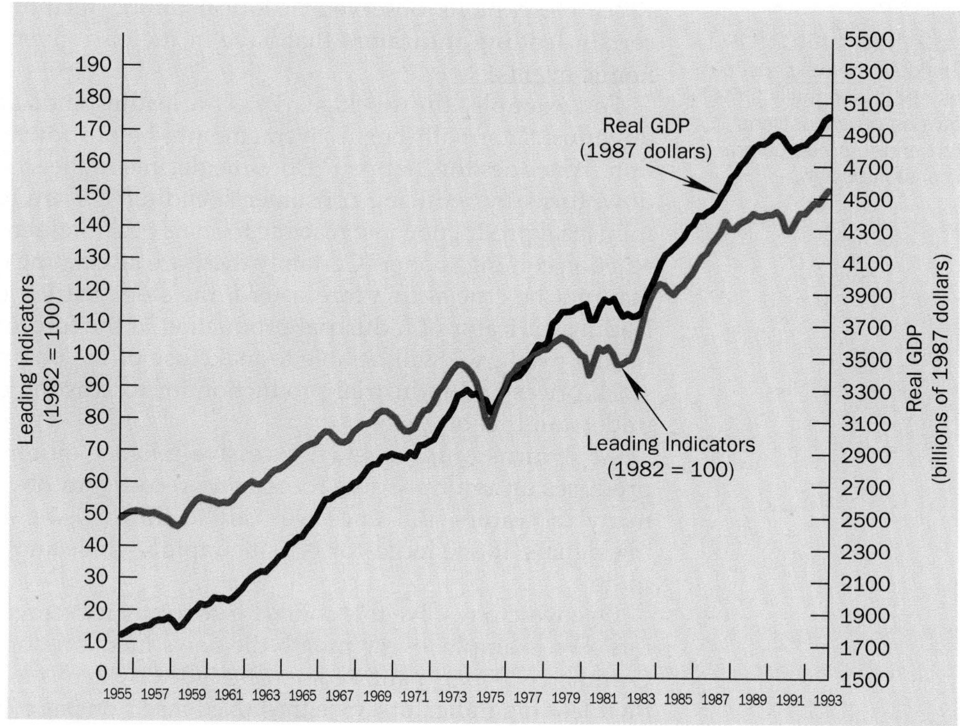


surveys. At times, it seems, they even gaze at the stars. Somehow, judgmental forecasters distill all this information in their heads and arrive at a forecast of GDP and other key variables. How do they go about it? An outside observer can never really tell, since the very nature of judgmental forecasting precludes the existence of a formula that can be written down or precisely described.

## THE ACCURACY OF ECONOMIC FORECASTS

Which method wins the prize for the most accurate forecasts? First, no technique is clearly superior all the time. If it were, no one would do it any other way. Second, because econometric forecasters use surveys, lead-lag patterns, and judgment in forming their predictions of exogenous variables, and since judgmental forecasters watch the models closely, a clean comparison is impossible. In recent years, however, it seems that the most accurate forecasts have been derived by judgmental adjustment of forecasts from econometric models.

How accurate are economic forecasts? That depends both on the variable being forecast (consumption, for example, is easier than investment) and on the time period (for example, the tumultuous years 1973–1983 were difficult times for forecasters; the placid 1984–1989 period was much easier).

To give a rough idea of magnitudes, forecasts of the inflation rate for the year ahead typically err by plus or minus 1 to $1\frac{1}{2}$ percentage points. But in a bad year

### *The Index of Leading Indicators*

The Commerce Department's widely publicized index of leading indicators is a weighted average of 11 economic variables that have been shown to be useful in predicting business fluctuations. While the components of the index sometimes change, at the time of this writing they are:

1. Stock market prices.
2. The money supply ($M2$), expressed in 1987 dollars.
3. An index of consumer expectations.
4. The percentage change in sensitive materials prices.
5. The average work week of production workers in manufacturing.
6. Initial claims for unemployment insurance. (This component enters negatively since rising unemployment is a sign of bad times.)
7. New building permits.
8. New orders for consumer goods and materials, in 1982 dollars.
9. Contracts and orders for investment goods, in 1982 dollars.
10. The change in manufacturers' unfilled orders for durable goods, in 1982 dollars.
11. Vendor performance (an indicator of how easy or difficult it is for firms to get deliveries of inputs).

for forecasters, errors of 3 percentage points or so are common. Forecasts of real GDP for the coming year made during the 1970s and 1980s also typically erred by between 1 and $1\frac{1}{2}$ percent. The biggest errors by far came in recession years such as 1974 and 1982. Apart from these periods, errors of under 1 percent have been typical.[3]

Is this record good enough? That depends on what the forecasts are used for. It is certainly not good enough to support so-called fine tuning, that is, attempts to keep the economy always within a hair's breadth of full employment. But it probably is good enough if our interest in using discretionary stabilization policy is to close persistent and sizable gaps between actual and potential GDP.

## OTHER DIMENSIONS OF THE RULES-VERSUS-DISCRETION DEBATE

While lags and forecasting play major roles in the debate between advocates of rules and advocates of discretionary policy, these are not the only battlegrounds.

### THE SIZE OF GOVERNMENT

One bogus argument that is nonetheless often heard is that an activist fiscal policy must inevitably lead to a growing public sector. Since proponents of fixed rules tend also to be opponents of big government, they view this as undesirable. Of

[3]See, for example, Victor Zarnowitz, "The Record and Improvability of Economic Forecasting," National Bureau of Economic Research, Working Paper No. 2099, December 1986, or Stephen K. McNees, "How Accurate Are Macroeconomic Forecasts?" *New England Economic Review*, July/August 1988, pp. 15–36.

course, others think that a larger public sector is just what society needs. This argument, however, is completely beside the point because, as we pointed out in Chapter 28 (page 701): *One's opinion about the proper size of government should have nothing to do with one's view on stabilization policy.* For example, President Ronald Reagan was as conservative as they come and devoted to *shrinking* the size of the public sector. But his tax-cutting initiatives in the early 1980s constituted an extremely *activist* policy to spur the economy.

## UNCERTAINTIES CAUSED BY GOVERNMENT POLICY

Advocates of rules are on stronger ground when they argue that frequent changes in tax laws, government spending programs, or monetary conditions make it difficult for firms and consumers to formulate and carry out rational plans. They argue that the authorities can provide a more stable environment for the private sector by adhering to fixed rules, which are known to businesses and consumers.

While no one disputes that a more stable environment is better for private planning, supporters of discretionary policy point out the difference between stability in the government budget (or in Federal Reserve operations) and stability in the economy. The goal of stabilization policy is to help *prevent* gyrations in the pace of economic activity by *causing* timely gyrations in the government budget (or in monetary policy). Which atmosphere is better for business, they ask, one in which fiscal and monetary rules keep things peaceful on Capitol Hill and at the Federal Reserve System while recessions and inflations rack the economy, or one in which policy instruments are changed abruptly on occasion but the economy grows more steadily? They think that the answer is self-evident.

## A POLITICAL BUSINESS CYCLE?

A final argument used by advocates of rules is political rather than economic in nature. Fiscal policy, they note, is decided upon by elected politicians: the president and members of Congress. When elections are on the horizon (and for members of the House of Representatives they *always* are), these men and women may be as concerned with keeping their offices as with doing what is right for the economy. This leaves fiscal policy subject to all sorts of "political manipulations," meaning that inappropriate actions may be taken to attain short-run political goals. A system of purely automatic stabilization, its proponents argue, would eliminate this peril by replacing the rule of men by the rule of law.

It is certainly *possible* that politicians could deliberately *cause* economic instability to help their own reelection. And some observers of these "political business cycles" have claimed that several American presidents have taken full advantage of the opportunity. Furthermore, even if there is no insidious intent, politicians may take the wrong actions for perfectly honorable reasons. Decisions in the political arena are never clear-cut, and it certainly is easy to find examples of grievous errors in the history of U.S. fiscal policy.

So, taken as a whole, the political argument against discretionary policy seems to have a great deal of merit. But what are we to do about it? It is foolhardy to believe that fiscal and monetary decisions could or should be made by a group of objective and nonpartisan technicians. Steering the economy is not like steering a rocket to the moon. Because policy actions that help on the employment front normally do harm on the inflation front, and vice versa, the "correct" policy action is almost always an inherently political matter. In a democracy, if we take such decisions out of the hands of elected officials, in whose hands shall we put them?

This harsh fact may seem worrisome in view of the possibilities for political chicanery. But it should not bother us any more (or any less!) than similar maneuvering in other areas of policy making. After all, the same problem besets international relations, issues of national defense, formulation and enforcement of the law, and so on. Politicians make all these decisions for us, subject only to sporadic accountability at election times. Is there really any reason why economic decisions should be different?

## CONCLUSION: WHAT SHOULD BE DONE?

Where do all these considerations leave us? On balance, is it better to conduct the best discretionary policy we can, knowing full well that we will never do it perfectly? Or is it wiser to rely on fixed rules and the automatic stabilizers?

In weighing the pros and cons that we have discussed in this chapter, one's basic view of the economy is central. Some economists believe that the economy, if left unmanaged, would generate a series of ups and downs that are hard to predict, but that it would correct each of them by itself in a relatively short period of time. They conclude that, because of long lags and poor forecasts, our ability to anticipate whether the economy will be heading up or down by the time policy actions have their effects is quite limited. And so they are led to advocate fixed rules.

Other economists liken the economy to a giant glacier with a great deal of inertia. This means that if we observe an inflationary or recessionary gap today, it is likely still to be there a year or two from now because the self-correcting mechanism works so slowly. In such a world, accurate forecasting is not imperative, even if policy lags are long. If we base policy on a forecast of a $200 billion gap between actual and potential GDP a year from now, and the gap turns out to be only $100 billion, then we still will have done the right thing despite the inaccurate forecast. Holders of this view of the economy, then, are likely to advocate the use of discretionary policy.

While there is no consensus on this issue either among economists or among politicians, a prudent view might be that:

The case for active discretionary policy is strong when the economy has a serious deficiency or excess of aggregate demand. However, advocates of fixed rules are right that it is unwise to try to iron out every little wiggle in the growth path of GDP.

But the decision cannot be made solely on economic grounds. Political judgments enter as well. In the end:

The question of whether the government should take an active hand in managing the economy, which is a major debate among economists today, is as much a matter of ideology as of economics. Liberals have always looked to government activism to solve social problems, while conservatives have consistently pointed out that many efforts of government fail despite the best intentions.

Since no one can decide whether liberal or conservative political attitudes are the "correct" ones on purely objective criteria, the rules-versus-discretion debate is likely to go on for quite some time.

## *Summary*

1. Monetarist and Keynesian analyses are two different ways of studying the determination of aggregate demand. Neither is a complete theory of the behavior of the economy until aggregate supply is brought into the picture.

2. **Velocity** ($V$) is the ratio of nominal GDP to the stock of money ($M$). It indicates how quickly money circulates, that is, how many times money changes hands in a year.

3. Among the determinants of velocity is the rate of interest ($r$). At higher interest rates, people find it less attractive to hold money because money pays no or little interest. Thus, when $r$ rises, money circulates faster, and $V$ rises.

4. **Monetarism** is a type of analysis that focuses attention on velocity and the money supply ($M$). Though monetarists realize that $V$ is not constant, they believe that it is predictable enough to make it a useful tool for policy analysis and forecasting.

5. Because it raises output and prices, and hence increases the demand for money, expansionary fiscal policy pushes interest rates higher. This is how a monetarist explains the effect of fiscal policy. Because higher $r$ leads to higher velocity, it leads to a higher product $M \times V$ even if $M$ is unchanged.

6. Because fiscal policy actions affect aggregate demand either directly through $G$ or indirectly through $C$, the expenditure lags between fiscal actions and their effects on aggregate demand are probably fairly short. By contrast, monetary policy operates mainly on investment, $I$, which responds slowly to changes in interest rates.

7. However, the policy-making lag normally is much longer for fiscal policy than for monetary policy. Hence, when the two lags are combined, it is not clear which type of policy acts more quickly.

8. Because it cannot control the demand curve for money, the Federal Reserve cannot control *both* $M$ and $r$. If the demand for money changes, the Fed must decide whether it wants to hold $M$ steady, hold $r$ steady, or adopt some compromise position.

9. Monetarists emphasize the importance of stabilizing the growth path of the money supply while many Keynesians put more emphasis on keeping interest rates on target.

10. In practice, the Fed has changed its views on this issue several times. For decades, it attached primary importance to interest rates. Between 1979 and 1982, it stressed its commitment to stable growth of the money supply. But since 1982 it has deemphasized money growth.

11. When the aggregate supply curve is very flat, increases in aggregate demand will add much to the nation's real output and add little to the price level. Under those circumstances, stabilization policy has much to recommend it as an antirecession device; but it has little power to combat inflation.

12. When the aggregate supply curve is steep, increases in aggregate demand increase real output rather little and succeed mostly in pushing up prices. In such a case, stabilization policy can do much to fight inflation but is not a very effective way to cure unemployment.

13. The aggregate supply curve is likely to be relatively flat in an economy with much unemployment but relatively steep in an economy producing near capacity levels.

14. When there are long **lags in the operation of fiscal and monetary policy**, it becomes possible that attempts to stabilize economic activity may actually succeed in destabilizing it.

15. The U.S. economy has a number of **automatic stabilizers** which make it less vulnerable to shocks than it would otherwise be. Among these are the personal income tax and unemployment benefits.

16. Economic forecasts are made by **econometric models**, by exploiting **leading indicators**, and by judgment. Each method seems to play a role in arriving at good forecasts. But no method is foolproof, and economic forecasts are not as accurate as we would like.

17. Some economists believe that our imperfect knowledge of the channels through which stabilization policy works, and the long lags involved, make it unlikely that discretionary stabilization policy can succeed.

18. Other economists recognize these difficulties but do not believe they are quite as serious. They also place much less faith in the economy's ability to cure recessions and inflations on its own. They therefore think that **discretionary policy** is not only advisable, but essential.

19. Stabilizing the economy by fiscal policy need *not* imply a tendency toward "big government."

## *Key Concepts and Terms*

Quantity theory of money
Velocity
Equation of exchange
Effect of interest rate on velocity
Monetarism
Effect of fiscal policy on interest rates
Lags in stabilization policy
Shape of the aggregate supply curve
Controlling *M* versus controlling *r*
Automatic stabilizers
Econometric models
Leading indicators
Judgmental forecasts
Rules versus discretionary policy

## *Questions for Review*

1. How much money (including cash and checking account balances) do you typically have at any particular moment? Divide this into your total income over the past 12 months to obtain your own personal velocity. Are you typical of the nation as a whole?

2. Just below, you will find data on nominal gross national product and the money supply (M1 definition) for selected years. Compute velocity in each year. Can you see any trend?

| YEAR | MONEY SUPPLY (M1) (billions of dollars) (end of year) | NOMINAL GNP (billions of dollars) |
|---|---|---|
| 1972 | 249 | 1207 |
| 1982 | 475 | 3150 |
| 1992 | 1027 | 6039 |

3. Use the concept of opportunity cost to explain why velocity is higher at higher interest rates.

4. How does monetarism differ from the quantity theory of money? How does it differ from Keynesian analysis?

5. Given the behavior of velocity shown in Figure 31–1, does it make more sense for the Federal Reserve to formulate targets for M1 or M2?

6. Distinguish between the expenditure lag and the policy lag in stabilization policy. Does monetary or fiscal policy have the shorter expenditure lag? What about the policy lag?

7. Explain why their contrasting views on the shape of the aggregate supply curve lead some economists to argue much more strongly for stabilization policies to fight unemployment and others to argue much more strongly for stabilization policies to fight inflation.

8. Use a supply and demand diagram similar to Figure 31–2 (page 772) to show the choices open to the Fed following an unexpected decline in the demand for money. If the Fed is following a monetarist policy rule, what will happen to the rate of interest?

9. Explain why lags make it possible for policy actions intended to stabilize the economy actually to destabilize it instead.

10. Which of the following events would strengthen the argument for the use of discretionary policy, and which would strengthen the argument for rules?
    a. Structural changes make the economy's self-correcting mechanism work more quickly and reliably than before.
    b. New statistical methods are found that improve the accuracy of economic forecasts.
    c. A Republican president is elected when there is an overwhelmingly Democratic Congress. The Congress and the president differ sharply on what should be done about the national economy.

11. (More difficult) Use the following hypothetical econometric model of the U.S. economy to obtain a forecast of the GDP in 1996:

$$C = 300 + 0.75DI$$
$$DI = Y - T$$
$$Y = C + I + G + (X - IM)$$

$T$, $I$, $G$, and $(X - IM)$ are the exogenous variables, and their forecasted values for 1996 are $T = 1200$, $I = 900$, $G = 1300$, $(X - IM) = -100$.

12. (More difficult) Answer the same question for an economy described by:

$$C = 18 + 0.9DI$$
$$DI = Y - T$$
$$T = 10 + \tfrac{1}{3}Y$$
$$Y = C + I + G + (X - IM)$$

with forecasts $I = 200$, $G = 880$, $(X - IM) = 0$.

13. Some observers think that from 1987 to 1990 the Federal Reserve under Alan Greenspan succeeded in using deft applications of monetary policy to "fine tune" the U.S. economy into the full-employment zone without worsening inflation. Use the data on money supply, interest rates, real GDP, unemployment, and the price level given on the inside rear cover of this book to evaluate this claim. What happened after 1990? Is our discussion of lags in monetary policy relevant here?

Chapter 32

# BUDGET DEFICITS AND THE NATIONAL DEBT: FACT AND FICTION

*Blessed are the young,*
*for they shall inherit*
*the national debt.*

HERBERT HOOVER

There is a belief that runs deep in the American character that there is something inherently wrong with government budget deficits. Opinion polls consistently show that the public wants smaller deficits. Yet for more than a decade our political process failed to produce them. Somehow, President Clinton seemed to change all that with his February 1993 State of the Union address, and deficit reduction became Washington's latest political fad. What is the economic substance in this debate? What kinds of problems do large deficits pose for the economy, both now and in the future? Should we strive to balance the budget? And if so, by what means? These are the questions for this chapter. ¶ We begin by explaining why the principles of stabilization policy that we have been learning in Part 7 do not imply that the budget should always be balanced. (Neither, however, do they lead to the conclusion that it should always have a massive deficit!) Next we look at the facts: we discuss the size of the national debt, how it grew so large, and why some economists claim that the federal budget deficit is mismeasured.

With the facts established, we examine the alleged ill effects of deficits. We shall see that many popular arguments against deficits are based on faulty reasoning. But not all are. In particular, we devote special attention to two potentially severe costs of deficit spending: it can be inflationary, and it can "crowd out" private investment spending.

## THE PARTISAN POLITICAL DEBATE OVER THE BUDGET DEFICIT

President Clinton's economic plan pushed deficit reduction to the top of the national agenda. Whatever else you think of the president's economic policies, it is clear that they focussed attention on the deficit in a way that had not been done in a long time. The political battle that ensued from the winter to the summer of 1993 showed just how contentious these issues are. After all, deficit reduction is about raising taxes and cutting spending—neither of which holds much appeal to politicians who must face the voters.

"The 'Twilight Zone' will not be seen tonight, so that we may bring you the following special on the federal budget."

Critics of President Clinton complained that he relied too heavily on tax increases and did not cut civilian spending enough. The proposed energy tax was a particular target of the critics because some of it fell on the middle class; and, ultimately, it was replaced by a small increase in the gasoline tax. The president's supporters replied that it was unrealistic to expect substantial deficit reduction without higher taxes. They noted that the president's tax plan placed most of the burden on upper income groups, and that the overall plan was well balanced between higher taxes and lower spending.

When the partisan political dust settled, Congress and the president had agreed on a five-year plan that is estimated to reduce the federal budget deficit in fiscal year 1998 by $146 billion (compared to what it otherwise would have been). Over the five year period 1994–1998, the new budget cuts $255 billion from spending and raises $250 billion in higher taxes. If all goes according to plan—which, of course, it never does—the federal budget deficit will fall from $285 billion in fiscal 1993 to around $180 billion in fiscal 1998. That is a big improvement. But $180 billion is still a long way from zero.

## SHOULD THE BUDGET BE BALANCED?

It is commonly believed that the government budget should be balanced. Indeed, most of the 50 states *require* their governments to have balanced budgets. Is a zero deficit an appropriate target for fiscal policy?

The basic principles that we discussed in Chapter 28 certainly do not lead to this conclusion. Instead, they point to the desirability of budget *deficits* when private demand, $C + I + (X - IM)$, is too weak and budget *surpluses* when private demand is too strong. The budget should be balanced, according to these principles, only when $C + I + G + (X - IM)$ under a balanced-budget policy approximately equals full-employment levels of output. This may sometimes occur, but it will not necessarily be the norm.

In brief, according to this approach, the focus of fiscal policy should be on *balancing aggregate supply and aggregate demand*, not on balancing the budget. But why do these two criteria differ? The reason should be clear from our earlier discussion of stabilization policy.

Consider the fiscal policy that would be followed under a balanced-budget policy. If private spending sagged for some reason, the multiplier would pull

GDP down. Since personal and corporate tax receipts fall sharply when GDP declines, the budget would swing into the red. That would require either lower spending or higher taxes—exactly the opposite of the appropriate policy response. Thus:

Attempts to balance the budget—as done, say, by President Herbert Hoover during the Great Depression—will prolong and deepen recessions.

Budget balancing can also lead to inappropriate fiscal policy under boom conditions. If rising tax receipts induce a budget-balancing government to spend more or cut taxes, fiscal policy will "boom the boom"—with disastrous inflationary consequences. Fortunately, believers in budget balancing usually are not alarmed by surpluses.

Actually, the issue is even more complicated than we have indicated so far. As we learned in Chapter 30, fiscal policy is not the only way the government affects aggregate demand. The government also influences aggregate demand through its monetary policy. For this reason:

The appropriate fiscal policy depends, among other things, on the stance of monetary policy. While a balanced budget may be appropriate under one monetary policy, a deficit or a surplus may be appropriate under another monetary policy.

An example will illustrate the point. Suppose Congress and the president believe that the aggregate supply and demand curves will intersect approximately at full employment if the budget is balanced. Then a balanced budget would seem to be the appropriate fiscal policy.

But suppose now that monetary policy turns contractionary, pulling the aggregate demand curve inward to the left as shown in Figure 32–1 and creating a recessionary gap. If the fiscal authorities wish to restore real GDP to its original level, they must shift the aggregate demand curve back to its original position, $D_0D_0$. To do this, they must either raise spending or cut taxes, thereby opening up a budget deficit. Thus the change in monetary policy changes the appropriate fiscal policy from a balanced budget to a deficit.

By the same token, a given target for aggregate demand implies that any change in fiscal policy will alter the appropriate monetary policy. For example, suppose Figure 32–1 indicates the effects of reducing the budget deficit by cutting government spending. If the authorities do not want real GDP to fall, monetary policy must become sufficiently more expansionary to restore the aggregate demand curve to $D_0D_0$. Indeed, it was precisely this mix of policy changes—a smaller budget deficit balanced by easier money—that the Clinton administration sought in 1993.

So a balanced budget should not be expected to be the norm. How, then, can we tell whether any particular deficit is too large or too small? That is a good question, but a complicated one. Before attempting an answer, we should get some facts straight.

## DEFICITS AND DEBT: SOME TERMINOLOGY

First some critical terminology. The title of this chapter contains two terms that seem similar but mean different things: *budget deficits* and the *national debt*. We must learn to distinguish between the two.

*Figure* **32–1** **THE INTERACTION OF MONETARY AND FISCAL POLICY**

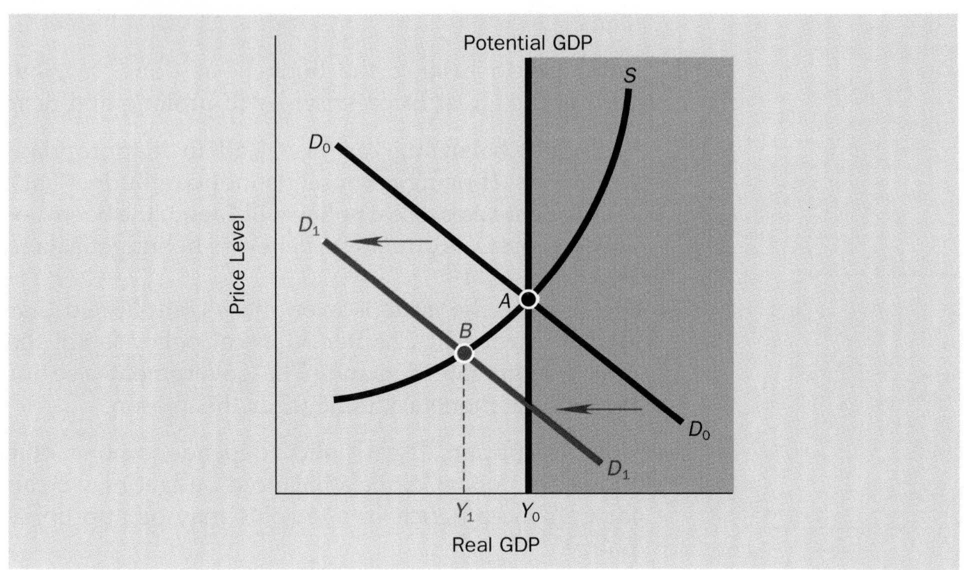


Both monetary and fiscal policy affect the aggregate demand curve. If monetary policy turns contractionary, the aggregate demand curve shifts inward from $D_0D_0$ to $D_1D_1$ thereby lowering real GDP from $Y_0$ *to* $Y_1$. If $Y_0$ represented full employment with a balanced budget, then $Y_1$ represents an economy with a recessionary gap. Expansionary fiscal policy can push the aggregate demand curve back to $D_0D_0$, but only by opening up a deficit in the government budget.

The **BUDGET DEFICIT** is the amount by which the government's expenditures exceed its receipts during a specified period of time, usually one year.

The **NATIONAL DEBT** is the federal government's total indebtedness at a moment in time. It is the result of previous deficits.

The **budget deficit** is the amount by which the government's expenditures exceed its receipts during some specified period of time, usually one year. For example, during fiscal year 1993, the government raised about $1140 billion in taxes but spent almost $1425 billion, leaving a deficit of about $285 billion.[1]

The **national debt**, also called the public debt, is the total value of the government's indebtedness at a moment in time. Thus, for example, the national debt at the end of fiscal year 1993 was about $4.4 trillion.

These two concepts—debt and deficits—are closely related because the government accumulates *debt* by running *deficits* or reduces its debt by running surpluses. The relationship between the debt and the deficit can be explained by a simple analogy. As you run water into a bathtub ("run a deficit"), the accumulated volume of water in the tub ("the debt") rises. Alternatively, if you let water out of the tub ("run a surplus"), the level of the water ("the debt") falls. Analogously, budget deficits raise the national debt while budget surpluses lower it.

Having made this distinction, let us look first at the size and nature of the accumulated public debt, and then at the annual budget deficit.

## SOME FACTS ABOUT THE NATIONAL DEBT

How large a public debt do we have? How did we get it? Who owns it? Is it really growing rapidly?

[1]*Reminder:* The fiscal year of the U.S. government ends on September 30. Thus, fiscal year 1993 ran from October 1, 1992, to September 30, 1993.

To begin with the simplest question, the public debt is enormous. At the end of 1993 it amounted to over $4.4 trillion, about $17,000 for every man, woman, and child in America. But over 30 percent of this outstanding debt was owned by agencies of the U.S. government—in other words, one branch of the government owed it to another. If we deduct this portion, the net national debt was just about $3 trillion, or around $11,600 per person.

Furthermore, when we compare the debt with the gross domestic product—the volume of goods and services our economy produces in a year—it does not seem so large after all. With a GDP of about $6.5 trillion in late 1993, the net debt was under one-half of the nation's yearly income. By contrast, many families who own homes owe *several years'* worth of income to the bank that granted them a mortgage. Many U.S. corporations also owe their bondholders much more than one-half of a year's sales.

But before these analogies make you feel too comfortable, we should point out that simple analogies between public and private debt are almost always misleading. A family with a large mortgage debt also owns a home with a value that presumably exceeds the mortgage. A solvent business firm has assets (factories, machinery, inventories, and so forth) that far exceed its outstanding bonds in value.

Is the same thing true of the U.S. government? No one knows for sure. How much is the White House worth? Or the national parks? And what about military bases, both here and abroad? Simply because these government assets are *not* sold on markets, no one knows for sure whether or not the federal government's assets exceed its debt. However, one heroic attempt to measure the value of the government's assets concluded that they fell slightly below the national debt by 1984.[2] And since then the government has accumulated debt much faster than it has accumulated assets.

Figure 32–2 charts the irregular increase in the national debt from 1915 to 1992. Until the 1980s, most of the debt was acquired either during wars, especially World War II, or during recessions. When economic activity falls, tax receipts of the federal government fall because of the heavy reliance on income taxes. As we shall see later, the *cause* of the debt is quite germane to the question of whether or not the debt is a burden. So it is important to remember that:

Until about 1983, almost all of the U.S. national debt stemmed from financing wars and from losses of tax revenues that accompany recessions.

The growth of the debt looks enormous in Figure 32–2. But we must remember that everything grows in a growing economy. Private debt and business debt have grown rapidly since 1915; it would be surprising indeed if the public debt had not grown also. The fact is that federal debt grew *less* rapidly than private debt for most of the period from World War II until about 1980.

In addition, the debt is measured in dollars and, in an inflationary environment, the amount of purchasing power that each dollar represents declines each year. A good way to put the numbers into perspective is to express each year's national debt as a fraction of that year's nominal GDP. This is done in Figure 32–3. Here, in contrast to Figure 32–2, we see an unmistakable downward trend from the dizzying heights of World War II until the recession of 1974–1975. In 1945, the national debt was the equivalent of 13 months' national income. By 1974, this

[2]Robert Eisner, *How Real Is the Federal Deficit?* (New York: Free Press, 1986), page 29.

Figure 32-2 THE U.S. NATIONAL DEBT, 1915–1993

This graph charts the behavior of the public debt in the United States, after subtracting out the portion of the debt that is held by government agencies. It is clear that, prior to the 1980s, just about all the increases could be accounted for by wars and recessions. Few people realize that the public debt was about the same in 1972 as it was in 1945. But since 1975, it has grown rapidly.

SOURCE: Constructed by the authors from data in *Historical Statistics of the United States* and *Economic Report of the President.*

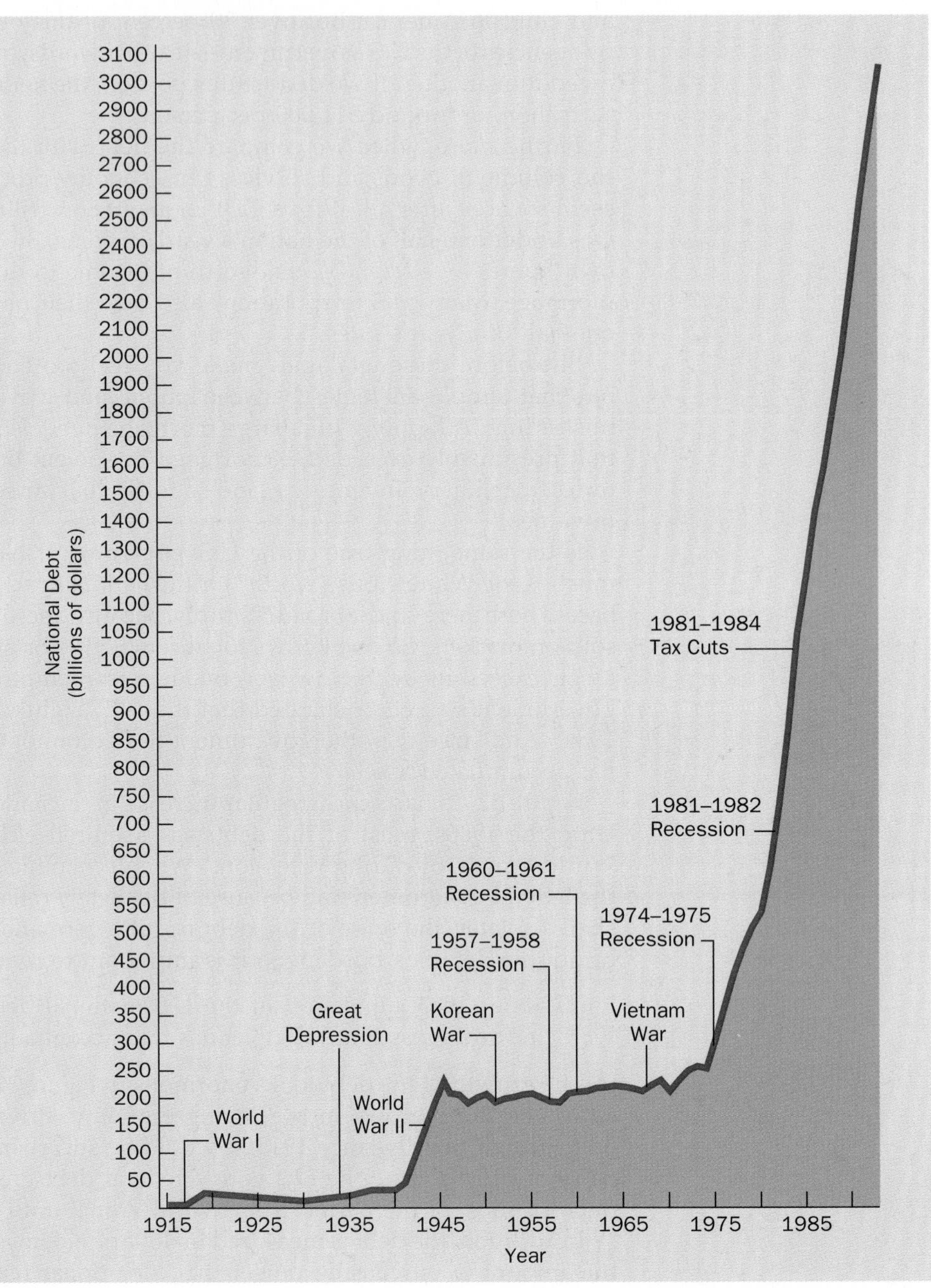


figure had been whittled down to two months. If we use this as a crude indicator of the nation's ability to "pay off" its debt, then the burden of the debt was certainly far smaller in 1974 than it was in 1945.

This last graph also calls attention to a disturbing fact: the national debt grew faster than GDP during the 1980s and early 1990s, reversing the pattern that had

Figure 32–3 **RATIO OF PUBLIC DEBT TO GROSS DOMESTIC PRODUCT**

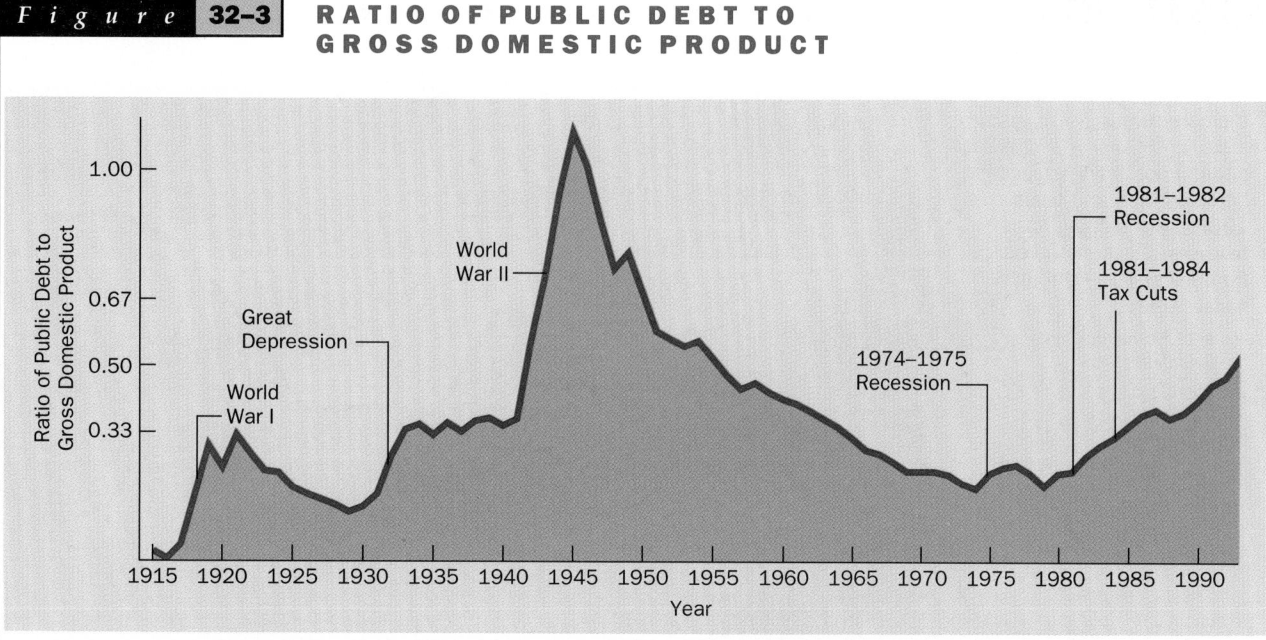


This graph takes the data from Figure 32–2 and divides each year's debt by the gross domestic product of that year. We can see that the debt grew relative to GDP during the two world wars, during the Great Depression, during the 1974–1975 recession, and since 1981. Other than that, the debt generally has fallen relative to GDP.

prevailed since 1945. By 1993, the debt exceeded five months' GDP—nearly triple its value in 1974. This is one reason why many economists are alarmed by continued large budget deficits.

## INTERPRETING THE BUDGET DEFICIT

We have observed that the federal government's annual budget deficits have been extremely large under the Reagan administration. As Figure 32–4 shows, the budget deficit ballooned from $79 billion in fiscal year 1981 to $208 billion by fiscal year 1983—setting a record which has subsequently been eclipsed several times. The budget for fiscal year 1993, which ended just as this edition went to press, is expected to show a deficit of $285 billion. These are enormous, even mind-boggling, numbers. But what do they mean? How are they to be interpreted?

### THE STRUCTURAL DEFICIT

First, it is important to understand that the same fiscal program can lead to a large or small deficit, depending on the state of the economy. Failure to appreciate this point has led many people to assume that a larger deficit always signifies a more expansionary fiscal policy. But that is not always true.

Think, for example, about what happens to the budget when the economy experiences a recession and GDP falls. The government's most important sources

*Figure* **32–4** **OFFICIAL BUDGET DEFICITS SINCE 1981 (FISCAL YEARS)**

The budget deficit almost tripled between fiscal year 1981 and fiscal year 1983 and did not change much between then and fiscal 1986. After dipping for a few years, it then soared from fiscal 1989 through fiscal 1993.

SOURCE: *Economic Report of the President.*

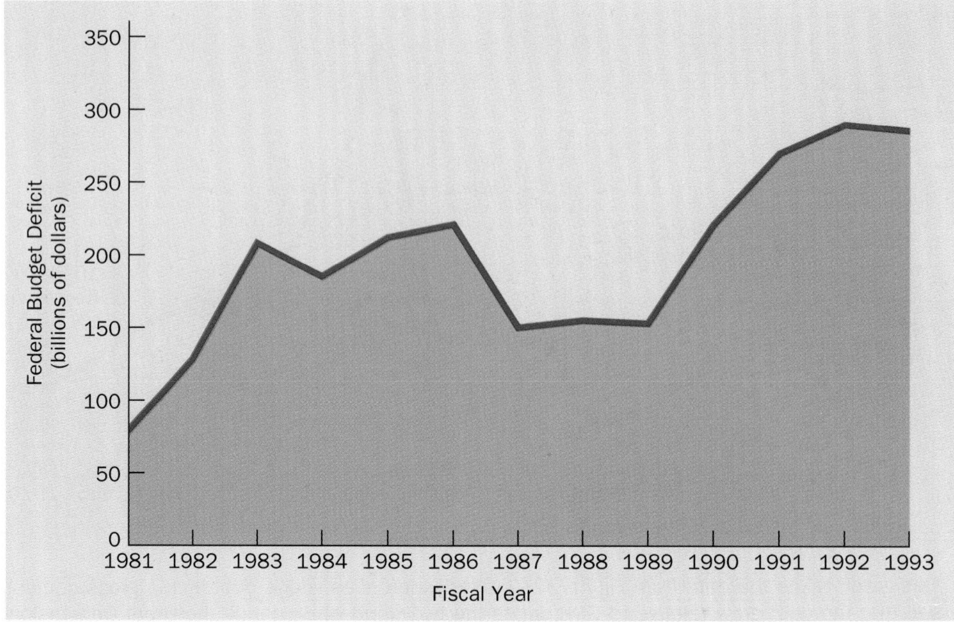


of tax revenue—income taxes, corporate taxes, and payroll taxes—all shrink because firms and people pay lower taxes when they earn less. Similarly, some types of government spending, notably transfer payments like unemployment benefits, rise when GDP falls because more people are out of work.

Remember that the deficit is the difference between government expenditures, which are either purchases or transfer payments, and tax receipts:

$$\text{Deficit} = G + \text{Transfers} - \text{Taxes}.$$

Since a falling GDP means higher expenditures and lower tax receipts:

The deficit rises in a recession and falls in a boom, even with no change in fiscal policy.

Figure 32–5 depicts the relationship between GDP and the budget deficit. The government's fiscal program is summarized by the blue and black lines. The horizontal black line labeled $G$ indicates that federal purchases of goods and services are approximately unaffected by GDP. The rising blue line labeled "Taxes minus Transfers" indicates that taxes rise and transfer payments fall as GDP rises. Notice that the same fiscal policy (that is, the same two lines) can lead to a large deficit if GDP is $Y_1$, a small deficit if GDP is $Y_2$, a balanced budget if GDP is $Y_3$, or even a surplus if GDP is as high as $Y_4$. Clearly, the deficit itself cannot be a good measure of the government's fiscal policy.

The **STRUCTURAL BUDGET DEFICIT** is the hypothetical deficit we *would have* under current fiscal policies if the economy were operating near full employment.

For this reason, many economists pay less attention to the *actual* deficit or surplus and more attention to what is called the **structural deficit or surplus**. This is a hypothetical construct that replaces both the spending and taxes in the *actual* budget by estimates of how much the government *would be* spending and

Figure 32–5 **THE EFFECT OF THE ECONOMY ON THE BUDGET**

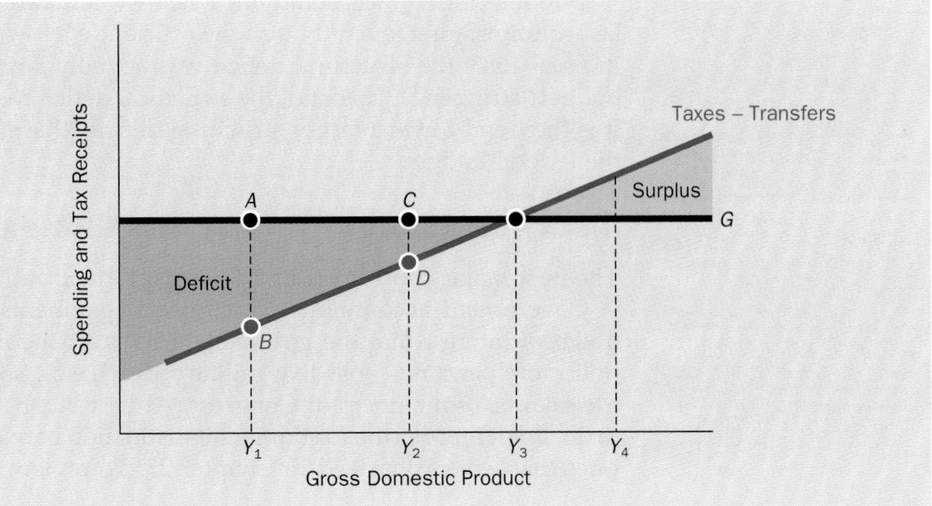


Since government purchases (*G*) do not depend on GDP, but taxes and transfer payments do, the deficit shrinks as GDP rises—even for a fixed fiscal policy. In this figure, the deficit is *AB* if GDP is $Y_1$, but only *CD* if GDP is $Y_2$. At still higher levels of GDP, the same policies could produce a balanced budget (at $Y_3$) or even a surplus (at $Y_4$).

receiving, given current tax rates and expenditure rules, if the economy were operating at some fixed high-employment level. For example, if the high-employment benchmark in Figure 32–5 was $Y_2$, while actual GDP was only $Y_1$, the actual deficit would be *AB* while the structural deficit would be only *CD*.

Because it is based on the spending and taxing the government would be doing at some fixed level of GDP, rather than on actual expenditures and receipts, the structural deficit is insensitive to the state of the economy. It changes only when policy changes. That is why most economists view it as a better measure of the thrust of fiscal policy than the actual deficit.

This new concept helps us understand the changing nature of the large budget deficits of the 1980s. Table 32–1 displays both the actual deficit and the structural deficit every other year since 1981. Because of recessions in 1983 and 1991, the

Table 32–1 **UNEMPLOYMENT AND THE DEFICIT**

| FISCAL YEAR | OFFICIAL DEFICIT (billions of dollars) | + | ADJUSTMENT TO HIGH EMPLOYMENT (billions of dollars) | = | STRUCTURAL DEFICIT (billions of dollars) |
|---|---|---|---|---|---|
| 1981 | –79 | | +42 | | –37 |
| 1983 | –208 | | +103 | | –105 |
| 1985 | –212 | | +35 | | –177 |
| 1987 | –150 | | +31 | | –119 |
| 1989 | –153 | | +7 | | –146 |
| 1991 | –270 | | +90 | | –180 |
| 1993 | –285 | | +79 | | –206 |

SOURCE: Congressional Budget Office, except for fiscal 1993, which is an estimate from the Office of Management and Budget.

difference between the two budgets was particularly large in those years. But it was negligible in 1989, when the economy was at full employment.

Two interesting facts stand out when we compare the numbers in the first and last columns. First, even though the official deficit was smaller in fiscal 1989 than in fiscal 1983, the structural deficit was actually larger in 1989—despite years of budget "stringency." Second, the structural deficit rose steadily from 1989 to 1993. It is the trend toward larger structural deficits that most alarms keen students of the federal budget.

## INFLATION ACCOUNTING FOR INTEREST PAYMENTS[3]

The next major problem is one of measurement rather than interpretation.

Government accountants treat interest payments in the obvious way: every dollar of interest that the government pays on the national debt is counted as a dollar of spending—just like military purchases, social security payments, and the salaries of members of Congress. At first blush, this seems the natural thing to do. But it ignores the fundamental distinction between real and nominal interest rates that we emphasized in Chapter 23. To review the analysis:

The real interest rate tells us the amount of purchasing power the borrower turns over to the lender for the privilege of borrowing. To this we must add an *inflation premium*, equal to the expected rate of inflation, to get the **nominal interest rate**. The inflation premium compensates the lender for the expected erosion of the purchasing power of her money and is best thought of as repayment of principal.[4]

The last sentence has important implications for the government budget—implications that few people understand.

From an economic point of view, the portion of the government's interest payments that merely compensates lenders for inflation should be counted as *repayment of principal*, not as *interest expense*, because it simply returns to lenders the purchasing power of their original loans. Only the *real* interest that the government pays should be treated as an expenditure item in the budget. Breaking up interest payments in this way is called **inflation accounting**. Since so few people understand inflation accounting, it is worth taking the time to illustrate the idea with an analogy and a simple example.

**INFLATION ACCOUNTING** means adjusting standard accounting procedures for the fact that inflation lowers the purchasing power of money.

Imagine that you lend a roommate, who is enrolled in a chemistry course, a bar of radium that you happen to own. Your roommate uses the radioactive bar (carefully!) in experiments for a year, and then returns it to you. Has your loan been repaid in full? Certainly not. Because of the natural process of radioactive decay, the bar you get back is smaller than the bar you originally loaned. To pay you back in full, your roommate would have to give you enough additional radium to replace the portion that eroded during the year.

The analogy to interest rates on loans is straightforward: inflation erodes the purchasing power of money just as radioactive decay erodes radium. So, in figuring out how many dollars constitutes repayment of principal, we must take inflation into account. Let's illustrate this by a concrete example: comparing a loan made at zero inflation (no decay) with a loan made at 10 percent inflation (rapid decay).

---

[3]This section contains difficult material which may be skipped in shorter courses.

[4]If you need review, see pages 576–77.

First, suppose the government borrows $1000 for a year when the inflation rate is zero, paying 2 percent interest. At the end of the year it must pay back $1000 in principal and $20 in interest, for a total of $1020. Of this, only $20—the interest payment—is an expenditure item in the budget. The repayment of principal does not appear in the budget since it is not spending. The loan transaction is summarized simply in column 1 of Table 32–2.

Now let us see how inflation (radioactive decay of money) complicates the accountant's job. Suppose the same transaction takes place when the rate of inflation is 10 percent. If the real rate of interest is still 2 percent, the nominal rate of interest must be about 12 percent.

More precisely, to compensate the lender for 10 percent inflation, and nothing more, the government must return $1.10 for each dollar originally borrowed. A real interest rate of 2 percent means that the government must return 2 percent more than this, or 1.02 × $1.10 = $1.122 per dollar borrowed. Since each dollar of lending earns 12.2 cents in interest, the nominal interest rate is 12.2 percent.

At a nominal interest rate of 12.2 percent, a government that borrows $1000 at the start of the year will have to repay $1,122 at year's end. Conventional accounting procedures will treat $1000 of this as repayment of principal (and hence not as an expenditure) and $122 as interest (which *is* an expenditure). This conventional accounting treatment is indicated in column 2 of Table 32–2.

But these numbers are misleading since $1000 at the end of the year is not full repayment of principal because inflation has eroded the real value of money. The correct inflation accounting treatment recognizes that it takes $1100 at the end of the year to buy what $1000 bought at the beginning of the year. So $1100 is treated as repayment of principal, leaving only $22 ($1122 − $1100) to be treated as interest. The correct inflation accounting treatment of the loan is shown in column 3 of Table 32–2.

To recapitulate, the proper economic treatment of a loan in an inflationary environment must recognize that more dollars (in our example, $1100) must be returned to the lender in order to give back the purchasing power of the original loan ($1000). Only the excess of the nominal interest payment ($122) over the compensation for inflation ($100) should be counted as interest.

**Table 32–2 ACCOUNTING FOR A $1000 LOAN AT A 2 PERCENT REAL INTEREST RATE**

| ITEM | (1) AT ZERO INFLATION | (2) AT 10% INFLATION CONVENTIONAL ACCOUNTING | (3) AT 10% INFLATION INFLATION ACCOUNTING |
|---|---|---|---|
| Interest (included in budget) | $ 20 | $ 122 | $ 22 |
| plus Principal (excluded from budget) | 1,000 | 1,000 | 1,100 |
| equals Total payment | $1,020 | $1,122 | $1,122 |
| *Addendum:* Purchasing power of principal repayment | $ 1000 | $ 909 | $1,000 |

This example holds the following lesson for interpreting budget deficit figures:

Inflation distorts the government budget under conventional accounting procedures by exaggerating interest expenses.

The example also suggests how this error can be corrected:

To correct the deficit for inflation, we must subtract the inflation premium from the interest paid on the national debt, thereby counting only *real* interest payments.

This treatment, by the way, corresponds exactly to the way inflation accounting is done by major corporations.

As Table 32–3 shows, making the inflation adjustment to interest payments would have reduced reported deficits by $80–90 billion in recent years, a sizable adjustment.

## OTHER MEASUREMENT ISSUES

There are other complicated issues in measuring and interpreting the federal budget deficit. We conclude this section by mentioning just two.

1. ***State and local budget surpluses.*** Part of the reason for the federal deficit is that the federal government gives a good deal of money (over $150 billion in recent years) to state and local governments in the form of *grants-in-aid* each year. These funds have helped state and local governments run small annual surpluses in recent years. Thus, the *combined* deficits of governments at *all* levels has been smaller than the *federal* deficit.
2. ***Capital expenditures.*** Some federal spending goes to purchase capital of various sorts—government buildings, military equipment, and so on. There is nothing unusual about borrowing to purchase assets. Private businesses and individuals do it all the time. For this reason, many people have suggested that the federal government compile a separate capital budget, just as most state and local governments now do.

## CONCLUSION: WHAT HAPPENED SINCE 1981?

Table 32–4 puts our two major adjustments—for inflation accounting and for unemployment—together and compares the official deficits recorded since 1981

**Table 32–3 INFLATION ACCOUNTING AND THE DEFICIT**

| FISCAL YEAR | OFFICIAL DEFICIT (billions of dollars) | + | INFLATION ADJUSTMENT FOR INTEREST PAID (billions of dollars) | = | INFLATION ADJUSTED DEFICIT (billions of dollars) |
|---|---|---|---|---|---|
| 1981 | –79 | | +62 | | –17 |
| 1983 | –208 | | +32 | | –176 |
| 1985 | –212 | | +43 | | –169 |
| 1987 | –150 | | +50 | | –100 |
| 1989 | –153 | | +80 | | –73 |
| 1991 | –270 | | +90 | | –180 |
| 1993 | –285 | | +83 | | –202 |

SOURCE: Congressional Budget Office, Office of Management and Budget, and authors' estimates.

**Table 32–4 ACTUAL AND ADJUSTED BUDGET DEFICITS**

| FISCAL YEAR | (1) OFFICIAL DEFICIT (billions of dollars) | + | (2) ADJUSTMENT FOR INFLATION (billions of dollars) | + | (3) ADJUSTMENT TO HIGH EMPLOYMENT (billions of dollars) | = | (4) ADJUSTED DEFICIT (–) OR SURPLUS (+) (billions of dollars) |
|---|---|---|---|---|---|---|---|
| 1981 | –79 | | +62 | | +42 | | +25 |
| 1983 | –208 | | +32 | | +103 | | – 73 |
| 1985 | –212 | | +43 | | +35 | | –134 |
| 1987 | –150 | | +50 | | +31 | | –69 |
| 1989 | –153 | | +80 | | +7 | | –66 |
| 1991 | –270 | | +90 | | +90 | | –90 |
| 1993 | –285 | | +83 | | +79 | | –123 |

SOURCE: Congressional Budget Office, Office of Management and Budget, and authors' estimates.

(column 1) with the corresponding figures for the structural, inflation-corrected deficit (column 4). The difference between the two columns is startling in some years. For example, the apparently substantial budget deficit of 1981 was actually a surplus on a structural, inflation-corrected basis. But since fiscal year 1983 even the structural, inflation-corrected budget has been in substantial deficit. And this concept of the deficit has grown alarmingly in recent years.

But what does this all mean? It certainly does *not* mean that in 1991, for example, only $90 billion in additional tax revenue (column 4) would have balanced the budget. What the numbers *do* mean is this. Of the $270 billion deficit in 1991 (column 1), about $90 billion was an artifact of poor accounting procedures and another $90 billion was attributable to the fact that the unemployment rate was well above full employment. This does not make the deficit disappear, but it does put it into some perspective.

## BOGUS ARGUMENTS ABOUT THE BURDEN OF THE DEBT

Having gained some perspective on the facts, let us now turn to some of the arguments advanced by those who claim that budget deficits place an intolerable burden on future generations.

**Argument 1:** Our children and grandchildren will be burdened by heavy interest payments. Higher taxes will be necessary to make these payments.

**Answer:** It is certainly true that a higher debt will necessitate higher interest payments and, other things being equal, this will force our children and grandchildren to pay higher taxes. But think who will receive the higher interest payments as income: our children and grandchildren! Thus one group of future Americans will be making interest payments to another group of future Americans. While some people will gain and others will lose, the future generation as a whole will come out even. We conclude that:

As long as the national debt is owned by domestic citizens, as the bulk of the U.S. debt is, future interest payments will merely shuffle money from one group of Americans to another. These transfers may or may not be desirable, but they hardly constitute a burden to the nation as a whole.

However, this argument *is* valid—and worrisome—for the 18 percent of our debt that is held by foreigners. Paying interest on this portion of the debt will burden future Americans in a concrete way: in the 21st century, a portion of America's GDP will have to be sent abroad to pay interest on the debts we incurred in the 1980s. For this reason, many thoughtful observers are more concerned about the amount America is borrowing from abroad than they are about the total budget deficit.[5]

**Argument 2:** It will ruin the nation when we repay the enormous debt.

**Answer:** A first answer to this merely rephrases the answer to the previous argument: only the part owned by foreigners involves any burden; the rest is paid by one group of Americans to another. But there is an even more fundamental point. *Unlike a private family, the nation need never pay off its debt.* Instead, each time the principal is due, the U.S. Treasury can simply "roll it over" by floating more debt. Indeed, this is precisely what the Treasury does.

Is this a bit of chicanery? How can the U.S. government get away with making loans that it never intends to pay back? The answer lies in the fallacy of comparing the U.S. government to a family or an individual. People cannot be extended credit in perpetuity because they will not live that long. Sensible lenders will not extend long-term credit to very old people because their heirs cannot be forced to pay up. But the U.S. government will never "die"; at least, we hope not! So this problem does not arise. In this respect, the government is in much the same position as a large corporation. The American Telephone and Telegraph Company never worries about paying off its debt. It too rolls it over by floating new debt all the time.

**Argument 3:** Like any family or any business firm, a nation has a limited capacity to borrow. If it exceeds this limit, it is in danger of being unable to pay its creditors. It may go bankrupt with calamitous consequences for everyone.

**Answer:** This is another example of a false analogy. What is claimed about private debtors is certainly true. But the U.S. government need never fear defaulting on its debt. Why? First, because it has enormous power to raise revenues by taxation. If you had such power, you would never have to fear bankruptcy either.

But there is a more fundamental point—one that distinguishes the U.S. debt from that of most other nations. *The American national debt is an obligation to pay U.S. dollars:* each debt certificate obligates the Treasury to pay the holder so many U.S. dollars on a prescribed date. But the U.S. government is the source of these dollars. It prints them! *No nation need ever fear defaulting on debts that call for repayment in its own currency.* At the very worst, it can always print whatever money it needs to pay off its creditors. This is not an option open to countries like Mexico, Brazil, and Argentina, whose debts generally call for payment in U.S. dollars.

---

[5]We will discuss the linkages between the federal budget deficit and foreign borrowing in greater detail in Chapter 37.

It does not follow, however, that acquiring more foreign debt through budget deficits is necessarily a good idea for the U.S. government. Sometimes it is clearly a bad idea. As we know, printing money to pay the debt will expand aggregate demand and cause inflation. In addition, as we will learn in Chapter 36, printing more dollars will make the international value of the dollar fall. We may not relish either of these outcomes. The point is not that budget deficits are either good or bad; they can be either under the appropriate circumstances. Rather, the point is that worrying about a possible default on the national debt is unnecessary and even foolish.

Having cleared the air of these fallacious arguments, we are now in a position to explore some genuine problems that may arise when the government spends more than it takes in through taxation.

## BUDGET DEFICITS AND INFLATION

One indictment of deficit spending that certainly *does* have validity under most circumstances is the charge that it is inflationary. Why? Because when government policy pushes up aggregate demand, firms may find themselves unwilling or unable to produce the higher quantities that are being demanded at the going prices. Prices will therefore have to rise.

Figure 32–6 is an aggregate supply and demand diagram that shows this analysis graphically. Initially, equilibrium is at point $E_0$—where demand curve $D_0D_0$ and supply curve *SS* intersect. Output is $6000 billion, and the price index is at 100. The diagram indicates that the economy is operating below full employment; there is a recessionary gap. If the government does nothing to reduce the

### Figure 32–6 THE INFLATIONARY EFFECTS OF DEFICIT SPENDING

In this diagram, expansionary fiscal policy pushes the aggregate demand curve out from $D_0D_0$ to $D_1D_1$, causing equilibrium to move from $E_0$ (where there is unemployment) to $E_1$ (where there is full employment). But because aggregate supply curve *SS* slopes upward, the price level is pushed up from 100 to 106; that is, there is a 6 percent inflation.

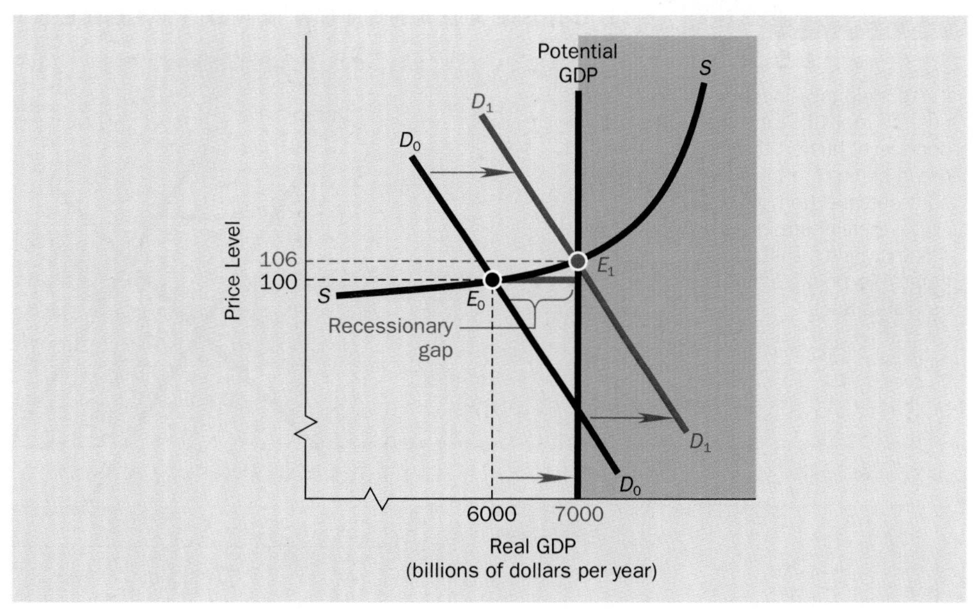

resulting unemployment, we know from Chapter 27 that this recessionary gap will linger for a long time. The economy will suffer through a prolonged period of unemployment.

Rather than permit such a long recession, we know the government can raise its spending or cut its taxes enough to shift the aggregate demand schedule upward from $D_0D_0$ to $D_1D_1$. Such a policy can wipe out the recessionary gap and the associated unemployment—but not without an inflationary cost. The diagram shows the new equilibrium price level at 106, or 6 percent higher than before the government acted.

Thus the cries that budget deficits are "inflationary" have the ring of truth. How much truth, of course, depends on the slope of the aggregate supply curve. Deficit spending will not cause much inflation if the economy has lots of slack and the aggregate supply curve consequently is flat. But deficit spending will be highly inflationary in a fully-employed economy with a steep aggregate supply curve.

## THE MONETIZATION ISSUE

Some people worry about the inflationary consequences of deficits for a rather different reason. They fear that the Federal Reserve may have to "monetize" part of the deficit, by which they mean that the Fed may feel compelled to purchase some of the newly issued government debt. Let us explain, first, why the Fed might make such purchases, and second, why these purchases are called **monetizing the deficit**.

The central bank is said to **MONETIZE THE DEFICIT** when it purchases the bonds that the government issues.

Deficit spending, we have just noted, normally drives up both real GDP and the price level. As we have emphasized before, such an economic expansion shifts the demand curve for money outward to the right—as depicted in Figure 32–7. The figure shows that, if the Federal Reserve takes no actions to shift the money supply curve, interest rates will rise.

*Figure* **32–7** **FISCAL EXPANSION AND INTEREST RATES**

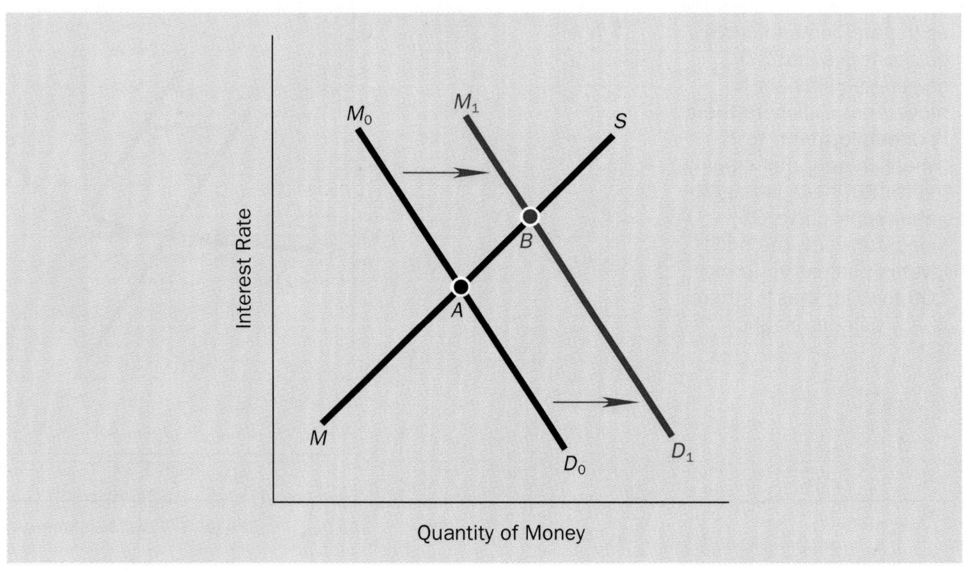


If expansionary fiscal policy pushes real GDP and the price level higher, the demand curve for money will shift outward from $M_0D_0$ to $M_1D_1$. Equilibrium in the money market shifts from point *A* to point *B*, so interest rates rise.

Figure 32–8 **MONETIZATION AND INTEREST RATES**

If the Federal Reserve does not want a fiscal expansion to raise interest rates, it must increase the money supply. In this diagram, the fiscal expansion shifts the demand curve for money from $M_0D_0$ to $M_1D_1$, precisely as it did in Figure 32–7. To keep the rate of interest constant, the Fed will have to shift the money supply curve outward from $M_0S_0$ to $M_1S_1$. Points *A* and *C* correspond to the same rate of interest.

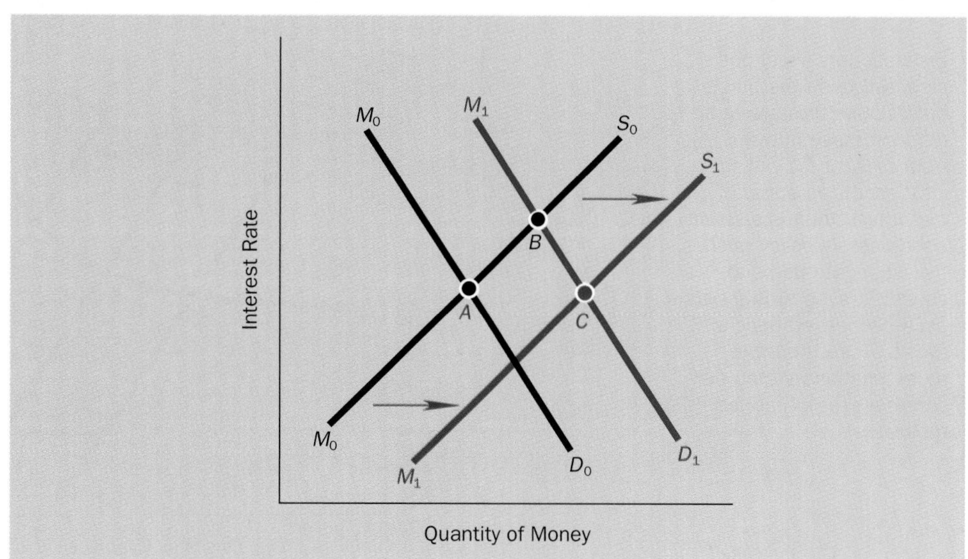


Suppose now that the Fed does not want interest rates to rise. What can it do? To prevent the incipient rise in *r*, it must engage in *expansionary monetary policies* that shift the supply curve for money outward to the right—as indicated in Figure 32–8. As noted in Chapter 30, expansionary monetary policies normally take the form of open-market purchases of government bonds. So deficit spending might induce the Federal Reserve to increase its purchases of government bonds, that is, to buy up some of the newly issued debt.

But why is this called *monetizing* the deficit? The reason is simple. As we learned in Chapter 30, open-market purchases of bonds by the Fed give banks more reserves, which leads, eventually, to an increase in the money supply. This is also shown in Figure 32–8: The outward shift of the money supply schedule from $M_0S_0$ to $M_1S_1$ leads to an increase in the money supply. By this indirect route, then, larger budget deficits may lead to an expansion of the money supply. To summarize:

If the Federal Reserve takes no countervailing actions, an expansionary fiscal policy that increases the budget deficit will raise real GDP and prices, thereby shifting the demand curve for money outward and driving up interest rates. If the Fed does not want interest rates to rise, it can engage in expansionary open-market operations, that is, purchase more government debt. If the Fed does this, the money supply will increase. In this case, we say that part of the deficit is *monetized*.

Monetized deficits are more inflationary than nonmonetized deficits for the simple reason that expansionary monetary and fiscal policy *together* are more inflationary than expansionary fiscal policy *alone*. Figure 32–9 illustrates this simple conclusion. The aggregate supply curve and aggregate demand curves $D_0D_0$ and $D_1D_1$ are carried over without change from Figure 32–6. The shift from $D_0D_0$ to $D_1D_1$ represents the effect of expansionary fiscal policy (raising the budget

Figure 32-9 MONETIZED DEFICIT SPENDING

Expansionary fiscal policies that raise the budget deficit push the aggregate demand curve outward from $D_0D_0$ to $D_1D_1$. If the Fed monetizes some of the deficit, then expansionary monetary policy pushes the aggregate demand curve out even further—to $D_2D_2$. Monetized deficits (point *C*) are therefore more inflationary than deficits that are not monetized (point *B*).

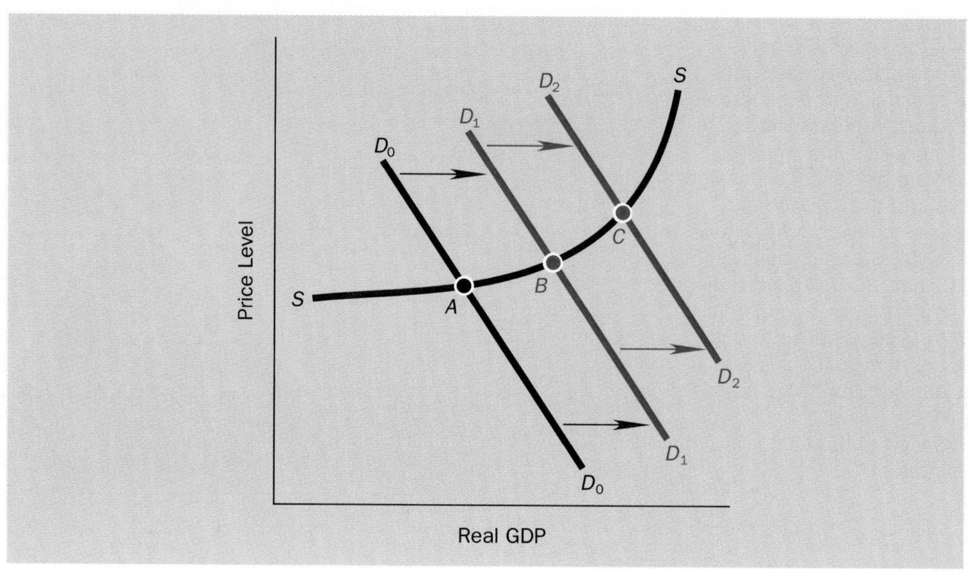


deficit). If, in addition, the Fed monetizes part of the deficit, the aggregate demand curve will shift out still further—perhaps to the position indicated by $D_2D_2$. Thus the price level will rise even more (compare points *B* and *C*).

Is this a real worry? Does the Fed actually monetize any substantial portion of the deficit? Sometimes it does, but normally it does not. For example, during the decade ending in 1992, the total federal debt held outside the government increased by a bit more than $2 trillion, but the Federal Reserve's holdings of government bonds increased by only about $160 billion. By this crude measure, only about eight percent of the typical deficit was monetized.

Nonetheless, many economists and business leaders are concerned about the long-run dangers of monetization when deficits are large and chronic. The reason is simple arithmetic. When budget deficits are extremely large, even a small percentage of monetization can lead to substantial increases in bank reserves and the money supply. While monetization of deficits has not been much of a problem for the United States, it has long been a major source of inflation in Latin America and lately has been the root cause of a ruinous hyperinflation in Russia.

## DEFICITS, INTEREST RATES, AND CROWDING OUT

So far we have been looking for possible burdens of the national debt on the *demand* side of the economy. But the more serious burden probably comes on the *supply* side because large budget deficits discourage investment and therefore retard the growth of our nation's capital stock. The mechanism is easy to understand.

We have just seen that budget deficits tend to raise interest rates unless the Fed engages in substantial monetization. But the rate of interest ($r$) is a major determinant of investment spending ($I$). In particular, higher $r$ leads to lower $I$. And if we spend less on $I$ today, we will have a smaller capital stock tomorrow. This, according to most economists, is the true sense in which a large national debt may burden future generations:

Because of the large national debt, we may bequeath less physical capital to future generations. If they inherit less plant and equipment, these generations will be burdened by a lower productive capacity—a lower potential GDP.

**CROWDING OUT** occurs when deficit spending by the government forces private investment spending to contract.

There is another way of looking at this problem—a way that explains why it is called the **crowding-out effect**. Consider what happens in financial markets when the government engages in deficit spending. When it spends more than it takes in through tax revenues, the government must borrow the balance from private citizens. It does this by issuing bonds, which compete with corporate bonds and other financial instruments for the available supply of funds. If some private savers decide to buy government bonds, the funds remaining to invest in private bonds must be smaller. Thus some private borrowers will get "crowded out" of the financial markets as the government claims an increasing share of the economy's total saving. (For a dissenting view, see the accompanying boxed insert.)

Some critics of deficits have taken this lesson to its illogical extreme and argued that each $1 of deficit spending by government crowds out exactly $1 of private spending, so that expansionary fiscal policy has no net effect on total demand. In their view, when $G$ rises, $I$ falls by the same amount, so that the total of $C + I + G + (X - IM)$ is unchanged.

Under normal circumstances, this would not be expected to occur. Why? First, moderate budget deficits push up interest rates only slightly. Second, the sensitivity of private spending to interest rates is modest. Even at the higher interest rates that government deficits cause, most corporations will continue to borrow to finance their investments.

**CROWDING IN** occurs when government spending, by raising real GDP, induces increases in private investment spending.

Furthermore, there is a counterforce that might be called the **crowding-in effect**. Deficit spending in time of economic slack presumably quickens the pace of economic activity; that, at least, is its purpose. As the economy expands, businesses find it both necessary and profitable to add to their capacity in order to meet the greater demands of consumers. Because of this *induced investment*, as we called it in earlier chapters, any increase in $G$ tends to *increase* investment rather than *decrease* it as predicted by the crowding-out hypothesis.

The strength of the crowding-in effect depends on how much additional real GDP is stimulated by government spending (that is, on the size of the multiplier) and on how sensitive investment spending is to the improved profit opportunities that accompany rapid growth. It is even conceivable that the crowding-in effect can dominate the crowding-out effect, so that $I$ rises on balance when $G$ rises.

But how can this be true in view of the crowding-out argument? Certainly, if government is borrowing more *and the total volume of private saving is fixed*, then private industry must be borrowing less. This little bit of arithmetic is indisputable. But the fallacy in the strict crowding-out argument comes in supposing that the economy's flow of saving is really fixed. If government deficits succeed in their goal of raising production, there will be more income and therefore more saving. In that way, *both* government *and* industry can borrow more.

Which effect dominates, crowding out or crowding in? Crowding out stems from the increases in interest rates caused by deficits, while crowding in derives from the faster real economic growth that deficits sometimes promote. Under

*At The* **FRONTIER**

### THE THEORY OF DEBT NEUTRALITY

Most economists, politicians, and business people worry that continuing large deficits will lead to high interest rates, weak investment, and perhaps higher inflation. But a vocal minority of economists subscribes to the new theory of **debt neutrality**, which implies that deficits do nothing at all. Why? Because rational citizens save more whenever the government deficit increases.

The argument is straightforward. When the government runs a deficit, it issues bonds. Each bond is a pledge to make specified interest and principal payments in the future. But it is also a promise to raise enough future tax revenue to meet those obligations. Advocates of debt neutrality insist that these two aspects of government bonds must cancel out precisely. Deficits are therefore mere bookkeeping operations that cut taxes now and raise them in the future. If the government cuts John Q. Citizen's 1993 tax bill by $1000, he can simply save the $1000, let it accumulate at compound interest, and use the proceeds to pay his future taxes.

Some economists question this conclusion on the grounds that people are less farsighted and rational than the theory supposes. If your friend Joe lends you $50 from Monday to Friday, this five-day loan may not change your plans significantly. But government bonds last much longer than five days. If you receive $50 now rather than five *years* from now, it may well change your behavior. Farsighted individuals should also know that they will not live long enough to pay back the government's debt. Since some of the future tax burden falls on their children, a tax cut financed by issuing bonds makes the currently living generations richer.

Or does it? A part of the theory proposed by Professor Robert Barro of Harvard argues that the same analysis applies when taxes are shifted from one generation to the next.* People care about their children. So, if the government cuts their taxes and raises their children's taxes, private citizens can easily undo the fiscal operation. They need only save the tax cut, let it accumulate at compound interest, and leave the money in their wills.

The model works in theory. Does it work in practice? Most economists think not. But no one is sure because we have no person-by-person data on how bequests relate to taxes. Instead, economists must deduce what the theory implies for *macroeconomic* behavior and compare that to what actually happens. Here serious problems arise because there are no controlled experiments in economics. When many things are changing at once, it is difficult to isolate the economic effects of the deficit. For example, as the text points out (page 816), a recession *raises* the deficit but *lowers* interest rates. But that does not mean that larger deficits cause lower interest rates.

Because budget deficits, private saving, and interest rates are subject to a variety of influences, research on the theory of debt neutrality continues at the frontier. The Reagan tax cuts of 1981–1984 may have provided something close to a controlled experiment. If debt is neutral, Americans should have saved their tax cuts. Most studies of the episode, however, conclude that consumers spent most of their tax cuts, just as the mainstream view predicts. But proponents of debt neutrality are not convinced that this is conclusive evidence.

*Robert J. Barro, "Are Government Bonds Net Wealth?," *Journal of Political Economy*, 1974, pages 1095–1117.

different sets of circumstances, one or the other force may prove to be the stronger. Near the bottom of a recession, for example, a surge in $G$ will probably produce a considerable rise in real output because the economy will be in the flat region of the aggregate supply curve (see Region I in Figure 32–10). Then crowding in will be strong. On the other hand, when resources are more fully employed, the economy will be operating in the steep portion of its aggregate supply curve

*Figure* 32–10 **A TYPICAL AGGREGATE SUPPLY CURVE**

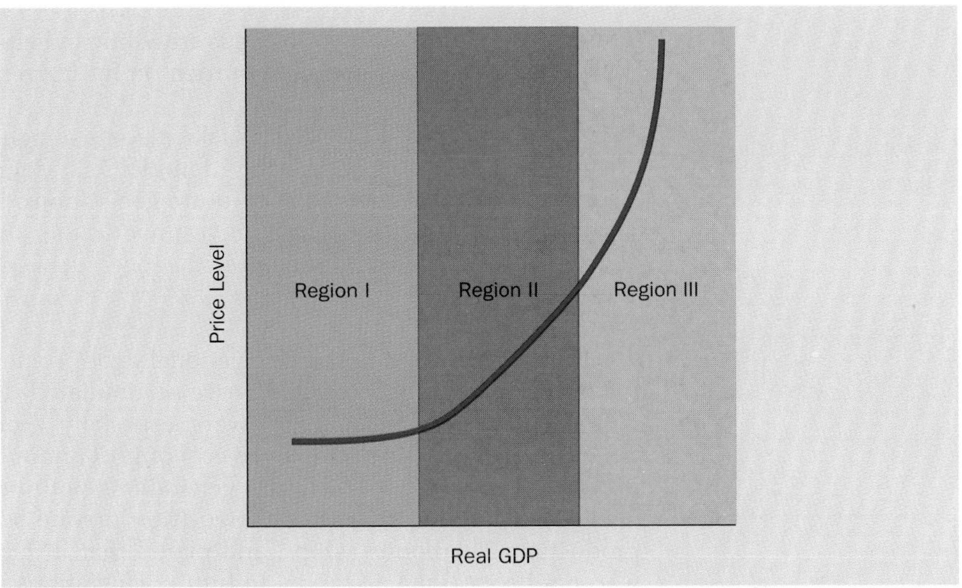


The aggregate supply curve depicted here has three regions. In Region I, output can increase with almost no change in prices because there is a great deal of unused labor and spare industrial capacity. Thus the supply curve is virtually horizontal. In Region III, resources are more or less fully employed, so even rather small increases in output necessitate substantial price increases; the supply curve is very steep. Region II is intermediate between these two extremes.

(Region III in Figure 32–10). Then a rise in aggregate demand will mainly push up the price level, raise the demand for cash balances, and crowd out private borrowers.[6]

Let us summarize what we have learned about the crowding-out controversy.

**SUMMARY**

1. The basic argument of the crowding-out hypothesis is sound: *unless there is enough additional saving,* more government borrowing will force out some private borrowers who are discouraged by the high interest rates. This will reduce investment spending and cancel out some of the expansionary effects of higher government spending.
2. This force is rarely strong enough to cancel out the *entire* expansionary thrust of government spending, however. Some net stimulus to the economy remains.
3. If the deficit spending induces substantial growth in GDP, then there will be more saving. There might even be so much more that private industry could borrow *more* than before, despite the increase in government borrowing.
4. The crowding-out effect is likely to dominate when the economy is operating near full employment. The crowding-in effect is likely to dominate when there is a great deal of slack.

[6]EXERCISE: Show that any given horizontal shift in the aggregate demand curve has a smaller effect on real GDP in Region III than it does in Region I.

## THE TRUE BURDEN OF THE NATIONAL DEBT

This analysis of crowding out versus crowding in helps us to understand whether or not budget deficits impose a burden on future generations:

When government budget deficits take place in a high-employment economy, the crowding-out effect will probably dominate. So deficits will exact a burden by leaving a smaller capital stock to future generations. However, deficits in a slack economy may well lead to *more* investment rather than *less*. In this case, where the crowding-in effect dominates, the new debt is a blessing rather than a burden.

Which case applies to the U.S. national debt? To answer this, let us go back to the historical facts and recall how we accumulated debt prior to the 1980s. The first cause was the financing of wars, especially World War II. Since this debt was contracted in a fully-employed economy, it undoubtedly constituted a burden in the formal sense. It left future generations with less capital because some of our nation's resources were diverted from private investment into government production. The bombs, ships, and planes that it financed were used up in the war, not bequeathed as capital to future generations.

"Would you mind explaining again how high interest rates and the national deficit affect my allowance?"

Yet what were the alternatives? We could have financed the entire war by taxation and thus placed the burden on consumption rather than on investment. But that would truly have been ruinous, and probably impossible, given the colossal wartime expenditures. Or we could have printed money. But that would have unleashed an inflation that nobody wanted. Or we could have done much less government spending and perhaps not have won the war. So, in retrospect, the generations alive today and in the future may not feel unduly burdened by the decisions of the people in power in the 1940s. One need only imagine the sort of burden we would have inherited had the United States not won the war.

A second major contributor to the national debt was a series of recessions. But these are precisely the circumstances under which increasing the debt might prove to be a blessing rather than a burden. So, if we look for the classic type of deficit to which the valid burden-of-the-debt argument applies—deficits acquired in a fully-employed peacetime economy—we do not find many in the U.S. record.

It is in this context that the budget deficits of the past decade or so are a sharp departure from the past. The tax cuts of 1981–1984 blew a large hole in the government budget. And the recession of 1981–1982 ballooned the deficit even further. By the late 1980s, the U.S. economy had recovered to full-employment, but a structural deficit of around $150 billion per year remained. This was something that had never happened before. Then, in the early 1990s, the structural deficit racheted up again—to above $200 billion per year. Such large structural deficits pose a real threat of crowding out and a serious potential burden on future generations.

Let us now summarize our evaluation of the burden of the national debt and thereby clarify one of the **12 Ideas for Beyond the Final Exam** introduced in Chapter 1.

**THE BURDEN OF THE NATIONAL DEBT**

First, the arguments that a large national debt may lead the nation into bankruptcy, or unduly burden future generations who have to make onerous payments of interest and principal, are mostly bogus. ¶ Second, the national debt *will* be a burden if it is sold to foreigners or contracted in a fully-employed peacetime economy. In the latter case, it will reduce the nation's capital stock. ¶ Third, there are circumstances in which budget deficits are appropriate for stabilization reasons. ¶ Fourth, until the 1980s, the actual public debt of the U.S. government was mostly contracted as a result of wars and recessions—precisely the circumstances under which the valid burden-of-the-debt argument does not apply. However, the large deficits of recent years cannot all be attributed to recessions, and are therefore worrisome.

## THE ECONOMIC EFFECTS OF BUDGET DEFICITS: CAUSATION VERSUS CORRELATION

Anyone who has followed the debate over budget deficits in the press is bound to have been confused by the contradictory claims and counter-claims. Do deficits lead to high interest rates? Some say yes, others say no. Are deficits inflationary? Some say yes, others say no. Are large deficits a roadblock to economic expansion? Some say yes, others say no. Some even claim that deficit reduction is the key to growth. And somehow each participant in the debate finds data to support his or her view.

Who is right? Let us use what we have learned about the economic effects of budget deficits to make some sense of this confusion. We can do so by contrasting two imaginary case studies which, however, bear a certain resemblance to events in the United States in the 1980s and early 1990s.

### CASE 1: A TAX CUT

Suppose the government opens up a budget deficit by reducing taxes. What should happen? According to the theory we have developed, aggregate demand should increase. And that, in turn, should raise both real GDP ($Y$) and the price level ($P$), as Figure 32–6 (page 807) shows. The rise in $Y$ and $P$ should shift the demand curve for money outward, thereby raising the rate of interest ($r$)—as in Figure 32–7 (page 808)—and subsequently lowering investment. Thus, in response to the large deficit, the economy should experience rapid GDP growth, high inflation, and high interest rates. The general conclusion is:

If the government deliberately undertakes expansionary fiscal policies, like cutting taxes or raising spending, the deficit should rise and:

1. Real GDP should grow faster;
2. Interest rates should rise (which harms investment);
3. Inflation should rise.

This conclusion is recorded for future reference in the first column of Table 32–5.

Table 32–5 DEFICITS AND THE ECONOMY: A SUMMARY

| EXPECTED EFFECT ON: | CASE 1 FISCAL POLICY ACTIONS RAISE THE DEFICIT | CASE 2 A RECESSION RAISES THE DEFICIT |
|---|---|---|
| Real GDP growth | Up | Down |
| Interest rate | Up | Down |
| Inflation rate | Up | Down |

## CASE 2: A RECESSION

Now suppose the budget deficit increases for an entirely different reason. For example, suppose consumer spending declines sharply. What will happen? The decline in aggregate demand will lower both real GDP and prices. With both $Y$ and $P$ falling, the quantity of money demanded will decline. And the decrease in the demand for money will pull down interest rates, which will stimulate investment. Finally, as we have noted in this chapter, when GDP falls so do tax receipts; so the deficit will widen.[7] Thus, in this case, we expect larger deficits to be accompanied by weaker GDP growth, slower inflation, and lower interest rates. The general conclusion is:

If the economy experiences a recession for reasons unconnected with fiscal policy, the deficit should rise and:

1. Real GDP should fall;
2. Interest rates should fall;
3. Inflation should fall.

This conclusion is recorded in the second column of Table 32–5.

Table 32–5 shows just how different the two cases are. The deficit rises in both cases. But in the first case $Y$, $P$, and $r$ all rise, while in the second case they all fall.[8] In the real world, of course, deficits are sometimes caused by fiscal policy actions (as in Case 1) and sometimes caused by other factors (as in Case 2). And that is why different people, looking at the same facts, can reach different conclusions about deficits.

The point is that "looking at the facts" is not enough. Simple correlations between the budget deficit and some other economic variable are not terribly informative. You must be able to distinguish between *cause* and *effect*. In Case 1, changes in fiscal policy were the driving force; in a very real sense, a higher deficit *caused* $Y$, $P$, and $r$ to rise. But in Case 2, there was no change in fiscal policy; a higher deficit was an *effect* of a recession.

The U.S. in recent years has displayed examples of both cases. In 1981–1984, President Reagan's tax cuts increased the deficit substantially and helped propel the economy forward—as in Case 1. In 1981–1982, and then again in 1990–1991, the U.S. economy suffered through recessions which raised the deficit while the

[7]EXERCISE: Test your understanding by working out the diagrams for this example.

[8]EXERCISE: To test your understanding, construct a version of Table 32–5 that applies to *falling* deficits caused by (a) a tax increase or (b) an autonomous increase in consumer spending. Be sure you can explain each entry in the table.

economy sagged—as in Case 2. No wonder the charges and countercharges were so confused, and the evidence so confusing. (See Question 10 at the end of the chapter.)

## CONCLUSION: THE ECONOMICS AND POLITICS OF THE BUDGET DEFICIT

Given what we have learned about the theory and facts of budget deficits, we are now in a position to address some of the issues that have been debated in the political arena for a decade or more.

1. ***How did we get such a large deficit?*** Triple-digit deficits began in 1982. At first, the most important cause was the steep recession, not President Reagan's budget policies. As we saw in Table 32–1 (page 801), the structural deficit was far smaller than the actual deficit in, say, 1983.

   But by the mid-1980s, with the economy improved and the tax cuts fully effective, the structural deficit was tremendous. By the late 1980s, deliberate fiscal policy actions (and inactions) accounted for virtually all of the deficit. Whether the blame for failing to address the deficit problem rests with the two Republican presidents or the Democratic Congress is a matter of politics, not economics. But the fact is that little was done to mitigate the problem.
2. ***Is the deficit really a problem?*** Once again, the answer to the question was different in 1981–1983 from what it has been since. In 1981–1982, the economy went through a deep recession. And in 1983, the first year of the recovery, unemployment was still far above full employment. Under these circumstances, crowding out would not be expected to be a serious problem and actions to close the deficit would have threatened the recovery. According to the basic principles of fiscal policy, a large deficit was probably appropriate.

   But things were much different by the late 1980s. Crowding out became a more serious issue as the economy neared full employment. So budget deficits should have fallen. But the actual deficit did not fall and the structural deficit actually rose. Since the mid-1980s, we have had persistently large structural deficits regardless of whether the economy was strong or weak. So worries about the burden of the national debt, once mostly myths, have become all too realistic.
3. ***What can be done about the deficit?*** There is no magic in the Clinton approach to deficit reduction. It is a matter of simple arithmetic that you close a budget deficit by raising taxes and/or by reducing spending, and President Clinton proposed (and Congress enacted) some of each. (See the accompanying boxed insert.) Either of these routes is a contractionary fiscal policy that reduces aggregate demand.

Is that a problem? Not necessarily, if fiscal and monetary policies are well coordinated. If fiscal policy turns contractionary to reduce the deficit, monetary policy can turn expansionary to counteract the effects on aggregate demand. In this way, we can hope to shrink the deficit without shrinking the economy. Such a change in the policy "mix" should also bring down interest rates, since both tighter budgets and easier money tend to push interest rates down. This, indeed, was the central hope of Clintonomics. And, at least initially, it appeared to be working. Interest rates fell dramatically while the plan was announced, debated, and enacted and, as of the time of this writing, have remained low.

## The Politics and Economics of Deficit Reduction: The Clinton Program

The structural budget deficit ballooned during the presidency of George Bush (see Table 32–1 on page 801). But neither President Bush nor challenger Bill Clinton ran on a platform of heavy deficit reduction in 1992. (Third-party candidate Ross Perot did.) After all, the political wisdom of the day was that deficit reduction—which means raising people's taxes or cutting government programs—was political death. Much of the nation was therefore surprised when President Clinton proposed a tough deficit-reduction program in February 1993.

The White House document *A Vision of Change for America* and the new president's first State of the Union address altered the terms of the deficit debate fundamentally—and somewhat incredibly. What was once political suicide was somehow transformed into political elixir. Deficit reduction became all the rage. Within weeks, Congress was vying with the President over who could cut the deficit more! In fact, the anti-deficit momentum grew so strong so quickly that it threatened other parts of the president's program. It is said that the American Congress and body politic can only concentrate on one thing at a time. For most of 1993, that one thing was deficit reduction.

President Clinton's original economic plan had three components:*

1. a small stimulus package—about $15 billion a year for two years—designed to spur the sluggish economy. This was killed by a Republican filibuster in the Senate, partly because it would have increased the deficit. Senators apparently forgot that you get fiscal stimulus only by raising the deficit.
2. a five-year program of new public investment initiatives, which was scheduled to grow to $55 billion annually by the fourth year. This program was scaled back during the Congressional appropriations process. Here, again, the president's requests to replace old spending with new spending ran head-on into the deficit-reduction tide. "How can you propose new spending when we need to cut the deficit?"
3. a large, multi-year deficit reduction program that would have pared the annual deficit by about $140 billion by fiscal year 1997.** To the amazement of many, the president's deficit-reduction program not only sailed through but was actually enlarged by Congress. When it became law in August 1993, the deficit reduction program was slightly larger than President Clinton's proposal and composed slightly more of spending cuts and slightly less of tax increases. But, on the whole, it closely resembled what the president had asked for in February.

Had the economics of deficit reduction changed between 1992 and 1993? Hardly. It was the politics of the issue that was somehow transformed, as political taboo turned into political virtue. Indeed, some economists worried that a Congress that had once been allergic to deficit reduction was taking a good thing too far.

*One of the authors of this book participated in the design of the Clinton plan.
**Reducing the deficit by $140 billion while adding $55 billion in new spending required a total of $195 billion in proposed spending cuts and tax increases.

## *Summary*

1. Rigid adherence to budget balancing would make the economy less stable by reducing aggregate demand (via tax increases and reductions in government spending) when private spending is low, and raising aggregate demand when private spending is high.
2. Since both monetary and fiscal policy influence aggregate demand, the appropriate **budget deficit** or surplus depends on monetary policy. Similarly, the appropriate monetary policy depends on budget policy.
3. The **national debt** has grown dramatically relative to GDP since the early 1980s, reversing the previous postwar trend.
4. One major reason for the large budget deficits of the early 1980s and early 1990s was the fact that the economy operated well below full employment. The **structural deficit**, which uses estimates of what the government's receipts and outlays would be at full employment, was much smaller than the official deficit.
5. Inflation exaggerates the deficit because all **nominal interest payments** are counted as expenditures. Under **inflation accounting**, only **real interest payments** would count as expenditures, and the deficit would be seen to be much smaller.
6. If we correct the official deficit for inflation and adjust it to high levels of employment, we find that deficits in the structural, inflation-corrected budget began only around 1983. Before that, there were balanced budgets or surpluses.
7. Arguments that the public debt will burden future generations, who will have to make huge payments of interest and principal, are based on false analogies. In fact, most of these payments are simply transfers from some Americans to other Americans. However, there is a legitimate worry about the portion of the national debt that is owned by foreigners.
8. The bogus argument that a large national debt can bankrupt a country like the United States ignores the fact that our national debt consists of obligations to pay U.S. dollars—a currency the government can raise by taxation or create by printing money.
9. Under normal circumstances, budget deficits are somewhat inflationary because they expand aggregate demand. They are even more inflationary if they are **monetized**, that is, if the Federal Reserve buys some of the newly issued government debt in the open market.
10. Unless the deficit is substantially monetized, deficit spending forces interest rates higher and discourages private investment spending. This is called the **crowding-out effect**. If there is a great deal of crowding out, then deficits really do impose a **burden on future generations** by leaving them a smaller capital stock to work with.
11. But there is also a **crowding-in effect** from higher government spending ($G$). If expansionary fiscal policy succeeds in raising real output ($Y$), more investment will be induced by the higher $Y$.
12. Whether crowding out or crowding in dominates depends mainly on the state of the economy. When unemployment is high, crowding in is probably the stronger force, so higher $G$ does not cause lower investment. But when the economy is near full employment, the proponents of the crowding-out hypothesis are probably right: high government spending mainly displaces private investment.
13. Whether or not deficits are a burden therefore depends on how and why the government ran these deficits in the first place. If deficits are contracted to fight recessions, it is possible that more investment is crowded in by the increases in income that these deficits make possible than is crowded out by the increases in interest rates. Deficits contracted to carry on wars certainly impair the future capital stock, though they may not be considered a burden for noneconomic reasons. Since these two cases account for most of the debt the U.S. government contracted until the mid-1980s, that debt cannot reasonably be considered a serious burden. However, recent deficits are more worrisome on this score. This is one of the **12 Ideas for Beyond the Final Exam**.
14. If deficits arise from deliberate fiscal policy actions, then larger deficits should lead to more rapid growth of real output, higher prices, and higher interest rates.
15. But if deficits arise from a recession, we should find larger deficits accompanied by declining GDP, lower inflation, and lower interest rates.

## Key Concepts and Terms

Budget deficit
National debt
Real versus nominal interest rates
Inflation accounting
Structural deficit or surplus
Monetization of deficits
Crowding out
Crowding in
Burden of the national debt
Mix of monetary and fiscal policy

## Questions for Review

1. Explain the difference between the budget deficit and the national debt. If we reduce the deficit, will the debt stop growing?
2. Explain how the U.S. government has managed to accumulate a debt of over $4 trillion. To whom does it owe this debt? Can the debt be considered a burden on future generations?
3. Comment on the following: "Deficit spending paves the road to ruination. If we keep it up, the whole nation will go bankrupt. Even if things do not go this far, what right have we to burden our children and grandchildren with these debts while we live high on the hog?"
4. Calculate the budget deficit and the inflation-corrected deficit for an economy with the following data:

   Government expenditures other than interest = 180
   Tax receipts = 200
   Interest payments = 60
   Interest rate = 6 percent
   Inflation rate = 3 percent
   National debt at start of year = 1000
   (*Note*: 6 percent interest on a $1000 debt is $60.)
5. Explain in words why the structural budget might show a surplus while the actual budget is in deficit. Illustrate this with a diagram like Figure 32–5.
6. If the Federal Reserve begins to increase the money supply more slowly than before, what will happen to the government budget deficit? (*Hint:* What will happen to tax receipts and interest expenses?) If the government wants to offset the effects of the Fed's actions on aggregate demand, what might it do? How will this affect the deficit?
7. Newspaper reports have suggested that the Clinton administration has pressured the Fed to expand the money supply faster. (The administration has denied it.) In view of your answer to Question 6, why do you think that might be?
8. Given the current state of the economy, do you think the Fed should monetize more of the deficit? (*Note:* There is no one correct answer to this question. It is a good question to discuss in class.)
9. Explain the difference between crowding out and crowding in. Given the current state of the economy, which effect would you expect to be dominant right now?
10. Evaluate each of the following statements. (*Note:* The facts in each case are correct; concentrate on the conclusion that is reached.)
    a. "In 1993, the deficit was larger than in 1991. But interest rates were lower. Therefore, larger deficits do not cause higher interest rates."
    b. "In 1991, we had a huge deficit and a recession. In 1988 and 1989, we had smaller deficits and a stronger economy. Therefore, deficit spending does not stimulate the economy."
    c. "If we compare 1980–1981 with 1991–1992, we find much larger deficits but much lower inflation in the last two years than in the first two. Therefore, it is clear that deficit spending is not inflationary."

Chapter 33

# THE TRADE-OFF BETWEEN INFLATION AND UNEMPLOYMENT

*We must seek to reduce inflation at a lower cost in lost output and unemployment.*

**JIMMY CARTER**

Inflation is now extremely low throughout the industrialized world: about 3 percent in the United States, about 2 percent in France, and about 1 percent in Japan, for example. The early 1990s were also characterized by extremely weak economic performance in most of the advanced economies: the U.S stubbornly refused to snap back from the 1990–1991 recession, Japan suffered its worst slowdown in decades, and Western Europe was mired in a steep slump. ¶ Most economists believe that this conjunction of events is no coincidence. Rather, they insist, the period of slow growth and high unemployment was the price we paid to reduce the rate of inflation. Although some optimists claim that it is possible to reduce inflation without suffering from unemployment, the world clearly paid a heavy price for the disinflation of the early 1990s. Was this price inevitable, or could we have avoided it? That is the question for this chapter. ¶ You may recall from Chapter 1 that the existence of an agonizing trade-off between inflation and unemployment is one of the **12 Ideas For Beyond the Final Exam**. The importance of this trade-off can hardly be overestimated. It is probably the one area of macroeconomics where confusion is most widespread. And because this confusion can have disastrous consequences for the conduct of stabilization policy, the trade-off merits the comprehensive examination that we give it in this chapter.

We begin the chapter by reviewing briefly what we have already learned about inflation. Then we contrast the differing empirical implications of inflation that emanates from rapid growth of aggregate demand versus from slow growth in aggregate supply. We next examine how people's expectations about inflation affect the nature of the trade-off, and consider the special things that can happen if these expectations are "rational"—a term that will be defined precisely. Finally, we discuss some of the political and economic aspects of the trade-off between inflation and unemployment and look into some suggested remedies.

## DEMAND-SIDE INFLATION VERSUS SUPPLY-SIDE INFLATION: A REVIEW

Since this chapter is the capstone of Part 7, we should begin by reviewing some of what we learned about inflation in earlier chapters.

One major cause of inflation, though certainly not the only one, is *excessive growth of aggregate demand*. We know, first of all, that any autonomous increase in spending—whether by consumers, investors, the government, or foreigners—will have a multiplier effect on aggregate demand. So each additional \$1 of $C$ or $I$ or $G$ or $(X - IM)$ will lead to more than \$1 of additional demand. Second, we know that firms normally find it profitable to supply the additional output only at higher prices. Hence, such a stimulus to aggregate demand will normally pull up *both* real output *and* prices.

**Figure 33–1** INFLATION FROM THE DEMAND SIDE

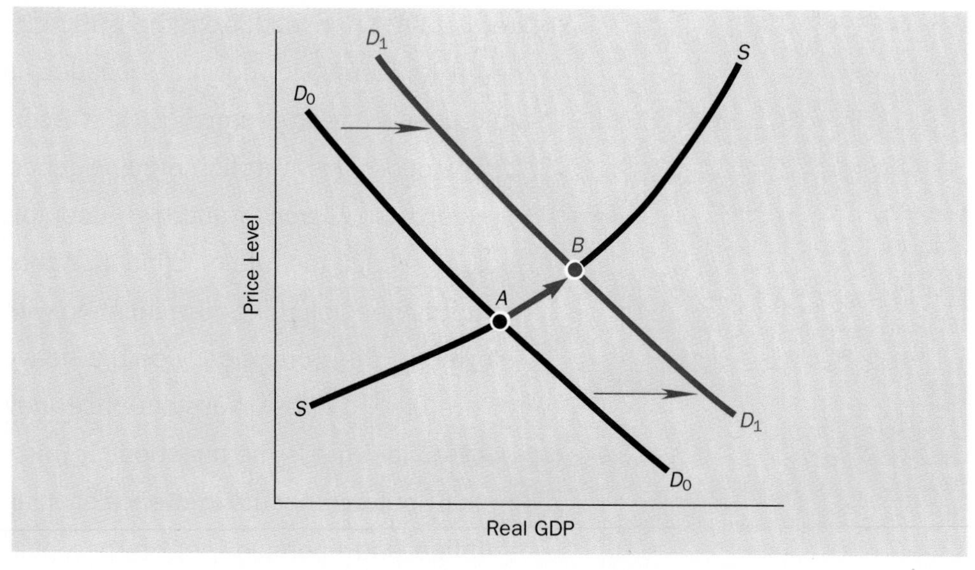


An increase in aggregate demand, whether it comes from consumers, investors, foreigners, or the government, shifts the aggregate demand curve outward from $D_0D_0$ to $D_1D_1$. The economy's equilibrium moves from point $A$ to point $B$. Since point $B$ corresponds to a higher price level than does point $A$, there is inflation (that is, a rising price level) as the economy moves from $A$ to $B$.

Figure 33–2 **INFLATION FROM THE SUPPLY SIDE**

A decrease in aggregate supply—which can be caused by such factors as an autonomous increase in wages, or by an increase in the price of foreign oil—can cause inflation. When the aggregate supply curve shifts to the left, from $S_0S_0$ to $S_1S_1$, the equilibrium point moves from *A* to *B*. Comparing *B* with *A*, we see that the price level is higher, which means there must have been *inflation* (rising prices) in the interim. Notice also that adverse supply shifts make real output decline while prices are rising; that is, they produce *stagflation*.

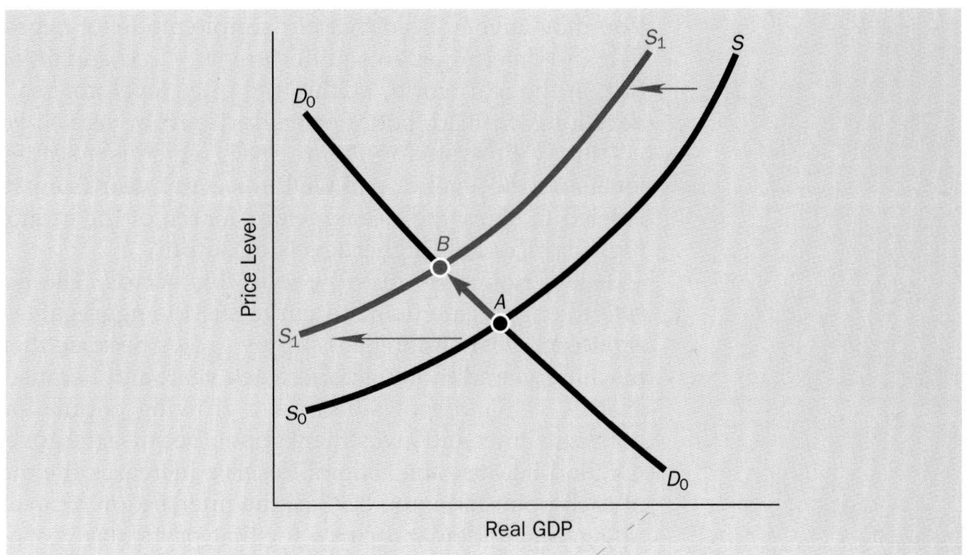


Figure 33–1, which is familiar from earlier chapters, reviews this conclusion. Initially, the economy is at point *A*, where aggregate demand curve $D_0D_0$ intersects aggregate supply curve *SS*. Then something happens to increase demand, and the aggregate demand curve shifts horizontally to $D_1D_1$. The new equilibrium is at point *B*, where both prices and output are higher than they were at *A*.

The slope of the aggregate supply curve measures the amount of inflation that accompanies any specified rise in output and therefore embodies the trade-off between unemployment and inflation. We concluded in the last chapter that this trade-off will be favorable when the economy is operating with underutilized resources of capital and labor. Under such circumstances, firms can expand their operations substantially without running into higher costs. On the other hand, if the stimulus to demand occurs in a fully employed economy, firms will find it difficult to raise output and so will respond mostly by raising prices. Thus, the tradeoff is unfavorable when unemployment is low.

But we have learned in this book (especially in Chapter 27) that inflation need not always emanate from the demand side. Restrictions in the growth of aggregate supply—caused, for example, by an increase in the price of foreign oil—can shift the economy's aggregate supply curve inward. This is illustrated in Figure 33–2, where the aggregate supply curve shifts from $S_0S_0$ to $S_1S_1$, and the economy's equilibrium consequently moves from point *A* to point *B*. Prices rise as output falls. We have *stagflation*.

Thus, while inflation can be initiated from either the *demand* side or the *supply* side of the economy, there is a crucial difference. Demand-side inflation is normally accompanied by rising real GDP (see Figure 33–1), while supply-side inflation may well be accompanied by falling GDP (see Figure 33–2). This is a crucial distinction, as we shall see in this chapter.

## APPLYING THE MODEL TO A GROWING ECONOMY

You may have noticed that our simple model of aggregate supply and aggregate demand determines an equilibrium *price level* and an equilibrium *level of real GDP*. But, in the real world, neither the price level nor real GDP remains constant for very long. Instead, both normally rise from year to year.

This is illustrated in Figure 33–3, which is a scatter diagram of the U.S. price level and the level of real GDP for every year from 1970 to 1992. The points are labeled to show the clear upward march of the economy through time—toward higher prices and higher levels of output.

It is certainly no mystery why this occurs. The normal state of affairs is for *both* the aggregate demand curve *and* the aggregate supply curve to shift to the right each year. Aggregate supply grows because there are more workers, more machinery, and more factories each year, and because technology improves. Aggregate demand grows because a growing population means more demand for both consumer and investment goods, because the government increases its spending, and because the Federal Reserve increases the money supply. We can think of each point in Figure 33–3 as the intersection of an aggregate supply curve and an aggregate demand curve for that particular year. To help you visualize this, the curves for 1980 are sketched in the diagram.

*Figure* **33–3** **THE PRICE LEVEL AND REAL OUTPUT IN THE UNITED STATES, 1970–1992**

This scatter diagram shows, for each year from 1970 to 1992, the price level (GDP deflator) and real GDP for the United States. Clearly the normal state of affairs is for both variables to rise from one year to the next.

SOURCE: U.S. Department of Commerce, Bureau of Economic Analysis.

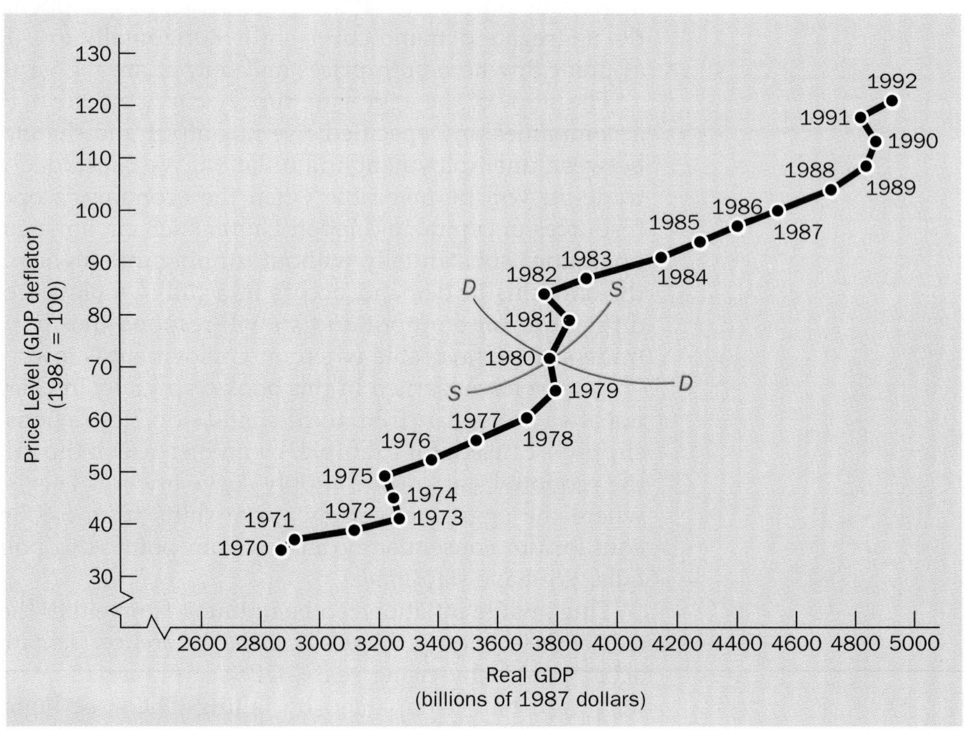

Figure 33–4

**AGGREGATE SUPPLY AND DEMAND ANALYSIS OF A GROWING ECONOMY**

This diagram illustrates how the aggregate supply and demand analysis of earlier chapters can be applied to a real-world economy, in which both the supply curve and the demand curve normally shift outward from one year to the next. In this example, demand curve $D_0D_0$ and supply curve $S_0S_0$ represent the U.S. economy in 1991. Equilibrium was at point *A*, with a price level of 118 and real GDP of \$4860 billion. Demand curve $D_1D_1$ and supply curve $S_1S_1$ represent 1992. During the year, the price index rose by 3 points (about 2.5 percent) and output increased by \$130 billion (or 2.7 percent).

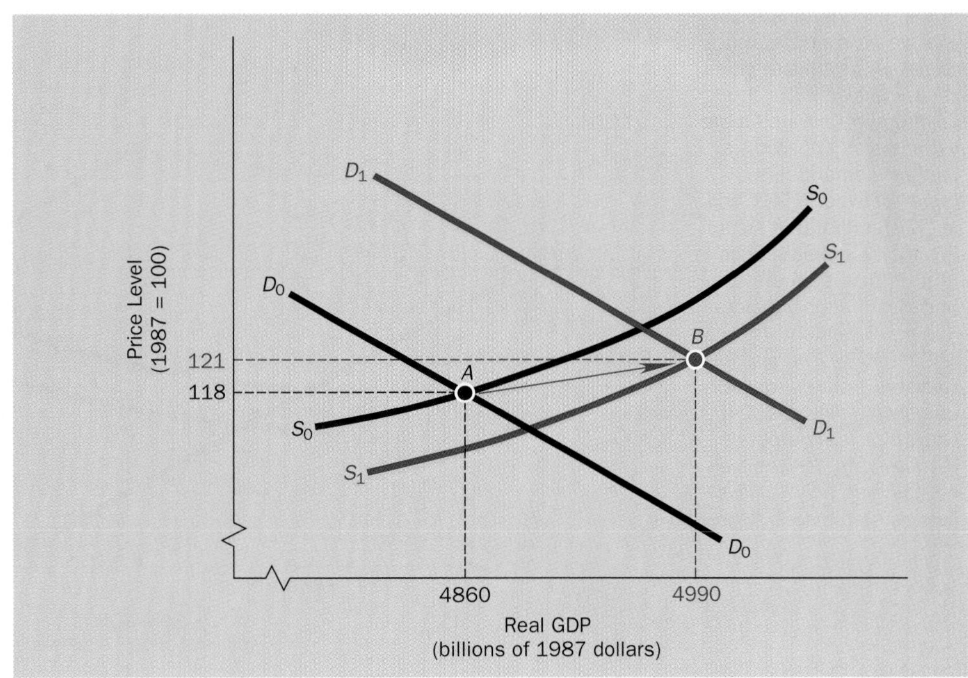


Figure 33–4 illustrates how our theoretical model of aggregate supply and aggregate demand applies to a growing economy. The numbers are chosen so that curves $D_0D_0$ and $S_0S_0$ roughly represent the year 1991, and the curves $D_1D_1$ and $S_1S_1$ roughly represent 1992, except that nice round numbers are used. Thus the equilibrium in 1991 was at point *A*, with a real GDP of \$4860 billion (in 1987 dollars) and a price level of 118, while the equilibrium a year later was at point *B*, with real GDP at \$4990 billion and the price level at 121, or 2.5 percent higher. The blue arrow in the diagram shows how equilibrium moved from 1991 to 1992. It points upward and to the right, meaning that both prices and output increased.

## DEMAND-SIDE INFLATION AND THE PHILLIPS CURVE

Let us now use our theoretical model to rerun history. Suppose that between 1991 and 1992 the aggregate demand curve grew *faster* than it actually did. What difference would this have made for the performance of the national economy? Figure 33–5 provides the answers. Here the demand curve $D_0D_0$ and both supply curves are exactly as they were in the previous diagram, but the demand curve $D_2D_2$ is farther to the right than the demand curve $D_1D_1$ in Figure 33–4. Equilibrium is at point *A* in 1991 and point *C* in 1992. Comparing point *C* in Figure 33–5 with point *B* in Figure 33–4, we see that output would have increased more over the year (\$260 billion versus \$130 billion) and prices would also have increased more

Figure 33–5 THE EFFECTS OF FASTER GROWTH OF AGGREGATE DEMAND

In this hypothetical example, we imagine that because either private citizens spent more or the government pursued more expansionary policies, aggregate demand grew faster between 1991 and 1992 than it did in Figure 33–4. The consequence is that, in this diagram, the price level rises 7 points (almost 6 percent) from 1991 to 1992 compared with the 3 points (or 2.5 percent) in Figure 33–4. Growth of real output is also greater: $260 billion here versus only $130 billion in the previous figure.

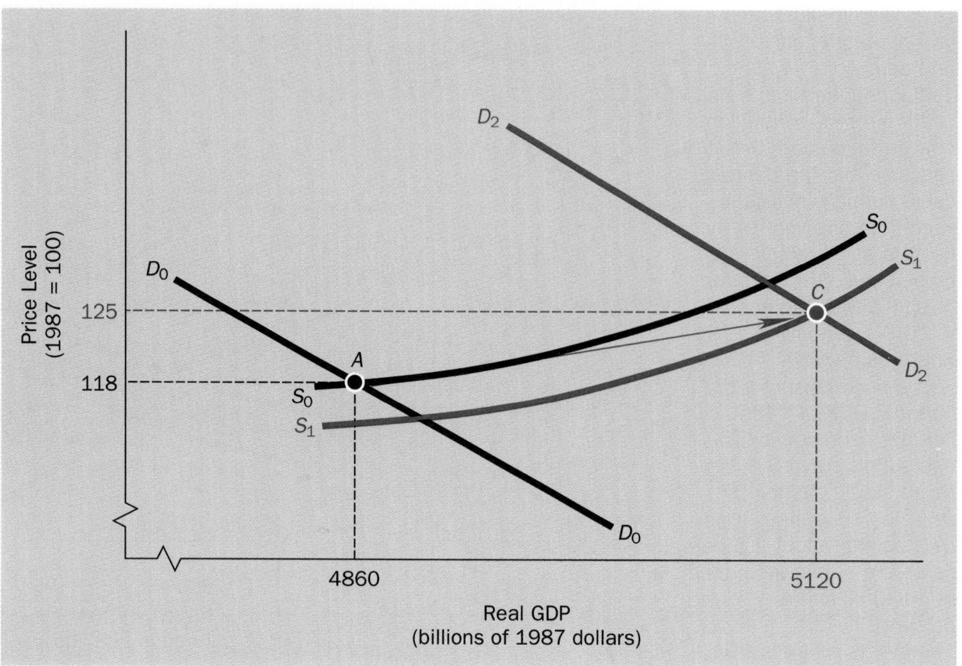


(to 125 instead of 121); that is, there would have been more *inflation*. This is generally what happens when the growth rate of aggregate demand speeds up.

For any given rate of growth of the aggregate supply curve, a faster rate of growth of the aggregate demand curve will lead to more inflation and faster growth of real output.

Figure 33–6 illustrates the opposite case. Here we imagine that the aggregate demand curve shifted out *less* than in Figure 33–4. That is, demand curve $D_3D_3$ in Figure 33–6 is to the left of demand curve $D_1D_1$ in Figure 33–4. The consequence, we see, is that the shift of the economy's equilibrium from 1991 to 1992 (from point *A* to point *E*) would have entailed *less inflation* and *slower growth of real output* than actually took place. This again is generally the case.

For any given rate of growth of the aggregate supply curve, a slower rate of growth of the aggregate demand curve will lead to less inflation and slower growth of real output.

If we put these two findings together, we have a clear prediction from our theory:

If fluctuations in the economy's real growth rate from year to year are caused primarily by variations in the rate at which aggregate demand increases, then the data should show the most rapid inflation occurring when output expands most rapidly and the slowest inflation occurring when output expands most slowly.

Does the theory fit the facts? We will put it to the test in a moment, but first let us translate it into a prediction about the relationship between inflation and unemployment. Faster growth of real output naturally means faster growth in the number of jobs and, hence, *lower unemployment*. Conversely, slower growth of real output means slower growth in the number of jobs and, hence, *higher unemployment*. So we conclude that, if business fluctuations emanate from the demand side, unemployment should be low when inflation is high and inflation should be low when unemployment is high.

Figure 33–7 illustrates this idea. The actual unemployment rate in the United States in 1992 averaged 7.3 percent, and the inflation rate from 1991 to 1992 was about 2.5 percent. This is point *b* in Figure 33–7, which corresponds to equilibrium point *B* in Figure 33–4. The faster growth rate of demand depicted by point *C* in Figure 33–5 would have led to higher inflation and lower unemployment. For the sake of a concrete example, we suppose that unemployment would have been 6.3 percent and inflation would have been 5.9 percent; this is point *c* in Figure 33–7. Point *E* in Figure 33–6 summarized the results of slower growth of aggregate demand: unemployment would have been higher and inflation lower. In Figure 33–7, this is represented by point *e*, with an unemployment rate of 8.3 percent and an inflation rate of 1.3 percent. This figure shows graphically the principal empirical implication of our theoretical model:

If fluctuations in economic activity are primarily caused by variations in the rate at which the aggregate demand curve shifts outward from year to year, then the data should show an inverse relationship between unemployment and inflation, as in Figure 33–7.

**Figure 33–6** **THE EFFECTS OF SLOWER GROWTH OF AGGREGATE DEMAND**

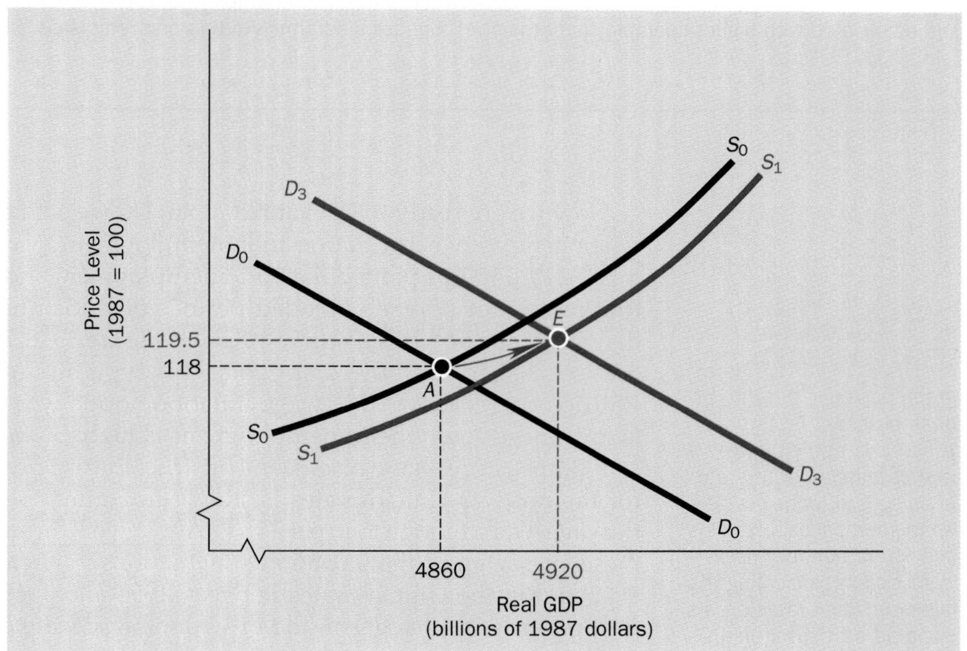


Here, the aggregate demand curve is assumed to shift outward less than it did in Figure 33–4. Consequently, the movement from equilibrium point *A* to equilibrium point *E* from 1991 to 1992 entails a smaller rise in the price level and a smaller increase in real output than actually occurred.

Figure 33–7 ORIGINS OF THE PHILLIPS CURVE

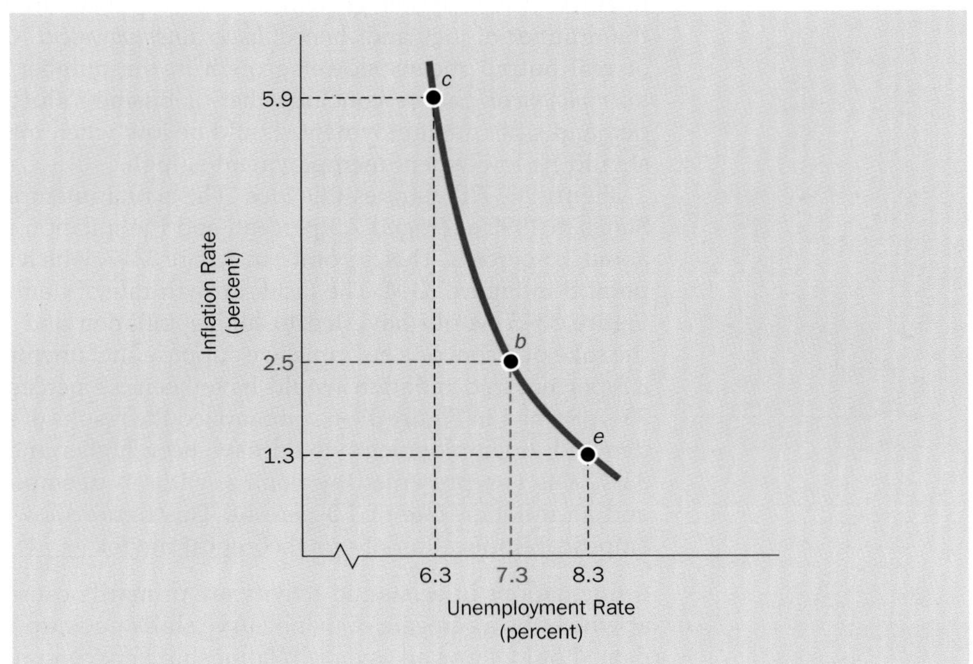


The three previous diagrams indicated three different rates of growth of real GDP between 1991 and 1992 and three different inflation rates. Since each different real growth rate corresponds to a different rate of unemployment, we can put the information contained in the three preceding diagrams together in a scatter diagram to show the relationship between inflation and unemployment. Points *b*, *c*, and *e* in this figure correspond to points *B*, *C*, and *E* in Figures 33–4, 33–5, and 33–6, respectively. The inflation numbers are read directly from the previous three graphs. The unemployment numbers are indicative of the fact that faster growth (Figure 33–5) is associated with lower unemployment (point *c*), while slower growth (Figure 33–6) is associated with higher unemployment (point *e*). Scatter diagrams like this one are called "Phillips curves," after their inventor, A.W. Phillips.

Now we are ready to look at real data. Do we actually observe such an inverse relationship between inflation and unemployment? More than 30 years ago, economist A. W. Phillips plotted data on unemployment and the rate of change of *wages* (not prices) for several extended periods of British history on a series of scatter diagrams, one of which is reproduced as Figure 33–8. He then sketched in a curve that seemed to "fit" the data well. This type of curve, which is now called a **Phillips curve,** shows that wage inflation normally is high when unemployment is low and is low when unemployment is high. So far, so good.

A **PHILLIPS CURVE** is a graph depicting the rate of unemployment on the horizontal axis and either the rate of inflation or the rate of change of money wages on the vertical axis. Phillips curves are normally downward sloping, indicating that higher inflation rates are associated with lower unemployment rates.

Phillips curves have also been constructed for *price* inflation, and one of these for the postwar United States is shown in Figure 33–9. The curve appears to fit the data well, though not perfectly. As viewed through the eyes of our theory, these facts suggest that economic fluctuations in Great Britain between 1861 and 1913 and in the United States between 1954 and 1969 probably were accounted for primarily by changes in the growth of aggregate demand. The simple model of demand-side inflation really does seem to describe what happened.

**Figure 33-8** THE ORIGINAL PHILLIPS CURVE

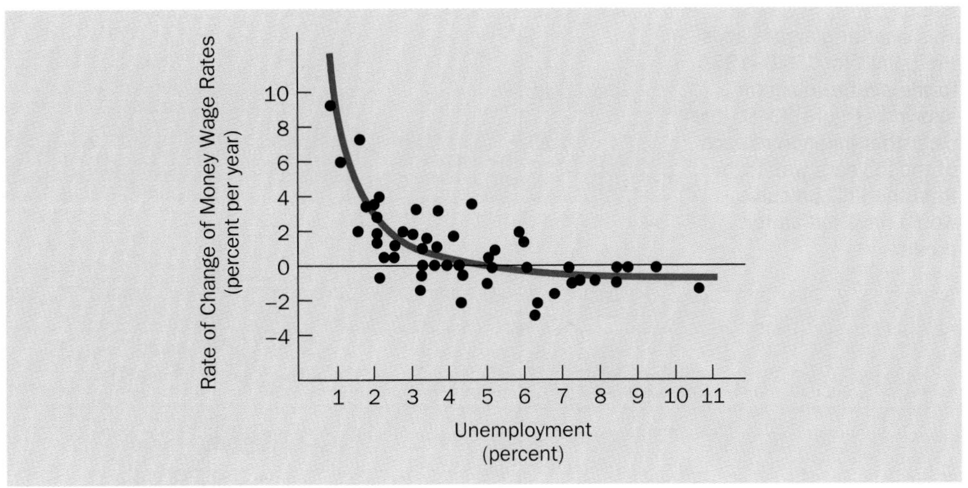


This scatter diagram, reproduced from the original article by A.W. Phillips, shows the rate of change of money wages and the rate of unemployment in Great Britain between 1861 and 1913. Each year is represented by a point in the diagram.

SOURCE: A.W. Phillips, "The Relation Between Unemployment and the Rate of Change of Money Wages in the United Kingdom, 1861–1957." *Economica*, New Series, vol. 25, November 1958.

During the 1960s and early 1970s, economists often thought of the Phillips curve as a "menu" of the choices available to policymakers. In this view, policymakers could opt for low unemployment and high inflation—as in 1969. Or they might prefer higher unemployment coupled with lower inflation—as, for example, in 1961. The Phillips curve, it was thought, described the *quantitative* trade-off between inflation and unemployment. And, for a number of years, it worked rather well.

**Figure 33-9** A PHILLIPS CURVE FOR THE UNITED STATES

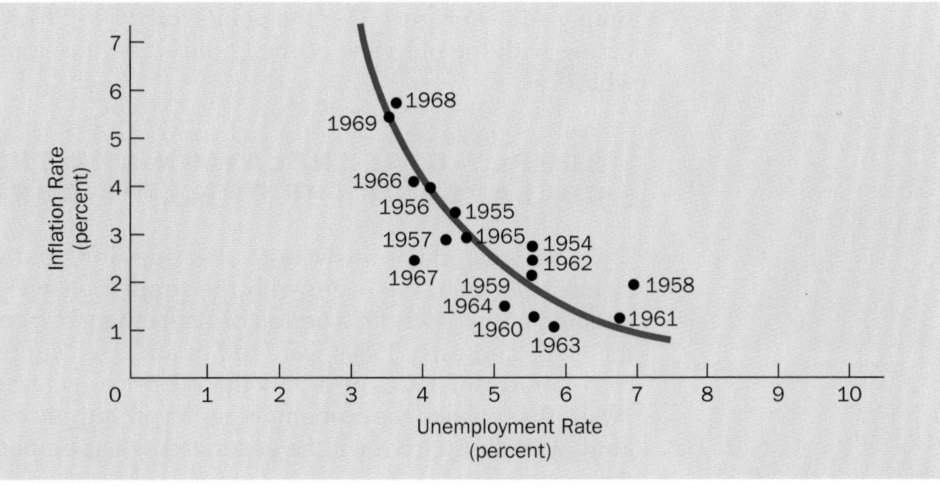


This Phillips curve relates *price* inflation (rather than wage inflation) to the unemployment rate in the United States for the years 1954–1969. Though it misses badly in a few instances (for example, 1958), it generally "fits" the data well.

**A PHILLIPS CURVE FOR THE UNITED STATES?**

This scatter diagram adds the points for 1970–1984 to the scatter diagram shown in Figure 33–9. It is clear that inflation in each of those years was higher than the Phillips curve would have led us to predict.

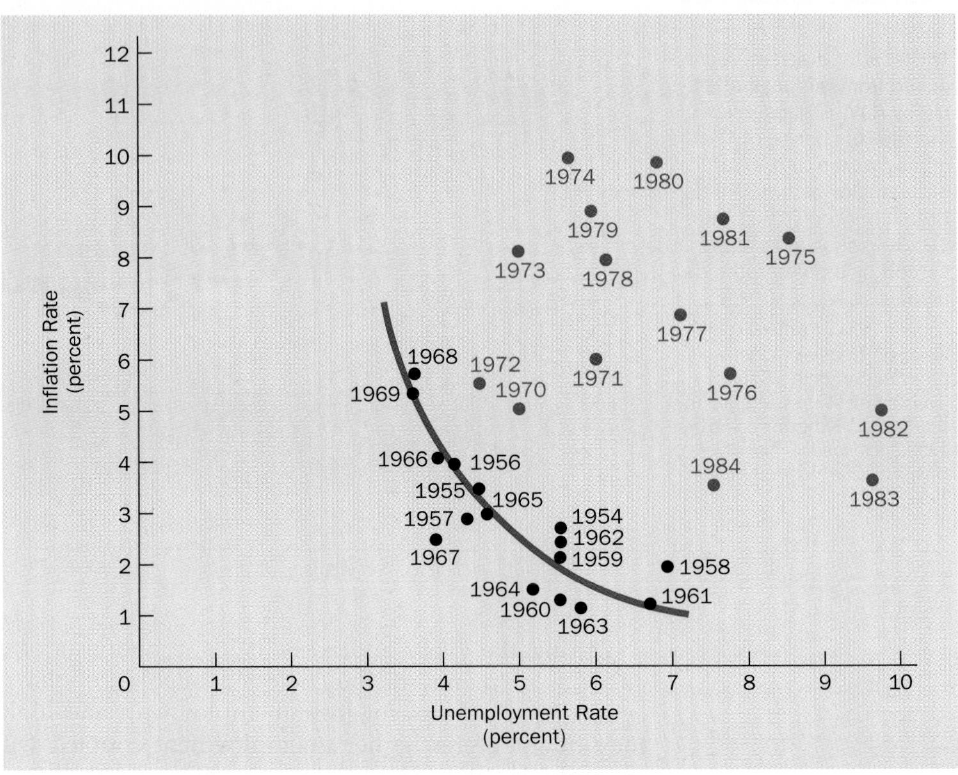


Then something happened. The economy in the 1970s and early 1980s behaved far worse than the Phillips curve shown in Figure 33–9 led economists to expect. In particular, given the unemployment rates in each of those years, inflation was astonishingly high by historical standards. This is shown in Figure 33–10, which simply adds to Figure 33–9 the points for 1970–1984. Clearly something had gone wrong with the old view of the Phillips curve as a menu for policy choices. But what?

## SUPPLY-SIDE INFLATION AND THE COLLAPSE OF THE PHILLIPS CURVE

There are two major answers to this question, and a full explanation contains elements of each. We begin with the simpler answer, which is that much of the inflation of the 1972–1982 period did not emanate from the demand side. Instead, the 1970s and early 1980s were full of adverse "supply shocks"—events like the crop failures of 1972–1973 and the oil price increases of 1973–1974 and 1979–1980—that pushed the economy's aggregate supply curve inward to the left. What kind of Phillips curve will be generated when economic fluctuations come from the supply side?

To find out, let us take the events of 1979 and 1980 as an example. In Figure 33–11, aggregate demand curve $D_0D_0$ and aggregate supply curve $S_0S_0$ represent the economic situation in 1979. Equilibrium was at point *A*, with a price level of 66 and real output of $3797 billion. By 1980, the aggregate demand curve had shifted out to the position indicated by $D_1D_1$, and, under normal conditions, the aggregate supply curve would have shifted out as well. But 1979–1980 was anything but normal. The Iranian revolution led to a shutdown of Iran's oilfields for months and a doubling of the price of oil.

Thus, instead of shifting *outward* as it normally does from one year to the next, the aggregate supply curve shifted *inward* from 1979 to 1980, to $S_1S_1$. The equilibrium for 1980 (point *B* in the figure) therefore wound up to the left of the equilibrium point for 1979. Real output declined slightly and prices—led by energy costs—rose rapidly.

Now, in a growing population with more people looking for jobs each year, a stagnant economy that is not generating new jobs suffers a rise in the unemployment rate. This is precisely what happened in the United States; the unemployment rate averaged 5.8 percent in 1979 and 7.1 percent in 1980. Thus, inflation and unemployment increased at the same time: the Phillips curve basically shifted upward. A general conclusion is that:

If fluctuations in economic activity emanate from the supply side, higher rates of inflation will be associated with higher rates of unemployment, and lower rates of inflation will be associated with lower rates of unemployment.

The instances of major supply shocks during the 1970s stand out clearly in Figure 33–10. (Remember these are *real* data, not textbook examples.) Food prices boomed in 1972–1974 and again in 1978. Energy prices soared in 1973–1974 and again in 1979–1980. Clearly, the inflation and unemployment data generated by the U.S. economy in 1972–1974, and again in 1978–1980, are consistent with our model of supply-side inflation. It was supply shocks, many economists believe, that made the Phillips curve shift.

**Figure 33–11** **STAGFLATION FROM A SUPPLY SHOCK**

Instead of shifting outward as it normally does, the aggregate supply curve shifted inward—from $S_0S_0$ to $S_1S_1$—between 1979 and 1980. Coupled with fairly slow growth of the aggregate demand curve—from $D_0D_0$ in 1979 to $D_1D_1$ in 1980—equilibrium moved from point *A* to point *B*. There was a slight decline of real output, and prices rose rapidly.

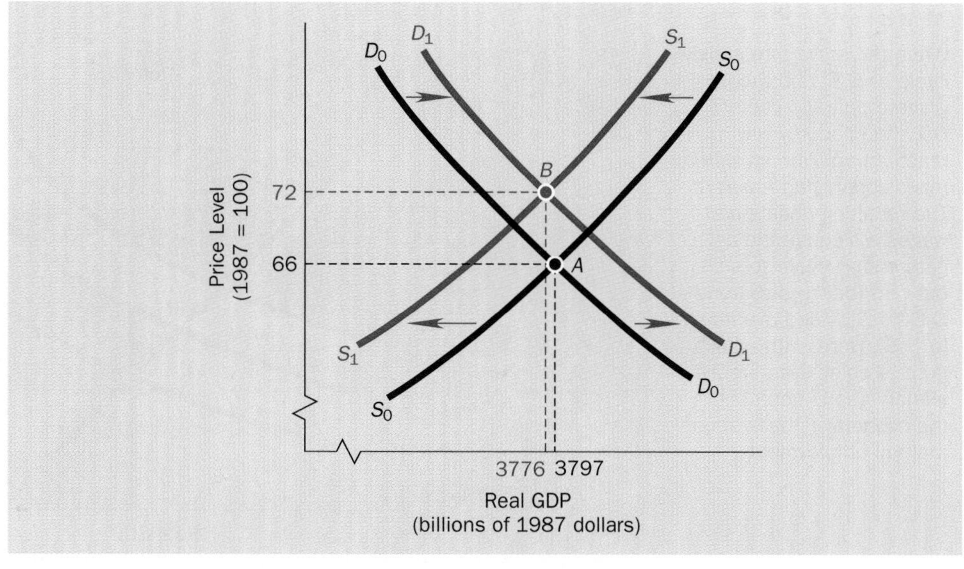

## WHAT THE PHILLIPS CURVE IS NOT

But there is another view of what went wrong in the 1970s. This one holds that policymakers misinterpreted the Phillips curve and tried to pick unsustainable combinations of inflation and unemployment.

Specifically, the Phillips curve is a *statistical relationship* between inflation and unemployment that we expect to emerge *if changes in the growth of aggregate demand are the predominant factor accounting for economic fluctuations*. But the curve was widely misinterpreted as depicting a number of *alternative equilibrium points* that the economy could achieve and from which policymakers could choose.

We can understand the flaw in this reasoning by quickly reviewing an earlier lesson. We know from Chapter 27 that the economy has a **self-correcting mechanism** that will cure both inflations and recessions *eventually* even if the government does nothing. Why is this relevant here? Because it tells us that many combinations of output and prices cannot be maintained indefinitely. Some will "self-destruct." For example, if the economy finds itself far away from the normal full-employment level of unemployment, forces will be set in motion that tend to erode the inflationary or recessionary gap.

Figure 33–12 depicts the case of a recessionary gap where aggregate supply curve $S_0S_0$ intersects aggregate demand curve *DD* at point *A*. With equilibrium output well below potential GDP, there is unused industrial capacity and unsold output. So firms will not raise prices much. At the same time, the availability of unemployed workers eager for jobs limits the rate at which labor can push up wage rates. But wages are the main component of business costs, so when wages decline (relative to what they would have been without a recession) so do costs. And lower costs stimulate greater production. This idea is shown in Figure 33–12 as an outward shift of the aggregate supply curve—from $S_0S_0$ to $S_1S_1$.

**Figure 33–12** THE ELIMINATION OF A RECESSIONARY GAP

When the aggregate supply curve is $S_0S_0$ and the aggregate demand curve is *DD*, the economy will reach an equilibrium with a recessionary gap (point *A*). The resulting deflation of wages will cause the aggregate supply curve to shift outward (downward) from $S_0S_0$ to $S_1S_1$ and eventually to $S_2S_2$. Here, with equilibrium at point *C*, the recessionary gap is gone and the economy is back at normal full employment.

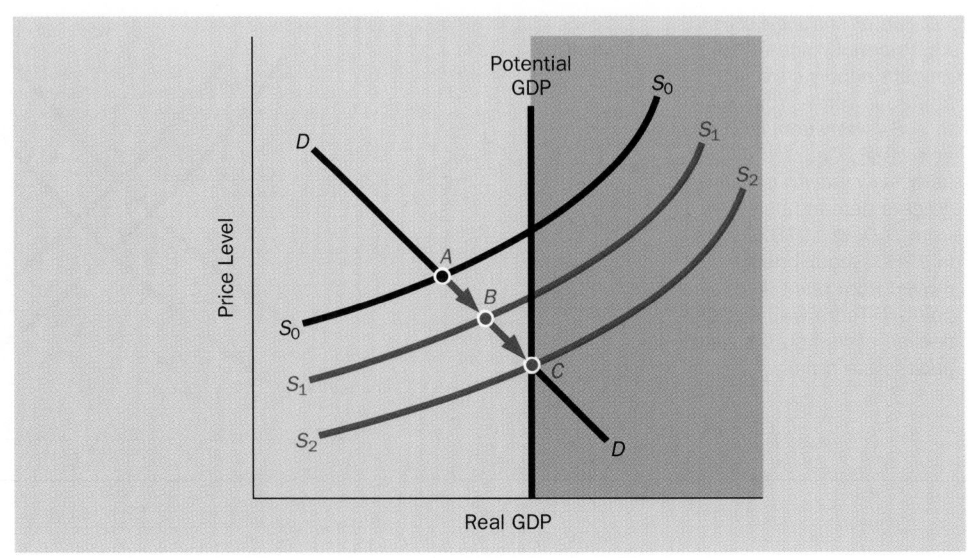

Figure 33–13 **THE VERTICAL LONG-RUN PHILLIPS CURVE**

In the long run, points like *a*, where unemployment is above the normal "full-employment" unemployment rate, are unsustainable. The economy's natural self-correcting mechanism (which was described in Figure 33–12) will erode the recessionary gap by reducing both inflation and unemployment. In the diagram, this will force the economy toward a point like *c*. The long-run choices, therefore, are among points like *c* and *f*, which constitute what is called the vertical (long-run) Phillips curve, not among points like *d* and *a* on the downward-sloping (short-run) Phillips curve.

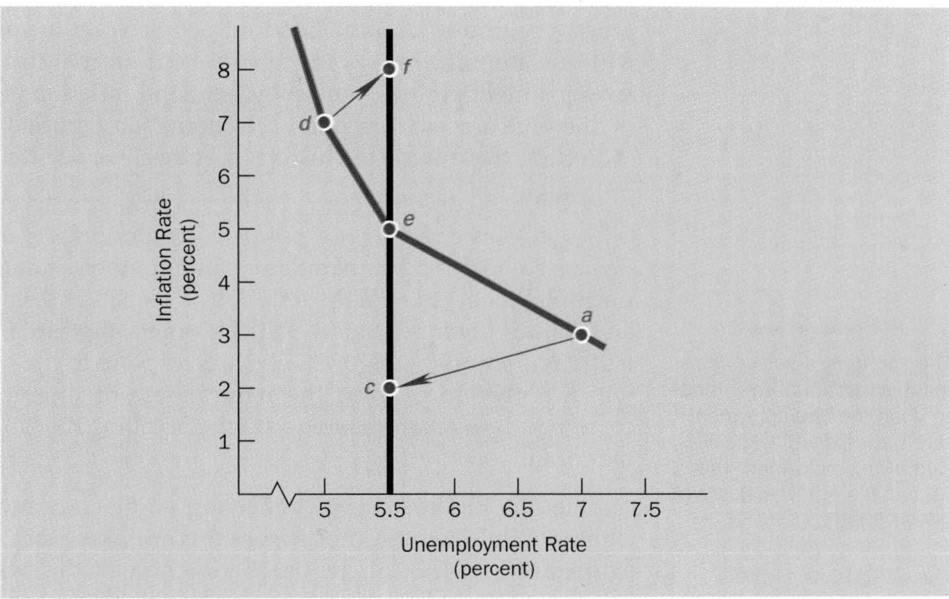


As can be seen in the figure, the outward shift of the aggregate supply curve brought on by the recession pushes equilibrium output up as the economy moves from point *A* to point *B*. Thus the size of the recessionary gap begins to shrink. This process continues until the aggregate supply curve reaches the position indicated by $S_2S_2$ in Figure 33–12. Here wages have fallen enough to eliminate the recessionary gap, and the economy has reached a full-employment equilibrium at point *C*.[1]

We can relate this to our discussion of the origins of the Phillips curve with the help of Figure 33–13, which is a hypothetical Phillips curve. Point *a* in Figure 33–13 corresponds to point *A* in Figure 33–12: it shows the initial recessionary gap with unemployment (assumed to be 7 percent) above full employment, which we assume to occur at 5.5 percent.

But we have just seen that point *A* in Figure 33–12—and therefore also point *a* in Figure 33–13—is not sustainable. The economy tends to rid itself of the recessionary gap through the disinflation process we have just described. The adjustment path from *A* to *C* depicted in Figure 33–12 would appear on our Phillips curve diagram as a movement toward less inflation and less unemployment—something like the blue arrow from point *a* to point *c* in Figure 33–13.

Similarly, points representing inflationary gaps—such as point *d* in Figure 33–13—are not sustainable. They are also gradually eliminated by the self-correcting mechanism that we studied in Chapter 27. Wages are forced up by the

[1]This simple analysis assumes that the aggregate demand curve does not move during the adjustment period. If it is shifting to the right, the recessionary gap will disappear even faster, but inflation will not slow down as much. EXERCISE: Construct the diagram for this case by adding a shift in the aggregate demand curve to Figure 33–12.

abnormally low unemployment, and this in turn pushes prices higher. Higher prices deter investment spending by forcing up interest rates and deter consumer spending by lowering the purchasing power of consumer wealth. The inflationary process continues until the amount people want to spend is brought into balance with the amount firms want to supply at normal full employment. During such an adjustment period, unemployment and inflation are both rising—as indicated by the blue arrow from point *d* to point *f* in Figure 33–13.

Putting these two conclusions together, we see that:

On a Phillips curve diagram, neither points corresponding to an inflationary gap (like *d* in Figure 33–13) nor points corresponding to a recessionary gap (like *a* in Figure 33–13) can be maintained indefinitely. Inflationary gaps lead to rising unemployment and rising inflation. Recessionary gaps lead to falling inflation and falling unemployment. All the points that are sustainable in the long run (such as *c*, *e*, and *f* in Figure 33–13) correspond to the same rate of unemployment, which is therefore called the **natural rate of unemployment**. The natural rate corresponds to what we have so far been calling the "full-employment" unemployment rate.

The economy's self-correcting mechanism always tends to push the unemployment rate back toward a specific rate of unemployment that we call the **NATURAL RATE OF UNEMPLOYMENT**.

The **VERTICAL (LONG-RUN) PHILLIPS CURVE** shows the menu of inflation/unemployment choices available to society in the long run. It is a vertical straight line at the natural rate of unemployment.

Thus the Phillips curve connecting points *d*, *e*, and *a* is not a menu of policy choices. While we can move from a point like *e* to a point like *d* by stimulating aggregate demand sufficiently, there is no way that we can stay at point *d*. Unemployment cannot be kept this low indefinitely. Instead, policymakers must choose from among points like *c*, *e*, and *f*, all of which are vertically above one another at the natural rate of unemployment. For rather obvious reasons, the line connecting these points has been dubbed the **vertical (long-run) Phillips curve**. It is this vertical Phillips curve, connecting points like *e* and *f*, that represents the true long-run menu of policy choices. We thus conclude:

**THE TRADE-OFF BETWEEN INFLATION AND UNEMPLOYMENT**

In the short-run, it is possible to "ride up the Phillips curve" toward lower levels of unemployment by stimulating aggregate demand. Conversely, by restricting the growth of demand, it is possible to "ride down the Phillips curve" toward lower rates of inflation (see, for example, point *a* in Figure 33–13). Thus there is a *trade-off between unemployment and inflation* in the short run. Stimulating demand will improve the unemployment picture but worsen inflation; restricting demand will lower inflation but aggravate the unemployment problem. ¶ However, *there is no such trade-off in the long run.* The economy's self-correcting mechanism ensures that unemployment eventually returns to the "natural rate," no matter what happens to aggregate demand. In the long run, faster growth of demand leads only to higher inflation, not to lower unemployment; and slower growth of demand leads only to lower inflation, not to higher unemployment.

## FIGHTING UNEMPLOYMENT WITH FISCAL AND MONETARY POLICY

Now let us apply this analysis to a concrete policy problem, one that has troubled many presidents including Ronald Reagan in 1981 and Bill Clinton in 1993. How, if at all, should the government's ability to manage aggregate demand through fiscal and monetary policy be used to combat unemployment?

To create an example that comes close to the one inherited by President Clinton in early 1993, imagine that a new president takes office when the inflation rate is about 3 percent and the unemployment rate is about 7 percent—point *a* in Figure 33–13. Suppose he views 7 percent unemployment as intolerably high. Should he adopt a policy of boosting the growth of aggregate demand by expansionary fiscal and monetary policies? Let us consider the costs and benefits.

Suppose first that nothing is done. The economy's self-correcting mechanism will start into motion and gradually erode the recessionary gap that point *a* represents. Both unemployment and inflation will decline gradually as the economy moves along the blue arrow from point *a* to point *c* in Figure 33–13. Eventually, the diagram shows, the economy will return to the natural rate of unemployment (5.5 percent) and inflation will fall from 3 percent to 2 percent.

The eventual outcome is quite satisfactory—lower unemployment and lower inflation. But it may take an agonizingly long time to get there. Suppose now that the president is impatient and wants to see unemployment decline faster. Some combination of expansionary fiscal and monetary policy can push the economy up the short-run Phillips curve from point *a* toward point *e* in Figure 33–13. Faster economic growth will push unemployment down to 5.5 percent more rapidly, which will make the president (and the voters) happy. But it will also short-circuit the disinflation process that would otherwise take place. So inflation will remain near 3 percent.

This, then, is the choice: Wait patiently while the economy's self-correcting mechanism pulls unemployment down to the natural rate—leading to a long-run equilibrium like point *c* in Figure 33–13. Or rush the process along with expansionary stabilization policy—and wind up with the same unemployment rate but higher inflation. In what sense, then, do policymakers face a *trade-off* between inflation and unemployment? The answer is that:

The cost of reducing unemployment more rapidly by expansionary fiscal and monetary policies is a permanently higher inflation rate.

Figures 33–14 and 33–15 are intended to give the flavor of what the real menu of choices looks like to a president considering whether or not to fight unemployment aggressively. Figure 33–14 contrasts the behavior of the unemployment rate over time under a "passive policy," which simply relies on the economy's self-correcting mechanism, with the behavior under an extremely "activist policy," which makes the unemployment rate jump down to 5.5 percent immediately.

If nothing is done, unemployment will gradually decline from 7 percent to 5.5 percent, as shown by the black "passive policy" path in Figure 33–14. This corresponds to the case where the economy moves from point *a* to point *c* in Figure 33–13.

On the other hand, if a super-activist stabilization policy raises aggregate demand so much that unemployment drops to the natural rate immediately, the economy will follow the blue "activist policy" path in Figure 33–14.[2]

The shaded area in the figure summarizes the difference between these two paths and therefore depicts the payoff to anti-unemployment policy. But there are also costs.

---

[2]This option is unrealistic. More realistic options would lie between the two paths shown in Figure 33–14.

*Figure* **33–14** **THE PAYOFF TO ANTI-UNEMPLOYMENT POLICY**

If expansionary fiscal and monetary policy are used to speed up economic growth ("activist policy" path), the unemployment rate will fall more quickly than if we just rely on the economy's self-correcting mechanism ("passive policy" path). In this example, both paths wind up at 5.5 percent unemployment, the presumed natural rate, but the blue "activist policy" path gets there sooner. The shaded area indicates the gains that the policy has reaped on the unemployment front.

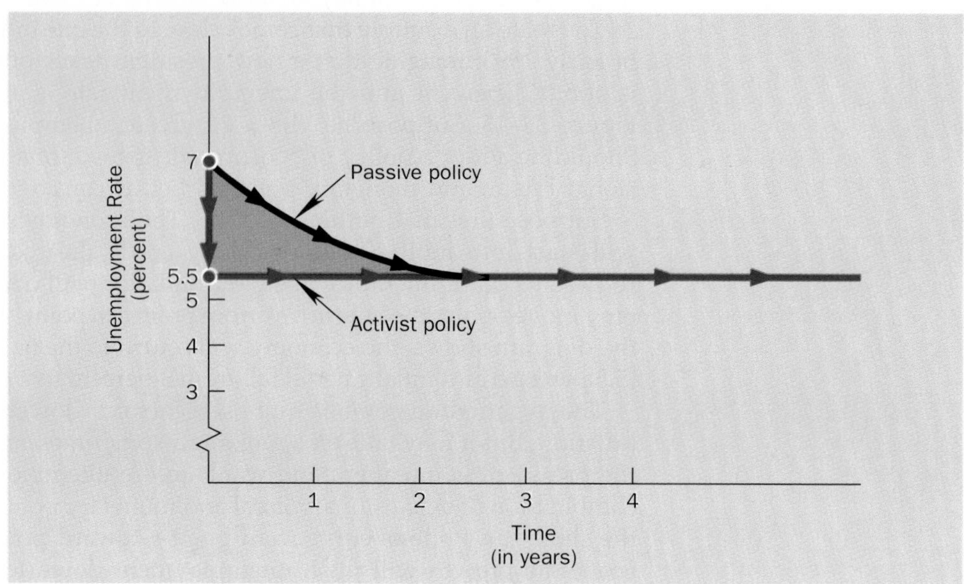


Figure 33–15 gives a rough impression of how the inflation rate might behave under the two alternative policies. The "passive policy" shows inflation drifting down because the unemployment rate remains above 5.5 percent, which is the natural rate, for a long time. The activist policy pushes the unemployment rate down to 5.5 percent immediately, so inflation does not decline. The shaded area therefore measures the inflationary costs of getting unemployment down faster.

Notice the differences in timing between the shaded areas of Figures 33–14 and 33–15. The gains on the unemployment front are transitory—though that does not necessarily make them unimportant, for it may mean that millions of people find work sooner. But the inflationary costs are permanent.

## WHAT SHOULD BE DONE?

Should the government pay the inflationary costs of fighting unemployment? When the benefits depicted in Figure 33–14 are balanced against the costs shown in Figure 33–15, have we made a good bargain? The Clinton administration apparently did not think so. Perhaps because the budget deficit it inherited was already so high, it decided not to use fiscal policy to expand demand.

How do policymakers make such decisions? Our analysis highlights three critical issues on which the answer depends.

### THE COSTS OF INFLATION AND UNEMPLOYMENT

We spent an entire chapter (Chapter 23) examining the social costs of inflation and unemployment. Most of the costs of the extra unemployment depicted in Figure 33–14, we concluded, are easily translated into dollars and cents. Basically, we need only estimate the real GDP that is lost each year. However, the costs of

*Figure* 33–15 **THE COST OF ANTI-UNEMPLOYMENT POLICY**

The unemployment gains depicted in the preceding figure do not come to us without cost. The expansionary policy prevents inflation from falling (blue "activist policy" path) as it would under the "passive policy" of relying on the self-correcting mechanism. The shaded area indicates the legacy of extra inflation that we inherit as a side-effect of bringing unemployment down sooner.

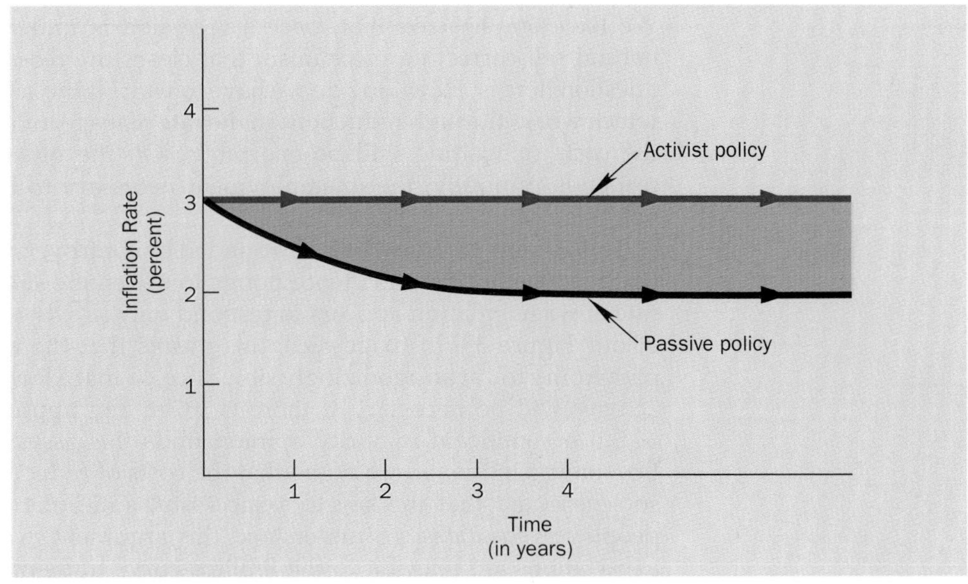


the higher inflation shown in Figure 33–15 are harder to measure. Thus there is considerable controversy over the costs and benefits of using demand management to fight unemployment.

Some economists and public figures, including Federal Reserve Chairman Alan Greenspan, believe that inflation is extremely costly. They may therefore deem it unwise to accept the trade-off embodied in Figures 33–14 and 33–15 in order to get the unemployment rate down faster. As just noted, the Clinton administration apparently agreed in 1993.[3] But politicians tend to have different attitudes when elections are near.

## THE POSITION OF THE ECONOMY

We have stated several times in this book that the shape of the economy's aggregate supply curve, and hence the shape of the short-run Phillips curve, depends on the degree of resource utilization. If resources are virtually fully employed, the aggregate supply curve (and thus the Phillips curve) will be steep, which means that the inflationary costs of expansionary policy will be substantial and the unemployment gains minimal. On the other hand, if there is a great deal of unemployed labor and unutilized industrial capacity, the aggregate supply curve (and hence the short-run Phillips curve) may be nearly horizontal. In that case, unemployment can be reduced a great deal with little cost in terms of higher inflation. The Phillips curves we have drawn in this chapter have this characteristic shape.

Because the Phillips curve is shaped this way, the trade-off for unemployment-fighters looks more favorable when markets are slack and less favorable when they are tight.

---

[3]In fact, the large budget deficit undoubtedly played a bigger role in the Clinton administration's decision not to use expansionary fiscal policy.

### THE EFFICIENCY OF THE ECONOMY'S SELF-CORRECTING MECHANISM

We have emphasized that, once a recession is underway, it is the economy's natural self-correcting mechanism that closes the recessionary gap. The obvious question here is: How long do we have to wait? If the self-correcting mechanism—which works through reductions in the rate of wage inflation—is slow and halting, the costs of waiting will be enormous. On the other hand, if wage inflation responds promptly, the unemployment necessary to bring down inflation may not be great.

This is another issue that is surrounded by controversy. Most economists believe that the weight of the evidence points to extremely sluggish wage behavior. The rate of wage inflation appears to respond only slowly to economic slack. In terms of our Figure 33–13 (page 833), this means that the economy will traverse the path from *a* to *c* at an agonizingly slow pace, so that a long period of weak economic activity will be necessary if there is to be any appreciable effect on inflation.

But a significant minority opinion finds this assessment far too pessimistic. Economists in this group argue that the costs of reducing inflation are not nearly so severe and that the key to a successful anti-inflation policy is its effects on people's *expectations*. To understand this argument, we must first examine why expectations are relevant to the Phillips-curve trade-off.

## INFLATIONARY EXPECTATIONS AND THE PHILLIPS CURVE

Recall from Chapter 27 that the main reason why the economy's aggregate supply curve slopes upward—that is, why output increases as the price level rises—is that businesses typically purchase labor and other inputs under long-term contracts that fix the cost of the input in *money* terms. (The money wage rate is the clearest example.) If such contracts are in force when prices of goods go up, then *real* wages fall. Labor therefore becomes cheaper in real terms, which persuades businesses to expand employment and output. Buying cheaply and selling dearly is, after all, the route to higher profits.

Table 33–1 illustrates how this works in a concrete example. We suppose that workers and firms agree today that the money wage to be paid a year from now

**Table 33–1 MONEY AND REAL WAGES UNDER UNEXPECTED INFLATION**

| INFLATION RATE (percent) | PRICE LEVEL ONE YEAR FROM NOW | MONEY WAGE ONE YEAR FROM NOW (dollars per hour) | REAL WAGE ONE YEAR FROM NOW (dollars per hour) |
|---|---|---|---|
| 0 | 100 | 10.00 | 10.00 |
| 2 | 102 | 10.00 | 9.80 |
| 4 | 104 | 10.00 | 9.62 |
| 6 | 106 | 10.00 | 9.43 |

*NOTE*: Each real wage figure is obtained by dividing the $10 nominal wage by the corresponding price level a year later and multiplying by 100. Thus, for example, when the inflation rate is 4 percent, the real wage at the end of the year is ($10/104) × 100 = $9.62.

**Table 33–2 MONEY AND REAL WAGES UNDER EXPECTED INFLATION**

| EXPECTED INFLATION RATE (percent) | EXPECTED PRICE LEVEL ONE YEAR FROM NOW | MONEY WAGE ONE YEAR FROM NOW (dollars per hour) | EXPECTED REAL WAGE ONE YEAR FROM NOW (dollars per hour) |
|---|---|---|---|
| 0 | 100 | 10.00 | 10.00 |
| 4 | 104 | 10.40 | 10.00 |
| 8 | 108 | 10.80 | 10.00 |
| 12 | 112 | 11.20 | 10.00 |

will be $10 per hour. The table then shows the real wage corresponding to each alternative rate of inflation. Clearly, the higher the inflation rate, the higher the price level at the end of the year and the lower the real wage.

Lower real wages provide an incentive for the firm to increase output, as we have just noted. But lower real wages also impose losses of purchasing power on workers. Thus, there is a sense in which workers are "cheated" by inflation if they sign a contract specifying a fixed money wage in an inflationary environment.

Many economists doubt that workers will sign such contracts *if they can see inflation coming*. Would it not be wiser, these economists ask, to insist on being compensated for inflation in advance? After all, firms should be willing to offer higher money wages if they expect inflation, because they realize that higher money wages need not imply higher *real* wages. Table 33–2 illustrates how this can be done. For example, if 4 percent inflation is expected, the contract could stipulate that the wage rate be increased to $10.40 (which is 4 percent more than $10) at the end of the year. That would keep the real wage at $10, the same as it would be under zero inflation. The other money wage figures in Table 33–2 are derived similarly.

If workers and firms behave this way, and forecast inflation accurately, then the real wage will not decline as the price level rises. Instead, prices and wages will go up together, leaving the real wage unchanged. Workers will not lose from inflation, and firms will not gain. (In the table, the expected future real wage is $10 per hour regardless of the expected rate of inflation.) But then there would be no reason for firms to raise production when the price level rises. In a word, the aggregate supply curve would become *vertical*. In general:

If workers can see inflation coming, and if they receive compensation for it in advance so that inflation does not erode *real* wages, then the economy's aggregate supply curve will not slope upward. It will be a vertical line at the level of output corresponding to potential GDP.

Such a curve is shown in part (a) of Figure 33–16. Since we derived the Phillips curve from the aggregate supply curve earlier in the chapter, it follows that even the *short-run* Phillips curve would be vertical under these circumstances (see part [b] of Figure 33–16).[4]

If this analysis is correct, it has profound implications for the costs and benefits of inflation fighting. To see this, refer back to Figure 33–13 on page 833, and use the graph to depict the strategy of fighting inflation by causing a recession. In order

[4]See Discussion Question 7 at the end of the chapter.

Figure 33–16 A VERTICAL AGGREGATE SUPPLY CURVE AND THE CORRESPONDING VERTICAL PHILLIPS CURVE

If workers foresee inflation, and if they also receive full compensation for it in advance, then inflation will no longer erode real wages. In that case, firms will have no incentive to raise production as prices rise, and the aggregate supply curve will be vertical as in part (a). Since we derived the short-run Phillips curve from the aggregate supply curve, the short-run Phillips curve will also become vertical (part [b]).

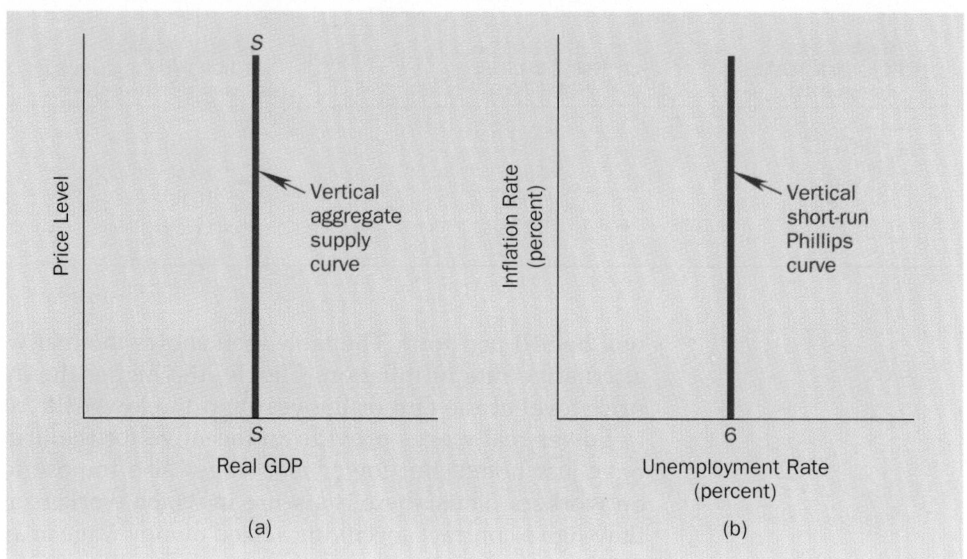


to move from point *e* (representing 5 percent inflation) to point *c* (representing 2 percent inflation), the economy must take a long and unpleasant detour through point *a*. Specifically, contractionary policies must push the economy down the Phillips curve toward point *a* before the self-correcting mechanism takes over and moves the economy from *a* to *c*. In other words, we must endure a recession to reduce inflation.

But what if even the *short-run* Phillips curve were *vertical* rather than downward sloping? Then this unpleasant recessionary detour would not be necessary. It would be possible for inflation to fall without unemployment rising. The economy could jump directly from point *e* to point *c*.

Is this analysis correct? Can we really slay the inflationary dragon so painlessly? Not necessarily, for our discussion of expectations so far has made at least one unrealistic assumption: that inflation can be predicted accurately. Under this assumption, as Table 33–2 shows, real wages are unaffected by inflation—leaving the aggregate supply curve vertical, even in the short run.

But forecasts of inflation are often inaccurate. Suppose workers underestimate inflation. For example, suppose they expect 4 percent inflation but actually get 6 percent. Then real wages will decline by 2 percent. More generally, real wages will fall if workers underestimate inflation *at all*. The effect of inflation on real wages will be somewhere in between that shown in Tables 33–1 and 33–2.[5] So firms will retain some incentive to raise production as the price level rises. The aggregate supply curve will remain upward sloping. We thus conclude that:

[5]To make sure you understand why, construct a version of Table 33–2 based on the assumption that workers expect 4 percent inflation (and hence set next year's wage at $10.40 per hour), regardless of what the actual rate of inflation is. If you do this correctly, your table will show that higher inflation leads to lower real wages, as in Table 33–1.

The short-run aggregate supply curve is *vertical* when inflation is predicted accurately, but *upward sloping* when inflation is underestimated. Thus, only an *unexpectedly* high inflation will raise output, because only unexpected inflation reduces real wages. (To see this, compare Tables 33–1 and 33–2.) Similarly, only an *unexpected* decline in inflation will lead to a recession.

Since people often fail to anticipate changes in inflation correctly, this seems to leave our earlier analysis of the Phillips curve almost intact. And, indeed, most economists nowadays believe that the Phillips curve is downward sloping in the short run but vertical in the long run.

## THE THEORY OF RATIONAL EXPECTATIONS

However, a vocal minority of economists disagrees. This group, believers in the hypothesis of *rational expectations,* insists that the Phillips curve is vertical even in the short run. To explain their point of view, we must first explain what rational expectations are. Then we will be in a position to understand why rational expectations have such radical implications for the trade-off between inflation and unemployment.

### WHAT ARE *RATIONAL* EXPECTATIONS?

In many economic contexts, people must formulate expectations about what the future will bring. For example, those who invest in the stock market need to forecast the future prices of the stocks they buy and sell. And we have just discussed why workers and businesses may want to forecast future prices before agreeing on a money wage. **Rational expectations** is a controversial hypothesis about how such forecasts are made.

**RATIONAL EXPECTATIONS** are forecasts which, while not necessarily correct, are the best that can be made given the available data. Rational expectations, therefore, cannot err systematically. If expectations are rational, forecasting errors are pure random numbers.

As used by economists, a forecast (an "expectation") of a future variable is considered rational if the forecaster makes *optimal* use of all relevant information that is *available.* Let us elaborate on the italicized words in this definition, using as an example a hypothetical stock market investor who has rational expectations.

First, proponents of rational expectations recognize that *information is limited.* An investor interested in buying General Motors stock would like to know how much profit the company will make in the coming years. Armed with such information, she could predict the future price of GM stock more accurately. But that information is simply not available. Her forecast of the future price of GM stock is not "irrational" just because she does not know GM's future profits. On the other hand, if GM stock normally goes down on Fridays and up on Mondays, she should be aware of this fact.

Next we have the word *optimal.* As used by economists, this means using proper statistical inference to process all the relevant information that is available before making a forecast. In a word, to have rational expectations, your forecasts do not have to be correct; but they cannot have systematic errors that could be avoided by applying better statistical methods. This requirement, while exacting, is not quite as outlandish as it may seem. A good billiards player makes expert use of the laws of physics even without understanding the theory. Similarly, an experienced stock market investor may make good use of information even without formal training in statistics.

## RATIONAL EXPECTATIONS AND THE TRADE-OFF

Let us now see how the hypothesis of rational expectations has been used to deny that there exists any trade-off between inflation and unemployment—even in the short run.

Although they recognize that inflation cannot always be predicted accurately, rational expectationists insist that workers will not make *systematic* errors. The preceding argument about expectations tacitly assumed that workers normally *underestimate* inflation when it is rising. Advocates of rational expectations deny that this is possible. Workers, they argue, will always make the best possible forecast of inflation, using all the latest data and the best available economic models. Such forecasts will sometimes be too high and sometimes be too low; but they will not err systematically in one direction or the other—regardless of whether inflation is rising or falling. Consequently:

If expectations are rational, the difference between the *actual* rate of inflation and the *expected* rate of inflation (the forecasting error) must be a pure random number.

Now recall that the argument in the previous section concluded that employment is affected by inflation only to the extent that inflation *differs* from what was expected. But, under rational expectations, no *predictable* change in inflation can make the *expected* rate of inflation deviate from the *actual* rate of inflation. Hence, according to the rational expectations hypothesis, unemployment will always remain at the natural rate—except for random, and therefore totally unpredictable, gyrations due to forecasting errors. Thus:

If expectations are rational, the inflation rate can be reduced without the need for a period of high unemployment because the short-run Phillips curve is vertical.

According to the rational expectations view, the government's ability to manipulate aggregate demand gives it no ability to control real output and unemployment because the aggregate supply curve is vertical—even in the short run. (To see why, experiment by moving an aggregate demand curve when the aggregate supply curve is vertical, as in Figure 33–16[a].) Any *predictable* change in aggregate demand will lead to a change in the expected rate of inflation, and hence will leave real wages unaffected.

The government therefore can influence output only by making *unexpected* changes in aggregate demand. But, according to the rational expectations hypothesis, this is not easy to do because people understand what policymakers are up to. If the monetary and fiscal authorities typically react to high inflation by reducing aggregate demand, people will soon come to anticipate this reaction. And anticipated reductions in aggregate demand do not cause *unexpected* changes in inflation.

## AN EVALUATION

Since proponents of rational expectations believe that inflation can be reduced without losses of output, they tend to be hawks in the war against inflation. Though the theory has attracted many adherents, most economists still believe there is a short-run trade-off between inflation and unemployment. There are several reasons for this.

1. Many contracts for labor and other raw materials cover such long periods of time that the expectations on which they were based, while rational at the time, may appear quite irrational from today's point of view. For example, when three-year labor contracts were drawn up late in 1980, inflation

was above 10 percent. It might therefore have been rational to expect the 1984 price level to be 30 percent above the 1981 price level and to have set 1984 wages accordingly. By late 1982, such an expectation would have been plainly irrational. But it might already have been written into contracts. If so, real wages wound up much higher than intended, giving firms a powerful incentive to reduce employment—even though no one behaved irrationally.

2. Many people believe that inflationary expectations do not adapt as quickly to changes in the economic environment as the rational expectations hypothesis assumes. If, for example, the government embarks on an anti-inflation policy, workers may continue to expect high inflation for quite a while. Thus they may continue to insist on rapid money wage increases. Then, if inflation actually slows down, real wages will end up rising faster than anyone expected, and unemployment will result. Such behavior may not be strictly *rational*. But, to many observers, it seems realistic.
3. The facts have not been kind to the rational expectations point of view. The theory suggests that unemployment should hover around the natural rate most of the time, with random gyrations in one direction or the other. Yet this does not seem to be the case. The theory also predicts that preannounced (and thus expected) anti-inflation programs should be relatively painless. Yet, in practice, inflation fighting looks to be very costly. Finally, many direct tests of the rationality of expectations have cast doubt on the hypothesis. For example, survey data on peoples' expectations rarely meet the exacting requirements of rationality.

As a piece of pure logic, then, the rational expectations argument is impeccable. But there is controversy over how best to apply the idea in practice. The issues are far from settled and research continues. But the evidence to date leads most economists to reject the extreme rational expectationist position for short-run analysis. In the long run, however, the rational expectations viewpoint should be more or less appropriate since people will not hold incorrect expectations indefinitely. As Abraham Lincoln said, you cannot fool all of the people all of the time.

## WHY ECONOMISTS (AND POLITICIANS) DISAGREE

This chapter has now taught us some of the reasons why economists often disagree about the proper conduct of national economic policy. And it also helps us understand some of the related political debates.

Should the government take stern actions to reduce inflation? You will say *yes* if you believe that (1) inflation is more costly than unemployment, (2) the short-run Phillips curve is steep, (3) expectations react quickly, and (4) the economy's self-correcting mechanism works smoothly and rapidly. These views on the economy tend to be held by monetarists and rational expectationists and by the (generally conservative) politicians who listen to them.

But you will say *no* if you believe that (1) unemployment is more costly than inflation, (2) the short-run Phillips curve is flat, (3) expectations react sluggishly, and (4) the self-correcting mechanism is slow and unreliable. These views are held by many Keynesian economists, so it is not surprising that the (generally liberal) politicians who follow their advice often oppose the use of recession to fight inflation.

The tables turn, however, when the question is whether to use demand management to bring a recession to a rapid end. The Keynesian view of the world—that unemployment is costly, that the short-run Phillips curve is flat, that expectations adjust slowly, and that the self-correcting mechanism is unreliable—leads to the conclusion that the benefits of fighting unemployment are high while the costs are low. And so Keynesians are eager to fight recessions. The monetarist and rational expectationist positions on these four issues are precisely the reverse, and so are the policy conclusions.

## THE DILEMMA OF DEMAND MANAGEMENT

So we have seen that the makers of monetary and fiscal policy face an agonizing trade-off. If they stimulate aggregate demand to reduce unemployment, they will aggravate inflation. If they restrict aggregate demand to fight inflation, they will cause higher unemployment.

But wait. Early in the chapter we learned that when inflation comes from the supply side, inflation and unemployment are *positively* associated: we suffer from more of both or enjoy less of each. Does this mean that monetary and fiscal policymakers can escape the trade-off between inflation and unemployment? Certainly not.

**THE TRADE-OFF BETWEEN INFLATION AND UNEMPLOYMENT**

Adverse shifts in the aggregate supply curve can cause both inflation and unemployment to rise together, and thus can destroy the statistical Phillips curve relationship. Nevertheless, anything that monetary and fiscal policy can do will make unemployment and inflation move in opposite directions because monetary and fiscal policy give the government control only over the *aggregate demand* curve, not over the *aggregate supply* curve. ¶ Thus, no matter what the source of inflation, and no matter what happens to the Phillips curve, the makers of monetary and fiscal policy must still face up to the disagreeable trade-off between inflation and unemployment. This is a principle that many policymakers have failed to recognize, and one of the **12 Ideas** that we hope you will remember well **Beyond the Final Exam.**

Naturally, the unpleasant nature of this trade-off has led to a vigorous search for a way out of the dilemma. Both economists and public officials have sought a policy that might offer improvements on both fronts simultaneously, or that might ease the pain of either unemployment or inflation. The rest of this chapter considers some of these ideas.

## ATTEMPTS TO IMPROVE THE TRADE-OFF DIRECTLY

One class of policies aims to reduce the natural rate of unemployment. For example, vocational training and retraining programs, if successful, help unemployed workers with obsolete skills acquire abilities that are currently in demand. By so doing, they help alleviate upward pressures on wage rates in jobs where qualified workers are in short supply.

For example, if an unemployed steelworker is taught to assemble computers, then progress is made against both inflation and unemployment, since one former steelworker leaves the ranks of the unemployed while one new worker helps alleviate the shortage of skilled labor in the computer industry. A similar role is played by the United States Employment Service and similar agencies at the state and local levels—which try to improve the match of workers to jobs by funneling information from prospective employers to prospective employees.

The idea sounds appealing and has many adherents; indeed, the Clinton administration has pledged to expand retraining programs for displaced workers. But, up to now, training and placement programs have achieved only modest successes. Too often, people are trained for jobs that do not exist by the time they finish their training—if indeed they ever existed. Even when they work, these programs are expensive, which restricts the number of workers that can be accommodated.

Over the last two decades, many government regulations over prices and provision of service were reduced or made more flexible in such industries as airlines, trucking, railroads, telecommunications, and energy. Presidents Ford, Carter, and Reagan all vigorously promoted deregulation, often citing the anti-inflationary impact as a reason.[6] Prices have generally fallen in the deregulated industries. However, even though most economists applaud deregulation on microeconomic grounds, they doubt that it has had a large effect on the economy-wide inflation rate.

## WAGE–PRICE CONTROLS

**WAGE–PRICE CONTROLS** are legal restrictions on the ability of industry and labor to raise wages and prices.

To many people, the most natural way to control inflation is to impose mandatory **wage–price controls**. After all, if we do not like something, why not just outlaw it? Wage–price controls have rarely been used in the United States, but some foreign countries have experimented with them much more.

Economists generally oppose controls for reasons we learned back in Chapter 4. When price ceilings are effective, they force the price below the equilibrium price, so that quantity demanded exceeds quantity supplied. This is shown in Figure 33–17, where the equilibrium price of hamburgers is assumed to be $1.50. If controls do not allow the price of hamburgers to rise above $1, quantity demanded will exceed quantity supplied by one million hamburgers per year.

With price no longer serving as the rationing device, some other method of rationing is necessary. One possibility is long lines of eager eaters waiting their turn for burgers. Scenes like this used to be typical in the former Soviet bloc and were seen in America when gasoline was rationed in the 1970s.

Another is government ration coupons, giving the owner the right to buy a hamburger—a device used successfully for many goods during World War II. Neither of these measures is likely to be popular with the electorate in peacetime. And both are likely to spawn black markets, which erode respect for law and order at the same time they abrogate the effects of controls. As critics are fond of pointing out, controls give perfectly law-abiding citizens incentives to break the law in an effort to circumvent the controls.

[6]For a full discussion of regulation and deregulation, see Chapter 18.

Figure 33–17 THE EFFECTS OF PRICE CONTROLS

This diagram portrays the market for hamburgers under an effective price control system. Since the equilibrium price is $1.50 per hamburger, a regulation that holds the price at $1 makes the quantity of hamburgers demanded (2,500,000 per year) exceed the quantity supplied (1,500,000 per year). There is a shortage of one million hamburgers per year, and some sort of rationing scheme probably is necessary.

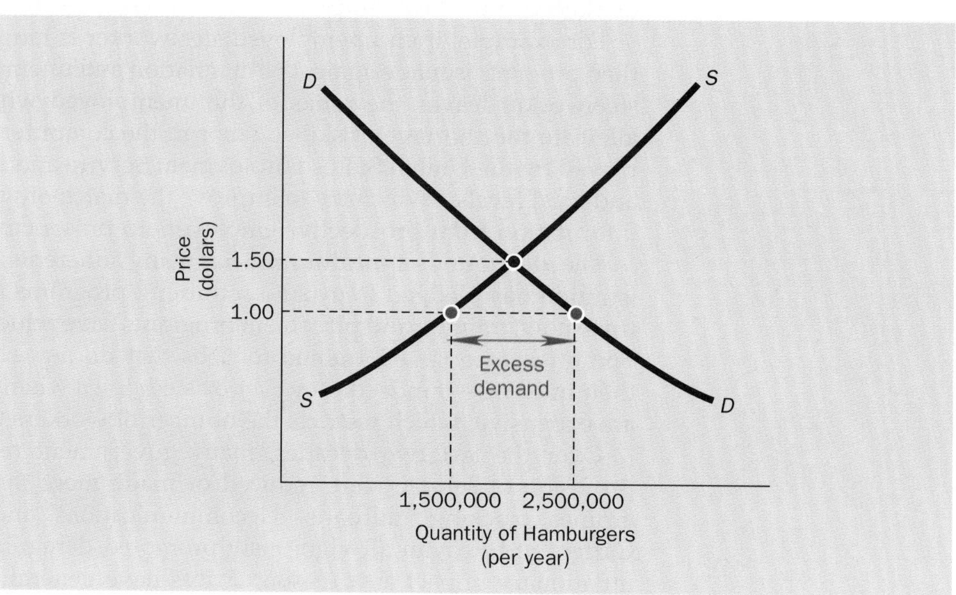


And the problems spawned by price controls go deeper than this. Among the principal factors determining the equilibrium price of hamburgers are the prices of raw agricultural commodities such as beef. But prices of raw agricultural commodities cannot be controlled by the government because they depend on the weather and other acts of nature. If price controls hold the price of hamburgers at $1 while the price of beef skyrockets, it may become unprofitable to sell hamburgers. If so, hamburgers will start disappearing from restaurant menus.

With hamburgers unavailable, consumers will turn to other goods, thereby putting upward pressure on the prices of items such as fish and soybeans. Thus, price controls on hamburgers will cause the hamburger industry to contract and necessitate additional price controls on fish and soybeans. And so it goes. Each extension of price controls to a new commodity requires additional controls to support it, in an ever-expanding chain. Thus, for price controls to be effective, they must be nearly universal—which is next to impossible. This, of course, is precisely the lesson the formerly socialist nations learned so painfully.

Nonetheless, there is an intellectually defensible case for wage–price controls under the right circumstances. Inflation gathers a substantial momentum once workers, consumers, and business managers begin to expect that it will continue. These **inflationary expectations** encourage workers to demand higher wage increases. Firms, in turn, are willing to grant the workers' demands because they believe they will be able to pass the cost increases on to consumers in a general inflationary environment. Thus, to a great extent, *inflation occurs because people expect it to occur*. Phrased in terms of our Phillips curve analysis, *inflationary expectations shift the Phillips curve upward*, so that any given rate of unemployment corresponds to a higher rate of inflation.

A tough and thorough program of wage and price controls, it is argued, can break the vicious cycle of inflationary expectations. By announcing controls, the government serves notice on workers that they do not need anticipatory wage increases to preserve their purchasing power. And firms are warned that they may not be able to pass on higher costs to consumers. By breaking inflationary expectations, supporters argue, a controls program can shift the Phillips curve down and reduce the rate of inflation.

Under the right conditions, this argument may be correct. Some economists, for example, believe that controls helped such countries as Argentina and Israel reduce galloping inflations in the 1980s. But these were extreme circumstances, and there was much more to the anti-inflation programs than merely controls. America's 1971–1974 experiment with wage–price controls under President Nixon, however, is generally considered to have failed. Most studies of the period conclude that the controls *lowered* inflation while they were in effect, but then *raised* it when they were lifted.

## INDEXING

**INDEXING** refers to provisions in a law or a contract whereby monetary payments are automatically adjusted whenever a specified price index changes. Wage rates, pensions, interest payments on bonds, income taxes, and many other things can be indexed in this way, and have been. Sometimes such contractual provisions are called *escalator clauses*.

**Indexing**—which refers to provisions in a law or contract whereby monetary payments are automatically adjusted whenever a specific price index changes—presents a very different approach to the inflation–unemployment dilemma. Whereas the other proposals discussed in this chapter are all designed *to lower the inflation rate*, the primary purpose of indexing is *to reduce the social costs of inflation*.

The mechanics of indexing are best explained by an example, and the most familiar example in the United States is an *escalator clause* in a wage agreement. An escalator clause provides for an automatic increase in money wages—without the need for new contract negotiations—any time the price level rises by more than a specified amount.

Suppose that with the Consumer Price Index (CPI) sitting at 150, a union and a firm agree on a three-year contract setting wages at $10 per hour this year, $11 next year, and $12 in the third year. They might then add an escalator clause stating that wages will be increased above these stipulated amounts by 5 cents per hour for each point by which the CPI exceeds 150 in any future year of the contract. Then, if the CPI reaches 160 in the third year of the contract, workers will receive an additional 50 cents per hour (5 cents for each point by which 160 exceeds 150), for a total wage of $12.50 per hour. In this way, workers are partly protected from inflation. Nowadays, less than half of all workers employed by large unionized firms in the United States are covered by some sort of escalator clause. And very few nonunion workers or employees of small firms enjoy such protection.

Interest payments on bonds or savings accounts can also be indexed, although this is not currently done in the United States.[7] The most extensive indexing to be found in the United States today is in government transfer payments. Social Security benefits, for instance, are indexed so that retirees are not victimized by inflation. Several other government income maintenance and social insurance programs also pay benefits that are tied directly to prices.

[7]Some other countries, with much higher inflation than ours, do extensive indexing of interest rates. Brazil and Israel are notable examples.

## INDEXING AND THE SOCIAL COSTS OF INFLATION

Some economists believe that the United States should follow the example of several foreign countries and adopt a much more widespread system of indexing. Why? Because, they argue, it would take most of the sting out of inflation. To see how indexing would accomplish this, let us review some of the social costs of inflation that we enumerated in Chapter 23.

One important cost is the capricious redistribution of income caused by unexpected inflation. We saw that borrowers and lenders normally incorporate an *inflation premium* equal to the *expected rate of inflation* into the nominal interest rate. Then, if inflation turns out to be higher than expected, the borrower has to pay to the lender only the agreed-upon nominal interest rate, including the premium for *expected* inflation; he does not have to compensate the lender for the (higher) *actual* inflation. Thus the borrower enjoys a windfall gain and the lender loses out. The opposite happens if inflation turns out to be lower than was expected. But if interest rates on loans were indexed, none of this would occur. Borrowers and lenders would agree on a fixed *real* rate of interest, and then the borrower would compensate the lender for whatever *actual inflation* occurred. No one would have to guess what the inflation rate would be.[8]

A second social cost we mentioned in Chapter 23 stems from the fact that our tax system levies taxes on nominal interest and nominal capital gains. As we learned, this flaw in the tax system leads to extremely high effective tax rates in an inflationary environment. But indexing could fix this problem easily. We need only rewrite the tax code so that only *real* interest payments and *real* capital gains are taxed.

A final problem noted in Chapter 23 is that uncertainty over future price levels makes it difficult to enter into long-term contracts—rental agreements, construction agreements, and so on. One way out of this problem is to write indexed contracts, which specify all future payments in real terms.

In the face of all these benefits, and others we have not mentioned here, why do many economists oppose indexing? Probably the major reason is the fear that indexing will lead to an acceleration of inflation. With the costs of inflation reduced so markedly, they argue, what will persuade governments to pay the price of fighting inflation? What will stop them from inflating more and more? They fear that the answer to these questions is, Nothing. Voters who stand to lose nothing from inflation are unlikely to pressure their legislators into stopping it. Opponents of indexing worry that a mild inflationary disease could turn into a ravaging epidemic in a highly indexed economy.

[8]For example, an indexed loan with a 2 percent real interest rate would require a 5 percent nominal interest payment if inflation were 3 percent, a 7 percent nominal interest payment if inflation were 5 percent, and so on.

## *Summary*

1. Inflation can be caused either by rapid growth of aggregate demand or by sluggish growth of aggregate supply.
2. When fluctuations in economic activity emanate from the demand side, prices will rise rapidly when real output grows rapidly. Since rapid growth means more jobs, unemployment and inflation will be inversely related.
3. This inverse relationship between unemployment and inflation is called the **Phillips curve**. U.S. data for the

1950s and 1960s display a Phillips curve relation, but data for the 1970s do not.

4. The Phillips curve is not a menu of *long-run* policy choices for the economy because the **self-correcting mechanism** guarantees that neither an inflationary gap nor a recessionary gap can last indefinitely.
5. Because of the self-correcting mechanism, the economy's true long-run choices lie along a **vertical Phillips curve**, which shows that the so-called **natural rate of unemployment** is the only unemployment rate that can persist indefinitely.
6. In the short run, the economy can move up or down its short-run Phillips curve. *Temporary* reductions in unemployment can be achieved at the cost of higher inflation. Similarly, *temporary* increases in unemployment can be used to fight inflation.
7. Whether it is advisable to use unemployment to fight inflation depends on four principal factors: the relative social costs of inflation versus unemployment, the efficiency of the economy's self-correcting mechanism, the current position of the economy, and how quickly inflationary expectations adjust.
8. If workers expect inflation to occur, and if they demand (and receive) compensation for inflation, output will be independent of the price level. Both the aggregate supply curve and the short-run Phillips curve are vertical in this case.
9. However, errors in predicting inflation will still change real wages and hence will still change the quantity of output that firms wish to supply. Thus, *unpredicted* movements in the price level will lead to a normal, upward-sloping aggregate supply curve.
10. According to the hypothesis of **rational expectations**, errors in predicting inflation are purely random. This means that, except for some random (and uncontrollable) gyrations, the aggregate supply curve is vertical even in the short run.
11. Many economists reject the rational expectations view of the world. Some deny that expectations are "rational" and believe instead that people tend, for example, to underpredict inflation when it is rising. Others point out that contracts signed years ago cannot possibly embody expectations that are "rational" in terms of what we know today.
12. When fluctuations in economic activity are caused by shifts of the aggregate supply curve, output will grow slowly (causing unemployment to rise) when inflation speeds up. Hence, the rates of unemployment and inflation will be positively related. Many observers feel that this sort of **stagflation** is why the Phillips curve collapsed in the 1970s.
13. Even if inflation is initiated by supply-side problems, so that inflation and unemployment occur together, the monetary and fiscal authorities still face this trade-off: anything they do to improve unemployment is likely to worsen inflation, and anything they do to reduce inflation is likely to aggravate unemployment. The reason is that monetary and fiscal policy mainly influence the aggregate demand curve, not the aggregate supply curve. This is one of our **12 Ideas for Beyond the Final Exam**.
14. Policies that improve the functioning of the labor market—including retraining programs and employment services—can lower the natural rate of unemployment. To date, however, the U.S. government has had only modest success with these measures.
15. Some small amount of progress against inflation may also be made by eliminating government regulations that keep prices high. Indeed, much of this has already been done.
16. One argument in favor of short-term **wage–price controls** is that they can reduce **inflationary expectations** and thereby rob inflation of some of its momentum.
17. However, legal limits on wage and price increases seriously interfere with the workings of a market economy.
18. **Indexing** is another way to approach the trade-off problem. Instead of trying to improve the trade-off, it concentrates on reducing the social costs of inflation—perhaps eliminating them, altogether. Opponents of indexing worry, however, that the economy's resistance to inflation may be lowered by indexing.

## *Key Concepts and Terms*

Demand-side inflation
Supply-side inflation
Phillips curve
Stagflation caused by supply shocks
Self-correcting mechanism
Natural rate of unemployment
Vertical (long-run) Phillips curve
Trade-off between unemployment and inflation in the short run and in the long run
Inflationary expectations
Rational expectations
Wage–price controls
Indexing (escalator clauses)
Real versus nominal interest rates

## Questions for Review

1. Some observers in the 1970s denied that policymakers faced a trade-off between inflation and unemployment. What made them say this? Were they correct?
2. "There is no sense in trying to shorten recessions through fiscal and monetary policy because the effects of these policies on the unemployment rate are sure to be temporary." Comment on both the truth of this statement and its relevance for policy formulation.
3. Why is it said that decisions on fiscal and monetary policy are, at least in part, political decisions that cannot be made on "objective" economic criteria?
4. What is a "Phillips curve"? Why did it seem to work so much better in the 1954–1969 period than it did in the 1970s?
5. Explain why expectations about inflation affect the wages that result from labor–management bargaining.
6. What is meant by "rational" expectations? Why does the hypothesis of rational expectations have such stunning implications for economic policy? Would believers in rational expectations want to shorten a recession by expanding aggregate demand? Would they want to fight inflation by reducing aggregate demand?
7. Show that, if the economy's aggregate supply curve is vertical, fluctuations in the growth of aggregate demand produce only fluctuations in inflation with no effect on output. Relate this to your answer to the previous question.
8. Suppose that a program of wage–price controls is under consideration by the government. What are the possible benefits to the nation from such a program? What are the possible costs? How would you balance the benefits against the costs?
9. Long-term government bonds now pay approximately 6 percent *nominal* interest. Would you prefer to trade yours in for an indexed bond that paid a 3 percent *real* rate of interest? What if the real interest rate offered were 2 percent? What if it were 1 percent? What do your answers to these questions reveal about your personal attitudes toward inflation?
10. In the late 1980s, the unemployment rate in the United States hovered in the 5–5.5 percent range and the inflation rate rose slightly. What do these facts suggest about the numerical value of the natural rate of unemployment?
11. It is said that the Federal Reserve Board typically cares more about inflation and less about unemployment than the administration. If this is true, why might President Clinton have been worried about what Fed Chairman Alan Greenspan would do in early 1993, when inflation increased for a few months?
12. The year 1993 opened with the unemployment rate around 7 percent, real GDP growing slowly, inflation about 3 percent, and the federal budget deficit over $300 billion.
    a. Make an argument for engaging in contractionary monetary or fiscal policies under these circumstances.
    b. Make an argument for engaging in expansionary monetary or fiscal policies under these circumstances.
    c. Which argument do you find more persuasive?

# PART VIII

# The United States in the World Economy

Chapter 34

# PRODUCTIVITY AND GROWTH IN THE WEALTH OF NATIONS

*The enormous wealth of Britain is attributable [primarily] to . . . the wonderful skill of her entrepreneurs . . . and the superiority of her workmen in rapid and masterly execution. . . . The English laborer . . . gives his work more care, attention and diligence, than the workmen of most other nations.*

**JEAN BAPTISTE SAY, 1819**

*Japan commercially, I regret to say, does not bear the best reputation for executing business. Inferior goods, irregularity and indifferent shipments have caused no end of worry . . . you are a very satisfied easy-going race . . . the habits of national heritage.*

**FROM A REPORT OF AN AUSTRALIAN EXPERT FOR THE JAPANESE GOVERNMENT, 1915**

This chapter introduces a major new topic, one of rapidly growing importance for all Americans: the place of the United States in the world economy. Exports and imports account for an ever-rising share of the country's output and consumption. We are conscious as never before of the effective competition the United States faces from other industrial economies. Our prosperity depends increasingly on that of other countries, and theirs, in turn, depends vitally on ours. ¶ This chapter takes a long-run view of such developments. It compares for a number of countries the growth in living standards and *productivity* (output per hour of work) over many decades; it seeks to provide some explanation for those growth patterns; and it indicates the directions in which the trends suggest we are going. ¶ Human history in the last two centuries has been unlike anything ever experienced before. In the world's industrial countries, the quantity and quality of food, clothing, and comforts have reached levels that were never dreamed possible by earlier generations. The change has been so revolutionary that it is difficult to grasp its magnitude. This chapter helps us envision how great the accomplishment has been. It also suggests that the transformation was made possible by productivity growth: the fact that a person in the United States today can produce in an hour perhaps 20 times as much as was possible in 1800. Just two figures will suggest the magnitude of the achievement. In 1800 about 90 percent of America's labor force had to work on farms, but all that farm labor barely managed to produce enough food to feed the country adequately. Today only about 3 percent of U.S. workers earn their living on farms. Yet those few farm workers provide an outpouring of surpluses which the U.S. government constantly struggles to contain.

## LIFE IN THE "GOOD OLD DAYS"

The United States, and the thirteen colonies before it, has always been a privileged land with relatively high levels of nutrition. In the eighteenth century, an average white, native-born male who reached the age of 10 could expect to live to somewhere between age 50 and 55. By contrast, an English *nobleman* at that time could expect to live only to something between age 39 and 46.

In the mid-nineteenth century, low incomes, local weather conditions, crop cycles, an almost complete lack of refrigeration, and limited transport of goods bound a large part of even the U.S. population to a minimal and nutritionally inferior variety of foods. Such uninspiring staples as potatoes, lard, cornmeal, and salt pork were the mainstays of diets, particularly outside the population centers. Most travelers' accounts of meals in nineteenth-century America mentioned the ubiquity of some kind of one-pot stew which constituted the main meal of the day for the family. According to one study, "There were, of course, a few people who knew what it was to . . . eat a meal that consisted of more than one course; but there were very, very few such people, and they were all very rich."[1]

Nevertheless, most Americans were right to feel that they lived in a land of unprecedented abundance, for that one-pot stew was quite sure to be there every day. For many centuries most Europeans had devoted nearly half their food budgets to breadstuffs (for example, in 1790 in France, "The price of bread [for a family of five], even in normal times . . . was half . . . the daily wage of common labor."[2] Often the bread took the form of gruel—a sort of cooked breakfast cereal—served in a single bowl with a single spoon, both passed around the table to the entire family.

In bad years, even gruel was unavailable. Famine continued to threaten Europe until the beginning of the nineteenth century, and earlier it had constituted a normal fact of existence. One historian writes,

> *. . . two consecutive bad harvests spelt disaster . . . . France, by any standards a privileged country, is reckoned to have experienced 10* general *famines during the tenth century; 26 in the eleventh; 2 in the twelfth; 4 in the fourteenth; 7 in the fifteenth; 13 in the sixteenth; 11 in the seventeenth and 16 in the eighteenth.*
>
> *The same could be said of any country in Europe. In Germany, famine was a persistent visitor to the towns and the flatlands . . .*

---

[1]Ruth Schwartz Cowan, *More Work for Mother: The Ironies of Household Technology from the Open Hearth to the Microwave* (New York: Basic Books, 1983), page 38.

[2]Robert Palmer, *The Age of Democratic Revolution*, Vol. 2, Princeton: Princeton University Press, 1964, page 49.

Late nineteenth century sod house in the Dakotas.

SOURCE: *New York Times Magazine,* March 18, 1990, page 34, which cites Bettman Archive.

> *... the countryside sometimes experienced far greater suffering. The peasants ... had no solution in case of famine except to turn to the town where they crowded together, begging in the streets and often dying in public squares, as in Venice and Amiens in the sixteenth century.*
>
> *The towns soon had to protect themselves against these regular invasions .... Beggars from distant provinces appeared in the fields and streets of the town(s) ... starving, clothed in rags and covered with fleas and vermin.*[3]

Food shortages were not the only manifestation of unimaginably poor living conditions:

> *It is difficult for anyone alive now to comprehend how appalling, as recently as a century ago, were the conditions of daily life in all the cities of the Western world, even in the wealthiest parts of town. The stupefying level of filth accepted as normal from the Middle Ages through the Enlightenment were augmented horribly by the Industrial Revolution.*[4]

Even in the United States, living conditions in the nineteenth century were far from ideal. Most of the homes that travelers saw in rural America were tiny and crudely built, with no glass windows, no lighting except the fireplace, no indoor plumbing, and scanty homemade furniture. Every winter it was expected that ink would freeze in the inkwells. Urban housing was not much better. In New York City in the 1860s, it was typical for six people to live in a ten-by-twelve room. In 1890 Jacob Riis wrote of the lower Manhattan tenements,

> *It is said that nowhere in the world are so many people crowded together on a square mile as here. In [one seven-story tenement building] there were 58 babies and 38 children that were over five years of age .... In Essex Street two small rooms in a six-story tenement were made to hold a "family" of father and mother, twelve children, and six boarders ....*[5]

The worst evils of these overcrowded slums were insufficient light and air—narrow airshafts conveyed foul air and disease and served as inflammatory flues when fire broke out. There were no private toilets or washing facilities in these buildings, and cellars and courtyards were foul.

---

[3]Fernand Braudel, *The Structures of Everyday Life: The Limits of the Possible,* Vol. 1, *Civilization and Capitalism, 15th-18th Century* (New York: Harper and Row, 1979), pages 73–75 (footnotes omitted, Braudel's emphasis).

[4]William L. Rathje, "Rubbish!," *The Atlantic Monthly,* Vol. 264, No. 6, December 1989, page 100.

[5]Jacob Riis, *How the Other Half Lives* (New York: Hill and Wang, Inc., 1957), page 77. Originally published by Charles Scribner's Sons, New York, 1890.

Like the common man, the rich have also gained much in terms of health and personal comfort in the course of two or three centuries. By the early 1900s, life expectancy at birth for a member of the British nobility had reached 65 years. But in the mid-sixteenth century, that figure was less than 40 years. More remarkable yet is the fact that longevity of the nobility in these centuries was no better than that of the population as a whole, despite the miserable living conditions of the bulk of the nation.

The dramatic improvement in the comforts enjoyed by the rich is illustrated by the development of home heating technology. The role of the draft in fireplace construction was not discovered until early in the eighteenth century. Until then, the huge fireplaces in the homes of the nobles, though beautiful, were extremely ineffective; they roasted nearby persons on one side and froze them on the other. Winter was a serious threat to rich and poor alike. "Cold weather . . . could be a public disaster, freezing rivers, halting mills [with little or no flour having been stored because preservation methods were largely unknown], bringing packs of dangerous wolves out into the countryside, multiplying epidemics."[6] Not even the highest nobility were spared. The Princess Palatine, the German sister-in-law of Louis XIV, reported that in February 1695 "in the Hall of Mirrors at Versailles at the King's table the wine and water froze in the glasses."[7]

Even the housing of relatively well-off nineteenth-century Americans was still primitive by modern standards. Baths, for example, were rare even in the cities. No homes had electricity and few had gas. Fewer still had hot running water, and not even 2 percent had indoor toilets and cold running water. Boston, with a population of nearly 200,000 in 1860, had only 31,000 sinks, 4,000 baths, and 10,000 water closets—about half of which were extremely primitive affairs. Albany, with a population in 1860 of 62,000, had only 19 private baths and 160 water closets. Outdoor privies were the norm and baths, for the great majority, a luxury.[8]

Though living conditions were vastly improved from earlier centuries, by today's standards, life in the United States just 100 years ago was hard and primitive.

## THE MAGNITUDE OF PRODUCTIVITY GROWTH

Today, of course, things are vastly different. By 1985 less than 2 percent of American housing units lacked complete plumbing—defined as hot and cold piped water, a flush toilet, and a bathtub or shower for the exclusive use of that housing unit. Less than 5 percent was occupied by more than one person per room. Of the new, privately owned, one-family houses built in 1991, nearly 60 percent had three bedrooms, 44 percent had two and a half or more bathrooms, and 75 percent had central air conditioning. Statistics for 1987 show that 93 percent of all households had a color television, virtually 100 percent were equipped with electric refrigerators, 75 percent had electric washing machines, 61 percent owned a microwave oven, and 54 percent had two or more vehicles.[9]

---

[6]Braudel, page 299.

[7]*Ibid.*

[8]Edgar W. Martin, *The Standard of Living in 1860* (Chicago: University of Chicago Press, 1942).

[9]U.S. Bureau of the Census, *Statistical Abstract of the United States, 1992* (112th edition) (Washington, D.C.: U.S. Government Printing Office, 1992).

By means such as technical improvement and heavier spending for the purpose, society has also been able to improve living standards in terms of *safety*—a subject usually ignored in discussions of economic progress. Figure 34–1 shows that in six decades the United States was able to cut the number of accidental deaths by more than half—despite the rise in miles traveled per person.

This revolution in manner of living was made possible by an unprecedented rate of growth in human efficiency in producing output. Before reporting the facts, it is necessary to describe the two basic concepts, *labor productivity* and *output per capita,* usually employed to measure first, the productive efficiency of the working population, and second, the resulting average level of economic well-being.

**LABOR PRODUCTIVITY** refers to the amount of output a worker turns out in an hour (or a week or a year) of labor. It can be measured as total national output (GDP) in a given year divided by the total number of hours of work performed for pay in the country during that year. That is, labor productivity is defined as GDP per hour of labor.

**Labor productivity** refers to the amount of output turned out by a *given* amount of labor (**gross domestic product [GDP] per labor hour**). Obviously, an increase in productivity means that a human being has become a more effective instrument of production. This can be the result of harder work, better training, more or better equipment, innovative technology, or a variety of other causes.

The **standard of living**, on the other hand, is more naturally measured by **GDP per capita**, that is, by total output (GDP) divided by the number of persons among whom it will be distributed. The more output there is for each person, the better off in economic terms the average person must be.

The fantastic magnitude of the increases in both labor productivity and output per capita since, say, 1800 is best appreciated by contrasting it with the dismal average record of many previous centuries. In Europe, after a long decline, living standards had been increasing intermittently since the eleventh century—the century in which William the Conqueror acquired England. Still, it is estimated

**Figure 34–1** **DEATHS FROM ACCIDENTS IN THE UNITED STATES, 1930–1990**

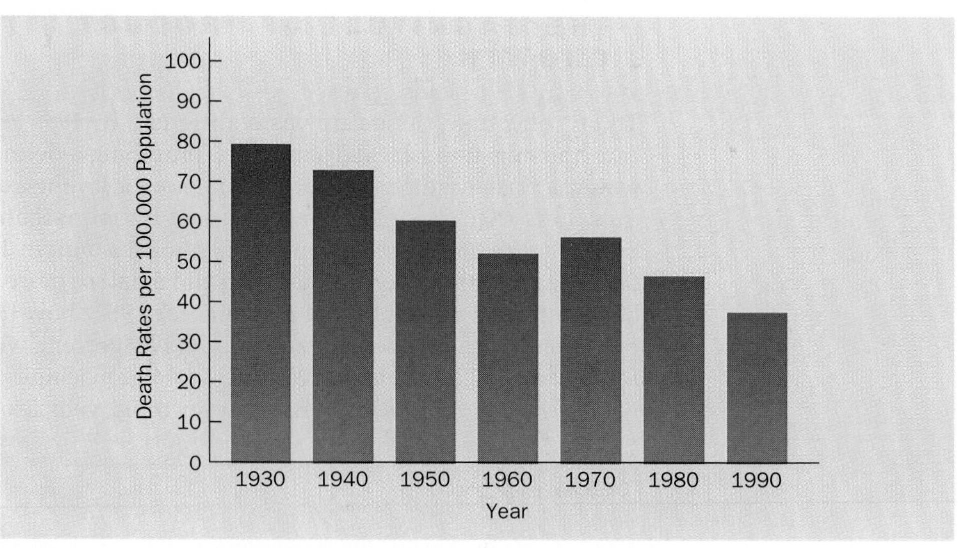


This graph reports the rate per 100,000 population of deaths from accidents in the United States. The graph shows that safety has increased dramatically, and that the number of deaths was reduced by more than half in six decades.

SOURCES: 1930–1960: U.S. Department of Commerce, Bureau of the Census, *Historical Statistics of the United States*, Washington, D.C.: U.S. Government Printing Office, 1975, page 58; 1970–1990: U.S. Department of Commerce, Bureau of the Census, *Statistical Abstract of the United States, 1992*, Washington, D.C.: U.S. Government Printing Office, 1992, page 82.

Figure 34–2 **LABOR PRODUCTIVITY, 1870–1989**

The productivity growth shown here for five industrial countries is typical of today's leading industrial economies. The explosive pattern of increase is unprecedented in previous history.

SOURCE: Angus Maddison, *Dynamic Forces in Capitalist Development* (New York: Oxford University Press, 1991).

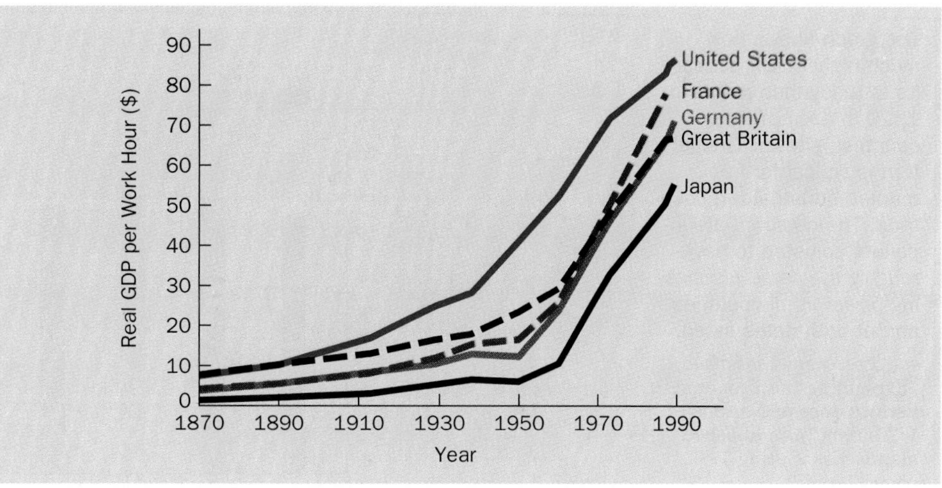


that even by the time of the American Civil War neither labor productivity nor GDP per capita had yet reattained the levels that had been achieved in ancient Rome—about 16 centuries earlier! Thus, on the average, productivity and GDP per capita did not grow at all over 1600 years. Even for those wealthy enough to buy them, the number of important new consumer goods introduced in those 16 centuries was remarkably small. Firearms, glass windowpanes, eyeglasses, mechanical clocks, tobacco, and printed books constitute almost the entire list of major new consumer products invented between the fall of the Roman Empire and the beginning of the nineteenth century. Indeed, some significant amenities, notably elaborate bathing facilities and efficient home heating devices, had disappeared since the fall of Rome.

In contrast, the period since, say, the 1830s has been characterized by an endless explosion of innovations. The railroad and the steamship revolutionized transportation. Steel-making technology changed drastically. The chemical and electronics industries were born and produced hundreds of new consumer products. The range of personal and household goods that we now take for granted—TV sets, dishwashers, cameras, automobiles, personal computers, and many, many others—appeared in an accelerating stream and became commonplace. This has reached a point where today our one unchanging expectation for the future is that it will be characterized by constant change.

Figure 34–2 shows, for five countries, the impressive growth of labor productivity over the past century.[10] For example, it indicates that in this period Japanese

[10]Throughout the chapter, as we compare output per capita or output per work hour (productivity) in different countries, we run into a problem. U.S. output is measured in dollars, and Japanese output in yen. It is *not* legitimate to compare them by looking up the number of yen that your bank will give you for a dollar, because that exchange rate changes from day to day, but relative productivity levels do not. Instead we try to measure the outputs of different countries in money (usually dollars) of constant purchasing power. That is, we ask how many yen does it cost to buy in Japan the same bundle of goods that one can buy for (say) $100 in the United States. This figure is referred to as a *purchasing power parity* exchange rate. Such numbers are used in all the international comparisons in this chapter.

*Figure* **34-3** **IMPROVEMENT IN LIVING STANDARDS, SIX COUNTRIES, 1820 VERSUS 1989**

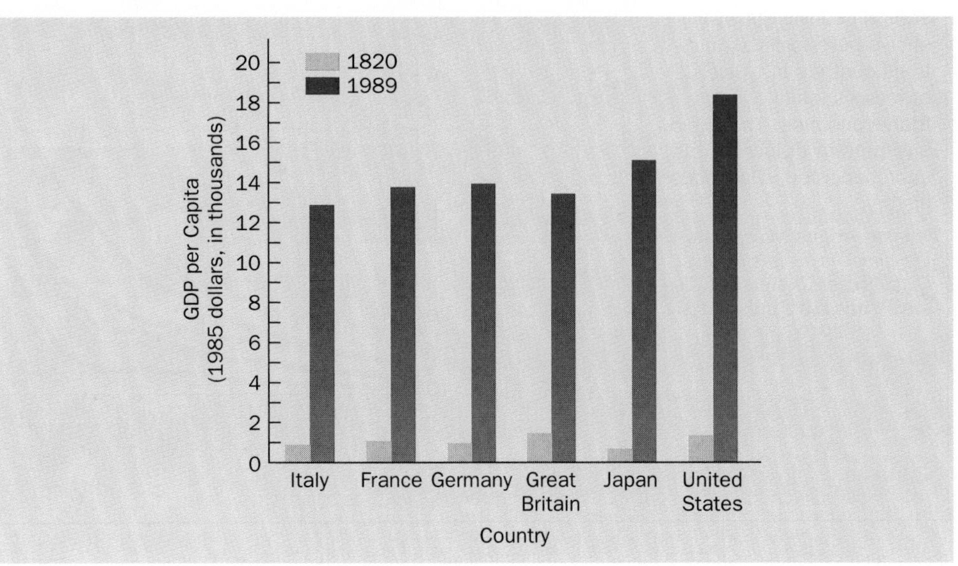


The graph shows how much higher GDP per capita is today than it was in 1820 in each of the six countries shown. The pattern is typical for free-market industrialized countries. The numbers are in dollars adjusted to have roughly the same purchasing power in all countries and at both dates listed.

SOURCE: Angus Maddison, "Explaining the Economic Performance of Nations, 1820–1989," unpublished manuscript, Spring 1992, pages 2 and 3.

productivity has risen about 2500 percent, French and German productivity levels each went up about 1500 percent, productivity in the United States increased about 1100 percent, and even British productivity jumped by an astonishing 600 percent.

To see the implications of this dramatic rise in productivity for living standards (as measured by output per capita) we must first note what has happened to labor time spent by the typical worker. In the industrialized free-market countries, the number of hours worked per year has fallen significantly—by about 40 percent on the average. This is partly the result of a fall in work hours per day—typically from about 12 hours in 1900 down to some $7\frac{1}{2}$ hours per day by 1979—and partly the result of a decline from six working days to five. But most surprising is the almost total absence of any vacations for most of the population before the twentieth century. The two- or four-week vacation is another luxury made possible by the rise in productivity.

Increases in output per person (or, average income per head) have also been spectacular. Over the 169-year period 1820–1989, output per capita went up almost 2500 percent in Japan, about 1400 percent in Germany and the United States, more than 1200 percent in Italy and France, and close to 900 percent in Great Britain.[11] In the United States, for example, average income measured in dollars

[11]It is important to notice that all of these numbers have been corrected to eliminate the effects of inflation. Thus, it is true, of course, that because of the subsequent inflation, a dollar in the mid-1800s could purchase much more bread or many more shoes than it can today, so that a $12 weekly salary then is not as low, in purchasing power, as it may seem. But the statistics reported here have been corrected to eliminate this source of confusion, using the standard statistical method employed for the purpose. That is, since the statistics indicate that U.S. consumer prices have risen by about 6 times since the mid-1800s, a $12 wage then is counted as $6 \times \$12 = \$72$ in dollars of today's purchasing power (for more details on the method for correction for inflation, see pages 587–88 in the appendix to Chapter 23).

of constant purchasing power was only about one-fifteenth as large in 1820 as it is today. To imagine what it is like to live on an income so small, one must think of *Egypt, Bolivia, or the Philippines,* whose per capita income today has been calculated to be on a par with that of an average American in the 19th century! Figure 34–3 translates the productivity growth since the beginning of the twentieth century into the resulting and very remarkable rise in living standards—in national output per capita. Obviously, the rise in economic well-being of an average American, and of an average resident of the other countries in Figures 34–2 and 34–3, has been substantial. Indeed, it represents a rise to a standard of living a person in an earlier century can hardly have imagined.

After some 1600 years of zero average growth in productivity and living standards, growth in both of these areas exploded in the world's industrial countries in the nineteenth and twentieth centuries, reaching levels previously unimaginable.

## SIGNIFICANCE OF THE GROWTH OF PRODUCTIVITY

**THE OVERWHELMING IMPORTANCE OF PRODUCTIVITY GROWTH IN THE LONG RUN**

As we pointed out in our list of **12 Ideas for Beyond the Final Exam**, it is hardly an exaggeration to say that, in the long run, almost nothing counts for the determination of a nation's standard of living but its rate of productivity growth—for only rising productivity can raise standards of living in the long run.

Over long periods of time, small differences in rates of productivity growth compound like interest in a bank account and can make an enormous difference to a society's prosperity. Nothing contributes more to reduction of poverty, to increases in leisure, and to the country's ability to finance education, public health, environmental improvement, and the arts.

Since 1800, productivity in the United States has increased at an average annual rate slightly less than 2 percent. An apparently small change in this figure would have enormous consequences over a long period. Had productivity grown at an average rate of only 1 percent per year instead, an average American today would command about 6.6 times as large a quantity of goods and services as his forebears did in 1800. Actually, though it is hard to believe, real per capita income has risen about 30-fold in this period. And if productivity had grown over the entire interval at an annual rate of 3 percent, average living standards would be an incredible 275 times as high as they were in 1800.

Productivity growth can make an enormous difference in a nation's standing in the hierarchy of the world's economies. It has been remarked that the success of the United States in keeping its annual productivity growth about 1 percent ahead of Great Britain for about a century transformed America from a minor, developing country into a superpower and transformed Great Britain from the world's preeminent power into a second-rate economy. It is Japan's 3-percent average annual productivity growth rate since 1870 that transformed it from one of the world's poorest countries into a nation with one of the highest GDP figures in the world.

## THE SECOND MAJOR DEVELOPMENT: CONVERGENCE

Not only has each of the industrial countries grown in productivity and income per capita, but these countries have also become more similar to one another both in terms of labor productivity and GDP per capita. In other words, among the industrial countries, those which were furthest behind in 1870 have been catching up with those that were ahead. For example, in 1870 the productivity level of the leading country (Australia) was about seven times as high as that of the least productive country (Japan). By 1989 that ratio had declined to about 1.5. That is, about three-quarters of the difference between the most productive and the least productive country were eliminated during the 119-year period.

Such a dramatic narrowing of productivity gaps among the industrial countries means that everyone else must be catching up with the leader, and that leader, ever since World War I, has been the United States. This is illustrated in Figure 34–4, which shows what happened to the *relative* labor productivity levels of four leading industrialized countries over the period 1950–1990. Specifically, it shows GDP per worker in each of those countries *as a percentage of the U.S. level.* (The U.S. figure is, therefore, always 100 percent). It indicates that, in 1950, per capita GDP for the average of the countries shown was about 35 percent of that of the United States. By 1990 the average was about 80 percent of the U.S. level. Figure 34–4 also shows that productivity in *each* of these countries has been moving closer to the United States in this 40-year period.[12]

These and other data indicate that levels of labor productivity are converging among the leading industrialized countries.[13]

Figure 34–4 also indicates that, as productivity levels in the other countries have come closer to those in the United States, the speed at which they have approached it has slowed. Note also that, despite the impression given in the press, Japan is still the lowest in this group, and that Germany is falling behind France (and several other countries).

## WHY INTERNATIONAL EQUALIZATION?

Why are all these countries growing more alike in productivity and average standards of living? No one has the entire answer, but a good part of the story is probably the speedup of the international spread of new technology. Better communications permit innovative techniques to move from one country to another far more quickly than in the past. Better and more widespread education permits countries to learn technical details from one another and to train their labor forces rapidly to make use of them. At the beginning of the eighteenth century when the Newcomen steam engine (the predecessor of Watt's steam

[12]To interpret the graph, remember that if the curve representing some country were to reach precisely the curve for the United States it would mean that this country's productivity per worker is equal to that of the United States.

[13]The reader should be warned that this conclusion has been challenged, at least for the years before World War II, on the grounds that the sample of countries studied happens to include those that have been converging toward the United States because they are the success stories for which statistics are available. Thus, the critics point out, Argentina is omitted from the sample of countries, even though in 1870 many observers would have predicted a brilliant economic future for that country.

Figure 34-4 LABOR PRODUCTIVITY LEVELS IN FIVE COUNTRIES AS A PERCENT OF U.S. LEVEL, 1950–1990

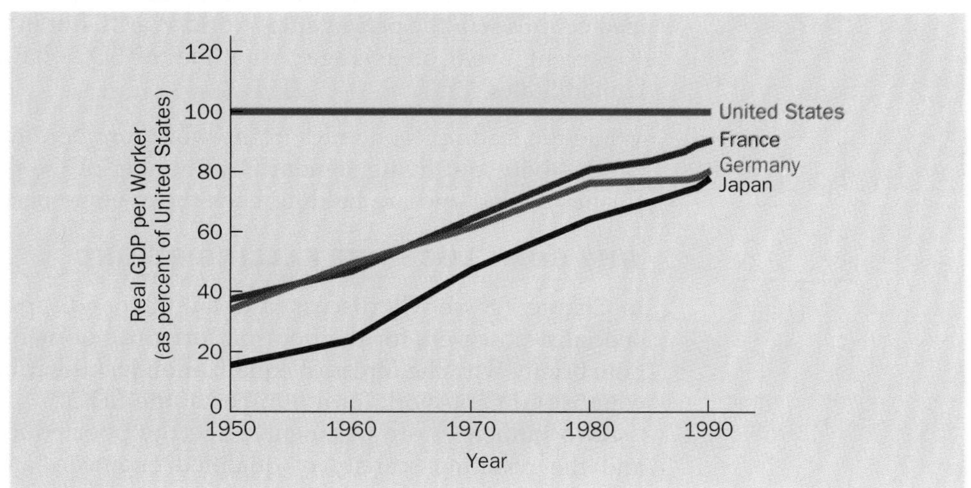


The graph shows that real GDP per worker in each of the countries is approaching the (growing) U.S. level. However, as productivity in those countries gets closer to our own, the catch-up process seems to have slowed. You may also be surprised to see that Japan still is at the bottom of the group and that France is ahead of Germany.

SOURCE: U.S. Department of Labor, Bureau of Labor Statistics, unpublished data.

engine) was invented in England, it took half a century for the engine to spread to Western European countries and to the American colonies. In contrast, the innovations in transistor and semiconductor technology since World War II have, on average, taken about two and one-half years to spread among countries.

All industrial countries benefit from the process of shared information; each learns from the innovations that occur in all the others. The British, the French, and the Germans benefit from American computer technology while the United States and others benefit from Japanese advances in robotics.

But there is one crucial asymmetry. Countries that are behind have a great deal to learn from countries that are ahead, but the leaders have less to learn from those that have lagged behind. This is generally believed to be a prime explanation of the convergence in living standards. Meanwhile, the growing speed and efficiency of communications speeds up the entire process.

Lagging countries have more to learn from leaders than leaders can learn from laggards. This fact, and the growing speed with which innovations are spread, help explain why the world's industrial economies are growing more equal.

## ARE ALL COUNTRIES PARTICIPATING IN EQUALIZATION?

So far we have seen that a considerable number of countries are growing increasingly similar to one another in terms of productivity and living standards. But we have yet to consider the world's poorest nations—usually referred to as "less developed countries," or LDCs. (See Chapter 38.) Have most of those countries also benefited from the spread of innovation and closed the gap between themselves and the world's economic leaders?

Unfortunately, among the LDCs, where equalization is most desperately needed, the picture is very mixed. Some economies, such as those of Taiwan and

South Korea, have achieved spectacular successes. But, as a group, the LDCs have grown less equal among themselves and have fallen further behind the United States. On average, GDP per capita grew about 3 percent per year in the industrialized countries in the period after World War II. But in the LDCs it rose only about $1\frac{1}{2}$ percent a year on average. A number of LDCs have fallen further behind the United States.

While the leading economies in the world are becoming more equal in terms of productivity and living standards, a number of the poorest countries are falling further behind and are holding back the average performance of the LDCs.

### WHY SOME LDCS ARE FALLING BEHIND

In Chapter 38 we will discuss in detail the handicaps that have been blamed by specialist observers for the poor performance of many LDCs. Here we will only note briefly why the forces of equalization just described for the more developed countries do not work for a number of the LDCs.

Two influences are pertinent. First, the poor educational levels in the LDCs and the resulting scarcity of qualified engineers and technicians is a serious impediment to imitation and effective use of the complex technological advances of the industrialized countries. So they do not benefit by learning from others to nearly the extent that the wealthier countries do.

Second, the absence of products to which sophisticated production techniques can readily be applied makes it hard to participate in the growth gains from learning and imitation. A country that depends on products such as bananas, peanuts, and sugar for most of its income has little use for new robot designs or automated manufacturing processes, though it can and often does benefit from agricultural innovations, some of substantial importance. As a result, while the LDCs can and do learn to some degree from the technology of the industrialized economies, they suffer from serious handicaps in this process, handicaps from which the industrial countries are largely immune.

## THE U.S. PRODUCTIVITY SLOWDOWN: IS AMERICAN ECONOMIC LEADERSHIP DOOMED?

Since the mid-1960s there has been a sharp decline in the rate of growth of productivity in the United States. From 1950 to 1973, productivity per worker grew at an average rate that has been estimated to be between 2 and $2\frac{1}{2}$ percent per year, which is probably somewhat faster than it had ever grown before over so long a period. Then, between 1973 and 1990 productivity growth fell sharply from its earlier postwar rate, back to between half a percent and one percent per year.

Some observers have concluded that the U.S. economy, and particularly its manufacturing sector, is in terrible trouble, and that the United States seems about to lose its leadership in both productivity and living standards. But these fears are, at the very least, exaggerated, for several reasons.

First, it should be noted carefully that throughout most of this period the *level* of U.S. productivity continued to improve. In almost every year it was higher than the last. It was the *rate of improvement* that slowed from a gallop to a walk, and finally to a crawl. Second, the United States is still by far the world's largest economy in terms of total production, wealth, and factors such as spending on research and development.

Figure 34–5

### FALL IN PRODUCTIVITY GROWTH RATES, 1950–1973 VERSUS 1973–1990

This graph confirms that productivity growth *did* decline in the period widely publicized as the "U.S. productivity slowdown." However, at the same time, it also fell throughout the industrial world and not just in the United States. The growth rates continued to be low throughout the 1980s.

SOURCE: U.S. Department of Labor, Bureau of Labor Statistics, unpublished data.

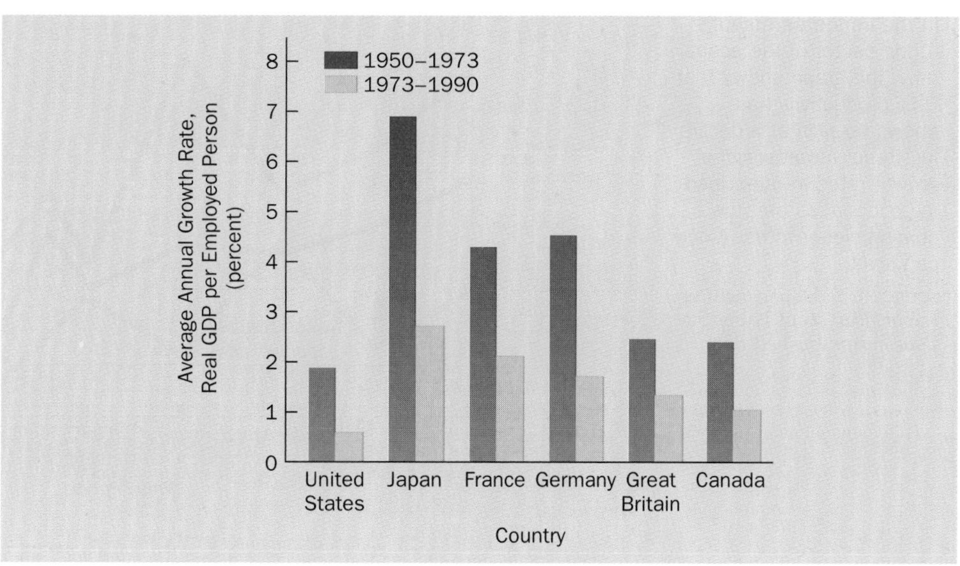


Third, some analysts question whether the U.S. productivity slowdown is as serious as it appears. They argue, first of all, that the United States is not alone in suffering a slowdown in productivity growth. The problem has affected virtually every industrial country. Figure 34–5 compares productivity growth rates for six industrial countries during 1950–1973 with those from 1973–1990—the years when the slowdown occurred. We find that the U.S. growth rate fell 65 percent, while Japan's declined 61 percent, Great Britain's rate fell 46 percent, France's declined 51 percent, Germany's fell 62 percent, and Canada's went down 58 percent. Compared with the others, the U.S. decline does not seem so far out of line.

In addition, very long-run data on U.S. productivity growth exhibit no downward long-term trend. The growth rate of productivity by decade in the United States was virtually constant at about 2 percent per year between about 1870 and 1930. Then, during the Great Depression of the 1930s, productivity growth plunged. With the advent of World War II and the postwar rebuilding of the devastated countries, U.S. productivity growth leaped upward. After this catch-up period, during which a great backlog of ideas for inventions and investment funds that accumulated during the war was gradually depleted, the growth rate fell from its postwar high. On this view of the matter, then, the deceleration of the 1970s, rather than being entirely a drop below its historical norms, was partly a return toward normalcy from a period of extraordinary growth which (in retrospect!) seems to have been predictably temporary.

Much more disturbing, however, is the fact that recently productivity growth in the United States has fallen well below its historical average and has so far shown only limited improvement: growth in American labor productivity fell from its average in the postwar period 1950–1973 to a figure estimated at between 0.6 and 1.1 percent per year in the period 1973–1990. No one has any idea how long this problem, which has beset much of the industrial world, is likely to last.

Figure 34–6 **ANNUAL GROWTH RATES, MANUFACTURING PRODUCTIVITY, THREE COUNTRIES, 1950–1990**

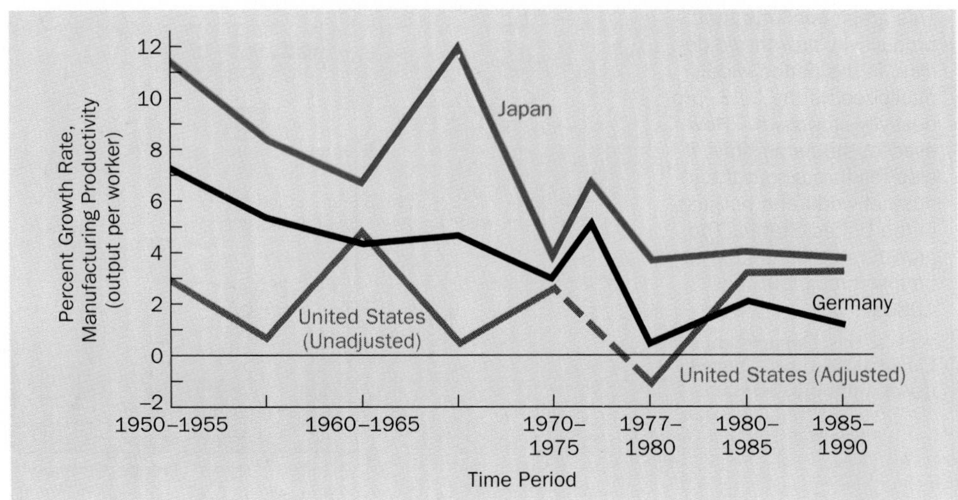


In the important manufacturing sector of the economy, the graph shows that U.S. productivity has shown no sign of a declining trend. Moreover, the growth rates in other leading economies are now coming closer to the American level.

SOURCE: U.S. Department of Labor, Bureau of Labor Statistics, unpublished data.

There is one other interesting aspect of the recent decline in the growth rate of *overall* U.S. productivity. Some sectors—such as construction, mining, and services—have had poor recent records. However, the main focus of public concern has been *manufacturing;* Americans seem to believe that this sector of our economy is most vulnerable to foreign competition because of its poor productivity performance. Yet the record shows something quite different: *U.S. manufacturing has experienced no trend toward a declining growth rate.* This is shown in Figure 34–6 which reports the growth rate of labor productivity in American manufacturing over the entire period since World War II. No downward trend is apparent. Moreover, we see that the growth rates of manufacturing productivity in Japan and Germany are no longer far out of line with those of the United States. Indeed, Germany has lately been the laggard of the group.

## THE U.S. PRODUCTIVITY GROWTH LAG BEHIND OTHER INDUSTRIAL COUNTRIES

What about the second disturbing fact about U.S. productivity growth—that it has recently been so much lower than that of other industrial countries? As a matter of fact that, too, is an old story. The growth rate of U.S. productivity has been just middling for the better part of a century. Between 1899 and 1913, the U.S. growth rate was already lower than that of Sweden, France, Germany, Italy, and Japan. Our growth rate was also below theirs (except for France) in 1924–1937. U.S. labor productivity grew rapidly relative to other nations only during both world wars, when many other countries were held back by the demands of their military activities.

There is a simple and plausible explanation for the comparatively slow growth of U.S. productivity. It is the equalization of productivity in the world's industrial countries—the convergence phenomenon we have already studied in this chapter.

If the forces making for equalization did in fact dominate the growth paths of those countries, it is necessarily true that productivity in the lagging countries *had* to grow more quickly than in the countries at the head of the line. Otherwise, they could never have grown more equal. The statistical evidence is consistent with the conjecture that the relative productivity growth rates of the various industrialized countries are largely explained by their distance behind the leader.

Viewed in this way, there is little to be alarmed about in the relatively slow growth rate of U.S. productivity compared with that of other countries. Indeed, if the higher growth rates of other countries is attributable in good part to their having much to copy from the United States as a productivity leader, we should not be surprised if the rapid growth rates of those countries were to slow as they approach the high American levels. There are, as a matter of fact, signs that this is beginning to happen. One sign of this is the fact that the high Japanese savings rates that seem to have contributed so much to that nation's productivity growth have fallen sharply in the past decade, perhaps by eight percent. And Japan's and Germany's productivity growth rates have continued on a mostly downward path, while the U.S. rate has recently been mostly rising, so that the gap has narrowed dramatically (see Figure 34–7).

Viewed in long-term perspective, the recent slowdown in U.S. productivity growth and its lag behind other industrial countries seems somewhat less serious than it appears from an examination of the decline from the mid-1960s.

## PRODUCTIVITY AND THE DEINDUSTRIALIZATION THESIS

Let us now turn to the popular notion that lagging productivity growth is turning the United States into a service economy, the "deindustrialization thesis." The trends are said to portend a future in which the United States suffers chronic

*Figure* **34–7**

**GROWTH RATES OF LABOR PRODUCTIVITY, FOUR COUNTRIES, 1950–1990**

Note the narrowing of the lead, in terms of greater rapidity of productivity growth in Germany and Japan relative to that of the United States.

SOURCE: U.S. Department of Labor, Bureau of Labor Statistics, unpublished data.

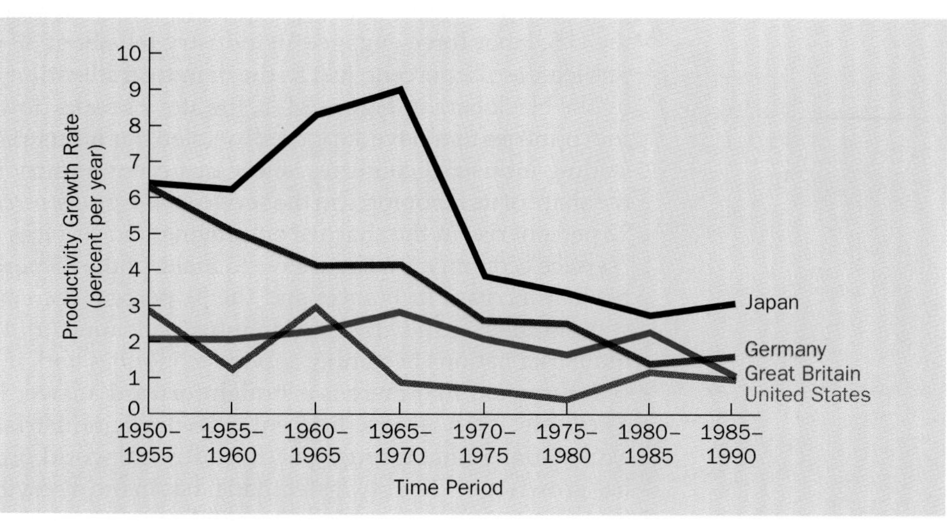

*Figure* **34–8** **GROWTH IN THE SHARE OF SERVICE SECTOR JOBS**

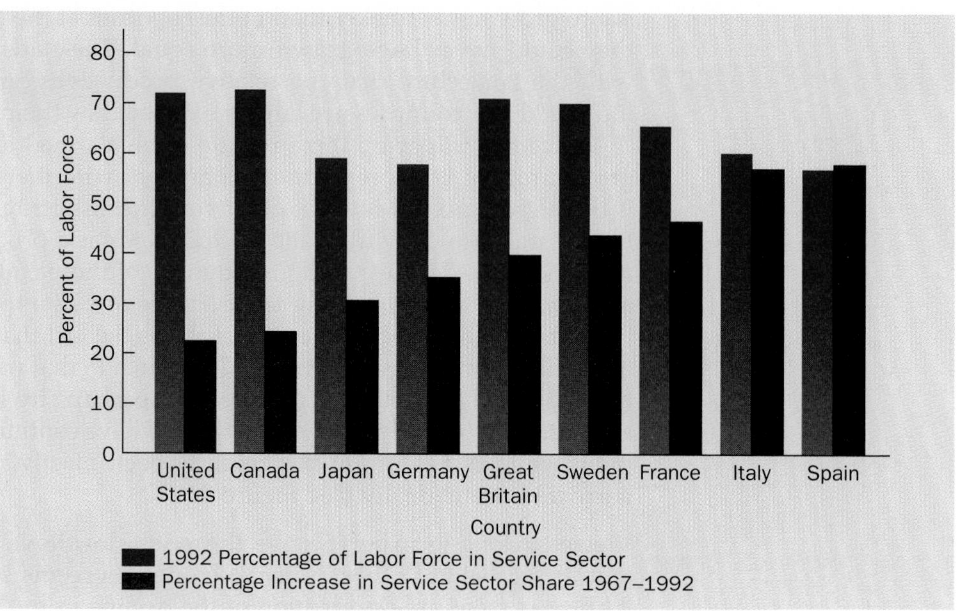


The black bars indicate the percentage growth of the share of employment in the service sector of nine industrial countries. It demonstrates that the United States is hardly the only country in which the proportion of labor employed in the services has been rising. Indeed many other countries have done so far more rapidly.

SOURCE: Organization for Economic Cooperation and Development, *Labour Force Statistics, 1970–1990*, and *Quarterly Labour Force Statistics*, No. 3, 1992.

and apparently incurable problems in its trade with other countries because its manufactured products are not competitive with those of foreign countries. As a result, it is argued, the United States will either be forced to bear heavy unemployment or to see its labor force driven into service-sector jobs at low pay, thus transforming the nation into a "service economy" in which people earn their living by flipping hamburgers and washing dishes. The "deindustrialization" story, oversimplified, asserts that slow productivity growth in manufacturing allows other countries to steal our industrial markets away.

At first glance, the data seem to confirm this. Between 1967 and 1992 the share of the U.S. labor force engaged in industry fell about 30 percent, whereas that in the services *rose* 22 percent, just as the deindustrialization thesis asserts. But, as shown by the black bars in Figure 34–8, the story breaks down when we seek to identify the countries that have supposedly stolen our industrial markets. The data, for nine leading industrial countries, show that *every* country in the sample has increased the share of its labor force in the services *by a greater percentage than ours*. If America's 22 percent rise in the share of employment in services represents a move toward a "service economy," what are we to make of the 35 percent rise in Germany, the 46 percent increase in France, and the 31 percent increase in Japan? Which country was "industrialized" by the "deindustrialization" of the United States? Or are all industrial nations becoming service economies and, if so, why?

It turns out that there is a straightforward answer in which productivity plays a key role; but it is very different from the deindustrialization parable. The simple explanation is that throughout the industrial world productivity in manufacturing has grown considerably faster than it has in most services. For example, productivity has grown far faster in automobile manufacturing than in selling real estate. This means that, though manufacturing outputs have grown, less and less of each nation's labor force has been needed to produce them, just as had happened previously in agriculture. So a declining share of each nation's jobs has been provided in the manufacturing sector.

Moreover, after correction for inflation, the ratio of the *outputs* of the manufacturing and service sectors of the industrial economies has remained roughly unchanged over the years, while national unemployment rates have shown no long-term tendency to rise. With manufacturing taking a declining share of the labor force and unemployment not rising, the share of employment in services naturally had to grow.

A hypothetical example makes the point clear. If, over a period of time when productivity in automobile manufacturing doubled, automobile sales rose only 50 percent, there must have been a 25 percent reduction in the number of workers employed in that industry. But if at the same time, productivity in the real estate industry stayed still, while sales volume rose 50 percent, this industry would need 50 percent more workers than before. Thus, with both industries expanding their outputs in exactly the same proportion, some labor must shift out of the auto industry with its high productivity growth, into the real estate industry, with its stagnant productivity. This is the true sense in which *all* the industrial nations are becoming service economies. The share of their outputs constituted by manufactures has generally not fallen, but the share of employment in the service sector has risen universally.

Thus, the growing share of service workers in U.S. employment is not attributable to lack of competitiveness of U.S. manufactures. On the contrary, between 1962 and 1990, years for which data are available, the U.S. share of the total industrial employment of the world's 25 most industrialized economies actually *increased* about 17 percent. (See Figure 34–9, which shows the near parallel growth

*Figure* **34–9** **SHARES OF WORLD INDUSTRIAL EMPLOYMENT OF FOUR INDUSTRIAL COUNTRIES, 1962–1990***

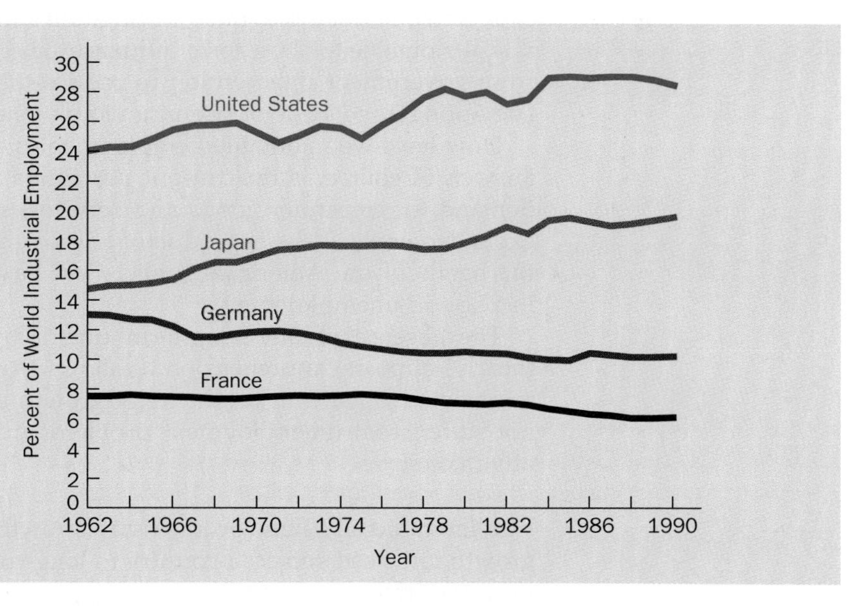


The graph shows that over the 28 years for which the data are available, Japan has steadily gained a larger share of the world's industrial jobs. But the U.S. share has risen significantly, at the expense of France and Germany.

SOURCE: Organization for Economic Cooperation and Development, *Indicators of Industrial Activity*, various issues, and *Labour Force Statistics*, various issues.

*World manufacturing here encompasses the 25 member-countries of the OECD, which includes the bulk of the free-market industrial economies of the world.

of U.S. and Japanese share of world industrial jobs.) That is hardly a picture of faltering competitiveness in our manufacturing sector.

## UNEMPLOYMENT AND PRODUCTIVITY GROWTH

Popular discussions of productivity growth often warn that rapid increases in labor productivity are not as beneficial as they are cracked up to be. We are told that each productivity increase reduces the demand for labor because it means that fewer work hours are needed to produce a given output. As a result, according to this view, productivity growth allegedly creates unemployment. Second, and perhaps somewhat inconsistently, it is argued that if an economy's productivity growth lags behind that of other countries, it will lose jobs to foreign workers, its industry will suffer, and its exports will fall. However, the data do not support either of these conclusions, at least for the long run.

If the spectre of growing long-run unemployment were a reality, we would expect that the 1100-percent increase in output per labor hour in the United States, its 600-percent increase in Great Britain, and its 1500-percent rise in Germany since 1870 would have had devastating effects on the demand for labor in these countries. After all, with productivity rising twelvefold during the last century, output per capita in the United States could have been kept about constant if employment were cut to one-twelfth its initial share of U.S. population. Even with a 50 percent fall in the number of hours an average person works per year, we might expect unemployment of perhaps five-sixths of the U.S. labor force by now.

In fact, nothing of the sort has happened. Unemployment rates for Great Britain, the United States, and Germany going back to the 1870s indicate that over this long period there was no upsurge in unemployment. Before 1914, unemployment in the three countries averaged about 4 percent of the labor force, while in the 1952–1973 period it averaged a bit more than 3 percent. Even though there has been a rise in unemployment throughout the industrial world recently, much of it is attributable to short-term influences and reorientation of public policy away from government intervention to reduce unemployment. There is no evidence suggesting any *long-term* rise in unemployment.

How have we maintained employment in the face of rising productivity? The answer, of course, is that output per capita has hardly remained constant. The demand for consumer goods and services, schools, hospitals, and factories has expanded explosively as productivity growth increased the purchasing power in the hands of the American public. That has sufficed to prevent any long-term increase in unemployment.

The absence of any long-term unemployment trend also undermines the (nearly) opposite apprehension. It shows that Great Britain, which has been the most noted laggard in productivity growth among industrialized countries, did not suffer from unemployment problems markedly more serious than those of other countries.

Neither rapid absolute productivity growth nor a slow relative productivity growth rate need subject a country to long-run and persistent increases in unemployment rates.

Before offering an explanation of this behavior of employment, we turn to the widely held view that a persistent lag in a nation's productivity growth will place it at an increasing competitive disadvantage in international trade, and that it will thereby be excluded increasingly from its export markets, with devastating effects upon its industries.

Here again we use Great Britain, with its relatively poor productivity record, to examine these claims. It is true that the British *share* of exports declined from over 40 percent of world trade in 1870 to less than 10 percent a century later. But that is only because other countries' foreign sales rose even more rapidly than Britain's. The fact is that the total exports of Great Britain have risen spectacularly. In about 100 years, the volume of British exports of goods and services increased about 900 percent.

## THE REAL COSTS OF LAGGING PRODUCTIVITY: LAGGING WAGES AND LIVING STANDARDS

From what has just been said, it may seem that it is not too bad to be a productivity laggard. After all, with no trend toward rising unemployment, with exports increasing, with the share of employment in manufacturing pretty well keeping up with other countries, what is so terrible about Great Britain's fate? Indeed, these observations may make one wonder how Britain was able to score these apparent successes despite its comparatively poor productivity performance.

The secret, which also shows the true price the British had to pay, is to be found in that country's lagging real wages. In the nineteenth century, British workers were the best paid in Europe. According to one estimate, which admittedly is not very reliable, in about 1860 an English worker's wages permitted the purchase of about $2\frac{1}{2}$ times the quantity of goods and services as a German worker's. Yet by the end of the 1980s, the purchasing power of a German worker's wages was almost twice as great as that of a British worker. In other words, in a little more than a century the relative position of workers in the two countries had almost been reversed.

How are lagging British wages related to its productivity lag? The answer is straightforward. If Britain cannot compete on world markets by virtue of growing efficiency (productivity), it still can sell its products by providing cheap British labor. Of course, Britain does not volunteer to adopt low real wages; rather, market forces make it happen automatically, because inefficiently produced goods cannot be sold on the international marketplace unless those goods are produced by cheaper inputs. Hence, the invisible hand forces British wages to lag behind. Labor simply cannot extract higher wages from an economy that has little to give.

A country with lagging productivity is likely to be condemned to become an exporter of cheap labor. That is the only way it can keep its industry viable, maintain its exports, and preserve domestic jobs. This is the real danger that the United States faces if its productivity performance is unsatisfactory for any substantial period of time.

More generally, despite everything that has been said in this chapter, there remain good reasons for concern about future U.S. productivity prospects. There certainly is no guarantee that productivity growth in the United States will return to its old historical pace of nearly 2 percent per year. To do so, the economy will require a continued flow of new and improving technology, new factories, new equipment, and the unslackening effort of engineers, scientists, technicians, management, and labor. None of this is easy or cheap, and none of it is guaranteed.

The costs of failure in this arena are very high. Above all, lagging productivity growth must slow or bring to an end the rising living standards and rising real wages which have so long been a prime accomplishment of the U.S. economy. If there is no rise in output per worker, then it will be impossible to keep increasing the quantity of goods and services provided to each consumer. Indeed, something of the sort has already happened. Since about the beginning of the 1970s, the purchasing power of an average American worker's hourly wage has not increased at all.

Though we do not know whether long-run U.S. productivity growth has declined, for the past few years it has fallen below its historical level. Failure to recoup threatens to hold back the growth in U.S. living standards.

## CONCLUDING COMMENT

Productivity growth is indeed the stuff of which prosperity is made. The persistent record of U.S. productivity growth is the source of its high standard of living, which is extraordinary both in terms of previous history and in comparison with that of most nations in the world. In the long run, nothing is more important than productivity growth for the economic welfare of the country and for the world. In Chapter 38 we will examine some of the things that can help stimulate this vital ingredient of long-run well-being, which in two centuries transformed the focus of popular and political concerns in many industrial countries from the threat of starvation to the fear of overabundance of products.

## *Summary*

1. Productivity growth over the past century has made a tremendous contribution to **standards of living**. Real U.S. per capita income is more than 8 times as large as it was in 1870. Never in previous history have economic conditions improved so much.

2. For the first time in history, famine is no longer a constant threat in the world's industrialized countries. That is because productivity in agriculture has increased greatly. In 1800 about 90 percent of the U.S. labor force was needed to feed the nation poorly. Today, only about 3 percent of the labor force works on farms and yet produces great abundance.

3. Because of compounding, over longer periods a small increase in rate of productivity growth can make an enormous difference in the economic well-being of a nation. This is one of the **12 Ideas for Beyond the Final Exam**.

4. There is evidence suggesting that at least a small set of the world's leading economies are converging toward similar living standards and similar productivity levels.

5. All nations learn about new technological developments from one another. The international spread of inventions means that research in one country also benefits inhabitants in much of the rest of the world.

6. Since the 1960s, there has been a substantial slowdown in productivity growth in most industrial countries.

7. Lagging productivity holds back real wages and per capita incomes in a country. However, in the long run it will generally not cause unemployment or inability to export enough to pay for the nation's imports.

8. The growth of productivity in U.S. manufacturing shows no sign of a long-term slowdown.

9. The growth rate of U.S. productivity has for many decades been slower than that of a number of other industrial countries. However, at least in part, that reflects the fact that the United States is still the world's productivity leader; so that while we have much to learn from others, they have even more to learn from us.
10. The share of the U.S. labor force employed in the services has increased substantially. But so has that of every industrial free-market economy. A major cause is probably the rapid rise of manufacturing productivity, which means that fewer workers are needed in that economic sector.
11. No one is sure whether or not the current slowdown in overall U.S. productivity is a temporary matter. If it persists, it can threaten relative U.S. living standards in the future.

## Key Concepts and Terms

Labor productivity
Standard of living
Gross Domestic Product (GDP)
GDP per labor hour
GDP per capita
Deindustrialization

## Questions for Review

1. Try to describe what family budgets were like 120 years ago when U.S. income per person (GDP per capita) was about one-eighth as high as it is today.
2. List some of the inventions that have increased agricultural output in the past century.
3. List some of the inventions that have increased manufacturing output in the last century.
4. List some of the new consumer products of the past century. Which of them became generally available only since World War II?
5. List some foreign inventions widely used in the United States.
6. List some American inventions widely used abroad.
7. If growing productivity has vastly reduced the amount of labor needed to produce a given output, why has it not caused massively growing unemployment?
8. If output per capita in a country doubles every 25 years, how much will it grow in a century?
9. Which do you think are more similar?
   a. Production methods in a U.S. and a German factory today.
   b. Production methods in a U.S. factory today and the methods used in that same U.S. factory 25 years ago.
10. Since the political upheavals in the communist bloc countries in Eastern Europe in 1989, it has been clear that one of their most urgent needs is productivity growth. What are they doing about it?

Chapter 35

# INTERNATIONAL TRADE AND COMPARATIVE ADVANTAGE

*No nation was ever ruined by trade.*

**BENJAMIN FRANKLIN**

International trade is vital to the health of any nation, and therefore to our study of economics. The world's major economies have always been linked in various ways. But dramatic improvements in transportation, telecommunications, and international relations in recent decades have pulled the industrial nations of the world ever closer together. We now truly live in "one world," at least in an economic sense. ¶ Economic events in other countries affect our economy for both macroeconomic and microeconomic reasons. For example, we learned in Parts 6 and 7 that the level of net exports is one important determinant of a nation's output and employment. But we did not delve very deeply into the factors that determine a nation's exports and imports. Chapters 36 and 37 will take up these *macroeconomic* linkages in greater detail. ¶ But, first, this chapter studies some of the reasons why international trade is important to a nation's *microeconomic* well-being. The central principle here is the *law of comparative advantage*, which plays a major role in determining the patterns of world trade. We will also learn how the prices of internationally traded goods are determined by supply and demand in a free world market. Finally, we will examine the effects of government interferences with foreign trade through quotas, tariffs, and other devices designed to protect domestic industries from foreign competition.

## ISSUE: THE COMPETITION OF "CHEAP FOREIGN LABOR"

Why do Americans (like the citizens of other nations) often want their government to limit or prevent import competition? One major reason is the common belief that imports take bread out of the mouths of American workers and depress standards of living in this country. According to this view, "cheap foreign labor" steals jobs from Americans and puts pressure on U.S. businesses to lower wages. Moreover, imports allegedly encourage foreign sweatshop operators, who can compete only on the basis of low wages.

Unfortunately, the facts are not consistent with this story. For one thing, wages in industrial countries that export to the United States rose spectacularly during the 1970s and 1980s. Table 35–1 shows that wages in seven leading industrial countries rose from an average of only 46 percent of American wages in 1970 to 122 percent by 1992. By 1992, labor costs in Sweden, the Netherlands, West Germany, and Italy far exceeded our own, and costs in Japan were about equal. Yet American imports of Toyotas from Japan, Volkswagens from Germany, and Volvos from Sweden grew as wages in those countries rose relative to American wages.

By comparison, European and Japanese wages were far below those in the United States in the 1950s, and yet American industry had no trouble marketing our products abroad. In fact, the main problem then was to bring our imports up to the level at which they roughly balanced our bountiful exports. Ironically, our position in the international marketplace deteriorated as wage levels in Europe and Japan began to rise closer to our own.

Clearly, then, cheap foreign labor need not serve as a crucial obstacle to U.S. sales abroad—as a "common sense" view of the matter suggests. In this chapter we will see what is wrong with that view.

# WHY TRADE?

The earth's resources are not equally distributed across the planet. While the United States can satisfy its own requirements for such goods as coal and wheat,

**Table 35–1 LABOR COSTS IN INDUSTRIALIZED COUNTRIES**

| | 1970 | 1992 |
|---|---|---|
| | (percentage of U.S. labor costs) | |
| France | 41 | 104 |
| United Kingdom | 35 | 91 |
| Italy | 42 | 120 |
| Japan | 24 | 100 |
| Netherlands | 51 | 128 |
| Sweden | 70 | 150 |
| (West) Germany | 56 | 160 |

Data are compensation estimates per hour and relate to production workers in the manufacturing sector.
SOURCE: U.S. Bureau of Labor Statistics.

it is almost *entirely* dependent on the rest of the world for other products, such as rubber and coffee. Similarly, Saudi Arabia has little land that is suitable for farming, but sits atop a huge pool of oil. Because of the seemingly whimsical distribution of vital resources, every nation must trade with others to acquire what it lacks.

Even if countries had all the resources they needed, other differences in natural endowments—such as climate, terrain, and so on—would lead them to engage in trade. Americans *could*, with great difficulty, grow their own banana trees and coffee shrubs in hothouses. But these crops are much more efficiently grown in Honduras and Brazil, where the climate is appropriate. On the other hand, corn grows well in the United States while mountainous Switzerland is not a good place to grow either bananas or corn.

The skills of a nation's labor force also play a role. If New Zealand has a large group of efficient farmers and few workers with industrial experience while the opposite is true in Japan, it makes sense for New Zealand to specialize in agriculture and let Japan concentrate on manufacturing.

Finally, a small country that tried to produce every product would end up with many industries too small to utilize mass-production techniques, specialized training facilities, and other methods that confer cost advantages on large-scale operations. For example, some countries operate their own international airlines or steel mills for reasons that can only be political, not economic. Inevitably, small nations that insist on competing in industries that are economical only when their scale of operation is large find that these enterprises can survive only with the aid of large government subsidies.

To summarize, the main reason why nations trade with one another is to exploit the many advantages of **specialization**.

**SPECIALIZATION** means that a country devotes its energies and resources to only a small proportion of the world's productive activities.

International trade is essential for the prosperity of the trading nations because:

1. every country lacks some vital resources that it can get only by trading with others;
2. each country's climate, labor force, and other endowments make it a relatively efficient producer of some goods and an inefficient producer of other goods; and
3. specialization permits larger outputs and can therefore offer economies of large-scale production.

## MUTUAL GAINS FROM TRADE

Many people believe that a nation can gain from trade only at the expense of another. Centuries ago, the early writers on international trade pointed out that nothing is produced by the act of trading; the total collection of goods in the hands of the two parties at the end of an exchange is the same as it was before. Therefore, they incorrectly argued, if one country gains from a swap, the other country must necessarily lose.

One of the consequences of this mistaken view was and is a policy prescription calling for each country to do its best to act to the disadvantage of its trading partners—in Adam Smith's terms, to "beggar its neighbors." The idea that one nation's gain must be another's loss means that a country can promote its own welfare only by harming others.

Yet, as Adam Smith and others after him emphasized, in any *voluntary exchange*, both parties *must* expect to gain something from the transaction unless there is misunderstanding or misrepresentation of the facts. Otherwise why would they agree to trade?

But how can mere exchange, with no increase in production, leave *both* parties better off? The answer is that while trade does not increase the physical quantities of the goods available, it does allow each party to acquire items better suited to their needs and tastes. Suppose Scott has four cookies and nothing to drink, while William has two glasses of milk and nothing to eat. A trade of two of Scott's cookies for one of William's glasses of milk does not increase the total supply of either milk or cookies, but it almost certainly improves the welfare of both boys.

By exactly the same logic, both the United States and Mexico must be better off if Mexico voluntarily ships tomatoes to the United States in return for chemicals.

**MUTUAL GAINS FROM VOLUNTARY EXCHANGE**

Both parties must expect to gain from any *voluntary exchange*. Trade brings about mutual gains by redistributing products in such a way that both parties end up holding a combination of goods that they prefer to the one they held before. This principle, which is one of our **12 Ideas for Beyond the Final Exam**, applies to nations just as it does to individuals.

## INTERNATIONAL VERSUS INTRANATIONAL TRADE

The 50 states of the United States may be the most eloquent testimony to the gains from specialization and free trade. Florida specializes in growing oranges, Iowa in growing corn, Pennsylvania makes steel, and Michigan builds cars. All these states trade freely with one another and enjoy great material prosperity. Try to imagine how much lower your standard of living would be if you could only consume items produced in your own state.

The logic of international trade is essentially no different from that underlying trade among different states; the basic reasons for trade are equally applicable *within* a country or *among* countries. Why, then, do we study international trade as a special subject? There are at least three reasons.

### POLITICAL FACTORS IN INTERNATIONAL TRADE

First, domestic trade takes place under a single national government, while foreign trade always involves at least two governments. At least in theory, a nation's government is concerned with the welfare of all its citizens. But governments are usually much less deeply concerned with the welfare of citizens of other countries. For example, the Constitution of the United States prohibits overt tariffs and other impediments to trade among states but does not prohibit the United States from imposing tariffs on imports from abroad. A major issue in the economic analysis of international trade, and therefore of this chapter, is the use and misuse of impediments to free international trade.

### THE MANY CURRENCIES INVOLVED IN INTERNATIONAL TRADE

Second, all trade within the borders of the United States is carried out in U.S. dollars. But trade across national borders must involve at least two currencies. Rates of exchange between different currencies can and do change. In 1985, it took about 250 Japanese yen to buy a dollar; now it takes only about 110. Variability in exchange rates brings with it a host of complications and policy problems that are discussed in Chapters 36 and 37.

### IMPEDIMENTS TO MOBILITY OF LABOR AND CAPITAL

Third, it is much easier for labor and capital to move about within a country than to move from one country to another. If there are jobs in Michigan but none in West Virginia, workers can move freely to follow the job opportunities. Of course, there are personal costs, including the financial cost of moving and the psychological cost of leaving friends and familiar surroundings. But such relocations are not inhibited by immigration quotas, by laws restricting the employment of foreigners, nor by the need to learn a new language.

There are also greater impediments to the transfer of capital across national boundaries than to its movement within a country. For example, many countries have rules limiting the share of foreign ownership in a company. Foreign investment is also subject to special political risks, such as the danger of outright expropriation after a change in government. But even if nothing so extreme occurs, capital invested abroad faces significant risks from variations in exchange rates. An investment valued at 250 million yen will be worth $1 million to American investors if the dollar is worth 250 yen, but $2 million if the dollar is worth just 125 yen.

While labor, capital, and other factors of production do move from country to country when offered an opportunity to increase their earnings abroad, they are less likely to do so than to move from one region of a country to another to gain similar increases.

## THE LAW OF COMPARATIVE ADVANTAGE

The gains from international specialization and trade are clear when one country is better at producing one item while its trading partner is better at producing another. For example, no one finds it surprising that Brazil sells coffee to the United States while America exports aircraft to Brazil. We know that coffee can be produced using less labor and other inputs in Brazil than in the United States. And America can produce passenger aircraft at a lower resource cost than can Brazil.

One country is said to have an **ABSOLUTE ADVANTAGE** over another in the production of a particular good if it can produce that good using smaller quantities of resources than can the other country.

We say that in such a situation Brazil has an **absolute advantage** in coffee production, and the United States has an absolute advantage in aircraft production. And, in such cases, it is obvious that both countries can gain by producing the item in which they have an absolute advantage, and then trading with one another.

What is much less obvious is the fact that two countries can generally gain from trade *even if one of them is more efficient than the other in producing everything.* A simple parable will help explain why.

Some lawyers are better typists than their secretaries. Should such a lawyer fire her secretary and do her own typing? Not likely. Even though the lawyer may be better than the secretary at both typing and arguing cases, good judgment tells her to concentrate her energies on the practice of law and leave the typing to a lower-paid secretary. Why? Because the *opportunity cost* of an hour devoted to typing is one hour less spent on her legal practice, which is a far more lucrative activity.

One country is said to have a **COMPARATIVE ADVANTAGE** over another in the production of a particular good relative to other goods if it produces that good least inefficiently as compared with the other country.

This is an example of the principle of **comparative advantage** at work. The lawyer specializes in arguing cases despite her absolute advantage in typing because she has a still greater absolute advantage as an attorney. She suffers some direct loss by not doing her own typing. But that loss is more than compensated for by the earnings she makes selling her legal services to clients.

Precisely the same principle applies to nations, and it underlies the economic analysis of patterns of international trade. The principle, called the *law of comparative advantage*, was discovered by David Ricardo, one of the giants in the history of economic analysis (see the Biographical Note box on page 878); and it is one of our **12 Ideas for Beyond the Final Exam**.

**THE LAW OF COMPARATIVE ADVANTAGE**

Even if one country is at an absolute disadvantage relative to another country in the production of *every* good, it is said to have a *comparative advantage* in making the good at which it is *least inefficient* (compared with the other country). ¶ Ricardo discovered that two countries can still gain by trading even if one country is more efficient than another in the production of *every* commodity—that is, has an absolute advantage in every commodity. ¶ In determining the most efficient patterns of production, it is *comparative* advantage, not *absolute* advantage, that matters. Thus a country can gain by importing a good even if that good can be produced at home more efficiently than it can be produced abroad. Such imports make sense because they enable the country to specialize in producing goods at which it is even more efficient.

## THE ARITHMETIC OF COMPARATIVE ADVANTAGE

Let's see precisely how this works using a hypothetical example that gives a somewhat exaggerated impression of the trading positions of the United States and Japan a few years ago. We imagine that labor is the only input used to produce microcomputers and television sets in the two countries. Suppose further that the U.S. has an absolute advantage in both goods, as indicated in Table 35–2. In this example, a year's worth of labor can produce either 50 computers or 50 TV sets in the U.S., but only 10 computers or 40 televisions in Japan. So

**Table 35–2 ALTERNATIVE OUTPUTS FROM ONE YEAR OF LABOR INPUT**

| | IN THE UNITED STATES | IN JAPAN |
|---|---|---|
| Computers | 50 | 10 |
| Televisions | 50 | 40 |

## *Biographical Note*

**DAVID RICARDO (1772–1823)**

David Ricardo was born four years before publication of Adam Smith's *Wealth of Nations.* Descended from a wealthy Jewish family of Portuguese origins, he had about twenty brothers and sisters. Ricardo's formal education ended at the age of 13, and so he was largely self-educated. He began his career by working in his father's stock brokerage firm. At age 21, Ricardo married a Quaker woman and decided to become a Unitarian, a sect then considered "little better than atheist." By Jewish custom, Ricardo's father broke with him, though apparently they remained friendly.

Ricardo then decided to go into the brokerage business on his own and was enormously successful. During the Napoleonic Wars he regularly scored business coups over leading British and foreign financiers, including the Rothschilds. After gaining a huge profit on government securities that he had bought just before the Battle of Waterloo, Ricardo decided to retire from business when he was just over 40 years old.

He purchased a country estate, Gatcomb (now owned by the royal family), where a brilliant group of intellectuals met regularly. Particularly remarkable for the period was the number of women included in the circle, among them Maria Edgeworth, the novelist (who wrote extravagant praise of Ricardo's mind), and Jane Marcet, an author of textbooks, one of which was probably the first textbook in economics. Ricardo's close friends included the economists T. R. Malthus and James Mill, father of John Stuart Mill, the noted philosopher-economist. Malthus remained a close friend of Ricardo even though they disagreed on many subjects and continued their arguments in personal correspondence and in their published works.

James Mill persuaded Ricardo to go into Parliament. As was then customary, Ricardo purchased his seat by buying a piece of land that entitled its owner to a seat in Parliament. There he proved to be a noteworthy advocate of many causes that were against his personal interests.

James Mill also helped persuade Ricardo to write his masterpiece, *The Principles of Political Economy and Taxation,* which may have been the first book of pure economic theory. It was noteworthy that Ricardo, the most practical of practical men, had little patience with empirical economics and preferred instead to rest his analysis explicitly and exclusively on theory. His book made considerable contributions to the analysis of pricing, wage determination, and the effects of various types of taxes, among many other subjects. It also gave us the law of comparative advantage.

Ricardo died in 1823 at the age of 51. He seems to have been a wholly admirable person—honest, charming, witty, conscientious, brilliant—altogether too good to be true.

America is the more efficient producer of both goods. Nonetheless, as our lawyer-secretary example suggests, it pays for the U.S. to specialize and trade with Japan.

We demonstrate this in two steps. First, we note that the U.S. has a comparative advantage in computers while Japan has a comparative advantage in TVs. Then we show that both countries can gain if the United States specializes in producing computers, Japan specializes in producing TVs, and the two countries trade.

The numbers in Table 35–2 show that the United States can produce 50 televisions with a year's labor while Japan can produce only 40; thus the U.S. is 25 percent more efficient than Japan in producing TV sets. However, the U.S. is five times as efficient as Japan in producing computers: it can produce 50 per year of labor rather than 10. Thus America's competitive edge is far greater in computers

**Table 35–3 EXAMPLE OF THE GAINS FROM TRADE**

| | THE UNITED STATES | JAPAN | TOTAL |
|---|---|---|---|
| Computers (thousands) | +25 | −10 | +15 |
| Televisions (thousands) | −25 | +40 | +15 |

than in televisions—which is precisely what we mean by saying that the U.S. has a *comparative advantage* in computers.

Looked at from the Japanese perspective, these same numbers indicate that Japan is only slightly less efficient than America in TV production but drastically less efficient in computer production. So Japan's comparative advantage is in the television industry. According to Ricardo's law of comparative advantage, then, the two countries can benefit if Japan makes TVs, America makes computers, and the two countries trade. Let us check that this is true.

Suppose Japan transfers 1000 years of labor out of the computer industry and into TV manufacturing. According to the figures in Table 35–2, its computer output falls by 10,000 units while its TV output rises by 40,000 units. (See Table 35–3.) Suppose, at the same time, the U.S. transfers 500 years of labor out of television manufacturing (thereby losing 25,000 TVs) and into computer making (thereby gaining 25,000 computers). Table 35–3 shows us that these transfers of resources in the two countries increase the world's production of both outputs! Together, the two countries now have 15,000 additional TVs and 15,000 additional computers—surely a nice outcome.

Was there some sleight of hand here? All that has taken place is an exchange. Yet, somehow the U.S. and Japan gain both computers and TVs. How can such gains in physical output be possible? The explanation is that the process we have just described involves more than just a swap of a fixed bundle of commodities. It is also a *change in the production arrangements*, with some of Japan's inefficient computer production taken over by more efficient American makers, and with some of America's TV production taken over by Japanese television companies who are *less* inefficient at making TVs than Japanese computer manufacturers are at making computers.

When every country does what it can do best, all countries can benefit because more of every commodity can be produced without increasing the amounts of labor used.

If this result still seems a bit mysterious, the concept of opportunity cost will help remove the remaining mystery. If the two countries do not trade, Table 35–2 shows that the United States can acquire a computer on its own by giving up a TV. Thus the opportunity cost of a computer in the U.S. is one television set. But in Japan the opportunity cost of a computer is four TVs (see, again, Table 35–2). Thus, in terms of real resources foregone, it is cheaper—for *either* country—to acquire computers in the United States. By a similar line of reasoning, the opportunity cost of TVs is higher in the U.S. than in Japan, so it makes sense for both countries to acquire their televisions in Japan.[1]

[1]As an exercise, provide this line of reasoning.

**Figure 35–1** **ABSOLUTE AND COMPARATIVE ADVANTAGE SHOWN BY TWO COUNTRIES' PRODUCTION POSSIBILITIES FRONTIERS**

The U.S.'s absolute advantage is shown by its ability to produce more of every commodity using the same quantity of labor as does Japan. Therefore, America's per-capita production possibilities frontier, *US*, is higher than Japan's, *JN*. But the U.S. has a comparative advantage in computer production, in which it is five times as productive as Japan. (It can produce 50 million computers, point *S*, compared with Japan's 10 million, point *N*.) On the other hand, the U.S. is only 25 percent more productive in TV production (point *U*) than Japan (point *J*). Thus, Japan is less inefficient in producing televisions, where it consequently has a comparative advantage.

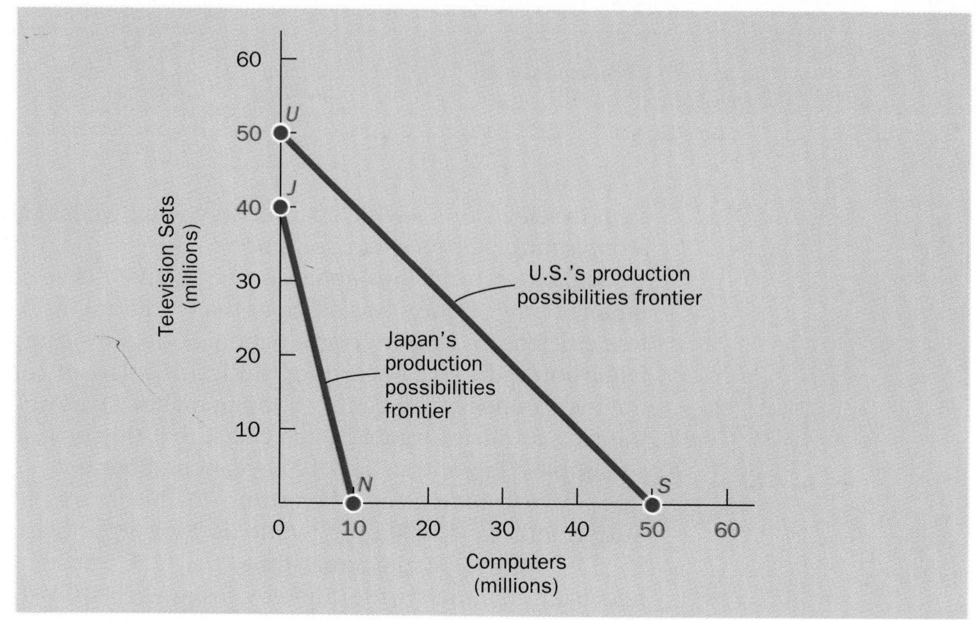


## THE GRAPHICS OF COMPARATIVE ADVANTAGE

The gains from trade can also be displayed graphically, and doing so helps us understand how these gains arise.

The lines *US* and *JN* in Figure 35–1 are closely related to the production possibilities frontiers of the two countries, but differ in that they pretend that each country has the same amount of labor available—in this case, a million person-years.[2] For example, Table 35–2 tells us that, for each million person-years of labor, the United States can produce 50 million TVs and no computers (point *U*), 50 million computers and no TVs (point *S*), or any combination between (the line *US*). Similar reasoning can be used to derive line *JN* for Japan.

America's actual production possibilities frontier would be even higher, relative to Japan's, than shown in Figure 35–1 because the U.S. population is larger. But Figure 35–1 is more useful to us because it highlights the differences in efficiency that determine both absolute and comparative advantage. Let us see how.

The fact than line *US* lies *above* line JN means that, with the same amount of labor, the U.S. can obtain more televisions and more computers than Japan. This reflects our assumption that America is the more efficient producer of *both* commodities; that is, that America has an *absolute* advantage in both TVs and computers.

[2]To review the concept of the production possibilities frontier, see Chapter 3.

America's comparative advantage in computer production and Japan's comparative advantage in TV production are shown in a different way—by the relative *slopes* of the two lines. America's frontier is not only higher than Japan's, it is also less steep. What does that mean economically? One way of looking at the difference is to remember that while America can produce five times as many computers per capita as Japan (compare points *S* and *N*), it can produce only 25 percent more TVs (compare points *U* and *J*). The U.S. is, relatively speaking, much better at computer production than at TV production. That is what we mean when we say it has a *comparative* advantage in computers.

We may express this difference more directly in terms of the slopes of the two lines. The slope of Japan's production possibilities frontier is $OJ/ON = 40/10 = 4$. This means that if Japan reduces its computer output by one unit, it will obtain four television sets. Thus, the *opportunity cost* of a computer in Japan is four TVs, as we observed earlier.

In the case of the U.S., the slope of the production possibilities frontier is $OU/OS = 50/50 = 1$. That is, if the U.S. reduces its computer output by one unit, it gets one additional television. So in the U.S., the *opportunity cost* of a computer is one TV.

A country's absolute advantage in production over another country is shown by its having a higher per-capita production possibilities frontier. The difference in the comparative advantages of the two countries is shown by the difference in the slopes of their frontiers.

Because opportunity costs differ in the two countries, gains from trade are possible. How these gains are divided between the two countries depends on the prices for televisions and computers that emerge from world trade, which is the subject of the next section. But we already know enough to see that world trade must leave a computer costing more than one TV and less than four. Why? Because, if a computer brought less than one TV (its opportunity cost in the U.S.) on the world market, America would produce its own TVs rather than buying them from Japan. Similarly, if a computer cost more than four TVs (its opportunity cost in Japan), Japan would prefer to produce its own computers rather than buy them from the U.S.

We conclude, therefore, that if both countries are to trade, the rate of exchange between TVs and computers must be somewhere between 4 to 1 and 1 to 1. To illustrate the gains from trade in a concrete example, suppose the world price ratio settles at 2 to 1; that is, one computer costs the same as two televisions. How much, precisely, do the U.S. and Japan gain from world trade?

Figure 35–2 is designed to help us see the answer. Production possibilities frontiers *US* in part (b) and *JN* in part (a) are the same as in Figure 35–1. But the U.S. can do better than line *US*. Specifically, with a world price ratio of 2 to 1, the U.S. can buy a TV by giving up only one-half of a computer, rather than one (which is the opportunity cost of TVs in the U.S.). Hence, if the U.S. produces only computers (point *S* in Figure 35–2[b]) and buys its TVs from Japan, America's *consumption possibilities* will be as indicated by the brown line that begins at point *S* and has a slope of 2—indicating that each computer it sells brings the U.S. two television sets. Since trade allows the U.S. to choose a point on *AS* rather than on *US*, trade opens up consumption possibilities that were simply not available before.

The story is similar for Japan. If the Japanese produce only televisions (point *J* in Figure 35–2[a]), they can acquire a computer from the U.S. for every two TVs

Figure 35–2 **THE GAINS FROM TRADE**

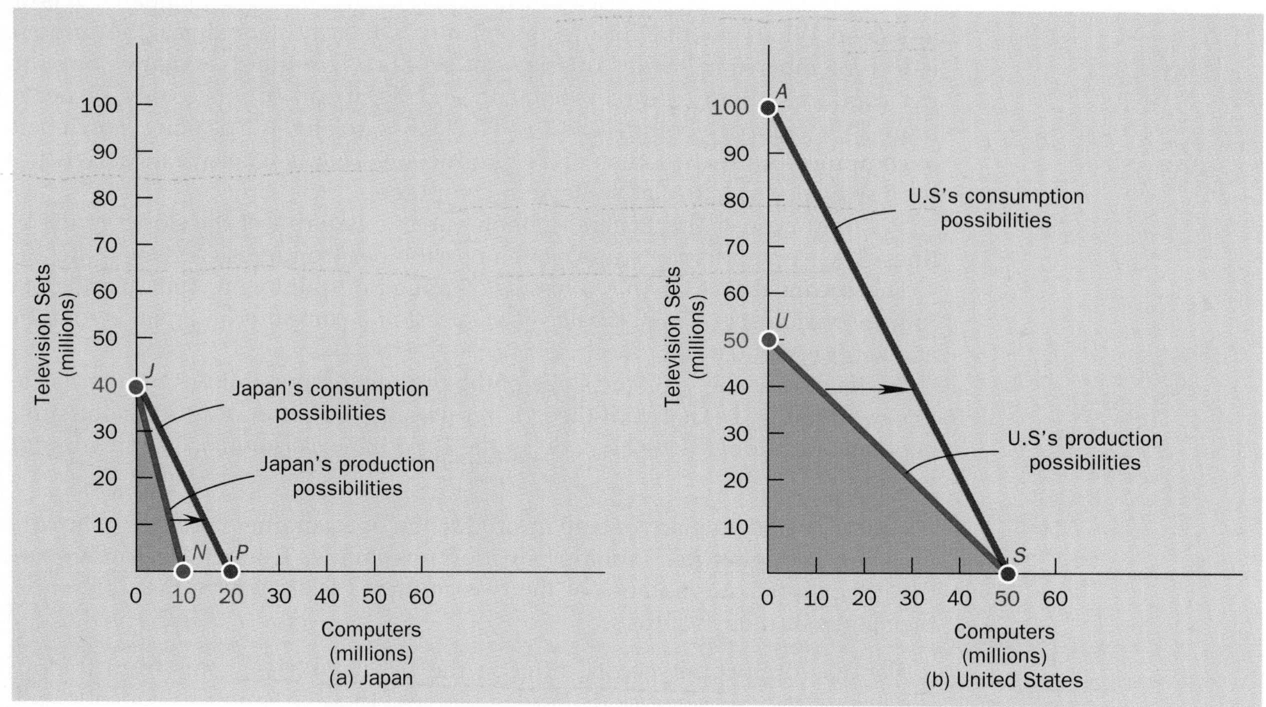


In this diagram, we suppose that trade opens up between the U.S. and Japan and that the world price of computers is twice the world price of TVs. Now the U.S.'s consumption possibilities are all the points on line *AS* (which starts at *S* and has a slope of 2), rather than just the points on its own production possibilities frontier, *US*. Similarly, Japan can choose any point on line *JP* (which begins at *J* and has a slope of 2), rather than just points on *JN*. Thus both nations gain from trade.

they give up as they move along the brown line *JP* (whose slope is 2). This is better than they can do on their own, since a sacrifice of two TVs in Japan yields only one-half of a computer. Hence world trade enlarges Japan's consumption possibilities from *JN* to *JP*.

Figure 35–2 shows graphically that gains from trade arise to the extent that world prices (2 to 1 in our example) differ from domestic opportunity costs (4 to 1 and 1 to 1 in our example). So it is a matter of some importance to understand how prices in international trade are established. This we shall do shortly.

## COMPARATIVE ADVANTAGE AND COMPETITION OF "CHEAP FOREIGN LABOR"

But first let us observe that the principle of comparative advantage takes us a good part of the way toward an explanation of the fallacy in the "cheap foreign labor" argument described earlier in the chapter. Given the assumed productive efficiency of American labor and the inefficiency of Japanese labor, we would expect wages to be much higher in the U.S. than in Japan. And, indeed, they were until recent years.

In these circumstances, one might expect American workers to be apprehensive about an agreement to permit open trade between the two countries—"How can we hope to meet the unfair competition of those underpaid Japanese workers?" And Japanese laborers might also be concerned—"How can we hope to meet the competition of those Americans, who are so efficient in producing everything?"

The principle of comparative advantage shows us that both fears are unjustified. As we have just seen, when trade is opened up between Japan and the United States, *workers in both countries will be able to earn higher real wages than before* because of the increased productivity that comes about through specialization.

Figure 35–2 shows this fact directly. We have seen from our illustration that, with trade, Japan can end up with more TVs and more computers than it had before. So the living standards of its workers can rise even though they have been left vulnerable to the competition of the superefficient Americans. The U.S. also can end up with more TVs and with more computers; so the living standards of its workers can rise even though they have been exposed to the competition of cheap Japanese labor. These higher standards of living are, of course, a reflection of the higher real wages earned by workers in both countries.

The lesson to be learned here is elementary: nothing helps raise standards of living more than does a greater abundance of goods.

## SUPPLY–DEMAND EQUILIBRIUM AND PRICING IN WORLD TRADE

How the gains from trade are shared depends on the prices that emerge from world trade. As usual, price determination in a free market depends on supply and demand.

When applied to international trade, the supply–demand model runs into several new complications. First, it involves at least two demand curves: that of the exporting country and that of the importing country. Second, it may also involve two supply curves, since the importing country may produce some part of its own consumption. Third, equilibrium does not take place at the intersection point of *either* pair of supply–demand curves. Why? Because if there is any trade, the exporting country's quantity supplied must be *greater* than its quantity demanded, while the quantity supplied by the importing country must be *less* than its quantity demanded.

These complications are illustrated in Figure 35–3, where we show the supply and demand curves of a country that exports wheat, in part (a), and those of one that imports wheat, in part (b). For simplicity, we assume that these countries do not deal in wheat with anyone else.

Where will the two-country wheat market reach equilibrium? The equilibrium price in a free market must satisfy two requirements:

1. The price of wheat must be the same in both countries.
2. The quantity of wheat exported must equal the quantity of wheat imported.

In Figure 35–3, this happens at a price of $2.50 per bushel. At that price, the distance *AB* between what the exporting country produces (point *B*) and what it consumes (point *A*) equals the distance *CD* between the quantity demanded of the importing country (point *D*) and its quantity supplied (point *C*). Thus, at a

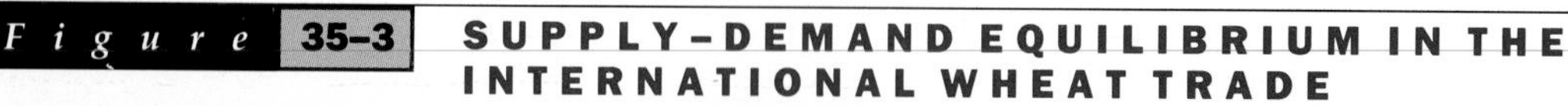

**Figure 35-3 SUPPLY–DEMAND EQUILIBRIUM IN THE INTERNATIONAL WHEAT TRADE**

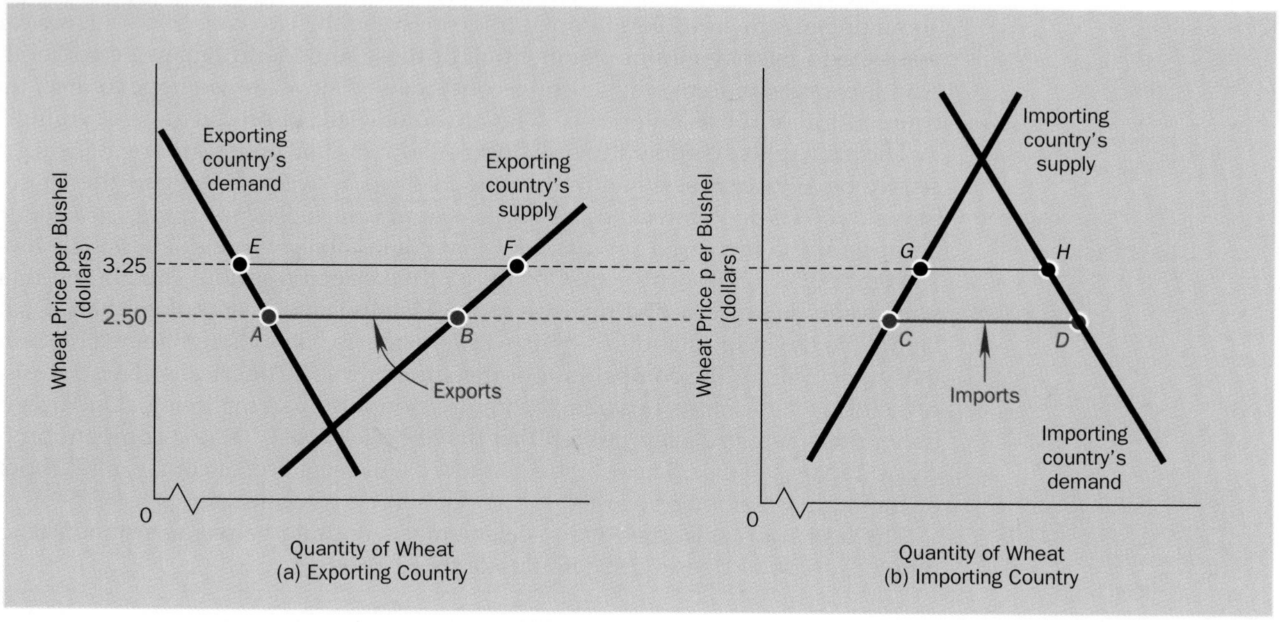


Equilibrium requires that exports, *AB* (which is the exporting nation's quantity supplied, *B*, minus the exporter's quantity demanded, *A*), exactly balance imports, *CD*, by the importing country. At $2.50 per bushel of wheat, there is equilibrium. But at a higher price, say $3.25, there is disequilibrium because export supply, *EF*, exceeds import demand, *GH*.

price of $2.50 per bushel, the amount the exporting country wants to sell is exactly equal to the amount the importing country wants to buy.

At any price above $2.50, producers in both countries will want to sell more and consumers in both countries will want to buy less. For example, if the price rises to $3.25 per bushel, the exporter's quantity supplied will rise from *B* to *F*, and the exporter's quantity demanded will fall from *A* to *E*, as shown in Figure 35–3(a). As a result, there will be more available for export—*EF* rather than *AB*. For exactly the same reason, the price increase will cause higher production and lower sales in the importing country, leading to a reduction in imports from *CD* to *GH* in part (b).

This means that the higher price, $3.25 per bushel, cannot be sustained if the international market is free and competitive. With export supply *EF* far greater than import demand *GH*, there must be downward pressure on price and a move back toward the $2.50 equilibrium price. Similar reasoning shows that prices below $2.50 also cannot be sustained.

We can now see the straightforward role of supply–demand equilibrium in international trade:

In international trade, the equilibrium price is the one that makes the exporting country want to export exactly the amount that the importing country wants to import. Equilibrium will thus occur at a price at which the horizontal distance *AB* in Figure 35–3(a) (the excess of the exporter's quantity supplied over its quantity demanded) is equal to the horizontal distance *CD* in Figure 35–3(b) (the excess of the importer's quantity demanded over its quantity supplied). At this price, the *world's* quantity demanded is equal to the *world's* quantity supplied.

## TARIFFS, QUOTAS, AND OTHER INTERFERENCES WITH TRADE

Despite the mutual gains from international trade, the countries of the world often interfere with the operation of free international markets. In fact, until the rise of the free-trade movement about 200 years ago (with such economists as Adam Smith and David Ricardo as its vanguard), it was taken for granted that one of the essential tasks of government was to impede trade—presumably in the national interest.

There were many who argued then (and some who still argue today) that a nation's wealth consists of the amount of gold or other monies at its command. According to this view, the proper aim of government policy was to promote exports and discourage imports, for that would increase the amount foreigners owed the nation.

Obviously, there are limits to which this policy can be pursued. A country *must* import vital foodstuffs or critical raw materials that it cannot supply for itself; for if it does not, it must suffer a severe fall in living standards as well as a deterioration in its military strength. Moreover, it is mathematically impossible for *every* country to sell more than it buys—one country's exports *must* be some other country's imports. If everyone competes in this game and cuts imports to the bone, then obviously exports must go the same way. The result will be that everyone is deprived of the mutual gains that trade can provide.

After the 1930s, the United States moved away from policies designed to reduce competition from foreign imports and gradually assumed a leading role in attempts to promote free trade. Over the course of several decades, tariffs and other trade barriers were reduced. However, a combination of high unemployment rates and a deterioration in America's competitive position since the 1980s have led to continuous political pressure to move back in the other direction. The decade of the 1980s, for example, witnessed new restrictions on U.S. trade in automobiles, lumber, semiconductors, and a variety of other products.

Three main devices are used by modern governments seeking to control trade: tariffs, quotas, and export subsidies.

A **TARIFF** is a tax on imports.

A **tariff** is simply a tax on imports. An importer of wheat, for example, may be charged $1 for each bushel he or she brings into the country. The United States is generally a low-tariff country, although there are a few notable exceptions. For example, a major controversy arose during 1993 over whether to raise the tariff on imported minivans from 2.5 percent to 25 percent. However, many other countries rely on heavy tariffs to protect their industries. Tariff rates of 100 percent or more are not unheard of.

A **QUOTA** specifies the maximum amount of a good that is permitted into the country from abroad per unit of time.

A **quota** is a legal limit on the amount of a good that may be imported. For example, the government might allow no more than 25 million bushels of wheat to be imported in a year. In some cases, governments ban the importation of certain goods outright—a quota of zero. (See the accompanying boxed insert for

## *Yes, Greeks Had No Bananas*

Import quotas are sometimes taken to extremes, producing strange results. Until recently, for example, they made bananas almost impossible to find in Greece—as the following newspaper story attests.

ATHENS—Are there no bananas in Olympia? Yes. Are there no bananas in Thebes? Yes. In Corinth? Yes. In Sparta, Marathon, Delphi? Yes, yes, yes.

Are there no bananas on Crete?

That depends on your definition of banana. Little green pods do grow on that Greek island, on scorched, drooping plants that look as though they want to be banana trees. They are called bananas, but they don't taste much like bananas—or, at least, that's what people say. A foreigner can't easily get a taste of a ripe Cretan banana. They are all sold secretly, on the black market. To buy a banana anywhere in Greece, you need a connection. All over the world, people take bananas for granted. A bunch of bananas off the boat from Panama isn't exactly what dreams are made of, right? Well, in this country, dreams *are* made of bananas. Alien bananas are contraband in Greece. For Greeks, a sweet, yellow, pulpy Panamanian banana is the forbidden fruit.

"Greece no banana," says the taxi driver at the Athens airport, ecstatically accepting an exotic beauty as a tip. A traveler has just slipped through customs with a bunch in a brown paper bag, defying a five-pound limit. The driver tenderly places his in the glove compartment. "I show it to my grandson," he says.

It has been 12 years now since the last banana boat sailed away from Piraeus. There are children in Greece today who don't even know what a banana is. Greece was a dictatorship in 1971, and dictatorships sometimes do strange things. The one in Greece outlawed the traffic in foreign bananas.

The head of internal security, Col. Stelios Pattakos, gave the order. He was born on Crete, a bone-dry island, and was friendly toward some farmers there who had it in their heads to try growing a fruit native to equatorial jungles. The colonel got rid of the competition. Still, the Cretan crop was so puny it couldn't satisfy a 50th of the Greek passion for bananas. The price went up. The government imposed controls. And then the banana peddlers went underground.

When the dictatorship collapsed in 1974, Col. Pattakos was sentenced to life imprisonment for nonbanana-related offenses. Democracy returned—but bananas didn't. Bureaucrats do strange things, too.

A banana avalanche, they determined, would hurt the Greek apple business. Everybody would suddenly stop eating apples and start eating bananas. It didn't do any good to argue that comparing apples and bananas was like comparing apples and oranges. So Col. Pattakos got life, and the Greek people got life without bananas.

SOURCE: *The Wall Street Journal*, July 28, 1983, page 1.

**EXPORT SUBSIDY** is a payment by the government to exporters to permit them to reduce the selling price of their goods so they can compete more effectively in foreign markets.

an example.) The United States now imposes quotas on a smattering of goods, including textiles, sugar, and meat. But most imports are free of quotas.

An **export subsidy** is a payment by the government to an exporter. By reducing the exporter's costs, such subsidies permit exporters to lower their selling prices and to compete more effectively in world trade. While export subsidies are minor in the United States, they are used extensively by some foreign governments to assist their industries—a practice that provokes bitter complaints from American manufacturers about "unfair competition." For example, years of heavy government subsidies helped the European Airbus consortium take a sizable share of the world market for commercial aircraft away from American manufacturers.

## HOW TARIFFS AND QUOTAS WORK

Both tariffs and quotas restrict supplies coming from abroad and drive up prices. A tariff works by raising prices and hence cutting the demand for imports, while the sequence associated with a quota is just the reverse—a restriction in supply forces prices up.

Let us use our international trade diagrams to see what a quota does. The supply and demand curves in Figure 35–4 are like those of Figure 35–3. Just as in Figure 35–3, equilibrium in a free international market occurs at a price of $2.50 per bushel (in both countries). At this price, the exporting country produces 125 million bushels (point *B* in part [a]) and consumes 80 million (point *A*); so its exports are 45 million bushels—the distance *AB*. Similarly, the importing country consumes 95 million bushels (point *D* in part [b]) and produces only 50 million (point *C*), so that its imports are also 45 million bushels—the distance *CD*.

Now suppose the government of the importing nation imposes an import quota of (no more than) 30 million bushels. The free-trade equilibrium is no longer possible. Instead, the market must equilibrate at a point where both exports and

*Figure* **35–4** **QUOTAS AND TARIFFS IN INTERNATIONAL TRADE**

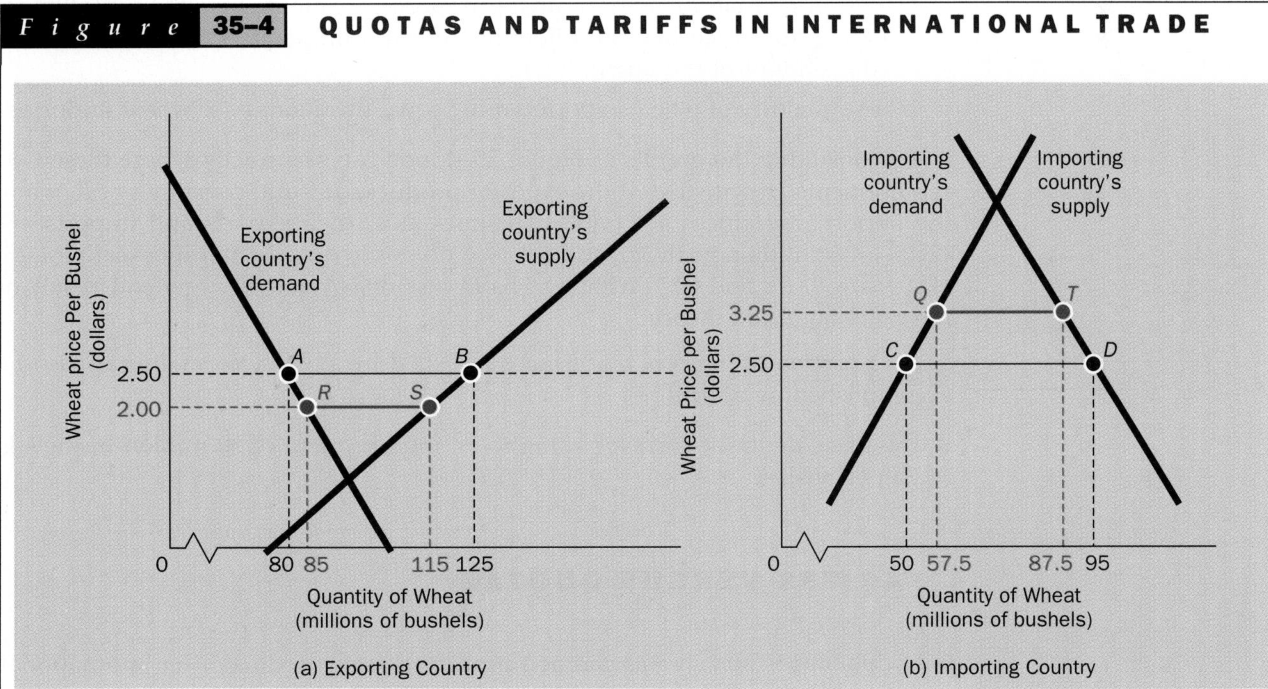


Under free trade, the equilibrium price of wheat is $2.50 per bushel. The exporting country, in part (a), sends *AB*, or 45 million bushels, to the importing country (distance *CD*). If a quota of 30 million bushels is imposed by the importing country, these two distances must shrink to 30 million bushels. The solution is shown by distance *RS* for exports and distance *QT* for imports. Exports and imports are equal, as must be the case, but the quota forces prices to be unequal in the two countries. Wheat sells for $3.25 per bushel in the importing country but only $2 per bushel in the exporting country. A tariff achieves the same result differently. It *requires* that the prices in the two countries be $1.25 apart. And this, as the graph shows, dictates that exports ( = imports) will be equal at 30 million bushels.

imports are 30 million bushels. As Figure 35–4 indicates, this requires different prices in the two countries.

Imports in part (b) will be 30 million—the distance *QT*—only when the price of wheat in the importing nation is $3.25 per bushel, because only at this price will quantity demanded exceed domestic quantity supplied by 30 million bushels. Similarly, exports in part (a) will be 30 million bushels—the distance *RS*—only when the price in the exporting country is $2 per bushel. At this price, quantity supplied exceeds domestic quantity demanded by 30 million bushels in the exporting country. Thus the quota *raises* the price in the importing country to $3.25 and *lowers* the price in the exporting country to $2. In general:

An import quota on a product normally will reduce the volume of that product traded, raise the price in the importing country, and reduce the price in the exporting country.

The same restriction of trade can be accomplished through a tariff. In the example we have just completed, a quota of 30 million bushels resulted in a price that was $1.25 higher in the importing country than in the exporting country ($3.25 versus $2). Suppose that, instead of a quota, the importing nation posts a $1.25 per bushel tariff. International trade equilibrium then must satisfy the following two requirements:

1. The price that consumers in the importing country pay for wheat must exceed the price that suppliers in the exporting country receive by $1.25 (the amount of the tariff).
2. The quantity of wheat exported must equal the quantity of wheat imported.

By consulting the graphs in Figure 35–4, you can see exactly where these two requirements are satisfied. If the exporter produces at *S* and consumes at *R*, while the importer produces at *Q* and consumes at *T*, then exports and imports are equal (at 30 million bushels), and the two domestic prices differ by exactly $1.25. (They are $3.25 and $2.) What we have just discovered is a general result of international trade theory:

Any restriction of imports that is accomplished by a quota normally can also be accomplished by a tariff.

In this case, the tariff corresponding to an import quota of 30 million bushels is $1.25 per bushel.

## TARIFFS VERSUS QUOTAS

But while tariffs and quotas can accomplish the same reduction in international trade and lead to the same domestic prices in the two countries, there *are* some important differences between the two types of restrictions.

First, under a quota, profits from the price increases in the importing country usually go into the pockets of the foreign and domestic sellers of the product. Because supplies are limited by quotas, customers in the importing country must pay more for the product. So the suppliers, whether foreign or domestic, receive more for every unit they sell. For example, it has been estimated that U.S. import quotas on Japanese cars in the early 1980s raised the profits of both American and Japanese automakers by billions of dollars per year.

On the other hand, when trade is restricted by a tariff, some of the profits go instead as tax revenues to the *government* of the importing country. In effect, the government increases its tax revenues partly at the expense of its citizens and partly at the expense of foreign exporters, who must accept a reduced price because of the resulting decrease in quantity demanded in the importing country. (Domestic producers again benefit, because they are exempt from the tariff.) In this respect, a tariff is certainly a better proposition than a quota from the viewpoint of the country that enacts it.

Another important distinction between the two measures is the difference in their implications for productive efficiency and prices in the long run. A tariff handicaps all foreign suppliers equally. It still awards sales to the firms and nations who are most efficient and can therefore supply the goods most cheaply.

A quota, on the other hand, necessarily awards its import licenses more or less capriciously—perhaps on a first-come, first-served basis or in proportion to past sales or even on political criteria. There is not the slightest reason to expect the most efficient and least costly suppliers to get the import permits. In the long run, the population of the importing country is likely to end up with significantly higher prices, poorer products, or both.

The U.S. quota on Japanese cars in the 1980s illustrates all of these effects. Japanese automakers responded to the limit on the number of cars by shipping bigger models equipped with more "optional" equipment. The "stripped down" Japanese car became a thing of the past. And the newer, smaller Japanese automakers—like Subaru and Mitsubishi—found it difficult at first to compete in the U.S. market because their quotas were so much smaller than those of Toyota, Nissan, and Honda.

If a country must inhibit imports, there are two important reasons for it to give preference to tariffs over quotas: (1) some of the resulting financial gains from tariffs go to the government of the importing country rather than to foreign and domestic producers; and (2) unlike quotas, tariffs offer no special benefits to inefficient exporters.

## WHY INHIBIT TRADE?

To state that tariffs are a better way to inhibit international trade than quotas leaves open a far more basic question, Why limit trade in the first place? There are two primary reasons for adopting measures that restrict trade: first, they may help the importing country get more advantageous prices for its goods, and second, they protect particular industries from foreign competition.

### SHIFTING PRICES IN YOUR FAVOR

How can a tariff make prices more advantageous for the importing country if it raises consumer prices there? The answer is that it forces foreign exporters to sell more cheaply by restricting their market. If they do not cut their prices, they will be left with unsold goods. Suppose, as in Figure 35–4(b), that a $1.25 tariff on wheat raises the price of a bushel in the importing country from $2.50 to $3.25 per bushel. This rise in price drives down imports from an amount represented by the length of the black line *CD* to the smaller amount represented by the blue line *QT*. And to the exporting country, this means an equal reduction in exports (see the change from *AB* to *RS* in Figure 35–4[a]).

## *An Eye for an Eye . . . and a Book for a Shingle?*

Trade wars have a way of gathering momentum and moving in unpredictable directions, as the following excerpt shows.

As the authorities in the United States prepare to announce a decision on whether to impose a duty on imports of softwood lumber from Canada, the Canadian Government is threatening retaliation.

The lumber dispute is by far the biggest trade battle between Canada and the United States, the world's largest trading partners. A tariff of the magnitude requested by the American lumber industry would add more than $1 billion to the $3.5 billion price of softwood lumber imported from Canada each year.

"I think you can expect a strong response, but I'm not going to tell you what it is," Pat Carney, Canada's Minister for International Trade, said in an interview today.

She called the American lumber producers' request for a duty "total harassment."

After Washington imposed a tariff on Canadian cedar shingles last May, Ottawa imposed duties on a number of imports from the United States ranging from books to Christmas trees. But trade experts say it is unclear what retaliatory steps the Canadians could take now.

SOURCE: *The New York Times*, October 9, 1986.

As a result, the price at which the exporting country can sell its wheat is driven down (from $2.50 to $2 in the example) while producers in the importing country—being exempt from the tariff—can charge $3.25 per bushel. In effect, such a tariff amounts to government intervention to rig prices in favor of domestic producers and to exploit foreign sellers by forcing them to sell more cheaply than they otherwise would.

However, this technique works only as long as foreigners accept tariff exploitation passively. And, as the boxed insert above suggests, they rarely do. Instead, they retaliate, usually by imposing tariffs or quotas of their own on their imports from the country that first began the tariff game. This can easily lead to a trade war in which no one gains in terms of more favorable prices and everyone loses in terms of the resulting reductions in overall trade. Something like this happened to the world economy in the 1930s and helped prolong the worldwide depression. At present, it is threatening to happen again.

Tariffs or quotas can benefit particular domestic industries in a country that is able to impose them without fear of retaliation. But when every country uses them, everyone is likely to lose in the long run.

### PROTECTING PARTICULAR INDUSTRIES

The second, and probably more frequent, reason why countries restrict trade is to protect particular industries from foreign competition. If foreigners can produce steel or watches or shoes more cheaply, domestic businesses and unions in these industries are quick to demand protection; and their governments are often reluctant to deny it to them. It is here that the cheap foreign labor argument is most likely to be invoked.

Protective tariffs and quotas are explicitly designed to rescue firms whose relative inefficiency does not permit them to compete with foreign exporters in an open world market. But it is precisely the harsh competition from abroad that gives consumers the benefits of international specialization. In our numerical example of comparative advantage, one can well imagine the complaints from Japanese computer makers as the opening of trade led to increased importation of U.S. computers. At the same time, American TV manufacturers would probably express equal concern over the flood of imported TVs from Japan. Yet it is Japanese specialization in televisions and U.S. specialization in computers that enables citizens of both countries to enjoy higher standards of living. If governments interfere with this process, consumers in both countries will lose out.

Often, industries threatened by foreign competition argue that some form of protection against imports is needed to prevent loss of jobs. We know from Part 7 that there are better ways to stimulate employment. But a program that limits foreign competition will do a better job of preserving employment *in the particular protected industry*. It will work, but often at a considerable cost to consumers in the form of higher prices and to the economy in the form of inefficient use of resources. Table 35–4 gives some estimates of the costs to American consumers of using tariffs and quotas to save jobs in selected industries. In every case, the costs far exceed the wages of the workers in the protected industries—ranging as high as a colossal $750,000 per job for quotas on steel products.

Nevertheless, complaints over proposals to reduce a tariff or a quota are justified unless something is done to ease the cost to individual workers of switching to the lines of production that trade makes profitable.

The argument for free trade between countries cannot be considered compelling if there is no adequate program to assist the minority of citizens in each country who will be harmed whenever patterns of production change drastically—as would happen, for example, if tariff and quota barriers were suddenly brought down.

Owners of television factories in the United States and of computer factories in Japan may see heavy investments suddenly rendered unprofitable. So would workers whose investments in acquiring special skills and training are no longer marketable. Nor are the costs to displaced workers only monetary. They may have to move to new locations as well as to new industries, uprooting

*Table* **35–4** **ESTIMATED COSTS OF PROTECTIONISM**

| INDUSTRY | COST PER JOB SAVED |
|---|---|
| Automobiles | $105,000 |
| Book manufacturing | 100,000 |
| Dairy products | 220,000 |
| Steel | 750,000 |
| Sugar | 60,000 |
| Textiles | 42,000 |

SOURCE: Gary C. Hufbauer, Diane T. Berliner, and Kimberly Ann Elliott, *Trade Protection in the United States: 31 Case Studies* (Washington: Institute for International Economic Studies), 1986, Table 1.2.

their families, losing old friends and neighbors, and so on. That the *majority* of citizens undoubtedly gain from free trade is no consolation to those who are its victims.

To help alleviate this problem, the United States (and other countries) has set up programs to assist workers who lose jobs because of changing patterns of world trade. In the United States such **trade adjustment assistance** is provided to firms or workers who suffer idle facilities, unprofitability, and unemployment because of sharp increases in imports.

**TRADE ADJUSTMENT ASSISTANCE** provides special unemployment benefits, loans, retraining programs, and other aid to workers and firms that are harmed by foreign competition.

Firms may be eligible for technical assistance designed to improve their efficiency, financial assistance in the form of government loans or government guarantees of private loans, and permission to delay tax payments. Workers are eligible for retraining programs, lengthened periods of eligibility for unemployment compensation, and allowances to help pay for the cost of moving to other jobs. Each form of assistance is designed to ease the burden on the victims of free trade so that the rest of us can enjoy its considerable benefits.

Trade adjustment assistance in the United States began in 1962, and benefits to displaced workers had grown to be extremely generous by the 1970s. However, the Reagan administration—objecting that the program put too much emphasis on *assistance* and not enough on *adjustment*—cut benefits drastically in 1981. One of the things President Clinton has proposed to do is to restore adjustment assistance to its former prominence, though not in the same forms it had taken in the past.

## OTHER ARGUMENTS FOR PROTECTION

### NATIONAL DEFENSE AND OTHER NONECONOMIC CONSIDERATIONS

There are times when a tariff or some other measure to interfere with trade may be justified on noneconomic grounds. If a country considers itself vulnerable to military attack, it may be perfectly rational to keep alive industries whose outputs can be obtained more cheaply abroad but whose supplies might be cut off in an emergency. For example, it has been argued that the United States must keep alive its semiconductor industry for precisely these reasons.

The argument has validity. The danger, however, is that industries with the most peripheral relationship to defense are likely to invoke this argument on their behalf. For instance, the U.S. watchmaking industry claimed protection for itself for many years on the grounds that its skilled craftsmen would be invaluable in wartime. Perhaps so, but a technicians' training program probably could have done the job more cheaply and even more effectively by teaching exactly the skills needed for military purposes.

Similarly, the United States has occasionally banned either exports to or imports from nations such as Cuba, Libya, and Afghanistan on political grounds. Such actions often have important economic effects, creating either bonanzas or disasters for particular American industries. But they are justified by politics, not by economics. Noneconomic reasons also explain quotas on importation of whaling products and on the furs of other endangered species.

## THE INFANT-INDUSTRY ARGUMENT

Another common argument for protectionism is the so-called **infant-industry argument**. Promising new industries, it is alleged, often need breathing room to flourish and grow. If we expose these infants to the rigors of international competition too soon, the argument goes, they may never develop to the point where they can survive on their own in the international marketplace.

The argument, while valid in certain instances, is less defensible than it seems. It only makes sense to protect an infant industry if the prospective future gains are sufficient to repay the social losses incurred while it is being protected. But if the industry is likely to be so profitable in the future, why doesn't private capital rush in to take advantage of the prospective net profits? The annals of business are full of cases in which a new product or a new firm lost money at first but profited handsomely later. The infant-industry argument for protection stands up to scrutiny only where funds are not available to a particular industry for some reason, despite its glowing profit prospects. And even then it may make more sense to provide a government loan than to provide trade protection.

It is hard to think of examples where the infant-industry argument applies. But even if such a case were found, one would have to be careful that the industry not remain in diapers forever. There are too many cases in which new industries were awarded protection when they were being established and, somehow, the time to withdraw that protection never arrived. One must beware of infant industries that never grow up.

## STRATEGIC TRADE POLICY

A stronger argument for (temporary) protection is beginning to have substantial influence on U.S. trade policy. Advocates of this argument, including some top officials in the Clinton administration, agree that free trade for all is the best system. But they point out that we live in an imperfect world in which many nations refuse to play by the rules of the free-trade game. And they fear that a nation that pursues free trade in a protectionist world is likely to lose out. It therefore makes sense, they argue, to *threaten* to protect your markets unless other nations agree to open theirs. (See the accompanying article by columnist William Safire.) And this is exactly what we have done in recent years to such countries as Japan, Korea, and Brazil.

The strategic argument for protection is a hard one for economists to deal with. While it accepts the superiority of free trade, it argues that threatening protectionism is the best way to establish free trade. Such a strategy might work, but it clearly involves great risks. If threats that America will turn protectionist induce other countries to scrap existing protectionist policies, then the gamble will have succeeded. But, if the gamble fails, the world ends up with even more protection than it started with.

The analogy to arms negotiations is pretty obvious. We used to periodically threaten to install new missiles unless the Russians agreed to dismantle some of theirs. When they did, both sides saved money and the world became a safer place. So everyone was better off. But, when they did not, the arms race accelerated and everyone was worse off. Was the threat to build new missiles therefore a wise or a foolish policy? There was never any agreement on this question, and so we should not expect agreement on the advisability of using protectionist measures in a strategic way.

## *Can Protectionism Save Free Trade?*

In this 1983 column, William Safire shook off his longstanding attachment to free trade and argued eloquently for retaliation against protectionist nations.

WASHINGTON—Free trade is economic motherhood. Protectionism is economic evil incarnate. . . Never should government interfere in the efficiency of international competition.

Since childhood, these have been the tenets of my faith. If it meant that certain businesses in this country went belly-up, so be it. . . If it meant that Americans would be thrown out of work by overseas companies paying coolie wages, that was tough. . .

The thing to keep in mind, I was taught, was the Big Picture and the Long Run. America, the great exporter, had far more to gain than to lose from free trade; attempts to protect inefficient industries here would ultimately cost more American jobs.

While playing with my David Ricardo doll and learning nursery rhymes about comparative advantage, I was listening to another laissez-fairy tale: Government's role in the world of business should be limited to keeping business honest and competitive. In God we antitrusted. Let businesses operate in the free marketplace.

Now American businesses are no longer competing with foreign companies. They are competing with foreign governments who help their local businesses. That means the world arena no longer offers a free marketplace; instead, most other governments are pushing a policy that can be called *helpfulism.*

Helpfulism works like this: A government like Japan decides to get behind its baseball-bat industry. It pumps in capital, knocks off marginal operators, finds subtle ways to discourage imports of Louisville Sluggers, and selects target areas for export blitzes. Pretty soon, the favored Japanese companies are driving foreign competitors batty.

How do we compete with helpfulism? One way is to complain that it is unfair; that draws a horselaugh. Another way is to demand a "Reagan Round" of trade negotiations under GATT, the Gentlemen's Agreement To Talk, which is equally laughable. Yet another way is to join the helpfuls by subsidizing our exports and permitting our companies to try monopolistic tricks abroad not permitted at home. But all that makes us feel guilty, with good reason.

The other way to deal with helpfulism is through—here comes the dreadful word—*protection.* Or, if you prefer a euphemism, *retaliation.* Or if that is still too severe, *reciprocity.* Whatever its name, it is a way of saying to the cutthroat cartelists we sweetly call our trading partners: "You have bent the rules out of shape. Change your practices to conform to the agreed-upon rules, or we will export a taste of your own medicine."

A little balance, then, from the free trade theorists. The demand for what the Pentagon used to call "protective reaction" is not demagoguery, not shortsighted, not self-defeating. On the contrary, the overseas pirates of protectionism and exemplars of helpfulism need to be taught the basic lesson in trade, which is: tit for tat.

SOURCE: William Safire, "Smoot-Hawley Lives," *The New York Times,* March 17, 1983. 

## WHAT IMPORT PRICES MOST BENEFIT A COUNTRY?

**DUMPING** means selling goods in a foreign market at lower prices than those charged in the home market.

One of the most curious features of the protectionist position is the fear of low prices charged by foreign sellers. Countries that subsidize exports are accused of **dumping**—of getting rid of their goods at unconscionably low prices. For example, Japan and Korea have frequently been accused of dumping a variety of goods on the U.S. market.

A moment's thought should indicate why this fear must be considered curious. As a nation of consumers, we should be indignant when foreigners charge us *high* prices, not *low* ones. That is the common-sense rule that guides every consumer, and the consumers of imported commodities should be no exception. Only from the topsy-turvy viewpoint of an industry seeking protection from competition are high prices seen as being in the public interest.

Ultimately, it must be in the best interest of a country to get its imports as cheaply as possible. It would be ideal for the United States if the rest of the world were willing to provide its exports to us free or virtually so. We could then live in luxury at the expense of the rest of the world.

But, of course, what benefits the United States as a whole does not necessarily benefit every single American. If quotas on, say, sugar imports were dropped, American consumers and industries that purchase sugar would gain from lower prices. But owners of and workers in sugar fields would suffer serious losses in the form of lower profits, lower wages, and lost jobs—losses they will fight hard to prevent. For this reason, politics often leads to the adoption of protectionist measures that would likely be rejected on strictly economic criteria.

The notion that low import prices are bad for a country is a fitting companion to the idea—so often heard—that it is good for a country to export much more than it imports. True, this means that foreigners will end up owing us a good deal of money. But it also means that we will have given them large quantities of our products and have gotten relatively little in foreign products in return. That surely is not an ideal way for a country to reap gains from international trade.

Our gains from trade do not consist of accumulations of gold or of heavy debts owed us by foreigners. Rather, our gains are composed of goods and services that others provide minus goods and services we must provide in return.

## CONCLUSION: A LAST LOOK AT THE "CHEAP FOREIGN LABOR" ARGUMENT

The preceding discussion should indicate the fundamental fallacy in the argument that American workers have to fear cheap foreign labor. If workers in other countries are willing to supply their products to us with little compensation, this must ultimately *raise* the standard of living of the average American worker. As long as the government's monetary and fiscal policies succeed in maintaining high levels of employment at home, how can we possibly lose by getting the products of the world at bargain prices?

There are, however, some important qualifications. First, our employment policy may not be effective. If workers who are displaced by foreign competition cannot find jobs in other industries, then American workers will indeed suffer from international trade. But that is a shortcoming of the government's employment program, not of its international trade policies.

Second, we have noted that an abrupt stiffening of foreign competition *can* hurt U.S. workers by not giving them an adequate chance to adapt gradually to the new conditions. The more rapid the change, the more painful it will be. If it occurs fairly gradually, workers can retrain and move on to the industries that now require their services. If the change is even more gradual, no one may have to move. People who retire or leave the threatened industry for other reasons simply need not be replaced. But competition that inflicts its damage overnight

## *Unfair Foreign Competition*

Satire and ridicule are often more persuasive than logic and statistics. Exasperated by the spread of protectionism under the prevailing Mercantilist philosophy, French economist Frédéric Bastiat decided to take the protectionist argument to its illogical conclusion. The fictitious petition of the French candlemakers to the Chamber of Deputies, written in 1845 and excerpted below, has become a classic in the battle for free trade.

We are subject to the intolerable competition of a foreign rival, who enjoys, it would seem, such superior facilities for the production of light, that he is enabled to inundate our national market at so exceedingly reduced a price, that, the moment he makes his appearance, he draws off all custom for us; and thus an important branch of French industry, with all its innumerable ramifications, is suddenly reduced to a state of complete stagnation. This rival is no other than the sun.

Our petition is, that it would please your honorable body to pass a law whereby shall be directed the shutting up of all windows, dormers, skylights, shutters, curtains, in a word, all openings, holes, chinks, and fissures through which the light of the sun is used to penetrate our dwellings, to the prejudice of the profitable manufactures which we flatter ourselves we have been enabled to bestow upon the country. . .

We foresee your objections, gentlemen; but there is not one that you can oppose to us . . . which is not equally opposed to your own practice and the principle which guides your policy. . .

Labor and nature concur in different proportions, according to country and climate, in every article of production. . . . If a Lisbon orange can be sold at half the price of a Parisian one, it is because a natural and gratuitous heat does for the one what the other only obtains from an artificial and consequently expensive one. . .

Does it not argue the greatest inconsistency to check as you do the importation of coal, iron, cheese, and goods of foreign manufacture, merely because and even in proportion as their price approaches *zero*, while at the same time you freely admit, and without limitation, the light of the sun, whose price is during the whole day at *zero*?

SOURCE: F. Bastiat, *Economic Sophisms* (New York: G. P. Putnam's Sons, 1922).

is certain to impose real costs upon the affected workers, costs that are no less painful for being temporary. That is why our trade laws make provisions for people and industries damaged by import surges. It is also why President Clinton has insisted that a side-agreement on import surges be made part of the North American Free Trade Agreement (NAFTA).

But these are, after all, only qualifications to an overwhelming argument. They call for intelligent monetary and fiscal policies and for transitional assistance to unemployed workers, not for abandonment of free trade. In general, the nation as a whole need not fear competition from cheap foreign labor.

In the long run, labor will be "cheap" only where it is not very productive. Wages will tend to be highest in countries in which high labor productivity keeps costs down and permits exporters to compete effectively despite high wages. It is thus misleading to say that the United States held its own in the international marketplace until recently *despite* the high wages of its workers. Rather it is much more illuminating to point out that the high wages of American workers were a result of high worker productivity, which gave the United States a heavy competitive edge.

We note that in this matter it is *absolute* advantage, not *comparative* advantage, that counts. The country that is most efficient in every output can pay its workers more in every industry.

## *Summary*

1. Countries trade because differences in their natural resources and other inputs create discrepancies in the efficiency with which they can produce different goods, and because **specialization** may offer them greater economies of large-scale production.
2. Voluntary trade will generally be advantageous to both parties in an exchange. This is one of our **12 Ideas for Beyond the Final Exam**.
3. International trade is more complicated than trade within a nation because of political factors, different national currencies, and impediments to the movement of labor and capital across national borders.
4. Both countries will gain from trade with one another if each exports goods in which it has a **comparative advantage**. That is, even a country that is generally inefficient will benefit by exporting the goods in whose production it is *least inefficient*. This is another of the **12 Ideas for Beyond the Final Exam.**
5. When countries specialize and trade, each can enjoy consumption possibilities that exceed its production possibilities.
6. The prices of goods traded between countries are determined by supply and demand, but one must consider explicitly the demand curve and the supply curve of *each* country involved. Thus, in international trade, the equilibrium price must be where the excess of the exporter's quantity supplied over its domestic quantity demanded is equal to the excess of the importer's quantity demanded over its quantity supplied.
7. The **"cheap foreign labor" argument** ignores the principle of comparative advantage, which shows that real wages can rise in both the importing and exporting countries as a result of specialization.
8. **Tariffs** and **quotas** are designed to protect a country's industries from foreign competition. Such protection may sometimes be advantageous to that country, but not if foreign countries adopt tariffs and quotas of their own as a means of retaliation.
9. While the same restriction of trade can be accomplished by either a tariff or a quota, tariffs offer at least two advantages to the country that imposes them: (1) some of the gains go to the government rather than to foreign producers; and (2) there is greater incentive for efficient production.
10. When a nation shifts from protection to free trade, some industries and their workers will lose out. Equity then demands that these people and firms be compensated in some way. The U.S. government offers various forms of **trade adjustment assistance** to do this.
11. Several arguments for protectionism can, under the right circumstances, have validity. These include the national defense argument, the **infant-industry argument**, and the use of trade restrictions for **strategic** purposes. But each of these arguments is frequently abused.
12. **Dumping** will hurt certain domestic producers; but it always benefits domestic consumers.

## *Key Concepts and Terms*

Imports
Exports
Specialization
Mutual gains from trade
Absolute advantage
Comparative advantage
"Cheap foreign labor" argument
Tariff
Quota
Export subsidy
Trade adjustment assistance
Infant-industry argument
Strategic trade protection
Dumping

## Questions for Review

1. You have a dozen eggs worth $1 and your neighbor has a pound of bacon worth about the same. You decide to swap six eggs for a half pound of bacon. In financial terms, neither of you gains anything. Explain why you are nevertheless both likely to be better off.
2. In the eighteenth century, some writers argued that one person in a trade could be made better off only by gaining at the expense of the other. Explain the fallacy in the argument.
3. Country A has mild weather with plenty of rain, plentiful land, but an unskilled labor force. What sorts of products do you think it is likely to produce? What are the characteristics of the countries with which you would expect it to trade?
4. Upon removal of a quota on semiconductors, a U.S. manufacturer of semiconductors goes bankrupt. Discuss the pros and cons of the tariff removal in the short and long runs.
5. Country A's government believes that it is best always to export more (in money terms) than the value of its imports. As a consequence, it exports more to country B every year than it imports from country B. After 100 years of this arrangement, both countries are destroyed in an earthquake. What were the advantages and disadvantages of the surplus to country A? To country B?
6. The table below describes the number of yards of cloth and barrels of wine that can be produced with a week's worth of labor in England and Portugal. Assume that no other inputs are needed.

| | IN ENGLAND | IN PORTUGAL |
|---|---|---|
| Cloth (yards) | 10 | 12 |
| Wine (barrels) | 1 | 6 |

   a. If there is no trade, what is the price of wine in terms of cloth in England?
   b. If there is no trade, what is the price of wine relative to cloth in Portugal?
   c. Suppose each country has 1 million weeks of labor available per year. Draw the production possibilities frontier for each country.
   d. Which country has an absolute advantage in the production of which good(s)? Which country has a comparative advantage in the production of which good(s)?
   e. If the countries start trading with each other, which country will specialize and export which good?
   f. What can be said about the price at which trade will take place?

7. Suppose that the United States and Mexico are the only two countries in the world, and that labor is the only productive input. In the United States, a worker can produce 12 bushels of wheat *or* 1 barrel of oil in a day. In Mexico, a worker can produce 2 bushels of wheat *or* 2 barrels of oil per day.
   a. What will be the price ratio between the two commodities (that is, the price of oil in terms of wheat) in each country if there is no trade?
   b. If free trade is allowed and there are no transportation costs, what commodity would the United States import? What about Mexico?
   c. In what range will the price ratio have to fall under free trade? Why?
   d. Picking one possible post-trade price ratio, show clearly how it is possible for both countries to benefit from free trade.
8. The table below presents the demand and supply curves for microcomputers in Japan and the United States.

| PRICE PER COMPUTER (thousands of dollars) | QUANTITY DEMANDED IN U.S. (thousands) | QUANTITY SUPPLIED IN U.S. (thousands) | QUANTITY DEMANDED IN JAPAN (thousands) | QUANTITY SUPPLIED IN JAPAN (thousands) |
|---|---|---|---|---|
| 0 | 100 | 0 | 100 | 0 |
| 1 | 90 | 10 | 90 | 25 |
| 2 | 80 | 20 | 80 | 50 |
| 3 | 70 | 30 | 70 | 70 |
| 4 | 60 | 40 | 60 | 80 |
| 5 | 50 | 50 | 50 | 90 |
| 6 | 40 | 60 | 40 | 100 |
| 7 | 30 | 70 | 30 | 110 |
| 8 | 20 | 80 | 20 | 120 |
| 9 | 10 | 90 | 10 | 130 |
| 10 | 0 | 100 | 0 | 140 |

   a. Draw the demand and supply curves for the United States on one diagram and those for Japan on another one.
   b. If there is no trade between the United States and Japan, what are the equilibrium price and quantity in the computer market in the United States? In Japan?
   c. Now suppose trade is opened up between the two countries. What will be the equilibrium price in the world market for computers? What has happened to the price of computers in the United States? In Japan?
   d. Which country will export computers? How many?
   e. When trade opens, what happens to the quantity of computers produced, and therefore employ-

ment, in the computer industry in the United States? In Japan? Who benefits and who loses *initially* from free trade?

9. Under current trade law, the president of the United States must report periodically to Congress on countries engaging in unfair trade practices that inhibit U.S. exports. How would you define an "unfair" trade practice? Suppose Country X exports much more to the United States than it imports, year after year. Does that constitute evidence that Country X's trade practices are unfair? What would constitute such evidence?

10. Suppose the United States finds Country X guilty of unfair trade practices and penalizes it with import quotas. So U.S. imports from Country X fall. Suppose, further, that Country X does not alter its trade practices in any way. Is the United States better or worse off? What about Country X?

Chapter 36

# THE INTERNATIONAL MONETARY SYSTEM: ORDER OR DISORDER?

*Cecily, you will read your Political Economy in my absence. The chapter on the Fall of the Rupee you may omit. It is somewhat too sensational.*

**MISS PRISM IN THE IMPORTANCE OF BEING EARNEST**

The last chapter discussed the reasons for international trade and the benefits that accrue to all nations when countries specialize in producing goods in which they have a comparative advantage. But when goods move across national borders, *money* must generally move in the opposite direction. When the United States buys coffee from Brazil, we must send money to the Brazilians. When Japan purchases petroleum from Saudi Arabia, it must send money to the Saudis, and so on. This chapter is about the system that has been set up to handle these international movements of money—the **international monetary system**. ¶ We begin by investigating a system in which rates of exchange among national currencies are determined in free markets by the laws of supply and demand. We shall see that the main macroeconomic variables studied in Parts 6 and 7—output, the price level, and the rate of interest—each play a role in the determination of a country's exchange rate. This discussion sets the stage for Chapter 37, where we will learn how movements of the exchange rate, in turn, affect the national economy.

Next, we turn to the opposite polar form—an international monetary system in which exchange rates are fixed by government authority, rather than by the market. We do not now live in such a world. Yet studying it will help us understand the current international monetary system, which is a curious hybrid of fixed and floating exchange rates. And it will also help us understand why some people believe that the world should move toward a system with greater fixity in exchange rates.

## WHAT ARE EXCHANGE RATES?

We noted in the previous chapter that international trade is more complicated than domestic trade. There are no national borders to be crossed when, say, California lettuce is shipped to Massachusetts. The consumer in Boston pays with *dollars*, just the currency that the farmer in Salinas wants. But if that same farmer ships his lettuce to Japan, consumers there will have only Japanese *yen* with which to pay, rather than the dollars the farmer in California wants. Thus if international trade is to take place, there must be a way to transform one currency into another. The rates at which such transformations are made are called **exchange rates**.

The **EXCHANGE RATE** states the price, in terms of one currency, at which another currency can be bought.

There is an exchange rate between every pair of currencies. For example, $1 is currently the equivalent of about 5.5 French francs. The exchange rate between the franc and the dollar, then, may be expressed as roughly "5.5 francs to the dollar" (meaning that it costs 5.5 francs to buy a dollar) or about "18 cents to the franc" (meaning that it costs 18 cents to buy a franc).

Although exchange rates change all the time, Table 36–1 gives an indication of exchange rates prevailing in July 1980, February 1985, and July 1993, showing how many dollars or cents it cost at each of those times to buy each unit of foreign currency. You will note some dramatic changes in the international value of the dollar over time. In a nutshell, the dollar soared in the period from mid-1980 to early 1985, fell against most major currencies from early 1985 until early 1988,

**Table 36–1 EXCHANGE RATES WITH THE U.S. DOLLAR (dollars per unit of foreign currency)**

| COUNTRY | CURRENCY UNIT | SYMBOL | COST IN DOLLARS JULY 1980 | COST IN DOLLARS FEBRUARY 1985 | COST IN DOLLARS JULY 1993 |
|---|---|---|---|---|---|
| Australia | dollar | $ | $1.16 | $0.74 | $.67 |
| Canada | dollar | $ | 0.87 | 0.74 | 0.78 |
| France | franc | FF | 0.25 | 0.10 | 0.17 |
| Germany | mark | DM | 0.57 | 0.30 | 0.59 |
| Italy | lira | L | 0.0012 | 0.00049 | 0.00065 |
| Japan | yen | ¥ | 0.0045 | 0.0038 | 0.0092 |
| Mexico | peso | $ | 0.044 | 0.0050 | 0.32* |
| Sweden | krona | Kr | 0.24 | 0.11 | 0.13 |
| Switzerland | franc | S. Fr. | 0.62 | 0.36 | 0.66 |
| United Kingdom | pound | £ | 2.37 | 1.10 | 1.50 |

*On January 1, 1993, the peso was redefined so that 1000 old pesos were equal to one new peso. Hence the 0.32 listed for July 1993 would be 0.00032 on the old basis.

SOURCE: International Financial Statistics and *The Wall Street Journal*.

and has generally fluctuated without any pronounced trend since. This chapter seeks to explain such currency movements.

A nation's currency is said to **APPRECIATE** when exchange rates change so that a unit of its own currency can buy more units of foreign currency.

The currency is said to **DEPRECIATE** when exchange rates change so that a unit of its currency can buy fewer units of foreign currency.

Under our present system, currency rates change frequently. When other currencies become more expensive in terms of dollars, we say that they have **appreciated** relative to the dollar. Alternatively, we can look at this same event as the dollar buying less foreign currency, meaning that the dollar has **depreciated** relative to another currency.

What is a depreciation to one country must be an appreciation to the other.

For example, if the dollar cost of a German mark rises from 50 cents to 60 cents, the cost of a U.S. dollar in terms of marks simultaneously falls from 2 marks to 1.67 marks. The Germans have had a currency *appreciation* while we have had a currency *depreciation*.

Notice also that, when many currencies are changing in value, the dollar may be appreciating with respect to one currency but depreciating with respect to another.

Table 36–1 shows that, between February 1985 and July 1993, the dollar *depreciated* sharply relative to the Japanese yen and most European currencies. For example, the British pound rose from $1.10 to $1.50. Yet during that same period the dollar *appreciated* dramatically relative to the Mexican peso; it bought about 200 pesos in 1985 but over 3000 in 1993.[1]

While this is the terminology used to describe movements of exchange rates in free markets, another set of terms is used to describe decreases and increases in currency values when those values are set by government decree. When an officially set exchange rate is altered so that a unit of a nation's currency can buy *fewer* units of foreign currency, we say there has been a **devaluation** of that currency. When the exchange rate is altered so that the currency can buy *more* units of foreign currency, we say there has been a **revaluation.**

A **DEVALUATION** is a reduction in the official value of a currency.

A **REVALUATION** is an increase in the official value of a currency.

## EXCHANGE RATE DETERMINATION IN A FREE MARKET

**FLOATING EXCHANGE RATES** are rates determined in free markets by the law of supply and demand.

Why is it that a German mark now costs about 60 cents and not 50 cents or 70 cents? In a world of **floating exchange rates**, with no government interferences, the answer would be straightforward. Exchange rates would be determined by the forces of supply and demand, just like the prices of apples, typewriters, and haircuts.

In a leap of abstraction, imagine that the United States and Germany were the only countries on earth, so there was only one exchange rate to be determined. Figure 36–1 depicts the determination of this exchange rate at the point (denoted *E* in the figure) where demand curve *DD* crosses supply curve *SS*. At this price (60 cents per mark), the number of marks demanded is equal to the number of marks supplied.

In a free market, exchange rates are determined by the law of supply and demand. If the rate were below the equilibrium level, the quantity of marks demanded would exceed the quantity of marks supplied, and the price of a mark would be bid up. If the rate were above the equilibrium level, quantity supplied would

[1]In fact, the dollar bought just over 3 pesos in 1993, but that is because the old peso was replaced by a new peso in January 1993, which moved the decimal point three places.

*Figure* **36–1** **DETERMINATION OF EXCHANGE RATES IN A FREE MARKET**

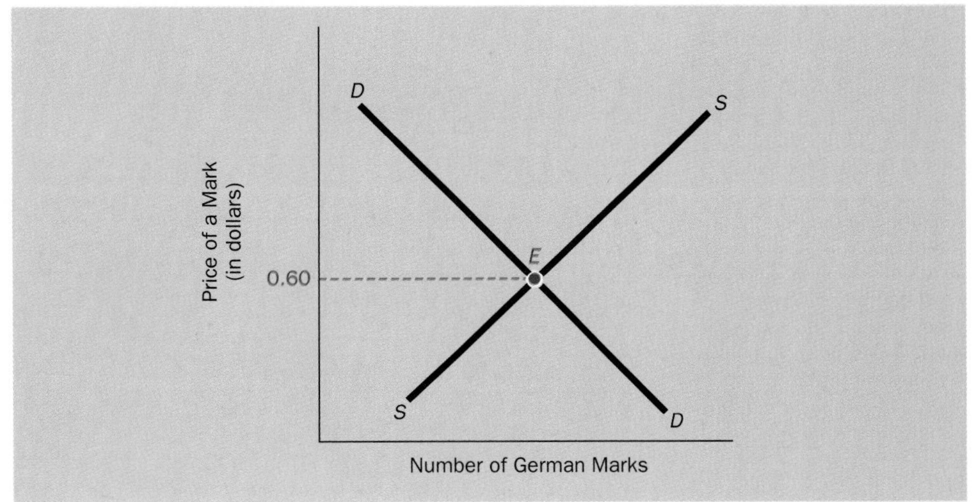


Like any price, an exchange rate will be determined by the intersection of the demand and supply curves in a free market. Point *E* depicts this point for the exchange rate between the U.S. dollar and the German mark, which settles at 60 cents per mark in this example.

exceed quantity demanded, and the price of a mark would fall. Only at the equilibrium exchange rate is there no tendency for the rate to change.

As usual, supply and demand determine price. What we must ask in this case is: Where do the supply and demand come from? Why does anyone demand a German mark? The answer comes in three parts:

1. *International trade in goods and services.* This was the subject of the last chapter. If, for example, Jane Doe, an American, wants to buy a German automobile, she will first have to buy marks with which to pay the dealer in Munich.[2] So Jane's demand for a German *car* leads to a demand for German *marks.* In general, *demand for a country's exports leads to a demand for its currency.*[3]
2. *International trade in financial instruments like stocks and bonds.* For example, if American investors want to purchase German stocks, they will first have to acquire the marks that the sellers will insist upon. In this way, demand for German financial assets leads to demand for German marks. Thus, *demand for a country's financial assets leads to a demand for its currency.*
3. *Purchases of physical assets like factories and machinery overseas.* If IBM wants to buy out a small German computer manufacturer, the owners will no doubt want to receive marks. So IBM will first have to acquire German currency. In general, *direct foreign investment leads to a demand for a country's currency.*

Now, where does the supply come from? To answer this, just turn all of these transactions around. Germans wanting to buy U.S. goods and services, or invest

[2]Actually, she will not do this because banks generally handle foreign exchange transactions for consumers. An American bank probably will buy the marks for her. But the effect is exactly the same as if Jane had done it herself.

[3]See Review Question 2 at the end of the chapter (page 923).

*Figure* **36–2** **THE EFFECT OF AN ECONOMIC BOOM ON THE EXCHANGE RATE**

If the U.S. economy suddenly booms, Americans will spend more on imports from Germany. Thus the demand curve for German marks will rise from $D_1D_1$ to $D_2D_2$ as Americans seek to acquire the marks they need. The diagram shows that this will cause the mark to appreciate, from 60 cents to 65 cents, as equilibrium shifts from point *E* to point *A*. Looked at from the U.S. perspective, the dollar will depreciate.

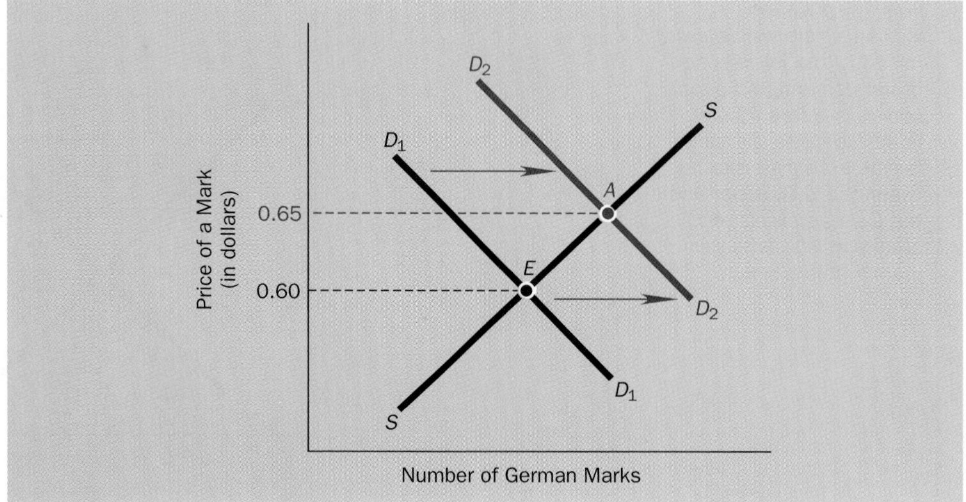


in U.S. financial markets, or make direct investments in America will have to offer their marks for sale in the foreign-exchange market (which is similar to the stock market) to acquire the needed dollars. To summarize:

The demand for a country's currency is derived from the demands of foreigners for its export goods and services and for its assets—including financial assets, like stocks and bonds, and real assets, like factories and machinery. The *supply* of a country's foreign currency arises from its imports, and from foreign investment by its own citizens.

To appreciate the usefulness of even this simple supply and demand analysis, let us consider how the exchange rate between the dollar and the mark would change if there were an economic boom in the United States. One important effect of such a boom would be to stimulate American demand for German products, such as automobiles, cameras, and wines. In terms of the supply–demand diagram shown in Figure 36–2, the increased desires of Americans for German goods would shift the demand curve for German marks out from $D_1D_1$ (the black line in the figure) to $D_2D_2$ (the blue line). Equilibrium would shift from point *E* to point *A*, and the exchange rate would rise from 60 cents per mark to 65 cents per mark. In a word, the increased demand for marks by U.S. citizens causes the mark to *appreciate* relative to the dollar.

**EXERCISE**

Test your understanding of the supply and demand analysis of exchange rates by showing why each of the following events would lead to an appreciation of the mark (a depreciation of the dollar) in a free market:

1. A recession in Germany cuts German purchases of American goods.

2. American investors are attracted by prospects for profit on the German stock market.
3. Interest rates on government bonds rise in Germany but are stable in the United States. (*Hint:* Which country's citizens will be attracted by high interest rates in the other country?)

To say that supply and demand determine exchange rates in a free market is at once to say everything and to say nothing. If we are to understand the reasons why some currencies appreciate while others depreciate, we must look into the factors that move the supply and demand curves. Economists believe that the principal determinants of exchange rate movements are rather different in the long, medium, and short runs. So we turn in the next three sections to the analysis of exchange rate movements over these three "runs," beginning with the long run.

## THE PURCHASING-POWER PARITY THEORY: THE LONG RUN

As long as there is free trade across national borders, exchange rates should eventually adjust so that the same product costs the same whether measured in dollars in the United States, marks in Germany, yen in Japan, and so on—except for differences in transportation costs and the like. This simple statement forms the basis of the major theory of exchange rate determination in the long run.

The **purchasing-power parity theory of exchange rate determination** holds that the exchange rate between any two national currencies adjusts to reflect differences in the price levels in the two countries.

An example will bring out the basic truth in this theory and also suggest some of its limitations. Suppose that German and American steel are identical and that these two nations are the only producers of steel for the world market. Suppose further that steel is the only tradable good that either country produces.

***Question:*** If American steel costs $180 per ton and German steel costs 300 marks per ton, what must be the exchange rate between the dollar and the mark?

***Answer:*** Since 300 marks or $180 each buys a ton of steel, they must be of equal value. Hence, each mark must be worth 60 cents. Why? Any higher price for a mark, like 75 cents, would mean that steel would cost $225 per ton (300 marks at 75 cents each) in Germany but only $180 per ton in the United States. In that case, all foreign customers would shop for their steel in the United States. Similarly, any exchange rate below 60 cents per mark would send all the steel business to Germany.

**EXERCISE**

Show why an exchange rate of 50 cents per mark is too low.

The purchasing-power parity theory is used to make long-run predictions about the effects of inflation on exchange rates. To continue our example, suppose that over a five-year period, prices in the United States rise by 25 percent while prices in Germany rise by 50 percent. The purchasing-power parity theory predicts that the mark will depreciate relative to the dollar. It also predicts the amount of the depreciation. After the inflation, American steel costs $225 per ton (one-fourth

## Purchasing-Power Parity and the Big Mac

Since 1986, *The Economist* magazine has been using a well-known international commodity—the Big Mac—to assess the purchasing-power parity theory of exchange rates, or as the magazine puts it, "to make exchange-rate theory more digestible." That famous hamburger is now sold in 66 countries, and *The Economist* included 25 of them in its latest survey.*

Here's how it works. In 1993, the average price of a Big Mac in the U.S.A. was $2.28, including sales tax. In Japan, that same commodity sold for ¥391. For those two amounts to be equal, a dollar would have had to have been worth about 391/2.28 = ¥171. In fact, however, the dollar was worth only ¥113 at the time of the survey. This large discrepancy means that, according to the Big Mac standard, the yen was 51 percent overvalued relative to the dollar.

Similar calculations at the time led to the conclusion that the British pound was 23 percent overvalued against the dollar. Since a Big Mac cost £1.79, the implied purchasing-power parity of the pound was 2.28/1.79 = $1.27, versus a market value of $1.56. The cheapest Big Macs in the world at the time were found in Russia, where the burger cost just $1.14 (780 roubles). That implied that the dollar was *under*valued by a whopping 50 percent against the rouble.

Such calculations, based as they are on a single commodity, are not known for their accuracy. Nonetheless, *The Economist* noted, more sophisticated estimates of the purchasing-power parity of the yen at the time were in the $1 = ¥140–180 range, and for the pound in the $1.30–$1.40 range. Not bad for a hamburger.

*"Big MacCurrencies," *The Economist*, April 17, 1993, page 79.

more than $180), while German steel costs 450 marks per ton (50 percent more than 300 marks). For these two prices to be equivalent, 450 marks must be worth $225, or one mark must be worth 50 cents. The mark, therefore, must have fallen from 60 cents to 50 cents.

According to the purchasing-power parity theory, differences in domestic inflation rates are a major cause of adjustments in exchange rates. If one country has higher inflation than another, then its exchange rate should be depreciating.

For many years, the theory seemed to work tolerably well. While precise numerical predictions based on purchasing-power parity calculations were never very accurate (see the accompanying boxed insert), nations with higher inflation did at least experience depreciating currencies. But in the 1980s, even this broke down. For example, while the U.S. inflation rate was higher than both Germany's and Japan's throughout the 1980s, the dollar nonetheless rose sharply relative to both the mark and the yen from 1980 to 1985 and again in 1988–1989. Clearly, the theory was missing something. What?

First, changes in any of the interferences with free trade, such as tariffs and quotas, can upset simple calculations based on purchasing-power parity. For example, if German prices rise faster than American prices but, at the same time, foreign countries erect tariff barriers to keep American (but not German) steel out, then the mark might not have to depreciate.

Second, some goods and services cannot be traded across national frontiers. Land and buildings are only the most obvious examples; most services can be traded only to a limited extent (as when tourists from one country rent hotel rooms in another). Inflation rates for goods and services that are *not tradable* have little bearing on exchange rates.

Third, few of the goods that different nations produce and trade are as uniform as the German and American steel in our example. A BMW and a Cadillac, for example, are not identical products. So the price of a BMW *in U.S. dollars* can rise faster than the price of a Cadillac without driving BMWs out of the market entirely. On balance:

Most economists believe that other factors are much more important than relative price levels for exchange rate determination in the short run. But in the long run, purchasing-power parity plays an important role.

## ECONOMIC ACTIVITY AND EXCHANGE RATES: THE MEDIUM RUN

Since consumer spending increases when income expands and decreases when income contracts, the same is likely to happen to spending on imported goods. For this reason:

A country's imports will rise quickly when its economy is booming and slowly when its economy is stagnating.

We have already illustrated this point with Figure 36–2. There we saw that a boom in the United States would shift the demand curve for marks outward as Americans bought more German goods. And that, in turn, would lead to an appreciation of the mark (depreciation of the dollar) as Americans sold dollars to buy marks. However, if Germany were booming at the same time, German citizens would be buying more American exports, which would shift the supply curve of marks outward. On balance, the value of the dollar might or might not fall. What matters is whether exports are growing faster than imports. The general lesson is that:

Holding other things equal, a country whose aggregate demand grows faster than the rest of the world's normally finds its currency depreciating because its imports grow faster than its exports. Thus its demand curve for foreign currency shifts outward more rapidly than its supply curve.

This is one reason why it is unwise to interpret a "strong currency" as an indication of a "strong economy." A nation that grows more rapidly than its trading partners may find itself with a depreciating currency.

## INTEREST RATES AND EXCHANGE RATES: THE SHORT RUN

While economic activity is important for exchange rate determination in the medium run, "other things" often are not equal in the short run. Specifically, one factor that often seems to call the tune in determining exchange rate movements in the short run is *interest rate differentials*. There is an enormous fund of so-called hot money—owned by banks, multinational corporations, and wealthy individuals of all nations, and amounting to several trillion dollars—that travels around the globe in search of the highest interest rates.

Thus suppose that British government bonds are paying a 6 percent rate of interest when yields on equally safe American government securities rise to 8 percent. British investors will be attracted by the high interest rates in the United

Figure 36–3 THE EFFECT OF A RISE IN U.S. INTEREST RATES

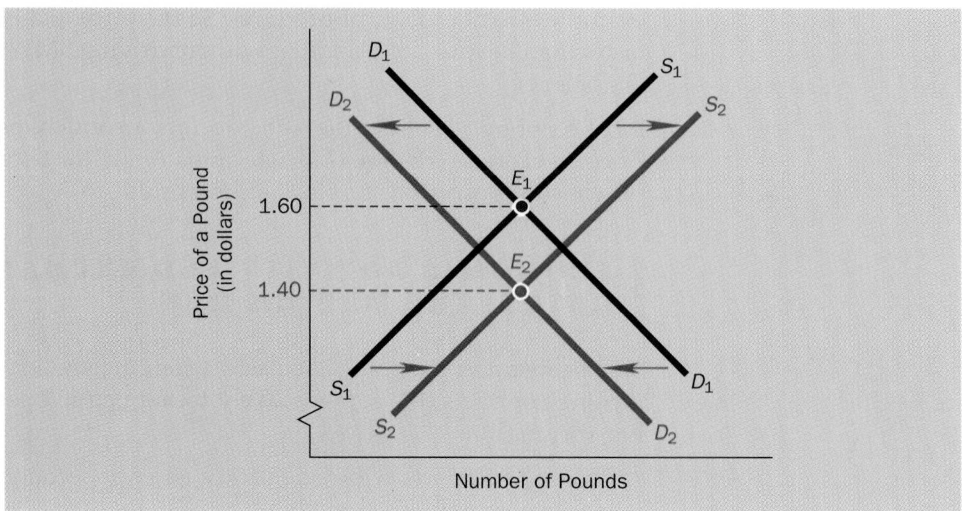


When the U.S. raises its interest rates, more English investors will want to buy American bonds, and so the supply curve of pounds will shift outward from $S_1S_1$ to $S_2S_2$. At the same time, fewer Americans will seek to buy British bonds, so the demand curve for pounds will shift inward from $D_1D_1$ to $D_2D_2$. The combined effect of these two shifts is to move the market equilibrium from point $E_1$ to point $E_2$. The British pound depreciates, and the dollar appreciates.

States and will offer pounds for sale in order to buy dollars, planning to use those dollars to buy American securities. At the same time, American investors will find investing in the United States more attractive than ever, so fewer pounds will be demanded by Americans.

When the demand schedule falls and the supply curve rises, the effect on price is predictable: the pound will depreciate, as Figure 36–3 shows. In the figure, the supply curve of pounds shifts outward from $S_1S_1$ to $S_2S_2$ when British investors seek to sell pounds in order to purchase U.S. securities. At the same time, American investors wish to buy fewer pounds because they no longer wish to invest in British securities. Thus the demand curve shifts inward from $D_1D_1$ to $D_2D_2$. The result, in our example, is a depreciation of the pound from \$1.60 to \$1.40. In general:

Holding other things equal, countries with high interest rates are able to attract more capital than are countries with low interest rates. Thus a rise in interest rates often will lead to an appreciation of the currency, and a drop in interest rates will lead to a depreciation.

Most experts in international finance agree that this factor is the major determinant of exchange rates in the short run. It certainly played a predominant role in the stunning movements of the U.S. dollar during the 1980s. Early in the decade, American interest rates rose well above comparable interest rates abroad. In consequence, foreign capital was attracted here, American capital stayed at home, and the dollar soared. Then, in the mid-1980s, the gap between U.S. and foreign interest rates narrowed and the dollar fell.

## MARKET DETERMINATION OF EXCHANGE RATES: SUMMARY

We can summarize this discussion of exchange rate determination in free markets as follows:

1. Currency values generally will be *appreciating* in countries whose inflation rates are lower than the rest of the world's because buyers in foreign countries will demand their goods, and thus drive up the currency.
2. Exchange rates would also be expected to rise in countries where aggregate demand is growing more slowly than average, because these countries will be importing rather little.
3. We expect to find appreciating currencies in countries whose interest rates are high because these countries will attract capital from all over the world.

Reversing each of these, we expect that currencies will be *depreciating* in countries with relatively high inflation rates, or rapid demand growth, or low interest rates.

## FIXED EXCHANGE RATES AND THE DEFINITION OF THE BALANCE OF PAYMENTS

Some exchange rates today are truly floating, determined by the forces of supply and demand without government interference. But many are not. Furthermore, some people claim that exchange-rate fluctuations are so troublesome that the world would be better off with fixed exchange rates. For these reasons, we turn our attention next to a system of **fixed exchange rates**, or rates that are set by government. Naturally, under such a system the exchange rate, being fixed, is not closely watched. Instead, international financial specialists focus on a country's *balance of payments*—a term we must now define.

**FIXED EXCHANGE RATES** are rates set by government decisions and maintained by government actions.

To understand what the balance of payments is, look at Figure 36–4, which depicts a situation that might represent, say, the United States just before the dollar fell in value in 1971—an *overvalued* currency. While the supply and demand

*Figure* **36–4** **A BALANCE OF PAYMENTS DEFICIT**

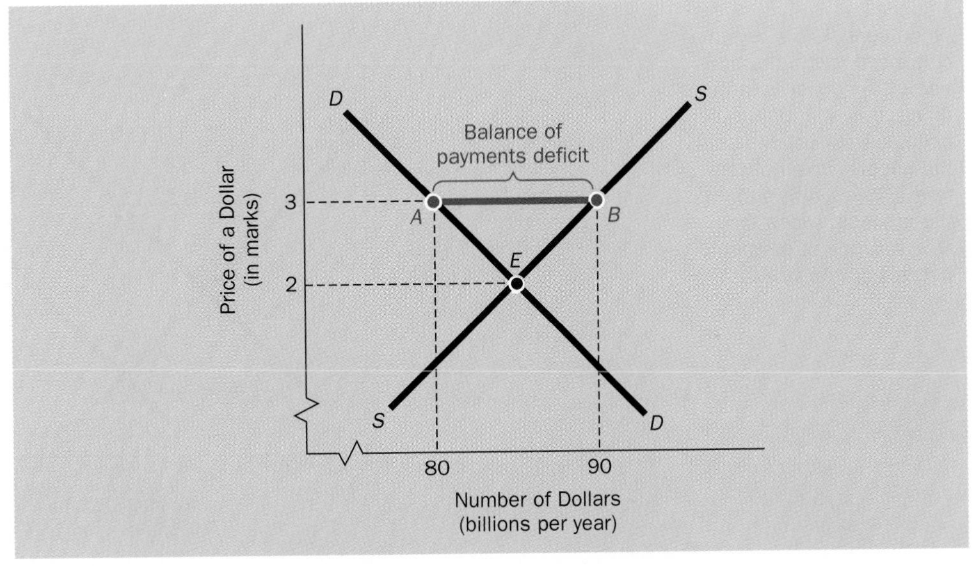


At a fixed exchange rate of 3 marks per dollar, which is well above the equilibrium level of 2 marks per dollar, America's currency is overvalued in this example. As a consequence, more dollars will be supplied (point *B*) than are demanded (point *A*). The difference—distance *AB*, or $10 billion per year—represents the U.S. balance of payments deficit.

curves for dollars indicate an equilibrium exchange rate of 2 marks to the dollar (point *E*), the U.S. government is keeping the rate at 3 marks. Notice that, at 3 marks to the dollar, more people are supplying dollars than are demanding them. In the example, suppliers are selling $90 billion per year, but demanders are purchasing only $80 billion.

The **BALANCE OF PAYMENTS DEFICIT** is the amount by which the quantity supplied of a country's currency (per year) exceeds the quantity demanded. Balance of payments deficits arise whenever the exchange rate is pegged at an artificially high level.

This gap between the $90 billion that some people sell and the $80 billion that other people buy is what we mean by America's **balance of payments deficit**—$10 billion per year in this case. It is shown by the horizontal distance between points *A* and *B* in Figure 36–4.

How can market forces be flouted in this way? Since sales and purchases on any market must be equal, as a simple piece of arithmetic, the excess of quantity supplied over quantity demanded of U.S. currency ($10 billion per year in this example) must be bought by the U.S. government. In buying these dollars, it must give up some of the gold and foreign currencies that it keeps as *reserves*. Thus the Federal Reserve would be losing $10 billion in reserves per year as the cost of keeping the dollar at 3 marks.

Naturally, this cannot go on forever; the reserves eventually will run out. And this was the fatal flaw in the system of fixed exchange rates. Once speculators became convinced that the exchange rate could be held for only a short while longer, they would sell dollars in massive amounts rather than hold on to a currency whose value they expected to fall. The supply curve of dollars would shift outward drastically, as shown in Figure 36–5, causing a sharp rise in the balance of payments deficit (from $10 billion to $20 billion in the example). Lacking sufficient reserves, the central bank would have to permit the exchange rate to fall to its equilibrium level, and this might amount to an even larger devaluation than would have been required before the speculative "run" on the dollar began. It was precisely the fear of such a run that induced the United States to end the system of fixed exchange rates in 1971.

**Figure 36–5 A SPECULATIVE RUN ON THE DOLLAR**

When speculators become convinced that a devaluation of the dollar is in the offing, they will rush to sell dollars. Their actions shift the supply curve outward from $S_1S_1$ to $S_2S_2$ and, in the process, widen the U.S. balance of payments deficit from *AB* to *AC*.

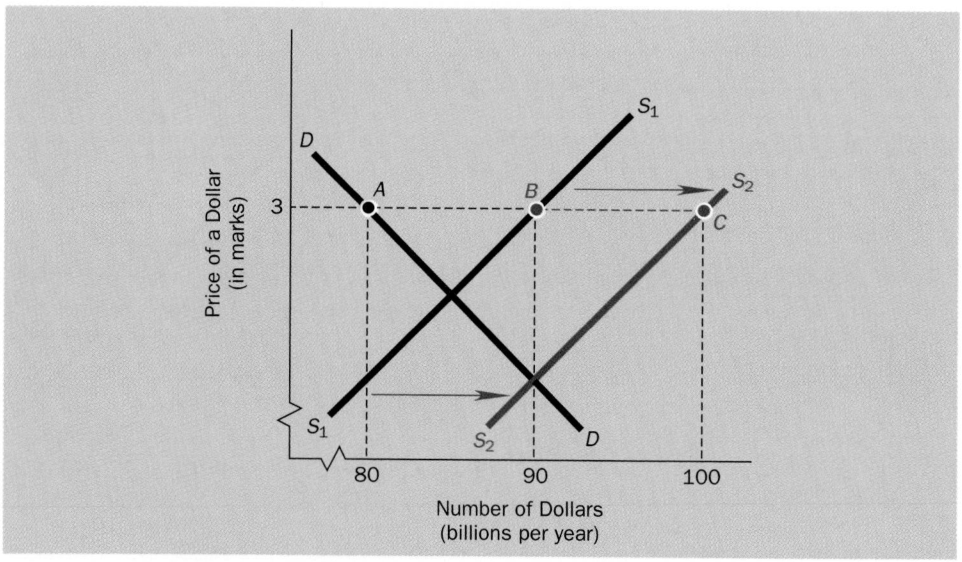

Figure 36–6 A BALANCE OF PAYMENTS SURPLUS

In this example, Germany's currency is undervalued at 33 cents per mark since the equilibrium exchange rate is 50 cents per mark. Consequently, more marks are being demanded (point *B*) than are being supplied (point *A*). The gap between quantity demanded and quantity supplied—distance *AB*, or 10 billion marks per year—measures Germany's balance of payments surplus.

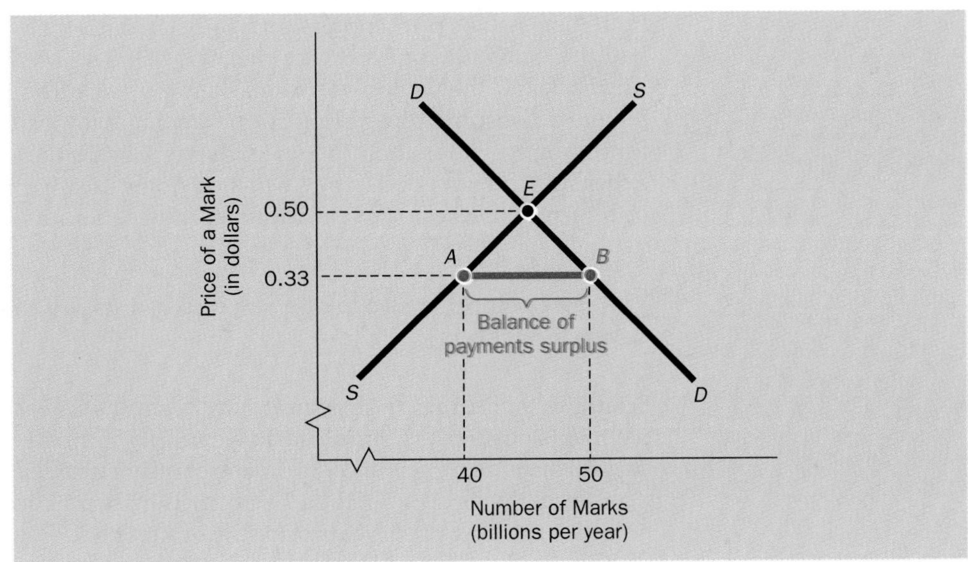


For an example of the reverse case, a severely *undervalued* currency, let us consider West Germany in 1973. Figure 36–6 depicts demand and supply curves for marks that intersect at an equilibrium price of 50 cents per mark (point *E* in the diagram). Yet, in the example, we suppose that the German authorities are holding the rate at 33 cents. At this rate, the quantity of marks demanded (50 billion) greatly exceeds the quantity supplied (40 billion). The difference is Germany's **balance of payments surplus**, and is shown by the horizontal distance *AB*.

The **BALANCE OF PAYMENTS SURPLUS** is the amount by which the quantity demanded of a country's currency (per year) exceeds the quantity supplied. Balance of payments surpluses arise whenever the exchange rate is pegged at an artificially low level.

Germany can keep the rate at 33 cents only by providing the marks that foreigners want to buy: 10 billion marks per year in this example. In return, it receives U.S. dollars, British pounds, French francs, gold, and so on. All of this serves to increase Germany's reserves of foreign currencies. But notice the important difference between this case and the overvalued U.S. dollar.

The accumulation of reserves rarely will *force* a central bank to revalue in the way that depletion of reserves can force a devaluation.

This was another weakness of the system of fixed exchange rates that prevailed between 1944 and 1971. In principle, imbalances in exchange rates could be cured either by a *devaluation* by the country with a balance of payments deficit or by an upward *revaluation* by the country with a balance of payments surplus. In practice, though, it was almost always the deficit countries that were forced to act.

Why did the surplus countries refuse to revalue? One reason was a stubborn refusal to recognize some basic economic realities. They viewed the disequilibrium as the problem of the deficit countries and believed that the deficit countries, therefore, should take the corrective steps. This, of course, is nonsense. Some currencies are overvalued *because* some other currencies are undervalued. In fact, the two statements mean exactly the same thing.

The other reason why exporters in Germany, Japan, and other surplus countries resisted upward revaluations is that such actions would have made their products more expensive to foreigners and thus cut into their sales. And these exporters had the political clout to make their views stick. Meanwhile, since the values of the mark and the yen on world markets were artificially held down, German and Japanese consumers were put in the unenviable position of having to pay more for imported goods than they need have paid. Rather than buy these excessively expensive foreign goods, they watched domestically produced goods go overseas in return for pieces of paper (dollars, francs, pounds, and so on).

## DEFINING THE BALANCE OF PAYMENTS IN PRACTICE

From the preceding discussion it may seem that measuring a nation's balance of payments position is a simple task: we simply count up the private demand for and supply of its currency and subtract quantity supplied from quantity demanded. Conceptually, this is all there is to it. But in practice the difficulties are great because we never observe directly the number of dollars demanded and supplied.

If we look at actual market transactions, we will see that the number of U.S. dollars actually *purchased* and the number of U.S. dollars actually *sold* are identical. Unless someone has made a bookkeeping error, this must always be so. How, then, can we recognize a balance of payments surplus or deficit? Easy, you say. Just look at the transactions of the central bank, whose purchases or sales must make up the difference between private demand and private supply. If the Federal Reserve is buying dollars, its purchases measure our balance of payments deficit. If it is selling, its sales represent our balance of payments surplus.

Thus the suggestion is to measure the balance of payments by *excluding official transactions among governments*. This is roughly how the balance of payments surplus or deficit is defined today, though, for a variety of complicated reasons, the U.S. government decided long ago to stop publishing any official statistic called "the balance of payments deficit." Instead, all foreign transactions are listed, and readers are invited to define the balance of payments in any way they wish. Let us now see just what data are published in these official accounts.

## THE U.S. BALANCE OF PAYMENTS ACCOUNTS

Using 1992 as an example, Table 36–2 shows the official U.S. balance of payments accounts. There is nothing that purports to measure America's overall balance of payments surplus or deficit. The top section of the table summarizes America's trade in currently produced goods and services—the so-called *current account*. The positive or negative sign attached to each entry indicates whether the transaction represented a *gain* (+) or a *loss* (−) of foreign currency.

Looking first at the top of the table, we see that in merchandise transactions, Americans imported about $96 billion more than they exported, leading to a whopping deficit in what is called the *balance of trade* (see lines 1–3). Because it is available on a monthly basis, this is the number reported most frequently by the news media. In the mid-1980s, America's trade deficits were the largest ever run by any nation. They have fallen substantially since then but are still a source

Table 36–2 U.S. BALANCE OF PAYMENTS ACCOUNTS, 1992 (billions of dollars)

| | | |
|---|---|---|
| **Current Account** | | |
| (1) Balance of trade | –$96.2 | |
| (2) Merchandise exports | | +440.1 |
| (3) Merchandise imports | | –536.3 |
| (4) Net military transactions | –2.8 | |
| (5) Travel and transportation (net) | +19.7 | |
| (6) Net income from investments and other services | +45.8 | |
| (7) Balance on goods and services | –33.5 | |
| (8) Unilateral transfers (net) | –32.9 | |
| (9) Private | | –14.5 |
| (10) U.S. Government (nonmilitary) | | –18.4 |
| (11) Balance on current account | –66.4 | |
| **Capital Account** | | |
| (12) Net private capital flows | +35.6 | |
| (13) Change in the U.S. assets abroad | | –53.3 |
| (14) Change in foreign assets in the U.S. | | +88.9 |
| (15) Net government capital flows | +43.0 | |
| (16) Change in U.S. government assets | | +2.3 |
| (17) Change in foreign official assets in the U.S. | | +40.7 |
| (18) Balance on capital account | +78.6 | |
| **Addendum** | | |
| (19) Sum of lines (11) and (18) | +12.2 | |
| (20) Statistical discrepancy | –12.2 | |

SOURCE: *Survey of Current Business*, June 1993. Organization of table changed by authors.

of some concern and considerable political controversy. For example, the trade deficit has been a major factor behind the drive for more protectionism that we discussed in Chapter 35.

The entry in line 4 indicates the net effect of a large number of dollars spent by U.S. military installations abroad (transactions that cost us foreign currency) and a large amount of foreign currency earned by selling armaments. On balance, these cost the United States about $2.8 billion in foreign currency. Line 5 shows that in 1992 American tourists and shippers spent $19.7 billion less on foreign services than foreign tourists and shippers spent here.

Line 6 displays a major source of foreign currency earnings for the United States: net income from our investments overseas and from selling other services. In 1992, America earned a net surplus of over $45 billion on this composite of services.

Line 7 gives the net result of all trading in goods and services—*the balance on goods and services*. The entry in line 7 means that the United States spent $33.5 billion more than it received during 1992. Lines 8–10 indicate the so-called unilateral transfers, including both private gifts to foreigners and official foreign aid. Together these cost us almost $33 billion in foreign currency. When these unilateral transfers are subtracted from the deficit on goods and services, we find (in line 11) a large deficit of $66.4 billion in America's *current account*. Many economists take the balance on current account to be the most basic measure of a nation's international transactions.

But this hardly represents our "balance of payments," as it leaves out all purchases and sales of assets. This group of transactions is shown in the *capital account* (lines 12–18) which, in recent years, is where our large foreign borrowing shows up. Line 12 shows that, on balance, foreign individuals and businesses bought about $36 billion more in assets here than private American investors bought from foreigners. The net entry is *plus* $35.6 billion because $53.3 billion dollars flowed *out of* the United States to buy foreign assets (line 13), while $88.9 billion in foreign money flowed into the United States to buy American assets (line 14).

This large surplus in private capital flows, coupled with a larger deficit in the current account, left the United States with a balance of payments deficit in 1992. How are such deficits financed? Mostly, by government capital flows in the opposite direction (such as when foreign governments buy U.S. government bonds). Foreign governments bought $40.7 billion worth of U.S. assets (line 17), while our government sold an additional $2.3 billion in foreign assets (line 16), leaving a surplus in governmental capital flows of $43 billion (line 15).

Thus the accounts do not balance. When we add up the current account (line 11) plus the overall (private plus government) capital account (line 18), we get a $12 billion surplus (line 19). But, of course, this is impossible. Since it is a simple matter of arithmetic that the two accounts together must balance (dollars purchased = dollars sold), the difference is considered a *statistical discrepancy* (line 20).

While part of this huge discrepancy simply comes from errors in data collection and computation, the lion's share reflects the U.S. government's inability to monitor all the flows of money, goods, and services across its borders. When we fail to record the cargo of a truck hauling U.S. goods to Canada, we overstate our current account deficit. When we fail to record foreign capital movements into the United States, we understate our capital account surplus. Such errors and omissions often leave big statistical discrepancies in the balance of payments accounts of the United States and other nations.

## A BIT OF HISTORY: THE GOLD STANDARD

It is hard to find examples of strictly fixed exchange rates in the historical record. About the only time exchange rates were truly fixed was under the old **gold standard**, at least when it was practiced in its ideal form.[4]

Under the gold standard, fixed exchange rates were maintained by an automatic equilibrating mechanism that went something like this: all currencies were defined in terms of gold; indeed, some were actually made of gold. When a nation had a deficit in its balance of payments, this meant, essentially, that more gold was flowing *out* than was flowing *in*. Since the domestic money supply was based on gold, losing gold to foreigners meant that the quantity of money fell *automatically*. This raised interest rates and attracted foreign capital. At the same time, the restrictive "monetary policy" pulled down output and prices, thus discouraging

[4]As a matter of fact, while the gold standard lasted (on and off) for hundreds of years, it was rarely practiced in its ideal form. Except for a brief period of fixed exchange rates in the late nineteenth and early twentieth centuries, there were periodic adjustments of exchange rates even under the gold standard.

imports and encouraging exports. The balance of payments problem quickly rectified itself. This meant, however, that:

Under the gold standard, no nation had control of its domestic monetary policy, and therefore no nation could control its domestic economy very well.

At least in principle, the effects on surplus countries were perfectly symmetrical under the gold standard. A balance of payments surplus led, via gold inflows, to an increase in the domestic money supply, whether the surplus country liked the idea or not. This raised prices and output, thereby increasing imports and decreasing exports. And it also lowered interest rates, thereby encouraging outflows of capital. Because of these automatic adjustments, nations rarely reached the point at which devaluations or revaluations were necessary. Exchange rates were fixed as long as countries abided by the rules of the gold standard game.

In addition to the loss of control over domestic monetary conditions, the gold standard posed one other serious difficulty.

A fundamental problem with the gold standard was that the world's commerce was at the mercy of gold discoveries.

Discoveries of gold meant higher prices in the long run and higher real economic activity in the short run, through the standard monetary-policy mechanisms that we studied in Part 7. And when the supply of gold did not keep pace with growth of the world economy, prices had to fall in the long run and employment had to fall in the short run.

## THE BRETTON WOODS SYSTEM AND THE INTERNATIONAL MONETARY FUND

The gold standard faltered many times and finally collapsed amid the financial chaos of the Great Depression of the 1930s and World War II. Without it, the world struggled through a serious breakdown in international trade.

Then, as World War II drew to a close, with much of Europe in ruins and with the United States holding the lion's share of the free world's reserves, officials of the industrial nations met at Bretton Woods, New Hampshire, in 1944. Their goal was to establish a stable monetary environment that would facilitate world trade. Since the dollar was the only "strong" currency at that time, it was natural for them to turn to the dollar as the basis of the new international economic order. And that is just what they did.

The Bretton Woods agreements reestablished a system of fixed exchange rates based not on the old gold standard but on the free convertibility of the U.S. dollar into gold. The United States agreed to buy or sell gold to maintain the $35 per ounce price that had been established by President Franklin Roosevelt in 1933. The other signatory nations, which had almost no gold in any case, agreed to buy and sell *dollars* to maintain their exchange rates at agreed-upon levels. Thus all currencies were indirectly on a modified "gold standard." A holder of French francs, for example, could exchange these for dollars at (roughly) 5 francs per dollar and then exchange these into gold at $35 per ounce. In this way, the value of the franc was fixed at 175 francs per ounce of gold (5 francs per dollar times 35 dollars per ounce). The new system was dubbed the **gold-exchange system**, and it was often referred to as the **Bretton Woods system**.

The **International Monetary Fund (IMF)** was set up to police and manage this new system. Using funds that had been contributed by member countries, the

IMF was empowered to make loans to countries that were running low on reserves. A change in exchange rates was to be permitted only in the case of a "fundamental disequilibrium" in a nation's balance of payments—for it was believed that only relatively fixed exchange rates could provide the stable climate needed to restore world trade.

Of course, the Bretton Woods conferees did not define clearly what a "fundamental disequilibrium" was, nor could they have. As the system evolved, it came to mean a chronic *deficit* in the balance of payments of sizable proportions. Such nations would then *devalue* their currencies relative to the dollar. So the system was not really one of fixed exchange rates but rather one where rates were "fixed until further notice."

Several flaws in the Bretton Woods system have already been mentioned in our discussion of the pure system of fixed exchange rates. First, since devaluations were permitted only after a long run of balance of payments deficits, these devaluations (a) could be clearly foreseen and (b) normally had to be large. Speculators then saw opportunities for profit and would "attack" weak currencies with a wave of selling.

This problem led many economists to question whether the system of fixed exchange rates was really providing the stable climate for world trade that had been intended. Was a system where rates were constant for long periods and then altered by large amounts really more conducive to international trade than one where overvalued currencies would gradually depreciate, as they would under a system of floating rates?

The second problem arose from the custom that deficit nations were expected to devalue when forced to, while surplus nations (at that time, mainly West Germany and Japan) could resist upward revaluations. Since the U.S. dollar defined the monetary value of gold (at $35 per ounce), America was the one nation in the world that had no way to devalue its currency relative to gold, no matter how "fundamental" the disequilibrium became. The only way exchange rates between the dollar and foreign currencies could change was if the surplus nations revalued their currencies upward relative to the dollar. They did not do this frequently enough, so the United States, with its chronically overvalued currency, ran persistent balance of payments deficits in the 1960s.

## ADJUSTMENT MECHANISMS UNDER THE BRETTON WOODS SYSTEM

Under the Bretton Woods system, devaluation was viewed as a last resort, to be used only after other methods of adjusting to payments imbalances had failed. What were these other methods?

We have already encountered most of them in our discussion of exchange rate determination in free markets (see pages 902–909). Any factor that increases the demand for, say, U.S. dollars or that reduces the supply will push the value of the dollar upward if it is free to adjust. If, however, the exchange rate is pegged, it is the balance of payments deficit rather than the exchange rate that will adjust when supply of or demand for a nation's money changes. Specifically, the U.S. balance of payments deficit will shrink if either the demand for dollars increases or the supply decreases.

The two panels of Figure 36–7 illustrate this adjustment. In each case, the U.S. has a payments deficit, since the official exchange rate (3 marks) exceeds the equilibrium rate (2 marks). The deficit starts at *AB* in each diagram. Then either

**Figure 36–7** ADJUSTING TO BALANCE OF PAYMENTS DEFICITS

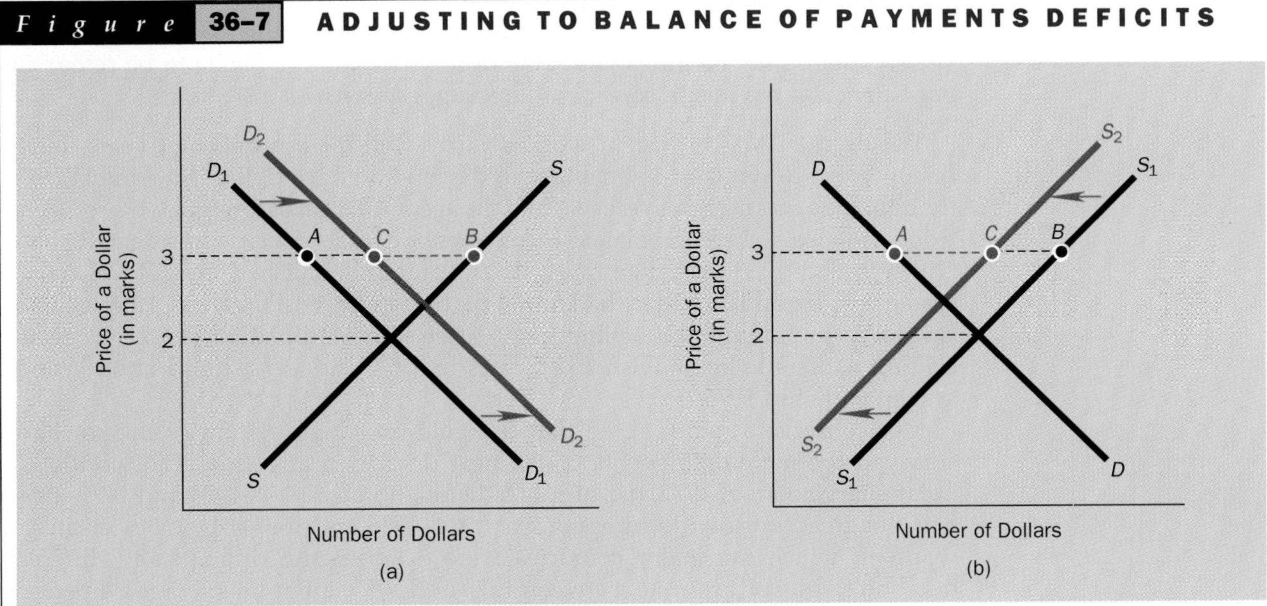


The two parts of this diagram illustrate alternative ways to cut America's balance of payments deficit while maintaining the exchange rate at 3 marks per dollar. Part (a) might represent a reduction in our inflation rate, which would increase world demand for U.S. export products. Or it could represent a rise in American interest rates, which would attract foreign capital. Part (b) might represent a reduction in domestic incomes, which would diminish American appetites for foreign goods. In either case, whether demand rises or supply falls, the balance of payments deficit is reduced: from *AB* to *CB* in part (a) and from *AB* to *AC* in part (b).

the demand curve moves outward as in part (a), or the supply curve moves inward as in part (b). With the exchange rate held at 3 marks to the dollar, the balance of payments deficit shrinks—to *CB* in part (a) or to *AC* in part (b).

Referring back to our earlier discussions of the factors that underlie the demand and supply curves, then, we see that one way a deficit nation can improve its balance of payments is to *reduce its aggregate demand*, thus discouraging imports and cutting down its demand for foreign currency. Another is to *slow its rate of inflation*, thus encouraging exports and discouraging imports. Finally, it can *raise its interest rates* in order to attract more foreign capital.

In a word, deficit nations were expected to follow restrictive monetary and fiscal policies *voluntarily* just as they would have done *automatically* under the old gold standard. However, just as under the gold standard, this medicine was often unpalatable—as it was to the United States in the 1960s.

Surplus nations could, of course, have taken the opposite measures: pursuing expansive monetary and fiscal policies to increase economic growth and lower interest rates. By increasing the supply of the country's currency and reducing the demand for it, such actions would have reduced the balance of payments surplus. But often the countries did not relish the inflation that accompanies expansionary policies; and so, once again, they left the burden of adjustment to the deficit nations. The general point about fixed exchange rates is that:

Under a system of fixed exchange rates, the government of a country loses some control over its domestic economy. There may be times when balance of payments considerations force it to contract its economy in order to cut down its demand for foreign currency, even though domestic needs are calling for expansion. Conversely, there may be times when the domestic economy needs to be reined in, but balance of payments considerations suggest expansion.

The Bretton Woods system worked fairly well for a number of years, but it finally broke down over its inability to devalue the U.S. dollar. By August 1971, the depletion of America's reserves and the accumulation of foreign debts resulting from America's chronic balance of payments deficits forced President Richard Nixon to end fixed exchange rates. He unilaterally abolished the gold exchange system by announcing that the United States would no longer peg the value of the dollar by buying and selling gold. After some futile attempts by the major trading nations to reestablish fixed rates in 1971 and 1972, the Bretton Woods system ended in 1973.

Most observers today agree that the gold-exchange system could not have survived the incredible events of the next decade in any case. The worldwide inflationary boom of 1972, the supply-side inflations of 1972–1974 and 1979–1980, and the great worldwide recessions of 1974–1976 and the early 1980s created a world in which the major countries were experiencing dramatically different inflation rates. For example, between 1975 and 1985, inflation averaged 4 percent per year in Germany, 7 percent in the United States, 11 percent in Great Britain, and 15 percent in Italy. As the purchasing-power theory reminds us, large differences in inflation rates call for *major* changes in currency values. The Bretton Woods system was ill-suited to handle such major changes.

## WHY TRY TO FIX EXCHANGE RATES?

In view of these and other severe problems with the Bretton Woods system, why did the international financial community work so hard to maintain fixed rates for so many years? And why do some people today want to return to fixed exchange rates? The answer is that floating exchange rates, determined in free markets by supply and demand, also pose problems.

Chief among these is the possibility that freely floating rates might prove to be highly variable rates, which add an unwanted element of risk to foreign trade. For example, if the exchange rate is 16 cents to the French franc, then a 2000-franc Parisian dress will cost $320. But should the franc appreciate to 20 cents, that same dress would cost $400. An American department store thinking of buying the dress may need to place its order far in advance and will want to know the cost *in dollars*. It may be worried about the possibility that the value of the franc will rise, so that the dress will cost more than $320. And such worries might inhibit trade.

"Then it's agreed. Until the dollar firms up, we let the clamshell float."

Drawing by Ed Fisher
© 1971, The New Yorker Magazine, Inc.

There are two answers to this concern. First, we might hope that freely floating rates would prove to be fairly stable. Prices of most ordinary goods and services, for example, are determined by supply and demand in free markets and yet do not fluctuate unduly. Unfortunately, experience since 1973 has dashed this hope. Exchange rates have been extremely volatile—much more volatile than advocates of floating rates anticipated. This volatility is a major reason why some observers want to move back toward fixed exchange rates.

A second possibility is that speculators might relieve business firms of exchange rate risks—for a fee, of course. Consider the department store example. If French francs cost 16 cents today, the department store manager can assure herself of paying exactly $320 for the dress several months from now by arranging for a speculator to deliver francs to her at 16 cents on the day she needs them. If the franc appreciates in the interim, it is the speculator, not the department store, that will take the financial beating. And, of course, if the franc depreciates, the speculator will pocket the profits. Thus speculators play an important role in a system of floating exchange rates.

The widespread fears that speculative activity in free markets will lead to wild gyrations in prices, while occasionally valid, are often unfounded. The reason is simple. To make profits, international currency speculators must buy a currency when its value is low (thus helping to support the currency by pushing up its demand curve) and sell it when its value is high (thus holding down the price by adding to the supply curve).

This means that, to be successful, speculators must come into the market as *buyers* when demand is weak (or when supply is strong), and come in as *sellers* when demand is strong (or supply is scant). In doing so, they will help limit price fluctuations. Looked at the other way around, speculators can destabilize prices only if they are systematically willing to lose money.[5]

Notice the stark contrast to the system of fixed exchange rates in which speculation often led to wild "runs" on currencies that were on the verge of devaluation. Speculative activity, which may well be destabilizing under fixed rates, is likely to be stabilizing under floating rates.

We do not mean to imply that speculation makes floating exchange rates trouble-free. At the very least, speculators will demand a fee for their services—a fee that adds to the costs of trading across national borders. In addition, not all exchange-rate risks can be eliminated through speculation. For example, few contracts on foreign currencies nowadays last more than, say, six months or a year. Thus no business can protect itself from exchange-rate changes over periods measured in years. Yet, despite this risk, international trade has flourished under floating exchange rates. Apparently, exchange-rate risk is not as burdensome as some people feared.

## THE CURRENT MIXED SYSTEM

Our current international financial system—where some currencies are still pegged in the old Bretton Woods manner, many are floating freely, and others are floating subject to government interferences—has evolved gradually since the United States severed the dollar's link to gold. Though it continues to change and adapt, at least three features have been evident.

The first is the decline in the notion that exchange rates should be fixed for long periods of time. The demand by many countries in the early 1970s that the world quickly return to fixed exchange rates had largely subsided by the mid-1970s. Even where rates are still pegged, devaluations and revaluations are now much more frequent—and smaller—than they were in the Bretton Woods era. Most free-world currency rates change slightly on a day-to-day basis, and market forces generally determine the basic trends, up or down. Even advocates of greater

---

[5]See Review Question 11 at the end of the chapter.

fixity in exchange rates generally propose that governments keep rates within certain *ranges*, rather than literally fix them.

Second, however, some central banks do not hesitate to intervene to moderate exchange movements whenever they feel that such actions are appropriate. Typically, these interventions are aimed at ironing out what are deemed to be transitory fluctuations. But there are times in which central banks oppose basic trends in exchange rates. For example, the Federal Reserve and other central banks sold dollars aggressively in 1985 to push the dollar down, and both the Fed and the Bank of Japan tried to arrest the rise of the yen in 1993. While we certainly no longer have many fixed exchange rates, most of the major currencies are floating less than freely. The terms **"dirty float"** or **"managed float"** have been coined to describe this mongrel system.

The third unmistakable feature of the present international monetary system is the virtual elimination of any role for gold. The trend away from gold actually began before 1971, and by now gold plays essentially no role in the world's financial system. Instead, there is a *free market* in gold in which dentists, jewelers, industrial users, speculators, and ordinary citizens who think of gold as a good store of value can buy or sell as they wish. The price of gold is determined each day by the law of supply and demand and has proved to be quite volatile.

## RECENT DEVELOPMENTS IN INTERNATIONAL FINANCIAL MARKETS

### THE DANCING DOLLAR

We mentioned earlier that floating exchange rates have not been stable exchange rates. No currency illustrates this better than the U.S. dollar. (See Figure 36–8.)

In 1977 and 1978, the international value of the dollar plummeted until a concerted effort by central banks to buy dollars stopped the fall. The dollar then stabilized for almost two years before starting to rise like a rocket for a period of almost five years. As Table 36–1 (page 901) shows, in 1980 a U.S. dollar bought less than 2 German marks, about 4 French francs, and about 830 Italian lira. By the time it peaked in February 1985, the mighty dollar could buy more than 3 German marks, about 10 French francs, and over 2000 Italian lira. Such major currency changes had dramatic effects on world trade.

The rising dollar was a blessing to Americans who traveled abroad or who bought foreign goods because foreign prices, when translated to dollars by the exchange rate, looked cheap to Americans.[6] But the arithmetic worked just the other way for U.S. firms seeking to sell their goods abroad; foreign buyers found everything American very expensive.[7] It was no surprise, therefore, that as the dollar climbed our exports fell, our imports rose, and our current account registered all-time record deficits. An expensive currency, Americans came to learn, is a mixed blessing.

From early 1985 until early 1988, the value of the dollar fell even faster than it had risen. The cheaper dollar curbed American appetites for imports and alleviated the plight of our export industries, many of which boomed. However, rising

[6]EXAMPLE: How much does a 600-franc hotel room in Paris cost in dollars when the franc is worth 20 cents? 16 cents? 10 cents?

[7]EXAMPLE: How much does a $55 American camera cost a German consumer when the mark is worth 55 cents? 44 cents? 33.33 cents?

*Figure* **36-8** **THE UPS AND DOWNS OF THE DOLLAR, 1974–1993**

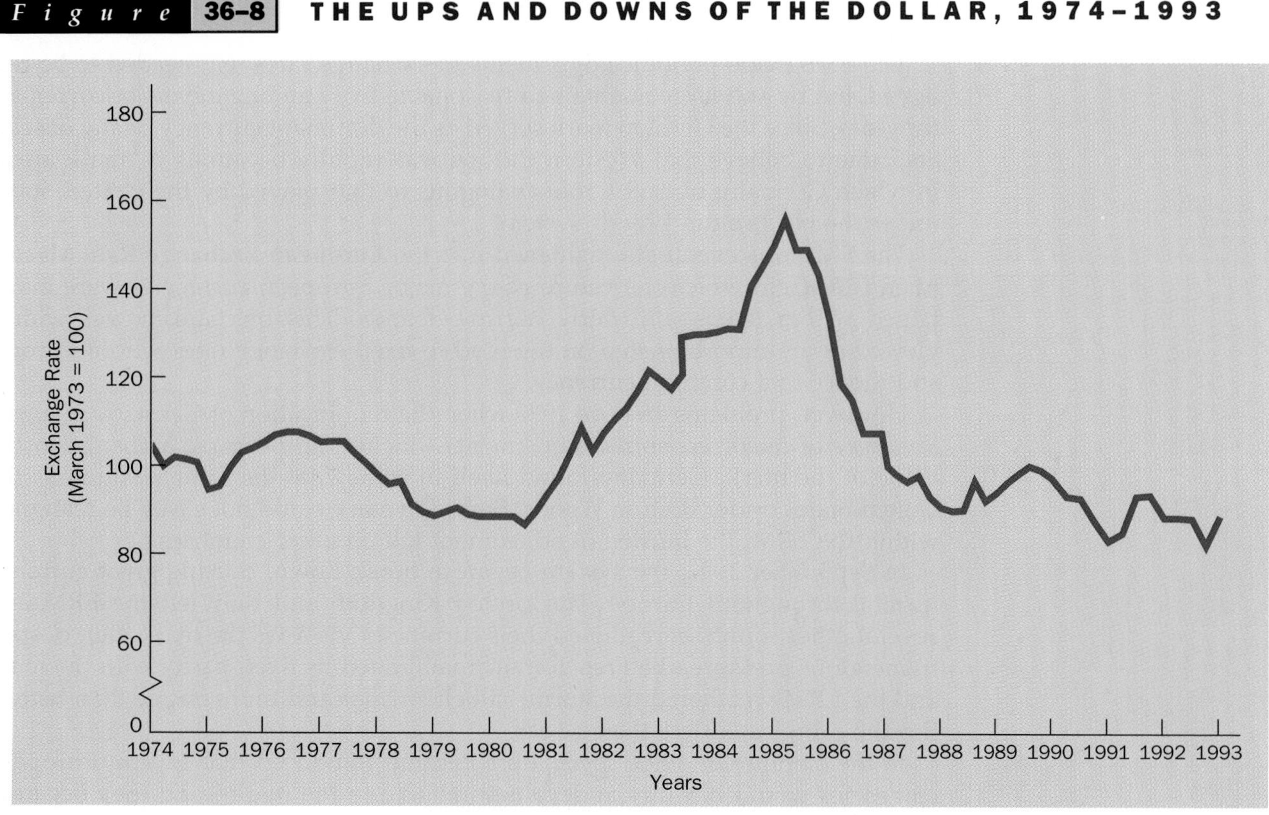


This graph charts the behavior of the international value of the dollar relative to a basket of ten major foreign currencies since 1974. (The index is based on March 1973 = 100.) The net change in the value of the dollar over the entire period is small, but the ups and downs have been pronounced. The stunning climb of the dollar from its 1980 low to its 1985 high stands out on the graph, as does the even more pronounced decline from 1985 to 1988.

SOURCE: Federal Reserve System.

prices for imported goods and foreign vacations were a source of consternation to many American consumers.

Then, in 1988 and 1989, the dollar rose sharply against most major currencies, renewing worries about America's ability to export. Since then, the overall value of the dollar has been relatively stable, but there have been notable movements against particular currencies. In particular, the yen appreciated sharply in 1993.

### THE EUROPEAN EXCHANGE RATE MECHANISM

As noted earlier, floating exchange rates are no magical cure-all. One particular problem beset the members of the European Economic Community (EC). These Common Market countries have pledged to create a unified market like the United States. As part of that pledge, they need eventually to establish a single currency for all member countries. Floating rates would make this goal unattainable. So in 1973 some of the member countries entered into an agreement whereby exchange rates among their currencies would remain relatively *fixed* while EC currencies as a group would rise or fall *relative to the rest of the world*. In 1979 this arrangement was strengthened and formalized, creating the *European Monetary System (EMS).*

The EMS made periodic adjustments to exchange rates that needed to be realigned, but by and large maintained reasonable fixity among the major currencies for years. Since the German mark served as the dominant currency, many observers came to believe that Western Europe was rapidly becoming a "mark area," in which Germany played a role analogous to that played by the United States under the old Bretton Woods system.

The EMS was eventually tightened into the **European Exchange Rate Mechanism (ERM)**, in which the values of the major European currencies were maintained within fixed—and fairly narrow—bands. This mechanism was widely viewed as an important step on the road to fixed exchange rates within Europe, and thence to a common currency.

However, problems arose in 1990 when the reunification of Germany required a variety of major economic adjustments—including, perhaps, a change in the value of the mark. Germany found itself in somewhat the same position as the United States under Bretton Woods: Since the mark could not easily be realigned within the ERM, the burden of adjustment fell on other countries.

In September 1992, the system began to break down, causing great currency turmoil throughout Europe. The United Kingdom and Italy left the ERM and several other countries realigned their currencies vis-a-vis the mark. But, despite tremendous pressure, the French franc maintained its fixed parity with the mark and the ERM weathered the storm—albeit smaller and more fragile than before. But the calm lasted less than a year.

In the summer of 1993, speculators became convinced that several European currencies would have to be devalued relative to the mark—and they began to sell these currencies and buy marks. Europe's central banks resisted for a while, but eventually succumbed to market forces. Currency bands were made so wide that the EC went on a *de facto* floating system even though the ERM remained intact in name. As of this writing, no one knows what might happen to the European Exchange Rate Mechanism next.

## *Summary*

1. **Exchange rates** state the value of one currency in terms of another and thus influence the patterns of world trade in important ways.
2. If governments do not interfere by buying or selling their currencies, exchange rates will be determined in free markets by the usual laws of supply and demand. Such a system is called **floating exchange rates**.
3. Demand for a nation's currency is derived from foreigners' desires to purchase that country's goods and services or to invest in its assets. Any change that increases the demand for a nation's currency will cause its exchange rate to **appreciate** under floating rates.
4. Supply of a nation's currency is derived from the desire of that country's citizens to purchase foreign goods and services or to invest in foreign assets. Any change that increases the supply of a nation's currency will cause its exchange rate to **depreciate** under floating rates.
5. In the long run, purchasing-power parity plays a major role in exchange rate movements. The **purchasing-power parity theory** states that relative price levels in any two countries determine the exchange rate between their currencies. Therefore, countries with relatively low inflation rates normally will have appreciating currencies.
6. Over shorter periods, purchasing-power parity has little influence over exchange-rate movements. The pace of economic activity and the level of interest rates exert greater influence. In particular, interest rate

movements are typically the dominant factor in the short run.

7. Exchange rates can be fixed at nonequilibrium levels by governments that are willing and able to mop up any excess of quantity supplied over quantity demanded, or provide any excess of quantity demanded over quantity supplied. In the first case, the country is suffering from a **balance of payments deficit** because of its overvalued currency. In the second, an undervalued currency has given it a **balance of payments surplus**.
8. In the early part of this century, the world was on a particular system of **fixed exchange rates** called the **gold standard**, in which the value of every nation's currency was fixed in terms of gold. But this created problems because nations could not control their own money supplies and because the world could not control its total supply of gold.
9. After World War II, the gold standard was replaced by the **gold-exchange (or Bretton Woods) system** where rates were again fixed, or rather, fixed until further notice. In this system, the U.S. dollar was the basis of international currency values.
10. The gold-exchange system served the world well and helped restore world trade, but it ran into trouble when the dollar became chronically overvalued since the system provided no way to remedy this situation.
11. Since 1971, the world has moved toward a system of relatively free exchange rates, though there are plenty of exceptions. We now have a thoroughly mixed system of **"dirty" or "managed" floating** which continues to evolve and adapt.
12. Floating rates are not without their problems. For example, importers and exporters justifiably worry about fluctuations in exchange rates. Though these problems seem manageable, some people think that a return to fixed exchange rates is desirable.
13. Under floating exchange rates, investors who speculate on international currency values provide a valuable service by assuming the risks of those who do not wish to speculate. Normally, speculators stabilize rather than destabilize exchange rates, because that is how they make profits.
14. The U.S. dollar rose dramatically in value from 1980 to 1985, making our imports cheaper and our exports more expensive. Then, from 1985 to 1988, the dollar tumbled, which had precisely the reverse effects.

## Key Concepts and Terms

International monetary system
Exchange rate
Appreciation
Depreciation
Devaluation
Revaluation
Supply of and demand for foreign exchange
Floating exchange rates
Purchasing-power parity theory
Fixed exchange rates
Balance of payments deficit and surplus
Current account
Capital account
Balance of trade
Gold standard
Gold-exchange system (Bretton Woods system)
International Monetary Fund (IMF)
"Dirty" or "managed" floating
The European Exchange Rate Mechanism (ERM)

## Questions for Review

1. What items do you own or routinely consume that are produced abroad? From what countries do these come? Suppose you decided to buy more of these things? How would that affect the exchange rates between the dollar and these currencies?
2. If the dollar depreciates relative to the Japanese yen, will the Sony Discman you have wanted become more or less expensive? What effect do you imagine this will have on American demands for Discmen? Does the American demand curve for yen, therefore, slope upward or downward? Explain.
3. During the first half of the 1980s, inflation in (West) Germany was consistently lower than in the United States. What, then, does the purchasing-power parity theory predict should have happened to the exchange rate between the mark and the dollar between 1980 and 1985? (Look at Table 36–1 to see what actually happened.)

4. Use supply and demand diagrams to analyze the effect on the exchange rate between the dollar and the British pound if:
   a. Britain's flow of North Sea oil increases.
   b. British dockworkers refuse to unload ships that arrive with cargo from America but continue to load ships that sail from Britain.
   c. The Federal Reserve raises interest rates in America.
   d. The U.S. government, to help settle the problems of the Middle East, gives huge amounts of foreign aid to Israel and her Arab neighbors.
   e. Both Britain and the United States recover from recessions, but the British recovery is more rapid.
   f. Polls suggest that Britain's conservative government will be replaced by radicals, who vow to nationalize all foreign-owned assets.
5. How are the problems of a country faced with a balance of payments deficit similar to those posed by a government regulation that holds the price of milk above the equilibrium level? (*Hint:* Think of each in terms of a supply-demand diagram.)
6. Look at the U.S. balance of payments accounts table in the text (Table 36–2 on page 913). Figure out where each of the following actions you could have taken in 1992 would have been recorded in these accounts:
   a. You spent the summer traveling in Europe.
   b. Your uncle in Canada sent you $20 as a birthday present.
   c. You bought a new Honda.
   d. You sold some stock you own on the Tokyo Stock Exchange.
   e. You came home from a trip to Canada carrying two cases of Canadian beer, which you sold to a friend. (*Hint*: Would your sale have been recorded anywhere?)
7. For each of the transactions listed in Question 6, indicate how it would affect:
   a. the U.S. balance of payments, if exchange rates were fixed;
   b. the international value of the dollar, if exchange rates were floating.
8. Under the old gold standard, what do you think happened to world prices when there was a huge gold strike in California in 1849? What do you think happened when the world went without any important new gold strikes for 20 years or so?
9. Explain why the members of the Bretton Woods conference in 1944 wanted to establish a system of fixed exchange rates. What was the flaw that led to the ultimate breakdown of the system in 1971?
10. Suppose you want to reserve a hotel room in London for the coming summer but are worried that the value of the pound may rise between now and then, making the rooms too expensive for your budget. Explain how a speculator could relieve you of this worry. (Don't actually try it. Speculators deal only in very large sums!)
11. On page 919, it is pointed out that successful speculators buy a currency when demand is weak and sell it when demand is strong. Use supply and demand diagrams for two different periods (one with weak demand, the other with strong demand) to show why this will limit price fluctuations.
12. Use the following statistics to produce a balance of payments table for the United States, identifying separately the current and capital accounts. (Assume no statistical discrepancy.)

| | |
|---|---|
| U.S. income on foreign investments (net) | 100 |
| U.S. government grants to foreigners | 25 |
| Merchandise exports | 750 |
| U.S. tourist expenditures abroad | 50 |
| U.S. private direct investment abroad | 80 |
| Foreign direct investment in the United States | 60 |
| Merchandise imports | 850 |

   a. Does the balance of payments show a surplus or a deficit?
   b. What would happen to the exchange rate under flexible exchange rates?
13. In 1993, market forces were pushing up the international value of the Japanese yen. What could the Bank of Japan (Japan's central bank) have done to try to prevent this appreciation? Why might it have failed? Could the Federal Reserve have done the job instead?

Chapter 37

# MACROECONOMICS IN A WORLD ECONOMY

*No man is an island,*
*entire of itself.*

JOHN DONNE

America is not an isolated economy immune from foreign influences. Today, more than ever before, the nations of the world are locked together in an uneasy economic union. Fluctuations in foreign GDP growth, foreign inflation, and foreign interest rates profoundly affect the U.S. economy. Similarly, economic events that originate in our country reverberate around the globe. Without a deeper understanding of these international linkages, we cannot hope to understand many of the most important economic developments of our time. ¶ What we learned in earlier chapters about the macroeconomics of international trade in goods and services was correct, but limited. In particular, it paid no attention to such crucial influences as exchange rates and international financial movements. Changes in exchange rates alter the prices of one country's goods in terms of the currency of another. In Chapter 36, we learned how major macroeconomic variables such as GDP, prices, and interest rates affect exchange rates. In this chapter, we complete the circle by studying how changes in the exchange rate affect the domestic economy. Then we bring international capital flows into the picture and learn how monetary and fiscal policy work in an **open economy**.

An **OPEN ECONOMY** is one that trades with other nations in goods and services, and perhaps also in financial assets.

## POLICY ISSUE: THE U.S. TRADE DEFICIT

Everybody knows that the United States has been importing much more than it has been exporting in recent years. In 1992, for example, our real imports of Japanese automobiles, Korean textiles, French wine, and other products amounted to $615 billion (in 1987 dollars) while our real exports of wheat, computers, banking services, and the like were just $573 billion—leaving a trade deficit of $42 billion. (See Figure 37–1.)

Naturally, deficits of this magnitude have attracted a great deal of attention not only from economists, but also from politicians, the business community, and the news media. Indeed, during the 1980s America's gaping trade deficit rivalled the federal budget deficit as *the* major economic news story. Some critics argue that the trade deficit illustrates the basic weakness of our national economy—though other observers argue that it actually shows our underlying strength! Many economists worry that, by continually buying more than we sell, America is piling up debts that we will live to regret.

**Figure 37–1**

### U.S. NET EXPORTS AND THE VALUE OF THE DOLLAR, 1981–1992

Real exports exceeded real imports in the United States in the early 1980s. Since then, however, our imports have exceeded our exports. The largest trade deficits occurred in 1985–1987; since 1986, our trade deficit has mostly been declining. The international value of the dollar rose a great deal in the first half of the 1980s, mostly fell in the second half, and has moved around with little trend so far in the 1990s.

SOURCE: U.S. Bureau of Economic Analysis and Federal Reserve System.

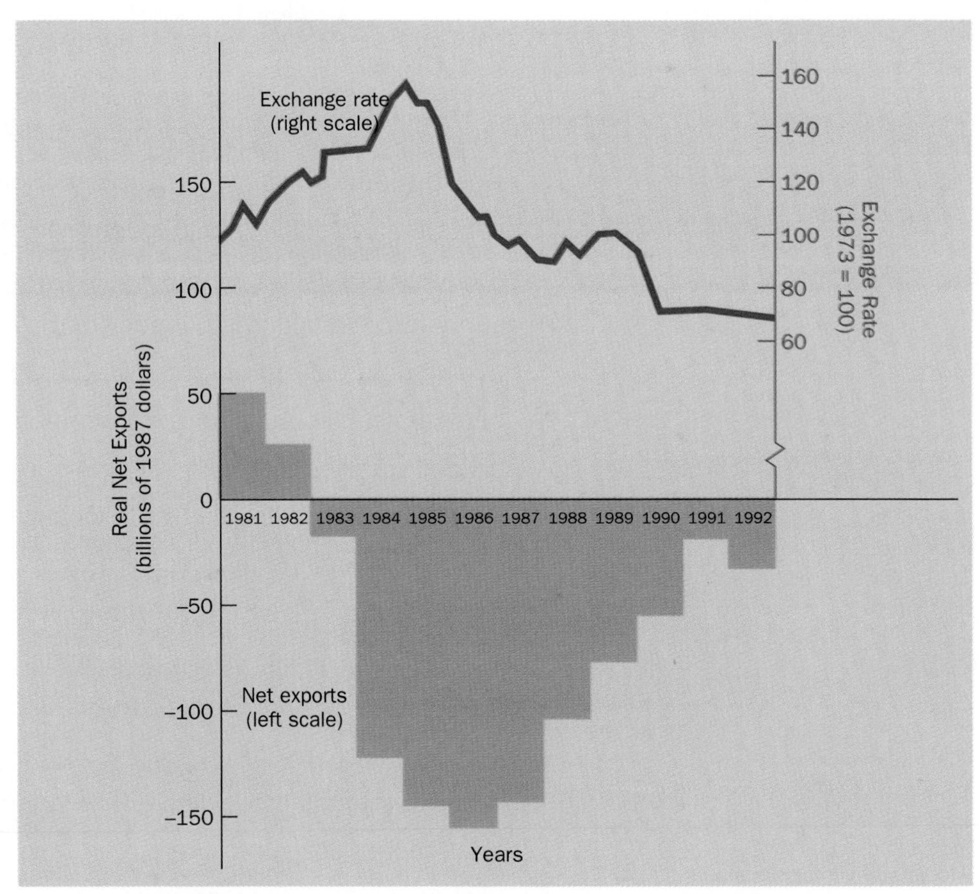

Figure 37–2 **THE EFFECTS OF HIGHER NET EXPORTS**

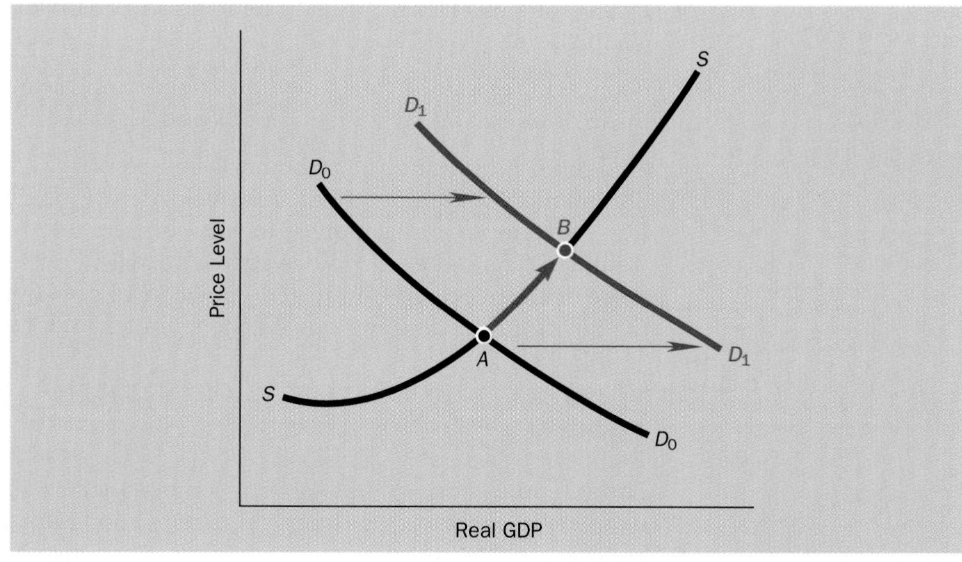


If real exports rise or real imports fall, the economy's aggregate demand curve shifts outward, from $D_0D_0$ to $D_1D_1$. Real GDP and the price level both rise as the equilibrium moves from point *A* to point *B*.

But few people realize that American foreign trade was roughly in balance as recently as a decade ago, as Figure 37–1 shows. And fewer still understand how we came to acquire a chronic trade deficit in so short a time. Lack of knowledge, however, has not prevented these same people from prescribing—and in some cases seeking to legislate—"cures" for our trade problems. By the end of this chapter, you will have a better understanding of the origins and implications of America's trade deficit, and you will be able to make up your own mind about how it can best be cured.

## INTERNATIONAL TRADE AND AGGREGATE DEMAND: A QUICK REVIEW

As we know from Part 6 (especially Chapters 25 and 26), a country's net exports, $(X - IM)$, are one component of its aggregate demand, $C + I + G + (X - IM)$. That implies, for example, that an autonomous increase in exports or decrease in imports has a multiplier effect on the economy, just like an increase in consumption, investment, or government purchases.[1] Figure 37–2 depicts this conclusion on an aggregate demand and supply diagram. A rise in net exports shifts the aggregate demand curve outward to the right, thereby raising both GDP and the price level.

But what can make net exports rise? One factor we mentioned in Chapter 25 was a rise in foreign incomes. If foreigners become richer, they are likely to spend more on a wide variety of products, some of which will be American. So America's

[1]An appendix to Chapter 26 showed that international trade lowers the numerical value of the multiplier. Nonetheless, autonomous changes in $C$, $I$, $G$, or $(X - IM)$ all have the same multiplier.

exports will rise. Thus Figure 37–2 illustrates the effect on the U.S. economy of a boom in Europe. Similarly, a recession abroad would reduce U.S. exports and hence shift the U.S. aggregate demand curve inward. Thus, as we learned in Chapter 26:

Booms or recessions in one country tend to be transmitted to other countries through international trade in goods and services.

One other important determinant of net exports was mentioned in Chapter 25, but not discussed in depth: the relative prices of foreign and domestic goods. The idea is a simple application of the law of demand: if the prices of the goods of Country X rise, then people everywhere will tend to buy fewer of them—and more of the goods of Country Y. As we shall see shortly, this simple idea holds the key to understanding how exchange rates affect international trade.

## RELATIVE PRICES, EXPORTS, AND IMPORTS

First assume—just for this short section—that exchange rates are *fixed*. What happens if the prices of American export goods fall while, say, Japanese prices are constant? With U.S. products now less expensive *relative to Japanese products*, both Japanese and American consumers will probably buy more American goods and fewer Japanese goods. So America's net exports will *rise*, adding to aggregate demand in this country—as shown in Figure 37–2. Conversely, a rise in American prices (relative to Japanese prices) will *decrease* our net exports and aggregate demand. Thus:

For given foreign prices, a fall in the prices of a country's exports will lead to an increase in that country's net exports, and hence to a rise in its real GDP. Analogously, a rise in the prices of a country's exports will decrease that country's net exports and GDP.

Precisely the same logic applies to changes in Japanese prices. If Japanese prices rise, Americans will export more and import less. So $(X - IM)$ will rise, boosting GDP in the United States. Figure 37–2 applies to this case without change. By similar reasoning, falling Japanese prices decrease U.S. net exports and depress our economy. Thus:

Price increases abroad raise a country's net exports and hence its GDP. Price decreases abroad have the opposite effects.

## THE EFFECTS OF CHANGES IN EXCHANGE RATES

From here it is a simple matter to figure out how changes in *exchange rates* affect a country's net exports, for currency appreciations or depreciations change international relative prices.

Recall that the basic role of an exchange rate is to convert one country's prices into the currency of another. Table 37–1 uses two examples of U.S.–Japanese trade to remind us of this role. Suppose the dollar depreciates from 150 yen to 120 yen. Then, from the viewpoint of American consumers, a television set that costs ¥60,000 in Japan goes up in price from $400 (that is, 60,000/150) to $500. To Americans, it is just as if TV prices in Japan had risen by 25 percent. Naturally,

**Table 37–1 EXCHANGE RATES AND HOME-CURRENCY PRICES**

| | 60,000 YEN JAPANESE TV SET | | $2000 U.S. HOME COMPUTER | |
|---|---|---|---|---|
| **EXCHANGE RATE** | **PRICE IN JAPAN** | **PRICE IN U.S.** | **PRICE IN U.S.** | **PRICE IN JAPAN** |
| $1 = 150 yen | ¥60,000 | $400 | $2,000 | ¥300,000 |
| $1 = 120 yen | ¥60,000 | $500 | $2,000 | ¥240,000 |

Americans react by purchasing fewer Japanese products. So American imports go down.

Now consider the implications for Japanese consumers interested in buying American microcomputers that cost $2000. When the dollar falls from 150 yen to 120 yen, they see the price of these computers falling from ¥300,000 (that is, 2,000 × 150) to ¥240,000. To them, it is just as if American producers had offered a 20 percent markdown. Under such circumstances, we expect U.S. sales to the Japanese to rise. So U.S. exports should increase. Putting these two findings together, we conclude that:

A currency depreciation should raise net exports and therefore increase aggregate demand. Conversely, a currency appreciation should reduce net exports and therefore decrease aggregate demand.

For later reference, this conclusion is recorded on an aggregate supply and demand diagram in Figure 37–3. If the currency depreciates, net exports rise and

**Figure 37–3 THE EFFECTS OF EXCHANGE RATE CHANGES ON AGGREGATE DEMAND**

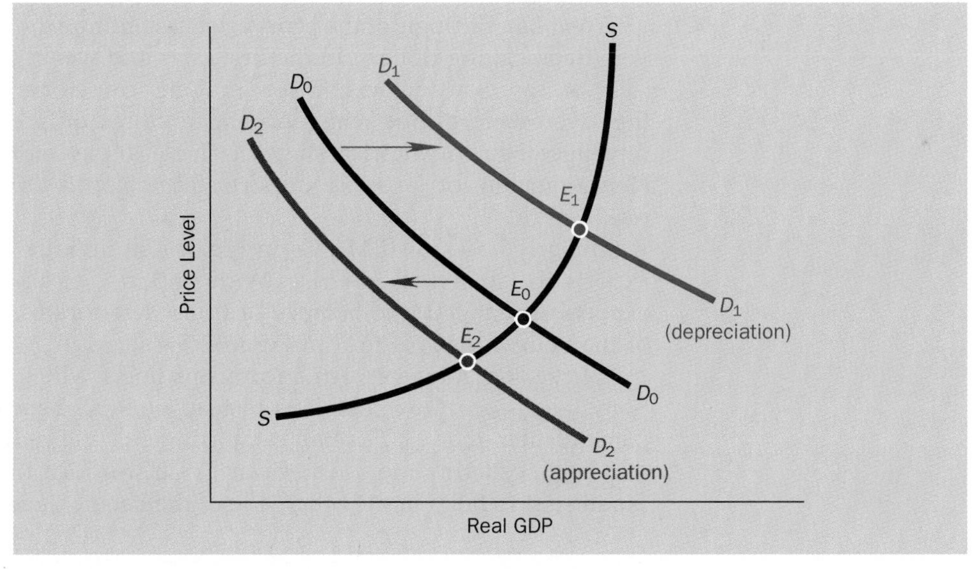


A depreciation of the exchange rate raises net exports and hence shifts the aggregate demand curve outward to the right, from $D_0D_0$ to $D_1D_1$ in the diagram. An appreciation of the currency shifts the aggregate demand curve inward to the left, to $D_2D_2$. Thus depreciations are expansionary and appreciations are contractionary.

the aggregate demand curve shifts outward from $D_0D_0$ to $D_1D_1$. Both prices and output rise as the economy's equilibrium moves from $E_0$ to $E_1$. If the currency appreciates, everything operates in reverse: net exports fall, the aggregate demand curve shifts inward to $D_2D_2$, and both prices and output decline.

Now we are in a position to understand one of the main reasons why the U.S. trade deficit grew so large in the 1980s. Figure 37–1 reminds us that the international value of the dollar soared in the first half of the 1980s. According to the analysis we have just completed, such a stunning appreciation of the dollar should have encouraged U.S. imports, damaged U.S. exports, and been a drag on aggregate demand. That is precisely what happened. In real 1987 dollars, American imports soared by 59 percent between 1981 and 1986, while American exports rose a scant 1 percent. The result is that a $22 billion net export *surplus* in 1981 turned into a $155 billion *deficit* by 1986.

## LAGS IN INTERNATIONAL TRADE AND THE J CURVE[2]

You may have noticed in Figure 37–1 that the highest exchange rate preceded the worst trade deficit. Specifically, the international value of the dollar hit its peak in early 1985; but our trade deficit continued to climb through most of 1986. Something seems wrong here. Since the dollar was falling during most of 1985 and 1986, our analysis predicts that America's net export position should have been improving. Instead, it continued to deteriorate. Why?

Actually, there is nothing wrong with our analysis. It is simply incomplete, for we have failed to note that international trade patterns take time to respond to changes in exchange rates. These lags in international trade give rise to a phenomenon known as the **J curve**. (See Figure 37–4.) The J curve indicates that, following a devaluation or depreciation, a country's trade deficit actually deteriorates for a while (from *A* to *B* in Figure 37–4) before improving (beyond point *B*). Thus a considerable period of time may elapse before any improvement in net exports is apparent. In the U.S. case, net exports first began to turn around late in 1986.

The **J CURVE** shows the typical pattern of response of net exports to a change in currency values. Following a depreciation or a devaluation, net exports usually decline at first and then rise.

To explain the logic of the J curve, let us continue the example of an appreciating yen (depreciating dollar). In the first days and weeks after the yen rises in value, sales of, say, Sony television sets in American stores will be about the same as they were before. But when American stores order more Japanese TV sets to replenish their inventories, they will have to pay more U.S. dollars for each set. Hence our bill for Japanese imports, *when measured in U.S. dollars*, will actually rise.

Similarly, sales of IBM PCs in Japan will initially be about the same; so our exports to Japan will not rise. With imports (measured in dollars) rising and exports unchanged, the balance of trade deteriorates. This is the falling portion of the J curve, from *A* to *B* in Figure 37–4.

Pretty soon, however, American consumers will start reacting to the fact that Sony televisions now cost $500 instead of $400. Their purchases will fall. After some further delay, U.S. retail establishments will reduce their orders from Sony and begin ordering more American TVs instead. At this point, U.S. imports from Japan start to fall. On the other side of the Pacific, Japanese consumers will begin

[2]This section can be deleted in shorter courses.

*Figure* **37–4** **THE J CURVE**

The response of a country's net exports to a decline in the value of its currency tends to follow a J-shaped pattern. In the period immediately following the depreciation or devaluation, everyone imports and exports about the same volume of goods as they did before. But imports cost more in terms of home currency, so net exports decline. This is the descending portion of the J curve, from point *A* to point *B*. After a while, however, imports decline and exports rise, so net exports improve. This is the rising portion of the curve, beyond point *B*.

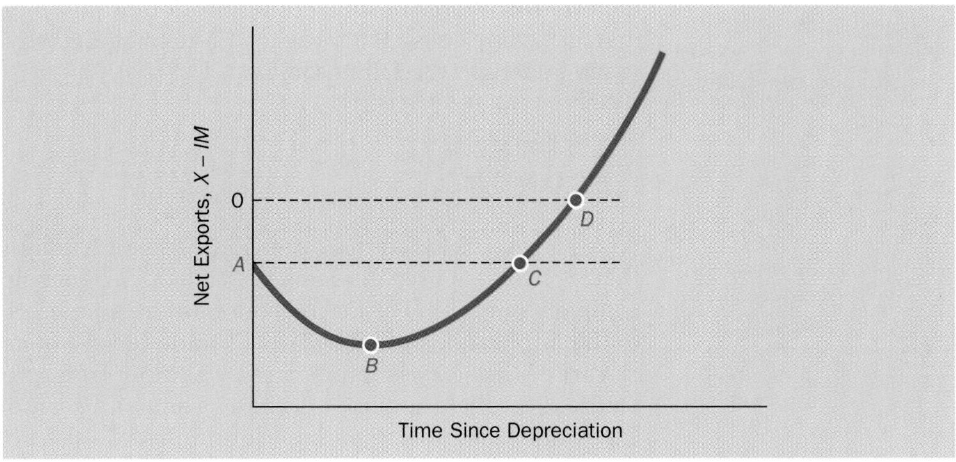


reacting to the fact that $2000 IBM computers now cost fewer yen. So U.S. exports to Japan start to rise. We are now on the rising portion of the J curve. But it takes some time (until point *C* in Figure 37–4) before trade patterns change enough to improve America's trade position with Japan.[3]

Some illustrative numbers will clarify the arithmetic behind the J curve. Suppose that, when the dollar was worth 150 yen, the United States was importing 1 million TV sets at $400 each and exporting 150,000 computers at $2000 each. Then the dollar value of our imports was $400 million and the dollar value of our exports was $300 million, leading to a trade deficit with Japan of $100 million.

Now the dollar depreciates to 120 yen and the dollar price of Japanese TVs rises to $500 (see Table 37–1). At first, purchases are unchanged; so our import bill for the 1 million Japanese TVs increases to $500 million. With exports remaining at $300 million, our trade deficit balloons to $200 million. We are on the downward portion of the J, between *A* and *B* in Figure 37–4.

After some time, however, Americans curtail their purchase of Japanese TVs and the Japanese buy more American computers. For the sake of concreteness, suppose that we now import 800,000 TVs and export 200,000 computers. At a price of $500 each, our TV imports cost $400 million. At a price of $2000 each, our computer exports earn us $400 million. Thus our trade with Japan is now balanced. In terms of Figure 37–4, we have reached point *D*.

Applying the J-curve analysis to U.S. experience in the 1980s is no easy matter. For one thing, the dollar did not decline all at once, but rather in stages beginning

[3]Actually, improvement occurs only if consumers in the two countries are sufficiently responsive to price changes. The changes in export and import volumes must be large enough to offset the fact that Japanese goods now cost more dollars.

in early 1985. Each depreciation set in motion its own little J curve, forming a complex pattern. For another, American firms seemed reluctant to cut their yen prices when the dollar fell, preferring to bolster their profit margins. And Japanese firms seemed even more reluctant to raise their dollar prices, preferring to maintain their market shares despite falling profit margins. Nonetheless, there is no doubt that the J curve goes a long way toward explaining why U.S. net exports responded so sluggishly to the falling dollar.

## AGGREGATE SUPPLY IN AN OPEN ECONOMY

So we have concluded that, after some (possibly long) delay, a currency depreciation increases aggregate demand while a currency appreciation decreases it. To complete our model of macroeconomics in an open economy, we must now turn to the implications of international trade for *aggregate supply*.

Part of the story is familiar. As we know from previous chapters, the United States, like all economies, purchases some of its productive inputs from abroad. Oil is only the most prominent example. We also rely on foreign suppliers for various metals (like titanium), many raw agricultural products (like coffee beans), and thousands of other items that are used by American industry. When the dollar depreciates, these imported inputs become more costly in terms of U.S. dollars—just as if foreign prices had risen.

The consequence is clear: with imported inputs more expensive, American firms will be forced to charge higher prices at any given level of output. Graphically, this means that *the aggregate supply curve will shift inward* (to the left).

When the dollar depreciates and the prices of foreign goods rise, the U.S. aggregate supply curve will shift inward, pushing up the prices of American-made goods and services. By exactly analogous reasoning, an appreciation of the dollar will make imported goods cheaper and shift the U.S. aggregate supply curve *outward*, thus pushing American prices down. (See Figure 37–5.)

Beyond this, a depreciating dollar has further inflationary effects that do not show up on the aggregate demand and supply diagram. Most obviously, prices of imported goods are included in American price indexes like the Consumer Price Index (CPI). So when dollar prices of Japanese cars, French wine, and Swiss watches increase, the CPI goes up even if no American price rises. For this and other reasons, the inflationary impact of a dollar depreciation is even greater than that indicated by Figure 37–5.[4]

## THE MACROECONOMIC EFFECTS OF EXCHANGE RATES

Let us now put aggregate demand and aggregate supply together and study the macroeconomic effects of changes in exchange rates.

First suppose that the international value of the dollar falls. Referring back to Figures 37–3 and 37–5, we see that this will shift the aggregate demand curve *outward* and the aggregate supply curve *inward*. The result, as Figure 37–6 shows,

[4]The diagram should be interpreted as showing the effects of currency depreciations and appreciations on the prices of *domestically-produced* goods.

Figure 37–5 **THE EFFECTS OF EXCHANGE RATE CHANGES ON AGGREGATE SUPPLY**

A depreciation of the currency pushes the aggregate supply curve inward, from $S_0S_0$ to $S_1S_1$ in the diagram, and is therefore inflationary. A currency appreciation has a deflationary effect because it pushes the aggregate supply curve outward, from $S_0S_0$ to $S_2S_2$.

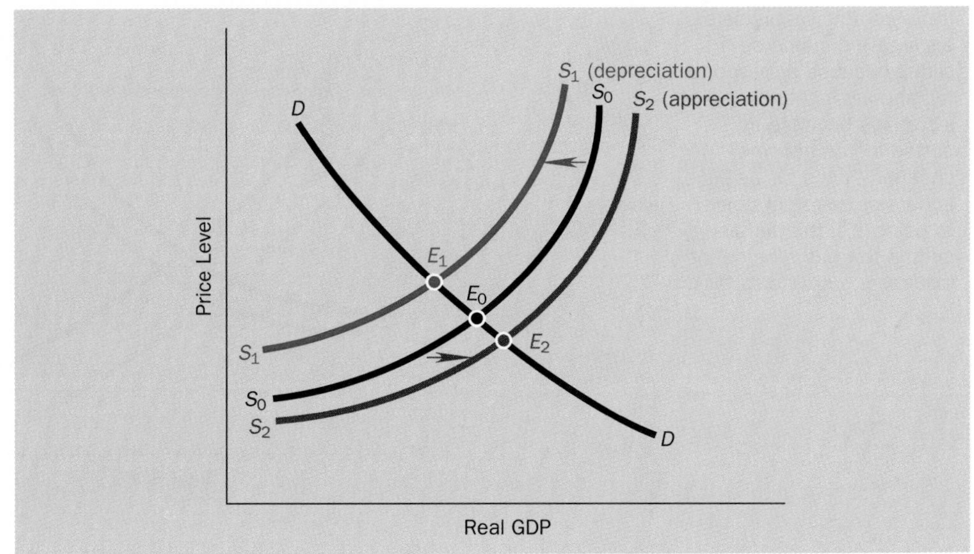


is that the U.S. price level certainly rises. Whether real GDP rises or falls depends on whether the supply or demand shift is the dominant influence. The evidence strongly suggests that aggregate *demand* shifts are usually more important, so we expect GDP to rise. Hence:

A currency depreciation is inflationary and probably also expansionary.

Figure 37–6 **THE EFFECTS OF A CURRENCY DEPRECIATION**

If the currency depreciates, aggregate demand increases because net exports are stimulated and aggregate supply decreases because imported inputs become more expensive. Prices rise as equilibrium moves from point $E$ to point $A$. If the demand shift is the more important influence, output increases, too.

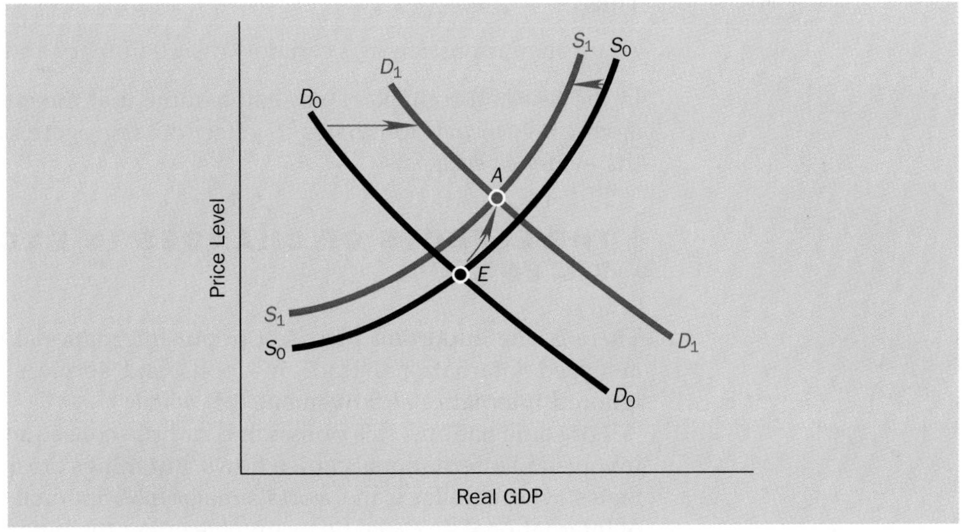

Figure 37–7 THE EFFECTS OF A CURRENCY APPRECIATION

If the currency appreciates, aggregate demand declines because net exports fall and aggregate supply increases because imported inputs become cheaper. Prices fall as equilibrium moves from point *E* to point *B*. If the demand shift is the more important influence, output also falls.

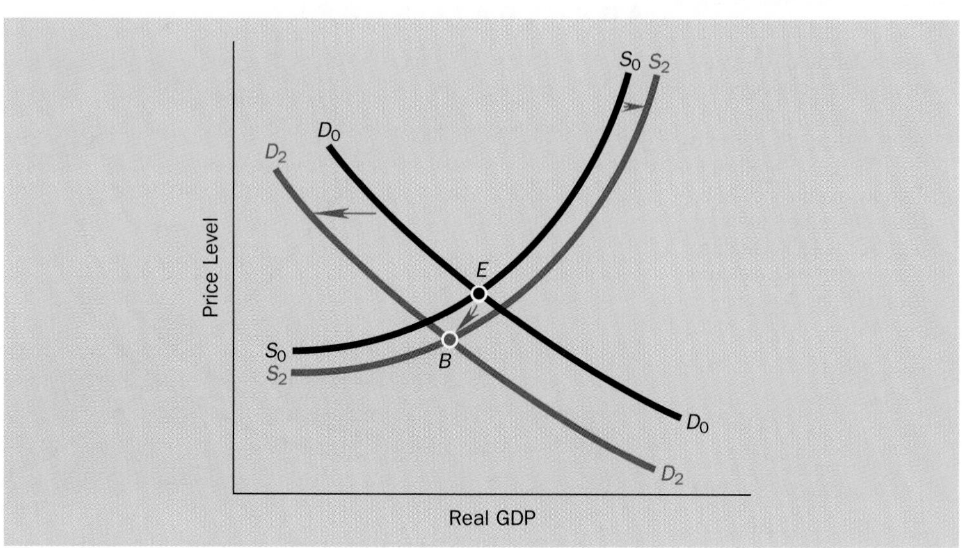


What is the intuitive explanation for this result? When the dollar falls, foreign goods become more expensive to Americans. That is directly inflationary. At the same time, aggregate demand in the United States is stimulated by rising net exports. As long as the expansion of demand outweighs the adverse shift of the aggregate supply curve brought on by the depreciation, real GDP should rise.

Now let's reverse things. Suppose the dollar *appreciates*. In this case, net exports *fall* so the aggregate demand curve shifts *inward*. At the same time, foreign goods become cheaper, so the aggregate supply curve shifts *outward*. (See Figure 37–7.) Once again, we can be sure of the movement of the price level: it falls. Output also falls if the demand shift is more important than the supply shift, as is likely. Thus:

A currency appreciation is certainly disinflationary and is probably contractionary.

In the rest of the chapter, we shall assume that the effect of the exchange rate on aggregate *demand* dominates its effect on aggregate *supply*, because that is what the evidence suggests.

## THE EFFECTS OF CHANGES IN EXCHANGE RATES

There is one important piece left in our international economic puzzle. We have analyzed international trade in goods and services rather fully, but we have ignored international movements of *capital*.

For some nations, this omission is of little consequence because they are rarely involved in international capital flows. But things are quite different for the United States, whose dollar is the world's major international currency. The vast majority of international financial flows involve either the buying or selling of assets whose values are stated in dollars. Fortunately, given what we have just learned about the effects of exchange rates, it is easy to add international capital flows to our analysis.

Recall from Chapter 36 that interest-rate differentials and capital flows are typically the most important determinants of exchange rate movements in the short run. Specifically, suppose interest rates in the United States rise while foreign interest rates remain unchanged. We learned in Chapter 36 that this will attract capital to the United States and cause the dollar to appreciate. This chapter has taught us that an appreciating dollar, in turn, will reduce net exports, prices, and output in the U.S.—as indicated in Figure 37–7. Thus:

A rise in interest rates tends to contract the economy by appreciating the currency and reducing net exports.

Notice that this conclusion has a familiar ring. In Chapter 30, while studying how monetary policy works, we observed that higher interest rates deter investment spending and hence reduce the $I$ component of $C + I + G + (X - IM)$. Now, in studying an open economy with international capital flows, we see that higher interest rates also reduce the $(X - IM)$ component. Thus *international capital flows strengthen the negative effects of interest rates on aggregate demand.*

If interest rates in the United States fall, or if those abroad rise, everything we have just said is turned in the opposite direction. There is no need to repeat the analysis. The conclusion is:[5]

A decline in interest rates tends to expand the economy by depreciating the exchange rate and raising net exports.

## FISCAL POLICY IN AN OPEN ECONOMY

Now we are ready to use our model to study how fiscal and monetary policy work when the exchange rate is floating and capital is internationally mobile. Doing so will teach us how international economic relations modify the effects of stabilization policies. Fortunately, no new theoretical apparatus is necessary; we only need remember what we have learned in the chapter up to this point. Specifically:

- A rise in the domestic interest rate leads to capital inflows and makes the exchange rate appreciate. A fall in the domestic interest rate leads to capital outflows and makes the exchange rate depreciate.
- A currency appreciation reduces aggregate demand and raises aggregate supply (see Figure 37–7). A currency depreciation raises aggregate demand and reduces aggregate supply (see Figure 37–6).

With this in mind, suppose the government cuts taxes or raises spending. Aggregate demand increases, which pushes up both real GDP and the price level in the usual manner. This is shown as the shift from $D_0D_0$ to blue line $D_1D_1$ in Figure 37–8. In a **closed economy**, that is the end of the story. But in an *open* economy with international capital flows, we must add in the macroeconomic effects of an increase in the exchange rate. We do this in two steps.

A **CLOSED ECONOMY** is one that does not trade with other nations in either goods or assets.

[5]EXERCISE: Provide the reasoning behind this conclusion.

**Figure 37–8 A FISCAL EXPANSION IN AN OPEN ECONOMY**

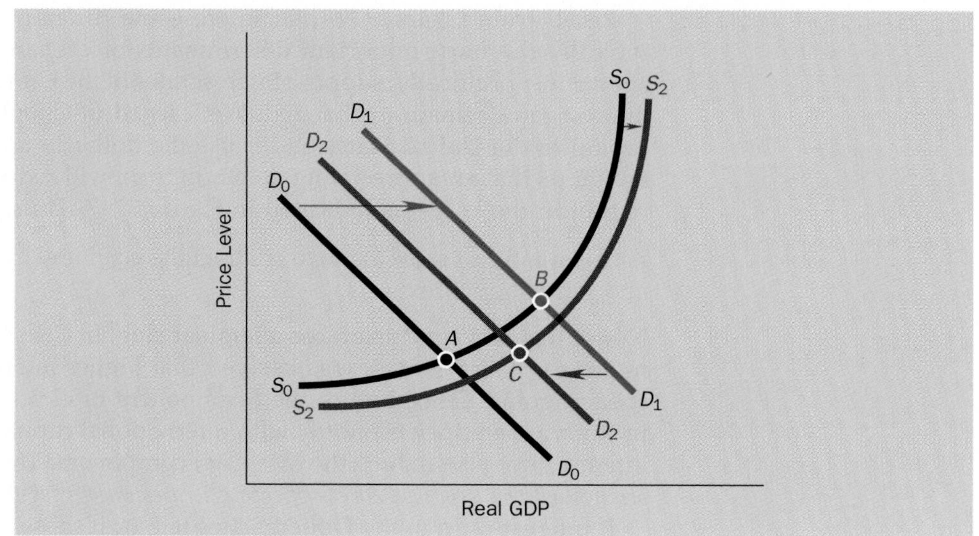


A fiscal expansion pushes the aggregate demand outward, from $D_0D_0$ to $D_1D_1$ in the diagram. But it also raises interest rates, which attracts international capital and appreciates the currency. The currency appreciation, in turn, reduces aggregate demand and raises aggregate supply—as shown by the brown curves $S_2S_2$ and $D_2D_2$. The result is that equilibrium occurs at point *C* rather than at point *B*. Output and prices both rise less than they would in a closed economy.

First, why will the exchange rate rise? We know from earlier chapters that a fiscal expansion pushes up interest rates—a fact that is sure to be noticed in international financial markets. At higher interest rates, American securities become more attractive to foreign investors, who go to the foreign exchange market to buy dollars for use in purchasing American securities. This buying pressure drives up the value of the dollar.

Second, what are the effects of a higher dollar? As we know, when the dollar rises in value, American goods become more expensive abroad and foreign goods become cheaper here. So exports fall and imports rise. The $(X - IM)$ component of aggregate demand therefore falls. The fiscal expansion thus winds up increasing both America's *capital account surplus* (by attracting foreign capital) and *current account deficit* (by reducing net exports). In fact, the two must rise by equal amounts because, under floating exchange rates, it is always true that:[6]

$$\text{current account surplus} + \text{capital account surplus} = 0.$$

Since a fiscal expansion leads in this way to a trade deficit, many economists believe that the U.S. trade deficit of the 1980s was a side-effect of the large tax cuts made early in the decade. We will come back to that issue shortly.

But first note that the induced rise in the dollar will shift the aggregate supply curve *outward* and the aggregate demand curve *inward*, as we saw in Figure 37–7. Figure 37–8 adds these two shifts (in brown) to the effect of the original fiscal expansion (in blue). The final equilibrium in an open economy is point *C*, whereas in a closed economy it would be point *B*. By comparing points *B* and *C*, we can see how international linkages change the picture of fiscal policy that we painted in Part 7.

[6]If you need review, turn back to Chapter 36, pages 912–14.

There are two main differences. First, a rising exchange rate offsets part of the inflationary effect of a fiscal expansion by making imports cheaper. Second, a rising exchange rate reduces the expansionary effect on real GDP by reducing $(X - IM)$. Here we have a new kind of "crowding out," different from the one we studied in Chapter 32. There we learned that an increase in $G$, by raising interest rates, will crowd out some private investment spending. Here a rise in $G$, by raising interest rates and the exchange rate, crowds out *net exports*. But the effect is the same: the fiscal multiplier is reduced. Thus, we conclude that:

International capital flows reduce the power of fiscal policy.

Table 37–2 suggests that this new international variety of crowding out was much more important than the traditional type of crowding out in the early 1980s. Between 1981 and 1986, the share of investment in GDP actually *increased* slightly (from 16.4 percent to 16.7 percent) despite the rise in the shares of both consumer spending and government purchases. Only the share of net exports, $(X - IM)$, fell—from 0.6 percent to −3.5 percent.

This was an important lesson that American economists learned in the 1980s. In 1980, many economists worried that large government budget deficits would crowd out private investment. By the end of the decade, most were more concerned that deficits were crowding out net exports. Similarly, when the Clinton administration announced its five-year deficit reduction program in February 1993, the expected benefits were split between higher investment and a smaller trade deficit.

## MONETARY POLICY IN AN OPEN ECONOMY

Now let us consider how monetary policy works in an open economy with floating exchange rates and international capital mobility. To remain consistent with the history of the 1980s, we consider a tightening, rather than a loosening, of monetary policy.

As we know from earlier chapters, contractionary monetary policy reduces aggregate demand, which lowers both $Y$ and $P$. This is shown in Figure 37–9 by the shift from $D_0D_0$ to blue line $D_1D_1$, and it looks like the exact opposite of a fiscal expansion. Without international capital flows, that would be the end of the story.

But, in the presence of internationally mobile capital, we must think through the consequences for interest rates and exchange rates. We know from previous chapters that a monetary contraction raises interest rates, just like a fiscal expansion. Hence tighter money attracts foreign capital into the United States in search of

**Table 37–2** PERCENTAGE SHARES OF REAL GDP IN THE UNITED STATES: 1981 AND 1986

| YEAR | C | I | G | X − IM |
|---|---|---|---|---|
| 1981 | 64.5% | 16.4% | 18.5% | 0.6% |
| 1986 | 67.4% | 16.7% | 19.4% | −3.5% |
| Change | +2.9 | +0.3 | +0.9 | −4.1 |

*Figure* **37–9** **A MONETARY CONTRACTION IN AN OPEN ECONOMY**

A monetary contraction pulls the aggregate demand inward, from $D_0D_0$ to $D_1D_1$, just like a fiscal contraction. But it raises, rather than lowers, interest rates, which leads to international capital inflows and a currency appreciation. The appreciation decreases net exports and therefore reduces aggregate demand— which shifts inward from $D_1D_1$ to $D_2D_2$. But it also reduces foreign prices and raises aggregate supply—as indicated by the shift from $S_0S_0$ to $S_2S_2$. The result is that output and prices both fall more in an open economy (point *C*) than they would in a closed economy (point *B*).

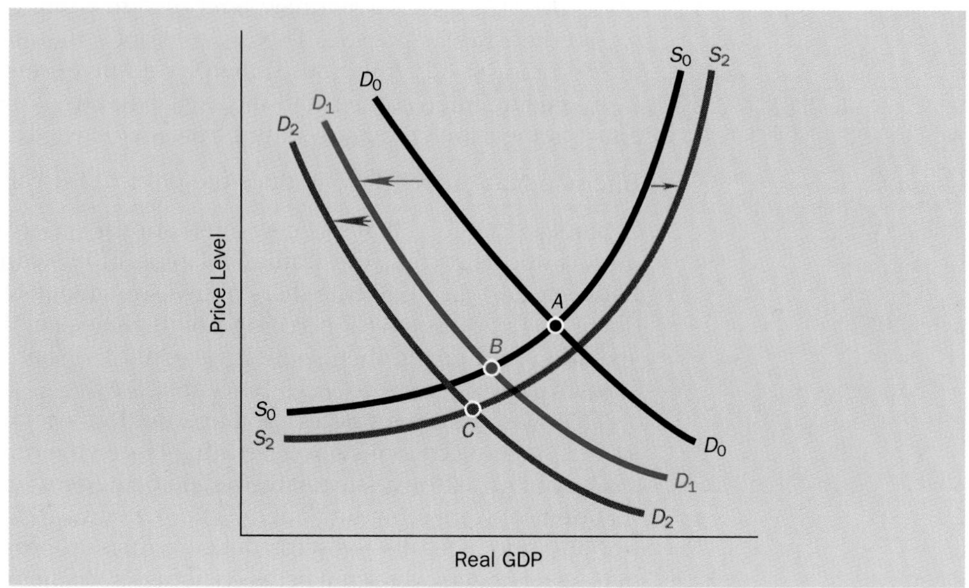


higher rates of return. The exchange rate rises. The appreciating dollar encourages imports and discourages exports; so $(X - IM)$ falls. America therefore winds up with capital flowing in (a surplus on capital account) and an increase in its trade deficit. This time, as you will notice from Figure 37–9:

International capital flows increase the power of monetary policy.

Why do capital flows *strengthen* monetary policy but *weaken* fiscal policy? The answer lies in their effects on interest rates. The main international repercussion of either a fiscal *expansion* or a monetary *contraction* is to raise interest rates and the exchange rate, thereby crowding out net exports. But that means that the initial effects of a fiscal expansion on aggregate demand are *weakened* while the initial effects of a monetary contraction are *strengthened*.

## INTERNATIONAL ASPECTS OF REAGANOMICS

This completes our theoretical analysis of the macroeconomics of open economies. Now let us put the theory through its paces by applying it to the changes in U.S. macroeconomic policy in the early 1980s. In the process, we will see that Reaganomics had important international implications that we did not mention in Part 7.

In broadest outline, the early years of the Reagan administration witnessed a dramatic change in the policy mix toward tighter money and much easier fiscal policy. The Federal Reserve's tight monetary policy was already in place when President Reagan was elected; the new administration simply encouraged the Fed to persevere. The expansionary fiscal policy was mainly the result of the tax cuts of 1981–1984, which led to large and persistent federal budget deficits.

Table 37–3 indicates what the theory predicts should have happened under such circumstances. Look first at column 1. We have just concluded that a fiscal expansion should raise real interest rates, make the dollar appreciate, raise real GDP, and be less inflationary than normal because of the rising dollar. This information is recorded by entering + signs for increases and − signs for decreases.

Similarly, our analysis of a monetary contraction says that the tight money component of Reaganomics should have raised real interest rates, made the dollar appreciate, reduced real GDP, and been more disinflationary than usual because of the rising dollar. All this is recorded in column 2.

Column 3 puts the two pieces together. We conclude that the policy mix of fiscal expansion and monetary contraction should have raised interest rates strongly, pushed the value of the dollar up dramatically, and devastated our foreign trade. But its effects on output and inflation are uncertain; the balance depends on whether fiscal expansion overwhelmed monetary contraction or vice-versa.

How well do these predictions square with the facts? Let us take them one at a time. We know from Figure 37–1 (page 926) that the international value of the dollar soared—rising about 80 percent from its low in mid-1980 to its high in early 1985—and that American foreign trade was clobbered. Real net exports fell from about +$22 billion in 1981 to about −$155 billion in 1986—a swing of $177 billion in just five years. These two facts are just what the theory predicts.

What about interest rates? Figure 37–10 shows an estimate of the real interest rate on long-term U.S. government bonds from 1978 to 1990. (The historic norm for this rate is between 2 and 3 percent.) The real rate of interest rose dramatically between the time of the 1980 election campaign and the time the Reagan economic program was enacted into law (September 1981). It then fell during the 1982 recession, but rose again to very high levels in mid-1984. Again, this is in accord with the theory: except for a brief recessionary interlude, the policy changes raised real interest rates.

What about real GDP? The U.S. economy suffered through a severe recession in 1981–1982. However, it then rebounded strongly and grew steadily for the remainder of the decade. To appraise the effects of Reaganomics on real output, we must consider a longer time frame. If we take the full eight-year period from 1981 to 1989, the average annual growth rate of real GDP was 2.9 percent. Since

**Table 37–3 EXPECTED EFFECTS OF POLICY**

| VARIABLE | (1) FISCAL EXPANSION | (2) MONETARY CONTRACTION | (3) REAGONOMICS |
|---|---|---|---|
| Real interest rate | + | + | + |
| Exchange rate | + | + | + |
| Net exports | − | − | − |
| Real GDP | + | − | ? |
| Inflation | + | − | ? |

**Figure 37–10 REAL INTEREST RATES IN THE UNITED STATES, 1978–1990**

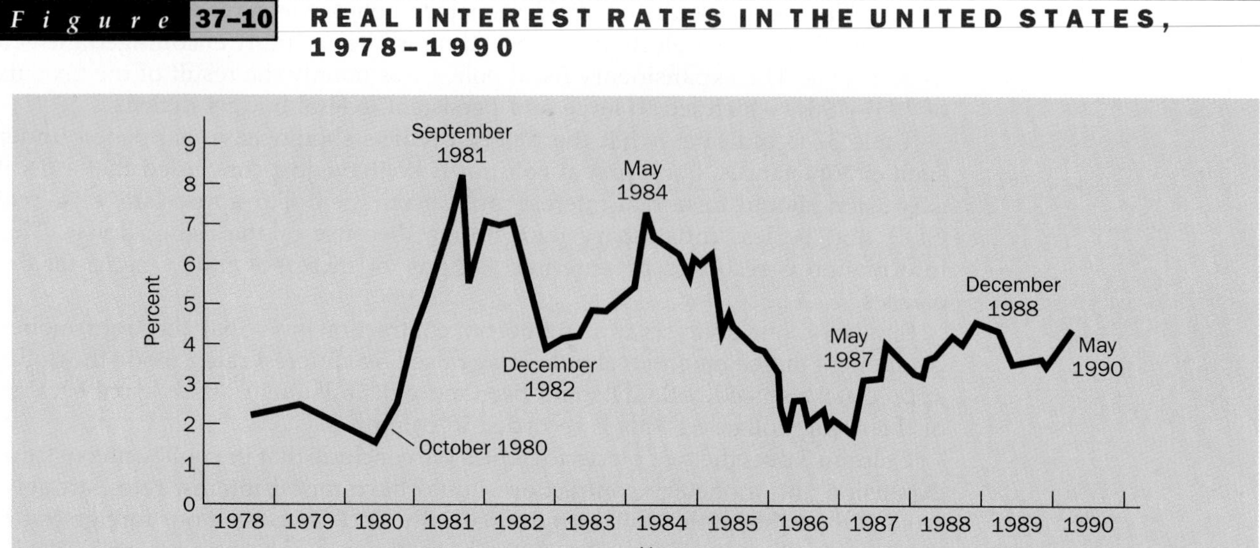


This figure charts the behavior of the real interest rate on ten-year U.S. government bonds on the basis of a survey of inflationary expectations. It rises steeply in 1980–1981.

SOURCE: Richard B. Hoey.

this is just a bit below the average growth rate achieved during the preceding 20 years, the conclusion seems to be that the monetary contraction and fiscal expansion combined had little net effect on the growth rate of aggregate demand.

If this is so, that would leave only the supply shifts caused by the appreciating dollar. Figures 37–8 and 37–9 show that both fiscal expansions and monetary contractions *increase* aggregate supply by appreciating the currency. The rising dollar certainly helped slow inflation in the early 1980s by holding down the prices of imported inputs. In addition, the fact that the deep recession came early in President Reagan's term of office meant that the economy had a recessionary gap throughout the 1981–1986 period. Finally, as we saw in earlier chapters, energy prices were falling rapidly. Each of these factors played a role in the rapid disinflation.

## THE LINK BETWEEN THE BUDGET DEFICIT AND THE TRADE DEFICIT

If the good news of the 1980s was the rapid decline in inflation, the bad news was the alarming deterioration of America's foreign trade position. We have already suggested that changes in the monetary–fiscal policy mix were largely responsible for the U.S. trade deficit. But to see the connection between the budget deficit and the trade deficit most clearly, we need to recall two simple pieces of arithmetic.

The first begins with the familiar equilibrium condition for GDP in an open economy:

$$Y = C + I + G + (X - IM).$$

Since GDP can either be spent, saved, or taxed away:

$$Y = C + S + T.^{7}$$

Equating these two expressions for $Y$ gives:

$$C + I + G + (X - IM) = C + S + T.$$

Finally, subtracting $C$ from both sides, and bringing terms involving the government to the lefthand side and terms involving the private sector to the right leads to an accounting relationship between the budget deficit and the trade deficit:

$$G - T = (S - I) - (X - IM).$$

In words, the government budget deficit, $G - T$, must be equal to the surplus of savings over investment plus the trade deficit, $-(X - IM)$.

This result may seem mechanical and not particularly interesting, but our second piece of arithmetic will bring out both the common sense behind this equation and its importance for understanding recent events.

As we have noted repeatedly, under floating exchange rates any deficit or surplus in the current account must be balanced by an equal and opposite surplus or deficit in the capital account. Thus, the current account *deficit*, which is $-(X - IM)$ in the previous equation, can be replaced by the capital account *surplus* to get:

$$G - T = (S - I) + \text{Net capital inflows.}$$

This last equation makes an obvious point. If the U.S. government runs a budget deficit $(G - T)$, that deficit must be financed either by an excess of saving over investment by American businesses and individuals $(S - I)$, or by borrowing from foreigners.

But what is the economic mechanism that makes the trade deficit follow the government budget deficit? There is no mystery. To attract the foreign capital that we must borrow, America must offer interest rates higher than those available abroad. As capital flows into the United States, the value of the dollar rises. And the more costly dollar leads to a larger trade deficit. Thus the adjustments of interest rates and exchange rates that we have been discussing are precisely the way a budget deficit leads to a trade deficit.

Our equation suggests a tight connection between the two deficits. Let us see how things worked out in the case of Reaganomics. Since the Reagan tax cuts led to a large budget deficit, the United States could have avoided a large trade deficit only by saving much more or investing much less. The latter is not a very appealing option and, in any case, generous business tax cuts shielded investment spending from the ravages of high real interest rates. As we saw in Table 37–2, the investment share of GDP hardly changed.

---

[7]If you do not see why, recall that GDP equals disposable income ($DI$) plus taxes ($T$), $Y = DI + T$, and that disposable income can either be consumed or saved, $DI = C + S$. These two definitions together imply that $Y = C + S + T$.

That leaves saving. Supply-siders did indeed promise that the tax cuts would raise savings by extraordinary amounts. Had their promises been redeemed, the budget deficit need not have caused a trade deficit. But they were not. With $S$ not rising and $I$ not falling, our fundamental equation leaves only one possibility: a rise in $G - T$ must be reflected in a fall in $(X - IM)$. The government budget deficit thus led to a massive trade deficit.

## IS THE TRADE DEFICIT A PROBLEM?

The preceding explanation suggests that America's large trade deficit is a symptom of a deeper trouble: the nation as a whole—including our government—has been spending more than it is producing and has been forced to borrow the difference from foreigners. The trade deficit is just the mirror image of the required capital inflows. Why do we worry about this? Because these capital inflows create debts on which interest and principal payments will have to be made in the future. Thus, on this view, Americans since the 1980s have been mortgaging their future to finance higher consumer spending.

But there is another, quite different, interpretation of the trade deficit. Suppose foreign investors in the 1980s began to see the United States as a much more attractive place to invest their capital. Then capital would have flowed in not because America needed to borrow it, but because foreigners were eager to lend it. In that case, the trade deficit would still be the mirror image of the capital inflows. But it would now signify America's economic strength, not its weakness.

The policy implications of these two views differ dramatically. The first view suggests that we should strive to reduce the trade deficit and, thereby, our need for foreign borrowing. The second view suggests that we should welcome the capital inflows and, therefore, not worry about the trade deficit. Which view is right?

The answer is in dispute. However, most economists ascribe to the first view—that the trade deficit is a problem, not a prize. At least two pieces of evidence persuade them. First, real interest rates in the 1980s were generally high, not low. This suggests that America was forced to pay high interest rates to attract the capital it needed, not that foreigners suddenly decided that America was the place to invest. Second, as we saw in Table 37–2 (page 937), it was the *consumption* share of GDP, not the *investment* share, that rose between 1981 and 1986. This suggests that America was borrowing to finance a consumption binge, not an investment boom.

## ON CURING THE TRADE DEFICIT

We now understand how the United States acquired its massive twin deficits and became the world's most indebted nation. And we have explained why many economists think the trade deficit is a problem. Next comes the hard question that we raised at the beginning of the chapter: What can be done about it? How can we cure our foreign trade problem and end our addiction to foreign borrowing?

The answer, of course, is highly controversial—and the controversies predate the presidency of Bill Clinton. Both economists and politicians disagree over the appropriate course of action. The best we can do here is outline some alternatives.

1. ***Change the Mix of Fiscal and Monetary Policy:*** The fundamental equation:

$$G - T = (S - I) - (X - IM)$$

suggests a *reduction in the budget deficit* as one good way to reduce the trade deficit. According to the analysis in this chapter, a reduction in $G$ or an increase in $T$ would lead to lower real interest rates in the United States, a depreciating dollar and, eventually, to a shrinking trade deficit.

This is the route that American economists have been urging for years. And, as a matter of fact, the dollar has come down considerably since the mid-1980s, and so has our trade deficit. However, partisan political bickering over how best to reduce the budget deficit made progress on this front agonizingly slow until President Clinton pushed through a comprehensive deficit-reduction plan in 1993.

When the government curtails its spending or raises taxes to reduce its budget deficit, aggregate demand falls. If we do not want deficit reduction to cause an economic contraction in the United States, we must therefore compensate for it by monetary stimulus. Like contractionary fiscal policy, expansionary monetary policy lowers interest rates, depreciates the dollar, and should therefore help reduce the trade deficit.

American policymakers have been pursuing this policy for years. Interest rates have generally been falling since mid-1984 (see Figure 37–10). In the late 1980s, however, the Fed became concerned about the possible inflationary consequences of easy money (and of the falling dollar) and grew more cautious. But when recession began in 1990, the Fed eased up again and interest rates fell.

Notice that these two remedies, in combination, amount to undoing the Reaganomics policy mix of tight money and loose budgets. Between 1980 and 1984, the United States experienced a monetary contraction followed by a fiscal expansion. What we have needed ever since to cure the trade deficit, according to many economists, is precisely the reverse: a monetary expansion coupled with a fiscal contraction. To some extent, this is the policy mix inherent in Clintonomics.

2. ***More Rapid Economic Growth Abroad:*** If foreign economies grew faster, residents of these countries would buy more American goods. That would raise American exports and reduce our trade deficit. Since the mid-1980s, the United States has been urging our major trading partners to stimulate their economies and to open their markets more to American goods—but with modest success. At first, foreign countries rightly asked why they should tailor their economic policies to America's needs. But more recently, with the European and Japanese economies slumping, domestic needs in those countries have also called for more expansionary policies.

3. ***Raise Domestic Savings or Reduce Domestic Investment:*** Our fundamental equation calls attention to two other routes to a smaller trade deficit: higher savings or lower investment.

U.S. personal saving rates have been near all-time lows in recent years. If Americans would save more, we could finance more of our government budget deficit at home and therefore would not need to borrow so much abroad. This, too, would lead to a cheaper dollar and a smaller trade deficit. The only trouble is that no one has yet found a reliable way to induce

## Saving Patterns and Trade Deficits: The Arithmetic of U.S.–Japanese Economic Relations

The huge U.S. trade deficit with Japan is a significant source of friction between the two countries and has led to frequent calls for protectionist measures here. Our fundamental equation,

$$G - T = (S - I) - (X - IM),$$

teaches us that part of the problem traces to different saving habits in the two countries. The Japanese people are among the biggest savers in the world. So $S - I$ is a large positive number in Japan. Furthermore, unlike the U.S. government, the Japanese government has a budget surplus. It therefore follows that, in order to balance the international books, Japan must generate a large trade *surplus*.

The contrast between the United States and Japan in this regard is marked. While the Japanese people and government together are big net *savers*, the American people and government together are big net *borrowers*. In an integrated world financial system, it is therefore natural that the Japanese should be lending to us. In short, Japan should have capital *outflows* and we should have capital *inflows*—which is just what has been happening in recent years. Remembering that:

$$\text{current account surplus} + \text{capital account surplus} = 0$$

the implication is that Japan should have a current account *surplus*, and we should have a current account *deficit*.

Once again this is only natural. In fact, the United States has had a trade deficit with Japan for a long time—even when our overall trade position and Japan's were nearly balanced. Being an island nation almost devoid of natural resources, Japan must run huge trade deficits in primary products. Much of this trade is with developing countries. To offset this trade deficit in primary products, Japan needs a surplus in trade in manufactured goods. And who are likely to be the leading customers for these goods? The biggest consumers on earth, of course—the Americans.

So it is natural for the United States to run a bilateral deficit in trading goods with Japan. However, that does not imply that an annual deficit of $50 billion or more is appropriate, nor that the Japanese are blameless. In fact, Japan has long been among the most protectionist of all the advanced industrial nations. Some of this protectionism takes the form of high tariffs and stiff quotas. But most is more subtle, coming instead through a variety of bureaucratic regulations that make importing difficult. So one possible solution to the U.S.–Japan trade problem is to persuade Japan to open its markets more. And the Clinton administration, like the Bush and Reagan administrations before it, is engaging the Japanese in talks on this subject. But no one really thinks that, even in a completely free market, we could sell in Japan nearly as much as they sell here.

Macroeconomic policy might be a more effective tool. Look once again at the fundamental equation:

$$G - T = (S - I) - (X - IM).$$

If Japan stimulated its economy by more expansionary fiscal policy, $G - T$ would rise and $(X - IM)$ would fall. If, at the same time, the United States reduced its budget deficit, $G - T$ would fall here and $(X - IM)$ would rise. In all likelihood, our bilateral trade deficit with Japan would narrow. That is precisely the "deal" that the two countries are trying to work out now.

Americans to save more. A variety of tax incentives for saving has been tried, and more are suggested every year. But there is not much evidence that these incentives have worked. We seem to be a nation of consumers.

If the other cures for our trade deficit fail to work in time, the trade deficit may cure itself in a particularly unpleasant way: by dramatically reducing U.S. domestic investment. Let us see how this might work. As our trade deficits and foreign borrowing persist, foreigners wind up holding more and more U.S. dollar assets. At some point, their willingness to acquire yet more dollar assets will begin to wear thin, and they will start charging us much higher interest rates. At best, higher interest rates lead to lower investment in the United States. At worst, foreigners cease lending to the United States, interest rates skyrocket, and we experience a severe recession. A recession, of course, would reduce our trade deficit substantially by curbing our appetite for imports. But it is a painful cure.

4. ***Protectionism:*** We have saved the worst remedy for last. One seemingly obvious way to cure our trade deficit is to limit imports by imposing stiff tariffs, strict quotas, and other protectionist devices. We discussed protectionism, and the reasons why almost all economists oppose it, in Chapter 35. Despite the economic arguments against it, protectionism has an undeniable political allure. It seems, superficially, to "save American jobs." And it conveniently shifts the blame for our trade problems onto foreigners.

   In addition to depriving us and other countries of the benefits of comparative advantage, there are reasons why protectionism might not even succeed in reducing our trade deficit. One is that other nations might retaliate. If we erect trade barriers to reduce our imports, $IM$ will fall. But if foreign countries erect corresponding barriers to our exports, $X$ will fall, too. On balance, our *net* exports, $(X - IM)$, may or may not improve. However, world trade will surely suffer. This is a game that may have no winners, only losers.

   Even if other nations do not retaliate, tariffs and quotas may not improve our trade deficit much. Why? If they succeed in reducing American spending on imports, tariffs and quotas will thereby reduce the supply of dollars on the world market. That would push the value of the dollar up. A rising dollar, of course, would hurt U.S. exports and encourage more imports. The fundamental equation,

$$G - T = (S - I) - (X - IM),$$

   reminds us that protectionism can raise $(X - IM)$ only if it reduces the budget deficit, raises saving, or reduces investment.[8]

## CONCLUSION: WE ARE NOT ALONE

We do indeed live in a world economy. The major trading nations of the world are linked by exports and imports, by capital flows, and by exchange rates. What happens to national income, prices, and interest rates in one country affects other nations.

Thus policymakers in Europe, Asia, and South America keep a watchful eye on developments in the U.S. economy. If the U.S. economy expands, these other countries have better markets for their exports. If we pursue policies that make the dollar depreciate, they find their currencies appreciating. If interest rates rise in the United States, they see capital flowing out of their countries into ours. Some observers think that, as the "big guy on the block," America bears a special responsibility for the health of the world economy.

[8]Here tariffs, which raise revenue for the government, have a clear advantage over quotas, which do not.

But we are not the *only* big guys on the block. Japan is also a giant economy with profound effects on the rest of the world. And, once fully unified, the European Economic Community will make Western Europe the biggest economy of all. What happens in Europe, Japan, and elsewhere often has important effects on the U.S. economy.

That the major economies of the world are linked suggests the need for greater policy coordination among nations. But since the national interests of particular countries often differ, countries are understandably reluctant to surrender any of their sovereignty. Hence international policy coordination remains an elusive goal. Economically speaking, we all live in one world. Politically, however, we live in a world of separate nation-states.

## *Summary*

1. The nations of the world are linked together economically because national income, prices, and interest rates in one country affect those in another. They are thus **open economies**.
2. Because one country's **imports** are another country's **exports**, rapid (or sluggish) economic growth in one country contributes to rapid (or sluggish) growth in other countries.
3. A country's **net exports** depend on whether its prices are high or low relative to those of other countries. Since exchange rates translate one country's prices into the currencies of other countries, the **exchange rate** is a key determinant of net exports.
4. If the currency depreciates, net exports rise and aggregate demand increases, thereby raising both real GDP and the price level. A depreciating currency also reduces aggregate supply by making imported inputs more costly.
5. If the currency appreciates, net exports fall and aggregate demand, real GDP, and the price level all decrease. But an appreciating currency also increases aggregate supply by making imported inputs cheaper.
6. Because there are lags in international trade, net exports follow a **J-curve** pattern after a currency depreciation; that is, the **trade deficit** gets worse before it gets better.
7. **International capital flows** respond strongly to interest rate differentials among countries. Hence higher domestic interest rates lead to currency **appreciations**, and lower interest rates lead to **depreciations**.
8. Contractionary monetary policies raise interest rates and therefore make the currency appreciate. Both the higher interest rates and the dearer currency reduce aggregate demand. Hence international capital flows make monetary policy more powerful than it would be in a **closed economy**.
9. Expansionary fiscal policies also raise interest rates and make the currency appreciate. But, in this case, the international repercussions cancel out part of the demand-expanding effects of the policies. Hence international capital flows make fiscal policy less powerful than it would be in a closed economy.
10. Since Reaganomics in the early 1980s combined tight money with highly expansionary fiscal policy, it raised interest rates, pushed the dollar up, and caused a large trade deficit in the United States.
11. **Budget deficits and trade deficits** are linked by the fundamental equation $G - T = (S - I) - (X - IM)$. This also implies that the budget deficit equals the sum of $S - I$ + capital inflows.
12. It follows from this equation that the U.S. trade deficit must be cured by some combination of lower budget deficits, higher savings, and lower investment.
13. A change in the policy mix toward easier monetary policy and smaller budget deficits is one way to reduce the U.S. trade deficit without contracting the U.S. economy.
14. Protectionist policies might not cure the U.S. trade deficit because (a) they will cause the dollar to appreciate and (b) they may provoke foreign retaliation.
15. International coordination of economic policies is important. But it is also elusive in a world of sovereign nations.

## Key Concepts and Terms

Exports
Imports
Net exports
Closed economy
Open economy
Exchange rate
Appreciation
Depreciation
Trade deficit
J curve
International capital flows
Budget deficits and trade deficits
$G - T = (S - I) - (X - IM)$

## Questions for Review

1. For years, the U.S. government has been trying to get Japan to expand its economy faster. Explain how more rapid growth in Japan would affect the U.S. economy.
2. If inflation is higher in Germany than in France, and the exchange rate between the two countries is fixed, what is likely to happen to the balance of trade between the two countries?
3. Explain why a currency depreciation leads to an improvement in a country's trade balance. If there is a "J curve," what happens in the short run? Why?
4. Explain why American fiscal policy is less powerful and American monetary policy is more powerful than indicated in the closed-economy model of Part 7.
5. Use an aggregate supply–demand diagram to analyze the effects of a currency appreciation.
6. Explain why $G - T = (S - I) - (X - IM)$.
7. Given what you now know, do you think it was a good idea for the United States to adopt a policy mix of tight money and large government budget deficits in the early 1980s? Why or why not?
8. What, in your view, is the best way for America to reduce its trade deficit?
9. During 1993, the international value of the yen rose sharply. This development worried the Japanese authorities. Why?
10. (More difficult) Suppose consumption and investment are described by:

$$C = 100 + .75DI \qquad (DI = \text{disposable income})$$
$$I = 500 + .2Y - 40r \qquad (Y = \text{GDP})$$

Here $r$, the interest rate, is measured in percentage points (for example, a 9 percent interest rate is $r = 9$). Exports and imports are as follows:

$$X = 150$$
$$IM = -100 + .2Y$$

Government purchases are $G = 750$, and taxes are 20 percent of income.

The price level is fixed and the central bank (called the "Fed") uses its monetary policy to peg the interest rate at $r = 10$.

a. Find equilibrium GDP, the budget deficit or surplus, and the trade deficit or surplus.

b. Suppose the currency depreciates and, as a result, exports and imports change to:

$$X = 200$$
$$IM = -150 + .2Y.$$

Now find equilibrium GDP, the budget deficit or surplus, and the trade deficit or surplus.

# PART IX

# Alternative Economic Systems

Chapter 38

# GROWTH IN DEVELOPED AND DEVELOPING COUNTRIES

*The three great causes most favorable to [growth in] production are, accumulation of capital, fertility of soil, and inventions to save labour.*

**T.R. MALTHUS**

The evidence indicates that a century ago an American could not afford to buy much more than a resident of the Philippines or Egypt consumes today. A few other countries have experienced comparable progress—spectacular growth in the productive powers of their economies. This chapter discusses what determines the rate at which an economy grows, and it examines the pros and cons of rapid growth. Then we turn to the special problems of the less developed countries (LDCs) and look at the measures that have been proposed to increase their rates of growth.

# SOME BASIC PRINCIPLES OF GROWTH ANALYSIS

## HOW TO MEASURE GROWTH: TOTAL OUTPUT OR OUTPUT PER CAPITA?

Adam Smith, like many of his successors, took it for granted that expansion of productive capacity is inherently desirable. But he also took it for granted, apparently without examining the matter very closely, that growth in the size of population is to be wished for. His reason was that a larger population provides a larger work force, and a larger work force makes a larger national output possible. Few economists since Smith's time have argued in this way. Nowadays we usually measure a nation's prosperity not in terms of its total output but in terms of its output *per person*. India has a GDP about six times as large as Sweden's. But with a population more than 100 times as large as Sweden's, India remains a poor country while Sweden is highly prosperous. The point is that:

If the objective of growth is the material welfare of the *individuals* who make up a country, then the proper measure of the success of a program of economic development is how much it adds to output per person. The relevant index is not total output. It is total output *divided by total population*—that is, **output per capita**.

From this point of view, the appropriate objective of growth is not, as the old cliché puts it, "the greatest good for the *greatest number*"—it is the greatest good *per person* in the economy. Per capita figures tell this story well. To make the appropriate comparison of well-being in Sweden and India, we note that per capita GDP in Sweden is nearly $18,000 a year, whereas in India, even after a generous adjustment to correct for lower prices in that country, the figure is about $1200 a year.[1]

Only where the objective of the government is grandeur or military strength may the number of inhabitants alone seem an appropriate part of its goal. A small country like Finland, for instance, cannot hope to overwhelm a giant neighbor like Russia, even if Finland has a much higher per capita GDP than Russia.[2] But where the goal of the government is not national power but the elimination of poverty, illiteracy, and inadequate medical care, sheer increase in population becomes a questionable pursuit.

[1]These per-capita GDP figures, expressed in U.S. dollars, were converted from the national currencies using purchasing-power-parity exchange rates. The source is the International Comparison Program, which is coordinated by the United Nations and supported by the World Bank and the Organization for Economic Cooperation and Development, and published by the World Bank as part of its *World Development Report 1993*, World Development Indicators, New York: Oxford University Press, 1993, p. 296. For an explanation of purchasing-power-parity exchange rates, see Chapter 34, footnote 10.

[2]Even where military power is the primary objective, a large but impoverished population may not be a very effective means to that end. China has long had an enormous population, but in the modern era its military presence is certainly quite recent.

## ON GROWTH IN POPULATION: IS LESS REALLY MORE?

In 1798, the Reverend Thomas R. Malthus (who was to become England's first professor of political economy) published *An Essay on the Principle of Population.* This book was to have a profound effect on people's attitudes toward population growth. Malthus argued that sexual drives and other influences induce people to reproduce themselves as rapidly as their means permit. Unfortunately, he said, when the number of humans increases, the production of food and other consumption goods generally cannot keep up.

The problem is the noted *law of diminishing returns* to additional labor used with a fixed supply of land, a relationship we encountered before (in Chapter 6). This states that if we use more and more labor to cultivate a fixed stock of land, we will eventually reach a point at which each additional laborer will contribute less additional output than the previous laborer. Ultimately, as the labor force increases, output per worker will decline.

Malthus and his followers concluded that the tendency of humankind to reproduce itself must constantly exert pressure on the economy to keep living standards from rising. Wages will gravitate toward some minimal subsistence level—the lowest income on which people are willing to marry and raise a family. If wages are above subsistence, the population can and will grow. Thus, a wage that is above subsistence will set forces into motion that will drive wages down toward subsistence because of diminishing returns.

Sometimes, according to Malthus, the population will grow beyond the capability of the economy to support it. Then the number of people will be brought back into line by means that are far more unpleasant than a decrease in wages—by starvation and disease or by wars that produce the required number of casualties.

Later in the nineteenth century and during the first half of the twentieth century, the gloomy Malthusian vision seemed to lose credibility. New technology and improved agricultural practices generally enabled the output of food and other agricultural products to increase faster than the population (at least in the wealthier, industrialized nations). In addition, it turned out that as living standards rose, people became less anxious to reproduce, and so the expansion of population slowed substantially. Figure 38–1 illustrates this trend in the United States for more than a century and a half. All in all, it began to look as though population growth constituted no significant threat—it was something with which human technological skills and ingenuity could cope.

More recently, however, there has been renewed concern over population. With improvements in medicine—notably, improved hygiene in hospitals, the use of such public health measures as swamp drainage, and the discovery of antibiotics—death rates have plunged in the developing countries, especially for infants. At the same time, birth control programs in most of these countries have, at least until quite recently, not been very successful. As a result, the populations of developing countries have continued to expand dramatically, eating up a good proportion of any output increases obtained through their governments' economic development programs.

It has been widely concluded that significant improvement in living standards in the developing areas is impossible without a substantial reduction in their population growth. But the "neo-Malthusians" go further than this, arguing that a rapid approach to birthrates so low that populations cease expanding—that is,

Figure 38–1 **AMERICAN BIRTHRATES, 1820–1990**

This chart shows that birthrates in the United States have generally been declining since 1820.

SOURCE: U.S. Bureau of the Census, *Historical Statistics of the United States, Colonial Times to 1970, Part I*, Washington, D.C.: U.S. Government Printing Office, 1975; and U.S. Bureau of the Census, *Statistical Abstract of the United States*, Washington, D.C.: U.S. Government Printing Office, various issues.

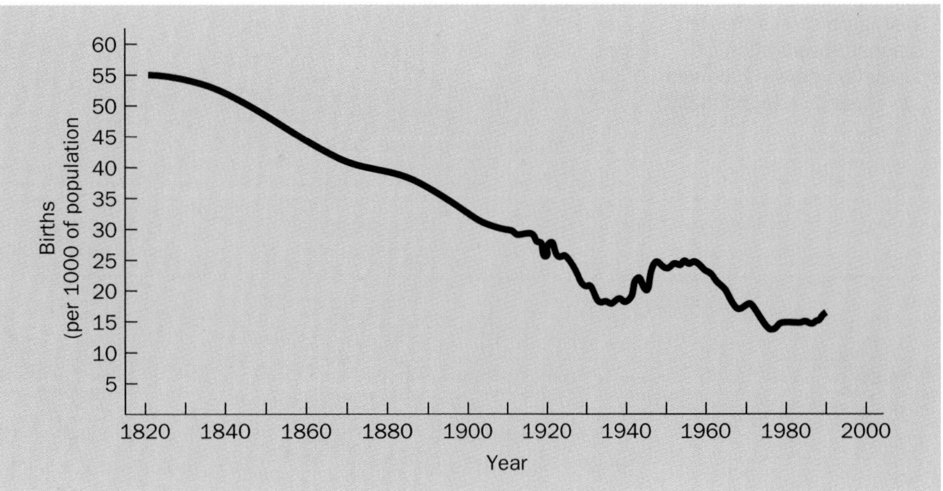


to *zero population growth*—is virtually a matter of life and death even for the most prosperous nations. It is illuminating to consider the logic of their argument.

## THE CROWDED PLANET: EXPONENTIAL POPULATION GROWTH

Malthus used an argument that has caught many imaginations ever since:

> *Population, when unchecked, increases in a geometrical ratio. Subsistence increases only in an arithmetical ratio. A slight acquaintance with numbers will shew the immensity of the first power in comparison of the second.*[3]

**EXPONENTIAL GROWTH** is growth at a constant percentage rate.

In modern discussions, such a "geometric" growth pattern is referred to as **exponential growth**, or "compounded growth" or "snowballing." Exponential growth is growth at a constant *percentage rate*. For example, at a 10 percent growth rate, a population of 100 persons will increase by 10 persons a year; but a population of a million persons will increase by 100,000 persons a year. Thus, although the *rate* of growth is the same for large and small populations, the *numbers* are dramatically different. The bigger the population, the more it will add annually. And each year's growth implies still faster growth in the following year. It is like a snowball rolling downhill, accumulating more snow the bigger it gets, thus expanding faster and faster all the time.

If the population doubles (grows 100 percent) in 35 years, it will quadruple (grow another 100 percent) in 70 years, increase 8-fold in 105 years, 16-fold in 140 years, and so on indefinitely. The doubling sequence 2, 4, 8, 16, 32, 64, and so on, is the basic pattern of exponential growth. Figure 38–2 shows how astronomical such a growth sequence is. Projecting the world's population 175 years into the future on the assumption that population will grow exponentially at about

[3]Thomas R. Malthus, *An Essay on the Principle of Population*, (London, 1798), page 20.

Figure 38-2

**PROJECTED GROWTH OF THE WORLD'S POPULATION IN 171 YEARS AT CURRENT RATE OF GROWTH**

This figure shows the sensational acceleration of population growth *if* population expands exponentially.

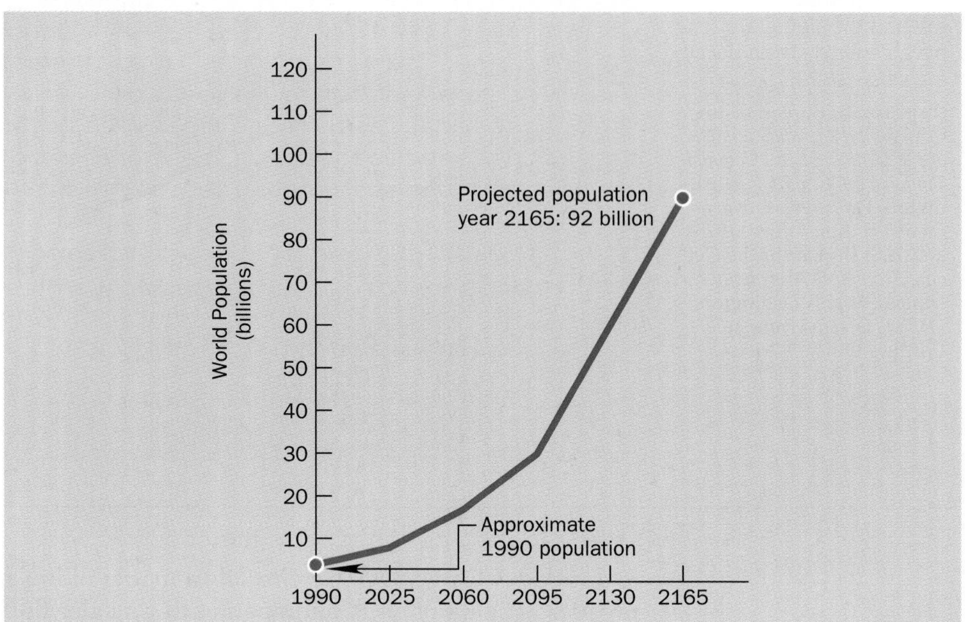


its current rate, the graph shows that by the year 2165 the population will exceed 90 billion—about 20 times as many people as there are today.

It turns out that in describing the consequences of exponential growth, Malthus was conservative. He did not begin to spell out the wonders and the horrors that his premise implied. Consider some calculations by one leading authority on population (who derived his conclusions simply by carrying through the arithmetic of exponential growth rates):

- *If population were to grow at today's rates for another 600–700 years, every square foot of the surface of the earth would contain a human being;*
- *If it were to expand at the same rate for 1200 years, the combined weight of the human population would exceed that of the earth itself;*
- *If that growth rate were to go on for 6000 years (a very short period of time in terms of biological history), the globe would constitute a sphere whose diameter was growing with the speed of light.*[4]

And none of this is conjecture. It is *sure* to come about *if* the present (exponential) rate of growth of the earth's population continues unabated.

Of course, none of this can really happen. Our finite earth just does not have room for that sort of expansion. The fate of humanity is not determined by the

[4]Ansley J. Coale, "Man and His Environment," *Science*, Vol. 179 (October 9, 1970), pages 132–36. Copyright 1970 by the American Association for the Advancement of Science.

rules of arithmetic—it depends on the course of nature and on the behavior of the human race. It is true that if the number of humans continues to swell until it presses upon the earth's capacity, the process will ultimately be brought to a halt in a Malthusian apocalypse. Disease, famine, and war must finally put a stop to the expansion process.

But there is a better alternative. People can choose to stop raising large families. There is no inevitability about the family of six or ten children. As we have just noted, there has in fact been a long-term decline in the rate of expansion in the wealthier societies such as the United States (see Figure 38–3). Even in the developing nations, as we will see later in this chapter, the birthrate has recently been declining.

A more balanced view of the matter recognizes the serious difficulties that rapid population growth can lead to, and suggests that its encouragement will not serve the interests of society. Yet, it does *not* imply that a great catastrophe is at hand or that the appropriate reaction is panic.

## REQUIREMENTS FOR INCREASED GROWTH

What can be done to increase the growth rate of production in an economy? Unfortunately, no one has a handy list of sure-fire recipes.

Growth can be attributed to a number of factors that no one knows how to explain: (1) *inventiveness*, which produces the new technology and other innovations that have contributed so much to economic expansion; (2) *entrepreneurship*, the leadership that recognizes no obstacles and undertakes the daring industrial ventures needed to move the economy ahead; and (3) *the work ethic* that leads a work force to high levels of productivity. No one really knows what features of

**Figure 38–3** ANNUAL PERCENTAGE GROWTH RATE OF THE U.S. POPULATION

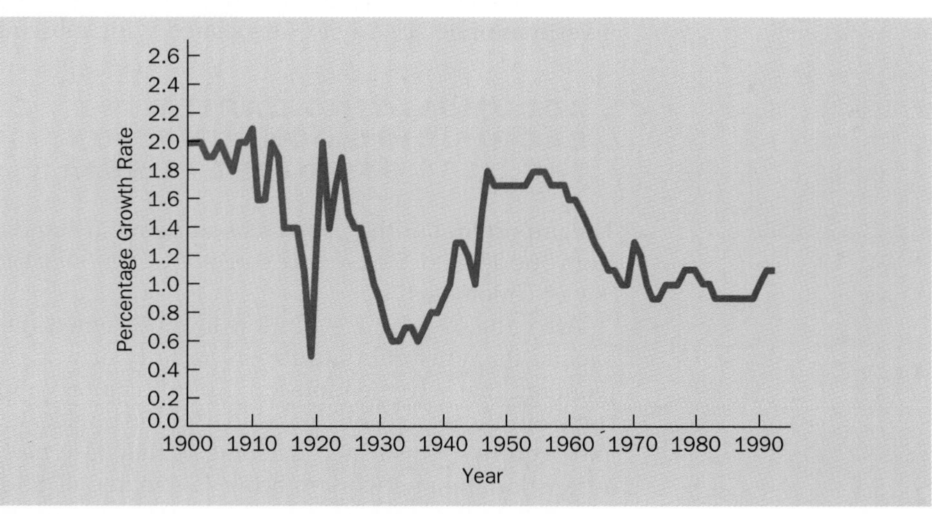


After falling rapidly during the first half of the 1980s, the population growth rate turned back up again after 1986. The U.S. Census Bureau projects that this trend will continue well into the next century. The recent growth rates are still far below the rates of the baby-boom years of the 1950s and early 1960s.

SOURCE: U.S. Bureau of the Census, *Current Population Reports*, Series P-25.

economic organization and social psychology actually lead a community to adopt these goals, as Great Britain is said to have done at the beginning of the nineteenth century, as the United States is reputed to have done in the first half of the twentieth century, and as Japan is apparently doing today. We do know, however, that:

Growth requires two things that people can influence directly:

1. A large expenditure on *capital equipment*: factories, machinery, transportation, and telecommunications equipment.
2. The devotion of considerable effort to research and development from which innovations are derived.

Both these types of expenditures help to increase the economy's ability to *supply* goods, which brings us back to the analysis of Parts 6–7. There we stressed that the level (and, consequently, the growth) of national income is determined by the interaction of *aggregate supply and aggregate demand*. It is the need for capital equipment in any growth process that provides a vital link between aggregate demand and aggregate supply, for an economy acquires a larger capital stock by investing. Recall that aggregate demand is the sum of consumption, investment, government spending, and net exports $Y = C + I + G + (X - IM)$. But $I$ is the only part of $Y$ that creates more capital for the future. Such investment can be carried out either by the private sector of the economy or by government. In free market economies government investment is, of course, a much smaller share of the total than it was in centrally directed economies.

The *composition* of aggregate demand is a major determinant of the rate of economic growth. If a larger fraction of total spending goes toward investment rather than toward consumption, government purchases, or net exports, the capital stock will grow faster and the aggregate supply schedule will shift more quickly to the right.

Figure 38–4 shows, for a set of 20 countries on four continents, how investment in one period (in this case, 1973) is related to subsequent growth (1973–1987) in per capita output. The graph confirms that the share of an economy's output devoted to investment does not, *by itself*, determine future growth. But higher investment rates clearly *are* associated with subsequently more-rapid growth.

## ACCUMULATING CAPITAL BY SACRIFICING CONSUMPTION: THE CASE OF SOVIET RUSSIA

The importance of the *composition* of demand stands out sharply if we turn away from the United States and consider a *centrally planned* economy, such as the Soviet Union was.

After the Russian Revolution in 1917, when the Soviet Union undertook to expand its industrial output very rapidly, it was clear from the earliest stage of planning that a tremendous amount of capital equipment would be required to carry out the expansion. Not only did the Soviets have to build modern factories and acquire sophisticated machinery, they also needed a **social infrastructure**—a transportation network to bring raw materials to the factories and take finished products to the markets, an efficient telecommunications system, and schools in which to train the population sufficiently to be an effective labor force. All this

Figure 38-4 **GROWTH AND INVESTMENT, 20 COUNTRIES**

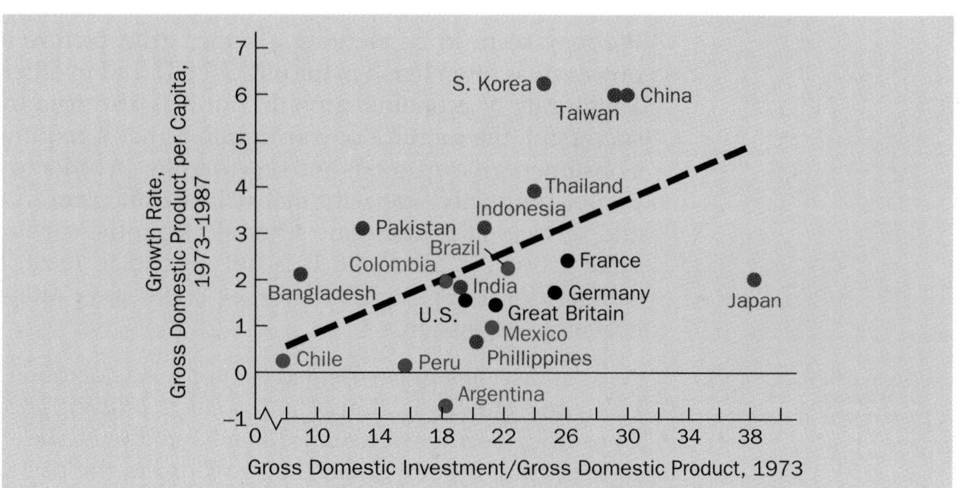


The graph shows, for twenty countries, how investment in 1973 is related to subsequent growth in per-capita GDP (1973–1987). It is clear that investment alone does not determine future economic growth, but higher investment rates are associated with more rapid growth rates.

SOURCE: Angus Maddison, *The World Economy in the 20th Century*, Paris: Organization for Economic Cooperation and Development, 1989.

and much more was needed, and all of it required labor, raw material, and fuel for its construction.

Obviously, such a use of resources has its *opportunity cost*. Fuel and steel that are employed to build a train become unavailable for the production of refrigerators and washing machines. The real price of accumulating plant, equipment, and infrastructure is paid in the form of consumer goods that must be given up in order to build that capital equipment. In other words:

Through saving, the public gives up some consumption, which is the price it must pay for the accumulation of plant, equipment, and infrastructure. Without this sacrifice, growth generally cannot occur.

This is the hard lesson that the inhabitants of the Soviet Union lived with for over seventy years. The Soviet leadership was determined to promote rapid economic growth and had imposed on the general public whatever sacrifices of current consumption were deemed necessary for the purpose. Only in the most recent decades was an increase in the supply of consumer goods assigned any priority. Yet, even shortly before its collapse, investment in the U.S.S.R. was still nearly one-third of GDP, while in the United States the figure is about half that amount. As a result, Soviet living standards rose very slowly, particularly because the demands of the military forces joined those of the growth planners in competing for the resources that might otherwise have gone into consumption. That is undoubtedly one of the main reasons for the demise of communism in the U.S.S.R. and the other countries of Eastern Europe.

The reason for this harsh trade-off is clear enough. If the economy is producing at its full potential, then real output $Y$ cannot be increased further. Since $Y = C + I + G + (X - IM)$, a decision to devote more resources to the production of heavy machinery (which is in $I$) or armaments (which are in $G$) is simultaneously a decision to forgo some consumption or to import more. Where resources are already fully employed, it is simply not possible to have both more guns *and* more butter.

## THE PAYOFF TO GROWTH: HIGHER CONSUMPTION IN THE FUTURE

We may seem to be painting a rather grim picture of growth, and indeed, the process was often harsh in the old U.S.S.R. and in other nations that have enforced a high rate of economic growth. But it is also true that if the growth process is successful, the sacrifice of consumption that it requires is only a temporary loss. Consumers give up goods and services now in order to make possible the construction of productive capacity that will permit them to consume even more goods and services at a later date. After all, from the consumers' point of view, that is what growth is all about. It is not an end in itself, but a means to an end—a standard of living higher than they could have attained without the process of economic expansion.

At least in a consumer-oriented economy, the decision to save in order to promote economic growth is simply an *exchange between present and future consumption.* Consumers sacrifice consumption now in order to be able to increase consumption in the future by more than they gave up in the past.

Of course, the payoff may never come if something goes wrong. An earthquake may destroy factories and roads, or a government with military ambitions may divert the increased productive capacity into the manufacture of armaments. So there is a risk in the decision to give up consumption now for increased consumption later. The growth process is a gamble—it means trading in a relatively sure thing (present consumption) for a risky future return (increased future consumption).

But betting on the future is not necessarily foolhardy. Economies would remain stagnant if people were unwilling to take the required chances. And some of the risk of investment plans can be reduced if decision makers understand fully the terms of the trade-off.

## GROWTH WITHOUT SACRIFICING CONSUMPTION: SOMETHING FOR NOTHING?

Some growth can be achieved without much sacrifice of present consumption. For at least one of the main engines of growth can be powered with relatively small increases in the nation's stock of factories, equipment, and infrastructure. Research and development can teach society new and more efficient ways of using the nation's productive resources. Thus, *innovation*—the process of putting inventions into operation—can permit an economy to get more output from the same input quantities, rather than by *expansion* of capital stock.

Everyone knows that this has in fact occurred. From the invention of the steam engine to that of the modern computer, our economy has benefited from a stream of inventions—some sensational, some more routine—which together have increased enormously the productivity of the nation's resources. Estimates of the relative contributions of innovation and accumulation to the growth process differ. A number of analysts attribute considerably more than half of the economic growth of the United States to research and invention. But whatever the correct figure, it is certainly large.

Another way of describing this conclusion is to say that while a substantial proportion of growth is **embodied** in increased quantities of plant, equipment, and infrastructure, a very large proportion of the economy's growth is **disembodied**. That is, it is attributable to better ideas—to improved methods of finding and using the same quantities of resources.

Embodied growth has two serious costs that disembodied growth avoids. First, embodied growth necessarily speeds up the use of society's depletable resources: its iron ore, its petroleum supplies, and its stocks of other minerals and fuels. Second, the resources that are used up in a process of embodied growth must ultimately end up on society's garbage heap. The physical laws of conservation of matter and energy tell us that no raw material can ever disappear. It can be transformed into smoke or solid waste, but unless it is recycled *entirely* (something that is both beyond the capability of our technology and impractical for other reasons), the greater the quantity of resources used in the productive process, the greater the quantity of wastes that must ultimately result.

Economist Kenneth Boulding has likened our planet to a spaceship hurtling through the solar system but constrained by terrestrial littering laws to keep its garbage on board. In spaceship Earth, we can transform waste materials into other forms—as by melting old bottles for reuse or converting them into energy, or by burning combustible garbage for heat—but we cannot simply toss them overboard.

So far, we have enjoyed substantial success in our efforts to achieve growth in output without commensurate increases in our use of resources. One statistical analysis, for example, attributes only about half of the growth in the United States to increased use of physical inputs. The remainder must be ascribed to improvements in technology as well as to increased education and skill of the labor force.[5]

One final remark on disembodied growth is in order. Economists are fond of pointing out that there is no such thing as a free lunch. Except in rare instances, improvements in technology are not "manna from heaven." They result, instead, from the work of scientists and technicians in government and industrial laboratories, from the labor of inventors in their basements or garages, and from the effort of management specialists studying the organization of factories and assembly lines. This means that labor (along with other resources) is diverted from other activities into the production of knowledge. *In a fully employed economy, the opportunity costs of investing in the discovery of new knowledge are the forgone consumption and physical investment of goods that would otherwise have been produced.* So even here, we cannot get something for nothing.

## IS MORE GROWTH REALLY BETTER?

A number of writers have raised questions about the desirability of faster economic growth as an end in itself, at least in the wealthier industrialized countries. Yet faster growth does mean more wealth, and to most people the desirability of wealth is beyond question. "I've been rich and I've been poor—and I can tell you, rich is better," a noted stage personality is said to have told an interviewer, and most people seem to have the same attitude about the economy as a whole. To those who hold this belief, a healthy economy is one that is capable of turning

[5]Edward F. Denison, *Accounting for United States Economic Growth 1929–1969* (Washington, D.C.: The Brookings Institution, 1974).

### *The Poverty of Affluence*

Does affluence make us better off? Psychologist Paul Wachtel argues that:

> . . . the growth economy . . . creates more needs than it satisfies and leaves us feeling more deprived than when we had "less". . . . It is ironic that the very kind of thinking which produces all our riches also renders them unable to satisfy us. Our restless desire for more and more has been a major dynamic for economic growth, but it has made the achievement of that growth largely a hollow victory. Our sense of contentment and satisfaction . . . depends upon our frame of reference, on how what we attain compares to what we expected. If we get farther than we expected we tend to feel good. If we expected to go farther than we have then even a rather high level of success can be experienced as disappointing.
>
> In America, we keep upping the ante. Our expectations keep accommodating to what we have attained. "Enough" is always just over the horizon, and like the horizon it recedes as we approach it. . . . The sense of economic distress and disappointment currently sweeping America has [little] to do with real deprivation and much [to do] with assumptions and expectations.

Paul L. Wachtel, *The Poverty of Affluence, A Psychological Portrait of the American Way of Life*, New York: The Free Press, 1983, pages 16–17.

out vast quantities of shoes, food, cars, and TV sets. An economy whose capacity to provide all these things is not expanding is said to have succumbed to the disease of *stagnation*.

Economists from Adam Smith to Karl Marx saw great virtue in economic growth. Marx argued that capitalism, at least in its earlier historical stages, was a vital form of economic organization by which society got out of the rut in which the medieval stage of history had trapped it. Marx believed that "the development of the productive powers of society . . . alone can form the real basis of a higher form of society. . . ." Marx went on to tell us that only where such great productive powers have been unleashed can one have "a society in which the full and free development of every individual forms the ruling principle."[6] In other words, only a wealthy economy can afford to give all individuals the opportunity for full personal satisfaction through the use of their special abilities in their jobs and through increased leisure activities.

Yet the desirability of further economic growth for a society that is already wealthy has been questioned on grounds that undoubtedly have a good deal of validity. It is pointed out that the sheer increase in quantity of products has imposed an enormous cost on society in the form of pollution, crowding, and proliferation of wastes that need disposal; some economists claim it has had unfortunate psychological and social effects. It is said that industry has transformed the satisfying and creative tasks of the artisan into the mechanical and dehumanizing routine of the assembly line. It has dotted our roadsides with

[6]Karl Marx, *Capital*, Vol. I (Chicago: Charles H. Kerr Publishing Co., 1906), page 649.

junkyards, filled our air with smoke, and poisoned our food with dangerous chemicals. The question is whether the outpouring of frozen foods, talking dolls, CD players, and headache remedies is worth its high cost to society. As one well-known economist put it:

> *The continued pursuit of economic growth by Western societies is more likely on balance to reduce rather than increase social welfare .... Technological innovations may offer to add to men's material opportunities. But by increasing the risks of their obsolescence it adds also to their anxiety. Swifter means of communications have the paradoxical effect of isolating people; increased mobility has led to more hours commuting; increased automobilization to increased separation; more television to less communication. In consequence, people know less of their neighbors than ever before in history.*[7]

Virtually every economist agrees that these concerns are valid, though many question whether economic growth is their major cause. Nevertheless, they all emphasize that pollution of air and water, noise and congestion, and the mechanization of the work process are very real and very serious problems. There is every reason for society to undertake programs that grapple with them. Chapter 21, which dealt with problems of the environment, examined these issues more closely and described some policies to deal with them.

Despite the costs of growth in terms of human and environmental damage, there is strong evidence that if the economy's total output were kept at its present level, the community would pay a high price over and above the loss of additional goods and services.

First, it is not easy to carry out a decision to prevent further economic growth. Mandatory controls are abhorrent to most Americans. We cannot *order* people to stop inventing means to expand productivity. Nor does it make any sense to order every firm and industry to freeze its output level, since changing tastes and needs require some industries to expand their outputs at the same time that others are contracting. But who is to decide which should grow and which should contract, and how shall such decisions be made? *The achievement of zero economic growth may very well require government intervention on a scale that becomes expensive and even repressive.*

Second, without continued growth it will be no easy matter to finance effective programs to improve the quality of life—programs such as environmental protection. To improve the purity of our air and water and to clean up urban neighborhoods, tens of billions of dollars must be made available every year. Continued growth would enable the required resources to be provided without any reduction in the availability of consumer goods. But without such growth, we may actually be forced to cut back on our programs to protect the environment. Society could thus end up with less goods and a worse environment.

Finally, zero economic growth may seriously hamper efforts to eliminate poverty both within our economy and throughout the world. Much of the earth's population today lives in a state of extreme want. And though wealthier nations have been reluctant to provide more than token amounts of help to the **less developed countries (LDCs)**, less wealth means there would be even less to share. So perhaps the only hope for improved living standards in the impoverished countries of Africa, Asia, and Latin America lies in continued increases in output.

---

[7]E. J. Mishan, *The Costs of Economic Growth* (New York: Frederick A. Praeger Publishers, 1967), pages 171, 175.

# PROBLEMS OF THE LESS DEVELOPED COUNTRIES

## LIVING IN THE LDCs

A substantial proportion of the world's population lives in areas whose average per capita GDP is $2,000 or less per year, evaluated (as well as it is possible to do) in terms of today's prices in the United States. Table 38–1 shows that there are countries in which annual per capita GDP is less than $600. Even after adjustment for differences in measurement of GDP in the United States and the poorer countries, this probably comes to an annual GDP figure under $1000.

To us, residents of an economy that offers an average GDP more than 20 times as high as this, such a figure is not only likely to seem incredible, it is all but incomprehensible. Few of us can *really* imagine what life would be like if our family income were reduced to $1000 per year. It is even hard to envision survival on such amounts. It must be emphasized that these figures do *not* represent the living standards of a small group of outcasts from their own societies. Rather, they are *typical* of many people who live in Asia, Africa, and Latin America.

What can life be like in such circumstances? No brief description can really bridge the gulf between our range of experience and theirs. Yet it can offer us a glimpse into a way of life that few of us will want to share.

Inhabitants of many of the less developed countries live with their large families in one-room shanties or apartments; their water supplies are scanty, polluted, and often miles from home; their only source of energy is that of human and beast; and their sparse harvests are wrung from miserable soil in good years,

Table 38–1 PER CAPITA GDP IN DEVELOPED AND LESS DEVELOPED COUNTRIES, 1991*

| | (measured in U.S. dollars)* |
|---|---|
| **Developed Countries** | |
| United States | $22,130 |
| United Kingdom | 16,340 |
| Sweden | 17,490 |
| **Less Developed Countries** | |
| Bolivia | 2,170 |
| China | 1,680 |
| Egypt | 3,600 |
| Ethiopia | 370 |
| Haiti | 1,220 |
| India | 1,150 |
| Tanzania | 570 |

SOURCE: The World Bank, *World Development Report* 1993, page 296.

*Using purchasing-power-parity exchange rates. See Chapter 34, footnote 10, for an explanation.

## *Starvation in Africa: A Recurring Tragedy*

Reporters assigned to cover events in Africa often find that one of their biggest journalistic challenges is to overcome the numbness and overfamiliarity engendered by the all too predictable cycles of drought, famine and human catastrophe in many parts of that continent. Less than a decade after the famine in Ethiopia in the mid-1980s, when a million people starved to death, newspapers of the world are once again filled with heart-rending photographs of skeletal, near-death Africans. And, once again, these nightmarish pictures are coming from the Horn of Africa.

Severe drought plays an important part in the latest food crisis. But totalitarian government, civil warfare, and economic collapse are bigger villains. *The Economist* magazine reports that, "The Horn is a catalogue of the malfeasance that drives millions to the brink. There, three countries embroiled in fighting (Ethiopia, Sudan and Somalia) contain more than half of Africa's hungry. Add in the victims of other civil wars (in Angola, Mozambique and Liberia) and the proportion rises to two-thirds." * The economies of these countries have suffered devastating effects from internal strife; according to the *1991 World Bank Annual Report*, GDP in Sudan fell by 5.8 percent in 1990, and output in Ethiopia dropped by about 2.5 percent. In Somalia, the economic situation continues to deteriorate.**

The end of the cold war may presage an end to the cycle of devastation. With the collapse of the Soviet Union, African conflicts are no longer the locus of superpower rivalry. The ex-Soviet Union is now virtually a nonpresence in African affairs, and the United States has adopted new attitudes toward aid in Africa, with amounts and timing starting to be contingent, for the first time, upon progress toward democracy. Experience in Botswana and Kenya, where universal suffrage has forced governments to protect the most at-risk and poor citizens during droughts, has shown that democracy may be the answer.

* "The Horn Is Empty," *The Economist*, May 11, 1991, pages 37–38.
**SOURCE: *The World Bank Annual Report 1991*, Washington, D.C.: The World Bank, 1991, page 113.

with starvation threatened perhaps every five years when the rains do not come and the crops fail. With no surplus in production, no food can be put into reserves, and the old, the infirm, and the very young are likely to perish. The box above describes the most recent manifestation of the recurring cycle of drought and famine in Africa.

The life of a man in an LDC is hard enough, with its low nutritional level, its lack of equipment to help him in his work, and its frequency of debilitating diseases. But his life is luxurious compared with that of a woman. She is usually married by the age of 14, bears 8 or 10 children with minimal medical assistance, and by 35 is often beset by chronic disease and aged far beyond her years. If (as is true of some 80 percent of the population) she inhabits a rural area, she may have to walk miles every day to fetch water for the family. She sews the family's clothes by hand and cooks its meals. There is not enough money for pre-ground flour, so part of a woman's daily work is to pound the grain by hand for food for the family—perhaps an additional two hours of hard labor. She also tends the gardens that produce food for the family, although, except in Moslem countries where women are sequestered, she is also expected to put in a full day in the fields during the six months of the agricultural season.

Another duty of the woman in an LDC is to bring produce, wood, or whatever she has to trade to market a couple of times a week, and she must often walk as

**Table 38–2 INFANT MORTALITY AND LIFE EXPECTANCY IN DEVELOPED AND LESS DEVELOPED COUNTRIES, 1992**

| | INFANT MORTALITY (deaths per 1000 live births) | LIFE EXPECTANCY AT BIRTH (years) (male/female) |
|---|---|---|
| **Developed Countries** | | |
| United States | 9.0 | 72/79 |
| Germany | 7.5 | 72/78 |
| Sweden | 6.0 | 75/80 |
| **Less Developed Countries** | | |
| Bolivia | 89 | 58/64 |
| China | 34 | 68/71 |
| Egypt | 73 | 58/61 |
| Ethiopia | 139 | 46/48 |
| Haiti | 106 | 53/56 |
| India | 91 | 58/59 |
| Tanzania | 105 | 49/54 |

SOURCE: Population Reference Bureau, Inc., *1992 World Population Data Sheet.*

many as 10 miles each way with bundles as heavy as she can carry on her back or on her head. She has no respite in the raising of her children, since they are likely not to have a school to attend when they are well or a hospital to go to when they are sick. It is no wonder that she ages so much faster than a woman in our society.

Table 38–2 gives the percentage of infant deaths for each 1000 live births and the average life expectancy of a newborn child in some countries ranging from the most underdeveloped to the most affluent. The contrasts are dramatic. In Bolivia, 89 babies die of every 1000 that are born, while the comparable figure in Sweden is six. In many countries people survive only until their 40s or 50s, while in Sweden the average life expectancy for men is 75 years and for women is 80 years. There is little question about the quality of life in less developed lands.

Most of the inhabitants of many LDCs are shockingly poor. Malnutrition and disease are widespread. The sheer process of living and surviving taxes the people to the utmost and makes them old before their time.

## RECENT TRENDS

Despite population increases, some LDCs, particularly in the Far East, have succeeded in breaking out of the stagnation trap. In those successful economies, if growth were to continue as it was in the 1970s, an average family could look forward to a doubling of its living standards in less than 30 years. Or put another way, in earlier decades standards of living were increasing faster than they did in the United States in the nineteenth century!

While in the 1970s such good news applied to a number of LDCs in several parts of the world, the 1980s were not so favorable. Aside from their debt problems, which will be discussed a bit later, there are several developments that can be considered either as merely unfortunate or as thoroughly ominous for the LDCs.

While the percentage rates of growth of per capita incomes in the LDCs have been impressive, the industrialized countries, with their initially high incomes, have not exactly been standing still. Indeed, largely because their population growth has been slower, the percentage growth rate in per capita incomes has been higher in the developed countries. But even if the *percentage* increases in their per capita incomes had been very similar, *absolute* incomes would have continued to rise more quickly in the richer lands. For example, where per capita income is \$100 a year, a $2\frac{1}{2}$ percent growth rate translates into a \$2.50 annual improvement; however, where per capita income is \$5000 a year, the same $2\frac{1}{2}$ percent rate of growth adds \$125 a year to the income of the average person.

A few numbers will indicate how discouraging the relative performance of the LDCs as a group has been. A study of some 70 countries by a group of noted economists[8] calculated a standard index of degree of inequality (called the "Gini index") for three subsets of these countries: the industrialized countries, the middle-income countries, and the LDCs. The study covered the 30-year period 1950–1980, which included the decade of the 1970s, usually considered an era of extraordinary progress for the LDCs. For the industrialized countries, the index of inequality fell by almost 60 percent over the 30-year period, meaning that the poorer of the industrial countries had done a very effective job of catching up with the richer ones. The countries of the middle-income group also came closer to one another, but only to a modest degree, with their inequality index falling 4 percent in 3 decades. But for the LDCs the index actually rose 9 percent, meaning that these poorest of countries were increasingly diverging among themselves into relatively richer and relatively poorer groups.

Even more important, the disparity between the LDCs and the other two groups has been increasing. The average annual growth rates of real GDP were 3.1 percent (compounded) for the industrial countries, 3.0 percent for the middle-income countries, and only 1.5 percent for the LDCs. With average growth rates half as big as those for the more-affluent economies, the LDCs as a group fell further behind the rest of the world for much of the period since World War II.

Figure 38–5 illustrates, for the case of Latin America, the poor growth performance of some of the LDCs in the 1980s. Of the nine countries whose records are reported, 7 actually experienced a *decline* in per capita GDP, with 4 of those falling substantially.

The purchasing power of the average family in an LDC is falling further behind that of a typical family in a wealthy economy.

Many critics, notably those on the left, emphasize that growth has been accompanied by a worsening distribution of income within some of the LDCs. The rise in population has worsened the living standards of people on marginal lands with inadequate rain (about 40 percent of Indian farmers and a large proportion of Africans). Add the massive explosion of urban unemployment, and one gets several hundred million people who are no better off and possibly worse off than ever before.

Another continuing problem within the LDCs is the relatively high growth rate of their populations.

---

[8]Robert Summers, Irving B. Kravis, and Alan Heston, "Changes in World Income Distribution," *Journal of Policy Modelling*, Vol. 6, May 1986, pages 237–69.

*Figure* **38-5** **FALLING PER CAPITA OUTPUTS IN LATIN AMERICA, 1981–1990**

Experience since the Industrial Revolution has led us to consider growth in per capita income to be the normal state of affairs for a country. However, this was true only for two of the nine countries in the graph. Four of them, Argentina, Peru, Venezuela, and Bolivia, actually experienced sharp drops in GDP per capita. .

SOURCE: Inter-American Development Bank, *Economic and Social Progress in Latin America, 1991*, Special Section: Social Security in Latin America, Washington, D.C.: Johns Hopkins University Press, October 1991, page 273.

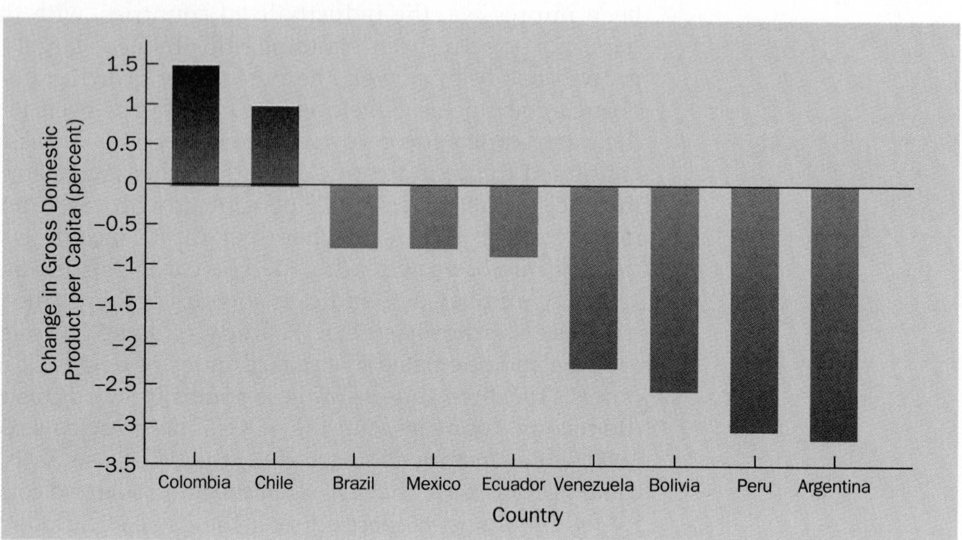


While net population growth has fallen almost to zero in the United States and some countries of Western Europe, the population explosion continues in some of the LDCs, particularly in Africa.

Table 38–3 tells the story. For the sample of LDCs shown, the annual growth rate of population continues about ten times as high as it is in the industrialized countries. Clearly, the more closely the growth in population approximates the growth in national income, the more slowly standards of living will rise, since there will be that many more persons among whom the additional product must be divided.

Finally, the LDCs have shown themselves highly vulnerable to such events as the oil crisis in 1979 and the high real interest rates of the 1980s. Much as the fall in Iranian oil exports and rise in oil prices affected the industrialized economies, it undoubtedly damaged the LDCs even more, leading to enormous deficits and foreign debts for the countries least able to afford them.

## IMPEDIMENTS TO DEVELOPMENT IN THE LDCs

No one has produced a definitive list of causes of the poverty of the LDCs, just as no one can pretend to have produced a foolproof prescription for its cure. Yet there is general agreement on the main conditions contributing to the economic problems of LDCs. These include lack of physical capital, rapid growth of population, lack of education, unemployment, and social and political impediments to business activity. Let us consider each of these.

## SCARCITY OF PHYSICAL CAPITAL

The LDCs are obviously handicapped by their lack of modern factories and machinery. In addition, they lack infrastructure—good roads, railroads, port facilities, and so on. But capital is not easy to acquire. If it is to be provided by the populations of the LDCs themselves, they must save the required resources—that is, as we saw earlier in this chapter, they must give up consumption in order to free the resources needed to build plants, equipment, and roads. That is comparatively easy in a rich community, where substantial saving still leaves the public well off in terms of current consumption. But in an LDC, where malnutrition is a constant threat, the bulk of the inhabitants cannot save except at enormous sacrifice to their families. Moreover, in many of the LDCs, tradition imputes little virtue to investment in business, so that even the wealthy are not terribly anxious to put their savings into productive equipment. Thus:

Because of poverty, which makes saving difficult, if not impossible, and because of traditions that do not encourage investment, the LDCs' growth rates of domestically financed capital are lower than those in the developed countries.

One way to help matters is to obtain the funds for investment from abroad. There is a long tradition of foreign investment in developing countries. For example, throughout the first half of the nineteenth century the United States almost constantly drew capital from abroad, though the amounts involved were only a small proportion of U.S. GDP. In recent decades a considerable share of the resources going to the LDCs from abroad has come from foreign governments as part of their aid programs. While some of the resources provided in this way have been used wastefully, informed observers generally agree that the waste incurred under these programs has not been spectacularly great, and they conclude that these capital transfers from the rich countries to the poor have at least worked in the right direction.

Capital can also be transferred to an LDC when a private firm chooses to invest money in such a country to build a factory or to explore for oil in order to increase

**Table 38–3 NATURAL INCREASE IN POPULATION (BIRTHRATE MINUS DEATH RATE) IN DEVELOPED AND LESS DEVELOPED COUNTRIES, 1992**

| | (births minus deaths as percent of population) |
|---|---|
| **Developed Countries** | |
| United States | 0.8 |
| Germany | −0.1 |
| Sweden | 0.3 |
| **Less Developed Countries** | |
| Bolivia | 2.7 |
| China | 1.3 |
| Egypt | 2.4 |
| Ethiopia | 2.8 |
| Haiti | 2.9 |
| India | 2.0 |
| Tanzania | 3.5 |

SOURCE: Population Reference Bureau, Inc., *1992 World Population Data Sheet*.

its own profits. This too seems to have been helpful to the LDCs. In earlier days, it sometimes gave an unacceptable degree of political influence to the foreign firms, particularly when the LDC was a colony of an industrial country. In recent years this difficulty may have become rarer. Nowadays, it is more often the outside firm that is afraid of the government of the LDC rather than vice versa, with foreign proprietors frequently fearful of rigid control by the government of the LDC in which it invests. Sometimes it even fears outright expropriation—that the government will simply take over its property in the LDC with, or even without, compensation because of the hostile attitudes that residents of many LDCs hold toward large foreign companies.

It is difficult for a resident of an industrialized country like the United States to realize how much hatred and resentment is felt in less developed countries toward the "northern imperialist powers." This resentment is focused in particular on **multinational corporations**—companies such as IBM, Royal Dutch Shell, Volkswagen, and Unilever—which have their headquarters in an industrialized country and their operations in a variety of less developed countries. Multinationals may first process their own raw materials in one country, ship them to another to make them into parts, and assemble them in still a third. Some of these corporations, among them the oil companies, specialize in the extraction and/or marketing of raw materials, while others, such as IBM and Volkswagen, specialize in manufacturing. Many LDCs regard these and other giant foreign corporations as instruments of imperialist exploitation, not as firms that happen to carry on their activities wherever the dictates of efficiency require, contributing benefits to each of the countries in which they operate.

It is true that foreign firms hope to make more money out of an LDC than they put into it, but that is only natural, since otherwise their investment would not have been expected to be profitable, and the funds would therefore not have been invested in the first place. But there are usually *mutual* gains from trade. Investment will be useful to the LDCs if, in the process of earning these profits, foreign firms build factories, infrastructure, and provide jobs that leave the community wealthier than it would otherwise have been. The evidence is that this is in fact what foreign private investment has typically accomplished in recent decades.

A problem with foreign business investment that is more serious is the danger that foreign firms will fail to train indigenous personnel in the skills necessary to run the factories built by those companies. Often the firms bring with them their own managers, engineers, and technicians, and the work force from the LDCs is kept in menial jobs in which on-the-job training is minimal. In recent years the LDCs have begun to deal with this problem by restricting immigration of foreign personnel, giving them work permits only for limited periods and requiring at least some minimum employment of indigenous personnel in key positions.

Another danger posed by foreign investment is that it may prevent future financial independence. Profits are a major source of the funds used for investment. If foreign investment takes over the LDCs' most profitable industries, then newly formed capital—new plants and equipment—will also be owned predominantly by foreigners.

## POPULATION GROWTH

Population growth is often described as the primary villain in the LDCs. We have already noted that their populations grow far more rapidly than those in the wealthier countries. And although the growth rate has recently been declining in many of the less developed countries, overall, the population of the LDCs is expanding at a rate that will double in less than 30 years, requiring a doubling of housing, schools, hospitals, and so on—a heavy real cost for an LDC.

The growth in population has been stimulated by improvements in medical care, which have reduced death rates spectacularly. Today, in some areas, death rates (ratio of deaths to population) are only one-quarter or one-fifth as high as birthrates. While formerly it was not unusual for half a nation's children to die before the age of 20, today in many countries this is true of only some 4 percent of those populations. This dramatic decline can be attributed primarily to inexpensive public health measures: reduction in intestinal diseases through purer water supplies; reduction in the incidence of malaria by the draining of swamps; insecticide spraying of the breeding grounds of disease-carrying mosquitoes; eradication of smallpox by vaccination; and so forth. The more expensive treatment of illness, using modern medical techniques and miracle drugs, seems to have contributed far less.

But not all LDCs suffer from serious population problems. India, Indonesia, and Egypt are frequently cited examples of population pressures. On the other hand, many African countries and parts of Latin America still have populations so small that they are denied economies of larger scale communication and transportation. The economy of a sparsely settled country whose electric power and telecommunication lines must traverse great unpopulated areas is under a costly handicap.

Governments in a number of LDCs have been struggling to find workable ways to cut population growth. Programs set up to distribute contraceptives and propaganda against large families have achieved modest success; but in some countries with particularly severe population problems the governments have been dissatisfied with the results of these voluntary efforts. In India, a program making use of compulsory sterilization aroused the anger of the public and finally led to the downfall of the government.

Ironically enough, it was communist China which, along with Singapore, decided to employ strong financial incentives for population control. In China, government support is provided for a first child. For a second, the support is withdrawn and some financial penalties imposed; and for a third child, the penalties are really prohibitive for most people. There is much more to the program, however, than such rather benign financial incentives. For example, in urban areas (where most of the citizens work in state-operated enterprises and are monitored more closely than rural residents), each factory is assigned a person or committee to keep track of birth control. Women workers are required to maintain a record of their menstrual cycles and submit the records to the monitor; a woman who misses a menstrual period is forced to have an abortion. According to a recent issue of *The Economist* magazine, "The *Ningxia Legal Daily* reports that ten couples in the south-western province of Sichuan refused to abort pregnancies which, if brought to term, would have violated the government's one-child family policy. To make them see sense, the men were caned on their bare buttocks, one stroke for each day of the pregnancy, and one of the women was threatened with caning, until all the couples agreed to abortions. 'A complete victory against the diehard elements,' noted the *Legal Daily* with satisfaction" (March 9, 1991, page 33).

Such coercive measures have, indeed, been successful in reducing average birthrates to a bit over one child per couple in the cities and a bit over two children per couple in rural areas (where five or six children used to be the norm). One population expert has warned, however, that the one-child program may prove disastrous for China's economy, because family enterprises have always played an important role, and because twenty years hence it can leave the support of a tremendous aging population to be borne by a depleted labor force.

## EDUCATIONAL AND TECHNICAL TRAINING

Everyone knows that educational levels in the LDCs are much lower than they are in the wealthier countries. There are fewer graduates of elementary schools, far fewer graduates of high schools, and enormously fewer college graduates. The percentage of the population that is literate is much lower than in industrialized nations. The issue is how much of a handicap this constitutes for economic growth.

If, by "education," we refer to general learning rather than technical (trade) schooling, the evidence is that it makes considerably less difference for economic growth than is often believed. For example, the number of jobs that clearly require secondary (high school) education rarely seems to exceed 10 percent of the labor force. Various studies that have investigated whether there is a statistical relationship between the economic growth of an economy and its typical educational level have found only weak correlations between the two. Other suggestive evidence can easily be cited. For example, in 1840 when Great Britain ruled the markets of the world, only 59 percent of the British adult population was literate, while in the United States, Scandinavia, and Germany, then all relatively undeveloped countries, the figure was about 80 percent.

All of this is not meant to imply that education is worthless. On the contrary, it obviously offers many benefits in and of itself, which need not be discussed here. But it does suggest that if a government invests in education *purely as a means to stimulate economic growth*, only a very limited outlay on *general* education beyond the achievement of literacy is justifiable on these grounds.

Matters are quite different when we turn to technical training. There is apparently a high payoff to the training of electricians, machinists, draftsmen, construction workers, and the like. While the number of persons involved need not be very high in proportion to the population, the role played by such specialists is crucial. However, the LDCs would find it a very heavy drain upon their scarce foreign currency to send young people abroad to learn these skills in the numbers called for by the needs of the economy. One of the main inhibitions to adequate training in these areas is that in many countries such skills are held in low esteem and considered inferior to training in the liberal arts. Consequently, technical education is often handicapped by low budgets, low teacher salaries—which discourage good people from entering the field—and the prejudice of potential students against such fields.

Training in improved farming methods also has a great deal to contribute. In many of the LDCs, agricultural methods produce yields far lower than the best of the known techniques can offer. As one leading observer, the late Nobel Prizewinner Sir W. Arthur Lewis, remarked:

> *If this gap could be closed, the economies of these countries would be unrecognizable. Indeed . . . no impact can be made on mass living standards without revolutionizing agricultural performance.*[9]

---

[9]W. A. Lewis, *Development Economics: An Outline* (Morristown, N.J.: General Learning Press, 1974), page 25.

There seem to be no easy ways to provide the necessary education to the farmers who cannot spare the time to attend schools, and training their children also involves a number of critical obstacles. Religious beliefs often lead parents to object to schooling of their children, particularly of girls; in areas where literacy is low (where the problem is generally most serious), truly literate and knowledgeable teachers are almost impossible to find in any substantial numbers; and children who do complete schooling have a tendency to leave the farms and move to the cities.

Programs to provide help to the peasants on their own farms have had only limited success. Indeed, lack of training is only part of the problem. Many other things are needed to make modern farming methods possible—farms larger than the five acres that are typical in a number of countries are required to permit the use of modern machinery where it is appropriate. Roads and storage facilities must be built. Credit must be made available to farmers. Financial arrangements must be changed so farmers need no longer give up half their crops to landlords and tax collectors whom farmers can surely regard as little more than parasites and who undermine incentives for improved productivity.

## UNEMPLOYMENT

One of the most noteworthy features of the growth of the LDCs has been an increase in unemployment as population shifted out of agriculture into the cities. Increased schooling has stimulated the migration out of the rural areas, as has unionization, which has often produced a huge gap between urban and rural wages. Government investment policies have also favored construction of schools, hospitals, and other facilities in the cities, and as a result, large numbers of migrants have entered the cities to swell the ranks of the unemployed. The unemployment rate among young urban workers has been particularly high; indeed, rates as high as 50 percent are not unheard of.

These figures are compounded by the phenomenon of **disguised unemployment**. For example, ten persons may do a job for which only six are needed. The statistics would show no unemployment among the ten workers, even though four of them really contribute nothing to output. Some observers believe that this is such a widespread problem in rural areas that even a substantial reverse migration of the urban unemployed back to the farms would add very little to production, at least in some of the LDCs.

An important consequence of all this is that in many LDCs unemployment may not be accompanied by any substantial reduction in output, in contrast to the situation in industrialized economies. But this does not mean that unemployment in the LDCs is not a serious problem. What it does mean is that it may sometimes be desirable for those economies to avoid the use of labor-saving equipment, partly because it will result in better use of an abundant resource and partly because it will contribute to the solution of a serious social problem. Thus, increased jobs are desirable perhaps primarily because they absorb unemployed labor. This is in contrast to the usual situation in the developed countries in which increased employment is desirable perhaps primarily because it increases income and output.

## SOCIAL IMPEDIMENTS TO ENTREPRENEURSHIP

As was noted earlier in this chapter, one of the magic ingredients of economic growth is **entrepreneurship**. It is clear that the LDCs need entrepreneurs if their economies are to grow rapidly. But in many of these economies there are serious inhibitions to entrepreneurship. Traditional social values often accord relatively low status to business activity. Indeed, those traditional values even prevent businesses from seeking ways to attract and please their customers and their work force. In addition, high positions in business in many LDCs are often determined by family connections and inheritance, not by ability.

In the LDCs, growth will be inhibited until customs can be modified to increase the social status of economic activity, to make it respectable for private business people and managers of public enterprises to do their best to attract business and increase productivity, and to assign responsibility on the basis of ability rather than family connections.

### GOVERNMENT INHIBITION OF BUSINESS ACTIVITY

In addition to social impediments to business, the political situation in the LDCs often is detrimental to business success. Business is not helped by unstable governments or by the uncertainty that accompanies such an environment, especially if there is a high likelihood of revolution. Foreign investment will be discouraged where there is fear of expropriation or of unstable currencies that may fall in value and wipe out hard-earned profits. And indigenous business people may live in fear of nationalization or even imprisonment—possibilities that are not likely to encourage investment.

In the normal course of events, governments in the LDCs are often inclined to interfere with business activity in a variety of ways that seem relatively innocuous—but whose effects can be deadly. Price controls are often imposed at levels that make the controlled activity totally unprofitable and cause it to wither. Licenses and other direct controls are frequently administered by incompetent bureaucrats, who tie up business activity in red tape. As a matter of prestige of the currency, exchange rates are often set so high that exports from the LDC cannot compete on the world market. The governments sometimes expropriate and seek to operate foreign firms before they have trained indigenous personnel to run them. In short:

Poorly conceived economic policies can impede business activity and hence economic growth in the LDCs. But, then, it must be admitted that the LDCs have no monopoly on foolish economic policies!

## HELP FROM INDUSTRIALIZED ECONOMIES

We have just seen that the two primary needs of the LDCs are technical skills and capital resources. Happily, these are precisely the things that the more prosperous nations are in a position to offer. We have the trained teachers, classrooms, laboratories, and equipment necessary to provide an education of the highest quality to students from the LDCs. However, there is a danger here that has received a great deal of attention, the so-called **brain drain**. This refers to the temptation for students from LDCs to try to stay in the countries where they have studied and enjoy the higher living standard, rather than to return home where their abilities are needed so badly.

There are several ways to deal with this. For example, one can require students to return to their homelands for at least some given number of years after completion of the educational program, or offer higher wages for trained persons in the

LDCs to make returning more attractive. Yet the problem is there, and the large number of doctors, teachers, and other skilled personnel from LDCs who are seeking jobs in the developed countries suggests that it is not negligible.

A second major contribution that the wealthier countries can make to the LDCs is to offer them trained technicians and technical advice from the wealthier countries' own populations. Such counseling and personnel can be very helpful as a temporary measure, but in the long run they can prove detrimental if provision for the training of local personnel for the ultimate replacement of the foreign technicians and advisers is not built into the program.

Third, the world can help the LDCs through research. One of the hardest problems for the developing world is what to do in the rural areas that suffer from inadequate rainfall, where several hundred million people live in both Asia and Africa. These people are badly in need of new dry-farming techniques. Until some are discovered, their poverty will increase as their numbers grow. An international research organization devoted to food production in problem areas in the LDCs would have much to contribute.

Fourth, the developed countries can help by encouraging freedom of trade and investment. This will help those LDCs whose exports are now being held back by barriers to trade. Exports of sugar, meat, cotton, and other agricultural products are inhibited by industrialized countries' tariffs and other restrictions. LDCs would also benefit substantially from a lifting of tariffs and quotas upon the import by industrial countries of processed or manufactured goods. Such restrictive measures make it difficult for LDCs to export anything but raw materials and impedes their industrialization and modernization. All in all, increased freedom of trade is a matter of highest priority for the LDCs. It will probably also prove beneficial to the wealthier countries, as improved incomes in the LDCs make the latter better customers for the exports of the former.[10]

A last, and very important, type of assistance from the developed to the less developed countries takes the form of money or physical resources provided either as loans made on favorable terms or as outright grants (gifts).

## LOANS AND GRANTS BY THE UNITED STATES AND OTHERS

Since World War II a number of countries have provided capital to the LDCs. An international organization, the International Bank for Reconstruction and Development (the **World Bank**), was created largely for this purpose. It has 155 member countries, each providing an amount of capital related to its wealth; for instance, the United States has contributed about 21 percent of the total, while Japan and West Germany have supplied 15 percent and 11 percent, respectively. The Bank makes loans that finance its bonds and has acted as guarantor of repayment to encourage some private lending. Since its inception the Bank has approved loans totalling $203.1 billion to 142 countries, mostly for infrastructure,

[10]Not everyone agrees with this conclusion. There are those who have argued that participation of LDCs in international trade is bad for them because it weakens their capacity to develop as self-reliant, mature economies. It is believed that new manufacturing industries in the LDCs will not take off without protection from foreign competition; that development of raw material exports creates a politically powerful vested interest that inhibits manufacturing; and that foreign participation in trade and production of exports inhibits domestic investment and the development of local entrepreneurship.

In this view, LDCs are therefore held back by international trade and they would do better to integrate regionally and develop their own home markets without foreigners, who also bring unsuitable habits, tastes, and technology, and impart a crippling inferiority complex to the LDCs.

dams, communications, and transportation. In addition, it provided technical assistance and planning advice.[11]

United States' loans and grants have exceeded the total given by all other countries and international agencies, with U.S. interest and repayment terms generally far more generous than those of other governments. However, the bulk of the assistance provided by the United States has gone to a small number of countries, such as India, Pakistan, South Korea, and Turkey.

During the 1960s, our expenditures on aid ran to more than $3 billion per year. In the past decade, expenditures on foreign aid have become less popular politically, and the amounts provided consequently have gone down sharply and steadily from about half a percent of U.S. GDP in 1965 to about 0.2 percent of GDP in 1990.[12]

France, Great Britain, West Germany, and other industrialized countries now provide about $70 billion per year, which is about one percent of their combined GDPs. Japan, too, has recently begun to make substantial contributions; in 1989 it appropriated about $24.1 billion, or 1.3 percent of its GDP.[13] The Soviet Union also used to be a major source of assistance to the LDCs, providing, along with its associated countries, more than $3 billion per year, or about 0.25 percent of their GDP. The recent economic troubles and political upheavals in the former Soviet bloc make it hard to foresee what will happen to contributions from this source.

Many economists have advocated greater generosity in our assistance to LDCs. It is argued that an effective aid program that really helps the growth of LDCs will also serve our own interests. By making those countries more stable economically and politically, we can contribute to our own economic tranquility. By increasing the LDCs' power to buy and sell, we contribute to the prosperity of the entire world.

## CAN LDCs BREAK AWAY FROM POVERTY?

It is easy to jump to the conclusion that the economic problems of the LDCs are staggering and that the prospects of their ever catching up with the industrialized countries are negligible. Yet a number of LDCs and former LDCs have made enormous progress. In Africa, Nigeria, Senegal, and Ghana increased their GDPs during the late 1980s at a rate of about 5 to 6 percent a year, which is considerably faster than their population growth.[14] In the Americas, Costa Rica's performance has been comparable. Even more striking is the expansion of output in a number of places in the Far East—particularly Hong Kong, Taiwan, South Korea, and Singapore, where prosperity is unprecedented and economic activity is expanding at an astonishing rate. Here, per capita GDPs have been growing at a rate of 6.5 percent a year and more. These economies have progressed to a point that makes it inappropriate to continue to classify them as LDCs.

---

[11]World Bank, *The World Bank Annual Report 1991*, Washington, D.C.: 1991.

[12]U.S. Bureau of the Census, *Statistical Abstract of the United States, 1992*, Washington, D.C.: U.S. Government Printing Office, 1992 and *Economic Report of the President, January 1993*, Washington, D.C.: U.S. Government Printing Office, 1993.

[13]*Ibid.*

[14]World Bank, *The World Bank Annual Report*, Washington, D.C.: various years

But the most impressive case is that of Japan. Many of your professors will remember clearly when U.S. business feared the flood of goods produced by cheap Japanese labor, and when the label "made in Japan" suggested inexpensive and shoddy merchandise. From one of the world's impoverished countries, Japan has risen to one of the world's richest. Its goods are now feared by American manufacturers not because they are produced and sold so cheaply, but because their quality is so high. Japanese cars and sophisticated electronic equipment find a ready market in the United States. And as a result, per capita income in Japan has surpassed that in Great Britain.

Clearly, a less developed country need not lag behind forever.

## *Summary*

1. If growth is evaluated in terms of its effect upon the well-being of individuals, a country's economic growth should be measured in terms of *per capita* income, not in terms of GDP or some other index of total output of the economy.
2. A rapidly rising population poses a threat to growth of per capita incomes.
3. On our finite planet, **exponential growth** (growth at a constant percentage rate) is, in general, impossible except for relatively brief periods.
4. Increases in growth depend heavily on entrepreneurship, accumulation of capital equipment, and research and development.
5. Saving is necessary for the accumulation of resources with which to produce factories, machinery, and other capital equipment. Thus, saving is a critical requisite for growth, particularly in less developed countries.
6. Many observers argue that even if continued growth does not lead to catastrophically rapid depletion of resources (as some have predicted), its desirability is nevertheless questionable because it produces pollution, overcrowding, and many other undesirable consequences.
7. Those who favor growth argue that without it there is no chance of ridding the world of poverty.
8. Standards of living in many **LDCs** are extremely low; per capita incomes that are equivalent to $1500 a year are not uncommon. Life expectancy is low and daily living is very difficult, particularly for women.
9. GDP and per capita incomes in the LDCs grew considerably in the 1970s, though in many cases they slowed in the 1980s.
10. Nevertheless, the gap between family incomes in the less developed and the industrialized countries has continued to widen.
11. In many LDCs, population continues to grow much faster than that in the industrialized countries.
12. Growth in the LDCs is impeded by shortages of capital caused by poverty, traditions that do not encourage investment, rapid population growth, poor education, unemployment, lack of **entrepreneurship**, and government impediments to business.
13. Industrialized countries can help the LDCs by providing capital through loans and grants, by offering training and education to people from those lands, and by encouraging freedom of trade with the LDCs.
14. In the period after World War II many countries, including the United States and the Soviet Union, provided large amounts of money to the LDCs in the form of loans and grants.
15. Several international organizations, most notably the **World Bank**, have been organized to provide economic assistance to the LDCs.

## *Key Concepts and Terms*

Output per capita
Exponential growth
Social infrastructure
Exchange between present and future consumption
Embodied growth
Disembodied growth
Less developed countries (LDCs)
Growth rate in GDP vs. per capita income
Multinational corporations
Disguised unemployment
Entrepreneurship
Brain drain
World Bank

## *Questions for Review*

1. Which do you think has the higher total GDP, Pakistan or Luxembourg? Which has the higher per capita GDP? In which do you think people are better off economically?
2. Suppose population grows at a constant exponential rate and doubles every 12 years. How many times will it have grown in 36 years? How many years does it require to expand to 32 times its initial level?
3. Can you think of any innovations that permit growth without proportionate increases in use of inputs?
4. Name as many undesirable consequences of growth as you can think of.
5. Are the undesirable consequences of growth more likely to be considered serious in a less developed country or in an industrialized country? Why?
6. To many families living in less developed countries, an income equivalent to $2000 per year is considered a high standard of living. Can you make up a budget for a U.S. family of four earning $2000 a year?
7. Explain how it is possible for the per capita income of an LDC to grow at a faster rate than that in the United States and yet for the dollar difference between the incomes of average families in both countries to increase. Can you give a numerical example showing how this happens?
8. Discuss the advantages and disadvantages to an LDC of a U.S. manufacturing company investing in that country.
9. If you were economic adviser to the president of an LDC, what might you suggest that he or she do to encourage increases in saving and investment?
10. No one knows what encourages or discourages the supply of entrepreneurs. Do you have any ideas about policies that may be capable of stimulating entrepreneurship?
11. Name some countries in which entrepreneurship seems to be abundant these days and some countries in which it seems to be scarce. What is your impression about what is happening to the supply of entrepreneurs in the United States?
12. It has been noted that crime overlords who organize drug empires and the managements of law firms that specialize in stimulation of litigation are often, in fact, successful entrepreneurs. Discuss whether these persons contribute to the growth of their economies.
13. What have you read in the newspapers and heard from other sources about the Japanese "growth miracle?" What does it portend for the future of the Japanese economy? For that of the United States?
14. Puerto Rico is reported to have the highest per capita income of any Latin American economy. What does this suggest about possible consequences of statehood for the island? How do you reconcile that statistic with the low economic status of many Puerto Ricans living in the continental United States?
15. Puerto Rico has a per-capita income far lower than that of any other state in the United States. What do you conclude by comparing this fact with those in the previous question?

Chapter 39

# COMPARATIVE ECONOMIC SYSTEMS: WHAT ARE THE CHOICES?

*They pretend to pay us, and we pretend to work.*

**POLISH FOLK DEFINITION OF COMMUNISM**

*There is no worthy alternative to the market mechanism as the method for coordinating economic activities.*

**LEONID ABALKIN (Deputy Prime Minister of the Soviet Union, 1989)**

On December 25, 1991, the unthinkable happened. The Soviet flag was lowered on the Kremlin in Moscow, signalling the end of the Soviet Union as a nation and the emergence of Russia and the Commonwealth of Independent States based upon the former Soviet republics. For decades, the rivalry between Western capitalism and Soviet-style socialism had dominated the world's geopolitical scene. This competition had important economic, political, and military dimensions. However, economic disarray in the planned socialist economic systems took its toll, and by the beginning of the 1990s, communism was dead in Eastern Europe and moribund in the former Soviet Union. The era of **transition**, began as one formerly socialist country after another began to replace its planned system with a market system. This transition process illustrates in a very stark way that a society can in fact *choose* an economic system. In a somewhat less dramatic way, the same thing is going in other parts of the world, such as Latin America. ¶ Here in the United States, we tend to take economic institutions as given and immutable. But they are not. In fact, there are many ways to practice capitalism, as the differing economic structures of Japan and Western Europe illustrate. A century ago, our country had no social security system, no income tax, no central bank, no antitrust laws, and hardly any labor unions. More than likely, the structure of the U.S. economy will change at least as much in the next century as it did in the last. But in which directions?

In this chapter we examine how a society might choose among *alternative economic systems.* The first parts of the chapter sketch out the elements of the two major choices that must be made by every society: Should economic activity be organized through *markets*, or by government *plan*? And should industry be *privately* or *publicly* owned? As we shall see, there are arguments on both sides of each question; so it is not surprising that different countries at different times have made different choices.

In the last sections of the chapter, we describe some of the actual choices that have been made in the contemporary world. We examine changes in the former Soviet Union and in the People's Republic of China, two socialist nations which are transforming themselves in quite different ways. Then we turn to a notable example of a successful capitalist country that does things rather differently than we do: Japan. Does the United States have much to learn from the experiences of these other countries? Read this chapter and then decide.

## ECONOMIC SYSTEMS: TWO IMPORTANT DISTINCTIONS

Economic systems can be distinguished along many lines, but two seem most important. The first is, *How is economic activity coordinated—by the market or by the plan?* The question does not, of course, demand an "either, or" answer. Rather the choice extends over a range running from laissez faire to rigid central planning, with many, many gradations in between.

Society must decide to what extent it wants decisions *decentralized*—that is, made by individual businesses and consumers, each acting in their own self-interest—and to what extent it wants decisions *centralized*, so that businesses and consumers act more "in the national interest." It is worth emphasizing that most types of planning involve some degree of *coercion*. But this term is not necessarily pejorative; all societies, for example, coerce people not to steal from their neighbors.

The second crucial distinction among economic systems concerns *who owns the means of production*. Specifically, are they privately owned by individuals or publicly owned by the state? Again, there is a wide range of choice and, to our knowledge, there are no examples of nations at either the **capitalist** extreme where all property is privately owned or at the **socialist** extreme where no private property whatever is permitted.

**CAPITALISM** is a method of economic organization in which private individuals own the means of production, either directly or indirectly through corporations.

**SOCIALISM** is a method of economic organization in which the state owns the means of production.

For example, while most industries are privately owned in the United States, a few are not. And owners of businesses often face restrictions on what they can do with their capital. Automobile companies must comply with environmental and safety regulations. Private communication and transportation companies may have both their prices and conditions of service regulated by the government. And even in China, where large enterprises are all publicly owned, anyone who can afford it can own a car, hold a bank account, or own small businesses.

People tend to merge the two distinctions and think of capitalist economies as those with both a great deal of privately owned property *and* heavy reliance on

## *East Meets West in Europe: Behind the Former Iron Curtain*

When the Soviet Union loosened its grip over Eastern Europe, both political democracy and free markets broke out with astonishing speed. Poland and Hungary were in the vanguard. By 1990, both had freely elected governments and were headed toward market capitalism, though by different routes.

**Poland's Big Bang**

The communists left behind an economy in which per-capita gross national product had declined to less than one-fifth of the Western European level. Inflation was raging at several thousand percent per year. The shops were empty.

Solidarity's economic team . . . eschewed piecemeal reform, in favor of a comprehensive program to create a market economy . . . In just 75 days, some stunning successes have been achieved. . . Hyperinflation has stopped dead. . . With prices now free to balance supply and demand, products returned to the shops . . . the six-hour gas lines of December have vanished. . . . In industry, scarce and vitally needed materals . . . are suddently arriving from Sweden, Finland, and Germany.

But these great successes are matched by grave risks. State firms are no longer coddled. . . Absenteeism has fallen in half as workers fear for their jobs. . . Yet, with much of the work force in uncompetitive companies and in unneeded sectors, unemployment and plant closings have started to soar. Unemployment could jump by as much as 10 percent of the labor force in the coming months. . .

Factories . . . have been cut off from markets for 40 years [and] know next to nothing about . . . export markets. Even when their technology is adequate and their workers skilled, after four decades of socialism, Poland's enterprises lack one key factor of production: skilled managers who know how to operate in a market environment. . . .

**Hungary's Dual System**

A thin brick wall dividing a big factory building still separates East from West in this light-industrial town near Hungary's border with Yugoslavia.

On one side of the building, two-thirds of state-owned Texcoop's obsolete knitting machines sit idle for lack of orders. The rest churn out frumpy 100%-acrylic sweaters for the Soviet Union. The plant, greasy and gloomy, has lost money ever since it opened.

On the other side of the building, a freshly scrubbed, brightly lit Levi Strauss factory hums to piped-in jazz. Dozens of women hunch over new American sewing machines and swiftly affix pockets, sew up inseams, and attach zippers. . . . The women, all of whom worked for Texcoop until last year, now earn more than twice as much money. The plant was profitable from Day One. Levi earned back its total investment in less than a year.

Eastern Europe still has far more factories like Texcoop's than like Levi's, but every day more ventures bringing Western management, cash and free-market fervor are being planned. Not only will they make jeans, light bulbs, and bicycles, but, economists say, the competition they create will eventually force state companies to either shape up, sell out or close. . . .

The test of this theory is furthest along in Hungary, the first East bloc country to allow joint ventures on realistic terms with the West, the first to allow its people to own private property, the first to establish an embryonic stock exchange. . . .

SOURCE: Jeffrey Sachs, "Management Positions Available: Call Warsaw," *The Wall Street Journal*, March 21, 1990.
NOTE: Professor Sachs was the major Western economic adviser to Solidarity.
SOURCE: Philip Rezvin, "Ventures in Hungary Test Theory that West Can Uplift East Bloc," *The Wall Street Journal*, April 5, 1990.

free markets. By the same token, socialist economics typically are thought of as highly planned. Recent events in the former Soviet bloc reinforced this view, since several of those countries rejected both public ownership and planning simultaneously. However:

Even though there is an undeniable association between the degree of socialism in a country and the degree to which it plans its economy, it is a mistake to regard these two features as equivalent. Socialism can exist with markets and capitalism can exist with rigid state planning. So, in *thinking* about a society's *choice* among economic systems, it is best to keep the two distinctions separate.

History also holds examples of planned, capitalist economies—such as Germany under Hitler and Italy under Mussolini. Argentina under Juan Peron was another example, though far less extreme. To a much lesser extent, Japan and the other "Asian tigers" also plan their capitalist economies—apparently with great success (see pages 993–97 below). And France has for years practiced a mild form of central planning which they call "indicative planning."

We are not trying to suggest that capitalist economies are typically as heavily planned as socialist ones. In fact, they are not. But it is useful to view the choices between planning and markets and between capitalism and socialism as two choices, not one. We take them up in turn.

In the real world, there are many systems which in fact would be appropriately termed "mixed systems" lying in the middle of our spectrum of system alternatives. Many of these systems have attracted considerable attention. For example, Yugoslavia once had a unique combination of social ownership via the Communist Party and a market economy with the added feature of **workers' management**. Sweden, on the other hand, is a quite traditional mix of market capitalist arrangements but often cast as a **welfare state** where many services are provided in the public sector through what by our standards are relatively high levels of taxation.

Under a system of **WORKERS' MANAGEMENT**, the employees of an enterprise make most of the decisions normally reserved for management.

## THE MARKET OR THE PLAN? SOME ISSUES

The choice between **planning** and reliance on **free markets** requires an understanding of just what the market accomplishes and where its strengths and weaknesses lie. Since these issues have been the focal point of much of this book, our review can be concise.

***What goods to produce and how much of each.*** In a market economy, consumers determine which goods and services shall be provided, and in what quantities, by registering their dollar votes. Items that are overproduced will fall in price, while items in short supply will rise in price. These price movements act as *signals* to profit-seeking firms, which then produce larger amounts of the goods whose prices rise and less of the goods whose prices fall. This mechanism is called **consumer sovereignty**.

**CONSUMER SOVEREIGNTY** means that consumer preferences determine what goods shall be produced and in what amounts.

Of course, consumers are not absolute monarchs, even in market economies. Governments interfere with the price mechanism in many ways—taxing some goods and services and subsidizing others. Such interferences certainly alter the bill of goods that the economy produces. We have also learned that in the presence of externalities the price system may send out false signals, leading to inappropriate levels of output for certain commodities.

***How to produce each good.*** In a market economy, firms decide on the production technique, guided once again by the price system. Inputs that are in short supply will be assigned high prices by the market. This will encourage producers to use them sparingly. Other inputs whose supply is more abundant will be priced lower, which will encourage firms to use them.

Once again, the same two qualifications apply: government taxes and subsidies alter relative prices, and externalities may make the price system malfunction. But on the whole, the market system has yet to meet its match as an engine of productive efficiency, as the formerly socialist economies learned.

***How income is distributed.*** The price system, by setting the levels of wages, interest rates, and profits, determines the distribution of income among individuals in a market economy. As we have stressed (especially in Chapter 17), there is no reason to expect the resulting income distribution to be "good" from an ethical point of view. And, in fact, the evidence shows that capitalist market economies produce a considerable degree of inequality.

This is certainly one of capitalism's weak points, though there are many ways for the government to alter the distribution of income without destroying either free markets or private property (for example, through progressive income taxation or a negative income tax, both of which were discussed in Chapter 17). It is also noteworthy that some planned economies have had rather unequal income distributions.

***Economic growth.*** The rate of economic growth depends fundamentally upon how much society decides to save and invest. In a free-market economy, these decisions are left to private firms and individuals, who determine how much of their current income they will consume today and how much they will invest for the future. Once again, however, government policies can influence these choices by, for example, making investment more or less attractive through tax incentives.

***Business fluctuations.*** A market economy is subject to periods of boom and bust, to inflation and unemployment. This holds not only in capitalist market economies like the United States, but also in socialist market economies. Interestingly, the highly planned but mostly capitalist economy of France showed little evidence of business cycle problems from 1958 until the mid-1970s. So it seems that the business cycle, which Marx dubbed one of the fundamental flaws of *capitalism*, is really a problem for *market economies*, be they capitalist or socialist.

Let us now go over this list again, seeing how each question is resolved in a planned economy, and comparing this to a market economy.

***What to produce and how much.*** Under central planning, the bill of goods that society produces is selected by planners rather than by consumers. Whether this is a strength or a weakness depends upon your point of view. Certainly, consumer sovereignty can lead to some bizarre products, the kinds of things that social reformers find offensive: designer jeans, junk food, low-quality television programming, and the like. But few of us would prefer the old Soviet-style system, which seemed incapable of providing the goods people wanted. Chronic shortages of ordinary consumer goods were a consistent feature of life in Eastern Europe and the Soviet Union—and one of the major causes of popular discontentment.

***How to produce.*** Planned economies can allow plant managers to choose a production technique, or they can let central planners do it instead. Under traditional Soviet-style planning, plant managers had little discretion; and this led to such monumental inefficiencies as production curtailments caused by lack of materials, poor quality, and high production costs. Indeed, this may have been the most serious weakness of socialist planning. The truth is that no incentive system has yet been designed that can match the profit motive of competitive firms for keeping costs down. Giving managers more freedom of choice and appropriate market incentives has been a consistent theme of economic reform, both in Russia and all over Eastern Europe.

***How income is distributed.*** The distribution of income is always influenced by government to some extent. Even in basically market economies like ours, the government taxes different people at different rates and pays transfer payments to others, seeking thereby to mitigate the inequality that capitalism and free markets tend to generate. Governments in planned economies do the same things, only more so. For instance, they may try to tamper directly with the income distribution by having planners, rather than the market, set relative wage rates. This, however, leads to shortages and surpluses of particular types of labor. So even in the former Soviet Union relative wages were established more or less by supply and demand.

***Economic growth.*** In general, planned economies have more direct control over their growth rates than do unplanned ones because the state can determine the volume of investment. They therefore can engineer very high growth rates, if they choose to—an option which both Stalin's Russia and Mao's China exercised successfully. Whether such rapid growth is a good idea, however, is another question, especially when it is paid for by sacrificing personal freedom or even by bloodshed. Furthermore, the growth performance of the U.S.S.R. and Eastern Europe was extremely poor in the in the 1970s and 1980s, while some of the fastest growth rates were turned in by the market economies of Japan, Taiwan, and Hong Kong.

***Business fluctuations.*** Business fluctuations are not much of a problem for highly planned economies. This is because total spending in such economies is controlled tightly by the planners and is not permitted to get far out of line with the economy's capacity to produce. So the business cycle was not traditionally a serious problem. However, under contemporary transition arrangements, macroeconomic issues have become dominant.

## THE MARKET OR THE PLAN: THE SCOREBOARD

As we look back over this list, what do we find? Concerning *what to produce*, adherents to Western values will give a clear edge to the market, though conceding the need to curb some of its more flagrant abuses. And, apparently, this view has now taken hold in the former Soviet bloc as well. As to *productive efficiency*, almost everyone now seems to recognize the superiority of the market mechanism—as the opening quotations of this chapter suggest. But when we consider the *distribution of income*, we find that all societies have decided to plan; they differ only in degree.

*High growth*, it seems, can be achieved with or without planning. Here an advanced nation will pause to question whether faster is always better. But among the less developed countries, which often lack the savings and the financial markets needed to channel funds into their most productive uses, the goal of rapid development is typically of paramount importance. These countries may have little choice but to plan. Finally, in managing *business fluctuations*, there is no question that planned economies can do much better.

The results of our scoreboard are clearly mixed. Do we therefore score the contest a tie? Hardly, as the switch of one country after another from planning to markets attests. What we do conclude is the following:

The market has both strengths and weaknesses. Different countries—with their different political systems, value judgments, traditions, and aspirations—will draw the boundaries between plan and market in different places. But it now appears that almost all countries believe that the market mechanism should bear the primary burden of deciding which products to produce and how best to produce them.

## CAPITALISM OR SOCIALISM?

Although the choice between capitalism and socialism seems to excite more ideological fervor, it is probably much less important than the choice between the market and the plan.

*If* it could design an appropriate incentive structure, a socialist *market* economy could do just as well as a capitalist market economy in terms of producing the right set of goods in the most efficient way. However, we have emphasized the word "if" to underscore the fact that designing such an incentive system may be quite difficult under socialism, even when markets are free.

Lacking the profit motive, a socialist society must provide incentives, material or otherwise, for its plant managers to perform well. This has proved difficult enough. But a still deeper problem caused by the absence of the profit motive is the need to maintain inventiveness, innovation, and risk-taking in an ever-changing world. Socialist nations, in which large accumulations of personal wealth are impossible, are noticeably low on "high rollers." This, many people feel, is why they were left behind in the 1980s. It may also be why Soviet President Mikhail Gorbachev felt a need to shake up his lethargic economy in the last 1980s.

Income distribution under socialism is naturally more equal than under capitalism simply because the profits of industry do not go to a small group of stockholders but instead are dispersed among the workers or among the populace as a whole. However, if supply and demand rules the labor market, a socialist nation may have as much inequality in the distribution of labor income as a capitalist economy does—and for the same reasons: to attract workers into risky, or highly skilled, or difficult occupations.

The capitalist–socialist cleavage is much more important in regard to the issue of economic growth. To oversimplify, under capitalism it is the capitalists who determine the growth rate, while under socialism it is the state. Still, government incentives can prod capitalists to invest more; and socialist bureaucrats cannot always get enterprises to pursue growth goals vigorously. Examples of both fast and slow growth can be found under both systems.

Finally, as we have said, the severity of business fluctuations in a country depends much more on whether its economy is planned or unplanned than on whether its industries are publicly or privately owned.

## SOCIALISM, PLANNING, AND FREEDOM

There is, however, a *noneconomic* aspect that is of the utmost importance in choosing between capitalism and socialism, or between the market and the plan, an issue whose importance was dramatized by the events in Eastern Europe in 1989 and in Russia in 1991: *individual freedom.*

Planning must by necessity involve some degree of coercion; if it does not, then the plan may amount to little more than wishful thinking. In the extreme case of a command economy (the U.S.S.R. under Stalin, Nazi Germany), the abridgment of personal freedom is both painful and obvious. Less rigid forms of planning involve commensurately smaller infringements of individual rights, infringements that many people find tolerable.

Even within a basic framework of free markets, some activities may be banned—such as prostitution and selling liquor to minors. Other economic activities may be compelled by law; safety devices in automobiles and labeling requirements on foods and drugs are two good examples. Each of these is a kind of planning, and each limits the freedom of some people. Yet most of these restrictions command broad public support in the United States.

Taxation is a still more subtle form of coercion. Most people do not view taxes as seriously impairing their personal freedom because, even though tax laws may make them pay for the privilege, they remain free to choose the courses of action that suit them best. Indeed, this is one major reason why economists generally favor taxes over quotas and outright prohibitions. It is true, however, that taxation can be a potent tool for changing individual behavior. As Chief Justice John Marshall pointed out with characteristic perspicacity, "The power to tax involves the power to destroy."

Individual freedom is also involved in the choice between capitalism and socialism. After all, under socialism there are many more restrictions on what a person can do with his or her wealth than there are under capitalism. On the other hand, the poorest people in a capitalist society may find little joy in their "freedom" to go homeless and hungry.

Once again, it would be a mistake to paint the issue in black and white. Under rigid authoritarian planning, the restrictions on individual liberties are so severe that they are probably intolerable to most people with Western values. That, presumably, is why many people in Eastern Europe reacted so strongly to the whiff of freedom. But more moderate and relaxed forms of planning—such as in France or Japan—seem compatible with personal freedoms.

Similarly, a doctrinaire brand of socialism that bans all private property (even the clothes on your back?) would entail a major loss of liberty. But a country with a large socialized sector can be basically free; the French, for example, do not feel notably less free than do Americans. And citizens of some countries with largely capitalist economies, such as South Korea or Taiwan, did not enjoy political freedom for years.

The real question is not *whether* we want to allow elements of socialism or planning to abridge our personal freedoms, but by *how much.*

Just as your freedom to extend your arm is limited by the proximity of your neighbor's chin, the freedom to build a factory need not extend to building it in the midst of a residential neighborhood. Just as freedom of speech does not justify yelling "Fire!" in a crowded movie theater when there is no fire, freedom of enterprise does not imply the right to monopolize trade. So, not surprisingly, different societies have struck the balance between the market and the plan, and between socialism and capitalism, in different places.

Up to now, we have emphasized the performance of different types of economic systems. But the world now faces a quite different set of issues. Since the end of the Soviet Union in December 1991 and the emergence of Russia and the Commonwealth of Independent States, the focus has been on *transition* from plan to market. But we cannot hope to understand this complex process unless we first learn how the old centrally planned systems functioned. To this end, we examine the former Soviet Union and China. Finally we discuss Japan as an important example of growth and prosperity under capitalism, but with interesting variations.

## THE ADMINISTRATIVE COMMAND ECONOMY: THE OLD SOVIET UNION

In November of 1917, a determined group of Bolsheviks led by V. I. Lenin overthrew a short-lived democratic government to establish a new government dominated by the Communist party. The Soviet Union was a relatively backward country, however, and its economy was exhausted by a civil war. So, seeing the new nation on the verge of both political and economic collapse by 1921, Lenin ushered in his New Economic Policy: a brief era of open discussion and dialogue in which markets returned and the economy prospered.

But this was not socialism, and Joseph Stalin chose a very different—and costly—course when he rose to power after Lenin's death. Starting in 1928, Stalin implemented what would be one of the most brutal regimes of modern times. Two major decisions were taken. First, Stalin forcibly introduced socialized agriculture in a process known as *collectivization*. Second, along with nationalization of the means of production, the market was eliminated and *central planning* was introduced as the mechanism for allocating resources.

### PLANNING AND THE COMMAND ECONOMY

The events of the early Stalinist era left a lasting mark on the Soviet economy, and indeed introduced changes that would plague transition efforts in the 1990s. Some of these characteristics are worth emphasizing:

- The economic system was *hierarchial* and *centralized*. The basic goals of economic activity were determined by the Communist party and left to be fulfilled by enterprise managers at the local level.
- Stalinist economic policies stressed maximal economic growth, with emphasis on *heavy industry* and, especially, on the *military*.
- The system was largely *quantity-directed*, with only limited use of the price mechanism and an attempt to replace private consumption by social consumption.
- Sectoral priorities were evident. Heavy industry was important, consumer goods and agriculture much less so.

### THE ROAD TO *PERESTROIKA:* WHY DID THE SOVIET ECONOMY FAIL?

Although we might well disagree with the priorities Stalin established and the brutal methods he used to achieve them, the Soviet economy did grow rapidly and the U.S.S.R. became a major world power with a significant military base in a relatively short span of time. Then things started to go wrong.

While historians have not yet rendered their verdict, we already know quite a lot about why the Soviet economic system failed. Indeed, many of the issues were discussed earlier in this chapter.

Soviet leaders used harsh methods to change priorities and raise production rapidly. Economic growth was in fact achieved, but at great cost, both in terms of human sacrifice and reduced attention to consumer well-being. While their leaders always argued that sacrifice in the present would bring well-being in the future, for most Soviet citizens the bright future never came. Why not?

We know from historical experience that many countries have gone through a period of rapid—and sometimes painful—economic development. But, ultimately, growth must be derived from better use of available resources rather than more and more inputs. The Soviet economy never achieved the sorts of efficiency that are commonplace in market economies.

Although the list of reasons is long, a few bear mentioning. The old Soviet system, largely because of its reliance on rules, did not adapt well to new technology. Thus the growth of productivity stagnated. Moreover, there were serious incentive failures. Many would argue that incentives cannot be socialized; and, as time passed, workers became irritated that money could not be translated into consumer goods and improved standards of living. The system, in a word, became ossified.

## CENTRAL PLANNING IN THE COMMAND ECONOMY

Let us see, briefly, how the old central planning system worked.

The structure of the Soviet economic system was in many ways similar to the hierarchy of a giant corporation.

At the top was a single strongman or a ruling clique. The political leadership functioned like the chairman of the board, setting overall policy objectives, but had much more absolute authority than the chairman of any corporation. Next came the State Planning Commission (*Gosplan*) which translated the goals and priorities established by the top echelons of the Communist party into Five-Year and One-Year Plans.

The **Five-Year Plans** set the nation's basic strategy for resource allocation: How much for investment? How much for military procurement and for scientific research? They also provided guidelines for the distribution of these totals among the various industries (Would there be more cars or more refrigerators?), and often included specific large construction projects, such as hydroelectric power plants. Much attention was paid, both in the West and the U.S.S.R., to the numerical goals posted by these plans and to the Soviet Union's failure to meet them.

The Five-Year Plans were too vague to serve as blueprints for action. This job was left to the **One-Year Plans**—enormous sets of documents that covered almost every facet of Soviet economic life. In fact, the One-Year Plans were so detailed and complex that they were rarely completed until well into the year. Sometimes they were never completed at all.

Planners translated broad national goals into specific directives for subordinate ministries, agencies, and regional authorities, which then would oversee the day-to-day management of particular industries and regions. As the plan passed down from one level of the hierarchy to the next, the lower level would constantly supply the higher level with both data and suggestions for changes in tactics.

Several more layers of bureaucracy intervened before reaching the level of the enterprise. Enterprise managers in the U.S.S.R. had less authority than their counterparts in the United States. They were expected to carry out directives handed down from above, fill their quotas, and send information back up the hierarchical ladder. They were bureaucrats, not entrepreneurs.

Communications within the hierarchy were predominantly vertical. Orders flowed down from top to bottom, while data flowed up from bottom to top. Since the data requirements were immense, and the number of layers within the bureacracy so large, the problems of accurate data transmission and processing were monumental. It is precisely this problem, of course, that the market mechanism solves so neatly: prices convey most of the information that anyone needs.

To see how difficult it is for a planner to accomplish what the market does routinely—consider the following simple example. Suppose three industries (called A, B, and C) use ball bearings. The output targets for each industry will imply a corresponding need for inputs of ball bearings. This quantity of ball bearings must, of course, be produced by the ball-bearing industry. This sounds simple until you realize that the ball-bearing industry itself needs input, and that some of these inputs may be the outputs of industries A, B, and C. So if, for example, the production of ball bearings is be increased, more steel and machinery may be required; and these additional outputs will require more ball bearings as inputs; and so on and so on.

To appreciate the complexity of the task faced by Soviet planners, try your hand at the following simple example. Suppose there are only three goods—ball bearings, steel, and automobiles—and that the national plan calls for consumers to get no ball bearings, $\frac{1}{2}$ unit of steel, and 1 unit of automobiles. How much must each of the three industries produce to achieve material balance?

To answer this, you must first know the input requirements of each industry. Suppose the inputs required *per unit of output* of each industry are as follows:

| OUTPUT | NECESSARY INPUTS |
|---|---|
| Ball bearings (one unit) | $\frac{1}{2}$ unit of steel *plus* |
| | $\frac{1}{4}$ unit of automobiles |
| Steel (one unit) | $\frac{1}{4}$ unit of ball bearings *plus* |
| | $\frac{1}{4}$ unit of steel *plus* |
| | $\frac{1}{4}$ unit of automobiles |
| Automobiles (one unit) | $\frac{1}{3}$ unit of ball bearings *plus* |
| | $\frac{1}{2}$ unit of steel *plus* |
| | $\frac{1}{6}$ unit of automobiles |

Use trial and error to figure out the necessary production levels for each industry. You will quickly see that the problem is quite difficult.[1]

The mathematical technique devised to solve problems like this is called *input–output analysis*,[2] and the preceding little problem is easily solved by this method. But Soviet planners faced a problem of this character with, literally, tens of thousands of commodities. Even a giant computer would be pressed to carry out the necessary calculations, even if all the data were available (which they were not). So a perfect solution to the problem was out of the question. In practice, planners relied on trial and error and sought to avoid as many shortages as they possibly could.

## CHANGING THE COMMAND ECONOMY

The economic system that we have just described was plagued by many problems. But they can all be summarized by pointing to the lack of productivity growth and the consequent slowing of the growth of output in the Soviet Union. While it is difficult to pinpoint the precise causes of the Soviet growth slowdown, several contributing factors are clear. First, central planning, while powerful, was also crude. It did not adapt well, for example, to changing technology nor to the increasing complexity of modern economic life.

Second, Soviet planning emphasized gross output, with little attention to issues of quality, cost minimization, and the like. So, where managerial bonuses depended upon fulfilling the plan, managers wanted "easy" targets and were quite willing to do dysfunctional things to achieve their quotas. For example, if materials were scarce, they would be hoarded, thus worsening the shortages. Often huge *buffer stocks* were used to absorb shocks and mistakes.

Third, the Soviet system inhibited change, since that might threaten fulfillment of the plan. The most critical aspect of this scenario was the limited attention accorded to *technological change*. Thus even when new technology could be imported, diffusion of these new ideas did not take place. There were no incentives, and the implementation of new ideas tended to disrupt plan fulfillment.

Attempts to reform the command economy go back as far as the Khrushchev era of the 1950s. But they were almost always superficial in character—designed to sustain the basic features of the command system. And they were always implemented on a limited scale. As a result, these waves of "reform" had little or no effect on the performance of the Soviet economy. Thus, from the 1950s onward, the rate of growth of output declined on an almost continuous basis—as did productivity growth.

Judged against this background, it is not surprising that there was genuine excitement when Mikhail Gorbachev assumed power in 1985 and announced ***perestroika*** (restructuring) and ***glasnost*** (openness). Both seemed to imply that there would be fundamental changes in the Soviet system. Cast against the authoritarian background of the Soviet Union, the concept of *glasnost*, which involved the expansion of democratic ideas in both the political and economic spheres seemed to be a major departure. Moreover, combined with *perestroika*, which involved major changes in the Soviet economy ranging from less planning to greater managerial autonomy to decentralization of foreign trade deci-

---

[1]The answer is: 2 units of ball bearings, 4 units of steel, and 3 units of automobiles.

[2]Input–output analysis was discussed in Chapter 10, pages 254–57.

sions, the Gorbachev concept of radical reform seemed to be an appropriate prescription.

But, in the end, *perestroika* failed. In a sense, *perestroika* was another partial reform designed to sustain the socialist economic system. Moreover, as with previous attempts at reform, implementation encountered resistance from the entrenched bureaucracy. Even the famous 500-day plans of the latter Gorbachev era failed. Only when Boris Yeltsin gradually asserted his authority and his support for the transition to markets did the old Soviet system come to an end. From that point, the operative concept became **transition**—the movement from plan to market. This process had, of course, begun in Eastern Europe several years earlier.

## ECONOMIC SYSTEMS IN THE 1990s: THE PROBLEM OF TRANSITION

The concept of transition implies not changing or modifying an existing system to make it work better, but rather replacing it with a different economic system. Typically, we have observed the replacement of plan by market. This process, as we shall see, is difficult and complex.

Although replacing planning by markets is a relatively new phenomenon, for which there is limited historical precedent and practical experience, the basic elements of change are nevertheless familiar, they can be categorized in four basic areas:

1. The microeconomy: privatization and markets;
2. The macroeconomy: money, budgets, and stabilization;
3. The international economy: trade liberalization; and
4. The safety net: social welfare policies.

**PRIVATIZATION** means transferring publicly owned property to private hands.

If planning is to be replaced by markets, assets must be placed in private hands—a process that came to be called **privatization**. But, in a country where the means of production had been confiscated from individual owners decades ago and held by the state, how is private ownership to be established? Whether by direct distribution of assets (for example, giving shares to workers or apartments to tenants) or more general voucher arrangements, privatization has been proceeding slowly and unevenly in Russia. Major problems include identification of ownership "rights," valuation of assets, unattractiveness of loss-making enterprises, and the shortage of managerial talent.

Developing a price system almost from scratch is also complicated. Most planned socialist economies had made minimal use of prices for allocating resources—even though economists had long agreed that prices are fundamental to the allocation process, and that such prices must reflect relative scarcities. What could be done in a formerly planned economy? Although it was agreed that privatization would eventually lead to the development of markets, intermediate steps were necessary. Thus prices were, to varying degrees, freed from control. Understandably, the result was overt inflation (which replaced the previously repressed inflation) and a sharp reduction in the real standard of living for most people. This was and remains a microeconomic issue with serious macroeconomic repercussions.

But, if privatization and the establishment of markets present complex problems, guiding the macroeconomy is no less difficult. Few of the formerly planned economies had used either monetary or fiscal policy in the manner typical of market economies. This led to some serious problems as the old systems began to disintegrate. Budget deficits increased because revenues could not be maintained with inappropriate tax systems and a collapsing political system. Since the vast bulk of employment had been in the state sector, a desire to avoid mass unemployment made it difficult to cut subsidies to loss-making enterprises. In the absence of financial markets as we know them, the reaction was generally inappropriate expansion of the money supply.

Although these issues seem to be inherently domestic in nature, there are also important international implications. One of the major features of the formerly planned socialist systems was their central control of both physical trade flows and their financing. When the planning system collapsed, trade decisions had to be removed from state control and decentralized to the enterprise level. It also became necessary to make the formerly nonconvertible currencies convertible to facilitate trade with the West.

The sorts of changes outlined above seem feasible, even if difficult to implement. But there are a variety of complicating issues.

- Probably the most dominant is that of *timing* and *complementarity*. Some countries, like Poland, followed the "big bang" philosophy and attempted to introduce the market regime as rapidly as possible. But Russia has followed a slower more *piecemeal* approach.
- Most economists agree that transition involves a reduction of output, and hence in standards of living, for some period of time. There must be limits to such a decline, however, even where there is initial popular support for change.
- Finally, the issue of **sequencing** must be considered. For example, it is evident that price controls must be removed, which will lead to rising prices. But, if markets are not yet established, and if enterprise managers have little if any experience in using prices to make allocational decisions, then will higher prices really call forth a greater quantity supplied? Or will the result be, instead, a lower level of living and, even worse, sudden rewards for those who are in a position to exercise monopoly power? Such problems are particularly acute where transition is taking place in a turbulent political setting.

**SEQUENCING** refers to the order in which changes are made.

Russia is now dealing with all these problems—and more.

## CHINA UNDER MAO: REVOLUTIONARY COMMUNISM

The People's Republic of China makes a good case study for this chapter because it has spent much of the last 40 years groping to find a suitable economic model. In this process, the Chinese have vividly confronted the fundamental questions of this chapter—socialism or capitalism? market or plan?—and have come up with different answers at different times.

Soon after the communist takeover in 1949, the Chinese economy was patterned on the Russian model and developed with Russian economic aid and technical expertise. In particular, China's leaders tried to institute a Soviet-style command economy with emphasis on rapid economic growth, particularly industrial growth.

But there were important differences stemming in part from ideology and in part from the fact that the Soviet model was not quite suitable for China. Probably the most important of these differences was the decision by Mao Tse-tung *not* to rely on **material incentives** to motivate the work force. Mao and the Chinese leadership looked with disdain at this "bourgeois" practice and preferred to motivate Chinese workers by exhortation, patriotism, and, where necessary, force.

Russian communism bent socialist doctrine to accommodate human nature. But Chinese communism for many years seemed determined to bend human nature to accommodate Maoist doctrine—to create "the new man in the new China," an effort that has now been abandoned.

A second, less important, difference is that Chinese planning was always less centralized than Russian planning. Provincial authorities have more power and discretion than they did in the U.S.S.R. This decentralization has deep roots in Chinese history, but may also have been due to China's immense size and economic backwardness in 1949. Without modern communications (and perhaps even *with* them), there was no way for planners in Beijing to control economic activity in the outlying provinces. Even today, this remains a problem for Beijing.

Chinese economic growth under the communist regime has proceeded in fits and starts.

The immediate problem after the Maoist takeover was to lift China out of wartime devastation and to establish communist institutions and values in a vast and semiliterate land. With Soviet assistance, the plan was apparently successful. But then Mao changed course.

China's next step, the **Great Leap Forward** (1958–1960), turned out to be a giant step backward—for several reasons. First, the Great Leap's production goals were unrealistically ambitious from the start. Second, because the ideologically pure "Reds" were in Mao's favor while the technocratic "experts" were not, the means selected for carrying out the Great Leap were more romantic than rational. Material incentives were deemphasized; China's vast economic planning structure was supposed to be decentralized, though controlled by the communist party; massive applications of brute labor were supposed to compensate for shortages of machinery and advanced technology.

In retrospect, the Great Leap Forward seems to have had three main effects. First, China's national income fell substantially (see Figure 39–1), particularly in the agricultural sector. It took years to make up for the losses of 1959–1962. Second, the ideological excesses of the period accelerated the growing schism between Russia and China. Third, it persuaded the Chinese leadership to throw out the "Reds" and bring back the "experts," signaling a return to rational economic calculation.

The early 1960s were marked by a return to the Soviet planning model, though some elements of decentralization from the Great Leap were retained. One departure from Soviet practice, however, was a greater emphasis on agriculture—no doubt a wise decision given China's resources. As a result, economic growth resumed.

Then, inexplicably, Mao changed China's course once again with the **Great Proletarian Cultural Revolution** (1965–1969). The "Reds" were in and the "experts" were out as never before. The infamous Red Guards were sent out to purge rightist elements from Chinese society, organize revolutionary cadres, and spread the teachings of Chairman Mao. If anyone worried about economic productivity in this environment, it did not show. By the summer of 1967, both the Chinese economy and other elements of Chinese society were in disarray. Output fell again, but recovered more quickly than it had from the Great Leap (see Figure 39–1).

**Figure 39-1** REAL NATIONAL INCOME IN THE PEOPLE'S REPUBLIC OF CHINA

While Chinese economic statistics are notoriously inaccurate, the official data are portrayed here. The Great Leap Forward and the Cultural Revolution stand out as major blemishes on the record of Chinese economic growth. Growth has been rapid and unbroken since 1976.

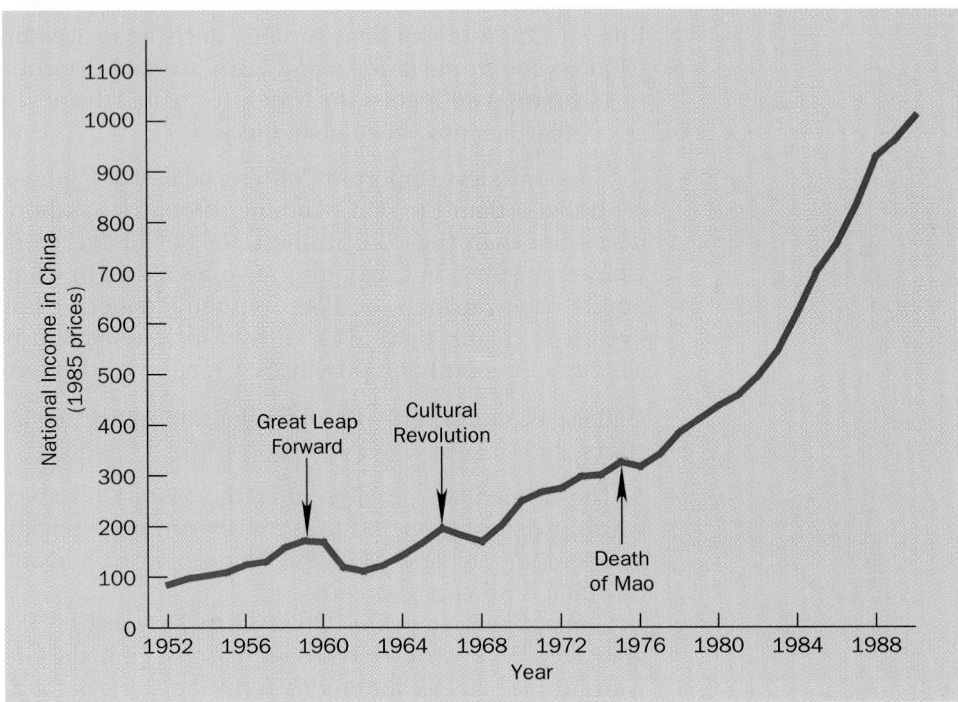


Things began to change in the 1970s. The period until Mao's death in 1976 was one of consolidation and economic growth. The Chinese revolutionary fever receded and, once again, the "experts" were rehabilitated. There was a restoration of material incentives and rational economic calculation—both of which were considered reactionary during the Cultural Revolution. In general, there was less politics and ideology and more economic growth.

## CHINA SINCE MAO: EXPLOSIVE GROWTH

After the death of Mao, the Chinese economic system again began to change rapidly. The leaders who succeeded Mao were less doctrinaire about their communism and far more interested in results. Both political and economic relations with the West were opened. Technicians and scientists who fell into disgrace in the Cultural Revolution were rehabilitated and put into positions of influence. In a startling reversal of roles, it was Mao and the revolutionaries whose wisdom was questioned.

Late in the 1970s, the Chinese began a series of reforms which amounted to stepping away from the Soviet model and adopting important features of the market economy in its place.

China began to welcome Western tourism, trade, and technology. Chinese managers, engineers, and economists came to the United States and other Western nations to study modern business techniques. Perhaps most important, material incentives were restored, and the Chinese showed themselves willing to experiment with a wide variety of different models of economic organization. Even small-scale capitalism was allowed back on the Chinese mainland.

These trends accelerated in the early 1980s, as market forces were allowed to supplant central planning more and more. Farmers were given land to do with as they pleased—once they paid a fixed amount of produce to the state. Markets, and even limited amounts of local entrepreneurship, were allowed to flourish in the form of private shops and other small businesses. Foreign companies were invited to set up operations in China, and the Chinese seemed eager to learn the ways of Western business.

In the late 1980s, however, two problems arose. As markets replaced planning, sound macroeconomic management was not put in place. So China experienced high inflation for the first time since the communist takeover. At about the same time, the Chinese people began to clamor—quite openly—for political freedoms to accompany their new-found economic freedoms. A struggle within the Chinese leadership ensued, which hardliner Li Peng and his supporters won after the bloody suppression of a popular revolt in Tiananmen Square in June 1989. Political dissent was surpressed, but economic liberalization continued. In recent years, Chinese growth rates have been among the highest in the world.

## THE AMAZING JAPANESE ECONOMY

People all over the world today view Japan the way they once viewed the United States—with a mixture of awe and resentment. The Japanese are admired as producers, feared as competitors. Their efficiency seems matchless; their ability to export seems boundless. "How do the Japanese do it?" is a question frequently asked, with barely concealed wonderment.

The reality is somewhat different. Economy-wide productivity in Japan is still below that in the United States. Average standards of living there lag even further behind our own, in part because so many Japanese live in tiny hovels. And Japan's retail and service industries are such marvels of inefficiency that some Japanese goods cost more in Tokyo than in New York!

Yet the Japanese economy is certainly *the* outstanding success story of the period after World War II. From 1955—when Japan began its productivity enhancement campaign—to 1989, real GNP in Japan rose by an astounding 836 percent. (The corresponding expansion of the U.S. economy was only 177 percent.) Its automobile, electronics, and semiconductor industries, to name just a few, lead the world in technological and manufacturing prowess. Its banks and other financial institutions are the world's largest. As an economic power, Japan has truly come of age.

But how? It is true, but far too simple, to say that Japan succeeded by adopting free-market capitalism—for both free markets and capitalism look quite different in Japan than in the United States. We devote most of the rest of this chapter to describing some of these differences.

### EXPORT-LED GROWTH

Japan is a crowded, island nation far removed from the world's major markets. Almost totally devoid of natural resources, it must import large amounts of raw materials, energy, and foodstuffs just to survive. And yet, by concentrating on manufacturing and exporting, it has managed not just to prosper but to propel itself into the forefront of nations.

**EXPORT-LED GROWTH** refers to the strategy of emphasizing the production of goods for export.

One secret to Japanese economic success has certainly been its emphasis on both high levels of investment and **export-led growth**. From 1955 to 1989, Japanese exports in real terms grew an astounding 3,227 percent. Indeed, Japan's export machine has been so successful that its trade surpluses are now causing international frictions. (See the boxed insert on page 995.)

How has Japan done it? There is no simple answer. High levels of investment have certainly facilitated the adoption of the latest technology. Japanese industry is clearly outward looking in a way that American industry is not. Many organizations, such as the fabled Ministry of International Trade and Industry (MITI) and the Japan External Trade Organization, work to promote exports. Japanese business has also shown a remarkable ability to adapt to changing world markets. As one industry (say, shipbuilding) declines, the Japanese shift into another (say, consumer electronics) whose star is rising. Above all, the major Japanese companies seek always to grow—and that means exporting.

## "JAPAN, INC."

Unlike the United States, but like much of Western Europe, Japan has no tradition of enforcing antitrust laws. Indeed, at times the government has seemed to promote rather than oppose bigness, perhaps as a way to catch up to the West. In consequence, Japanese industry is far more concentrated than American industry, especially in manufacturing and financial services. Industrial concentration, barriers to imports, and inefficient retailing combine to keep domestic prices of consumer goods high. The cozy relationship between the big Japanese corporations (*kaisha*) and the Japanese government has acquired the nickname "Japan, Inc.," to indicate that economic policy there is geared more to producer than to consumer interests.

Japanese industrial organization also looks different from *inside* the corporation. An industrial giant like Toyota may be surrounded by satellite companies that supply parts and help it operate its famous "just-in-time" inventory system (*kanban*), a highly efficient way of organizing the factory floor to minimize delays. These smaller companies live at the mercy of the large *kaisha* and act as shock absorbers when demand declines.

In addition, members of Japan's manufacturing combines (*keiretsu*) own chunks of each other's stock and forge tight links with the world's largest banks. This gives Japanese industry access to cheap, "patient" capital that is willing to wait for a return on its investment. Japanese managers pay scant attention to daily movements of the stock market and never worry about hostile takeovers. All this helps Japanese industry maintain its long-run focus.

## JAPAN'S SYSTEM OF LABOR–MANAGEMENT RELATIONS

Japan also differs from the United States in the way its workforce is organized and paid. For one thing, many employees of large Japanese corporations have *lifetime employment* guarantees and are never laid off. These features help align the interests of labor and management, build loyalty to the company, and make Japanese workers less resistant to change than their American counterparts. For example, if a Japanese plant automates, most employees know they will not only keep their jobs but share in any gains automation may bring.

### U.S.–Japanese Trade: Is Everyone Playing Fair?

Japan's huge trade surpluses with the United States now threaten friendly relations between the two countries. Several rounds of trade negotiations have failed to reduce the surplus. Why? One former trade negotiator believes that leaders of both nations incorrectly assume that the Japanese and U.S. economies are organized in the same way.

As long as this assumption is accepted, there are only two possible explanations for our problems: Someone is cheating or someone is performing poorly. . . .

There is a third explanation: The two sides do not share the same economic views. The U.S. runs its economy for the consumer, prevents or strictly regulates aggregation of corporate power, eschews industrial policy, views the government role as that of referee and calls for a laissez-faire brand of free trade. Japan emphasizes the interest of the producer, promotes agglomeration of corporate power, pursues an active industrial policy, sees the government as a coach and practices a mercantilistic brand of free trade.

In effect, Japan is playing football while the U.S. is playing baseball. Japan is not playing unfairly, and the U.S. team is trying as hard as it can. But football is a rougher game than baseball, and the baseball players are taking a beating. They will continue to do so as long as their leaders insist that the games are really the same.

SOURCE: Clyde Prestowitz, "George and Toshiki—The Odd Couple," *The New York Times*, March 10, 1990.

The Japanese workplace is also less hierarchical. Pay differentials between executives and production workers are much smaller than in the United States, so, naturally, the Japanese distribution of income is much more equal. Managers eat in the same cafeterias, drink in the same bars, and sometimes even wear the same uniforms as blue-collar workers. Japanese workers are also consulted closely on how the factory is to be run. Decision making is by consensus—even if consensus takes a long time to develop. American management, by contrast, exercises more top-down control.

For these reasons, and perhaps also because of strong conformist tendencies within Japanese society, labor–management relations are less adversarial and more cooperative than in the United States.

## IS JAPAN A PLANNED ECONOMY?

All this did not happen by the invisible hand alone. The system was consciously designed to raise industrial productivity, keep it growing, and turn Japan into an industrial powerhouse that would equal the Western nations. Many Japanese innovations, such as *kanban*, originated in the private sector. But the government—through the Japan Productivity Center, the Economic Planning Agency, the powerful Ministry of Finance, and MITI—played an active role in promoting what it saw as good ideas, discouraging bad ones and, in general, lending a helping and guiding hand.

## *Can America Import Japanese Manufacturing Methods?*

Most [Japanese] firms [in the United States] have adopted something like joint consultation and related Japanese practices, including an elaborate screening of job applicants . . . . some U.S. workers who were hired at Honda in Ohio were reportedly surprised both at the many questions they were asked that seemed unrelated to work and at the length of the interviews, which were attended by executives and vice presidents. . . . Once hired, these workers reported attending frequent meetings with the management on production matters. Such frequent meetings at the Honda plant in Ohio are signified by the slogan, "let's Y-gaya," which means in fractured Japanese, "let's have a bull session." In these operations management and workers share the same tables for lunch, thereby creating an informal setting for communication. . . .

Productivity at Nummi [a joint Toyota-General Motors factory in Fremont, California] after only one year of operation was reported to have increased by 48.5 percent over what it was at the old Fremont plant under GM management. Absenteeism and drug use, which plagued the old Fremont plant, dropped dramatically after Nummi took over. Nummi's efforts at productivity enhancement continue with the slogan "let's kaizen," or "let's improve." Also, in contrast to the old Fremont plant, the quality of the automobiles produced at Nummi has been rated highly. . . .

. . . Honda in Japan is known for its emphasis on nurturing the sense of cooperative teamwork among its workers. This emphasis was imported to Honda's operation in Ohio. At the Ohio plant workers, referred to as associates, are encouraged to acquire skills and training by continual interactions with one another on the shop floor rather than through formal training sessions. Productivity at the plant reportedly approaches that of Honda's plants in Japan, and the quality of the automobiles produced in Ohio is said to equal that of Japanese-made Hondas.

SOURCE: Masanori Hashimoto, "Employment and Wage Systems in Japan and Their Implications for Productivity," in Alan S. Blinder (ed.), *Paying for Productivity: A Look at the Evidence* (Washington, D.C.: The Brookings Institution), 1990, pp. 292–93.

The role of the government, and especially MITI, in Japan's economic success is highly controversial. Ardent free-marketeers downplay its contribution and point to episodes in which MITI clearly got in the way—such as its ill-conceived attempt to drive several companies out of the automobile business in the 1960s. Protectionists seeking to limit Japanese imports exaggerate the role of MITI and portray Japan, Inc., as a monolith, which it certainly is not. In their eyes, Japan's **industrial policy** is the key to its success.

A balanced view of the matter seems hard to strike, especially since few Westerners really fathom the clubby ways of Japanese businesses. But a few things seem clear. First the Ministry of Finance and the Bank of Japan (the central bank) have exercised more comprehensive control over the Japanese financial system than the Treasury and the Federal Reserve have done here. Second, Japanese industrial policy, while far from infallible, seems to have had considerable success in assisting winners and shutting down losers. Third, Japanese industry benefits enormously from a workforce that may be the best educated and most cooperative in the world; this is certainly a substantial achievement of government.

## WHAT CAN THE UNITED STATES LEARN FROM (AND TEACH) JAPAN?

Learning is a two-way street. The Japanese have learned much from American industry (their famed "quality circles," for example, orginated here) and continue to do so. Economy-wide productivity continues to be higher in the United States than in Japan. Nonetheless, there are important industries—such as automobiles and robotics, in which the Japanese seem to be the technological leader. There, we can "play catch up" by observing them, just as they did years ago by observing us.

Many people feel, however, that the most important things we can learn from the Japanese are not the latest innovations in robotics or chip manufacturing, but rather their ways of organizing and motivating people. This begins with an education system that has virtually abolished illiteracy, continues through Japan's unique labor-relations system, and includes *kanban* and other management techniques. And it seems to work, even when imported to America (see the boxed insert on page 996).

Some observers predict that, as the Japanese get richer, they will come to behave more like Americans. Already, for example, there are signs that Japanese households are saving less and Japanese workers are changing jobs more frequently than they used to. Others, however, stress basic cultural differences between the two societies that change very slowly, if at all.

A more general, and controversial, hypothesis is that the Japanese "corporatist" style of doing business is more suitable to the modern world of international competition than the American "individualist" style. The two brands of capitalism are indeed different. Is theirs the wave of the future and ours the wave of the past? Only time will tell.

## *Summary*

1. Economic systems differ in the amount of planning they do and in the extent to which they permit private ownership of property. However, **socialism** (state ownership of the means of production) need not go hand in hand with central planning, and **capitalism** need not rely on free markets. The two choices are distinct, at least conceptually.
2. **Free markets** seem to do a good job of selecting the bill of goods and services to be produced and at choosing the most efficient techniques for producing these goods and services. Planned systems have difficulties with both these choices.
3. Market economies, however, do not guarantee an equitable distribution of income and are often plagued by business fluctuations. In these two areas, **planning** seems to have clear advantages.
4. A major problem for socialism is how to motivate management to achieve maximal efficiency and to maintain inventiveness in the absence of the profit motive.
5. Individual freedom is a noneconomic goal that is of major importance in the choice among economic systems. Any element of planning or of socialism infringes upon the freedoms of some individuals. Yet complete freedom does not exist anywhere, and certain limitations on individual freedom command wide popular support.
6. From the days of Stalin until its dissolution in 1991, the Soviet Union followed a rigid system of **central planning** in which heavy industry and armaments were emphasized and consumer needs were deemphasized.
7. Planning in the U.S.S.R. was bureaucratic and hierarchical and encountered monumental difficulties in transmitting accurate information, equating supply and demand for the various inputs, motivating both

workers and managers, and achieving satisfactory agricultural productivity.

8. While Soviet consumers were free to spend their money as they pleased, there was no **consumer sovereignty**. Planners, not consumers, decided, what would be produced. The labor market, however, operated much as it does in America—using wage rates to equate supply and demand.

9. The Soviet Union came to an end in December of 1991, and the former Soviet republics became separate countries. (Russia is the largest.) All are moving in different degrees toward a market economic system.

10. With the end of centrally planned socialism in Eastern Europe and the former Soviet Union, planned systems are being replaced by market systems, a process generally described as **transition**.

11. **Transition** from plan to market involves macro issues (money and budgets), micro issues (**privatization**, markets, and prices), trade issues (decentralization and currency convertibility), and development of a social safety net.

12. The Chinese economic system has changed several times since the Communist takeover in 1949, passing through several periods of intense revolutionary fervor and little economic progress. Planning there has been similar to that in Russia, although somewhat less centralized.

13. Over the decade from the late 1970s to the late 1980s, the Chinese introduced important aspects of the market economy—and even bits of capitalism—into their economic system resulting in Chinese growth rates in the 1990s that are among the highest in the world.

14. Japan has used **export-led growth** to propel itself to the forefront of nations; but lately its single-minded concentration on exporting has been a source of international tension.

15. Japan has more industrial concentration than the United States, a less adversarial system of labor-management relations, tighter links between manufacturing companies and banks, and more active cooperation between government and industry. Observers disagree about the relative importance of each of these influences in accounting for Japan's industrial success.

## *Key Concepts and Terms*

Transition
Capitalism
Socialism
Workers' management
Welfare state
Planning
Free markets

Consumer sovereignty
Collectivization
Central planning
Soviet Five-Year and One-Year Plans
*Perestroika*
*Glasnost*
Privatization

Sequencing
Material incentives
Great Leap Forward
Great Proletarian Cultural Revolution
Export-led growth
Industrial policy

## *Questions for Review*

1. Explain why the choice between capitalism and socialism is not the same as the choice between markets and central planning. Cite an example of a socialist market economy and of a planned capitalist economy.

2. If you were the leader of a small, developing country, what are some of the factors that would weigh heavily in your choice of an economic system?

3. Which type of economic system generally has the most trouble achieving each of the following goals? In each case, explain why.

   a. An equal distribution of income
   b. Adequate incentives for industrial managers
   c. Eliminating business fluctuations
   d. Balancing supply and demand for inputs

4. If you were a plant manager under old-style Soviet planning, what are some of the things you might do to make your life easier and more successful? (Use your imagination. Russian plant managers did!)

5. What are some special problems encountered when a country tries to make the transition from central planning to markets? (*Hint:* What kinds of difficulties can arise when some markets are tightly controlled while others are free?)

6. What are the major differences between the speed and sequencing of transition in Russia, Poland, and Hungary?
7. Do you think the United States government should take a more active role in guiding American industry? If so, is Japan a good model? If not, why is Japan not a good model?
8. During the early 1990s, Japan and the United States engaged in talks on "structural impediments" to more balanced trade between the two nations. As part of these talks, U.S. government representatives told the Japanese how they could make their economy more like ours, while Japanese negotiators told their American counterparts how to make the United States more like Japan. Does this make sense to you? Who should be emulating whom?
9. What are the major issues involved in the transition from plan to market, and why is this transition so difficult in practice?

# GLOSSARY

The **ABILITY-TO-PAY PRINCIPLE** refers to the idea that people with greater ability to pay taxes should pay (503)

One country is said to have an **ABSOLUTE ADVANTAGE** over another in the production of a particular good if it can produce that good using smaller quantities of resources than can the other country. (876)

**ABSTRACTION** means ignoring many details in order to focus on the most important elements of a problem. (11)

**AFFIRMATIVE ACTION** refers to active efforts to locate and hire members of underrepresented groups. (444)

**AGGREGATE DEMAND** is the total amount that all consumers, business firms, and government agencies are willing to spend on final goods and services. (591)

The **AGGREGATE DEMAND CURVE** shows the quantity of domestic product that is demanded at each possible value of the price level. (548)

The **AGGREGATE SUPPLY CURVE** shows, for each possible price level, the quantity of goods and services that all the nation's businesses are willing to produce during a specified period of time, holding all other determinants of aggregate quantity supplied constant. (548, 668)

**AGGREGATION** means combining many individual markets into one overall market. (545)

The **ALLOCATION OF RESOURCES** refers to the decision on how to divide up the economy's scarce input resources among the different outputs produced in the economy and among the different firms or other organizations that produce those outputs. (59)

A nation's currency is said to **APPRECIATE** when exchange rates change so that a unit of its own currency can buy more units of foreign currency. (902)

An **ASSET** of an individual or business firm is an item of value that the individual or firm owns. (726)

An **AUTOMATIC STABILIZER** is any arrangement that automatically serves to support aggregate demand when it would otherwise sag and to hold down aggregate demand when it would otherwise surge ahead. In this way, an automatic stabilizer reduces the sensitivity of the economy to shifts in demand. (781)

An **AUTONOMOUS INCREASE IN CONSUMPTION** is an increase in consumer spending without any increase in incomes. It is represented on a graph as a shift of the entire consumption function. (654)

A firm's **AVERAGE COST (AC)** curve shows, for each output, the cost per unit, that is, total cost divided by output. (111)

The **AVERAGE PHYSICAL PRODUCT (APP)** is the total physical product (TPP) divided by the quantity of input used. Thus, APP = TPP/X where X = the quantity of input. (133)

**AVERAGE REVENUE (AR)** is total revenue (TR) divided by quantity. (109)

The **AVERAGE TAX RATE** is the ratio of taxes to income. (497)

The **BALANCE OF PAYMENTS DEFICIT** is the amount by which the quantity supplied of a country's currency (per year) exceeds the quantity demanded. Balance of payments deficits arise whenever the exchange rate is pegged at an artificially high level. (910)

The **BALANCE OF PAYMENTS SURPLUS** is the amount by which the quantity demanded of a country's currency (per year) exceeds the quantity supplied. Balance of payments surpluses arise whenever the exchange rate is pegged at an artificially low level. (911)

A **BALANCE SHEET** is an accounting statement listing the values of all the assets on the left-hand side and the values of all the liabilities and **net worth** on the right-hand side. (726)

**BARTER** is a system of exchange in which people directly trade one good for another, without using money as an intermediate step. (615)

An activity is said to generate a **BENEFICIAL OR DETRIMENTAL EXTERNALITY** if that activity causes incidental benefits or damages to others, and no corresponding compensation is provided to or paid by those who generate the externality. (313)

The **BENEFITS PRINCIPLE OF TAXATION** holds that people who derive the benefits from the service should pay the taxes that finance it. (504)

**BILATERAL MONOPOLY** is a market situation in which there is both a monopoly on the selling side and a monopsony on the buying side. (410)

A **BOND** is simply an IOU by a corporation that promises to pay the holder of the piece of paper a fixed sum of money at the specified *maturity* date and some other fixed amount of money (the *coupon* or the *interest payment*) every year up to the date of maturity. (341)

The **BUDGET DEFICIT** is the amount by which the government's expenditures exceed its receipts during a specified period of time, usually one year. (796)

The **BURDEN OF A TAX** to an individual is the amount he would have to be given to make him just as well off with the tax as he was without it. (505)

**CAPITAL** refers to an inventory (*a stock*) of plant, equipment, and other productive resources held by a business firm, an individual, or some other organization. (365)

A **CAPITAL GAIN** is the difference between the price at which an asset is sold and the price at which it was bought. (578)

A **CAPITAL GOOD** is an item that is used to produce other goods and services in the future, rather than being consumed today. Factories and machines are examples. (65)

**CAPITALISM** is a method of economic organization in which private individuals own the means of production, either directly or indirectly through corporations. (978)

A **CARTEL** is a group of sellers of a product who have joined together to control its production, sale, and price in the hope of obtaining the advantages of monopoly. (294)

A **CENTRAL BANK** is a bank for banks. America's central bank is the **Federal Reserve System**. (739)

A **CLOSED ECONOMY** is one that does not trade with other nations in either goods or assets. (935)

A **CLOSED SHOP** is an arrangement that permits only union members to be hired. (405)

A **COMMODITY MONEY** is an object in use as a medium of exchange, but which also has a substantial value in alternative (nonmonetary) uses. (718)

A **COMMON STOCK** of a corporation is a piece of paper that gives the holder of the stock a share of the ownership of the company. (341)

**COMPARABLE WORTH** refers to pay standards that assign equal wages to jobs judged "comparable." (444)

One country is said to have a **COMPARATIVE ADVANTAGE** over another in the production of a particular good relative to other goods if it produces that good least inefficiently as compared with the other country. (877)

Two goods are called **COMPLEMENTS** if an increase in the quantity consumed of one increases the quantity demanded of the other, all other things remaining constant. (180)

A **CONCENTRATION RATIO** is the percentage of an industry's output produced by its *four* largest firms. It is intended to measure the degree to which the industry is dominated by large firms. (41)

**CONSUMER EXPENDITURE**, symbolized by the letter **C**, is the total amount spent by consumers on newly produced goods and services (excluding purchases of new homes, which are considered investment goods). (591)

**CONSUMER SOVEREIGNTY** means that consumer preferences determine what goods shall be produced and in what amounts. (980)

**CONSUMER'S SURPLUS** is the difference between the amount that the quantity of commodity *X* purchased is worth to the consumer and the amount that the market requires the consumer to pay for that quantity of *X*. (199)

The **CONSUMPTION FUNCTION** is the relationship between total consumer expenditure and total disposable income in the economy, holding all other determinants of consumer spending constant. (600)

A **CONSUMPTION GOOD** is an item that is available for immediate use by households, and that satisfies wants of members of households without contributing directly to future production by the economy. (65)

A **CORPORATION** is a firm that has the legal status of a fictional individual. This fictional individual is owned by a number of persons, called its stockholders, and is run by a set of elected officers (usually headed by a president) and a board of directors. (38)

Two variables are said to be **CORRELATED** if they tend to go up or down together. But correlation need not imply causation. (14)

A **CRAFT UNION** represents a particular type of skilled worker, such as newspaper typographers or electricians, regardless of what industry they work in. (405)

**CREEPING INFLATION** refers to an inflation that proceeds for a long time at a moderate and fairly steady pace. (581)

The **CROSS ELASTICITY OF DEMAND** for product X to a change in the price of another product, Y, is the ratio of the percentage change in quantity demanded of product X to the percentage change in the price of product Y that brings about the change in quantity demanded. (180)

**CROSS-SUBSIDIZATION** means selling one product at a loss, which is balanced by higher profits on another product. (458)

**CROWDING IN** occurs when government spending, by raising real GDP, induces increases in private investment spending. (811)

**CROWDING OUT** occurs when deficit spending by the government forces private investment spending to contract. (811)

**CYCLICAL UNEMPLOYMENT** is the portion of unemployment that is attributable to a decline in the economy's total production. Cyclical unemployment rises during recessions and falls as prosperity is restored. (568)

**DEFLATION** refers to a sustained *decrease* in the general price level. (553)

A **DEMAND CURVE** is a graphical depiction of a demand schedule. It shows how the quantity demanded of some product during a specified period of time will change as the price of that product changes, holding all other determinants of quantity demanded constant. (78)

A **DEMAND SCHEDULE** is a table showing how the quantity demanded of some product during a specified period of time changes as the price of that product changes, holding all other determinants of quantity demanded constant. (77)

A commodity is **DEPLETABLE** if it is used up when someone consumes it. (318)

**DEPOSIT INSURANCE** is a system that guarantees that depositors will not lose money even if their bank goes bankrupt. (724)

The currency is said to **DEPRECIATE** when exchange rates change so that a unit of its currency can buy fewer units of foreign currency. (902)

A **DEVALUATION** is a reduction in the official value of a currency. (902)

**DIRECT TAXES** are taxes levied directly on people. (497)

The **DISCOUNT RATE** is the interest rate the Fed charges on loans it makes to banks. (746)

A **DISCOURAGED WORKER** is an unemployed person who gives up looking for work and is therefore no longer counted as part of the labor force. (568)

**DISPOSABLE INCOME** is the sum of the incomes of all the individuals in the economy after all taxes have been deducted and all transfer payments have been added. (592)

**DIVERSIFICATION** means including a number and variety of stocks, bonds, and other such items in an individual's portfolio. If the individual owns airline stocks, for example, diversification requires the purchase of a stock or bond in a very different industry, such as a breakfast cereal producer. (345)

**DIVISION OF LABOR** means breaking up a task into a number of smaller, more specialized tasks so that each worker can become more adept at a particular job. (68)

**DUMPING** means selling goods in a foreign market at lower prices than those charged in the home market. (894)

An **ECONOMETRIC MODEL** is a set of mathematical equations that embody the economist's model of the economy. (782)

**ECONOMIC DISCRIMINATION** occurs when equivalent factors of production receive different payments for equal contributions to output. (431)

**ECONOMIC GROWTH** occurs when an economy is able to produce more goods and services for each consumer. (65)

An **ECONOMIC MODEL** is a simplified, small-scale version of some aspect of the economy. Economic models are often expressed in equations, by graphs, or in words. (15)

**ECONOMIC PROFIT** equals net earnings, in the accountant's sense, minus the opportunity costs of capital and of any other inputs supplied by the firm's owners. (238)

**ECONOMIC RENT** is the portion of the earnings of a factor of production that exceeds the minimum amount necessary to induce any of that factor to be supplied. (379)

Production is said to involve **ECONOMIES OF SCALE,** also referred to as **INCREASING RETURNS TO SCALE**, if, when all input quantities are doubled, the quantity of output is more than doubled. (154)

**ECONOMIES OF SCALE** are savings that are acquired through increases in quantities produced. (454)

**ECONOMIES OF SCOPE** are savings that are acquired through simultaneous production of many different products. (454)

An **ECONOMY** is a collection of markets in a defined geographical area. (28)

An **EFFICIENT ALLOCATION OF RESOURCES** is one that takes advantage of every opportunity to make some individuals better off in their own estimation while not worsening the lot of anyone else. (246)

**ENTREPRENEURSHIP** is the act of starting new firms, introducing new products and technological innovations, and, in general, taking the risks that are necessary in seeking out business opportunities. (361)

The **EQUATION OF EXCHANGE** states that the money value of GDP transactions must be equal to the product of the average stock of money times velocity. That is:

$$M \times V = P \times Y. \qquad (762)$$

An **EQUILIBRIUM** is a situation in which there are no inherent forces that produce change. Changes away from an equilibrium position will occur only as a result of "outside events" that disturb the status quo. (81, 626)

The **EXCESS BURDEN** of a tax to an individual is the amount by which the burden of the tax exceeds the tax that is paid. (505)

**EXCESS RESERVES** are any reserves held in excess of the legal minimum. (727)

A commodity is **EXCLUDABLE** if someone who does not pay for it can be kept from enjoying it. (318)

The **EXCHANGE RATE** states the price, in terms of one currency, at which another currency can be bought. (901)

An **EXPENDITURE SCHEDULE** shows the relationship between national income (GDP) and total spending. (628)

**EXPONENTIAL GROWTH** is growth at a constant percentage rate. (953)

**EXPORT-LED GROWTH** refers to the strategy of emphasizing the production of goods for export. (994)

An **EXPORT SUBSIDY** is a payment by the government to exporters to permit them to reduce the selling price of their goods so they can compete more effectively in foreign markets. (886)

**FIAT MONEY** is money that is decreed as such by the government. It is of little value as a commodity, but it maintains its value as a medium of exchange because people have faith that the issuer will stand behind the pieces of printed paper and limit their production. (718)

**FINAL GOODS AND SERVICES** are those that are purchased by their ultimate users. (550)

**FISCAL FEDERALISM** refers to the system of grants from one level of government to the next. (503)

The government's **FISCAL POLICY** is its plan for spending and taxation. It is designed to steer aggregate demand in some desired direction. (691)

A **FIXED COST** is the cost of the inputs whose quantity does not rise when output goes up, and which are required to produce any output at all. The total cost of such indivisible inputs does not change when the output changes. Any other cost of the firm's operation is called a **VARIABLE COST**. (140)

**FIXED EXCHANGE RATES** are rates set by government decisions and maintained by government actions. (909)

**FIXED TAXES** are tax taxes that do not vary with the level of GDP. (691)

**FLOATING EXCHANGE RATES** are rates determined in free markets by the law of supply and demand. (902)

The **FLYPAPER THEORY OF INCIDENCE** holds that the burden of a tax always sticks where the government puts it. (507)

A **45° LINE** is a ray through the origin with a slope of +1. It marks off points where the variables measured on each axis have equal values.[3] (24)

**FRACTIONAL RESERVE BANKING** is a system under which bankers keep as reserves only a fraction of the funds they hold on deposit. (722)

**FRICTIONAL UNEMPLOYMENT** is unemployment that is due to normal turnover in the labor market. It includes people who are temporarily between jobs because they are moving or changing occupations, or for similar reasons. (568)

**GALLOPING INFLATION** refers to an inflation that proceeds at an exceptionally high rate, perhaps for only a relatively brief period. Galloping inflations are generally characterized by accelerating rates of inflation so that the rate of inflation is higher this month than it was last month. (581)

**GOVERNMENT PURCHASES**, symbolized by the letter **G**, refers to the goods (such as airplanes and paper clips) and services (such as school teaching and police protection) purchased by all levels of government. (591)

**GROSS DOMESTIC PRODUCT (GDP)** is a measure of the size of an economy. It is, roughly speaking, the money value of all the goods and services produced in a year. (30)

**GROSS DOMESTIC PRODUCT (GDP)** is the sum of the money values of all final goods and services produced in the domestic economy during a specified period of time, usually one year. (549)

**HORIZONTAL EQUITY** is the notion that equally situated individuals should be taxed equally. (503)

The **INCIDENCE OF A TAX** is an allocation of the burden of the tax to specific individuals or groups. (507)

The **INCOME EFFECT** is a *portion* of the change in quantity of a good demanded when its price changes. A rise in price cuts the consumer's purchasing power (real income), which leads to a change in the quantity demanded of that commodity. That change is the income effect. (201)

An **INCOME-EXPENDITURE DIAGRAM,** also called a **45° LINE DIAGRAM**, plots total real expenditure (on the vertical axis) against real income (on the horizontal axis). The 45° line marks off points where income and expenditure are equal. (631)

**INDEXING** refers to provisions in a law or a contract whereby monetary payments are automatically adjusted whenever a specified price index changes. Wage rates, pensions, interest payments on bonds, income taxes, and many other things can be indexed in this way, and have been. Sometimes such contractual provisions are called *escalator clauses*. (847)

**INDIRECT TAXES** are taxes levied on specific economic activities. (497)

An **INDUCED INCREASE IN CONSUMPTION** is an increase in consumer spending that stems from an increase in consumer incomes. It is represented on a graph as a movement along a fixed consumption function. (654)

**INDUCED INVESTMENT** is the part of investment spending that rises when GDP rises and falls when GDP falls. (628)

An **INDUSTRIAL UNION** represents all types of workers in a single industry, such as auto manufacturing or coal mining. (405)

An **INFERIOR GOOD** is a commodity whose quantity demanded falls when the purchaser's real income rises, all other things remaining equal. (201)

**INFLATION** refers to a sustained increase in the average level of prices. (33, 548)

**INFLATION ACCOUNTING** means adjusting standard accounting procedures for the fact that inflation lowers the purchasing power of money. (802)

The **INFLATIONARY GAP** is the amount by which equilibrium real GDP exceeds the full-employment level of GDP. (635)

**INNOVATION**, the next step, is the act of putting the new idea into practical use. (382)

**INTEREST** is the payment for the use of funds employed in the production of capital; it is measured as a percent per year of the value of the funds tied up in the capital. (367)

An **INTERMEDIATE GOOD** is a good purchased for resale or for use in producing another good. (550)

**INVENTION** is the act of generating an idea for a new product or a new method for making an old product. (382)

**INVESTMENT** is the *flow* of resources into the production of new capital. It is the labor, steel, and other inputs devoted to the *construction* of factories, warehouses, railroads, and other pieces of capital during some period of time. (365)

**INVESTMENT SPENDING**, symbolized by the letter **I**, is the sum of the expenditures of business firms on new plant and equipment and households on new homes. Financial "investments" are not included, nor are resales of existing physical assets. (591)

The **J CURVE** shows the typical pattern of response of net exports to a change in currency values. Following a depreciation or a devaluation, net exports usually decline at first and then rise. (930)

The **LABOR FORCE** is the number of people holding or seeking jobs. (568)

**LABOR PRODUCTIVITY** refers to the amount of output a worker turns out in an hour (or a week or a year) of labor. It can be measured as total national output (GDP) in a given year divided by the total number of hours of work performed for pay in the country during that year. That is, labor productivity is defined as GDP per hour of labor. (856)

**LAISSEZ FAIRE** refers to a program of minimal interference with the workings of the market system. The term means that people should be left alone in carrying out their economic affairs. (252)

The **"LAW" OF DEMAND** states that a lower price generally increases the amount of a commodity that people in a market are willing to buy. So, for most goods, demand curves have a negative slope. (204)

The **"LAW" OF DIMINISHING MARGINAL UTILITY** asserts that additional units of a commodity are worth less and less to a consumer in money terms. As the individual's consumption increases, the marginal utility of each additional unit declines. (193)

The **LAW OF SUPPLY AND DEMAND** states that, in a free market, the forces of supply and demand generally push the price toward the level at which quantity supplied and quantity demanded are equal. (83)

A **LEADING INDICATOR** is a variable that, experience has shown, normally turns down before recessions start and turns up before expansions begin. (785)

A **LIABILITY** of an individual or business firm is an item of value that the individual or firm owes. Many liabilities are known as "debts." (726)

**LIMITED LIABILITY** is a legal obligation of a firm's owners to pay back company debts only with the money they have already invested in the firm. (338)

An asset's **LIQUIDITY** refers to the ease with which it can be converted into cash. (721)

The **LONG RUN** is a period of time long enough for all the firm's sunk commitments to come to an end. (145)

The narrowly defined money supply, usually abbreviated **M1**, is the sum of all coins and paper money in circulation, plus certain checkable deposit balances at banks and savings institutions.[2] (720)

The broadly defined money supply, usually abbreviated **M2**, is the sum of all coins and paper money in circulation, plus all types of checking account balances, plus most forms of savings account balances, plus shares in money market mutual funds, and a few other minor items. (720)

A firm's **MARGINAL COST (MC)** curve shows, for each output, the increase in the firm's total cost required if it increases its output by an additional unit. (111)

Land that is just on the borderline of being used is called **MARGINAL LAND**. (373)

The **MARGINAL PHYSICAL PRODUCT (MPP)** of an input is the increase in total output that results from a one-unit increase in the input, holding the amounts of all other inputs constant. (133, 361)

**MARGINAL PROFIT** is the *addition* to total profit resulting from one more unit of output. (115)

The **MARGINAL PROPENSITY TO CONSUME** (or MPC for short) is the ratio of the change in consumption to the change in disposable income that produces the change in consumption. On a graph, it appears as the slope of the consumption function. (600)

**MARGINAL REVENUE,** often abbreviated MR, is the *addition* to total revenue resulting from the addition of one unit to total output. Geometrically, marginal revenue is the *slope* of the total revenue curve. Its formula is $MR_1 = TR_1 - TR_0$, and so on. (110)

The **MARGINAL REVENUE PRODUCT (MRP)** of an input is the additional revenue the producer earns from the increased sales when it uses an additional unit of the input. (136, 361)

The **MARGINAL SOCIAL COST** of an activity is the sum of **marginal private cost** plus the incidental cost (positive or negative) which is borne by others. (313)

The **MARGINAL TAX RATE** is the fraction of each *additional* dollar of income that is paid in taxes. (497)

The **MARGINAL UTILITY** of a commodity to a consumer (measured in money terms) is the maximum amount of money he or she is willing pay *for one more unit* of it. (192)

A **MARKET** refers to the set of all sale and purchase transactions that affect the price of some commodity. (221)

A **MARKET DEMAND CURVE** shows how the total quantity demanded of some product during a specified period of time changes as the price of that product changes, holding other things constant. (203)

**MARKET POWER** is the ability of a firm to raise its price significantly above the competitive price level and to maintain this high price profitably for a considerable period. (490)

A **MARKET SYSTEM** is a form of organization of the economy in which decisions on resource allocation are left to the independent decisions of individual producers and consumers acting in their own best interests without central direction. (70)

The **MAXIMIN CRITERION** means selecting the strategy that yields the maximum payoff, on the assumption that your opponent does as much damage to you as he or she can. (299)

A **MERGER** occurs when two previously independent firms are combined under a single owner or group of owners. A **horizontal merger** is the merger of two firms producing similar products, as when one toothpaste manufacturing firm purchases another. A **vertical merger** involves the joining of two firms, one of which supplies an ingredient of the other's product, as when an auto maker acquires a tire manufacturing firm. A **conglomerate merger** is the union of two unrelated firms, as when a defense industry firm joins a firm that produces video tapes. (482)

A **MIXED ECONOMY** is one in which there is some public influence over the workings of free markets. There may also be some public ownership mixed in with private property. (47)

**MONETARISM** is a mode of analysis that uses the equation of exchange to organize and analyze macroeconomic data. (766)

**MONETARY POLICY** refers to actions that the Federal Reserve System takes in order to change the equilibrium of the money market; that is, to alter the money supply, move interest rates, or both. (751)

The central bank is said to **MONETIZE THE DEFICIT** when it purchases the bonds that the government issues. (808)

**MONEY** is the standard object used in exchanging goods and services. In short, money is the **MEDIUM OF EXCHANGE**. (717)

A **MONEY FIXED ASSET** is an asset with a face value fixed in terms of dollars, such as money itself, government bonds, and corporate bonds. (603)

**MONOPOLISTIC COMPETITION** refers to a market in which products are heterogenous but which is otherwise the same as a market that is perfectly competitive. (287)

**MONOPSONY** refers to a market situation in which there is only one buyer. (410)

**MORAL HAZARD** refers to the tendency of insurance to discourage policyholders from protecting themselves from risk. (324)

**MORAL SUASION** refers to informal requests and warnings designed to persuade banks to limit their borrowings from the Fed. (747)

The **MULTIPLIER** is the ratio of the change in equilibrium GDP (*Y*) divided by the original change in spending that causes the change in GDP. (648)

The **NATIONAL DEBT** is the federal government's total indebtedness at a moment in time. It is the result of previous deficits. (796)

**NATIONAL INCOME** is the sum of the incomes of all the individuals in the economy earned in the forms of wages, interest, rents, and profits. It excludes transfer payments and is calculated before any deductions are taken for income taxes. (592)

A **NATURAL MONOPOLY** is an industry in which advantages of large-scale production make it possible for a single firm to produce the entire output of the market at lower average cost than a number of firms each producing a smaller quantity. (271)

The economy's self-correcting mechanism always tends to push the unemployment rate back toward a specific rate of unemployment that we call the **NATURAL RATE OF UNEMPLOYMENT**. (834)

**NEAR MONEYS** are liquid assets that are close substitutes for money. (721)

**NET EXPORTS**, symbolized by (X − IM), is the difference between U.S. exports and U.S. imports. It indicates the difference between what we sell to foreigners and what we buy from them. (592)

**NET WORTH** is the value of all assets minus the value of all liabilities. (726)

**NOMINAL GDP** is calculated by valuing all outputs at current prices. (549)

The **NOMINAL RATE OF INTEREST** is the percentage by which the money the borrower pays back exceeds the money that he borrowed, making no adjustment for any fall in the purchasing power of this money that results from inflation. (577)

An **OLIGOPOLY** is a market dominated by a few sellers at least several of which are large enough relative to the total market to be able to influence the market price. (292)

An economy is called relatively **OPEN** if its exports and imports constitute a large share of its GDP. An economy is considered relatively **CLOSED** if they constitute a small share. (31)

An **OPEN ECONOMY** is one that trades with other nations in goods and services, and perhaps also in financial assets. (925)

**OPEN-MARKET OPERATIONS** refer to the Fed's purchase or sale of government securities through transactions in the open market. (742)

The **OPPORTUNITY COST** of some decision is the value of the next best alternative which you have to give up because of that decision (for example, working instead of going to school). (7, 57)

An **OPTIMAL** decision is one which, among all the decisions that are actually possible, is best for the decision maker. For example, if profit is the sole objective of some firm, the price that makes the firm's profit as large as possible is optimal for that company. (105)

The lower left-hand corner of a graph where the two axes meet is called the **ORIGIN**. Both variables are equal to zero at the origin. (24)

**OUTPUTS** are the goods and services that consumers want to acquire. **INPUTS** or **FACTORS OF PRODUCTION** are the labor, machinery, buildings, and natural resources used to make these outputs. (28)

The **PARADOX OF THRIFT** is the fact that an effort by a nation to save more may simply reduce national income and fail to raise total saving. (658)

A **PARTNERSHIP** is a firm whose ownership is shared by a fixed number of partners. (40, 337)

A **PATENT** is a temporary grant of monopoly rights over an innovation. (488)

A market is **PERFECTLY CONTESTABLE** if entry and exit are costless and unimpeded. (303)

A **PHILLIPS CURVE** is a graph depicting the rate of unemployment on the horizontal axis and either the rate of inflation or the rate of change of money wages on the vertical axis. Phillips curves are normally downward sloping, indicating that higher inflation rates are associated with lower unemployment rates. (828)

**PLOWBACK** or **RETAINED EARNINGS** is the portion of a corporation's profits that management decides to keep and invest back into the firm's operations rather than to pay out directly to stockholders in the form of dividends. (341)

**POTENTIAL GROSS DOMESTIC PRODUCT** is the real GDP the economy would produce if its labor and other resources were fully employed. (566)

The **POVERTY LINE** is an amount of income below which a family is considered "poor." (424)

A **PRICE CEILING** is a legal maximum on the price that may be charged for a commodity. (91)

**PRICE DISCRIMINATION** occurs when different prices, relative to costs, are charged to different buyers of the same product. (479)

The **(PRICE) ELASTICITY OF DEMAND** is the ratio of the *percentage* change in quantity demanded to the *percentage* change in price that brings about the change in quantity demanded. (176)

A **PRICE FLOOR** is a legal minimum on the price that may be charged for a commodity. (93)

Under **PRICE LEADERSHIP,** one firm sets the price for the industry and the others follow. (295)

In a **PRICE WAR** each competing firm is determined to sell at a price that is lower than the prices of its rivals, usually regardless of whether that price covers the pertinent cost. Typically, in such a price war Firm A cuts its price below Firm B's; then B retaliates by undercutting A, and so on and on until one or more of the firms surrender and let themselves be undersold. (295)

The **PRINCIPLE OF INCREASING COSTS** states that as the production of a good expands, the opportunity cost of producing another unit generally increases. (61)

**PRIVATIZATION** means transferring publicly owned property to private hands. (989)

The **PRODUCTION FUNCTION** indicates the *maximum* amount of product that can be obtained from any specified *combination* of inputs, given the current state of knowledge. That is, it shows the *largest* quantity of goods that any particular collection of inputs is capable of producing. (152)

A **PRODUCTION POSSIBILITIES** frontier shows the different combinations of various goods that a producer can turn out, given the available resources and existing technology. (60)

**PRODUCTIVITY** is the amount of output produced by a unit of input. (672)

A tax is **PROGRESSIVE** if the ratio of taxes to income rises as income rises. (47)

A **PROGRESSIVE TAX** is one in which the average tax rate paid by an individual rises as income rises. (496)

A **PROPORTIONAL TAX** is one in which the average tax rate is the same at all income levels. (497)

A **PROPRIETORSHIP** is a business firm owned by a single person. (40, 336)

A **PUBLIC GOOD** is a commodity or service whose benefits are *not depleted* by an additional user and for which it is generally difficult or *impossible to exclude* people from its benefits, even if they are unwilling to pay for them. In contrast, a **private good** is characterized by both excludability and depletability. (318)

The **PURCHASING POWER** of a given sum of money is the volume of goods and services it will buy. (572)

A **PURE MONOPOLY** is an industry in which there is only one supplier of a product for which there are no close substitutes, and in which it is very hard or impossible for another firm to coexist. (269)

The **QUANTITY DEMANDED** is the number of units consumers want to buy over a specified period of time. (77)

The **QUANTITY SUPPLIED** is the number of units sellers want to sell over a specified period of time. (79)

A **QUOTA** specifies the maximum amount of a good that is permitted into the country from abroad per unit of time. (885)

The time path of a variable such as the price of a stock is said to constitute a **RANDOM WALK** if its magnitude in one period (say, May 2, 1994) is equal to its value in the preceding period (May 1, 1994) plus a completely random number. That is: Price on May 2, 1994 = Price on May 1, 1994 + Random number where the random number (positive or negative) might be obtained by a roll of dice or some such procedure. (354)

A **RATIONAL DECISION** is one that best serves the objective of the decision maker, whatever that objective may be. Such objectives may include a firm's desire to maximize its profits, a government's desire to maximize the welfare of its citizens, or another government's desire to maximize its military might. The term "rational" connotes neither approval nor disapproval of the objective itself. (57)

**RATIONAL EXPECTATIONS** are forecasts which, while not necessarily correct, are the best that can be made given the available data. Rational expectations, therefore, cannot err systematically. If expectations are rational, forecasting errors are pure random numbers. (841)

A straight line emanating from the origin, or zero point on a graph, is called a ray through the origin or, sometimes, just a **RAY**. (24)

**REAL GDP** is the value of all the goods and services produced by an economy in a year, evaluated in dollars of constant purchasing power. Hence, inflation does not raise real GDP. (33, 549)

The **REAL RATE OF INTEREST** is the percentage increase in purchasing power that the borrower pays to the lender for the privilege of borrowing. It indicates the increased ability to purchase goods and services that the lender earns. (577)

The **REAL WAGE RATE** is the wage rate adjusted for inflation. It indicates the volume of goods and services that money wages will buy. (572)

A **RECESSION** is a period of time during which the total output of the economy falls. (34)

The **RECESSIONARY GAP** is the amount by which the equilibrium level of real GDP falls short of potential GDP. (634)

A **REGRESSIVE TAX** is one in which the average tax rate falls as income rises. (497, 548)

**REGULATION OF INDUSTRY** is a process established by law which restricts or controls some specified decisions made by the affected firms. Regulation is usually carried out by a special government agency assigned the task of administering and interpreting the law. That agency also acts as a court in enforcing the regulatory laws. (451)

An item's **RELATIVE PRICE** is its price in terms of some other item, rather than in terms of dollars. (574)

**RENT SEEKING** refers to unproductive activity in the pursuit of economic profit—in other words, profit in excess of competitive earnings. (324)

**REQUIRED RESERVES** are the minimum amount of reserves (in cash or the equivalent) required by law. Normally, required reserves are proportional to the volume of deposits. (726)

**RESOURCES** are the instruments provided by nature or by people that are used to create the goods and services humans want. Natural resources include minerals, the soil (usable for agriculture, building plots, and so on), water, and air. Labor is a scarce resource partly because of time limitations (the day has only 24 hours), and partly because the number of skilled workers is limited. Factories and machines are resources made by people. These three types of resources are often referred to as "land," "labor," and "capital." They are also called the inputs used in production processes or **FACTORS OF PRODUCTION**. (56)

A **REVALUATION** is an increase in the official value of a currency. (902)

A **RUN ON A BANK** occurs when many depositors withdraw cash from their accounts all at once. (615)

A **SCATTER DIAGRAM** is a graph showing the relationship between two variables (such as consumption and disposable income). Each year is represented by a point in the diagram. The coordinates of each year's point show the value of the two variables in that year. (596)

**SENIORITY RULES** are rules that give special job-related advantages to workers who have held their jobs longest. In particular this usually requires that workers most recently hired be the first to be fired when a firm cuts employment. (406)

**SEQUENCING** refers to the order in which changes are made. (990)

A **SHORTAGE** is an excess of quantity demanded over quantity supplied. When there is a shortage, buyers cannot purchase the quantities they desire. (81)

The **SHORT RUN** is a shorter period of time than the long run, so that some, but not all, of the firm's commitments may have ended. (145)

**SOCIALISM** is a method of economic organization in which the state owns the means of production. (978)

**SPECIALIZATION** means that a country devotes its energies and resources to only a small proportion of the world's productive activities. (874)

Individuals who engage in **SPECULATION** deliberately invest in risky assets, hoping to obtain a profit from the expected changes in the prices of these assets. (352)

**STABILIZATION POLICY** is the name given to government programs designed to prevent or shorten recessions and to counteract inflation (that is, to *stabilize* prices). (559)

**STAGFLATION** is inflation that occurs while the economy is growing slowly ("stagnating") or having a recession. (558, 678)

**STATISTICAL DISCRIMINATION** is said to occur when the productivity of a particular worker is estimated to be low just because that worker belongs to a particular group (such as women). (434)

A **STORE OF VALUE** is an item used to store wealth from one point in time to another. (717)

The **STRUCTURAL BUDGET DEFICIT** is the hypothetical deficit we *would have* under current fiscal policies if the economy were operating near full employment. (800)

**STRUCTURAL UNEMPLOYMENT** refers to workers who have lost their jobs because they have been displaced by automation, because their skills are no longer in demand, or for similar reasons. (568)

Two goods are called **SUBSTITUTES** if an increase in the quantity consumed of one cuts the quantity demanded of the other, all other things remaining constant. (180)

The **SUBSTITUTION EFFECT** is the change in quantity demanded of a good resulting from a change in its relative price, exclusive of whatever change in quantity demanded may be attributable to the associated change in real income. (202)

A **SUNK COST** is a cost to which a firm is precommitted for some limited period, either because the firm has signed a contract to make the payments or because the firm has already paid for some durable item (such as a machine or a factory) and cannot get its money back except by using that item to produce output for some period of time. (145)

A **SUPPLY CURVE** is a graphical depiction of a supply schedule. It shows how the quantity supplied of some product during a specified period of time will change as the price of that product changes, holding all other determinants of quantity supplied constant. (79)

A **SUPPLY SCHEDULE** is a table showing how the quantity supplied of some product during a specified period of time changes as the price of that product changes, holding all other determinants of quantity supplied constant. (79)

A **SURPLUS** is an excess of quantity supplied over quantity demanded. When there is a surplus, sellers cannot sell the quantities they desire to supply. (81)

A **TAKEOVER** is the acquisition by an outside group (the raiders) of a controlling proportion of the company's stock. When the old management opposes the takeover attempt, it is called a hostile takeover attempt. (351)

A **TARIFF** is a tax on imports. (885)

A **TAX DEDUCTION** is a sum of money that may be subtracted before the taxpayer computes his or her taxable income. (499)

A particular source of income is **TAX EXEMPT** if income from that source is not taxable. (498)

A **TAX LOOPHOLE** is a special provision in the tax code that reduces taxation below normal rates (perhaps to zero) if certain conditions are met. (498)

**TAX SHIFTING** occurs when the economic reactions to a tax cause prices and outputs in the economy to change, thereby shifting part of the burden of the tax onto others. (508)

A **TIME SERIES GRAPH** is a type of two-variable diagram in which time is the variable measured along the horizontal axis. It shows how some variable changed as time passed. (32)

A **THEORY** is a deliberate simplification of relationships whose purpose is to explain how those relationships work. (14)

A firm's **TOTAL COST (TC)** curve shows, for each possible quantity of output at some given point in time, the total amount which the firm must spend for its inputs to produce that amount of output plus any opportunity cost incurred in the process. (110)

The firm's **TOTAL PHYSICAL PRODUCT (TPP) CURVE** shows what happens to output when the firm changes the quantity of one of its inputs while holding all other input quantities constant. (133)

The **TOTAL PROFIT** of a firm is its net earnings during some period of time. It is equal to the total amount of money the firm gets from the sale of its products (the firm's **total revenue**) minus the total amount it spends to make those products (**total cost**). (108)

The **TOTAL UTILITY** of a quantity of goods to a consumer (measured in money terms) is the maximum amount of money he or she is willing to give in exchange for it. (192)

**TRADE ADJUSTMENT ASSISTANCE** provides special unemployment benefits, loans, retraining programs, and other aid to workers and firms that are harmed by foreign competition. (892)

**TRANSFER PAYMENTS** are sums of money that certain individuals receive as outright grants from the government rather than as payments for services rendered. (47, 594)

The **UNEMPLOYMENT RATE** is the number of unemployed people, expressed as a percentage of the **labor force**. (565)

A **UNION SHOP** is an arrangement under which nonunion workers may be hired, but then must join the union within a specified period of time. (405)

The **UNIT OF ACCOUNT** is the standard unit for quoting prices. (717)

**UNLIMITED LIABILITY** is a legal obligation of a firm's owner(s) to pay back company debts with whatever resources he or she owns. (336)

A **USURY LAW** sets down a maximum permissible interest rate for a particular type of loan. Loans at rates above the usury ceiling are illegal. (578)

A **VARIABLE** is something, such as price, whose magnitude is measured by a number; it is used to analyze what happens to other things when the size of that number changes (varies). (24)

**VARIABLE TAXES** are taxes that do vary with the level of GDP. (691)

**VELOCITY** indicates the number of times per year that an "average dollar" is spent on goods and services. It is the ratio of nominal GDP to the number of dollars in the money stock. That is:

$$\text{Velocity} = \frac{\text{Nominal GDP}}{\text{Money stock}} \quad (762)$$

**VERTICAL EQUITY** refers to the notion that differently situated individuals should be taxed differently in a way that society deems to be fair. (503)

The **VERTICAL (LONG-RUN) PHILLIPS CURVE** shows the menu of inflation/unemployment choices available to society in the long run. It is a vertical straight line at the natural rate of unemployment. (834)

**WAGE–PRICE CONTROLS** are legal restrictions on the ability of industry and labor to raise wages and prices. (845)

Under a system of **WORKERS' MANAGEMENT**, the employees of an enterprise make most of the decisions normally reserved for management. (980)

# CREDITS

Page 1: © Francisco Villaflor/Photonica; p. 11: © H.M. Gousha, A division of Simon and Schuster Inc.; p. 12: © H.M. Gousha, A division of Simon and Schuster Inc.; p. 13: © H.M. Gousha, A division of Simon and Schuster Inc.; p. 16: London School of Economics and Political Science © David Burnett, Contact Press Images. p. 41: Courtesy of the U.S. Geological Survey; p. 47: © Butch Gemin; p. 69: © UPI/Bettmann; p. 75: Courtesy of the Metropolitan Museum of Art, Bequest of Charles Allen Munn, 1924. (24.90.1828); p. 82: © Philip Chalfant/The Image Bank; p. 97: © Chris Brown/Stock, Boston; p. 103: © Rudiuv Starrex/Photonica; p. 121: © Jeff Greenberg/Leo de Wys; p. 149: RIA-NOVOSTI/SOVFOTO; p. 151: © Dan Coffey/The Image Bank; p. 197: left: © Al Hamden/The Image Bank; p. 197: right: © G.K. & Vikki Hart/The Image Bank; p. 219: © Kazura Shimizu/Photonica; p. 248: © M. Richards/PhotoEdit; p. 251: Witold Skrypezak/Leo de Wys Inc.; p. 255: © *Krododil*, Sovfoto; p. 304: © Tony Stone Images; p. 323: Source: *The Fort Worth Star-Telegram*; p. 325: GROPPER, William. *The Senate*. (1935). Oil on Canvas, $25\frac{1}{8} \times 33\frac{1}{8}''$. The Museum of Modern Art, New York. Gift of A. Conger Goodyear; p. 346: Reprinted by permission of *The Wall Street Journal*, © 1993 Dow Jones and Company, Inc. All Rights Reserved Worldwide; p. 347: Reprinted by permission of *The Wall Street Journal*, © 1993 Dow Jones and Company, Inc. All Rights Reserved Worldwide; p. 355: © Reuters/Bettmann; p. 356: KAL © 1990 Cartoonist and Writers Syndicate; p. 359: © Jeff Spielman/The Image Bank; p. 376: © Chuck Mason/The Image Bank; p. 381: © Butch Gemin; p. 390: © Bob Englehart—*The Hartford Courant*/Copley News Service; p. 404: © UPI/Bettmann Newsphotos; p. 426: © Joe Rodriquez/Black Star; p. 435: © David Young-Wolff/PhotoEdit; p. 445: Reuters/Bettmann; p. 446: left © Wolfgang Spunbarg/PhotoEdit; right © Tom McCarthy/Photo Edit; p. 449: © Andy Post; p. 461: © UPI/Bettmann; p. 472: © Michael R. Schneps/The Image Bank; p. 477: © The Bettmann Archive; p. 492: © Mike Mazzaschi/Stock Boston; p. 506: © Reuters/Bettmann; p. 517: THE FAR SIDE copyright FARWORKS, INC./Dist. by UNIVERSAL PRESS SYNDICATE. Reprinted with permission. All rights reserved. p. 520: © Linda Wooton Miller; p. 530: © Christian Bossu-Pica/Tony Stone Images; p. 543: © Abrams Lacagnina; p. 551: © Mary Kate Denny/Photo Edit; p. 555: © UPI/Bettmann/British Information Service; p. 557: © UPI/Bettmann; p. 573: From *The Wall Street Journal*—Permission, Cartoon Features Syndicate; p. 582: NYT Pictures; p. 583: Camera Press-Photo Trends; p. 638: © 1989, Comstock; p. 689: © 1993, Westlight; p. 707: © 1993 Michael Geissinger/Comstock; p. 717: Used by permission of Johnny Hart and Creators Syndicate, Inc.; p. 719: University Museum, University of Pennsylvania; p. 725: © Tony Freeman/Photo Edit; p. 784: © A. Upitis/The Image Bank; p. 787: © Francesco Ruggeri/The Image Bank; p. 794: From *The Wall Street Journal*—Permission, Cartoon Features Syndicate. p. 814: From *The Wall Street Journal*—Permission, Cartoon Features. p. 818: © AP/Wide World Photos; p. 851: © Michael Medford/The Image Bank; p. 854: © Bettmann Newsphotos; p. 878: © Culver Pictures; p. 886: © Elena Rooraid/Photo Edit; p. 890: © Felicia Martinez/Photo Edit; p. 894: © Dennis Brady/Black Star; p. 896: © Culver Pictures; p. 918: Drawing by Ed Fisher, © 1971 *The New Yorker Magazine*; p. 949: © 1993, Sovfoto; p. 960: © D.E. Cox/Tony Stone Images; p. 979: © AP/Wide World Photos; p. 995: © Matthew Neal McVay/Stock Boston; p. 996: © M. Hayman/Stock, Boston.

# INDEX

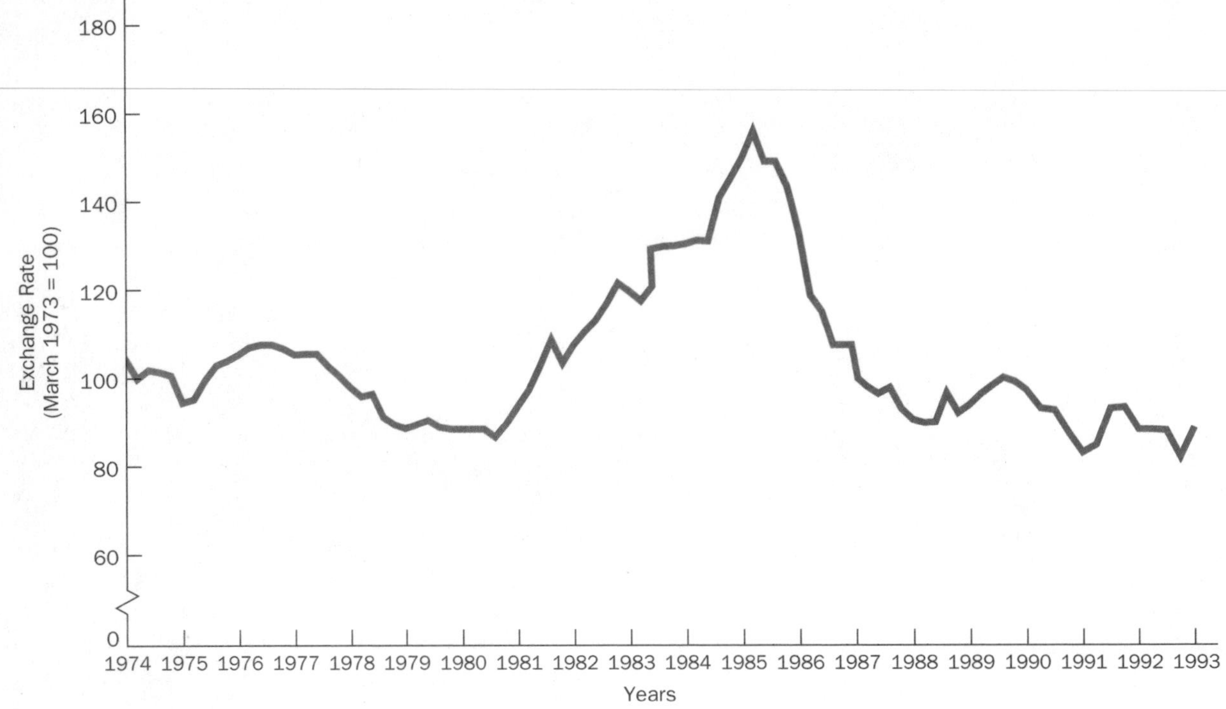


**INTERNATIONAL VALUE OF THE DOLLAR (MARCH 1973 = 100)**

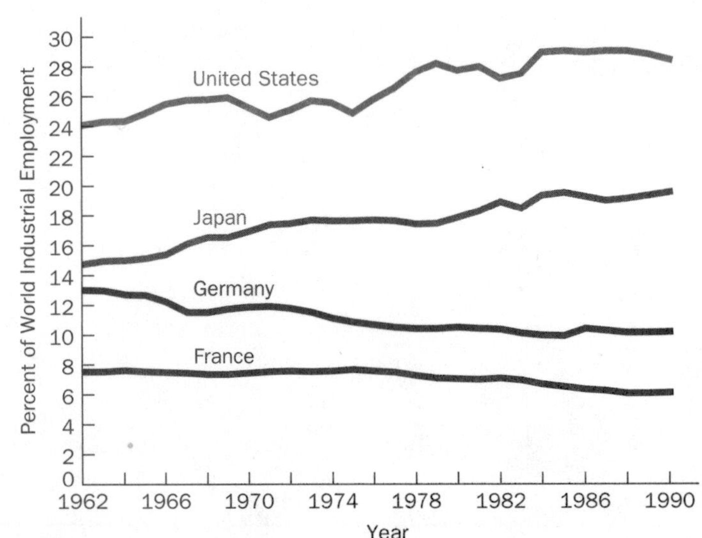


**SHARES OF WORLD INDUSTRIAL EMPLOYMENT OF FOUR INDUSTRIAL COUNTRIES, 1962–1990**